SOCIAL SECURITY LEGISLATION 2015/16

VOLUME IV:
TAX CREDITS AND HMRC-ADMINISTERED SOCIAL SECURITY BENEFITS

SOCIAL SECURITY LEGISLATION 2015/16

General Editor
Nick Wikeley, M.A. (Cantab)

VOLUME IV:
TAX CREDITS AND HMRC-ADMINISTERED SOCIAL SECURITY BENEFITS

Commentary By

Nick Wikeley, M.A. (Cantab)
*Temporary Chamber President, War Pensions
and Armed Forces Compensation Chamber,
Judge of the Upper Tribunal,
Emeritus Professor of Law, University of Southampton*

David W. Williams, LL.M., Ph.D., C.T.A.
*Judge of the Upper Tribunal,
Former Professor of Tax Law, Queen Mary College, London*

Ian Hooker, LL.B.
*Formerly Lecturer in Law, University of Nottingham,
Formerly Chairman, Social Security Tribunals*

Consultant Editor
Child Poverty Action Group

SWEET & MAXWELL

Published in 2015 by
Thomson Reuters (Professional) UK Limited
trading as Sweet & Maxwell,
Friars House, 160 Blackfriars Road, London, SE1 8EZ
(Registered in England & Wales, Company No 1679046.
Registered Office and address for service:
2nd floor, 1 Mark Square, Leonard Street, London EC2A 4EG

Typeset by Servis Filmsetting Ltd, Stockport, Cheshire
Printed and bound by CPI Group (UK) Ltd, Croydon, CR0 4YY

For further information on our products and services,
visit www.sweetandmaxwell.co.uk

No natural forests were destroyed to make this product.
Only farmed timber was used and re-planted.

A CIP catalogue record for this book is
available from the British Library

ISBN 978-0-414-03907-0

Crown copyright material is reproduced with the permission
of the Controller of HMSO and the Queen's Printer for
Scotland.

All rights reserved. No part of this publication may be reproduced or transmitted in any form or by any means, or stored in any retrieval system of any nature without prior written permission, except for permitted fair dealing under the Copyright, Designs and Patents Act 1988, or in accordance with the terms of a licence issued by the Copyright Licensing Agency in respect of photocopying and/or reprographic reproduction. Application for permission for other use of copyright material including permission to reproduce extracts in other published works shall be made to the publishers. Full acknowledgement of author, publisher and source must be given.
Material is contained in this publication for which publishing permission has been sought, and for which copyright is acknowledged. Permission to reproduce such material cannot be granted by the publishers and application must be made to the copyright holder.

Thomson Reuters and the Thomson Reuters Logo are trademarks of Thomson Reuters. Sweet & Maxwell® is a registered trademark of Thomson Reuters (Professional) UK Limited.

Commentators have asserted their moral rights under the Copyright, Designs and Patents Act 1988 to be identified as the authors of the commentary in this Volume.

© 2015 Thomson Reuters (Professional) UK Limited

CHILD POVERTY ACTION GROUP

The Child Poverty Action Group (CPAG) is a charity, founded in 1965, which campaigns for the relief of poverty in the United Kingdom. It has a particular reputation in the field of welfare benefits law derived from its legal work, publications, training and parliamentary and policy work, and is widely recognised as the leading organisation for taking test cases on social security law.

CPAG is therefore ideally placed to act as Consultant Editor to this 5-volume work—**Social Security Legislation 2015/16**. CPAG is not responsible for the detail of what is contained in each volume, and the authors' views are not necessarily those of CPAG. The Consultant Editor's role is to act in an advisory capacity on the overall structure, focus and direction of the work.

For more information about CPAG, its rights and policy publications or training courses, its address is 30 Micawber Street, London, N1 7TB (telephone: 020 7837 7979—website: *http://www.cpag.org.uk*).

FOREWORD

Changes in substantive law rarely lead to simplicity, often layer upon layer of complexity is added to deal with the unexpected and unintended consequences of earlier legislation. In a rapidly changing world further complexity is added because of a need to deal with the quickening pace of change. What is needed then is an authoritative guide allowing for both necessary detail and yet a clear and concise explanation. Hence the great value placed upon this series, an invaluable guide to legislation in this field. I and the Tribunal as a whole are greatly indebted to those who have contributed to these indispensable volumes and thus rendered such assistance to our work.

HH Judge John Aitken
President
Social Entitlement Chamber
First-tier Tribunal

PREFACE

Tax Credits and HMRC-administered Social Security Benefits is Volume IV of the 16th edition of what is now a five volume series: *Social Security Legislation 2015/16*. The companion volumes are Bonner, Hooker, Poynter, White, Wikeley, Williams and Wood, *Volume I: Non Means Tested Benefits and Employment and Support Allowance*; Wood, Poynter, Wikeley and Mesher, *Volume II: Income Support, Jobseeker's Allowance, State Pension Credit and the Social Fund*; and Rowland and White, *Volume III: Administration, Adjudication and the European Dimension*. The volumes are designed to be used in conjunction with *Social Security Legislation 2013/14, Volume V: Universal Credit*. Readers are accordingly reminded that the legislation and authoritative commentary on the decision-making and appeals legislation and on the tribunal procedural rules, are to be found in *Volume III* of this series (as are human rights aspects and European law issues).

Each of the volumes in the series provides a legislative text, clearly showing the form and date of amendments, and commentary up to date to April 13, 2015. The commentary sometimes includes references to some later case law.

The Tax Credits Act 2002, introducing Child Tax Credit (CTC) and Working Tax Credit (WTC) from April 2003, represented a radical shift for the benefits system and provided the initial impetus for this fourth volume in the series. This volume, designed in the same format as its companion volumes, covers CTC and WTC along with social security benefits administered and paid by Her Majesty's Revenue and Customs (HMRC, formerly the Inland Revenue), namely Child Benefit and Guardian's Allowance, as well as those administered by HMRC but paid by employers: statutory sick pay (SSP), statutory maternity pay (SMP), ordinary and additional statutory paternity pay (SPP), statutory adoption pay (SAP) and now the new statutory shared parental pay (ShPP). This volume also includes the statutory provisions relating to the child trust funds, including amendments introduced as the Coalition Government began the process of scaling back the scheme prior to its closure.

We have taken the opportunity in this year's 13th edn of *Volume IV* to cover significant recent Upper Tribunal decisions and to bring the statutory text up to date, reflecting the various amendments made by regulations to the scope of WTC and CTC. In addition, this year's volume includes commentary on the important changes to the statutory provisions governing the admission of late tax credits appeals, as well as analysis of Upper Tribunal decisions on evidential issues arising in tax credits appeals. As previously, given that there continues to be considerable public interest in the issue of overpayments of tax credits, we have included the text of leaflet WTC7 on Tax Credits penalties and HMRC's revised Code of Practice 26 (COP 26) on the recovery of overpayments.

Two years ago we noted the start of the "roll out" of the measures embodied in the Welfare Reform Act 2012, presaged in the 2010 Budget.

Preface

Under these reforms, CTC and WTC will be phased out of the legislation and merged into the new Universal Credit by stages. However, progress in introducing Universal Credit has been slower than originally planned. As a result, the tax credits regime remains very much alive for large numbers of claimants on low incomes. As noted above, Universal Credit is dealt with by a new fifth volume in the series, which was published for the first time in January 2014.

Users of these volumes in this series, and their predecessors, have over the years provided valuable comments which have invariably been helpful to the editors in ensuring that the selection of legislative material for inclusion and the commentary upon it reflect the sorts of difficulties encountered in practice. In doing so, readers have thus helped to shape the content of each of the volumes in the current series. We also hope that users of the work will continue to provide such helpful input and feedback. Please write to the General Editor of the series, Professor Nick Wikeley, c/o School of Law, University of Southampton, Highfield, Southampton SO17 1BJ (njw@soton.ac.uk) and he will pass on any comments received to the appropriate commentator.

Our gratitude also goes to the Chamber President of the Social Entitlement Chamber of the First-tier Tribunal and his staff for continuing the tradition of help and encouragement.

August 2015

Nick Wikeley
David Williams

CONTENTS

	Page
Foreword	vii
Preface	ix
Using this Book: An Introduction to Legislation and Case Law	xv
Major Changes to Credits and Benefits	xxv
Change of Name from Department of Social Security to Department for Work and Pensions	xxvii
Changes in Terminology Consequent upon the Entry into Force of the Treaty of Lisbon	xxix
The Marriage (Same Sex Couples) Act 2013	xxxi
Table of Cases	xxxiii
Table of Commissioners' Decisions 1948–2009	xxxvii
Table of Abbreviations used in this Series	xxxix

PART I
HM REVENUE AND CUSTOMS
TAX CREDITS AND SOCIAL SECURITY

	Paras
Taxes Management Act 1970	1.1
Social Security Contributions and Benefits Act 1992	1.29
Social Security Administration Act 1992	1.206
Social Security Act 1988	1.222
Social Security Contributions (Transfer of Functions, etc.) Act 1999	1.225
Tax Credits Act 2002	1.251
Employment Act 2002	1.445
Income Tax (Earnings and Pensions) Act 2003	1.475
Child Trust Funds Act 2004	1.599
Income Tax (Trading and Other Income) Act 2005	1.696
Commissioners for Revenue and Customs Act 2005	1.806
Income Tax Act 2007	1.829
Welfare Reform Act 2012	1.848

PART II
TAX CREDITS

	Paras
Tax Credits Act 2002 (Commencement No.3 and Transitional Provisions and Savings) Order 2003	2.1
Tax Credits Act 2002 (Commencement No.4, Transitional Provisions and Savings) Order 2003	2.8
Tax Credits Act 2002 (Transitional Provisions) Order 2008	2.12
Tax Credits Act 2002 (Transitional Provisions) Order 2010	2.15
Working Tax Credit (Entitlement and Maximum Rate) Regulations 2002	2.19

Tax Credits (Definition and Calculation of Income) Regulations 2002	2.103
Child Tax Credit Regulations 2002	2.192
Tax Credits (Income Thresholds and Determination of Rates) Regulations 2002	2.219
Tax Credits (Claims and Notifications) Regulations 2002	2.271
Tax Credits [(Payment by the Commissioners)] Regulations 2002	2.340
Tax Credits (Administrative Arrangements) Regulations 2002	2.368
The Tax Credits (Appeals) (No.2) Regulations 2002	2.375
Tax Credits (Interest Rate) Regulations 2003	2.388
Tax Credits (Immigration) Regulations 2003	2.394
Tax Credits (Residence) Regulations 2003	2.412
Tax Credits (Official Error) Regulations 2003	2.430
Tax Credits (Provision of Information) (Functions Relating to Health) Regulations 2003	2.436
The Tax Credits (Polygamous Marriages) Regulations 2003	2.441
Tax Credits (Provision of Information) (Functions Relating to Health) (No.2) Regulations 2003	2.454
Tax Credits (Provision of Information) (Function Relating to Employment and Training) Regulations 2003	2.458
Tax Credits Act 2002 (Child Tax Credit) (Transitional Provisions) Order 2003	2.462
Tax Credits (Provision of Information) (Evaluation and Statistical Studies) Regulations 2003	2.466
Tax Credits (Provision of Information) (Evaluation and Statistical Studies) (Northern Ireland) Regulations 2004	2.468
Tax Credits (Provision of Information) (Functions Relating to Health) (Scotland) Regulations 2004	2.470
Tax Credits (Provision of Information) (Function Relating to Employment and Training) Regulations 2005	2.472
The Tax Credits (Child Care Providers) Miscellaneous Revocation and Transitional Provisions) (England) Scheme 2007	2.474
The Loss of Tax Credits (Specified Day) Order 2013	2.480
The Loss of Tax Credits Regulations 2013	2.483
The Tax Credits (Late Appeals) Order 2014	2.487
The Tax Credits, Child Benefit and Guardian's Allowance Reviews and Appeals Order 2014	2.490
Tax Credits (Settlement of Appeals) Regulations 2014	2.495
Tax Credits (Exercise of Functions) Order 2014	2.498

PART III
CHILDREN AND GUARDIANS

	Paras
The Child Benefit (General) Regulations 2006	3.1
Child Benefit (Residence and Persons Abroad) Regulations 1976	3.54
The Child Benefit (Rates) Regulations 2006	3.56
Guardian's Allowance (General) Regulations 2003	3.62
Guardian's Allowance Up-rating Order 2015	3.78
Guardian's Allowance Up-rating Regulations 2015	3.80

Contents

PART IV
STATUTORY SICK PAY

	Paras
Statutory Sick Pay (General) Regulations 1982	4.1
Statutory Sick Pay (Mariners, Airmen and Persons Abroad) Regulations 1982	4.45
Statutory Sick Pay (Medical Evidence) Regulations 1985	4.66
Statutory Sick Pay (National Health Service Employees) Regulations 1991	4.73
Statutory Sick Pay and Statutory Maternity Pay (Decisions) Regulations 1999	4.80
Statutory Sick Pay Percentage Threshold (Revocations, Transitional and Saving Provisions) (Great Britain and Northern Ireland) Order 2014	4.85

PART V
STATUTORY MATERNITY PAY

	Paras
Statutory Maternity Pay (General) Regulations 1986	5.1
Statutory Maternity Pay (Medical Evidence) Regulations 1987	5.57
Statutory Maternity Pay (Persons Abroad and Mariners) Regulations 1987	5.62
Statutory Maternity Pay (National Health Service Employees) Regulations 1991	5.74
Statutory Maternity Pay (Compensation of Employers) and Miscellaneous Amendment Regulations 1994	5.81
Statutory Maternity Pay (General) (Modification and Amendment) Regulations 2000	5.93
Statutory Maternity Pay and Statutory Adoption Pay (Curtailment) Regulations 2014	5.100

PART VI
STATUTORY PATERNITY PAY
AND STATUTORY ADOPTION PAY

	Paras
Statutory Paternity Pay and Statutory Adoption Pay (Weekly Rates) Regulations 2002	6.1
Statutory Paternity Pay and Statutory Adoption Pay (National Health Service Employees) Regulations 2002	6.8
Statutory Paternity Pay and Statutory Adoption Pay (Administration) Regulations 2002	6.16
Statutory Paternity Pay and Statutory Adoption Pay (Persons Abroad and Mariners) Regulations 2002	6.33
Statutory Paternity Pay and Statutory Adoption Pay (Persons Abroad and Mariners) Regulations 2002	6.46
Statutory Paternity Pay and Statutory Adoption Pay (General) Regulations 2002	6.57
Social Security Contributions and Benefits Act 1992 (Application of Parts 12ZA and 12ZB to Adoptions from Overseas) Regulations 2003	6.112

Contents

Statutory Paternity Pay (Adoption) and Statutory Adoption Pay (Adoptions from Overseas) (Administration) Regulations 2003	6.120
Statutory Paternity Pay (Adoption) and Statutory Adoption Pay (Adoptions from Overseas) (No.2) Regulations 2003	6.125
Ordinary Statutory Paternity Pay (Adoption), Additional Statutory Paternity Pay (Adoption) and Statutory Adoption Pay (Adoptions from Overseas) (Persons Abroad and Mariners) Regulations 2010	6.146
Additional Statutory Paternity Pay (National Health Service Employees) Regulations 2010	6.152
Additional Statutory Paternity Pay (General) Regulations 2010	6.159
Additional Statutory Paternity Pay (Adoptions from Overseas) Regulations 2010	6.200
Additional Statutory Paternity Pay (Weekly Rates) Regulations 2010	6.213
Social Security Contributions and Benefits Act 1992 (Application of Parts 12ZA, 12ZB and 12ZC to Parental Order Cases) Regulations 2014	6.218
Statutory Paternity Pay and Statutory Adoption Pay (Parental Orders and Prospective Adopters) Regulations 2014	6.228

PART VII
STATUTORY SHARED PARENTAL PAY

	Paras
Statutory Shared Parental Pay (Administration) Regulations 2014	7.01
Statutory Shared Parental Pay (General) Regulations 2014	7.17
Statutory Shared Parental Pay (Parental Order Cases) Regulations 2014	7.109
Statutory Shared Parental Pay (Persons Abroad and Mariners) Regulations 2014	7.127

PART VIII
CHILD TRUST FUNDS

	Paras
Child Trust Funds Act 2004 (Commencement No.1) Order 2004	8.1
Child Trust Funds Act 2004 (Commencement No.2) Order 2004	8.3
Child Trust Funds Regulations 2004	8.5
Child Trust Funds (Insurance Companies) Regulations 2004	8.53
The Child Trust Funds (Non-tax Appeals) Regulations 2005	8.62
The Child Trust Funds (Appeals) Regulations 2005	8.68

PART IX
HMRC CODES OF PRACTICE AND GUIDANCE

	Paras
WTC7—Tax Credits Penalties	9.1
COP 26—What happens if we've paid you too much tax credit?	9.15

	Page
Index	1087

USING THIS BOOK: AN INTRODUCTION TO LEGISLATION AND CASE LAW

Introduction

This book is not a general introduction to, or general textbook on, the law relating to social security but it is nonetheless concerned with both of the principal sources of social security law—*legislation* (both primary and secondary) and *case law*. It sets out the text of the most important legislation, as currently in force, and then there is added commentary that refers to the relevant case law. Lawyers will be familiar with this style of publication, which inevitably follows the structure of the legislation.

This note is designed primarily to assist readers who are not lawyers to find their way around the legislation and to understand the references to case law, but information it contains about how to find social security case law is intended to be of assistance to lawyers too.

Primary legislation

Primary legislation of the United Kingdom Parliament consists of *Acts of Parliament* (also known as *statutes*). They will have been introduced to Parliament as *Bills*. There are opportunities for Members of Parliament and peers to debate individual clauses and to vote on amendments before a Bill is passed and becomes an Act (at which point the clauses become sections). No tribunal or court has the power to disapply, or hold to be invalid, an Act of Parliament unless it is inconsistent with European Union law.

An Act is known by its "short title", which incorporates the year in which it was passed (e.g. the Social Security Contributions and Benefits Act 1992), and is given a chapter number (abbreviated as, for instance, "c.4" indicating that the Act was the fourth passed in that year). It is seldom necessary to refer to the chapter number but it appears in the running heads in this book.

Each *section* (abbreviated as "s." or, in the plural, "ss.") of an Act is numbered and may be divided into *subsections* (abbreviated as "subs." and represented by a number in brackets), which in turn may be divided into *paragraphs* (abbreviated as "para." and represented by a lower case letter in brackets) and *subparagraphs* (abbreviated as "subpara." and represented by a small roman numeral in brackets). Subparagraph (ii) of para.(a) of subs.(1) of s.72 will usually be referred to simply as "s.72(1)(a)(ii)". Upper case letters may be used where additional sections or subsections are inserted by amendment and additional lower case letters may be used where new paragraphs and subparagraphs are inserted. This accounts for the rather ungainly s.171ZS of the Social Security Contributions and Benefits Act 1992 (in Vol.IV).

Sections of a large Act may be grouped into a numbered *Part*, which may even be divided into *Chapters*. It is not usual to refer to a Part or a Chapter unless referring to the whole Part or Chapter.

Where a section would otherwise become unwieldy because it is necessary to include a list or complicated technical provisions, the section may simply refer to a *Schedule* at the end of the Act. A Schedule (abbreviated as "Sch.") may be divided into paragraphs and subparagraphs and further divided into heads and subheads. Again, it is usual to refer simply to, say, "para.23(3)(b)(ii) of Schedule 3". Whereas it is conventional to speak of a section *of* an Act, it is usual to speak of a Schedule *to* an Act.

When Parliament wishes to change the law, it may do so by passing a new Act that amends a previous Act or it may do so by passing a freestanding Act, although even then consequential amendments to other legislation are usually required. Thus, for instance, when incapacity benefit was introduced by the Social Security (Incapacity for Work) Act 1994, the changes were largely made by inserting ss.30A to 30E and Pt XIIA into the Social Security Contributions and Benefits Act 1992 and repealing the provisions in that Act dealing with sickness and invalidity benefit. In contrast, when jobseeker's allowance was introduced by the Jobseekers Act 1995, it was decided that the main provisions relating to the new benefit would be found in the 1995 Act itself and the 1992 Act was amended only so as to repeal, or amend, the provisions dealing with, or referring to, unemployment benefit.

When there has been a proliferation of Acts or Acts have been very substantially amended, the legislation may be consolidated in a new Act, for which there is a fast track procedure in Parliament. Only limited amendments may be made by a consolidation Act but such an Act reorganises and tidies up the legislation. Because social security law is so frequently amended, it tends to be consolidated every decade or two. The last consolidation Acts relevant to this book were the Social Security Contributions and Benefits Act 1992 (in Vols I, II and IV) and the Social Security Administration Act 1992 (in Vol.III).

Secondary legislation

Secondary legislation (also known as *subordinate legislation* or *delegated legislation*) is made by *statutory instrument* in the form of a set of *Regulations* or a set of *Rules* or an *Order*. The power to make such legislation is conferred on ministers and other persons or bodies by Acts of Parliament. To the extent that a statutory instrument is made beyond the powers (in Latin, *ultra vires*) conferred by primary legislation, it may be held by a tribunal or court to be invalid and ineffective. Secondary legislation must be laid before Parliament. However, most secondary legislation is not debated in Parliament and, even when it is, it cannot be amended although an entire statutory instrument may be rejected.

A set of Regulations or Rules or an Order has a name indicating its scope and the year it was made and also a number, as in the Social Security (Disability Living Allowance) Regulations 1991 (SI 1991/2890) (the 2890th statutory instrument issued in 1991). Because there are over 3,000 statutory instruments each year, the number of a particular statutory instrument is important as a means of identification and it should usually be cited the first time reference is made to that statutory instrument.

Sets of Regulations or Rules are made up of individual *regulations* (abbreviated as "reg.") or *rules* (abbreviated as "r." or, in the plural, "rr."). An Order is made up of *articles* (abbreviated as "art."). Regulations, rules and articles may be divided into paragraphs, subparagraphs and heads. As in Acts, a set of Regulations or Rules or an Order may have one or more

Schedules attached to it. The style of numbering used in statutory instruments is the same as in sections of, and Schedules to, Acts of Parliament. As in Acts, a large statutory instrument may have regulations or rules grouped into Parts and, occasionally, Chapters. Statutory instruments may be amended in the same sort of way as Acts.

Northern Ireland legislation

Most of the legislation set out in this series applies only in Great Britain, social security not generally being an excepted or reserved matter in relation to Northern Ireland. However, Northern Irish legislation—both primary legislation, most relevantly in the form of *Orders in Council* (which, although statutory instruments, had the effect of primary legislation in Northern Ireland while there was direct rule from Westminster) and *Acts of the Northern Ireland Assembly*, and subordinate legislation, in the form of *statutory rules*—has, until recently, largely replicated legislation in Great Britain so that much of the commentary in this book will be applicable to equivalent provisions in Northern Ireland legislation. Latterly, there has been a greater reluctance to maintain parity with Great Britain and, in particular, the provisions in the Welfare Reform Act 2012 have not been replicated in Northern Ireland; although a Bill based on the 2012 Act was brought before the Assembly, it failed to pass its final stage in May 2015.

European Union legislation

The United Kingdom is a Member State of the European Union, and European Union legislation has effect within the United Kingdom. The primary legislation is in the form of the *Treaties* agreed by the Member States. Relevant subordinate legislation is in the form of *Regulations*, adopted to give effect to provisions of the Treaties, and *Directives*, addressed to Member States and requiring them to incorporate certain provisions into their domestic laws. Directives are relevant because, where a person brings proceedings against an organ of the State, as is invariably the case where social security is concerned, that person may rely on the Directive as having direct effect if the Member State has failed to comply with it. European Union Treaties, Regulations and Directives are divided into *Articles* (abbreviated as "art."). United Kingdom legislation that is inconsistent with European Union legislation may be disapplied. The most relevant provisions of European Union legislation are set out in Part III of *Vol.III: Administration, Appeals and the European Dimension*.

Finding legislation in this book

If you know the name of the piece of legislation for which you are looking, use the list of contents at the beginning of each volume of this series which lists the pieces of legislation contained in the volume. That will give you the paragraph reference to enable you to find the beginning of the piece of legislation. Then, it is easy to find the relevant section, regulation, rule, article or Schedule by using the running heads on the right-hand pages. If you do not know the name of the piece of legislation, you will probably need to use the index at the end of the volume in order to find the relevant paragraph number but will then be taken straight to a particular provision.

The legislation is set out as amended, the amendments being indicated by numbered sets of square brackets. The numbers refer to the numbered

Using this Book

entries under the heading "AMENDMENTS" at the end of the relevant section, regulation, rule, article or Schedule, which identify the amending statute or statutory instrument. Where an Act has been consolidated, there is a list of "DERIVATIONS" identifying the provisions of earlier legislation from which the section or Schedule has been derived.

Finding other legislation

Legislation in its unamended form may be found on *http://www.legislation. gov.uk* (although some primary legislation on this site now includes amendments). Obscure provisions of Great Britain social security legislation not included in this book may be found, as amended but without a commentary, at *http://lawvolumes.dwp.gov.uk/the-law-relating-to-social-security/*. Northern Ireland social security legislation may be found at *http://www. dsdni.gov.uk/law_relating_to_social_security*. European Union legislation may be found at *http://eur-lex.europa.eu/collection/eu-law.html*

Interpreting legislation

Legislation is written in English and generally means what it says. However, more than one interpretation is often possible. Most legislation itself contains definitions. Sometimes these are in the particular provision in which a word occurs but, where a word is used in more than one place, any definition will appear with others. In an Act, an interpretation section is usually to be found towards the end of the Act or of the relevant Part of the Act. In a statutory instrument, an interpretation provision usually appears near the beginning of the statutory instrument or the relevant Part of it. In the more important pieces of legislation in this series, there is included after every section, regulation, rule, article or Schedule a list of "DEFINITIONS", showing where definitions of words used in the provision are to be found.

However, not all words are statutorily defined and there is in any event more to interpreting legislation than merely defining its terms. Decision-makers and tribunals need to know how to apply the law in different types of situations. That is where case law comes in.

Case law and the commentary in this book

In deciding individual cases, courts and tribunals interpret the relevant law and incidentally establish legal principles. Decisions on questions of legal principle of the superior courts and appellate tribunals are said to be binding on decision-makers and the First-tier Tribunal, which means that decision-makers and the First-tier Tribunal must apply those principles. Thus the judicial decisions of the superior courts and appellate tribunals form part of the law. The commentary to the legislation in this series, under the heading "GENERAL NOTE" after a section, regulation, rule, article or Schedule, refers to this *case law*.

The largest part of the case law regarding social security benefits is still in the form of decisions of Social Security Commissioners and Child Support Commissioners. However, while there are still Commissioners in Northern Ireland, which has a largely separate judiciary and tribunal system, the functions of Commissioners in Great Britain were transferred to the Upper Tribunal and allocated to the Administrative Appeals Chamber of that tribunal on November 3, 2008. Consequently, social security case law is increasingly to be found in decisions of the Upper Tribunal.

Using this Book

The commentary in this series is not itself binding on any decision-maker or tribunal because it is merely the opinion of the author. It is what is actually said in the legislation or in the judicial decision that is important. The legislation is set out in this series, but it will generally be necessary to look elsewhere for the precise words used in judicial decisions. The way that decisions are cited in the commentary enables that to be done.

The reporting of decisions of the Upper Tribunal and Commissioners

About 50 of the most important decisions of the Administrative Appeals Chamber of the Upper Tribunal are selected to be "reported" each year in the Administrative Appeals Chamber Reports, using the same criteria as were formerly used for reporting Commissioners' decisions in Great Britain. The selection is made by an editorial board of judges and decisions are selected for reporting only if they are of general importance and command the assent of at least a majority of the relevant judges. The term "reported" simply means that they are published in printed form as well as on the Internet (see *Finding case law*, below) with headnotes (i.e. summaries) and indexes, but there are two other important consequences of a decision being reported. Reported decisions are available in some tribunal venues and can be consulted in local social security offices and some main libraries. They also have a greater precedential status than ordinary decisions (see *Judicial precedent* below).

A handful of Northern Ireland Commissioners' decisions are also selected for reporting in the Administrative Appeals Chamber Reports each year, the selection being made by the Chief Social Security Commissioner in Northern Ireland.

Citing case law

As has been mentioned, the largest part of social security case law is still to be found in decisions of Social Security Commissioners and Child Support Commissioners, even though the Commissioners have now effectively been abolished in Great Britain.

Reported decisions of Commissioners were known merely by a number or, more accurately, a series of letters and numbers beginning with an "R". The type of benefit in issue was indicated by letters in brackets (e.g. "IS" was income support, "P" was retirement pension, and so on) and the year in which the decision was selected for reporting or, from 2000, the year in which it was published as a reported decision, was indicated by the last two digits, as in *R(IS) 2/08*. In Northern Ireland there was a similar system until 2009, save that the type of benefit was identified by letters in brackets after the number, as in *R 1/07 (DLA)*.

Unreported decisions of the Commissioners in Great Britain were known simply by their file numbers, which began with a "C", as in *CIS/2287/2008*. The letters following the "C" indicated the type of benefit in issue in the case. Scottish and, at one time, Welsh cases were indicated by a "S" or "W" immediately after the "C", as in *CSIS/467/2007*. The last four digits indicated the calendar year in which the case was registered, rather than the year it was decided. A similar system operated in Northern Ireland until 2009, save that the letters indicating the type of benefit appeared in brackets after the numbers and, from April 1999, the financial year rather than the calendar year was identified, as in *C 10/06-07 (IS)*.

xix

Using this Book

Decisions of the Upper Tribunal, of courts and, since 2010, of the Northern Ireland Commissioners are generally known by the names of the parties (or just two of them in multi-party cases). Individuals are anonymised through the use of initials in the names of decisions of the Upper Tribunal and the Northern Ireland Commissioners and occasionally in the names of decisions of courts. In this series, the names of official bodies may also be abbreviated (e.g. "SSWP" for the Secretary of State for Work and Pensions, "HMRC" for Her Majesty's Revenue and Customs, "CMEC" for the Child Maintenance and Enforcement Commission and "DSD" for the Department for Social Development in Northern Ireland). Since 2010, decisions of the Upper Tribunal and of Northern Ireland Commissioners have also been given a "flag" in brackets to indicate the subject matter of the decision, which in social security cases indicates the principal benefit in issue in the case. Thus, the name of one jobseeker's allowance case is *SSWP v JB (JSA)*.

Any decision of the Upper Tribunal, of a court since 2001 or of a Northern Ireland Commissioner since 2010 that has been intended for publication has also given a *neutral citation number* which enables the decision to be more precisely identified. This indicates, in square brackets, the year the decision was made (although in relation to decisions of the courts it sometimes merely indicates the year the number was issued) and also indicates the court or tribunal that made the decision (e.g. "UKUT" for the Upper Tribunal, "NICom" for a Northern Ireland Commissioner, "EWCA Civ" for the Civil Division of the Court of Appeal in England and Wales, "NICA" for the Court of Appeal in Northern Ireland, "CSIH" for the Inner House of the Court of Session (in Scotland), "UKSC" for the Supreme Court and so on). A number is added so that the reference is unique and finally, in the case of the Upper Tribunal or the High Court in England and Wales, the relevant chamber of the Upper Tribunal or the relevant division or other part of the High Court is identified (e.g. "(AAC)" for the Administrative Appeals Chamber, "(Admin)" for the Administrative Court and so on). Examples of decisions of the Upper Tribunal and a Northern Ireland Commissioner with their neutral citation numbers are *SSWP v JB (JSA)* [2010] UKUT 4 (AAC) and *AR v DSD (IB)* [2010] NICom 6.

If the case is reported in the Administrative Appeals Chamber Reports or another series of law reports, a reference to the report usually follows the neutral citation number. Conventionally, this includes either the year the case was decided (in round brackets) or the year in which it was reported (in square brackets), followed by the volume number (if any), the name of the series of reports (in abbreviated form—see the Table of Abbreviations at the beginning of each volume of this series) and either the page number or the case number. However, before 2010, cases reported in the Administrative Appeals Chamber Reports or with Commissioners' decisions were numbered in the same way as reported Commissioners' decisions. *Abdirahman v Secretary of State for Work and Pensions* [2007] EWCA Civ 657; [2008] 1 W.L.R. 254 (also reported as *R(IS) 8/07*) is a Court of Appeal decision, decided in 2007 but reported in 2008 in volume 1 of the Weekly Law Reports at p.254 and also in the 2007 volume of reported Commissioners' decisions. *NT v SSWP* [2009] UKUT 37 (AAC), *R(DLA) 1/09* is an Upper Tribunal case decided in 2009 and reported in the Administrative Appeals Chamber Reports in the same year. *Martin v SSWP* [2009] EWCA Civ 1289; [2010] AACR 9 is a decision of the Court of Appeal that was decided in 2009 and was the ninth decision reported in the Administrative Appeals Chamber Reports in 2010.

Using this Book

It is usually necessary to include the neutral citation number or a reference to a series of reports only the first time a decision is cited in any document. After that, the name of the case is usually sufficient.

All decisions of the Upper Tribunal that are on their website have neutral citation numbers. If you wish to refer a tribunal or decision-maker to a decision of the Upper Tribunal that does not have a neutral citation number, contact the office of the Administrative Appeals Chamber (adminappeals@HMCTS.gsi.gov.uk) who will provide a number and add the decision to the website.

Decision-makers and claimants are entitled to assume that judges of both the First-tier Tribunal and the Upper Tribunal have immediate access to reported decisions of Commissioners or the Upper Tribunal and they need not provide copies, although it may sometimes be helpful to do so. However, where either a decision-maker or a claimant intends to rely on an unreported decision, it will be necessary to provide a copy of the decision to the judge and other members of the tribunal. A copy of the decision should also be provided to the other party before the hearing because otherwise it may be necessary for there to be an adjournment to enable that party to take advice on the significance of the decision.

Finding case law

The extensive references described above are used so as to enable people easily to find the full text of a decision. Most decisions of any significance since the late 1990s can be found on the Internet.

Decisions of the Upper Tribunal and of the Commissioners in Great Britain may be found on the HMCTS website at *http://www.osscsc.gov.uk/Decisions/decisions.htm*. This includes reported decisions since 1991 and other decisions considered likely to be of interest to tribunals and tribunal users since about 2000, together with a few older decisions. Decisions of Commissioners in Northern Ireland may be found on *http://www.dsdni.gov.uk/index/law_and_legislation.htm*.

The Administrative Appeals Chamber Reports, which include not only reported decisions of the Administrative Appeals Chamber of the Upper Tribunal but also reported decisions of the Northern Ireland Commissioners and decisions of the courts in related areas of law, are available on the HMCTS website at *http://www.osscsc.gov.uk/Decisions/adminAppealsChamberReports.htm*. They are also published by the Stationery Office in bound volumes which follow on from the bound volumes of Commissioners' decisions published from 1948.

Copies of decisions of the Administrative Appeals Chamber of the Upper Tribunal or of Commissioners that are otherwise unavailable may be obtained from the offices of the Upper Tribunal (Administrative Appeals Chamber) or, in Northern Ireland, from the Office of the Social Security and Child Support Commissioners.

Decisions of a wide variety of courts and tribunals in the United Kingdom may be found on the free website of the British and Irish Legal Information Institute, *http://www.bailii.org*. It includes all decisions of the Supreme Court and provides fairly comprehensive coverage of decisions given since about 1996 by the House of Lords and Privy Council and most of the higher courts in England and Wales, decisions given since 1998 by the Court of Session and decisions given since 2000 by the Court of Appeal and High Court in Northern Ireland. Some earlier decisions have been

Using this Book

included, so it is always worth looking and, indeed, those decisions dating from 1873 or earlier and reported in the English Reports may be found through a link to *http://www.commonlii.org/uk/cases/EngR/*.

Decisions of the European Court of Justice (concerned with the law of the European Union) are all to be found on *http://www.curia.europa.eu*.

Decisions of the European Court of Human Rights are available at *http://www.echr.coe.int*.

Most decisions of the courts in social security cases, including decisions of the European Court of Justice on cases referred by United Kingdom courts and tribunals, are reported in the Administrative Appeals Chamber Reports or with the reported decisions of Commissioners and may therefore be found on the same websites and in the same printed series of reported decisions. So, for example, *R(I) 1/00* contains Commissioner's decision *CSI/12/1998*, the decision of the Court of Session upholding the Commissioner's decision and the decision of the House of Lords in *Chief Adjudication Officer v Faulds*, reversing the decision of the Court of Session. The most important decisions of the courts can also be found in the various series of law reports familiar to lawyers (in particular, in the *Law Reports*, the *Weekly Law Reports*, the *All England Law Reports*, the *Public and Third Sector Law Reports*, the *Industrial Cases Reports* and the *Family Law Reports*) but these are not widely available outside academic or other law libraries, although the *All England Law Reports* are occasionally to be found in the larger public libraries. See the Table of Cases at the beginning of each volume of this series for all the places where a decision mentioned in that volume is reported.

If you know the name or number of a decision and wish to know where in a volume of this series there is a reference to it, use the Table of Cases or the Table of Commissioners' Decisions in the relevant volume to find the paragraph(s) where the decision is mentioned.

Judicial precedent

As already mentioned, decisions of the Upper Tribunal, the Commissioners and the higher courts in Great Britain become *case law* because they set binding precedents which must be followed by decision-makers and the First-tier Tribunal in Great Britain. This means that, where the Upper Tribunal, Commissioner or court has decided a point of legal principle, decision-makers and appeal tribunals must make their decisions in conformity with the decision of the Upper Tribunal, Commissioner or court, applying the same principle and accepting the interpretation of the law contained in the decision. So a decision of the Upper Tribunal, a Commissioner or a superior court explaining what a term in a particular regulation means, lays down the definition of that term in much the same way as if the term had been defined in the regulations themselves. The decision may also help in deciding what the same term means when it is used in a different set of regulations, provided that the term appears to have been used in a similar context.

Only decisions on points of law set precedents that are binding and, strictly speaking, only decisions on points of law that were necessary to the overall conclusion reached by the Upper Tribunal, Commissioner or court are binding. Other parts of a decision (which used to be known as obiter dicta) may be regarded as helpful guidance but need not be followed if a decision-maker or the First-tier Tribunal is persuaded that there is a better approach. It is particularly important to bear this in mind in relation to older decisions of Social Security Commissioners because, until 1987, the right of appeal to a Commissioner was not confined to points of law.

Where there is a conflict between precedents, a decision-maker or the First-tier Tribunal is generally free to choose between decisions of equal status. For these purposes, most decisions of the Upper Tribunal and decisions of Commissioners are of equal status. However, a decision-maker or First-tier Tribunal should generally prefer a reported decision to an unreported one unless the unreported decision was the later decision and the Commissioner or Upper Tribunal expressly decided not to follow the earlier reported decision. This is simply because the fact that a decision has been reported shows that at least half of the relevant judges of the Upper Tribunal or the Commissioners agreed with it at the time. A decision of a Tribunal of Commissioners (i.e. three Commissioners sitting together) or a decision of a three-judge panel of the Upper Tribunal must be preferred to a decision of a single Commissioner or a single judge of the Upper Tribunal.

A single judge of the Upper Tribunal will normally follow a decision of a single Commissioner or another judge of the Upper Tribunal, but is not bound to do so. A three-judge panel of the Upper Tribunal will generally follow a decision of another such panel or of a Tribunal of Commissioners, but similarly is not bound to do so, whereas a single judge of the Upper Tribunal will always follow such a decision.

Strictly speaking, the Northern Ireland Commissioners do not set binding precedent that must be followed in Great Britain but their decisions are relevant, due to the similarity of the legislation in Northern Ireland, and are usually regarded as highly persuasive with the result that, in practice, they are generally given as much weight as decisions of the Great Britain Commissioners. The same approach is taken in Northern Ireland to decisions of the Upper Tribunal on social security matters and to decisions of the Great Britain Commissioners.

Decisions of the superior courts in Great Britain and Northern Ireland on questions of legal principle are almost invariably followed by decision-makers, tribunals and the Upper Tribunal, even when they are not strictly binding because the relevant court was in a different part of the United Kingdom or exercised a parallel—but not superior—jurisdiction.

Decisions of the European Court of Justice come in two parts: the Opinion of the Advocate General and the decision of the Court. It is the decision of the Court which is binding. The Court is assisted by hearing the Opinion of the Advocate General before itself coming to a conclusion on the issue before it. The Court does not always follow its Advocate General. Where it does, the Opinion of the Advocate General often elaborates the arguments in greater detail than the single collegiate judgment of the Court. Decision-makers, tribunals and Commissioners must apply decisions of the European Court of Justice, where relevant to cases before them, in preference to other authorities binding on them.

The European Court of Human Rights in Strasbourg is quite separate from the European Court of Justice in Luxembourg and serves a different purpose: interpreting and applying the European Convention on Human Rights, which is incorporated into United Kingdom law by the Human Rights Act 1998. Since October 2, 2000, public authorities in the United Kingdom, including courts, Commissioners, tribunals and decision-makers, have been required to act in accordance with the incorporated provisions of the Convention, unless statute prevents this. They must take into account

Using this Book

the Strasbourg case law and are required to interpret domestic legislation, so far as it is possible to do so, to give effect to the incorporated Convention rights. Any court or tribunal may declare secondary legislation incompatible with those rights and, in certain circumstances, invalidate it. Only the higher courts can declare a provision of primary legislation to be incompatible with those rights, but no court, tribunal or Upper Tribunal can invalidate primary legislation. The work of the Strasbourg Court and the impact of the Human Rights Act 1998 on social security are discussed in the commentary in Part IV of *Vol III: Administration, Appeals and the European Dimension*.

See the note to s.3(2) of the Tribunals, Courts and Enforcement Act 2007 in Part V of *Vol III: Administration, Appeals and the European Dimension* for a more detailed and technical consideration of the rules of precedent.

Other sources of information and commentary on social security law

For a comprehensive overview of the social security system in Great Britain, CPAG's *Welfare Benefits and Tax Credits Handbook*, published annually each spring, is unrivalled as a practical introduction from the claimant's viewpoint.

From a different perspective, the Department for Work and Pensions publishes the 14-volume *Decision Makers' Guide* at *https://www.gov.uk/government/collections/decision-makers-guide-staff-guide* and the new *Advice for Decision Making*, which covers personal independence payment, universal credit and the "new" versions of Jobseeker's Allowance and Employment and Support Allowance, at *https://www.gov.uk/government/publications/advice-for-decision-making-staff-guide*. Similarly, Her Majesty's Revenue and Customs publish manuals relating to tax credits, child benefit and guardian's allowance, which they administer, see *http://www.hmrc.gov.uk/thelibrary/manuals-a-z.htm*. (Note that the *Child Benefit Technical Manual* also covers guardian's allowance). These guides and manuals are extremely useful but their interpretation of the law is not binding on tribunals and the courts, being merely internal guidance for the use of decision-makers.

There are a number of other sources of valuable information or commentary on social security case law: see in particular publications such as the *Journal of Social Security Law*, CPAG's *Welfare Rights Bulletin*, *Legal Action* and the *Adviser*. As far as online resources go there is little to beat *Rightsnet* (*http://www.rightsnet.org.uk*). This site contains a wealth of resources for people working in the welfare benefits field but of special relevance in this context are the Commissioners/Upper Tribunal Decisions section of the "Toolkit" area and also the "Briefcase" area which contains summaries of the decisions (with links to the full decisions). Sweet and Maxwell's online subscription service *Westlaw* is another valuable source (*http://www.westlaw.co.uk*), as is the Merrill Corporation's *Casetrack* (*http://www.casetrack.com/ct/casetrack.nsf/index?openframeset*) and LexisNexis *Lexis* (*http://www.lexis.com*).

Conclusion

The Internet provides a vast resource but a search needs to be focused. Social security schemes are essentially statutory and so in Great Britain the legislation which is set out in this series forms the basic structure of social security law. However, the case law shows how the legislation should be interpreted and applied. The commentary in this series should point the way to the case law relevant to each provision and the Internet can then be used to find it where that is necessary.

MAJOR CHANGES TO CREDITS AND BENEFITS

The Coalition Government announced major changes to the credits and benefits detailed in this volume in its 2010 Budget. Those that had taken effect beyond the extent of limited pilot measures by April 2013 are covered in this volume. Further measures are contained, in particular, in the Welfare Reform Act 2012 but are not to take effect, on a national basis, until later in 2013 or 2014. These are not covered in this volume.

Tax credits: general

The separate tax credits are being phased out of the legislation. The strategy that has been adopted is to merge them into the new universal credit by stages. The relevant legislation, including the prospective repeal of the Tax Credits Act 2002 and all regulations made under it, is in the Welfare Reform Act 2012. That Act also contains powers to transfer any relevant administrative powers and duties from HMRC to the Secretary of State for Work and Pensions. This process started in April 2013 with a very limited pilot scheme. It is currently expected that it will take a further four years for the process to be completed. At the time of writing we await the July 2015 budget of the newly elected UK Government and details of forthcoming cuts to benefits and tax credits. Given the lack of detail during the general election campaign, forward speculation is plainly of no value at this stage.

Other changes

Although the attempted integration of tax credits and income tax is coming to an end, the Government has not hesitated to use the personal tax system in parallel with the social security system to achieve other aims. One example of a new technique is the imposition, from January 2013, of income tax liability on higher rate earners who receive child benefit. The effective result under the relevant tax legislation is to remove any economic gain from an earner with earnings of over £60,000 who claims child benefit, with a reduction in economic value by means of the imposition of a 50 per cent tax rate on child benefit received by those earning over £50,000. By contrast, there have been linked changes to the tax treatment of childcare charges.

The real value of child benefit and some elements of tax credits is being eroded, as with some other social security benefits, by an absence of any cost of living increase for 2013/14 and, in the case of the income tax disregard for tax credits, a reduction of the figure from the previous year.

CHANGE OF NAME FROM DEPARTMENT OF SOCIAL SECURITY TO DEPARTMENT FOR WORK AND PENSIONS

The Secretaries of State for Education and Skills and for Work and Pensions Order 2002 (SI 2002/1397) makes provision for the change of name from the Department of Social Security to Department for Work and Pensions. Article 9(5) provides:

"(5) Subject to article 12 [which makes specific amendments], any enactment or instrument passed or made before the coming into force of this Order shall have effect, so far as may be necessary for the purposes of or in consequence of the entrusting to the Secretary of State for Work and Pensions of the social security functions, as if any reference to the Secretary of State for Social Security, to the Department of Social Security or to an officer of the Secretary of State for Social Security (including any reference which is to be construed as such as reference) were a reference to the Secretary of State for Work and Pensions, to the Department for Work and Pensions or, as the case may be, to an officer of the Secretary of State for Work and Pensions."

CHANGES IN TERMINOLOGY CONSEQUENT UPON THE ENTRY INTO FORCE OF THE TREATY OF LISBON

Note that The Treaty of Lisbon (Changes in Terminology) Order 2011 (SI 2011/1043) (which came into force on April 22, 2011) makes a number of changes to terminology used in primary and secondary legislation as a consequence of the entry into force of the Treaty of Lisbon. The Order accomplishes this by requiring certain terms in primary and secondary legislation to be read in accordance with the requirements of the Order. No substantive changes to the law are involved.

The changes are somewhat complex because of the different ways in which the term "Community" is used, and the abbreviations "EC" or "EEC" are used. References to the "European Community", "European Communities", "European Coal and Steel Communities", "the Community", "the EC" and "the EEC" are generally to be read as references to the "European Union."

The following table shows the more common usages involving the word "Community" in the first column which are now to be read in the form set out in the second column:

Original term	**To be read as**
Community treaties	EU treaties
Community institution	EU institution
Community instrument	EU instrument
Community obligation	EU obligation
Enforceable Community right	Enforceable EU right
Community law, or European Community law	EU law
Community legislation, or European Community legislation	EU legislation
Community provision, or European Community provision	EU provision

Provision is also made for changes to certain legislation relating to Wales in the Welsh language.

Relevant extracts from the Order can be found in Volume III, *Administration, Adjudication and the European Dimension*.

THE MARRIAGE (SAME SEX COUPLES) ACT 2013

The Marriage (Same Sex Couples) Act 2013 (c.30) provides in s.3 and Schedules 3 and 4 that the terms "marriage", "married couple" and being "married" in existing and future legislation in England and Wales are to be read as references to a marriage between persons of the same sex. The same approach is taken to any legislation about couples living together as if married. This is subject to certain specified exclusions contained in Schedule 4, and in any Order providing for a contrary approach to be taken.

Schedule 2 to The Marriage (Same Sex Couples) Act 2013 (Consequential and Contrary Provisions and Scotland) Order 2014 (SI 2014/560) contains a substantial list of contrary provisions to s.11(1) and (2) and paragraphs 1 to 3 of Schedule 3 to the 2013 Act. Most of these relate to specific enactments, but note that Part 2 of the Schedule provides that s.11(1) and (2) do not apply to "EU instruments". This term is defined in Schedule 1 to the European Communities Act 1972 (as amended) as "any instrument issued by an EU institution". It refers mainly to regulations, directives, decisions, recommendations and opinions issued by the institutions.

TABLE OF CASES

AA v HMRC (TC) [2012] UKUT 121 (AAC) **2.285, 2.406**
Abdirahman v Secretary of State for Work and Pensions [2007] EWCA Civ 657; [2008] 1 W.L.R. 254; [2007] 4 All E.R. 882; [2007] 3 C.M.L.R. 37; [2007] Eu. L.R. 814 .... 2.422
AD v Secretary of State for Work and Pensions [2009] UKUT 46 (AAC) 3.5
AG v HMRC (TC) [2013] UKUT 530 (AAC) **1.387**
Alabaster v Barclays Bank Plc and Secretary of State for Social Security. *See* Alabaster v Woolwich Plc (CA)
Alabaster v Woolwich Plc (C-147/02) [2005] All E.R. (EC) 490; [2004] E.C.R. I-3101; [2004] 2 C.M.L.R. 9; [2004] C.E.C. 261; [2005] I.C.R. 695; [2004] I.R.L.R. 486 ECJ 1.97, 5.37
Alabaster v Woolwich Plc; sub nom Alabaster v Barclays Bank Plc and Secretary of State for Social Security[2005] EWCA Civ 508; [2005] 2 C.M.L.R. 19; [2005] Eu. L.R. 824; [2005] I.C.R. 1246; [2005] I.R.L.R. 576 .... 1.98, 5.37
Alabaster v Woolwich Plc (Reference to ECJ) [2002] EWCA Civ 211; [2002] 1 C.M.L.R. 56; [2002] I.R.L.R. 420 .... **1–97**
Ali v Birmingham City Council; Tomlinson v Birmingham City Council [2010] UKSC 8; [2010] 2 A.C. 39; [2010] 2 W.L.R. 471; [2010] 2 All E.R. 175; [2010] P.T.S.R. 524; [2010] H.R.L.R. 18; [2010] U.K.H.R.R. 417; [2010] H.L.R. 22; [2010] B.L.G.R. 401; (2010) 154(7) S.J.L.B. 37 .... **1.319**
AR-L v HMRC (TC) [2015] UKUT 303 (AAC) 1.386
AS v HMRC (CB) [2013] NI Comm. 15 .... 3.37
Barber v Secretary of State for Social Security. *See* R. (on the application of Barber) v Secretary of State for Work and Pensions
Bressol v Gouvernement de la Communauté Française [2010] 3 C.M.L.R. 559 .... 3.37
Brown v Chief Adjudication Officer [1997] I.C.R. 266; [1997] I.R.L.R. 110; (1996) 93(42) L.S.G. 28; (1996) 140 S.J.L.B. 221 CA (Civ Div) **1.72**
Cenlon Finance Co Ltd v Ellwood (Inspector of Taxes) [1962] A.C. 782; [1962] 2 W.L.R. 871; [1962] 1 All E.R. 854; 40 T.C. 176; (1962) 41 A.T.C. 11; [1962] T.R. 1; (1962) 106 S.J. 280 HL 1.20
Centre Public d'Aide Sociale, Courcelles v Lebon (316/85) [1987] E.C.R. 2811; [1989] 1 C.M.L.R. 337 ECJ 1.613
Chester v Secretary of State for Social Security. *See* R. (on the application of Chester) v Secretary of State for Social Security
Chief Adjudication Officer v Ellis. *See* R(IS) 22/95
CI v HMRC (TC) [2014] UKUT 158 (AAC) **1.320**
Clixby v Pountney [1968] Ch. 719; [1968] 2 W.L.R. 865; [1968] 1 All E.R. 802; 44 T.C. 575; (1967) 46 A.T.C. 398; [1967] T.R. 383; 117 N.L.J. 1343; (1968) 112 S.J. 16 Ch D 1.362
CM v HMRC (TC) [2010] UKUT 400 (AAC) 2.199
Customs and Excise Commrs v Medway Draughting and Technical Services Ltd [1989] S.T.C. 346; [1989] B.T.C. 5070; [1989] C.O.D. 497 QBD 1.363
DG v HMRC (TC) [2013] UKUT 0631 (AAC) **1.275**
Edwards (Inspector of Taxes) v Clinch [1982] A.C. 845; [1981] 3 W.L.R. 707; [1981] 3 All E.R. 543; [1981] S.T.C. 617; 56 T.C. 367; [1981] T.R. 393; (1981) 125 S.J. 762 HL 2.129
EG v HMRC (TC) [2011] UKUT 467 .... **1.273**, 2.406
EM v HMRC (TC) [2010] UKUT 323 (AAC) **1.272**
Ensign Tankers (Leasing) Ltd v Stokes (Inspector of Taxes) [1992] 1 A.C. 655; [1992] 2 W.L.R. 469; [1992] 2 All E.R. 275; [1992] S.T.C. 226; 64 T.C. 617; [1992] S.T.I. 364; (1992) 89(17) L.S.G. 49; (1992) 136 S.J.L.B. 89 HL 2.147
Fitzpatrick v Sterling Housing Association Ltd [2001] 1 A.C. 27; [1999] 3 W.L.R. 1113; [1999] 4 All E.R. 705; [2000] 1 F.L.R. 271; [1999] 2 F.L.R. 1027; [2000] 1

xxxiii

Table of Cases

F.C.R. 21; [2000] U.K.H.R.R. 25; 7 B.H.R.C. 200; (2000) 32 H.L.R. 178; [2000] L. & T.R. 44; [2000] Fam. Law 14; [1999] E.G. 125 (C.S.); (1999) 96(43) L.S.G. 3; [1999] N.P.C. 127; (2000) 79 P. & C.R. D4 HL 6.72
FK v HMRC [2009] UKUT 134 (AAC)..**2.407**
Flemming v Secretary of State for Work and Pensions. *See* R(G) 2/02
GC v HMRC (TC) [2014] UKUT 251 (AAC) 2.32, **2.424**
Ghaidan v Godin-Mendoza [2004] UKHL 30; [2004] 2 A.C. 557; [2004] 3 W.L.R. 113; [2004] 3 All E.R. 411; [2004] 2 F.L.R. 600; [2004] 2 F.C.R. 481; [2004] H.R.L.R. 31; [2004] U.K.H.R.R. 827; 16 B.H.R.C. 671; [2004] H.L.R. 46; [2005] 1 P. & C.R. 18; [2005] L. & T.R. 3; [2004] 2 E.G.L.R. 132; [2004] Fam. Law 641; [2004] 27 E.G. 128 (C.S.); (2004) 101(27) L.S.G. 30; (2004) 154 N.L.J. 1013; (2004) 148 S.J.L.B. 792; [2004] N.P.C. 100; [2004] 2 P. & C.R. DG17........6.72
Gillespie v Northern Health and Social Services Board (No.2) [1997] N.I. 190; [1997] Eu. L.R. 566; [1997] I.R.L.R. 410 CA (NI) 1.97
GJ v HMRC (TC) [2013] UKUT 561 (AAC)..**2.197**
Gladders v Prior (Inspector of Taxes) [2003] S.T.C. (S.C.D.) 245; [2003] S.T.I. 946 Sp Commrs 1.363
Gray (Inspector of Taxes) v Matheson [1993] 1 W.L.R. 1130; [1993] S.T.C. 178; 65 T.C. 577; [1993] S.T.I. 214; (1993) 90(10) L.S.G. 36; (1993) 137 S.J.L.B. 46 Ch D 1.20
Great Western Railway Co v Bater (Surveyor of Taxes) [1920] 3 K.B. 266 BD.............2.129
Grzelczyk v Centre Public d'Aide Sociale d'Ottignies Louvain la Neuve (C-184/99) [2003] All E.R. (EC) 385; [2001] E.C.R. I-6193; [2002] 1 C.M.L.R. 19; [2002] I.C.R. 566 ECJ...1.613
Hillenbrand v IRC, 1966 S.L.T. 213; 42 T.C. 617; (1966) 45 A.T.C. 224; [1966] T.R. 201 IH (1 Div) 1.362
Hinchy v Secretary of State for Work and Pensions [2005] UKHL 16; [2005] 1 W.L.R. 967; [2005] 2 All E.R. 129; (2005) 102(17) L.S.G. 32; (2005) 149 S.J.L.B. 299 .... 1.289, 1.318
HMRC v CB (TC) [2013] UKUT 484 (AAC)...**2.79**
HMRC v DH [2005] UKUT 24 (AAC)..2.196
HMRC v DH [2009] UKUT 24 (AAC).. **1.304**, 2.199
HMRC v PD (TC) [2012] UKUT 230 (AAC)................................ **1.272, 1.275**, 1.277
HMRC v Ruas [2010] EWCA Civ 291; [2010] AACR 31 .... **1.58**, 3.31
Hudson v Humbles (1965) 42 T.C. 380; (1965) 44 A.T.C. 124; [1965] T.R. 135; (1965) 109 S.J. 315 ....1.362
Humphreys v Revenue and Customs Commrs [2012] UKSC 18; [2012] 1 W.L.R. 1545; [2012] P.T.S.R. 1024; [2012] Eq. L.R. 714; [2012] S.T.I. 1664; (2012) 162 N.L.J. 712; (2012) 156(20) S.J.L.B. 31 ....**1.304**
IRC v Lysaght [1928] A.C. 234; [1928] All E.R. Rep. 575; 13 T.C. 511 HL.................2.418
JI v HMRC [2013] UKUT 199 (AAC) **1.19, 1.272, 1.394**, 2.198, **2.280, 2.386**
JL v HMRC (TC) [2013] UKUT 325 (AAC) 1.274, **2.316**
JN v HMRC (TC) [2010] UKUT 288 (AAC)...**2.212**
Jones v Leeming [1930] A.C. 415 HL..2.147
JP v HMRC (TC) [2013] UKUT 519 (AAC) **1.388, 2.435**
JR v HMRC [2009] UKUT 18 (AAC) 3.31
JR v HMRC [2015] UKUT 192 (AAC)... **1.328**, 1.388
King v United Kingdom (13881/02) [2005] S.T.C. 438; (2005) 41 E.H.R.R. 2; 76 T.C. 699; [2007] B.T.C. 85; 7 I.T.L. Rep. 339; [2004] S.T.I. 2396 ECHR................1.363
KN v HMRC [2009] UKUT 79 (AAC)..**2.198**
KT v HMRC [2013] UKUT 0151 (AAC) **1.58**
Leeves v Chief Adjudication Officer [1999] E.L.R. 90 CA (Civ Div) 2.160
Levene v IRC [1928] A.C. 217; [1928] All E.R. Rep. 746; 13 T.C. 486 HL.................2.418
LV v HMRC (TC) [2010] UKUT 483 (AAC) **2.313, 2.318**
Martinez Sala v Freistaat Bayern (C–85/96) [1998] E.C.R. I–2691 .... 1.58, 1.613
Meyers v Adjudication Officer (C–116/94) [1995] All E.R. (E.C.) 705; [1995] E.C.R. I-2131; [1996] 1 C.M.L.R. 461; [1995] I.R.L.R. 498 ECJ (4th Chamber)..............1.314
MI v HMRC [2009] UKUT 73 (AAC)..**2.407**
ML v HMRC (TC) [2015] UKUT 166 (AAC) **2.212**
Morrell v Secretary of State for Work and Pensions [2003] EWCA Civ 526................2.160
Moxon v Ipsos-RSL Ltd [2002] All E.R. (D) 109 EAT 4.13
Mulvey v Secretary of State for Social Security, 1997 S.C. (H.L.) 105; 1997 S.L.T. 753; 1997 S.C.L.R. 348; [1997] B.P.I.R. 696 HL 1.629

Table of Cases

Nethermere (St Neots) Ltd v Gardiner [1984] I.C.R. 612; [1984] I.R.L.R. 240; (1984) 81 L.S.G. 2147; (1984) 134 N.L.J. 544; CA (Civ Div)..**2.34**
North Yorkshire Police Authority v Revenue and Customs Commrs; sub nom Wade and North Yorkshire Police Authority v HMRC [2011] I.R.L.R. 393 UT (TC) 1.95, **5.6**
Nu-Swift International Ltd v Mallinson [1979] I.C.R. 157; [1978] I.R.L.R. 537 EAT....1.92
OFCOM v Morrissey and Information Commr [2011] UKUT 116 (AAC) 1.387
Oxfam v Revenue and Customs Commrs [2009] EWHC 3078 (Ch); [2010] S.T.C. 686; [2010] B.V.C. 108; [2010] A.C.D. 50; [2010] S.T.I. 556 ....1.387
Patmalniece v Secretary of State for Work and Pensions [2011] UKSC 11; [2011] 1 W.L.R. 783; [2011] 3 All E.R. 1; [2011] P.T.S.R. 680; [2011] 2 C.M.L.R. 45; [2011] Eq. L.R. 508; (2011) 108(13) L.S.G. 23; (2011) 155(11) S.J.L.B. 31............3.37
PD v HMRC and CD (TC) [2010] UKUT 159 (AAC).................................... 1.296, 2.378
PM v United Kingdom (6638/03) [2005] S.T.C. 1566; [2005] 3 F.C.R. 101; (2006) 42 E.H.R.R. 45; 18 B.H.R.C. 668; 7 I.T.L. Rep. 970 ECHR................................**1.363**
R. v Allen (Brian Roger) [2001] UKHL 45; [2002] 1 A.C. 509; [2001] 3 W.L.R. 843; [2001] 4 All E.R. 768; [2001] S.T.C. 1537; [2002] 1 Cr. App. R. 18; [2002] H.R.L.R. 4; 74 T.C. 263; [2001] B.T.C. 421; 4 I.T.L. Rep. 140; [2001] S.T.I. 1348..1.363
R. v Barnet LBC Ex p Shah (Nilish); sub nom Shah v Barnet LBC [1983] 2 A.C. 309; [1983] 2 W.L.R. 16; [1983] 1 All E.R. 226; 81 L.G.R. 305; (1983) 133 N.L.J. 61; (1983) 127 S.J. 36 HL...2.418
R. v Secretary of State for the Home Department Ex p Saleem; sub nom R. (on the application of Saleem) v Secretary of State for the Home Department [2001] 1 W.L.R. 443; [2000] 4 All E.R. 814; [2000] Imm. A.R. 529; [2000] I.N.L.R. 413 CA (Civ Div) 2.380
R. (on the application of Barber) v Secretary of State for Social Security; sub nom Barber v Secretary of State for Social Security [2002] EWHC 1915 (Admin); [2002] 2 F.L.R. 1181; [2002] Fam. Law 888; (2002) 99(36) L.S.G. 40...... 1.181, 1.182
R. (on the application of Bidar) v Ealing LBC (C-209/03) [2005] Q.B. 812; [2005] 2 W.L.R. 1078; [2005] All E.R. (EC) 687; [2005] E.C.R. I-2119; [2005] 2 C.M.L.R. 3; [2005] C.E.C. 607; [2005] E.L.R. 404 ECJ.. 1.613, 1.614
R. (on the application of Chester) v Secretary of State for Social Security; sub nom Chester v Secretary of State for Social Security [2001] EWHC Admin 1119.. 1.181, 1.182
R. (on the application of D) v Secretary of State For Work and Pensions [2004] EWCA Civ 1468 ....3.37
R. (on the application of Ford) v Revenue and Customs Commrs [2005] EWHC 1109 (Admin) 1.181
R. (on the application of Saleem) v Secretary of State for the Home Department. *See* R. v Secretary of State for the Home Department Ex p Saleem
R. (on the application of Sier) v Cambridge City Council HBRB [2001] EWCA Civ 1523..2.435
Ransom (Inspector of Taxes) v Higgs [1974] 1 W.L.R. 1594; [1974] 3 All E.R. 949; [1974] S.T.C. 539; [1974] T.R. 281; (1974) 118 S.J. 849 HL.................................2.147
Reina v Landeskreditbank Baden-Württemberg (C–65/81) [1982] E.C.R. 33; [1982] 1 C.M.L.R. 744 ECJ (3rd Chamber)..1.613
Revenue and Customs Commrs v Spiridonova [2014] NICA 63 ....3.31, 3.37
Revenue and Customs Commrs v Thorn Baker Ltd [2007] EWCA Civ 626; [2008] I.C.R. 46; 79 T.C. 1; (2007) 104(28) L.S.G. 29; (2007) 151 S.J.L.B. 890.............**1.194**
SB v HMRC [2013] UKUT 24 (AAC) **1.48**
Scorer (Inspector of Taxes) v Olin Energy Systems Ltd [1985] A.C. 645; [1985] 2 W.L.R. 668; [1985] 2 All E.R. 375; [1985] S.T.C. 218; (1985) 82 L.S.G. 1943; (1985) 129 S.J. 248 HL...1.20
Seaton v HMRC Commrs [2011] UKUT 297 (TCC)................................**1.72**, 1.90, **1.194**
Secretary of State for Social Services v Smith [1983] 1 W.L.R. 1110; [1983] 3 All E.R. 173; (1983) 80 L.S.G. 2684; (1983) 127 S.J. 663 CA (Civ Div) 1.61, 1.181
Secretary of State for Work and Pensions v Deane [2010] EWCA Civ 699; [2011] 1 W.L.R. 743; [2011] P.T.S.R. 289; [2010] E.L.R. 662; (2010) 107(27) L.S.G. 17..... 3.5
Secretary of State for Work and Pensions v HMRC (TC) [2014] UKUT 383 (AAC) ...1.278
Secretary of State for Work and Pensions v TB and HMRC (RP) [2010] UKUT 88 (AAC); [2010] AACR 38 ....1.228
SG v HMRC (TC) [2011] UKUT 199 ....1.319, 1.330, 1.387

Table of Cases

SH v HMRC and SC (TC) [2013] UKUT 0297 (AAC) **1.386, 1.388**
Shah v Barnet LBC. *See* R. v Barnet LBC Ex p Shah (Nilish)
Sharkey v De Croos. *See* Sharkey v Revenue and Customs Commr
Sharkey v Revenue and Customs Commr; sub nom Sharkey v De Croos [2005] S.T.C.
    (S.C.D.) 336; [2005] S.T.I. 223 Sp Commrs 1.363
Shilton v Wilmshurst (Inspector of Taxes) [1991] 1 A.C. 684; [1991] 2 W.L.R. 530;
    [1991] 3 All E.R. 148; [1991] S.T.C. 88; 64 T.C. 78; (1991) 135 S.J. 250 HL 2.35
SP v HMRC [2009] UKUT (AAC) 2.292
Spence v HMRC Commrs [2012] UKFTT 213 .... 1.90, 4.38
SW v Secretary of State for Work and Pensions (IS) [2011] UKUT 145 (AAC) 1.275
Taylor Gordon & Co Ltd (t/a Plan Personnel) v Timmons [2004] I.R.L.R. 180; (2003)
    100(44) L.S.G. 32 EAT 1.63, **1.228**
TM v HMRC (TC) [2013] UKUT 444 (AAC) **1.388**
Tomlinson v Birmingham City Council. *See* Ali v Birmingham City Council
W v L [1974] Q.B. 711; [1973] 3 W.L.R. 859; [1973] 3 All E.R. 884; 72 L.G.R. 36;
    (1973) 4 Fam. Law 134; (1973) 117 S.J. 775 CA (Civ Div) 2.99
Wade and North Yorkshire Police Authority v HMRC. *See* North Yorkshire Police
    Authority v Revenue and Customs Commrs
Whelan v Chief Adjudication Officer, *Independent*, 14 November 1994 .... 2.198
WW v HM Revenue and Customs [2011] UKUT 11 (AAC) **1.289**
Zalewska v Department for Social Development [2008] UKHL 67; [2008] 1 W.L.R.
    2602; [2009] 2 All E.R. 319; [2009] N.I. 116; [2009] 1 C.M.L.R. 24; [2009] Eu.
    L.R. 344; (2008) 158 N.L.J. 1643; (2008) 152(45) S.J.L.B. 27 .... **2.422, 3.37**
ZB v HMRC [2015] UKUT 198 (AAC) **1.328**, 1.388
ZM and AB v HMRC (TC) [2013] UKUT 547 (AAC) **1.319**

TABLE OF COMMISSIONERS' DECISIONS 1948–2009

C6/05–06(IS)	2.422	CTC/244/2008	1.319, 1.347
CCS/6302/1999	2.380	CTC/2878/2008	2.292
CCS/2288/2005	2.380	CTC/3611/2008	1.295
CDWA/3123/1997	2.92, 2.93	CTC/3692/2008	1.319, 1.401, 2.407
CF/3348/2002	1.48, 1.180	CTC/1853/2009	1.272
CF/1968/2007	3.41	CTC/616/2011	2.326
CF/2266/2007	1.58	CTC/0838/2011	2.407
CF/2826/2008	1.180	CTC/3443/2012	2.37
CFC/1537/1995	2.197, 2.198	CTC/135/2013	2.197
CG/60/92	1.34, 1.35	CTC/2409/2013	2.199
CG/2973/2004	2.380	R3/74 (P)	1.34
CIB/303/1999	2.380	R3/75 (P)	1.34
CIS/49/1991	2.198	R(A) 2/92	2.99, 2.100
CIS/995/2004	1.269, 1.321, 2.275, 2.277	R(A) 2/06	2.378
CIS/2559/2005	2.422	R(DLA) 3/05	2.380
CIS/2680/2005	2.422	R(F) 3/60	3.9
CIS/3573/2005	2.422	R(F) 2/79	1.48, 2.197
CIS/1813/2007	2.316	R(F) 2/81	1.48, 2.197
CIS/2457/2008	1.181	R(F) 3/81	1.180, 3.46
CPC/2920/2005	2.422	R(F) 1/82(S)	1.61
CSG/8/92	1.35	R(F) 4/85	1.180, 3.46
CSIS/48/1992	1.268	R(F) 1/93	3.5
CSTC/326/2003	1.264	R(F) 1/08	1.61, 1.181
CSTC/76/2006	2.57, 2.81	R(FC) 2/90	1.307
CSTC/724/2006	1.272	R(FC) 1/92	2.37
CTC/2090/2004	1.277, 2.378	R(FIS) 1/86	2.35
CTC/2576/2004	1.327	R(G) 3/68	1.34, 1.35
CTC/3059/2004	1.276, 1.276	R(G) 2/83	1.34, 1.35
CTC/3543/2004	1.277	R(G) 4/83(T)	1.40
CTC/3864/2004	1.272, 1.276	R(G) 2/02	3.5
CTC/4390/2004	1.326, 2.199, 2.378	R(IB) 2/04	1.319
CTC/262/2005	2.435	R(IS) 12/92	1.307
CTC/643/2005	2.57	R(IS) 22/95	2.35, 2.37
CTC/2612/2005	2.378	R(IS) 9/98	2.407
CTC/2662/2005	1.332, 1.355	R(IS) 8/07	2.422
CTC/3981/2005	1.327	R(M) 1/85	2.418
CTC/31/2006	1.319, 1.387	R(M) 2/89	2.91
CTC/1594/2006	1.330, 1.388	R(S) 11/51	2.90
CTC/2103/2006	2.37	R(S) 24/54	4.5, 4.6
CTC/2113/2006	1.293, 1.332, 2.133, 2.223	R(S) 1/72	4.5
CTC/3981/2006	1.355	R(S) 4/93	4.5, 4.6
CTC/1586/2007	2.378	R(SB) 17/81	1.276
CTC/1686/2007	2.199	R(SB) 19/83	2.380
CTC/1907/2007	1.355	R(SB) 55/83	2.380
CTC/2270/2007	1.296, 1.355, 2.254	R(SSP) 1/85	4.13
CTC/3096/2007	2.199	R(SSP) 1/86	1.195
CTC/3646/2007	2.75	R(SSP) 1/89	4.38
		R(TC) 2/05	1.277

TABLE OF ABBREVIATIONS USED IN THIS SERIES

1975 Act	Social Security Act 1975
1977 Act	Marriage (Scotland) Act 1977
1979 Act	Pneumoconiosis (Workers' Compensation) Act 1979
1986 Act	Social Security Act 1986
1996 Act	Employment Rights Act 1996
1998 Act	Social Security Act 1998
2002 Act	Tax Credits Act 2002
2004 Act	Gender Recognition Act 2004
2006 Act	Armed Forces Act 2006
2008 Act	Child Maintenance and Other Payments Act 2008
2013 Act	Marriage (Same Sex Couples) Act 2013
2014 Act	Marriage and Civil Partnership (Scotland) Act 2014
A1P1	Art.1 of Protocol 1 to the European Convention on Human Rights
AA	Attendance Allowance
AA 1992	Attendance Allowance Act 1992
AAC	Administrative Appeals Chamber
AACR	Administrative Appeals Chamber Reports
A.C.	Law Reports, Appeal Cases
A.C.D.	Administrative Court Digest
Admin	Administrative Court
Admin L.R.	Administrative Law Reports
Administration Act	Social Security Administration Act 1992
Administration Regulations	Statutory Paternity Pay and Statutory Adoption Pay (Administration) Regulations 2002
AIP	assessed income period
All E.R.	All England Reports
All E.R. (E.C.)	All England Reports (European Cases)
AMA	Adjudicating Medical Authorities
AO	Adjudication Officer; Authorised Officer
AOG	*Adjudication Officers Guide*
art.	article
Art.	Article
ASD	Autistic Spectrum Disorder
ASPP	Additional Statutory Paternity Pay

Table of Abbreviations used in this Series

A.T.C.	Annotated Tax Cases
Attendance Allowance Regulations	Social Security (Attendance Allowance) Regulations 1991
AWT	All Work Test
BA	Benefits Agency
Benefits Act	Social Security Contributions and Benefits Act 1992
B.H.R.C.	Butterworths Human Rights Cases
B.L.G.R.	Butterworths Local Government Reports
Blue Books	*The Law Relating to Social Security*, Vols 1–11
B.P.I.R.	Bankruptcy and Personal Insolvency Reports
B.T.C.	British Tax Cases
BTEC	Business and Technology Education Council
B.V.C.	British Value Added Tax Reporter
B.W.C.C.	Butterworths Workmen's Compensation Cases
c.	chapter
C	Commissioner's decision
C&BA 1992	Social Security Contributions and Benefits Act 1992
CAA 2001	Capital Allowances Act 2001
CAB	Citizens Advice Bureau
CAO	Chief Adjudication Officer
CB	Child Benefit
CBA 1975	Child Benefit Act 1975
CBJSA	Contribution-Based Jobseeker's Allowance
C.C.L. Rep.	Community Care Law Reports
CCM	HMRC *New Tax Credits Claimant Compliance Manual*
C.E.C.	European Community Cases
CERA	cortical evoked response audiogram
CESA	Contribution-based Employment and Support Allowance
CFS	chronic fatigue syndrome
Ch.	Chancery Division Law Reports; Chapter
Citizenship Directive	Directive 2004/38/EC of the European Parliament and of the Council of April 29, 2004
CJEC	Court of Justice of the European Communities
CJEU	Court of Justice of the European Union
Claims and Payments Regulations	Social Security (Claims and Payments) Regulations 1987
Claims and Payments Regulations 1979	Social Security (Claims and Payments) Regulations 1979
CM	Case Manager
CMA	Chief Medical Adviser
CMEC	Child Maintenance and Enforcement Commission

Table of Abbreviations used in this Series

C.M.L.R.	Common Market Law Reports
C.O.D.	Crown Office Digest
COLL	*Collective Investment Schemes Sourcebook*
Community, The	European Community
Computation of Earnings Regulations	Social Security Benefit (Computation of Earnings) Regulations 1978
Computation of Earnings Regulations 1996	Social Security Benefit (Computation of Earnings) Regulations 1996
Consequential Provisions Act	Social Security (Consequential Provisions) Act 1992
Contributions and Benefits Act	Social Security Contributions and Benefits Act 1992
Contributions Regulations	Social Security (Contributions) Regulations 2001
CP	Carer Premium; Chamber President
CPAG	Child Poverty Action Group
CPR	Civil Procedure Rules
Cr. App. R.	Criminal Appeal Reports
CRCA 2005	Commissioners for Revenue and Customs Act 2005
Credits Regulations 1974	Social Security (Credits) Regulations 1974
Credits Regulations 1975	Social Security (Credits) Regulations 1975
Crim. L.R.	Criminal Law Review
CRU	Compensation Recovery Unit
CSA 1995	Children (Scotland) Act 1995
CSIH	Inner House of the Court of Session (Scotland)
CSM	Child Support Maintenance
CS(NI)O 1995	Child Support (Northern Ireland) Order 1995
CSOH	Outer House of the Court of Session (Scotland)
CSPSSA 2000	Child Support, Pensions and Social Security Act 2000
CTA	Common Travel Area
CTA 2009	Corporation Tax Act 2009
CTA 2010	Corporation Tax Act 2010
CTB	Council Tax Benefit
CTC	Child Tax Credit
CTC Regulations	Child Tax Credit Regulations 2002
CTF	child trust fund
CTS	Carpal Tunnel Syndrome
DAT	Disability Appeal Tribunal
dB	decibels
DCA	Department for Constitutional Affairs
DCP	Disabled Child Premium
Decisions and Appeals Regulations 1999	Social Security Contributions (Decisions and Appeals) Regulations 1999

xli

Table of Abbreviations used in this Series

Dependency Regulations	Social Security Benefit (Dependency) Regulations 1977
DfEE	Department for Education and Employment
DHSS	Department of Health and Social Security
Disability Living Allowance Regulations	Social Security (Disability Living Allowance) Regulations
DIY	do it yourself
DLA	Disability Living Allowance
DLA Regs 1991	Social Security (Disability Living Allowance) Regulations 1991
DLAAB	Disability Living Allowance Advisory Board
DLADWAA 1991	Disability Living Allowance and Disability Working Allowance Act 1991
DM	Decision Maker
DMA	Decision-making and Appeals
DMG	*Decision Makers' Guide*
DMP	Delegated Medical Practitioner
DP	Disability Premium
DPTC	Disabled Person's Tax Credit
DRO	Debt Relief Order
DSD	Department for Social Development (Northern Ireland)
DSS	Department of Social Security
DTI	Department of Trade and Industry
DWA	Disability Working Allowance
DWP	Department for Work and Pensions
DWPMS	Department for Work and Pensions Medical Service
EAA	Extrinsic Allergic Alveolitis
EAT	Employment Appeal Tribunal
EC	European Community
ECHR	European Convention on Human Rights
ECJ	European Court of Justice
E.C.R.	European Court Reports
ECSC	European Coal and Steel Community
ECSMA	European Convention on Social and Medical Assistance
EEA	European Economic Area
EEC	European Economic Community
EESSI	Electronic Exchange of Social Security Information
E.G.	Estates Gazette
E.G.L.R.	Estates Gazette Law Reports
EHC plan	education, health and care plan
EHIC	European Health Insurance Card

Table of Abbreviations used in this Series

EHRC	European Human Rights Commission
E.H.R.R.	European Human Rights Reports
EL	employers' liability
E.L.R	Education Law Reports
EMA	Education Maintenance Allowance
EMP	Examining Medical Practitioner
Employment and Support Allowance Regulations	Employment and Support Allowance Regulations 2008
EPS	extended period of sickness
Eq. L.R.	Equality Law Reports
ERA	evoked response audiometry
ERA scheme	Employment, Retention and Advancement scheme
ES	Employment Service
ESA	Employment and Support Allowance
ESA Regs 2013	Employment and Support Allowance Regulations 2013
ESA Regulations	Employment and Support Allowance Regulations 2008
ESA WCAt	Employment and Support Allowance Work Capability Assessment
ESE Scheme	Employment, Skills and Enterprise Scheme
ESE Regulations	Jobseeker's Allowance (Employment, Skills and Enterprise Scheme) Regulations 2011
ESES Regulations	Jobseeker's Allowance (Employment, Skills and Enterprise Scheme) Regulations 2011
ETA 1973	Employment and Training Act 1973
ETA(NI) 1950	Employment and Training Act (Northern Ireland) 1950
ETS	European Treaty Series
EU	European Union
Eu.L.R.	European Law Reports
EWCA Civ	Civil Division of the Court of Appeal (England and Wales)
EWHC Admin	Administrative Court Division of the High Court (England and Wales)
FA 1993	Finance Act 1993
FA 1996	Finance Act 1996
FA 2004	Finance Act 2004
Fam. Law	Family Law
FAS	Financial Assistance Scheme
F.C.R.	Family Court Reporter
FIS	Family Income Supplement
FISMA 2000	Financial Services and Markets Act 2000
F.L.R.	Family Law Reports
FME	further medical evidence

Table of Abbreviations used in this Series

F(No.2)A 2005	Finance (No.2) Act 2005
FOTRA	Free of Tax to Residents Abroad
FRAA	flat rate accrual amount
FSCS	Financial Services Compensation Scheme
FTT	First-tier Tribunal
General Benefit Regulations 1982	Social Security (General Benefit) Regulations 1982
General Regulations	Statutory Shared Parental Pay (General) Regulations 2014
GMP	Guaranteed Minimum Pension
GNVQ	General National Vocational Qualification
GP	General Practitioner
GRA	Gender Recognition Act 2004
GRB	Graduated Retirement Benefit
GRP	Graduated Retirement Pension
HB	Housing Benefit
HBRB	Housing Benefit Review Board
HCD	House of Commons Debates
HCP	healthcare professional
HCV	Hepatitis C virus
Health Service Act	National Health Service Act 2006
Health Service (Wales) Act	National Health Service (Wales) Act 2006
HIV	Human Immunodeficiency Virus
HL	House of Lords
H.L.R.	Housing Law Reports
HMIT	Her Majesty's Inspector of Taxes
HMRC	Her Majesty's Revenue and Customs
HMSO	Her Majesty's Stationery Office
Hospital In-Patients Regulations 1975	Social Security (Hospital In-Patients) Regulations 1975
HP	Health Professional
HPP	Higher Pensioner Premium
HRA 1998	Human Rights Act 1998
H.R.L.R.	Human Rights Law Reports
HRP	Home Responsibilities Protection
HSE	Health and Safety Executive
IAC	Immigration and Asylum Chamber
IAP	Intensive Activity Period
IB	Incapacity Benefit
IB PCA	Incapacity Benefit Personal Capability Assessment
IB Regs	Social Security (Incapacity Benefit) Regulations 1994
IB Regulations	Social Security (Incapacity Benefit) Regulations 1994

Table of Abbreviations used in this Series

IB/IS/SDA	Incapacity Benefits Regime
IBJSA	Income-Based Jobseeker's Allowance
IBS	Irritable Bowel Syndrome
ICA	Invalid Care Allowance
I.C.R.	Industrial Cases Reports
ICTA 1988	Income and Corporation Taxes Act 1988
IFW Regulations	Incapacity for Work (General) Regulations 1995
IH	Inner House of the Court of Session
I.I.	Industrial Injuries
IIAC	Industrial Injuries Advisory Council
IIDB	Industrial Injuries Disablement Benefit
ILO	International Labour Organization
Imm. A.R.	Immigration Appeal Reports
Incapacity for Work Regulations	Social Security (Incapacity for Work) (General) Regulations 1995
Income Support General Regulations	Income Support (General) Regulations 1987
IND	Immigration and Nationality Directorate of the Home Office
I.N.L.R.	Immigration and Nationality Law Reports
I.O.	Insurance Officer
IPPR	Institute of Public Policy Research
IRESA	Income-Related Employment and Support Allowance
I.R.L.R.	Industrial Relations Law Reports
IS	Income Support
IS Regs	Income Support Regulations
IS Regulations	Income Support (General) Regulations 1987
ISA	Individual Savings Account
ISBN	International Standard Book Number
ITA 2007	Income Tax Act 2007
ITEPA 2003	Income Tax, Earnings and Pensions Act 2003
I.T.L. Rep.	International Tax Law Reports
I.T.R.	Industrial Tribunals Reports
ITS	Independent Tribunal Service
ITTOIA 2005	Income Tax (Trading and Other Income) Act 2005
IVB	Invalidity Benefit
IW (General) Regs	Social Security (Incapacity for Work) (General) Regulations 1995
IW (Transitional) Regs	Incapacity for Work (Transitional) Regulations
Jobseeker's Allowance Regulations	Jobseeker's Allowance Regulations 1996
Jobseeker's Regulations 1996	Jobseeker's Allowance Regulations 1996
JSA	Jobseeker's Allowance
JSA 1995	Jobseekers Act 1995

xlv

Table of Abbreviations used in this Series

JSA (NI) Regulations	Jobseeker's Allowance (Northern Ireland) Regulations 1996
JSA (Transitional) Regulations	Jobseeker's Allowance (Transitional) Regulations 1996
JSA Regs 1996	Jobseeker's Allowance Regulations 1996
JSA Regs 2013	Jobseeker's Allowance Regulations 2013
JS(NI)O 1995	Jobseekers (Northern Ireland) Order 1995
J.S.S.L.	Journal of Social Security Law
J.S.W.L.	Journal of Social Welfare Law
K.B.	Law Reports, King's Bench
L.& T.R.	Landlord and Tenant Reports
LCW	limited capability for work
LCWA	Limited Capability for Work Assessment
LCWRA	limited capability for work and work-related activity
LEA	local education authority
LEL	Lower Earnings Limit
LET	low earnings threshold
L.G. Rev.	Local Government Review
L.G.L.R.	Local Government Reports
L.J.R.	Law Journal Reports
LRP	liable relative payment
L.S.G.	Law Society Gazette
Luxembourg Court	Court of Justice of the European Union (also referred to as CJEC and ECJ)
MA	Maternity Allowance
MAF	Medical Assessment Framework
Maternity Allowance Regulations	Social Security (Maternity Allowance) Regulations 1987
ME	myalgic encephalomyelitis
Medical Evidence Regulations	Social Security (Medical Evidence) Regulations 1976
MEN	Mandatory Employment Notification
Mesher and Wood	*Income Support, the Social Fund and Family Credit: the Legislation* (1996)
M.H.L.R.	Mental Health Law Reports
MHP	mental health problems
MIG	minimum income guarantee
Migration Regulations	Employment and Support Allowance (Transitional Provisions, Housing Benefit and Council Tax Benefit (Existing Awards) (No.2) Regulations 2010
MP	Member of Parliament
MRSA	methicillin-resistant Staphylococcus aureus
MS	Medical Services
MWA Regulations	Jobseeker's Allowance (Mandatory Work Activity Scheme) Regulations 2011

Table of Abbreviations used in this Series

MWAS Regulations	Jobseeker's Allowance (Mandatory Work Activity Scheme) Regulations 2011
NCB	National Coal Board
NDPD	Notes on the Diagnosis of Prescribed Diseases
NHS	National Health Service
NI	National Insurance
N.I..	Northern Ireland Law Reports
NICA	Northern Ireland Court of Appeal
NICom	Northern Ireland Commissioner
NICs	National Insurance Contributions
NINO	National Insurance Number
NIRS 2	National Insurance Recording System
N.L.J.	New Law Journal
NMC	Nursing and Midwifery Council
Northern Ireland Contributions and Benefits Act	Social Security Contributions and Benefits (Northern Ireland) Act 1992
N.P.C.	New Property Cases
NTC Manual	Clerical procedures manual on tax credits
NUM	National Union of Mineworkers
NUS	National Union of Students
Ogus, Barendt and Wikeley	A. Ogus, E. Barendt and N. Wikeley, *The Law of Social Security* (1995)
Old Cases Act	Industrial Injuries and Diseases (Old Cases) Act 1975
OPB	One Parent Benefit
O.P.L.R.	Occupational Pensions Law Reports
OPSSAT	Office of the President of Social Security Appeal Tribunals
Overlapping Benefits Regulations	Social Security (Overlapping Benefits) Regulations 1975
P	retirement pension case
P. & C.R.	Property and Compensation Reports
para.	paragraph
Pay Regulations	Statutory Paternity Pay and Statutory Adoption Pay (General) Regulations 2002; Statutory Shared Parental Pay (General) Regulations 2014
PAYE	Pay As You Earn
PC	Privy Council
PCA	Personal Capability Assessment
PD	Practice Direction; prescribed disease
Pens. L.R.	Pensions Law Reports
Pensions Act	Pension Schemes Act 1993
PEP	Personal Equity Plan
Persons Abroad Regulations	Social Security Benefit (Persons Abroad) Regulations 1975

xlvii

Table of Abbreviations used in this Series

Persons Residing Together Regulations	Social Security Benefit (Persons Residing Together) Regulations 1977
PIE	Period of Interruption of Employment
PILON	pay in lieu of notice
PIP	Personal Independence Payment
P.I.Q.R.	Personal Injuries and Quantum Reports
Polygamous Marriages Regulations	Social Security and Family Allowances (Polygamous Marriages) Regulations 1975
PPF	Pension Protection Fund
Prescribed Diseases Regulations	Social Security (Industrial Injuries) (Prescribed Diseases) Regulations 1985
PSCS	Pension Service Computer System
Pt	Part
PTA	pure tone audiometry
P.T.S.R.	Public and Third Sector Law Reports
PTWR 2000	Part-time Workers (Prevention of Less Favourable Treatment) Regulations 2000
PVS	private and voluntary sectors
Q.B.	Queen's Bench Law Reports
QBD	Queen's Bench Division
QEF	qualifying earnings factor
QYP	qualifying young person
r.	rule
R	Reported Decision
R.C.	Rules of the Court of Session
REA	Reduced Earnings Allowance
reg.	regulation
RIPA	Regulation of Investigatory Powers Act 2000
RMO	Responsible Medical Officer
rr.	rules
RR	reference rate
RSI	repetitive strain injury
R.V.R.	Rating & Valuation Reporter
s.	section
S	Scottish Decision
SAP	Statutory Adoption Pay
SAPOE Regulations	Jobseeker's Allowance (Schemes for Assisting Persons to Obtain Employment) Regulations 2013
SAWS	Seasonal Agricultural Work Scheme
SAYE	Save As You Earn
SB	Supplementary Benefit
SBAT	Supplementary Benefit Appeal Tribunal
SBC	Supplementary Benefits Commission
S.C.	Session Cases

Table of Abbreviations used in this Series

S.C. (H.L.)	Session Cases (House of Lords)
S.C. (P.C.)	Session Cases (Privy Council)
S.C.C.R.	Scottish Criminal Case Reports
S.C.L.R.	Scottish Civil Law Reports
Sch.	Schedule
SDA	Severe Disablement Allowance
SDP	Severe Disability Premium
SEC	Social Entitlement Chamber
SEN	special educational needs
SERPS	State Earnings Related Pension Scheme
ShPP	statutory shared parental pay
ShPP Regulations	Statutory Shared Parental Pay (General) Regulations 2014
SI	Statutory Instrument
SIP	Share Incentive Plan
S.J.	Solicitors Journal
S.J.L.B.	Solicitors Journal Law Brief
S.L.T.	Scots Law Times
SMP	Statutory Maternity Pay
SMP (General) Regulations 1986	Statutory Maternity Pay (General) Regulations 1986
SPC	State Pension Credit
SPC Regulations	State Pension Credit Regulations 2002
SPCA 2002	State Pension Credit Act 2002
SPL Regulations	Shared Parental Leave Regulations 2014
SPP	Statutory Paternity Pay
ss.	sections
SS (No.2) A 1980	Social Security (No.2) Act 1980
SSA 1975	Social Security Act 1975
SSA 1977	Social Security Act 1977
SSA 1978	Social Security Act 1978
SSA 1979	Social Security Act 1979
SSA 1981	Social Security Act 1981
SSA 1986	Social Security Act 1986
SSA 1988	Social Security Act 1988
SSA 1989	Social Security Act 1989
SSA 1990	Social Security Act 1990
SSA 1998	Social Security Act 1998
SSAA 1992	Social Security Administration Act 1992
SSAC	Social Security Advisory Committee
SSAT	Social Security Appeals Tribunal
SSCBA 1992	Social Security Contributions and Benefits Act 1992

Table of Abbreviations used in this Series

SSCB(NI)A 1992	Social Security Contributions and Benefits (Northern Ireland) Act 1992
SSCPA 1992	Social Security (Consequential Provisions) Act 1992
SSD	Secretary of State for Defence
SSHBA 1982	Social Security and Housing Benefits Act 1982
SSHD	Secretary of State for the Home Department
SSI	Scottish Statutory Instrument
SS(MP)A 1977	Social Security (Miscellaneous Provisions) Act 1977
SSP	Statutory Sick Pay
SSP (General) Regulations	Statutory Sick Pay (General) Regulations 1982
SSPA 1975	Social Security Pensions Act 1975
SSPP	statutory shared parental pay
SSWP	Secretary of State for Work and Pensions
State Pension Credit Regulations	State Pension Credit Regulations 2002
S.T.C.	Simon's Tax Cases
S.T.C. (S.C.D.)	Simon's Tax Cases: Special Commissioners' Decisions
S.T.I.	Simon's Tax Intelligence
STIB	Short-Term Incapacity Benefit
subpara.	subparagraph
subs.	subsection
T	Tribunal of Commissioners' Decision
T.C.	Tax Cases
TCA 1999	Tax Credits Act 1999
TCA 2002	Tax Credits Act 2002
TCC	Technology and Construction Court
TCEA 2007	Tribunals, Courts and Enforcement Act 2007
TCGA 1992	Taxation of Chargeable Gains Act 2002
TCTM	*Tax Credits Technical Manual*
TEC	Treaty Establishing the European Community
TEU	Treaty on European Union
TFEU	Treaty on the Functioning of the European Union
TIOPA 2010	Taxation (International and Other Provisions) Act 2010
TMA 1970	Taxes Management Act 1970
T.R.	Taxation Reports
Transfer of Functions Act	Social Security Contributions (Transfer of Functions etc.) Act 1999
Tribunal Procedure Rules	Tribunal Procedure (First-tier Tribunal)(Social Entitlement Chamber) Rules 2008
UB	Unemployment Benefit
UC	Universal Credit

Table of Abbreviations used in this Series

UC Regs 2013	Universal Credit Regulations 2013
UC Regulations	Universal Credit Regulations 2013
UCITS	Undertakings for Collective Investments in Transferable Securities
UKAIT	UK Asylum and Immigration Tribunal
UKBA	UK Border Agency of the Home Office
UKCC	United Kingdom Central Council for Nursing, Midwifery and Health Visiting
UKFTT	United Kingdom First-tier Tribunal Tax Chamber
UKHL	United Kingdom House of Lords
U.K.H.R.R.	United Kingdom Human Rights Reports
UKSC	United Kingdom Supreme Court
UKUT	United Kingdom Upper Tribunal
UN	United Nations
URL	uniform resource locator
USI Regs	Social Security (Unemployment, Sickness and Invalidity Benefit) Regulations 1983
USI Regulations	Social Security (Unemployment, Sickness and Invalidity Benefit) Regulations 1983
UT	Upper Tribunal
VAT	Value Added Tax
VCM	vinyl chloride monomer
Vol.	Volume
VWF	Vibration White Finger
W	Welsh Decision
WCA	Work Capability Assessment
WCAt	limited capability for work assessment
WFHRAt	Work-Focused Health-Related Assessment
WFI	work-focused interview
WFTC	Working Families Tax Credit
Wikeley, Annotations	N. Wikeley, "Annotations to Jobseekers Act 1995 (c.18)" in *Current Law Statutes Annotated* (1995)
Wikeley, Ogus and Barendt	Wikeley, Ogus and Barendt, *The Law of Social Security* (2002)
W.L.R.	Weekly Law Reports
Workmen's Compensation Acts	Workmen's Compensation Acts 1925 to 1945
WP	Widow's Pension
WPS	War Pensions Scheme
WRA 2007	Welfare Reform Act 2007
WRA 2009	Welfare Reform Act 2009
WRA 2012	Welfare Reform Act 2012
W-RA Regulations	Employment and Support Allowance (Work-Related Activity) Regulations 2011
WRAAt	Work-Related Activity Assessment

Table of Abbreviations used in this Series

WRPA 1999	Welfare Reform and Pensions Act 1999
WRP(NI)O 1999	Welfare Reform and Pensions (Northern Ireland) Order 1999
WTC	Working Tax Credit
WTC Regulations	Working Tax Credit (Entitlement and Maximum Rate) Regulations 2002

PART I

HM REVENUE AND CUSTOMS
TAX CREDITS AND SOCIAL SECURITY

Taxes Management Act 1970

(1970 C.9)

ARRANGEMENT OF SELECTED SECTIONS

PART I

ADMINISTRATION

1.   Responsibility for certain taxes   1.1

PART II

RETURNS OF INCOME AND GAINS

Income tax

- 8.   Personal return
- 9.   Returns to include self-assessment
- 9ZA. Amendment of personal or trustee return by taxpayer
- 9ZB. Correction of personal or trustee return by Revenue
- 9A.   Notice of enquiry
- 9B.   Amendment of return by taxpayer during enquiry
- 9C.   Amendment of self-assessment during enquiry to prevent loss of tax

Records

12B.   Records to be kept for purposes of returns

PART IV

ASSESSMENTS AND CLAIMS

- 28A. Completion of enquiry into personal or trustee return
- 29.   Assessment where loss of tax discovered

Relief for excessive assessments

- 32.   Double assessment
- 33.   Error or mistake

Taxes Management Act 1970

Time-limits

34. Ordinary time-limit of four years
36. Loss of tax brought about carelessly or deliberately, etc.

PART V

APPEALS AND OTHER PROCEEDINGS

Proceedings before Commissioners

54. Settling of appeals by agreement

PART X

PENALTIES, ETC.

105. Evidence in cases of fraud and wilful default

PART XI

MISCELLANEOUS AND SUPPLEMENTAL

Documents

112. Loss, destruction or damage to assessments, returns, etc.
114. Want of form or errors not to invalidate assessments, etc.

Interpretation

118. Interpretation

INTRODUCTION AND GENERAL NOTE

1.2 The TMA 1970 was a consolidation measure, but it has been extensively and repeatedly amended since 1970. Only two sections apply directly to tax credits: s.1 (read to include tax credits) and s.54. For the express application of s.54, see Tax Credits (Appeals) Regulations 2002 reg.3. But TCA 2002 refers to several other sections. Set out below are the key sections of the TMA 1970 that apply for the purposes of the income tax assessments, alongside which tax credit calculations will be made in most cases.

In addition, the selection includes other provisions setting out the power of HMRC to investigate and deal with income tax assessments, the scope for a taxpayer to amend a self-assessment or request an amendment of an assessment, and formal sections dealing with evidence and documentation.

As s.1 indicates, this Act also deals with assessments and administration of capital gains tax and corporation tax, but all provisions relating only to those taxes have been excluded from this selection, as have provisions dealing with other taxes or past taxes.

Part I

Administration

Responsibility for certain taxes

1.—The Commissioners for Her Majesty's Revenue and Customs shall be responsible for the collection and management of—
   (a) income tax,
   (b) corporation tax, and
   (c) capital gains tax.

Part II

Returns of Income and Gains

Income tax

Personal return

8.—(1) For the purpose of establishing the amounts in which a person is chargeable to income tax and capital gains tax for a year of assessment, . . . he may be required by a notice given to him by an officer of the Board—
   (a) to make and deliver to the officer, a return containing such information as may reasonably be required in pursuance of the notice, and
   (b) to deliver with the return such accounts, statements and documents, relating to information contained in the return, as may reasonably be so required.

(1A) The day referred to in subsection (1) above is—
(a) the 31st January next following the year of assessment, or
(b) where the notice under this section is given after the 31st October next following the year, the last day of the period of three months beginning with the day on which the notice is given.

(1AA) For the purposes of subsection (1) above—
(a) the amounts in which a person is chargeable to income tax and capital gains tax are net amounts, that is to say, amounts which take into account any relief or allowance a claim for which is included in the return; and
(b) the amount payable by a person by way of income tax is the difference between the amount in which he is chargeable to income tax and the aggregate amount of any income tax deducted at source and any tax credits to which section 397(1) or 397A(1) of ITTOIA 2005 applies.

Taxes Management Act 1970

(1B) In the case of a person who carries on a trade, profession, or business in partnership with one or more other persons, a return under this section shall include each amount which, in any relevant statement, is stated to be equal to his share of any income, loss, tax, credit or charge for the period in respect of which the statement is made.

(1C) In subsection (1B) above "relevant statement" means a statement which, as respects the partnership, falls to be made under section 12AB of this Act for a period which includes, or includes any part of, the year of assessment or its basis period.

(1D) A return under this section for a year of assessment (Year 1) must be delivered—
   (a) in the case of a non-electronic return, on or before 31st October in Year 2, and
   (b) in the case of an electronic return, on or before 31st January in Year 2.

(1E) But subsection (1D) is subject to the following two exceptions.

(1F) Exception 1 is that if a notice in respect of Year 1 is given after 31st July in Year 2 (but on or before 31st October), a return must be delivered—
   (a) during the period of 3 months beginning with the date of the notice (for a non-electronic return), or
   (b) on or before 31st January (for an electronic return).

(1G) Exception 2 is that if a notice in respect of Year 1 is given after 31st October in Year 2, a return (whether electronic or not) must be delivered during the period of 3 months beginning with the date of the notice.

(1H) The Commissioners—
   (a) shall prescribe what constitutes an electronic return, and
   (b) may make different provision for different cases or circumstances.

(2) Every return under this section shall include a declaration by the person making the return to the effect that the return is to the best of his knowledge correct and complete.

(3) A notice under this section may require different information, accounts and statements for different periods or in relation to different descriptions of source of income.

(4) Notices under this section may require different information, accounts and statements in relation to different descriptions of person.

(5) In this section and sections 8A, 9 and 12AA of this Act, any reference to income tax deducted at source is a reference to income tax deducted or treated as deducted from any income or treated as paid on any income.

Returns to include self-assessment

1.5

9.—(1) Subject to subsections (1A) and (2) below, every return under section 8 or 8A of this Act shall include a self-assessment, that is to say—
   (a) an assessment of the amounts in which, on the basis of the information contained in the return and taking into account any relief or allowance a claim for which is included in the return, the person making the return is chargeable to income tax and capital gains tax for the year of assessment; and
   (b) an assessment of the amount payable by him by way of income tax, that is to say, the difference between the amount in which he is

assessed to income tax under paragraph (a) above and the aggregate amount of any income tax deducted at source and any tax credits to which section 397(1) or 397A(1) of ITTOIA 2005 applies

but nothing in this subsection shall enable a self-assessment to show as repayable any income tax treated as deducted or paid by virtue of section 246D(1) of the principal Act, section 626 of ITEPA or section 399(2), 400(2), 414(1), 421(1) or 530(1) of ITTOIA 2005.

(1A) The tax to be assessed on a person by a self-assessment shall not include any tax which—
  (a) is chargeable on the scheme administrator of a registered pension scheme under Part 4 of the Finance Act 2004,
  (ab) is chargeable on the sub-scheme administrator of a sub-scheme under Part 4 of the Finance Act 2004 as modified by the Registered Pensions (Splitting of Schemes) Regulations 2006, or
  (b) is chargeable on the person who is (or persons who are) the responsible person in relation to an employer-financed retirement benefits scheme under section 394(2) of ITEPA 2003.

(2) A person shall not be required to comply with subsection (1) above if he makes and delivers his return for a year of assessment—
  (a) on or before the 31st October next following the year; or
  (b) where the notice under section 8 or 8A of this Act is given after the 31st August next following the year, within the period of two months beginning with the day on which the notice is given.

(3) Where, in making and delivering a return, a person does not comply with subsection (1) above, an officer of the Board shall, if subsection (2) above applies, and may in any other case—
  (a) make the assessment on his behalf on the basis of the information contained in the return; and
  (b) send him a copy of the assessment so made.

(3A) An assessment under subsection (3) above is treated for the purposes of this Act as a self-assessment and as included in the return.

Amendment of personal or trustee return by taxpayer

9ZA.—(1) A person may amend his return under section 8 or 8A of this Act by notice to an officer of the Board.

(2) An amendment may not be made more than 12 months after the filing date.

(3) In this section "the filing date", in respect of a return for a year of assessment (Year 1), means—
  (a) 31st January of Year 2, or
  (b) if the notice under section 8 or 8A is given after 31st October of Year 2, the last day of the period of three months beginning with the date of the notice.

Correction of personal or trustee return by Revenue

9ZB.—(1) An officer of the Board may amend a return under section 8 or 8A of this Act so as to correct—
  (a) obvious errors or omissions in the return (whether errors of principle, arithmetical mistakes or otherwise), and
  (b) anything else in the return that the officer has reason to believe is incorrect in the light of information available to the office.

(2) A correction under this section is made by notice to the person whose return it is.

(3) No such correction may be made more than nine months after—

(a) the day on which the return was delivered, or

(b) if the correction is required in consequence of an amendment of the return under section 9ZA of this Act, the day on which that amendment was made.

(4) A correction under this section is of no effect if the person whose return it is gives notice rejecting the correction.

(5) Notice of rejection under subsection (4) above must be given—

(a) to the officer of the Board by whom the notice of correction was given,

(b) before the end of the period of 30 days beginning with the date of issue of the notice of correction.

Notice of enquiry

9A.—(1) An officer of the Boardmay enquire into a return under section 8 or 8A of this Act if he gives notice of his intention to do so ("notice of enquiry")—

(a) to the person whose return it is ("the taxpayer"),

(b) within the time allowed.

(2) The time allowed is—

(a) if the return was delivered on or before the filing date, up to the end of the period of twelve months after the filing date;

(b) if the return was delivered after the filing date, up to and including the quarter day next following the first anniversary of the day on which the return was delivered;

(c) if the return is amended under section 9ZA of this Act, up to and including the quarter day next following the first anniversary of the day on which the amendment was made.

For this purpose, the quarter days are 31st January, 30th April, 31st July and 31st October.

(3) A return which has been the subject of one notice of enquiry may not be the subject of another, except one given in consequence of an amendment (or another amendment) of the return under section 9ZA of this Act.

(4) An enquiry extends to—

(a) anything contained in the return, or required to be contained in the return, including any claim or election included in the return,

(b) consideration of whether to give the taxpayer a transfer pricing notice under section 168(1) of TIOPA 2010 (provision not at arm's length: medium-sized enterprise),

(c) consideration of whether to give the taxpayer a notice under section 81(2) of TIOPA 2010 (notice to counteract scheme or arrangement designed to increase double taxation relief),

but this is subject to the following limitation.

(5) If the notice of enquiry is given as a result of an amendment of the return under section 9ZA of this Act—

(a) at a time when it is no longer possible to give notice of enquiry under subsection (2)(a) or (b) above, or

(b) after an enquiry into the return has been completed, the enquiry into the return is limited to matters to which the amendment relates or which are affected by the amendment.

(6) In this section "the filing date" means, in relation to a return, the last day for delivering it in accordance with section 8 or section 8A.

Amendment of return by taxpayer during enquiry

9B.—(1) This section applies if a return is amended under section 9ZA of this Act (amendment of personal or trustee return by taxpayer) at a time when an enquiry is in progress into the return.

(2) The amendment does not restrict the scope of the enquiry but may be taken into account (together with any matters arising) in the enquiry.

(3) So far as the amendment affects the amount stated in the self-assessment included in the return as the amount of tax payable, it does not take effect while the enquiry is in progress and—
- (a) if the officer states in the closure notice that he has taken the amendment into account and that—
  - (i) the amendment has been taken into account in formulating the amendments contained in the notice, or
  - (ii) his conclusion is that the amendment is incorrect, the amendment shall not take effect;
- (b) otherwise, the amendment takes effect when the closure notice is issued.

(4) For the purposes of this section the period during which an enquiry is in progress is the whole of the period—
- (a) beginning with the day on which notice of enquiry is given; and
- (b) ending with the day on which the enquiry is completed.

Amendment of self-assessment during enquiry to prevent loss of tax

9C.—(1) This section applies where an enquiry is in progress into a return as a result of notice of enquiry by an officer of the Board under section 9A(1) of this Act.

(2) If the officer forms the opinion—
- (a) that the amount stated in the self-assessment contained in the return as the amount of tax payable is insufficient; and
- (b) that unless the assessment is immediately amended there is likely to be a loss of tax to the Crown,

he may by notice to the taxpayer amend the assessment to make good the deficiency.

(3) In the case of an enquiry which under section 9A(5) of this Act is limited to matters arising from an amendment of the return, subsection (2) above only applies so far as the deficiency is attributable to the amendment.

(4) For the purposes of this section the period during which an enquiry is in progress is the whole of the period—
- (a) beginning with the day on which notice of enquiry is given, and
- (b) ending with the day on which the enquiry is completed.

Taxes Management Act 1970

Records

Records to be kept for purposes of returns

1.11
12B.—(1) Any person who may be required by a notice under section 8, 8A, or 12AA of this Act to make and deliver a return for a year of assessment or other period shall—
- (a) keep all such records as may be requisite for the purpose of enabling him to make and deliver a correct and complete return for the year or period; and
- (b) preserve those records until the end of the relevant day, that is to say, the day mentioned in subsection (2) below or, where a return is required by a notice given on or before that day, whichever of that day and the following is the latest, namely—
  - (i) where enquiries into the return are made by an officer of the Board, the day on which, by virtue of section 28A(1) or 28B(1) of this Act, those enquiries are completed; and
  - (ii) where no enquiries into the return are so made, the day on which such an officer no longer has power to make such enquiries.

(2) The day referred to in subsection (1) above is—
- (a) in the case of a person carrying on a trade, profession or business alone or in partnership or a company, the fifth anniversary of the 31st January next following the year of assessment or (as the case may be) the sixth anniversary of the endof the period;
- (b) [otherwise], the first anniversary of 31st January next following the year of assessment . . .

or (in either case) such earlier day as may be specified in writing by the Commissioners for Her Majesty's Revenue and Customs (and different days may be specified for different cases).

(2A) Any person who—
- (a) is required, by such a notice as is mentioned in subsection (1) above given at any time after the end of the day mentioned in subsection (2) above, to make and deliver a return for a year of assessment or other period; and
- (b) has in his possession at that time any records which may be requisite for the purpose of enabling him to make and deliver a correct and complete return for the year or period,

shall preserve those records until the end of the relevant day, that is to say, the day which, if the notice had been given on or before the day mentioned in subsection (2) above, would have been the relevant day for the purposes of subsection (1) above.

(3) In the case of a person carrying on a trade, profession or business alone or in partnership—
- (a) the records required to be kept and preserved under subsection (1) or (2A) above shall include records of the following, namely—
  - (i) all amounts received and expended in the course of the trade, profession or business and the matters in respect of which the receipts and expenditure take place, and
  - (ii) in the case of a trade involving dealing in goods, all sales and purchases of goods made in the course of the trade . . .

(3A) The Commissioners for Her Majesty's Revenue and Customs may by regulations—

(1970 c.9 s.12B)

(a) provide that the records required to be kept and preserved under this section include, or do not include, records specified in the regulations, and
(b) provide that those records include supporting documents so specified.

(4) The duty under subsection (1) or (2A) to preserve records may be discharged—
(a) by preserving them in any form and by any means, or
(b) by preserving the information contained in them in any form and by any means,

subject to subsection (4A) and any conditions or further exceptions specified in writing by the Commissioners for Her Majesty's Revenue and Customs.

(4A) Subsection (4)(b) does not apply in the case of the following kinds of records—
(a) any statement in writing such as is mentioned in—
   (i) subsection (1) of section 1100 of CTA 2010 (amount of qualifying distribution and tax credit); or
   (ii) section 495(1) or 975(2) or (4) of ITA 2007 (statements about deduction of income tax),

which is furnished by the company or person there mentioned, whether after the making of a request or otherwise;
(b) any record (however described) which is required by regulations under section 70(1)(c) of the Finance Act 2004 to be given to a sub-contractor (within the meaning of section 58 of that Act) on the making of a payment to which section 61 of that Act (deductions on account of tax) applies;
(c) any such record as may be requisite for making a correct and complete claim in respect of, or otherwise requisite for making a correct and complete return so far as relating to, an amount of tax—
   (i) which has been paid under the laws of a territory outside the United Kingdom, or
   (ii) which would have been payable under the law of a territory outside the United Kingdom ("territory F") but for a development relief.

(4B) In subsection (4A)(c) "development relief" means a relief—
(a) given under the law of territory F with a view to promoting industrial, commercial, scientific, educational or other development in a territory outside the United Kingdom, and
(b) about which provision is made in arrangements that have effect under section 2(1) of TIOPA 2010 (double taxation relief by agreement with territories outside the United Kingdom).

(5) Subject to subsections (5A) and (5B) below any person who fails to comply with subsection (1) or (2A) above in relation to a year of assessment or accounting period shall be liable to a penalty not exceeding £3,000.

(5A) Subsection (5) above does not apply where the records which the person fails to keep or preserve are records which might have been requisite only for the purposes of claims, elections or notices which are not included in the return.

(5B) Subsection (5) above also does not apply where—

Taxes Management Act 1970

(a) the records which the person fails to keep or preserve are records falling within paragraph (a) of subsection (4A) above; and
(b) an officer of the Board is satisfied that any facts which he reasonably requires to be proved, and which would have been proved by the records, are proved by other documentary evidence furnished to him.
(5C) Regulations under this section may—
(a) make different provision for different cases, and
(b) make provision by reference to things specified in a notice published by the Commissioners for Her Majesty's Revenue and Customs in accordance with the regulations (and not withdrawn by a subsequent notice).
(6) For the purposes of this section—
(a) a person engaged in the letting of property shall be treated as carrying on a trade; and
(b) "supporting documents" includes accounts, books, deeds, contracts, vouchers and receipts.

PART IV

ASSESSMENT AND CLAIMS

Completion of enquiry into personal or trustee return

1.12 **28A.**—(1) An enquiry under section 9A(1) of this Act is completed when an officer of the Boardby notice (a "closure notice") informs the taxpayer that he has completed his enquiries and states his conclusions. In this section "the taxpayer" means the person to whom notice of enquiry was given.
(2) A closure notice must either—
(a) state that in the officer's opinion no amendment of the return is required; or
(b) make the amendments of the return required to give effect to his conclusions.
(3) A closure notice takes effect when it is issued.
(4) The taxpayer may apply to the tribunal for a direction requiring an officer of the Board to issue a closure notice within a specified period.
(5) Any such application is to be subject to the relevant provisions of Part 5 of this Act (see, in particular, section 48(2)(b)).
(6) The tribunal shall give the direction applied for unless . . . satisfied that there are reasonable grounds for not issuing a closure notice within a specified period.

Assessment where loss of tax discovered

1.13 **29.**—(1) If an officer of the Board or the Board discover, as regards any person (the taxpayer) and a year of assessment—
(a) that income which ought to have been assessed to income tax, or chargeable gains which ought to have been assessed to capital gains tax, have not been assessed, or
(b) that an assessment to tax is or has become insufficient, or
(c) that any relief which has been given is or has become excessive,

the officer or, as the case may be, the Board may, subject to subsections (2) and (3) below, make an assessment in the amount, or the further amount, which ought in his or their opinion to be charged in order to make good to the Crown the loss of tax.

(2) Where—
  (a) the taxpayer has made and delivered a return under section 8 or 8A of this Act in respect of the relevant year of assessment, and
  (b) the situation mentioned in subsection (1) above is attributable to an error or mistake in the return as to the basis on which his liability ought to have been computed,

the taxpayer shall not be assessed under that subsection in respect of the year of assessment there mentioned if the return was in fact made on the basis or in accordance with the practice generally prevailing at the time when it was made.

(3) Where the taxpayer has made and delivered a return under section 8 or 8A of this Act in respect of the relevant year of assessment, he shall not be assessed under subsection (1) above—
  (a) in respect of the year of assessment mentioned in that subsection; and
  (b) in the same capacity as that in which he made and delivered the return,

unless one of the two conditions mentioned below is fulfilled.

(4) The first condition is that the situation mentioned in subsection (1) above was brought about carelessly or deliberately by the taxpayer or a person acting on his behalf.

(5) The second condition is that at the time when an officer of the Board—
  (a) ceased to be entitled to give notice of his intention to enquire into the taxpayer's return under section 8 or 8A of this Act in respect of the relevant year of assessment; or
  (b) informed the taxpayer that he had completed his enquiries into that return,

the officer could not have been reasonably expected, on the basis of the information made available to him before that time, to be aware of the situation mentioned in subsection (1) above.

(6) For the purposes of subsection (5) above, information is made available to an officer of the Board if—
  (a) it is contained in the taxpayer's return under section 8 or 8A of this Act in respect of the relevant year of assessment (the return), or in any accounts, statements or documents accompanying the return;
  (b) it is contained in any claim made as regards the relevant year of assessment by the taxpayer acting in the same capacity as that in which he made the return, or in any accounts, statements or documents accompanying any such claim;
  (c) it is contained in any documents, accounts or particulars which, for the purposes of any enquiries into the return or any such claim by an officer of the Board, are produced or furnished by the taxpayer to the officer; or
  (d) it is information the existence of which, and the relevance of which as regards the situation mentioned in subsection (1) above—
    (i) could reasonably be expected to be inferred by an officer of

the Board from information falling within paragraphs (a)–(c) above; or

(ii) are notified in writing by the taxpayer to an officer of the Board.

(7) In subsection (6) above—

(a) any reference to the taxpayer's return under section 8 or 8A of this Act in respect of the relevant year of assessment includes—
   (i) a reference to any return of his under that section for either of the two immediately preceding years of assessment; and
   (ii) where the return is under section 8 and the taxpayer carries on a trade, profession or business in partnership, a reference to any partnership return with respect to the partnership for the relevant year of assessment or either of those periods; and
(b) any reference in paragraphs (b) to (d) to the taxpayer includes a reference to a person acting on his behalf.

(7A) The requirement to fulfil one of the two conditions mentioned above does not apply so far as regards any income or chargeable gains of the taxpayer in relation to which the taxpayer has been given, after any enquiries have been completed into the taxpayer's return, a notice under section 81(2) of TIOPA 2010 (notice to counteract scheme or arrangement designed to increase double taxation relief).

(8) An objection to the making of an assessment under this section on the ground that neither of the two conditions mentioned above is fulfilled shall not be made otherwise than on an appeal against the assessment.

(9) Any reference in this section to the relevant year of assessment is a reference to—

(a) in the case of the situation mentioned in paragraph (a) or (b) of subsection (1) above, the year of assessment mentioned in that subsection; and
(b) in the case of the situation mentioned in paragraph (c) of that subsection, the year of assessment in respect of which the claim was made.

Relief for excessive assessments

Double assessment

1.14   **32.**—(1) If on a claim made to the Board it appears to their satisfaction that a person has been assessed to tax more than once for the same cause and for the same chargeable period, they shall direct the whole, or such part of any assessment as appears to be an overcharge, to be vacated, and thereupon the same shall be vacated accordingly.

(2) An appeal may be brought against the refusal of a claim under this section.

(3) Notice of appeal under subsection (2) must be given—

(a) in writing;
(b) within 30 days after the day on which notice of the refusal is given;
(c) to the officer of Revenue and Customs by whom that notice was given.

Recovery of overpaid tax etc

1.15   **33.**—Schedule 1AB contains provision for and in connection with claims for the recovery of overpaid income tax and capital gains tax.

(1970 c.9 s.34)

Time limits

Ordinary time-limit of four years

34.—(1) Subject to the following provisions of this Act, and to any other provisions of the Taxes Acts allowing a longer period in any particular class of case, an assessment to income tax or capital gains tax may be made at any time not more than 4 years after the end of the year of assessment to which it relates.

(2) An objection to the making of any assessment on the ground that the time-limit for making it has expired shall only be made on an appeal against the assessment.

Loss of tax brought about carelessly or deliberately etc.

36.—(1) An assessment on a person in a case involving a loss of income tax or capital gains tax brought about carelessly by the person may be made at any time not more than 6 years after the end of the year of assessment to which it relates (subject to subsection (1A) and any other provision of the Taxes Acts allowing a longer period).

(1A) An assessment on a person in a case involving a loss of income tax or capital gains tax —
(a) brought about deliberately by the person,
(b) attributable to a failure by the person to comply with an obligation under section 7, or
(c) attributable to arrangements in respect of which the person has failed to comply with an obligation under section 309, 310 or 313 of the Finance Act 2004 (obligation of parties to tax avoidance schemes to provide information to Her Majesty's Revenue and Customs),

may be made at any time not more than 20 years after the end of the year of assessment to which it relates (subject to any provision of the Taxes Acts allowing a longer period).

(1B) In subsections (1) and (1A) references to a loss brought about by the person who is the subject of the assessment include a loss brought about by another person acting on behalf of that person.

(2) Where the person mentioned in subsection (1) or (1A) ("the person in default") carried on a trade, profession or business with one or more other persons at any time in the period for which the assessment is made, an assessment in respect of the profits or gains of the trade, profession or business for the purpose mentioned in subsection (1A) or (1B) may be made not only on the person in default but also on his partner or any of his partners.

(3) If the person on whom the assessment is made so requires, in determining the amount of the tax to be charged for any chargeable period in any assessment made for the purpose mentioned in subsection (1) or (1A) above, effect shall be given to any relief or allowance to which he would have been entitled for that chargeable period on a claim or application made within the time allowed by the Taxes Acts.

(3A) In subsection (3) above, "claim or application" does not include an election under section 257BA of the principal Act (elections as to transfer of married couple's allowance).

(4) Any act or omission such as is mentioned in section 98B below on

Taxes Management Act 1970

the part of a grouping (as defined in that section) or member of a grouping shall be deemed for the purposes of subsections (1) and (1A) to be the act or omission of each member of the grouping.

Part V

Appeals and Other Proceedings

Proceedings before the Commissioners

Setting of appeals by agreement

1.18   54.—(1) Subject to the provisions of this section, where a person gives notice of appeal and, before the appeal is determined by the [¹ [² [³ [⁴ First-tier Tribunal]]]], [¹ [⁴ an officer of Revenue and Customs]] and the appellant come to an agreement, whether in writing or otherwise, that the [⁴ determination] or decision under appeal should be treated as upheld without variation, or as varied in a particular manner or as discharged or cancelled, the like consequences shall ensue for all purposes as would have ensued if, at the time when the agreement was come to, the tribunal had determined the appeal and had upheld the [⁴ determination] or decision without variation, had varied it in that manner or had discharged or cancelled it, as the case may be.

(2) Subsection (1) of this section shall not apply where, within thirty days from the date when the agreement was come to, the appellant gives notice in writing to [¹ [⁴ an officer of Revenue and Customs]] that he desires to repudiate or resile from the agreement.

[¹ [⁴ (3) Where an agreement is not in writing—
 (a) the preceding provisions of this section shall not apply unless the Board give notice, in such form and manner as they consider appropriate, to the appellant of the terms agreed between the officer of Revenue and Customs and the appellant; and
 (b) the references in those preceding provisions to the time when the agreement was come to shall be construed as references to the date of that notice.]]

(4) Where—
 (a) a person who has given a notice of appeal notifies [¹ [⁴ an officer of Revenue and Customs]], whether orally or in writing, that he desires not to proceed with the appeal; and
 (b) thirty days have elapsed since the giving of the notification without [¹ [⁴ an officer of Revenue and Customs]] giving to the appellant notice in writing indicating that he is unwilling that the appeal should be treated as withdrawn,
the preceding provisions of this section shall have effect as if, at the date of the appellant's notification, the appellant and [¹ [⁴ an officer of Revenue and Customs]] had come to an agreement, orally or in writing, as the case may be, that the [⁴ determination] or decision under appeal should be upheld without variation.

(5) The references in this section to an agreement being come to with an appellant and the giving of notice or notification to or by an appellant

include references to an agreement being come to with, and the giving of notice or notification to or by, a person acting on behalf of the appellant in relation to the appeal.

[¹(6) In subsection (1) "appeal tribunal" means an appeal tribunal [² . . .] constituted in Northern Ireland under Chapter 1 of Part 2 of the Social Security (Northern Ireland) Order 1998 (social security appeals: Northern Ireland).]

AMENDMENTS AND MODIFICATIONS

1. Modifications made to tax credit cases by the Tax Credits (Appeals) Regulations 2002 (SI 2002/2926) reg.3 (December 17, 2002).
2. Amendments made by the Tribunals, Courts and Enforcement Act 2007 (Transitional and Consequential Provisions) Order 2008 (SI 2008/2683) art.6 and Sch.1 para.193 (November 3, 2008).
3. Amendments made by the Transfer of Tribunal Functions and Revenue and Customs Appeals Order 2009 (SI 2009/56) art.3 and Sch.1 para.33 (April 1, 2009).
4. Modifications made to tax credits cases by the Tax Credits (Settlement of Appeals) Regulations 2014 (SI 2014/1933) reg.3 (August 12, 2014).

DEFINITIONS

"appeal tribunal"—see subs.(6).
"the Board"—see s.67 of the Tax Credits Act 2002 but note that the functions of the Board have now been transferred to the Commissioners for Her Majesty's Revenue and Customs (Commissioners for Revenue and Customs Act 2005 s.5(2)).

GENERAL NOTE

The major modifications made to s.54 by the Tax Credits (Settlement of Appeals) Regulations 2014 (SI 2014/1933) should be read with the close and careful decision of Upper Tribunal Judge Rowland in *JI v HMRC* [2013] UKUT 199 (AAC). As that decision makes clear, the previous state of s.54 as applied (if it was applied) to tax credits was a mess. The 2014 amendments update, clarify and tidy up the previously messy and incomplete provisions. In particular they confirm that the general settlement powers used by HMRC to deal with income tax and similar disputes apply to the settlement of tax credits appeals. Section 54 is also subject to modifications for child trust funds appeals made by the Child Trust Funds (Non-tax Appeals) Regulations 2005 (SI 2005/191), along parallel lines to those in the Tax Credits (Appeals) Regulations 2002, subject to some very minor consequential adjustments (however, the modifications exclusive to child trust fund appeals are not captured in the text of s.54 as set out above).

1.19

Subsection (1)
This allows the parties to compromise an appeal and reach an agreement that is as final as a decision of a tribunal. Indeed, it is more final because, not actually being a decision of a tribunal, there can be no appeal to the Upper Tribunal. Note that the agreement must be reached before the appeal tribunal determines the appeal. Therefore, this sort of agreement cannot put an end to an appeal to the Upper Tribunal, notwithstanding the definition of "tax credit appeal" in reg.2 of the Tax Credits (Appeals) Regulations 2002, although a Judge or registrar would no doubt have regard to any agreement when deciding whether or not to allow an appeal to be withdrawn under r.17 of the Tribunal Procedure (Upper Tribunal) Rules 2008. If a Judge sets aside a decision of an appeal tribunal and refers the case to another tribunal, it again becomes possible for an agreement to be made.

The effect of an agreement is to prevent an officer of Revenue and Customs

1.20

from making any further decision in respect of the same issue and the same period (*Cenlon Finance Co Ltd v Ellwood* [1961] Ch.50). However, an officer is not barred from making a new decision if it is discovered that the agreement was based on incorrect information supplied by the appellant (*Gray v Matheson* [1993] 1 W.L.R. 1130). It is suggested that an officer is also not barred from making a decision under s.18 of the Tax Credits Act 2000 if the agreement related to a s.14 decision and it may also not be inappropriate to revise, under, says s.15 or s.16, an agreed award, depending on what exactly had been the scope of the agreement. In the context of tax credit cases there will not often be any doubt as to the scope of the agreement but where there was more than one issue between the parties—perhaps where the amount of earnings from self-employment is in dispute—the test is whether, looking objectively at all the relevant circumstances (including, in particular, the issues raised by the appellant and all the material known to have been in the possession of Her Majesty's Revenue and Customs), a reasonable man would conclude that the officer had accepted all the appellant's contentions (*Scorer v Olin Energy Systems Ltd* [1984] 1 W.L.R. 675). If the agreement is not in writing, see subs.(3).

Subsection (2)

1.21 This provides a 30-day cooling-off period for an appellant (but not an officer of Revenue and Customs) and may be particularly relevant in the light of subs.(5). It could give rise to delay if a hearing date is cancelled in the light of an agreement from which an appellant later resiles. On the other hand, the delay is no greater than can arise in a social security case where the Secretary of State makes a new decision, causing an appeal to lapse under s.9(6) of the Social Security Act 1998 but generating a new right of appeal.

Subsection (3)

1.22 If an agreement is not in writing, Her Majesty's Revenue and Customs must set out in writing their understanding of the agreement and give the appellant 30 days to object. This ensures a reasonable degree of certainty as to the terms of the agreement. The appellant is not required expressly to accept the written version.

Subsection (4)

1.23 There is no provision in the Tax Credits (Appeals) (No.2) Regulations 2002 allowing an appellant to withdraw an appeal by giving notice to the clerk to the tribunal (compare r.17 of the Tribunal Procedure (First-tier Tribunal)(Social Entitlement Chamber) Rules 2008. Instead, an appellant may give notice of his desire to abandon the appeal to the officer of Revenue and Customs and the officer has 30 days in which to object. If the officer signifies agreement within the 30 days, subss.(1)–(3) will be brought into operation, as will be the case if the officer does nothing for 30 days. If the officer objects within the 30 days, the appeal proceeds. Presumably that means that any attempt to withdraw an appeal is ineffective for 30 days unless the officer consents. This provision applies only to appeals. The 2008 Rules permit the unilateral withdrawal of an application for a direction or penalty proceedings where a tribunal has a first instance jurisdiction.

Subsection (5)

1.24 By virtue of this subsection, an agreement under subs.(1) may be entered into by an appellant's representative. However, such an agreement may be repudiated by the appellant under subs.(2).

(1970 c. 9 s. 105)

Part X

Penalties, etc.

Admissibility of evidence not affected by offer of settlement etc

105.—(1) Statements made or documents produced by or on behalf of a person shall not be inadmissible in any such proceedings as are mentioned in subsection (2) below by reason only that it has been drawn to his attention—
  (a) that where serious tax fraud has been committed the Board may accept a money settlement and that the Board will accept such a settlement, and will not pursue a criminal prosecution, if he makes a full confession of all tax irregularities, or
  (b) that the extent to which he is helpful and volunteers information is a factor that will be taken into account in determining the amount of any penalty,
and that he was or may have been induced thereby to make the statements or produce the documents.
  (2) The proceedings mentioned in subsection (1) above are—
  (a) any criminal proceedings against the person in question for any form of fraudulent conduct in connection with or in relation to tax; and
  (b) any proceedings against him for the recovery of any tax due from him and
  (c) any proceedings for a penalty or on appeal against the determination of a penalty.

1.25

Part XI

Miscellaneous and Supplemental

Documents

Loss, destruction or damage to assessments, returns, etc.

112.—(1) Where any assessment to tax, or any duplicate of assessment to tax, or any return or other document relating to tax, has been lost or destroyed, or been so defaced or damaged as to be illegible or otherwise useless, HMRC may, notwithstanding anything in any enactment to the contrary, do all such acts and things as they might have done, and all acts and things done under or in pursuance of this section shall be as valid and effectual for all purposes as they would have been, if the assessment or duplicate of assessment had not been made, or the return or other document had not been made or furnished or required to be made or furnished.
  Provided that, where any person who is charged with tax in consequence or by virtue of any act or thing done under or in pursuance of this section proves to the satisfaction of the tribunal that he has already paid any tax for the

1.26

same chargeable period in respect of the subject matter and on the account in respect of and on which he is so charged, relief shall be given to the extent to which the liability of that person has been discharged by the payment so made either by abatement from the charge or by repayment, as the case may require.

...

(3) The references in subsection (1) above to assessments to tax include references to determinations of penalties; and in its application to such determinations the proviso to that subsection shall have effect with the appropriate modifications.

Want of form or errors not to invalidate assessments, etc.

114.—(1) An assessment or determination, warrant or other proceeding which purports to be made in pursuance of any provision of the Taxes Acts shall not be quashed, or deemed to be void or voidable, for want of form, or be affected by reason of a mistake, defect or omission therein, if the same is in substance and effect in conformity with or according to the intent and meaning of the Taxes Acts, and if the person or property charged or intended to be charged or affected thereby is designated therein according to common intent and understanding.

(2) An assessment or determination shall not be impeached or affected—
   (a) by reason of a mistake therein as to—
      (i) the name or surname of a person liable, or
      (ii) the description of any profits or property, or
      (iii) the amount of the tax charged, or
   (b) by reason of any variance between the notice and the assessment or determination.

Interpretation

Interpretation

118.—(1) In this Act, unless the context otherwise requires—
"Act" includes an Act of the Parliament of Northern Ireland; and
"enactment" shall be construed accordingly;
"the Board" means the Commissioners of Inland Revenue;
"body of persons" means any body politic, corporate or collegiate, and any company, fraternity, fellowship and society of persons, whether corporate or not corporate;
"chargeable gain" has the same meaning as in the 1992 Act;
"chargeable period" means a year of assessment or a company's accounting period;
"collector" means any collector of taxes;
"company" has the meaning given by section 1121(1) of CTA 2010 (with section 617 of that Act);
"CTA 2009" means the Corporation Tax Act 2009,
"CTA 2010" means the Corporation Tax Act 2010,
...
"HMRC" means Her Majesty's Revenue and Customs;
"incapacitated person" means any infant, person of unsound mind, lunatic, idiot or insane person;

"infant", in relation to Scotland, except in section 73 of this Act, means a person under legal disability by reason of nonage, and, in the said section 73, means a person under the age of 18 years;

"inspector" means any inspector of taxes;

"ITEPA 2003" means the Income Tax (Earnings and Pensions) Act 2003;

"ITTOIA 2005" means the Income Tax (Trading and Other Income) Act 2005;

"ITA 2007" means the Income Tax Act 2007;

"partnership return" has the meaning given by section 12AA(10A) of this Act;

"the principal Act" means the Income and Corporation Taxes Act 1988;

"the relevant trustees", in relation to a settlement, shall be construed in accordance with section 7(9) of this Act;

"return" includes any statement or declaration under the Taxes Acts;

. . .

"successor", in relation to a person who is required to make and deliver, or has made and delivered, a partnership return, and "predecessor" and "successor", in relation to the successor of such a person, shall be construed in accordance with section 12AA(11) of this Act;

"tax", where neither income tax nor capital gains tax nor corporation tax is specified, means any of those taxes except that in sections 20, 20A, 20B and 20D it does not include development land tax;

"the Taxes Acts" means this Act and—
   (a) the Tax Acts; and
   (b) the Taxation of Chargeable Gains Act 1992 and all other enactments relating to capital gains tax;

"the TCEA 2007" means the Tribunals, Courts and Enforcement Act 2007;

"the 1992 Act" means the Taxation of Chargeable Gains Act 1992;

"TIOPA 2010" means the Taxation (International and other Provisions) Act 2010;

"trade" includes every trade, manufacture, adventure or concern in the nature of trade.

"the tribunal" is to be read in accordance with section 47C;

(2) For the purposes of this Act, a person shall be deemed not to have failed to do anything required to be done within a limited time if he did it within such further time, if any, as the Board or the tribunal or officer concerned may have allowed; and where a person had a reasonable excuse for not doing anything required to be done he shall be deemed not to have failed to do it unless the excuse ceased and, after the excuse ceased, he shall be deemed not to have failed to do it if he did it without unreasonable delay after the excuse had ceased.

. . .

(4) For the purposes of this Act, the amount of tax covered by any assessment shall not be deemed to be finally determined until that assessment can no longer be varied, whether by the tribunal on an appeal notified to it or by the order of any court.

(5) For the purposes of this Act a loss of tax or a situation is brought about carelessly by a person if the person fails to take reasonable care to avoid bringing about that loss or situation.

(6) Where—
   (a) information is provided to Her Majesty's Revenue and Customs,
   (b) the person who provided the information, or the person on whose

Taxes Management Act 1970

    behalf the information was provided, discovers some time later that the information was inaccurate, and
  (c) that person fails to take reasonable steps to inform Her Majesty's Revenue and Customs,
any loss of tax or situation brought about by the inaccuracy shall be treated for the purposes of this Act as having been brought about carelessly by that person.

    (7) In this Act references to a loss of tax or a situation brought about deliberately by a person include a loss of tax or a situation that arises as a result of a deliberate inaccuracy in a document given to Her Majesty's Revenue and Customs by or on behalf of that person.

Social Security Contributions and Benefits Act 1992

(1992 c.4)

SECTIONS REPRODUCED

PART III

NON-CONTRIBUTORY BENEFITS

1.29   77.   Guardian's allowance

PART IX

CHILD BENEFIT

141. Child benefit
142. "Child" and "qualifying young person"
143. Meaning of person responsible for child or qualifying young person
144. Exclusions and priority
145. Rate of child benefit
145A. Entitlement after death of child or qualifying young person
146. Presence in Great Britain
146A. Persons subject to immigration control
147. Interpretation of Part IX and supplementary provisions

(1992 c.4)

Part XI

Statutory Sick Pay

Employer's liability

151. Employer's liability

The qualifying conditions

152. Period of incapacity for work
153. Period of entitlement
154. Qualifying days

Limitations on entitlement, etc.

155. Limitations on entitlement
156. Notification of incapacity for work

Rates of payment, etc.

157. Rates of payment
158. Recovery by employers of amounts paid by way of statutory sick pay (*repealed*)
159. Power to substitute provisions for section 158(2) (*repealed*)
159A. Power to provide for recovery by employers of sums paid by way of statutory sick pay

Miscellaneous

160. Relationship with benefits and other payments, etc.
161. Crown employment—Part XI
162. Special classes of persons
163. Interpretation of Part XI and supplementary provisions

Part XII

Statutory Maternity Pay

164. Statutory maternity pay—entitlement and liability to pay
165. The maternity pay period
166. Rate of statutory maternity pay
167. Funding of employers' liabilities in respect of statutory maternity pay
168. Relationship with benefits and other payments, etc.
169. Crown employment—Part XII
170. Special classes of persons
171. Interpretation of Part XII and supplementary provisions

Part XIIZA

Statutory Paternity Pay

171ZA.	Entitlement: birth
171ZB.	Entitlement: adoption
171ZC.	Entitlement: general
171ZD.	Liability to make payments
171ZE.	Rate and period of pay
s.171ZEA.	Entitlement to additional statutory paternity pay: birth
s.171ZEB.	Entitlement to additional statutory paternity pay: adoption
s.171ZEC.	Entitlement to additional statutory paternity pay: general
s.171ZED.	Liability to make payments of additional statutory paternity pay
s.171ZEE.	Rate and period of pay: additional statutory paternity pay
171ZF.	Restrictions on contracting out
171ZG.	Relationship with contractual remuneration
171ZH.	Crown employment—Part XIIZA
171ZI.	Special classes of person
171ZJ.	Part XIIZA: supplementary
171ZK.	Power to apply Part XIIZA to adoption cases not involving placement

Part XIIZB

Statutory Adoption Pay

171ZL.	Entitlement
171ZM.	Liability to make payments
171ZN.	Rate and period of pay
171ZO.	Restrictions on contracting out
171ZP.	Relationship with benefits and other payments, etc.
171ZQ.	Crown employment—Part XIIZB
171ZR.	Special classes of person
171ZS.	Part XIIZB: supplementary
171ZT.	Power to apply Part XIIZB to adoption cases not involving placement

Part XIIZC

Statutory Shared Parental Pay

171ZU.	Entitlement: birth
171ZV.	Entitlement: adoption
171ZW.	Entitlement: general
171ZX.	Liability to make payments
171ZY.	Rate and period of pay
171ZZ.	Restrictions on contracting out
171ZZ1.	Relationship with contractual remuneration
171ZZ2.	Crown employment
171ZZ3.	Special classes of person
171ZZ4.	Part XIIZC: supplementary
171ZZ5.	Power to apply Part XIIZC

(1992 c.4)

Part XIII

General

Interpretation

172. Application of Act in relation to territorial waters
173. Age
174. References to Acts

Schedules

Schedule 9—Exclusions from entitlement to child benefit
Schedule 10—Priority between persons entitled to child benefit
Schedule 11—Circumstances in which periods of entitlement to statutory sick pay do not arise
Schedule 12—Relationship of statutory sick pay with benefits and other payments, etc.
Schedule 13—Relationship of statutory maternity pay with benefits and other payments, etc.

Guardian's allowance

Guardian's allowance

77.—(1) A person shall be entitled to a guardian's allowance in respect of a child [³ or qualifying young person] if—
- (a) he is entitled to child benefit in respect of that child [³ or qualifying young person], and
- (b) the circumstances are any of those specified in subsection (2) below; [¹ . . .]

(2) The circumstances referred to in subsection (1)(b) above are—
- (a) that both of the [³ parents of the child or qualifying young person] are dead; or
- (b) that one of the [³ parents of the child or qualifying young person] is dead and the person claiming a guardian's allowance shows that he was at the date of the death unaware of, and has failed after all reasonable efforts to discover, the whereabouts of the other parent; or
- (c) that one of the [³ parents of the child or qualifying young person] is dead and the other is in prison.

(3) There shall be no entitlement to a guardian's allowance in respect of a child [³ or qualifying young person] unless at least one of the [³ parents of the child or qualifying young person] satisfies, or immediately before his death satisfied, such conditions as may be prescribed as to nationality, residence, place of birth or other matters.

(4) Where, apart from this subsection, a person is entitled to receive, in respect of a particular child [³ or qualifying young person], payment of an amount by way of a guardian's allowance, that amount shall not be payable unless one of the conditions specified in subsection (5) below is satisfied.

(5) Those conditions are—
- (a) that the beneficiary would be treated for the purposes of Part IX of this Act as having the child [³ or qualifying young person] living with him; or

1.30

25

(b) that the requisite contributions are being made to the cost of providing for the child [³ or qualifying young person].

(6) The condition specified in subsection (5)(b) above is to be treated as satisfied if, but only if—
- (a) such contributions are being made at a weekly rate not less than the amount referred to in subsection (4) above—
  - (i) by the beneficiary; or
  - (ii) where the beneficiary is one of two spouses [² or civil partners] residing together, by them together; and
- (b) except in prescribed cases, the contributions are over and above those required for the purpose of satisfying section 143(1)(b) below.

(7) A guardian's allowance in respect of a child [³ or qualifying young person] shall be payable at the weekly rate specified in Schedule 4, Part III, paragraph 5.

(8) Regulations—
- (a) may modify subsection (2) or (3) above in relation to cases in which a child [³ or qualifying young person] has been adopted or is illegitimate, or the marriage of [³ the parents of a child or qualifying young person] has been terminated by divorce [² or the civil partnership of the child's parents has been dissolved];
- (b) shall prescribe the circumstances in which a person is to be treated for the purposes of this section as being in prison (by reference to his undergoing a sentence of imprisonment for life or of a prescribed minimum duration, or to his being in legal custody in prescribed circumstances); and
- (c) may, for cases where entitlement to a guardian's allowance is established by reference to a person being in prison, provide—
  - (i) for requiring him to pay to the National Insurance Fund sums paid by way of a guardian's allowance;
  - (ii) for suspending payment of an allowance where a conviction, sentence or order of a court is subject to appeal, and for matters arising from the decision of an appeal;
  - (iii) for reducing the rate of an allowance in cases where the person in prison contributes to the cost of providing for the child [³ or qualifying young person].

(9) Where a husband and wife are residing together and, apart from this subsection, they would each be entitled to a guardian's allowance in respect of the same child [³ or qualifying young person], only the wife shall be entitled, but payment may be made either to her or to him unless she elects in the prescribed manner that payment is not to be made to him.

(10) Subject to subsection (11) below, no person shall be entitled to a guardian's allowance in respect of a child [³ or qualifying young person] of which he or she is the parent.

(11) Where a person—
- (a) has adopted a child [³ or qualifying young person]; and
- (b) was entitled to guardian's allowance in respect of the child [³ or qualifying young person] immediately before the adoption,

subsection (10) above shall not terminate his entitlement.

(1992 c.4 s.77)

AMENDMENTS

1. Tax Credits Act 2002 s.60 and Sch.6 (April 6, 2003).
2. Civil Partnership Act 2004 s.254 and Sch.24 para.34 (December 5, 2005).
3. Child Benefit Act 2005 s.1 and Sch.1 para.4 (April 10, 2006).

DEFINITIONS

"child"—s.122.
"entitled"—*ibid.*
"Great Britain"—by art.1 of the Union with Scotland Act 1706, this means England, Scotland and Wales.
"United Kingdom"—by Sch.1 of the Interpretation Act 1978, this means Great Britain and Northern Ireland.
"week"—s.122.

GENERAL NOTE

Since April 2003 responsibility for the administration of Guardian's Allowance has lain with HMRC. Arrangements for claims, payments, decisions and appeals are now to be found in the Child Benefit and Guardian's Allowance (Administration) Regulations (SI 2003/492), the Child Benefit and Guardian's Allowance (Administrative Arrangements) Regulations (SI 2003/494), and the Child Benefit and Guardian's Allowance (Decisions and Appeals) Regulations (SI 2003/916). These regulations may be found in Vol.III of this work. 1.31

Subsection (1)
Guardian's Allowance is a benefit paid to those caring for children who are, or are in effect, orphans. The claimant does not have to be in any legal sense the guardian of the child (e.g. under the Children Act 1989), but they must be entitled to child benefit in respect of the child (whether or not they actually receive it) or be treated as if they are entitled. 1.32

Subsection (2)
A claim for Guardian's Allowance can only succeed if it is shown that either: 1.33

(a) both of the child's parents are dead,

(b) that one of them is dead and the whereabouts of the other is and has been unknown since the date of that death, or

(c) that one of them is dead and the other is in prison.

Proof of death will normally be supplied by production of a death certificate though death might be presumed in circumstances similar to those for bereavement benefits.

In showing that the whereabouts of a surviving parent are unknown it is necessary for the claimant to show that this has always been the situation since the death of the other, and remains the situation despite having made all reasonable efforts of discovery.

In considering whether the whereabouts of a surviving parent can reasonably be discovered under (b) above, a tribunal may take into account information which came to light after the claim had been made but before the decision maker had come to a decision, even where the whereabouts of the surviving parent became known otherwise than through the efforts of the claimant. The operative date is the date of decision by the DM. The tribunal must consider the case on the basis of the facts known as at the date of the decision (*R(G) 3/68*). Once the whereabouts of the parent have become known, the claim to the allowance cannot be resurrected on the subsequent disappearance of that parent (*R(G)2/83*). This was a case where 1.34

the surviving parent attended the funeral of the dead parent but then disappeared and his whereabouts could not be ascertained. The claim to the allowance failed. In the same case the Commissioner said that "all reasonable efforts" means the efforts someone could reasonably be expected to make if they wished to find the person for whom they were searching. "Whereabouts" is not the same as residence, so knowing the town but not the address where the missing parent lives may be enough to defeat the claim to benefit. It should be noted that Commissioners in Northern Ireland have taken a different view, saying that in an urban environment "whereabouts" must mean a place identifiable with "some particularity" (*R3/74(P)*). Indeed, Commissioners in Northern Ireland have taken an altogether more generous view of the conditions to be satisfied, holding that knowledge that a parent is alive does not defeat a claim if the whereabouts of the living parent cannot be ascertained after reasonable efforts (*R3/74/(P)* and *R3/75/(P)*, a decision of a Tribunal of Commissioners). In *R3/75/(P)*, the Tribunal of Commissioners suggested that the Commissioners in Great Britain appeared to be regarding the inquiries as being directed to whether the other parent was alive rather than where that parent was living. In an obiter statement in *R(G) 2/83* the Commissioner appears to share this view, suggesting that mere evidence that the second parent is alive will not amount to knowledge of whereabouts so as to defeat a claim, but this does not, of course, overrule the earlier decisions noted above. It seems that the Northern Ireland Commissioners have viewed the benefit as one payable in the absence of a parent able to assume financial responsibility for the child, whereas the British Commissioners see it as concerned primarily with those rendered orphans.

Two unreported Commissoners' decisions demonstrate just how difficult it has become to interpret this subsection where the underlying philosophy of the provisions is unclear.

In the first of them (*CG/60/92*), the claimant grandmother had custody of a child whose mother had died. The father was known and had visited the child at the grandmother's house on four occassions since the death of the mother. As well, he had been served notice of custody proceedings either at, or through, his parents' address, though subsequently they denied knowledge of his whereabouts. The Commissioner held that the claimant must be taken to have known of the father's whereabouts when she had him in her house and could talk to him. An argument was pressed that knowing the whereabouts of someone must mean knowing an address of residence, or of employment, or at any rate of regular attendance, at which something like service of process could be accomplished. If the reason behind GA has indeed shifted to the idea of a resource for maintenance of the child then there would be something to be said for this argument, but the Commissioner thought that the essence of knowing the whereabouts of a person meant no more than being able in some way to communicate with him, and that was clearly achieved here on the four occasions of his visits. The Commissioner relied in this case on the view expressed in *R(G) 2/83* (where the claimant was visited once, and knew of an address that was valid for a week) which also seems to accept that an ability to communicate with the parent is the touchstone.

1.35 In the other case (*CSG/8/92*), the claimant, again a grandmother with the custody of her deceased daughter's child, had had no contact with the child's father, but she had provided an address for service in custody proceedings, she had said that she knew where the other parent was living at the time of her daughter's death, and that she had been told that he was at the funeral, though she had not seen him herself. There was no suggestion that the custody address had been effective and it would appear that at a subsequent SSAT appeal the claimant must have given evidence suggesting that the other matters were based only on rumour. The Commissioner allowed an appeal by the adjudication officer on the ground that the SSAT had failed to explain adequately why they were rejecting the original statements and preferring her later accounts, and he sent the matter back for consideration by another tribunal. In doing so he gave further attention to the meaning of reasonable steps to discover the whereabouts of a parent. First, he seems to accept that actual contact with the

(1992 c.4 s.77)

other parent, or even a chance to communicate, is a conclusive block to the claimant; she cannot in those circumstances say that at all times since the death she has been unaware of the whereabouts of the other parent. Seeing the other parent at the funeral is probably enough to preclude her claim because she could have taken the opportunity to establish contact. It is not enough for the claimant to say that she had no wish to speak to the other (probably estranged) parent, because the test suggested in *R(G) 2/83*, and adopted in these cases, is that reasonable efforts to discover the whereabouts of another person mean the steps that would be reasonable for a person who *wanted* to find that other person. (Though, quaere, it might be possible to argue that one could want to find another person and yet reasonably refrain from making inquiries upon an occasion of particular emotion and distress such as the funeral.)

Both cases (and *R(G) 2/83*), therefore, agree that where actual contact has been made, even though transitory, the claimant knows (or rather has known) the whereabouts of the other parent and the claim must fail. The Commissioner goes on to consider, however, the question of how much knowledge of the other parent's location will suffice if no contact is made. Put another way, the question is what is meant by "whereabouts" when someone is being sought, and how much do you have to know in order to say you have found him? Knowing that the parent is somewhere in the world cannot be sufficient because, as has been pointed out, this equates to knowing that he is alive, whereas the statute requires knowledge of his whereabouts. There seems much good sense in the observation of the Northern Ireland Commissioner that while the name of a village may suffice to locate someone living there, something more must be known of someone in an urban environment. *R(G) 3/68* held that knowing an address (in Russia) from which letters had purported to have been sent, but from which no reply was obtained, did amount to knowing the whereabouts of that person. *CG/60/92* rejects the argument that "whereabouts" should be equated with address for service, but only in the context of a claimant who had actual, if transitory, contact. In *CSG/8/92*, the Commissioner seemed ready to accept that "whereabouts" should now be taken to mean knowledge of the person's residence, of employment, or place of attendance by habit (such as a public house) by which he could be located without undue further difficulty. An unresponsive address in Russia would fail this test. This seems a workable and common sense approach and is one step towards rationalising GA, at least in part, as a benefit for the replacement of parental maintenance.

The circumstances in which a child is regarded as "orphaned" by the surviving parent being in prison are defined in reg.7 of the Guardian's Allowance (General) Regulations 2003. 1.36

Where a child has been adopted the adopted parents are put for all purposes in the place of the child's parents. Where a child has been adopted by only one parent a claim may be made in respect of that child when only that parent has died (see reg.4 of the Guardian's Allowance (General) Regulations 2003).

Where a child's parents are not married to each other a claim may be made following the death of the mother if paternity of the child has not been established by a court and is not regarded as having been established by the determining authority (reg.4 of the Guardian's Allowance (General) Regulations 2003).

Where a child's parents have been divorced a claim may be made following the death of the parent with whom the child was living if there is no residence order in favour of the surviving parent and no liability for that parent to maintain the child either under a court order or a decision in force under the Child Support Act 1991 (reg.6 of the Guardian's Allowance (General) Regulations 2003).

Subsections (3)

Conditions as to residence of the child's parents are to be found in reg.9 of the Guardian's Allowance (General) Regulations 2003. 1.37

Subsections (4), (5) and (6)

1.38 A claim for GA can only succeed if the claimant is either:

(a) treated as having the child living with them for the purpose of a claim for Child Benefit, or

(b) is contributing (or if living with their spouse, the spouse is contributing) to the cost of maintaining the child to an extent equal to the amount of GA that is payable. This contribution must be in addition to any contribution necessary to qualify for the payment of child benefit.

Subsection (9)

1.39 This is a curiously worded provision. Where husband and wife are living together and, but for this provision, they would each be entitled to claim GA, only the wife is to be entitled. Nevertheless HMRC could make payment to the husband unless his wife has elected in the proper way to deny payment to her husband.

Subsection (10)

1.40 This prevents a claim for GA by a parent of the child. But for this purpose a step-parent is not regarded as a parent and such a claim could also succeed if it is made by the natural parent of a child whose adoptive parents have died—the effect of the adoption is to substitute the adoptive parents as the child's "parents" for this purpose. (*R(G)4/83(T)*)—and see reg.4 Guardian's Allowance (General) Regulations 2003.)

PART IX

CHILD BENEFIT

Child benefit

1.41 **141.**—A person who is responsible for one or more children [1 or qualifying young persons] in any week shall be entitled, subject to the provisions of this Part of this Act, to a benefit (to be known as "child benefit") for that week in respect of the [1 child or qualifying young person, or each of the children or qualifying young persons] for whom he is responsible.

AMENDMENT

1. Child Benefit Act 2005 s.1 (April 10, 2006).

GENERAL NOTE

1.42 Since April 2003 administration of Child Benefit has lain with HMRC, but the structure of the benefit remains substantially unchanged.

The administrative arrangements for claims, payments, decisions and appeals are now to be found in Child Benefit and Guardian's Allowance (Administration) Regulations (SI 2003/492), the Child Benefit and Guardian's Allowance (Administrative Arrangements) Regulations (SI 2003/494) and the Child Benefit and Guardian's Allowance (Decisions and Appeals) Regulations 2003 (SI 2003/916). All of these are to be found in Vol.III of this work.

1.43 Child Benefit is a benefit paid to those responsible for a child or qualifying young person. Under the new definitions adopted from 2006 a "child" is a person under the age of 16 (whether or not they are in education) and a "qualifying young person" will be defined by regulation generally as a young person who remains in non advanced education or in certain forms of training up to the age of 20 (see s.142 below). Those responsible for a child include not only those with whom the child is living, but also those contributing sufficiently to the cost of maintaining that child.

Child Benefit is paid at a higher rate in respect of the first or only child and at a lower rate for all other children in the family.

1.44

Claimants for Child Benefit are also subject to conditions as to residence and presence (including the presence of the child) and are disqualified while they are subject to immigration control—see s.146A.

Most of those responsible for children who receive child benefit also receive or are entitled to child tax credit. See s.8 of the Tax Credits Act 2002 para.1.250.

Section 8 of, and Sch.1 to, the Finance Act 2012 introduce a new High Income Child Benefit Charge. This took initial effect from January 7, 2013 and full effect for the tax year 2013/14 under Sch.1 para.7 of that Act. The charge is detailed in what are now ss.681B–681H of the Income Tax (Earnings and Pensions) Act 2003. The detail of those provisions is beyond the scope of this work. The effect is to impose an income tax charge equal to all child benefit received on any taxpayer whose income exceeds £60,000 with a 50 per cent charge imposed on a taxpayer where income exceeds £50,000 to the extent that that taxpayer's income exceeds £50,000. In other words, a taxpayer over the higher limit receives no long-term advantage from child benefit while there is a tapered removal of advantage where income is below £60,000.

Amendments to s.7 of the Taxes Management Act 1970 (not contained in this work) and the addition of s.13A of the Social Security Administration Act 1992 (see para.1.178 below) allow individuals who would lose all advantage from child benefit under these provisions to elect not to receive child benefit.

[¹ "Child" and "qualifying young person"

142.—(1) For the purposes of this Part of this Act a person is a child if he has not attained the age of 16.

1.45

(2) In this Part of the Act "qualifying young person" means a person, other than a child, who—
  (a) Has not attained such age (greater than 16) as is prescribed by regulations made by the Treasury, and
  (b) satisfies conditions so prescribed.]

AMENDMENT

1. Child Benefit Act 2005 s.1 (April 10, 2006).

Meaning of "person responsible for [³ child or qualifying young person]"

143.—(1) For the purposes of this Part of this Act a person shall be treated as responsible for a child [³ or qualifying young person] in any week if—
  (a) he has the child [³ or qualifying young person] living with him in that week; or
  (b) he is contributing to the cost of providing for the child [³ or qualifying young person] at a weekly rate which is not less than the weekly rate of child benefit payable in respect of the child [³ or qualifying young person] for that week.

1.46

(2) Where a person has had a child [⁴ or qualifying young person] living with him at some time before a particular week he shall be treated for the purposes of this section as having the child [⁴ or qualifying young person] living with him in that week notwithstanding their absence from one

another unless, in the 16 weeks preceding that week, they were absent from one another for more than 56 days not counting any day which is to be disregarded under subsection (3) below.

(3) Subject to subsection (4) below, a day of absence shall be disregarded for the purposes of subsection (2) above if it is due solely to the [4 the fact that the child or qualifying young person is]—

(a) receiving [4 education or training of a description prescribed by regulations made by the Treasury];
(b) undergoing medical or other treatment as an in-patient in a hospital or similar institution; or
(c) [4 . . .], in such circumstances as may be prescribed, in residential accommodation pursuant to arrangements made under—
   [1[5(i) [6 . . .] paragraph 2 of Schedule 15 to the National Health Service (Wales) Act 2006]
   (ii) the Children Act 1989;]
   [2 (iii) the Social Work (Scotland) Act 1968;
   (iv) the National Health Service (Scotland) Act 1978;
   (v) the Education (Scotland) Act 1980;
   (vi) the Mental Health (Scotland) Act 1984; or
   (vii) the Children (Scotland) Act 1995.]

(4) The number of days that may be disregarded by virtue of subsection (3)(b) or (c) above in the case of any child [4 or qualifying young person] shall not exceed such number as may be prescribed unless the person claiming to be responsible for the child [4 or qualifying young person] regularly incurs expenditure in respect [4 of him].

(5) Regulations may prescribe the circumstances in which a person is or is not to be treated—

(a) as contributing to the cost of providing for a child [4 or qualifying young person] as required by subsection (1)(b) above; or
(b) as regularly incurring expenditure in respect of a child [4 or qualifying young person] as required by subsection (4) above;

and such regulations may in particular make provision whereby a contribution made or expenditure incurred by two or more persons is to be treated as made or incurred by one of them or whereby a contribution made or expenditure incurred by one of two spouses [3 or civil partners] residing together is to be treated as made or incurred by the other.

AMENDMENTS

1. Social Security (Consequential Provisions) Act 1992 s.6 and Sch.4 para.5 (April 1, 1993).
2. Child Support Pensions and Social Security Act 2000 s.72 (October 9, 2000).
3. Civil Partnership Act 2004 s.254 and Sch.24 para.47 (December 5, 2005).
4. Child Benefit Act 2005 s.1 and Sch.1 para.9 (April 10, 2006).
5. National Health Service (Consequential Provisions) Act 2006 Sch.1 para.146 (March 1, 2007).
6. Care Act 2014 and Children and Families Act 2014 (Consequential Amendments) Order 2015 (SI 2015/914) Sch. art.54 (April 1, 2015).

GENERAL NOTE

1.47   The provisions in this section are to be compared with the equivalent (but different) rules for child tax credit. See Child Tax Credit Regulations 2002 reg.3 (para.2.194 below).

(1992 c.4 s.143)

Subsection (1)

A person is regarded as being "responsible for a child or qualifying young person" if they either have the child living with them, or if they are contributing to the upkeep of that child a weekly sum not less that the amount of Child Benefit payable for that week. See reg.11 of the Child Benefit (General) Regulations 2006. To be "living with" the claimant in this context requires that the child resides in the same house in a "settled course of daily living". In *R(F) 2/81* the claimant failed because his daughter spent only the day time hours each weekend in his home. Mere residence on its own may be insufficient if the child is normally living elsewhere (as for example where a child spends its holidays living away from home). But where the child is living with a parent who has rights of care and control it may be regarded as living with that parent even though at other times it may be living with the other parent *(R(F) 2/79)*.

1.48

The importance of focusing on the right question in deciding whether a child is living with the claimant is demonstrated by *SB v HMRC* [2013] UKUT 24 (AAC). The claimant, who was a Polish national, had come to this country together with her four-year-old daughter. Shortly after arrival, and when she was in employment, she claimed both Child Benefit and Child Tax Credit (CTC). The claimant was asked to provide documentary evidence of the fact that the child was attending school and was registered at a GP surgery. At first both benefits were refused because the claimant had not provided that documentation. However, after appealing, the documents were received by the section dealing with CTC and that claim was allowed. An electronic file dealing with that claim was stored on the HMRC computer system. But the Child Benefit appeal was rejected and an appeal to the FTT was also dismissed. At the tribunal hearing the claimant produced a letter from the school confirming attendance, but no GP documentation. The FTT regarded the school letter as deficient and the absence of the other as significant.

In the Upper Tribunal, Judge Wikeley was critical of the approach adopted both within HMRC and the FTT. As he pointed out, the sole relevant question was whether the child was "living with" her mother. No questions were asked by the FTT that addressed that issue. The documents requested could be evidence of the child's existence, but, unless they recorded the child's address as being the same as that of the claimant, they really said nothing about the living arrangements. It does appear, however, that in practice such evidence is all that is required by HMRC, because on the basis of the documents that had been received, the claim to CTC had been accepted. Judge Wikeley also pointed out that the existence of the CTC appeal was revealed on the papers relating to the claim for Child Benefit and he had been assured by HMRC's representative that it would be easy for each section to access the information used by the other—as he put it, a lamentable failure by the left hand to know of what was done by the right. This is a prime example of what an FTT should have done in exercising its inquisitorial function. The appeal was allowed.

The interaction of subss.(1) and (2) together with s.144(3) and Sch.10 referred to there is applied in *CF/3348/2002*. There the child remained with the wife when her husband, who had been in receipt of Child Benefit, left her. In accordance with s.144(3) and Sch.10, he nevertheless remained entitled to receive the benefit for the next three weeks.

Subsection (2)

A child may continue to live with the claimant even though one or other of them may be absent provided that the absence is not more than 56 days in a period of 16 weeks. Where the absence is continuous, therefore, entitlement will cease after 8 weeks.

1.49

Subsection (3)

In counting days of absence certain days are disregarded. These include days away at boarding school, days in hospital or otherwise undergoing medical

1.50

33

treatment, or days in local authority care on disability or health grounds—reg.9 of the Child Benefit (General) Regulations 2006.

Subsection (4)

1.51 Where the child is absent for medical treatment or in care on grounds of disability or health the period of permitted absence is extended to 12 weeks— reg.10 of the Child Benefit (General) Regulations 2006.

But entitlement may be continued further provided that the claimant can show that they are regularly incurring expenditure in respect of the child.

Subsection (5)

1.52 Regulation 11 of the Child Benefit (General) Regulations 2006 provides for the aggregation of amounts where two or more persons are contributing to the cost of maintaining a child and for either agreement between them or, failing that, a determination by the Board as to which of them will be treated as entitled to benefit. Where spouses are residing together a contribution made by one of them may be treated as having been made by the other.

Exclusions and priority

1.53 **144.**—(1) [1 . . .]

(2) Schedule 9 to this Act shall have effect for excluding entitlement to child benefit [1 . . .].

(3) Where, apart from this subsection, two or more persons would be entitled to child benefit in respect of the same child [1 or qualifying young person] for the same week, one of them only shall be entitled; and the question which of them is entitled shall be determined in accordance with Schedule 10 to this Act.

AMENDMENT

1. Child Benefit Act 2005 s.1 and Sch.1 para.10 (April 10, 2006).

GENERAL NOTE

1.54 Note that recourse to Sch.10 is appropriate only where two or more people are entitled to Child Benefit in respect of the same child for the same week. If, therefore, only one of them remains entitled under s.143 there is no recourse to Sch.10. But where, for example, a child has ceased to reside with one parent (s.143(1)) that parent may remain entitled for a period by the application of the other provisions of s.143 and by the effect of s.13(2) of the SSAA 1992. See *CF/2826/2008* and the notes following Sch.10. Compare the different approach taken for child tax credit in Child Tax Credit Regulations 2002 reg.3 (see para.2.186 below) to that in Sch.10.

Rate of child benefit

1.55 **145.**—(1) Child benefit shall be payable at such weekly rate as may be prescribed.

(2) Different rates may be prescribed in relation to different cases, whether by reference to the age of the child [2 or qualifying young person] in respect of whom the benefit is payable or otherwise.

(3) The power to prescribe different rates under subsection (2) above shall be exercised so as to bring different rates into force on such day as the Secretary of State may by order specify.

(4) No rate prescribed in place of a rate previously in force shall be lower than the rate that it replaces.

(5) [1 . . .]

(1992 c.4 s.145)

(6) An order under subsection (3) above may be varied or revoked at any time before the date specified thereby.

(7) An order under that subsection shall be laid before Parliament after being made.

AMENDMENTS

1. Tax Credits Act 2002 s.60 and Sch.6 (April 1, 2003).
2. Child Benefit Act 2005 s.1 and Sch.1 para.11 (April 10, 2006).

[1 Entitlement after death of child [3 or qualifying young person]

145A.—(1) If a child [3 or qualifying young person] dies and a person is entitled to child benefit in respect of him for the week in which his death occurs, that person shall be entitled to child benefit in respect of the child [3 or qualifying young person] for a prescribed period following that week.

(2) If the person entitled to child benefit under subsection (1) dies before the end of that prescribed period and, at the time of his death, was—
  (a) a member of a married couple [2 or civil partnership] and living with the person to whom he was married [2 or who was his civil partner], or
  (b) a member of an unmarried couple [2 or a cohabiting same sex couple],
that other member of the [2 couple or partnership] shall be entitled to child benefit for the period for which the dead person would have been entitled to child benefit under subsection (1) above but for his death.

(3) If a child [3 or qualifying young person] dies before the end of the week in which he is born, subsections (1) and (2) apply in his case as if references to the person entitled to child benefit in respect of a child [3 or qualifying young person] for the week in which his death occurs were to the person who would have been so entitled if the child had been alive at the beginning of that week (and if any conditions which were satisfied, and any facts which existed, at the time of his death were satisifed or existed then).

(4) Where a person is entitled to child benefit in respect of a child under this section, section 77 applies with the omission of subsections (4) to (6).

(5) In this section—
[2 "civil partnership" means two people of the same sex who are civil partners of each other and are neither—
  (a) separated under a court order, nor
  (b) separated in circumstances in which the separation is likely to be permanent,
"cohabiting same-sex couple" means two people of the same sex who are not civil partners of each other but are living together as if they were civil partners.]
"married couple" means a man and a woman who are married to each other and are neither—
  (a) separated under a court order, nor
  (b) separated in circumstances in which the separation is likely to be permanent, and
"unmarried couple" means a man and a woman who are not a married couple but are living together as husband and wife.]

[2 (6) For the purposes of this section, two people of the same sex are to be regarded as living together as if they were civil partners if, but only if, they would be regarded as living together as husband and wife were they instead two people of the opposite sex.]

1.56

Amendments

1. Tax Credits Act 2002 s.56 (April 1, 2003).
2. Civil Partnership Act 2004 s.254 and Sch.24 para.48 (December 5, 2005).
3. Child Benefit Act 2005 s.1 and Sch.1 para.12 (April 10, 2006).

[¹Presence in Great Britain

146.—(1) No child benefit shall be payable in respect of a child [² or qualifying young person] for a week unless he is in Great Britain in that week.

(2) No person shall be entitled to child benefit for a week unless he is in Great Britain in that week.

(3) Circumstances may be prescribed in which [² any] person is to be treated for the purposes of [² subsection (1) or (2) above] as being, or as not being, in Great Britain.]

Amendments

1. Tax Credits Act 2002 s.56 (April 1, 2003).
2. Child Benefit Act 2005 s.1 and Sch.1 para.13 (April 10, 2006).

General Note

This section was inserted with effect from April 2003. It replaces an earlier version, but the effect of this section when combined with the Child Benefit (General) Regulations is largely the same. See the notes to those Regulations. For questions that involve persons either coming from, or going to, another country that is a part of the European Union, reference should be made to the relevant sections of Vol.III of this work.

In *Commissioners for HMRC v Ruas* [2010] EWCA Civ 291; [2010] AACR 31, the claimant, a Portuguese national, had come to the UK from Portugal in 2000 with his wife and youngest child. His two elder children had remained living in Portugal with a relative. The claimant worked in the UK and paid national insurance contributions until he became unable to work due to ill-health in 2004. He remained living in the UK and in 2006 applied for child benefit for all three of his children, when he was in receipt of DLA and income support and qualified for national insurance credits on the ground of incapacity for work. The Court of Appeal held (dismissing the appeal of the Secretary of State against the decision of Judge Mesher in *CF/2266/2007*) that the claimant was entitled to claim child benefit in the UK for his children resident in Portugal. The effect of s.146, which restricts child benefit to children resident in Great Britain, had to be disapplied by virtue of art.73 of Regulation 1408/71, which was directly effective in the UK, conferring on the claimant an entitlement to UK child benefit (*Martinez Sala v Freistaat Bayern* (C-85/96) [1998] E.C.R. I-2691 followed).

Further consideration has been given to Regulation 1408/71 and to its successor 883/2004 in *KT v HMRC* [2013] UKUT 0151 (AAC). Regulation 1408/71 was replaced by 883/2004 with effect from May 1, 2010, but the claim in this case had been made in late April of that year. The judge dealt with entitlement under both regulations because a new claim could have been brought under 883/2004, but he thought the outcome would be the same. The claimant was a Polish national living and working in this country and making payments in respect of two children, his nephew and niece, who were living with their mother in Poland. These children seem to fall awkwardly between two stools; if they had been his children the claim would succeed in accordance with the *Martinez Sala* case above (and now under 883/2004 as well), and if they had been living in this country (even though not with the claimant) it would succeed under s.143 so long as he was providing for them at the requisite rate. However, the judge holds that neither of these Regulations can provide for them. This was because in each case it was necessary to find that the claim was in respect of a child who was "a member of the family", In each of the Regulations above member of the family is defined (in part) as

> "any person defined or recognised as a member of the family or designated as a member of the household by the legislation under which benefits are provided;"

The relevant provision of UK law does not refer to "family" or "household" using instead the concept of "person responsible for a child" under s.143 above. In relation to Regulation 1408/71, therefore, the Judge found that he should fall back upon interpreting family and household as ordinary words of English law neither of which, he thought, could encompass these children. In relation to Regulation 883/2004 the definition was extended to specific persons, but in this context, would cover only children of the claimant. The claim therefore failed under both regulations. The only way it seems that such a claim could succeed would be if s.143 were treated as defining the family for the purposes of the definition above.

Persons subject to immigration control

[¹ **146A.**—[² . . .]]

1.59

AMENDMENTS

1. Asylum and Immigration Act 1996 s.10 (August 19, 1996).
2. Immigration and Asylum Act 1999 s.169(3) and Sch.16 (April 3, 2000).

Interpretation of Part IX and supplementary provisions

147.—(1) In this Part of this Act—

1.60

"prescribed" means prescribed by regulations;

"recognised educational establishment" [² omitted]

"voluntary organisation" means a body, other than a public or local authority, the activities of which are carried on otherwise than for profit; and

"week" means a period of 7 days beginning with a Monday.

(2) Subject to any provision made by regulations, references in this Part of this Act to any condition being satisfied or any facts existing in a week shall be construed as references to the condition being satisfied or the facts existing at the beginning of that week.

(3) References in this Part of this Act to a parent, father or mother of a child [² or qualifying young person] shall be construed as including references to a step-parent, step-father or step-mother.

(4) Regulations may prescribe the circumstances in which persons are or are not to be treated for the purposes of this Part of this Act as residing together.

(5) Regulations may make provision as to the circumstances in which [¹ a marriage during the subsistence of which a party to it is at any time married to more than one person is to be treated for the purposes of this Part of this Act as having, or not having, the same consequences as any other marriage.]

(6) Nothing in this Part of this Act shall be construed as conferring a right to child benefit on any body corporate; but regulations may confer such a right on voluntary organisations and for that purpose may make such modifications as the Secretary of State thinks fit—

(a) of any provision of this Part of this Act; or
(b) of any provision of the Administration Act relating to child benefit.

Social Security Contributions and Benefits Act 1992

AMENDMENTS

1. Private International Law (Miscellaneous Provisions) Act 1995 the Schedule para.4(3) (January 8, 1996).
2. Child Benefit Act 2005 s.1 and Sch.1 para.14 (April 10, 2006).

GENERAL NOTE

"week"

1.61   A week is defined as a period of seven days beginning on a Monday. Falling short of a full week by a few hours can be ignored: *R(F) 1/82(S)*. The provision in subs.(2) is a trap for the unwary. It means that, subject to provisions in regulations imposing a different rule, a condition to be satisfied or circumstances existing on a Monday (which, of course, begins at midnight on Sunday) are taken as subsisting for the whole week.

The meaning of parent is also extended by the effect of the Children Act 1989, to include any person in whose favour a residence order has been made. This is because the "parental responsibility" conferred by the order made under that Act is defined to include all the rights which, by law, a parent has in relation to that child. For the purposes of the Contributions and Benefits Act, the word parent is to be construed as the "legal parent" of the child. (See *Secretary of State for Social Services v Smith* [1983] 1 W.L.R. 1110, where the effect of an order made under equivalent legislation then in force, was to include an adoptive parent of the child and at the same time to exclude the natural parent.) The same reasoning was applied by Commissioner Howell in *R(F) 1/08* where a lesbian couple had two children with the assistance of artificial insemination and after they had separated a residence order had been made in favour of both of them. The Commissioner held that both must be regarded as parents, not just the biological mother, and consequently it became necessary for HMRC to exercise the discretion provided for in para.5.

PART XI

STATUTORY SICK PAY

GENERAL NOTE

1.62   Statutory Sick Pay (SSP) was originally introduced in April 1983 by the Social Security and Housing Benefits Act 1982. The main primary legislation is now to be found in Pt XI, annotated here; there are also various sets of regulations, principally the SSP (General) Regulations 1982 (SI 1982/894), which are contained in Pt III of this volume. Section 151(1) of the SSCBA 1992 provides that an employer is liable to pay to an employee for any day of incapacity for work in relation to the employee's contract of service with that employer, where the day in question is a qualifying day (see s.154) which forms part of a period of incapacity to work (see s.152) and falls within a period of entitlement as between that employer and that employee (s.153 and Sch.11). Incapacity must be duly notified to the employer, and SSP may be withheld in the event of non-existent or late notification (see s.156). Those who are self-employed (who by definition lack an employer) and those who are unemployed are excluded from entitlement to SSP. Some employees are also excluded from SSP. Section 153(3) and Sch.11 prevent the requisite period of entitlement arising as between employer and employees in various types of case (e.g. low earners, women at a certain stage of pregnancy, some persons affected by trade disputes).

Statutory Sick Pay is payable at a weekly rate. The daily rate will depend on the number of qualifying days in the week (see s.157). Statutory Sick Pay is not payable in respect of the first three qualifying days (or "waiting days") in any period of entitlement (see s.155(1)). Statutory Sick Pay cannot be paid in kind or by the provision of board and lodging or other services or facilities (SSP (General) Regulations 1982 (SI 1982/894) reg.8). Any day of incapacity for work in relation to a contract of service which falls within a period of entitlement to SSP precludes concurrent entitlement to incapacity benefit (Sch.12 para.1). Employees reach their maximum entitlement to SSP as against any one employer in any one period of entitlement when they have been entitled in that period to 28 times the appropriate weekly rate of SSP (see s.155(4)). This is typically after 28 weeks of continuous incapacity. If the person remains incapacitated after that, he or she must look to incapacity benefit or, failing that, a means-tested benefit.

At the start of the SSP scheme in 1983, employers were able to recoup the entire amount paid from the National Insurance contributions and the PAYE tax that they were required to collect and account for to the Inland Revenue. The initial effect of SSP was thus to transfer the cost of administration from the State to the employer. The Statutory Sick Pay Act 1991 limited employers to recouping 80 per cent of the cost of SSP payments, but "small employers" were still able to claim full reimbursement. This was followed by the Statutory Sick Pay Act 1994, which abolished employers' general right to recover (some of) the costs of SSP. The special rules for reimbursing small employers were then repealed (although they remain for the purposes of SMP). Instead, in principle any employer—not just small employers— can recover the costs of SSP payments under the Percentage Threshold Scheme. However, this reimbursement is only available where the employer's expenditure on SSP exceeds 13 per cent of their gross National Insurance contributions liability—in other words, only where there is an epidemic of illness in the workforce (see further Statutory Sick Pay Threshold Order 1995 (SI 1995/512)).

In certain circumstances, where an employer does not, or because of insolvency, cannot, discharge their statutory liability to pay SSP, that liability became that of the Board of Inland Revenue (s.151(6) of the SSP (General) Regulations 1982 (SI 1982/894) regs 9A–9C). This liability was transferred from the Secretary of State to the Board of the Inland Revenue with effect from April 1, 1999, under the Social Security Contributions (Transfer of Functions, etc.) Act 1999 s.1(2) and Sch.2, along with those functions under SSP (General) Regulations 1982 regs 10 and 14.

1.63

The arrangements for resolving disputes about entitlement to SSP were changed with effect from April 1, 1999. Before that date, certain questions could be referred to an AO, thus opening up the usual channels of appeal to SSATs, Commissioners and ultimately the courts. Since that date the Social Security Contributions (Transfer of Functions, etc.) Act 1999 and the Statutory Sick Pay and Statutory Maternity Pay (Decisions) Regulations 1999 (SI 1999/776) have replaced the AO with an officer of Revenue and Customs. Consequently, decision-making and appeals are now governed by Pt II of the 1999 Act, with the right of appeal lying to the tax chamber of the First-tier Tribunal. An employment tribunal has no jurisdiction under the Employment Rights Act 1996 to entertain an employee's complaint that SSP has not been paid: (per Mr Recorder Luba QC in *Taylor Gordon & Co Ltd v Timmons* ([2004] I.R.L.R. 180, at [43])).

Employer's liability

Employer's liability

151.—(1) Where an employee has a day of incapacity for work in relation to his contract of service with an employer, that employer shall, if the conditions set out in sections 152 to 154 below are satisfied, be liable to make him, in accordance with the following provisions of this Part of this Act, a payment (to be known as "statutory sick pay") in respect of that day.

1.64

(2) Any agreement shall be void to the extent that it purports—
  (a) to exclude, limit or otherwise modify any provision of this Part of this Act; or

Social Security Contributions and Benefits Act 1992

(b) to require an employee to contribute (whether directly or indirectly) towards any costs incurred by his employer under this Part of this Act.

(3) For the avoidance of doubt, any agreement between an employer and an employee authorising any deductions from statutory sick pay which the employer is liable to pay to the employee in respect of any period shall not be void by virtue of subsection (2)(a) above if the employer—
- (a) is authorised by that or another agreement to make the same deductions from any contractual remuneration which he is liable to pay in respect of the same period, or
- (b) would be so authorised if he were liable to pay contractual remuneration in respect of that period.

(4) For the purposes of this Part of this Act [[1]a day of incapacity for work in relation to a contract of service means a day on which] the employee concerned is, or is deemed in accordance with regulations to be, incapable by reason of some specific disease or bodily or mental disablement of doing work which he can reasonably be expected to do under that contract.

(5) In any case where an employee has more than one contract of service with the same employer the provisions of this Part of this Act shall, except in such cases as may be prescribed and subject to the following provisions of this Part of this Act, have effect as if the employer were a different employer in relation to each contract of service.

(6) Circumstances may be prescribed in which, notwithstanding the provisions of subsections (1) to (5) above, the liability to make payments of statutory sick pay is to be a liability of the [[2]Commissioners of Inland Revenue].

[[2](7) Regulations under subsection (6) above must be made with the concurrence of the Commissioners of Inland Revenue.]

AMENDMENTS

1. Social Security (Incapacity for Work) Act 1994 s.11(1) and Sch.1 para.34 (April 13, 1995).
2. Social Security Contributions (Transfer of Functions, etc.) Act 1999 s.1(1) and Sch.1 para.9 (April 1, 1999).

DEFINITIONS

"contract of service"—see s.163(1).
"employee"—*ibid.* and SSP (General) Regulations 1982 reg.16.
"employer"—see s.163(1).
"prescribed"—*ibid.*

GENERAL NOTE

Subsections (1)–(3)

1.65 The general liability on employers to pay SSP—where the qualifying conditions are fulfilled by the employee—is set out in subs.(1). Employers cannot contract out of this liability (subs.(2), but note the qualification in subs.(3)).

Subsection (4)

1.66 For the purposes of SSP, a day of incapacity for work in relation to any contract of service may arise in either of two ways. The first is where the employee is actually incapable by reason of some specific disease or bodily or mental disablement of doing work which he or she can reasonably be expected to do under that contract.

(1992 c.4 s.151)

On "incapable of work" and "by reason of some specific disease or bodily or mental disablement", see the annotations to SSCBA 1992 s.171B(2) in Vol.I to this series. The second, and alternative, possibility is where the employee, although not actually incapable, falls within the protection of regulations which deem a day to be one of incapacity for work. On deemed incapacity, see SSP (General) Regulations 1982 (SI 1982/894) reg.2.

Subsection (5)
This contemplates that an employee who has more than one contract of service with the same employer could get SSP in respect of each contract of service, where the eligibility conditions were satisfied with respect to each contract. This provision is modified by SSP (General) Regulations 1982 (SI 1982/894) reg.21.

1.67

Subsection (6)
See SSP (General) Regulations 1982 (SI 1982/894) regs 9A–9C and see also General Note to Pt XI of this Act, above.

1.68

The qualifying conditions

Period of incapacity for work

152.—(1) The first condition is that the day in question forms part of a period of incapacity for work.

1.69

(2) In this Part of this Act "period of incapacity for work" means any period of four or more consecutive days, each of which is a day of incapacity for work in relation to the contract of service in question.

(3) Any two periods of incapacity for work which are separated by a period of not more than 8 weeks shall be treated as a single period of incapacity for work.

(4) The Secretary of State may by regulations direct that a larger number of weeks specified in the regulations shall be substituted for the number of weeks for the time being specified in subsection (3) above.

(5) No day of the week shall be disregarded in calculating any period of consecutive days for the purposes of this section.

(6) A day may be a day of incapacity for work in relation to a contract of service, and so form part of a period of incapacity for work, notwithstanding that—
   (a) it falls before the making of the contract or after the contract expires or is brought to an end; or
   (b) it is not a day on which the employee concerned would be required by that contract to be available for work.

DEFINITIONS

"contract of service"—see s.163(1).
"employee"—*ibid.* and SSP (General) Regulations 1982 reg.16.
"period of incapacity for work"—see subs.(2).
"week"—see s.163(1).

GENERAL NOTE

Liability to pay SSP can only arise if the qualifying day which is one of incapacity for work also forms part of a period of incapacity for work (subs.(1)). A period of incapacity for work is formed by any period of four or more consecutive days of incapacity for work in relation to the contract of service in question (subs.(2)). Every day of the

1.70

week counts for determining periods of consecutive days (subs.(4)). Any two periods of incapacity "link" to form a single period where they are not separated by more than eight weeks, counting the separation period from the end of the "first" period. Note that under subs.(5), a day can still be one of incapacity for work in relation to the contract of service and thus be part of a period of incapacity for work where it is not one on which the contract would require the employee to be available for work, or where it falls before the contract was made or after it expires or is otherwise brought to an end.

Period of entitlement

1.71

153.—(1) The second condition is that the day in question falls within a period which is, as between the employee and his employer, a period of entitlement.

(2) For the purposes of this Part of this Act a period of entitlement, as between an employee and his employer, is a period beginning with the commencement of a period of incapacity for work and ending with whichever of the following first occurs—

(a) the termination of that period of incapacity for work;
(b) the day on which the employee reaches, as against the employer concerned, his maximum entitlement to statutory sick pay (determined in accordance with section 155 below);
(c) the day on which the employee's contract of service with the employer concerned expires or is brought to an end;
(d) in the case of an employee who is, or has been, pregnant, the day immediately preceding the beginning of the disqualifying period.

(3) Schedule 11 to this Act has effect for the purpose of specifying circumstances in which a period of entitlement does not arise in relation to a particular period of incapacity for work.

(4) A period of entitlement as between an employee and an employer of his may also be, or form part of, a period of entitlement as between him and another employer of his.

(5) The Secretary of State may by regulations—

(a) specify circumstances in which, for the purpose of determining whether an employee's maximum entitlement to statutory sick pay has been reached in a period of entitlement as between him and an employer of his, days falling within a previous period of entitlement as between the employee and any person who is or has in the past been an employer of his are to be counted; and
(b) direct that in prescribed circumstances an employer shall provide a person who is about to leave his employment, or who has been employed by him in the past, with a statement in the prescribed form containing such information as may be prescribed in relation to any entitlement of the employee to statutory sick pay.

(6) Regulations may provide, in relation to prescribed cases, for a period of entitlement to end otherwise than in accordance with subsection (2) above.

(7) In a case where the employee's contract of service first takes effect on a day which falls within a period of incapacity for work, the period of entitlement begins with that day.

(8) In a case where the employee's contract of service first takes effect between two periods of incapacity for work which by virtue of section 152(3) above are treated as one, the period of entitlement begins with the first day of the second of those periods.

(1992 c.4 s.153)

(9) In any case where, otherwise than by virtue of section 6(1)(b) above, an employee's earnings under a contract of service in respect of the day on which the contract takes effect do not attract a liability to pay secondary Class 1 contributions, subsections (7) and (8) above shall have effect as if for any reference to the contract first taking effect there were substituted a reference to the first day in respect of which the employee's earnings attract such a liability.

(10) Regulations shall make provision as to an employer's liability under this Part of this Act to pay statutory sick pay to an employee in any case where the employer's contract of service with that employee has been brought to an end by the employer solely, or mainly, for the purpose of avoiding liability for statutory sick pay.

(11) Subsection (2)(d) above does not apply in relation to an employee who has been pregnant if her pregnancy terminated, before the beginning of the disqualifying period, otherwise than by confinement.

(12) In this section—

"confinement" is to be construed in accordance with section 171(1) below;

"disqualifying period" means—
   (a) in relation to a woman entitled to statutory maternity pay, the maternity pay period; and
   (b) in relation to a woman entitled to maternity allowance, the maternity allowance period;

"maternity allowance period" has the meaning assigned to it by section 35(2) above; and

"maternity pay period" has the meaning assigned to it by section 165(1) below.

DEFINITIONS

"confinement"—see subs.(12).
"contract of service"—see s.163(1).
"disqualifying period"—see subs.(12).
"employee"—see s.163(1) and SSP (General) Regulations 1982 reg.16.
"employer"—*ibid.*
"maternity allowance"—*ibid.*
"maternity allowance period"—subs.(12).
"maternity pay period"—*ibid.*
"period of incapacity for work"—see s.163(1).
"prescribed"—see *ibid.*
"week"—see *ibid.*

GENERAL NOTE

Subsections (1) and (2)
   There can be no liability to pay SSP unless the qualifying day, being one of incapacity for work forming part of a period of incapacity for work, also falls within a period of entitlement as between the employee and his employer (subs.(1)). Such a period of entitlement generally begins on the first day of a period of incapacity for work (subs. (2)), but note the modifications effected by subss.(7), (8), and (9). A period of entitlement ends with whichever of the circumstances set out in subs.(2)(a)–(d) first occurs. Note that subs.2(d) does not apply in the circumstances set out in subs.(11).
   The position of "regular casual" workers was dealt with by the Court of Appeal in *Brown v Chief Adjudication Officer* [1997] I.R.L.R. 110. So long as such workers have worked continuously for a period of three months, or for a series of periods

1.72

totalling three months in aggregate and not separated by more than eight weeks, they become entitled to the minimum periods of notice provided for by s.86 of Employment Rights Act 1996, and their contract of employment will not terminate unless it is frustrated or is terminated by their employer. See further the commentary to Sch.11 para.2 below.

The First-tier Tribunal (Tax Chamber) has held that where a person has no weekly earnings for a period, owing to the default of her employer, then a "period of entitlement" does not arise within subs.(2) and so there is no entitlement to SSP. This was because the words "the average weekly earnings which in the relevant period have been paid to him" in s.163(2) referred to actual payments of wages and did not cover subsequent payments made in respect of the relevant period, e.g. as a result of a claim in the employment tribunal for unlawful deduction of wages: *Seaton v Revenue and Customs Commissioners* [2010] UKFTT 270 (TC).

Subsection (3)

1.73   In the circumstances set out in Sch.11 below, no period of entitlement arises with respect to the particular period of incapacity for work there referred to, thus excluding certain employees from SSP in respect of that period of incapacity for work.

Subsection (4)

1.74   An employee may have a period of entitlement with more than one employer at the same time, albeit that the length of the period with each is not coterminous.

Subsection (5)

1.75   See SSP (General) Regulations 1982 (SI 1982/894) reg.3A.

Subsection (6)

1.76   See SSP (General) Regulations 1982 (SI 1982/894) reg.3 dealing with prisoners, pregnant women entitled neither to SMP nor to maternity allowance, and setting a maximum three-year limit on any one period of entitlement.

Subsection (10)

1.77   See SSP (General) Regulations 1982 (SI 1982/894) reg.4.

Qualifying days

1.78   **154.**—(1) The third condition is that the day in question is a qualifying day.

(2) The days which are for the purposes of this Part of this Act to be qualifying days as between an employee and an employer of his (that is to say, those days of the week on which he is required by his contract of service with that employer to be available for work or which are chosen to reflect the terms of that contract) shall be such day or days as may, subject to regulations, be agreed between the employee and his employer or, failing such agreement, determined in accordance with regulations.

(3) In any case where qualifying days are determined by agreement between an employee and his employer there shall, in each week (beginning with Sunday), be at least one qualifying day.

(4) A day which is a qualifying day as between an employee and an employer of his may also be a qualifying day as between him and another employer of his.

DEFINITIONS

"contract of service"—see s.163(1).
"employee"—*ibid.* and SSP (General) Regulations 1982 reg.16.

"employer"—see s.163(1).
"week"—*ibid.*

GENERAL NOTE

In order to attract SSP liability, the day of incapacity which forms part of a period of incapacity for work and falls within a period of entitlement must also be a qualifying day (subs.(1)). Under subs.(2) an employer and employee are permitted a degree of freedom to determine by agreement which days of the week will for them rank as such, although subs.(3) stipulates that such agreements must specify at least one qualifying day per week. Furthermore SSP (General) Regulations 1982 (SI 1982/894) reg.5(3) renders ineffective an agreement treating as qualifying days any day identified expressly or otherwise by reference to it being a day of incapacity for work in relation to the employee's contract of service with an employer, or by reference to a period of incapacity for work or to a period of entitlement. Where there is no agreement on qualifying days or the only agreement is one rendered ineffective by reg.5(3), qualifying days are determined in accordance with SSP (General) Regulations 1982 reg.5(2).

1.79

Limitations on entitlement, etc.

Limitations on entitlement

155.—(1) Statutory sick pay shall not be payable for the first three qualifying days in any period of entitlement.

1.80

(2) An employee shall not be entitled, as against any one employer, to an aggregate amount of statutory sick pay in respect of any one period of entitlement which exceeds his maximum entitlement.

(3) The maximum entitlement as against any one employer is reached on the day on which the amount to which the employee has become entitled by way of statutory sick pay during the period of entitlement in question first reaches or passes the entitlement limit.

(4) The entitlement limit is an amount equal to 28 times [¹the weekly rate applicable in accordance with] section 157 below.

(5) Regulations may make provision for calculating the entitlement limit in any case where an employee's entitlement to statutory sick pay is calculated by reference to different weekly rates in the same period of entitlement.

AMENDMENT

1. Social Security (Incapacity for Work) Act 1994 s.8 (April 6, 1995).

DEFINITIONS

"employee"—see s.163(1) and SSP (General) Regulations 1982 reg.16.
"employer"—see s.163(1).
"period of entitlement"—*ibid.*
"qualifying day"—*ibid.*

Notification of incapacity for work

156.—(1) Regulations shall prescribe the manner in which, and the time within which, notice of any day of incapacity for work is to be given by or on behalf of an employee to his employer.

1.81

(2) An employer who would, apart from this section, be liable to pay an

amount of statutory sick pay to an employee in respect of a qualifying day (the "day in question") shall be entitled to withhold payment of that amount if—
  (a) the day in question is one in respect of which he has not been duly notified in accordance with regulations under subsection (1) above; or
  (b) he has not been so notified in respect of any of the first three qualifying days in a period of entitlement (a "waiting day") and the day in question is the first qualifying day in that period of entitlement in respect of which the employer is not entitled to withhold payment—
    (i) by virtue of paragraph (a) above; or
    (ii) in respect of an earlier waiting day by virtue of this paragraph.
(3) Where an employer withholds any amount of statutory sick pay under this section—
  (a) the period of entitlement in question shall not be affected; and
  (b) for the purposes of calculating his maximum entitlement in accordance with section 155 above the employee shall not be taken to have become entitled to the amount so withheld.

Rates of payment, etc.

Rates of payment

1.82   **157.**—(1) Statutory sick pay shall be payable by an employer at the weekly rate of [²£88.45].
(2) The Secretary of State may by order—
[¹(a) amend subsection (1) above so as to substitute different provision as to the weekly rate or rates of statutory sick pay; and]
  (b) make such consequential amendments as appear to him to be required of any provision contained in this Part of this Act.
(3) The amount of statutory sick pay payable by any one employer in respect of any day shall be the weekly rate applicable on that day divided by the number of days which are, in the week (beginning with Sunday) in which that day falls, qualifying days as between that employer and the employee concerned.

AMENDMENTS

1. Social Security (Incapacity for Work) Act 1994 s.8 (April 6, 1995).
2. Welfare Benefits Up-rating Order 2015 (SI 2015/30) art.3 (April 6, 2015).

Recovery by employers of amounts paid by way of statutory sick pay

1.83   **158.**—[¹ . . .]

AMENDMENT

1. Statutory Sick Pay Percentage Threshold Order 1995 (SI 1995/512) reg.5(a) (April 6, 1995).

Power to substitute provisions for section 158(2)

1.84   **159.**—[¹ . . .]

AMENDMENT

1. Statutory Sick Pay Percentage Threshold Order 1995 (SI 1995/512) reg.5(a) (April 6, 1995).

[¹Power to provide for recovery by employers of sums paid by way of statutory sick pay

159A.—(1) The Secretary of State may by order provide for the recovery by employers, in accordance with the order, of the amount (if any) by which their payments of, or liability incurred for, statutory sick pay in any period exceeds the specified percentage of the amount of their liability for contributions payments in respect of the corresponding period.

(2) An order under subsection (1) above may include provision—
(a) as to the periods by reference to which the calculation referred to above is to be made;
(b) for amounts which would otherwise be recoverable but which do not exceed the specified minimum for recovery not to be recoverable;
(c) for the rounding up or down of any fraction of a pound which would otherwise result from a calculation made in accordance with the order; and
(d) for any deduction from contributions payments made in accordance with the order to be disregarded for such purposes as may be specified,

and may repeal sections 158 and 159 above and make any amendments of other enactments which are consequential on the repeal of those sections.

(3) In this section—

"contributions payments" means payments which a person is required by or under any enactment to make in discharge of any liability of his as an employer in respect of primary or secondary Class 1 contributions; and

"specified" means specified in or determined in accordance with an order under subsection (1).

(4) The Secretary of State may by regulations make such transitional and consequential provision, and such savings, as he considers necessary or expedient for or in connection with the coming into force of any order under subsection (1) above.]

AMENDMENT

1. Statutory Sick Pay Act 1994 s.3 (February 10, 1994).

Miscellaneous

Relationship with benefits and other payments, etc.

160.—Schedule 12 to this Act has effect with respect to the relationship between statutory sick pay and certain benefits and payments.

Crown employment—Part XI

161.—(1) Subject to subsection (2) below, the provisions of this Part of this Act apply in relation to persons employed by or under the Crown as they apply in relation to persons employed otherwise than by or under the Crown.

(2) The provisions of this Part of this Act do not apply in relation to persons serving as members of Her Majesty's forces, in their capacity as such.

(3) For the purposes of this section Her Majesty's forces shall be taken to consist of such establishments and organisations as may be prescribed [¹by regulations made by the Secretary of State with the concurrence of the Treasury], being establishments and organisations in which persons serve under the control of the Defence Council.

AMENDMENT

1. Social Security Contributions (Transfer of Functions, etc.) Act 1999 s.1(1) and Sch.1 para.10 (April 1, 1999).

Special classes of persons

162.—(1) The Secretary of State [¹may with the concurrence of the Treasury] make regulations modifying this Part of this Act in such manner as he thinks proper in their application to any person who is, has been or is to be—

(a) employed on board any ship, vessel, hovercraft or aircraft;
(b) outside Great Britain at any prescribed time or in any prescribed circumstances; or
(c) in prescribed employment in connection with continental shelf opeations, as defined in section 120(2) above.

(2) Regulations under subsection (1) above may in particular provide—

(a) for any provision of this Part of this Act to apply to any such person, notwithstanding that it would not otherwise apply;
(b) for any such provision not to apply to any such person, notwithstanding that it would otherwise apply;
(c) for excepting any such person from the application of any such provision where he neither is domiciled nor has a place of residence in any part of Great Britain;
(d) for the taking of evidence, for the purposes of the determination of any question arising under any such provision, in a country or territory outside Great Britain, by a British consular official or such other person as may be determined in accordance with the regulations.

AMENDMENT

1. Social Security Contributions (Transfer of Functions, etc.) Act 1999 s.1(1) and Sch.1 para.11 (April 1, 1999).

Interpretation of Part XI and supplementary provisions

163.—(1) In this Part of this Act—

"contract of service" (except in paragraph (a) of the definition below of "employee") includes any arrangement providing for the terms of appointment of an employee;

"employee" means a person who is—

(a) gainfully employed in Great Britain either under a contract of service or in an office (including elective office) with [⁴ general earnings (as defined by section 7 of the Income Tax (Earnings and Pensions) Act 2003)];

(1992 c.4 s.163)

[⁵...]
but subject to regulations, which may provide for cases where any such person is not to be treated as an employee for the purposes of this Part of this Act and for cases where any person who would not otherwise be an employee for those purposes is to be treated as an employee for those purposes;

[⁵"employer", in relation to an employee and a contract of service of his, means a person who—
(a) under section 6 above is liable to pay secondary Class 1 contributions in relation to any earnings of the employee under the contract, or
(b) would be liable to pay such contributions but for—
  (i) the condition in section 6(1)(b), or
  (ii) the employee being under the age of 16:]

"period of entitlement" has the meaning given by section 153 above;
"period of incapacity for work" has the meaning given by section 152 above;
[¹...]
"prescribed" means prescribed by regulations;
"qualifying day" has the meaning given by section 154 above;
"week" means any period of seven days.

(2) For the purposes of this Part of this Act an employee's normal weekly earnings shall, subject to subsection (4) below, be taken to be the average weekly earnings which in the relevant period have been paid to him or paid for his benefit under his contract of service with the employer in question.

(3) For the purposes of subsection (2) above, the expressions "earnings" and "relevant period" shall have the meaning given to them by regulations.

(4) In such cases as may be prescribed an employee's normal weekly earnings shall be calculated in accordance with regulations.

(5) Without prejudice to any other power to make regulations under this Part of this Act, regulations may specify cases in which, for the purposes of this Part of this Act or such of its provisions as may be prescribed—
(a) two or more employers are to be treated as one;
(b) two or more contracts of service in respect of which the same person is an employee are to be treated as one.

(6) Where, in consequence of the establishment of one or more National Health Service trusts under [⁶the National Health Service Act 2006, the National Health Service (Wales) Act 2006] or the National Health Service (Scotland) Act 1978, a person's contract of employment is treated by a scheme under [⁶any of those Acts] as divided so as to constitute two or more contracts, [³or where an order [⁶paragraph 26(1) of Schedule 3 to the National Health Service Act 2006] provides that a person's contract of employment is so divided,] regulations may make provision enabling him to elect for all of those contracts to be treated as one contract for the purposes of this Part of this Act or of such provisions of this Part of this Act as may be prescribed; and any such regulations may prescribe—
(a) the conditions that must be satisfied if a person is to be entitled to make such an election;
(b) the manner in which, and the time within which, such an election is to be made;
(c) the persons to whom, and the manner in which, notice of such an election is to be given;

Social Security Contributions and Benefits Act 1992

(d) the information which a person who makes such an election is to provide, and the persons to whom, and the time within which, he is to provide it;
(e) the time for which such an election is to have effect;
(f) which one of the person's employers under the two or more contracts is to be regarded for the purposes of statutory sick pay as his employer under the one contract;

and the powers conferred by this subsection are without prejudice to any other power to make regulations under this Part of this Act.

(7) Regulations may provide for periods of work which begin on one day and finish on the following day to be treated, for the purposes of this Part of this Act, as falling solely within one or other of those days.

AMENDMENTS

1. Jobseekers Act 1995 s.41(5) and Sch.3 (April 1, 1996).
2. Social Security Act 1998 s.86 and Sch.7 para.74 (April 6, 1999).
3. Health Act 1999 (Supplementary, Consequential etc. Provisions) Order 2000 (SI 2000/90) art.3(1) and Sch.1 para.27 (February 8, 2000).
4. Income Tax (Earnings and Pensions) Act 2003 s.722 and Sch.6 para.181 (April 6, 2003).
5. Employment Equality (Age) Regulations 2006 (SI 2006/1031) reg.49(1) and Sch.8 para.9 (October 1, 2006).
6. National Health Service (Consequential Provisions) Act 2006 s.2 and Sch.1 para.147 (March 1, 2007).

GENERAL NOTE

1.90 *Normal weekly earnings*: see subs.(2)–(4) and also *Seaton v Commissioners for HMRC* [2011] UKUT 297 (TCC) and *Spence v Commissioners for HMRC* [2012] UKFTT 213 (TC).

PART XII

STATUTORY MATERNITY PAY

Statutory maternity pay—entitlement and liability to pay

1.91 **164.**—(1) Where a woman who is or has been an employee satisfies the conditions set out in this section, she shall be entitled, in accordance with the following provisions of this Part of this Act, to payments to be known as "statutory maternity pay".

(2) The conditions mentioned in subsection (1) above are—
(a) that she has been in employed earner's employment with an employer for a continuous period of at least 26 weeks ending with the week immediately preceding the 14th week before the expected-week of confinement but has ceased to work for him, [³. . .];
(b) that her normal weekly earnings for the period of eight weeks ending with the week immediately preceding the 14th week before the expected week of confinement are not less than the lower earnings limit in force under section 5(1)(a) above immediately before the commencement of the 14th week before the expected week of confinement; and
(c) that she has become pregnant and has reached, or been confined before reaching, the commencement of the 11th week before the expected week of confinement.

(3) The liability to make payments of statutory maternity pay to a woman is a liability of any person of whom she has been an employee as mentioned in subsection (2)(a) above.

[³(4) A woman shall be entitled to payments of statutory maternity pay only if—
  (a) she gives the person who will be liable to pay it notice of the date from which she expects his liability to pay her statutory maternity pay to begin; and
  (b) the notice is given at least 28 days before that date or, if that is not reasonably practicable, as soon as is reasonably practicable.]

(5) The notice shall be in writing if the person who is liable to pay the woman statutory maternity pay so requests.

(6) Any agreement shall be void to the extent that it purports—
  (a) to exclude, limit or otherwise modify any provision of this Part of this Act; or
  (b) to require an employee or former employee to contribute (whether directly or indirectly) towards any costs incurred by her employer or former employer under this Part of this Act.

(7) For the avoidance of doubt, any agreement between an employer and an employee authorising any deductions from statutory maternity pay which the employer is liable to pay to the employee in respect of any period shall not be void by virtue of subsection (6)(a) above if the employer—
  (a) is authorised by that or another agreement to make the same deductions from any contractual remuneration which he is liable to pay in respect of the same period; or
  (b) would be so authorised if he were liable to pay contractual remuneration in respect of that period.

(8) Regulations shall make provision as to a former employer's liability to pay statutory maternity pay to a woman in any case where the former employer's contract of service with her has been brought to an end by the former employer solely, or mainly, for the purpose of avoiding liability for statutory maternity pay.

(9) The Secretary of State may by regulations—
  (a) specify circumstances in which, notwithstanding subsections (1) to (8) above, there is to be no liability to pay statutory maternity pay in respect of a week;
  (b) specify circumstances in which, notwithstanding subsections (1) to (8) above, the liability to make payments of statutory maternity pay is to be a liability [²of the Commissioners of Inland Revenue];
  (c) specify in what circumstances employment is to be treated as continuous for the purposes of this Part of this Act;
  (d) provide that a woman is to be treated as being employed for a continuous period of at least 26 weeks where—
    (i) she has been employed by the same employer for at least 26 weeks under two or more separate contracts of service; and
    (ii) those contracts were not continuous;
  (e) provide that any of the provisions specified in subsection (10) below shall have effect subject to prescribed modifications [³in such cases as may be prescribed]
[³(ea) provide that subsection (4) above shall not have effect, or shall have effect subject to prescribed modifications, in such cases as may be prescribed;]

(f) provide for amounts earned by a woman under separate contracts of service with the same employer to be aggregated for the purposes of this Part of this Act; and

(g) provide that—
 (i) the amount of a woman's earnings for any period; or
 (ii) the amount of her earnings to be treated as comprised in any payment made to her or for her benefit,

shall be calculated or estimated in such manner and on such basis as may be prescribed and that for that purpose payments of a particular class or description made or falling to be made to or by a woman shall, to such extent as may be prescribed, be disregarded or, as the case may be, be deducted from the amount of her earnings.

(10) The provisions mentioned in subsection (9)(e) above are—

(a) subsection (2)(a) and (b) above; and

(b) [⁴ section 166(1) and (2)], [¹. . .] below.

[²(11) Any regulations under subsection (9) above which are made by virtue of paragraph (b) of that subsection must be made with the concurence of the Commissioners of Inland Revenue.]

AMENDMENTS

1. Maternity Allowance and Statutory Maternity Pay Regulations 1994 (SI 1994/1230) reg.6 (October 16, 1994).

2. Social Security Contributions (Transfer of Functions, etc.) Act 1999 s.1(1) and Sch.1 para.12 (April 1, 1999).

3. Employment Act 2002 s.20 (April 6, 2003).

4. Employment Act 2002 s.53 and Sch.7 para.6 (April 6, 2003).

DEFINITIONS

"confined"—see s.171(1).
"confinement"—see *ibid*.
"earnings"—see *ibid*. and reg.20 of the Statutory Maternity Pay (General) Regulations 1986.
"employee"—see s.171 and reg.17 of the Statutory Maternity Pay (General) Regulations 1986.
"employed earner"—see s.2.
"employer"—see s.171(1).
"modifications"—see *ibid*.
"normal weekly earnings"—see s.171(4).
"prescribed"—see s.171(1).
"week"—see *ibid*.

GENERAL NOTE

1.92 Statutory Maternity Pay (SMP) provides an income for employees and former employees during a period of maternity leave. In order to qualify for SMP a woman must have worked for an employer for 26 weeks continuously into the week (known as the qualifying week) preceding the 14th week before the expected date of her confinement (subs.(2)(a)). Part III of the SMP (General) Regulations 1986 (SI 1986/1960) defines the concept of continuous employment. The woman must also have been earning during the last eight weeks of her employment an amount at least equal to the lower earnings limit for contribution purposes (subs.(2)(b)). She must, moreover, have become pregnant and have reached (or given birth before reaching) the start of the 11th week before the expected week of confinement (subs.(2)(c)). The further requirement that she must actually have left that employment because of her pregnancy or confinement was repealed by the Employment Act 2002. This repeal itself effectively supersedes reg.2 of the Statutory Maternity Pay (General) (Modification and Amendment) Regulations 2000 (SI 2000/2883), which modified the original version of subs.(2)(a) of the Act in relation to pregnant women who were dismissed or whose employment was otherwise terminated without consent.

Where a woman leaves her employment earlier than 11 weeks before the expected week of confinement she loses her entitlement to SMP (unless she has given birth), but if her employer has dismissed her solely or mainly for the purpose of avoiding the liability to pay SMP she will remain entitled. This applies even if she has been working for that employer for only a short period, so long as it is at least eight continuous weeks (see reg.3 of the SMP General Regulation 1986 (SI 1986/1960)). If a woman qualifies for SMP from more than one employer she is entitled to receive it from each of them (*ibid.*, reg.18).

It is a precondition of entitlement to SMP that the woman has given notice of her intention to leave by reason of pregnancy or confinement at least 28 days (21 days before the Employment Act 2002) before leaving, unless it is not reasonably practicable to do so and she gives it thereafter as soon as it is reasonably practicable to do so (subs.(4); see further SMP (General) Regulations 1986 (SI 1986/1960) reg.23). This would be so if the baby arrives unexpectedly early, but may also extend to a woman who did not know of the notice requirement and had not been put on inquiry about it. (That was the position taken by the Employment Appeal Tribunal in *Nu-Swift International Ltd v Mallinson* [1979] I.C.R. 157 in relation to maternity pay.) The notice must be in writing if the employer so requests (subs.(5)).

A woman is not entitled to SMP if at any time during the maternity pay period (on which see s.165) she is imprisoned or sentenced to imprisonment (other than suspended). Statutory Maternity Pay is lost for the remainder of the period whether or not she is imprisoned for the whole period (see reg.9 of the SMP (General) Regulations 1986 (SI 1986/1960)).

1.93

The liability to pay SMP rests with the employer (subs.(3)). In certain circumstances, where an employer does not, or because of insolvency, cannot discharge his liability to pay SMP, that liability is discharged by the Board, now HMRC (at least since April 1, 1999; see subs.(9)(b), SMP (General) Regulations 1986 (SI 1986/1960) reg.7 and Social Security Contributions (Transfer of Functions, etc.) Act 1999 s.1(2) and Sch.2.; the same applies to the Secretary of State's functions under SMP (General) Regulations regs 25, 30 and 31).

Statutory Maternity Pay, therefore, like Statutory Sick Pay, is administered by the employer whilst HMRC is responsible for the resolution of certain disputes about entitlement. Until April 1, 1999, this was achieved by enabling the reference of certain questions to an AO, thereby opening up the usual channels of appeal to SSATs, Commissioners and the courts. With effect from April 1, 1999, the Social Security Contributions (Transfer of Functions, etc.) Act 1999, and the Statutory Sick Pay and Statutory Maternity Pay (Decisions) Regulations 1999 (SI 1999/776) replaced the role of AO with that of an officer of the Board of Inland Revenue (now HMRC). Consequently decision-making and appeals relating to SMP are governed by Pt II of the 1999 Act, with the right of appeal lying to the Tax Chamber of the First-tier Tribunal.

The maternity pay period

165.—(1) Statutory maternity pay shall be payable, subject to the provisions of this Part of this Act, in respect of each week during a prescribed period ("the maternity pay period") of a duration not exceeding [²52 weeks].

1.94

[³(2) Subject to subsections (3) and (7), the maternity pay period shall begin with the 11th week before the expected week of confinement.

(3) Cases may be prescribed in which the first day of the period is to be a prescribed day after the beginning of the 11th week before the expected week of confinement, but not later than the day immediately following the day on which she is confined.]

[⁵ (3A) Regulations may provide for the duration of the maternity pay period as it applies to a woman to be reduced, subject to prescribed restrictions and conditions.

(3B) Regulations under subsection (3A) are to secure that the reduced period ends at a time—
   (a) after a prescribed period beginning with the day on which the woman is confined, and
   (b) when at least a prescribed part of the maternity pay period remains unexpired.

(3C) Regulations under subsection (3A) may, in particular, prescribe restrictions and conditions relating to—
   (a) the end of the woman's entitlement to maternity leave;
   (b) the doing of work by the woman;
   (c) the taking of prescribed steps by the woman or another person as regards leave under section 75E of the Employment Rights Act 1996 in respect of the child;
   (d) the taking of prescribed steps by the woman or another person as regards statutory shared parental pay in respect of the child.

(3D) Regulations may provide for a reduction in the duration of the maternity pay period as it applies to a woman to be revoked, or to be treated as revoked, subject to prescribed restrictions and conditions.]

(4) [³Except in such cases as may be prescribed,] statutory maternity pay shall not be payable to a woman by a person in respect of any week during any part of which she works under a contract of service with him.

(5) It is immaterial for the purposes of subsection (4) above whether the work referred to in that subsection is work under a contract of service which existed immediately before the maternity pay period or a contract of service which did not so exist.

(6) Except in such cases as may be prescribed, statutory maternity pay shall not be payable to a woman in respect of any week after she has been confined and during any part of which she works for any employer who is not liable to pay her statutory maternity pay.

(7) Regulations may provide that this section shall have effect subject to prescribed modifications in relation—
   (a) to cases in which a woman has been confined before the 11th week before the expected week of confinement; and
   (b) to cases in which—
      (i) a woman is confined [¹ at any time after the end of the week immediately preceding the 11th week] before the expected week of confinement; and
      (ii) the maternity pay period has not then commenced for her.

[³(8) In subsections (1), (4) and (6) "week" means a period of seven days beginning with the day of the week on which the maternity pay period begins.]

AMENDMENTS

1. Maternity Allowance and Statutory Maternity Pay Regulations 1994 (SI 1994/1230) reg.3 (October 16, 1994).
2. Employment Act 2002 s.18 (April 6, 2003).
3. Work and Families Act 2006 s.1 (October 1, 2006).
4. Work and Families Act 2006 s.11 and Sch.1 para.7 (October 1, 2006).
5. Children and Families Act 2014 s.120(4) (June 30, 2014).

(1992 c.4 s.165)

DEFINITIONS

"confined"—see s.171(1).
"confinement"—*ibid.*
"employer"—*ibid.*
"maternity pay period"—*ibid.*
"modifications"—*ibid.*
"prescribed"—*ibid.*
"week"—*ibid.*

GENERAL NOTE

Statutory Maternity Pay is now payable for a period of 39 weeks (previously 26 weeks as a result of the Employment Act 2002, in force in April 2003, before which the maximum period was 18 weeks). As a general rule, the maternity pay period begins with the 11th week before the expected week of confinement (subs.(2)). Regulations provide for this period to be varied when the woman gives birth early (see SMP (General) Regulations 1986 (SI 1986/1960) reg.2).

The normal rule under subs.(4) that a woman is not entitled to receive SMP for any week in which she works for the employer who is liable to pay her SMP has now been relaxed. A woman may now work for her employer for a maximum of 10 days without losing entitlement to SMP (see reg.9A of the SMP (General) Regulations 1986 (SI 1986/1960)). A woman is not entitled to SMP if she works for another employer after her confinement (subs.(6)) unless she had worked for two or more employers up to her qualifying week, one of whom was not liable to pay her SMP, and it is now that employer for whom she is working after confinement (see reg.8 of the SMP (General) Regulations 1986 (SI 1986/1960)). But where she works for a new employer after her confinement, even if she works only briefly, she loses her entitlement for the remainder of the maternity pay period. Apparently there is no restriction on working for another employer before confinement.

On some of the difficulties in establishing the start of the maternity pay period, see *Wade and North Yorkshire Police Authority v HMRC* (FTC/35/2009, FTC/42/2009 and FTC/43/2009) [2011] I.R.L.R. 393.

1.95

[¹Rate of statutory maternity pay

166.—(1) Statutory maternity pay shall be payable to a woman—
 (a) at the earnings-related rate, in respect of the first six weeks in respect of which it is payable; and
 (b) at whichever is the lower of the earnings-related rate and such weekly rate as may be prescribed, in respect of the remaining portion of the maternity pay period.

[²(1A) In subsection (1) "week" means any period of seven days.]

(2) The earnings-related rate is a weekly rate equivalent to 90 per cent of a woman's normal weekly earnings for the period of eight weeks immediately preceding the 14th week before the expected week of confinement.

(3) The weekly rate prescribed under subsection (1)(b) above must not be less than the weekly rate of statutory sick pay for the time being specified in section 157(1) above or, if two or more such rates are for the time being so specified, the higher or highest of those rates.]

[²(4) Where for any purpose of this Part of this Act or of regulations it is necessary to calculate the daily rate of statutory maternity pay, the amount payable by way of statutory maternity pay for any day shall be taken as one seventh of the weekly rate.]

1.96

55

AMENDMENTS

1. Employment Act 2002 s.19 (April 6, 2003).
2. Work and Families Act 2006 s.11 and Sch.1 para.8 (October 1, 2006).

DEFINITIONS

"confinement"—see s.171(1).
"maternity pay period"—*ibid.*
"normal weekly earnings"—*ibid.*
"prescribed"—*ibid.*
"week—*ibid.*

GENERAL NOTE

1.97   A new s.166 was substituted by s.19 of the Employment Act 2002. This preserved the pre-existing position so far as the rate of payment for the first six weeks of the maternity pay period is concerned. During this initial period SMP is paid at the earnings-related rate of 90 per cent of the woman's average weekly earnings in the eight weeks preceding the qualifying week (subss.(1)(a) and (2)). Thereafter, SMP is paid at either the standard prescribed rate (£139.58 per week in 2015/16) or the earnings-related rate, whichever is the lower (subs.(1)(b)), for the balance of 20 weeks. Previously the balance of the maternity pay period was just 12 weeks, but the then lower rate was always payable, irrespective of whether the earnings-related rate was lower.

There remains an important issue relating to the SMP earnings calculation and the extent to which this takes into account pay rises. As a result of the decision of the European Court of Justice in *Gillespie v Northern Health and Social Services Board* [1996] I.R.L.R. 214, the earnings calculation for SMP purposes must take into account any pay rise which is backdated into the "relevant period" (on the meaning of which see SSCBA 1992 s.171(4) and (5) and SMP (General) Regulations 1986 (SI 1986/1960 reg.21)). The *Gillespie* decision led to a limited amendment to the relevant regulations (SMP (General) Regulations 1986 reg.21(7), inserted by the SMP (General) Amendment Regulations 1996 (SI 1996/1335)). The question remains whether a woman on maternity leave should receive the benefit of any pay rise which has been implemented after the qualifying week and before the end of paid maternity leave. The original reg.21(7), it was argued, failed to give full effect to the ruling in *Gillespie* by limiting it to cases in which the pay increase is backdated into the relevant period. The Court of Appeal referred a series of questions on this point to the European Court of Justice in *Alabaster v Woolwich Plc* [2002] EWCA Civ. 211; [2002] 1 C.M.L.R. 56; [2002] I.R.L.R. 420. On the request for a preliminary ruling, the ECJ ruled as follows:

> "Article 119 of the Treaty must be interpreted as requiring that, in so far as the pay received by the worker during her maternity leave is determined, at least in part, on the basis of the pay she earned before her maternity leave began, any pay rise awarded between the beginning of the period covered by the reference pay and the end of the maternity leave must be included in the elements of pay taken into account in calculating the amount of such pay. This requirement is not limited to cases where the pay rise is back-dated to the period covered by the reference pay."

Alabaster v Woolwich Plc and Secretary of State for Social Security (C-147/02) [2004] I.R.L.R. 486 at [50].

1.98   A new reg.21(7) was subsequently inserted with effect from April 6, 2005, to ensure that a woman's entitlement (or potential entitlement) to statutory maternity pay reflects any pay rise that the woman would have received, but for her maternity leave, and which is effective at any time between the start of the period used to calculate her entitlement and the end of her maternity leave. See further Statutory Maternity Pay (General) (Amendment) Regulations 2005 (SI 2005/729) reg.3. A month later (May 3, 2005), the Court of Appeal delivered its judgment following

(1992 c.4 s.166)

the decision of the ECJ: see *Alabaster v Barclays Bank Plc and the Secretary of State for Social Security* [2005] EWCA Civ 508. The Court of Appeal held that in order to give effect to the appellant's rights under EU law it was necessary to disapply those parts of Equal Pay Act 1970 s.1 which imposed the requirement for a male comparator.

[[1]Funding of employers' liabilities in respect of statutory maternity pay

167.—(1) Regulations shall make provision for the payment by employers of statutory maternity pay to be funded by the Commissioners of Inland Revenue to such extent as may be prescribed.

(2) Regulations under subsection (1) shall—
- (a) make provision for a person who has made a payment of statutory maternity pay to be entitled, except in prescribed circumstances, to recover an amount equal to the sum of—
    - (i) the aggregate of such of those payments as qualify for small employers' relief; and
    - (ii) an amount equal to 92 per cent of the aggregate of such of those payments as do not so qualify; and
- (b) include provision for a person who has made a payment of statutory maternity pay qualifying for small employers' relief to be entitled, except in prescribed circumstances, to recover an additional amount, determined in such manner as may be prescribed—
    - (i) by reference to secondary Class 1 contributions paid in respect of statutory maternity pay;
    - (ii) by reference to secondary Class 1 contributions paid in respect of statutory sick pay; or
    - (iii) by reference to the aggregate of secondary Class 1 contributions paid in respect of statutory maternity pay and secondary Class 1 contributions paid in respect of statutory sick pay.

(3) For the purposes of this section a payment of statutory maternity pay which a person is liable to make to a woman qualifies for small employers' relief if, in relation to that woman's maternity pay period, the person liable to make the payment is a small employer.

(4) For the purposes of this section "small employer", in relation to a woman's maternity pay period, shall have the meaning assigned to it by regulations, and, without prejudice to the generality of the foregoing, any such regulations—
- (a) may define that expression by reference to the amount of a person's contributions payments for any prescribed period; and
- (b) if they do so, may in that connection make provision for the amount of those payments for that prescribed period—
    - (i) to be determined without regard to any deductions that may be made from them under this section or under any other enactment or instrument; and
    - (ii) in prescribed circumstances, to be adjusted, estimated or otherwise attributed to him by reference to their amount in any other prescribed period.

(5) Regulations under subsection (1) may, in particular, make provision—
- (a) for funding in advance as well as in arrear;
- (b) for funding, or the recovery of amounts due under provision made by virtue of subsection (2)(b), by means of deductions from such

1.99

amounts for which employers are accountable to the Commissioners of Inland Revenue as may be prescribed, or otherwise;

(c) for the recovery by the Commissioners of Inland Revenue of any sums overpaid to employers under the regulations.

(6) Where in accordance with any provision of regulations under subsection (1) an amount has been deducted from an employer's contributions payments, the amount so deducted shall (except in such cases as may be prescribed) be treated for the purposes of any provision made by or under any enactment in relation to primary or secondary Class 1 contributions—

(a) as having been paid (on such date as may be determined in accordance with the regulations); and

(b) as having been received by the Commissioners of Inland Revenue, towards discharging the employer's liability in respect of such contributions.

(7) Regulations under this section must be made with the concurrence of the Commissioners of Inland Revenue.

(8) In this section, "contributions payments", in relation to an employer, means any payments which the employer is required, by or under any enactment, to make in discharge of any liability in respect of primary or secondary Class 1 contributions.]

AMENDMENT

1. Employment Act 2002 s.21 (April 6, 2003).

DEFINITIONS

"contributions payments"—see subs.(8).
"employer"—see s.171(1).
"maternity pay period"—*ibid.*
"prescribed"—*ibid.*

GENERAL NOTE

1.100   The new s.167, substituted by s.21 of the Employment Act 2002, is different from its predecessor in two main respects. First, it allows regulations to be made which enable employers to recover SMP from tax and other payments due to HMRC (see subs.(5)(b) and now Statutory Maternity Pay (Compensation of Employers) and Miscellaneous Amendment Regulations 1994 (SI 1994/1882) reg.6), and not just from payments of national insurance contributions, as was previously the case. Secondly, as with the tax credits regime, it provides for regulations to be made enabling employers to apply to HMRC for advance funding (*ibid.*, reg.5). Formerly employers could only deduct, in arrears, the amount of SMP payments from contributions payments due to the Revenue.

Relationship with benefits and other payments, etc.

1.101   **168.**—Schedule 13 to this Act has effect with respect to the relationship between statutory maternity pay and certain benefits and payments.

GENERAL NOTE

1.102   As a general rule, entitlement to SMP precludes any entitlement to maternity allowance, SSP or incapacity benefit for the same period. Where SMP is paid, it is treated as going towards the employer's contractual obligation (if any) to pay maternity pay for the same period. If a woman receives maternity allowance because she does not earn enough to qualify for SMP, but then receives a backdated pay increase, making her then entitled to SMP, the employer is required to meet the difference between the maternity allowance paid and the SMP due (SMP (General) Regulations 1986 (SI 1986/1960) reg.21B).

Crown employment—Part XII

169.—The provisions of this Part of this Act apply in relation to women employed by or under the Crown as they apply in relation to women employed otherwise than by or under the Crown.

1.103

Special classes of persons

170.—(1) The Secretary of State may [¹with the concurrence of the Treasury] make regulations modifying this Part of this Act in such manner as he thinks proper in their application to any person who is, has been or is to be—
  (a) employed on board any ship, vessel, hovercraft or aircraft;
  (b) outside Great Britain at any prescribed time or in any prescribed circumstances; or
  (c) in prescribed employment in connection with continental shelf operations, as defined in section 120(2) above.
(2) Regulations under subsection (1) above may in particular provide—
  (a) for any provision of this Part of this Act to apply to any such person, notwithstanding that it would not otherwise apply;
  (b) for any such provision not to apply to any such person, notwithstanding that it would otherwise apply;
  (c) for excepting any such person from the application of any such provision where he neither is domiciled nor has a place of residence in any part of Great Britain;
  (d) for the taking of evidence, for the purposes of the determination of any question arising under any such provision, in a country or territory outside Great Britain, by a British consular official or such other person as may be determined in accordance with the regulations.

1.104

AMENDMENT

1. Social Security Contributions (Transfer of Functions, etc.) Act 1999 s.1(1) and Sch.1 para.14 (April 1, 1999).

DEFINITIONS

"Great Britain"—see s.172(a).
"prescribed"—see s.171(1).

Interpretation of Part XII and supplementary provisions

171.—(1) In this Part of this Act—
"confinement" means—
  (a) labour resulting in the issue of a living child; or
  (b) labour after [¹24 weeks] of pregnancy resulting in the issue of a child whether alive or dead;
and "confined" shall be construed accordingly; and where a woman's labour begun on one day results in the issue of a child on another day she shall be taken to be confined on the day of the issue of the child or, if

1.105

Social Security Contributions and Benefits Act 1992

labour results in the issue of twins or a greater number of children, she shall be taken to be confined on the day of the issue of the last of them;

"dismissed" is to be construed in accordance with [³Part X of the Employment Rights Act 1996];

"employee" means a woman who is—
  (a) gainfully employed in Great Britain either under a contract of service or in an office (including elective office) with [⁵ general earnings (as defined by section 7 of the Income Tax (Earnings and Pensions) Act 2003)]

[⁷. . .]

but subject to regulations [⁴made with the concurrence of [⁵Her Majesty's Revenue and Customs] which may provide for cases where any such woman is not to be treated as an employee for the purposes of this Part of this Act and for cases where a woman who would not otherwise be an employee for those purposes is to be treated as an employee for those purposes;

[⁷"employer", in relation to a woman who is an employee, means a person who—
(a) under section 6 above is liable to pay secondary Class 1 contributions in relation to any of her earnings; or
(b) would be liable to pay such contributions but for—
    (i) the condition in section 6(1)(b), or
    (ii) the employee being under the age of 16;]

"maternity pay period" has the meaning assigned to it by section 165(1) above;

"modifications" includes additions, omissions and amendments, and related expressions shall be construed accordingly;

"prescribed" means specified in or determined in accordance with regulations;

[⁸. . .]

[⁸(1A) In this Part, except section 165(1), (4) and (6), section 166(1) and paragraph 3(2) of Schedule 13, "week" means a period of 7 days beginning with Sunday or such other period as may be prescribed in relation to any particular case or class of case.]

(2) Without prejudice to any other power to make regulations under this Part of this Act, regulations may specify cases in which, for the purposes of this Part of this Act or of such provisions of this Part of this Act as may be prescribed—
  (a) two or more employers are to be treated as one;
  (b) two or more contracts of service in respect of which the same woman is an employee are to be treated as one.

(3) Where, in consequence of the establishment of one or more National Health Service trusts [⁹the National Health Service Act 2006, the National Health Service (Wales) Act 2006] or the National Health Service (Scotland) Act 1978, a woman's contract of employment is treated by a scheme under [⁹any of those Acts] as divided so as to constitute two or more contracts, [²or where an order under [⁹paragraph 26(1) of Schedule 3 to the National Health Service Act 2006] provides that a woman's contract of employment is so divided,] regulations may make provision enabling her to elect for all of those contracts to be treated as one contract for the purposes of this Part of this Act or of such provisions of this Part of this Act as may be prescribed; and any such regulations may prescribe—

(1992 c.4 s.171)

(a) the conditions that must be satisfied if a woman is to be entitled to make such an election;
(b) the manner in which, and the time within which, such an election is to be made;
(c) the persons to whom, and the manner in which, notice of such an election is to be given;
(d) the information which a woman who makes such an election is to provide, and the persons to whom, and the time within which, she is to provide it;
(e) the time for which such an election is to have effect;
(f) which one of the woman's employers under the two or more contracts is to be regarded for the purposes of statutory maternity pay as her employer under the one contract;

and the powers conferred by this subsection are without prejudice to any other power to make regulations under this Part of this Act.

(4) For the purposes of this Part of this Act a woman's normal weekly earnings shall, subject to subsection (6) below, be taken to be the average weekly earnings which in the relevant period have been paid to her or paid for her benefit under the contract of service with the employer in question.

(5) For the purposes of subsection (4) above "earnings" and "relevant period" shall have the meanings given to them by regulations.

(6) In such cases as may be prescribed a woman's normal weekly earnings shall be calculatedin accordance with regulations.

[4(7) Regulations under any of subsections (2) to (6) above must be made with the concurrence of the Commissioners of Inland Revenue.]

AMENDMENTS

1. Still-Birth (Definition) Act 1992 s.2 (October 1, 1992).
2. Health Act 1999 (Supplementary, Consequential etc. Provisions) Order 2000 art.3 Sch.1 para.27 (SI 2000/90) (February 8, 2000).
3. Employment Rights Act 1996 s.240 and Sch.1 para.51(5) (August 23, 1996).
4. Social Security Contributions (Transfer of Functions, etc.) Act 1999 s.1(1) and Sch.1 para.15 (April 1, 1999).
5. Income Tax (Earnings and Pensions) Act 2003 s.722 and Sch.6 para.182 (April 6, 2003).
6. Commissioners for Revenue and Customs Act 2005 s.50 and Sch.4 para.43 (April 18, 2005).
7. Employment Equality (Age) Regulations 2006 (SI 2006/1031) reg.49(1) and Sch.8 para.10 (October 1, 2006).
8. Work and Families Act 2006 s.11 and Sch.1 para.9 (October 1, 2006).
9. National Health Service (Consequential Provisions) Act 2006 s.2 and Sch.1 para.148 (March 1, 2007).

[1PART XIIZA

[2 ORDINARY AND ADDITIONAL STATUTORY PATERNITY PAY]

AMENDMENTS

1. Part XIIZA was inserted by the Employment Act 2002 s.2 (December 8, 2002).
2. Work and Families Act 2006 s.11(1) Sch.1 para.10 (April 6, 2010).

GENERAL NOTE

1.106 Part XIIZA of the SSCBA 1992 was inserted by the Employment Act 2002. The 2002 Act followed the Employment Relations Act 1999, which itself included a number of "family friendly" employment measures (e.g. new rights to 13 weeks' unpaid parental leave and to unpaid time off to deal with family crises). The ordinary period of maternity leave was also increased in 1999 from 14 to 18 weeks (this period was extended to 26 weeks in April 2003 by other provisions in the Employment Act 2002), along with several other reforms designed to simplify the notoriously complex rules governing maternity leave and pay. A further review was announced in the 2000 Budget statement, which led to the publication of a Green Paper, *Work and Parents: Competitiveness and Choice* (DTI, December 2000). The Government's decisions on that review were announced at or around the time of the 2001 Budget statement, and were followed by the issue of three further consultation documents on the frameworks for maternity, paternity and adoption leave and pay. In November 2001 the DTI published a summary of responses to these various papers in the *Government's Response on Simplification of Maternity Leave, Paternity Leave and Adoption Leave*.

The Government's proposals were then brought forward in the Bill which became the Employment Act 2002. Part I of the 2002 Act dealt with statutory leave and pay. Thus, s.1 introduced a right to paternity leave in the Employment Rights Act 1996 (inserting ss.80A–80E), while s.2 inserted this Pt XIIZA into the SSCBA 1992 to make provision for statutory paternity pay (SPP). Sections 3 and 4 dealt with adoption leave and statutory adoption pay (SAP) respectively (on the latter see SSCBA 1992 Pt XIIZB). The procedural provisions relating to SPP and SAP were contained in ss.5–16 of the 2002 Act. (The 2002 Act also included measures to establish statutory minimum dismissal, disciplinary and grievance procedures and changes to employment tribunal procedures.)

The amendments made by c.1 of Pt I of the Employment Act 2002 relating to paternity and adoption, including the insertion of Pt XIIZA into the SSCBA 1992, came into force on December 8, 2002 (Employment Act 2002 (Commencement No.3 and Transitional and Saving Provisions) Order 2002 art.2(2) and Sch.1, Pt II). However, art.3 and Sch.3, para.1 of the same Order provide that Pt XIIZA shall have effect only in relation to a person who satisfies the prescribed conditions of entitlement in respect of a child who is either: (a) born on or after April 6, 2003 (or whose expected week of birth begins on or after that date); or (b) matched for the purposes of adoption with a person who is notified of having been matched on or after April 6, 2003 (or placed for adoption on or after that date).

1.106A Statutory Paternity Pay is payable for a two-week period only (SSCBA 1992 s.171ZE(2)). Such paid paternity leave must be taken in a single block within the first eight weeks after the child's birth (SSCBA 1992 s.171ZE(3)). There are, in fact, two forms of SPP, known in the regulations (the Statutory Paternity Pay and Statutory Adoption Pay (General) Regulations 2002 (SI 2002/2822)) as SPP (birth) and SPP (adoption), although these terms do not appear in the primary legislation. The principal eligibility criteria for SPP (birth) are set out in SSCBA 1992 s.171ZA and for SPP (adoption) in s.171ZB. Entitlement to SPP (birth) arises in respect of children born on or after April 6, 2003, or whose expected week of birth begins on or after that date (SPP and SAP (General) Regulations 2002 reg.3(1)(a); see also (Employment Act 2002 (Commencement No.3 and Transitional and Saving Provisions) Order 2002 art.3 and Sch.3). Similarly, entitlement to SPP (adoption) arises where the adoptive parent is notified of having been matched on or after April 6, 2003 or the child is placed for adoption on or after that date (SPP and SAP (General) Regulations 2002 reg.3(1)(b)). Section 171ZC contains general conditions of entitlement (e.g. as to giving the requisite notice to the employer). Section 171ZD places the liability to make payments of SPP on employers (the recovery mechanisms are the same as for SMP), while s.171ZE, with the associated regulations, deals with matters such as the rate and period of pay. Although paid for a shorter period than

(1992 c.4 s.171)

SMP, SPP is paid at the same rate as SMP. Sections 171ZF–171ZK make provision for various types of special cases and matters of interpretation, etc.

[¹ Ordinary statutory paternity pay]

Entitlement: birth

171ZA.—(1) Where a person satisfies the conditions in subsection (2) below, he shall be entitled in accordance with the following provisions of this Part to payments to be known as [¹ ordinary statutory paternity pay].

(2) The conditions are—
(a) that he satisfies prescribed conditions—
  (i) as to relationship with a newborn child; and
  (ii) as to relationship with the child's mother;
(b) that he has been in employed earner's employment with an employer for a continuous period of at least 26 weeks ending with the relevant week;
(c) that his normal weekly earnings for the period of eight weeks ending with the relevant week are not less than the lower earnings limit in force under section 5(1)(a) above at the end of the relevant week; and
(d) that he has been in employed earner's employment with the employer by reference to whom the condition in para.(b) above is satisfied for a continuous period beginning with the end of the relevant week and ending with the day on which the child is born.

(3) The references in subsection (2) above to the relevant week are to the week immediately preceding the 14th week before the expected week of the child's birth.

(4) A person's entitlement to [¹ ordinary statutory paternity pay] under this section shall not be affected by the birth, or expected birth, of more than one child as a result of the same pregnancy.

(5) In this section, "newborn child" includes a child stillborn after 24 weeks of pregnancy.

AMENDMENT

1. Work and Families Act 2006 s.11(1) Sch.1 paras 11 and 12 (April 6, 2010).

DEFINITIONS

"employer"—see s.171ZJ(1).
"newborn child"—see subs.(5).
"prescribed"—see s.171ZJ(1).
"the relevant week"—see subs.(3).
"week"—see s.171ZJ(5).

GENERAL NOTE

Subsection (2)(a)

The entitlement conditions referred to in subs.(2)(a) are those prescribed in regs 4(2)(b) and (c) of the Paternity and Adoption Leave Regulations 2002 (SI 2002/2788), which are incorporated by the cross-reference in reg.4 of the SPP and SAP (General) Regulations 2002 (SI 2002/2822). These requirements are that the employee is, first, either: (i) the father of the child, or (ii) married to or the partner of the child's mother, but not the child's father (reg.4(2)(b)); and, secondly, has, or expects to have: (i) responsibility for the upbringing of the child (if he is the child's father); or (ii) the main responsibility (apart from any responsibility of the mother) for the upbringing of the child (if he is the mother's husband or partner but not the child's father) (reg.4(2)(c)).

Subsection (2)(b)

1.109
On the extended meaning of continuous employment, see SPP and SAP (General) Regulations 2002 regs 33–37.

Subsection (2)(c)

1.110
The minimum threshold requirement that the claimant's earnings are not less than the National Insurance lower earnings limit necessarily excludes those fathers on very low incomes, and typically in part-time work, from SPP. Arguably this is the group of men whose families are most at risk of social exclusion and thus most in need of support such as SPP. The problem is exacerbated by the fact that the National Insurance scheme, unlike the income tax system, does not aggregate earnings from, e.g. two part-time jobs with different employers. (But note the special case of associated employers: see SPP and SAP (General) Regulations 2002 reg.38.) Women who do not meet the lower earnings limit requirement do not qualify for SMP (SSCBA 1992 s.164(2)(b)) but may qualify for maternity allowance (SSCBA 1992 s.35—see Vol.I of this series). There is, at present, no such alternative form of income maintenance for fathers in a similar position. This was the one aspect in relation to this part of the Employment Act 2002 which caused considerable disquiet amongst Government back-benchers during the Standing Committee debates on the Bill (Standing Committee F, January 10, 2002, cols 333–360). The minister promised members that the DWP and Department of Health were actively considering how to provide support for low-wage adoptive parents with some form of support equivalent to maternity allowance.

Subsection (2)(b)–(d)

1.111
The entitlement conditions are modified if a person fails to meet the conditions set out in subs.(2)(b)–(d) because the child's birth occurred earlier than the 14th week before the expected week of the birth: see SPP and SAP (General) Regulations 2002 reg.5. This modification is in exercise of the regulation-making powers under s.171ZC(3)(a).

Subsection (4)

1.112
Thus, SPP is not paid for twice as long in the case of a father of twins.

Entitlement: adoption

1.113
171ZB.—(1) Where a person satisfies the conditions in subsection (2) below, he shall be entitled in accordance with the following provisions of this Part to payments to be known as [¹ ordinary statutory paternity pay].

(2) The conditions are—
(a) that he satisfies prescribed conditions—
   (i) as to relationship with a child who is placed for adoption under the law of any part of the United Kingdom, and
   (ii) as to relationship with a person with whom the child is so placed for adoption;
(b) that he has been in employed earner's employment with an employer for a continuous period of at least 26 weeks ending with the relevant week;
(c) that his normal weekly earnings for the period of 8 weeks ending with the relevant week are not less than the lower earnings limit in force under section 5(1)(a) at the end of the relevant week;
(d) that he has been in employed earner's employment with the

employer by reference to whom the condition in paragraph (b) above is satisfied for a continuous period beginning with the end of the relevant week and ending with the day on which the child is placed for adoption; and

(e) where he is a person with whom the child is placed for adoption, that he has elected to receive statutory paternity pay.

(3) The references in subsection (2) to the relevant week are to the week in which the adopter is notified of being matched with the child for the purposes of adoption.

(4) A person may not elect to receive [¹ ordinary statutory paternity pay] if he has elected in accordance with section 171ZL below to receive statutory adoption pay.

(5) Regulations may make provision about elections for the purposes of subsection (2)(e) above.

(6) A person's entitlement to [¹ ordinary statutory paternity pay] under this section shall not be affected by the placement for adoption of more than one child as part of the same arrangement.

(7) In this section, "adopter", in relation to a person who satisfies the condition under subsection (2)(a)(ii) above, means the person by reference to whom he satisfies that condition.

[² (8) This section has effect in a case involving a child placed under section 22C of the Children Act 1989 by a local authority in England with a local authority foster parent who has been approved as a prospective adopter with the following modifications—

(a) the references in subsection (2) to a child being placed for adoption under the law of any part of the United Kingdom are to be treated as references to a child being placed under section 22C in that manner;
(b) the reference in subsection (3) to the week in which the adopter is notified of being matched with the child for the purposes of adoption is to be treated as a reference to the week in which the prospective adopter is notified that the child is to be, or is expected to be, placed with the prospective adopter under section 22C;
(c) the reference in subsection (6) to placement for adoption is to be treated as a reference to placement under section 22C;
(d) the definition in subsection (7) is to be treated as if it were a definition of "prospective adopter".

(9) Where, by virtue of subsection (8), a person becomes entitled to statutory paternity pay in connection with the placement of a child under section 22C of the Children Act 1989, the person may not become entitled to payments of statutory paternity pay in connection with the placement of the child for adoption.]

AMENDMENTS

1. Work and Families Act 2006 s.11(1) Sch.1 para.13 (April 6, 2010).
2. Children and Families Act 2014 s.121(3) (June 30, 2014).

DEFINITIONS

"adopter"—see subs.(7).
"employer"—see s.171ZJ(1).
"normal weekly earnings"—see s.171ZJ(6).
"prescribed"—see s.171ZJ(1).

Social Security Contributions and Benefits Act 1992

"the relevant week"—see subs.(3).
"week"—see s.171ZJ(5).

GENERAL NOTE

1.114   The conditions prescribed under subs.(2)(a) are, first, that the claimant is married to or the partner of a child's adopter (or in a case where there are two adopters, married to or the partner of the other adopter) and, secondly, has, or expects to have, the main responsibility for the upbringing of the child (apart from the responsibility of the child's adopter, or in a case where there two adopters, together with the other adopter): SPP and SAP (General) Regulations 2002 (SI 2002/2822) reg.11. Note that, unusually, reg.11 specifically includes same-sex partners. "Partner" is defined by reg.11(2) as meaning a person (excluding certain defined relatives) "who lives with the adopter and the child in an enduring family relationship", irrespective of whether the relationship between the adults is heterosexual or same-sex in nature.

Entitlement: general

1.115   **171ZC.**—(1) A person shall be entitled to payments of [¹ ordinary statutory paternity pay] in respect of any period [² only if he gives the person who will be liable to pay it notice of the week or weeks in respect of which he expects there to be liability to pay him statutory paternity pay.]

[² (1A) Regulations may provide for the time by which notice under subsection (1) is to be given.]

(2) The notice shall be in writing if the person who is liable to pay the [¹ ordinary statutory paternity pay] so requests.

(3) The Secretary of State may by regulations—
(a) provide that subsection (2)(b), (c) or (d) of section 171ZA or 171ZB above shall have effect subject to prescribed modifications in such cases as may be prescribed;
(b) provide that subsection (1) above shall not have effect, or shall have effect subject to prescribed modifications, in such cases as may be prescribed;
(c) impose requirements about evidence of entitlement;
(d) specify in what circumstances employment is to be treated as continuous for the purposes of section 171ZA or 171ZB above;
(e) provide that a person is to be treated for the purposes of section 171ZA or 171ZB above as being employed for a continuous period of at least 26 weeks where—
  (i) he has been employed by the same employer for at least 26 weeks under two or more separate contracts of service; and
  (ii) those contracts were not continuous;
(f) provide for amounts earned by a person under separate contracts of service with the same employer to be aggregated for the purposes of section 171ZA or 171ZB above;
(g) provide that—
  (i) the amount of a person's earnings for any period; or
  (ii) the amount of his earnings to be treated as comprised in any payment made to him or for his benefit,
shall be calculated or estimated for the purposes of section 171ZA or 171ZB above in such manner and on such basis as may be prescribed and that for that purpose payments of a particular class or description made or falling to be made to or by a person shall, to such extent as may be prescribed,

be disregarded or, as the case may be, be deducted from the amount of his earnings.

AMENDMENTS

1. Work and Families Act 2006 s.11(1) Sch.1 para.14 (April 6, 2010).
2. Children and Families Act 2014 s.123(2) (June 30, 2014).

DEFINITIONS

"employer"—see s.171ZJ(1).
"modifications"—see *ibid.*
"prescribed"—see *ibid.*
"week"—see s.171ZJ(5).

GENERAL NOTE

See further regs 6 and 7 of the SPP and SAP (General) Regulations 2002 (SI 2002/2822) on the period of payment and notice requirements for SPP (birth). The requirements relating to evidence of entitlement are in reg.9. The equivalent provisions for SPP (adoption) are in regs 12, 13 and 15.

1.116

Liability to make payments

171ZD.—(1) The liability to make payments of [¹ ordinary] statutory paternity pay under section 171ZA or 171ZB above is a liability of any person of whom the person entitled to the payments has been an employee as mentioned in subsection (2)(b) and (d) of that section.

1.117

(2) Regulations shall make provision as to a former employer's liability to pay [¹ ordinary statutory paternity pay] to a person in any case where the former employee's contract of service with him has been brought to an end by the former employer solely, or mainly, for the purpose of avoiding [¹ liability for ordinary statutory paternity pay or additional statutory paternity pay (or both)].

(3) The Secretary of State may, with the concurrence of the Board, by regulations specify circumstances in which, notwithstanding this section, liability to make payments of statutory paternity pay is to be a liability of the Board.

AMENDMENT

1. Work and Families Act 2006 s.11(1) Sch.1 para.15 (April 6, 2010).

DEFINITIONS

"the Board"—see s.171ZJ(1).
"employer"—see *ibid.*

GENERAL NOTE

This section, placing the liability to make payments of SPP on employers, follows the same approach as the provisions governing SMP (ss.164(3) and (8)). Note that there is no liability to pay SPP in respect of any week during which the claimant either is entitled to SSP or is detained in custody (or sentenced to imprisonment): SPP and SAP (General) Regulations 2002 (SI 2002/2822) reg.18. Similarly, there is no liability to pay SPP in the week that the person entitled dies.

The rules governing the funding of SPP and employers' responsibilities in connection with SPP payments are contained in the SPP and SAP (Administration) Regulations 2002 (SI 2002/2820). The special circumstances in which the Board is liable to pay SPP under subs.(3) are set out in SPP and SAP (General) Regulations 2002 reg.43.

1.118

Rate and period of pay

1.119   **171ZE.**—(1) [² ordinary statutory paternity pay] shall be payable at such fixed or earnings-related weekly rate as may be prescribed by regulations, which may prescribe different kinds of rate for different cases.

(2) [² ordinary statutory paternity pay] shall be payable in respect of—
   (a) a period of two consecutive weeks within the qualifying period beginning on such date within that period as the person entitled may choose in accordance with regulations; or
   (b) if regulations permit the person entitled to choose to receive [² ordinary statutory paternity pay] in respect of—
      (i) a period of a week, or
      (ii) two non-consecutive periods of a week,
   such week or weeks within the qualifying period as he may choose in accordance with regulations.

(3) For the purposes of subsection (2) above, the qualifying period shall be determined in accordance with regulations, which shall secure that it is a period of at least 56 days beginning—
   (a) in the case of a person to whom the conditions in section 171ZA(2) above apply, with the date of the child's birth, and
   (b) in the case of a person to whom the conditions in section 171ZB(2) above apply, with the date of the child's placement for adoption.

[³ (3A) Statutory paternity pay is not payable to a person in respect of a statutory pay week if—
   (a) statutory shared parental pay is payable to that person in respect of any part of that week or that person takes shared parental leave in any part of that week, or
   (b) statutory shared parental pay was payable to that person or that person has taken shared parental leave in respect of the child before that week.]

(4) [² Ordinary statutory paternity pay] shall not be payable to a person in respect of a statutory pay week if it is not his purpose at the beginning of the week—
   (a) to care for the child by reference to whom he satisfies the condition in sub-paragraph (i) of section 171ZA(2)(a) or 171ZB(2)(a) above; or
   (b) to support the person by reference to whom he satisfies the condition in sub-paragraph (ii) of that provision.

(5) A person shall not be liable to pay [² ordinary statutory paternity pay] to another in respect of a statutory pay week during any part of which the other works under a contract of service with him.

(6) It is immaterial for the purposes of subsection (5) above whether the work referred to in that subsection is work under a contract of service which existed immediately before the statutory pay week or a contract of service which did not so exist.

(7) Except in such cases as may be prescribed, [² ordinary statutory paternity pay] shall not be payable to a person in respect of a statutory pay week during any part of which he works for any employer who is not liable to pay him [² ordinary statutory paternity pay].

(8) The Secretary of State may by regulations specify circumstances in which there is to be no liability to pay [² ordinary statutory paternity pay] in respect of a statutory pay week.

(9) Where more than one child is born as a result of the same pregnancy,

(1992 c.4 s.171ZE)

the reference in subsection (3)(a) to the date of the child's birth shall be read as a reference to the date of birth of the first child born as a result of the pregnancy.

(10) Where more than one child is placed for adoption as part of the same arrangement, the reference in subsection (3)(b) to the date of the child's placement shall be read as a reference to the date of placement of the first child to be placed as part of the arrangement.

[¹(10A) Where for any purpose of this Part of this Act or of regulations it is necessary to calculate the daily rate of ordinary statutory paternity pay, the amount payable by way of ordinary statutory paternity pay for any day shall be taken as one seventh of the weekly rate.]

(11) In this section—

"statutory pay week", in relation to a person entitled to statutory paternity pay, means a week chosen by him as a week in respect of which statutory paternity pay shall be payable;

"week" means any period of seven days.

[³ (12) Where statutory paternity pay is payable to a person by virtue of section 171ZB(8), this section has effect as if—

(a) the references in subsections (3)(b) and (10) to placement for adoption were references to placement under section 22C of the Children Act 1989;

(b) the references in subsection (10) to being placed for adoption were references to being placed under section 22C.]

AMENDMENTS

1. Work and Families Act 2006 s.11 and Sch.1 para.16(1) and (3) (October 1, 2006).
2. Work and Families Act 2006 s.11(1) Sch.1 para.16(1) and (2) (April 6, 2010).
3. Children and Families Act 2014 ss.120(5) and 121(4) (June 30, 2014).

DEFINITIONS

"employer"—see s.171ZJ(1).
"statutory pay week"—see subs.(11).
"week"—see *ibid.*

GENERAL NOTE

The weekly rate of SPP for 2014–15 is the lesser of £139.58 and 90 per cent of normal weekly earnings (on which see SPP and SAP (General) Regulations 2002 (SI 2002/2822) reg.40): SPP and SAP (Weekly Rates) Regulations 2002 (SI 2002/2818) reg.2.

The qualifying period for SPP (birth), i.e. the period within which the SPP period must occur, is the period of 56 days from the date of the child's birth (SPP and SAP (General) Regulations 2002 reg.8). For SPP (adoption), the 56 days runs from the date of the child's placement for adoption: see reg.14.

Regulation 18 of the SPP and SAP (General) Regulations 2002, made under para.(8), sets out the circumstances in which there is no liability to pay SPP (where SSP is payable, or the person has died or is in legal custody).

The rules governing the time for paying SPP are set out in reg.42 of the SPP and SAP (General) Regulations 2002. SPP may be paid in the same way as ordinary remuneration but must not include payment in kind or by way of board and lodging: reg.41.

1.120

[1 Entitlement to additional statutory paternity pay: birth

1.121   **¹171ZEA.**— (1) The Secretary of State may by regulations provide that, where all the conditions in subsection (2) are satisfied in relation to a person ("the claimant"), the claimant shall be entitled, in accordance with the following provisions of this Part, to payments to be known as "additional statutory paternity pay".
(2) Those conditions are—
- (a) that the claimant satisfies prescribed conditions—
    - (i) as to relationship with a child, and
    - (ii) as to relationship with the child's mother;
- (b) that the claimant has been in employed earner's employment with an employer for a continuous period of at least the prescribed length ending with a prescribed week;
- (c) that the claimant's normal weekly earnings for a prescribed period ending with a prescribed week are not less than the lower earnings limit in force under section 5(1)(a) at the end of that week;
- (d) if regulations so provide, that the claimant continues in employed earner's employment (whether or not with that employer) until a prescribed time;
- (e) that the mother of the child by reference to whom the condition in paragraph (a) is satisfied became entitled, by reference to the birth of the child—
    - (i) to a maternity allowance, or
    - (ii) to statutory maternity pay;
- (f) that the mother has, in relation to employment as an employed or self-employed earner, taken action that is treated by regulations as constituting for the purposes of this section her return to work;
- (g) that the day on which the mother is treated as returning to work falls—
    - (i) after the end of a prescribed period beginning with the birth of the child, but
    - (ii) at a time when at least a prescribed part of her maternity allowance period or maternity pay period remains unexpired;
- (h) that it is the claimant's intention to care for the child during a period beginning not later than a prescribed time.

(3) The regulations may—
- (a) exclude the application of the conditions mentioned in paragraphs (f) and (g) of subsection (2) in cases where the child's mother has died, and
- (b) provide that the condition mentioned in paragraph (e) of that subsection shall have effect with prescribed modifications in such cases.

(4) A person's entitlement to additional statutory paternity pay under this section shall not be affected by the birth of more than one child as a result of the same pregnancy.]

AMENDMENT

1. Work and Families Act 2006 s.6 (March 3, 2010).

[1 Entitlement to additional statutory paternity pay: adoption

1.122   **¹171ZEB.**— (1) The Secretary of State may by regulations provide that, where all the conditions in subsection (2) are satisfied in relation to a

(1992 c.4 s.171ZEB)

person ("the claimant"), the claimant shall be entitled in accordance with the following provisions of this Part to payments to be known as "additional statutory paternity pay".

(2) Those conditions are—
- (a) that the claimant satisfies prescribed conditions—
    - (i) as to relationship with a child who has been placed for adoption under the law of any part of the United Kingdom, and
    - (ii) as to relationship with a person with whom the child is so placed for adoption ("the adopter");
- (b) that the claimant has been in employed earner's employment with an employer for a continuous period of at least the prescribed length ending with a prescribed week;
- (c) that the claimant's normal weekly earnings for a prescribed period ending with a prescribed week are not less than the lower earnings limit in force under section 5(1)(a) at the end of that week;
- (d) if regulations so provide, that the claimant continues to work in employed earner's employment (whether or not with that employer) until a prescribed time;
- (e) that the adopter became entitled to statutory adoption pay by reference to the placement of the child for adoption;
- (f) that the adopter has, in relation to employment as an employed or self-employed earner, taken action that is treated by regulations as constituting for the purposes of this section the adopter's return to work;
- (g) that the day on which the adopter is treated as returning to work falls—
    - (i) after the end of a prescribed period beginning with the placement of the child for adoption, but
    - (ii) at a time when at least a prescribed part of the adopter's adoption pay period remains unexpired;
- (h) that it is the claimant's intention to care for the child during a period beginning not later than a prescribed time.

(3) The regulations may—
- (a) exclude the application of the conditions mentioned in paragraphs (f) and (g) of subsection (2) in cases where the adopter has died, and
- (b) provide that the condition mentioned in paragraph (e) of that subsection shall have effect with prescribed modifications in such cases.

(4) A person may not elect to receive additional statutory paternity pay if he has elected in accordance with section 171ZL to receive statutory adoption pay.

(5) A person's entitlement to additional statutory paternity pay under this section shall not be affected by the placement for adoption of more than one child as part of the same arrangement.]

AMENDMENT

1. Work and Families Act 2006 s.7 (March 3, 2010).

[1 Entitlement to additional statutory paternity pay: general

¹171ZEC.— (1) A person shall not be entitled to payments of additional statutory paternity pay in respect of any period unless—
- (a) he gives the person who will be liable to pay it notice of the date from which he expects the liability to pay him additional statutory

1.123

paternity pay to begin and the date on which he expects that liability to end, and

(b) the notice is given by such time as may be prescribed.

(2) The notice shall be in writing if the person who is liable to pay the additional statutory paternity pay so requests.

(3) The Secretary of State may by regulations—

(a) provide that the conditions mentioned in subsection (2)(b) or (c) of section 171ZEA or 171ZEB shall have effect subject to prescribed modifications in such cases as may be prescribed;

(b) provide that subsection (1) of this section shall not have effect, or shall have effect subject to prescribed modifications, in such cases as may be prescribed;

(c) impose requirements about evidence of entitlement;

(d) specify in what circumstances employment is to be treated as continuous for the purposes of section 171ZEA or 171ZEB;

(e) provide that a person is to be treated for the purposes of section 171ZEA or 171ZEB as being employed for a continuous period of the length prescribed under that section where—

   (i) he has been employed by the same employer for a period of at least that length under two or more contracts of service, and

   (ii) those contracts were not continuous;

(f) provide for amounts earned by a person under separate contracts of service with the same employer to be aggregated for the purposes of section 171ZEA or 171ZEB;

(g) provide that—

   (i) the amount of a person's earnings for any period, or

   (ii) the amount of his earnings to be treated as comprised in any payment made to him or for his benefit,

shall be calculated or estimated for the purposes of section 171ZEA or 171ZEB in such manner and on such basis as may be prescribed, and that, for that purpose, payments of a particular class or description made or falling to be made to or by a person, shall, to such extent as may be prescribed, be disregarded or, as the case may be, be deducted from the amount of his earnings.]

AMENDMENT

1. Work and Families Act 2006 s.8 (March 3, 2010).

[1 Liability to make payments of additional statutory paternity pay

1171ZED.— (1) The liability to make payments of additional statutory paternity pay under section 171ZEA or 171ZEB is a liability of any person of whom the person entitled to the payments has been an employee as mentioned in subsection (2)(b) of that section.

(2) Regulations shall make provision as to a former employer's liability to pay additional statutory paternity pay to a person in any case where the former employee's contract of service with him has been brought to an end solely, or mainly, for the purpose of avoiding liability for additional statutory paternity pay or ordinary statutory paternity pay, or both.

(3) The Secretary of State may, with the concurrence of the Commissioners for Her Majesty's Revenue and Customs, by regulations specify circumstances in which, notwithstanding this section, liability to make payments of additional statutory paternity pay is to be a liability of the Commissioners.]

(1992 c.4 s.171ZED)

AMENDMENT

1. Work and Families Act 2006 s.9 (March 3, 2010).

[1 Rate and period of pay: additional statutory paternity pay

¹**171ZEE.**— (1) Additional statutory paternity pay shall be payable at such fixed or earnings-related weekly rate as may be prescribed by regulations, which may prescribe different kinds of rate for different cases.

(2) Subject to the following provisions of this section, additional statutory paternity pay shall be payable in respect of a period ("the additional paternity pay period") —
- (a) beginning with such day as may (subject to subsection (3)) be determined in accordance with regulations, and
- (b) ending with—
    - (i) the day on which the additional statutory pay period is ended by virtue of subsection (4) or (8), or
    - (ii) such earlier day as the employee may choose in accordance with regulations.

(3) The first day of the additional paternity pay period must not be earlier than the day on which the child's mother or the person with whom the child is placed for adoption ("the mother or adopter") is treated for the purpose of section 171ZEA or 171ZEB as returning to work; but this subsection does not apply in a case where the mother or adopter has died.

(4) The additional paternity pay period—
- (a) shall not last longer than any prescribed number of weeks,
- (b) shall not continue after the end of the period of 12 months beginning with the relevant date, and
- (c) shall not continue after the end—
    - (i) in a case falling within section 171ZEA, of the mother's maternity allowance period or maternity pay period, or
    - (ii) in a case falling within section 171ZEB, of the adoption pay period of the person with whom the child is placed for adoption.

(5) In subsection (4)(b), "the relevant date" means—
- (a) in the case of a person to whom the conditions in section 171ZEA(2) apply, the date of the child's birth (or, where more than one child is born as a result of the same pregnancy, the date of birth of the first child born as a result of the pregnancy), and
- (b) in the case of a person to whom the conditions in section 171ZEB(2) apply, the date of the child's placement for adoption (or, where more than one child is placed for adoption as part of the same arrangement, the date of placement of the first child to be placed as part of the arrangement).

(6) Additional statutory paternity pay shall not be payable to a person in respect of a week if it is not his purpose at the beginning of the week to care for the child by reference to whom he satisfies the condition in subparagraph (i) of section 171ZEA(2)(a) or 171ZEB(2)(a).

(7) Except in such cases as may be prescribed, additional statutory paternity pay shall not be payable to a person in respect of a week during any part of which he works for any employer.

(8) Where subsection (6) or (7) prevents additional statutory paternity pay being payable to a person in respect of any week, the person's

1.125

Social Security Contributions and Benefits Act 1992

additional paternity pay period shall be taken to have ended at the end of the previous week.

(9) Where for any purpose of this Part of this Act or of regulations it is necessary to calculate the daily rate of additional statutory paternity pay, the amount payable by way of additional statutory paternity pay for that day shall be taken to be one-seventh of the weekly rate.

(10) In this section "week" means a period of seven days beginning with the day of the week on which the additional paternity pay period began.]

AMENDMENT

1. Work and Families Act 2006 s.10 (March 3, 2010).

[¹ *Ordinary and additional statutory paternity pay: supplementary provisions*]

Restrictions on contracting out

1.126   **171ZF.**—(1) Any agreement shall be void to the extent that it purports—
(a) to exclude, limit or otherwise modify any provision of this Part of this Act; or
(b) to require an employee or former employee to contribute (whether directly or indirectly) towards any costs incurred by his employer or former employer under this Part of this Act.

(2) For the avoidance of doubt, any agreement between an employer and an employee authorising any deductions from [¹ ordinary statutory paternity pay or additional statutory paternity pay] which the employer is liable to pay to the employee in respect of any period shall not be void by virtue of subsection (1)(a) above if the employer—
(a) is authorised by that or another agreement to make the same deductions from any contractual remuneration which he is liable to pay in respect of the same period; or
(b) would be so authorised if he were liable to pay contractual remuneration in respect of that period.

AMENDMENT

1. Work and Families Act 2006 s.11(1) Sch.1 paras 17 and 18 (April 6, 2010).

DEFINITION

"employer"—see s.171ZJ(1).

GENERAL NOTE

1.127   These restrictions on contracting out follow the equivalent provisions for SSP (s.151(2)–(3)) and SMP (s.164(6)–(7)).

Relationship with contractual remuneration

1.128   **171ZG.**—(1) Subject to subsections (2) and (3) below, any entitlement to statutory paternity pay shall not affect any right of a person in relation to remuneration under any contract of service ("contractual remuneration").

(2) Subject to subsection (3) below—
(a) any contractual remuneration paid to a person by an employer of his

(1992 c.4 s.171ZG)

in respect of any period shall go towards discharging any liability of that employer to pay statutory paternity pay to him in respect of that period; and

(b) any statutory paternity pay paid by an employer to a person who is an employee of his in respect of any period shall go towards discharging any liability of that employer to pay contractual remuneration to him in respect of that period.

(3) Regulations may make provision as to payments which are, and those which are not, to be treated as contractual remuneration for the purposes of subsections (1) and (2) above.

[1 (4) In this section "statutory paternity pay" means ordinary statutory paternity pay or additional statutory paternity pay.]

AMENDMENT

1. Work and Families Act 2006 s.11(1) Sch.1 para.19 (April 6, 2010).

DEFINITIONS

"contractual remuneration"—see subs.(1).
"employer"—see s.171ZJ(1).

GENERAL NOTE

This section mirrors Sch.12, para.2 the equivalent provision in relation to SSP, and Sch.13 para.3, which governs SMP to the same effect. The basic principle is that entitlement to SPP does not affect a claimant's rights to any contractual remuneration (subs.(1)), subject to the significant exception that any payment of contractual remuneration can be regarded as the discharge of SPP liability and vice versa (subs.(2)). Regulations made under subs.(3) provide that the payments to be treated as contractual remuneration are sums payable under a contract of service (a) by way of remuneration, (b) for incapacity for work due to sickness or injury, or (c) by reason of the birth or adoption of a child (SPP and SAP (General) Regulations 2002 (SI 2002/2822) reg.19).

1.129

Crown employment—Part XIIZA

171ZH. The provisions of this Part of this Act apply in relation to persons employed by or under the Crown as they apply in relation to persons employed otherwise than by or under the Crown.

1.130

GENERAL NOTE

This mirrors s.169, the equivalent provision for SMP.

1.131

Special classes of person

171ZI.—(1) The Secretary of State may with the concurrence of the Treasury make regulations modifying any provision of this Part of this Act in such manner as he thinks proper in its application to any person who is, has been or is to be—

(a) employed on board any ship, vessel, hovercraft or aircraft;
(b) outside Great Britain at any prescribed time or in any prescribed circumstances; or
(c) in prescribed employment in connection with continental shelf operations, as defined in section 120(2) above.

1.132

(2) Regulations under subsection (1) above may, in particular, provide—
(a) for any provision of this Part of this Act to apply to any such person, notwithstanding that it would not otherwise apply;
(b) for any such provision not to apply to any such person, notwithstanding that it would otherwise apply;
(c) for excepting any such person from the application of any such provision where he neither is domiciled nor has a place of residence in any part of Great Britain;
(d) for the taking of evidence, for the purposes of the determination of any question arising under any such provision, in a country or territory outside Great Britain, by a British consular official or such other person as may be determined in accordance with the regulations.

DEFINITIONS

"Great Britain"—see s.172(a).
"prescribed"—see s.171ZJ(1).

GENERAL NOTE

1.133 This enabling provision is in the same terms as s.162, which applies to SSP. See further the Statutory Paternity Pay and Statutory Adoption Pay (Persons Abroad and Mariners) Regulations 2002 (SI 2002/2821).

Part XIIZA: supplementary

1.134 171ZJ.—(1) In this Part of this Act—
"the Board" means the Commissioners of Inland Revenue;
[²"employer", in relation to a person who is an employee, means a person who—
(a) under section 6 above is, liable to pay secondary Class 1 contributions in relation to any of the earnings of the person who is an employee; or
(b) would be liable to pay such contributions but for—
    (i) the condition in section 6(1)(b), or
    (ii) the employee being under the age of 16;]
[⁵ "local authority" has the same meaning as in the Children Act 1989 (see section 105(1) of that Act);
"local authority foster parent" has the same meaning as in the Children Act 1989 (see section 22C(12) of that Act);]
"modifications" includes additions, omissions and amendments, and related expressions are to be read accordingly;
"prescribed" means prescribed by regulations.
(2) In this Part of this Act, "employee" means a person who is—
(a) gainfully employed in Great Britain either under a contract of service or in an office (including elective office) with [¹general earnings (as defined by section 7 of the Income Tax (Earnings and Pensions) Act 2003)]
[². . .]
(3) Regulations may provide—
(a) for cases where a person who falls within the definition in subsection (2) above is not to be treated as an employee for the purposes of this Part of this Act; and
(b) for cases where a person who would not otherwise be an employee

for the purposes of this Part of this Act is to be treated as an employee for those purposes.

(4) Without prejudice to any other power to make regulations under this Part of this Act, regulations may specify cases in which, for the purposes of this Part of this Act or of such provisions of this Part of this Act as may be prescribed—
(a) two or more employers are to be treated as one;
(b) two or more contracts of service in respect of which the same person is an employee are to be treated as one.

(5) In this Part, except [4 sections 171ZE and 171ZEE], "week" means a period of seven days beginning with Sunday or such other period as may be prescribed in relation to any particular case or class of cases.

(6) For the purposes of this Part of this Act, a person's normal weekly earnings shall, subject to subsection (8) below, be taken to be the average weekly earnings which in the relevant period have been paid to him or paid for his benefit under the contract of service with the employer in question.

(7) For the purposes of subsection (6) above, "earnings" and "relevant period" shall have the meanings given to them by regulations.

(8) In such cases as may be prescribed, a person's normal weekly earnings shall be calculated in accordance with regulations.

(9) Where—
(a) in consequence of the establishment of one or more National Health Service trusts under [3the National Health Service Act 2006, the National Health Service (Wales) Act 2006], or the National Health Service (Scotland) Act 1978 a person's contract of employment is treated by a scheme under [3any of those Acts] as divided so as to constitute two or more contracts; or
(b) an order under [3paragraph 26(1) of Schedule 3 to the National Health Service Act 2006] provides that a person's contract of employment is so divided;

regulations may make provision enabling the person to elect for all of those contracts to be treated as one contract for the purposes of this Part of this Act or such provisions of this Part of this Act as may be prescribed.

(10) Regulations under subsection (9) above may prescribe—
(a) the conditions that must be satisfied if a person is to be entitled to make such an election;
(b) the manner in which, and the time within which, such an election is to be made;
(c) the persons to whom, and the manner in which, notice of such an election is to be given;
(d) the information which a person who makes such an election is to provide, and the persons to whom, and the time within which, he is to provide it;
(e) the time for which such an election is to have effect;
(f) which one of the person's employers under two or more contracts is to be regarded for the purposes of [4 ordinary statutory paternity pay or additional statutory paternity pay] as his employer under the contract.

(11) The powers under subsections (9) and (10) are without prejudice to any other power to make regulations under this Part of this Act.

(12) Regulations under any of subsections (4) to (10) above must be made with the concurrence of the Board.

AMENDMENTS

1. Income Tax (Earnings and Pensions) Act 2003 s.722 and Sch.6 para.183 (April 6, 2003).
2. Employment Equality (Age) Regulations 2006 (SI 2006/1031) reg.49(1) and Sch.8 Pt 1 para.11(2) (October 1, 2006).
3. National Health Service (Consequential Provisions) Act 2006 s.2 and Sch.1 para.149 (March 1, 2007).
4. Work and Families Act 2006 s.11(1) Sch.1 para.20 (April 6, 2010).
5. Children and Families Act 2014 s.121(7)(a) (June 30, 2014).

GENERAL NOTE

1.135   "*Earnings*": The definition and enabling power under subss.(6) and (7) should be read with reg.39 of the SPP and SAP (General) Regulations 2002 (SI 2002/2822), which defines this term.

"*Employee*": The definition under subs.(2) is modified by regulations made under subs.(3). Thus those who are treated as employed earners under the Social Security (Categorisation of Earners) Regulations 1978 (SI 1978/1689) are also treated as employees for the purpose of SPP: SPP and SAP (General) Regulations 2002 reg.32(1). Apprentices are also covered (reg.32(2)). Employed earners who do not meet the residence or presence requirements under the rules governing National Insurance contributions are excluded from the definition of employee for these purposes (reg.32(3)). Continuous employment is dealt with by regs 33–37. Employment with more than one employer (subs.(4)) is covered by reg.38.

"*National Health Service trusts*": The special position of NHS employees with more than one contract of employment (e.g. with different NHS trusts) is dealt with by the SPP and SAP (National Health Service Employees) Regulations 2002 (SI 2002/2819). These regulations enable such employees to elect to treat two or more such contracts as one contract of employment.

"*Normal weekly earnings*": The definition and enabling power under subss.(6) and (7) should be read with reg.40 of the SPP and SAP (General) Regulations 2002, which defines this term.

Power to apply Part XIIZA to adoption cases not involving placement

1.136   **171ZK.**—The Secretary of State may by regulations provide for this Part to have effect in relation to cases which involve adoption, but not the placement of a child for adoption under the law of any part of the United Kingdom, with such modifications as the regulations may prescribe.

DEFINITIONS

"modifications"—see s.171ZJ(1).
"United Kingdom"—see s.172(b).

GENERAL NOTE

1.137   See further the Social Security Contributions and Benefits Act 1992 (Application of Pts 12ZA and 12ZB to Adoptions from Overseas) Regulations 2003 (SI 2003/499) and the Statutory Paternity Pay (Adoption) and Statutory Adoption Pay (Adoptions from Overseas) (No.2) Regulations 2003 (SI 2003/1194).

(1992 c.4 s.171ZK)

[¹Part XIIZB

Statutory Adoption Pay

Amendment

1. Part XIIZB was inserted by the Employment Act 2002 s.4 (December 8, 2002).

General Note

Part XIIZB of the SSCBA 1992 was inserted by the Employment Act 2002. On the background to the introduction of statutory adoption pay (SAP), see the General Note to Pt XIIZA on statutory paternity pay (SPP), introduced at the same time. The amendments made by c.1 of Pt I of the Employment Act 2002 relating to paternity and adoption, including the insertion of Pt XIIZB into the SSCBA 1992, came into force on December 8, 2002 (Employment Act 2002 (Commencement No.3 and Transitional and Saving Provisions) Order 2002 art.2(2) and Sch.1 Pt 2). However, art.3 and Sch.3 para.2 of the same Order provide that Pt XIIZB shall have effect only in relation to a person with whom a child is, or is expected to be, placed for adoption on or after April 6, 2003.

Adoptive parents have a right under employment legislation to 26 weeks' ordinary adoption leave with the option of 26 weeks' additional adoption leave, mirroring the arrangements now in place for maternity leave. Statutory Adoption Pay is payable for 26 weeks (SSCBA 1992 s.171ZN(2)), as with SMP (but unlike the mere two weeks for SPP). The rules governing entitlement to SAP are set out in SSCBA 1992 s.171ZL: employees must have completed 26 weeks' service with their employer by the time they are matched with the child to be adopted and their earnings, on average, must be at least equal to the lower earnings limit for the purpose of National Insurance contributions. The liability to make payments of SAP is placed on employers (SSCBA 1992 s.171ZM), with the recovery arrangements being as for SMP. Provision for various types of special cases and for matters of interpretation is to be found in SSCBA 1992 ss.171ZO–171ZT.

1.138

Entitlement

171ZL.—(1) Where a person who is, or has been, an employee satisfies the conditions in subsection (2) below, he shall be entitled in accordance with the following provisions of this Part to payments to be known as "statutory adoption pay".

1.139

(2) The conditions are—
(a) that he is a person with whom a child is, or is expected to be, placed for adoption under the law of any part of the United Kingdom;
(b) that he has been in employed earner's employment with an employer for a continuous period of at least 26 weeks ending with the relevant week;
(c) that he has ceased to work for the employer;
(d) that his normal weekly earnings for the period of 8 weeks ending with the relevant week are not less than the lower earnings limit in force under section 5(1)(a) at the end of the relevant week; and
(e) that he has elected to receive statutory adoption pay.

(3) The references in subsection (2)(b) and (d) above to the relevant week are to the week in which the person is notified that he has been matched with the child for the purposes of adoption.

(4) A person may not elect to receive statutory adoption pay if—

(a) he has elected in accordance with section 171ZB above to receive statutory paternity pay, or
[¹(b) he falls within subsection (4A);
(4A) A person falls within this subsection if—
(a) the child is, or is expected to be, placed for adoption with him as a member of a couple;
(b) the other member of the couple is a person to whom the conditions in subsection (2) above apply; and
(c) the other member of the couple has elected to receive statutory adoption pay.
(4B) For the purposes of subsection (4A), a person is a member of a couple if—
(a) in the case of an adoption or expected adoption under the law of England and Wales, he is a member of a couple within the meaning of section 144(4) of the Adoption and Children Act 2002;
(b) in the case of an adoption or an expected adoption under the law [² . . .] of Northern Ireland, he is a member of a married couple;]
[² (c) in the case of an adoption or expected adoption under the law of Scotland he is a member of a relevant couple within the meaning of section 29(3) of the Adoption and Children (Scotland) Act 2007.]
(5) A person's entitlement to statutory adoption pay shall not be affectedby the placement, or expected placement, for adoption of more than one childas part of the same arrangement.
(6) A person shall be entitled to payments of statutory adoption pay only if—
(a) he gives the person who will be liable to pay it notice of the date from which he expects the liability to pay him statutory adoption pay to begin; and
(b) the notice is given at least 28 days before that date or, if that is not reasonably practicable, as soon as is reasonably practicable.
(7) The notice shall be in writing if the person who is liable to pay the statutory adoption pay so requests.
(8) The Secretary of State may by regulations—
(a) provide that subsection (2)(b), (c) or (d) above shall have effect subject to prescribed modifications in such cases as may be prescribed;
(b) provide that subsection (6) above shall not have effect, or shall have effect subject to prescribed modifications, in such cases as may be prescribed;
(c) impose requirements about evidence of entitlement;
(d) specify in what circumstances employment is to be treated as continuous for the purposes of this section;
(e) provide that a person is to be treated for the purposes of this section as being employed for a continuous period of at least 26 weeks where—
(i) he has been employed by the same employer for at least 26 weeks under two or more separate contracts of service; and
(ii) those contracts were not continuous;
(f) provide for amounts earned by a person under separate contracts of service with the same employer to be aggregated for the purposes of this section;
(g) provide that—
(i) the amount of a person's earnings for any period; or
(ii) the amount of his earnings to be treated as comprised in any payment made to him or for his benefit;

(1992 c.4 s.171ZL)

shall be calculated or estimated for the purposes of this section in such manner and on such basis as may be prescribed and that for that purpose payments of a particular class or description made or falling to be made to or by a person shall, to such extent as may be prescribed, be disregarded or, as the case may be, be deducted from the amount of his earnings;
(h) make provision about elections for statutory adoption pay.

[³ (9) This section has effect in a case involving a child who is, or is expected to be, placed under section 22C of the Children Act 1989 by a local authority in England with a local authority foster parent who has been approved as a prospective adopter with the following modifications—
(a) the references in subsections (2)(a) and (4A)(a) to a child being placed for adoption under the law of any part of the United Kingdom are to be treated as references to a child being placed under section 22C in that manner;
(b) the reference in subsection (3) to the week in which the person is notified that he has been matched with the child for the purposes of adoption is to be treated as a reference to the week in which the person is notified that the child is to be, or is expected to be, placed with him under section 22C;
(c) the references in subsection (4B)(a) to adoption are to be treated as references to placement under section 22C;
(d) the reference in subsection (5) to placement, or expected placement, for adoption is to be treated as a reference to placement, or expected placement, under section 22C.

(10) Where, by virtue of subsection (9), a person becomes entitled to statutory adoption pay in respect of a child who is, or is expected to be, placed under section 22C of the Children Act 1989, the person may not become entitled to payments of statutory adoption pay as a result of the child being, or being expected to be, placed for adoption.]

AMENDMENTS

1. Adoption and Children Act 2002 (Consequential Amendment to Statutory Adoption Pay) Order 2006 (SI 2006/2012) art.3 (October 1, 2006).
2. Adoption and Children (Scotland) Act 2007 (Consequential Modifications) Order 2011 (SI 2011/1740) art.2 and Sch.1 para.4 and Pt 3 (July 15, 2011).
3. Children and Families Act 2014 s.121(5) (June 30, 2014).

DEFINITIONS

"employee"—see s.171ZS(2).
"employer"—see s.171ZS(1).
"modifications"—see *ibid.*
"normal weekly earnings"—see s.171ZS(6).
"prescribed"—see s.171ZS(1).
"relevant week"—see subs.(3).
"United Kingdom"—see s.172(b).
"week"—see s.171ZS(5).

GENERAL NOTE

This section sets out the qualifying conditions for receipt of SAP. A person is entitled to SAP if he or she meets each of five conditions (subs.(2)). First, the claimant must have an approved match with the child. Secondly, the person must be an employee who has satisfied the service qualification of continuous service with

1.140

the same employer for at least 26 weeks by the week in which the approved match is made. Thirdly, the person must have actually stopped working for that employer (see also s.171ZN(3) (and (4)). Fourthly, the employee's average weekly earnings must be not less than the lower earnings limit for National Insurance contributions. Finally, the person must have elected to receive SAP, which requires that he or she provide the employer with an appropriate notification (see subss.(6) and (7); see also reg.23 of the SPP and SAP (General) Regulations 2002 (SI 2002/2822)) and evidence of entitlement (SPP and SAP (General) Regulations 2002 reg.24).

Statutory Adoption Pay is available to an adoptive parent of a child newly placed for adoption, whether the child is being adopted within the UK or from overseas. There are, however, some slight differences in the provisions for SAP for domestic and overseas adoptions respectively: see further SSCBA 1992 s.171ZT. It is also important to note that entitlement to SAP arises only for children who are newly placed for adoption. It is therefore not possible to receive SAP for a step-family adoption or where the child is adopted by his or her existing foster carers.

Liability to make payments

1.141 **171ZM.**—(1) The liability to make payments of statutory adoption pay is a liability of any person of whom the person entitled to the payments has been an employee as mentioned in section 171ZL(2)(b) above.

(2) Regulations shall make provision as to a former employer's liability to pay statutory adoption pay to a person in any case where the former employee's contract of service with him has been brought to an end by the former employer solely, or mainly, for the purpose of avoiding liability for statutory adoption pay.

(3) The Secretary of State may, with the concurrence of the Board, by regulations specify circumstances in which, notwithstanding this section, liability to make payments of statutory adoption pay is to be a liability of the Board.

DEFINITIONS

"the Board"—see s.171ZS(1).
"employee"—see s.171ZS(2).
"employer"—see s.171ZS(1).

GENERAL NOTE

1.142 This section, placing the liability to make payments of SAP on employers, follows the same approach as the provisions governing SMP (ss.164(3) and (8)) and SPP (s.171ZD). Note that there is no liability to pay SAP in respect of any week during which the claimant either is entitled to SSP or is detained in custody (or sentenced to imprisonment): SPP and SAP (General) Regulations 2002 (SI 2002/2822) reg.27 (but note that, unlike with SPP, there are exceptions to the latter preclusionary rule: reg.27(2)). As with SPP, however, there is no liability to pay SAP in the week that the person entitled dies.

The rules governing the funding of SAP and employers' responsibilities in connection with SAP payments are contained in the SPP and SAP (Administration) Regulations 2002 (SI 2002/2820). The special circumstances in which HMRC is liable to pay SAP under subs.(3) are set out in SPP and SAP (General) Regulations 2002 regs 43 and 44 (the latter applying solely to SAP and not SPP).

Rate and period of pay

1.143 **171ZN.**—(1) Statutory adoption pay shall be payable at such fixed or earnings-related weekly rate as the Secretary of State may prescribe

(1992 c.4 s.171ZN)

by regulations, which may prescribe different kinds of rate for different cases.

(2) Statutory adoption pay shall be payable, subject to the provisions of this Part of this Act, in respect of each week during a prescribed period ("the adoption pay period") of a duration not exceeding [¹52 weeks].

[³ (2A) Regulations may provide for the duration of the adoption pay period as it applies to a person ("A") to be reduced, subject to prescribed restrictions and conditions.

(2B) Regulations under subsection (2A) are to secure that the reduced period ends at a time—
  (a) after a prescribed part of the adoption pay period has expired, and
  (b) when at least a prescribed part of the adoption pay period remains unexpired.

(2C) Regulations under subsection (2A) may, in particular, prescribe restrictions and conditions relating to—
  (a) the end of A's entitlement to adoption leave;
  (b) the doing of work by A;
  (c) the taking of prescribed steps by A or another person as regards leave under section 75G of the Employment Rights Act 1996 in respect of the child;
  (d) the taking of prescribed steps by A or another person as regards statutory shared parental pay in respect of the child.

(2D) Regulations may provide for a reduction in the duration of the adoption pay period as it applies to a person to be revoked, or to be treated as revoked, subject to prescribed restrictions and conditions.]

(3) [¹Except in such cases as may be prescribed,] a person shall not be liable to pay statutory adoption pay to another in respect of any week during any part of which the other works under a contract of service with him.

(4) It is immaterial for the purposes of subsection (3) above whether the work referred to in that subsection is work under a contract of service which existed immediately before the adoption pay period or a contract of service which did not so exist.

(5) Except in such cases as may be prescribed, statutory adoption pay shall not be payable to a person in respect of any week during any part of which he works for any employer who is not liable to pay him statutiory adoption pay.

(6) The Secretary of State may by regulations specify circumstances in which there is to be no liability to pay statutory adoption pay in respect of a week.

[²(6A) Where for any purpose of this Part of this Act or of regulations it is necessary to calculate the daily rate of statutory adoption pay, the amount payable by way of statutory adoption pay for any day shall be taken as one seventh of the weekly rate.]

(7) In subsection (2) above, "week" means any period of seven days.

(8) In subsection (3), (5) and (6) above, "week" means a period of seven days beginning with the day of the week on which the adoption pay period begins.

[³ (9) Where statutory adoption pay is payable to a person by virtue of section 171ZL(9), this section has effect as if the reference in subsection (2F) to the week in which the person is notified that he has been matched with a child for the purposes of adoption were a reference to the week in

Social Security Contributions and Benefits Act 1992

which the person is notified that a child is to be, or is expected to be, placed with him under section 22C of the Children Act 1989.]

AMENDMENTS

1. Work and Families Act 2006 s.2 (October 1, 2006).
2. Work and Families Act 2006 s.11 and Sch.1 para.21 (October 1, 2006).
3. Children and Families Act 2014 ss.120(6) and 121(6) (June 30, 2014).

DEFINITIONS

"adoption pay period"—see subs.(2).
"employer"—see s.171ZS(1).
"prescribed"—see *ibid.*
"week"—see subss.(7) and (8).

GENERAL NOTE

1.144 This section provides that SAP is payable for a period of up to 52 weeks (the "adoption pay period" under subs.(2)). The rate of SAP is the same as that for SMP, namely (from April 2015) the lesser of £139.58 a week or 90 per cent of the employee's average weekly earnings: SPP and SAP (Weekly Rates) Regulations 2002 (SI 2002/2818) reg.3. More detailed rules relating to the adoption pay period are set out in regs 21 and 22 of the SPP and SAP (General) Regulations 2002 (SI 2002/2822).

Restrictions on contracting out

1.145 **171ZO.**—(1) Any agreement shall be void to the extent that it purports—
  (a) to exclude, limit or otherwise modify any provision of this Part of this Act; or
  (b) to require an employee or former employee to contribute (whether directly or indirectly) towards any costs incurred by his employer or former employer under this Part of this Act.

(2) For the avoidance of doubt, any agreement between an employer and an employee authorising any deductions from statutory adoption pay which the employer is liable to pay to the employee in respect of any period shall not be void by virtue of subsection (1)(a) above if the employer—
  (a) is authorised by that or another agreement to make the same deductions from any contractual remuneration which he is liable to pay in respect of the same period; or
  (b) would be so authorised if he were liable to pay contractual remuneration in respect of that period.

DEFINITIONS

"employee"—see s.171ZS(2).
"employer"—see s.171ZS(1).

GENERAL NOTE

1.146 These restrictions on contracting out are in the same terms as the equivalent provisions for SSP (s.151(2)–(3)), SMP (s.164(6)–(7)) and SPP (s.171ZF). See also SPP and SAP (General) Regulations 2002 (SI 2002/2822) reg.30.

(1992 c.4 s.171ZP)

Relationship with benefits and other payments etc.

171ZP.—(1) Except as may be prescribed, a day which falls within the adoption pay period shall not be treated as a day of incapacity for work for the purposes of determining, for this Act, whether it forms part of a period of incapacity for work for the purposes of incapacity benefit.

(2) Regulations may provide that in prescribed circumstances a day which falls within the adoption pay period shall be treated as a day of incapacity for work for the purposes of determining entitlement to the higher rate of short-term incapacity benefit or to long-term incapacity benefit.

(3) Regulations may provide that an amount equal to a person's statutory adoption pay for a period shall be deducted from any such benefit in respect of the same period and a person shall be entitled to such benefit only if there is a balance after the deduction and, if there is such a balance, at a weekly rate equal to it.

(4) Subject to subsections (5) and (6) below, any entitlement to statutory adoption pay shall not affect any right of a person in relation to remuneration under any contract of service ("contractual remuneration").

(5) Subject to subsection (6) below—
(a) any contractual remuneration paid to a person by an employer of his in respect of a week in the adoption pay period shall go towards discharging any liability of that employer to pay statutory adoption pay to him in respect of that week; and
(b) any statutory adoption pay paid by an employer to a person who is an employee of his in respect of a week in the adoption pay period shall go towards discharging any liability of that employer to pay contractual remuneration to him in respect of that week.

(6) Regulations may make provision as to payments which are, and those which are not, to be treated as contractual remuneration for the purposes of subsections (4) and (5) above.

(7) In subsection (5) above, "week" means a period of seven days beginning with the day of the week on which the adoption pay period begins.

1.147

DEFINITIONS

"adoption pay period"—see s.171ZN(2).
"contractual remuneration"—see subs.(4).
"employee"—see s.171ZS(2).
"employer"—see s.171ZS(1).
"prescribed"—see *ibid.*
"week"—see subs.(7).

GENERAL NOTE

The basic principle is that entitlement to SAP does not affect a claimant's rights to any contractual remuneration (subs.(4)), subject to the significant exception that any payment of contractual remuneration can be regarded as the discharge of SAP liability and vice versa (subs.(5)). Regulations made under subs.(6) provide that the payments to be treated as contractual remuneration are sums payable under a contract of service: (a) by way of remuneration, (b) for incapacity for work due to sickness or injury, or (c) by reason of the adoption of a child (SPP and SAP (General) Regulations 2002 (SI 2002/2822) reg.28).

1.148

Crown employment—Part XIIZB

1.149   **171ZQ.**— The provisions of this Part of this Act apply in relation to persons employed by or under the Crown as they apply in relation to persons employed otherwise than by or under the Crown.

GENERAL NOTE

1.150   This mirrors s.169, the equivalent provision for SMP, and s.171ZH, which deals with SPP.

Special classes of person

1.151   **171ZR.**—(1) The Secretary of State may with the concurrence of the Treasury make regulations modifying any provision of this Part of this Act in such manner as he thinks proper in its application to any person who is, has been or is to be—
(a) employed on board any ship, vessel, hovercraft or aircraft;
(b) outside Great Britain at any prescribed time or in any prescribed circumstances; or
(c) in prescribed employment in connection with continental shelf operations, as defined in section 120(2) above.
(2) Regulations under subsection (1) above may, in particular, provide—
(a) for any provision of this Part of this Act to apply to any such person, notwithstanding that it would not otherwise apply;
(b) for any such provision not to apply to any such person, notwithstanding that it would otherwise apply;
(c) for excepting any such person from the application of any such provision where he neither is domiciled nor has a place of residence in any part of Great Britain;
(d) for the taking of evidence, for the purposes of the determination of any question arising under any such provision, in a country or territory outside Great Britain, by a British consular official or such other person as may be determined in accordance with the regulations.

DEFINITIONS

"Great Britain"—see s.172(a).
"prescribed"—see s.171ZS(1).

GENERAL NOTE

1.152   This enabling provision is in the same terms as s.162, which applies to SSP, and s.171ZI, which deals with SPP. See further the Statutory Paternity Pay and Statutory Adoption Pay (Persons Abroad and Mariners) Regulations 2002 (SI 2002/2821).

Part XIIZB: supplementary

1.153   **171ZS.**—(1) In this Part of this Act—
"adoption pay period" has the meaning given by section 171ZN(2) above;
"the Board" means the Commissioners of Inland Revenue;
[2"employer", in relation to a person who is an employee, means a person who—
(a) under section 6 above is liable to pay secondary Class 1 contributions in relation to any of the earnings of the person who is an employee; or

(1992 c.4 s.171ZS)

   (b) would be liable to pay such contributions but for—
      (i) the condition in section 6(1)(b), or
      (ii) the employee being under the age of 16;]
[⁴ "local authority" has the same meaning as in the Children Act 1989 (see section 105(1) of that Act);
"local authority foster parent" has the same meaning as in the Children Act 1989 (see section 22C(12) of that Act);]
"modifications" includes additions, omissions and amendments, and related expressions are to be read accordingly;
"prescribed" means prescribed by regulations.
(2) In this Part of this Act, "employee" means a person who is—
(a) gainfully employed in Great Britain either under a contract of service or in an office (including elective office) with [¹general earnings (as defined by section 7 of the Income Tax (Earnings and Pensions) Act 2003)]
[². . .]
(3) Regulations may provide—
(a) for cases where a person who falls within the definition in sub-section (2) above is not to be treated as an employee for the purposes of this Part of this Act; and
(b) for cases where a person who would not otherwise be an employee for the purposes of this Part of this Act is to be treated as an employee for those purposes.
(4) Without prejudice to any other power to make regulations under this Part of this Act, regulations may specify cases in which, for the purposes of this Part of this Act or of such provisions of this Part of this Act as may be prescribed—
(a) two or more employers are to be treated as one;
(b) two or more contracts of service in respect of which the same person is an employee are to be treated as one.
(5) In this Part, except sections 171ZN and 171ZP, "week" means a period of seven days beginning with Sunday or such other period as may be prescribed in relation to any particular case or class of cases.
(6) For the purposes of this Part of this Act, a person's normal weekly earnings shall, subject to subsection (8) below, be taken to be the average weekly earnings which in the relevant period have been paid to him or paid for his benefit under the contract of service with the employer in question.
(7) For the purposes of subsection (6) above, "earnings" and "relevant period" shall have the meanings given to them by regulations.
(8) In such cases as may be prescribed, a person's normal weekly earnings shall be calculated in accordance with regulations.
(9) Where—
(a) in consequence of the establishment of one or more National Health Service trusts under [³the National Health Service Act 2006, the National Health Service (Wales) Act 2006] or the National Health Service (Scotland) Act 1978, a person's contract of employment is treated by a scheme under [³any of those Acts] as divided so as to constitute two or more contracts; or
(b) an order under [³paragraph 26(1) of Schedule 3 to the National Health Service Act 2006] provides that a person's contract of employment is so divided;

regulations may make provision enabling the person to elect for all of those contracts to be treated as one contract for the purposes of this Part of this Act or such provisions of this Part of this Act as may be prescribed.

(10) Regulations under subsection (9) above may prescribe—
(a) the conditions that must be satisfied if a person is to be entitled to make such an election;
(b) the manner in which, and the time within which, such an election is to be made;
(c) the persons to whom, and the manner in which, notice of such an election is to be given;
(d) the information which a person who makes such an election is to provide, and the persons to whom, and the time within which, he is to provide it;
(e) the time for which such an election is to have effect;
(f) which one of the person's employers under two or more contracts is to be regarded for the purposes of statutory adoption pay as his employer under the contract.

(11) The powers under subsections (9) and (10) are without prejudice to any other power to make regulations under this Part of this Act.

(12) Regulations under any of subsections (4) to (10) above must be made with the concurrence of the Board.

AMENDMENTS

1. Income Tax (Earnings and Pensions) Act 2003 s.722 and Sch.6 para.184 (April 6, 2003).
2. Employment Equality (Age) Regulations 2006 (SI 2006/1031) reg.49(1) and Sch.8 Pt 1 para.12 (October 1, 2006).
3. National Health Service (Consequential Provisions) Act 2006 s.2 and Sch.1 para.150 (March 1, 2007).
4. Children and Families Act 2014 s.121(7)(b) (June 30, 2014).

DEFINITIONS

"Earnings"—see General Note to s.171ZJ.
"Employee"—see General Note to s.171ZJ.
"National Health Service trusts"—see General Note to s.171ZJ.
"Normal weekly earnings"—see General Note to s.171ZJ.

Power to apply Part XIIZB to adoption cases not involving placement

1.154   **171ZT.**— The Secretary of State may by regulations provide for this Part to have effect in relation to cases which involve adoption, but not the placement of a child for adoption under the law of any part of the United Kingdom, with such modifications as the regulations may prescribe.

GENERAL NOTE

1.155   See further the Social Security Contributions and Benefits Act 1992 (Application of Pts 12ZA and 12ZB to Adoptions from Overseas) Regulations 2003 (SI 2003/499) and the Statutory Paternity Pay (Adoption) and Statutory Adoption Pay (Adoptions from Overseas) (No.2) Regulations 2003 (SI 2003/1194).

(1992 c.4 s.171ZU)

[¹ PART 12ZC

STATUTORY SHARED PARENTAL PAY

Entitlement: birth

171ZU.—(1) Regulations may provide that, where all the conditions in subsection (2) are satisfied in relation to a person who is the mother of a child ("the claimant mother"), the claimant mother is to be entitled in accordance with the following provisions of this Part to payments to be known as "statutory shared parental pay".

(2) The conditions are—
(a) that the claimant mother and another person ("P") satisfy prescribed conditions as to caring or intending to care for the child;
(b) that P satisfies prescribed conditions—
  (i) as to employment or self-employment,
  (ii) as to having earnings of a prescribed amount for a prescribed period, and
  (iii) as to relationship either with the child or with the claimant mother;
(c) that the claimant mother has been in employed earner's employment with an employer for a continuous period of at least the prescribed length ending with a prescribed week;
(d) that at the end of that prescribed week the claimant mother was entitled to be in that employment;
(e) that the claimant mother's normal weekly earnings for a prescribed period ending with a prescribed week are not less than the lower earnings limit in force under section 5(1)(a) at the end of that week;
(f) if regulations so provide, that the claimant mother continues in employed earner's employment (whether or not with the employer by reference to whom the condition in paragraph (c) is satisfied) until a prescribed time;
(g) that the claimant mother became entitled to statutory maternity pay by reference to the birth of the child;
(h) that the claimant mother satisfies prescribed conditions as to the reduction of the duration of the maternity pay period;
(i) that the claimant mother has given the person who will be liable to pay statutory shared parental pay to her notice of—
  (i) the number of weeks in respect of which she would be entitled to claim statutory shared parental pay in respect of the child if the entitlement were fully exercised (disregarding for these purposes any intention of P to claim statutory shared parental pay in respect of the child),
  (ii) the number of weeks in respect of which she intends to claim statutory shared parental pay, and
  (iii) the number of weeks in respect of which P intends to claim statutory shared parental pay;
(j) that the claimant mother has given the person who will be liable to pay statutory shared parental pay to her notice of the period or periods during which she intends to claim statutory shared parental pay in respect of the child;

(k) that a notice under paragraph (i) or (j)—
   (i) is given by such time as may be prescribed, and
   (ii) satisfies prescribed conditions as to form and content;
(l) that P consents to the extent of the claimant mother's intended claim for statutory shared parental pay;
(m) that it is the claimant mother's intention to care for the child during each week in respect of which statutory shared parental pay is paid to her;
(n) that the claimant mother is absent from work during each week in respect of which statutory shared parental pay is paid to her;
(o) that, where she is an employee within the meaning of the Employment Rights Act 1996, the claimant mother's absence from work during each such week is absence on shared parental leave.

(3) Regulations may provide that, where all the conditions in subsection (4) are satisfied in relation to a person ("the claimant"), the claimant is to be entitled in accordance with the following provisions of this Part to payments to be known as "statutory shared parental pay".

(4) The conditions are—
(a) that the claimant and another person ("M") who is the mother of a child satisfy prescribed conditions as to caring or intending to care for the child;
(b) that the claimant satisfies—
   (i) prescribed conditions as to relationship with the child, or
   (ii) prescribed conditions as to relationship with M;
(c) that M satisfies prescribed conditions—
   (i) as to employment or self-employment, and
   (ii) as to having earnings of a prescribed amount for a prescribed period;
(d) that the claimant has been in employed earner's employment with an employer for a continuous period of at least the prescribed length ending with a prescribed week;
(e) that at the end of that prescribed week the claimant was entitled to be in that employment;
(f) that the claimant's normal weekly earnings for a prescribed period ending with a prescribed week are not less than the lower earnings limit in force under section 5(1)(a) at the end of that week;
(g) if regulations so provide, that the claimant continues in employed earner's employment (whether or not with the employer by reference to whom the condition in paragraph (d) is satisfied) until a prescribed time;
(h) that M became entitled, by reference to the birth of the child, to—
   (i) a maternity allowance, or
   (ii) statutory maternity pay;
(i) that M satisfies prescribed conditions as to—
   (i) the reduction of the duration of the maternity allowance period, or
   (ii) the reduction of the duration of the maternity pay period, as the case may be;
(j) that the claimant has given the person who will be liable to pay statutory shared parental pay to the claimant notice of—
   (i) the number of weeks in respect of which the claimant would be entitled to claim statutory shared parental pay in respect of

the child if the entitlement were fully exercised (disregarding for these purposes any intention of M to claim statutory shared parental pay in respect of the child),
   (ii) the number of weeks in respect of which the claimant intends to claim statutory shared parental pay, and
   (iii) the number of weeks in respect of which M intends to claim statutory shared parental pay;
(k) that the claimant has given the person who will be liable to pay statutory shared parental pay to the claimant notice of the period or periods during which the claimant intends to claim statutory shared parental pay in respect of the child;
(l) that a notice under paragraph (j) or (k)—
   (i) is given by such time as may be prescribed, and
   (ii) satisfies prescribed conditions as to form and content;
(m) that M consents to the extent of the claimant's intended claim for statutory shared parental pay;
(n) that it is the claimant's intention to care for the child during each week in respect of which statutory shared parental pay is paid to the claimant;
(o) that the claimant is absent from work during each week in respect of which statutory shared parental pay is paid to the claimant;
(p) that, where the claimant is an employee within the meaning of the Employment Rights Act 1996, the claimant's absence from work during each such week is absence on shared parental leave.

(5) Regulations may provide for—
(a) the determination of the extent of a person's entitlement to statutory shared parental pay in respect of a child;
(b) when statutory shared parental pay is to be payable.

(6) Provision under subsection (5)(a) is to secure that the number of weeks in respect of which a person is entitled to payments of statutory shared parental pay in respect of a child does not exceed the number of weeks of the maternity pay period reduced by—
(a) where the mother of the child takes action that is treated by regulations as constituting for the purposes of this section her return to work without satisfying conditions prescribed under subsection (2)(h) or, as the case may be, subsection (4)(i)—
   (i) the number of relevant weeks in respect of which maternity allowance or statutory maternity pay is payable to the mother, or
   (ii) if that number of relevant weeks is less than a number prescribed by regulations, that prescribed number of weeks, or
(b) except where paragraph (a) applies, the number of weeks to which the maternity allowance period is reduced by virtue of section 35(3A) or, as the case may be, the maternity pay period is reduced by virtue of section 165(3A).

(7) In subsection (6)(a) "relevant week" means—
(a) where maternity allowance is payable to a mother, a week or part of a week falling before the time at which the mother takes action that is treated by regulations as constituting for the purposes of this section her return to work;
(b) where statutory maternity pay is payable to a mother, a week falling before the week in which the mother takes action that is so treated.

Social Security Contributions and Benefits Act 1992

For these purposes "week" has the meaning given by section 122(1), in relation to maternity allowance, or the meaning given by section 165(8), in relation to statutory maternity pay.

(8) In determining the number of weeks for the purposes of subsection (6)(b)—
  (a) "week" has the same meaning as in subsection (7), and
  (b) a part of a week is to be treated as a week.

(9) Provision under subsection (5)(a) is to secure that, where two persons are entitled to payments of statutory shared parental pay in respect of a child, the extent of one's entitlement and the extent of the other's entitlement do not, taken together, exceed what would be available to one person (see subsection (6)).

(10) Provision under subsection (5)(b) is to secure that no payment of statutory shared parental pay may be made to a person in respect of a child after the end of such period as may be prescribed.

(11) Provision under subsection (5)(b) is to secure that no payment of statutory shared parental pay in respect of a child may be made to a person who is the mother of the child before the end of the mother's maternity pay period.

(12) Regulations may provide that, where the conditions in subsection (13) are satisfied in relation to a person who is entitled to statutory shared parental pay under subsection (1) or (3) ("V"), V may vary the period or periods during which V intends to claim statutory shared parental pay in respect of the child in question, subject to complying with provision under subsection (14) where that is relevant.

(13) The conditions are—
  (a) that V has given the person who will be liable to pay statutory shared parental pay to V notice of an intention to vary the period or periods during which V intends to claim statutory shared parental pay;
  (b) that a notice under paragraph (a)—
    (i) is given by such time as may be prescribed, and
    (ii) satisfies prescribed conditions as to form and content.

(14) Regulations may provide that, where the conditions in subsection (15) are satisfied in relation to a person who is entitled to statutory shared parental pay under subsection (1) or (3) ("V"), V may vary the number of weeks in respect of which V intends to claim statutory shared parental pay.

(15) The conditions are—
  (a) that V has given the person who will be liable to pay statutory shared parental pay to V notice of—
    (i) the extent to which V has exercised an entitlement to statutory shared parental pay in respect of the child,
    (ii) the extent to which V intends to claim statutory shared parental pay in respect of the child,
    (iii) the extent to which another person has exercised an entitlement to statutory shared parental pay in respect of the child, and
    (iv) the extent to which another person intends to claim statutory shared parental pay in respect of the child;
  (b) that a notice under paragraph (a)—
    (i) is given by such time as may be prescribed, and
    (ii) satisfies prescribed conditions as to form and content;
  (c) that the person who is P or, as the case may be, M in relation to V consents to that variation.

(1992 c.4 s.171ZU)

(16) A person's entitlement to statutory shared parental pay under this section is not affected by the birth of more than one child as a result of the same pregnancy.]

AMENDMENT

1. Children and Families Act 2014 s.119 (June 30, 2014).

[¹ Entitlement: adoption

171ZV.—(1) Regulations may provide that, where all the conditions in subsection (2) are satisfied in relation to a person with whom a child is, or is expected to be, placed for adoption under the law of any part of the United Kingdom ("claimant A"), claimant A is to be entitled in accordance with the following provisions of this Part to payments to be known as "statutory shared parental pay".

(2) The conditions are—
- (a) that claimant A and another person ("X") satisfy prescribed conditions as to caring or intending to care for the child;
- (b) that X satisfies prescribed conditions—
  - (i) as to employment or self-employment,
  - (ii) as to having earnings of a prescribed amount for a prescribed period, and
  - (iii) as to relationship either with the child or with claimant A;
- (c) that claimant A has been in employed earner's employment with an employer for a continuous period of at least the prescribed length ending with a prescribed week;
- (d) that at the end of that prescribed week claimant A was entitled to be in that employment;
- (e) that claimant A's normal weekly earnings for a prescribed period ending with a prescribed week are not less than the lower earnings limit in force under section 5(1)(a) at the end of that week;
- (f) if regulations so provide, that claimant A continues in employed earner's employment (whether or not with the employer by reference to whom the condition in paragraph (c) is satisfied) until a prescribed time;
- (g) that claimant A became entitled to statutory adoption pay by reference to the placement for adoption of the child;
- (h) that claimant A satisfies prescribed conditions as to the reduction of the duration of the adoption pay period;
- (i) that claimant A has given the person who will be liable to pay statutory shared parental pay to claimant A notice of—
  - (i) the number of weeks in respect of which claimant A would be entitled to claim statutory shared parental pay in respect of the child if the entitlement were fully exercised (disregarding for these purposes any intention of X to claim statutory shared parental pay in respect of the child),
  - (ii) the number of weeks in respect of which claimant A intends to claim statutory shared parental pay, and
  - (iii) the number of weeks in respect of which X intends to claim statutory shared parental pay;
- (j) that claimant A has given the person who will be liable to pay statutory shared parental pay to claimant A notice of the period or periods

1.157

Social Security Contributions and Benefits Act 1992

during which claimant A intends to claim statutory shared parental pay in respect of the child;
(k) that a notice under paragraph (i) or (j)—
   (i) is given by such time as may be prescribed, and
   (ii) satisfies prescribed conditions as to form and content;
(l) that X consents to the extent of claimant A's intended claim for statutory shared parental pay;
(m) that it is claimant A's intention to care for the child during each week in respect of which statutory shared parental pay is paid to claimant A;
(n) that claimant A is absent from work during each week in respect of which statutory shared parental pay is paid to claimant A;
(o) that, where claimant A is an employee within the meaning of the Employment Rights Act 1996, claimant A's absence from work during each such week is absence on shared parental leave.

(3) Regulations may provide that, where all the conditions in subsection (4) are satisfied in relation to a person ("claimant B"), claimant B is to be entitled in accordance with the following provisions of this Part to payments to be known as "statutory shared parental pay".

(4) The conditions are—
(a) that claimant B and another person ("Y") who is a person with whom a child is, or is expected to be, placed for adoption under the law of any part of the United Kingdom satisfy prescribed conditions as to caring or intending to care for the child;
(b) that claimant B satisfies—
   (i) prescribed conditions as to relationship with the child, or
   (ii) prescribed conditions as to relationship with Y;
(c) that Y satisfies prescribed conditions—
   (i) as to employment or self-employment, and
   (ii) as to having earnings of a prescribed amount for a prescribed period;
(d) that claimant B has been in employed earner's employment with an employer for a continuous period of at least the prescribed length ending with a prescribed week;
(e) that at the end of that prescribed week claimant B was entitled to be in that employment;
(f) that claimant B's normal weekly earnings for a prescribed period ending with a prescribed week are not less than the lower earnings limit in force under section 5(1)(a) at the end of that week;
(g) if regulations so provide, that claimant B continues in employed earner's employment (whether or not with the employer by reference to whom the condition in paragraph (d) is satisfied) until a prescribed time;
(h) that Y became entitled to statutory adoption pay by reference to the placement for adoption of the child;
(i) that Y satisfies prescribed conditions as to the reduction of the duration of the adoption pay period;
(j) that claimant B has given the person who will be liable to pay statutory shared parental pay to claimant B notice of—
   (i) the number of weeks in respect of which claimant B would be entitled to claim statutory shared parental pay in respect of the

child if the entitlement were fully exercised (disregarding for these purposes any intention of Y to claim statutory shared parental pay in respect of the child),
  (ii) the number of weeks in respect of which claimant B intends to claim statutory shared parental pay, and
  (iii) the number of weeks in respect of which Y intends to claim statutory shared parental pay;
(k) that claimant B has given the person who will be liable to pay statutory shared parental pay to claimant B notice of the period or periods during which claimant B intends to claim statutory shared parental pay in respect of the child;
(l) that a notice under paragraph (j) or (k)—
  (i) is given by such time as may be prescribed, and
  (ii) satisfies prescribed conditions as to form and content;
(m) that Y consents to the extent of claimant B's intended claim for statutory shared parental pay;
(n) that it is claimant B's intention to care for the child during each week in respect of which statutory shared parental pay is paid to claimant B;
(o) that claimant B is absent from work during each week in respect of which statutory shared parental pay is paid to claimant B;
(p) that, where claimant B is an employee within the meaning of the Employment Rights Act 1996, claimant B's absence from work during each such week is absence on shared parental leave.

(5) Regulations may provide for—
(a) the determination of the extent of a person's entitlement to statutory shared parental pay in respect of a child;
(b) when statutory shared parental pay is to be payable.

(6) Provision under subsection (5)(a) is to secure that the number of weeks in respect of which a person is entitled to payments of statutory shared parental pay in respect of a child does not exceed the number of weeks of the adoption pay period reduced by—
(a) where the person who became entitled to receive statutory adoption pay takes action that is treated by regulations as constituting for the purposes of this section the person's return to work without satisfying conditions prescribed under subsection (2)(h) or, as the case may be, subsection (4)(i)—
  (i) the number of relevant weeks in respect of which statutory adoption pay is payable to the person, or
  (ii) if that number of relevant weeks is less than a number prescribed by regulations, that prescribed number of weeks, or
(b) except where paragraph (a) applies, the number of weeks to which the adoption pay period has been reduced by virtue of section 171ZN(2A).

(7) In subsection (6)(a) "relevant week" means a week falling before the week in which a person takes action that is treated by regulations as constituting for the purposes of this section the person's return to work, and for these purposes "week" has the meaning given by section 171ZN(8).

(8) In determining the number of weeks for the purposes of subsection (6)(b)—
(a) "week" has the same meaning as in subsection (7), and

(b) a part of a week is to be treated as a week.

(9) Provision under subsection (5)(a) is to secure that, where two persons are entitled to payments of statutory shared parental pay in respect of a child, the extent of one's entitlement and the extent of the other's entitlement do not, taken together, exceed what would be available to one person (see subsection (6)).

(10) Provision under subsection (5)(b) is to secure that no payment of statutory shared parental pay may be made to a person in respect of a child after the end of such period as may be prescribed.

(11) Provision under subsection (5)(b) is to secure that no payment of statutory shared parental pay in respect of a child may be made to a person who became entitled to receive statutory adoption pay in respect of the child before the end of the person's adoption pay period.

(12) Regulations may provide that, where the conditions in subsection (13) are satisfied in relation to a person who is entitled to statutory shared parental pay under subsection (1) or (3) ("V"), V may vary the period or periods during which V intends to claim statutory shared parental pay in respect of the child in question, subject to complying with provision under subsection (14) where that is relevant.

(13) The conditions are—
(a) that V has given the person who will be liable to pay statutory shared parental pay to V notice of an intention to vary the period or periods during which V intends to claim statutory shared parental pay;
(b) that a notice under paragraph (a)—
  (i) is given by such time as may be prescribed, and
  (ii) satisfies prescribed conditions as to form and content.

(14) Regulations may provide that, where the conditions in subsection (15) are satisfied in relation to a person who is entitled to statutory shared parental pay under subsection (1) or (3) ("V"), V may vary the number of weeks in respect of which V intends to claim statutory shared parental pay.

(15) The conditions are—
(a) that V has given the person who will be liable to pay statutory shared parental pay to V notice of—
  (i) the extent to which V has exercised an entitlement to statutory shared parental pay in respect of the child,
  (ii) the extent to which V intends to claim statutory shared parental pay in respect of the child,
  (iii) the extent to which another person has exercised an entitlement to statutory shared parental pay in respect of the child, and
  (iv) the extent to which another person intends to claim statutory shared parental pay in respect of the child;
(b) that a notice under paragraph (a)—
  (i) is given by such time as may be prescribed, and
  (ii) satisfies prescribed conditions as to form and content;
(c) that the person who is X or, as the case may be, Y in relation to V consents to that variation.

(16) A person's entitlement to statutory shared parental pay under this section is not affected by the placement for adoption of more than one child as part of the same arrangement.

(17) Regulations are to provide for entitlement to statutory shared parental pay in respect of a child placed, or expected to be placed, under section 22C of the Children Act 1989 by a local authority in England with a local

authority foster parent who has been approved as a prospective adopter.

(18) This section has effect in relation to regulations made by virtue of subsection (17) as if—
- (a) references to a child being placed for adoption under the law of any part of the United Kingdom were references to being placed under section 22C of the Children Act 1989 with a local authority foster parent who has been approved as a prospective adopter;
- (b) references to placement for adoption were references to placement under section 22C with such a person.]

AMENDMENT

1. Children and Families Act 2014 s.119 (June 30, 2014).

[¹ **Entitlement: general**

171ZW.—(1) Regulations may—
- (a) provide that the following do not have effect, or have effect subject to prescribed modifications, in such cases as may be prescribed—
   - (i) section 171ZU(2)(a) to (o),
   - (ii) section 171ZU(4)(a) to (p),
   - (iii) section 171ZU(13)(a) and (b),
   - (iv) section 171ZU(15)(a) to (c),
   - (v) section 171ZV(2)(a) to (o),
   - (vi) section 171ZV(4)(a) to (p),
   - (vii) section 171ZV(13)(a) and (b), and
   - (viii) section 171ZV(15)(a) to (c);
- (b) impose requirements about evidence of entitlement and procedures to be followed;
- (c) specify in what circumstances employment is to be treated as continuous for the purposes of section 171ZU or 171ZV;
- (d) provide that a person is to be treated for the purposes of section 171ZU or 171ZV as being employed for a continuous period of at least the prescribed period where—
   - (i) the person has been employed by the same employer for at least the prescribed period under two or more separate contracts of service, and
   - (ii) those contracts were not continuous;
- (e) provide for amounts earned by a person under separate contracts of service with the same employer to be aggregated for the purposes of section 171ZU or 171ZV;
- (f) provide that—
   - (i) the amount of a person's earnings for any period, or
   - (ii) the amount of the person's earnings to be treated as comprised in any payment made to the person or for the person's benefit,

are to be calculated or estimated for the purposes of section 171ZU or 171ZV in such manner and on such basis as may be prescribed and that for that purpose payments of a particular class or description made or falling to be made to or by a person are, to such extent as may be prescribed, to be disregarded or, as the case may be, to be deducted from the amount of the person's earnings.

(2) The persons upon whom requirements may be imposed by virtue of subsection (1)(b) include—

1.158

Social Security Contributions and Benefits Act 1992

(a) a person who, in connection with another person's claim to be paid statutory shared parental pay, is required to satisfy conditions prescribed under section 171ZU(2)(b) or (4)(c) or 171ZV(2)(b) or (4)(c);
(b) an employer or former employer of such a person.
(3) In subsection (1)(d) "the prescribed period" means the period of the length prescribed by regulations under section 171ZU(2)(c) or (4)(d) or 171ZV(2)(c) or (4)(d), as the case may be.]

AMENDMENT

1. Children and Families Act 2014 s.119 (June 30, 2014).

[¹ Liability to make payments

1.159 **171ZX.**—(1) The liability to make payments of statutory shared parental pay under section 171ZU or 171ZV is a liability of any person of whom the person entitled to the payments has been an employee as mentioned in section 171ZU(2)(c) or (4)(d) or 171ZV(2)(c) or (4)(d), as the case may be.
(2) Regulations must make provision as to a former employer's liability to pay statutory shared parental pay to a person in any case where the former employee's contract of service with the person has been brought to an end by the former employer solely, or mainly, for the purpose of avoiding liability for statutory shared parental pay.
(3) The Secretary of State may, with the concurrence of the Commissioners for Her Majesty's Revenue and Customs, by regulations specify circumstances in which, notwithstanding this section, liability to make payments of statutory shared parental pay is to be a liability of the Commissioners.]

AMENDMENT

1. Children and Families Act 2014 s.119 (June 30, 2014).

[¹ Rate and period of pay

1.160 **171ZY.**—(1) Statutory shared parental pay is payable at such fixed or earnings-related weekly rate as may be prescribed by regulations, which may prescribe different kinds of rate for different cases.
(2) Subject to the following provisions of this section, statutory shared parental pay is payable to a person in respect of each week falling within a relevant period, up to the number of weeks determined in the case of that person in accordance with regulations under section 171ZU(5) or 171ZV(5).
(3) Except in such cases as may be prescribed, statutory shared parental pay is not payable to a person in respect of a week falling within a relevant period if it is not the person's intention at the beginning of the week to care for the child by reference to whom the person satisfies—
(a) the condition in section 171ZU(2)(a) or (4)(a), or
(b) the condition in section 171ZV(2)(a) or (4)(a).
(4) Except in such cases as may be prescribed, statutory shared parental pay is not payable to a person in respect of a week falling within a relevant period during any part of which week the person works for any employer.
(5) The Secretary of State may by regulations specify circumstances

in which there is to be no liability to pay statutory shared parental pay in respect of a week falling within a relevant period.

(6) Where for any purpose of this Part or of regulations it is necessary to calculate the daily rate of statutory shared parental pay, the amount payable by way of statutory shared parental pay for any day shall be taken as one seventh of the weekly rate.

(7) For the purposes of this section a week falls within a relevant period if it falls within a period specified in a notice under—

(a) section 171ZU(2)(j), (4)(k) or (13)(a), or
(b) section 171ZV(2)(j), (4)(k) or (13)(a),

and is not afterwards excluded from such a period by a variation of the period or periods during which the person in question intends to claim statutory shared parental pay.

(8) In this section "week", in relation to a relevant period, means a period of seven days beginning with the day of the week on which the relevant period starts.]

AMENDMENT

1. Children and Families Act 2014 s.119 (June 30, 2014).

[¹ Restrictions on contracting out

171ZZ.—(1) An agreement is void to the extent that it purports—

(a) to exclude, limit or otherwise modify any provision of this Part, or
(b) to require a person to contribute (whether directly or indirectly) towards any costs incurred by that person's employer or former employer under this Part.

(2) For the avoidance of doubt, an agreement between an employer and an employee, authorising deductions from statutory shared parental pay which the employer is liable to pay to the employee in respect of any period, is not void by virtue of subsection (1)(a) if the employer—

(a) is authorised by that or another agreement to make the same deductions from any contractual remuneration which the employer is liable to pay in respect of the same period, or
(b) would be so authorised if the employer were liable to pay contractual remuneration in respect of that period.]

1.161

AMENDMENT

1. Children and Families Act 2014 s.119 (June 30, 2014).

[¹ Relationship with contractual remuneration

171ZZ1.—(1) Subject to subsections (2) and (3), any entitlement to statutory shared parental pay is not to affect any right of a person in relation to remuneration under any contract of service ("contractual remuneration").

(2) Subject to subsection (3)—

(a) any contractual remuneration paid to a person by an employer of that person in respect of any period is to go towards discharging any liability of that employer to pay statutory shared parental pay to that person in respect of that period; and
(b) any statutory shared parental pay paid by an employer to a person who is an employee of that employer in respect of any period is to go

1.162

towards discharging any liability of that employer to pay contractual remuneration to that person in respect of that period.

(3) Regulations may make provision as to payments which are, and those which are not, to be treated as contractual remuneration for the purposes of subsections (1) and (2).]

AMENDMENT

1. Children and Families Act 2014 s.119 (June 30, 2014).

[¹ Crown employment

1.163   171ZZ2.—The provisions of this Part apply in relation to persons employed by or under the Crown as they apply in relation to persons employed otherwise than by or under the Crown.]

AMENDMENT

1. Children and Families Act 2014 s.119 (June 30, 2014).

[¹ Special classes of person

1.164   171ZZ3.—(1) The Secretary of State may with the concurrence of the Treasury make regulations modifying any provision of this Part in such manner as the Secretary of State thinks proper in its application to any person who is, has been or is to be—
(a) employed on board any ship, vessel, hovercraft or aircraft;
(b) outside Great Britain at any prescribed time or in any prescribed circumstances; or
(c) in prescribed employment in connection with continental shelf operations, as defined in section 120(2).

(2) Regulations under subsection (1) may, in particular, provide—
(a) for any provision of this Part to apply to any such person, notwithstanding that it would not otherwise apply;
(b) for any such provision not to apply to any such person, notwithstanding that it would otherwise apply;
(c) for excepting any such person from the application of any such provision where the person neither is domiciled nor has a place of residence in any part of Great Britain;
(d) for the taking of evidence, for the purposes of the determination of any question arising under any such provision, in a country or territory outside Great Britain, by a British consular official or such other person as may be determined in accordance with the regulations.]

AMENDMENT

1. Children and Families Act 2014 s.119 (June 30, 2014).

[¹ Part 12ZC: supplementary

1.165   171ZZ4.—(1) In this Part—
"adoption pay period" has the meaning given in section 171ZN(2);
"employer", in relation to a person who is an employee, means a person who—
(a) under section 6 is liable to pay secondary Class 1 contributions in relation to any of the earnings of the person who is an employee, or

(b) would be liable to pay such contributions but for—
  (i) the condition in section 6(1)(b), or
  (ii) the employee being under the age of 16;
"local authority" has the same meaning as in the Children Act 1989 (see section 105(1) of that Act);
"local authority foster parent" has the same meaning as in the Children Act 1989 (see section 22C(12) of that Act);
"maternity allowance period" has the meaning given in section 35(2);
"maternity pay period" has the meaning given in section 165(1);
"modifications" includes additions, omissions and amendments, and related expressions are to be read accordingly;
"prescribed" means prescribed by regulations.

(2) In this Part "employee" means a person who is gainfully employed in Great Britain either under a contract of service or in an office (including elective office) with general earnings (as defined by section 7 of the Income Tax (Earnings and Pensions) Act 2003).

(3) Regulations may provide—
(a) for cases where a person who falls within the definition in subsection (2) is not to be treated as an employee for the purposes of this Part, and
(b) for cases where a person who would not otherwise be an employee for the purposes of this Part is to be treated as an employee for those purposes.

(4) Without prejudice to any other power to make regulations under this Part, regulations may specify cases in which, for the purposes of this Part or of such provisions of this Part as may be prescribed—
(a) two or more employers are to be treated as one;
(b) two or more contracts of service in respect of which the same person is an employee are to be treated as one.

(5) In this Part, except where otherwise provided, "week" means a period of seven days beginning with Sunday or such other period as may be prescribed in relation to any particular case or class of cases.

(6) For the purposes of this Part, a person's normal weekly earnings are, subject to subsection (8), to be taken to be the average weekly earnings which in the relevant period have been paid to the person or paid for the person's benefit under the contract of service with the employer in question.

(7) For the purposes of subsection (6) "earnings" and "relevant period" have the meanings given to them by regulations.

(8) In such cases as may be prescribed, a person's normal weekly earnings are to be calculated in accordance with regulations.

(9) Where—
(a) in consequence of the establishment of one or more National Health Service trusts under the National Health Service Act 2006, the National Health Service (Wales) Act 2006 or the National Health Service (Scotland) Act 1978, a person's contract of employment is treated by a scheme under any of those Acts as divided so as to constitute two or more contracts, or
(b) an order under paragraph 26(1) of Schedule 3 to the National Health Service Act 2006 provides that a person's contract of employment is so divided,
regulations may make provision enabling the person to elect for all of

those contracts to be treated as one contract for the purposes of this Part or such provisions of this Part as may be prescribed.

(10) Regulations under subsection (9) may prescribe—
(a) the conditions that must be satisfied if a person is to be entitled to make such an election;
(b) the manner in which, and the time within which, such an election is to be made;
(c) the persons to whom, and the manner in which, notice of such an election is to be given;
(d) the information which a person who makes such an election is to provide, and the persons to whom, and the time within which, the person is to provide it;
(e) the time for which such an election is to have effect;
(f) which one of the person's employers under two or more contracts is to be regarded for the purposes of statutory shared parental pay as the person's employer under the contract.

(11) The powers under subsections (9) and (10) are without prejudice to any other power to make regulations under this Part.

(12) Regulations under any of subsections (4) to (10) must be made with the concurrence of the Commissioners for Her Majesty's Revenue and Customs.]

AMENDMENT

1. Children and Families Act 2014 s.119 (June 30, 2014).

[¹ Power to apply Part 12ZC

171ZZ5.—(1) The Secretary of State may by regulations provide for this Part to have effect in relation to cases which involve adoption, but not the placement of a child for adoption under the law of any part of the United Kingdom, with such modifications as the regulations may prescribe.

(2) The Secretary of State may by regulations provide for this Part to have effect in relation to cases which involve a person who has applied, or intends to apply, with another person for a parental order under section 54 of the Human Fertilisation and Embryology Act 2008 and a child who is, or will be, the subject of the order, with such modifications as the regulations may prescribe.

(3) Where section 171ZW(1)(b) has effect in relation to such cases as are described in subsection (2), regulations under section 171ZW(1)(b) may impose requirements to make statutory declarations as to—
(a) eligibility to apply for a parental order;
(b) intention to apply for such an order."

(2) In section 176 of the Social Security Contributions and Benefits Act 1992 (Parliamentary control of subordinate legislation), in subsection (1) (affirmative procedure), in paragraph (a), at the appropriate place there is inserted— "any of sections 171ZU to 171ZY;".]

AMENDMENT

1. Children and Families Act 2014 s.119 (June 30, 2014).

(1992 c.4 s.172)

PART XIII

GENERAL

Interpretation

Application of Act in relation to territorial waters

172.— In this Act—
(a) any reference to Great Britain includes a reference to the territorial waters of the United Kingdom adjacent to Great Britain;
(b) any reference to the United Kingdom includes a reference to the territorial waters of the United Kingdom.

1.167

Age

173.— For the purposes of this Act a person—
(a) is over or under a particular age if he has or, as the case may be, has not attained that age; and
(b) is between two particular ages if he has attained the first but not the second;
and in Scotland (as in England and Wales) the time at which a person attains a particular age expressed in years is the commencement of the relevant anniversary of the date of his birth.

1.168

References to Acts

174. In this Act—
"the 1975 Act" means the Social Security Act 1975;
"the 1986 Act" means the Social Security Act 1986;
"the Administration Act" means the Social Security Administration Act 1992;
"the Consequential Provisions Act" means the Social Security (Consequential Provisions) Act 1992;
"the Northern Ireland Contributions and Benefits Act" means the Social Security Contributions and Benefits (Northern Ireland) Act 1992;
"the Old Cases Act" means the Industrial Injuries and Diseases (Old Cases) Act 1975; and
"the Pensions Act" means the [¹ Pensions Schemes Act 1993].

1.169

AMENDMENT

1. Pension Schemes Act 1993 s.190 and Sch.8 para.41 (February 7, 1994).

SCHEDULE 9

EXCLUSIONS FROM ENTITLEMENT TO CHILD BENEFIT

Children [³ and qualifying young persons] in detention, care, etc.

1.—Except where regulations otherwise provide, no person shall be entitled to child benefit in respect of a child [³ or qualifying young person] for any week if in that week the child [³ or qualifying young person]—

1.170

(a) is undergoing imprisonment or detention in legal custody;
(b) is subject to a supervision requirement made under section 44 of the Social Work (Scotland) Act 1968 and is residing in a residential establishment within the meaning of that section; or
(c) is in the care of a local authority in such circumstances as may be prescribed.
[³ . . .]

Married children [³ and qualifying young persons]

1.171 3.—Except where regulations otherwise provide, no person shall be entitled to child benefit in respect of a child [³ or qualifying young person] who is married.

Persons exempt from tax

1.172 4.—[² . . .].

Children entitled to severe disablement allowance

1.173 5.—[¹ . . .].

DEFINITIONS

"child"—s.142.
"week"—s.147.

AMENDMENTS

1. Welfare Reform and Pensions Act 1999 Sch.13 part IV (April 6, 2001)
2. Tax Credits Act 2002 s.57 Sch.6 (April 7, 2003).
3. Child Benefit Act 2005 s.1 and Sch.1 para.17 (April 10, 2006).

SCHEDULE 10

PRIORITY BETWEEN PERSONS ENTITLED TO CHILD BENEFIT

Person with prior award

1.174 1.—(1) Subject to sub-paragraph (2) below, as between a person claiming child benefit in respect of a child [¹ or qualifying young person] for any week and a person to whom child benefit in respect of that child [¹ or qualifying young person] for that week has already been awarded when the claim is made, the latter shall be entitled.
(2) Sub-paragraph (1) above shall not confer any priority where the week to which the claim relates is later than the third week following that in which the claim is made.

Person having child [¹ and qualifying young person] living with him

1.175 2.—Subject to paragraph 1 above, as between a person entitled for any week by virtue of paragraph (a) of subsection (1) of section 143 above and a person entitled by virtue of paragraph (b) of that subsection the former shall be entitled.

Husband and wife

1.176 3.—Subject to paragraphs 1 and 2 above, as between a husband and wife residing together the wife shall be entitled.

Parents

1.177 4.—(1) Subject to paragraphs 1 to 3 above, as between a person who is and one who is not a parent of the child [¹ or qualifying young person] the parent shall be entitled.
(2) Subject as aforesaid, as between two persons residing together who are parents of the child [¹ or qualifying young person] but not husband and wife, the mother shall be entitled.

(1992 c.4 Sch.10)

Other cases

5.—As between persons not falling within paragraphs 1 to 4 above, such one of them shall be entitled as they may jointly elect or, in default of election, as the Secretary of State may in his discretion determine.

1.178

Supplementary

6.—(1) Any election under this Schedule shall be made in the prescribed manner.

1.179

(2) Regulations may provide for exceptions from the modifications of the provisions of paragraphs 1 to 5 above in relation to such cases as may be prescribed.

AMENDMENT

1. Child Benefit Act 2005 s.1 and Sch.7 para.18 (April 10, 2006).

DEFINITIONS

"child"—s.142.
"parent, father or mother"—s.147(3).
"week"—s.147.

GENERAL NOTE

Under s.143 it is possible for more than one person to be entitled to claim Child Benefit. For example, the child may live with one parent while being maintained to the requisite extent by the other; or the child may live with a parent in the home of a grandparent. In such cases only one award of Child Benefit can be made and Sch.10 determines the order of priority between multiple claimants. Note that s.144 and Sch.10 apply only where more than one person is entitled to benefit for the same child in respect of that week. Where the child has ceased to live with one parent as provided for in s.143, and a claim is not precluded by the effect of s.13(2) of SSAA 1992 (which prevents a claim being made where payment of benefit has been made already to another claimant, and the decision to make such payment has not been revised, nor has the payment been repaid voluntarily) then Sch.10 does not apply. In that case the DM should decide the case on the basis of s.143 alone. For an explanation of these provisions and their interaction see *CF/2826/2008*.

1.180

In the first place no payment will be made unless there has been a claim, so that if only one claim is made, even by a person of lower priority, that claim will be met. Where, however, there are multiple claims priority will be given in the following order:

(1) The person with whom the child is living.

(2) The wife, as between a husband and wife who are residing together.

(3) A parent, as between a person who is a parent and one who is not.

(4) The mother, as between parents who are residing together but are not married.

(5) The person agreed by them, as between any other persons.

(6) The person determined by a decision maker of HMRC, where such other persons cannot agree.

Where there is an existing award of Child Benefit in payment at the time a rival claim is made, the existing award will continue to be paid for a period of three weeks (provided the claimant continues to satisfy the other conditions of entitlement), even though the new claimant may be entitled thereafter by priority. The reservation of entitlement to the current claimant for a period of three weeks was applied in *CF/3348/2002*.

The meaning of "residing together" for the purposes of Child Benefit is dealt with largely by reg.34 of the Child Benefit (General) Regulations, and is not the same as in other benefit contexts. Spouses and parents who are not married to each other are treated as residing together if their separation is not likely to be permanent and, in the case of spouses only, if it is for the purposes of medical treatment. In *R(F) 4/85* it was held that a couple who married while the husband was in prison, and who had never lived together, had to be treated under this regulation as if they were residing together because their separation was not likely to be permanent—they could be expected to commence cohabitation when the husband was released from prison. (The effect in this case was to deprive the claimant of the increase for one parent benefit.) It has also been accepted in this context that parties may not be residing together if they maintain separate households under the same roof (*R(F) 3/81*).

1.181 Where the parents of a child are residing together (whether married or not) and the mother of the child obtains a certificate of gender recognition as a man he will continue to be regarded as the mother of their child for this purpose because s.12 of the Gender Recognition Act 2004, provides that the acquired status does not affect the status of a person as the mother or father of a child.

A "parent" for the purposes of Child Benefit is given an extended meaning by s.147(3) to include a step parent. The meaning of parent is also extended by the effect of the Children Act 1989, to include any person in whose favour a residence order has been made. This is because the parental responsibility conferred by the order made under that Act is defined to include all the rights which, by law, a parent has in relation to that child. For the purposes of the Contributions & Benefits Act, the word parent is to be construed as the "legal parent" of the child. (See *Secretary of State v Smith* [1983] 1 W.L.R. 1110, where the effect of an order made under equivalent legislation then in force, was to include an adoptive parent of the child and at the same time to exclude the natural parent.) The same reasoning was applied by Commissioner Howell in *R(F) 1/08* where a lesbian couple had two children with the assistance of artificial insemmination and after they had separated a residence order had been made in favour of both of them. The Commissioner held that both must be regarded as parents, not just the biological mother and, consequently it became necessary for HMRC to exercise the discretion provided for in [5].

The particular problem that arises when the parents of a child have separated and the care of the child is then shared between them (e.g. in holidays and at weekends) is referred to by Judge Wikeley in *CIS/2457/2008*. The issue arose only indirectly in that case, which was a determination of the claimant's entitlement to Income Support, but that entitlement depended, in turn, on her right to receive Child Benefit, and the judge added an appendix to his decision that covers earlier cases (*Chester v Secretary of State for Social Security* [2001] EWHC Admin 1119; (*Barber v Secretary of State for Social Security* [2002] EWHC 1915 (Admin) and *R. (on the relation of Ford) v Board of Inland Revenue* [2005] EWHC 1109 (Admin)) where decisions awarding all of the Child Benefit to one parent had been quashed on review.

1.182 A decision by HMRC in default of agreement is not appealable but an application for revision or review may be made. In *Chester v Secretary of State for Social Security* [2001] EWHC Admin 1119, (approved in *Barber* [2002] EWHC 1915) it was held that such a default decision engaged the right to private and family life in art.8 ECHR though in that case there was no need for the claimant to rely upon it. Note too, that it is now possible for an application for judicial review to be transferred to the Upper Tribunal.

The procedure for making an election as to priority, and for waiving priority, is provided for in regs 14 and 15 of the Child Benefit (General) Regulations 2006.

Section 153(3)   SCHEDULE 11

CIRCUMSTANCES IN WHICH PERIODS OF ENTITLEMENT TO
STATUTORY SICK PAY DO NOT ARISE

1.183 1. A period of entitlement does not arise in relation to a particular period of incapacity for work in any of the circumstances set out in para.2 below or in such other circumstances as may be prescribed.

(1992 c.4 Sch.11)

[⁴**1A.** — Regulations made under paragraph 1 must be made with the concurrence of the Treasury.] 1.184

2.—The circumstances are that— 1.185
  (a) [⁶. . .]
  (b) [⁵. . .];
  (c) at the relevant date the employee's normal weekly earnings are less than the lower earnings limit then in force under section 5(1)(a) above;
[¹(d) in the period of 57 days ending immediately before the relevant date the employee had at least one day on which—
    (i) he was entitled to incapacity benefit (or would have been so entitled had he satisfied the contribution conditions mentioned in section 30A(2)(a) above); or
    (ii) [³. . .]
    (iii) he was entitled to a severe disablement allowance;]
[⁸ (dd) in the period of 85 days ending immediately before the relevant date the employee had at least one day on which he was entitled to an employment and support allowance (or would have been so entitled had he satisfied the requirements in section 1(2) of the Welfare Reform Act 2007.]
  (e) [¹. . .]
  (f) the employee has done no work for his employer under his contract of service;
  (g) on the relevant date there is [². . .] a stoppage of work due to a trade dispute at the employee's place of employment;
  (h) the employee is, or has been, pregnant and the relevant date falls within the disqualifying period (within the meaning of section 153(12) above).

3.—In this Schedule, "relevant date" means the date on which a period of entitlement would begin in accordance with section 153 above if this Schedule did not prevent it arising. 1.186

4.— [⁵. . .] 1.187
5.— [¹. . .] 1.188

[⁷**5A.** —(1) Paragraph 2(d)(i) above does not apply if, at the relevant date, the employee is over pensionable age and is not entitled to incapacity benefit. 1.189

(2) Paragraph 2(d)(i) above ceases to apply if, at any time after the relevant date, the employee is over pensionable age and is not entitled to incapacity benefit.

(3) In this paragraph "pensionable age" has the meaning given by the rules in paragraph 1 of Schedule 4 to the Pensions Act 1995.]

6.—For the purposes of paragraph 2(f) above, if an employee enters into a contract of service which is to take effect not more than eight weeks after the date on which a previous contract of service entered into by him with the same employer ceased to have effect, the two contracts shall be treated as one. 1.190

7.—Paragraph 2(g) above does not apply in the case of an employee who proves that at no time on or before the relevant date did he have a direct interest in the trade dispute in question. 1.191

8.—Paragraph 2(h) above does not apply in relation to an employee who has been pregnant if her pregnancy terminated, before the beginning of the disqualifying period, otherwise than by confinement (as defined for the purposes of statutory maternity pay in section 171(1) above). 1.192

AMENDMENTS

1. Social Security (Incapacity for Work) Act 1994 s.11(1) and Sch.1 para.43 (April 6, 1995).

2. Jobseekers Act 1995 s.41(5) and Sch.3 (October 7, 1996).

3. Social Security Act 1998 s.73 (April 6, 1999).

4. Social Security Contributions (Transfer of Functions, etc.) Act 1999 s.1(1) and Sch.1 para.20 (April 1, 1999).

5. Fixed-term Employees (Prevention of Less Favourable Treatment) Regulations 2002 (SI 2002/2034) reg.11 and Sch.2 para.1 (October 1, 2002).

6. Employment Equality (Age) Regulations 2006 (SI 2006/1031) reg.49(1) and Sch.8 Pt 1 para.13(1) (October 1, 2006).

7. Employment Equality (Age) (Consequential Amendments) Regulations 2007 (SI 2007/825) reg.2 (April 6, 2007).

8. Employment and Support Allowance (Consequential Provisions) (No.2) Regulations 2008 (SI 2008/1554) reg.44 (October 27, 2008).

DEFINITIONS

"contract of service"—see s.163(1).
"disqualifying period"—see s.153(12).
"employee"—see s.163(1) and SSP (General) Regulations 1982 reg.16.
"employer"—see s.163(1).
"period of entitlement"—see *ibid*.
"period of incapacity for work"—see s.163(1).
"prescribed"—see *ibid*.
"relevant date"—see para.(3).

GENERAL NOTE

Paragraph 1

1.193 The general rule, stated here, is that no period of entitlement to SSP can arise in any of the circumstances set out in para.2 or in such circumstances as are prescribed by regulations. The relevant regulation is reg.3 of the SSP (General) Regulations 1982 (SI 1982/894), which excludes prisoners and women entitled neither to SMP nor to maternity allowance who have reached a particular stage in their pregnancy or have been confined before reaching that stage.

Paragraph 2

1.194 This sets out the categories of persons for whom a period of entitlement does not arise for the purposes of para.1, and so who are excluded from the scope of SSP. The "relevant date" is the date on which a period of entitlement would otherwise begin were it not for the provisions of this Schedule (para.3). Thus the relevant date will usually be the first day of incapacity for work in the period of incapacity for work in question (s.153(2), but note the modifying provisions in (7), (8) and (9)). Those persons who are excluded from SSP by virtue of this paragraph may be able to claim incapacity benefit or, in the case of pregnant women, SMP or maternity allowance. The particular exclusions are:

(1) employees whose earnings are below the National Insurance lower earnings limit (sub-para.2(c)). Note that if, irrespective of contractual entitlement, the employer pays nothing during the relevant period, then the exclusion in sub-para.(2)(c) does not come into play at all: *Seaton v Commissioners for HMRC* [2011] UKUT 297 (TCC) at [29] and [31];

(2) claimants whose day of incapacity links back to a recent entitlement to incapacity benefit (sub-para.2(d)). But note also para.5A, which ensures that employees who cannot return to incapacity benefit as they are now over pensionable age, but who would have returned to IB rather than becoming entitled to SSP had they been under pensionable age, are now entitled to SSP;

(3) employees who have yet to start work under the contract of service (sub-para.2(f), but note the linking rule in para.6);

(4) employees who are subject to a stoppage of work due to a trade dispute at their place of employment (sub-para.2(g), but note the exception in para.7); and

(5) employees who are or have been pregnant and where the relevant date falls within the disqualifying period for persons entitled to SMP or maternity allowance (sub-para.2(h), but note the exception in para.8).

In addition, under the original para.(2)(b), employees with a contract of service for a specified period of not more than three months were excluded from entitlement to SSP. This exclusion was repealed by the Fixed-term Employees (Prevention of Less Favourable Treatment) Regulations 2002 (SI 2002/2034) as from October 1, 2002. The effect of this amendment was considered by Lewison J in *Commissioners for HMRC v Thorn Baker Ltd* [2006] EWHC 2190 (Ch), who held that the 2002

Social Security Contributions and Benefits Act 1992

Regulations had no impact on employees working under fixed-term contracts who were agency workers. The effect of that decision is that SSP is not payable to agency workers whose contract with the agency is for a specified period of three months or less. The Court of Appeal has dismissed HMRC's appeal ([2007] EWCA Civ 626).

Paragraph 7
The effect of the wording of this exception is that if the employee has at some time before the relevant date had a direct interest in the trade dispute, he or she cannot take advantage of this provision and so is caught by the exclusion in sub-para.2(g): see *R(SSP)1/86*.

1.195

Section 160   SCHEDULE 12

Relationship of Statutory Sick Pay with Benefits
and Other Payments, etc.

The general principle

1. Any day which—
    (a) is a day of incapacity for work in relation to any contract of service; and
    (b) falls within a period of entitlement (whether or not it is also a qualifying day);
shall not be treated for the purposes of this Act as a day of incapacity for work for the purposes of determining whether a period is [^{1} . . .] [^{2} a period of incapacity for work for the purposes of incapacity benefit].

1.196

Contractual remuneration

2.—(1) Subject to sub-paragraphs (2) and (3) below, any entitlement to statutory sick pay shall not affect any right of an employee in relation to remuneration under any contract of service ("contractual remuneration").
  (2) Subject to sub-para.(3) below—
    (a) any contractual remuneration paid to an employee by an employer of his in respect of a day of incapacity for work shall go towards discharging any liability of that employer to pay statutory sick pay to that employee in respect of that day; and
    (b) any statutory sick pay paid by an employer to an employee of his in respect of a day of incapacity for work shall go towards discharging any liability of that employer to pay contractual remuneration to that employee in respect of that day.
  (3) Regulations may make provision as to payments which are, and those which are not, to be treated as contractual remuneration for the purposes of sub-paragraph (1) or (2) above.

1.197

[^{2}*Incapacity benefit*

3.—(1) This paragraph and paragraph 4 below have effect to exclude, where a period of entitlement as between an employee and an employer of his comes to an end, the provisions by virtue of which short-term incapacity benefit is not paid for the first three days.
  (2) If the first day immediately following the day on which the period of entitlement came to an end—
    (a) is a day of incapacity for work in relation to that employee; and
    (b) is not a day in relation to which paragraph 1 above applies by reason of any entitlement as between the employee and another employer,
that day shall, except in prescribed cases, be or form part of a period of incapacity for work notwithstanding section 30C(1)(b) above (by virtue of which a period of incapacity for work must be at least 4 days long).
  (3) Where each of the first two consecutive days, or the first three consecutive days, following the day on which the period of entitlement came to an end is a day to which paragraph (a) and (b) of sub-paragraph (2) above apply, that sub-paragraph has effect in relation to the second day or, as the case may be, in relation to the second and third days, as it has effect in relation to the first.
  4.—(1) Where a period of entitlement as between an employee and an employer of his comes to an end, section 30A(3) above (exclusion of benefit for first three days of period) does not apply in relation to any day which—
    (a) is or forms part of a period of incapacity for work (whether by virtue of paragraph 3 above or otherwise); and

1.198

109

Social Security Contributions and Benefits Act 1992

(b) falls within the period of 57 days immediately following the day on which the period of entitlement came to an end.

(2) Where sub-paragraph (1) above applies in relation to a day, section 30A(3) above does not apply in relation to any later day in the same period of incapacity for work.]

[²*Incapacity benefit for widows and widowers*

1.199
5. Paragraph 1 above does not apply for the purpose of determining whether the conditions specified in section 40(3) or (4) or section 41(2) or (3) above are satisfied.]

Unemployability supplement

1.200
6. Paragraph 1 above does not apply in relation to paragraph 3 of Schedule 7 to this Act and accordingly the references in paragraph 3 of that Schedule to a period of interruption of employment shall be construed as if the provisions re-enacted in this Part of this Act had not been enacted.

AMENDMENTS

1. Jobseekers Act 1995 s.41(5) and Sch.3 para.1 (October 7, 1996).
2. Social Security (Incapacity for Work) Act 1994 s.11(1) and Sch.1 para.44 (April 13, 1995).

GENERAL NOTE

Paragraph 1

1.201
No day which falls within a period of entitlement for the purposes of SSP (whether or not it is a qualifying day) can count as a day of incapacity for the purposes of establishing entitlement to incapacity benefit.

Paragraphs 3 and 4

1.202
These paragraphs assist certain persons, not caught by para.1, who have days of incapacity subsequent to the end of a period of entitlement, to qualify for incapacity benefit by not applying the normal rules, e.g. on waiting days. See further SSP (General) Regulations 1982 (SI 1982/894) reg.12.

Section 168   SCHEDULE 13

RELATIONSHIP OF STATUTORY MATERNITY PAY WITH BENEFITS AND OTHER PAYMENTS, ETC.

The general principle

1.203
[²1.—Except as may be prescribed, a day which falls within the maternity pay period shall not be treated as a day of incapacity for work for the purposes of determining, for this Act, whether it forms part of a period of incapacity for work for the purposes of incapacity benefit.]

[¹*Incapacity benefit*

1.204
2.—(1) Regulations may provide that in prescribed circumstances a day which falls within the maternity pay period shall be treated as a day of incapacity for work for the purpose of determining entitlement to the higher rate of short-term incapacity benefit or to long-term incapacity benefit.

(2) Regulations may provide that an amount equal to a woman's statutory maternity pay for a period shall be deducted from any such benefit in respect of the same period and a woman shall be entitled to such benefit only if there is a balance after the deduction and, if there is such a balance, at a weekly rate equal to it.]

(1992 c.4 Sch.13)

Contractual remuneration

3.—(1) Subject to sub-paragraphs (2) and (3) below, any entitlement to statutory maternity pay shall not affect any right of a woman in relation to remuneration under any contract of service ("contractual remuneration").

(2) Subject to sub-paragraph (3) below—
  (a) any contractual remuneration paid to a woman by an employer of hers in respect of a week in the maternity pay period shall go towards discharging any liability of that employer to pay statutory maternity pay to her in respect of that week; and
  (b) any statutory maternity pay paid by an employer to a woman who is an employee of his in respect of a week in the maternity pay period shall go towards discharging any liability of that employer to pay contractual remuneration to her in respect of that week.

[³(2A) In sub-paragraph (2) "week" means a period of seven days beginning with the day of the week on which the maternity pay period begins.]

(3) Regulations may make provision as to payments which are, and those which are not, to be treated as contractual remuneration for the purposes of sub-paragraphs (1) and (2) above.

1.205

AMENDMENTS

1. Social Security (Incapacity for Work) Act 1994 s.11(1) and Sch.1 para.45(3) (April 6, 1995).
2. Jobseekers Act 1995 s.41(4) and Sch.2 para.37 (October 7, 1996).
3. Work and Families Act 2006 s.11 and Sch.1 para.23 (October 1, 2006).

Social Security Administration Act 1992

(1992 c.5)

SECTIONS REPRODUCED

PART I

CLAIMS FOR PAYMENTS AND GENERAL ADMINISTRATION OF BENEFIT

Child benefit

13A.   Election not to receive child benefit

1.206

Statutory sick pay

14.   Duties of employees, etc. in relation to statutory sick pay

Statutory maternity pay

15.   Duties of women etc. in relation to statutory maternity pay

Social Security Administration Act 1992

PART III

OVERPAYMENTS AND ADJUSTMENTS OF BENEFIT

Misrepresentation etc

71. Overpayments—general

PART VI

ENFORCEMENT

113A. Statutory sick pay and statutory maternity pay: breach of regulations
113B. Statutory sick pay and statutory maternity pay: fraud and negligence

PART VII

INFORMATION

Information held by tax authorities

122A. Disclosure of contributions etc. information by [Her Majesty's Revenue and Customs]

Statutory sick pay and other benefits

129. Disclosure by Secretary of State for purpose of determination of period of entitlement to statutory sick pay
130. Duties of employers—statutory sick pay and claims for other benefits

Statutory maternity pay and other benefits

131. Disclosure by Secretary of State for purpose of determination of period of entitlement to statutory maternity pay
132. Duties of employers—statutory maternity pay and claims for other benefits

PART I

CLAIMS FOR AND PAYMENTS AND GENERAL ADMINISTRATION OF BENEFIT

Child benefit

[¹ **Election not to receive child benefit**

1.207   **13A.** — (1) A person ("P") who is entitled to child benefit in respect of one or more children may elect for all payments of the benefit to which P is entitled not to be made.
    (2) An election may be made only if P reasonably expects that, in the

(1992 c.5 s.13A)

absence of the election, P or another person would be liable to a high income child benefit charge in respect of the payments to which the election relates made for weeks in the first tax year.

(3) An election has effect in relation to payments made for weeks beginning after the election is made.

(4) But where entitlement to child benefit is backdated, an election may have effect in relation to payments for weeks beginning in the period of three months ending immediately before the claim for the benefit was made.

(5) An election may be revoked.

(6) A revocation has effect in relation to payments made for weeks beginning after the revocation is made.

(7) But if—
 (a) P makes an election which results in all payments, in respect of child benefit, to which P is entitled for one or more weeks in a tax year not being paid, and
 (b) had no election been made, neither P nor any other person would have been liable to a high income child benefit charge in relation to the payments,

P may, no later than two years after the end of the tax year, revoke the election so far as it relates to the payments.

(8) Subsections (2) to (7) are subject to directions under subsection (9).

(9) The Commissioners for Her Majesty's Revenue and Customs may give directions as to—
 (a) the form of elections and revocations under this section, the manner in which they are to be made and the time at which they are to be treated as made, and
 (b) the circumstances in which, if child benefit is not being paid to a person at the full rate or the Commissioners are satisfied that there are doubts as to a person's entitlement to child benefit for a child, an election or revocation is not to have effect or its effect is to be postponed.

(10) For the purposes of this section—
"child" includes a qualifying young person;
"first tax year", in relation to an election, means the tax year in which the first week beginning after the election is made falls;
"week" means a period of 7 days beginning with a Monday; and a week is in a tax year if (and only if) the Monday with which it begins is in the tax year.]

AMENDMENT

1. Finance Act 2012 Sch.1 para.3 (April 6, 2013).

GENERAL NOTE

See the note to s.143 SSCBA about the imposition from 2013/14 of the High Income Child Benefit Charge. This provision was introduced so that high earners who will no longer receive any economic benefit from receiving child benefit can elect not to receive the benefit. But note that this provision allows the election to be revoked if, with the benefit of hindsight, some economic benefit would have been received from a claim. The wording of the provision suggests that the election is not to receive payment. It is not clear whether it is therefore necessary for someone to

1.208

claim the benefit and then exercise the election in order to protect this prospective right.

Statutory Sick Pay

Duties of employees, etc. in relation to statutory sick pay

1.209   **14.**—(1) Any employee who claims to be entitled to statutory sick pay from his employer shall, if so required by his employer, provide such information as may reasonably be required for the purpose of determining the duration of the period of entitlement in question or whether a period of entitlement exists as between them.

(2) The Secretary of State may by regulations [¹ made with the concurrence of the Inland Revenue] direct—
- (a) that medical information required under subsection (1) above shall, in such cases as may be prescribed, be provided in a prescribed form;
- (b) that an employee shall not be required under subsection (1) above to provide medical information in respect of such days as may be prescribed in a period of incapacity for work.

(3) Where an employee asks an employer of his to provide him with a written statement, in respect of a period before the request is made, of one or more of the following—
- (a) the days within that period which the employer regards as days in respect of which he is liable to pay statutory sick pay to that employee;
- (b) the reasons why the employer does not so regard the other days in that period;
- (c) the employer's opinion as to the amount of statutory sick pay to which the employee is entitled in respect of each of those days,

the employer shall, to the extent to which the request was reasonable, comply with it within a reasonable time.

AMENDMENT

1. Social Security Contributions (Transfer of Functions, etc.) Act 1999 s.2 and Sch.3 para.42 (April 1, 1999).

Statutory maternity pay

Duties of women, etc. in relation to statutory maternity pay

1.210   **15.**—(1) A woman shall provide the person who is liable to pay her statutory maternity pay—
- (a) with evidence as to her pregnancy and the expected date of confinement in such form and at such time as may be prescribed; and
- (b) where she commences work after her confinement but within the maternity pay period, with such additional information as may be prescribed.

[¹(1A) Any regulations for the purposes of subsection (1) above must be made with the concurrence of the Inland Revenue.]

(2) Where a woman asks an employer or former employer of hers to

provide her with a written statement, in respect of a period before the request is made, of one or more of the following—
  (a) the weeks within that period which he regards as weeks in respect of which he is liable to pay statutory maternity pay to the woman;
  (b) the reasons why he does not so regard the other weeks in that period; and
  (c) his opinion as to the amount of statutory maternity pay to which the woman is entitled in respect of each of the weeks in respect of which he regards himself as liable to make a payment;
the employer or former employer shall, to the extent to which the request was reasonable, comply with it within a reasonable time.

AMENDMENT

1. Social Security Contributions (Transfer of Functions, etc.) Act 1999 s.2 and Sch.3 para.43 (April 1, 1999).

PART III

OVERPAYMENTS AND ADJUSTMENTS OF BENEFIT

Misrepresentation etc

Overpayments – general

71.—(1) Where it is determined that, whether fraudulently or otherwise, any person has misrepresented, or failed to disclose, any material fact and in consequence of the misrepresentation or failure–
  (a) a payment has been made in respect of a benefit to which this section applies; or
  (b) any sum recoverable by or on behalf of the Secretary of State in connection with any such payment has not been recovered,
the Secretary of State shall be entitled to recover the amount of any payment which he would not have made or any sum which he would have received but for the misrepresentation or failure to disclose.

(2) Where any such determination as is referred to in subsection (1) above is made, the person making the determination shall in the case of the Secretary of State or a First- tier Tribunal, and may in the case of the Upper Tribunal or court—
  (a) determine whether any, and if so what, amount is recoverable under that subsection by the Secretary of State, and
  (b) specify the period during which that amount was paid to the person concerned.

(3) An amount recoverable under subsection (1) above is in all cases recoverable from the person who misrepresented the fact or failed to disclose it.

(4) In relation to cases where payments of benefit to which this section applies have been credited to a bank account or other account under arrangements made with the agreement of the beneficiary or a person acting

1.211

Social Security Administration Act 1992

for him, circumstances may be prescribed in which the Secretary of State is to be entitled to recover any amount paid in excess of entitlement; but any such regulations shall not apply in relation to any payment unless before he agreed to the arrangements such notice of the effect of the regulations as may be prescribed was given in such manner as may be prescribed to the beneficiary or to a person acting for him.

(5) . . .

(5A) Except where regulations otherwise provide, an amount shall not be recoverable under subsection (1) or under regulations under subsection (4) above unless the determination in pursuance of which it was paid has been reversed or varied on an appeal or has been revised under section 9 or superseded under section 10 of the Social Security Act 1998.

(6) Regulations may provide—
  (a) that amounts recoverable under subsection (1) above or regulations under subsection (4) above shall be calculated or estimated in such manner and on such basis as may be prescribed;
  (b) for treating any amount paid to any person under an award which it is subsequently determined was not payable—
    (i) as properly paid; or
    (ii) as paid on account of a payment which it is determined should be or should have been made,
    and for reducing or withholding any arrears payable by virtue of the subsequent determination;
  (c) for treating any amount paid to one person in respect of another as properly paid for any period for which it is not payable in cases where in consequence of a subsequent determination—
    (i) the other person is himself entitled to a payment for that period; or
    (ii) a third person is entitled in priority to the payee to a payment for that period in respect of the other person,
    and for reducing or withholding any arrears payable for that period by virtue of the subsequent determination.

(7) . . .

(8) Where any amount paid other than an amount paid in respect of child benefit or guardian's allowance is recoverable under—
  (a) subsection (1) above;
  (b) regulations under subsection (4) above; or
  (c) section 74 below,
it may, without prejudice to any other method of recovery, be recovered by deduction from prescribed benefits.

(9) . . .
(9A) . . .
(9B) . . .
(9C) . . .
(10) . . .
(10A) . . .
(11) This section applies to the following benefits—
  (a) benefits as defined in section 122 of the Contributions and Benefits Act;
    . . .
  (f) child benefit.
(12) . . .

(1992 c.5 s.71)

GENERAL NOTE

Section 71 of the Administration Act is a much amended and much litigated section. For a full commentary on the section, its amendments and the extensive case law see the detailed analysis in Volume III of this work. The extracts included in this volume are of those parts of the section that apply specifically to the benefits administered by HMRC, namely child benefit and guardian's allowance. These benefits are included within the scope of the section by subs.(12). The regime for tax credit overpayments is entirely separate and is dealt with in the Tax Credits Act 2002. The extracts above do not refer to the many amendments to the section or the alternative wording operating for different benefits for different purposes, nor to provisions not relevant to the two benefits stated. Full details are in Volume III. There were provisions amending this section in the Tax Credits Act 1999 and applying this section to those tax credits. However, the provisions were fully repealed by the 2002 Act and may now be regarded as entirely spent.

Note that subs.(8) expressly prevents overpayments of these benefits being collected by deduction from other benefits.

1.212

PART VI

ENFORCEMENT

[¹**Statutory sick pay and statutory maternity pay: breach of regulations**

113A.—(1) Where a person fails to produce any document or record, or provide any information, in accordance with—
  (a) regulations under section 5(1)(i) and (5), so far as relating to statutory sick pay or statutory maternity pay,
  (b) regulations under section 130 or 132, or
  (c) regulations under section 153(5)(b) of the Contributions and Benefits Act,
that person is liable to the penalties mentioned in subsection (2).

(2) The penalties are—
  (a) a penalty not exceeding £300, and
  (b) if the failure continues after a penalty is imposed under paragraph (a), a further penalty or penalties not exceeding £60 for each day on which the failure continues after the day on which the penalty under that paragraph was imposed (but excluding any day for which a penalty under this paragraph has already been imposed).

(3) Where a person fails to maintain a record in accordance with regulations under section 130 or 132, he is liable to a penalty not exceeding £3,000.

(4) No penalty may be imposed under subsection (1) at any time after the failure concerned has been remedied.

(5) But subsection (4) does not apply to the imposition of a penalty under subsection (2)(a) in respect of a failure to produce any document or record in accordance with regulations under section 130(5) or 132(4).

(6) Where, in the case of any employee, an employer refuses or repeatedly fails to make payments of statutory sick pay or statutory maternity pay in accordance with any regulations under section 5, the employer is liable to a penalty not exceeding £3,000.

(7) Section 118(2) of the Taxes Management Act 1970 (extra time for compliance etc) applies for the purposes of subsections (1), (3) and (6) as it applies for the purposes of that Act.

1.213

117

(8) Schedule 1 to the Employment Act 2002 (penalties relating to statutory paternity pay and statutory adoption pay: procedures and appeals) applies in relation to penalties imposed under this section (with the modifications set out in subsection (9)).

(9) That Schedule applies as if—
(a) references to a penalty under section 11 or 12 of that Act were to a penalty under this section,
(b) in paragraph 1(2), the reference to section 11(2)(a) of that Act were to subsection (2)(a) of this section, and
(c) the provisions of the Taxes Management Act 1970 having effect in relation to an appeal mentioned in paragraph 3(2) of that Schedule did not include section 50(9) of that Act.]

AMENDMENT

1. National Insurance Contributions and Statutory Payments Act 2004 s.9(5) (April 6, 2005).

GENERAL NOTE

1.214 This provision brings in a compliance regime based on civil penalties, as with the administration of tax. Section 113A provides for civil penalties for failures to keep records, to produce records, to provide information or to pay either statutory sick pay or statutory maternity pay. The appeals procedures for such penalties are governed by Sch.1 to the Employment Act 2002 (see ss.113A(8) and (9)). Section 113B below is concerned with breaches by commission, and provides for penalties in cases of fraud or negligence which involve employers making incorrect statements or declarations, producing incorrect documents or records, making incorrect payments of statutory sick pay and statutory maternity pay and receiving incorrect advances of statutory maternity pay. HMRC has stated that penalties will be reserved for "serious situations such as where there has been a deliberate manipulation of the schemes, where a failure has continued after we have put the employer right and where the employer has failed to pay after the appeal period against a formal decision on liability" (*Regulatory Impact Assessment*, Annex E, para.7).

[¹**Statutory sick pay and statutory maternity pay: fraud and negligence**

1.215 **113B.**—(1) Where a person fraudulently or negligently—
(a) makes any incorrect statement or declaration in connection with establishing entitlement to statutory sick pay or statutory maternity pay, or
(b) produces any incorrect document or record or provides any incorrect information of a kind mentioned in—
   (i) regulations under section 5(1)(i) and (5), so far as relating to statutory sick pay or statutory maternity pay,
   (ii) regulations under section 130 or 132, or
   (iii) regulations under section 153(5)(b) of the Contributions and Benefits Act,
he is liable to a penalty not exceeding £3,000.

(2) Where an employer fraudulently or negligently makes an incorrect payment of statutory sick pay or statutory maternity pay, he is liable to a penalty not exceeding £3,000.

(3) Where an employer fraudulently or negligently receives an overpayment

(1992 c.5 s.113B)

in pursuance of regulations under section 167 of the Contributions and Benefits Act (statutory maternity pay: advance payments to employers), he is liable to a penalty not exceeding £3,000.

(4) Schedule 1 to the Employment Act 2002 (penalties relating to statutory paternity pay and statutory adoption pay: procedures and appeals) applies in relation to penalties imposed under this section (with the modifications set out in subsection (5)).

(5) That Schedule applies as if—
(a) references to a penalty under section 11 or 12 of that Act were to a penalty under this section, and
(b) the provisions of the Taxes Management Act 1970 having effect in relation to an appeal mentioned in paragraph 3(2) of that Schedule did not include section 50(9) of that Act.]

AMENDMENT

1. National Insurance Contributions and Statutory Payments Act 2004 s.9(5) (April 6, 2005).

PART VII

[1INFORMATION

Information held by tax authorities 1.216

[1**Disclosure of contributions etc. information by [4 Her Majesty's Revenue and Customs]**

122AA. —(1) No obligation as to secrecy imposed by statute or otherwise on [4 Revenue and Customs officials (within the meaning of section 18 of the Commissioners for Revenue and Customs Act 2005 (confidentiality)] shall prevent information held for the purposes of the functions of [4 Her Majesty's Revenue and Customs] in relation to contributions, statutory sick pay [2, statutory maternity pay, [7 statutory paternity pay,] statutory adoption pay [6 or statutory shared parental pay]] from being disclosed— 1.217
(a) to any of the authorities to which this paragraph applies, or any person authorised to exercise any function of that authority, for the purposes of the functions of that authority, or
(b) in a case where the disclosure is necessary for the purpose of giving effect to any agreement to which an order under section 179(1) below relates.

(2) The authorities to which subsection(1)(a) above applies are—
(a) the Health and Safety Executive,
(b) the Government Actuary's Department,
(c) the [5 Statistics Board], and
(d) the [3 Pensions Regulator.]

AMENDMENTS

1. Social Security Contributions (Transfer of Functions, etc.) Act 1999 s.6 and Sch.6 para.3 (April 1, 1999).
2. Employment Act 2002 s.53 and Sch.7 paras 8 and 13 (December 8, 2002).
3. Pensions Act 2004 s.319 and Sch.12 para.7 (April 6, 2005).
4. Commissioners for Revenue and Customs Act 2005 s.50(4) and Sch.4 para.46 (April 18, 2005).
5. Statistics and Registration Service Act 2007 s.46 and Sch.2 para.5 (April 1, 2008).
6. Children and Families Act 2014 s.126(1) and Sch.7 paras 23 and 25(b) (December 1, 2014).
7. Children and Families Act 2014 s.126(1) and Sch.7 paras 23 and 25(a) (April 5, 2015).

Statutory sick pay and other benefits

Disclosure by Secretary of State for purpose of determination of period of entitlement to statutory sick pay

1.218 **129.** Where the Secretary of State considers that it is reasonable for information held by him to be disclosed to an employer, for the purpose of enabling that employer to determine the duration of a period of entitlement under Part XI of the Contributions and Benefits Act in respect of an employee, or whether such a period exists, he may disclose the information to that employer.

Duties of employers—statutory sick pay and claims for other benefits

1.219 **130.**—(1) Regulations may make provision requiring an employer, in a case falling within subsection (3) below to furnish information in connection with the making, by a person who is, or has been, an employee of that employer, of a claim for—
[^{6} (za) universal credit;]
  [^{1}(a) short-term incapacity benefit;]
  (b) a maternity allowance;
  [^{1}(c) long-term incapacity benefit;]
  (d) industrial injuries benefit; [^{3}. . .]
  (e) [^{3}. . .].
[^{5}(f) an employment and support allowance.]
(2) Regulations under this section shall prescribe—
  (a) the kind of information to be furnished in accordance with the regulations;
  (b) the person to whom information of the prescribed kind is to be furnished; and
  (c) the manner in which, and period within which, it is to be furnished.
(3) The cases are—
  (a) where, by virtue of paragraph 2 of Schedule 11 to the Contributions and Benefits Act or of regulations made under paragraph 1 of that Schedule, a period of entitlement does not arise in relation to a period of incapacity for work;
  (b) where a period of entitlement has come to an end but the period of incapacity for work which was running immediately before the period of entitlement came to an end continues; and

(c) where a period of entitlement has not come to an end but, on the assumption that—
  (i) the period of incapacity for work in question continues to run for a prescribed period; and
  (ii) there is no material change in circumstances;
the period of entitlement will have ended on or before the end of the prescribed period.

(4) Regulations [²made with the concurrence of the Inland Revenue]—
(a) may require employers to maintain such records in connection with statutory sick pay as may be prescribed;
(b) may provide for—
  (i) any person claiming to be entitled to statutory sick pay; or
  (ii) any other person who is a party to proceedings arising under Part XI of the Contributions and Benefits Act;
to furnish to the Secretary of State [² or the Inland Revenue (as the regulations may require)], within a prescribed period, any information required for the determination of any question arising in connection there with; and
(c) may require employers who have made payments of statutory sick pay to furnish to the Secretary of State [² or the Inland Revenue (as the regulations may require)] such documents and information, at such times, as may be prescribed.

[⁴(5) Regulations made with the concurrence of the Inland Revenue may require employers to produce wages sheets and other documents and records to officers of the Inland Revenue, within a prescribed period, for the purpose of enabling them to satisfy themselves that statutory sick pay has been paid, and is being paid, in accordance with regulations under section 5 above, to employees or former employees who are entitled to it.]

AMENDMENTS

1. Social Security (Incapacity for Work) Act 1994 s.11(1) and Sch.1 para.49 (April 6, 1995).
2. Social Security Contributions (Transfer of Functions, etc.) Act 1999 s.6 and Sch.6 para.3 (April 1, 1999).
3. Welfare Reform and Pensions Act 1999 s.88 and Sch.13 Pt IV (April 6, 2001).
4. National Insurance Contributions and Statutory Payments Act 2004 s.9(2) (January 1, 2005).
5. Welfare Reform Act 2007 s.28(1) and Sch.3 para.10(1) and (19) (October 27, 2008).
6. Welfare Reform Act 2012 s.31 and Sch.2 paras 3 and 20 (April 29, 2013).

Statutory maternity pay and other benefits

Disclosure by Secretary of State for purpose of determination of period of entitlement to statutory maternity pay

131.—Where the Secretary of State considers that it is reasonable for information held by him to be disclosed to a person liable to make payments of statutory maternity pay for the purpose of enabling that person to determine—
(a) whether a maternity pay period exists in relation to a woman who is or has been an employee of his; and

(b) if it does, the date of its commencement and the weeks in it in respect of which he may be liable to pay statutory maternity pay,

he may disclose the information to that person.

Duties of employers—statutory maternity pay and claims for other benefits

1.221 **132.**—(1) Regulations may make provision requiring an employer in prescribed circumstances to furnish information in connection with the making of a claim by a woman who is or has been his employee for—

[6 (za) universal credit;]
 (a) a maternity allowance;
[5(aa) an employment and support allowance.]
 (b) [1short-term incapacity benefit;]
 (c) [1long-term incapacity benefit under section 30A], 40 or 41 of the Contributions and Benefits Act; [3. . .]
 (d) [3. . .].

(2) Regulations under this section shall prescribe—
 (a) the kind of information to be furnished in accordance with the regulations;
 (b) the person to whom information of the prescribed kind is to be furnished; and
 (c) the manner in which, and period within which, it is to be furnished.

(3) Regulations [2made with the concurrence of the Inland Revenue]—
 (a) may require employers to maintain such records in connection with statutory maternity pay as may be prescribed;
 (b) may provide for—
  (i) any woman claiming to be entitled to statutory maternity pay; or
  (ii) any other person who is a party to proceedings arising under Part XII of the Contributions and Benefits Act,
 to furnish to the Secretary of State [2or the Inland Revenue (as the regulations may require)], within a prescribed period, any information required for the determination of any question arising in connection there with; and
 (c) may require persons who have made payments of statutory maternity pay to furnish to the Secretary of State [2or the Inland Revenue (as the regulations may require)] such documents and information, at such time, as may be prescribed.

[4(4) Regulations made with the concurrence of the Inland Revenue may require employers to produce wages sheets and other documents and records to officers of the Inland Revenue, within a prescribed period, for the purpose of enabling them to satisfy themselves that statutory maternity pay has been paid, and is being paid, in accordance with regulations under section 5 above, to employees or former employees who are entitled to it.]

AMENDMENTS

1. Social Security (Incapacity for Work) Act 1994 s.11(1) and Sch.1 para.50 (April 6, 1995).
2. Social Security Contributions (Transfer of Functions, etc.) Act 1999 s.6 and Sch.1 para.27 (April 1, 1999).

(1992 c.5 s.132)

3. Welfare Reform and Pensions Act 1999 s.88 and Sch.13 Pt IV (April 6, 2001).
4. National Insurance Contributions and Statutory Payments Act 2004 s.9(3) (January 1, 2005).
5. Welfare Reform Act 2007 s.28(1) and Sch.3 para.10(1) and (20) (October 27, 2008).
6. Welfare Reform Act 2012 s.31 and Sch.2 paras 3 and 21 (April 29, 2013).

Social Security Act 1998

(1998 C.14)

An Act to make provision as to the making of decisions and the determination of appeals under enactments relating to social security, child support, vaccine damage payments and war pensions; to make further provision with respect to social security; and for connected purposes.

Appeal to [²First-tier Tribunal]

12.— (1) [¹ . . .]
(2) [¹ . . .]
(3) [¹ . . .]
(4) [¹ . . .]
(5) [¹ . . .]
(6) [¹ . . .]
(7) Regulations may [³ . . .]
[³ (a) make provision as to the manner in which, and the time within which, appeals are to be brought;
(b) provide that, where in accordance with regulations under subsection (3A) there is no right of appeal against a decision, any purported appeal may be treated as an application for revision under section 9.]
(8) In deciding [¹ a child trust fund appeal], [² the First-tier Tribunal]—
(a) [¹ . . .]
(b) shall not take into account any circumstances not obtaining at the time when the decision appealed against was made.
(9) [¹ . . .].

AMENDMENTS

1. Child Trust Funds (Non-tax Appeals) Regulations 2005 (SI 2005/191) reg.6 (February 25, 2005).
2. Transfer of Tribunal Functions Order 2008 (SI 2008/2833) art.9(1) and Sch.3 para.149 (November 3, 2008).
3. Welfare Reform Act 2012 s.102(4) (February 25, 2013).

GENERAL NOTE

This is the version of s.12 of the 1998 Act as modified for the purposes of child trust fund appeals.

Social Security Contributions (Transfer of Functions, etc.) Act 1999

Social Security Contributions (Transfer of Functions, etc.) Act 1999

(1999 c.2)

1.225   An Act to transfer from the Secretary of State to the Commissioners of Inland Revenue or the Treasury certain functions relating to national insurance contributions, the National Insurance Fund, statutory sick pay, statutory maternity pay or pension schemes and certain associated functions relating to benefits; to enable functions relating to any of those matters in respect of Northern Ireland to be transferred to the Secretary of State, the Commissioners of Inland Revenue or the Treasury; to make further provision, in connection with the functions transferred, as to the powers of the Commissioners of Inland Revenue, the making of decisions and appeals; to provide that rebates payable in respect of members of money purchase contracted-out pension schemes are to be payable out of the National Insurance Fund; and for connected purposes.

ARRANGEMENT OF SECTIONS

PART II

DECISIONS AND APPEALS

1.226
8. Decisions by officers of Board
9. Regulations with respect to decisions
10. Decisions varying or superseding earlier decisions
11. Appeals against decisions of Board
12. Exercise of right of appeal
13. Regulations with respect to appeals
14. Matters arising as respects decisions
15. (*Omitted*)
16. (*Omitted*)
17. Arrangements for discharge of decision-making functions
18. Amendments relating to decisions and appeals
19. Interpretation of Part II

PART III

MISCELLANEOUS AND SUPPLEMENTAL

27. Interpretation

PART II

DECISIONS AND APPEALS

Decisions by officers of Board

1.227   **8.**—(1) Subject to the provisions of this Part, it shall be for an officer of the Board—

(a) to decide whether for the purposes of Parts I to V of the Social Security Contributions and Benefits Act 1992 a person is or was an earner and, if so, the category of earners in which he is or was to be included;
(b) to decide whether a person is or was employed in employed earner's employment for the purposes of Part V of the Social Security Contributions and Benefits Act 1992 (industrial injuries);
(c) to decide whether a person is or was liable to pay contributions of any particular class and, if so, the amount that he is or was liable to pay,
(d) to decide whether a person is or was entitled to pay contributions of any particular class that he is or was not liable to pay and, if so, the amount that he is or was entitled to pay,
(e) to decide whether contributions of a particular class have been paid in respect of any period,
[5 (ea) to decide whether a person is or was entitled to make a deduction under section 4 of the National Insurance Contributions Act 2014 (deductions etc of employment allowance) and, if so, the amount the person is or was entitled to deduct,
(eb) to decide whether a person is or was entitled to a repayment under that section and, if so, the amount of the repayment,]
(f) subject to and in accordance with regulations made for the purposes of this paragraph by the Secretary of State with the concurrence of the Board, to decide any issue arising as to, or in connection with, entitlement to statutory sick pay, [4, statutory maternity pay, [7 statutory paternity pay,] statutory adoption pay]] [6 or statutory shared parental pay],
(g) to make any other decision that falls to be made [4under Parts XI to [5 12ZC] of the Social Security Contributions and Benefits Act 1992 (statutory sick pay, statutory maternity pay, [7 statutory paternity pay,] statutory adoption pay]] [6 or statutory shared parental pay])],
[4(ga) to make any decision that falls to be made under regulations under section 7 of the Employment Act 2002 (funding of employers' liabilities to make payments of [7 statutory paternity pay,] statutory adoption pay]] [6 or statutory shared parental pay],];
(h) to decide any question as to the issue and content of a notice under subsection (2) of section 121C of the Social Security Administration Act 1992 (liability of directors etc. for company's contributions);
(i) to decide any issue arising under section 27 of the Jobseekers Act 1995 (employment of long-term unemployed: deductions by employers), or under any provision of regulations under that section, as to—
   (i) whether a person is or was an employee or employer of another;
   (ii) whether an employer is or was entitled to make any deduction from his contributions payments in accordance with regulations under section 27 of that Act;
   (iii) whether a payment falls to be made to an employer in accordance with those regulations;
   (iv) the amount that falls to be so deducted or paid; or
   (v) whether two or more employers are, by virtue of regulations under section 27 of that Act, to be treated as one,
[3(ia) to decide whether to give or withdraw an approval for the purposes of para.3B(1)(b) of Sch.1 to the Social Security Contributions and Benefits Act 1992,];

Social Security Contributions (Transfer of Functions, etc.) Act 1999

(j) [² . . .];
(k) to decide whether a person is liable to a penalty under—
   (i) paragraph 7A(2) or 7B(2)(h) of Schedule 1 to the Social Security Contributions and Benefits Act 1992; or
   (ii) section 113(1)(a) of the Social Security Administration Act 1992;
(l) to decide the [² . . .] penalty payable under any of the provisions mentioned in [²paragraph (k)] above; and
(m) to decide such issues relating to contributions, other than the issues specified in paragraphs (a) to (l) above or in paragraphs 16 and 17 of Schedule 3 to the Social Security Act 1998, as may be prescribed by regulations made by the Board.

[⁵ (1A) No decision in respect of Class 2 contributions under section 11(2) of the Social Security Contributions and Benefits Act 1992 may be made under subsection (1) in relation to an issue specified in paragraph (c) or (e) of that subsection if the person to whom the decision would relate—
(a) has appealed under Part 5 of the Taxes Management Act 1970 in relation to that issue,
(b) can appeal under that Part in relation to that issue, or
(c) might in the future, without the agreement of Her Majesty's Revenue and Customs or permission of the tribunal, be able to appeal under that Part in relation to that issue.]

(2) Subsection (1)(c) and (e) above do not include any decision relating to Class 4 contributions other than a decision falling to be made—
(a) under subsection (1) of section 17 of the Social Security Contributions and Benefits Act 1992 as to whether by regulations under that subsection a person is or was excepted from liability for Class 4 contributions, or his liability is or was deferred; or
(b) under regulations made by virtue of subsection (3) or (4) of that section or section 18 of that Act.

(3) Subsection (1)(g) above does not include—
(a) any decision as to the making of subordinate legislation; or
(b) any decision as to whether the liability to pay statutory sick pay [⁴, statutory maternity pay, [⁷ statutory paternity pay,] statutory adoption pay]] [⁶ or statutory shared parental pay] is a liability of the Board rather than the employer.

(4) [¹ . . .].

AMENDMENTS

1. Welfare Reform and Pensions Act 1999 s.88 and Sch.13 Pt VI (April 6, 2000).
2. Child Support, Pensions and Social Security Act 2000 ss.76(6) and 85 and Sch.9 Pt VIII (July 28, 2000).
3. Child Support, Pensions and Social Security Act 2000 ss.77(5) (July 28, 2000).
4. Employment Act 2002 ss.9(2) and (3) (December 8, 2002).
5. National Insurance Contributions Act 2014 s.6(1) (April 6, 2014).
6. Children and Families Act 2014 s.126(1) Sch.7 paras 44 and 45(1), (2)(b) (c) and (e) (December 1, 2014).
7. Children and Families Act 2014 s.126(1) Sch.7 paras 44 and 45(1)(2)(a) and (d) (April 5, 2015).

DEFINITIONS

"Board"—see s.27.
"contributions"—*ibid.*

"employed earner"—see SSCBA 1992 s.2(1)(a).
"employment"—see SSCBA 1992 s.122.

GENERAL NOTE

This section provides for HMRC to take decisions on a range of specified questions in relation to SMP, SSP, NICs, employment status and related matters. The extensive list of such decisions, set out in subs.(1), covers much of the former jurisdiction of the Secretary of State for Social Security under SSAA 1992 s.17(1), with the addition of some further matters. For example, the function of making decisions as to entitlement to SMP or SSP (subs.(1)(f)) was traditionally a function of an adjudication officer (SSAA 1992 s.20(3)) but was then transferred to the Secretary of State (SSA 1998 s.8(1)(d)) before now moving to an officer of the Board (now HMRC). This is one of the areas in which the power to make regulations still rests with the Secretary of State (albeit with the agreement of HMRC), as the policy responsibility for these benefits is retained by the DWP (see General Note to s.2). However, in terms of decision-making on matters of entitlement to SSP (and, by analogy, to SMP, SPP and SAP), HMRC has an "exclusive and exhaustive jurisdiction" (per Mr Recorder Luba QC in *Taylor Gordon & Co Ltd v Timmons* ([2004] I.R.L.R. 180, at [£43]). Thus an employment tribunal has no jurisdiction under the Employment Rights Act 1996 to entertain an employee's complaint that SSP has not been paid.

For the relevant regulation-making powers, see s.9 and for provision for variation and supersession of decisions made under s.8, see s.10. From April 6, 2009 appeals go to the First-tier Tribunal Tax Chamber. One result of the tribunal reforms introduced then is that a number of judges now sit both to hear tax appeals and appeals under this section as well as appeals on social security matters in the Social Entitlement Chamber.

For the procedure to be adopted where a national insurance contributions issue arises in relation to a benefit appeal, see *Secretary of State for Work and Pensions v TB and HMRC (RP)* [2010] UKUT 88 (AAC), [2010] AACR 38.

Section 126 of the Welfare Reform Act 2012 provides legislative powers to transfer any tax credit function exercised by the Treasury or HMRC to the Secretary of State, or for any such function to be exercised jointly. The policy is to provide that during the staged transfer of claimants from tax credits to universal credits the administration is transferred across from HMRC to the DWP. This is being done in part by transferring (and in some cases transferring back) the relevant staff from HMRC to DWP.

1.228

Regulations with respect to decisions

9.—(1) Subject to the provisions of this Part and of the Social Security Administration Act 1992, provision may be made by the Board by regulations as to the making by their officer of any decision under or in connection with the Social Security Contributions and Benefits Act 1992, the Social Security Administration Act 1992 or the Jobseekers Act 1995 which falls to be made by such an officer.

(2) Where it appears to an officer of the Board that a matter before him involves a question of fact requiring special expertise, he may direct that in dealing with that matter he shall have the assistance of one or more experts.

(3) In subsection (2) above "expert" means a person appearing to the officer of the Board to have knowledge or experience which would be relevant in determining the question of fact requiring special expertise.

1.229

DEFINITIONS

"Board"—see s.27.
"expert"—see subs.(3).

General Note

1.230   Subsection (1), modelled on SSA 1998 s.11, provides for HMRC to make regulations governing procedural matters relating to decisions made by HMRC staff under s.8.

Subsections (2) and (3) enable HMRC to seek specialist advice before making a decision (e.g. as to medical evidence relevant to a claim for SSP). In the first instance SMP or SSP decisions are made by the employer, and only referred for a formal decision where the parties are unable to reach agreement. There are only about 500 referrals each year concerning SMP or SSP; most of these cases concern the linking or employment rules, with perhaps no more than 50 involving a medical issue (*per* Baroness Hollis of Heigham, Parliamentary Under-Secretary of State for Social Security, *Hansard*, H.L. Debs. Vol.596, col.322 (January 14, 1999)).

Decisions varying or superseding earlier decisions

1.231   **10.**—(1) [¹ Subject to subsection (2A) below,] the Board may by regulations make provision—
(a) for any decision of an officer of the Board under section 8 of this Act (including a decision superseding an earlier decision) to be varied either within the prescribed period or in prescribed cases or circumstances;
(b) for any such decision to be superseded, in prescribed circumstances, by a subsequent decision made by an officer of the Board; and
(c) for any such decision as confirmed or varied by the [² First-tier Tribunal or Upper Tribunal] on appeal to be superseded, in the event of a material change of circumstances since the decision was made, by a subsequent decision made by an officer of the Board.
(2) The date as from which—
(a) any variation of a decision, or
(b) any decision superseding an earlier decision,
is to take effect shall be determined in accordance with the regulations.
[¹(2A) The decisions in relation to which provision may be made by regulations under this section shall not include decisions falling within section 8(1)(ia) above.]
(3) In this section "prescribed" means prescribed by regulations under this section.

Amendments

1. Child Support, Pensions and Social Security Act 2000 s.77(6) (July 28, 2000).
2. Transfer of Tribunal Functions and Revenue and Customs Appeals Order 2009 (SI 2009/56) art.3 and Sch.1 (April 1, 2009).

Definitions

"Board"—s.27.
"prescribed"—subs.(3).

General Note

1.232   This enabling provision reflects similar powers, governing Secretary of State decisions, contained in SSA 1998 ss.9 (revision) and 10 (supersession).

Appeals against decisions of Board

1.233   **11.**—(1) This section applies to any decision of an officer of the Board under section 8 of this Act or under regulations made by virtue of section

(1999 c.2 s.11)

10(1)(b) or (c) of this Act (whether as originally made or as varied under regulations made by virtue of section 10(1)(a) of this Act).

(2) In the case of a decision to which this section applies—
(a) if it relates to a person's entitlement to statutory sick pay [¹, statutory maternity pay, [⁴ statutory paternity pay,] statutory adoption pay]] [³ or statutory shared parental pay], the employee and employer concerned shall each have a right to appeal to the [² tribunal], and
(b) in any other case, the person in respect of whom the decision is made and such other person as may be prescribed shall have a right to appeal to the [² tribunal].

(3) In subsection (2)(b) above "prescribed" means prescribed by the Board by regulations.

(4) This section has effect subject to section 121D of the Social Security Administration Act 1992 (appeals in relation to personal liability notices).

AMENDMENTS

1. Employment Act 2002 s.9(4) (December 8, 2002).
2. Transfer of Tribunal Functions and Revenue and Customs Appeals Order 2009 (SI 2009/56) art.3 and Sch.1 (April 1, 2009).
3. Children and Families Act 2014 s.126(1) Sch.7 paras 44, 46(b) (December 1, 2014).
4. Children and Families Act 2014 s.126(1) Sch.7 paras 44, 46(a) (April 5, 2015).

DEFINITIONS

"Board"—see s.27.
"prescribed"—see subs.(3)
[² tribunal]

GENERAL NOTE

This provides a right of appeal to the First-tier Tribunal. It will normally go to the Tax Chamber (but see First-tier Tribunal and Upper Tribunal (Chambers) (Amendment No.3) Order 2009 (SI 2009/1590) with effect from September 1, 2009). Tribunal reforms allow this to be dealt with by a judge familiar with both tax law and social security law, so allowing consideration to be given to the problem that a s.8 appeal may be considered while removed from its social security context. Both employees and employers have a right of appeal in relation to decisions on SMP and SSP entitlement (subs.(2)(a)). Note also that subs.(2)(b) contains a broader regulation-making power to give interested parties in other decisions a right of appeal. This provision only provides for additional rights of appeal; unlike SSA 1998 s.12(2), there is no power to prescribe in regulations for cases in which there is to be no right of appeal.

1.234

Exercise of right of appeal

12.—(1) Any appeal against a decision must be brought by a notice of appeal in writing given within 30 days after the date on which notice of the decision was issued.

1.235

(2) The notice of appeal shall be given to the officer of the Board by whom notice of the decision was given.

[¹ (3) The notice of appeal shall specify the grounds of appeal.]
(4) [¹. . .]
(5) [¹. . .]

AMENDMENT

1. Transfer of Tribunal Functions and Revenue and Customs Appeals Order 2009 (SI 2009/56) art.3 and Sch.1 (April 1, 2009) and Sch.

DEFINITIONS

"Board"—see s.27.

GENERAL NOTE

1.236 This section, governing rights of appeal, is modelled on the provisions governing tax appeals (Taxes Management Act 1970 s.31) rather than those for social security matters (SSA 1998 s.12).

Subsection (1)
1.237 This provision adopts the standard 30-day appeal deadline in s.31(1) of the Taxes Management Act 1970.

Subsection (2)
1.238 This requirement mirrors s.31(2) of the Taxes Management Act 1970.

Regulations with respect to appeals

1.239   13.—(1) The Board may, by regulations made with the concurrence of the Lord Chancellor and the [Secretary of State], make provision with respect to appeals to the [¹tribunal] under this Part.
    (2) Regulations under subsection (1) above may, in particular—
    (a) make provision with respect to any of the matters dealt with in the following provisions of the Taxes Management Act 1970—
        (i) [². . .]
        (ii) sections 48 to 54 (appeals to the [²tribunal] under the Taxes Acts); and
        (iii) [² section 56 (payment of tax where there is a further appeal)] or
    (b) provide for any of those provisions of that Act to apply, with such modifications as may be specified in the regulations, in relation to an appeal to the [²tribunal] under this Part.
    [³ (2A) Regulations under subsection (1) above may provide for sections 11(2) and 13(2) of the Tribunals, Courts and Enforcement Act 2007 to apply with such modifications as may be specified in the regulations in relation to an appeal to the tribunal under this Part.]
    [². . .]

AMENDMENTS

1. Transfer of Functions (Lord Advocate and Secretary of State) Order 1999 (SI 1999/678) art.2(1).
2. Transfer of Tribunal Functions and Revenue and Customs Appeals Order 2009 (SI 2009/56) art.3 and Sch.1 (April 1, 2009).
3. Revenue and Customs Appeals Order 2009 (SI 2009/777) art.3 (April 1, 2009).

DEFINITIONS

"Board"—see s.27.

GENERAL NOTE

1.240 This section enables HMRC to make regulations about the procedures to apply for appeals to the tax appeal Commissioners against decisions under s.8. Such regulations can only be made with the concurrence of the Lord Chancellor and the Lord Advocate, who are responsible for funding the tax appeal Commissioners. In general terms, most of the provisions about appeals in Pt V of the Taxes Management Act 1970 are adopted for the purposes of such appeals. However, given that there are material differences between tax and matters such as SSP and SMP, subs.(2)(b) provides for appropriate modifications to be made to these appellate procedures. This reflects the existing arrangements for appeals to the Tax Chamber of the First-tier Tribunal in relation to Class 4 NICs, under SSCBA 1992 Sch.2 para.8.

Matters arising as respects decisions

14.—(1) The Board may by regulations make provision as respects matters arising—

  (a) pending any decision of an officer of the Board under section 8 of this Act which relates to—

    (i) statutory sick pay [[1], statutory maternity pay, [[4] statutory paternity pay,] statutory adoption pay]] [[3] or statutory shared parental pay], or

    (ii) any person's liability for contributions;

  (b) pending the determination by the [[2]tribunal] of an appeal against any such decision,

  (c) out of the variation, under regulations made under section 10 of this Act or on appeal, of any such decision, or

  (d) out of the making of a decision which, under regulations made under that section, supersedes an earlier decision.

(2) Regulations under this section may, in particular—

  (a) make provision making a person liable to pay contributions pending the determination by the [[2]tribunal] of an appeal against a decision of an officer of the Board; and

  (b) make provision as to the repayment in prescribed circumstances of contributions paid by virtue of the regulations.

(3) Regulations under this section must be made with the concurrence of the Secretary of State in so far as they relate to statutory sick pay [[1], statutory maternity pay, [[4] statutory paternity pay,] statutory adoption pay]] [[3] or statutory shared parental pay].

1.241

AMENDMENTS

1. Employment Act 2002 s.9(5) (December 8, 2002).
2. Transfer of Tribunal Functions and Revenue and Customs Appeals Order 2009 (SI 2009/56) art.3 and Sch.1 (April 1, 2009).
3. Children and Families Act 2014 s.126(1) Sch.7 paras 44, 47(1) and (2)(b) (June 30, 2014).
4. Children and Families Act 2014 s.126(1) Sch.7 paras 44, 47(1) and (2)(a) (April 5, 2015).

DEFINITIONS

  "Board"—see s.27.
  "contributions"—*ibid.*

GENERAL NOTE

This section is modelled on SSA 1998 s.18. It vests HMRC with a parallel regulation-making power to deal with matters arising before a decision is made or an appeal is heard (subss.(1)(a) and (b)), or concerning the consequences of varying

1.242

Social Security Contributions (Transfer of Functions, etc.) Act 1999

or superseding a previous decision (including a variation following an appeal) (subss.(1)(c) and (d)). As such regulations may have implications for benefit rights in relation to SMP and SSP, in those instances the power can only be exercised with the agreement of the Secretary of State for Work and Pensions (subs.(3)).

Arrangements for discharge of decision-making functions

1.243

17.—(1) The Secretary of State may make arrangements with the Board for any of his functions under Chapter II of Part I of the Social Security Act 1998 in relation to—
  (a) a decision whether a person was (within the meaning of regulations) precluded from regular employment by responsibilities at home; or
  (b) a decision whether a person is entitled to be credited with earnings or contributions in accordance with regulations made under section 22(5) of the Social Security Contributions and Benefits Act 1992;
to be discharged by the Board or by officers of the Board.

(2) No such arrangements shall affect the responsibility of the Secretary of State or the application of Chapter II of Part I of the Social Security Act 1998 in relation to any decision.

(3) Until the commencement of Chapter II of Part I of the Social Security Act 1998, the references to that chapter in subsections (1) and (2) above shall have effect as references to Part II of the Social Security Administration Act 1992.

DEFINITION

"Board"—see s.27.

GENERAL NOTE

1.244

This section enables decisions on home responsibilities protection or credits to be performed by HMRC as agents for the Secretary of State for Work and Pensions. This arrangement is appropriate as such decisions primarily impact upon entitlement to social security benefits.

Amendments relating to decisions and appeals

1.245

18.—Schedule 7 to this Act (which contains amendments relating to decisions and appeals) shall have effect.

GENERAL NOTE

1.246

Schedule 7 provides for the detailed responsibilities of existing legislation relating to decision-making and appeals (Taxes Management Act 1970, SSCBA 1992, SSAA 1992, Pensions Schemes Act 1993, Employment Rights Act 1996 and SSA 1998).

[1 Interpretation of Part II

1.247

19.—In this Part—
"tribunal" means the First-tier Tribunal or, where determined by or under Tribunal Procedure Rules, the Upper Tribunal.]

AMENDMENT

1. Transfer of Tribunal Functions and Revenue and Customs Appeals Order 2009 (SI 2009/56) art.3 and Sch.1 (April 1, 2009).

(1999 c.2 s.20)

PART III

MISCELLANEOUS AND SUPPLEMENTAL

20.–26. [*Omitted.*]

Interpretation

27.—In this Act, unless a contrary intention appears—
"the Board" means the Commissioners of Inland Revenue;
"contributions" means contributions under Part I of the Social Security Contributions and Benefits Act 1992.
28.—[*Omitted.*]

GENERAL NOTE

The provisions in Pt III (with the exception of s.27) fall outside the scope of this volume and so are omitted. Section 20 provides that rebates in respect of money purchase contracted-out pension schemes should be funded from the National Insurance Fund. Sections 21 and 22 deal with the transfer of contracts and property from the former DSS to the Inland Revenue. Section 23 provides for the transfer of functions by Order in Council. Section 24 enables provision to be made for Northern Ireland by Order in Council while s.25 concerns regulation and Order making powers generally; s.26 introduces Schs 8 (savings and transitional provisions), 9 (consequential amendments) and 10 (repeals and revocations). Section 28 governs the short title, commencement and extent of the Act.

Tax Credits Act 2002

(2002 C.21)

ARRANGEMENT OF SECTIONS

PART I

TAX CREDITS

General

1. Introductory
2. Functions of Commissioners
3. Claims
4. Claims: supplementary
5. Period of awards
6. Notifications of changes of circumstances
7. Income test

133

Tax Credits Act 2002

Child tax credit

8. Entitlement
9. Maximum rate

Working tax credit

10. Entitlement
11. Maximum rate
12. Childcare element

Rate

13. Rate

Decisions

14. Initial decisions
15. Revised decisions after notifications
16. Other revised decisions
17. Final notice
18. Decisions after final notice
19. Power to enquire
20. Decisions on discovery
21. Decisions subject to official error
21A. Reviews of decisions
21B. Late application for a review
22. Information, etc. requirements: supplementary
23. Notice of decisions

Payment

24. Payments
25. Payments of working tax credit by employers (*omitted*)
26. Liability of officers for sums paid to employers (*omitted*)
27. Rights of employees
28. Overpayments
29. Recovery of overpayments
30. Underpayments

Penalties

31. Incorrect statements, etc.
32. Failure to comply with requirements
33. Failure by employers to make correct payments (*omitted*)
34. Supplementary

Fraud

35. Offence of fraud
36. Powers in relation to documents

(2002 c.21)

36A. Loss of working tax credit in case of conviction etc. for benefit offence
36B. Section 36A: supplementary
36C. Loss of working tax credit for repeated benefit fraud
36D. Section 36C: supplementary

Interest

37. Interest

Appeals

38. Appeals
39. Exercise of right of appeal
39A. Late appeals

Supplementary

40. Annual reports
41. Annual review
42. Persons subject to immigration control
43. Polygamous marriages
44. Crown employment
45. Inalienability
46. Giving of notices by Board
47. Consequential amendments
48. Interpretation

PART II

CHILD BENEFIT AND GUARDIAN'S ALLOWANCE

49.–57. (*Omitted*)

PART III

SUPPLEMENTARY

Information etc.

58. Administrative arrangements
59. Use and disclosure of information

Other supplementary provisions

60. Repeals
61. Commencement
62. Transitional provisions and savings
63. Tax credits appeals etc.: temporary modifications
64. Northern Ireland

65. Regulations, orders and schemes
66. Parliamentary etc. control of instruments
67. Interpretation
68. Financial provision (*omitted*)
69. Extent (*omitted*)
70. Short title (*omitted*)

Schedule 1—Rights of employees (*omitted*)
Schedule 2—Penalties: supplementary
Schedule 3—Tax credits: consequential amendments (*omitted*)
Schedule 4—Transfer of functions: consequential amendments (*omitted*)
Schedule 5—Use and disclosure of information (*omitted*)
Schedule 6—Repeals and revocations (*omitted*)

GENERAL NOTE

Scope and scheme of the Act

1.252 The Tax Credits Bill 2001 was introduced to the House of Commons as a Treasury measure. It was subject to minimal amendment as it went through its parliamentary proceedings in the House of Commons. The Speaker ruled that it was not a Money Bill (possibly because of Pt II of the Act). It was subject to rigorous challenge in the House of Lords. The criticisms ranged from normal political confrontations about tax and social security measures to a challenge to the fundamental approach, even the title, of the Bill itself. It was at that stage also (after strong protests from the opposition parties and an apology from the minister piloting the Bill through the House) that important government technical and drafting amendments were tabled. The main focus of opposition criticism was on the issue whether tax credits counted as public expenditure or as tax uncollected. In fact, that issue did not feature in the Bill at all as it does not require legislation. The answer (after a disagreement about the right approach, recorded in the note) was published in the Red Book (the Financial Statement) published by the Treasury to accompany the Chancellor 2002 Budget (See *2002 Financial Statement*, Box C2, p.216). It is that tax credits count as public expenditure in so far as they exceed the income tax due from the claimant, and as negative taxation in so far as they do not. Tax credits under the Tax Credits Act 1999 are classified as public expenditure. During Parliamentary debates, it was said that as a ball-park figure, 90 per cent of the amount was public expenditure and 10 per cent tax foregone.

The Tax Credits Act 2002 ("this Act") repeals and replaces the Tax Credits Act 1999 ("TCA 1999") in its entirety and carries further the reforms started by that Act. The Act is structured in three Parts. Part I (Tax credits) provides the necessary primary legislative framework to introduce the child tax credit and working tax credit. It also provides a common procedure for those tax credits. Schedules 1–3 to the Act are associated with this Part. Part II (Child benefit and guardian's allowance) makes provision for the transfer of functions concerning child benefit and guardian's allowance to the Treasury and HMRC, and the associated minor amendments to entitlement. Schedule 4 is associated with this Part. Part III (Supplementary) makes additional provision for both other Parts. Schedules 5 and 6 are associated with this Part.

Repeal of the 2002 Act

1.253 Schedule 14 Pt 1 to the Welfare Reform Act 2012 contains the legislation necessary to repeal the whole of the Tax Credits Act 2002 with the exception of Schs 1 and 3 to the 2002 Act. Paragraphs 1 and 6 of Sch.6 to the 2012 Act contain wide powers to allow the staged transfer of claimants from tax credits to universal credit. Government policy is to introduce the transfer by initial pilots and then by stages. As at April 2013 only a small initial pilot transfer had taken place. This volume does not therefore take account of the pilots and staged transfers.

Tax credits under the Tax Credits Act 2002

The introduction of the current reforms was announced by the Chancellor of the Exchequer, Gordon Brown, in his 1999 Budget and confirmed in his 2000 Budget. The detailed shape of the proposals was first announced in an HMRC consultation paper published in July 2001: *New Tax Credits: Supporting families, making work pay and tackling poverty*. This received significant comment from many sources and the HMRC published its *Response* in November 2001.

1.254

Child tax credit

CTC is a means-tested social security benefit for all those responsible for children and qualifying young persons, although it is presented as a tax credit.

Support for children through the tax and social security systems was previously provided in several ways. The first and most important provision was child benefit. The second line of support for children in poorer families was by way of an addition or increase to individual means-tested benefits (or tax credits). Thirdly, and separately from the income-related benefits, contributory and other social security benefits also made provision for dependent children (e.g. the child dependency increases under SSCBA 1992 ss.80 and 85 and the child increase for carer's allowance under SSCBA 1992 s.90). There were further provisions in the Social Security (Dependency) Regulations 1977 (SI 1977/343). Moreover, a few individuals looking after children as their guardians can claim guardian's allowance, under SSCBA 1992 s.77. Finally, and separately again from these sources of assistance for those bringing up children, the Finance Act 2000 introduced the children's tax credit as s.257AA of the ICTA 1988, supported by Sch.13B to that Act. Despite its name, this was not a tax credit, but an income tax reduction. It only overlapped with the social security benefits in so far as the claimants of those benefits were also income tax payers. This Act sweeps away all mention of SSCBA 1992 ss.80 and 90 (but *not* s.85, which allows for increases for retirement pensioners for an adult caring for children for whom the pensioner is receiving child credit). With them go the relevant regulations. Section 257AA of ICTA 1988 also goes. So also, by regulation, does the overlap between child benefit and CTC. Any overlap with WTC is also avoided by regulation. Further regulations under s.1 were intended to transfer all child elements from all income-related benefits to CTC. That proved far harder than was anticipated. The provisions originally intended to be in place in 2004 were repeatedly postponed, and are now being phased in for new claims from 2009 as detailed in the note to s.1.

1.255

Working tax credit

Until 2012, WTC was not strictly a social security benefit. This is because, from the introduction of WTC, one element of the tax credit replaced an employment-related payment known as New Deal 50 Plus. This was an employment credit under the Employment and Training Act 1973. As its name suggests, this was a cash incentive designed to encourage those over 50 to go back to work. Further, it was paid not by the DWP but by the former Department for Education and Employment. The 50 Plus element of WTC was abolished from April 6, 2012 and the relevant legislation has been repealed or revoked from then. There is, however, a partial replacement of a credit entitlement for some individuals over 60. Arguably, what is left is now a social security payment.

1.256

WTC is stated to be a general provision for all in "qualifying remunerative work", though tantalisingly the Act does not define that central term. Rather, regulations specify what work will qualify. That specification was tightened in 2012. The definition is by reference to hours worked in a week. The requirement is:

(1) 16 hours in total from one person if the claimant is a lone parent responsible for a child or young person; or a couple responsible for a child where one partner is over 60 or qualifies for the disability element of WTC; or a couple responsible for a child where one partner is working and the other partner is incapacitated or unable to work for other specified reasons.

(2) 24 hours in total from both joint claimants if the claim is by a couple

responsible for a child and one of the partners is working 16 hours a week. (This was increased from 16 hours in 2012.)
(3) 30 hours in total if the claimant (or joint claimants) have no responsibility for children and is (or are) aged 25 or over.

How CTC and WTC developed

1.257 The tax credit system was designed as a redistributive system, with lower paid families as particular beneficiaries but also with other lower paid workers and families more generally put within its original scope. Over the decade that followed the elements of the system that helped lower paid families were increased, while those helping better paid families were allowed to reduce in level by inflation-based erosion. They have now been reduced deliberately following the emergency budget in 2010. But Chancellors gave undertakings that the main elements of CTC would be increased in line with earnings rather than inflation in the cost of living, and this has occurred. The childcare element of the system is part of WTC, not CTC, and so was not within this undertaking. At first the maximum amount payable towards child care expenses was increased, but this was later put into reverse. The effect is a reduction in the potential value of the system to lower paid working families, while those who are not required to work and can claim income support, or who are claiming jobseeker's allowance, are still assisted to the original levels set within the system.

Commencement

1.258 Section 61 (Commencement) and subsequent sections came into effect on Royal Assent (8 July 2002). Pt I (ss.1–48) is brought into effect under the Tax Credits Act 2002 (Commencement No.1) Order 2002 (SI 2002/1727) made that day. The balance of the Act was brought in by the Tax Credits Act 2002 (Commencement No.2) Order 2003 (SI 2003/392) (Pt II), the Tax Credits Act 2002 (Commencement No.3 and Transitional Provisions and Savings) Order 2003 (SI 2003/938) (the abolition of the child additions and benefits under s.1(3) of the Act) and Tax Credits Act 2002 (Commencement No.4, Transitional Provisions and Savings) Order 2003 (SI 2003/962) (the remainder).

The pattern of introduction of tax credits is as follows:

General:
July 9, 2002 regulation-making powers

For all claimants except those on income support and jobseeker's allowance:
August 1, 2002 making claims and relevant provisions
January 1, 2003 making decisions on claims
April 6, 2003 entitlements to payment of awards and abolition of child additions from all benefits save as below.

For claimants over 60 transferring to or qualifying for state pension credit:
October 1, 2003 making claims and awards.

For other claimants of income support or jobseeker's allowance:
December 31, 2008 phased introduction of CTC to all claimants.

However, tax credits are being phased out before the full introduction has been completed. See the note on *Repeal of the 2002 Act* above.

General problems with the 2002 Act

1.259 The first two years of the operation of the Tax Credits Act 2002 cannot, by any stretch of imagination, be called an outstanding success. Overall, it proved far harder to start the system than anticipated. However, the Government was proved right on one aspect of the new tax credits. Some claimed that the take-up rates for the credits would be low. This was a longstanding problem with family credit. But

(2002 c.21)

the estimated take-up for child tax credit in its first year was 80 per cent, compared to 65 per cent and 57 per cent in the first years of working families' tax credit and family credit respectively. In addition, no less than 480,000 claimants claimed nil credits (i.e. they put in protective claims in 2004–05 but did not receive anything).

General administration of tax credits proved far more complex than planned. Indeed, the government was forced to abandon its intentions of having the credits paid through people's pay packets. This was an aim of government as long ago as 1973 when family income supplement was turned into family credit. It was a firm aim of government in 2002, following the approach of s.6 of the Tax Credits Act 1999. But the 2002 Act contained a more limited measure than the original proposals. Section 25 provides for payment of working tax credit, or prescribed elements, by employers. This was never used to pay the full credit, as the childcare element was paid direct to the family. In 2004 the Chancellor announced that even the partial payment was to cease. And by April 2006 all payments by employers ceased. From then, payment is made only by HMRC.

Changes since enactment

Four aspects of the original scheme have been delayed, watered-down or abandoned: (1) all payments are made direct by HMRC and none through the pay packet; (2) CTC is yet to be made payable to all claimants of income related benefits under s.1 of the 2002 Act; (3) the power to make shared awards of CTC where there is shared responsibility for a child has not been used; and (4) despite the terms of s.7, awards are based almost entirely on income of the previous year.

1.260

Two underlying aims have been achieved. There is a significantly greater take-up of tax credits compared with previous benefits. Behind this is a regime that redistributes greater help to lower-income families. As at April 2011 6.3 million families with 10.3 million children were benefiting. At the same time the number of in-work families without children receiving WTC rose from 240,000 in 2004 to 590,000 in April 2011. However, the removal and reduction of elements of the credits combined with changes to the income thresholds have been reflected in a significant reduction in the number of tax credit claimants from 2012.

Statistics for take-up of tax credits in 2011–12 have been published by HMRC. They show a central estimate of take-up of working tax credit of 65 per cent but a continuing low take-up (33 per cent) by households with no children. Take-up of child tax credit remains high at 85 per cent claiming an estimated 93 per cent of total national entitlement.

Problems with error and fraud have abated but still remain significant. The HMRC *Error and Fraud Statistics 2012–2013* are estimates but show a central estimate of 1.5 million finalised entitlement decisions in excess of the correct amounts due to error or fraud, or 7 per cent of all finalised entitlement decisions, with 380,000 underpaid (or 0.7 per cent).

Welfare Reform Act 2012 and anti-fraud measures

The Welfare Reform Act 2012 amends the Secretary of State's powers as regards investigating benefit fraud. Previously tax credits were not classed as relevant social security benefits, and so the definition of "benefit offence" did not apply to them under the SSAA 1992.

1.261

Section 122 of WRA 2012 extends the Secretary of State's powers of investigation to cover investigations in respect of the commission, or suspected commission, of tax credit fraud by inserting a new s.109A(9) into SSAA 1992 (authorisations for investigators).

Section 123 of WRA 2012 amends s.122B of SSAA 1992 (supply of government information for fraud prevention, etc.), enabling the DWP to receive information for use in the prevention, detection, investigation or prosecution of offences relating to tax credits.

Section 125 of WRA 2012 amends Sch.4 to the SSAA 1992 (persons employed in social security administration or adjudication) so as to provide further safeguards

1.262

against inappropriate disclosure of information that DWP staff receive during the course of their employment.

These amendments were brought into force with effect from June 6, 2012 (art.2 of the Welfare Reform Act 2012 (Commencement No.2) (Amendment) Order 2012 (SI 2012/1440), amending art.2(2) of the Welfare Reform Act 2012 (Commencement No.2) Order 2012 (SI 2012/1246). Section 124 of the WRA 2012 amends s.35 of the Tax Credits Act 2002 (tax credit fraud: prosecution and penalties), but to date these amendments have not been brought into force.

PART I

TAX CREDITS

General

Introductory

1.263

1.—(1) This Act makes provision for—
 (a) a tax credit to be known as child tax credit, and
 (b) a tax credit to be known as working tax credit.

(2) In this Act references to a tax credit are to either of those tax credits and references to tax credits are to both of them.

(3) The following (which are superseded by tax credits) are abolished—
 (a) children's tax credit under section 257AA of the Income and Corporation Taxes Act 1988 (Chapter 1),
 (b) working families' tax credit,
 (c) disabled person's tax credit,
 (d) the amounts which, in relation to income support and income-based jobseeker's allowance, are prescribed as part of the applicable amount in respect of a child or young person, the family premium, the enhanced disability premium in respect of a child or young person and the disabled child premium,
 (e) increases in benefits in respect of children under sections 80 and 90 of the Social Security Contributions and Benefits Act 1992 (Chapter 4) and sections 80 and 90 of the Social Security Contributions and Benefits (Northern Ireland) Act 1992 (Chapter 7), and
 (f) the employment credit under the schemes under section 2(2) of the Employment and Training Act 1973 (Chapter 50) and section 1 of the Employment and Training Act (Northern Ireland) 1950 (Chapter 29 (NI)) known as "New Deal 50 Plus".

DEFINITIONS

"child tax credit"—see s.8.
"tax credit"—see subs.2.
"working tax credit"—see s.10.

(2002 c.21 s.1)

GENERAL NOTE

1.264

Section 1 is, as its title states, purely an introductory section. Strictly it adds nothing to the enacting provisions of Pt I, but it flags up the two kinds of tax credit payable under the Act and also the benefits repealed (by s.60 and Sch.6). Subsection (1) lists the two tax credits introduced by the Act, but (as with the rest of Pt I) is drafted so that other tax credits could be added to the list in the sub, and the machinery sections of the Act (which apply to "tax credits" as defined in subs. (2)) would then apply to the new tax credits also. At the date of writing, no specific further tax credits have been suggested. The abolition of the child premiums to income support and JSA were deferred to December 31, 2008, and deferred again to December 31, 2011, and then to December 2014 and finally indefinitely.

Indeed, it has proved harder than anticipated to introduce child tax credits for those on income support and jobseeker's allowance. It is understood that there are many cases where one parent of a child is claiming one of these benefits with child addition while the other parent is claiming child tax credit for the same child or children. In *CSTC/326/2003* Commissioner Parker considered an argument that the measures taken to postpone the introduction of s.1(3)(d) discriminated against those receiving income support as against those who received the tax credits direct. The appellant's wife received income support. Entitlement to child tax credit was higher than to income support. But under the transitional legislation the appellant could claim CTC only from the date of his claim. No backdating was allowed. The appellant argued that either this was ultra vires the TCA 2002 or it was discriminatory under the European Convention on Human Rights. The Commissioner rejected both arguments. In dealing with somewhat unfocussed arguments about the European Convention on Human Rights, the Commissioner took the view that CTC is a means-tested social security benefit but assumed for the purposes of argument that both art.8 of, and art.1, Protocol 1 to, the Convention were engaged. She then considered if there was discrimination within the meaning of art.14 but found none. Her decision reveals that the process of suspending s.1(3)(d) while benefit claimants are "migrated" to it as being in some confusion. Of the relevant subordinate legislation (in particular SI 2005/773, SI 2005/776 and SI 2005/1106), she comments (at [16]):

"the last minute nature of the amendment order, the curiosity of two substantially overlapping measures produced on the same day (the transitional provisions order 2005 and the second transitional provisions order), a draft order which was never laid, and the failure to enact a consistent statutory scheme of backdating to prevent double recovery, indicate a history of some haste and confusion by the legislators. There has been a complex web of measures, note always successful, necessitated because the prospects for the completion of intended migration seem ever to recede."

[¹Function of Commissioners

2. The Commissioners for Her Majesty's Revenue and Customs shall be responsible for the payment and management of tax credits.]

1.265

AMENDMENT

1. Commissioners for Revenue and Customs Act 2005 Sch.4 para.88 (April 6, 2005).

DEFINITIONS

"tax credits"—see s.1(2).
"the Commissioners for Revenue and Customs"—see CRCA 2005 s.4.

Tax Credits Act 2002

GENERAL NOTE

1.266   This short section replaced its lengthy predecessor as CRCA 2005 came into effect. That Act repealed and replaced the Inland Revenue Regulation Act 1890 to which this section previously referred. All necessary provisions for both the payment of tax credits (and repayment) and management and administration are now either in the CRCA 2005 or this Act. The wording of this section reflects the similar wording in CRCA 2005 applying also to taxes, duties and benefits. See the general note to CRCA 2005 about the powers to transfer these functions back to the Treasury and HMRC as part of the staged abolition of tax credits.

The Tax Credits (Exercise of Functions) Order 2014 (SI 2014/3280), made on December 10, 2014, empowers the Secretary of State to exercise some tax credit functions concurrently with HMRC. From April 1, 2015 those functions are the recovery of overpayments and of any penalty imposed.

Claims

1.267   **3.**—(1) Entitlement to a tax credit for the whole or part of a tax year is dependent on the making of a claim for it.

(2) Where the Board—
  (a) decide under section 14 not to make an award of a tax credit on a claim, or
  (b) decide under section 16 to terminate an award of a tax credit made on a claim,
(subject to any appeal) any entitlement, or subsequent entitlement, to the tax credit for any part of the same tax year is dependent on the making of a new claim.

(3) A claim for a tax credit may be made—
  (a) jointly by the members of a [²couple] both of whom are aged at least sixteen and are in the United Kingdom [(and neither of whom are members of a polygamous unit)]¹; or
  [(aa) jointly by the members of a polygamous unit all of whom are aged at least sixteen and are in the United Kingdom, or]¹;
  (b) by a person who is aged at least sixteen and is in the United Kingdom but is not entitled to make a claim under paragraph (a) (jointly with another).

(4) Entitlement to a tax credit pursuant to a claim ceases—
  (a) in the case of a joint claim, if the persons by whom it was made could no longer jointly make a joint claim; and
  [(aa) in the case of a joint claim under subsection (3)(a), if a member of the [²couple] becomes a member of a polygamous unit, and
  (ab) in the case of a joint claim under subsection (3)(aa), if there is any change in the persons who comprise the polygamous unit, and]¹
  (b) in the case of a single claim, if the person by whom it was made could no longer make a single claim.

(5) [² . . .

(5A) In this Part "couple" means—
  (a) a man and woman who are married to each other and are neither—
    (i) separated under a court order, nor
    (ii) separated in circumstances in which the separation is likely to be permanent,
  (b) a man and woman who are not married to each other but are living together as husband and wife,

(c) two people of the same sex who are civil partners of each other and are neither—
  (i) separated under a court order, nor
  (ii) separated in circumstances in which the separation is likely to be permanent, or
(d) two people of the same sex who are not civil partners of each other but are living together as if they were civil partners.]
(6) [². . .]
[(6A) In this Part, "polygamous unit" has the meaning given by regulation 2 of the Tax Credits (Polygamous Marriages) Regulations 2003.]¹
(7) Circumstances may be prescribed in which a person is to be treated for the purposes of this Part as being, or as not being, in the United Kingdom.
(8) In this Part—
  "joint claim" means a claim under paragraph (a) [or (aa)]¹ of subsection (3), and
  "single claim" means a claim under paragraph (b) of that subsection.

AMENDMENTS

1. Modifications for the purposes of application to polygamous units by Tax Credits (Polygamous Marriages) Regulations 2003 (SI 2003/742) reg.4 (April 6, 2003).
2. Civil Partnership Act 2004 s.254 and Sch.24 para.144 (December 5, 2005).

DEFINITIONS

"award"—see s.14(1).
"the Board"—see s.67.
"claim"—see subs.(1), s.4.
"couple"—see subs.(5A).
"entitlement"—see s.18(1).
"joint claim"—see subs.(8).
"prescribed"—see s.67.
"single claim"—see subs.(8).
"tax credit"—see s.1(2).
"tax year"—see s.47.

GENERAL NOTE

This is the first of the sections in the Act that create the necessary compromise for tax credits between the general approach of income tax administration and the general approach of social security administration. Subsection (1) adopts and adapts the requirement from SSAA 1992 s.1(1), that there can be no entitlement to a tax credit without a claim. Subsection (2) reinforces this. Subsections (3) and following set out both the main conditions for making a claim and the requirement that both (or all) those who are partners to a marriage (or equivalent) join in making the claim. Subsection (8) adopts appropriate definitions for joint and single claims. There is also a definition of "claimant" in s.9(8), which would be better placed here in subs.(8).

Determining when a claim is made is important because of the operation of the "three month" rule for a new claim following some changes of circumstances. The ability to make claims by telephone or email in addition to the traditional posted claim means that this may be a matter to be determined on appeal in the light of conflicting evidence from the claimants and HMRC. See *CSIS/48/1992* for the presumption that a document that can be served by post is delivered in ordinary course of post. HMRC treat the rule with a little generosity because it directs staff to assume that for these purposes three months is always 91 days and a single month always has 31 days.

1.268

Subsection (1)

1.269 This requires a claim before any award can be made under s.14. If no valid claim is made, then HMRC cannot make an award. HMRC take the view that it is for HMRC to decide if a claim is valid in accordance with reg.5(1) of the Tax Credits (Claims and Notifications) Regulations 2002 (see below), and that the decision is not appealable. On the latter argument, see note to s.38 (Appeals) below.

The standard claim form is TC600 for new claims. In practice claims can be made over the telephone. See TC(Claims and Notifications) Regs 2002 reg.5 and *CIS/995/2004* discussed at para.2.276 below. Further, although renewal claims are needed each year, a renewal claim may be treated as being made as the procedure for checking a past claim takes place at the end of that year of claim.

HMRC have accepted that it is appropriate in some cases to make protective claims where a claim will lead to a nil award on the then current information about income, but where a claimant may later in the tax year be entitled to tax credits. In such cases, nil awards will be made. See *Tax Adviser*, June 2003, p.13. HMRC statistics show that in December 2006 there were about 0.8 million claimants with zero awards. This suggests that these claims have become standard practice for many advisers, as the total number of recipients of credit had not risen in the previous two years while the number of zero awards doubled. Another explanation is that 0.6 million lower paid individuals (perhaps self-employed) without children now receive zero awards, and the number of such claimants also doubled in that period. Another reason is that HMRC may revise an award to zero rather than cancel it when a claimant is no longer entitled to receive a positive award. However, the abolition of the family element from 2012 will now have affected these figures.

Subsection (2)

1.270 This adopts in part a policy of SSA 1998 s.8, that a claim ceases to have effect when a decision has been made on it. A new claim is required if the Board refuses or ends a tax credit award for a tax year and for any reason the claimant wants that decision revisited. In practice, however, the Board may choose to make a "nil" award, so leaving the matter open to review if circumstances change, rather than a reclaim.

Subsection (3)

1.271 This is the primary provision entitling a claim to be made. It imposes a series of conditions on all claimants:
   (a) if a claimant is one of a married or unmarried couple (or of a polygamous unit) then the claim can only be made in the names of both (or all) of them;
   (b) the claimant or claimants must be over 16; and
   (c) the claimant or claimants (and if more than one, all) must be "in the UK".

The following subsections make provisions for those conditions. But s.42 excludes those subject to immigration control from entitlement except in specified cases. The approach of requiring joint claims is also reinforced by s.4(1)(g), which enables regulations to treat a single claim as a joint claim. This has been extended by regulations under s.43 to cover polygamous units, the policy again being that all the members of a polygamous unit must be linked to the claim.

Following the enactment of the Gender Recognition Act 2004, HMRC have issued guidance that if an individual has gender recognition certificate issues under the Act, then this will or affect the status of the individual as a single or joint claimant: see TCTM 06100. However, there will be a potential interaction with the new definition of "couple" following the enactment of the Civil Partnership Act 2004. See below.

1.272 In *CSTC/724/2006* the Commissioner considered the application of subs.(3)(a) and (b) to an entitlement decision under s.19. The Commissioner followed the comments of the deputy Commissioner in *CTC/3864/2004* (an appeal about a s.16 decision) in confirming that the paragraphs are mutually exclusive. An individual cannot acquire entitlement to a tax credit if he or she did not claim it. The

Commissioner rejected a decision of a tribunal that took the view that HMRC had the power to amend an award to take into account that the claimant became one of a couple. The appropriate single and joint claims must remain exclusive. Therefore a member of a couple who made a claim as a single claimant could have no entitlement to tax credits in either capacity. The other member of the couple could not be made liable for any overpayment in respect of any such decision if he or she was not a claimant.

For discussion of the importance of proper fact-finding in cases of separating spouses, see *HMRC v PD (TC)* [2012] UKUT 230 (AAC). Judge Lane held on the facts that although a separating married couple were living in the same house, they were no longer living in the same household at the material time. And see also the comments of Judge Rowland in *JI v HMRC* [2013] UKUT 199 (AAC) about the scope for treating notification of a breakup of a relationship as a new claim for child tax credits for children of the household.

In *CTC/1853/2009* it was held that claimants resident not in the UK but elsewhere in the European Union could not claim child tax credit under art.77 of Council Regulation (EEC) 1408/71. This was agreed in *EM v HMRC (TC)* [2010] UKUT 323 (AAC), although it was commented that in some circumstances there might be a claim under other European legislation. However, both judges noted that the Regulation was replaced by Council Regulation (EC) 883/2004 from May 2010. HMRC will now pay child tax credit to claimants such as those in these appeals (payment having been stopped in both cases).

HMRC is reminding all claimants by letter of the need to report a change of circumstances, including in particular whether a claim should be a joint claim or single claim. This followed recognition that in 2008-09 150,000 claims (2.5 per cent of the total) were incorrect single claims.

1.273

One situation not expressly covered by this provision is that of a married couple who are not formally separated but only one of whom is "in the United Kingdom" as defined in the Tax Credits (Residence) Regulations 2003 (see para.2.408 below). If one of a married couple is ordinarily resident in the UK but the other is not, then the resident spouse should make a single claim. For that purpose, the non-resident spouse's income is not relevant to the claim.

For cases with an EU dimension, see *EG v HMRC (TC)* [2011] UKUT 467 (AAC). The two joint claimants, who were both UK nationals, were a married couple, and neither legally separated or estranged. However, they maintained separate residences: the husband throughout being both resident and ordinarily resident in the UK, but the wife, who received UK incapacity benefit, being resident in Spain and not ordinarily resident in the UK. The claim was in respect of their children, who at all times lived with their mother in Spain. Judge Howell QC held that she was within the provision in art.73 of Council Regulation 1408/71/EEC, namely that an "employed person subject to the legislation of a member state" is to be entitled to family benefits (which include child tax credits) in respect of members of his or her family residing in another Member State. The UK was the competent member state in relation to her social insurance for the relevant year as she was neither employed or self-employed in Spain at that time. It followed that she was entitled to participate in the joint claim by virtue of art.73 of EU Regulation 1408/71, disapplying the national condition about her own residence, and a decision was accordingly given confirming their entitlement to the child tax credits for that year. For discussion of art.73 and its replacement by arts 67 and following of Regulation 883/2004 of Vol.III of this work.

Subsection (4)

This is designed to stop the claim under subs.(3) continuing if the identity of the claimant(s) changes because an individual gains a partner, a couple breaks up, or a polygamous unit changes membership. But it deals with *entitlement* not *award*, and its inclusion at this point in this section is a little obscure. It links with the provisions on joint claims (or deemed joint claims) to withdraw *entitlement* where joint claimants are no longer *entitled to make* a joint claim, thus stopping both joint claims and claims

1.274

deemed to be joint. Nonetheless its interaction with ss.17 and 18 and with a continuing *award* is not clear. It appears to suggest that an award can continue without underlying entitlement. However, under the Tax Credits (Claims and Notifications) Regulations 2002 (SI 2002/2014) reg.21, notification must be given whenever a joint claim should become a single claim, or the reverse. In practice, this applies to awards as much as to entitlement. See further *JL v HMRC (TC)* [2013] UKUT 325, discussed in the commentary to reg.21 of the Claims and Notifications Regulations.

Subsections (5A), (6A)

1.275 The original subs.(5) defined "married couple" and subs.(6) defined "unmarried couple". Both definitions have been replaced under the Civil Partnership Act 2004, but the new subsections reflect the former compromise between the income tax definition of a married couple (see ICTA s.282) and the social security definition (see Vol.II of this work for SSCBA 1992 s.137).

If the couple are husband and wife, the explicit questions in subs.(5A)(a) are whether they are separated, and if so in what way. As Judge Lane emphasised in *HMRC v PD* [2012] UKUT 230 (AAC), behind the statutory language is the determination whether the couple are sharing a household. In that case the judge found as fact that the married couple who were appealing against a decision that they had to make a joint claim were separated although living in the same building, and a joint claim was not required. This follows from the jurisprudence in family law establishing that couples may be living apart—that is, not as members of one household—although they are under the same roof. See also the decision of Judge Lane in *SW v SSWP* [2011] UKUT 145 (AAC).

In *DG v HMRC (TC)* [2013] UKUT 0631 (AAC) Judge Wikeley emphasised that the statutory definition of a married couple is deliberately phrased in a different way to the standard social security definition. He also cautioned against adopting from family law the definition in the Matrimonial Causes Act 1973. He concluded on the facts of the case that a woman who was living both in the same house and in the same household as her husband was, nonetheless, separated from him for tax credit purposes. Consequently, he upheld the wife's appeal against a First-tier Tribunal decision to the opposite effect. More generally, he declined to follow the decision in *HMRC v PD (TC)* [2012] UKUT 230 (AAC) insofar as it took a contrary view. He also commented on HMRC guidance about any necessity for a separation between spouses to be formalised.

1.276 Decisions by HMRC that two individuals are a couple and should be making a joint claim continue to cause disputes. Commissioners have commented in several decisions on the approach to be taken. In *CTC/3059/2004* a deputy Commissioner decided that an appellant and her husband-to-be were not, on the facts, living together as wife and husband before their marriage although both HMRC and the tribunal had found that they were. (HMRC later supported the appeal to the Commissioner on the basis that the tribunal's findings of fact had gone beyond the evidence.) Deputy Commissioner White held:

> "12. Though the term 'unmarried couple' is defined in the Tax Credits Act 2002, the concept of 'living together as husband and wife' is not defined in the legislation. There appears to be no dispute that it is appropriate to use the guidance provided in Commissioners' decisions in relation to other benefits in considering such questions when they arise in relation to tax credits. I agree that the framework established in relation to other benefits is helpful.
> 13. That framework (*the Commissioner referred to Volume II*) indicates that a number of factors should be considered as a whole in deciding whether, on the balance of probabilities, a man and a woman are living together as husband and wife."

The Deputy Commissioner then examined the facts by reference to: where the husband-to-be lived; financial support; sexual relationship; stability of relationship; care of the children of the wife-to-be; and public acknowledgement. He accepted that there were difficulties in using the latter three factors with regard to an engaged couple. However, he concluded on the evidence that the engaged couple were not living together.

In *CTC/3864/2004* Deputy Commissioner Green held that HMRC and another tribunal had erred on the same question, and again HMRC supported the claimant's appeal. It is to be noted that one ground on which HMRC supported the appeal was that the tribunal failed to provide an explanation why they did not find all the claimant's evidence reliable. The Deputy Commissioner agreed, commenting that the tribunal had on one point rejected the claimant's evidence although that was the only evidence before the tribunal on that point. It may be that the HMRC support on this point reflects an HMRC expectation that it might expect to have to meet more exacting standards of evidence as to truth and credibility when appearing before the tax tribunals. More generally, Deputy Commissioner Green took the same approach as in *CTC/3059/2004* (although without reference to it) in adopting the decisions of social security commissioners on the question of living together and referring to the guidance formerly in the *Supplementary Benefits Handbook* and in *R(SB) 17/81*.

In *R(TC) 2/05* a deputy Commissioner considered the importance in what has become subs.(5A) of the test of "separated in circumstances in which the separation is likely to be permanent". The context was a claim by a wife whose marriage to her husband was in difficulties. Divorce proceedings had been put on hold after they were started. HMRC decided that the claim she made should have been a joint claim. The tribunal agreed, but that decision was set aside. The deputy Commissioner emphasised the importance in cases such as this of making proper decisions about the credibility of a claimant. In this case the tribunal failed to deal adequately with the claimant's oral evidence and also with correspondence produced by her from others about the status of the marriage. But he does not deal with the question of obtaining evidence from the husband. In *HMRC v PD (TC)* [2012] UKUT 230 (AAC) Judge Lane emphasised that although there is no express mention of a common household in s.3(5A) this was implicit in determining if a couple were living together.

1.277

In *CTC/2090/2004* Commissioner Bano dealt with some of the consequences of competing claims for child tax credit. He resisted an argument put by HMRC that the appeal tribunal should have summonsed the mother to give evidence before finding for the father on a claim made by him. He also raised issues about the duty on HMRC itself in such a situation. In *CTC/3543/2004* Commissioner Jacobs considered who are the parties to proceedings in cases where there are joint claims. In his view where there is a joint claim both the claimants must be parties to any proceedings against one of them. The Commissioner referred to both SSA 1998 s.14(3)(d) and the Social Security and Child Support (Decisions and Appeals) Regulations 1999 reg.1(2) to decide that if there is an overpayment relating to a joint claim then both the claimants must be parties to the proceedings even if only one has appealed. Conversely it would follow that where a claim should be a joint claim but is not, the non-claimant is not automatically subject to a decision against the claimant.

See the note to s.6 for the effect of the introduction of the potential change of status of couples who become civil partners after December 5, 2005 while one or both of them is receiving tax credits, or who are to be treated as if they are living together as civil partners from that date while one or both is claiming tax credits. Anyone making a new claim after that date must disclose if she or he has a civil partner or is living together with another person as civil partners.

HMRC issues extensive guidance about identifying couples and related questions. See *Tax Credits Claims Compliance Manual* paragraphs CCM 15000–CCM 15350. This guidance is of course not binding on tribunals. CCM 15040 follows the standard DWP approach to identifying who are a couple, save that the reference to sexual relationships is omitted. CCM 15120 confirms the policy and gives officials the following guidance:

1.278

"Appeal tribunals sometimes ask claimants about their sexual relationships, however, it remains our policy that you must not ask such questions. If a tribunal asks you why you have not established the position you should say that our

Tax Credits Act 2002

internal policy, in common with that in DWP, is not to ask about this side of the relationship."

CCM 15045 stresses the nature of "modern-day relationships":

"By 2004, 70% of first domestic partnerships involved unmarried couples and it is now common for each party in a couple to work full-time, keep their own incomes and bank accounts and perhaps only pay money into a joint account for items of joint responsibility. Often because of demands on time both parties share childcare and domestic tasks."

In *SS v HMRC (TC)* [2014] UKUT 383 (AAC) Judge Rowley gives a close and critical analysis of the conduct of decision-making by HMRC officers and a First-tier Tribunal about whether two adults were a couple. The decision is critical of both HMRC and the tribunal but in discussion the judge examines the evidence that both parties put and should have put before the tribunal and the approach the tribunal should have taken.

Subsection (7)

1.279　This allows jurisdictional limits to be placed on entitlement to tax credit. Again, this breaks away from social security practice (which deals with Great Britain and Northern Ireland separately) to adopt income tax practice. It is supplemented by s.42 (persons subject to immigration control) and regulations made under that section. The main regulations under this subsection are the Tax Credits (Residence) Regulations 2003 (SI 2003/642). These impose a test of "ordinary residence" on most claimants.

Claims: supplementary

1.280　**4.**—(1) Regulations may—
 (a) require a claim for a tax credit to be made in a prescribed manner and within a prescribed time,
 (b) provide for a claim for a tax credit made in prescribed circumstances to be treated as having been made on a prescribed date earlier or later than that on which it is made,
 (c) provide that, in prescribed circumstances, a claim for a tax credit may be made for a period wholly or partly after the date on which it is made,
 (d) provide that, in prescribed circumstances, an award on a claim for a tax credit may be made subject to the condition that the requirements for entitlement are satisfied at a prescribed time,
 (e) provide for a claim for a tax credit to be made or proceeded with in the name of a person who has died,
 (f) provide that, in prescribed circumstances, one person may act for another in making a claim for a tax credit,
 (g) provide that, in prescribed circumstances, a claim for a tax credit made by one member of a [². . .] couple is to be treated as also made by the other member of [² the couple]¹, and
 (h) provide that a claim for a tax credit is to be treated as made by a person or persons in such other circumstances as may be prescribed.
 (2) The Board may supply to a person who has made a claim for a tax credit (whether or not jointly with another)—
 (a) any information relating to the claim, to an award made on the claim or to any change of circumstances relevant to the claim or such an award,
 (b) any communication made or received relating to such an award or any such change of circumstances, and
 (c) any other information which is relevant to any entitlement to tax credits

(2002 c.21 s.4)

pursuant to the claim or any such change of circumstances or which appeared to be so relevant at the time the information was supplied.

AMENDMENTS

1. Tax Credits (Polygamous Marriages) Regulations 2003 (SI 2003/742) amends s.4(1)(g) as follows for the purposes of polygamous marriages:
"In section 4(1)(g)—
  (a) for 'member of a married couple or an unmarried couple' substitute 'or more members of a polygamous unit';
  (b) for 'of the married couple or unmarried couple' substitute 'or members'."
2. Civil Partnership Act 2004 s.254 and Sch.24 para.145 (December 5, 2005).

DEFINITIONS

"award"—see s.14(1).
"the Board"—see s.67.
"claim"—see s.3(1).
"couple"—see s.3(5A).
"entitlement"—see s.18(1).
"joint claim"—see s.3(8).
"prescribed"—see s.67.
"single claim"—see s.3(8).
"tax credit"—see s.1(2).
"tax year"—see s.47.

GENERAL NOTE

Regulations for the purposes of subs.(1) are made by HMRC by negative procedure: ss.65(2) and 66(3). The main regulations made are the Tax Credits (Claims and Notifications) Regulations 2002 (SI 2002/2014). References to "the Board" are now references to the Commissioners for Revenue and Customs: CRCA 2005 s.4.

The most important point relevant to this section is that, from 2012/13, a claim must be made not later than 31 days after the date on which it can operate. For a claim to be effective from the beginning of a tax year, it must therefore be made not later than May 6 in that year. If made later, it will operate back only 31 days from the date of claim. There is no discretion to extent this back-dating rule, although it was previously 93 days, and the only exception applies to claims where there is a disability element. See regs 7 and 8 of those regulations.

Subsection (2) gives HMRC power that it would otherwise not have to inform a claimant of information of which it knows that is relevant to a claim, or to an award or entitlement continuing. This will ensure that either member of a joint claiming couple can be informed of anything that the other member of the couple tells HMRC. This cuts across the privacy as between members of a couple that was respected by HMRC following the introduction of individual self-assessment for income tax.

1.281

Period of awards

5.—(1) Where a tax credit is claimed for a tax year by making a claim before the tax year begins, any award of the tax credit on the claim is for the whole of the tax year.

(2) An award on any other claim for a tax credit is for the period beginning with the date on which the claim is made and ending at the end of the tax year in which that date falls.

(3) Subsections (1) and (2) are subject to any decision by the Board under section 16 to terminate an award.

1.282

DEFINITIONS

"award"—see s.14(1).
"the Board"—see s.67.
"claim"—see s.3(1).
"tax credit"—see s.1(2).
"tax year"—see s.47.

GENERAL NOTE

1.283   This section applies to both CTC and WTC. It confirms the import of s.3(1), namely that a claim is for one tax year at a time, and provides that any award is for that tax year (or, if made during the year, for what is left of it). This is subject to the power in s.16 to end an award, after which a new claim must be made (s.3(2)). Effect is given to these provisions by the Tax Credits (Claims and Notifications) Regulations 2002 (SI 2002/2014) regs 4–11. Regulations 11 and 12 of those regulations provide a mechanism whereby a reply to a notice relating to one year of claim under s.17 of this Act can be treated as a claim for the following year.

Subsection (2), on its face, prevents retrospective claims, but it must be read with reg.4 and following of the Tax Credits (Claims and Notifications) Regulations 2002. These make provision for the "date on which a claim is made". Under reg.7, the general rule is that a claim is treated as made for the purposes of this subsection up to three months before the date on which the claim is received by an appropriate office, if *entitlement* extends that far back. This, like other issues about *award* and *entitlement*, seems to conflate the making of an award with entitlement (see the note to s.6). It will only be known that a person is entitled once a final decision is made under s.17 of this Act after the end of the year, while the award operates on the basis that the person is probably entitled.

See also Tax Credits Act 2002 (Transitional Provisions) Order 2005 (SI 2005/773) art.6.

Notifications of changes of circumstances

1.284   **6.**—(1) Regulations may provide that any change of circumstances of a prescribed description which may increase the maximum rate at which a person or persons may be entitled to a tax credit is to do so only if notification of it has been given.

(2) Regulations under subsection (1) may—
(a) provide for notification of a change of circumstances given in prescribed circumstances to be treated as having been given on a prescribed date earlier or later than that on which it is given,
(b) provide that, in prescribed circumstances, a notification of a change of circumstances may be given for a period wholly or partly after the date on which it is given, and
(c) provide that, in prescribed circumstances, an amendment of an award of a tax credit in consequence of a notification of a change of circumstances may be made subject to the condition that the requirements for entitlement to the amended amount of the tax credit are satisfied at a prescribed time.

(3) Regulations may require that, where a person has or persons have claimed a tax credit, notification is to be given if there is a change of circumstances of a prescribed description which may decrease the rate at which he is or they are entitled to the tax credit or mean that he ceases or they cease to be entitled to the tax credit.

[1(3A) For the purposes of this section, a change of circumstances shall

(2002 c.21 s.6)

be treated as having occurred where by virtue of the coming into force of Part 14 of Schedule 24 to the Civil Partnership Act 2004 (amendments of the Tax Credits Act 2002) two people of the same sex are treated as a couple.

(3B) In subsection (3A), "couple" has the meaning given in paragraph 144(3) of Part 14 of Schedule 24 to the Civil Partnership Act 2004.]

(4) Regulations under this section may—
(a) require a notification to be given in a prescribed manner and within a prescribed time,
(b) specify the person or persons by whom a notification may be, or is to be, given, and
(c) provide that, in prescribed circumstances, one person may act for another in giving a notification.

AMENDMENT

1. Tax Credits Notification of Changes of Circumstances (Civil Partnership) (Transitional Provisions) Order 2005 (SI 2005/828) art.2 (April 8, 2005). Note that these provisions have effect only for the tax year 2005/06.

DEFINITIONS

"award"—see s.14(1).
"claim"—see s.3(1).
"entitlement"—see s.18(1).
"maximum rate"—see ss.9 and 11.
"prescribed"—see s.67.
"tax credit"—see s.1(2).

GENERAL NOTE

The Bill on which this Act was based was tabled in, and passed through, the House of Commons without a clear distinction being drawn between the measures relating to *award* of a tax credit on a claim and the later issue of *entitlement* to that credit. As a result, there is no clear progression in the sections of the Act from claims to award to entitlement. This section might from context appear to be about awards, but subs.(1) is drafted to cover only entitlement issues. The link is provided partly under subs.(2) and partly by s.15, which links changes in awards to the rate at which someone *may be* entitled to a tax credit.

"Change of circumstances" is, of course, a familiar social security concept on which the SSA 1998 relies heavily for powers to change decisions after they are made but where they have continuing effect. There is also a general duty on claimants to report changes of circumstances of relevance to benefit awards. This section allows a similar duty to be imposed on tax credit claimants. The section is purely empowering. Regulations may be made by the Revenue by negative procedure: ss.65(2) and 66(3). The relevant regulations are the Tax Credits (Claims and Notifications) Regulations 2002 (SI 2002/2014) regs 19–29. Those regulations, however, take a substantially different approach to changes of circumstances to those operated for social security benefits.

The nature of a "change of circumstances" and the treatment adopted for making and dealing with changes of circumstance requires some further explanation because of the differences in the ways in which the rules operate compared with those for income support or jobseeker's allowance. The main differences are:
(a) not all changes of circumstances during a year will result in a change of circumstances affecting the award or entitlement;
(b) the duty to notify changes of circumstances is limited in scope and applies only to some changes;

1.285

(c) failure to notify when there is a duty to do so may make the person failing to notify liable to penalties and penalty proceedings under ss.31(1) and 32(3).

Relevant changes of circumstances

1.286 Because the income test under s.7 is applied to the tax year (or period of award) as a whole, a change in income levels during a year may be irrelevant to award or entitlement levels, and so not constitute a change of circumstances. This will be particularly so towards the end of a tax year. Further, because of the "buffer" built into the income test by s.7(3), any increase of income over the year as a whole of less than £10,000 is irrelevant in any event. Changes in capital are also immaterial, as it is only the (taxable) income from capital that affects the level of award and entitlement. For similar reasons, a change of job (with a gap of under seven days between jobs) will also not affect an award or entitlement unless either it changes the income level significantly over the year as a whole or it decreases the hours worked below 16, or—for WTC only—it increases or decreases the hours above or below 30.

The changes that are relevant are significant income changes, as noted above, and other changes that will stop entitlement or cause its overall level to be changed. This may apply differently to CTC and WTC. But not all those changes must be reported. Nonetheless, this remains a very wide provision, and notification may affect the start date for an award even if it does not affect the weekly amount. For example, take the case of disablement leading to a claim for disability living allowance and for a disability element to a tax credit claim. Regulation 26A of the Tax Credits (Claims and Notifications) Regulations 2002 (para.2.324 below) assumes that the date of claim for DLA and the date on which it is first payable both represent changes of circumstances, as will the date of award or of any increase or decrease in award, and the date on which an individual becomes disabled or more or less disabled.

Changes that must be reported

1.287 There is no general duty to report all changes of circumstances, although it may be in a claimant's interest to do so. See Code of Practice 26 at the end of this volume.

HMRC handle the issue of changes by requiring some changes to be reported within one month of the change. The list of items that must be reported within one month is in reg.21 of the Tax Credits (Claims and Notifications) Regulations 2002. See para.2.307 below.

Changes that may be reported

1.288 Under regs 20 and 25 of the Tax Credits (Claims and Notifications) Regulations 2002, a change of circumstances that may increase an award or entitlement to either WTC or CTC will only do so if notification of the change has been given to HMRC within three months of the date when the change occurred. Later notice will be backdated not more than three months. This time limit is, however, extended under reg.26 for those claiming the disability or severe disability elements of WTC. In all other cases, notification of any change of circumstances that will or may benefit the claimant should be made within the three months' limit to prevent both loss of award and loss of entitlement.

Current HMRC guidance on voluntary reporting is:

"You do not have to tell us about the following changes, but it is in your interest to do so because they may increase the amount of tax credits you are due. Please tell us if:

- A young person over 16 continues in full time education, registers with a careers service, Connexions, or equivalent, or joins an approved Government

(2002 c.21 s.6)

training scheme. If you do not tell us, their Child Tax Credit will stop on 1st September after their 16th birthday.
- Your income goes down.
- Your income goes up. This may not affect your current tax credits, but it will affect how much we should pay you for next year. If we pay you too much because you delay telling us about any changes, you will be asked to pay back any tax credits overpaid.
- Your child care costs go up by £10 a week or more.
- Your usual working hours change from less than 16 hours a week to 16 or more.
- Your usual working hours change from less than 30 hours a week to 30 or more. For couples with children, it is your joint working hours that count towards the 30 hours.
- To report a change please call the tax credits Helpline on 0845 300 3900. The lines are open from 8.00am–8.00pm seven days a week."

Where changes are reported, HMRC practice is to issue a new award notice based on the details reported. Claimants are asked to check the award notice and report any errors. They are also asked to enquire if they do not receive a new award notice within one month of notifying the changes. See s.15 and COP 26 below.

Automatic notification?

Part II of this Act transfers responsibility for child benefit to HMRC. The decision of the House of Lords in *Hinchy v Secretary of State for Work and Pensions* [2005] UKHL 16 confirms the traditional view that a claimant must tell the relevant office about changes of circumstances. It is therefore not enough that, for example, a claimant tells the HMRC Child Benefit Office but not the tax credits office or the local social security office or housing benefit authority of the changed position of one of the claimant's children. However, the growth of public computer-based records and the interlinking of records between departments under the Generalised Matching Service increasingly notifies one department of information known to another. That is no defence under the tax credit scheme to liability to repay any overpaid tax credit. It will be for consideration whether this is relevant to any penalty proceedings under ss.31 or 32. It is understood that HMRC is notified automatically about decisions of the termination of disability living allowance awards.

1.289

See also *WW v HM Revenue and Customs* [2011] UKUT 11 (AAC), where an Upper Tribunal judge held that a DWP officer had ostensible authority to make oral representations to a claimant about onward transmission to HMRC of changes of circumstances about child benefit entitlement. However, as the judge pointed out, there is also a continuing duty to disclose where a change of circumstances continues.

Failure to report

Leaving aside fraudulent or other cases of deliberate non-disclosure, if a change of circumstances is not reported when it happens it will be picked up directly or indirectly when the claimant replies to HMRC's final notice issued under s.17. This is because of the declaration necessary under s.17. If it is a relevant change, then the entitlement to WTC and/or CTC will be confirmed at a different rate to that of the award. This will result in an overpayment (see s.28) if the level of award is, as a result, higher than the level of entitlement. It could also result in an underpayment (see s.30), but only to the extent that the notification is regarded as in time for any part of the relevant tax year. In most cases, if the notification is more than three months after the end of the tax year then the right to an increased entitlement will have been lost.

1.290

HMRC has announced that it will not seek penalties from a taxpayer who has a nil award following a claim and who then fails to make a mandatory notification of a change of circumstances. See *Tax Adviser*, June 2003, p.13.

Tax Credits Act 2002

Both the Parliamentary Ombudsman and the Citizens Advice Bureaux published further reports about tax credits in October 2007. *Tax Credits: Getting it wrong?* was published as the 5th Report of the Parliamentary Ombudsman (HC 1010, Session 2006–07). The report contains detailed case studies about, in particular, overpayments and their recovery, and notes that complaints about tax credits continue to form a growing part of the workload of the Ombudsman. In the year starting on April 1, 2007 to the end of August, tax credits complaints formed 26 per cent of the Ombudsman's workload, and three quarters of those complaints were upheld either in whole or in part. It also comments on the complaints and appeals procedures. Nearly all current complaints are about overpayments.

The National Association of Citizens Advice Bureaux published a report at the same time entitled *Tax Credits: the current picture*. This summarises the comments of 1,500 respondents to a survey on their experiences of tax credits—drawn from 186,000 people helped by CABs in handling their tax credits in the last year. The report notes as worrying the number of respondents who stopped claiming tax credits because of the problems involved.

Income test

1.291

7.—(1) The entitlement of a person or persons of any description to a tax credit is dependent on the relevant income—
- (a) not exceeding the amount determined in the manner prescribed for the purposes of this paragraph in relation to the tax credit and a person or persons of that description (referred to in this Part as the income threshold), or
- (b) exceeding the income threshold by only so much that a determination in accordance with regulations under section 13(2) provides a rate of the tax credit in his or their case.

(2) Subsection (1) does not apply in relation to the entitlement of a person or persons to a tax credit for so long as the person, or either of the persons, is entitled to any social security benefit prescribed for the purposes of this subsection in relation to the tax credit.

(3) In this Part "the relevant income" means—
- (a) if an amount is prescribed for the purposes of this paragraph and the current year income exceeds the previous year income by not more than that amount, the previous year income,
- (b) if an amount is prescribed for the purposes of this paragraph and the current year income exceeds the previous year income by more than that amount, the current year income reduced by that amount,
- (c) if an amount is prescribed for the purposes of this paragraph and the previous year income exceeds the current year income by not more than that amount, the previous year income,
- (d) if an amount is prescribed for the purposes of this paragraph and the previous year income exceeds the current year income by more than that amount, the current year income increased by that amount, and
- (e) otherwise, the current year income.

(4) In this Part "the current year income" means—
- (a) in relation to persons by whom a joint claim for a tax credit is made, the aggregate income of the persons for the tax year to which the claim relates, and

(b) in relation to a person by whom a single claim for a tax credit is made, the income of the person for that tax year.

(5) In this Part "the previous year income" means—

(a) in relation to persons by whom a joint claim for a tax credit is made, the aggregate income of the persons for the tax year preceding that to which the claim relates, and

(b) in relation to a person by whom a single claim for a tax credit is made, the income of the person for that preceding tax year.

(6) Regulations may provide that, for the purposes of this Part, income of a prescribed description is to be treated as being, or as not being, income for a particular tax year.

(7) In particular, regulations may provide that income of a prescribed description of a person for the tax year immediately before the preceding tax year referred to in subsection (5) is to be treated as being income of that preceding tax year (instead of any actual income of that description of the person for that preceding tax year).

(8) Regulations may for the purposes of this Part make provision—

(a) as to what is, or is not, income, and

(b) as to the calculation of income.

(9) Regulations may provide that, for the purposes of this Part, a person is to be treated—

(a) as having income which he does not in fact have, or

(b) as not having income which he does in fact have.

(10) The Board may estimate the amount of the income of a person, or the aggregate income of persons, for any tax year for the purpose of making, amending or terminating an award of a tax credit; but such an estimate does not affect the rate at which he is, or they are, entitled to the tax credit for that or any other tax year.

AMENDMENTS

1. Subsection (2) is amended as it applies to polygamous units by Tax Credits (Polygamous Marriages) Regulations 2003 (SI 2003/742) reg.6.

2. References to "the Board" are now references to the Commissioners for Revenue and Customs: CRCA 2005 s.4.

DEFINITIONS

"award"—see s.14(1).
"the Board"—see s.67.
"claim"—see s.3(1).
"couple"—see s.3(5A).
"entitlement"—see s.18(1).
"joint claim"—see s.3(8).
"prescribed"—see s.67.
"single claim"—see s.3(8).
"tax credit"—see s.1(2).
"tax year"—see s.47.

GENERAL NOTE

This is a framework and empowering section making provision for the imposition of an income test on all claimants for both CTC and WTC. The relevant regulations are the Tax Credits (Definition and Calculation of Income) Regulations 2002 (SI 2002/2006) and the Tax Credits (Income Thresholds and Determination of Rates) Regulations 2002 (SI 2002/2008). The powers to make regulations are

1.292

Tax Credits Act 2002

Treasury powers requiring affirmative procedures. Further, the regulations link the income test closely to income tax rules, thus breaking away from the separate social security means tests.

Subsection (1)

1.293 This is worded to refer "a tax credit" so that different amounts may be prescribed for different tax credits. Regulation 3 of the Tax Credits (Income Thresholds and Determination of Rates) Regulations 2002 sets a threshold for WTC of £6,420, and for CTC of £15,910 with a further higher threshold for the family element only of CTC of £40,000 in reg.8 of those Regulations. See para.2.224.

Although this section defines the amounts of income above which tax credits are reduced by reference to income as "income threshold", HMRC literature, including formal papers, refers to them instead as "taper start points". A Commissioner criticised this change of language, without any accompanying explanation, in *CTC/2113/2006*. In that case, which concerned the operation of these start points or threshold, the Commissioner criticised the failure of HMRC to explain how its language fitted in with the statutory language. This left a claimant unable to understand the HMRC submissions and the appeal tribunal's decision agreeing with the submission (but using the statutory language also without explanation).

Subsection (2)

1.294 This disapplies the income test, so allowing payment of a tax credit without reference to separate means-testing, where the prescribed benefits are in payment. The benefits are prescribed by Tax Credits (Income Thresholds and Determination of Rates) Regulations 2002 reg.4 as covering only some claimants for income support, employment and support allowance, state pension credit and jobseeker's allowance.

Subsections (3)–(5)

1.295 These provisions are intended to enable a practical way of moving between the current year assessment rules that apply to all income tax assessments and a previous year assessment that would allow an award to be made ahead of the year in question. However, implementing the rules proved more problematic than anticipated and the rules were only fully implemented from 2012/13. Until that year no figures were set under s.7(3)(c) and (d) so stopping that aspect of the rule working. From 2012/13 the figure has been set at £2,500 (see the Tax Credits (Income Thresholds and Determination of Rates) Regulations 2002 reg.5. That regulation sets the figure for s.7(3)(a) and (b) at £10,000. This was reduced from £10,000 to £5,000 for 2013/14. However, as was emphasised in *CTC/3611/2008* these apply to entitlement decisions rather than awards. See further the comment on that regulation.

Subsection (4)

1.296 *CTC/2270/2007* confirmed HMRC's interpretation on an important aspect of subs.(7)(a). Where two individuals become a couple during a year and make a joint claim, this requires that the aggregate income for the year is the income for the entire year of both of the couple. The Deputy Commissioner rejected the argument of a man whose partner, and later wife, moved in with him during the year that her income before she moved in was irrelevant to the joint claim made after she moved in. The plain language of Parliament required that the full income for the year of both of them was to be calculated, and then apportioned to the part of the year during which they made the joint claim. It followed that part of the wife's income was to be taken into account in respect of the joint income even though she had earned nothing since she moved in with her husband. The Deputy Commissioner reasoned that:

"... the position is that Parliament in passing the Act and the Treasury in making the Regulations have chosen a method of determining income that may be criticised as somewhat rough and ready and as such producing anomalous outcomes in cases like the present, but is nevertheless relatively simple to operate compared with the alternative of enquiring into the actual income of each single and joint claimant in respect of claim periods of less than a year."

The result of this interpretation is that in every case the full year income of any individual must be taken into account under subs.(4)(b), with the amount relevant to any claim being apportioned. The subsection as a whole is anomalous. The result where A and B became partners during a year and then split up again during that year is that the incomes of both A and B are to be taken into account from the beginning of the year to the time they split up, but then apportioned to the period of the joint claim. But after the couple split up their incomes must be disaggregated and any claim by either A or B is then to be based only on her or his income for that year. *CTC/2270/2007* was followed by an Upper Tribunal Judge in *PD v HMRC and CD (TC)* [2010] UKUT 159 (AAC).

Subsections (6)–(9)
See the Tax Credits (Definition and Calculation of Income) Regulations 2002, as amended.

1.297

Subsection (10)
This is a wide power to deal with awards. It allows HMRC to make, change or stop an award during the tax year on the basis of an estimate only. That estimate will be the decision made under ss.14(1), 15(1) or 16(1). Any of these decisions are subject to appeal and, on appeal, it will be for the appeal tribunal to make the estimate (subject to any settlement of the appeal under s.54 of the TMA 1970). See further the note to s.39 below. It is understood that the standard practice of HMRC is to make all initial decisions on the basis of the previous year's income using this power. Where a claim form indicates that the current year's income should be used, HMRC then makes an immediate revision under s.15.

1.298

Child tax credit

Entitlement

8.—(1) The entitlement of the person or persons by whom a claim for child tax credit has been made is dependent on him, or either of them, being responsible for one or more children or qualifying young persons.

1.299

(2) Regulations may make provision for the purposes of child tax credit as to the circumstances in which a person is or is not responsible for a child or qualifying young person.

(3) For the purposes of this Part a person is a child if he has not attained the age of sixteen; but regulations may make provision for a person who has attained that age to remain a child for the purposes of this Part after attaining that age for a prescribed period or until a prescribed date.

(4) In this Part "qualifying young person" means a person, other than a child, who—
(a) has not attained such age (greater than 16) as is prescribed, and
(b) satisfies prescribed conditions.

(5) Circumstances may be prescribed in which a person is to be entitled to child tax credit for a prescribed period in respect of a child or qualifying young person who has died.

Tax Credits Act 2002

AMENDMENT

1. Subsection (1) is amended as it applies to polygamous units by Tax Credits (Polygamous Marriages) Regulations 2003 (SI 2003/742) reg.7.

DEFINITIONS

"child"—see subs.(3).
"prescribed"—see s.67.
"qualifying young person"—see subs.(4).

GENERAL NOTE

1.300   This section sets the central tests for claiming child tax credits, namely that there be a child or young person for whom the claimant is, or joint claimants are, responsible. Subsection (1) provides that entitlement to child tax credit is dependent on these tests. It is deliberately parallel to SSCBA 1992 s.141, the section entitling claimants to child benefit for each of the children for whom a claimant is responsible. Subsection (2) makes provision for regulations defining responsibility for a child. This is covered by SSCBA 1992 s.143 and supporting regulations. The regulations also deal with competing claims for child tax credit for the same child. See paras 2.194–2.198. Subsection (3) defines a child as someone who has not reached the age of 16, but also allows the age to be extended by regulation. Child benefit is payable for all children who have not reached 16 (SSCBA 1992 s.142(1)). Child benefit is also payable for certain children over 16, but for child tax credit purposes they are known as "qualifying young persons". Subsection (4) allows regulations to define that category. The intention is, as with child benefit, to include certain young persons over 16 but not over 19, depending on ongoing education (but not covering students undergoing higher education). The effect confirms a general policy to exclude those over 16 from being "children" for state benefit purposes, but to include them, along with students, in a separate category. This is because those over 16 can claim some benefits in their own right. See further the Child Tax Credit Regulations 2002 (SI 2002/2007).

The question whether claimants caring for children elsewhere in the European Union were entitled to child tax credit has been considered by the Upper Tribunal in two appeals. See note to s.3(3) above.

Subsection (5)

1.301   This makes identical provision as that in s.54 of this Act, ensuring that both child benefit and child tax credit remain payable for a period (set by regulations at eight weeks) after the death of a child or, in the case of child tax credit, qualifying young person.

Maximum rate

1.302   **9.**—(1) The maximum rate at which a person or persons may be entitled to child tax credit is to be determined in the prescribed manner.

(2) The prescribed manner of determination must involve the inclusion of—
  (a) an element which is to be included in the case of all persons entitled to child tax credit, and
  (b) an element in respect of each child or qualifying young person for whom the person is, or either of them is or are, responsible.

(3) The element specified in paragraph (a) of subsection (2) is to be known as the family element of child tax credit and that specified in paragraph (b) of that subsection is to be known as the individual element of child tax credit.

(2002 c.21 s.9)

(4) The prescribed manner of determination may involve the inclusion of such other elements as may be prescribed.

(5) The prescribed manner of determination—

(a) may include provision for the amount of the family element of child tax credit to vary according to the age of any of the children or qualifying young persons or according to any such other factors as may be prescribed,

(b) may include provision for the amount of the individual element of child tax credit to vary according to the age of the child or qualifying young person or according to any such other factors as may be prescribed, and

(c) must include provision for the amount of the individual element of child tax credit to be increased in the case of a child or qualifying young person who is disabled and to be further increased in the case of a child or qualifying young person who is severely disabled.

(6) A child or qualifying young person is disabled, or severely disabled, for the purposes of this section only if—

(a) he satisfies prescribed conditions, or

(b) prescribed conditions exist in relation to him.

(7) If, in accordance with regulations under section 8(2), more than one claimant may be entitled to child tax credit in respect of the same child or qualifying young person, the prescribed manner of determination may include provision for the amount of any element of child tax credit included in the case of any one or more of them to be less than it would be if only one claimant were so entitled.

(8) "Claimant" means—

(a) in the case of a single claim, the person who makes the claim; and

(b) in the case of a joint claim, the persons who make the claim.

AMENDMENT

1. Subsection (2) is amended as it applies to polygamous units by Tax Credits (Polygamous Marriages) Regulations 2003 (SI 2003/742) reg.8.

DEFINITIONS

"child"—see s.8(3).
"child tax credit"—see s.8.
"claimant"—see subs.(8).
"disabled"—see subs.(6).
"prescribed"—see s.67.
"qualifying young person"—see s.8(4).
"severely disabled"—see subs.(6).

GENERAL NOTE

This section is again a mixture of defining provisions and empowering provisions. Subsection (1) provides that the way in which entitlement to CTC is to be calculated is to be set out in regulations. The regulations for this purpose are the Child Tax Credit Regulations 2002 (SI 2002/2007). Subsections (2) and (3) provide that in every case an award of CTC must involve both a "family element" for the claimant and an "individual element" for each child or young person. The amount of the individual element must be higher for children or young persons who are disabled, and higher again if they are seriously disabled, but definition of those

1.303

Tax Credits Act 2002

conditions is left to regulations: subss.(5)(c) and (6). The other provisions in the section are permissive.

Subsection (7)

1.304   As with child benefit, both HMRC and the appeal tribunals are regularly faced with disputes between two estranged parents or others both claiming child tax credit for the same child or children. The rules giving HMRC a discretion to decide to whom to pay child benefit do not apply to child tax credits. And the power to divide a single award in this subsection has not been used. In some cases the optimal approach where there is more than one child is for the parents (or other carers) to agree to split the award, or to have it paid to the claimant who can claim most. For the rules that apply where they cannot agree see Child Tax Credit Regulations reg.3.

In *HMRC v DH* [2009] UKUT 24 (AAC) Judge Jacobs found that any breach of the human rights of a claimant for CTC who had a substantial minority responsibility for the shared care of a child because HMRC declined to share an award was justified by HMRC's evidence. This is set out at length in the decision. A further appeal against that decision was dismissed by the Court of Appeal in *Humphreys v HM Revenue and Customs* [2010] EWCA Civ 56, where the Court ruled at [66] that:

> "taking into account everything we have said about the similarities and differences between this case and *Hockenjos*, and allowing for the broad margin of appreciation, we have come to the conclusion that the Commissioners have established a sufficient justification for drawing the line where they have and adhering to a system of single payment of CTC. There may well be a better or fairer way of distributing CTC, but a particular policy choice has been made and it cannot in our judgment be characterised as unreasonable or as being manifestly without reasonable foundation."

The Supreme Court has endorsed the decisions of Judge Jacobs and the Court of Appeal in a single judgment that looks closely at the Government's approach to the policy of paying tax credit to one parent only both by reference to Parliamentary record and to the post-*Hockenjos* review. See *Humphreys v HMRC* [2012] UKSC 18.

Working tax credit

Entitlement

1.305   **10.**—(1) The entitlement of the person or persons by whom a claim for working tax credit has been made is dependent on him, or either of them, being engaged in qualifying remunerative work.

(2) Regulations may for the purposes of this Part make provision—
  (a) as to what is, or is not, qualifying remunerative work, and
  (b) as to the circumstances in which a person is, or is not, engaged in it.

(3) The circumstances prescribed under subsection (2)(b) may differ by reference to—
  (a) the age of the person or either of the persons,
  (b) whether the person, or either of the persons, is disabled,
  (c) whether the person, or either of the persons, is responsible for one or more children or qualifying young persons, or
  (d) any other factors.

(4) Regulations may make provision for the purposes of working tax credit as to the circumstances in which a person is or is not responsible for a child or qualifying young person.

(2002 c.21 s.10)

AMENDMENT

1. Subsections (1) and (3) are amended as they apply to polygamous units by Tax Credits (Polygamous Marriages) Regulations 2003 (SI 2003/742) reg.9.

DEFINITIONS

"child"—see s.8(3).
"disabled"—see s.11(7).
"engaged"—see subs.(2).
"qualifying remunerative work"—see subs.(2).
"qualifying young person"—see s.8(4).
"responsible for a child"—see subs.(4).

GENERAL NOTE

This section is the parallel to s.8, laying down the central test for claiming WTC by single or joint claimants, and defining or providing for definition of the key terms.

1.306

Subsection (1)

This makes the central test for WTC "being engaged in qualifying remunerative work". It is used in the regulations defining entitlement to income support and jobseeker's allowance. See the notes to Income Support (General) Regulations 1987 reg.4, and Jobseeker's Allowance Regulations 1996 reg.51, in Vol.II of this work. The test of "work" has been held by Commissioners to be wider than "employment" (*R(FC) 2/90*), although the requirement that it be "remunerative"—defined as work done for payment or in expectation of payment—excludes volunteers (*R(IS) 12/92*).

Although the test is the same both for tax credits and for income support and JSA, experience has shown that gaps can occur between one award ending and the other starting, particularly where work ends near the end of a tax year for example because of ill health or disablement. HMRC has no powers to assist someone who stops being a credit claimant in these circumstances and is under no duty to forward a claim to the Department for Work and Pensions. Nor can an appeal assist such a claimant.

1.307

Subsection (2)

This provides for further definition of what is "qualifying" work, and also when someone is "engaged" in work. This is used to set the number of hours that must be worked in order to count for WTC purposes, but it also allows the start and finish of a period of work to be defined and intermittent work patterns to be subject to regulation.

See the WTC (Entitlement and Maximum Rate) Regulations 2002 (SI 2002/2005) reg.4.

1.308

Subsection (3)

This permits the qualifying conditions for WTC to be varied between different claimants. Regulation 4 of the Working Tax Credit (Entitlement and Maximum Rate) Regulations 2002 provides that the minimum work level is 16 hours a week for single claimants with children and those suffering from disabilities, 24 hours for couples with children, and 30 hours for other claimants over 25. No WTC is payable to those under 25 unless they can claim on another basis.

1.309

Subsection (4)

This provides that responsibility for a child or qualifying young person may be defined differently for WTC purposes to the definition under s.8 for CTC purposes. This links with s.12, the childcare element of WTC. However, the regulations have not to date adopted any distinction.

1.310

161

Maximum rate

1.311

11.—(1) The maximum rate at which a person or persons may be entitled to working tax credit is to be determined in the prescribed manner.

(2) The prescribed manner of determination must involve the inclusion of an element which is to be included in the case of all persons entitled to working tax credit.

(3) The prescribed manner of determination must also involve the inclusion of an element in respect of the person, or either or both of the persons, engaged in qualifying remunerative work—
   (a) having a physical or mental disability which puts him at a disadvantage in getting a job, and
   (b) satisfying such other conditions as may be prescribed.

(4) The element specified in subsection (2) is to be known as the basic element of working tax credit and the element specifiedin subsection (3) is to be known as the disability element of working tax credit.

(5) The prescribed manner of determination may involve the inclusion of such other elements as may be prescribed.

(6) The other elements may (in particular) include—
   (a) an element in respect of the person, or either of the persons or the two taken together, being engaged in qualifying remunerative work to an extent prescribed for the purposes of this paragraph;
   (b) an element in respect of the persons being the members of [^{1} a couple],
   (c) an element in respect of the person not being a member of [^{1} a couple] but being responsible for a child or qualifying young person;
   (d) an element in respect of the person, or either or both of the persons, being severely disabled; and
   (e) an element in respect of the person, or either or both of the persons, being over a prescribed age, satisfying prescribed conditions and having been engaged in qualifying remunerative work for not longer than a prescribed period.

(7) A person has a physical or mental disability which puts him at a disadvantage in getting a job, or is severely disabled, for the purposes of this section only if—
   (a) he satisfies prescribed conditions, or
   (b) prescribed conditions exist in relation to him.

AMENDMENTS

1. For the purposes of applying this section to polygamous units, Tax Credits (Polygamous Marriages) Regulations 2003 (SI 2003/742) reg.10 omits subs.(6)(c) and introduces alternative wording to subss.(3) and (6).
2. Civil Partnership Act 2004 s.254 and Sch.24 para.145 (December 5, 2005).

DEFINITIONS

"child"—see s.8(3).
"couple"—see s.3(5A).
"physical or mental disability"—see subs.(7).
"prescribed"—see s.67.
"qualifying young person"—see s.8(4).
"severely disabled"—see subs.(7).

(2002 c.21 s.11)

GENERAL NOTE

This parallels s.9 for WTC. Subsection (1) allows the determination of WTC rates to be set by regulations, but subss.(2) and (4) require that anyone entitled to WTC must receive a basic element of credit. There must also be an additional disability element in appropriate cases (carrying forward the policy of DPTC): subss. (3) and (4). Subsection (7) sets the test for the disability element. There may also be a childcare element, but this is provided for in s.12. Subsections (5) and (6) are purely permissive. Effect is given to these provisions by the WTC (Entitlement and Maximum Rate) Regulations 2002 (SI 2002/2005).

Childcare element

12.—(1) The prescribed manner of determination of the maximum rate at which a person or persons may be entitled to working tax credit may involve the inclusion, in prescribed circumstances, of a childcare element.

(2) A childcare element is an element in respect of a prescribed proportion of so much of any relevant childcare charges as does not exceed a prescribed amount.

(3) "Childcare charges" are charges of a prescribed description incurred in respect of childcare by the person, or either or both of the persons, by whom a claim for working tax credit is made.

(4) "Childcare", in relation to a person or persons, means care provided—
 (a) for a child of a prescribed description for whom the person is responsible, or for whom either or both of the persons is or are responsible, and
 (b) by a person of a prescribed description.

(5) The descriptions of persons prescribed under subsection (4)(b) may include descriptions of persons approved in accordance with a scheme made by the appropriate national authority under this subsection.

(6) "The appropriate national authority" means—
 (a) in relation to care provided in England, the Secretary of State,
 (b) in relation to care provided in Scotland, the Scottish Ministers,
 (c) in relation to care provided in Wales, the [² Welsh Ministers], and
 (d) in relation to care provided in Northern Ireland, the Department of Health, Social Services and Public Safety.

(7) The provision made by a scheme under subsection (5) must involve the giving of approvals, in accordance with criteria determined by or under the scheme, by such of the following as the scheme specifies—
 (a) the appropriate national authority making the scheme;
 (b) one or more specified persons or bodies or persons or bodies of a specified description, and
 (c) persons or bodies accredited under the scheme in accordance with criteria determined by or under it.

(8) A scheme under subsection (5) may authorise—
 (a) the making of grants or loans to, and
 (b) the charging of reasonable fees by, persons and bodies giving approvals.

1.312

1.313

AMENDMENTS

1. Subsections (3) and (4) are modified, as they apply to polygamous units, by Tax Credits (Polygamous Marriages) Regulations 2003 (SI 2003/742) reg.11.
2. Child Minding and Day Care (Wales) Regulations 2010 (SI 2010/2574) Sch.1 (April 1, 2011).

DEFINITIONS

"appropriate national authority"—see subs.(6).
"child"—see s.8(3).
"childcare"—see subs.(4).
"childcare charges"—see subs.(3).
"maximum rate"—see s.11(1).
"prescribed"—see s.67.
"tax credit"—see s.1(2).

GENERAL NOTE

1.314 The childcare element was introduced to family credit in response to a successful discrimination challenge to the previous law before the European Court of Justice in *Meyers v Adjudication Officer* (C-116/94) [1995] All E.R. (EC) 705. Successive governments have made it more generous, and it is now given further prominence by its own section in this Act. However, the section is in form entirely permissive, even if the failure to implement it at all might invite a further challenge to the European Court. Subsections (2)–(4) provide that the element is a credit for a part of the charges incurred by a claimant for "childcare" provided for prescribed children by prescribed persons. Regulation 7 of the Tax Credits (Income Thresholds and Determination of Rates) Regulations 2002 (SI 2002/2008) specifies the proportion as 80 per cent from April 2006. The important issue here is the identity of those who may provide the childcare. Government policy is that childcare providers should be licensed or supervised. But the way in which that is to be done is a devolved matter for the separate governments of England, Scotland, Wales and Northern Ireland. This reflects the fact that both education and social welfare functions are now functions of the separate national authorities. Subsections (5)–(8) give effect to this. Responsibility for both policy and operation of the childcare registration rules is therefore outside the responsibilities of HMRC and outside the jurisdiction of the appeal tribunals.

Parents are often able to secure free or subsidised childcare through their employers or from national or local schemes. In these cases, the childcare element is only paid for costs not met by the other scheme. For example if a nursery place is free for the child but the parent has to meet costs such as food, then those costs alone may be claimed.

Employers can provide employees with free childcare places or vouchers for childcare, often in exchange for a salary sacrifice. See ss.318–318C of ITEPA (set out below). Where there are such schemes, parents may be able to choose between receiving employer vouchers or the childcare element of working tax credit, but they cannot receive both. It is a matter for individual calculation as to which is better.

Rate

Rate

1.315 **13.**—(1) Where, in the case of a person or persons entitled to a tax credit, the relevant income does not exceed the income threshold (or his or their entitlement arises by virtue of section 7(2)), the rate at which he is or they are entitled to the tax credit is the maximum rate for his or their case.

(2) Regulations shall make provision as to the manner of determining the rate (if any) at which a person is, or persons are, entitled to a tax credit in any other case.

(3) The manner of determination prescribed under subsection (2)—
  (a) may involve the making of adjustments so as to avoid fractional amounts, and
  (b) may include provision for securing that, where the rate at which a person or persons would be entitled to a tax credit would be less than a prescribed rate, there is no rate in his or their case.

DEFINITIONS
  "the income threshold"—see s.7(1)(a).
  "maximum rate"—see ss.9(1) and 11(1).
  "prescribed"—see s.67.
  "relevant income"—see s.7(3).
  "tax credit"—see s.1(2).

GENERAL NOTE

This short section supplements s.7 in defining the maximum rate of WTC for a claimant, and a minimum level of payment, and provides for regulations to determine these. See the Tax Credits (Income Thresholds and Determination of Rates) Regulations 2002 (SI 2002/2008), which set out a multi-stage formula.

Decisions

Initial decisions

14.—(1) On a claim for a tax credit the Board must decide—
  (a) whether to make an award of the tax credit, and
  (b) if so, the rate at which to award it.
(2) Before making their decision the Board may by notice—
  (a) require the person, or [either or both][any or all][1] of the persons, by whom the claim is made to provide any information or evidence which the Board consider they may need for making their decision, or
  (b) require any person of a prescribed description to provide any information or evidence of a prescribed description which the Board consider they may need for that purpose, by the date specified in the notice.
(3) The Board's power to decide the rate at which to award a tax credit includes power to decide to award it at a nil rate.

AMENDMENTS

1. Subsection (2) is modified in its application to polygamous units by Tax Credits (Polygamous Marriages) Regulations 2003 (SI 2003/742) reg.12.
2. References to "the Board" are now references to the Commissioners for Revenue and Customs: CRCA 2005 s.4.

Tax Credits Act 2002

3. The section is disapplied for claimants subject to immigration control. See Tax Credits (Immigration) Regulations 2003 (SI 2003/623) regs 3 and 4.

DEFINITIONS

"claim"—see s.3(8).
"the Board"—see s.67.
"tax credit"—see s.1(2).

GENERAL NOTE

1.318
This section imposes a duty on HMRC to decide a claim properly made under s.3 by making an award (or not), but it sets no time limit on that decision. An award is a decision to pay the tax credit. It is not a decision on entitlement. That is made later, under s.18. This explains the section title "initial decisions" (in the first draft of the Bill it was "provisional decisions"). Section 7(10) provides that HMRC may make this decision on the basis of an estimate. A decision under subs.(1) can be appealed (s.38). HMRC terms these notices "award notices".

This imposes the formal duty to deal with a claim by making or refusing an award. HMRC may use the power to estimate the income of claimants under s.7(10) rather than wait for information from an examination of the claim. Or it may make an award and examine the claim more thoroughly afterwards. A decision to award or refuse under this subsection is subject to appeal: s.38(1). However, HMRC practice is to attempt to deal with any such appeal by a settlement under the terms of s.54 of the Taxes Managements Act 1970. See the note to s.39 below. If HMRC take the view that a valid claim has not been made then no decision will be made under this section. For discussion about whether that is an appealable decision, see commentary to s.38 below.

HMRC has now automated most of the process. There is no "ownership" of a tax credits decision. One team run the computers that make the initial award decisions, then other teams take over to deal with other aspects of the case. There is also no "local office" culture in HMRC tax credit administration. That being so, it would appear to be arguable that the recognition of that aspect of DWP administration by the House of Lords in *Hinchy* would have no application to HMRC.

1.319
For judicial criticism of the practice of HMRC issuing informal decisions and then, sometimes after several months, later issuing formal decisions see *CTC/244/2008*, para.3. In *CTC/3692/2008* a social security commissioner applied *R(IB) 2/04*, a decision of a Tribunal of three Commissioners, to HMRC tax credit decisions in the same way as to social security decisions. He decided that an HMRC decision was so faulty that the only proper course was to allow the appeal and send the issue back to HMRC to take the decision properly.

ZM and AB v HMRC (TC) [2013] UKUT 547 (AAC) is the decision of the Upper Tribunal in a test case brought by the Child Poverty Action Group about the meaning of s.14. The case concerned a joint claim refused by HMRC because of a query about the identity of one of the couple. This turned in part on reg.5 of the Tax Credits (Claims and Notifications) Regulations 2002. HMRC argued that a decision whether a claim was properly made under that regulation was not subject to any statutory procedure.

Judge Ward accepted that argument with regard to UK domestic legislation but then turned to an argument based by CPAG on the Human Rights Act 1988, ss.3 and 6, and art.6 of the European Convention on Human Rights. It was not in dispute before him that determination of a claim for tax credits was a determination of the claimant's civil rights. That must follow from the decision of the Supreme Court in *Tomlinson v Birmingham CC* [2010] UKSC 8. Judge Ward considered in detail whether the availability of judicial review was an art.6-compliant remedy for this kind of case. He decided that it was not, drawing support from the reasoning about the scope of judicial review of a First-tier Tribunal in the decision of Judge

(2002 c.21 s.14)

Turnbull in *SG v HMRC (TC)* [2011] UKUT 199 (AAC) and the decision of (then) Commissioner Levenson in *CTC/31/2006* (unreported) which he cited at some length. He concluded that he was required by the Human Rights Act 1998 to read s.14(1):

> "as if it said 'On a claim for a tax credit or on what would constitute such a claim but for the Board's view that the person or one of the persons making the claim could not avail themselves of regulation 5(8) of the Tax Credits (Claims and Notifications) Regulations 2002 where that provision is in issue . . .'"

Judge Ward noted that reg.5(8) had been introduced by amending regulations without any certificate of compliance with the 1998 Act and that it was not in contemplation when the 2002 Act was passed. He concluded that his approach was a proper approach to be taken as a matter of rights-compliant interpretation and was not in effect judicial legislation. 1.320

While the judge carefully kept his focus on the specific issue in dispute, the strength of the arguments suggest that they might be applied to any other "decision" that is not regarded by HMRC as appealable save where (as with overpayments) there is clear legislative authority that the determination is not appealable.

The decision in that case, but not the full reasoning, was followed by Judge Mark in *CI v HMRC (TC)* [2014] UKUT 158 (AAC). Judge Mark agreed that judicial review was not an adequate remedy in dealing with rejection of a claim. But he emphasised that the fact that a claim was bound to fail did not prevent it being justiciable. So in that case the failure to provide a NINO for the claimant's wife would probably mean that the claim would fail but did not prevent the claimant appealing against a refusal by HMRC. There may have been questions about immigration control that should have been investigated but were not.

Subsection (2)

This empowers HMRC to require further information before making the decision by notice (see s.45 as to the notice). Penalties attach to failure to reply to a notice or to wrong replies (ss.31 and 32). The subsection also permits information to be required from others. This has been applied by the Tax Credits (Claims and Notifications) Regulations 2002 (SI 2002/2014) regs 30–32 to employers and those providing childcare. 1.321

HMRC practice appears not to be using this section and those that follow as drafted. Subsection (2) gives the Revenue powers to seek information "before making their decision". There are separate powers once an award is made. HMRC practice is to examine claims both before and during the award in the same way. In other words, the award is often made and then examined. This is possible for tax credits, as they are based on a full year's claim at a time, in a way that is not possible for most social security benefits, to which individuals have entitlements on a daily or weekly basis. Rather, it follows the approach long used by HMRC under the PAYE system for taxing employment income.

In decision *CIS/995/2004* Commissioner Mesher confirmed the view stated above that the power in this section is available to deal with enquiries only *before* a decision is made. The Commissioner also criticises the standard letter TC602 used by HMRC in connection with these enquiries. It follows that HMRC have no power to impose a penalty under s.32 for failure to answer an enquiry that is purportedly made under this section but not in accordance with its terms. However, the power cited by HMRC in its notices to claimants about both enquiries and examinations cite s.19 powers, not s.14 powers (see WTC/FS1 and WTC/FS2 issued in 2013). But the power under s.19 is available only after a s.18 decision has been taken. If *CIS/995/2004* is correct, it would seem there is no power to impose a penalty for a failure to respond to a check made between the issue of the initial award under this section and the final decision under s.18 save where HMRC can show reasonable grounds for using its s.16 powers. This provides a limit on HMRC checking powers that may not have been intended but nonetheless removes liability to penalties.

167

Subsection (3)

1.322	This allows the award of a nil rate, so awarding a tax credit without payment. This "has the effect of keeping an entitlement going even though no money is in payment or in process. It makes it easier for the claimant and it makes it easier for us" (Baroness Hollis, House of Lords Grand Committee, May 23, 2002, CWH 146). This again reflects the fact that at this stage the decision is an initial decision only. It also means that a claimant with a nil award can ask for a review to deal with a change of circumstances rather than having to make a new claim. This gives a practical solution to a recurring problem under the SSAA 1992 and the SSA 1998 of reviews, revisions and supersessions. The adoption of this practice will, in particular, avoid some of the more awkward aspects of supersession.

Revised decisions after notifications

1.323	**15.**—(1) Where notification of a change of circumstances increasing the maximum rate at which a person or persons may be entitled to a tax credit is given in accordance with regulations under section 6(1), the Board must decide whether (and, if so, how) to amend the award of the tax credit made to him or them.

(2) Before making their decision the Board may by notice—
   (a) require the person by whom the notification is given to provide any information or evidence which the Board consider they may need for making their decision; or
   (b) require any person of a prescribed description to provide any information or evidence of a prescribed description which the Board consider they may need for that purpose,
by the date specified in the notice.

AMENDMENT

1. The section is disapplied for claimants subject to immigration control. See Tax Credits (Immigration) Regulations 2003 (SI 2003/623) regs 3 and 4.

DEFINITIONS

"the Board"—see s.67.
"maximum rate"—see ss.9(1) and 11(1).
"prescribed"—see s.67.
"tax credit"—see s.1(2).

GENERAL NOTE

1.324	Section 6 makes provision for a claimant to tell HMRC of a change of circumstances that should or may increase the tax credit to be awarded. This section imposes a duty on HMRC to consider if the award made under s.14 should be amended if such a notification is given (subs.(1)). The decision, including a decision not to amend, is appealable (s.38). Subsection (2) gives HMRC the same powers to enquire as s.14(2). The same provisions about notice (s.45) and penalties (ss.31 and 32) apply. Following the comment in s.14, it may be noted that although the heading of the section refers to revision, the text of the section does not. The power in this section is to "amend". That is the term used in the TMA 1970 when either the taxpayer or HMRC changes a tax return (see ss.9ZA and 9ZB of the TMA 1970).

(2002 c.21 s.16)

Other revised decisions

16.—(1) Where, at any time during the period for which an award of a tax credit is made to a person or persons, the Board have reasonable grounds for believing—
   (a) that the rate at which the tax credit has been awarded to him or them for the period differs from the rate at which he is, or they are, entitled to the tax credit for the period; or
   (b) that he has, or they have, ceased to be, or never been, entitled to the tax credit for the period,
the Board may decide to amend or terminate the award.

(2) Where, at any time during the period for which an award of a tax credit is made to a person or persons, the Board believe—
   (a) that the rate at which a tax credit has been awarded to him or them for the period may differ from the rate at which he is, or they are, entitled to it for the period, or
   (b) that he or they may have ceased to be, or never been, entitled to the tax credit for the period,
the Board may give a notice under subsection (3).

(3) A notice under this subsection may—
   (a) require the person, or either or both of the persons, to whom the tax credit was awarded to provide any information or evidence which the Board consider they may need for considering whether to amend or terminate the award under subsection (1); or
   (b) require any person of a prescribed description to provide any information or evidence of a prescribed description which the Board consider they may need for that purpose,
by the date specified in the notice.

1.325

AMENDMENTS

1. Subsection (3) is modified as it appplies to polygamous units by Tax Credits (Polygamous Marriages) Regulations 2003 (SI 2003/742) reg.13.
2. The section is disapplied for claimants subject to immigration control. See Tax Credits (Immigration) Regulations 2003 (SI 2003/623) regs 3 and 4.

DEFINITIONS

"the Board"—see s.67.
"tax credit"—see s.1(2).

GENERAL NOTE

The procedure laid down in this section gives the Board flexibility to alter a decision at any time because HMRC has "reasonable grounds to believe" that a change is appropriate (subs.(1)). These general terms reflect the flexibility given to the Secretary of State under the SSA 1998, and transferred to the Board by the TCA 1999. But it is clear that, unlike that under the TCA 1999, the procedure is not a mirror of the 1998 Act procedure. As noted in s.15, the drafter has deliberately avoided the revision and supersession language of both the SSAA 1992 and the SSA 1998. Despite the heading of the section, the operative power is to "amend" or "terminate" an award. Both this section and s.15 also avoid introducing the troublesome distinction between revisions and supersessions under the SSA 1998.

Again in contrast to the 1998 procedures, this section provides a power, not a duty. In *CTC/4390/2004* the Commissioner noted that on an appeal against a s.16 decision the tribunal also had a power, not a duty, to act. The express right to appeal

1.326

169

a s.16 decision is granted in s.38(1). In such cases it is for the tribunal to decide for itself if there are reasonable grounds to make the decision, and if so it whether a decision is to be made.

The Board has power to give notice if it "believes" that the award of a tax credit may be wrong (subs.(2)). As might be expected, this is wider than the power to amend or terminate. The notice may require information or evidence from claimants and others, as defined in regulations (subs.(3)). Current regulations empower HMRC to seek information from employers and childcare providers (see note to s.14). Penalties attach to the failure to respond or to a false response (ss.31 and 32).

1.327 A standard HMRC use of the section is, somewhat obscurely, announced as a footnote to the regular series of official statistics on tax credits. They explain by way of a note to the table of total awards why, every year, there has been a reduction in the total number of awards made for both forms of tax credit in December as compared with the previous April as follows:

"Note: between each April and December families' awards are stopped at (a) 31 August if their only qualifying child falls out of entitlement at that date, or (b) in the autumn if they fail to return their Annual Declaration for the previous year. This introduces some seasonality into the figures."

In *CTC/2576/2004* the Commissioner set aside a decision of a tribunal confirming a decision of HMRC under s.16. The Commissioner also set aside the s.16 decision and referred the matter back to HMRC. HMRC could not produce the actual decision made, and had contradicted itself in letters to the claimant. The tribunal considered this in the same way as a revision or supersession under the SSA 1998. The Commissioner found that the tribunal erred in this approach and should have relied on the TCA 2002 procedures. In addition, HMRC had erred in both its versions of its original decision. The Commissioner commented that "the decision of the Board was not properly articulated in that the intimations of it to the claimant were contradictory". It is not clear from the decision whether s.23 of this Act was also considered, as HMRC conceded that its decisions were in error.

In *CTC/3981/2005* the Commissioner analysed both the s.16 procedure and the effectiveness of appeals against s.16 decisions.

1.328 Recent decisions of the Upper Tribunal highlight a lack of focus both by HMRC and by the First-tier Tribunal on the requirements of this section. Indeed, some decisions reflect a failure both by HMRC and by the tribunal to identify specifically which provisions are used in decisions changing an initial award of tax credits to a claimant. For example, in *JR v HMRC* [2015] UKUT 192 (AAC) the Upper Tribunal judge commented in a decision setting aside both the decision of the First-tier Tribunal and of HMRC (with the agreement of the latter):

"[4] The HMRC submission to the FTT is, to put it mildly, light if not slight. There is no reference or citation of any legislation relied on by HMRC. Presumably (but this is supposition on my part) HMRC was relying on section 16 of the Tax Credits Act 2002. HMRC plainly has the power to terminate a tax credits awards under s.16(1) where it has reasonable grounds for believing certain matters to be the case. Alternatively, if it thinks that such matters in s.16(1) "may" be the case, then by s.16(2) and (3)(a) HMRC may issue the claimant with a notice requiring information or evidence. However, as I understand it, there is no power to disallow tax credits for a simple failure to provide information—rather, the HMRC decision maker must actually decide the issue arising under s.16(1)."

See also *ZB v HMRC* [2015] UKUT 198 (AAC), a decision made by the same judge the following day.

In that context, it is to be emphasised that it is not sufficient for the exercise of the powers in s.16(1) that HMRC has some reason to doubt the accuracy of an award it has made. The first issue must be the basis of the underlying award decision under s.14. Did this merely accept the claim made by the claimant or was it on some other basis? The second issue is whether there has been any notification giving rise to the power to revise upon changes of circumstance under s.15. The powers under s.16 only arise if those two powers have not triggered the necessary power to decide or revise. Also, they arise only if HMRC has some reasonable ground other than notification of a change of circumstances to call into question the award decision. The power in s.16(2) arises if there is a "belief" that the decision may be wrong for unnotified reasons. While the wording of the subsection does not require that belief to have "reasonable grounds", there must be some basis. HMRC cannot therefore engage in a "fishing expedition" or random investigation. It can only act on that investigation if, after receiving any response from the request for information, there are then reasonable grounds for making the s.16 decision. That must be decided expressly even if there is no reply from the claimant.

As was emphasised in the decisions noted above, that decision is then appealable and if appealed must be expressly decided by the tribunal. Further, the tribunal must decide the appeal on the evidence before it and on the balance of probabilities. That will of course include any evidence before it that relates to the circumstances at the date of the original decision. There is a further source of confusion here because of the process of mandatory reconsideration. If the request for evidence is only made *after* HMRC has taken the s.16 decision and the claimant has asked for reconsideration, then it is not a request made under s.16—that power has already become spent by the decision. Further, that will mean that HMRC has to establish its reasonable grounds before the tribunal without reference to any further evidence. That must be done, in the ordinary course of events, by a submission to the tribunal that gives the factual basis on which HMRC has established those reasonable grounds. Otherwise the decision cannot without more be confirmed. The burden of proof under s.16 is on HMRC and therefore HMRC must offer evidence and submissions to show that it is probably right in making the decision. To confirm such a decision otherwise may also be a breach of the principles of natural justice, in that it does not allow the claimant to challenge the evidential basis for the decision and may inadvertently reverse the burden of proof. In the worst case, as Judge Wikeley commented in *ZB v HMRC* [2015] UKUT 198 (AAC), a claimant is faced with an unidentified decision made on unidentified evidence and that "is the stuff of Kafka (para.[8])."

Final notice

17.—(1) Where a tax credit has been awarded for the whole or part of a tax year—
  (a) for awards made on single claims, the Board must give a notice relating to the tax year to the person to whom the tax credit was awarded, and
  (b) for awards made on joint claims, the Board must give such a notice to the persons to whom the tax credit was awarded (with separate copies of the notice for each of them if the Board consider appropriate).
(2) The notice must either—
  (a) require that the person or persons must, by the date specified for the purposes of this subsection, declare that the relevant circumstances were as specified or state any respects in which they were not, or
  (b) inform the person or persons that he or they will be treated as having declared in response to the notice that the relevant circumstances were as specified unless, by that date, he states or they state any respects in which they were not.

(3) "Relevant circumstances" means circumstances (other than income) affecting—
- (a) the entitlement of the person, or joint entitlement of the persons, to the tax credit, or
- (b) the amount of the tax credit to which he was entitled, or they were jointly entitled, for the tax year.

(4) The notice must either—
- (a) require that the person or persons must, by the date specified for the purposes of this subsection, declare that the amount of the current year income or estimated current year income (depending on which is specified) was the amount, or fell within the range, specified or comply with subsection (5), or
- (b) inform the person or persons that he or they will be treated as having declared in response to the notice that the amount of the current year income or estimated current year income (depending on which is specified) was the amount, or fell within the range, specified unless, by that date, he complies or they comply with subsection (5).

(5) To comply with this subsection the person or persons must either—
- (a) state the current year income or his or their estimate of the current year income (making clear which); or
- (b) declare that, throughout the period to which the award related, subsection (1) of section 7 did not apply to him or them by virtue of subsection (2) of that section.

(6) The notice may—
- (a) require that the person or persons must, by the date specified for the purposes of subsection (4), declare that the amount of the previous year income was the amount, or fell within the range, specified or comply with subsection (7), or
- (b) inform the person or persons that he or they will be treated as having declared in response to the notice that the amount of the previous year income was the amount, or fell within the range, specified unless, by that date, he complies or they comply with subsection (7).

(7) To comply with this subsection the person or persons must either—
- (a) state the previous year income, or
- (b) make the declaration specified in subsection (5)(b).

(8) The notice must inform the person or persons that if he or they—
- (a) makes or make a declaration under paragraph (a) of subsection (4), or is or are treated as making a declaration under paragraph (b) of that subsection, in relation to estimated current year income (or the range within which estimated current year income fell); or
- (b) states or state under subsection (5)(a) his or their estimate of the current year income;

he or they will be treated as having declared in response to the notice that the amount of the (actual) current year income was as estimated unless, by the date specified for the purposes of this subsection, he states or they state the current year income.

(9) "Specified", in relation to a notice, means specified in the notice.

(10) Regulations may—
- (a) provide that, in prescribed circumstances, one person may act for another in response to a notice under this section, and
- (b) provide that, in prescribed circumstances, anything done by one

(2002 c.21 s.17)

member of a [²couple] in response to a notice given under this section is to be treated as also done by the other member of [²the couple].

AMENDMENTS

1. Subsection (10) is modified as it applies to polygamous units by Tax Credits (Polygamous Marriages) Regulations 2003 (SI 2003/742) reg.14.
2. Civil Partnership Act 2004 s.254 and Sch.24 para.145 (December 5, 2005).
3. The section is disapplied for claimants subject to immigration control. See Tax Credits (Immigration) Regulations 2003 (SI 2003/623) regs 3 and 4.

DEFINITIONS

"the Board"—see s.67.
"couple"—see s.3(5A).
"current year income"—see s.7(4).
"joint claims"—see s.3(8).
"prescribed"—see s.67.
"previous year income"—see s.7(5).
"relevant circumstances"—see subs.(3).
"specified"—see subs.(9).
"tax credit"—see s.1(2).
"tax year"—see s.47.

GENERAL NOTE

What are now ss.17 and 18 were originally drafted as one clause. It was divided by amendments in the House of Lords into the notice provisions (s.17) and the decision provisions (s.18), to avoid it being overlong. Together the two sections provide the regime for checking the s.14 initial decision on an award before turning it into an entitlement, and then for making the entitlement decision. The underlying pattern is that the award decision must be made in response to a claim. Payment is then made under the award decision for a tax year. At the end of the tax year, HMRC uses the s.17 powers to check whether the claimant is, or remains, entitled to the tax credit awarded, or to some higher or lower rate of tax credit. After checking, a "final decision" is made on entitlement.

1.330

The effect of subs.(1) is that all awards of tax credit must be checked. In every case a notice must be sent to a claimant (or joint claimants). Notices must take one of two forms. One is a demand for a declaration that there has been no change of relevant circumstances (subs.(2)(a)). It can also demand details (or an estimate) of the current year's income (subs.(4)(a)). The other is a notice telling people that it will be assumed that there is no change of circumstances unless any changes are reported by a given date (subs.(2)(b)). It can also tell people that it is assumed that their income is of an assumed level or range unless a declaration is made stating otherwise (subs.(4)(b)). The notice may also take either of those approaches about the previous year's income (subs.(6)). Further provisions are laid down in the Tax Credits (Claims and Notifications) Regulations 2002 (SI 2002/2014). The section also states the ways in which people must comply with these notices. Penalties may be imposed on failures to reply and wrong replies (ss.31 and 32).

HMRC calls the notices issued under this section "Annual Declarations". The annual declarations may also constitute claims under s.3. The point may arise as to which years the declaration and claim relate to. In *CTC/1594/2006* the Commissioner accepted HMRC's argument that it was for HMRC to decide this, subject to judicial review rather than appeal, but also suggested it might depend on the wording used. And see *SG v HM Revenue and Customs (TC)* [2011] UKUT 199 about the effects of failing to respond to a final notice.

Decisions after final notice

18.—(1) After giving a notice under section 17, the Board must decide —
  (a) whether the person was entitled, or the persons were jointly entitled, to the tax credit, and
  (b) if so, the amount of the tax credit to which he was entitled, or they were jointly entitled, for the tax year.

(2) But, subject to subsection (3), that decision must not be made before a declaration or statement has been made in response to the relevant provisions of the notice.

(3) If a declaration or statement has not been made in response to the relevant provisions of the notice on or before the date specified for the purposes of section 17(4), that decision may be made after that date.

(4) In subsections (2) and (3) "the relevant provisions of the notice" means—
  (a) the provision included in the notice by virtue of subsection (2) of section 17,
  (b) the provision included in the notice by virtue of subsection (4) of that section, and
  (c) any provision included in the notice by virtue of subsection (6) of that section.

(5) Where the Board make a decision under subsection (1) on or before the date referred to in subsection (3), they may revise it if a new declaration or statement is made on or before that date.

(6) If the person or persons to whom a notice under section 17 is given is or are within paragraph (a) or (b) of subsection (8) of that section, the Board must decide again—
  (a) whether the person was entitled, or the persons were jointly entitled, to the tax credit, and
  (b) if so, the amount of the tax credit to which he was entitled, or they were jointly entitled, for the tax year.

(7) But, subject to subsection (8), that decision must not be made before a statement has been made in response to the provision included in the notice by virtue of subsection (8) of section 17.

(8) If a statement has not been made in response to the provision included in the notice by virtue of that subsection on or before the date specified for the purposes of that subsection, that decision may be made after that date.

(9) Where the Board make a decision under subsection (6) on or before the date referred to in subsection (8), they may revise it if a new statement is made on or before that date.

(10) Before exercising a function imposed or conferred on them by subsection (1), (5), (6) or (9), the Board may by notice require the person, or either or both of the persons, to whom the notice under section 17 was given to provide any further information or evidence which the Board consider they may need for exercising the function by the date specified in the notice.

(11) Subject to sections [³19, 20, 21A and 21B] and regulations under section 21 (and to any revision under subsection (5) or (9) and any appeal)—
  (a) in a case in which a decision is made under subsection (6) in relation

to a person or persons and a tax credit for a tax year, that decision, and

(b) in any other case, the decision under subsection (1) in relation to a person or persons and a tax credit for a tax year,

is conclusive as to the entitlement of the person, or the joint entitlement of the persons, to the tax credit for the tax year and the amount of the tax credit to which he was entitled, or they were jointly entitled, for the tax year.

AMENDMENTS

1. Subsection (10) is modified as it applies to polygamous units by Tax Credits (Polygamous Marriages) Regulations 2003 (SI 2003/742) reg.15.
2. The section is modified for claimants subject to immigration control. See Tax Credits (Immigration) Regulations 2003 (SI 2003/623) regs 3 and 4.
3. Tax Credits, Child Benefit and Guardian's Allowance Reviews and Appeals Order 2014 (SI 2014/886) art.2(2) (April 6, 2014).

DEFINITIONS

"the Board"—see s.67.
"prescribed"—see s.67.
"relevant provisions of the notice"—see subs.(4).
"tax credit"—see s.1(2).
"tax year"—see s.47.

GENERAL NOTE

HMRC calls these notices "finalised awards". In *CTC/2113/2006* a Commissioner criticised this use of language, and a more general failure to distinguish between awards and entitlements, in HMRC notices and literature in the case papers.

See the note to s.17 for the general scheme of which this is part. Subsection (1) of this section imposes the duty on HMRC to make a decision on entitlement in every case, but only after the s.17 notice procedure has been followed (subs.(2)) or the full time to comply has been allowed (subs.(3)). Subsection (4) links the procedures under this section with the relevant notice provisions in s.17. Subsection (5) allows an entitlement decision under subs.(1) to be revised if there is a reply or further reply from a claimant after a decision has been made. The use of "revise" was avoided in earlier sections in favour of "amend" (despite their headings: see ss.15 and 16), but is here applied to changes to a final decision. Such revisions can be of the whole or only part of the decision. The language avoids attaching formalities or threshold conditions to the process. Subsections (6)–(9) repeat the substance of subss.(1)–(5) for claimants who estimated their current year income in their claims or initial responses to the s.17 notice. In either case, HMRC may require further information (subs.(10)). The standard penalty regime applies to subs.(10). Subsection (11) makes a subs.(1) or subs.(6) decision conclusive unless it is revised under subss.(5) or (9), or it is appealed under s.38, or it is altered under any of the powers in ss.19–21. The Claimant Compliance Manual (CCM) (on the CCM, see note to TCA 2002 s.31 below) emphasises that a decision under subs.(6) should be taken by an officer as a "best judgment" decision, not just a guess. "You can use some guess-work but it must be honest guess-work" (at para.10270). HMRC literature emphasises that the procedure under ss.17 and 18 does not provide a mechanism to take into account a change of circumstances that would lead to an increase in tax credits for the year. Such changes must be notified through the change of circumstances procedure. It is understood that this view is thought by some to be open to challenge, and that the procedure should operate in both ways. However, that would cut across the provisions for notification in s.15 and linked regulations.

1.332

For an analysis of the procedure under s.18, see *CTC/2662/2005*.

The addition of the references to ss.21A and 21B in para.(11) ensures that this regulation is compatible with the provisions about reviews added by those sections.

Power to enquire

1.333 **19.**—(1) The Board may enquire into—
(a) the entitlement of a person, or the joint entitlement of persons, to a tax credit for a tax year, and
(b) the amount of the tax credit to which he was entitled, or they were jointly entitled, for the tax year,
if they give notice to the person, or each of the persons, during the period allowed for the initiation of an enquiry.

(2) As part of the enquiry the Board may by notice—
(a) require the person, or either or both of the persons, to provide any information or evidence which the Board consider they may need for the purposes of the enquiry, or
(b) require any person of a prescribed description to provide any information or evidence of a prescribed description which the Board consider they may need for those purposes, by the date specified in the notice.

(3) On an enquiry the Board must decide—
(a) whether the person was entitled, or the persons were jointly entitled, to the tax credit, and
(b) if so, the amount of the tax credit to which he was entitled, or they were jointly entitled,
for the tax year.

(4) The period allowed for the initiation of an enquiry is the period beginning immediately after the relevant section 18 decision and ending—
(a) if the person, or either of the persons, to whom the enquiry relates is required by section 8 of the Taxes Management Act 1970 (c.9) to make a return, with the day on which the return becomes final (or, if both of the persons are so required and their returns become final on different days, with the later of those days), or
(b) in any other case, one year after the beginning of the relevant section 17 date.

(5) "The relevant section 18 decision" means—
(a) in a case in which a decision must be made under subsection (6) of section 18 in relation to the person or persons and the tax year to which the enquiry relates, that decision; and
(b) in any other case, the decision under subsection (1) of that section in relation to the person or persons and that tax year.

(6) "The relevant section 17 date" means—
(a) in a case in which a statement may be made by the person or persons in response to provision included by virtue of subsection (8) of section 17 in the notice given to him or them under that section in relation to the tax year, the date specified in the notice for the purposes of that subsection, and
(b) in any other case, the date specified for the purposes of subsection (4) of that section in the notice given to him or them under that section in relation to the tax year.

(7) A return becomes final—
(a) if it is enquired into under section 9A of the Taxes Management Act

(2002 c.21 s.19)

1970 (c.9), when the enquiries are completed (within the meaning of section 28A of that Act), or

(b) otherwise, at the end of the period specified in subsection (2) of that section in relation to the return.

(8) An enquiry is completed at the time when the Board give notice to the person or persons of their decision under subsection (3); but if the Board give notice to the persons at different times the enquiry is completed at the later of those times.

(9) The person, or either of the persons, to whom the enquiry relates may at any time before such notice is given apply for a direction that the Board must give such a notice.

[4 (10) Any such application is to be subject to the relevant provisions of Part 5 of the Taxes Management Act 1970 (see, in particular, section 48(2)(b) of that Act), and the tribunal must give the direction applied for unless satisfied that the Board have reasonable grounds for not making the decision or giving the notice.]

(11) Where the entitlement of a person, or the joint entitlement of persons, to a tax credit for a tax year has been enquired into under this section, it is not to be the subject of a further notice under subsection (1).

(12) Subject to [5sections 20, 21A and 21B] and regulations under section 21 (and to any appeal), a decision under subsection (3) in relation to a person or persons and a tax credit for a tax year is conclusive as to the entitlement of the person, or the joint entitlement of the persons, to the tax credit for the tax year and the amount of the tax credit to which he was entitled, or they were jointly entitled, for the tax year.

AMENDMENTS

1. Subsections (2), (4) and (9) are modified for polygamous units by Tax Credits (Polygamous Marriages) Regulations 2003 (SI 2003/742) reg.16.
2. Subsection (10) is modified by TCA 2002 s.63(5)(a), the modification being indicated by square brackets.
3. The section is modified for claimants subject to immigration control. See Tax Credits (Immigration) Regulations 2003 (SI 2003/623) regs 3 and 4.
4. Transfer of Tribunal Functions and Revenue and Customs Appeals Order 2009 (SI 2009/56) art.3(1) and Sch.1 para.313 (April 1, 2009).
5. Tax Credits, Child Benefit and Guardian's Allowance Reviews and Appeals Order 2014 (SI 2014/886) art.2(3) (April 6, 2014).

DEFINITIONS

"the Board"—see s.67.
"General Commissioners"—see s.47.
"prescribed"—see s.67.
"Special Commissioners"—see s.47.
"the relevant section 17 date"—see subs.(6).
"the relevant section 18 decision"—see subs.(5).
"tax credit"—see s.1(2).

GENERAL NOTE

This provision gives HMRC a broad general power similar to that in s.9A of the TMA 1970 (power to enquire into self-assessment returns) to enquire into the correctness of a s.18 entitlement decision. An enquiry under this section can be opened at any time after the s.18 decision is made until a year after the final

1.334

date for replying to a s.17 notice, unless HMRC uses its power to issue a demand for a personal tax return under s.8 of the TMA 1970 on the claimant. A return for a year must be made by January 31 next after the tax year ends (each April) or, if demanded later, three months after it is required. Section 9A (which entitles HMRC to issue a notice of enquiry into a return under s.8) allows about a year (the period is defined precisely) for a HMRC enquiry to follow a personal return.

An individual who is the subject of an enquiry has the same power to apply to a tribunal to stop the enquiry as exists for the equivalent income tax provisions, save that the application goes to the appeal tribunal (see s.63), not a tax tribunal.

Subsections (9) and (10) allow an individual to ask a tribunal to close an HMRC enquiry. This power has been created because there is otherwise no time limit to end an enquiry provided that it is started by HMRC within the correct time limits. The practice of tax tribunals, approved by the courts, is to deal with many applications by setting a time limit on HMRC rather than closing the enquiry immediately. It is also clear that rejection by a tribunal of one application to close an enquiry does not prevent an individual later making another application if the enquiry continues. The amended version of subs.(10) aligns the procedure with the new procedure for reviewing all tax decisions introduced by the Finance Act 2008 by way of amendments now in the Taxes Management Act 1970 from s.48. HMRC is given the right to review any decision before it goes forward to a tribunal, unless the appellant directly notifies the tribunal of the decision that is subject to appeal.

1.335   The addition of the references to ss.21A and 21B in para.(12) ensures that this regulation is compatible with the provisions about reviews added by those sections.

The power to look into a decision about entitlement to tax credits is referred to both in this section and in practice as an enquiry. This is to be distinguished from an investigation into a claim for, or award of, a tax credit, which is referred to by HMRC as an examination. The key difference is that an award is provisional, while an enquiry relates to an award that has been or is being finalised to give rise to entitlement.

HMRC have issued a short series of factsheets about its powers and practices for claimants: WTC/FS1 on enquiries; WTC/FS2 on examinations; WTC/FS3 on formal requests for information; and WTC/FS4 on meetings with an officer of Revenue and Customs.

Decisions on discovery

1.336   **20.**—(1) Where in consequence of a person's income tax liability being revised the Board have reasonable grounds for believing that a conclusive decision relating to his entitlement to a tax credit for a tax year (whether or not jointly with another person) is not correct, the Board may decide to revise that decision.

(2) A person's income tax liability is revised—
(a) on the taking effect of an amendment of a return of his under section 9ZA(1) of the Taxes Management Act 1970,
(b) on the issue of a notice of correction under section 9ZB of that Act amending a return of his (provided that he does not give a notice of rejection before the end of the period of thirty days beginning with the date of issue of the notice of correction),
(c) on the amendment of an assessment of his by notice under section 9C of that Act,
(d) on the amendment of a return of his under section 12ABA(3)(a) of that Act,
(e) on the amendment of a return of his under subsection (6)(a) of

section 12ABB of that Act after the correction of a partnership return under that section (provided that the amendment does not cease to have effect by reason of the rejection of the correction under subsection (4) of that section),
(f) on the issue of a closure notice under section 28A of that Act making amendments of a return of his;
(g) on the amendment of a return of his under section 28B(4)(a) of that Act,
(h) on the making of an assessment as regards him under section 29(1) of that Act,
(i) on the vacation of the whole or part of an assessment of his under section 32 of that Act,
(j) on giving him relief under section 33 of that Act, or
(k) on the determination (or settlement) of an appeal against the making, amendment or vacation of an assessment or return, or a decision on a claim for relief, under any of the provisions mentioned in paragraphs (c), (f) and (h) to (j).

(3) But no decision may be made under subsection (1)—
(a) unless it is too late to enquire into the person's entitlement under section 19, or
(b) after the period of one year beginning when the person's income tax liability is revised.

(4) Where the Board have reasonable grounds for believing that—
(a) a conclusive decision relating to the entitlement of a person, or the joint entitlement of persons, to a tax credit for a tax year is not correct, and
(b) that is attributable to fraud or neglect on the part of the person, or of either of the persons, or on the part of any person acting for him, or either of them,
the Board may decide to revise that decision.

(5) But no decision may be made under subsection (4)—
(a) unless it is too late to enquire into the entitlement, or joint entitlement, under section 19, or
(b) after the period of five years beginning with the end of the tax year to which the conclusive decision relates.

(6) "Conclusive decision", in relation to the entitlement of a person, or joint entitlement of persons, to a tax credit for a tax year, means—
(a) a decision in relation to it under section 18(1), (5), (6) or (9) or 19(3) or a previous decision under this section, or
(b) a decision under regulations under section 21 relating to a decision within paragraph (a),[² . . .]
[²(c) a decision within paragraph (a) or (b) as varied under section 21A(5)(b), or
(d) a decision on an appeal against a decision within paragraph (a), (b) or (c).]

(7) Subject to any subsequent decision under this section and to regulations under section 21 [²and to any review under section 21A] (and to any appeal), a decision under subsection (1) or (4) in relation to a person or persons and a tax credit for a tax year is conclusive as to the entitlement of the person, or the joint entitlement of the persons, to the tax credit for the tax year and the amount of the tax credit to which he was entitled, or they were jointly entitled, for the tax year.

Tax Credits Act 2002

AMENDMENTS

1. Subsection (4) is modified as it applies to polygamous units by Tax Credits (Polygamous Marriages) Regulations 2003 (SI 2003/742) reg.17.
2. Tax Credits, Child Benefit and Guardian's Allowance Reviews and Appeals Order 2014 (SI 2014/886) art.2(4) and (5) (April 6, 2014).

CROSS-REFERENCES

TMA 1970:
s.9ZA	Amendment of personal or trustee return by taxpayer
s.9ZB	Correction of personal return by taxpayer
s.9C	Amendment of self-assessment during enquiry to prevent loss of tax
s.12ABA	Amendment of partnership return by taxpayer
s.12ABB	Correction of partnership return by Revenue
s.28A	Completion of enquiry into personal or trustee return
s.28B	Completion of enquiry into partnership return
s.29	Assessment where loss of tax discovered
s.32	Double assessment
s.33	Error or mistake

DEFINITIONS

"conclusive decision"—see subs.(6).
"income tax"—see ICTA 1988 s.1.
"prescribed"—see s.67.
"tax credit"—see s.1(2).

GENERAL NOTE

1.337
Discovery is the traditional term used for finding out or taking informed guesses about undisclosed income for income tax purposes. The power to make assessments where loss of tax is discovered is in s.29 of the TMA 1970. This section is wider than that, although in part it flows from it. Section 29 allows an officer who discovers unassessed tax or excessive relief to make an assessment of the amount which, in the officer's opinion, ought to be charged to tax, and also imposes other conditions before the power can be used. This section, by contrast, allows action by HMRC in two sets of circumstances.

The first is if HMRC has reasonable grounds for believing an otherwise conclusive decision about tax credit (defined in subs.(6)) is not correct because of a revision of income tax liability (subs.(1)). HMRC may act if one of the TMA 1970 powers listed in subs.(2) has been used for a revision. These include s.29 and also the powers to revisit personal and partnership tax returns and decisions made by settlement or on appeal. Revisions under this power can be made only if it is too late to use s.19. And they cannot be made unless the revision is made within a year of the income tax revision (subs.(3)).

The second power (in subs.(4)) arises where HMRC has reasonable grounds to believe that an otherwise conclusive decision is wrong because of "fraud or neglect". "Fraud or neglect" are not defined in the Act. They are based on the version of s.29(4) of the Taxes Management Act 1970 in force when this Act was enacted. From April 6, 2009 s.29(4) is amended to refer to "carelessly or deliberately" and those terms are given definitions. The new terms apply to all tax penalties but have not been applied to tax credits.

A decision made under this section is itself conclusive, subject only to further decisions under this section or on appeal or because of official error (subs.(7)).

(2002 c.21 s.21)

Decisions subject to official error

21.—Regulations may make provision for a decision under section 14(1), 15(1), 16(1), 18(1), (5), (6) or (9), 19(3) or 20(1) or (4) to be revised in favour of the person or persons to whom it relates if it is incorrect by reason of official error (as defined by the regulations).

GENERAL NOTE

"Official error" is defined by the Tax Credits (Official Error) Regulations 2003 (SI 2003/692). See the note on those regulations. The provision is significantly narrower than the equivalent provision for income tax in s.33 of the TMA 1970 (error or mistake), which applies to any error or mistake.

[¹ Review of decisions

21A.—(1) The Commissioners for Her Majesty's Revenue and Customs must review any decision within section 38(1) if they receive a written application to do so that identifies the applicant and decision in question, and—
  (a) that application is received within 30 days of the date of the notification of the original decision or of the date the original decision was made if not notified because of section 23(3), or
  (b) it is received within such longer period as may be allowed under section 21B.

(2) The Commissioners must carry out the review as soon as is reasonably practicable.

(3) When the review has been carried out, the Commissioners must give the applicant notice of their conclusion containing sufficient information to enable the applicant to know—
  (a) the conclusion on the review,
  (b) if the conclusion is that the decision is varied, details of the variation, and
  (c) the reasons for the conclusion.

(4) The conclusion on the review must be one of the following—
  (a) that the decision is upheld;
  (b) that the decision is varied;
  (c) that the decision is cancelled.

(5) Where—
  (a) the Commissioners notify the applicant of further information or evidence that they may need for carrying out the review, and
  (b) the information or evidence is not provided to them by the date specified in the notice,
the review may proceed without that information or evidence.]

AMENDMENT

1. Section added by Tax Credits, Child Benefit and Guardian's Allowance Reviews and Appeals Order 2014 (SI 2014/886) art.2(6) (April 6, 2014).

GENERAL NOTE

This new section and s.21B give effect from April 6, 2014 to the Government's announced policy of requiring any potential appellant to apply for mandatory reconsideration by HMRC of any decision made about tax credits before an appeal may be made to a tribunal. A footnote to the Order introducing this review power specifically notes that "in practice, this review will be known as a 'mandatory reconsideration'". That makes the language actually used consistent with that used by the Secretary of State for Work and Pensions since October 2013 when considering revision of decisions made about social security benefits. The social security changes were implemented by statutory instruments made under Social Security Act 1998 s.12(3A) and (3B) (see Vol. III of this series). An equivalent set of legislative provisions for revision applying to income tax decisions are optional. A taxpayer may apply for reconsideration of a decision before going to a tribunal, but is not required to do so.

Subsection (1) requires HMRC to review any appealable decision (as listed in s.38(1)) once a written application to do so is received. There is a 30-day time limit of the date of the notification of the decision. That period may be extended under limited circumstances as defined by s.21B below, subject to an absolute time limit of 13 months.

It is not clear why the language of this section does not echo the language of the original Act in referring to "the date on which notice of the decision was given" and so tying the timing of the service of the notice in with s.23 of the Act (notice of decisions). Is the date on which a decision is notified the same as the date on which notice is given? In any event, it is arguable that if notice is not given then the time limit for applying for a review cannot start.

HMRC itself is not subject to any specific time limit in conducting the mandatory reconsideration. It has powers to seek further information while doing so but is not required to await a reply when information is requested. It is required to give reasons for the conclusion it reaches on the reconsideration.

Only when the reconsideration has been completed can an appellant take the matter forward to a tribunal.

[¹ Late application for a review

1.342

21B.— (1) The Commissioners for Her Majesty's Revenue and Customs may in a particular case extend the time limit specified in section 21A(1)(a) for making an application for a review if all of the following conditions are met.

(2) The first condition is that the person seeking a review has applied to the Commissioners for an extension of time.

(3) The second condition is that the application for the extension—
  (a) explains why the extension is sought, and
  (b) is made within 13 months of the notification of the original decision or of the date the original decision was made if not notified because of section 23(3).

(4) The third condition is that the Commissioners are satisfied that due to special circumstances it was not practicable for the application for a review to have been made within the time limit specified in section 21A(1)(a).

(5) The fourth condition is that the Commissioners are satisfied that it is reasonable in all the circumstances to grant the extension.

(6) In determining whether it is reasonable to grant an extension, the Commissioners must have regard to the principle that the greater the amount of time that has elapsed between the end of the time limit specified in section 21A(1)(a) and the date of the application, the more compelling should be the special circumstances on which the application is based.

(7) An application to extend the time limit specified in section 21A(1)(a) which has been refused may not be renewed.]

(2002 c.21 s.21B)

AMENDMENT

1. Section added by Tax Credits, Child Benefit and Guardian's Allowance Reviews and Appeals Order 2014 (SI 2014/886) art.2(6) (April 6, 2014).

GENERAL NOTE

See the note to section 21A above. 1.343

Information, etc. requirements: supplementary

22.—(1) Regulations may make provision as to the manner and form in which— 1.344
 (a) information or evidence is to be provided in compliance with a requirement imposed by a notice under section 14(2), 15(2), 16(3), 18(10) or 19(2), or
 (b) a declaration or statement is to be made in response to a notice under section 17.

(2) Regulations may make provision as to the dates which may be specified in a notice under section 14(2), 15(2), 16(3), 17, 18(10) or 19(2).

GENERAL NOTE

These regulation-making powers are necessary because the standard regulations applying to social security decision-making (the Social Security and Child Support (Decisions and Appeals) Regulations 1999 (SI 1999/991)) do not apply and there are no equivalents in the TMA 1970. The regulations made under these powers are the Tax Credits (Claims and Notifications) Regulations 2002 (SI 2002/2014). 1.345

Notice of decisions

23.—(1) When a decision is made under section 14(1), 15(1), 16(1), 18(1), (5), (6) or (9), 19(3) or 20(1) or (4) or regulations under section 21, the Board must give notice of the decision to the person, or each of the persons, to whom it relates. 1.346

(2) Notice of a decision must state the date on which it is given and include details of any right [¹to a review under section 21A and of any subsequent right] to appeal against the decision under section 38.

(3) Notice need not be given of a decision made under section 14(1) or 18(1) or (6) on the basis of declarations made or treated as made by the person or persons in response to the notice given to him or them under section 17 if—
 (a) that notice, or
 (b) in the case of a decision under subsection (6) of section 18, that notice or the notice of the decision under subsection (1) of that section,
stated what the decision would be and the date on which it would be made.

AMENDMENT

1. Tax Credits, Child Benefit and Guardian's Allowance Reviews and Appeals Order 2014 (SI 2014/886) art.2(7) (April 6, 2014).

DEFINITION

"the Board"—see s.67.

GENERAL NOTE

1.347 This section requires HMRC to adopt the same approach as for social security decisions of giving formal notice of every decision (save in limited cases where notice has already been given). The notice must set out any appeal rights. Section 45 makes provision for the form of a notice. Further details are laid down in the Tax Credits (Claims and Notifications) Regulations 2002 (SI 2002/2014). However, it may be viewed as significant that this provision is in primary legislation, while the equivalent for social security purposes (Social Security and Child Support (Decisions and Appeals) Regulations 1999 (SI 1999/991) reg.28) is made by regulation only. It is suggested therefore that the mandatory terms of subs.(1) (the Board *must* give notice) and subs.(2) (the notice *must* state) are not amenable to the somewhat relaxed approach to formalities applied to the social security equivalent (see the note to reg.28 of those Regulations). In particular, if no notice is given, it is arguable that no effective decision has been made, or alternatively that the decision is not final and the appeal period cannot start running.

The resulting effect on appeal rights is compounded by HMRC practice to give informal decisions before giving decisions to which this provision applies. See for example the criticism in *CTC/244/2008*, para.3.

Payment

Payments

1.348 **24.**—(1) Where the Board have made an award of a tax credit, the amount of the tax credit awarded must be paid to the person to whom the award is made, subject to subsections (2) and (3).

(2) Where an award of a tax credit is made to the members of [²a couple], payments of the tax credit, or of any element of the tax credit, are to be made to whichever of them is prescribed.

(3) Where an award of a tax credit is made on a claim which was made by one person on behalf of another, payments of the tax credit, or of any element of the tax credit, are to be made to whichever of those persons is prescribed.

(4) Where an award of a tax credit has been made to a person or persons for the whole or part of a tax year, payments may, in prescribed circumstances, continue to be made for any period, after the tax year, within which he is or they are entitled to make a claim for the tax credit for the next tax year.

(5) Payments made under subsection (4) are to be treated for the purposes of this section and the following provisions of this Part as if they were payments of the tax credit for the next tax year.

(6) Subject to section 25, payments of a tax credit must be made by the Board.

(7) Regulations may make provision about the time when and the manner in which a tax credit, or any element of a tax credit, is to be paid by the Board.

(8) If the regulations make provision for payments of a tax credit, or any element of a tax credit, to be made by the Board by way of a credit to a bank account or other account notified to the Board, the regulations may provide that entitlement to the tax credit or element is dependent on an account having been notified to the Board in accordance with the regulations.

(2002 c.21 s.24)

AMENDMENTS

1. Subsection (2) is modified as it applies to polygamous units by Tax Credits (Polygamous Marriages) Regulations 2003 (SI 2003/742) reg.18.
2. Civil Partnership Act 2004 s.254 and Sch.24 para.145 (December 5, 2005).

DEFINITIONS

"claim"—see s.3(8).
"couple"—see s.3(5A).
"the Board"—see s.67.
"prescribed"—see s.67.
"tax credit"—see s.1(2).
"tax year"—see s.47.

GENERAL NOTE

From April 2006 HMRC makes all WTC and CTC payments. Payment by employers has been discontinued. Sections 25 (Payment by employers), 26 (liability of officers for sums paid to employers) and 33 (failure by employers to make correct payments) and the related regulations therefore have no current relevance and are not set out in this volume. For the texts see the volume for previous years.

1.349

Rights of employees

27. Schedule 1 (rights of employees not to suffer unfair dismissal or other detriment) has effect.

1.350

DEFINITIONS

"employee"—see s.25(5).

GENERAL NOTE

This section introduces Sch.1. Both this section and the Schedule are based on s.7 of, and Sch.3 to, the TCA 1999. The aim is to provide employees with direct rights to ensure that employers do not discriminate against them because of WTC. The underlying fear is that employers would rather get rid of employees than implement the WTC process. Schedule 1 makes the necessary amendments to the Employment Rights Act (GB) and Order (NI) to give employees a right not to suffer detriment and a right not to be unfairly dismissed because of tax credits. The text of Sch.1 is not included here as it is a matter of employment law.

1.351

Overpayments

28.—(1) Where the amount of a tax credit paid for a tax year to a person or persons exceeds the amount of the tax credit to which he is entitled, or they are jointly entitled, for the tax year (as determined in accordance with the provision made by and by virtue of sections 18 to [21B]), the Board may decide that the excess, or any part of it, is to be repaid to the Board.

1.352

(2) In this Part such an excess is referred to as an overpayment.

(3) For overpayments made under awards on single claims, the person to whom the tax credit was awarded is liable to repay the amount which the Board decide is to be repaid.

(4) For overpayments made under awards on joint claims, the persons to whom the tax credit was awarded are jointly and severally liable to repay the amount which the Board decide is to be repaid unless the Board decide that each is to repay a specified part of that amount.

(5) Where it appears to the Board that there is likely to be an overpayment of a tax credit for a tax year under an award made to a person or persons, the Board may, with a view to reducing or eliminating the overpayment, amend the award or any other award of any tax credit made to the person or persons; but this subsection does not apply once a decision is taken in relation to the person or persons for the tax year under section 18(1).

(6) Where the Board decide under section 16 to terminate an award of a tax credit made to a person or persons on the ground that at no time during the period to which the award related did the person or persons satisfy—

(a) section 8(1) (if the award related to child tax credit), or

(b) section 10(1) (if it related to working tax credit),

the Board may decide that the amount paid under the award, or any part of it, is to be treated for the purposes of this Part (apart from subsection (5)) as an overpayment.

AMENDMENT

1. Tax Credits, Child Benefit and Guardian's Allowance Reviews and Appeals Order 2014 (SI 2014/886) art.2(8) (April 6, 2014).

DEFINITIONS

"the Board"—see s.67.
"joint claim"—see s.3(8).
"overpayment"—see subs.(2).
"single claim"—see s.3(8).
"tax credit"—see s.1(2).
"tax year"—see s.47.

GENERAL NOTE

1.353 An overpayment is an excess of a tax credit awarded and paid as against the amount of tax credit to which a claimant is entitled under a final decision about entitlement (subs.(2)). This will usually arise where the final decision on entitlement is for a lesser amount than the amount awarded. It may also arise under a later revision under ss.19 or 20, or when an award was made that should not have been made (subs.(6)). Subsection (1) gives a power to (but does not impose a duty on) HMRC to collect overpayments. The decision of HMRC whether or not to collect an overpayment is not subject to appeal, and is not conditional on the fulfilment of any test by the claimant. This is a different approach from that taken for social security purposes, and by the previous tax credits regime, where it had to be shown in most cases that the claimant had caused the overpayment by a failure to disclose, or a misrepresentation of, a material fact. In addition, the decision on recoverability for social security purposes is subject to appeal.

The government has consistently failed to act on the recommendations of the Parliamentary Ombudsman and others that there be a right of appeal against overpayment decisions. Dispute about the underlying entitlement to tax credits are appealable, though such disputes do not often reach tribunals. Disputes about the amount of overpayments are dealt with as recovery questions. See further s.29.

Recovery of overpayments

1.354 **29.**—(1) Where an amount is liable to be repaid by a person or persons under section 28, the Board must give him, or each of them, a notice specifying the amount.

(2002 c.21 s.29)

(2) The notice must state which of subsections (3) to (5) is to apply in relation to the amount or any specifiedpart of the amount; and a notice may at any time be replaced by another notice containing a different statement.

(3) Where a notice states that this subsection applies in relation to an amount (or part of an amount), it is to be treated for the purposes of Part 6 of the Taxes Management Act 1970 (c.9) (collection and recovery) as if it were tax charged in an assessment and due and payable by the person or persons to whom the notice was given at the end of the period of 30 days beginning with the day on which the notice is given.

(4) Where a notice states that this subsection applies in relation to an amount (or part of an amount), it may, subject to provision made by regulations, be recovered by deduction from payments of any tax credit under an award made for any period to the person, or either or both of the persons, to whom the notice was given.

(5) Where a notice states that this subsection applies in relation to an amount (or part of an amount), [1 PAYE regulations] apply to it as if it were an under payment of [2 income tax] for a previous year of assessment by the person or persons to whom the notice was given [2 that is not a relevant debt (within the meaning of section 684 of the Income Tax (Earnings and Pensions) Act 2003))].

AMENDMENT

1. Words amended by ITEPA 2003 Sch.6 para.266 (April 6, 2003). Subsection (4) is modified by the Tax Credits (Polygamous Marriages) Regulations 2003 (SI 2003/742) reg.12 as it applies to polygamous units.
2. Finance Act 2009 s.110 and Sch.58 para.8 (July 21, 2009).

DEFINITIONS

"the Board"—see s.67.
"overpayment"—see s.28(2).

GENERAL NOTE

There is no appeal against a decision about either recovery or recoverability under this Act. The absence of a right of appeal has been consistently confirmed by Commissioners. See *CTC/2662/2005*, *CTC/3981/2006* and *CTC/2270/2007*. As that last decision emphasises, the approach is not the same as that applied to the former WFTC (as illustrated by *CTC/1907/2007*). The decision that can be appealed is the entitlement decision under which the overpayment arises. That decision must be notified to the claimant under s.23, save where one of the exceptions in s.23(3) applies. It may be anticipated that, following equivalent experience in social security cases, some recipients will only object, and attempt to appeal, when they receive notice of an overpayment under this section rather than notice of the decision that gives rise to the overpayment. Whether this can amount to an effective and timely appeal against the entitlement decision will depend on part on how and when the required notices are given, and is for decision under s.39.

This section is the equivalent of s.30 of the TMA 1970. HMRC may give a formal notice to someone whom it has decided has been overpaid tax credit. The notice may activate all or any of three alternative methods of recovering the overpaid tax credit. The first, under subs.(3), is by using ss.60–70A of the TMA 1970. These empower HMRC's collection and recovery powers for unpaid income tax demands. These allow distraint and action in both civil courts and magistrates' courts. Subsection (4) entitles

1.355

Tax Credits Act 2002

HMRC to collect the overpayment by deducting it from other payments of tax credit: see further Tax Credits (Payments by the Board) Regulations 2002 (SI 2002/2173) reg.12A, inserted by the Tax Credits (Miscellaneous Amendments) Regulations 2004 (SI 2004/762) reg.18. Subsection (5) allows overpayments of tax credits to be collected with income tax and NI contributions but this power is not used.

The way in which HMRC decides on the recovery of overpayments and then collects them continues to be a matter of controversy as there is no direct appeal to the First-tier Tribunal against an overpayment or recovery decision. HMRC however publicises this as an appeal against the overpayment (see form TC846). Only the underlying entitlement decision may be appealed. The way in which overpayments are collected is set out in Code of Practice 26, now updated annually, the most recent version of which is set out in full at the end of this volume.

1.356 The Income Tax (Pay as You Earn) (Amendment No 4) Regulations 2014 (SI 2014/2689) empower Her Majesty's Revenue and Customs to start recovering tax credit debts by using the PAYE coding and tax deduction machinery to collect such debts. Separate legislation increases the HMRC power to use tax coding in this way to a total debt of £17,000. These regulations allow that maximum to be used for tax credit debts. This starts with codings for the tax year 2015–16.

Someone wishing to dispute recovery of an overpayment should send a copy of form TC846 (available on the HMRC website) to the Overpayments Dispute Team, Tax Credits Office, Preston PR1 0SB (or Belfast BT2 7WF).

Note also that s.684(7A) of ITEPA was amended by Finance Act 2009 s.110 and Sch.58 para.7 to permit HMRC to agree with a payer of PAYE income to collect amounts other than tax. Section 684(7AA) of ITEPA defines a relevant debt as a sum payable by the payee to the Commissioners either under or by virtue of an enactment (other than an excluded debt) or under a contract settlement. Subsection (7AB)(a) provides that for the purposes of subs.(7AA) child tax credit or working tax credit that the payee is liable to repay is an excluded debt. These amendments allow HMRC to recover overpaid tax credits through the PAYE system with the consent of the individual.

HMRC has published detailed guidance for intermediaries and advisers in a new leaflet *How HMRC handle tax credit overpayments*.

Underpayments

1.357 **30.**—(1) Where it has been determined in accordance with the provision made by and by virtue of sections 18 to [21B] that a person was entitled, or persons were jointly entitled, to a tax credit for a tax year and either—
   (a) the amount of the tax credit paid to him or them for that tax year was less than the amount of the tax credit to which it was so determined that he is entitled or they are jointly entitled, or
   (b) no payment of the tax credit was made to him or them for that tax year,
the amount of the difference, or of his entitlement or their joint entitlement, must be paid to him or to whichever of them is prescribed.

(2) Where the claim for the tax credit was made by one person on behalf of another, the payment is to be made to whichever of those persons is prescribed.

AMENDMENT

1. Tax Credits, Child Benefit and Guardian's Allowance Reviews and Appeals Order 2014 (SI 2014/886) art.2(8) (April 6, 2014).

(2002 c.21 s.30)

DEFINITIONS

"prescribed"—see s.67.
"tax credit"—see s.1(2).
"tax year"—see s.47.

GENERAL NOTE

This provision is the converse of s.28. However, the procedure that triggers it is not a mirror of the provisions giving rise to an overpayment. In particular, see the note to s.6 on notifications of changes of circumstances. If there is an underpayment, this section requires HMRC to make it good. However underpayments, unlike repayments of income tax, or overpayments of tax credit, do not carry interest. Nor does the section impose any time-limit on the payment.

Penalties

Incorrect statements, etc.

31.—(1) Where a person fraudulently or negligently—
  (a) makes an incorrect statement or declaration in or in connection with a claim for a tax credit or a notification of a change of circumstances given in accordance with regulations under section 6 or in response to a notice under section 17, or
  (b) gives incorrect information or evidence in response to a requirement imposed on him by virtue of section 14(2), 15(2), 16(3), 18(10) or 19(2) or regulations under section 25 [²or in response to a notification under section 21A(5)],
a penalty not exceeding £3,000 may be imposed on him.

(2) Where a person liable to a penalty under subsection (1) is a person making, or who has made, a claim for a tax credit for a period jointly with another and the penalty is imposed—
  (a) under paragraph (a) of that subsection in respect of the claim, a notification relating to the tax credit claimed or a notice relating to the tax credit awarded on the claim, or
  (b) under paragraph (b) of that subsection in respect of a requirement imposed on him with respect to the tax credit for the period,
a penalty of an amount not exceeding £3,000 may be imposed on the other person unless subsection (3) applies.

(3) This subsection applies if the other person was not, and could not reasonably have been expected to have been, aware that the person liable to the penalty under subsection (1) had fraudulently or negligently made the incorrect statement or declaration or given the incorrect information or evidence.

(4) Where penalties are imposed under subsections (1) and (2) in respect of the same statement, declaration, information or evidence, their aggregate amount must not exceed £3,000.

(5) Where a person acts for another—
  (a) in or in connection with a claim or notification referred to in subsection (1), or
  (b) in response to a notice so referred to,
subsection (1) applies to him (as well as to any person to whom it applies apart from this subsection).

1.358

1.359

Tax Credits Act 2002

AMENDMENTS

1. Subsection (2) is modified as it applies to polygamous units by Tax Credits (Polygamous Marriages) Regulations 2003 (SI 2003/742) reg.20.
2. Tax Credits, Child Benefit and Guardian's Allowance Reviews and Appeals Order 2014 (SI 2014/886) art.2(9) (April 6, 2014).

DEFINITIONS

"change of circumstances"—see s.6(1).
"claim"—see s.3(8).
"joint claim"—*ibid.*
"tax credit"—see s.1(2).

GENERAL NOTE

1.360 This Act reflects a concern about potential fraud with regard to claims and payments. There were originally several sources of concern. One—abuse by employers in payments through the wage packet—no longer applies. All payments are made by HMRC. Concern about the payment process itself is dealt with in part by ensuring that most payments are made direct to bank accounts. The remaining original concern was fraud by claimants. Events showed that another, unanticipated, source of fraud proved a big problem. This was the fraudulent use by third parties of the facility to make claims online. This resulted in the online facility being closed down some years ago. It has yet to be reinstated. The focus of ss.31–34 and Sch.2 is now mainly claimants. The powers are wide enough to catch anyone else involved, such as someone providing childcare on the basis of false information.

Sections 31–34 draw on the then regime applying for income tax. This was in Pt X of the TMA 1970. After full consultation, HMRC secured a complete rewrite of tax penalty powers in the Finance Act 2008. This came into effect on April 1, 2009. It applies to all direct and indirect taxes. It does not apply to tax credits. There have been no changes to these sections equivalent to the changes for tax purposes, so the "old" law continues to apply here.

This section deals with the problem where anyone required to make a declaration, statement or notification or to give information or evidence does so "incorrectly" and where the person does so "fraudulently or negligently". It applies both to the person making the declaration, etc., and to anyone acting for that person (subs.(5)), and both could be subject to penalty proceedings in connection with the same matter.

1.361 HMRC have published two leaflets of guidance about the exercise of their penalty powers: WTC3, *Tax Credit Penalties, How tax credit examinations are settled*, and WTC4, *Tax Credit penalties, How tax credit enquiries are settled.* They apply to penalties under both this section and s.32. These reflect the differences between examinations (taking place about current claims or awards) and enquiries (taking place when an award is finalised or after entitlement has been established). They are now combined with WTC7, which is set out at the end of this volume. The leaflets set out the procedure for dealing with the imposition of penalties and the basis on which HMRC decide at what level a penalty will be set. HMRC's practice follows that applying for similar income tax examinations and enquiries. Discounts to the maximum penalty will be applied to reflect: the extent to which the error was disclosed voluntarily by the claimant; the extent to which the claimant has co-operated with HMRC in the examination or enquiry; the seriousness of the errors or omissions; and whether this is a first or subsequent occasion on which there has been an error or omission. All penalty decisions are open to appeal. Appeals go to the First-tier Tribunal and then the Upper Tribunal. Since the introduction of the new appeal system an appellant must obtain leave to appeal to take the appeal to the Upper Tribunal. Under the original system no leave was needed to appeal against a penalty to the social security commssioners. No such appeal was considered by them, and few were considered by the social security tribunals. This is in part because HMRC were reluctant at first to

Fraudulently or negligently

The former penalty provisions in TMA 1970 had been subject to consideration in the courts on a number of occasions, and it is to be expected that the common phraseology of those sections and these (such as "fraudulently or negligently") will receive a similar interpretation. On this basis, the fraud or neglect of an agent will be regarded as the fraud or neglect of the claimant: *Clixby v Pountney* (1968) 44 T.C. 575. It is clearly established in income tax law that the onus of proving fraud or neglect is on HMRC. *Hillenbrand v IRC* (1966) 42 T.C. 617 established that there is no presumption of fraud or neglect because of an omission, although the omission might give a factual basis for a decision on this point. However, if HMRC establish the fraud or neglect, then the burden shifts to the taxpayer to show that any assessment made by HMRC as a result is incorrect. It is also established that HMRC does not have to show the precise nature of discovered income: *Hudson v Humbles* (1965) 42 T.C. 380. That is part of the process of making and appealing an assessment. It is suggested that the same approaches would be appropriate here, save that in addition HMRC and appeal tribunal will be able to take account of evidence gathered for income tax purposes in deciding the outcome of a s.20 review.

1.362

Additionally, since the Human Rights Act 1998 came into effect, it is arguable that this section imposes a "criminal" liability under art.6(3) of the European Convention on Human Rights. (For the text, see Vol.III of this work). Courts have applied the criminal standard to equivalent provisions in income tax and VAT legislation. If art.6(3) applies then close consideration needs to be given to the burden of proof under this section, the evidence available for establishing or resisting the application of the section and the availability of legal aid.

A penalty under this section bears interest under s.37. It is treated as unpaid tax for the purposes of recovery and collection (Sch.2 para.7). Appeals against penalty decisions are dealt with in Sch.2 (see s.34).

Subsections (2) and (3) deal with a problem that is no longer relevant to income tax, namely the case where one of a couple making a joint claim has failed fully to co-operate with the other, so that the declaration is wrong but one of the joint claimants is not aware that this is so. In such cases responsibility remains joint and several unless one of the claimants can show that the defence in subs.(3) applies. This imposes a double test of both fact and reasonableness.

The conduct of penalty cases

Appeals under s.31 are "criminal" in the sense that arts 6(2) and (3) of the European Convention on Human Rights apply in addition to art.6(1). This is clear from the decision of the European Court of Human Rights in *King v United Kingdom (No.2)*, Application 13881/02, of February 17, 2004, [2004] S.T.C. 911. See Vol.III of this work for the text of the article and commentary. That approach will be strengthened by the decision of that court in *PM v United Kingdom*, Application 6638/03, [2005] S.T.C. 1566. In that case a taxpayer was held entitled to invoke the scope of art.1, Protocol 1 (rights of property) in alleging discrimination about the terms of entitlement to a deduction for maintenance payments under s.347 of the Income and Corporation Taxes Act 1988. As there was no internal remedy for discrimination caused by primary legislation, the European Court awarded damages to the appellant.

1.363

The HMRC Claimant Compliance Manual (CCM) refers to s.31 as being a power to punish. But this does not apply to s.32. See the detailed analysis of the equivalent income tax provisions in *Gladders v Prior* [2003] S.T.C. (S.C.D.) 245 (decision of Special Commissioner of Income Tax, not appealed). A notice requiring information does not breach the rule on self-incrimination. See *Sharkey v De*

Croos [2005] S.T.C. (S.C.D.) 336 citing *R. v Allen* [2002] A.C. 509 on a similar income tax provision.

There is authority that receipt of a relevant notice is crucial to the activation of the sections, and that the Interpretation Act presumptions do not apply: Macpherson J in *CEC v Medway Draughting and Technical Services Ltd* [1989] S.T.C. 346 dealing with a similar VAT provision.

The burden of proof rests with HMRC, who should open any appeal. The degree of proof remains the civil burden, namely that something is "more likely than not". Removal of the unused open power to appeal against the decision of the first tribunal leaves questions of fact entirely in the control, now, of the judges of the First-tier Tribunal. This will include issues about setting the specific level of any penalty.

The level of penalties

1.364 The procedure to be followed by HMRC officers when imposing or applying for tax credits penalties are set out in the *New Tax Credits Claimant Compliance Manual* (abbreviated as CCM). This is available on the HMRC website at http://www.hmrc.gov.uk/manuals/ccmmanual/Index.htm. However, some parts of CCM have been withheld from publication under the Freedom of Information Act 2000. See, for example CCM 10070 (even the number of that paragraph is withheld, but it is referred to in cross-references not withheld as covering "Penalties: calculation of penalties in incorrect claims"). The main issue withheld in that paragraph is the calculation of the amount of a penalty to be imposed under subs.(4) of this section. CCM 10080 on the calculation of a percentage of an overpaid claim is not withheld, although it makes little sense in the absence of CCM 10070. This is in contrast to the approach adopted by HMRC with regard to penalties under the income tax penalty regime, and in which percentages play a major role. See now the recently published *Code of Practice 9 (2005)* on civil investigation into cases of suspected serious fraud. This specifically details reductions of maximum penalties by the following percentages:

— up to 20 per cent for voluntary disclosure (or 30 per cent for full disclosure with no risk of discovery);

— up to 40 per cent for cooperation with an investigation, including full disclosures of information requested; and

— up to 40 per cent for seriousness of errors and omissions.

Withholding information under the 2000 Act does not apply when HMRC must explain to an appeal tribunal how it reaches the level of penalty it has selected. As a result, various parts of the withheld information have come to the attention of individual appeal tribunals. That is not a satisfactory situation.

It would seem that the approach broadly follows the income tax penalty approach save that in the case of tax penalties the maximum amount of the penalty is a set figure and not a percentage of the income tax under-declared. For example, CCM 10080 shows that an officer should look at the percentage of the overclaimed credits as compared with total credits originally claimed. CCM 10090 refers to "the relatively small amount of penalties for first offences". CCM 10100 refers to an abatement of a maximum of 50 per cent for full and prompt co-operation with an enquiry or examination. These statements, and the examples at CCM 10110, all point to the same broad approach as that used for income tax. CCM also emphasises that penalties for second and subsequent incorrect statements are likely to be significantly higher than initial penalties. Officers are required to notify claimants of this when imposing an initial penalty.

1.365 That aside, CCM sets out in considerable detail the procedures to be used by individual HMRC officers in the process of imposing or requesting penalties.

(2002 c.21 s.31)

CCM 10040 emphasises that the penalty power related to s.17 notifications applies only once although the information applies to two years. However, if there are incorrect s.17 notices at both ends of a year, HMRC may levy two penalties. In addition, there may be separate penalties up to the maximum where there is an incorrect s.17 notification and some other "offence" as the CCM terms it.

Failure to comply with requirements

32.—(1) Where a person fails—
(a) to provide any information or evidence which he is required to provide by virtue of section 14(2), 15(2), 16(3), 18(10) or 19(2) or regulations under section 25, or
(b) to comply with a requirement imposed on him by a notice under section 17 by virtue of subsection (2)(a), (4)(a) or (6)(a) of that section,

the penalties specified in subsection (2) may be imposed on him.

(2) The penalties are—
(a) a penalty not exceeding £300, and
(b) if the failure continues after a penalty is imposed under paragraph (a), a further penalty or penalties not exceeding £60 for each day on which the failure continues after the day on which the penalty under that paragraph was imposed (but excluding any day for which a penalty under this paragraph has already been imposed).

(3) Where a person fails to give a notification required by regulations under section 6(3), a penalty not exceeding £300 may be imposed on him.

(4) No penalty under subsection (2) may be imposed on a person in respect of a failure after the failure has been remedied.

(5) For the purposes of this section a person is to be taken not to have failed to provide information or evidence, comply with a requirement or give a notification which must be provided, complied with or given by a particular time—
(a) if he provided, complied with or gave it within such further time (if any) as the Board may have allowed,
(b) if he had a reasonable excuse for not providing, complying with or giving it by that time, or
(c) if, after having had such an excuse, he provided, complied with or gave it without unreasonable delay.

(6) Where the members of [¹ a couple] both fail as mentioned in subsection (1)(b), the aggregate amount of any penalties under subsection (2) imposed on them in relation to their failures must not exceed the amounts specified in that subsection; and where the members of [¹ a couple] both fail as mentioned in subsection (3), the aggregate amount of any penalties imposed on them in relation to their failures must not exceed £300.

AMENDMENT

1. Civil Partnership Act 2004 s.254 and Sch.24 para.145 (December 5, 2005).

DEFINITIONS
"the Board"—see s.67.
"couple"—see s.3(5A).

GENERAL NOTE

1.367
See the note to s.31 on the penalty regime as a whole. This section imposes penalties on those who fail to comply with any notices under s.17, who fail to provide information or evidence under any of the powers to require this, or who fail to give notification of a change of circumstances under s.6. It imposes a potential penalty on all failures, regardless of the reason for the failure. There is no test of fraud or negligence. The policy of all these measures is to impose a relatively low initial maximum penalty (£300 in all cases), but then to provide a cumulatively daily penalty as a strong deterrent to those who choose to ignore not only the notices and requirements but also the initial penalty. In each case, the maximum daily rate is £60. But the daily rate stops when the failure is remedied.

A penalty under this section bears interest under s.37. It is treated as unpaid tax for the purposes of recovery and collection (Sch.2 para.7). Appeals against penalty decisions are dealt with in Sch.2 (see s.34). By contrast with s.31, this section does not demand proof of fraud or negligence, and may therefore impose a civil penalty rather than a criminal penalty for the purposes of the European Convention on Human Rights.

For details of HMRC's practice in setting and dealing with penalties, see the note to s.31 and HMRC. The full text of WTC7 is set out at the end of the volume. HMRC has announced that it will, on a concessionary basis, not seek penalties from those who fail to comply with the mandatory provisions in this section when the award made to the individual is a nil award.

.368–1.369
Subsection (1) lists the powers under which HMRC can demand information within the penalty regime. It is important to note that those powers are not all-embracing but are subject to clear time limits laid down in primary legislation. See further the notes to ss.14 and 19 above.

The CCM (Claimant Compliance Manual—see note to p.161 above) states that:

"Penalties under s.32(1) are not intended to punish a person who will not provide information. The penalties are intended to encourage the person to comply with the notice and if you do not think the penalties will achieve this result you should not normally begin penalty action." (CCM 10230).

The guidance also states that s.32 penalties will not normally be needed for s.14(2) or s.15(2) failures. In-year challenges will normally only be those under s.16 (CCM 10235, 10240). Similarly, CCM discourages s.32 penalties for s.17 notices.

Supplementary

1.370
34.—Schedule 2 (penalties: supplementary) has effect.

Fraud

Offence of fraud

1.371
35.—(1) A person commits an offence if he is knowingly concerned in any fraudulent activity undertaken with a view to obtaining payments of a tax credit by him or any other person.

(2) A person who commits an offence under subsection (1) is liable—
(a) on summary conviction, to imprisonment for a term not exceeding six months, or a fine not exceeding the statutory maximum, or both, or
(b) on conviction on indictment, to imprisonment for a term not exceeding seven years, or a fine, or both.

DEFINITION

"tax credit"—see s.1(2).

GENERAL NOTE

Like the penalties provisions, this section reflects the fear of fraud by claimants and others abusing the tax credits system. There is no equivalent of this section in the TCA 1999. The new offence is briefly stated and is clearly intended to have a wide reach. It is not confined to claimants or employers and could be applied, for example, to a childcare provider.

Section 124 of the Welfare Reform Act 2012 contains detailed provisions to amend this section to increase the penalties. That is not yet in effect. That Act contains related measures, some of which are in effect since June 2012 but are beyond the scope of this work, to increase DWP and HMRC powers to investigate tax credit frauds. In particular, a series of amendments to other legislation treat tax credits as social security benefits for the purposes of benefit offences and their investigation.

Powers in relation to documents

36.—(1) Section 20BA of the Taxes Management Act 1970 (c.9) (orders for delivery of documents) applies (with Schedule 1AA and section 20BB) in relation to offences involving fraud in connection with, or in relation to, tax credits as in relation to offences involving serious fraud in connection with, or in relation to, tax.

(2) [1 . . .]

(3) [1 . . .]

(4) Any regulations under Schedule 1AA to the Taxes Management Act 1970 which are in force immediately before the commencement of subsection (1) apply, subject to any necessary modifications, for the purposes of that Schedule as they apply by virtue of that subsection (until amended or revoked).

AMENDMENT

1. Finance Act 2007 s.84(4) and Sch.22 para.14 (December 1, 2007).

DEFINITION

"tax credit"—see s.1(2).

GENERAL NOTE

This applies specific powers available to HMRC for dealing with tax fraud to tax credit fraud. Sections 20BA and 20BB of the TMA 1970 deal with orders for delivery of documents and offences of fraud respectively. The statutory instrument currently made under Sch.1AA is the Orders for the Delivery of Documents (Procedure) Regulations 2000 (SI 2000/2875).

Loss of tax credit provisions

[¹ Loss of working tax credit in case of conviction etc for benefit offence

36A. — (1) Subsection (4) applies where a person ("the offender")—
(a) is convicted of one or more benefit offences in any proceedings, or
(b) after being given a notice under subsection (2) of the appropriate penalty provision by an appropriate authority, agrees in the manner specified by the appropriate authority to pay a penalty under the appropriate penalty provision to the appropriate authority, in a case where the offence to which the notice relates is a benefit offence, or
(c) is cautioned in respect of one or more benefit offences.
(2) In subsection (1)(b)—
(a) "the appropriate penalty provision" means section 115A of the Social Security Administration Act 1992 (penalty as alternative to prosecution) or section 109A of the Social Security Administration (Northern Ireland) Act 1992 (the corresponding provision for Northern Ireland);
(b) "appropriate authority" means—
(i) in relation to section 115A of the Social Security Administration Act 1992, the Secretary of State or an authority which administers housing benefit or council tax benefit, and
(ii) in relation to section 109A of the Social Security Administration (Northern Ireland) Act 1992, the Department (within the meaning of that Act) or the Northern Ireland Housing Executive.
(3) Subsection (4) does not apply by virtue of subsection (1)(a) if, because the proceedings in which the offender was convicted constitute the current set of proceedings for the purposes of section 36C, the restriction in subsection (3) of that section applies in the offender's case.
(4) If this subsection applies and the offender is a person who would, apart from this section, be entitled (whether pursuant to a single or joint claim) to working tax credit at any time within the disqualification period, then, despite that entitlement, working tax credit shall not be payable for any period comprised in the disqualification period—
(a) in the case of a single claim, to the offender, or
(b) in the case of a joint claim, to the offender or the other member of the couple.
(5) Regulations may provide in relation to cases to which subsection (4)(b) would otherwise apply that working tax credit shall be payable, for any period comprised in the disqualification period, as if the amount payable were reduced in such manner as may be prescribed.
(6) For the purposes of this section, the disqualification period, in relation to any disqualifying event, means the relevant period beginning with such date, falling after the date of the disqualifying event, as may be determined by or in accordance with regulations.
(7) For the purposes of subsection (6) the relevant period is—
(a) in a case falling within subsection (1)(a) where the benefit offence, or one of them, is a relevant offence, the period of three years,
(b) in a case falling within subsection (1)(a) (but not within paragraph (a) above), the period of 13 weeks, or

(c) in a case falling within subsection (1)(b) or (c), the period of 4 weeks.

(8) The Treasury may by order amend subsection (7)(a), (b) or (c) to substitute a different period for that for the time being specified there.

(9) This section has effect subject to section 36B.

(10) In this section and section 36B—

"benefit offence" means any of the following offences committed on or after the day specified by order made by the Treasury—
  (a) an offence in connection with a claim for a disqualifying benefit;
  (b) an offence in connection with the receipt or payment of any amount by way of such a benefit;
  (c) an offence committed for the purpose of facilitating the commission (whether or not by the same person) of a benefit offence;
  (d) an offence consisting in an attempt or conspiracy to commit a benefit offence;

"disqualifying benefit" has the meaning given in section 6A(1) of the Social Security Fraud Act 2001;

"disqualifying event" means—
  (a) the conviction falling within subsection (1)(a);
  (b) the agreement falling within subsection (1)(b);
  (c) the caution falling within subsection (1)(c);

"relevant offence" has the meaning given in section 6B of the Social Security Fraud Act 2001.]

AMENDMENT

1. Welfare Reform Act 2012 s.120 (April 6, 2013) (see Welfare Reform Act 2012 (Commencement No.7) Order 2013 (SI 2013/178) art.2).

DEFINITIONS

"caution"—see s.67
"disqualifying benefit—see Social Security Fraud Act 2001 s.6A(1) as amended by Welfare Reform Act 2012 s.117.
"joint claim"—see s.3(3).
"working tax credit"—see s.8.

GENERAL NOTE

The Welfare Reform Act 2012 introduced this section and ss.36B–36D in parallel with equivalent provisions for social security benefits. They provide the legislation necessary to carry forward the Government's policy of penalising by loss of benefit those who commit benefit frauds. This is separate from any criminal penalty imposed and any recovery of wrongly paid benefit. The provisions apply to working tax credit, but not to child tax credit. Where the working tax credit is paid on a joint claim, these sections apply to both joint claimants save as specified by or under this section. The effect of the section is to stop the tax credit being payable for a stated period despite any continuing entitlement to the credit. That is normally a complete stop to payment for a "disqualification period", but a reduced level of payment applies in some cases, as noted below.

As subs.(1) makes clear, these sections apply not only to cases where a claimant has been convicted of a benefit offence, but also where a claimant has agreed to pay a penalty to the Secretary of State or any other relevant authority or has accepted a caution. And they apply regardless of the specific benefit for which the conviction, penalty or caution is imposed. So, for example, the loss of tax credits could apply because of an accepted fraud with regard to housing benefit.

1.376

Tax Credits Act 2002

Where the offender is one of a couple and the other member of the couple is not subject to a disqualification period at the same time, provision is made by regulation that payment of the working tax is to continue at a 50 per cent rate. See Loss of Tax Credit Regulations 2013 (SI 2013/715) reg.3 (para.2.491, below).

For the date from which subs.(6) operates see the Loss of Tax Credit Regulations 2013 (SI 2013/715) reg.2 (para.2.490, below).

[¹ **Supplementary**

1.377   **36B.**—(1) Where—
(a) the conviction of any person of any offence is taken in account for the purposes of the application of section 36A in relation to that person, and
(b) that conviction is subsequently quashed,
all such payments and other adjustments shall be made as would be necessary if no restriction had been imposed by or under section 36A that could not have been imposed if the conviction had not taken place.

(2) Where, after the agreement of any person ("P") to pay a penalty under the appropriate penalty provision is taken into account for the purposes of the application of section 36A in relation to that person—
(a) P's agreement to pay the penalty is withdrawn under subsection (5) of the appropriate penalty provision, or
(b) it is decided on an appeal or in accordance with regulations under the Social Security Act 1992 or the Social Security (Northern Ireland) Order 1998 (S.I. 1998/1506 (N.I. 10)) that the overpayment to which the agreement relates is not recoverable or due,
all such payments and other adjustments shall be made as would be necessary if no restriction had been imposed by or under section 36A that could not have been imposed if P had not agreed to pay the penalty.

(3) Where, after the agreement ("the old agreement") of any person ("P") to pay a penalty under the appropriate penalty provision is taken into account for the purposes of the application of section 36A in relation to P, the amount of any overpayment made to which the penalty relates is revised on an appeal or in accordance with regulations under the Social Security Act 1998 or the Social Security (Northern Ireland) Order 1998—
(a) section 36A shall cease to apply by virtue of the old agreement, and
(b) subsection (4) shall apply.

(4) Where this subsection applies—
(a) if there is a new disqualifying event consisting of—
(i) P's agreement to pay a penalty under the appropriate penalty regime in relation to the revised overpayment, or
(ii) P being cautioned in relation to the offence to which the old agreement relates,
the disqualification period relating to the new disqualifying event shall be reduced by the number of days in so much of the disqualification period relating to the old agreement as had expired when subsection 36A ceased to apply by virtue of the old agreement, and
(b) in any other case, all such payments and other adjustments shall be made as would be necessary if no restriction had been imposed by or under section 36A that could not have been imposed if P had not agreed to pay the penalty.

(2002 c.21 s.36B)

(5) For the purposes of section 36A—
(a) the date of a person's conviction in any proceedings of a benefit offence shall be taken to be the date on which the person was found guilty of that offence in those proceedings (whenever the person was sentenced) or in the case mentioned in paragraph (b)(ii) the date of the order for absolute discharge, and
(b) references to a conviction include references to—
  (i) a conviction in relation to which the court makes an order for absolute or conditional discharge,
  (ii) an order for absolute discharge made by a court of summary jurisdiction in Scotland under section 246(3) of the Criminal Procedure (Scotland) Act 1995 without proceeding to a conviction, and
  (iii) a conviction in Northern Ireland.
(6) In this section "the appropriate penalty provision" has the meaning given by section 36A(2)(a).]

AMENDMENT

1. Welfare Reform Act 2012 s.120 (April 6, 2013) (see Welfare Reform Act 2012 (Commencement no.7) Order 2013 (SI 2013/178) art.2).

DEFINITIONS

"benefit offence"—see s.36A(10).
"caution"—see s.67.

GENERAL NOTE

See the note to s.36A above. This section makes provision where either the imposition of a disqualifying period becomes inappropriate either because an event ceases to be a disqualifying event or because of a new disqualifying event.

1.378

[1 Loss of working tax credit for repeated benefit fraud

36C.—(1) If—

1.379

(a) a person ("the offender") is convicted of one or more benefit offences in a set of proceedings ("the current set of proceedings"),
(b) within the period of five years ending on the date on which the benefit offence was, or any of them were, committed, one or more disqualifying events occurred in relation to the offender (the event, or the most recent of them, being referred to in this section as "the earlier disqualifying event"),
(c) the current set of proceedings has not been taken into account for the purposes of any previous application of this section in relation to the offender,
(d) the earlier disqualifying event has not been taken into account as an earlier disqualifying event for the purposes of any previous application of this section in relation to the offender, and
(e) the offender is a person who would, apart from this section, be entitled (whether pursuant to a single or joint claim) to working tax credit at any time within the disqualification period, then, despite that entitlement, the restriction in subsection (3) shall apply in relation to the payment of that benefit in the offender's case.

(2) The restriction in subsection (3) does not apply if the benefit offence referred to in subsection (1)(a), or any of them, is a relevant offence.

(3) Working tax credit shall not be payable for any period comprised in the disqualification period—
  (a) in the case of a single claim, to the offender, or
  (b) in the case of a joint claim, to the offender or the other member of the couple.

(4) Regulations may provide in relation to cases to which subsection (3)(b) would otherwise apply that working tax credit shall be payable, for any period comprised in the disqualification period, as if the amount payable were reduced in such manner as may be prescribed.

(5) For the purposes of this section the disqualification period, in an offender's case, means the relevant period beginning with a prescribed date falling after the date of the conviction in the current set of proceedings.

(6) For the purposes of subsection (5) the relevant period is—
  (a) in a case where, within the period of five years ending on the date on which the earlier disqualifying event occurred, a previous disqualifying event occurred in relation to the offender, the period of three years;
  (b) in any other case, 26 weeks.

(7) In this section and section 36D—
"appropriate penalty provision" has the meaning given in section 36A(2)(a);
"benefit offence" means any of the following offences committed on or after the day specified by order made by the Treasury—
  (a) an offence in connection with a claim for a disqualifying benefit;
  (b) an offence in connection with the receipt or payment of any amount by way of such a benefit;
  (c) an offence committed for the purpose of facilitating the commission (whether or not by the same person) of a benefit offence;
  (d) an offence consisting in an attempt or conspiracy to commit a benefit offence;
"disqualifying benefit" has the meaning given in section 6A(1) of the Social Security Fraud Act 2001;
"disqualifying event" has the meaning given in section 36A(10);
"relevant offence" has the meaning given in section 6B of the Social Security Fraud Act 2001.

(8) Where a person is convicted of more than one benefit offence in the same set of proceedings, there is to be only one disqualifying event in respect of that set of proceedings for the purposes of this section and—
  (a) subsection (1)(b) is satisfied if any of the convictions take place in the five year period there;
  (b) the event is taken into account for the purposes of subsection (1)(d) if any of the convictions have been taken into account as mentioned there;
  (c) in the case of the earlier disqualifying event mentioned in subsection (6)(a), the reference there to the date on which the earlier disqualifying event occurred is a reference to the date on which any of the convictions take place;
  (d) in the case of the previous disqualifying event mentioned in subsection (6)(a), that provision is satisfied if any of the convictions take place in the five year period mentioned there.

(9) The Treasury may by order amend subsection (6) to substitute different periods for those for the time being specified there.

(10) An order under subsection (9) may provide for different periods to apply according to the type of earlier disqualifying event or events occurring in any case.

(11) This section has effect subject to section 36D.]

AMENDMENT

1. Welfare Reform Act 2012 s.120 (April 6, 2013) (Welfare Reform Act 2012 (Commencement no.7) Order 2013 (SI 2013/178) art.2).

DEFINITIONS

"benefit offence"—see s.36A(10).
"caution"—see s.67.
"disqualifying benefit—see Social Security Fraud Act 2001 s.6A(1) as amended by Welfare Reform Act 2012 s.117.
"joint claim"—see s.3(3).
"working tax credit—see s.8.

GENERAL NOTE

See the note to s.36A above. As the title to this section indicates, this deals with repeat cases that result or may result or could have resulted in loss of tax credit, including past events.

For regulations under subss.(3) and (4) see the Loss of Tax Credit Regulations 2013 (SI 2013/715) reg.3 (see para.2.491, below). This provides for a 50 per cent reduction rather than a total loss of tax credit where these provisions are triggered by actions or failures of one of a couple making a joint claim but not by the other member of the couple.

[¹ **Section 36C: supplementary**

36D.—(1) Where—
 (a) the conviction of any person of any offence is taken into account for the purposes of the application of section 36C in relation to that person, and
 (b) that conviction is subsequently quashed,
all such payments and other adjustments shall be made as would be necessary if no restriction had been imposed by or under section 36C that could not have been imposed if the conviction had not taken place.

(2) Subsection (3) applies where, after the agreement of any person ("P") to pay a penalty under the appropriate penalty provision is taken into account for the purposes of the application of section 36C in relation to that person—
 (a) P's agreement to pay the penalty is withdrawn under subsection (5) of the appropriate penalty provision,
 (b) it is decided on an appeal or in accordance with regulations under the Social Security Act 1998 or the Social Security (Northern Ireland) Order 1998 (S.I. 1998/1506 (N.I. 10)) that any overpayment made to which the agreement relates is not recoverable or due, or
 (c) the amount of any over payment to which the penalty relates is revised on an appeal or in accordance with regulations under the Social Security Act 1998 or the Social Security (Northern Ireland) Order 1998 and there is no new agreement by P to pay a penalty under the appropriate penalty provision in relation to the revised overpayment.

(3) In those circumstances, all such payments and other adjustments

shall be made as would be necessary if no restriction had been imposed by or under section 36C that could not have been imposed if P had not agreed to pay the penalty.

(4) For the purposes of section 36C—
(a) the date of a person's conviction in any proceedings of a benefit offence shall be taken to be the date on which the person was found guilty of that offence in those proceedings (whenever the person was sentenced) or in the case mentioned in paragraph (b)(ii) the date of the order for absolute discharge, and
(b) references to a conviction include references to—
  (i) a conviction in relation to which the court makes an order for absolute or conditional discharge,
  (ii) an order for absolute discharge made by a court of summary jurisdiction in Scotland under section 246(3) of the Criminal Procedure (Scotland) Act 1995 without proceeding to a conviction, and
  (iii) a conviction in Northern Ireland.

(5) In section 36C references to any previous application of that section—
(a) include references to any previous application of a provision having an effect in Northern Ireland corresponding to provision made by that section, but
(b) do not include references to any previous application of that section the effect of which was to impose a restriction for a period comprised in the same disqualification period.]

AMENDMENT

1. Welfare Reform Act 2012 s.120 (April 6, 2013) (Welfare Reform Act 2012 (Commencement No.7) Order 2013 (SI 2013/178) art.2).

DEFINITIONS

"appropriate penalty provision"—see s.36A(2).
"benefit offence"—see s.36A(10).
"caution"—see s.67.
"disqualifying benefit—see Social Security Fraud Act 2001 s.6A(1) as amended by Welfare Reform Act 2012 s.117.
"joint claim"—see s.3(3).
"working tax credit—see s.8.

GENERAL NOTE

1.382 See the note to s.36A above.

Interest

Interest

1.383 **37.**—(1) If an overpayment of a tax credit for a period is attributable to fraud or neglect on the part of the person, or either or both of the persons, to whom the award of the tax credit was made (or a person acting for him, or for either or both of them, in making the claim for the tax credit), the Board may decide that the whole or any part of the overpayment is to carry interest.

(2) Where the Board so decide the overpayment (or part of the overpayment) carries interest at a prescribed rate from the date 30 days after the appropriate date.

(3) "The appropriate date" is—

(a) in the case of an amount treated as an overpayment by virtue of section 28(6), the date of the decision under section 16 to terminate the award; and

(b) in any other case, the date specified for the purposes of subsection (4) of section 17 in the notice given to the person or persons under that section in relation to the tax credit.

(4) The Board must give notice of a decision under subsection (1) to the person, or each of the persons, to whom it relates; and the notice must state the date on which it is given and include details of the right to appeal against the decision under section 38.

(5) A penalty under any of sections 31 to 33 carries interest at the prescribed rate from the date on which it becomes due and payable; but the Board may in their discretion mitigate any interest or entirely remit any interest which would otherwise be carried by a penalty.

(6) Any interest carried under this section by an overpayment or penalty is to be regarded for the purposes of section 29(3) to (5) or paragraph 7 of Schedule 2 as if it were part of the overpayment or penalty.

AMENDMENT

Subsection (1) is modified as it applies to polygamous units by Tax Credits (Polygamous Marriages) Regulations 2003 (SI 2003/742) reg.21.

DEFINITIONS

"the Board"—see s.67.
"prescribed"—*ibid.*
"overpayment"—see s.28.
"tax credit"—see s.1(2).

GENERAL NOTE

Interest has long been imposed on taxpayers who do not make timely payments of income tax. This includes an underpayment (or repayment) of tax reliefs and deductions (see TMA 1970 s.86). By contrast, interest is not imposed on those required to repay an overpayment of social security benefits. Interest was not imposed on overpayments under the TCA 1999, although penalties under s.9 of that Act carried interest (Sch.4 para.8 to that Act).

This section adopts a compromise in imposing interest payments on overpayments caused by fraud or neglect, but not generally. It also imposes again an interest charge on payments of penalties. Interest does not run unless a decision is made to impose it, and that cannot start until either the date on which the award of tax credit was terminated under s.16 or the closing date of a notice issued under s.17.

The "prescribed rate" is set out in the Tax Credits (Interest Rate) Regulations 2003 (SI 2003/123).

1.384

Appeals

1.385   **38.**—(1) An appeal may [² , subject to subsection (1A),] be brought against—
(a) a decision under section 14(1), 15(1), 16(1), 19(3) or 20(1) or (4) or regulations under section 21,
(b) the relevant section 18 decision in relation to a person or persons and a tax credit for a tax year and any revision of that decision under that section,
(c) a determination of a penalty under paragraph 1 of Schedule 2, [¹. . .]
[¹ (ca) a decision under section 36A or 36C that working tax credit is not payable (or is not payable for a particular period), and]
(d) a decision under section 37(1).
[²(1A) An appeal may not be brought by virtue of subsection (1) against a decision unless a review of the decision has been carried out under section 21A and notice of the conclusion on the review has been given under section 21A(3).
(1B) If in any case the conclusion of a review under section 21A is to uphold the decision reviewed, an appeal by virtue of subsection (1) in that case may be brought only against the original decision.
(1C) If in any case the conclusion of a review under section 21A is to vary the decision reviewed, an appeal by virtue of subsection (1) in that case may be brought only against the decision as varied.]
(2) "The relevant section 18 decision" means—
(a) in a case in which a decision must be made under subsection (6) of section 18 in relation to the person or persons and the tax credit for the tax year, that decision, and
(b) in any other case, the decision under subsection (1) of that section in relation to the person or persons and the tax credit for the tax year.

AMENDMENTS

1. Welfare Reform Act 2012 s.120 (April 6, 2013).
2. Tax Credits, Child Benefit and Guardian's Allowance Reviews and Appeals Order 2014 (SI 2014/886) art.2(10) and (11) (April 6, 2014).

DEFINITIONS

"tax credit"—see s.1(2).
"tax year"—see s.47.

GENERAL NOTE

1.386   This section creates a series of specific rights of appeal. The following decisions or actions of HMRC are subject to the appeal process:

(a) an initial decision to award or refuse tax credits under s.14(1);

(b) a decision whether (and if so, how) to amend a s.14 decision under s.15(1);

(c) a decision amending or terminating a s.14 decision under s.16(1);

(d) a decision on entitlement made under s.18(1) or (6);

(e) a decision after an enquiry under s.19(3);

(f) a decision revising a previous decision on entitlement under s.20(1);

(2002 c.21 s.38)

(g) a decision revising a previous decision on entitlement on the grounds of fraud or neglect under s.20(4);

(h) a decision to revise a decision on entitlement because of official error under s.21;

(i) a determination of a penalty under Sch.2 para.1; and

(j) a decision to impose interest under s.37(1).

As is emphasised above in the note to s.16, HMRC must in all cases identify under which provision any final decision is made. In practice, the only decision that will fall out with the jurisdiction of the First-tier Tribunal will be an overpayment decision. The underlying decision causing the overpayment will be appealable and must have been identified to the claimant.

Upper Tribunal Judge Jacobs has recently issued the following guidance to any First-tier Tribunal faced with a submission from HMRC that failed to make clear the decision under appeal:

"The proper course ... to have taken was not to struggle on to make the best sense ... of what was presented ..., it was to remit the case back to the Commissioners with directions on how to remedy the deficiencies in their submission" (*AR-L v HMRC (TC)* [2015] UKUT 303 (AAC), para.8).

In *SH v HMRC and SC (TC)* [2013] UKUT 0297 (AAC) Judge Wikeley drew attention to the sensitivity of appeals involving the relationships of two separated parents to a child or children, particularly where there was a dispute between them about a child. Allowing an appeal, he gave careful directions to the First-tier Tribunal requiring anonymity for all aspects of the further hearing of the appeal by that tribunal.

In *CTC/31/2006* the Commissioner rejected as outside his jurisdiction an attempt to appeal a decision of HMRC that a claim was not properly made. The claim had been made on an income tax return, and HMRC had refused to accept it. The Commissioner held that this was not within the terms of s.38. He also held that it could not be read into the section by reference to the European Convention on Human Rights. In the view of the Commissioner judicial review was an adequate means of challenging a decision to refuse a claim that was alleged to be unlawful. However, this decision predated the creation of the new tribunal system and the broader powers now given to tribunals to deal with issues that are in effect judicial review. The Upper Tribunal, if not the First-tier Tribunal, now has express power to deal with judicial review. And, in the light of that, a broad approach to jurisdiction such as that taken on a tax issue by Sales J in *Oxfam v HMRC* [2009] EWHC 3078, Ch D., may suggest that the matter should be within s.38. But see also *OFCOM v Morrissey and Information Commissioner* [2011] UKUT 116 (AAC).

1.387

In *SG v HM Revenue and Customs (TC)* [2011] UKUT 199 subs.1(a) was interpreted to include an appeal where the dispute was about whether there had been a valid claim.

In a robust decision criticising both HMRC's submissions to a First-tier Tribunal and the failure of that tribunal to note their deficiencies, Judge Ward sets out in some detail in his decision in *AG v HMRC (TC)* [2013] UKUT 530 (AAC) the extent to which HMRC is required to provide a First-tier Tribunal with evidence about a tax credit appeal. The case concerned a claim by an appellant that he had provided information to HMRC about a change of circumstances. A First-tier Tribunal had directed HMRC to produce further details about the case. HMRC had produced nothing relevant and had failed to respond to part of the direction, but a second First-tier Tribunal ignored the failure and found against the appellant. In the Upper Tribunal, Judge Ward directed full disclosure. In response he was given details of the telephone conversations recorded by HMRC from its helpline.

Tax Credits Act 2002

He rules that this should have been provided to the First-tier Tribunal, noting that the failure to do so was a breach of r.24(3) of the First-tier Tribunal's procedural rules. It followed that the decision of that tribunal was in error of law for failure to consider the full case. The judge helpfully scheduled to his decision part of an affidavit of evidence from HMRC about the evidence it records and how it is recorded.

1.388   See also the criticisms about the failure of HMRC to provide First-tier Tribunal hearings with full papers in the decisions of Judge Wikeley in *SH v HMRC (TC)* [2013] UKUT 297 (AAC) and Judge Turnbull in *JP v HMRC (TC)* [2013] UKUT 519 (AAC), where he commented that this was not the first time on which he had noted a reluctance of HMRC to put all potentially relevant documents before a First-tier Tribunal. In *TM v HMRC (TC)* [2013] UKUT 444 (AAC) Judge Wright set aside a First-tier Tribunal decision in a case where HMRC produced its submission only at the last minute to the tribunal. The appellant had not been given an adequate time to consider it as HMRC had not issued it to the appellant. The failure to issue to the appellant was a breach of the duty on HMRC under the tribunal procedure rules, unless a tribunal had expressly waived the requirement.

See also the decisions of Upper Tribunal Judge Wikeley in *JR v HMRC* [2015] UKUT 192 (AAC) and *ZB v HMRC* [2015] UKUT 198 (AAC) endorsing these decisions but adding a comment from HMRC (recorded at [17] of the decision) that:

> "HMRC's approach in the present case, and others like it, does not reflect the current approach which is that full details of the case are always included in the written response, and the response itself is accompanied by all relevant documents, in compliance with Tribunal Procedure Rules. The current and compliant approach has been in place since May 2014."

CTC/1594/2006 illustrates the importance of checking for which year or years an appeal is made. This is potentially more of a problem for tax credits than most benefits because of the effect of having an award decision during the same year as the entitlement decision for the previous year. The Commissioner accepted the arguments for HMRC in that case that a claimant could not use an appeal to challenge more than the specific decisions challenged. As Commissioners have observed on more than one occasion, this means that challenges against award decisions may be of limited value. HMRC is no more debarred from altering a tribunal decision about an award at the end of the year than any other award decision. This issue is not always easy to clarify as HMRC uses terminology in its literature that conflates awards and entitlement decisions. See para.1.294.

1.389   It is to be emphasised that this section gives the right of appeal, and s.39 as amended by s.63 is concerned only with how the appeal is made. It is often said that the appeal is to HMRC and not an appeal tribunal. That is not correct. The appeal is to the tribunal ,while notification is to HMRC. The importance of this used to be that it was for HMRC to deal with passing a tribunal a case for listing. There was a major change of approach adopted for all tax cases when the Special and General Commissioners were abolished and replaced by the Tax Chamber of the First-tier Tribunal. It was agreed that listing was no longer for HMRC but is now a function of the Tribunals Service, operating through its Tax Chamber offices. The trigger in direct tax cases is notification of the appeal directly to the Tribunals Service by the appellant. The same should therefore apply to all tax credit appeals. These should therefore be listed by the Tribunals Service for hearing or decision as it considers appropriate when an appellant notifies the tribunal of the appeal. This change may deal with some of the recurring complaints that appeals about tax credits entitlement (as against unappealable decisions about overpayments) do not reach the tribunals.

The absence of appeals undoubtedly reflects the power of the Inland Revenue and now the HMRC to settle cases under s.54 of the TMA 1970. This is a power not possessed by the Department for Work and Pensions or local authorities (or the former Customs and Excise Commissioners). That power is particularly useful in dealing with questions of disputed income and with penalty cases, although it is of limited use in cases such as whether two individuals should be making a joint claim. But on one view HMRC is making too wide a use of that power. In *Tax Credits Agenda for Improvement*, published in September 2004 jointly by the Chartered Institute of Taxation, Citizens Advice, CPAG, The Institute of Chartered Accountants of England and Wales, the Low Income Tax Reform Group, and One Parent Families, the approach of HMRC to settlement was criticised. The bodies jointly asked for:

> "adherence to proper procedures when the IR decide to settle an appeal, rather than 'cancelling' the appeal and issuing revised decisions outside the appeal process."

While HMRC have, as noted, a power to settle under s.54 of the TMA it is a process with its own safeguards (see para.1.19, above). Similarly, once an appeal has been made it cannot be "cancelled" otherwise than by a properly reached settlement or as part of the appeal process. Any attempt to interfere with the appeal process outside those protective limits is an interference by one party in the appeal process and as such is likely to be in breach of the "equality of arms" principle laid down by the European Court of Human Rights. That principle demands that all parties have equal access to a court or tribunal as part of the fundamental principle of fair hearings laid down in art.6 of the European Convention on Human Rights. (See Vol.III of this series for that provision and the Human Rights Act 1998 that introduces it into United Kingdom law.)

This section clearly gives separate appeal rights against s.14 decisions as against s.18 decisions. The automated process, followed by checks, that is used for awards (see the notes to s.14) would suggest that the administrative approach adopted by HMRC, while undoubtedly efficient in many cases, may be the reason why the joint protest has arisen.

1.390

Separately from these, the appellate authorities can be invoked in two other situations. HMRC cannot itself make a determination of daily penalties under s.32(2) and must instead start proceedings for such penalties before the appellate authorities. This is not technically an appeal (see Sch.2 para.3). An individual subject to an enquiry under s.19 can, under s.19(8), apply to the appellate authorities to direct the enquiry to end. Such an application is to be treated as if it was an appeal (s.19(10)).

The 2007 special report of the Parliamentary Ombudsman noted above continues to recommend that appeal rights should be given to an independent tribunal in connection with overpayments. It also sets out the government response to that recommendation, which is an enhanced complaints procedure. This procedure is now applied by both HMRC and the Ombudsman to all tax credits complaints, including appeals. In effect, a complaint only gets to the Ombudsman or an appeal to a tribunal as a fourth level of review.

Exercise of right of appeal

39.— (1) [¹. . .]

1.391

(2) [¹ . . .]

(6) Part 5 of the Taxes Management Act 1970 (appeals and other proceedings) applies in relation to appeals under section 38 (as in relation to appeals under the Taxes Acts, within the meaning of that Act), but subject to such modifications as are prescribed.

AMENDMENT

1. Tax Credits, Child Benefit and Guardian's Allowance Reviews and Appeals Order 2014 (SI 2014/886) art.2(12) (April 6, 2014).

Tax Credits Act 2002

GENERAL NOTE

1.392 This section, as amended, has to be read subject to two very large health warnings. The first is that the version as set out above, with the repeal of paras (1) and (2), applies in relation to HMRC decisions made on or after April 6, 2014. See further s.39A below and the General Note to that new provision. For the version of s.39 which applied to HMRC decisions before that date, please see previous editions of this Volume. The second health warning is that the first health warning applies only to England, Wales and Scotland. However, with regard to the second health warning, the Tax Credits, Child Benefit and Guardian's Allowance Appeals (Appointed Day) (Northern Ireland) Order 2014 (SI 2014/2881) apply the provisions in SI 2014/886 to Northern Ireland from March 2, 2015.

[² **Late appeals**

1.393 **39A.**— (1) The Commissioners for Her Majesty's Revenue and Customs may treat a late appeal under section 38 as made in time where the conditions specified in subsections (2) to (6) are satisfied, except that the Commissioners may not do so in the case of an appeal made more than one year after the expiration of the time (original or extended) for appealing.

(2) An appeal may be treated as made in time if the Commissioners are satisfied that it is in the interests of justice to do so.

(3) For the purposes of subsection (2) it is not in the interests of justice to treat an appeal as made in time unless—
  (a) the special circumstances specified in subsection (4) are relevant; or
  (b) some other special circumstances exist which are wholly exceptional and relevant, and as a result of those special circumstances it was not practicable for the appeal to be made in time.

(4) The special circumstances mentioned in subsection (3)(a) are—
  (a) the appellant or a partner or dependant of the appellant has died or suffered serious illness;
  (b) the appellant is not resident in the United Kingdom; or
  (c) normal postal services were disrupted.

(5) In determining whether it is in the interests of justice to treat an appeal as made in time, regard shall be had to the principle that the greater the amount of time that has elapsed between the expiration of the time for appealing and the submission of the notice of appeal, the more compelling should be the special circumstances.

(6) In determining whether it is in the interests of justice to treat an appeal as made in time, no account shall be taken of the following—
  (a) that the appellant or any other person acting for the appellant was unaware of or misunderstood the law applicable to the appellant's case (including ignorance or misunderstanding of any time limit); or
  (b) that the Upper Tribunal or a court has taken a different view of the law from that previously understood and applied.

(7) If in accordance with the preceding provisions of this section the Commissioners for Her Majesty's Revenue and Customs treat a late appeal under section 38 as made in time, it is to be treated as having been brought within any applicable time limit.]

(2002 c.21 s.39A)

AMENDMENT

1. Text of section added by Tax Credits (Late Appeals) Order 2014 (SI 2014/885) art.2 (April 1, 2014).

GENERAL NOTE

HMRC offered the following explanation for the new section in its explanatory note for the draft Order to the Joint Committee on Statutory Instruments:

1.394

"Article 2 makes provision which mirrors that provided by regulation 5 (late appeals) of the Tax Credits (Appeals) (No. 2) Regulations 2002 (S.I. 2002/3196). Regulation 5 of S.I. 2002/3196 was made under powers contained in section 12(7) (appeal to First-tier Tribunal) of the Social Security Act 1998 (c. 14) which applied (as modified) to tax credit appeals by virtue of regulation 4 of the Tax Credits (Appeals) Regulations 2002 (S.I. 2002/2926). S.I. 2002/2926, made under the power in section 63(8) of the 2002 Act (tax credits appeals etc: temporary modifications), lapsed in respect of its application in Great Britain, as a result of amendments to section 63 by the Transfer of Tribunal Functions and Revenue and Customs Appeals Order 2009 (S.I. 2009/56) ("the 2009 Order") following the transfer of the functions of the tax tribunals to the new tribunals established under the Tribunals, Courts and Enforcement Act 2007 (c. 15). Tax credits appeals in Great Britain were transferred from the Social Security and Child Support Appeals Tribunal to the Social Entitlement Chamber of the First-tier Tribunal and amendments were made to section 63 by S.I. 2009/56 to reflect these changes. Article 3 of, and paragraph 316 of Schedule 1 to, the 2009 Order amended section 63 by substituting references to the "appeal tribunal", defined by reference to Northern Ireland legislation, which did not include the First-tier Tribunal in Great Britain. As a result of those amendments to the regulation-making power in section 63 was that S.I. 2002/2926, and therefore S.I. 2002/3196 (which applied only in respect of appeals in Great Britain), no longer applied in respect of appeals in Great Britain (but continued to apply in respect of appeals in Northern Ireland). The Revenue and Customs Appeals Order 2012 (S.I. 2012/533) amended sections 63(5) and (8) by inserting a reference to the First-tier Tribunal to correct this defect."

That explanation fails to note that Judge Rowland held that the provision dealing with late appeals in the No.2 Regulations to be invalid in *JI v HMRC* [2013] UKUT 199 (AAC). See para.2.389.

There has clearly been both confusion and inconsistency in dealing with late appeals notwithstanding the introduction of the new provisions of s.39A from April 1, 2014. This is in part because the general view appears now to be that s.39A only achieved part of its purpose, notwithstanding the views expressed to Parliament in the explanatory note to the statutory instrument introducing it. Historically, it is clear that both HMRC (and its predecessor) and tribunals had power to deal with late appeals before November 4, 2008. A minor result—presumably unintended—of the major reforms in 2008 is now accepted to be that from that date while HMRC continued to have power to deal with late appeals, the relevant tribunal (the First-tier Tribunal) did not have that power. Then on April 1, 2009 – again presumably without any specific intention so to do—other legislative changes took away the power of HMRC to deal with late appeals. While it has been argued that the decision of Judge Rowland is open to criticism for failure to deal with human rights issues and is limited in its binding effect to the position before the introduction of s.39A and supporting provisions, those are arguably arguments that must be set against the plainly binding authority of the central elements of the decision and the close reasoning of the whole decision. The position for any period before April 1, 2014 must therefore be that set out in that decision.

Unfortunately, and notwithstanding the careful rehearsal of the legislative history

1.395

of this topic in Judge Rowland's decision, a third set of errors appear to have been made—yet again it is assumed unintentionally—when the new provisions incorporated in s.39A took effect on April 1, 2014. Here the result appears to be that HMRC again has power to deal with late appeals both before and after the new provisions take effect. However, there is nothing to give the power back to tribunals retrospectively and the effect of the one-year absolute time limit in s.39A(1) is to bar consideration of any late appeal made before April 1, 2013. So it appears that old late appeals may still be caught by the unintended bar against late appeals and more recent appeals made before the new rules came in may enter a limbo where a tribunal has no jurisdiction to consider the matter. In such a case if HMRC does not agree to admit a late appeal, then tribunals cannot deal with it.

There is often an additional kind of confusion in these cases. Bearing in mind that there are at least two separate operative decisions for each tax year (and often more), it is always necessary to check against which decision or decisions a claimant is seeking to appeal. It may be that the result is that some decisions can be admitted late and considered while others remain late and outside the jurisdiction of a tribunal. A final point is that the time limit only starts when the notice provisions in s.23(2) of the Act are met. See paras 1.307–308 above. If there has been no proper notice of decision, then time cannot start running.

The explanation for the draft Order also noted that:

"Article 2(3) [of the 2014 Order] deals with cases that are in the pipeline, and sometimes have been pending and in uncertainty for a very long time. HMRC have not opposed late appeals of late, relying on their management function in section 2 of the Tax Credits Act 2002 to forward them to the tribunal. So article 2(3) simply validates, going forward, HMRC decisions to allow such late appeals."

Supplementary

Annual reports

1.396

40.—(1) The Board must make to the Treasury an annual report about—

(a) [¹ . . .]
(b) the number of awards of child tax credit and of working tax credit,
(c) the number of enquiries conducted under section 19,
(d) the number of penalties imposed under this Part, and
(e) the number of prosecutions and convictions for offences connected with tax credits.

(2) The Treasury must publish each annual report made to it under subsection (1) and lay a copy before each House of Parliament.

AMENDMENTS

1. Commissioners for Revenue and Customs Act 2005 s.50 and Sch.4 para.89 (April 18, 2005).
2. References to "the Board" are now references to the Commissioners for Revenue and Customs: CRCA 2005 s.4.

DEFINITIONS

"the Board"—see s.67.
"child tax credit"—see s.8.

"tax credits"—see s.1(2).
"working tax credit"—see s.10.

GENERAL NOTE

This section derives from a clause adopted by the House of Lords against the wishes of government, and represents the one major amendment in the Act not moved by the Government itself. The aim is to ensure a specific report that would be put before Parliament each year about both the scale of the tax credits system and the extent of fraud within it. The wording of the section comes from a government amendment moved to replace the Lords clause in the House of Commons. It was recognised that to some extent it duplicates figures already published by HMRC in its more general reports.

The report for 2012–13 is brief but states that there were 67,000 s.19 enquiries in the year, of which 8,020 led to penalties and 83 criminal convictions.

Annual review

41.—(1) The Treasury must, in each tax year, review the amounts specified in subsection (2) in order to determine whether they have retained their value in relation to the general level of prices in the United Kingdom as estimated by the Treasury in such manner as it considers appropriate.

(2) The amounts are monetary amounts prescribed—
  (a) under subsection (1)(a) of section 7;
  (b) for the purposes of any of paragraphs (a) to (d) of subsection (3) of that section;
  (c) under section 9;
  (d) under section 11, otherwise than by virtue of section 12, or
  (e) under subsection (2) of section 13, otherwise than by virtue of subsection (3) of that section.

(3) The Treasury must prepare a report of each review.

(4) The report must include a statement of what each amount would be if it had fully retained its value.

(5) The Treasury must publish the report and lay a copy of it before each House of Parliament.

DEFINITION

"prescribed"—see s.67.

GENERAL NOTE

This provides for the annual uprating review of the monetary amounts used in awarding tax credits.

Persons subject to immigration control

42.—(1) Regulations may make provision in relation to persons subject to immigration control or in relation to prescribed descriptions of such persons—
  (a) for excluding entitlement to, or to a prescribed element of, child tax credit or working tax credit (or both), or
  (b) for this Part to apply subject to other prescribed modifications.

(2) "Person subject to immigration control" has the same meaning as in section 115 of the Immigration and Asylum Act 1999 (c.33).

DEFINITIONS

"child tax credit"—see s.8.
"modifications"—see s.67.
"persons subject to immigration control"—see Immigration and Asylum Act 1999 s.115.
"prescribed"—see s.67.
"working tax credit"—see s.10.

GENERAL NOTE

1.401   Although listed in the "supplementary" part of Pt I of the Act, this makes provision for excluding anyone from entitlement to tax credits if he or she is "subject to immigration control", a phrase derived from the Immigration and Asylum Act 1999. The definition covers those who are not nationals of an EEA state and who require leave to enter the United Kingdom or have certain forms of conditional leave. For the detailed application of this section, see the Tax Credits (Immigration) Regulations 2003 (SI 2003/653). An attempt to challenge the regulations made under this section as discriminatory by reference to the Human Rights Act 1999 failed in *CTC/3692/2008*.

Polygamous marriages

1.402   **43.**—(1) Regulations may make provision for this Part to apply in relation to persons who are parties to polygamous marriages subject to prescribed modifications.

(2) A person is a party to a polygamous marriage if—
(a) he is a party to a marriage entered into under a law which permits polygamy, and
(b) either party to the marriage has a spouse additional to the other party.

DEFINITION

"modifications"—see s.67.

GENERAL NOTE

1.403   This is another of the necessary compromises between the general approach to income tax and the general approach to social security. Social security benefits have long contained special provisions dealing with polygamous marriages, if only to prevent more than two of the marriage partners benefiting for a particular benefit as a married couple. In contrast, the point is not so significant in the context of income tax as there is now individual assessment. The standard treatment of monogamous marriages is set out in s.3.

Effect is given to this section by the Tax Credits (Polygamous Marriages) Regulations 2003 (SI 2003/742). Where those regulations provide for a modification of the sections of this Act, that is noted in this volume as an amendment to the section.

Crown employment

1.404   **44.**—This Part applies in relation to persons employed by or under the Crown (as in relation to other employees).

DEFINITIONS

"Crown"—see Interpretation Act 1978 Sch.1.
"employed"—see s.25(5).

GENERAL NOTE

This section avoids any unintended exclusion of civil and other public servants by reason of the Crown Proceedings Act 1947 or otherwise. The Tax Credits (Residence) Regulations 2003 (SI 2003/642) extend this further by applying the Act to Crown Servants working overseas and their partners. The main concern of both this section and those regulations is that Crown servants receive full entitlement to CTC.

Inalienability

45.—(1) Every assignment of or charge on a tax credit, and every agreement to assign or charge a tax credit, is void; and, on the bankruptcy of a person entitled to a tax credit, the entitlement to the tax credit does not pass to any trustee or other person acting on behalf of his creditors.

(2) In the application of subsection (1) to Scotland—
(a) the reference to assignment is to assignation ("assign" being construed accordingly), and
(b) the reference to the bankruptcy of a person is to the sequestration of his estate or the appointment on his estate of a judicial factor under section 41 of the Solicitors (Scotland) Act 1980 (c.46).

DEFINITION

"tax credit"—see s.1(2).

GENERAL NOTE

This mirrors (and repeats much of the wording of) SSAA 1992 s.187. While informal pledges of both benefit and benefit books occur, that section renders any such arrangement unenforceable in the courts or as against government departments. This section ensures that this also applies to tax credits.

Giving of notices by Board

46. The Board may give any notice which they are required or permitted to give under this Part in any manner and form which the Board consider appropriate in the circumstances.

DEFINITION

"the Board"—see s.67.

GENERAL NOTE

No provision is made in this section for regulations or for deemed notice. There is no equivalent of TMA 1970 s.114 (want of form not to invalidate assessments) or 115 (delivery and service of documents) provided for in the Act. However, it is suggested that this does not discharge HMRC from the duty of complying with specific provisions as to content in this Act, in the Tax Credits (Claims and Notifications) Regulations 2002 (SI 2002/2014), or elsewhere. HMRC is also required, by reason of the art.6 of the European Convention on Human Rights and the Human Rights Act 1998 (see Vol.III in this series), to ensure that proper notice is given of any appeal to the appeal tribunals or the appellant as the case may be.

Consequential amendments

47. Schedule 3 (consequential amendments) has effect.

General Note

1.411 This section gives effect to Sch.3 (not included in this volume). Section 68(1) ensures that those provisions are co-extensive with the provisions they affect. Most of the provisions are concerned to replace WFTC with WTC and to substitute a reference to CTC in place of references to the various previous child benefits and credits. Paragraph 25 amends s.30C of the SSCBA 1992, and para.30 amends s.42 of that Act. Both deal with transfers between benefit and tax credit.

Interpretation

1.412 **48.**—[¹(1)] In this Part—

"child" has the meaning given by section 8(3),

[¹"couple" has the meaning given by section 3(5A)],

"the current year income" has the meaning given by section 7(4),

"employee" and "employer" have the meaning given by section 25(5),

[² . . .]

"the income threshold" has the meaning given by section 7(1)(a),

"joint claim" has the meaning given by section 3(8),

[¹ . . .],

"overpayment" has the meaning given by section 28(2) and (6),

"the previous year income" has the meaning given by section 7(5),

"qualifying remunerative work", and being engaged in it, have the meaning given by regulations under section 10(2),

"qualifying young person" has the meaning given by section 8(4),

"the relevant income" has the meaning given by section 7(3),

"responsible", in relation to a child or qualifying young person, has the meaning given by regulations under section 8(2) (for the purposes of child tax credit) or by regulations under section 10(4) (for the purposes of working tax credit),

"single claim" has the meaning given by section 3(8),

[² . . .]

"tax year" means a period beginning with 6th April in one year and ending with 5th April in the next, and

[¹ . . .].

[¹(2) For the purposes of this Part, two people of the same sex are to be regarded as living together as if they were civil partners if, but only if, they would be regarded as living together as husband and wife were they instead two people of the opposite sex.]

Amendments

1. Civil Partnership Act 2004 ss.254 and 261(4) and Sch.24 para.147 and Sch.30 (December 5, 2005).
2. Transfer of Tribunal Functions and Revenue and Customs Appeals Order 2009 (SI 2009/56) art.3(1) and Sch.1 para.315 (April 1, 2009).

General Note

1.413 See also s.67 for further definitions.

(2002 c.21 s.49)

Part II

Child Benefit and Guardian's Allowance

49.–57. (*Omitted*)

Part III

Supplementary

Information etc.

Administrative arrangements

58.—(1) This section applies where regulations under—
(a) section 4 or 6 of this Act,
(b) section 5 of the Social Security Administration Act 1992 (c.5), or
(c) section 5 of the Social Security Administration (Northern Ireland) Act 1992 (c.8),
permit or require a claim or notification relating to a tax credit, child benefit or guardian's allowance to be made or given to a relevant authority.

(2) Where this section applies, regulations may make provision—
(a) for information or evidence relating to tax credits, child benefit or guardian's allowance to be provided to the relevant authority (whether by persons by whom such claims and notifications are or have been made or given, by the Board or by other persons),
(b) for the giving of information or advice by a relevant authority to persons by whom such claims or notifications are or have been made or given, and
(c) for the recording, verification and holding, and the forwarding to the Board or a person providing services to the Board, of claims and notifications received by virtue of the regulations referred to in sub-section (1) and information or evidence received by virtue of paragraph (a).

(3) "Relevant authority" means—
(a) the Secretary of State,
(b) the Northern Ireland Department, or
(c) a person providing services to the Secretary of State or the Northern Ireland Department.

Definitions

"child benefit"—see SSCBA 1992 s.141.
"claim"—see s.3(8).
"guardian's allowance"—see SSCBA 1992 s.77.
"relevant authority"—see subs.(3).
"tax credit"—see s.1(2).

GENERAL NOTE

1.416 Section 5 of the SSAA 1992 and its Northern Ireland equivalent provide the authority for the Social Security (Claims and Payments) Regulations 1987 (SI 1987/1968) under which regulations for all aspects of claiming benefits are detailed. This section enables claims and notifications for tax credits and child benefit being validly given to both HMRC and the social security authorities, and to anyone acting under contract to the social security authorities. It will, for example, allow claims for child benefit and CTC to be made together to one authority. See also the Tax Credits (Administrative Arrangements) Regulations 2002 (SI 2002/3036).

CRCA 2005 contains a wide general power for HMRC to use for all its statutory purposes all the information that comes into its possession for any purpose. This is subject to limits in Sch.2 of that Act. There are no limits in the Schedule relevant to the management and payment of tax credits.

Use and disclosure of information

1.417 **59.** Schedule 5 (use and disclosure of information) has effect.

GENERAL NOTE

1.418 This section incorporates Sch.5 into the Act. The Schedule adds further provisions to the statutory authority already available so that tax authorities, social security authorities, other government departments, and local authorities can exchange information. The widest power is the power to give information to anyone for the purposes of the Learning and Skills Act 2000 (para.10). This wide power is linked to a new criminal offence if it is misused (para.10(4)). Paragraph 11 includes disclosures about tax credits in the general offence of disclosing information held by a person in connection with tax, tax credit and social security functions unless the information is disclosed with lawful authority or certain other conditions are met. This replaces the inclusion of tax credits within that section under s.12 of the TCA 1999. Paragraph 9 of the Schedule has given effect by the Tax Credits (Provision of Information) (Functions Relating to Health) Regulations 2003 (SI 2003/731) and the Tax Credits (Provision of Information) (Functions Relating to Health) (No.2) Regulations 2003 (SI 2003/1650) and a series of other short specific provisions.

Other supplementary provisions

Repeals

1.419 **60.** Schedule 6 (repeals) has effect.

GENERAL NOTE

1.420 This section incorporates the standard repeals Schedule into the Act. It provides the authority for the abolitions flagged up in s.1(3). It confirms that this Act replaces the whole of the TCA 1999.

Commencement

1.421 **61.** Apart from section 54(1) and (2), the preceding provisions of this Act come into force in accordance with orders made by the Treasury.

GENERAL NOTE

1.422 See end of the introductory General Note to the Act as a whole.

Transitional provisions and savings

62.—(1) The Secretary of State may by order make as respects England and Wales and Scotland, and the Northern Ireland Department may by order make as respects Northern Ireland, any transitional provisions or savings which appear appropriate in connection with the commencement of the abolition of the increases referred to in section 1(3)(e).

(2) Subject to any provision made by virtue of subsection (1), the Treasury may by order make any transitional provisions or savings which appear appropriate in connection with the commencement of any provision of this Act.

GENERAL NOTE

See the note to the previous section.

Tax credits appeals etc.: temporary modifications

63.—(1) Until such day as the Treasury may by order appoint, Part I of this Act has effect subject to the modifications specified in this section; and an order under this subsection may include any transitional provisions or savings which appear appropriate.

[² (2) Except in the case of an appeal against an employer penalty, an appeal under section 38 is to—
(a) in Great Britain, the First-tier Tribunal; or
(b) in Northern Ireland, the appeal tribunal;
and in either case section 39(6) shall not apply.]

[² (3) The function of giving a direction under section 19(10) is a function of—
(a) in Great Britain, the First-tier Tribunal; or
(b) in Northern Ireland, the appeal tribunal;
and in either case the relevant provisions of Part 5 of the Taxes Management Act 1970 shall not apply.]

[² (4) In Northern Ireland, except in the case of an employer information penalty, proceedings under paragraph 3 of Schedule 2 are by way of information in writing, made to the appeal tribunal (rather than to the tribunal), and upon summons issued by them to the defendant to appear before them at a time and place stated in the summons; and they must hear and decide each case in a summary way.]

(5) So far as is appropriate in consequence of subsections (2) to (4)—
  (a) the references to the [² tribunal in section 19(10)] and paragraphs 2 and 3(2) of Schedule 2 are to the [³ the First-tier Tribunal or] [² appeal tribunal], [² . . .]
  (b) [² . . .]

[² (6) In Northern Ireland, an appeal under paragraph 2(2) or 4(1) of Schedule 2 from a decision of, or against the determination of a penalty by, the appeal tribunal lies to the Northern Ireland Social Security Commissioner (rather than to the Upper Tribunal).]

(7) So far as is appropriate in consequence of subsection (6), the references in paragraphs 2(2) and 4 of Schedule 2 [² to the Upper Tribunal are to the Northern Ireland Social Security Commissioner].

(8) Regulations may apply any provision contained in—
  (a) Chapter 2 of Part I of the Social Security Act 1998 (c.14) (social security appeals: Great Britain),
  (b) Chapter 2 of Part II of the Social Security (Northern Ireland) Order

1998 (SI 1998/1506 (N.I. 10)) (social security appeals: Northern Ireland), or

(c) section 54 of the Taxes Management Act 1970 (c.9) (settling of appeals by agreement),

in relation to appeals which, by virtue of this section, are to [³ the First-tier Tribunal or] [¹ the appeal tribunal or lie to] [[¹a]Northern Ireland Social Security Commissioner], but subject to such modifications as are prescribed. [² . . .]

([¹ (10) "Appeal tribunal" means an appeal tribunal constituted under Chapter 1 of Part 2 of the Social Security (Northern Ireland) Order 1998.]

(11) "Employer penalty" means—

(a) a penalty under section 31 or 32 relating to a requirement imposed by virtue of regulations under section 25, or

(b) a penalty under section 33.

(12) "Employer information penalty" means a penalty under section 32(2)(a) relating to a requirement imposed by virtue of regulations under section 25.

(13) ["Northern Ireland Social Security Commissioner" means] the Chief Social Security Commissioner or any other Social Security Commissioner appointed under the Social Security Administration (Northern Ireland) Act 1992 (c.8) or a tribunal of two or more Commissioners constituted under Article 16(7) of the Social Security (Northern Ireland) Order 1998 (SI 1998/1506 (N.I. 10)).

[¹ (14) "tribunal" (other than in the expression "appeal tribunal") shall have the meaning in section 47C of the Taxes Management Act 1970.]

AMENDMENTS

1. Transfer of Tribunals Functions Order 2008 (SI 2008/2833) art.9(1) Sch.3 para.191 (November 3, 2008).
2. Transfer of Tribunal Functions and Revenue and Customs Appeals Order 2009 (SI 2009/56) art.3(1) Sch.1 para.316 (April 1, 2009).
3. Revenue and Customs Appeals Order 2012 (SI 2012/533) art.2 (March 1, 2012).

DEFINITIONS

"appeal tribunal"—see subs.(10).
"employer information penalty"—see subs.(12).
"employer penalty"—see subs.(11).
"General Commissioners"—see s.47.
"modifications"—see s.67.
"Social Security Commissioner"—see subs.(13).
"Special Commissioners"—see s.47.

GENERAL NOTE

The original aim of this section was to introduce what was said to be a temporary transfer of tax credits from the General and Special Commissioners to the social security tribunals. No such transfer took place, and events have been overtaken by the more general reforms of both tribunals. The choice is now between the Social Entitlement Chamber of the First-tier Tribunal, where appeals are now heard, and the Tax Chamber of the same tribunal, where it is still the policy intention to have the appeals heard. In practice, the distinction matters little as the rules and practices are now substantially the same and there are, in any event, few tax credits appeals. A major focus of difficulty in the appeals now heard are on the issue of whether a claim should have been a joint claim (that is, the claimant is living with a partner). That is a kind of appeal in which the social entitlement tribunals have considerable experience and the tax tribunals have none.

(2002 c.21 s.63)

The "temporary modifications" to s.63 are unlikely to be modified before the whole Act is itself repealed when tax credits are replaced, as provided for the Welfare Reform Act 2012 by the universal credit. Under that Act power is given to transfer tax credits functions in whole or in part from Her Majesty's Revenue and Customs to the relevant Secretary of State.

As part of those reforms, the procedure on appeals is now the standard First-tier Tribunal procedure. See Vol.III of this work. Again as part of those reforms, appeals from the tax tribunals no longer go to the High Court or Court of Session, but now go to the Upper Tribunal, as do all social entitlement appeals.

There was no equivalent reform of the Northern Ireland system. The section therefore provides that appeals go to the "old" tribunals and Commissioners there.

Northern Ireland

64.—(1) The Northern Ireland Act 1998 (c.47) has effect subject to the amendments in subsections (2) and (3).

(2) In Schedule 2 (excepted matters), after paragraph 10 insert—

"**10A.** Tax credits under Part 1 of the Tax Credits Act 2002.
10B. Child benefit and guardian's allowance."

(3) In section 87 (consultation and co-ordination on social security matters), after subsection (6) insert—

"(6A) But this section does not apply to the legislation referred to in subsection (6) to the extent that it relates to child benefit or guardian's allowance."

(4) For the purposes of that Act, a provision of—
(a) an Act of the Northern Ireland Assembly; or
(b) a Bill for such an Act,
which amends or repeals any of the provisions of the Employment Rights (Northern Ireland) Order 1996 (SI 1996/1919 (N.I. 16)) dealt with in Schedule 1 shall not be treated as dealing with tax credits if the Act or Bill deals with employment rights conferred otherwise than by that Schedule in the same way.

1.427

DEFINITION

"tax credits"—see s.1(2).

GENERAL NOTE

The provisions on Northern Ireland are necessary because of the transfer of the administration of child benefit and guardian's allowance from the Northern Ireland authorities to the Home Civil Service. The amendments also confirm the effect of s.16 of the Tax Credits Act 1999 in reserving tax credits as excepted matters.

1.428

Regulations, orders and schemes

65.—(1) Any power to make regulations under sections 3, 7 to 13, 42 and 43, and any power to make regulations under this Act prescribing a rate of interest, is exercisable by the Treasury.

(2) Any other power to make regulations under this Act is exercisable by the Board.

(3) Subject to subsection (4), any power to make regulations, orders or schemes under this Act is exercisable by statutory instrument.

(4) The power—

1.429

Tax Credits Act 2002

    (a) of the Department of Health, Social Services and Public Safety to make schemes under section 12(5), and

    (b) of the Northern Ireland Department to make orders under section 62(1),

is exercisable by statutory rule for the purposes of the Statutory Rules (Northern Ireland) Order 1979 (S.I. 1979/1573 (N.I. 12)).

(5) Regulations may not be made under section 25 or 26 in relation to appeals in Scotland without the consent of the Scottish Ministers.

(6) Regulations may not be made under section 39(6) or 63(8) without the consent of the Lord Chancellor [1, the Department of Justice in Northern Ireland] and the Scottish Ministers.

(7) Any power to make regulations under this Act may be exercised—

    (a) in relation to all cases to which it extends, to all those cases with prescribed exceptions or to prescribed cases or classes of case,

    (b) so as to make as respects the cases in relation to which it is exercised the full provision to which it extends or any less provision (whether by way of exception or otherwise),

    (c) so as to make the same provision for all cases in relation to which it is exercised or different provision for different cases or classes of case or different provision as respects the same case or class of case for different purposes,

    (d) so as to make provision unconditionally or subject to any prescribed condition,

    (e) so as to provide for a person to exercise a discretion in dealing with any matter.

(8) Any regulations made under a power under this Act to prescribe a rate of interest may—

    (a) either themselves specify a rate of interest or make provision for any such rate to be determined by reference to such rate or the average of such rates as may be referred to in the regulations,

    (b) provide for rates to be reduced below, or increased above, what they otherwise would be by specified amounts or by reference to specified formulae,

    (c) provide for rates arrived at by reference to averages to be rounded up or down,

    (d) provide for circumstances in which alteration of a rate of interest is or is not to take place, and

    (e) provide that alterations of rates are to have effect for periods beginning on or after a day determined in accordance with the regulations in relation to interest running from before that day as well as from or from after that day.

(9) Any power to make regulations or a scheme under this Act includes power to make any incidental, supplementary, consequential or transitional provision which appears appropriate for the purposes of, or in connection with, the regulations or scheme.

AMENDMENT

1. Northern Ireland Act 1998 (Devolution of Policing and Justice Functions) Order 2010 (SI 2010/ 976) art.15(5) and Sch.18 para.60 (April 12, 2010).

(2002 c.21 s.65)

DEFINITIONS

"the Board"—see s.67, but note that the functions of the Board have been transferred to Her Majesty's Revenue and Customs by the Commissioners for Revenue and Customs Act 2005.
"prescribe"—see s.67.

Parliamentary etc. control of instruments

66.—(1) No [¹ order or] regulations to which this subsection applies may be made unless a draft of the instrument containing [¹ the order or regulations] (whether or not together with other provisions) has been laid before, and approved by a resolution of, each House of Parliament.

(2) Subsection (1) applies to—
[¹(za) an order made by the Treasury under section 36A(8) or 36C(9),
(zb) regulations made under section 36A(5) or 36C(4),]
  (a) regulations prescribing monetary amounts that are required to be reviewed under section 41,
  (b) regulations made by virtue of subsection (2) of section 12 prescribing the amount in excess of which charges are not taken into account for the purposes of that subsection, and
  (c) the first regulations made under sections 7(8) and (9), 9, 11, 12 and 13(2).
(3) [¹ An order or] a statutory instrument containing—
  (a) regulations under this Act,
  (b) a scheme made by the Secretary of State under section 12(5), or
  (c) an Order in Council under section 52(7),
is (unless a draft of the instrument has been laid before, and approved by a resolution of, each House of Parliament) subject to annulment in pursuance of a resolution of either House of Parliament.

(4) A statutory instrument containing a scheme made by the Scottish Ministers under section 12(5) is subject to annulment in pursuance of a resolution of the Scottish Parliament.

(5) A statutory rule containing a scheme made by the Department of Health, Social Services and Public Safety under section 12(5) is subject to negative resolution within the meaning of section 41(6) of the Interpretation Act (Northern Ireland) 1954 (c. 33 (N.I.)).

1.430

AMENDMENT

1. Welfare Reform Act 2012 s.120(4) (April 6, 2013).

Interpretation

67.—In this Act—
"the Board" means the Commissioners of Inland Revenue,
[¹ "cautioned", in relation to any person and any offence, means cautioned after the person concerned has admitted the offence; and "caution" is to be interpreted accordingly;]
"modifications" includes alterations, additions and omissions, and "modifies" is to be construed accordingly,
"the Northern Ireland Department" means the Department for Social Development in Northern Ireland,
"prescribed" means prescribed by regulations, and
"tax credit" and "tax credits" have the meanings given by section 1(2).

1.431

Tax Credits Act 2002

AMENDMENT

1. Welfare Reform Act 2012 s.120(3) (April 6, 2013).

GENERAL NOTE

1.432 For references to "the Board" see now s.2 above and CRCA 2005 s.1.

1.433 **68.—70.** *Omitted.*

1.434 **Sch.1.**—*Omitted.*

SCHEDULE 2
PENALTIES: SUPPLEMENTARY

Determination of penalties by Board

1.435 **1.**—(1) The Board may make a determination—
  (a) imposing a penalty under section 31, 32(2)(b) or (3) or 33; and
  (b) setting it at such amount as, in their opinion, is appropriate.
(2) The Board must give notice of a determination of a penalty under this paragraph to the person on whom the penalty is imposed.
(3) The notice must state the date on which it is given and give details of the right to appeal against the determination under section 38.
(4) After the notice of a determination under this paragraph has been given the determination must not be altered except on appeal.
(5) A penalty determined under this paragraph becomes payable at the end of the period of 30 days beginning with the date on which the notice of determination is given.

2.—(1) On an appeal [· . . .] under section 38 against the determination of a penalty under [¹ paragraph 1 that is notified to the First-tier Tribunal, the tribunal] may—
  (a) if it appears that no penalty has been incurred, set the determination aside,
  (b) if the amount determined appears to be appropriate, confirm the determination,
  (c) if the amount determined appears to be excessive, reduce it to such other amount (including nil) as [¹ the First-tier Tribunal considers] appropriate, or
  (d) if the amount determined appears to be insufficient, increase it to such amount not exceeding the permitted maximum [¹ the First-tier Tribunal considers] consider appropriate.

[¹ (2) In addition to any right of appeal on a point of law under section 11(2) of the Tribunals, Courts and Enforcement Act 2007, the person liable to the penalty may appeal to the Upper Tribunal against the amount of the penalty which has been determined under sub-paragraph (1), but not against any decision which falls under section 11(5)(d) or (e) of that Act and was made in connection with the determination of the amount of the penalty.

(2A) Section 11(3) and (4) of the Tribunals, Courts and Enforcement Act 2007 applies to the right of appeal under sub-paragraph (2) as it applies to the right of appeal under section 11(2) of that Act.

(2B) On an appeal under this paragraph the Upper Tribunal has the same powers as are conferred on the First-tier Tribunal by virtue of this paragraph.]

Penalty proceedings before [¹ tribunal]

1.436 **3.**—(1) The Board may commence proceedings for a penalty under section 32(2)(a) [¹ before the tribunal].
[¹ (2) The person liable to the penalty shall be a party to the proceedings.
(3) "tribunal" is to be read in accordance with section 47C of the Taxes Management Act 1970.]

4.—[¹ (1) In addition to any right of appeal on a point of law under section 11(2) of the Tribunals, Courts and Enforcement Act 2007, the person liable to the penalty may appeal to the Upper Tribunal against the determination of a penalty in proceedings under paragraph 2(1), but not against any decision which falls under section 11(5)(d) or (e) of that Act and was made in connection with the determination of the amount of the penalty.

(1A) Section 11(3) and (4) of the Tribunals, Courts and Enforcement Act 2007 applies to the right of appeal under sub-paragraph (1) as it applies to the right of appeal under section 11(2) of that Act.]

(2) On any such appeal the [¹Upper Tribunal] may—

(a) if it appears that no penalty has been incurred, set the determination aside,
(b) if the amount determined appears to be appropriate, confirm the determination,
(c) if the amount determined appears to be excessive, reduce it to such other amount (including nil) as the [¹Upper Tribunal] considers appropriate, or
(d) if the amount determined appears to be insufficient, increase it to such amount not exceeding the permitted maximum as the [¹Upper Tribunal] considers appropriate.

Mitigation of penalties

5.—The Board may in their discretion mitigate any penalty under this Part or stay or compound any proceedings for any such penalty and may also, after judgment, further mitigate or entirely remit any such penalty.

1.437

Time limits for penalties

6.—(1) In the case of a penalty under s.31 relating to a tax credit for a person or persons for the whole or part of a tax year (other than a penalty to which sub-paragraph (3) applies), the Board may determine the penalty at any time before the latest of—
(a) the end of the period of one year beginning with the expiry of the period for initiating an enquiry under section 19 into the entitlement of the person, or the joint entitlement of the persons, for the tax year,
(b) if such an enquiry is made, the end of the period of one year beginning with the day on which the enquiry is completed, and
(c) if a decision relating to the entitlement of the person, or the joint entitlement of the persons, for the tax year is made under section 20(1) or (4), the end of the period of one year beginning with the day on which the decision is made.
(2) In the case of a penalty under section 32 relating to a tax credit for a person or persons for the whole or part of a tax year (other than a penalty to which sub-paragraph (3) applies), the Board may determine the penalty, or commence proceedings for it, at any time before—
(a) if an enquiry into the entitlement of the person, or the joint entitlement of the persons, for the tax year is made under section 19, the end of the period of one year beginning with the day on which the enquiry is completed, and
(b) otherwise, the end of the period of one year beginning with the expiry of the period for initiating such an enquiry.
(3) In the case of—
(a) a penalty under section 31 or 32 relating to a requirement imposed by virtue of regulations under section 25; or
(b) a penalty under section 33,
the Board may determine the penalty, or commence proceedings for it, at any time before the end of the period of six years after the date on which the penalty was incurred or began to be incurred.

1.438

Recovery of penalties

7.—(1) A penalty payable under this Part is to be treated for the purposes of Part VI of the Taxes Management Act 1970 (c.9) (collection and recovery) as if it were tax charged in an assessment and due and payable.
(2) Regulations under section 203(2)(a) of the Income and Corporation Taxes Act 1988 (c.1) (PAYE) apply to a penalty payable under this Part as if it were an underpayment of tax for a previous year of assessment.

1.439

AMENDMENT

1. Transfer of Tribunal Functions and Revenue and Customs Order 2009 (SI 2009/56) Sch.1 paras 312, 317 and 318 (April 1, 2009).

DEFINITIONS

"appeal tribunal"—s.63(10).
"the Board"—s.57 but note that the functions of the Board have been transferred to HMRC by CRCA 2005.
"Social Security Commissioner"—s.63(13).

"tax credit"—by virtue of s.67, see s.1(2).
"tax year"—s.47.

GENERAL NOTE

1.440 This Schedule is set out as modified by s.63, which has the effect that, except in cases involving employer penalties or employer information penalties (neither of which can arise since payment by employers was abolished from April 6, 2006), the jurisdiction of the General Commissioners and Special Commissioners was exercised by appeal tribunals and the jurisdiction of the High Court and the Court of Session as the Court of Exchequer in Scotland was exercised by Social Security Commissioners. Since April 2009 all appeals now go to the First-tier Tribunal and then the Upper Tribunal. For more general information, see the note to s.39.

Paragraph 2

1.441 Initial penalty determinations are by HMRC under para.1 except where the penalty is an initial penalty for failing to provide information to be imposed under s.32(2)(a). Section 38 provides a right of appeal against determinations under para.1 and s.39 provides for its exercise. Paragraph 2 makes provision for the powers of the tribunal and, as modified by ss.63(6) and (7) for an appeal to the Upper Tribunal on issues of quantum. In other words, the appeal is not confined to points of law. But the power to appeal without first obtaining permission to appeal has been removed.

Paragraphs 3 and 4

1.442 Paragraph 3 provides for HMRC to bring proceedings before a tribunal for an initial information penalty under s.32(2)(a). See para.6(2) for the time limit for bringing such proceedings. Paragraph 4 provides a right of appeal to the Upper Tribunal. It is similar to that provided in para.2 but see the note to s.63(8).

Paragraph 5

1.443 Section 54 of the Taxes Management Act 1970 would enable an appeal to a tribunal under para.2 to be compromised but this provision also allows proceedings under para.3 to be abandoned and for an appeal to the Upper Tribunal to be compromised. Note that HMRC may reduce a penalty imposed by a tribunal but may not increase it. There is no provision for an appeal by HMRC against the amount of any reduction in a penalty.

1.444 **Sch.3–Sch.6**—*Omitted.*

(2002 c.22)

Employment Act 2002

(2002 c.22)

Arrangement of Sections

Part I

Statutory Leave and Pay

Chapter 1

Paternity and Adoption

Rights to leave and pay

1. Paternity leave [*omitted*]   1.445
2. Statutory paternity pay [*omitted*]★
3. Adoption leave [*omitted*]
4. Statutory adoption pay [*omitted*]★

Administration and enforcement: pay

5. [*repealed*]
6. Financial arrangements [*omitted*]
7. Funding of employers' liabilities
8. Regulations about payment
9. Decisions and appeals [*omitted*]
10. Powers to require information
11. Penalties: failures to comply
12. Penalties: fraud, etc.
13. Supply of information held by the Board
14. Supply of information held by the Secretary of State
15. Use of information by the Board
16. Interpretation

Chapter 2

Maternity

17. Rights during and after maternity leave [*omitted*]
18. Maternity pay period [*omitted*]★
19. Rate of statutory maternity pay [*omitted*]★
20. Entitlement to statutory maternity pay [*omitted*]★
21. Funding of employers' liabilities: statutory maternity pay [*omitted*]★

225

Employment Act 2002

Part II

Tribunal Reform

22–28. [*Omitted*]

Part III

Dispute Resolution, etc.

29–40. [*Omitted*]

Part IV

Miscellaneous and General

41–55. [*Omitted*]

Schedule 1—Penalties: procedure and appeals
Schedules 2–8 [*Omitted*]

*These sections make amendments to SSCBA 1992 which are incorporated in the text of that legislation elsewhere in this volume.

General Note

1.446   On the background to the Employment Act 2002, see the General Note to SSCBA 2002 Pt 12ZA.

Part I

Statutory Leave and Pay

Chapter 1

Paternity and Adoption

Administration and enforcement: pay

Financial arrangements

1.447   **6.**—[*Omitted.*]

(2002 c.22 s.6)

GENERAL NOTE

This section amends SSAA 1992 and SSCBA 1992 to ensure that SPP and SAP are treated in the same was as SPP and SMP in terms of their administration.

1.448

Funding of employers' liabilities

7.—(1) The Secretary of State shall by regulations make provision for the payment by employers of [¹ ordinary statutory paternity pay, additional statutory paternity pay] and statutory adoption pay to be funded by the Board to such extent as the regulations may specify.

1.449

(2) Regulations under subsection (1) shall—
  (a) make provision for a person who has made a payment of [¹ ordinary statutory paternity pay, additional statutory paternity pay] or statutory adoption pay to be entitled, except in such circumstances as the regulations may provide, to recover an amount equal to the sum of—
    (i) the aggregate of such of those payments as qualify for small employers' relief; and
    (ii) an amount equal to 92 per cent of the aggregate of such of those payments as do not so qualify; and
  (b) include provision for a person who has made a payment of [¹ ordinary statutory paternity pay, additional statutory paternity pay] or statutory adoption pay qualifying for small employers' relief to be entitled, except in such circumstances as the regulations may provide, to recover an additional amount equal to the amount to which the person would have been entitled under section 167(2)(b) of the Social Security Contributions and Benefits Act 1992 (corresponding provision for statutory maternity pay) had the payment been a payment of statutory maternity pay.

(3) For the purposes of subsection (2), [¹ a payment of ordinary statutory paternity pay, additional statutory paternity pay] or statutory adoption pay qualifies for small employers' relief if it would have so qualified were it a payment of statutory maternity pay, treating the period for which the payment is made, [¹ in the case of ordinary statutory paternity pay or additional statutory paternity pay], or the payee's adoption pay period, in the case of statutory adoption pay, as the maternity pay period.

(4) Regulations under subsection (1) may, in particular—
  (a) make provision for funding in advance as well as in arrear;
  (b) make provision for funding, or the recovery of amounts due under provision made by virtue of subsection (2)(b), by means of deductions from such amounts for which employers are accountable to the Board as the regulations may provide, or otherwise;
  (c) make provision for the recovery by the Board of any sums overpaid to employers under the regulations.

(5) Where in accordance with any provision of regulations under subsection (1) an amount has been deducted from an employer's contributions payments, the amount so deducted shall (except in such cases as the Secretary of State may by regulations provide) be treated for the purposes of any provision made by or under any enactment in relation to primary or secondary Class 1 contributions—
  (a) as having been paid (on such date as may be determined in accordance with the regulations), and

227

Employment Act 2002

(b) as having been received by the Board, towards discharging the employer's liability in respect of such contributions.

(6) Regulations under this section must be made with the concurrence of the Board.

(7) In this section, "contributions payments", in relation to an employer, means any payments which the employer is required, by or under any enactment, to make in discharge of any liability in respect of primary or secondary Class 1 contributions.

AMENDMENT

1. Work and Families Act 2006 s.11(1) Sch.1 para.50 (April 6, 2010).

DEFINITIONS

"the Board"—see s.16.
"contributions payments"—see subs.(7).
"employer"—see *ibid*.

GENERAL NOTE

1.450 See further the SPP and SAP (Administration) Regulations 2002, especially regs 3–8.

Regulations about payment

1.451 **8.**—(1) The Secretary of State may make regulations with respect to the payment by employers of [¹ ordinary statutory paternity pay, additional statutory paternity pay] and statutory adoption pay.

(2) Regulations under subsection (1) may, in particular, include provision—

(a) about the records to be kept by employers in relation to payments of [¹ ordinary statutory paternity pay, additional statutory paternity pay] and statutory adoption pay, including the length of time for which they are to be retained;

(b) for the production of wages sheets and other documents and records to officers of the Board for the purpose of enabling them to satisfy themselves that [¹ ordinary statutory paternity pay, additional statutory paternity pay] and statutory adoption pay have been paid and are being paid, in accordance with the regulations, to employees who are entitled to them;

(c) for requiring employers to provide information to employees (in their itemised pay statements or otherwise);

(d) for requiring employers to make returns to the Board containing such particulars with respect to payments of [¹ ordinary statutory paternity pay, additional statutory paternity pay] and statutory adoption pay as the regulations may provide.

(3) Regulations under subsection (1) must be made with the concurrence of the Board.

AMENDMENT

1. Work and Families Act 2006 s.11(1) and Sch.1 para.51 (April 6, 2010).

(2002 c.22 s.8)

DEFINITIONS

"the Board"—see s.16.
"employer"—see *ibid.*

GENERAL NOTE

See further the SPP and SAP (Administration) Regulations 2002 regs 9 and 10.   1.452

Decisions and appeals

9.—[*Omitted.*]

GENERAL NOTE

This section amends ss.8, 11 and 14 of the Social Security Contributions (Transfer of Functions, etc.) Act 1999; the relevant amendments are incorporated elsewhere in this volume.   1.453

Powers to require information

10.—(1) The Secretary of State may by regulations make provision enabling an officer of the Board authorised by the Board for the purposes of this section to require persons of a description specified in the regulations to provide, or produce for inspection, within such period as the regulations may require, such information or documents as the officer may reasonably require for the purpose of ascertaining whether [1 ordinary statutory paternity pay, additional statutory paternity pay] or statutory adoption pay is or was payable to or in respect of any person.   1.454

(2) The descriptions of person which may be specified by regulations under subsection (1) include, in particular—

(a) any person claiming to be entitled to [1 ordinary statutory paternity pay, additional statutory paternity pay] or statutory adoption pay,
(b) any person who is, or has been, the spouse or partner of such a person as is mentioned in paragraph (a),
(c) any person who is, or has been, an employer of such a person as is mentioned in paragraph (a),
(d) any person carrying on an agency or other business for the introduction or supply to persons requiring them of persons available to do work or to perform services, and
(e) any person who is a servant or agent of any such person as is specified in paragraphs (a) to (d).

(3) Regulations under subsection (1) must be made with the concurrence of the Board.

AMENDMENT

1. Work and Families Act 2006 s.11(1) and Sch.1 para.52 (April 6, 2010).

DEFINITIONS

"the Board"—see s.16.
"employer"—see *ibid.*

GENERAL NOTE

See further the SPP and SAP (Administration) Regulations 2002, especially regs 11–14.   1.455

Penalties: failures to comply

1.456
11.—(1) Where a person—
(a) fails to produce any document or record, provide any information or make any return, in accordance with regulations under section 8, or
(b) fails to provide any information or document in accordance with regulations under section 10,
he shall be liable to the penalties mentioned in subsection (2) below (subject to subsection (4)).

(2) The penalties are—
(a) a penalty not exceeding £300, and
(b) if the failure continues after a penalty is imposed under paragraph (a), a further penalty or penalties not exceeding £60 for each day on which the failure continues after the day on which the penalty under that paragraph was imposed (but excluding any day for which a penalty under this paragraph has already been imposed).

(3) Where a person fails to keep records in accordance with regulations under section 8, he shall be liable to a penalty not exceeding £3,000.

(4) Subject to subsection (5), no penalty shall be imposed under subsection (2) or (3) at any time after the failure concerned has been remedied.

(5) Subsection (4) does not apply to the imposition of a penalty under subsection (2)(a) in respect of a failure within subsection (1)(a).

(6) Where, in the case of any employee, an employer refuses or repeatedly fails to make payments of [1 ordinary statutory paternity pay, additional statutory paternity pay] or statutory adoption pay in accordance with any regulations under section 8, the employer shall be liable to a penalty not exceeding £3,000.

(7) Section 118(2) of the Taxes Management Act 1970 (c.9) (extra time for compliance, etc.) shall apply for the purposes of subsections (1), (3) and (6) as it applies for the purposes of that Act.

(8) Schedule 1 to this Act (penalties: procedure and appeals) has effect in relation to penalties under this section.

AMENDMENT

1. Work and Families Act 2006 s.11(1) and Sch.1 para.53 (April 6, 2010).

DEFINITIONS

"the Board"—see s.16.
"employer"—see *ibid.*

GENERAL NOTE

1.457
This provision, imposing penalties on employers who fail to comply with the requirements of the SPP and SAP schemes, is modelled on the equivalent provision for tax credits: TCA 2002 s.32.

Penalties: fraud, etc.

1.458
12.—(1) Where a person fraudulently or negligently—
(a) makes any incorrect statement or declaration in connection with establishing entitlement to [1 ordinary statutory paternity pay], or
(b) provides any incorrect information or document of a kind mentioned

in regulations under section 10(1) so far as relating to [¹ ordinary statutory paternity pay],

he shall be liable to a penalty not exceeding £300.

(2) Where a person fraudulently or negligently—
  (a) makes any incorrect statement or declaration in connection with establishing entitlement to statutory adoption pay [¹ or additional statutory paternity pay], or
  (b) provides any incorrect information or document of a kind mentioned in regulations under section 10(1) so far as relating to statutory adoption pay [¹ or additional statutory paternity pay],

he shall be liable to a penalty not exceeding £3,000.

(3) Where an employer fraudulently or negligently makes incorrect payments of [¹ ordinary statutory paternity pay], he shall be liable to a penalty not exceeding £300.

(4) Where an employer fraudulently or negligently makes incorrect payments of statutory adoption pay, he shall be liable to a penalty not exceeding £3,000.

(5) Where an employer fraudulently or negligently—
  (a) produces any incorrect document or record, provides any incorrect information or makes any incorrect return, of a kind mentioned in regulations under section 8; or
  (b) receives incorrect payments in pursuance of regulations under section 7;

he shall be liable to a penalty not exceeding £3,000 or, if the offence relates only to [¹ ordinary statutory paternity pay], £300.

(6) Schedule 1 (penalties: procedure and appeals) has effect in relation to penalties under this section.

AMENDMENT

1. Work and Families Act 2006 s.11(1) and Sch.1 para.54 (April 6, 2010).

DEFINITIONS

"the Board"—see s.16.
"employer"—see *ibid.*

GENERAL NOTE

This provision, imposing penalties on employers who act fraudulently in connection with the SPP and SAP schemes, is modelled on the equivalent provision for tax credits: TCA 2002 s.31.

Supply of information held by the Board

13.—(1) This section applies to information which is held for the purposes of functions relating to [² ordinary statutory paternity pay, additional statutory paternity pay] or statutory adoption pay—
  (a) by the Board, or
  (b) by a person providing services to the Board, in connection with the provision of those services.

(2) Information to which this section applies may be supplied—
  (a) to the Secretary of State [¹, the Child Maintenance and Enforcement Commission] or the Department; or

(b) to a person providing services to the Secretary of State or the Department;

for use for the purposes of functions relating to social security, child support or war pensions [¹ and in relation to the Child Maintenance and Enforcement Commission, any function of that Commission].

AMENDMENTS

1. Child Support (Consequential Provisions) (No. 2) Regulations 2008 (SI 2008/2656) reg.2 (November 1, 2008).
2. Work and Families Act 2006 s.11(1) and Sch.1 para.55 (April 6, 2010).

DEFINITIONS

"the Board"—see s.16.
"the Department"—see *ibid.*

Supply of information held by the Secretary of State

1.461   **14.**—(1) This section applies to information which is held for the purposes of functions relating to [¹ ordinary statutory paternity pay, additional statutory paternity pay] or statutory adoption pay—
  (a) by the Secretary of State or the Department, or
  (b) by a person providing services to the Secretary of State or the Department, in connection with the provision of those services.
(2) Information to which this section applies may be supplied—
  (a) to the Board, or
  (b) to a person providing services to the Board,
for use for the purposes of functions relating to [¹ ordinary statutory paternity pay, additional statutory paternity pay] or statutory adoption pay.

AMENDMENT

1. Work and Families Act 2006 s.11(1) and Sch.1 para.56 (April 6, 2010).

DEFINITIONS

"the Board"—see s.16.
"the Department"—see *ibid.*

Use of information by the Board

1.462   **15.**—(1) Information which is held—
  (a) by the Board, or
  (b) by a person providing services to the Board, in connection with the provision of those services,
for the purposes of any functions specified in any paragraph of subsection (2) below may be used for the purposes of, or for any purposes connected with, the exercise of any functions specified in any other paragraph of that subsection, and may be supplied to any person providing services to the Board for those purposes.
(2) The functions referred to in subsection (1) above are—
  (a) the functions of the Board in relation to [¹ ordinary] statutory paternity pay;
[¹(aa) their functions in relation to additional statutory paternity pay;]
  (b) their functions in relation to statutory adoption pay, and

(2002 c.22 s.15)

(c) their functions in relation to tax, contributions, statutory sick pay, statutory maternity pay or tax credits, or functions under Part III of the Pension Schemes Act 1993 (c.48) (certification of pension scheme, etc.) or Part III of the Pension Schemes (Northern Ireland) Act 1993 (c.49) (corresponding provisions for Northern Ireland).

(3) In subsection (2)(c) above, "contributions" means contributions under Part I of the Social Security Contributions and Benefits Act 1992 (c.4) or Part I of the Social Security Contributions and Benefits (Northern Ireland) Act 1992 (c.7).

AMENDMENT

1. Work and Families Act 2006 s.11(1) and Sch.1 para.57 (April 6, 2010).

DEFINITION

"the Board"—see s.16.

Interpretation

16. In sections 5 to 15— 1.463
"the Board" means the Commissioners of Inland Revenue;
"the Department" means the Department for Social Development or the Department for Employment and Learning;
"employer" and "employee" have the same meanings as in Parts 12ZA and 12ZB of the Social Security Contributions and Benefits Act 1992.

CHAPTER 2

MATERNITY

17.–21—[*Omitted.*] 1.464

GENERAL NOTE

Section 17 amends the provisions governing the right to maternity leave under the Employment Rights Act 1996. Sections 18–20 amend ss.164 and 165 of the SSCBA 1992, and substitutes a new s.166 of that Act, while s.21 substitutes a new s.167 of the same Act. These amendments are incorporated elsewhere in this volume. 1.465

SCHEDULE 1

PENALTIES: PROCEDURE AND APPEALS

Determination of penalties by officer of Board

1.—(1) Subject to sub-paragraph (2) and except where proceedings have been instituted under paragraph 5, an officer of the Board authorised by the Board for the purposes of this paragraph may make a determination— 1.466
    (a) imposing a penalty under section 11 or 12, and
    (b) setting it at such amount as, in his opinion, is correct or appropriate.
(2) Sub-paragraph (1) does not apply to the imposition of such a penalty as is mentioned in section 11(2)(a).
(3) Notice of a determination of a penalty under this paragraph shall be served on the person liable to the penalty and shall state the date on which it is issued and the time within which an appeal against the determination may be made.
(4) After the notice of a determination under this paragraph has been served the determination shall not be altered except in accordance with this paragraph or on appeal.

Employment Act 2002

(5) If it is discovered by an officer of the Board authorised by the Board for the purposes of this paragraph that the amount of a penalty determined under this paragraph is or has become insufficient, the officer may make a determination in a further amount so that the penalty is set at the amount which, in his opinion, is correct or appropriate.

Provisions supplementary to paragraph 1

1.467

2.—(1) A penalty determined under paragraph 1 above shall be due and payable at the end of the period of thirty days beginning with the date of the issue of the notice of determination.

(2) Part 6 of the Taxes Management Act 1970 (c.9) shall apply in relation to a penalty determined under para.1 as if it were tax charged in an assessment and due and payable.

Appeals against penalty determinations

1.468

3.—(1) An appeal may be brought against the determination of a penalty under paragraph 1.

(2) The provisions of the Taxes Management Act 1970 relating to appeals, except section 50(6) to (8), shall have effect in relation to an appeal against such a determination as they have effect in relation to an appeal against an assessment to tax [1 except that references to the tribunal shall be taken to be references to the First-tier Tribunal].

(3) On an appeal by virtue of sub-paragraph (2) against the determination of a penalty under paragraph 1, the [1 First-tier Tribunal] may—
  (a) if it appears [1 . . .] that no penalty has been incurred, set the determination aside,
  (b) if the amount determined appears [1. . .] to be appropriate, confirm the determination,
  (c) if the amount determined appears [1 . . .] to be excessive, reduce it to such other amount (including nil) as [1 the tribunal considers] appropriate,
  (d) if the amount determined appears [1 . . .] to be insufficient, increase it to such amount not exceeding the permitted maximum as [1 the tribunal considers] appropriate.

[1(4) In addition to any right of appeal on a point of law under section 11(2) of the Tribunals, Courts and Enforcement Act 2007, the person liable to the penalty may appeal to the Upper Tribunal against the amount of the penalty which had been determined under sub-paragraph (3), but not against any decision which falls under section 11(5)(d) or (e) of that Act and was made in connection with the determination of the amount of the penalty.

(4A) Section 11(3) and (4) of the Tribunals, Courts and Enforcement Act 2007 applies to the right of appeal under sub-paragraph (4) as it applies to the right of appeal under section 11(2) of that Act.

(4B) On an appeal under this paragraph the Upper Tribunal has the like jurisdiction as is conferred on the First-tier Tribunal by virtue of this paragraph.]

Penalty proceedings before [1 First-tier Tribunal]

1.469

4.—(1) An officer of the Board authorised by the Board for the purposes of this paragraph may commence proceedings for any penalty to which sub-paragraph (1) of paragraph 1 does not apply by virtue of sub-paragraph (2) of that paragraph.

[1 (2) The person liable to the penalty shall be a party to the proceedings.]

(3) Part 6 of the Taxes Management Act 1970 (c.9) shall apply in relation to a penalty determined in proceedings under this paragraph as if it were tax charged in an assessment and due and payable.

[1 (4) In addition to any right of appeal on a point of law under section 11(2) of the Tribunals, Courts and Enforcement Act 2007, the person liable to the penalty may appeal to the Upper Tribunal against the determination of a penalty in proceedings under sub-paragraph (1), but not against any decision which falls under section 11(5)(d) or (e) of that Act and was made in connection with the determination of the amount of the penalty.

(4A) Section 11(3) and (4) of the Tribunals, Courts and Enforcement Act 2007 applies to the right of appeal under sub-paragraph (4) as it applies to the right of appeal under section 11(2) of that Act.]

(5) On any such appeal the [1Upper Tribunal] may—
  (a) if it appears that no penalty has been incurred, set the determination aside;
  (b) if the amount determined appears to be appropriate, confirm the determination;
  (c) if the amount determined appears to be excessive, reduce it to such other amount (including nil) as the [1Upper Tribunal] considers appropriate;
  (d) if the amount determined appears to be insufficient, increase it to such amount not exceeding the permitted maximum as the [1Upper Tribunal] considers appropriate.

Penalty proceedings before court

5.—(1) Where in the opinion of the Board the liability of any person for a penalty under section 11 or 12 arises by reason of the fraud of that or any other person, proceedings for the penalty may be instituted before the High Court or, in Scotland, the Court of Session as the Court of Exchequer in Scotland.

(2) Subject to sub-paragraph (3), proceedings under this paragraph shall be instituted—
 (a) in England and Wales, in the name of the Attorney General; and
 (b) in Scotland, in the name of the Advocate General for Scotland.

(3) Sub-paragraph (2) shall not prevent proceedings under this paragraph being instituted in England and Wales under the Crown Proceedings Act 1947 (c.44) by and in the name of the Board as an authorised department for the purposes of that Act.

(4) Any proceedings under this paragraph instituted in England and Wales shall be deemed to be civil proceedings by the Crown within the meaning of Part II of the Crown Proceedings Act 1947.

(5) If in proceedings under this paragraph the court does not find that fraud is proved but considers that the person concerned is nevertheless liable to a penalty, the court may determine a penalty notwithstanding that, but for the opinion of the Board as to fraud, the penalty would not have been a matter for the court.

1.470

Mitigation of penalties

6.—The Board may in their discretion mitigate any penalty under section 11 or 12, or stay or compound any proceedings for a penalty, and may also, after judgment, further mitigate or entirely remit the penalty.

1.471

Time-limits for penalties

7.—A penalty under section 11 or 12 may be determined by an officer of the Board, or proceedings for the penalty may be commenced before the [1Tribunal] or the court, at any time within six years after the date on which the penalty was incurred or began to be incurred.

1.472

Interest on penalties

8.—(1) After paragraph (p) of section 178(2) of the Finance Act 1989 (c.26) (setting rates of interest) there shall be inserted—

"(q) paragraph 8 of Schedule 1 to the Employment Act 2002."

(2) A penalty under section 11 or 12 shall carry interest at the rate applicable under section 178 of the Finance Act 1989 from the date on which it becomes due and payable until payment.

1.473

Interpretation

9.—In this Schedule—
"the Board" means the Commissioners of Inland Revenue;
[1. . .]

1.474

AMENDMENT

1. Transfer of Tribunal Functions and Revenue and Customs Order 2009 (SI 2009/56) Sch.1 paras 322–325 (April 1, 2009).

Income Tax (Earnings and Pensions) Act 2003

Income Tax (Earnings and Pensions) Act 2003

(2003 c.1)

Arrangement of Selected Sections

Part 1

Overview

1.475
1. Overview of contents of this Act
2. Abbreviations and general index in Schedule 1

Part 2

Employment Income: Charge to Tax

Chapter 1

Introduction

3. Structure of employment income Parts
4. "Employment" for the purposes of the employment income Parts
5. Application to offices and officeholders

Chapter 2

Tax on Employment Income

6. Nature of charge to tax on employment income
7. Meaning of "employment income", "general earnings" and "specific employment income"
8. Meaning of "exempt income"

Chapter 3

Operation of Tax Charge

9. Amount of employment income charged to tax
10. Meaning of "taxable earnings" and "taxable specific income"

11. Calculation of "net taxable earnings"
12. Calculation of "net taxable specific income"
13. Person liable for tax

CHAPTER 7

APPLICATION OF PROVISIONS TO AGENCY WORKERS

Agency workers

44. Treatment of workers supplied by agencies

PART 3

EMPLOYMENT INCOME: EARNINGS AND BENEFITS, ETC. TREATED AS EARNINGS

CHAPTER 1

EARNINGS

62. Earnings

CHAPTER 2

TAXABLE BENEFITS: THE BENEFITS CODE

The benefits code

63. The benefits code
64. Relationship between earnings and benefits code
65. Dispensations relating to benefits within provisions not applicable to lower-paid employment

General definitions for benefits code

66. Meaning of "employment" and related expressions

CHAPTER 3

TAXABLE BENEFITS: EXPENSES PAYMENTS

70. Sums in respect of expenses
71. Meaning of paid or put at disposal by reason of the employment
72. Sums in respect of expenses treated as earnings

Income Tax (Earnings and Pensions) Act 2003

Chapter 4

Taxable Benefits: Vouchers and Credit-tokens

Cash vouchers: introduction

73. Cash vouchers to which this chapter applies
74. Provision for, or receipt by, member of employee's family

Meaning of "cash voucher"

75. Meaning of "cash voucher"
76. Sickness benefits-related voucher

Benefit of cash voucher treated as earnings

81. Benefit of cash voucher treated as earnings

Non-cash vouchers: introduction

82. Non-cash vouchers to which this chapter applies

Meaning of "non-cash voucher"

84. Meaning of "non-cash voucher"

Benefit of non-cash voucher treated as earnings

87. Benefit of non-cash voucher treated as earnings

Credit-tokens: introduction

90. Credit-tokens to which this chapter applies

Meaning of "credit-token"

92. Meaning of "credit-token"

Benefit of credit-token treated as earnings

94. Benefit of credit-token treated as earnings

General supplementary provisions

95. Disregard for money, goods or services obtained

(2003 c.1)

CHAPTER 10

TAXABLE BENEFITS: RESIDUAL LIABILITY TO CHARGE

Introduction

201. Employment-related benefits
202. Excluded benefits

Cash equivalent of benefit treated as earnings

203. Cash equivalent of benefit treated as earnings

Determination of the cost of the benefit

204. Cost of the benefit: basic rule
210. Exemption of minor benefits

CHAPTER 11

TAXABLE BENEFITS: EXCLUSION OF LOWER-PAID EMPLOYMENTS FROM PARTS OF BENEFIT CODE

Introduction

216. Provisions not applicable to lower-paid employments

What is lower-paid employment?

217. Meaning of "lower-paid employment"
218. Calculation of earnings rate for a tax year
219. Extra amounts to be added in connection with a car

PART 4

EMPLOYMENT INCOME: EXEMPTIONS

CHAPTER 11

MISCELLANEOUS EXEMPTIONS

318. Childcare: exemption for employer-provided care
318A. Childcare: exemption for other care

Income Tax (Earnings and Pensions) Act 2003

318AA. Meaning of "relevant earnings amount" and "required time"
318B. Childcare: meaning of "care", "child" and "parental responsibility"
318C. Childcare: meaning of "qualifying child care"

Part 5

Employment Income: Deductions Allowed from Earnings

Chapter 1

Deductions Allowed from Earnings: General Rules

Introduction

327. Deductions from earnings: general

General rules

328. The income from which deductions may be made
329. Deductions from earnings not to exceed earnings
330. Prevention of double deductions
331. Order for making deductions
332. Meaning of "the deductibility provisions"

Chapter 2

Deductions for Employee's Expenses

Introduction

333. Scope of this chapter: expenses paid by the employee
334. Effect of reimbursement, etc.

General rule for deduction of employee's expenses

336. Deductions for expenses: the general rule

Travel expenses

337. Travel in performance of duties
338. Travel for necessary attendance
339. Meaning of "workplace" and "permanent workplace"

(2003 c.1)

PART 9

PENSION INCOME

CHAPTER 1

INTRODUCTION

565. Structure of Part 9

CHAPTER 2

TAX ON PENSION INCOME

566. Nature of charge to tax on pension income and relevant definitions
567. Amount charged to tax
568. Person liable for tax

CHAPTER 3

UNITED KINGDOM PENSIONS: GENERAL RULES

569. United Kingdom pensions
570. "Pension": interpretation
571. Taxable pension income
572. Person liable for tax

CHAPTER 5

UNITED KINGDOM SOCIAL SECURITY PENSIONS

577. United Kingdom social security pensions
578. Taxable pension income
579. Person liable for tax

PART 10

SOCIAL SECURITY INCOME

CHAPTER 1

INTRODUCTION

655. Structure of Part 10

Income Tax (Earnings and Pensions) Act 2003

CHAPTER 2

TAX ON SOCIAL SECURITY INCOME

656. Nature of charge to tax on social security income
657. Meaning of "social security income", "taxable benefits", etc.
658. Amount charged to tax
659. Person liable for tax

CHAPTER 3

TAXABLE UK SOCIAL SECURITY BENEFITS

660. Taxable benefits: UK benefits—Table A
661. Taxable social security income
662. Person liable for tax

CHAPTER 4

TAXABLE UK SOCIAL SECURITY BENEFITS: EXEMPTIONS

Incapacity benefit

663. Long-term incapacity benefit: previous entitlement to invalidity benefit
664. Short-term incapacity benefit not payable at the higher rate

Income support

665. Exempt unless payable to member of couple involved in trade dispute
666. Child maintenance bonus
667. Amounts in excess of taxable maximum
668. Taxable maximum
669. Interpretation

Jobseeker's allowance

670. Child maintenance bonus
671. Amounts in excess of taxable maximum
672. Taxable maximum: general
673. Taxable maximum: income-based jobseeker's allowance
674. Taxable maximum: contribution-based jobseeker's allowance
675. Interpretation

Increases in respect of children

676. Increases in respect of children

(2003 c.1)

CHAPTER 5

UK SOCIAL SECURITY BENEFITS WHOLLY EXEMPT FROM INCOME TAX

677. UK social security benefits wholly exempt from tax: Table B

CHAPTER 6

TAXABLE FOREIGN BENEFITS

678. Taxable benefits: foreign benefits
679. Taxable social security income
680. Person liable for tax

PART 13

SUPPLEMENTARY PROVISIONS

Interpretation

720. [*repealed*]
721. Other definitions

INTRODUCTION AND GENERAL NOTE

This Act (destined to be known as ITEPA or ITEPA 2003) is the second of the major income tax Acts produced by the Tax Law Rewrite Project. (The first was the Capital Allowances Act 2001.) It took effect from and including the start of the 2003–04 income tax year, April 6, 2003, the same day that the TCA 2002 came fully into effect. It is of considerable importance to tax credits because it entirely rewrites the income tax rules dealing with earnings from employments and offices, pension income, and social security income. The time-hallowed "Schedule E" and its charge to tax on "offices and employments on emoluments therefrom" has at last been relegated to history and a codified set of provisions taxing employment income, pension income and social security income put in its place. The approach of TCA 2002 is to rely on income tax rules for the calculation of income for tax credits purposes. The provisions of ITEPA are therefore the rules that will apply to the great majority of claimants for tax credits.

ITEPA is of considerable length and detail, running to 725 sections and 8 Schedules on enactment. It has been drafted in the form of a code, and therefore includes signposting provisions and a far stronger internal structure than the previous legislation.

ITEPA also uses, where possible, plain English. Its language is therefore updated from the "old" language of "Sch.E" and "emoluments".

The Tax Credits (Definition and Calculation of Income) Regulations 2002, as amended to take into account ITEPA, refer to a considerable number of provisions of ITEPA. This selection of sections from ITEPA includes the more important of those sections, together with the sections that set out the internal signposting of ITEPA and its definitions. It is not a complete reproduction of all ITEPA sections, as some of the anti-avoidance provisions that are applied to tax credits are highly

1.476

1.477

technical and, in practice, sometimes quite controversial in application, while others will, it is anticipated, rarely be directly relevant to tax credits claims. In particular, the following parts are entirely omitted:
Part 4: Employment income: Exemptions
Part 6: Employment Income: Income which is not earnings or share-related
Part 7: Employment income: Share-related income and exemptions
Part 8: Former employees: Deductions for liabilities
Part 9: Pay As You Earn
Schs 2–8

Part 2, Chapter 8 of ITEPA (ss.48–61) deal with the so-called IR35 provisions, namely the provisions under which income of a "pocket book" company could be treated as the employment income of the individual who owned the company so that income was not diverted so as to be excluded from income tax. It was understood that these sections would apply to tax credits and they were therefore included in the 2003–04 edition of this volume. However, amendments to the Working Tax Credit (Entitlement and Maximum Rate) Regulations 2002 were made by the Tax Credits (Miscellaneous Amendments No.2) Regulations 2003 (SI 2003/2815) to clarify the intended policy that these provisions do not apply to tax credits. They are therefore no longer of relevance to this volume.

Part 7 of ITEPA was repealed completely and replaced by new provisions by the Finance Act 2003 s.140 and Sch.22 with effect from April 15, 2003. The original Pt 7 was outside the scope of tax credits income calculations. The new Pt 7 is not, by reason of amendment of the Tax Credits (Definition and Calculation of Income) Regulations 2002 (SI 2002/2006) reg.4. See the note to that regulation. The text of the new Pt 7 is not reproduced in this volume.

But particular attention has been paid to sections making special provision for those who are sick or disabled, and to the taxation of state pensions and social security benefits.

ITEPA and the Commissioners for Revenue and Customs Act 2005

1.478 The merger of the Inland Revenue and HM Customs and Excise, and the creation of the new joint HMRC (the new Commissioners and its officers under the new title "officer of Revenue and Customs"), requires textual amendment to most sections in ITEPA. The approach taken by the Rewrite team was to replace previous references—in many forms to "the Commissioners", "the Board", or "an inspector" or "an officer" with either "the Board" (if the function was unlikely to be delegated) or "an officer of the Board" in all other cases. CRCA 2005 adopts a different approach not entirely consistent with this. This is of limited importance in ITEPA. But, for example, the reference to the Board of Inland Revenue in s.343 should now be read as a reference to "the Commissioners", but probably "the Inland Revenue" in s.344 should now be "an officer of Revenue and Customs"—although that is not clear. This lack of clarity is emphasised by the repeal of the definition of those terms as part of the repeal of the definitions in s.720 (which formerly defined "the Inland Revenue" as meaning any officer of the Board. The old text—save for s.720—has not been amended by CRCA 2005 expressly and has been left in this edition.

PART 1

OVERVIEW

Overview of contents of this Act

1.479 **1.**—(1) This Act imposes charges to income tax on—
(a) employment income (see Parts 2 to 7),

(b) pension income (see Part 9), and
(c) social security income (see chapters 1 to 7 of Part 10)
(2) *Repealed*
(3) This Act also—
(a) confers certain reliefs in respect of liabilities of former employees (see Part 8);
(aa) makes provision for the high income child benefit charge (see chapter 8 of Part 10);
(b) provides for the assessment, collection and recovery of income tax in respect of employment, pension or social security income that is PAYE income (see Part 2); and
(c) allows deductions to be made from such income in respect of payroll giving (see Part 12).

Abbreviations and general index in Schedule [1]

2.—(1) Schedule 1 (abbreviations and defined expressions) applies for the purposes of this Act.

1.480

(2) In Schedule 1—
(a) Part 1 gives the meaning of the abbreviated references to Acts and instruments used in this Act; and
(b) Part 2 lists the places where expressions used in this Act are defined or otherwise explained.
(3) *Omitted.*

PART 2

EMPLOYMENT INCOME: CHARGE TO TAX

CHAPTER 1

INTRODUCTION

Structure of employment income Parts

3.—(1) The structure of the employment income Parts is as follows—
This Part imposes the charge to tax on employment income, and sets out—

1.481

(a) how the amount charged to tax for a tax year is to be calculated; and
(b) who is liable for the tax charged;

Part 3 sets out what are earnings and provides for amounts to be treated as earnings;

Part 4 deals with exemptions from the charge to tax under this Part (and, in some cases, from other charges to tax);

Part 5 deals with deductions from taxable earnings;

Part 6 deals with employment income other than earnings or share-related income; and

Part 7 deals with share-related income and exemptions.

Income Tax (Earnings and Pensions) Act 2003

(2) In this Act "the employment income Parts" means this Part and Parts 3 to 7.

GENERAL NOTE

1.482 Part 4 (Employment income: Exemptions)—ss.227–326—is entirely omitted from this work. It comprises a codified list of all exemptions from the charge to income tax otherwise imposed by ITEPA on various earnings and benefits, under the following chapter heads: mileage allowances and passenger payments; transport travel and subsistence; education and training; recreational benefits; non-cash vouchers and credit-tokens; removal benefits and expenses; special kinds of employee; pension provision; termination of employment; and miscellaneous. The general rule of income tax law is that it is for a claimant to claim for, and show that he or she is entitled to, the benefit of an exemption.

Part 6 is also entirely omitted. It comprises ss.386–416, and deals with payments to, and benefits from, non-approved pension schemes, and payments on termination of employment.

Part 7 is also entirely omitted. It is a lengthy part—ss.417–564 and Schs 2–5. They deal with the detail of the various kinds of tax charge on, and exemption of, share-related income including all forms of benefits obtained by shares or interests in shares.

"Employment" for the purposes of the employment income Parts

1.483 **4.**—(1) In the employment income Parts "employment" includes in particular—
  (a) any employment under a contract of service,
  (b) any employment under a contract of apprenticeship, and
  (c) any employment in the service of the Crown.

(2) In those Parts, "employed", "employee" and "employer" have corresponding meanings.

GENERAL NOTE

1.484 There are no general income tax (or, more generally, tax) rules defining whether an individual is an employee or self-employed, or whether a relationship is an employment relationship. That is a matter to be decided by general law. There is considerable case law on the subject, some of it deriving from income tax and some from social security cases. Under the Social Security Contributions (Transfer of Functions) Act 1999 s.8, decisions about the same question for the purposes of the Social Security Contributions and Benefits Act 1992 were transferred to the Inland Revenue and, on appeal, to the tax appeal tribunals. There is, however, no equivalent provision in the TCA 2002. It would seem, therefore, that appeals about Revenue decisions about employment for tax credit purposes go to appeal tribunals, not tax appeal tribunals.

Application to offices and office-holders

1.485 **5.**—(1) The provisions of the employment income Parts that are expressed to apply to employments apply equally to offices, unless otherwise indicated.

(2) In those provisions as they apply to an office—
  (a) references to being employed are to being the holder of the office;
  (b) "employee" means the office-holder;
  (c) "employer" means the person under whom the office-holder holds office.

(2003 c.1 s.5)

(3) In the employment income Parts "office" includes in particular any position which has an existence independent of the person who holds it and may be filled by successive holders.

Chapter 2

Tax on Employment Income

Nature of charge to tax on employment income

6.—(1) The charge to tax on employment income under this Part is a charge to tax on—
(a) general earnings; and
(b) specific employment income.
The meaning of "employment income", "general earnings" and "specific employment income" is given in section 7.

(2) The amount of general earnings or specific employment income which is charged to tax in a particular tax year is set out in section 9.

(3) The rules in Chapters 4 and 5 of this Part, which are concerned with—
(a) the residence and domicile of an employee in a tax year; and
(b) the tax year in which amounts are received or remitted to the United Kingdom;
apply for the purposes of the charge to tax on general earnings but not that on specific employment income.

(4) The person who is liable for any tax charged on employment income is set out in section 13.

(5) Employment income is not charged to tax under this Part if it is within the charge to tax under Part 2 of ITTOIA by virtue of section 15 of that Act (divers and diving supervisors).

1.486

Meaning of "employment income", "general earnings" and "specific employment income"

7.—(1) This section gives the meaning for the purposes of the Tax Acts of "employment income", "general earnings" and "specific employment income".

(2) "Employment income" means—
(a) earnings within Chapter 1 of Part 3;
(b) any amount treated as earnings (see subsection (5)); or
(c) any amount which counts as employment income (see subsection (6)).

(3) "General earnings" means—
(a) earnings within Chapter 1 of Part 3; or
(b) any amount treated as earnings (see subsection (5));
excluding in each case any exempt income.

(4) "Specific employment income" means any amount which counts as employment income (see subsection (6)), excluding any exempt income.

1.487

247

(5) Subsection (2)(b) or (3)(b) refers to any amount treated as earnings under—
  (a) Chapters 7 and 8 of this Part (application of provisions to agency workers and workers under arrangements made by intermediaries),
  (b) Chapters 2 to 11 of Part 3 (the benefits code),
  (c) Chapters 12 of Part 3 (payments treated as earnings), or
  (d) section 262 of CAA 2001 (balancing charges to be given effect by treating them as earnings).
(6) Subsection (2)(c) or (4) refers to any amount which counts as employment income by virtue of—
  (a) Part 6 (income which is not earnings or share-related),
  (b) Part 7 (share-related income and exemptions), or
  (c) any other enactment.

Meaning of "exempt income"

1.488　**8.**—For the purposes of the employment income Parts, an amount of employment income within paragraph (a), (b) or (c) of section 7(2) is "exempt income" if, as a result of any exemption in Part 4 or elsewhere, no liability to income tax arises in respect of it as such an amount.

Chapter 3

Operation of Tax Charge

Amount of employment income charged to tax

1.489　**9.**—(1) The amount of employment income which is charged to tax under this Part for a particular tax year is as follows.
(2) In the case of general earnings, the amount charged is the net taxable earnings from an employment in the year.
(3) That amount is calculated under section 11 by reference to any taxable earnings from the employment in the year (see section 10(2)).
(4) In the case of specific employment income, the amount charged is the net taxable specific income from an employment for the year.
(5) That amount is calculated under section 12 by reference to any taxable specific income from the employment for the year (see section 10(3)).
(6) Accordingly, no amount of employment income is charged to tax under this Part for a particular tax year unless—
  (a) in the case of general earnings, they are taxable earnings from an employment in that year; or
  (b) in the case of specific employment income, it is taxable specific income from an employment for that year.

Meaning of "taxable earnings" and "taxable specific income"

1.490　**10.**—(1) This section explains what is meant by "taxable earnings" and "taxable specific income" in the employment income Parts.
(2) "Taxable earnings" from an employment in a tax year are to be determined in accordance with—

(a) Chapter 4 of this Part (rules applying to employees resident, ordinarily resident and domiciled in the UK); or
(b) Chapter 5 of this Part (rules applying to employees resident, ordinarily resident or domiciled outside the UK).

(3) "Taxable specific income" from an employment for a tax year means the full amount of any specific employment income which, by virtue of Part 6 or 7 or any other enactment, counts as employment income for that year in respect of the employment.

Calculation of "net taxable earnings"

11.—(1) For the purposes of this Part, the "net taxable earnings" from an employment in a tax year are given by the formula—

$$TE - DE,$$

where—

TE means the total amount of any taxable earnings from the employment in the tax year; and

DE means the total amount of any deductions allowed from those earnings under provisions listed in sections 327(3) to (5) (deductions from earnings: general).

(2) If the amount calculated under subsection (1) is negative, the net taxable earnings from the employment in the year are to be taken to be nil instead.

(3) Relief may be available under section 128 of ITA 2007 (set-off against general income)—
(a) where TE is negative; or
(b) in certain exceptional cases where the amount calculated under subsection (1) is negative.

(4) If a person has more than one employment in a tax year, the calculation under subsection (1) must be carried out in relation to each of the employments.

Calculation of "net taxable specific income"

12.—(1) For the purposes of this Part the "net taxable specific income" from an employment for a tax year is given by the formula—

$$TSI - DSI,$$

where—

TSI means the amount of any taxable specific income from the employment for the tax year; and

DSI means the total amount of any deductions allowed from that income under provisions of the Tax Acts not included in the lists in section 327(3) and (4) (deductions from earnings: general).

(2) If the amount calculated under subsection (1) is negative, the net taxable specific income from the employment for the year is to be taken to be nil instead.

(3) If a person has more than one kind of specific employment income from an employment for a tax year, the calculation under subsection (1) must be carried out in relation to each of those kinds of specific employment income; and in such a case the "net taxable specific income"

from the employment for that year is the total of all the amounts so calculated.

Person liable for tax

1.493

13.—(1) The person liable for any tax on employment income under this Part is the taxable person mentioned in subsection (2) or (3). This is subject to subsection (4).

(2) If the tax is on general earnings, "the taxable person" is the person to whose employment the earnings relate.

(3) If the tax is on specific employment income, "the taxable person" is the person in relation to whom the income is, by virtue of Part 6 or 7 or any other enactment, to count as employment income.

(4) If the tax is on general earnings received, or remitted to the United Kingdom, after the death of the person to whose employment the earnings relate, the person's personal representatives are liable for the tax.

(5) In that event the tax is accordingly to be assessed on the personal representatives and is a debt due from and payable out of the estate.

CHAPTER 7

APPLICATION OF PROVISIONS TO AGENCY WORKERS

Agency workers

Treatment of workers supplied by agencies

1.494

44.—(1) This section applies if—
  (a) an individual ("the worker") personally provides, or is under an obligation personally to provide, services (which are not excluded services) to another person ("the client");
  (b) the services are supplied by or through a third person ("the agency") under the terms of an agency contract;
  (c) the worker is subject to (or to the right of) supervision, direction or control as to the manner in which the services are provided; and
  (d) remuneration receivable under or in consequence of the agency contract does not constitute employment income of the worker apart from this chapter.

(2) If this section applies—
  (a) the services which the worker provides, or is obliged to provide, to the client under the agency contract are to be treated for income tax purposes as duties of an employment held by the worker with the agency; and
  (b) all remuneration receivable under or in consequence of the agency contract (including remuneration which the client pays or provides in relation to the services) is to be treated for income tax purposes as earnings from that employment.

(2003 c.1 s.62)

Part 3

Employment Income: Earnings and Benefits, etc. Treated as Earnings

Chapter 1

Earnings

Earnings

62.—(1) This section explains what is meant by "earnings" in the employment income Parts.

(2) In those Parts, "earnings", in relation to an employment, means—
(a) any salary, wages or fee;
(b) any gratuity or other profit or incidental benefit of any kind obtained by the employee if it is money or money's worth; or
(c) anything else that constitutes an emolument of the employment.

(3) For the purposes of subsection (2), "money's worth" means something that is—
(a) of direct monetary value to the employee; or
(b) capable of being converted into money or something of direct monetary value to the employee.

(4) Subsection (1) does not affect the operation of statutory provisions that provide for amounts to be treated as earnings (and see section 721(7)).

1.495

Chapter 2

Taxable Benefits: The Benefits Code

The benefits code

The benefits code

63.—(1) In the employment income Parts "the benefits code" means—
this chapter,
Chapter 3 (expenses payments),
Chapter 4 (vouchers and credit-tokens),
Chapter 5 (living accommodation),
Chapter 6 (cars, vans and related benefits),
Chapter 7 (loans),
Chapter 10 (residual liability to charge), and
Chapter 11 (exclusion of lower-paid employments from parts of benefits code).

(2) If an employment is an excluded employment, the general effect of section 216(1) (provisions not applicable to lower-paidemployments) is that only the following chapters apply to the employment—
this chapter,

1.496

Chapter 4 (vouchers and credit-tokens),
Chapter 5 (living accommodation), and
Chapter 11 (exclusion of lower-paidemployments from parts of benefits code).

(3) Section 216(5) and (6) explain and restrict the effect of section 216(1).

(4) In the benefits code, "excluded employment" means an employment to which the exclusion in section 216(1) applies.

Relationship between earnings and benefits code

1.497   **64.**—(1) This section applies if, apart from this section, the same benefit would give rise to two amounts ("A" and "B")—
   (a) A being an amount of earnings as defined in Chapter 1 of this Part; and
   (b) B being an amount to be treated as earnings under the benefits code.
(2) In such a case—
   (a) A constitutes earnings as defined in Chapter 1 of this Part; and
   (b) the amount (if any) by which B exceeds A is to be treated as earnings under the benefits code.
(3) This section does not apply in connection with living accommodation to which Chapter 5 of this Part applies.
(4) In that case section 109 applies to determine the relationship between that chapter and Chapter 1 of this Part.

Dispensations relating to benefits within provisions not applicable to lower-paid employment

1.498   **65.**—(1) This section applies for the purposes of the listed provisions where a person ("P") supplies the Inland Revenue with a statement of the cases and circumstances in which—
   (a) payments of a particular character are made to or for any employees; or
   (b) benefits or facilities of a particular kind are provided for any employees,
whether they are employees of P or some other person.

(2) The "listed provisions" are the provisions listed in section 216(4) (provisions of the benefits code which do not apply to lower-paid employments).

(3) If the Inland Revenue are satisfied that no additional tax is payable by virtue of the listed provisions by reference to the payments, benefits or facilities mentioned in the statement, they must give P a dispensation under this section.

(4) A "dispensation" is a notice stating that an officer of Revenue and Customs agrees that no additional tax is payable by virtue of the listed provisions by reference to the payments, benefits or facilities mentioned in the statement supplied by P.

(5) If a dispensation is given under this section, nothing in the listed provisions applies to the payments, or the provision of the benefits or facilities, covered by the dispensation or otherwise has the effect of imposing any additional liability to tax in respect of them.

(6) If in their opinion there is reason to do so, the Inland Revenue may revoke a dispensation by giving a further notice to P.

(7) That notice may revoke the dispensation from—
(a) the date when the dispensation was given; or
(b) a later date specified in the notice.
(8) If the notice revokes the dispensation from the date when the dispensation was given—
(a) any liability to tax that would have arisen if the dispensation had never been given is to be treated as having arisen; and
(b) P and the employees in question must make all the returns which they would have had to make if the dispensation had never been given.
(9) If the notice revokes the dispensation from a later date—
(a) any liability to tax that would have arisen if the dispensation had ceased to have effect on that date is to be treated as having arisen; and
(b) P and the employees in question must make all the returns which they would have had to make if the dispensation had ceased to have effect on that date.

General definitions for benefits code

Meaning of "employment" and related expressions

66.—(1) In the benefits code—   1.499
(a) "employment" means a taxable employment under Part 2; and
(b) "employed", "employee" and "employer" have corresponding meanings.
(2) Where a chapter of the benefits code applies in relation to an employee—
(a) references in that chapter to "the employment" are to the employment of that employee; and
(b) references in that chapter to "the employer" are to the employer in respect of that employment.
(3) For the purposes of the benefits code an employment is a "taxable employment under Part 2" in a tax year if the earnings from the employment for that year are (or would be if there were any) general earnings to which the charging provisions of Chapter 4 or 5 of Part 2 apply.
(4) In subsection (3)—
(a) the reference to an employment includes employment as a director of a company; and
(b) "earnings" means earnings as defined in Chapter of this Part.

CHAPTER 3

TAXABLE BENEFITS: EXPENSES PAYMENTS

Sums in respect of expenses

70.—(1) This chapter applies to a sum paid to an employee in a tax year   1.500
if the sum—

(a) is paid to the employee in respect of expenses; and
(b) is so paid by reason of the employment.

(2) This chapter applies to a sum paid away by an employee in a tax year if the sum—
(a) was put at the employee's disposal in respect of expenses;
(b) was so put by reason of the employment; and
(c) is paid away by the employee in respect of expenses.

(3) For the purposes of this chapter it does not matter whether the employment is held at the time when the sum is paid or paidaway so long as it is held at some point in the tax year in which the sum is paid or paidaway.

(4) References in this chapter to an employee accordingly include a prospective or former employee.

(5) This chapter does not apply to the extent that the sum constitutes earnings from the employment by virtue of any other provision.

Meaning of paid or put at disposal by reason of the employment

1.501   **71.**—(1) If an employer pays a sum in respect of expenses to an employee it is to be treated as paid by reason of the employment unless—
(a) the employer is an individual, and
(b) the payment is made in the normal course of the employer's domestic, family or personal relationships.

(2) If an employer puts a sum at an employee's disposal in respect of expenses it is to be treated as put at the employee's disposal by reason of the employment unless—
(a) the employer is an individual, and
(b) the sum is put at the employee's disposal in the normal course of the employer's domestic, family or personal relationships.

Sums in respect of expenses treated as earnings

1.502   **72.**—(1) If this chapter applies to a sum, the sum is to be treated as earnings from the employment for the tax year in which it is paid or paidaway.

(2) Subsection (1) does not prevent the making of a deduction allowed under any of the provisions listed in subsection (3).

(3) The provisions are—
section 336 (deductions for expenses: the general rule);
section 337 (travel in performance of duties);
section 338 (travel for necessary attendance);
section 340 (travel between group employments);
section 341 (travel at start or finish of overseas employment);
section 342 (travel between employments where duties performed abroad);
section 343 (deduction for professional membership fees);
section 344 (deduction for annual subscriptions);
section 346 (deduction for employee liabilities);
section 353 (deductions from earnings charged on remittance).

(2003 c.1 s.73)

CHAPTER 4

TAXABLE BENEFITS: VOUCHERS AND CREDIT-TOKENS

Cash vouchers: introduction

Cash vouchers to which this chapter applies

73.—(1) This chapter applies to a cash voucher provided for an employee by reason of the employment which is received by the employee.

(2) A cash voucher provided for an employee by the employer is to be regarded as provided by reason of the employment unless—
  (a) the employer is an individual; and
  (b) the provision is made in the normal course of the employer's domestic, family or personal relationships.

(3) A cash voucher provided for an employee and appropriated to the employee—
  (a) by attaching it to a card held for the employee; or
  (b) in any other way;
is to be treated for the purposes of this chapter as having been received by the employee at the time when it is appropriated.

1.503

Provision for, or receipt by, member of employee's family

74.—For the purposes of this chapter any reference to a cash voucher being provided for or received by an employee includes a reference to it being provided for or received by a member of the employee's family.

1.504

Meaning of "cash voucher"

Meaning of "cash voucher"

75.—(1) In this chapter "cash voucher" means a voucher, stamp or similar document capable of being exchanged for a sum of money which is—
  (a) greater than;
  (b) equal to; or
  (c) not substantially less than,
the expense incurred by the person at whose cost the voucher, stamp or similar document is provided.

(2) For the purposes of subsection (1) it does not matter whether the document—
  (a) is also capable of being exchanged for goods or services;
  (b) is capable of being exchanged singly or together with other vouchers, stamps, or documents;
  (c) is capable of being exchanged immediately or only after a time.

(3) Subsection (1) is subject to section 76 (sickness benefits-related voucher).

1.505

Sickness benefits-related voucher

76.—(1) This section applies where—
  (a) the expense incurred by the person at whose cost a voucher, stamp

1.506

or similar document is provided ("the provision expense") includes costs to that person of providing sickness benefits ("sickness benefits costs"),

(b) the voucher, stamp or document would be a cash voucher (apart from this section) but for the fact that the sum of money for which it is capable of being exchanged ("the exchange sum") is substantially less than the provision expense, and

(c) the whole or part of the difference between the exchange sum and the provision expense represents the sickness benefits costs.

(2) The voucher, stamp or document is a cash voucher within the meaning of this chapter if—

$$E = \frac{PE}{D}$$

or

E is not substantially less than $\frac{PE}{D}$,

where—

E is the exchange sum;

PE is the provision expense; and

D is the amount of the difference between E and PE which represents the sickness benefits costs.

(3) In this section "sickness benefits" mean benefits in connection with sickness, personal injury or death.

Benefit of cash voucher treated as earnings

Benefit of cash voucher treated as earnings

1.507 **81.**—(1) The cash equivalent of the benefit of a cash voucher to which this chapter applies is to be treated as earnings from the employment for the tax year in which the voucher is received by the employee.

(2) The cash equivalent is the sum of money for which the voucher is capable of being exchanged.

Non-cash vouchers: introduction

Non-cash vouchers to which this chapter applies

1.508 **82.**—(1) This chapter applies to a non-cash voucher provided for an employee by reason of the employment which is received by the employee.

(2) A non-cash voucher provided for an employee by the employer is to be regarded as provided by reason of the employment unless—

(a) the employer is an individual; and

(b) the provision is made in the normal course of the employer's domestic, family or personal relationships.

(3) A non-cash voucher provided for an employee and appropriated to the employee—

(2003 c.1 s.82)

  (a) by attaching it to a card held for the employee; or
  (b) in any other way,
is to be treated for the purposes of this chapter as having been received by the employee at the time when it is appropriated.

Meaning of "non-cash voucher"

Meaning of "non-cash voucher"

  84.—(1) In this chapter "non-cash voucher" means—
  (a) a voucher, stamp or similar document or token which is capable of being exchanged for money, goods or services;
  (ab) a childcare voucher
  (b) a transport voucher, or
  (c) a cheque voucher,
but does not include a cash voucher.

  (2) For the purposes of subsection (1)(a) it does not matter whether the document or token is capable of being exchanged—
  (a) singly or together with other vouchers, stamps, documents or tokens;
  (b) immediately or only after a time.

  (2A) In this chapter "childcare voucher" means a voucher, stamp or similar document or token intended to enable a person to obtain the provision of case for a child (whether or not in exchange for it).

  (3) In this chapter "transport voucher" means a ticket, pass or other document or token intended to enable a person to obtain passenger transport services (whether or not in exchange for it).

  (4) In this chapter "cheque voucher" means a cheque—
  (a) provided for an employee; and
  (b) intended for use by the employee wholly or mainly for payment for—
    (i) particular goods or services; or
    (ii) goods or services of one or more particular classes;
and, in relation to a cheque voucher, references to a voucher being exchanged for goods or services are to be read accordingly.

1.509

Benefit of non-cash voucher treated as earnings

Benefit of non-cash voucher treated as earnings

  87.—(1) The cash equivalent of the benefit of a non-cash voucher to which this chapter applies is to be treated as earnings from the employment for the tax year in which the voucher is received by the employee.

  (2) The cash equivalent is the difference between—
  (a) the cost of provision; and
  (b) any part of that cost made good by the employee to the person incurring it.

  (3) In this chapter the "cost of provision" means, in relation to a non-cash voucher, the expense incurred in or in connection with the provision of—

1.510

(a) the voucher, and
(b) the money, goods or services for which it is capable of being exchanged,

by the person at whose cost they are provided.

(3A) In the case of a childcare voucher, the reference in subsection (3)(b) to the services for which the voucher is capable of being exchanged is to the provision of care for a child which may be obtained by using it.

(4) In the case of a transport voucher, the reference in subsection (3)(b) to the services for which the voucher is capable of being exchanged is to the passenger transport services which may be obtained by using it.

(5) If a person incurs expense in or in connection with the provision of non-cash vouchers for two or more employees as members of a group or class, the expense incurred in respect of one of them is to be such part of that expense as is just and reasonable.

(6) This section is subject to section 89 (reduction for meal vouchers).

Credit-tokens: introduction

Credit-tokens to which this chapter applies

1.511   **90.**—(1) This chapter applies to a credit-token provided for an employee by reason of the employment which is used by the employee to obtain money, goods or services.

(2) A credit-token provided for an employee by the employer is to be regarded as provided by reason of the employment unless—
(a) the employer is an individual; and
(b) the provision is made in the normal course of the employer's domestic, family or personal relationships.

Meaning of "credit-token"

Meaning of "credit-token"

1.512   **92.**—(1) In this chapter "credit-token" means a credit card, debit card or other card, a token, a document or other object given to a person by another person ("X") who undertakes—
(a) on the production of it, to supply money, goods or services on credit; or
(b) if a third party ("Y") supplies money, goods or services on its production, to pay Y for what is supplied.

(2) A card, token, document or other object can be a credit-token even if—
(a) some other action is required in addition to its production in order for the money, goods or services to be supplied;
(b) X in paying Y may take a discount or commission.

(3) For the purposes of this section—
(a) the use of an object given by X to operate a machine provided by X is to be treated as its production to X, and
(b) the use of an object given by X to operate a machine provided by Y is to be treated as its production to Y.

(4) A "credit-token" does not include a cash voucher or a non-cash voucher.

Benefit of credit-token treated as earnings

Benefit of credit-token treated as earnings

94.—(1) On each occasion on which a credit-token to which this chapter applies is used by the employee in a tax year to obtain money, goods or services, the cash equivalent of the benefit of the token is to be treated as earnings from the employment for that year.

(2) The cash equivalent is the difference between—
   (a) the cost of provision; and
   (b) any part of that cost made good by the employee to the person incurring it.

(3) In this section the "cost of provision" means the expense incurred—
   (a) in or in connection with the provision of the money, goods or services obtained on the occasion in question; and
   (b) by the person at whose cost they are provided.

(4) If a person incurs expense in or in connection with the provision of credit-tokens for two or more employees as members of a group or class, the expense incurred in respect of one of them is to be such part of that expense as is just and reasonable.

General supplementary provisions

Disregard for money, goods or services obtained

95.—(1) This section applies if the cash equivalent of the benefit of a cash voucher, a non-cash voucher or a credit-token—
   (a) is to be treated as earnings from an employee's employment under this chapter; or
   (b) would be so treated but for a dispensation given under section 96.

(2) Money, goods or services obtained—
   (a) by the employee or another person in exchange for the cash voucher or non-cash voucher; or
   (b) by the employee or a member of the employee's family by use of the credit-token,

are to be disregarded for the purposes of the Income Tax Acts.

(3) But the goods or services are not to be disregarded for the purposes of applying sections 362 and 363 (deductions where non-cash voucher or credit-token provided).

(3A) In the case of a childcare voucher, the reference in subsection (2)(a) to the services obtained in exchange for the voucher is to the provision of care for a child which may be obtained by using it.

(4) In the case of a transport voucher, the reference in subsection (2)(a) to the services obtained in exchange for the voucher is to the passenger transport services obtained by using it.

Income Tax (Earnings and Pensions) Act 2003

Chapter 10

Taxable Benefits: Residual Liability to Charge

Introduction

Employment-related benefits

1.515　　201.—(1) This chapter applies to employment-related benefits.
(2) In this chapter—
"benefit" means a benefit or facility of any kind;
"employment-related benefit" means a benefit, other than an excluded benefit, which is provided in a tax year—
 (a) for an employee; or
 (b) for a member of an employee's family or household;
  by reason of the employment.
For the definition of "excluded benefit" see section 202.
(3) A benefit provided by an employer is to be regarded as provided by reason of the employment unless—
 (a) the employer is an individual; and
 (b) the provision is made in the normal course of the employer's domestic, family or personal relationships.
(4) For the purposes of this chapter it does not matter whether the employment is held at the time when the benefit is provided so long as it is held at some point in the tax year in which the benefit is provided.
(5) References in this chapter to an employee accordingly include a prospective or former employee.

Excluded benefits

1.516　　202.—(1) A benefit is an "excluded benefit" for the purposes of this chapter if—
 (a) any of Chapters 3 to 9 of the benefits code applies to the benefit;
 (b) any of those chapters would apply to the benefit but for an exception; or
 (c) the benefit consists in the right to receive, or the prospect of receiving, sums treated as earnings under section 221 (payments where employee absent because of sickness or disability).
(2) In this section, "exception", in relation to the application of a chapter of the benefits code to a benefit, means any enactment in the chapter which provides that the chapter does not apply to the benefit. But for this purpose section 86 (transport vouchers under pre-26th March 1982 arrangements) is not an exception.

Cash equivalent of benefit treated as earnings

Cash equivalent of benefit treated as earnings

1.517　　203.—(1) The cash equivalent of an employment-related benefit is to be treated as earnings from the employment for the tax year in which it is provided.

(2003 c.1 s.203)

(2) The cash equivalent of an employment-related benefit is the cost of the benefit less any part of that cost made good by the employee to the persons providing the benefit.

(3) The cost of an employment-related benefit is determined in accordance with section 204 unless—
  (a) section 205 provides that the cost is to be determined in accordance with that section; or
  (b) section 206 provides that the cost is to be determined in accordance with that section.

Determination of the cost of the benefit

Cost of the benefit: basic rule

204. The cost of an employment-related benefit is the expense incurred in or in connection with provision of the benefit (including a proper proportion of any expense relating partly to provision of the benefit and partly to other matters).

1.518

Exemption of minor benefits

210.—(1) The Treasury may make provision by regulations for exempting from the application of this Chapter such minor benefits as may be specified by regulation.

1.519

(2) An exemption conferred by such regulations is conditional on the benefit being made available to the employer's employees generally on similar terms.

GENERAL NOTE

For regulations made under this section see the Income Tax (Exemption of Minor Benefits) Regulations 2002 (SI 2002/205) as amended by the Income Tax (Exemption of Minor Benefits)(Amendment) Regulations 2003 (SI 2003/1434). These regulations are not included in this volume. They remove taxation from minor benefits, such as free meals, provided by employers that would otherwise be liable to taxation.

1.520

For revocations to some minor benefits exempted from this section by regulations see Income Tax (Exemption of Minor Benefits) (Revocation) Regulations 2009 (SI 2009/695). This follows the enactment of the main extra-statutory concessions by other statutory instruments.

CHAPTER 11

TAXABLE BENEFITS: EXCLUSION OF LOWER-PAID EMPLOYMENT FROM PARTS OF BENEFITS CODE

Introduction

Provisions not applicable to lower-paid employments

216.—(1) The chapters of the benefits code listed in subsection (4) do not apply to an employment in relation to a tax year if—

1.521

261

(a) it is lower-paid employment in relation to that year (see section 217); and
(b) condition A or B is met.

(2) Condition A is that the employee is not employed as a director of a company.

(3) Condition B is that the employee is employed as a director of a company but has no material interest in the company and either—
  (a) the employment is as a full-time working director; or
  (b) the company is non-profit-making or is established for charitable purposes only.

"Non-profit-making" means that the company does not carry on a trade and its functions do not consist wholly or mainly in the holding of investments or other property.

(4) The chapters referred to in subsection (1) are—
Chapter 3 (taxable benefits: expenses payments);
Chapter 6 (taxable benefits: cars, vans and related benefits);
Chapter 7 (taxable benefits: loans);
Chapter 10 (taxable benefits: residual liability to charge).

(5) Subsection (1)—
  (a) means that in any of those chapters a reference to an employee does not include an employee whose employment is within the exclusion in that subsection, if the context is such that the reference is to an employee in relation to whom the chapter applies; but
  (b) does not restrict the meaning of references to employees in other contexts.

(6) Subsection (1) has effect subject to—
section 188(2) (discharge of loan: where employment becomes lower-paid);
and
section 220 (employment in two or more related employments).

What is lower-paid employment?

Meaning of "lower-paid employment"

1.522   **217.**—(1) For the purposes of this chapter an employment is "lower-paid employment" in relation to a tax year if the earnings rate for the employment for the year (calculated under section 218) is less than £8,500.

(2) Subsection (1) is subject to section 220 (employment in two or more related employments).

Calculation of earnings rate for a tax year

1.523   **218.**—(1) For any tax year the earnings rate for an employment is to be calculated as follows—

Step 1

Find the total of the following amounts—
  (a) the total amount of the earnings from the employment for the year within Chapter 1 of this Part;

(b) the total of any amounts that are treated as earnings from the employment for the year under the benefits code (see subsections (2) and (3));
(c) the total of any amounts that are treated as earnings from the employment for the year under Chapter 12 of this Part (payments treated as earnings); and
(d) in the case of an employment within section 56(2) (deemed employment of worker by intermediary), the amount of the deemed employment payment for the year (see section 54), excluding any exempt income.

Step 2

Add to that total any extra amount required to be added for the year by section 219 (extra amounts to be added in connection with a car).

Step 3

Subtract the total amount of any authorised deductions (see subsection (4)) from the result of step 2.

Step 4

The earnings rate for the employment for the year is given by the formula—

$$\frac{Y}{R \times E}$$

where—
R is the result of step 3;
Y is the number of days in the year; and
E is the number of days in the year when the employment is held.

(2) Section 216(1) (provisions not applicable to lower-paid employment) is to be disregarded for the purpose of determining any amount under step 1.

(3) If the benefit of living accommodation is to be taken into account under step 1, the cash equivalent is to be calculated in accordance with section 105 (even if the cost of providing the accommodation exceeds £75,000).

(4) For the purposes of step 3, "authorised deduction" means any deduction that would (assuming it was an amount of taxable earnings) be allowed from any amount within step 1 under—
section 346 (employee liabilities);
section 352 (agency fees paid by entertainers);
section 355 (corresponding payments by non-domiciled employees with foreign employers);
section 368 (fixed sum deductions from earnings payable out of public revenue);
section 370 (travel costs and expenses where duties performed abroad: employee's travel);
section 371 (travel costs and expenses where duties performed abroad: visiting spouse's, civil partner's or child's travel);

section 373 (non-domiciled employee's travel costs and expenses where duties performed in United Kingdom);

section 374 (non-domiciled employee's spouse's, civil partner's or child's travel costs and expenses where duties performed in United Kingdom);

section 376 (foreign accommodation and subsistence costs and expenses (overseas employments));

section 377 (costs and expenses in respect of personal security assets and services);

section 713 (payroll giving to charities); section 592(7) of ICTA (contributions to exempt approved schemes); section 594 of ICTA (contributions to exempt statutory schemes); or section 262 of CAA 2001 (capital allowances to be given effect by treating them as deductions).

Extra amounts to be added in connection with a car

1.524   **219.**—(1) The provisions of this section apply for the purposes of section 218(1) in the case of a tax year in which a car is made available as mentioned in section 114(1) (cars, vans and related benefits) by reason of the employment.

(2) Subsection (3) applies if in the tax year—
(a) an alternative to the benefit of the car is offered; and
(b) the amount that would be earnings within Chapter 1 of this Part if the benefit of the car were to be determined by reference to the alternative offered exceeds the benefit code earnings (see subsection (4)).

(3) The amount of the excess is an extra amount to be added under step 2 in section 218(1).

(4) For the purposes of subsection (2) "the benefit code earnings" is the total for the year of—
(a) the cash equivalent of the benefit of the car (calculated in accordance with Chapter 6 of this Part); and
(b) the cash equivalent (calculated in accordance with that chapter) of the benefit of any fuel provided for the car by reason of the employment.

(7) Section 216(1) (provisions not applicable to lower-paid employment) is to be disregarded for the purpose of determining any amount under this section.

PART 4

EMPLOYMENT INCOME: EXEMPTIONS

CHAPTER 11

MISCELLANEOUS EXEMPTIONS

Childcare: exemption for employer-provided care

1.525   **318.**—(1) No liability to income tax arises in respect of the provision for an employee of care for a child if conditions A to D are met. For the meaning of "care" and "child", see section 318B.

(2003 c.1 s.318)

(2) If those conditions are met only as respects part of the provision, no such liability arises in respect of that part.

(3) Condition A is that the child—
 (a) is a child or stepchild of the employee and is maintained (wholly or partly) at the employee's expense,
 (b) is resident with the employee, or
 (c) is a person in respect of whom the employee has parental responsibility.
For the meaning of "parental responsibility", see section 318B.

(4) Condition B is that—
 (a) the premises on which the care is provided are not used wholly or mainly as a private dwelling, and
 (b) any applicable registration requirement is met.

(5) The registration requirements are—
 (za) in England, that under ... Part 3 of the Childcare Act 2006;
 (a) in ...Wales, that under Part 2 of the Children and Families (Wales) Measure 2010;
 (b) in Scotland, that under Part 1 or 2 of the Regulation of Care (Scotland) Act 2001;
 (c) in Northern Ireland, that under Part XI of the Children (Northern Ireland) Order 1995.

(6) Condition C is that—
 (a) the premises on which the care is provided are made available by the scheme employer alone, or
 (b) the partnership requirements are met.
In this section "scheme employer" means the employer operating the scheme under which the care is provided (who need not be the employer of the employee).

(7) The partnership requirements are—
 (a) that the care is provided under arrangements made by persons who include the scheme employer,
 (b) that the premises on which it is provided are made available by one or more of those persons, and
 (c) that under the arrangements the scheme employer is wholly or partly responsible for financing and managing the provision of the care.

(8) Condition D is that the care is provided under a scheme that is open—
 (a) to the scheme employer's employees generally, or
 (b) generally to those of the scheme employer's employees at a particular location,
and that the employee to whom it is provided is either an employee of the scheme employer or is an employee working at the same location as employees of the scheme employer to whom the scheme is open.

GENERAL NOTE

This and the following sections are inserted into ITEPA by Finance Act 2004 s.78 and Sch.13 from April 6, 2005. They are set out here as they are seen by some as alternatives to the provision of childcare in return for payment by an individual using the childcare element of WTC.

Section 318C was amended from April 6, 2007 for England by the Income Tax (Qualifying Child Care) Regulations 2007 (SI 2007/849). The formal introduction to the regulations makes clear that these changes were made in coordination with changes to the equivalent regulations for the childcare element of tax credits.

1.526

Income Tax (Earnings and Pensions) Act 2003

Childcare: limited exemption for other care

1.527

318A.—(1) If conditions A to C and D are met in relation to the provision for an employee of care for a child—
   (a) no liability to income tax arises under section 62 (general definition of earnings), and
   (b) liability to income tax by virtue of Chapter 10 of Part 3 (taxable benefits: residual liability to charge) arises only in respect of so much of the cash equivalent of the benefit as exceeds the exempt amount.
For the meaning of "care" and "child", see section 318B.
   (2) If those conditions are met only as respects part of the provision, subsection (1) applies in respect of that part.
   (3) Condition A is that the child—
   (a) is a child or stepchild of the employee and is maintained (wholly or partly) at the employee's expense, or
   (b) is resident with the employee and is a person in respect of whom the employee has parental responsibility.
For the meaning of "parental responsibility", see section 318B.
   (4) Condition B is that the care is qualifying child care.
For the meaning of "qualifying child care", see section 318C.
   (5) Condition C is that the care is provided under a scheme that is open—
   (a) to the employer's employees generally, or
   (b) generally to those at a particular location.
   (5A) Where the scheme under which the care is provided involves—
   (a) relevant salary sacrifice arrangements, or
   (b) relevant flexible remuneration arrangements,
Condition C is not prevented from being met by reason only that the scheme is not open to relevant low-paid employees.
   (5B) In subsection (5A)—
"relevant salary sacrifice arrangements" means arrangements (whenever made) under which the employees for whom the care is provided give up the right to receive an amount of general earnings or specific employment income in return for the provision of the care;
"relevant flexible remuneration arrangements" means arrangements (whenever made) under which the employees for whom the care is provided agree with the employer that they are to be provided with the care rather than receive some other description of employment income;
"relevant low-paid employees" means any of the employer's employees who are remunerated by the employer at a rate such that, if the relevant salary sacrifice arrangements or relevant flexible remuneration arrangements applied to them, the rate at which they would then be so remunerated would be likely to be lower than the national minimum wage.
   (5C) Condition D is that the employer has, at the required time, made an estimate of the employee's relevant earnings amount for the tax year in respect of which the care is provided (see section 318AA).
   (6) For the purposes of this section the "exempt amount", in any tax year, is the appropriate amount for each qualifying week in that year.
   (6A) In subsection (6) "the appropriate amount", in the case of an employee, means—
   (a) if the relevant earnings amount in the case of the employee for the tax year, as estimated in accordance with subsection (5C), exceeds the higher rate limit for the tax year, £22,

(b) if the relevant earnings amount in the case of the employee for the tax year, as so estimated, exceeds the basic rate limit for the tax year but does not exceed the higher rate limit for the tax year, £28, and
(c) otherwise, £55.

(7) A "qualifying week" means a tax week in which care is provided for a child in circumstances in which conditions A to C are met. "tax week" means one of the successive periods in a tax year beginning with the first day of that year and every seventh day after that (so that the last day of a tax year or, in the case of a tax year ending in a leap year, the last two days is treated as a separate week).

(8) An employee is only entitled to one exempt amount even if care is provided for more than one child. It does not matter that another person may also be entitled to an exempt amount in respect of the same child.

(9) An employee is not entitled to an exempt amount under this section and under section 270A (limited exemption for childcare vouchers) in respect of the same tax week.

GENERAL NOTE

The amendments made to s.318A have effect for the tax year 2011–12, save for those made by inserting subss.(5A) and (5B), which have effect for the tax year 2005-06 and subsequent tax years.

Meaning of "relevant earnings amount" and "required time"

318AA.— (1) For the purposes of section 318A, "relevant earnings amount", in the case of an employee provided with care by an employer for any qualifying week in a tax year, means—
(a) the aggregate of—
   (i) the amount of any relevant earnings for the tax year from employment by the employer, and
   (ii) any amounts treated under Chapters 2 to 12 of Part 3 as earnings from such employment, less
(b) the aggregate of any excluded amounts.

(2) But if the employee becomes employed by the employer during the tax year, what would otherwise be the amount of the aggregate mentioned in subsection (1)(a) is the relevant multiple of that amount; and the relevant multiple is—

$$\frac{365}{RD}$$

where RD is the number of days in the period beginning with the day on which the employee becomes employed by the employer and ending with the tax year.

(3) In subsection (1)—
"relevant earnings" has the same meaning as in subsection (1)(a) of section 270B (see subsection (3) of that section), and
"excluded amounts" has the same meaning as in subsection (1)(b) of section 270B (see subsection (4) of that section).

(4) In section 318A "the required time", in the case of an employee, means—
(a) if the employee joins the scheme under which the care is provided at a time during the tax year, that time, and
(b) otherwise, the beginning of the tax year.

Income Tax (Earnings and Pensions) Act 2003

(5) For the purposes of subsection (5)(a) the employee is taken to join the scheme as soon as—
(a) the employer has agreed that care will be provided under the scheme for the employee, and
(b) there is a child falling within section 318A(3)(a) or (b) in relation to the employee.
(6) The Treasury may by order amend this section.

Childcare: meaning of "care", "child" and "parental responsibility"

1.530   **318B.**—(1) For the purposes of sections 318 and 318A (exemptions for employer-provided or employer-contracted childcare) "care" means any form of care or supervised activity that is not provided in the course of the child's compulsory education.
(2) For the purposes of those sections a person is a "child" until the last day of the week in which falls the 1st September following the child's fifteenth birthday (or sixteenth birthday if the child is disabled).
(3) For the purposes of subsection (2) a child is disabled if—
(a) a disability living allowance or personal injury payment is payable in respect of him, has ceased to be payable solely because he is a patient,
(b) he—
  (i) is registered as blind in a register compiled by a local authority under section 29 of the National Assistance Act 1948 (welfare services),
  (ii) has been certified as blind in Scotland and in consequence is registered as blind in a register maintained by or on behalf of a local authority in Scotland, or
  (iii) has been certified as blind in Northern Ireland and in consequence is registered as blind in a register maintained by or on behalf of a Health and Social Services Board, or
(c) he ceased to be so registered as blind within the previous 28 weeks.
(4) In subsection (3)(a) "patient" means a person (other than a person who is serving a sentence imposed by a court in a prison or custody institution or, in Scotland, a young offenders' institution) who is regarded as receiving free in-patient treatment within the meaning of the Social Security (Hospital In-Patients) Regulations 1975 or the Social Security (Hospital In-Patients) Regulations (Northern Ireland) 1975.
(5) For the purposes of sections 318 and 318A "parental responsibility" means all the rights, duties, powers, and authority which by law a parent of a child has in relation to the child and the child's property.
(6) In this section and section 318C "local authority" means—
(a) in relation to England, the council of a county or district, a metropolitan district, a London Borough, the Common Council of the City of London or the Council of the Isles of Scilly;
(b) in relation to Wales, the council of a county or county borough;
(c) in relation to Scotland, a council constituted under section 2 of the Local Government etc. (Scotland) Act 1994.

Childcare: meaning of "qualifying child care"

1.531   **318C.**—(1) For the purposes of section 318A "qualifying child care" means registered or approved care within any of subsections (2) to (6) below that is not excluded by subsection (7) below.

(2) Care provided for a child in England is registered or approved care if it is provided—
- (a) ...
- (b) ...
- (ba) by a person registered under Part 3 of the Childcare Act 2006,
- (c) by or under the direction of the proprietor of a school on the school premises (subject to subsection (2B)), or
- (d) ...
- (e) ...
- (ea) ...
- (eb) ...
- (f) by a domiciliary care worker under the Domiciliary Care Agencies Regulations 2002 ...

(2A) In subsection (2)(c)—

"proprietor", in relation to a school, means—
- (a) the governing body incorporated under section 19 of the Education Act 2002, or
- (b) if there is no such body, the person or body of persons responsible for the management of the school;

"school" means a school that Her Majesty's Chief Inspector of Education, Children's Services and Skills (the "Chief Inspector") is or may be required to inspect;

"school premises" means premises that may be inspected as part of an inspection of the school by the Chief Inspector.

(2B) Care provided for a child in England is not registered or approved care under subsection (2)(c) if—
- (a) it is provided during school hours for a child who has reached compulsory school age, or
- (b) it is provided in breach of a requirement to register under Part 3 of the Childcare Act 2006.

(3) Care provided for a child in Wales is registered or approved care if it is provided—
- (a) by a person registered under Part 2 of the Children and Families (Wales) Measure 2010,
- (b) by a person in circumstances where, but for article 11, 12 or 14 of the Child Minding and Day Care Exceptions (Wales) Order 2010, the care would be day care for the purposes of Part 2 of the Children and Families (Wales) Measure 2010,
- (c) in the case of care provided for a child out of school hours, by a school on school premises or by a local authority,
- (d) by a child care provider approved by an organisation accredited under the Tax Credit (New Category of Child Care Provider) Regulations 1999,
- (e) by a domiciliary care worker under the Domiciliary Care Agencies (Wales) Regulations 2004,
- (f) by a child care provider approved under the Tax Credits (Approval of Child Care Providers) (Wales) Scheme 2007, or
- (g) by a foster parent in relation to a child (other than one whom the foster parent is fostering) in circumstances where, but for the fact that the child is too old, the care would be–
  - (i) child minding, or day care, for the purposes of Part 2 of the Children and Families (Wales) Measure 2010, or

(ii) qualifying child care for the purposes of the Tax Credits (Approval of Child Care Providers) (Wales) Scheme 2007.

(4) Care provided for a child in Scotland is registered or approved care if it is provided—
 (a) by a person in circumstances where the care service provided by him—
   (i) consists of child minding or of day care of children within the meaning of section 2 of the Regulation of Care (Scotland) Act 2001, and
   (ii) is registered under Part 1 of that Act, or
 (b) by a local authority in circumstances where the care service provided by the local authority—
   (i) consists of child minding or of day care of children within the meaning of section 2 of the Regulation of Care (Scotland) 2001, and
   (ii) is registered under Part 2 of that Act.

(5) Care provided for a child in Northern Ireland is registered approved care if it is provided—
 (a) by a person registered under Part XI of the Children (Northern Ireland) Order 1995, or
 (b) by an institution or establishment that does not need to be registered under that Part to provide the care because of an exemption under Article 121 of that Order, or
 (c) in the case of care provided for a child out of school hours, by a school on school premises or by an education and library board or an HSS trust.

(6) Care provided for a child outside the United Kingdom is registered or approved child care if it is provided by a child care provider approved by an organisation accredited under the Tax Credit (New Category of Child Care Provider) Regulations 2002.

(7) Child care is excluded from section 318A—
 (a) if it is provided by the partner of the employee in question,
 (b) if it is provided by a relative of the child wholly or mainly in the child's home or (if different) the home of a person having parental responsibility for the child, or
 (c) in the case of care falling within subsection (2)(ea) or (3)(f) if—
   (i) it is provided wholly or mainly in the home of a relative of the child, and
   (ii) the provider usually provides care there solely in respect of one or more children to whom the provider is a relative.

(8) In subsection (7)—
"partner" means one of a couple (within the meaning given by section 137(1) of Social Security Contributions and Benefits Act 1992 or section 133(1) of SSCB(NI)A 1992); and
"relative" means parent, grandparent, aunt, uncle, brother or sister, whether by blood, half blood or marriage or civil partnership.

(9) In subsection (7)(c), "relative in relation to a child, also includes—
(a) a local authority foster parent in relation to the child,
(b) a foster parent with whom the child has been placed by a voluntary organisation,
(c) a person who fosters the child privately (within the meaning of section 66 of the Children Act 1989, or
(d) a step-parent of the child.

(2003 c.1 s.327)

Part 5

Employment Income: Deductions Allowed from Earnings

Chapter 1

Deductions Allowed from Earnings: General Rules

Introduction

Deductions from earnings: general

327.—(1) This Part provides for deductions that are allowed from the taxable earnings from an employment in a tax year in calculating the net taxable earnings from the employment in the tax year for the purposes of Part II (see section 11(1)).

(2) In this Part, unless otherwise indicated by the context—
(a) references to the earnings from which deductions are allowed are references to the taxable earnings mentioned in subsection (1); and
(b) references to the tax year are references to the tax year mentioned there.

(3) The deductions for which this Part provides are those allowed under—

Chapter 2 (deductions for employee's expenses);
Chapter 3 (deductions from benefits code earnings);
Chapter 4 (fixed allowances for employee's expenses);
Chapter 5 (deductions for earnings representing benefits or reimbursed expenses); and
Chapter 6 (deductions from seafarers' earnings).

(4) Further provision about deductions from earnings is made in—
section 232 (giving effect to mileage allowance relief);
section 619 of ICTA (contributions under retirement annuity contracts); and
section 262 of CAA 2001 (capital allowances to be given effect by treating them as deductions from earnings).

(5) Further provision about deductions from income including earnings is made in—
Part 12 (payroll giving);
section 592(7) of ICTA (contributions to exempt approved schemes); and
section 594(1) of ICTA (contributions to exempt statutory schemes).

1.532

General rules

The income from which deductions may be made

328.—(1) The general rule is that deductions under this Part are allowed—

1.533

(a) from any earnings from the employment in question; and
(b) not from earnings from any other employment. This is subject to subsections (2) to (4).

(2) Deductions under section 351 (expenses of ministers of religion) are allowed from earnings from any employment as a minister of a religious denomination.

(3) Deductions under section 368 (fixed sum deductions from earnings payable out of public revenue) are allowed only from earnings payable out of the public revenue.

(4) Deductions limited to specified earnings (see subsection (5)) are allowed—
(a) only from earnings from the employment that are taxable earnings under certain of the charging provisions of Chapters 4 and 5 of Part 2; and
(b) not from other earnings from it.

(5) "Deductions limited to specified earnings" are deductions under—
sections 336 to 342 (deductions from earnings charged on receipt: see sections 335(2) and 354);
section 353 (deductions from earnings charged on remittance);
sections 370 to 374 (travel deductions from earnings charged on receipt), and Chapter 6 of this Part (deductions from seafarers' earnings: see section 378(1)(a)).

Deductions from earnings not to exceed earnings

1.534   **329.**—(1) The amount of a deduction allowed under this Part may not exceed the earnings from which it is deductible.

If two or more deductions allowed under this Part are deductible from the same earnings, the amounts deductible may not in aggregate exceed those earnings.

(3) If deductions allowed otherwise than under this Part fall to be allowed from the same earnings as amounts deductible under this Part, the amounts deductible under this Part may not exceed the earnings remaining after the other deductions.

(4) Subsections (1) and (2) do not apply to a deduction under section 351 (expenses of ministers of religion), and subsection (3) applies as if such a deduction were allowed otherwise than under this Part.

(5) This section is to be disregarded for the purposes of the deductibility provisions (see section 332).

(6) See also section 380 of ICTA (which provides that where a loss in an employment is sustained, relief may be given against other income).

Prevention of double deductions

1.535   **330.**—(1) A deduction from earnings under this Part is not allowed more than once in respect of the same costs or expenses.

(2) If apart from this subsection—
(a) a deduction would be allowed under Chapter 4 of this Part (fixed allowances for employee's expenses) for a sum fixed by reference to any kind of expenses; and
(b) the employee would be entitled under another provision to a deduction for an amount paid in respect of the same kind of expenses;

only one of those deductions is allowed.

Order for making deductions

331.—(1) This Part needs to be read with section 835(3) and (4) of ICTA (general rule that deductions are to be allowed in the order resulting in the greatest reduction of liability to income tax).

In the case of deductions under this Part, the general rule in that section is subject to—
  (a) section 23(3) (which requires certain deductions to be made in order to establish "chargeable overseas earnings"); and
  (b) section 381 (which requires deductions under other provisions to be taken into account before deductions under Chapter 6 of this Part (seafarers)).

Meaning of "the deductibility provisions"

332. For the purposes of this Part, "the deductibility provisions" means the following provisions (which refer to amounts or expenses that would be deductible if they were incurred and paid by an employee)—

the definition of "business travel" in section 171(1) (definitions for Chapter 6 of Part 3),

section 179(6) (exception for certain advances for necessary expenses), the definition of "business travel" in section 236(1) (definitions for Chapter 2 of Part 4),

section 240(1)(c) and (5) (exemption of incidental overnight expenses and benefits),

section 252(3) (exception from exemption of work-related training provision for non-deductible travel expenses),

section 257(3) (exception from exemption for individual learning account training provision for non-deductible travel expenses),

section 305(5) (offshore oil and gas workers: mainland transfers),

section 310(6)(b) (counselling and other outplacement services),

section 311(5)(b) (retraining courses),

section 361(b) (scope of Chapter 3 of this Part: cost of benefits deductible as if paid by employee),

section 362(1)(c) and (2)(b) (deductions where non-cash voucher provided),

section 363(1)(b) and (2)(b) (deductions where credit-token provided),

section 364(1)(b) and (2) (deductions where living accommodation provided),

section 365(1)(b) and (2) (deductions where employment-related benefit provided).

CHAPTER 2

DEDUCTIONS FOR EMPLOYEE'S EXPENSES

Introduction

Scope of this chapter: expenses paid by the employee

333.—(1) A deduction from a person's earnings for an amount is allowed under the following provisions of this chapter only if the amount—

(a) is paid by the person; or
(b) is paid on the person's behalf by someone else and is included in the earnings.

(2) In the following provisions of this chapter, in relation to a deduction from a person's earnings, references to the person paying an amount include references to the amount being paid on the person's behalf by someone else if or to the extent that the amount is included in the earnings.

(3) Subsection (1)(b) does not apply to the deductions under—
(a) section 351(2) and (3) (expenses of ministers of religion); and
(b) section 355 (deductions for corresponding payments by non-domiciled employees with foreign employers),

and subsection (2) does not apply in the case of those deductions.

(4) Chapter 3 of this Part provides for deductions where—
(a) a person's earnings include an amount treated as earnings under Chapter 4, 5 or 10 of Part 3 (taxable benefits: vouchers, etc., living accommodation and residual liability to charge); and
(b) an amount in respect of the benefit in question would be deductible under this chapter if the person had incurred and paid it.

Effect of reimbursement, etc.

1.539   **334.**—(1) For the purposes of this chapter, a person may be regarded as paying an amount despite—
(a) its reimbursement; or
(b) any other payment from another person in respect of the amount.

(2) But where a reimbursement or such other payment is made in respect of an amount, a deduction for the amount is allowed under the following provisions of this chapter only if or to the extent that—
(a) the reimbursement; or
(b) so much of the other payment as relates to the amount; is included in the person's earnings.

(3) *Omitted.*

General rule for deduction of employee's expenses

Deductions for expenses: the general rule

1.540   **336.**—(1) The general rule is that a deduction from earnings is allowed- for an amount if—
(a) the employee is obliged to incur and pay it as holder of the employment; and
(b) the amount is incurred wholly, exclusively and necessarily in the performance of the duties of the employment.

(2) The following provisions of this chapter contain additional rules allowing deductions for particular kinds of expenses and rules preventing particular kinds of deductions.

(3) No deduction is allowed under this section for an amount that is deductible under sections 337 to 342 (travel expenses).

(2003 c.1 s.337)

Travel expenses

Travel in performance of duties

337.—(1) A deduction from earnings is allowed for travel expenses if— 1.541
   (a) the employee is obliged to incur and pay them as holder of the employment; and
   (b) the expenses are necessarily incurred on travelling in the performance of the duties of the employment.

(2) This section needs to be read with section 359 (disallowance of travel expenses: mileage allowances and reliefs).

Travel for necessary attendance

338.—(1) A deduction from earnings is allowed for travel expenses if— 1.542
   (a) the employee is obliged to incur and pay them as holder of the employment; and
   (b) the expenses are attributable to the employee's necessary attendance at any place in the performance of the duties of the employment.

(2) Subsection (1) does not apply to the expenses of ordinary commuting or travel between any two places that is for practical purposes substantially ordinary commuting.

(3) In this section, "ordinary commuting" means travel between—
   (a) the employee's home and a permanent workplace; or
   (b) a place that is not a workplace and a permanent workplace.

(4) Subsection (1) does not apply to the expenses of private travel or travel between any two places that is for practical purposes substantially private travel.

(5) In subsection (4), "private travel" means travel between—
   (a) the employee's home and a place that is not a workplace; or
   (b) two places neither of which is a workplace.

(6) This section needs to be read with section 359 (disallowance of travel expenses: mileage allowances and reliefs).

Meaning of "workplace" and "permanent workplace"

339.—(1) In this Part, "workplace", in relation to an employment, 1.543
means a place at which the employee's attendance is necessary in the performance of the duties of the employment.

(2) In this Part "permanent workplace", in relation to an employment, means a place which—
   (a) the employee regularly attends in the performance of the duties of the employment; and
   (b) is not a temporary workplace.
This is subject to subsections (4) and (8).

(3) In subsection (2), "temporary workplace", in relation to an employment, means a place which the employee attends in the performance of the duties of the employment—
   (a) for the purpose of performing a task of limited duration; or
   (b) for some other temporary purpose.
This is subject to subsections (4) and (5).

(4) A place which the employee regularly attends in the performance of the duties of the employment is treated as a permanent workplace and not a temporary workplace if—
   (a) it forms the base from which those duties are performed; or
   (b) the tasks to be carried out in the performance of those duties are allocated there.

(5) A place is not regarded as a temporary workplace if the employee's attendance is—
   (a) in the course of a period of continuous work at that place—
      (i) lasting more than 24 months, or
      (ii) comprising all or almost all of the period for which the employee is likely to hold the employment; or
   (b) at a time when it is reasonable to assume that it will be in the course of such a period.

(6) For the purposes of subsection (5), a period is a period of continuous work at a place if over the period the duties of the employment are performed to a significant extent at the place.

(7) An actual or contemplated modification of the place at which duties are performed is to be disregarded for the purposes of subsections (5) and (6) if it does not, or would not, have any substantial effect on the employee's journey, or expenses of travelling, to and from the place where they are performed.

(8) An employee is treated as having a permanent workplace consisting of an area if—
   (a) the duties of the employment are defined by reference to an area (whether or not they also require attendance at places outside it);
   (b) in the performance of those duties the employee attends different places within the area;
   (c) none of the places the employee attends in the performance of those duties is a permanent workplace; and
   (d) the area would be a permanent workplace if subsections (2), (3), (5), (6) and (7) referred to the area where they refer to a place.

PART 9

PENSION INCOME

CHAPTER 1

INTRODUCTION

Structure of Part 9

565. The structure of this Part is as follows—
Chapter 2—
   (a) imposes the charge to tax on pension income; and
   (b) provides for deductions to be made from the amount of income chargeable;
Chapters 3 to 15 set out the types of income which are charged to tax under this Part and, for each type of income, identify—
   (a) the amount of income chargeable to tax for a tax year; and

(b) the person liable to pay any tax charged;

Chapter 15A makes provision about exemptions and charges in relation to lump sums under registered pension schemes; Chapters 17 and 18 deal with other exemptions from the charge to tax (whether under this Part or any other provision).

GENERAL NOTE

In the ICTA, most forms of pension income were taxed in the same way as emoluments under Schedule E. One of the main changes undertaken as part of the Tax Law Rewrite Project was to extract all the various provisions relating to the taxation of pensions of employees and office holders (both in the UK and overseas) and put them together in a single code. That code now forms Pt 9 of ITEPA 2003. It contains all the primary legislation from the ICTA 1988 and successive Finance Acts on the taxation of state pensions (including social security pensions), occupational pensions payable to officeholders and employees, and personal pensions. It recognises the division between earnings and pensions, but prevails over the separate provisions in Pt 10, dealing with social security income. It includes provisions in separate chapters dealing with foreign pension income.

The Tax Credits (Definition and Calculation of Income) Regulations 2002 rely on that code for defining pension income for the purposes of the tax credits income test. This selection of sections sets out the key provisions from that code. Foreign pensions, are not, however, included as pension income for tax credits purposes, so no reference is made to those chapters of Pt 9 of ITEPA. Foreign pensions should therefore be considered as foreign income, not pension income, for tax credits purposes. The Finance Act 2004 Pt 4 and associated Schedules, completely replaced the taxation rules applying to pensions and pension funds (though not the taxation of ordinary social security pension income) with a fundamentally new regime. As part of that, much of Pt 9 of this Act was repealed and replaced. But the new provisions are beyond the scope of this volume and are omitted. Only the general rules and social security pension rules are included.

1.545

CHAPTER 2

TAX ON PENSION INCOME

Nature of charge to tax on pension income and relevant definitions

566.—(1) The charge to tax on pension income under this Part is a charge to tax on that income excluding any exempt income.

(2) "Pension income" means the pensions, annuities and income of other types to which the provisions listed in subsection (4) apply.

This definition applies for the purposes of the Tax Acts.

(3) "Exempt income" means pension income on which no liability to income tax arises as a result of any provision of Chapters 16 to 18 of this Part.

This definition applies for the purposes of this Part.

(4) These are the provisions referred to in subsection (2)—

1.546

Provision	Income	Chapter (of this Part)
Section 569	United Kingdom pensions	Chapter 3
Section 573	Foreign pensions	Chapter 4
Section 577	United Kingdom social security pensions	Chapter 5

Provision	Income	Chapter (of this Part)
Section 579A	Pensions under registered pension schemes	Chapter 5A
Section 609	Annuities for the benefit of dependants	Chapter 10
Section 610	Annuities under sponsored superannuation schemes	Chapter 10
Section 611	Annuities in recognition of another's services	Chapter 10
Section 615	Certain overseas government pensions paid in the United Kingdom	Chapter 11
Section 619	The House of Commons Members' Fund	Chapter 12
Section 629	Pre-1973 pensions paid under OPA 1973	Chapter 14
Section 633	Voluntary annual payments	Chapter 15
Section 636B	Pensions treated as arising from payment of trivial commutation lump sums and winding-up lump sums under registered pension schemes	Chapter 15A
Section 636C	Pensions treated as arising from payment of trivial commutation lump sum death benefits and winding-up lump sum death benefits under registered pension schemes	Chapter 15A

Amount charged to tax

567.—(1) The amount of pension income which is charged to tax under this Part for a particular tax year is as follows.

(2) In relation to each pension, annuity or other item of pension income, the amount charged to tax is the "net taxable pension income" for the tax year.

(3) The net taxable pension income for a pension, annuity or other item of pension income for a tax year is given by the formula—

$$\frac{TPI}{DPI}$$

where—
TPI means the amount of taxable pension income for that pension, annuity or item of pension income for that year (see subsection (4)); and
DPI means the total amount of any deductions allowed from the pension, annuity or item of pension income (see subsection (5)).
(4) For the purposes of this Act—
(a) the amount of taxable pension income for a pension, annuity or other item of pension income for a tax year is determined in accordance with Chapters 13 to 15A of this Part (which contain provisions relating to this amount for each type of pension income); and

(b) in determining the amount of taxable pension income for a pension, annuity or other item of pension income, any exempt income is to be excluded.

(5) The deductions allowed from a pension, annuity or other item of pension income are those under—

section 617 (10% deduction from an overseas government pension to which section 615 applies);

Part 22 (payroll giving).

Person liable for tax

568.—For the provision identifying which person is liable for any tax charged under this Part on a pension, annuity or other item of pension income, see Chapters 3 to 15.

1.548

Chapter 3

United Kingdom Pensions: General Rules

United Kingdom pensions

569.—(1) This section applies to any pension paid by or on behalf of a person who is in the United Kingdom.

(2) But this section does not apply to a pension if any provision of Chapters 5 to 14 of this Part applies to it.

(3) For pensions paid by or on behalf of a person who is outside the United Kingdom, see Chapter 4 of this Part.

1.549

General Note

Most UK pensions will be caught under the new Chapter 5A ss.579A–D, taxing pensions under registered pension schemes on the same basis as ss.571 and 572 below, subject to the exceptions for some lump sums and other payments detailed in the FA 2004 provisions. The detailed new provisions are omitted as they will be of limited importance to most tax credit claimants.

1.550

"Pension": interpretation

570.—In this chapter, "pension" includes a pension which is paid voluntarily or is capable of being discontinued.

1.551

Taxable pension income

571.—If section 569 applies, the taxable pension income for a tax year is the full amount of the pension accruing in that year, irrespective of when any amount is actually paid.

1.552

Person liable for tax

572.—If section 569 applies, the person liable for any tax charged under this Part is the person receiving or entitled to the pension.

1.553

Income Tax (Earnings and Pensions) Act 2003

CHAPTER 5

UNITED KINGDOM SOCIAL SECURITY PENSIONS

United Kingdom social security pensions

1.554   577.—(1) This section applies to—
the state pension;
graduated retirement benefit;
industrial death benefit;
widowed mother's allowance;
widowed parent's allowance; and
widow's pension.

(1A) But this section does not apply to any social security pension lump sum (within the meaning of section 7 of F(No.2)A 2005).

(2) In this section—
"state pension" means any pension payable under—
   (a) section 44, 48A, 48B, 48BB, 51 or 78 of SSCBA 1992; or
   (b) section 44, 48, 48B, 48BB, 51 or 78 of SSCB(NI)A 1992;
"graduated retirement benefit" means any benefit payable under—
   (a) section 36 or 37 of the National Insurance Act 1965 (Chapter 51); or
   (b) section 35 or 36 of the National Insurance Act (Northern Ireland) 1966 (Chapter 6 (NI));
"industrial death benefit" means any benefit payable under—
   (a) section 94 of, and Part 6 of Schedule 7 to SSCBA 1992; or
   (b) section 94 of, and Part 6 of Schedule 7 to SSCB(NI)A 1992;
"widowed mother's allowance" means any allowance payable under—
   (a) section 37 of SSCBA 1992; or
   (b) section 37 of SSCB(NI)A 1992;
"widowed parent's allowance" means any allowance payable under—
   (a) section 39A of SSCBA 1992; or
   (b) section 39A of SSCB(NI)A 1992;
"widow's pension" means any pension payable under—
   (a) section 38 of SSCBA 1992; or
   (b) section 38 of SSCB(NI)A 1992.

(3) In subsection (2), in paragraph (b) of the definition of state pension, the reference to section 48 of SSCB(NI)A 1992 is a reference to the section 48 inserted by paragraph 3(1) of Schedule 2 to the Pensions (Northern Ireland) Order 1995 (SI 1995/3213 (NI 22)).

(4) Chapter 17 of this Part provides a partial exemption for a pension to which this section applies in respect of any part of the pension which is attributable to an increase in respect of a child (see section 645).

GENERAL NOTE

1.555   This section lists forms of state pension to be brought within the charge to tax in s.578. The exclusion of social security lump sums is because separate provision is made to tax those sums in ss.7 and 8 of F(No.2)A 2005. Lump sums are treated as income for income tax purposes but are given special treatment to prevent the recipients losing their age-related personal allowances. They are also to be taxed regardless of the residence or domicile of the recipients. Section 8 sets the date on which the tax charge is to apply. It is usually in the tax year in which the right to the pension starts.

(2003 c.1 s.578)

Taxable pension income

578.—If section 577 applies, the taxable pension income for a tax year is the full amount of the pension, benefit or allowance accruing in that year, irrespective of when any amount is actually paid.

1.556

Person liable for tax

579.—If section 577 applies, the person liable for any tax charged under this Part is the person receiving or entitled to the pension, benefit or allowance.

1.557

PART 10

SOCIAL SECURITY INCOME

CHAPTER 1

INTRODUCTION

Structure of Part 10

655.—(1) The structure of this Part is as follows—
Chapter 2—
  (a) imposes the charge to tax on social security income; and
  (b) provides for deductions to be made from the amount of income chargeable;
Chapter 3 sets out the United Kingdom social security benefits which are charged to tax under this Part and identifies—
  (a) the amount of income chargeable to tax for a tax year; and
  (b) the person liable to pay any tax charged;
Chapters 4 and 5 deal with exemptions from the charge to tax on United Kingdom social security benefits (whether under this Part or any other provision);
Chapters 6 and 7 make provisions about foreign benefits.
Chapter 8 makes provision for the high income child benefit charge.
(2) For other provisions about the taxation of social security benefits see—
section 151 of FA 1996 (power for the Treasury to make orders about the taxation of benefits payable under Government pilot schemes);
section 781 of ITA 2007 (exemption of payments under New Deal 50plus);
section 782 of ITA 2007 (exemption of payments under Employment Zones programme).
(3) For the charge to tax on social security pensions see Part 9.

1.558

GENERAL NOTE

"Social security income" is another head of charge created from the Tax Law Rewrite Project. Previously, all forms of social security income were fitted, sometimes somewhat uncomfortably, in Schedule E. Part 10 of ITEPA is now used to codify the charge to income tax on all forms of social security benefit and allowance other than pensions. As this section records, Pt 9 deals with pensions. The

1.559

opportunity has also been taken to set out the various provisions in a systematic way, and dealing with both UK and other benefits.

Because of the general importance of these provisions for social security purposes, the Part has been included more extensively than other Parts of ITEPA for social security purposes, and not restricted to those relevant only for tax credits purposes.

Subsection (1) is a signposting provision.

Subsection (2) lists the three sections (not included in this volume) under which limited exemptions from income tax may be made for social security benefits. The power under s.151 of FA 1996 is used to exempt payments made to claimants under pilot schemes. For current exemptions under this provision, see: the Taxation of Benefits under Government Pilot Schemes (Return to Work Credit and Employment Retention and Advancements Schemes) Order 2003 (SI 2003/2339) (not reproduced in this volume), in effect from October 1, 2003; and the Taxation of Benefits under government Pilot Schemes (Working Neighbourhoods Pilot and In Work Credit) Order 2004 (SI 2004/575), in effect from April 6, 2004. Both orders fully exempt payments under those schemes form income tax. The reference to s.84 of FA 2000 is superseded from the start of working tax credit as New Deal payments have now been incorporated into the credit.

Subsection (3) is a signpost to s.577 (UK social security pensions).

CHAPTER 2

TAX ON SOCIAL SECURITY INCOME

Nature of charge to tax on social security income

1.560   **656.**—(1) The charge to tax on social security income is a charge to tax on that income excluding any exempt income.

(2) "Exempt income" is social security income on which no liability to income tax arises as a result of any provision of Chapters 4, 5 or 7 of this Part.

This definition applies for the purposes of this Part.

DEFINITIONS

"social security income"—see s.657(2).
"tax"—see ICTA s.832(3).

GENERAL NOTE

1.561   This section is extremely important because it emphasises that the exemption provisions in the Part override the charges to tax. In practice, very few forms of UK social security income are chargeable to tax under this Part. Remember that pensions are chargeable under Pt 9. In most cases statutory sick pay and the other statutory payments are chargeable to tax under Pt 2. Any such payments that are not caught by Pt 3 are caught by a "safety net" provision in this Part.

Provisions in this part exempt child benefit, guardian's allowance and child tax credit and so exclude all child-related benefit. Other provisions exempt all disablement related benefits payable to the disabled or incapacitated individual.

Tax credits under the TCA 2002 are themselves exempted from tax under this Part. So are the local government benefits of housing benefit and council tax benefit. Benefits received from the national health service, in kind or in cash, are not income for any income tax purpose, and are not affected by this Part. Welfare benefits in kind, such as welfare foods and publicly provided accommodation, are not within the definition of "social security income" in s.657 and so are excluded from the charge to tax under this Part. They do not fall to be charged under any other part of ITEPA 2003.

This leaves income tax payable only on some parts of some payments of income support, jobseeker's allowance and incapacity benefit, and also on bereavement allowance (in practice linked with pension entitlements but not a form of pension income) and carer's allowance (formerly known as invalid care allowance).

The equivalent approach is adopted for foreign social security payments.

Meaning of "social security income", "taxable benefits", etc.

657.—(1) This section defines—
"social security income" for the purposes of the Tax Acts; and
"taxable benefits", "Table A" and "Table B" for the purposes of this Part.
(2) "Social security income" means—
(a) the United Kingdom social security benefits listed in Table A;
(b) the United Kingdom social security benefits listed in Table B;
(c) the foreign benefits to which section 678 applies; and
(d) the foreign benefits to which section 681(2) applies.
(3) "Taxable benefits" means—
(a) the United Kingdom social security benefits listed in Table A; and
(b) the foreign benefits to which section 678 applies.
(4) Subsections (2) and (3) are subject to section 660(2).
(5) "Table A" means Table A in section 660.
(6) "Table B" means Table B in section 677.

GENERAL NOTE

This section defines the term "social security income" used in s.656, which is the charging section. Unless a form of income is within the scope of the definition in subs.(2), it is not liable to income tax under this Part. Nor will it be liable to income tax under any other general provision in the Taxes Act. However, the interpretation of the scope of this section must take into account the very wide provisions dealing with benefits provided by employers in Pt 2, which in practice covers some forms of payments that are in principle social security payments (such as statutory maternity pay). Further, anything that is a "pension" is taxable under Pt 9 and is removed from this Part by s.655(3).

Amount charged to tax

658.—(1) The amount of social security income which is charged to tax under this Part for a particular tax year is as follows.
(2) In relation to a taxable benefit, the amount charged to tax is the net taxable social security income for the tax year.
(3) The net taxable social security income for a taxable benefit for a tax year is given by the formula—

$$TSSI - PGD$$

where—
TSSI means the amount of taxable social security income for that benefit for that year (see subsections (4) to (7)); and
PGD means the amount of the deduction (if any) allowed from the benefit under Part 12 (payroll giving).
(4) In relation to bereavement allowance, carer's allowance, contributory employment and support allowance, incapacity benefit and income support (which are listed in Table A), the amount of taxable social security income is determined in accordance with section 661.

(5) In relation to any other benefit listed in Table A, the amount of taxable social security income is the amount of the benefit that falls to be charged to tax.

(6) In relation to foreign benefits to which section 678 applies, the amount of taxable social security income is determined in accordance with section 679.

(7) In determining for the purposes of this Act the amount of taxable social security income, any exempt income is to be excluded.

DEFINITIONS

"exempt income"—see s.656(2).
"social security income"—see s.657(2).
"tax year"—see s.721(1).
"taxable benefit"—see s.657(3).

Person liable for tax

1.565   659.—The person liable for any tax charged under this Part is identified in—
(a) section 662 (United Kingdom benefits); or
(b) section 680 (foreign benefits).

CHAPTER 3

TAXABLE UNITED KINGDOM SOCIAL SECURITY BENEFITS

Taxable benefits: United Kingdom benefits—Table A

1.566   660.—(1) This is Table A:

1.567

TABLE A

TAXABLE UK BENEFITS

Social security benefit	Payable under	
Bereavement allowance	SSCBA 1992	Section 39B
	SSCB(NI)A 1992	Section 39B
Carer's allowance	SSCBA 1992	Section 70
	SSCB(NI)A 1992	Section 70
Contributory employment and support allowance	WRA 2007	Section 1(2) (a)
	Any provision made for Northern Ireland which corresponds to section 1(2)(a) of WRA 2007	
Incapacity benefit	SSCBA 1992	Section 30A(1) or (5), 40 or 41
	SSCB(NI)A 1992	Section 30A(1) or (5), 40 or 41

(2003 c.1 s.660)

Social security benefit	Payable under	
Income support	SSCBA 1992	Section 123
	SSCB(NI)A 1992	Section 124
Jobseeker's allowance	JSA 1995	Section 1
	JS(NI)O 1995	Article 3
Statutory adoption pay	SSCBA 1992	Section 171ZL
	Any provision made for Northern Ireland which corresponds to section 171ZL of SSCBA 1992	
Statutory maternity pay	SSCBA 1992	Section 164
	SSCB(NI)A 1992	Section 160
Statutory paternity pay	SSCBA 1992	Section 171ZA or 171ZB
	Any provision made for Northern Ireland which corresponds to section 171ZA or section 171ZB of SSCBA 1992	
Statutory sick pay	SSCBA 1992	Section 151
	SSCB(NI)A 1992	Section 147.

(2) A benefit listed below is not "social security income" or a "taxable benefit" if it is charged to tax under another Part of this Act—
statutory adoption pay;
statutory maternity pay;
statutory paternity pay;
statutory sick pay.

DEFINITIONS
"social security income"—see s.657(2).
"taxable benefit"—see s.657(3).

GENERAL NOTE

This section and those that follow need updating to take account of the changes made to social security benefits by the Welfare Reform Act 2012. See the note on that Act below. For the full forms of the abbreviations in Table A see Sch.1 Pt 1 to the Act. Subsection (2) provides that a charge to tax under Pt 2 of the Act takes priority over this Part, but the section ensures that all statutory payments are taxable.

1.568

Taxable social security income

661.—(1) This section applies in relation to each of the following taxable benefits listed in Table A—
bereavement allowance;
carer's allowance;
contributory employment and support allowance.
incapacity benefit; and
income support.
(2) The amount of taxable social security income for a taxable benefit for a tax year is the full amount of the benefit accruing in the tax year irrespective of when any amount is actually paid.

1.569

DEFINITIONS
"tax year"—see s.721(1).
"taxable benefit"—see s.675(3).

GENERAL NOTE

1.570 This is a new rule under ITEPA introduced to replace both inconsistent previous legislation and a lack of legislation, the rules apparently varying from one benefit to another for no good reason. "Accrued" is standard income tax language not normally used for social security purposes. In social security terms, as the section makes clear, it means payable not paid.

Person liable for tax

1.571 **662.**—The person liable for any tax charged under this Part on a taxable benefit listed in Table A is the person receiving or entitled to the benefit.

GENERAL NOTE

1.572 "Received or entitled" is familiar income tax language applied to social security income by ITEPA in place of a lack of any clear previous rule. As the wording indicates it covers both the person for whom the benefit is payable and the person who actually receives it. The wording will make joint claimants for jobseeker's allowance both liable for any income tax on the allowance. It is, however, not clear how this is applied to appointees appointed to receive income support for a claimant.

CHAPTER 4

TAXABLE UK SOCIAL SECURITY BENEFITS: EXEMPTIONS

Incapacity benefit

Long-term incapacity benefit: previous entitlement to invalidity benefit

1.573 **663.**—(1) No liability to income tax arises on long-term incapacity benefit if—
 (a) a person is entitled to the benefit for a day of incapacity for work which falls in a period of incapacity for work which is treated for the purposes of that benefit as having begun before April 13, 1995; and
 (b) the part of that period which is treated as having fallen before that date includes a day for which that person was entitled to invalidity benefit.
(2) In this section—
"invalidity benefit" means invalidity benefit under—
 (a) Part 2 of SSCBA 1992; or
 (b) Part 2 of SSCB(NI)A 1992;
"long-term incapacity benefit" means incapacity benefit payable under—
 (a) section 30A(5), 40 or 41 of SSCBA 1992; or
 (b) section 30A(5), 40 or 41 of SSCB(NI)A 1992.

Short-term incapacity benefit not payable at the higher rate

1.574 **664.**—(1) No liability to income tax arises on short-term incapacity benefit unless it is payable at the higher rate.

(2) In this section—
(a) "short-term incapacity benefit" means incapacity benefit payable under—
   (i) section 30A(1) of SSCBA 1992; or
   (ii) section 30A(1) of SSCB(NI)A 1992;
(b) the reference to short-term incapacity benefit payable at the higher rate is to be construed in accordance with—
   (i) section 30B of SSCBA 1992; or
   (ii) section 30B of SSCB(NI)A 1992.

Income support

Exempt unless payable to member of couple involved in trade dispute

665.—(1) No liability to income tax arises on income support unless—
(a) the income support is payable to one member of a couple ("the claimant"); and
(b) section 126 of SSCBA 1992 or section 125 of SSCB(NI)A 1992 (trade disputes) applies to the claimant but not to the other member of the couple.

(2) In this section, couple has the same meaning as in section 137(1) of SSCBA 1992 or section 133(1) of SSCB(NI)A 1992.

Child maintenance bonus

666.—No liability to income tax arises on a part of income support which is attributable to a child maintenance bonus (within the meaning of section 10 of CSA 1995 or Article 4 of CS(NI)O 1995).

Amounts in excess of taxable maximum

667.—(1) If the amount of income support paid to a person ("the claimant") for a week or a part of a week exceeds the claimant's taxable maximum for that period, no liability to income tax arises on the excess.

(2) The claimant's taxable maximum for a period is determined under section 668.

Taxable maximum

668.—(1) A claimant's taxable maximum for a week is determined under this subsection if the applicable amount for the purpose of calculating the income support consists only of an amount in respect of the relevant couple.

The taxable maximum is equal to one half of the applicable amount.

(2) A claimant's taxable maximum for a week is determined under this subsection if the applicable amount includes amounts that are not in respect of the relevant couple.

The taxable maximum is equal to one half of the amount which is included in the applicable amount in respect of the relevant couple.

(3) A claimant's taxable maximum for a part of a week is determined as follows—

Step 1

Assume that the income support is paid to the claimant for the whole of, rather than part of, the week.

Step 2

Determine under subsection (1) or (2) what the claimant's taxable maximum for that week would be on that assumption.

Step 3

Determine the claimant's taxable maximum for the part of the week using this formula—

$$\frac{N}{7} \times TMW$$

where—
N is the number of days in the part of the week for which the claimant is actually paid the income support; and
TMW is the taxable maximum for the whole week determined under step 2.

Interpretation

669.—(1) In section 668, except in relation to Northern Ireland—
"applicable amount" means the amount prescribed in relation to income support in regulations made under section 135 of SSCBA 1992;
"couple" has the same meaning as in section 137(1) of Social Security Contributions and Benefits Act 1992;
(2) In section 668, in relation to Northern Ireland—
"applicable amount" means the amount prescribed in relation to income support in regulations made under section 131 of SSCB(NI)A 1992;
"couple" has the same meaning as in section 133(1) of Social Security Contributions and Benefits (Northern Ireland) Act 1992;
(3) In section 668, "relevant couple", in relation to a claimant, means the couple of which the claimant is a member.

GENERAL NOTE

This section applies the definition of "couple" adopted for social security purposes following the replacement by the Civil Partnership Act 2004 of all references to "married couples" and "unmarried couples" for the purposes of ITEPA. The effect is to impose the social security meaning of "couple" on the income tax treatment of social security income, and not the income tax definition.

Jobseeker's allowance

Child maintenance bonus

670.—No liability to income tax arises on a part of a jobseeker's allowance which is attributable to a child maintenance bonus (within the meaning of section 10 of CSA 1995 or Article 4 of CS(NI)O 1995).

(2003 c.1 s.671)

Amounts in excess of taxable maximum

671.—(1) If the amount of jobseeker's allowance paid to a person ("the claimant") for a week or a part of a week exceeds the claimant's taxable maximum for that period, no liability to income tax arises on the excess.

(2) The claimant's taxable maximum for a period is determined under sections 672 to 674.

Taxable maximum: general

672.—(1) A claimant's taxable maximum for a week is determined—
- (a) under section 673, if the claimant is paid an income-based jobseeker's allowance for that week; or
- (b) under section 674, if the claimant is paid a contribution-based jobseeker's allowance for that week.

(2) A claimant's taxable maximum for a part of a week is determined as follows—

Step 1

Assume that the jobseeker's allowance is paid to the claimant for the whole of, rather than part of, the week.

Step 2

Determine under section 673 or 674 what the claimant's taxable maximum for that week would be on that assumption.

Step 3

Determine the claimant's taxable maximum for the part of the week using this formula—

$$\frac{N}{7} \times TMW$$

where—
N is the number of days in the part of the week for which the claimant is actually paid the jobseeker's allowance; and
TMW is the taxable maximum for the whole week determined under step 2.

Taxable maximum: income-based jobseeker's allowance

673.—(1) A claimant's taxable maximum for a week is determined under this section if—
- (a) the claimant is paid an income-based jobseeker's allowance for that week, or
- (b) the claimant is assumed under section 672(2) to be paid an income-based jobseeker's allowance for that week.

(2) If the claimant is not a member of a couple, the claimant's taxable maximum for the week is equal to the age-related amount which would be applicable to the claimant if a contribution based jobseeker's allowance were payable to the claimant for that week.

(3) If the claimant is a member of a couple, the claimant's taxable maximum for the week is equal to the portion of the applicable amount which is included in the jobseeker's allowance in respect of the couple for that week.

(4) But if—
- (a) the claimant is a member of a couple; and
- (b) the other member of that couple is prevented by section 14 of JSA

1995 or Article 16 of JS(NI)O 1995 (trade disputes) from being entitled to a jobseeker's allowance;

the claimant's taxable maximum for that week is equal to half the portion of the applicable amount which is included in the jobseeker's allowance in respect of the couple for that week.

Taxable maximum: contribution-based jobseeker's allowance

1.585   **674.**—(1) A claimant's taxable maximum for a week is determined under this section if—
  (a) the claimant is paid a contribution-based jobseeker's allowance for that week; or
  (b) the claimant is assumed under section 672(2) to be paid a contribution-based jobseeker's allowance for that week.

(2) If the claimant is not a member of a couple, the claimant's taxable maximum for the week is equal to the age-related amount which is applicable to the claimant for that week.

(3) If the claimant is a member of a couple, the claimant's taxable maximum for the week is equal to the portion of the applicable amount which would be included in the jobseeker's allowance in respect of the couple if an income-based jobseeker's allowance were payable to the claimant for that week.

Interpretation

1.586   **675.**—(1) In sections 671 to 674, except in relation to Northern Ireland—
"age-related amount" and "applicable amount" mean the amounts determined as such in accordance with regulations made under section 4 of JSA 1995;
"contribution-based jobseeker's allowance" and "income-based jobseeker's allowance" have the same meaning as in section 1(4) of JSA 1995;
"married couple" and "unmarried couple" have the same meaning as in section 35(1) of JSA 1995.

(2) In sections 671 to 674, in relation to Northern Ireland—
"age-related amount" and "applicable amount" mean the amounts determined as such in accordance with regulations made under Article 6 of JS(NI)O 1995;
"contribution-based jobseeker's allowance" and "income-based jobseeker's allowance" have the same meaning as in Article 3(4) of JS(NI)O 1995;
"couple" has the same meaning as in s.351(1) of JSA 1995.

Increases in respect of children

Increases in respect of children

1.587   **676.**—No liability to income tax arises on a part of a taxable benefit listed in Table A which is attributable to an increase in respect of a child.

General Note

1.588   This is superseded from 2003/04 for incapacity benefit and carer's allowance, by the introduction of child tax credit, which is exempt from tax.

(2003 c.1 s.677)

CHAPTER 5

UK SOCIAL SECURITY BENEFITS WHOLLY EXEMPT FROM INCOME TAX

UK social security benefits wholly exempt from tax: Table B

677.—(1) No liability to income tax arises on the United Kingdom social security benefits listed in Table B.

TABLE B—PART I

BENEFITS PAYABLE UNDER PRIMARY LEGISLATION

Social security benefit	Payable under
Attendance allowance	SSCBA 1992, s.64
	SSCB(NI)A 1992, s.64
Back to work bonus	JSA 1995, s.26
	JS(NI)O 1995, Article 28
Bereavement payment	SSCBA 1992, s.36
	SSCB(NI)A 1992, s.36
Child benefit	SSCBA 1992, s.141
	SSCB(NI)A 1992, s.137
Child's special allowance	SSCBA 1992, s.56
	SSCB(NI)A 1992, s.56
Child tax credit	TCA 2002, Part 1
Council tax benefit	SSCBA 1992, s.131
Disability living allowance	SSCBA 1992, s.71
	SSCB(NI)A 1992, s.71
Guardian's allowance	SSCBA 1992, s.77
	SSCB(NI)A 1992, s.77
Health in Pregnancy Grant	SSCBA 1992, s.140A
	SSCB(NI)A 1992, s.136A
Housing benefit	SSCBA 1992, s.130
	SSCB(NI)A 1992, s.129
Income-related employment and support allowance	WRA 2007 s.1(2)(b)
	Any provision made for Northern Ireland which corresponds to section 1(2)(b) of WRA 2007
In-work credit	ETA 1973, S.2
	ETA(NI) 1950, s.1
In-work emergency discretion fund payment	ETA 1973, s.2
In-work emergency fund payment	ETA(NI) 1950, s.1
Industrial injuries benefit (apart from industrial death benefit)	SSCBA 1992, s.94
	SSCB(NI)A 1992, s.94
Pensioner's Christmas bonus	SSCBA 1992, s.148
	SSCB(NI)A 1992, s.144
Payments out of the social fund	SSCBA 1992, s.138

Income Tax (Earnings and Pensions) Act 2003

Social security benefit	Payable under
Return to work credit	SSCB(NI)A 1992, s.134 ETA 1973, s.2 ETA(NI) 1950, s.1
Severe disablement allowance	SSCBA 1992, s.68 SSCB(NI)A 1992, s.68
State maternity allowance	SSCBA 1992, s.35 or 35B Any provision made for Northern Ireland which corresponds to s.35 or 35B of SSCBA 1992
State pension credit	SPCA 2002, s.1 SPCA(NI) 2002, s.1
Universal Credit	WRA 2012
Working tax credit	TCA 2002, Part 1

TABLE B—PART 2

1.591   BENEFITS PAYABLE UNDER REGULATIONS

Social security benefit	Payable under regulations made under
Payments to reduce under-occupation by housing benefit claimants	WRPA 1999, s.79 WRP(NI)O 1999, Article 70

(2) Industrial death benefit is charged to tax under Part 9 (see section 577).
(3) In this section "industrial death benefit" means any benefit payable under—
 (a) section 94 of, and Part 6 of Schedule 7 to, SSCBA 1992; or
 (b) section 94 of, and Part 6 of Schedule 7 to, SSCB(NI)A 1992.

GENERAL NOTE

1.592   The provisions in both tables need amending to deal with the changes to social security benefits and the replacement of council tax benefit with council tax reduction under the Welfare Reform Act 2012. It may, however, be argued that council tax reductions are no longer in a form that can be regarded as a social security benefit and therefore as income and do not need any exempting provision.

A revised definition of "state maternity allowance" was inserted by reg.3 of the Social Security (Maternity Allowance) (Participating Wife or Civil Partner of Self-employed Earner) Regulations 2014 (SI 2014/606).

CHAPTER 6

TAXABLE FOREIGN BENEFITS

Taxable benefits: foreign benefits

1.593   **678.**—(1) This section applies to any benefit which is payable under the law of a country or territory outside the United Kingdom if—
 (a) it is substantially similar in character to a benefit listed in Table A, and

292

(b) it is payable to a person resident in the United Kingdom.

(2) But this section does not apply to a benefit which is charged to tax under Pt 9 (pension income).

GENERAL NOTE

This is a new statutory provision in ITEPA. Until its enactment, the Revenue and Customs refrained from taxing foreign social security benefits on the basis of an extra-statutory concession. The only real problem area is the divide between social security income, exempt under this provision, and pension income, taxed under Pt 9.

Taxable social security income

679.—(1) If section 678 applies, the taxable social security income for a taxable benefit for a tax year is the amount on which tax would be chargeable if the benefit were chargeable to tax under Case V of Schedule D (see in particular the provisions of ICTA listed in subsection (2)).

(2) Those provisions of ICTA are—
(a) sections 65 and 68 (calculation of the amount of the income on which tax is to be charged in the tax year);
(b) section 584 (relief for unremittable overseas income);
(c) section 585 (relief on delayed remittances).

Person liable for tax

680.—The person liable for any tax charged under this Part on a benefit to which section 678 applies is the person receiving or entitled to the benefit.

PART 13

SUPPLEMENTARY PROVISIONS

Interpretation

Other definitions

721.—(1) In this Act—
"cash voucher" has the same meaning as in Chapter 4 of Part 3 (see section 75);
"credit-token" has the same meaning as in Chapter 4 of Part 3 (see section 92);
"foreign employer" means—
  (a) in the case of an employee resident in the United Kingdom, an individual, partnership or body of persons resident outside the United Kingdom and not resident in the United Kingdom or the Republic of Ireland, and
  (b) in the case of an employee not resident in the United Kingdom, an individual, partnership or body of persons resident outside and not resident in the United Kingdom;
"non-cash voucher" has the same meaning as in Chapter 4 of Part 3 (see section 84);

(3) Any reference in this Act to being domiciled in the United Kingdom is to be read as a reference to being domiciled in any part of the United Kingdom.

(4) For the purposes of this Act the following are members of a person's family—
   (a) the person's spouse [¹or civil partner],
   (b) the person's children and their spouses [¹or civil partners],
   (c) the person's parents, and
   (d) the person's dependants.

(5) For the purposes of this Act the following are members of a person's family or household—
   (a) members of the person's family,
   (b) the person's domestic staff, and
   (c) the person's guests.

(6) The following provisions (which relate to the legal equality of illegitimate children) are to be disregarded in interpreting references in this Act to a child or children—
   (a) section 1 of the Family Law Reform Act 1987 (Chapter 42),
   (b) the paragraph inserted in Schedule 1 to the Interpretation Act 1978 (Chapter 30) by paragraph 73 of Schedule 2 to the 1987 Act,
   (c) section 1(2) of the Law Reform (Parent and Child) (Scotland) Act 1986 (Chapter 9),
   (d) Article 155 of the Children (Northern Ireland) Order 1995 (SI 1995 No.755 (NI 2)).

(7) In the employment income Parts any reference to earnings which is not limited by the context—
   (a) to earnings within Chapter 1 of Part 3, or
   (b) to any other particular description of earnings; includes a reference to any amount treated as earnings by any of the provisions mentioned in section 7(5) (meaning of "employment income" etc.).

GENERAL NOTE

1.598   See further for definitions ITA 2007 Sch.4 of which (not included in this work) includes an index of terms defined for the Income Tax Acts.

Child Trust Funds Act 2004

(2004 c.6)

ARRANGEMENT OF SECTIONS

Introductory

1.599
1. Child trust funds
2. Eligible children
3. Requirements to be satisfied
4. Inalienability

(2004 c.6)

Opening and transfers

5. Opening by responsible person or child
6. Opening by Inland Revenue
7. Transfers
7A. Transfers to other accounts for children
7B. Transfers on child reaching 18
7C. Powers to safeguard interests of children

Contributions and subscriptions

8. Initial contribution by Inland Revenue
9. Supplementary contribution by Inland Revenue
10. Further contributions by Inland Revenue
11. Recouping Inland Revenue contributions
12. Subscription limits

Tax

13. Relief from income tax and capital gains tax
14. Insurance companies and friendly societies

Information etc.

15. Information from account providers, etc.
16. Information about children in care of authority
17. Use of information
18. Disclosure of information

Payments after death

19. Payments after death of child

Penalties

20. Penalties
21. Decisions, appeals, mitigation and recovery

Appeals

22. Rights of appeal
23. Exercise of rights of appeal
24. Temporary modifications

Supplementary

25. Northern Ireland
26. Money
27. Commencement
28. Regulations and orders
29. Interpretation

30. Extent
31. Short title

An Act to make provision about child trust funds and for connected purposes.

INTRODUCTION AND GENERAL NOTE

1.600 The basic scheme of the Child Trust Fund Act 2004 is that all children in the UK born after August 31, 2002 will have a "child trust fund account", which will in effect be a universal savings policy. Building societies and other financial institutions will have to seek HMRC approval to be an "account provider" under this Act. It is a condition of approval that account providers offer equity-based stakeholder accounts (although cash accounts may also be offered). The Treasury provides an initial endowment of £250 for each child at the point when the account is opened, or £500 in the case of children in low income families or those who are being looked after by a local authority. The Government subsequently approved a further endowment (of £250, or £500 for children in low income families) when every child reaches the age of seven. Parents, relatives and family friends are able to make further contributions to the child trust fund account at any time. The minimum such investment is £10 (unless the account provider permits smaller deposits) and the maximum annual aggregate contribution by family and friends is £1,200. Subject to some very narrow exceptions, no withdrawals will be permitted until the child is 18, so that the child reaches adulthood with a "nest-egg" which can then be re-invested, spent on education or setting up in business, etc. The cost of the scheme is estimated to be in the order of £4 billion over 18 years.

The Government has set out four objectives for child trust fund accounts. These are "to help people understand the benefits of saving and investing; to encourage parents and children to develop the savings habit; to ensure that all children have a financial asset at the start of their adult life; and to build on financial education and help people make better financial choices throughout their lives" (Lord McIntosh of Haringey, Parliamentary Under-Secretary of State, *Hansard* HL Debates Vol.658, col.351, February 26, 2004). The Child Trust Fund Act may thus be seen as an example of the Government's commitment to the principles of "asset-based welfare" and "progressive universalism". It will, of course, take some time to assess whether the scheme fulfils its goals.

The idea of child trust funds emerged through the work of the Institute of Public Policy Research (IPPR) in 2000 and was canvassed by the Treasury in its consultation paper *Savings and Assets for All*, The Modernisation of Britain's Tax and Benefit System, Number 8 (April 2001). The proposal also appeared in the Labour Party's 2001 general election manifesto. The Government set out its proposals more fully in the Treasury papers *Delivering Saving and Assets* (November 2001) and especially in *Detailed proposals for the Child Trust Fund* (October 2003). The House of Commons Treasury Committee has issued a report supporting the initiative, although making some further recommendations: *Child Trusts Funds* (Second Report of Session 2003–04, HC 86), and see further *Government Response to the Committee's Second Report on Child Trust Funds* (HC 86) (First Special Report of Session 2003–04, HC 387). In the 2003 Budget the Chancellor of the Exchequer announced the Government's intention that the scheme should commence operations in April 2005 (but confirming that it would also apply to all children born after August 31, 2002). For a full analysis of the scheme, see N. Wikeley, "Child Trust Funds—asset-based welfare or a recipe for increased inequality?" (2004) 11 *Journal of Social Security Law* 189.

Section 1 of the Act explains what is meant by a child trust fund, whilst s.2 defines the crucial qualifying category of "eligible children". The nature and management of child trust fund accounts is governed by s.3. Funds in such accounts are inalienable (s.4). The expectation is that accounts will be opened by a "responsible person", typically a parent, or by the child (in the case of a child aged 16 or over, who, for example, has just arrived in the country); see s.5, which makes the award of child benefit the trigger for entitlement to a child trust fund account. The fallback position is that HMRC will open an account (s.6) for any child lacking a child trust fund. Accounts may be transferred to another financial institution (s.7). The initial and supplementary Treasury contributions to be made at the opening of the account are governed by ss.8 and 9. All children receive the initial contribution under s.8 (children being looked after by local authorities receive a higher rate) and children in low income families qualify for the supplementary contribution under s.9. Section 10 makes provision for further Treasury contributions to be made at some late date (or dates). Where Treasury contributions have been credited in error, they can be recovered by virtue of s.11. Section 12 deals with contributions by parents and others to child trust fund accounts. The tax position is covered by ss.13 and 14 while ss.15–18 make provision for the disclosure and exchange of information relating to accounts. Section 19 makes special provision for the situation where a payment is due after a child beneficiary has died. Sections 20 and 21 concern penalties and ss.22–24 set out appeal rights. The remaining sections of the Act are supplementary in nature (ss.25–31). The first regulations under the Act are the Child Trust Funds Regulations 2004 (SI 2004/1450).

The future of child trust funds

On May 24, 2010, the coalition Government announced that as part of its package of saving £6.2 billion in 2010/11, it would save £320 million from reducing and then stopping government contributions to the Child Trust Fund. The Government proposed to scale back payments from August 2010 and then to stop payments from January 1, 2011. Section 1 of the Savings Accounts and Health in Pregnancy Grant Act 2010 subsequently implemented the second phase of the cancellation of the scheme by stopping all government payments altogether. It did this by amending s.2 of the 2004 Act to remove eligibility from children born after January 2, 2011 and from certain children who would otherwise become eligible on or after that date.

1.601

Commencement and extent

The supplementary provisions in this Act (ss.25–31) came into force on Royal Assent (May 13, 2004): see s.27. Various procedural provisions came into force on January 1, 2005: Child Trust Funds Act 2004 (Commencement No.1) Order 2004 (SI 2004/2422 (C.103). The remainder of the Act was brought into force by the Child Trust Funds Act 2004 (Commencement No.2) Order 200 (SI 2004/3369 (C.158). The Child Trust Funds Regulations 2004 (SI 2004/1450) came into force for various purposes on January 1, 2005 and for remaining purposes on "the appointed day", namely April 6, 2005. The Act extends to the whole of the UK (see further ss.25 and 30).

1.602

Introductory

Child trust funds

1.—(1) This Act makes provision about child trust funds and related matters.

(2) In this Act "child trust fund" means an account which—
(a) is held by a child who is or has been an eligible child (see section 2),
(b) satisfies the requirements imposed by and by virtue of this Act (see section 3), and
(c) has been opened in accordance with this Act (see sections 5 and 6).

(3) The matters dealt with by and under this Act are to be under the care and management of the Inland Revenue.

1.603

Definitions
"child"—s.29.
"child trust fund"—subs.(2) and s.29.
"eligible child"—ss.2 and 29.
"Inland Revenue"—s.29.

General Note

1.604 This is a genuinely introductory section.

Subsection (1)
1.605 This provision is no more illuminating than the long title to the Act.

Subsection (2)
1.606 This is more helpful than subs.(1) in that it stipulates the three defining characteristics of a child trust fund—that it be held by an "eligible child" (see s.2), that it meet the statutory requirements (see s.3) and that it has been opened in the appropriate manner (either by a "responsible person" (typically a parent) under s.5 or by HMRC under s.6).

Subsection (3)
1.607 This reflects a standard principle of revenue law (see, e.g. Taxes Management Act 1970 s.1(1)), namely that such matters are "under the care and management of the Inland Revenue". The only difference is one of nomenclature in the reference to "the Inland Revenue", rather than the more usual statutory formula of "the Board". This principle enables the Revenue to apply the law with a degree of administrative flexibility in appropriate cases. For example, in the context of taxation, this is the basis upon which the Revenue has traditionally promulgated extra-statutory concessions and reached settlements in disputes with taxpayers.

Eligible children

1.608 2.—(1) For the purposes of this Act a child is an "eligible child" if the child was born after 31st August 2002 [² and before 3rd January 2011] and either—
  (a) a person is entitled to child benefit in respect of the child, or
  (b) entitlement to child benefit in respect of the child is excluded by the provisions specified in subsection (2)(a) or (b) (children in care of authority),
but subject as follows.
(2) The provisions referred to in subsection (1)(b) are—
  (a) paragraph 1(c) of Schedule 9 to the Social Security Contributions and Benefits Act 1992 (c. 4) and regulations made under it, and
  (b) paragraph 1(1)(f) of Schedule 9 to the Social Security Contributions and Benefits (Northern Ireland) Act 1992 (c. 7) and regulations made under it.
(3) Where entitlement to child benefit in respect of a child is excluded because of a directly applicable Community provision or an international agreement, subsection (1) applies as if that exclusion did not apply.
(4) Where a person is entitled to child benefit in respect of a child only because of a directly applicable Community provision or an international agreement, subsection (1) applies as if the person were not so entitled.
(5) A child who—
  (a) does not have the right of abode in the United Kingdom within the meaning given by section 2 of the Immigration Act 1971 (c.77),

[¹(b) is not entitled to enter or remain in the United Kingdom by virtue of an enforceable Community right or any provision made under section 2(2) of the European Communities Act 1972, and]
(c) is not settled in the United Kingdom within the meaning given by section 33(2A) of the Immigration Act 1971,

is not an eligible child.

[² (5A) A child born before 3rd January 2011 who would otherwise have become an eligible child on or after that date is not an eligible child unless subsection (5B) or (5C) applies to the child.

(5B) This subsection applies to a child (who accordingly is an eligible child by virtue of subsection (1)(a)) if—
(a) a person is entitled to child benefit in respect of the child,
(b) the first day for which child benefit is paid falls on or before 3rd January 2011, and
(c) either subsection (5) does not apply to the child at the beginning of 3rd January 2011, or that subsection applies to the child at that time but ceases to apply to the child before 3rd April 2011.

(5C) This subsection applies to a child (who accordingly is an eligible child by virtue of subsection (1)(b)) if—
(a) the child is in the United Kingdom at the beginning of 3rd January 2011,
(b) the provisions specified in subsection (2)(a) or (b) apply in relation to the child before 3rd April 2011, and
(c) either subsection (5) does not apply to the child at the beginning of 3rd January 2011, or that subsection applies to the child at that time but ceases to apply to the child before 3rd April 2011.]

(6) A person is not to be regarded for the purposes of subsection (1)(a) [or 5B(a)] as entitled to child benefit in respect of a child (otherwise than by virtue of subsection (3)) unless it has been decided in accordance with—
(a) Chapter 2 of Part 1 of the Social Security Act 1998 (c.14), or
(b) Chapter 2 of Part 2 of the Social Security (Northern Ireland) Order 1998 (SI 1998/1506 (N.I. 10)),

that the person is so entitled (and that decision has not been overturned).

(7) Regulations may amend subsection (1) by substituting for the reference to 31st August 2002 a reference to an earlier date.

AMENDMENTS

1. Immigration (European Economic Area) (Amendment) Regulations 2009 (SI 2009/1117) reg.3 and Sch.2 para.1 (June 1, 2009).

2. Savings Accounts and Health in Pregnancy Grant Act 2010 s.1 (December 16, 2010).

DEFINITIONS

"child"—s.29.
"eligible child"—subs.(1) and s.29.

GENERAL NOTE

This section defines the concept of an "eligible child", the first of the three fundamental features of a child trust fund. The basic definition is to be found in subs.(1), as expanded by subs.(2) to deal with the special case of children being looked after by a local authority. Cases that have an international dimension are covered by subss.(3)–(5). Subsection (6) acts as a definition provision for subs.(1).

1.609

Subsection (7) provides the potential for the scope of the child trust fund scheme to be expanded to include children born before the cut-off date for eligibility for a child trust fund.

Subsection (1)

1.610 This is the core definition of who is an "eligible child". There are two basic rules. First, the child must have been born *after* August 31, 2002. This date was chosen to align entitlement with the school year (at least in England and Wales), so that all pupils in any given school year (after that date) would be equally entitled. There will, however, be cases involving siblings born either side of the eligibility date: for the position of children who were born *before* September 1, 2002, see further the annotation to subs.(7) below. Secondly, the child must have been born *before* January 3, 2011. This reflects the coalition Government's decision to close down access to the child trust fund scheme. Thirdly, *either* someone must be entitled to child benefit for that child (subs.(1)(a); see further subs.(6)) *or* that person's entitlement is excluded because the child is being looked after by a local authority (subs.(1)(b) and (2)). Thus in general terms, and subject to that special case, entitlement to child benefit is employed as a gateway to eligibility for a child trust fund. Subsections (3)–(5) make special provision for cases with an international dimension.

Subsection (2)

1.611 The case of a child being looked after by a local authority is the only situation in which the rule requiring that a person be entitled to child benefit in respect of the child is waived. It must follow that in the other situations set out in SSCBA 1992 Sch.9 in which there is no entitlement to child benefit, there is also no entitlement to a child trust fund. These situations include children in detention (but see s.10(4)) and married children. These exclusions, and particularly the latter, may eventually affect a handful of children who are recent immigrants to the country.

Subsection (3)

1.612 There will be some children who live in the UK but in respect of whom child benefit is not payable because of EU law or an international agreement. This provision ensures that such children remain eligible for a child trust fund, notwithstanding that there is no child benefit entitlement. In practice this will apply most commonly to some children who live in Northern Ireland but whose parent works in the Republic of Ireland. In such circumstances, under the EU rules governing the benefit entitlement of migrant workers in Regulation 1408/71, child benefit is payable by the benefit authorities in the Republic. As a result of subs.(3) such children are eligible for a child trust fund account.

Subsection (4)

1.613 This deals with the converse position to that in subs.(3). In some cases there is entitlement to child benefit in the UK solely because of provisions in EU law or under an international agreement. This would apply where a citizen and resident of the Republic of Ireland (or any other EU country) works in the UK but his or her child lives in the Republic (or other Member State). Again, EU Regulation 1408/71 provides that child benefit is payable by the UK authorities. This subsection provides, in effect, that children in this type of case will not be eligible for a child trust fund, unless and until they come to live in the UK. This will affect fewer than 500 children, according to official estimates. The Government's view is that "there is no case for the UK Government to pay endowments to encourage saving for and by children whose ties are not within the UK" (Ruth Kelly, Financial Secretary to the Treasury, Standing Committee A, col.37, January 6, 2004). This exclusion will not affect the special position of the children of Crown servants, such as army personnel, who are entitled to child benefit when stationed overseas by virtue of a provision in purely domestic law (Child Benefit (General) Regulations 2003 (SI 2003/493) reg.30).

However, it is by no means certain that the exclusion of EU workers (and their children) who reside outside but work in the UK from eligibility for child trust funds will necessarily survive legal scrutiny. There are a number of different avenues that might be used to challenge the validity of this provision under EU law. First, art.7(2) of EU Regulation 1612/68 requires migrant workers to "enjoy the same social and tax advantages as national workers". Of course, one of the fundamental purposes of the child trust fund scheme is to benefit the child, rather than the worker. Indeed, case law demonstrates that the social or tax advantage must be of some direct or indirect benefit to the worker, and not just to a family member (*Centre Public d'Aide Sociale de Courcelles v Lebon* (316/85) [1987] E.C.R. 2811). But a broad view of the child trust fund scheme might meet this requirement. See also *Reina v Landeskredit Bank Baden-Württemberg* (65/81) [1982] E.C.R. 33, in which it was held that an interest-free childbirth loan granted only to German nationals was a social advantage within art.7(2), and so could not be denied to an Italian couple. Although one of the fundamental objectives of the child trust fund scheme is to benefit *children* by providing them with a valuable asset on attaining their majority, it does not require too much imagination to see that the scheme might be construed as being of indirect benefit to the parent-worker. Yet the other purposes of the 2004 Act are framed in terms of domestic policy imperatives, such as encouraging savings, which have no obvious linkage with the free movement of labour. Moreover, the ECJ jurisprudence on art.7(2) has typically concerned the migrant worker who goes both to work and *live* in another Member State, and not merely to work there; the problem identified in this note is strictly more to do with "frontier workers" than "migrant workers". On that basis, therefore, it may be that s.2(4) is not inconsistent with art.7(2) of Regulation 1612/68.

Even if this is the case, it does not necessarily follow that s.2(4) is EU-compliant. A second or parallel type of challenge might be made on the basis that the child trust fund scheme confers a "family benefit" within the scope of Regulation 1408/71, so bringing into play Ch.7 of that Regulation. Given the linkage between entitlement to child benefit and eligibility for a child trust fund payment, this point is at least arguable. Finally, there remains the broader argument that this provision in the 2004 Act is in breach of art.12 of the Treaty itself, which prohibits "within the scope of the application" of the Treaty "any discrimination on grounds of nationality". Section 2(4) makes no express reference to parents' nationality, but may be viewed as indirectly discriminatory in that its operation in practice is more likely to affect (for example) Irish nationals than British nationals. In recent years the ECJ has demonstrated greater willingness to invoke art.12 for the benefit of citizens of other Member States (see e.g. *Martinez Sala* [1998] E.C.R. I-2691 and *Grzelczyk* (C-184/99) [2001] E.C.R. I-6193; *R. (Bidar) v Ealing London BC* (C-209/03) [2005] 2 W.L.R. 1078; and see further R.C.A. White, "Residence, Benefit Entitlement and Community Law" [2005] 12 *Journal of Social Security Law* 10).

Subsection (5)

A child who lacks a proper immigration status cannot be an "eligible child". This covers children who, under the Immigration Act 1971, have no right of abode or are not settled in the UK. However, subs.(5)(c) may give rise to problems in the context of citizenship of the Union: see further the Advocate General's Opinion of November 11, 2004 in *Bidar* (C-209/03). Children who have no entitlement to reside in the UK under EEA law are likewise excluded from access to the child trust fund scheme.

Subsections (5A)–(5C)

Subsection (5A) provides that a child born *before* January 3, 2011 who would otherwise become eligible *on or after* that date may not be an eligible child unless either subs.(5B) or (5C) applies.

Subsection (5B)(a) and (b) reflect the processes involved in claiming child benefit and the fact that entitlement can only commence on a Monday and can only be backdated for up to three months. Subsection (5B)(c) reflects the fact that a child who is subject to immigration control is not an eligible child under subs.(5), even though child benefit may be being received in respect of that child. To provide parity with the possibility of backdating for three months under the child benefit regime, the same window of three months will apply to such children born before January 3, 2011.

Subsection (5C) provides that a looked-after child born before January 3, 2011 will still be an eligible looked-after child if the conditions set out there are met. The requirement that the child becomes a looked-after child before April 3, 2011 provides parity with the child qualifying under the usual child benefit route.

Subsection (6)

1.616 This provides that a person is not entitled to child benefit until a decision has been taken to that effect (and has not been overturned) in accordance with the SSA Act 1998 (or its Northern Ireland equivalent). Thus HMRC decision to award child benefit acts as the trigger for eligibility for a child trust fund account.

Subsection (7)

1.617 For the purposes of this Act a child is only an "eligible child" if born after August 31, 2002 (subs.(1)). This provision allows the Government to use secondary legislation to substitute an earlier date for the purpose of this definition, thus bringing older children into the scope of eligibility for a child trust fund account. Given the effect of the 2010 amendments, requiring that an eligible child must have been born *before* January 3, 2011, and thereafter closing the child trust funds scheme, there is clearly no prospect of this power being exercised.

Requirements to be satisfied

1.618 **3.**—(1) A child trust fund may be held only with a person (referred to in this Act as an "account provider") who has been approved by the Inland Revenue in accordance with regulations.

(2) An account is not a child trust fund unless it is an account of one of the descriptions prescribed by regulations.

(3) The provision which may be made by regulations under subsection (1) includes making approval of an account provider dependent on the person undertaking to provide accounts of such of the descriptions for which provision is made by regulations under subsection (2) as is prescribed by the regulations.

(4) The terms of a child trust fund must—
(a) secure that it is held in the name of a child,
(b) secure that the child is beneficially entitled to the investments under it,
(c) secure that all income and gains arising on investments under it constitute investments under it,
(d) prevent withdrawals from it except as permitted by regulations [¹ under this section or any other provision of this Act], and
(e) provide that instructions may be given to the account provider with respect to its management only by the person who has the authority to manage it.

(5) Regulations may impose other requirements which must be satisfied in relation to child trust funds.

(6) The person who has the authority to manage a child trust fund held by a child—
(a) if the child is 16 or over, is the child, and

(b) if the child is under 16, is the person who has that authority by virtue of subsection (7) (but subject to subsection (10)).

(7) If there is one person who is a responsible person in relation to the child, that person has that authority; and if there is more than one person who is such a person, which of them has that authority is to be determined in accordance with regulations.

(8) For the purposes of this Act a person is a responsible person in relation to a child under 16 if the person has parental responsibility in relation to the child and is not—
  (a) a local authority or, in Northern Ireland, an authority within the meaning of the Children (Northern Ireland) Order 1995 (S.I. 1995/755 (N.I. 2)), or
  (b) a person under 16.

(9) "Parental responsibility" means—
  (a) parental responsibility within the meaning of the Children Act 1989 (c.41) or the Children (Northern Ireland) Order 1995, or
  (b) parental responsibilities within the meaning of the Children (Scotland) Act 1995 (c.36).

(10) Regulations may provide that, in circumstances prescribed by the regulations, the person who has the authority to manage a child trust fund held by a child under 16 is to be the Official Solicitor (in England and Wales or Northern Ireland) or the Accountant of Court (in Scotland).

(11) A person who has the authority to manage a child trust fund by virtue of subsection (10) is entitled to give any instructions to the account provider with respect to its management which appear to the person who has that authority to be for the benefit of the child.

(12) Where a contract is entered into by or on behalf of a child who is 16 or over in connection with a child trust fund—
  (a) held by the child, or
  (b) held by another child in relation to whom the child has parental responsibility,

the contract has effect as if the child had been 18 or over when it was entered into.

AMENDMENT

1. Deregulation Act 2015 s.62(4) (March 26, 2015 for purposes of making regulations, April 6, 2015 for other purposes).

DEFINITIONS

"account provider"—subs.(1) and s.29.
"child"—s.29.
"child trust fund"—*ibid.*
"Inland Revenue"—*ibid.*
"parental responsibility"—subs.(9).
"responsible person"—subs.(8).

GENERAL NOTE

This section sets out various administrative and procedural requirements which must be satisfied in order for a child trust fund account to come into existence. Only authorised financial institutions may offer child trust fund accounts (subs.(1)) and such accounts must meet a number of criteria (subss.(2)–(5)). This section also

1.619

defines who has the authority to manage the child's account. This will usually be a person with parental responsibility or, in the case of a child aged at least 16, the child him or herself (subss.(6)–(12)).

Subsection (1)

1.620   Financial institutions, known as "account providers" in this Act, must be approved by HMRC before they can offer child trust fund accounts. The details of the approval process, which are set out in regulations, are modelled on those that apply to Individual Savings Accounts (ISAs) (see Child Trust Funds Regulations 2004 regs 14–17 and 19–20). Institutions denied approval have a right of appeal (see s.22(1)).

Subsection (2)

1.621   Approval operates at two levels. First, the account provider itself must be approved by HMRC under subs.(1). Secondly, by virtue of this subsection, only certain types of accounts may qualify as child trust fund accounts. In order to qualify an account must meet the criteria which are set out in regulations and are based on the arrangements governing ISAs (see Child Trust Funds Regulations 2004 reg.8).

Subsection (3)

1.622   This provision means that the regulations governing the approval of financial institutions may require account providers to provide particular types of account as a condition of such approval. The general rule is that, in order to be authorised as an account provider for the purposes of the child trust fund scheme, institutions must offer stakeholder accounts to the general public (see Child Trust Funds Regulations 2004 reg.14(2)(b)(i)). The characteristics of a stakeholder account are defined in the Schedule to the Regulations. The policy justification for this requirement is that it will enable beneficiaries to gain from the potentially higher returns from equities as a long-term investment. Further, the risk of a fall in the value of equities is reduced by the requirement to spread the investment over a number of companies (*ibid.*, para.2(2)(c)) and to transfer the investment to other assets (e.g. cash or gilts) as the maturity date nears.

Subsection (4)

1.623   This provision sets out the core requirements which must be met in order for an account to qualify for the purposes of the child trust fund scheme. For further details, see Child Trust Funds Regulations 2004 reg.8.

The general rule is that no withdrawals are permitted from a child trust fund account before the child attains 18 (subs.(4)(d)). The Government's argument is that this restriction is essential if such accounts are to achieve their long-term goals. The only exceptions to this principle in the regulations as originally drafted related to withdrawals on closure in the event of the child's death and to deductions for management charges due (Child Trust Funds Regulations 2004 reg.18; there is a cap of 1.5 per cent on administration fees: *ibid.*, Sch. para.3(2)). However, following sustained pressure in Parliament, the Government conceded that a further exception should be made in the case of children suffering from a terminal illness. See now Child Trust Funds Regulations 2004 reg.18A. In contrast to the tight restrictions on withdrawals before the age of 18, there are no controls whatsoever on how young adults apply their child trust fund account holdings on reaching that age.

Subsection (5)

1.624   For further details, see Child Trust Funds Regulations 2004 reg.8.

Subsection (6)

The effect of this provision, taken together with the definitions and qualifications in the following subsections, is that the child trust fund account is managed by the child, if he or she is 16 or over, and otherwise by the person with parental responsibility in respect of that child. This provision was inserted as a government amendment to the original Bill, which had given 16 and 17 year olds in Scotland the right to manage their accounts, but not their peers south of the border (reflecting the special rules in Scots law relating to the age of majority). Following debate, the Government accepted that it was difficult to sustain this distinction in the context of the child trust fund, and so brought forward this provision to ensure that all 16 and 17 year olds in the UK have the right to manage their child trust fund account. Such individuals are deemed to have full contractual authority to manage their accounts by virtue of subs.(12). They will not be able to withdraw funds until they reach the age of 18 (see subs.(4)(d)).

1.625

Subsections (7)–(9)

In the case of children under the age of 16, the "responsible person" is designated as the individual with the authority to manage the child trust fund account (subs.(7)). The basic rule is that the "responsible person" in respect of a child under 16 is the person with parental responsibility for that child under the Children Act 1989 (or the relevant legislation for other parts of the UK: see subs. (9)). There are two exceptions to this rule (subs.(8))—first, a local authority (which may have parental responsibility by virtue of a care order) cannot be a "responsible person"; secondly, a young parent under the age of 16 cannot assume that role. It follows, for example, that the child trust fund accounts of both a 15-year-old mother and her baby will have to be managed by a third party.

1.626

It is common, of course, for two individuals to share parental responsibility for a child, as in the case of a married couple (Children Act 1989 s.2(1)). In such cases voucher will be sent to the holder of the child benefit award (see s.5 and Child Trust Funds Regulations 2004 reg.3(2)). Moreover, there can be only one person with authority to manage the child trust fund account, known as the "registered contact" (*ibid.*, reg.8(1)(d)). Typically this will be a "single responsible person", i.e. a person with parental responsibility (see further *ibid.*, reg.13).

Subsection (10)

This was another government amendment to the original Bill. It is designed to deal with the problem created by the lack of a "responsible person" for some children in local authority care. A local authority cannot be a responsible person (subs. (8)(a)). In the case of most children being looked after by a local authority, this will not matter, as the child's parent will retain parental responsibility and so be a responsible person. However, there will be a minority of cases in which no individual person holds parental responsibility (e.g. some orphans in care). The Government has announced that the Official Solicitor (in England, Wales and Northern Ireland) or the Accountant of Court (in Scotland) will undertake the function of managing the accounts of children in care for whom there is no one with parental responsibility. See now Child Trust Funds Regulations 2004 reg.33A.

1.627

Inalienability

4.—(1) Any assignment of, or agreement to assign, investments under a child trust fund, and any charge on or agreement to charge any such investments, is void.

1.628

(2) On the bankruptcy of a child by whom a child trust fund is held, the entitlement to investments under it does not pass to any trustee or other person acting on behalf of the child's creditors.

(3) "Assignment" includes assignation; and "assign" is to be construed accordingly.

(4) "Charge on or agreement to charge" includes a right in security over or an agreement to create a right in security over.

(5) "Bankruptcy", in relation to a child, includes the sequestration of the child's estate.

DEFINITIONS

"assign"—subs.(3).
"assignment"—*ibid.*
"bankruptcy"—subs.(5)
"charge on or agreement to charge"—subs.(4).
"child trust fund"—s.29.

GENERAL NOTE

1.629 The principle of the inalienability of social security benefits is enshrined in SSAA 1992 s.187 (see also Tax Credits Act 2002 s.45). This section provides, in similar fashion, for the inalienability of investments held under a child trust fund. The parallel provision in SSAA 1992 s.187 was applied (in the Scottish context) in *Mulvey v Secretary of State for Social Security* 1997 S.C. (HL) 105, where the House of Lords held that the bankrupt's right to income support could not be owed to the permanent trustee (the Scottish equivalent of a trustee in bankruptcy). However, the House of Lords held that deductions could lawfully be made from income support to pay a social fund debt incurred prior to sequestration.

Opening and transfers

Opening by responsible person or child

1.630 **5.**—(1) In the case of each child who is first an eligible child by virtue of section 2(1)(a) the Inland Revenue must issue, in a manner prescribed by regulations, a voucher in such form as is so prescribed.

(2) The voucher must be issued to the person who is entitled to child benefit in respect of the child (or, in the case of a child who is such an eligible child because of section 2(3), to a responsible person).

(3) An application may be made—
   (a) if the child is 16 or over, by the child, or
   (b) otherwise, by a responsible person,
to open for the child with an account provider a child trust fund of any description provided by the account provider.

(4) The application is to be made—
   (a) within such period beginning with the day on which the voucher is issued as is prescribed by regulations, and
   (b) in accordance with regulations.

(5) When the application has been made the account provider must—
   (a) open, in accordance with regulations, a child trust fund of that description for the child, and
   (b) inform the Inland Revenue in accordance with regulations.

DEFINITIONS

"account provider"—s.29.
"child"—*ibid.*
"child trust fund"—*ibid.*

"eligible child"—s.2(1) and s.29.
"Inland Revenue"—s.29.
"responsible person"—ss.3(8) and 29.

GENERAL NOTE

This section sets out the framework within which child trust fund accounts are to be opened, typically by the "responsible person" (as defined by s.3(8)) and in exceptional cases by the child (assuming he or she is 16 or over). The default position is that an account must be opened by HMRC (see further s.6).

Subsection (1)

This places a duty on HMRC to issue a voucher in respect of any eligible child (within the normal definition in s.2(1)(a)). The issue of the voucher will be triggered by the award of child benefit (which, as a result of the Tax Credits Act 2002, is now administered by HMRC rather than the Department for Work and Pensions). See further Child Trust Funds Regulations 2004 reg.3.

Subsection (2)

The voucher must be issued to the individual who is entitled to child benefit. The voucher is in the amount of the initial Treasury contribution to be paid to all eligible children (£250). It should be noted that the process of issuing vouchers is designed to be an automatic process—there is no requirement in the legislation for the parent or other responsible person to make an independent claim for a child trust fund account voucher. In the special cross-border situation where the child lives in the UK but the parent works in another EU Member State (e.g. the Republic of Ireland) there will be no child benefit recipient in this jurisdiction (see annotation to s.2(3)). Accordingly in such cases the voucher must be issued to a responsible person for that child.

Subsection (3)

This enables the "responsible person" to apply to open a child trust fund account with an approved account provider (see further subs.(4)). As originally drafted, the Bill would have required the responsible person physically to present the voucher to the account provider. As a result of a government amendment, the details of this procedure are now left to regulations. The Child Trust Funds Regulations 2004 still envisage a physical transfer of the voucher (reg.5(1), condition 1), but may in the future make provision for an entirely on-line application process. The "responsible person" is not, as such, under a statutory duty to make such an application. If he or she fails to do so, the default position is that ultimately HMRC will step in (see further s.6). In exceptional cases a child aged 16 or 17 may make an application to open a child trust fund account in his or her own name. The most likely circumstance in which this will arise is in the future where a child (born after August 31, 2002) moves to the UK at the age of 16 having never previously had an entitlement to a child trust fund account.

Subsection (4)

The application procedure is set out in regulations (see Child Trust Funds Regulations 2004 regs 5 and 13). The responsible person can select both the account provider and the type of account for the child trust fund. The voucher issued by HMRC will be valid for one year from the date of issue (*ibid.*, reg.3(2)), so applicants have a year in which to make the application. If they fail to do so, HMRC's default duty under s.6 arises.

Subsection (5)

1.636 Once a valid application has been made, an account provider is required to open a child trust fund account for the child in question and to inform the Revenue that it has done so. The Child Trust Funds Regulations 2004 require institutions to make both fortnightly and annual returns of such information to the Revenue (regs 30 and 32).

Opening by Inland Revenue

1.637 **6.**—(1) In the case of each child to whom this section applies, the Inland Revenue must apply to open for the child with an account provider selected in accordance with regulations a child trust fund of a description so selected.

(2) The application is to be made in accordance with regulations.

(3) The account provider must—

(a) open, in accordance with regulations, a child trust fund of that description for the child, and

(b) inform the Inland Revenue in accordance with regulations.

(4) This section applies—

(a) to a child in respect of whom a voucher is issued under section 5(1) but in whose case subsection (5) is satisfied, and

(b) to a child who is first an eligible child by virtue of section 2(1)(b).

(5) This subsection is satisfied in the case of a child if—

(a) the period prescribed under section 5(4) expires without a child trust fund having been opened for the child, or

(b) the child is under 16 and it appears to the Inland Revenue that there is no-one who is a responsible person in relation to the child.

(6) No liability is to arise in respect of the selection of an account provider, or a description of child trust fund, in accordance with regulations under this section.

DEFINITIONS

"account provider"—s.29.
"child"—*ibid*.
"child trust fund"—*ibid*.
"eligible child"—s.2(1) and s.29.
"Inland Revenue"—s.29.
"responsible person"—ss.3(8) and 29.

GENERAL NOTE

1.638 Normally a child's parent (or other adult who is the child benefit recipient), as a "responsible person", will make an application for a child trust fund account in accordance with s.5. There will inevitably be cases where no such application is made. This section therefore performs a "mop-up" function, placing the onus on HMRC to ensure that accounts are opened for such children who would otherwise miss out. HMRC's obligation under subs.(1) to open a child trust fund account arises in two types of case. The first is where either, following an award of child benefit, a voucher has been issued to the "responsible person" but no application has been made to open a child trust fund account for that child within the required period (12 months) or there appears to be no "responsible person" for that child (subss.(4)(a) and (5)). The second is where the child is being looked after by a local authority and so there is no individual entitled to child benefit (subs.(4)(b)).

Subsection (1)

In cases to which this section applies (see subss.(4) and (5) and the General Note), HMRC *must* take the initiative and apply to open a child trust fund account for the child in question. The details of the procedure to be adopted are set out in the Child Trust Funds Regulations 2004 reg.6. Account providers are not required to offer these default HMRC-allocated accounts under this arrangement. However, *if* institutions do agree to offer such accounts, they must then accept any HMRC application to open such an account (see subs.(3) and Child Trust Funds Regulations 2004 reg.6(2)). HMRC will maintain a list of account providers willing to offer such accounts, and select account holders in rotation to ensure parity of treatment (*ibid.* reg.6(3)). If account holders offer more than one type of stakeholder account, the account will likewise be chosen in rotation (*ibid.*, reg.6(4)). The legislation expressly exempts HMRC from any liability in respect of such decisions (subs.(6)). In these cases HMRC's role is furthermore limited to *opening* the account; it will have no role in *managing* the account in such a case. It will always be open to parents to transfer the account to another provider (s.7).

1.639

Subsection (2)

See further Child Trust Funds Regulations 2004 reg.6.

1.640

Subsection (3)

This is in parallel terms to the obligation imposed on account providers by s.5(5).

1.641

Subsections (4) and (5)

See the General Note to this section.

1.642

Subsection (6)

See the annotation to subs.(1).

1.643

Transfers

7.—Regulations may make provision about the circumstances in which—

(a) a child trust fund which is an account of one of the descriptions prescribed by regulations may become an account of another of those descriptions, and

(b) a child trust fund held with one account provider may be transferred to another.

1.644

DEFINITIONS

"account provider"—s.29.
"child trust fund"—*ibid.*

GENERAL NOTE

This allows regulations to be made which permit the responsible person to change the type of child trust fund account (e.g. from a cash to a stakeholder account) and to move from one provider to another. The procedural rules for transfers are similar to those relating to transfers of ISA accounts, but require transfers to be free of charge (save for share dealing costs); see further Child Trust Funds Regulations 2004 reg.21.

1.645

[¹ 7A. Transfers to other accounts for children

1.646 (1) Regulations may make provision requiring an account provider, at the request of a person who has the authority to manage a child trust fund, to—
(a) transfer all the investments under the fund, or an amount representing their value in cash, to a protected child account that is provided by a person chosen by the person making the request, and
(b) when all the investments have been transferred, close the child trust fund.
(2) An account is a protected child account if—
(a) there is relief from income tax and capital gains tax in respect of investments under it,
(b) it may be held only by a child, and
(c) it satisfies any other conditions prescribed in regulations under this section.]

AMENDMENT

1. Deregulation Act 2015 s.62(2) (March 26, 2015 for purposes of making regulations, April 6, 2015 for other purposes).

DEFINITIONS

"account provider" —s.29.
"child trust fund" —*ibid*.

[¹ 7B. Transfers on child reaching 18

1.647 (1) Regulations may make provision requiring an account provider to transfer all the investments under a child trust fund held by a person immediately before his or her 18th birthday to a protected account of a description prescribed in the regulations.
(2) Regulations under subsection (1) must include provision that the requirement does not apply if the person gives instructions, in accordance with the regulations, to the account provider as to what is to be done with the investments.
(3) An account is a protected account if—
(a) there is relief from income tax and capital gains tax in respect of investments under it, and
(b) it satisfies any other conditions prescribed in regulations under this section.]

AMENDMENT

1. Deregulation Act 2015 s.62(3) (March 26, 2015 for purposes of making regulations, April 6, 2015 for other purposes).

DEFINITIONS

"account provider" —s.29.
"child trust fund" —*ibid*.
"protected account" —subs.(3).

(2004 c. 6 s. 7C)

[¹ Powers to safeguard interests of children

7C. Powers to safeguard interests of children

(1) The Treasury may make regulations under this section if the Treasury think it appropriate to do so for the purpose of safeguarding the financial interests of children, or any group of children, who hold child trust funds.

(2) The regulations may authorise the Treasury to permit withdrawals from—
 (a) any child trust funds;
 (b) any child trust funds held with an account provider that is prescribed, or of a description prescribed, in the regulations.

(3) The regulations may authorise the Treasury to require any account provider or any account provider that is prescribed, or of a description prescribed, in the regulations to take one or more of the following steps in relation to every child trust fund held with it—
 (a) to seek to transfer the fund to another account provider;
 (b) to seek to transfer all the investments under the fund to a protected child account that can be used for investments of that kind and is provided by a person chosen by the account provider;
 (c) to seek to transfer an amount in cash representing the value of all the investments under the fund (whether consisting of cash or stocks and shares) to a protected child account that can be used for investments in cash and is provided by a person chosen by the account provider;
 (d) to transfer an amount in cash representing the value of all the investments under the fund (whether consisting of cash or stocks and shares) to a protected child account that can be used for investments in cash and is provided by a person specified by the Treasury.

(4) The regulations may provide—
 (a) that child trust funds held with an account provider that is prescribed, or of a description prescribed, in the regulations are to be treated for all purposes as if they were protected child accounts of a description so prescribed;
 (b) that, where child trust funds are (under the regulations) to be treated as protected child accounts of a particular description, the account provider is to be treated, for such purposes as may be prescribed in the regulations, as a person who lawfully provides protected child accounts of that description.

(5) If the regulations authorise the Treasury to require that one or more of the steps mentioned in subsection (3)(b) to (d) be taken, the regulations may also authorise the Treasury to require an account provider who, in pursuance of such a requirement, transfers all the investments under a child trust fund, or an amount representing the value of all the investments, to close the child trust fund.

(6) If the regulations authorise the Treasury to require an account provider to take more than one of the steps mentioned in subsection (3), the regulations must also—
 (a) authorise the Treasury to specify the order in which the steps are to be taken, and
 (b) provide that if (as a result of complying with a requirement to take a particular step) an account holder no longer holds investments

under any child trust fund, any requirement imposed on that provider to take another step lapses.

(7) The Treasury is not liable in respect of—
(a) the selection by an account provider of a person to whom to make a transfer in response to a requirement of a kind mentioned in subsection (3)(a) to (c), or
(b) a decision made by it as to the person to be specified in a requirement of a kind mentioned in subsection (3)(d).

(8) In this section, "protected child account" means an account which is a protected child account for the purposes of section 7A.]

AMENDMENT

1. Deregulation Act 2015 s.63 (March 26, 2015 for purposes of making regulations, April 6, 2015 for other purposes).

Contributions and subscriptions

Initial contribution by Inland Revenue

1.649   8.—(1) The Inland Revenue must pay to an account provider such amount as is prescribed by regulations if the account provider has—
(a) informed the Inland Revenue under section 5(5) or 6(3) that a child trust fund has been opened, and
(b) made a claim to the Inland Revenue in accordance with regulations.

(2) On receipt of the payment the account provider must credit the child trust fund with the amount of the payment.

DEFINITIONS

"account provider"—s.29.
"child trust fund"—*ibid.*
"Inland Revenue"—*ibid.*

GENERAL NOTE

1.650   This section explains how the initial Treasury contribution of £250 stated on the voucher issued to the child benefit recipient is actually converted, albeit indirectly, into cash (the voucher itself cannot be exchanged for money: see Child Trust Funds Regulations 2004 reg.3(1)). Once a child trust fund account has been opened, either in the normal way (s.5) or through the process of HMRC allocation (s.6), the account provider is required to notify HMRC. Account providers then make a claim to HMRC (these are to be made on a fortnightly basis—see Child Trust Funds Regulations 2004 reg.30. HMRC must in turn pay the account holder "such amount as is prescribed by regulations" by way of an initial contribution (subs.(1)), which the account holder must credit to the relevant account (subs.(2)). Children born into the poorest families may also qualify for a "supplementary contribution" under s.9. There is, moreover, a further Treasury contribution for all eligible children when they reach the age of seven (see s.10).

The regulations describe the "initial" and "supplementary" contributions as "Government contributions" (Child Trust Funds Regulations 2004 reg.7). The basic rule for children born on or after the appointed day (April 6, 2005) is that the initial contribution will be £250, or £500 for those in local authority care (*ibid.*, reg.7(4)). Slightly higher amounts have been prescribed for those born on or after September 1, 2002 (the first date on which a child could qualify as an eligible child under s.2(1)) but before the appointed day. These higher amounts are designed to reflect the fact that these children have not had the benefit of interest on their investments to date. The rates are £277 for children born after August 31, 2002 but before the end of the 2002/03 tax year, £268 for those born in the 2003/04 tax year, and £256 for those born between April 6, 2004 and the appointed day (*ibid.*, reg.7(2)). For children in care, the equivalent figures are £554, £536 and £512.

Supplementary contribution by Inland Revenue

9.—(1) If this section applies to a child the Inland Revenue must inform the account provider with whom a child trust fund is held by the child that this section applies to the child.

(2) If the account provider makes a claim to the Inland Revenue in accordance with regulations, the Inland Revenue must pay to the account provider such amount as is prescribed by regulations.

(3) On receipt of the payment the account provider must credit the child trust fund with the amount of the payment.

(4) This section applies to a child if—
(a) a child trust fund is held by the child,
(b) the child was first an eligible child by virtue of section 2(1)(a), and
(c) the condition in subsection (5) is satisfied in relation to the child.

(5) That condition is that it has been determined in accordance with the provision made by and by virtue of sections 18 to 21 of the Tax Credits Act 2002 (c. 21)—
(a) that a person was, or persons were, entitled to child tax credit in respect of the child for the child benefit commencement date, and
(b) that either the relevant income of the person or persons for the tax year in which that date fell does not exceed the income threshold or the person, or either of the persons, was entitled to a relevant social security benefit for that date,

and that determination has not been overturned.

(6) In subsection (5)(b)—
"the income threshold" has the meaning given by section 7(1)(a) of the Tax Credits Act 2002,
"the relevant income", in relation to a person or persons and a tax year, has the meaning given by section 7(3) of that Act in relation to a claim by the person or persons for a tax credit for the tax year,
"relevant social security benefit" means any social security benefit prescribed for the purposes of section 7(2) of that Act, and
"tax year" means a period beginning with 6th April in one year and ending with 5th April in the next.

(7) If the child benefit commencement date is earlier than 6th April 2005, this section applies in relation to the child even if the condition in subsection (5) is not satisfied in relation to the child provided that the condition in subsection (8) is so satisfied.

(8) That condition is that—
(a) income support, or income-based jobseeker's allowance, was paid for the child benefit commencement date to a person whose applicable amount included an amount in respect of the child, or
(b) working families' tax credit, or disabled person's tax credit, was paid for that date to a person whose appropriate maximum working

1.651

families' tax credit, or appropriate maximum disabled person's tax credit, included a credit in respect of the child.

(9) If the child benefit commencement date is earlier than 6th April 2003, subsection (5) has effect as if—
  (a) the reference in paragraph (a) to the child benefit commencement date were to any date in the tax year beginning with 6th April 2003,
  (b) the reference in paragraph (b) to the tax year in which the child benefit commencement date fell were to the tax year beginning with 6th April 2003, and
  (c) the reference in paragraph (b) to being entitled to a relevant social security benefit for the child benefit commencement date were to being so entitled for any date in that tax year for which the person was, or the persons were, entitled to child tax credit in respect of the child.

(10) "Child benefit commencement date", in relation to a child, means—
  (a) the first day for which child benefit was paid in respect of the child (otherwise than because of a directly applicable Community provision or an international agreement), or
  (b) in the case of a child to whom section 2(3) applies or section 2(5) has applied, such day as is prescribed by regulations.

DEFINITIONS

"account provider"—s.29.
"child"—*ibid.*
"child benefit commencement date"—subs.(10).
"child trust fund"—s.29.
"eligible child"—ss.2(1) and 29.
"income threshold"—subs.(6).
"Inland Revenue"—s.29.
"relevant income"—subs.(6).
"relevant social security benefit"—*ibid.*
"tax year"—*ibid.*

GENERAL NOTE

1.652 In addition to the initial contribution under s.8, children born into families on low incomes will be eligible for a "supplementary contribution" to boost their child trust fund account investment at the outset. This section sets out the rules governing the award of the supplementary contribution. Subsections (1)–(3) specify the procedure to be followed. Subsection (4) spells out the criteria for receipt of the supplementary condition. Children being looked after in local authority care will *not* qualify for this extra amount (see subs.(4)(b)), but they will in any event qualify for an equivalent amount under s.8 by virtue of their status. The means-test is explained in subs.(5), with various terms defined by subss.(6) and (10). Subsections (7)–(9) deal with various awkward transitional cases.

Subsection (1)

1.653 There is no need for parents on low incomes to claim the supplementary contribution; indeed, there is no facility for them to do so. Instead, the legislation requires HMRC to inform the account provider if a child is eligible for the supplementary contribution. HMRC will have this information as it is responsible for administering child tax credit under the Tax Credits Act 2002, which acts as the trigger for entitlement to the extra Treasury contribution (see subss.(4)(c) and (5)).

Subsections (2) and (3)

Having been informed that the child in question is eligible for the supplementary contribution, the account provider may then make a claim for that extra amount (subs.(2); see Child Trust Funds Regulations 2004 reg.30(6)(b)). This section then requires HMRC to pay the account provider the appropriate amount by way of a supplementary contribution. In the case of children born after the appointed day, this is a further £250 (*ibid.*, reg.7(7)), making £500 in total. The amounts are increased for those born on or after September 1, 2002 but before the appointed day (*ibid.*, reg.7(6)). The account provider must then credit the extra amount to the child's account (subs.(3)). Subsequent regulations amending the amount of the supplementary contribution under subs.(2) will be subject to the affirmative procedure (see ss.28(5) and (6)(b)).

1.654

Subsection (4)

This sets out the criteria for the award of the supplementary contribution. The child must have a child trust fund account, have qualified on the basis of an award of child benefit and meet the child tax credit means-test set out in subs.(5). The second of these requirements has the effect of excluding children who initially qualified for an account because they were in care (see s.2(1)(b)), as they will, in any event, receive the higher initial contribution (see annotation to s.8).

1.655

Subsection (5)

This provision sets out the means-test which determines whether a child is eligible to receive the supplementary as well as the initial Treasury contribution. Two separate conditions must each be satisfied. In the case of both these requirements, the determination of entitlement must have been a final one in accordance with ss.18–21 of the Tax Credits Act 2002 and must not have been overturned.

1.656

The first condition is that someone was entitled to child tax credit for the child in question at the date when child benefit was first paid (known as the "child benefit commencement date": see subs.(10)). The second requirement is that *either* their income does not exceed the child tax credit income threshold for the tax year in issue *or* that person is entitled to a "relevant social security benefit". The statutory authority for the child tax credit income threshold is Tax Credits Act 2002 s.7(1)(a) (see subs.(6)). The annual amount of this threshold is prescribed in regulations, and for the 2015/16 tax year is £16,105 (Tax Credits (Income Threshold and Determination of Rates) Regulations 2002 (SI 2002/2008) reg.3(3), as amended by Tax Credits Up-rating Regulations 2010 (SI 2010/981) reg.4(2)). The expression "relevant social security benefit" is defined by reference to Tax Credits Act 2002 s.7(2)) (see subs.(6)), and so includes only income support, income-based jobseeker's allowance, income-related employment and support allowance and pension credit (Tax Credits (Income Threshold and Determination of Rates) Regulations 2002 (SI 2002/2008) reg.4).

These tests require some modification so that they operate in the desired fashion for eligible children born in the transitional period between August 31, 2002 and April 6, 2005. There are two sets of special transitional rules contained in subss. (7)–(9).

Subsections (7) and (8)

The first transitional problem relates to the phasing in of child tax credit for families in receipt of income support or income-based jobseeker's allowance. Child tax credit, payable under the Tax Credits Act 2002, came into force on April 6, 2003, at least so far as new claimants and those claiming working tax credit (the successor to working families' tax credit) were concerned. Originally it was anticipated that

1.657

315

families already in receipt of income support or income-based jobseeker's allowance would move over to child tax credit a year later on April 6, 2004. In fact, only new claimants of these benefits have received child tax credit from that date. The revised plan was that the process of "migration" for existing benefits cases would then start in October 2004, with a view to such transfers being completed by the end of the 2004–05 tax year. (In the meantime all such families have received the cash equivalent of child tax credit through their existing benefits). Some families have therefore not met the strict terms of subs.(5) because, although they were getting income support or income-based jobseeker's allowance at the material time, they were not yet, as a result of this phasing process, receiving child tax credit. Subsections (7) and (8) deal with this by disapplying the means-test based on entitlement to child tax credit in subs.(5). Instead, they provide alternatively that it is sufficient that a child born before April 6, 2005 was in a household which received one of the means-tested benefits or tax credits listed in subs.(8) in respect of that child.

As matters have transpired, this process of migration has been further delayed and had not been commenced, let alone completed, by the end of the 2004–05 tax year. The plan was to have this process completed by December 31, 2014: see Tax Credits Act 2002 (Commencement No.4, Transitional Provisions and Savings) Order 2003 (SI 2003/962 (c.51)) as amended. As the commentary to that provision notes, this target has now been abandoned.

Subsection (9)

1.658 This deals with a separate transitional problem relating to children born between September 1, 2002 and April 5, 2003. The first condition in the means-test (subs.(5)(a)) is that a person was entitled to child tax credit in respect of the child when child benefit was first paid. However, child tax credit did not come into operation until April 6, 2003, and so subs.(5)(a) cannot be satisfied if child benefit was payable *before* that date. There are also knock-on problems in terms of complying with subs.(5)(b) in such cases. This subsection resolves these problems by deeming the child benefit commencement date (and hence the entitlement to child tax credit) as having been in the 2003–04 tax year.

Further contributions by Inland Revenue

1.659 **10.**—(1) Regulations may make provision for the making by the Inland Revenue in the circumstances mentioned in subsection (2) of payments to account providers of child trust funds held by—
  (a) eligible children, or
  (b) any description of eligible children,
of amounts prescribed by, or determined in accordance with, regulations.
  (2) The circumstances referred to in subsection (1) are—
  (a) the children attaining such age as may be prescribed by the regulations, or
  (b) such other circumstances as may be so prescribed.
  (3) The regulations must include provision—
  (a) for making account providers aware that such amounts are payable,
  (b) about the claiming of such payments by account providers, and
  (c) about the crediting of child trust funds by account providers with the amount of such payments.
  (4) For the purposes of this section, a child is to be treated as being an eligible child if entitlement to child benefit in respect of the child is excluded by—
  (a) paragraph 1(a) of Schedule 9 to the Social Security Contributions and Benefits Act 1992 (c. 4) (children in custody), or
  (b) paragraph 1(1)(a) to (d) of Schedule 9 to the Social Security

(2004 c.6 s.10)

Contributions and Benefits (Northern Ireland) Act 1992 (c. 7) (corresponding provision for Northern Ireland).

DEFINITIONS

"account provider"—s.29.
"child"—*ibid.*
"child trust fund"—*ibid.*
"eligible child"—ss.2(1) and 29.
"Inland Revenue"—s.29.

GENERAL NOTE

This is an enabling measure, allowing regulations to be made which may provide for a further Treasury contribution to be credited to the child's account at a later date. Any regulations made under subs.(1) or (2) will be subject to the affirmative procedure (see s.28(5) and (6)(a)). 　1.660

Subsections (1) and (2)
The powers enshrined in the section are expressed in broad terms—thus regulations may provide that further contributions are made to all eligible children, or just to a subset of them (subs.(1)). The trigger for a further contribution may be when the child attains a particular age, as set out in regulations, or some other factor (subs.(2)). The Government's stated intention is that there will be one further contribution which will be payable to all eligible children at the age of seven (rather than three payments at ages 5, 11 and 16, as suggested in *Savings and Assets for All*). It follows that the first such payments will not become due until 2009 (see now Child Trust Funds Regulations 2004 reg.7A). In its 2004 Pre-Budget Report the Government announced a consultation process on the appropriate levels for such further contributions. The consultation paper suggested that there be a further universal payment of £250 at age seven, with an extra £250 for children in low-income families (Treasury Press Notice 5, December 2, 2004). A further consultation was initiated by the 2005 Budget, with a view to seeing whether there is support for a further contribution to children of secondary school age and, if so, at what age and in what amounts. In both consultations the Government has invited views on the appropriate ratio of progressivity (currently 1:2, i.e. £250 universal and £500 means-tested). The rationale for further contributions is that they will enable additional endowment funds to be targeted on those most in need. It will also help to keep the accounts "live" by reminding both children and their parents of the existence and growth of such funds. Note also that account providers will have to issue annual account statements (Child Trust Funds Regulations 2004 reg.10). 　1.661

Subsection (3)
As well as specifying matters such as the amount of the further contribution and the age at which it becomes payable, the regulations which are to be made nearer the time must also address the various procedural matters referred to in this subsection. 　1.662

Subsection (4)
A child will remain an eligible child for these purposes even if there is no child benefit entitlement at the date when the further contribution becomes payable because he or she is detained in custody. Clearly children aged seven are not going to be in custody. However, a future government might decide to make further Treasury contributions to children at the age of 12 or over, when this could become an issue. The Government's view, as a matter of principle, was that it was not justifiable "to disadvantage such children on the grounds that they were in custody on a particular birthday". Such an exclusion from the further contribution might also 　1.663

result in anomalies depending on the length of time the child was in custody and when their birthday fell.

Recouping Inland Revenue contributions

11.—(1) Regulations may make provision requiring that, in circumstances prescribed by the regulations, a person of a description so prescribed is to account to the Inland Revenue for amounts credited to a child trust fund in respect of Inland Revenue contributions (together with any income and gains arising in consequence of the crediting of those amounts).

(2) "Inland Revenue contributions" means payments made by the Inland Revenue which were required to be made under or by virtue of sections 8 to 10 or which the Inland Revenue considered were required to be so made.

DEFINITIONS

"child trust fund"—s.29.
"Inland Revenue"—*ibid.*
"Inland Revenue contributions"—subs.(2).

GENERAL NOTE

In some cases payments will be made under ss.8, 9 or 10 which should not have been so credited; in social security parlance these would be described as overpayments. This section allows the Treasury to make regulations governing the recovery of such payments, e.g. where more than one account has been opened or where the child in question was never an eligible child within s.2. The intention is that recovery will be possible from the account provider, the child, the registered contact (typically the parent) and anyone into whose hands the funds have come.

Subscription limits

12.—(1) No subscription may be made to a child trust fund otherwise than by way of a monetary payment.

(2) Regulations may prescribe the maximum amount that may be subscribed to a child trust fund in each year (otherwise than by way of credits made under or by virtue of this Act or income or gains arising on investments under the child trust fund).

(3) "Year", in relation to a child trust fund held by a child, means—
(a) the period beginning with the day on which the child trust fund is opened and ending immediately before the child's next birthday, and
(b) each succeeding period of twelve months.

DEFINITIONS

"child trust fund"—s.29.
"year"—subs.(3).

GENERAL NOTE

Whereas ss.8–11 are all concerned with Treasury contributions to a child trust fund account, this section deals with contributions to such accounts by others, for example a child's family and friends. Such non-governmental contributions may only be in money terms (subs.(1)), and so shares cannot be transferred to a child trust fund account. There will also be an annual aggregate limit on such non-governmental contributions, prescribed by regulations made under subs.(2). This cap is to be £1,200 a year at the outset (Child Trust Fund Regulations 2004 reg.9(2); there is no facility to carry over any unused allowance to a following year (*ibid.*, reg.9(3)). A year, in this context, means each year from the date of the individual child's birthday (subs.(3)), not each calendar year or each tax year. The minimum contribution on any one transaction is £10, unless the account provider permits a smaller amount (Child Trust Fund Regulations 2004 Sch. para.2(4)).

There is no provision in the Act for automatic indexation of the annual aggregate limit; the Government intends to treat the cap in the same way as the ISA limit, so any uprating will be announced in the Budget or simply through regulations.

Tax

Relief from income tax and capital gains tax

13.—(1) Regulations may make provision for and in connection with giving relief from—
(a) income tax, and
(b) capital gains tax,
in respect of investments under child trust funds.

(2) The regulations may, in particular, include—
(a) provision for securing that losses are disregarded for the purposes of capital gains tax where they accrue on the disposal of investments under child trust funds, and
(b) provision dealing with anything which, apart from the regulations, would have been regarded for those purposes as an indistinguishable part of the same asset.

(3) The regulations may specify how tax relief is to be claimed by persons entitled to it or by account providers on their behalf.

(4) The regulations may include provision requiring that, in circumstances prescribed by the regulations, the person prescribed by the regulations is to account to the Inland Revenue for—
(a) tax from which relief has been given under the regulations, and
(b) income or gains arising in consequence of the giving of relief under the regulations,
or for an amount determined in accordance with the regulations in respect of such tax.

(5) Provision made by virtue of this section may disapply, or modify the effect of, any enactment relating to income tax or capital gains tax.

DEFINITIONS
"account provider"—s.29.
"child trust fund"—*ibid.*
"Inland Revenue"—*ibid.*

GENERAL NOTE

This section is concerned with the tax treatment of investments held in child trust funds. It allows regulations to make provision for relief in respect of income tax and capital gains tax (subs.(1)), and how such tax relief should be claimed

1.668

1.669

(subs.(3)). Such regulations may effectively ring-fence child trust fund investments from any other investments held by the child concerned; this will mean that any capital losses arising on the disposal of child trust fund investments will not be deductible from any capital gains outside the child trust fund (subs.(2)(a)). Regulations will also provide for the separate identification of disposals of shares within and outside a child trust fund (subs.(2)(b)). Regulations may provide for the repayment of tax relief that is given in circumstances where it should not have been (subs.(4)). Subsection (5) is a general power that enables regulations to modify income tax and capital gains tax legislation for child trust fund accounts (see generally Child Trust Funds Regulations 2004 Pt 3 and especially regs 24 and 36).

Insurance companies and friendly societies

1.670   **14.**—[¹ . . .]

AMENDMENT

1. Finance Act 2007 s.114 and Sch.27 pt 2 (July 19, 2007).

Information, etc.

Information from account providers, etc.

1.671   **15.**—(1) Regulations may require [¹ . . .] any [¹person who is or has been the account provider in relation to a child trust fund]—
   (a) to make documents available for inspection on behalf of the Inland Revenue, or
   (b) to provide to the Inland Revenue any information,
relating to, or to investments which are or have been held under, [¹the child trust fund].
   (2) [¹ . . .]
   (3) The regulations may include provision requiring documents to be made available or information to be provided—
   (a) in the manner and form, and
   (b) by the time and at the place,
prescribed by or under the regulations.

AMENDMENT

1. Finance Act 2009 s.96 and Sch.48 (Appointed Day, Savings and Consequential Amendments) Order 2009 (SI 2009/3054) art.3 and Sch. para.12 (April 1, 2010).

DEFINITIONS

"account provider"—s.29.
"child"—*ibid.*
"child trust fund"—*ibid.*
"Inland Revenue"—*ibid.*
"relevant person"—subs.(2).

General Note

This section enables the Treasury to make regulations requiring account providers and other "relevant persons" (as defined by subs.(2)) to supply information or make documents available for inspection (and subject to requirements stipulated under subs.(3)). The Child Trust Funds Regulations 2004 require account holders to supply HMRC with both fortnightly and annual returns (regs 30 and 32). The fortnightly returns will both act as a claim for payment of the government contributions and enable HMRC to identify children for whom accounts have not been opened.

1.672

Information about children in care of authority

16.—(1) Regulations may require, or authorise officers of the Inland Revenue to require, an authority—
 (a) to make documents available for inspection on behalf of the Inland Revenue, or
 (b) to provide to the Inland Revenue any information,
which the Inland Revenue may require for the discharge of any function relating to child trust funds and which is information to which subsection (2) applies.

1.673

(2) This subsection applies to information relating to a child who falls or has fallen within—
 (a) paragraph 1(c) of Schedule 9 to the Social Security Contributions and Benefits Act 1992 (c. 4), or
 (b) paragraph 1(1)(f) of Schedule 9 to the Social Security Contributions and Benefits (Northern Ireland) Act 1992 (c. 7),
by reason of being, or having been, in the care of the authority in circumstances prescribed by regulations under that provision.

(3) The regulations may include provision requiring documents to be made available or information to be provided—
 (a) in the manner and form, and
 (b) by the time and at the place,
prescribed by or under the regulations.

Definitions

 "child"—s.29.
 "child trust fund"—*ibid.*
 "Inland Revenue"—*ibid.*

General Note

The normal rule is that a child is an "eligible child" if child benefit is payable in respect of him or her (s.2(1)(a)). Receipt of child benefit thus acts as a passport to entitlement to the child trust fund. HMRC is also responsible for administering child benefit and accordingly has access to all the relevant information in such cases. However, child benefit cannot be claimed for children in local authority care, for whom special provision has to be made to make them "eligible children" (ss.2(1)(b) and 2(2)). As these children will not appear in the records of current child benefit payments, HMRC will have to obtain the necessary information direct from local authorities. This section accordingly enables the Treasury to make regulations requiring local authorities to provide the information necessary to arrange for a child trust fund account to be opened or for further contributions to be made. Local authorities are required to make monthly returns (Child Trust Funds Regulations 2004 reg.33).

1.674

Use of information

1.675   **17.**—(1) Information held for the purposes of any function relating to child trust funds—
  (a) by the Inland Revenue, or
  (b) by a person providing services to the Inland Revenue, in connection with the provision of those services,
may be used, or supplied to any person providing services to the Inland Revenue, for the purposes of, or for any purposes connected with, the exercise of any such function.

(2) Information held for the purposes of any function relating to child trust funds—
  (a) by the Inland Revenue, or
  (b) by a person providing services to the Inland Revenue, in connection with the provision of those services,
may be used, or supplied to any person providing services to the Inland Revenue, for the purposes of, or for any purposes connected with, the exercise of any other function of the Inland Revenue.

(3) Information held for the purposes of any function other than those relating to child trust funds—
  (a) by the Inland Revenue, or
  (b) by a person providing services to the Inland Revenue, in connection with the provision of those services,
may be used, or supplied to any person providing services to the Inland Revenue, for the purposes of, or for any purposes connected with, the exercise of any function of the Inland Revenue relating to child trust funds.

(4) Information held by the Secretary of State or the Department for Social Development in Northern Ireland, or any person providing services to the Secretary of State or that Department, may be supplied to—
  (a) the Inland Revenue, or
  (b) a person providing services to the Inland Revenue, in connection with the provision of those services,
for use for the purposes of, or for any purposes connected with, the exercise of any function of the Inland Revenue relating to child trust funds.

DEFINITIONS

  "child trust fund"—s.29.
  "Inland Revenue"—*ibid.*

GENERAL NOTE

1.676   This section allows information relating to child trust funds to be shared both within government and between government departments and their contractors (typically their IT providers). Subsection (1) allows information relating to child trust funds to be used for purposes relating to such funds. Subsection (2), on the other hand, enables such information to be used for other (non-child trust fund) purposes by HMRC (e.g. official evaluations of savings policies). Subsection (3) permits information held by HMRC in connection with other purposes to be used for child trust fund purposes. This allows HMRC to access information about a person's child tax credit status in order to determine eligibility for the supplementary contribution (see s.9(5)). Finally, subs.(4) allows other government departments to provide information to HMRC (or its contractors) for reasons connected with child trust funds. In particular, this will enable HMRC to obtain information from the Department for Work and Pensions about a person's benefit status. This will be relevant to determining entitlement to the supplementary condition in respect of children born on or after September 1, 2002 but before child tax credit became payable to the household in question.

Disclosure of information

18.—[*Section omitted.*]

General Note

This section amends the Finance Act 1989 s.182 and so brings the child trust fund scheme within the existing statutory provisions which deal with the confidentiality of personal information held by HMRC, and the exceptions to that principle.

Payments after death

Payments after death of child

19.—(1) Where a relevant child dies, the Inland Revenue may make a payment to the personal representatives of the child if any one or more of the conditions specified in subsection (3) is satisfied.

(2) "Relevant child" means a child who is or has been an eligible child (or would have been had this Act come into force on the date referred to in section 2(1)).

(3) The conditions are—
(a) that either no payment had been made under section 8 by the Inland Revenue or, if one had, the amount of the payment had not been credited to the child trust fund held by the child,
(b) that section 9 applied to the child (or would have had this Act come into force on the date referred to in section 2(1)) but either no payment had been made under that section by the Inland Revenue or, if one had, the amount of the payment had not been credited to the child trust fund held by the child, and
(c) that the Inland Revenue was required by regulations under section 10 to make a payment in respect of the child but either the payment had not been made or, if it had, the amount of the payment had not been credited to the child trust fund held by the child.

(4) The amount of the payment is to be equal to the amount of the payment or payments which had not been made or credited.

Definitions

"child"—s.29.
"child trust fund"—*ibid.*
"eligible child"—*ibid.*
"Inland Revenue"—*ibid.*
"relevant child"—subs.(2).

General Note

1.680 This section gives HMRC the power to make child trust fund payments in respect of children born after August 31, 2002 but who have died before such payments have been credited to an account. Any one (or more) of three requirements must be satisfied. These are: (1) that no initial contribution has been paid under s.8 (or it has not been credited to the account); (2) that the child was entitled to a supplementary contribution under s.9 but this had not been paid or credited to the account; or (3) that a further contribution was due under s.10 but again had not been paid or credited (subs.(3)). The amount payable is a sum equal to the amount of the outstanding payment(s) (subs.(4)) and is payable to the child's personal representatives (subs.(1)). Note that there is no absolute right to such a payment; HMRC *may* make such a payment. The element of discretion has been inserted to allow HMRC to refuse to make payments in cases where the child has been unlawfully killed by the parent. The personal representatives have a right of appeal in the event of a dispute about payment (s.22(5)).

Penalties

Penalties

1.681 **20.**—(1) A penalty of £300 may be imposed on any person who fraudulently—
  (a) applies to open a child trust fund,
  (b) makes a withdrawal from a child trust fund otherwise than as permitted by regulations under section 3(4)(d), or
  (c) secures the opening of a child trust fund by the Inland Revenue.
(2) A penalty not exceeding £3,000 may be imposed on—
  (a) an account provider who fraudulently or negligently makes an incorrect statement or declaration in connection with a claim under section 8 or 9 or regulations under section 10 or 13, and
  (b) any person who fraudulently or negligently provides incorrect information in response to a requirement imposed by or under regulations under section 15.
(3) Penalties may be imposed on—
  (a) an account provider who fails to make a claim under section 8 or 9 or regulations under section 10 by the time required by regulations under the section concerned, and
  (b) any person who fails to make a document available, or provide information, in accordance with regulations under section 15.
(4) The penalties which may be imposed under subsection (3) are—
  (a) a penalty not exceeding £300, and
  (b) if the failure continues after a penalty under paragraph (a) is imposed, a further penalty or penalties not exceeding £60 for each day on which the failure continues after the day on which the penalty under that paragraph was imposed (but excluding any day for which a penalty under this paragraph has already been imposed).
(5) No penalty under subsection (3) may be imposed on a person in respect of a failure after the failure has been remedied.
(6) For the purposes of subsection (3) a person is to be taken not to have failed to make a claim, make available a document or provide information which must be made, made available or provided by a particular time—

(a) if the person made it, made it available or provided it within such further time (if any) as the Inland Revenue may have allowed,
(b) if the person had a reasonable excuse for not making it, making it available or providing it by that time, or
(c) if, after having had such an excuse, the person made it, made it available or provided it without unreasonable delay.

(7) A penalty may be imposed on an account provider in respect of—
(a) the provision by the account provider, as a child trust fund, of an account which does not meet the condition in subsection (8),
(b) a failure by the account provider to comply with section 8(2) or 9(3) or with a requirement imposed on the account provider by regulations under section 5(5), 6(3), 7 [¹, 7A, 7B] or 10(3), or
(c) a breach of section 12(1), or regulations under section 12(2), in relation to a child trust fund held with the account provider.

(8) An account meets the condition referred to in subsection (7)(a) if—
(a) it is of one of the descriptions prescribed by regulations under section 3(2),
(b) section 3(4) is complied with in relation to it, and
(c) the requirements imposed by regulations under section 3(5) are satisfied in relation to it.

(9) The penalty which may be imposed under subsection (7) on the account provider is a penalty not exceeding—
(a) £300, or
(b) £1 in respect of each account affected by the matter, or any of the matters, in respect of which the penalty is imposed,
whichever is greater.

AMENDMENT

1. Deregulation Act 2015 s.62(5) (March 26, 2015 for purposes of making regulations, April 6, 2015 for other purposes).

DEFINITIONS

"account provider"—s.29.
"child trust fund"—*ibid.*
"Inland Revenue"—*ibid.*

GENERAL NOTE

This section makes provision for penalties to be imposed in connection with child trust fund applications and related matters. Individuals who fraudulently apply to open or secure the opening of an account, or make an account withdrawal, are subject to a penalty of £300 (subs.(1)). Account providers and others who make fraudulent or negligent statements or declarations are liable to a penalty not exceeding £3,000 (subs.(2)). Account providers and others are also liable to a £300 penalty (and £60 per day thereafter for continued non-compliance) for failing to make claims in respect of reimbursements or for failing to provide information or produce documentation (subss.(3) and (4); see further subss.(5) and (6)). Subsections (7)–(9) make further provision for penalties to be imposed on account providers in respect of non-compliance with various statutory requirements.

Any penalties under this section are imposed by HMRC (s.21(1)), subject to the various procedural requirements in s.21. There is a right of appeal against any decision to impose a penalty, or its amount (s.22(6)).

Decisions, appeals, mitigation and recovery

21.—(1) It is for the Inland Revenue to impose a penalty under section 20.

(2) If the Inland Revenue decide to impose such a penalty the decision must (subject to the permitted maximum) set it at such amount as, in their opinion, is appropriate.

(3) A decision to impose such a penalty may not be made after the end of the period of six years beginning with the date on which the penalty was incurred or began to be incurred.

(4) The Inland Revenue must give notice of such a decision to the person on whom the penalty is imposed.

(5) The notice must state the date on which it is given and give details of the right to appeal against the decision under section 22.

(6) After the notice has been given, the decision must not be altered except on appeal.

(7) But the Inland Revenue may, in their discretion, mitigate any penalty under section 20.

(8) A penalty under section 20 becomes payable at the end of the period of 30 days beginning with the date on which notice of the decision is given.

(9) On an appeal under section 22 against a decision under this section, the [1 appropriate tribunal] may—
 (a) if it appears that no penalty has been incurred, set the decision aside,
 (b) if the amount set appears to be appropriate, confirm the decision,
 (c) if the amount set appears to be excessive, reduce it to such other amount (including nil) as [1 the tribunal considers] appropriate, or
 (d) if the amount set appears to be insufficient, increase it to such amount not exceeding the permitted maximum as [1 the tribunal considers] appropriate.

[1(10) In addition to any right of appeal on a point of law under section 11(2) of the Tribunals, Courts and Enforcement Act 2007, the person liable to the penalty may appeal to the Upper Tribunal against the amount of a penalty which has been determined under subsection (9), but not against any decision which falls under section 11(5)(d) and (e) of that Act and was made in connection with the determination of the amount of the penalty.

(10A) Section 11(3) and (4) of the Tribunals, Courts and Enforcement Act 2007 applies to the right of appeal under subsection (10) as it applies to the right of appeal under section 11(2) of that Act.

(10B) On an appeal under this section the Upper Tribunal has a similar jurisdiction to that conferred on the First-tier Tribunal by virtue of this section.

(10C) In Northern Ireland, an appeal from a decision of the appropriate tribunal lies, at the instance of the person on whom the penalty was imposed to a Northern Ireland Social Security Commissioner, who shall have a similar jurisdiction on such an appeal to that conferred on the appeal tribunal by subsection (9).]

(11) A penalty is to be treated for the purposes of Part 6 of the Taxes Management Act 1970 (c. 9) (collection and recovery) as if it were tax charged in an assessment and due and payable.

(2004 c.6 s.21)

AMENDMENT

1. Transfer of Tribunal Functions and Revenue and Customs Appeals Order 2009 (SI 2009/56) art.3(1) and Sch.1 para.415 (April 1, 2009).

DEFINITIONS

"appeal tribunal"—s.24(6).
"the Inland Revenue"—s.29 but note that the functions of the Inland Revenue have been transferred to HMRC by CRCA 2005.

Appeals

Rights of appeal

22.—(1) A person may appeal against—
(a) a decision by the Inland Revenue not to approve the person as an account provider, or
(b) a decision by the Inland Revenue to withdraw the person's approval as an account provider.

(2) A person who is a relevant person in relation to a child may appeal against a decision by the Inland Revenue—
(a) not to issue a voucher under section 5 in relation to the child,
(b) not to open a child trust fund for the child under section 6,
(c) not to make a payment under section 8 or 9 in respect of the child, or
(d) not to make a payment under regulations under section 10 in respect of the child.

(3) "Relevant person", in relation to a child, means—
(a) the person (if any) entitled to child benefit in respect of the child,
(b) anyone who applied to open a child trust fund for the child, and
(c) anyone who has, at any time, given instructions with respect to the management of the child trust fund held by the child.

(4) A person who is required by the Inland Revenue to account for an amount under regulations under section 11 or 13 may appeal against the decision to impose the requirement.

(5) The personal representatives of a child who has died may appeal against a decision by the Inland Revenue not to make a payment to them under section 19.

(6) A person on whom a penalty under section 20 is imposed may appeal against the decision to impose the penalty or its amount.

1.684

DEFINITIONS

"account provider"—s.29.
"child"—*ibid.*
"child trust fund"—*ibid.*
"Inland Revenue"—*ibid.*
"relevant person"—subs.(3).

GENERAL NOTE

This section sets out the categories of person who can appeal against a decision relating to the child trust fund. In so far as there are any appeals, most appeals will presumably be brought by individuals and will concern the entitlement to child

1.685

trust fund payments in individual cases (subs.(2)). However, companies who are refused permission by HMRC to act as account providers also have a right of appeal (subs.(1)). Subsections (4)–(6) ensure that various other persons have a right of appeal as appropriate. In particular, subs.(6) provides that any person on whom a penalty is imposed has a right of appeal against both the decision to levy the penalty and also the amount. The tribunal's powers on hearing appeals under this section are set out in s.21(9). In the short to medium term, child trust fund appeals will be heard by the First-tier Tribunal and, on further appeal, by the Upper Tribunal (s.24, temporarily modifying s.23: see General Note to s.21).

Exercise of rights of appeal

1.686
23.—(1) Notice of an appeal under section 22 against a decision must be given to the Inland Revenue in the manner prescribed by regulations within the period of thirty days after the date on which notice of the decision was given.

(2) Notice of such an appeal must specify the grounds of appeal.

[¹ (3) An appeal under section 22 is to the appropriate tribunal.]

(4) [¹. . .]

(5) On the hearing of an appeal under section 22 the [¹appeal tribunal] may allow the appellant to put forward grounds not specified in the notice, and take them into consideration if satisfied that the omission was not wilful or unreasonable.

[¹ (6) Regulations may apply (with or without modifications) any provision contained in—
  (a) the Social Security Act 1998 (c. 14) (social security appeals: Great Britain),
  (b) the Social Security (Northern Ireland) Order 1998 (SI 1998/1506 (NI 10))(social security appeals: Northern Ireland), or
  (c) section 54 of the Taxes Management Act 1970 (settling of appeals by agreement),
in relation to appeals which by virtue of this section are to the appropriate tribunal or in relation to appeals under this Act which lie to a Social Security Commissioner.]

(7) [¹. . .]

AMENDMENT

1. Transfer of Tribunal Functions and Revenue and Customs Appeals Order 2009 (SI 2009/56) art.3(1) and Sch.1 para.416 (April 1, 2009).

DEFINITION

"the Inland Revenue"—s.29 but note that the functions of the Inland Revenue have been transferred to HMRC by CRCA 2005.

Temporary modifications

1.687
24.—[¹. . .]

AMENDMENT

1. Transfer of Tribunal Functions and Revenue and Customs Appeals Order 2009 (SI 2009/56) art.3(1) and Sch.1 para.417 (April 1, 2009).

(2004 c.6 s.25)

Supplementary

Northern Ireland

25.—In Schedule 2 to the Northern Ireland Act 1998 (c. 47) (excepted matters), after paragraph 9 insert—
"9A Child Trust Funds."

1.688

GENERAL NOTE

The child trust fund scheme is added to the Schedule of excepted matters in the Northern Ireland Act 1998, so ensuring that the Fund is governed by legislation common to the whole of the UK (see also s.30).

1.689

    26.—[*Omitted.*]   1.690

    27.—[*Omitted.*]   1.691

    28.—[*Omitted.*]   1.692

Interpretation

29. — In this Act—
"account provider" is to be construed in accordance with section 3(1),
[1 "appropriate tribunal" means
(a) the First-tier Tribunal, or
(b) in Northern Ireland, an appeal tribunal constituted under Chapter 1 of Part 2 of the Social Security (Northern Ireland) Order 1998,]
"child" means a person under the age of 18,
"child trust fund" has the meaning given by section 1(2),
"eligible child" is to be construed in accordance with section 2,
[1 . . .]
"the Inland Revenue" means the Commissioners of Inland Revenue,
[1 "Northern Ireland Social Security Commissioner" means the Chief Social Security Commissioner or any other Social Security Commissioner appointed under the Social Security Administration (Northern Ireland) Act 1992 (c. 8) or a tribunal of three or more Commissioners constituted under article 16(7) of the Social Security (Northern Ireland) Order 1998,]
"responsible person" has the meaning given by section 3(8), and
[1 . . .]

1.693

AMENDMENT

1. Transfer of Tribunal Functions and Revenue and Customs Appeals Order 2009 (SI 2009/56) art.3(1) and Sch.1 para.418 (April 1, 2009).

    30.—[*Omitted.*]   1.694

    31.—[*Omitted.*]   1.695

Income Tax (Trading and Other Income) Act 2005

Income Tax (Trading and Other Income) Act 2005

(2005 c.5)

CONTENTS

PART 1

OVERVIEW

1. Overview of Act
2. Overview of priority rules

PART 2

TRADING INCOME

CHAPTER 1

INTRODUCTION

3. Overview of Part 2
4. Provisions which must be given priority over Part 2

CHAPTER 2

INCOME TAXED AS TRADE PROFITS

Charge to tax on trade profits

5. Charge to tax on trade profits
6. Territorial scope of charge to tax
7. Income charged
8. Person liable

Trades and trade profits

9. Farming and market gardening

Starting and ceasing to trade

17. Effect of becoming or ceasing to be a UK resident

(2005 c.5)

Rent-a-room and qualifying care relief

23. Rent-a-room and foster-care relief

CHAPTER 3

TRADE PROFITS: BASIC RULES

24. Professions and vocations
25. Generally accepted accounting practice
26. Losses calculated on same basis as profits
27. Receipts and expenses
28. Items treated under CAA 2001 as receipts and expenses
29. Interest
31. Relationship between rules prohibiting and allowing deductions

CHAPTER 4

TRADE PROFITS: RULES RESTRICTING DEDUCTIONS

Introduction

32. Professions and vocations

Capital expenditure

33. Capital expenditure

Wholly and exclusively and losses rules

34. Expenses not wholly and exclusively for trade and unconnected losses

Bad and doubtful debts

35. Bad and doubtful debts

Unpaid remuneration

36. Unpaid remuneration

Business entertainment and gifts

45. Business entertainment and gifts: general rule

Income Tax (Trading and Other Income) Act 2005

Social security contributions

53. Social security contributions

CHAPTER 6

TRADE PROFITS: RECEIPTS

Introduction

95. Professions and vocations

Capital receipts

96. Capital receipts

Debts released

97. Debts incurred and later released

CHAPTER 15

BASIS PERIODS

INTRODUCTION

196. Professions and vocations
197. Meaning of "accounting date"
198. General rule

(2005 c.5)

PART 3

PROPERTY INCOME

CHAPTER 1

INTRODUCTION

260. Overview of Part 3
261. Provisions which must be given priority over Part 3
262. Priority between Chapters within Part 3

CHAPTER 2

PROPERTY BUSINESSES

Introduction

263. Introduction

Basic meaning of UK and overseas property business

264. UK property business
265. Overseas property business

Generating income from land

266. Meaning of "generating income from land"

CHAPTER 3

PROFITS OF PROPERTY BUSINESSES: BASIC RULES

Charge to tax on profits of a property business

268. Charge to tax on profits of a property business
269. Territorial scope of charge to tax
270. Income charged
271. Person liable

Calculation of profits

272. Profits of a property business: application of trading income rules

Income Tax (Trading and Other Income) Act 2005

PART 4

SAVINGS AND INVESTMENT INCOME

CHAPTER 1

INTRODUCTION

365. Overview of Part 4
366. Provisions which must be given priority over Part 4
367. Priority between Chapters within Part 4
368. Territorial scope of Part 4 charges

CHAPTER 2

INTEREST

Charge to tax on interest

369. Charge to tax on interest
370. Income charged
371. Person liable

Other income taxed as interest

372. Building society dividends

CHAPTER 3

DIVIDENDS ETC. FROM UK RESIDENT COMPANIES ETC.

Introduction

382. Contents of Chapter

Charge to tax on dividends and other distributions

383. Charge to tax on dividends and other distributions
384. Income charged
385. Person liable

Chapter 4

Dividends from Non-UK Resident Companies

Charge to tax on dividends from non-UK resident companies

- 402. Charge to tax on dividends from non-UK resident companies
- 403. Income charged
- 404. Person liable

Chapter 7

Purchased Life Annuity Payments

- 422. Charge to tax on purchased life annuity payments
- 423. Meaning of "purchased life annuity"
- 424. Income charged
- 425. Person liable

Part 5

Miscellaneous Income

Chapter 1

Introduction

- 574. Overview of Part 5
- 575. Provisions which must be given priority over Part 5
- 576. Priority between Chapters within Part 5

Chapter 5

Settlements: Amounts Treated as Income of Settlor

Charge to tax under Chapter 5

- 619. Charge to tax under Chapter 5
- 620. Meaning of "settlement" and "settlor"

Income charged and person liable

- 621. Income charged
- 622. Person liable

Chapter 8

Income not Otherwise Charged

687. Charge to tax on income not otherwise charged
688. Income charged
689. Person liable

Part 6

Exempt Income

Chapter 1

Introduction

690. Overview of Part 6

Chapter 2

National Savings Income

691. National Savings Bank ordinary account interest [*omitted*]
692. Income from savings certificates [*omitted*]

Chapter 8

Other Annual Payments

Certain annual payments by individuals

730. Foreign maintenance payments

Periodical payments of personal injury damages etc.

731. Periodical payments of personal injury damages
732. Compensation awards
733. Persons entitled to exemptions for personal injury payments etc.
734. Payments from trusts for injured persons

Health and employment insurance payments

735. Health and employment insurance payments
736. Health and employment risks and benefits

Payments to adopters

744. Payments to adopters etc.: England and Wales

CHAPTER 9

OTHER INCOME

751. Interest on damages for personal injury
753. Interest on repayment of student loan
776. Scholarship income
780. Disabled person's vehicle maintenance grant

CHAPTER 10

GENERAL

783. General disregard of exempt income for income tax purposes

PART 7

INCOME CHARGED UNDER THIS ACT: RENT-A-ROOM AND QUALIFYING CARE RELIEF

CHAPTER 1

RENT-A-ROOM RELIEF

Introduction

784. Overview of Chapter 1
785. Person who qualifies for relief

Basic definitions

786. Meaning of "rent-a-room receipts"
787. Meaning of "residence"
788. Meaning of "total rent-a-room amount"

Individual's limit

789. The individual's limit

Income Tax (Trading and Other Income) Act 2005

CHAPTER 2

QUALIFYING-CARE RELIEF

Introduction

803.   Overview of Chapter 2
804.   Person who qualifies for relief
804A. Shared lives care: further condition for relief

Basic definitions

805.   Meaning of "qualifying-care receipts"
805A. Meaning of providing qualifying care
806.   Meaning of providing foster care
806A. Meaning of providing shared lives care
806B. Meaning of "residence"
807.   Calculation of "total foster-care receipts" [*omitted*]

PART 10

GENERAL PROVISIONS

CHAPTER 1

INTRODUCTION

864.   Overview of Part 10

CHAPTER 2

GENERAL CALCULATON RULES ETC.

868.   Social security contributions: non-trades, etc.

INTRODUCTION AND GENERAL NOTE

1.697   ITTOIA is the third of the series of Acts produced under the Tax Law Rewrite Project. It came into effect on April 6, 2005. Together with ITEPA it has rewritten all the main charging provisions of income tax as they apply to individuals, partnerships and trusts. Provisions applying to companies have not been rewritten, but they are not relevant to tax credits.
ITTOIA completes the abolition of all the former income tax schedules as its provisions replace the old Sch.A (taxation of income from land in the UK) and Sch.D, Cases I to VI (trading and professional income, investment income, and foreign source income). Following the approach adopted in ITEPA it also merges provisions about the taxation of UK-source income with the taxation of foreign source income. The relevance here is that assessment of income for tax credits purposes includes worldwide income. With effect from the tax year 2006–07 no reference therefore need be made to the old law for tax credits purposes.

The pattern adopted by ITTOIA is as follows. The charges to tax under the various Schedules and other separate charging sections have been converted into charges on different classes of income, and the rules relating to each kind of income are set out in separate Parts of the Act. These are then followed by general exemptions and other provisions. Each part has "signposts" in it, including an initial overview and provisions dealing with priorities between charging provisions.

The most important difference between kinds or classes of income is the one that lies between ITEPA and ITTOIA: is an individual employed or self-employed? ITTOIA operates if ITEPA does not, but the decision whether someone is employed or not in that narrower sense is left outside both Acts and for the ordinary law—and in the social security context is usually to be determined under the provisions of s.8 of the Social Security (Transfer of Functions) Act 1999.

The new charges to tax, exemptions and reliefs are:

Part 2 Trading income (including professions and vocations)

Part 3 Property income (including both UK and foreign land)

Part 4 Savings and investment income (including interest and dividends)

Part 5 Miscellaneous income (the "sweeper")

Part 6 Exempt income

Part 7 Rent-a-room and qualifying care reliefs

1.698

Trading income replaces the old Sch.D Cases I and II and part of Case VI. Property income replaces the old Sch.A and part of Sch.D Case V. Savings and investment income replaces the old Sch.D Case III and Case IV, part of Case V and part of Case VI. It also replaces Sch.F. (It also includes the former Sch.C, which was repealed and replaced by provisions included in Sch.D some years ago). As the former Sch.B was repealed many years ago, this completes the repeal for income tax (and therefore tax credits) purposes of all the old 1803 income tax schedules.

A consistent pattern within each part is to place the most important provisions at the start of the Part. For example, in the savings and investment income part the charge on interest comes first, then dividends, with less commonly used provisions following in decreasing order of importance. The Act also seeks to put all the important measures in the main text of the Act, rather than in schedules. This explains the need for a lengthy Pt 7, dealing with the important but inevitably detailed provisions that exempt small incomes from income tax if drawn from renting rooms in the individual's only or main residence or from foster care payments (or both).

The sections selected for inclusion

The sections set out in this work are selected for two reasons: first, they are the main sections of the Act and the ones to which reference is most likely to be made, directly or indirectly, in straightforward tax credits cases involving either the self-employed or forms of savings and investment income. Secondly, sections are included where they deal expressly with social security income or the kinds of income received in particular by those with disabilities. Provisions providing exemption from two specific kinds of income widely received by those with entitlement to tax credits are also included: tax relief under the rent-a-room scheme exempting income where a resident owner lets part of his or her house to a lodger; and the exemption of income paid to foster parents and other carers under qualifying care relief.

1.699

The law is as applied for 2013–14 after any amendments in the Finance Acts. No history of amendments is set out. However, the full history of the original ITTOIA provisions (to which as yet little amendment has been made) are in the full explanatory notes to ITTOIA issued by the Tax Law Rewrite Project.

Income Tax (Trading and Other Income) Act 2005

PART 1

OVERVIEW

Overview of Act

1.700

1.—(1) This Act imposes charges to income tax under—
(a) Part 2 (trading income),
(b) Part 3 (property income),
(c) Part 4 (savings and investment income), and
(d) Part 5 (certain miscellaneous income).
(2) *Repealed.*
(3) Exemptions from those charges are dealt with in Part 6 (exempt income) but any Part 6 exemptions which are most obviously relevant to particular types of income are also mentioned in the provisions about those types of income.
(4) What is or is not mentioned in those provisions does not limit the effect of Part 6.
(5) This Act also contains—
(a) provision about rent-a-room relief and qualifying care relief (see Part 7),
(b) special rules for foreign income (see Part 8),
(c) special rules for partnerships (see Part 9), and
(d) certain calculation rules and general provisions (see Part 10).
(6) For abbreviations and defined expressions used in this Act, see 885 and Sch.4.

Overview of priority rules

1.701

2.—(1) This Act contains some rules establishing an order of priority in respect of certain amounts which would otherwise—
(a) fall within a charge to income tax under two or more Chapters or Parts of this Act, or
(b) fall within a charge to income tax under a Chapter or Part of this Act and ITEPA 2003.
(2) See, in particular—
section 4 (provisions which must be given priority over Part 2),
section 261 (provisions which must be given priority over Part 3),
section 262 (priority between Chapters within Part 3),
section 366 (provisions which must be given priority over Part 4),
section 367 (priority between Chapters within Part 4),
section 575 (provisions which must be given priority over Part 5), and
section 576 (priority between Chapters within Part 5).
(3) But the rules in those sections need to be read with other rules law (whether in this Act or otherwise) about the scope of particular provisions or the order of priority to be given to them.
(4) Section 171(2) of FA 1993 (profits of Lloyd's underwriters charged only under Chapter 2 of Part 2 of this Act) is one example of another rule of law.

(2005 c.5 s.3)

Part 2

Trading Income

Chapter 1

Overview of Part 2

3.—(1) This Part imposes charges to income tax under—
(a) Chapter 2 (the profits of a trade, profession or vocation which meet the territorial conditions mentioned in section 6),
(b) Chapter 17 (amounts treated as adjustment income under section 228), and
(c) Chapter 18 (post-cessation receipts that are chargeable under this Part).
(2) Part 6 deals with exemptions from the charges under this Part.
(3) See, in particular, the exemptions under sections 777 (VAT repayment supplements) and 778 (incentives to use electronic communications).
(4) The charges under this Part apply to non-UK residents as well as UK residents but this is subject to sections 6(2) and (3) and 243(3) and (4) (charges on non-UK residents only on UK income).
(5) The rest of this Part contains rules relevant to the charges to tax under this Part.
(6) This section needs to be read with the relevant priority rules (see sections 2 and 4).

1.702

General Note

Part 2 rewrites (and to some extent also codifies) the previous provisions in Sch.D Case I (income from trade wholly or partly in the UK) and Case II (income from professions and vocations) and aspects of Case IV (other income) previously in ICTA 1988 and subsequent Finance Acts. But the definition of "trade" remains in ICTA 1988 s.832. The charges under this Part on non-UK residents are not covered in this work.

1.703

Provisions which must be given priority over Part 2

4.—(1) Any receipt or other credit item, so far as it falls within—
(a) Chapter 2 of this Part (receipts of trade, profession or vocation), and
(b) Chapter 3 of Part 3 so far as it relates to a UK property business,
is dealt with under Part 3.
(2) Any receipt or other credit item, so far as it falls within—
(a) this Part, and
(b) Part 2, 9 or 10 of ITEPA 2003 (employment income, pension income or social security income),
is dealt with under the relevant Part of ITEPA 2003.

1.704

Income Tax (Trading and Other Income) Act 2005

CHAPTER 2

INCOME TAXED AS TRADE PROFITS

Charge to tax on trade profits

Charge to tax on trade profits

1.705   **5.**—Income tax is charged on the profits of a trade, profession or vocation.

Territorial scope of charge to tax

1.706   **6.**—(1) Profits of a trade arising to a UK resident are chargeable to tax under this Chapter wherever the trade is carried on.
(2) Profits of a trade arising to a non-UK resident are chargeable to tax under this Chapter only if they arise—
   (a) from a trade carried on wholly in the United Kingdom, or
   (b) in the case of a trade carried on partly in the United Kingdom and partly elsewhere, from the part of the trade carried on in the United Kingdom.
(3) This section applies to professions and vocations as it applies to trades.

Income charged

1.707   **7.**—(1) Tax is charged under this Chapter on the full amount of the profits of the tax year.
(2) For this purpose the profits of a tax year are the profits of the basis period for the tax year.
(3) For the rules identifying the basis period for a tax year, see Chapter 15.
(4) This section is subject to Part 8 (foreign income: special rules).
(5) And, for the purposes of section 830 (meaning of "relevant foreign income"), the profits of a trade, profession or vocation arise from a source outside the United Kingdom only if the trade, profession or vocation is carried on wholly outside the United Kingdom.

Person liable

1.708   **8.**—The person liable for any tax charged under this Chapter is the person receiving or entitled to the profits.

Trades and trade profits

Farming and market gardening

1.709   **9.**—(1) Farming or market gardening in the United Kingdom is treated for income tax purposes as the carrying on of a trade or part of a trade (whether or not the land is managed on a commercial basis and with a view to the realisation of profits).
(2) All farming in the United Kingdom carried on by a person, other

than farming carried on as part of another trade, is treated for income tax purposes as one trade.

(3) In the case of farming carried on by a firm, this rule is explained by section 859(1).

Starting and ceasing to trade

Effect of becoming or ceasing to be a UK resident

17.—(1) This section applies if—
(a) an individual carries on a trade wholly or partly outside the United Kingdom otherwise than in partnership, and
(b) the individual becomes or ceases to be UK resident.
(2) The individual is treated for income tax purposes—
(a) as permanently ceasing to carry on the trade at the time of the change of residence, and
(b) so far as the individual continues to carry on the trade, as starting to carry on a new trade immediately afterwards.
(3) But subsection (2) does not prevent a loss made before the change of residence from being deducted under section 831 of ITA 2007 against profits arising after the change.
(4) This section applies to professions and vocations as it applies to trades.
(5) In the case of a trade carried on by a firm, see sections 852(6) (7) and 854(5).

1.710

Rent-a-room and qualifying care relief

Rent-a-room and qualifying care relief

23.—(1) The rules for calculating the profits of a trade carried on by an individual are subject to Chapter 1 of Part 7 (rent-a-room relief).
(2) That Chapter provides relief on income from the use of furnished accommodation in the individual's only or main residence (see, in particular, sections 792 and 796).
(3) The rules for calculating the profits of a trade, profession or vocation carried on by an individual are subject to Chapter 2 of Part 7 (qualifying care relief).
(4) That Chapter provides relief on income from the provision by the individual of qualifying care (see, in particular, sections 813, 816, 822 and 823).

1.711

CHAPTER 3

TRADE PROFITS: BASIC RULES

Professions and vocations

24.—Apart from section 30 (animals kept for trade purposes), the provisions of this Chapter apply to professions and vocations as they apply to trades.

1.712

Income Tax (Trading and Other Income) Act 2005

Generally accepted accounting practice

1.713   **25.**—(1) The profits of a trade must be calculated in accordance with generally accepted accounting practice, subject to any adjustment required or authorised by law in calculating profits for income tax purposes.
(2) This does not—
  (a) require a person to comply with the requirements of the Companies Act 1985 (c. 6) or the Companies (Northern Ireland) Order 1986 (S.I. 1986/1032 (N.I. 6)) except as to the basis of calculation, or
  (b) impose any requirements as to audit or disclosure.
(3) This section is subject to section 160 (barristers and advocates in early years of practice).
(4) This section does not affect provisions of the Income Tax Acts relating to the calculation of the profits of Lloyd's underwriters.

Losses calculated on same basis as profits

1.714   **26.**—(1) The same rules apply for income tax purposes in calculating losses of a trade as apply in calculating profits.
(2) This is subject to any express provision to the contrary.

Receipts and expenses

1.715   **27.**—(1) In the Income Tax Acts, in the context of the calculation of the profits of a trade, references to receipts and expenses are to any items brought into account as credits or debits in calculating the profits.
(2) There is no implication that an amount has been actually received or paid.
(3) This section is subject to any express provision to the contrary.

Items treated under CAA 2001 as receipts and expenses

1.716   **28.**—The rules for calculating the profits of a trade need to be read with—
  (a) the provisions of CAA 2001 which treat charges as receipts of a trade, and
  (b) the provisions of CAA 2001 which treat allowances as expenses of a trade.

Interest

1.717   **29.**—For the purpose of calculating the profits of a trade, interest is an item of a revenue nature, whatever the nature of the loan.

Relationship between rules prohibiting and allowing deductions

1.718   **31.**—(1) Any relevant permissive rule in this Part—
  (a) has priority over any relevant prohibitive rule in this Part, but
  (b) is subject to sections 48 (car hire) and 55 (crime-related payments).
(2) In this section "any relevant permissive rule in this Part" means any provision of—
  (a) Chapter 5 (apart from sections 60 to 67),
  (b) Chapter 11, or
  (c) Chapter 13,
which allows a deduction in calculating the profits of a trade.
(3) In this section "any relevant prohibitive rule in this Part", in relation to any deduction, means any provision of this Part (apart from sections 48 and 55) which might otherwise be read as—

(2005 c.5 s.31)

(a) prohibiting the deduction, or
(b) restricting the amount of the deduction.

CHAPTER 4

TRADE PROFITS: RULES RESTRICTING DEDUCTIONS

Introduction

Professions and vocations

32. The provisions of this Chapter apply to professions and vocations as they apply to trades. 1.719

Capital expenditure

Capital expenditure

33. In calculating the profits of a trade, no deduction is allowed for items of a capital nature. 1.720

Wholly and exclusively and losses rules

Expenses not wholly and exclusively for trade and unconnected losses

34.—(1) In calculating the profits of a trade, no deduction is allowed for— 1.721
  (a) expenses not incurred wholly and exclusively for the purposes of the trade, or
  (b) losses not connected with or arising out of the trade.
(2) If an expense is incurred for more than one purpose, this section does not prohibit a deduction for any identifiable part or identifiable proportion of the expense which is incurred wholly and exclusively for the purposes of the trade.

Bad and doubtful debts

Bad and doubtful debts

35.—(1) In calculating the profits of a trade, no deduction is allowed for a debt owed to the person carrying on the trade, except so far as— 1.722
  (a) the debt is bad,
  (b) the debt is estimated to be bad, or
  (c) the debt is released wholly and exclusively for the purposes of the trade as part of a statutory insolvency arrangement.
(2) If the debtor is bankrupt or insolvent, the whole of the debt is estimated to be bad for the purposes of subsection (1)(b), except so far as any amount may reasonably be expected to be received on the debt.

Unpaid remuneration

Unpaid remuneration

1.723 **36.**—(1) This section applies if, in calculating the profits of a trade of a period of account—
(a) an amount is charged in the accounts for the period in respect of employees' remuneration, and
(b) a deduction for the remuneration would otherwise be allowable for the period.
(2) No deduction is allowed for the remuneration for the period of account unless it is paid before the end of the period of 9 months immediately following the end of the period of account.
(3) If the remuneration is paid after the end of that 9 month period, deduction for it is allowed for the period of account in which it is paid.

Business entertainment and gifts

Business entertainment and gifts: general rule

1.724 **45.**—(1) The general rule is that no deduction is allowed in calculating the profits of a trade for expenses incurred in providing entertainment or gifts in connection with the trade.
(2) A deduction for expenses which are incurred—
(a) in paying sums to or on behalf of an employee of the person carrying on the trade ("the trader"), or
(b) in putting sums at the disposal of an employee of the trader,
is prohibited by the general rule if (and only if) the sums are paid, or put at the employee's disposal, exclusively for meeting expenses incurred or to be incurred by the employee in providing the entertainment or gift.
(3) The general rule is subject to exceptions—
for entertainment (see section 46), and
for gifts (see section 47).
(4) For the purposes of this section and those two sections—
(a) "employee", in relation to a company, includes a director of the company and a person engaged in the management of the company,
(b) "entertainment" includes hospitality of any kind, and
(c) the expenses incurred in providing entertainment or a gift include expenses incurred in providing anything incidental to the provision of entertainment or a gift.

Social security contributions

Social security contributions

1.725 **53.**—(1) In calculating the profits of a trade, no deduction is allowed for any contribution paid by any person under—

(2005 c.5 s.53)

(a) Part 1 of the Social Security Contributions and Benefits Act 1992 (c. 4), or
(b) Part 1 of the Social Security Contributions and Benefits (Northern Ireland) Act 1992 (c.7).
(2) But this prohibition does not apply to an employer's contribution.
(3) For this purpose "an employer's contribution" means—
(a) a secondary Class 1 contribution,
(b) a Class 1A contribution, or
(c) a Class 1B contribution,
within the meaning of Part 1 of the Social Security Contributions and Benefits Act 1992 or of the Social Security Contributions and Benefits (Northern Ireland) Act 1992.

CHAPTER 6

TRADE PROFITS: RECEIPTS

Introduction

Professions and vocations

95.—Apart from section 105 (industrial development grants), the provisions of this Chapter apply to professions and vocations as they apply to trades.

1.726

Capital receipts

Capital receipts

96.—(1) Items of a capital nature must not be brought into account as receipts in calculating the profits of a trade.
(2) But this does not apply to items which, as a result of any provision of this Part, are brought into account as receipts in calculating the profits of the trade.

1.727

Debts released

Debts incurred and later released

97.—(1) This section applies if—
(a) in calculating the profits of a trade, a deduction is allowed for the expense giving rise to a debt owed by the person carrying on the trade,
(b) all or part of the debt is released, and
(c) the release is not part of a statutory insolvency arrangement.
(2) The amount released—
(a) is brought into account as a receipt in calculating the profits of the trade, and
(b) is treated as arising on the date of the release.

1.728

347

Chapter 15

Basis Periods

Introduction

Professions and vocations

1.729 **196.**—The provisions of this Chapter apply to professions and vocations as they apply to trades.

Accounting date

Meaning of "accounting date"

1.730 **197.**—(1) In this Chapter "accounting date", in relation to a tax year, means—
 (a) the date in the tax year to which accounts are drawn up, or
 (b) if there are two or more such dates, the latest of them.
(2) This is subject to—
 (a) section 211(2) (middle date treated as accounting date), and
 (b) section 214(3) (date treated as accounting date if date changed in tax year in which there is no accounting date).

The normal rules

General rule

1.731 **198.**—(1) The general rule is that the basis period for a tax year is the period of 12 months ending with the accounting date in that tax year.
(2) This applies unless a different basis period is given by one of the following sections—
 section 199 (first tax year),
 section 200 (second tax year),
 section 201 (tax year in which there is no accounting date),
 section 202 (final tax year),
 section 209 or 210 (first accounting date shortly before end of tax year),
 section 212 (tax year in which middle date treated as accounting date),
 section 215 (change of accounting date in third tax year), and
 section 216 (change of accounting date in later tax year).

(2005 c.5 s.260)

PART 3

PROPERTY INCOME

CHAPTER 1

INTRODUCTION

Overview of Part 3

260.—(1) This Part imposes charges to income tax under— 1.732
 (a) Chapter 3 (the profits of a UK property business or an overseas property business),
 (b) Chapter 7 (amounts treated as adjustment income under section 330),
 (c) Chapter 8 (rent receivable in connection with a UK section 12(4) concern),
 (d) Chapter 9 (rent receivable for UK electric-line wayleaves),
 (e) Chapter 10 (post-cessation receipts arising from a UK property business), and
 (f) Chapter 11 (overseas property income of a person to whom the remittance basis applies).

(2) Part 6 deals with exemptions from the charges under this Part.

(3) See, in particular, the exemptions under sections 769 (housing grants), 777 (VAT repayment supplements) and 778 (incentives to use electronic communications).

(4) The charges under Chapters 3, 7, 8, 9 and 10 apply to non-UK residents as well as UK residents but this is subject to section 269 (charges on non-UK residents only on UK source income).

(5) This section needs to be read with the relevant priority rules (see sections 2 and 261).

GENERAL NOTE

Part 3 brings together and rewrites the income tax rules formerly in Sch.A (applying 1.733
to income from UK land) and Sch.D Case V (applying to income from overseas land) formerly in ICTA 1988 as amended. The way in which income from land has been taxed has varied over the years. The most recent approach, adopted here, is to align the income of landlords and others receiving income from the exploitation of land closely to the taxation of income from trade, and therefore to the rules now set out in Pt 2.

Provisions which must be given priority over Part 3

261.—Any receipt or other credit item, so far as it falls within— 1.734
 (a) Chapter 3 of this Part so far as it relates to an overseas property business or Chapter 8 or 9 of this Part (rent receivable in connection with a UK section 12(4) concern or for UK electric-line wayleaves), and
 (b) Chapter 2 of Part 2 (receipts of a trade, profession or vocation),
is dealt with under Part 2.

Priority between Chapters within Part 3

262.—(1) Any receipt, so far as it falls within— 1.735
 (a) Chapter 3 so far as it relates to a UK property business, and

(b) Chapter 8 (rent receivable in connection with a UK section 12(4) concern),

is dealt with under Chapter 8.

(2) Any receipt, so far as it falls within—
 (a) Chapter 3 so far as it relates to a UK property business, and
 (b) Chapter 9 (rent receivable for UK electric-line wayleaves),

is dealt with under Chapter 9.

(3) Any receipt, so far as it falls within Chapter 8 (rent receivable in connection with a UK section 12(4) concern) and Chapter 9 (rent receivable for UK electric-line wayleaves), is dealt with under Chapter 9.

CHAPTER 2

PROPERTY BUSINESSES

Introduction

Introduction

1.736   **263.**—(1) This Chapter explains for the purposes of this Act what is meant by—
 (a) a person's UK property business (see section 264), and
 (b) a person's overseas property business (see section 265).

(2) Both those sections need to be read with—
 (a) section 266 (which explains what is meant by generating income from land), and
 (b) section 267 (which provides that certain activities do not count as activities for generating income from land).

(3) In the case of the property business of a firm, the basic rules in sections 264 and 265 are explained in section 859(2) and (3).

(4) References in this Act to an overseas property business are to an overseas property business so far as any profits of the business are chargeable to tax under Chapter 3 (as to which see, in particular, section 269).

(5) Accordingly, nothing in Chapter 4 or 5 is to be read as treating an amount as a receipt of an overseas property business if the profits concerned would not be chargeable to tax under Chapter 3.

(6) In this Act "property business" means a UK property business or an overseas property business.

Basic meaning of UK and overseas property business

UK property business

1.737   **264.**—A person's UK property business consists of—
 (a) every business which the person carries on for generating income from land in the United Kingdom, and
 (b) every transaction which the person enters into for that purpose otherwise than in the course of such a business.

(2005 c.5 s.265)

Overseas property business

265.—A person's overseas property business consists of—
(a) every business which the person carries on for generating income from land outside the United Kingdom, and
(b) every transaction which the person enters into for that purpose otherwise than in the course of such a business.

Generating income from land

Meaning of "generating income from land"

266.—(1) In this Chapter "generating income from land" means exploiting an estate, interest or right in or over land as a source of rents or other receipts.
(2) "Rents" includes payments by a tenant for work to maintain or repair leased premises which the lease does not require the tenant to carry out.
(3) "Other receipts" includes—
(a) payments in respect of a licence to occupy or otherwise use land,
(b) payments in respect of the exercise of any other right over land, and
(c) rentcharges and other annual payments reserved in respect of, or charged on or issuing out of, land.
(4) For the purposes of this section a right to use a caravan or houseboat at only one location is treated as a right deriving from an estate or interest in land.

CHAPTER 3

PROFITS OF PROPERTY BUSINESSES: BASIC RULES

Charge to tax on profits of a property business

Charge to tax on profits of a property business

268.—Income tax is charged on the profits of a property business.

Territorial scope of charge to tax

269.—(1) Profits of a UK property business are chargeable to tax under this Chapter whether the business is carried on by a UK resident or a non-UK resident.
(2) Profits of an overseas property business are chargeable to tax under this Chapter only if the business is carried on by a UK resident.
(3) But, in the case of an overseas property business carried on by a UK resident to whom the remittance basis applies, the only profits of the business chargeable to tax under this Chapter are those in respect of land in the Republic of Ireland.
(4) For a UK resident to whom the remittance basis applies, see also Chapter 11 (charge to tax on overseas property income other than income arising in Republic of Ireland).

Income charged

1.742 **270.**—(1) Tax is charged under this Chapter on the full amount of the profits arising in the tax year.
(2) Subsection (1) is subject to Part 8 (foreign income: special rules).

Person liable

1.743 **271.**—The person liable for any tax charged under this Chapter is the person receiving or entitled to the profits.

Calculation of profits

Profits of a property business: application of trading income rules

1.744 **272.**—(1) The profits of a property business are calculated in the same way as the profits of a trade.
(2) *Omitted.*
(3) *Omitted.*

PART 4

SAVINGS AND INVESTMENT INCOME

CHAPTER 1

INTRODUCTION

Overview of Part 4

1.745 **365.**—(1) This Part imposes charges to income tax under—
(a) Chapter 2 (interest),
(b) Chapter 3 (dividends etc. from UK resident companies etc.),
(c) Chapter 4 (dividends from non-UK resident companies),
(d) Chapter 5 (stock dividends from UK resident companies),
(e) Chapter 6 (release of loan to participator in close company),
(f) Chapter 7 (purchased life annuity payments),
(g) Chapter 8 (profits from deeply discounted securities),
(h) Chapter 9 (gains from contracts for life insurance etc.),
(i) Chapter 10 (distributions from unauthorised unit trusts),
(j) Chapter 11 (transactions in deposits),
(k) Chapter 12 (disposals of futures and options involving guaranteed returns), and
(l) Chapter 13 (sales of foreign dividend coupons).
(2) Part 6 deals with exemptions from the charges under this Part.

(3) See, in particular, any exemptions mentioned in the particular Chapters.

(4) The charges under this Part apply to non-UK residents as well as UK residents but this is subject to section 368(2) (charges on non-UK residents only on UK source income).

(5) This section needs to be read with the relevant priority rules (see sections 2 and 366).

GENERAL NOTE

Part 4 brings together a number of separate charges to income tax on what used to be termed unearned income: interest and similar income from the former Sch.D Cases III (UK source) and IV (foreign securities) and V (foreign possessions), with dividends from the former Sch.F (distributions from UK companies) and again Sch.D Case V (dividends from foreign companies), and other payments such as annuities and income gains from life assurance policies and other forms of investment. Originally to be called investment income, it was given a wider flavour by adding "savings" to the heading. However, it is not all-encompassing because other forms of unearned income are included in Pt 5. In practice, wide use is made of tax-exempt forms of saving and investment. The details of the exemptions are in Pt 6 of the Act, which—along with pension savings under Pt 9 of ITEPA and the treatment of capital gains under the separate regime under the Taxation of Chargeable Gains Act 1992—mean that many people pay only limited income tax on their savings income. Most of these exemptions also apply for tax credits. Tax credits also take no account of capital gains. As a result, claimants can protect their savings from tax credits as well as income tax.

Provisions which must be given priority over Part 4

366.—(1) Any income, so far as it falls within—
(a) any Chapter of this Part, and
(b) Chapter 2 of Part 2 (receipts of a trade, profession or vocation),
is dealt with under Part 2.

(2) Any income, so far as it falls within—
(a) any Chapter of this Part, and
(b) Chapter 3 of Part 3 so far as the Chapter relates to a UK property business,
is dealt with under Part 3.

(3) Any income, so far as it falls within—
(a) any Chapter of this Part other than Chapter 3 or 6, and
(b) Part 2, 9 or 10 of ITEPA 2003 (employment income, pension income or social security income),
is dealt with under the relevant Part of ITEPA 2003.

(4) Nothing in this section prevents amounts both—
(a) being counted as income for the purposes of Chapter 9 of this Part (gains from contracts for life insurance etc.), and
(b) being taken into account in calculating income, or counting as income, for the purposes of other Parts of this Act,
but see section 527 (reduction for sums taken into account otherwise than under Chapter 9).

Priority between Chapters within Part 4

367.—(1) Any income, so far as it falls within Chapter 2 (interest) and Chapter 8 (profits from deeply securities), is dealt with under Chapter 8.

(2) Any income, so far as it falls within Chapter 3 (dividends etc. UK resident companies etc.) and another Chapter, is dealt with under Chapter 3 (but this is subject to subsection (3)).

(3) Any income, so far as it falls within—

(a) Chapter 2 (interest) as a result of section 372 (building society dividends) or 379 (industrial and provident society payments), and

(b) Chapter 3,

is dealt with under Chapter 2.

Territorial scope of Part 4 charges

1.749   **368.**—(1) Income arising to a UK resident is chargeable to tax under this Part whether or not it is from a source in the United Kingdom.

(2) Income arising to a non-UK resident is chargeable to tax under this Part only if it is from a source in the United Kingdom.

(3) References in this section to income which is from a source in the United Kingdom include, in the case of any income which does not have a source, references to income which has a comparable connection to the United Kingdom.

(4) This section is subject to any express or implied provision to the contrary in this Part (or elsewhere in the Income Tax Acts).

CHAPTER 2

INTEREST

Charge to tax on interest

Charge to tax on interest

1.750   **369.**—(1) Income tax is charged on interest.

(2) The following sections extend what is treated as interest for certain purposes—

    section 372 (building society dividends),
    section 373 (open-ended investment company interest distributions),
    section 376 (authorised unit trust interest distributions),
    section 378A (offshore fund distributions)
    section 379 (industrial and provident society payments),
    section 380 (funding bonds),
    section 380A (FSCS payments representing interest), and
    section 381 (discounts).

(3) For exemptions, see in particular—

(a) Chapter 2 of Part 6 (national savings income),

(b) Chapter 3 of Part 6 (income from individual investment plans),

(c) Chapter 4 of Part 6 (SAYE interest),

(d) Chapter 6 of Part 6 (income from FOTRA securities),

(2005 c.5 s.369)

(e) sections 749 to 756A (interest arising from repayment supplements, reserve certificates, damages for personal injury, employees' share schemes, repayments of student loans, the redemption of funding bonds, certain foreign currency securities and interest on certain deposits of victims of National-Socialist persecution, and interest on certain foreign currency securities), and
(f) sections 757 to 767 (interest and royalty payments).

(4) Subsection (1) is also subject to Chapter 3 of Part 12 of ITA 2007 (exemptions for interest on securities to which Chapter 2 of that Part applies).

Income charged

370.—(1) Tax is charged under this Chapter on the full amount of the interest arising in the tax year. 1.751

(2) Subsection (1) is subject to Part 8 (foreign income: special rules).

Person liable

371.—The person liable for any tax charged under this Chapter is the person receiving or entitled to the interest. 1.752

Other income taxed as interest

Building society dividends

372.—(1) Any dividend paid by a building society is treated as interest for the purposes of this Act. 1.753

(2) In this section "dividend" includes any distribution (whether or not described as a dividend).

CHAPTER 3

DIVIDENDS ETC. FROM UK RESIDENT COMPANIES ETC.

Introduction

Contents of Chapter

382.—(1) This Chapter— 1.754
(a) imposes a charge to income tax on dividends and other distributions of UK resident companies (see section 383),
(b) treats dividends as paid in some circumstances (see sections 386 to 391), and
(c) makes special provision where the charge is in respect of shares awarded under an approved share incentive plan (see sections 392 to 396).

355

(2) This Chapter also makes provision about tax credits, tax being treated as paid and reliefs available in respect of certain distributions which applies whether or not the distributions are otherwise dealt with under this Chapter (see sections 397 to 401).

(3) For exemptions from the charge under this Chapter, see in particular—

Chapter 3 of Part 6 (income from individual investment plans),

Chapter 5 of that Part (venture capital trust dividends),

section 770 (amounts applied by SIP trustees acquiring dividend shares or retained for reinvestment), and

section 498 of ITEPA 2003 (no charge on shares ceasing to be subject to SIP in certain circumstances).

(4) In this Chapter "dividends" does not include income treated as arising under section 410 (stock dividends).

Charge to tax on dividends and other distributions

Charge to tax on dividends and other distributions

1.755　　**383.**—(1) Income tax is charged on dividends and other distributions of a UK resident company.

(2) For income tax purposes such dividends and other distributions are to be treated as income.

(3) For the purposes of subsection (2), it does not matter that those dividends and other distributions are capital apart from that subsection.

Income charged

1.756　　**384.**—(1) Tax is charged under this Chapter on the amount or value of the dividends paid and other distributions made in the tax year.

(2) Subsection (1) is subject to—

section 393(2) and (3) (later charge where cash dividends retained in SIPs are paid over), and

section 394(3) (distribution when dividend shares cease to be subject to SIP).

(3) See also section 398 (under which the amount or value of the dividends or other distributions is treated as increased if any person is entitled to a tax credit in respect of them).

Person liable

1.757　　**385.**—(1) The person liable for any tax charged under this Chapter is—

(a) the person to whom the distribution is made or is treated as made (see Part 6 of ICTA and sections 386(3) and 389(3)), or

(b) the person receiving or entitled to the distribution.

(2) Subsection (1) is subject to—

section 393(4) (later charge where cash dividends retained in SIPs are paid over), and

section 394(4) (distribution when dividend shares cease to be subject to SIP).

(2005 c.5 s.402)

CHAPTER 4

DIVIDENDS FROM NON-UK RESIDENT COMPANIES

Charge to tax on dividends from non-UK resident companies

Charge to tax on dividends from non-UK resident companies

402.—(1) Income tax is charged on dividends of a non-UK resident company.

(2) For exemptions, see in particular section 770 (amounts applied by SIP trustees acquiring dividend shares or retained for reinvestment).

(3) Subsection (1) is also subject to section 498 of ITEPA 2003 (no charge on shares ceasing to be subject to SIP in certain circumstances).

(4) In this Chapter "dividends" does not include dividends of a capital nature.

1.758

Income charged

403.—(1) Tax is charged under this Chapter on the full amount of the dividends arising in the tax year.

(2) Subsection (1) is subject to—

section 406(2) and (3) (later charge where cash dividends retained in SIPs are paid over),

section 407(3) (dividend payment when dividend shares cease to be subject to SIP), and

Part 8 (foreign income: special rules).

1.759

Person liable

404.—(1) The person liable for any tax charged under this Chapter is the person receiving or entitled to the dividends.

(2) Subsection (1) is subject to—

section 406(4) (later charge where cash dividends retained in SIPs are paid over), and

section 407(4) (dividend payment when dividend shares cease to be subject to SIP).

1.760

CHAPTER 7

PURCHASED LIFE ANNUITY PAYMENTS

Charge to tax on purchased life annuity payments

422.—(1) Income tax is charged on annuity payments made under a purchased life annuity.

(2) For exemptions, see in particular—

1.761

(a) section 717 (exemption for part of purchased life annuity payments),
(b) section 725 (annual payments under immediate needs annuities),
(c) section 731 (periodical payments of personal injury damages), and
(d) section 732 (compensation awards).

Meaning of "purchased life annuity"

1.762   **423.**—(1) In this Chapter "purchased life annuity" means an annuity—
(a) granted for consideration in money or money's worth in the ordinary course of a business of granting annuities on human life, and
(b) payable for a term ending at a time ascertainable only by reference to the end of a human life.

(2) For this purpose it does not matter that the annuity may in some circumstances end before or after the life.

Income charged

1.763   **424.**—(1) Tax is charged under this Chapter on the full amount of the annuity payments arising in the tax year.

(2) Subsection (1) is subject to Part 8 (foreign income: special rules).

Person liable

1.764   **425.**—The person liable for any tax charged under this Chapter is the person receiving or entitled to the annuity payments.

PART 5

MISCELLANEOUS INCOME

CHAPTER 1

INTRODUCTION

Overview of Part 5

1.765   **574.**—(1) This Part imposes charges to income tax under—
(a) Chapter 2 (receipts from intellectual property),
(b) Chapter 3 (films and sound recordings: non-trade businesses),
(c) Chapter 4 (certain telecommunication rights: non-trading income),
(d) Chapter 5 (settlements: amounts treated as income of settlor),
(e) Chapter 6 (beneficiaries' income from estates in administration),
(f) Chapter 7 (annual payments not otherwise charged), and

(g) Chapter 8 (income not otherwise charged).

(2) Part 6 deals with exemptions from the charges under this Part.

(3) See, in particular, any exemptions mentioned in the Chapters of this Part.

(4) The charges under this Part apply to non-UK residents as well as UK residents but this is subject to section 577(2) (charges on non-UK residents only on UK source income).

(5) This section needs to be read with the relevant priority rules (see sections 2, 575 and 576).

Provisions which must be given priority over Part 5

575.—(1) Any income, so far as it falls within—
  (a) any Chapter of this Part, and
  (b) Chapter 2 of Part 2 (receipts of a trade, profession or vocation),
is dealt with under Part 2.

(2) Any income, so far as it falls within—
  (a) any Chapter of this Part, and
  (b) Chapter 3 of Part 3 so far as the Chapter relates to a UK property business,
is dealt with under Part 3.

(3) Any income, so far as it falls within—
  (a) any Chapter of this Part, and
  (b) Chapter 2 or 3 of Part 4 (interest and dividends etc. from UK resident companies etc.),
is dealt with under the relevant Chapter of Part 4.

(4) Any income, so far as it falls within—
  (a) any Chapter of this Part, and
  (b) Part 2, 9 or 10 of ITEPA 2003 (employment income, pension income or social security income),
is dealt with under the relevant Part of ITEPA 2003.

Priority between Chapters within Part 5

576.—Any income, so far as it falls within Chapter 2 (receipts from intellectual property) and Chapter 3 (films and sound recordings: non-trade businesses), is dealt with under Chapter 3.

CHAPTER 5

SETTLEMENTS: AMOUNTS TREATED AS INCOME OF SETTLOR

Charge to tax under Chapter 5

Charge to tax under Chapter 5

619.—(1) Income tax is charged on—
  (a) income which is treated as income of a settlor as a result of section 624 (income where settlor retains an interest),

(b) income which is treated as income of a settlor as a result of section 629 (income paid to unmarried minor children of settlor),
(c) capital sums which are treated as income of a settlor as a result of section 633 (capital sums paid to settlor by trustees of settlement), and
(d) capital sums which are treated as income of a settlor as a result of section 641 (capital sums paid to settlor by body connected with settlement).

(2) The charge on the settlor under subsection (1)(a) or (b) above operates on distribution income by treating the income as if it were income to which Chapter 2 of Part 2 of ITA 2007 (rates at which income tax is charged) applies as a result of subsection (2)(b) that section (income chargeable under Chapter 3, 5 or 6 of Part 4: etc. from UK resident companies etc. and release of loan to participator in close company).

(3) In subsection (2) "distribution income" means income which represents income received by the trustees of the settlement, or any other person to whom it is payable, which is—
(a) income chargeable under Chapter 3 of Part 4 (dividends etc. from UK resident companies etc.),
(b) income chargeable under Chapter 4 of Part 4 (dividends from non-UK resident companies),
(c) income chargeable under Chapter 5 of Part 4 (stock dividends from UK resident companies),
(d) income chargeable under Chapter 6 of Part 4 (release of loan to participator in close company), or
(e) a relevant foreign distribution chargeable under Chapter 8 of this Part (income not otherwise charged).

(4) In subsection (3) "relevant foreign distribution" means any distribution of a non-UK resident company which—
(a) is not chargeable under Chapter 4 of Part 4, but
(b) would be chargeable under Chapter 3 of that Part if the company were UK resident.

GENERAL NOTE

1.769 The provisions in this chapter are complex but important as they include very wide anti-avoidance provisions that can affect income earners at all levels. They are all applied to the calculation of income for tax credit purposes, and therefore now have a double effect on many middle range income earners who seek to use trusts to cut their incomes. Sections 624–628 contain provisions designed to stop tax avoidance by putting money into a form of trust where the settlor has an interest in the trust, unless it is a trust between spouses or partners, or it is to a charity. Section 629 is a very widely drawn provision that has the effect of transferring back to a settlor any income given by the settlor to an unmarried minor child of the settlor (for example, by putting money in a building society account in the name of the child, or buying National Savings Certificates in the child's name). But see now the tax provisions designed to assist child trust funds, which allow all these provisions to be sidestepped to a limited extent if a child trust fund is used.

Meaning of "settlement" and "settlor"

1.770 **620.**—(1) In this Chapter—
"settlement" includes any disposition, trust, covenant, agreement, or transfer of assets (except that it does not include a charitable loan arrangement), and

"settlor", in relation to a settlement, means any person by whom the settlement was made.

(2) A person is treated for the purposes of this Chapter as having made a settlement if the person has made or entered into the settlement directly or indirectly.

(3) A person is, in particular, treated as having made a settlement if the person—
  (a) has provided funds directly or indirectly for the purpose of the settlement,
  (b) has undertaken to provide funds directly or indirectly for the purpose of the settlement, or
  (c) has made a reciprocal arrangement with another person for the other person to make or enter into the settlement.

(4) This Chapter applies to settlements wherever made.

(5) In this section—

"charitable loan arrangement" means any arrangement so far as it consists of a loan of money made by an individual to a charity either—
  (a) for no consideration, or
  (b) for a consideration which consists only of interest, and

"charity" includes—
  (a) trustees of the National Heritage Memorial Fund
  (b) Historical Buildings and Monuments Commission for England
  (c) National Endowment for Science, Technology and the Arts.

Income charged and person liable

Income charged

621.—Tax is charged under this Chapter on all income and capital sums to which section 619(1) applies.

1.771

Person liable

622.—The person liable for any tax charged under this Chapter is the settlor.

1.772

CHAPTER 8

INCOME NOT OTHERWISE CHARGED

Charge to tax on income not otherwise charged

687.—(1) Income tax is charged under this Chapter on income from any source that is not charged to income tax under or as a result of any other provision of this Act or any other Act.

1.773

(2) Subsection (1) does not apply to annual payments.

(3) Subsection (1) does not apply to income that would be charged to income tax under or as a result of another provision but for an exemption.

(4) The definition of "income" in section 878(1) does not apply for the purposes of this section.

(5) For exemptions from the charge under this Chapter, see in particular—
section 768 (commercial occupation of woodlands), and
section 779 (gains on commodity and financial futures).

Income charged

1.774   **688.**—(1) Tax is charged under this Chapter on the full amount of the income arising in the tax year.
(2) Subsection (1) is subject to—
(a) Chapter 1 of Part 7 (which provides relief on income from the use of furnished accommodation in an individual's only or main residence: see, in particular, sections 794 and 798),
(b) Chapter 2 of that Part (which provides relief on income from the provision by an individual of qualifying care: see, in particular, sections 814 and 817), and
(c) Part 8 (foreign income: special rules).

Person liable

1.775   **689.**—The person liable for any tax charged under this Chapter is the person receiving or entitled to the income.

PART 6

EXEMPT INCOME

CHAPTER 1

INTRODUCTION

Overview of Part 6

1.776   **690.**—(1) This Part provides for certain exemptions from charges to income tax under this Act.
(2) The exemptions are dealt with in—
(a) Chapter 2 (national savings income),
(b) Chapter 3 (income from individual investment plans),
(c) Chapter 4 (SAYE interest),
(d) Chapter 5 (venture capital trust dividends),
(e) Chapter 6 (income from FOTRA securities),
(f) Chapter 7 (purchased life annuity payments),
(g) Chapter 8 (other annual payments), and
(h) Chapter 9 (other income).
(3) Chapter 10 explains that, in general, the effect of the exemptions is that the exempt amounts are ignored for other income tax purposes.
(4) Other exemptions, such as exemptions relating to particular categories of persons, may also be relevant to the charges to income tax under this Act.
(5) And the exemptions dealt with in this Part may themselves be relevant to charges to income tax outside this Act.

(2005 c.5 s.730)

CHAPTER 8

OTHER ANNUAL PAYMENTS

Certain annual payments by individuals

Foreign maintenance payments

730.—(1) No liability to income tax arises under Part 5 in respect of an annual payment if—
(a) it is a maintenance payment,
(b) it arises outside the United Kingdom, and
(c) had it arisen in the United Kingdom it would be exempt from income tax under section 727 (certain annual payments by individuals).

(2) In subsection (1) "maintenance payment" means a periodical payment which meets conditions A and B.

(3) Condition A is that the payment is made under a court order or a written or oral agreement.

(4) Condition B is that the payment is made by a person—
(a) as one of the parties to a marriage [1 or civil partnership] to, or for the benefit of, and for the maintenance of, the other party,
(b) to any person under 21 for that person's own benefit, maintenance or education, or
(c) to any person for the benefit, maintenance or education of a person under 21.

(5) In subsection (4) "marriage" includes a marriage that has been dissolved or annulled, and "civil partnership" includes a civil partnership that has been dissolved or annulled.

(6) Subsection (1) also applies to a payment made by an individual's personal representatives if—
(a) the individual would have been liable to make it, and
(b) that subsection would have applied if the individual had made it.

Periodical payments of personal injury damages etc.

Periodical payments of personal injury damages

731.—(1) No liability to income tax arises for the persons specified in section 733 in respect of periodical payments to which subsection (2) or annuity payments to which subsection (3) applies.

(2) This subsection applies to periodical payments made pursuant to—
(a) an order of the court, so far as it is made in reliance on section 2 of the Damages Act 1996 (c. 48) (periodical payments) (including an order as varied),
(b) an order of a court outside the United Kingdom which is similar to an order made in reliance on that section (including an order as varied),

363

(c) an agreement, so far as it settles a claim or action for damages in respect of personal injury (including an agreement as varied),
(d) an agreement, so far as it relates to making payments on account of damages that may be awarded in such a claim or action (including an agreement as varied), or
(e) a Motor Insurers' Bureau undertaking in relation to a claim or action in respect of personal injury (including an undertaking as varied).

(3) This subsection applies to annuity payments made under an annuity purchased or provided—
(a) by the person by whom payments to which subsection (2) applies would otherwise fall to be made, and
(b) in accordance with such an order, agreement or undertaking as is mentioned in subsection (2) or a varying order, agreement or undertaking.

(4) In this section "damages in respect of personal injury" includes in respect of a person's death from personal injury.

(5) In this section "personal injury" includes disease and impairment of physical or mental condition.

(6) In this section "a Motor Insurers' Bureau undertaking" means an undertaking given by—
(a) the Motor Insurers' Bureau (being the company of that name incorporated on 14th June 1946 under the Companies Act 1929 (c. 23)), or
(b) an Article 75 insurer under the Bureau's Articles of Association.

Compensation awards

1.779

732.—(1) No liability to income tax arises for the persons specified in section 733 in respect of annuity payments if they are made under an annuity purchased or provided under an award of compensation made under the Criminal Injuries Compensation Scheme.

(2) The Treasury may by order provide for sections 731, 733 and 734 to apply, with such modifications as they consider necessary, to periodical payments by way of compensation for personal injury for which provision is made under a scheme or arrangement other than the Criminal Injuries Compensation Scheme.

(3) In this section—
"the Criminal Injuries Compensation Scheme" means—
(a) the schemes established by arrangements made under the Criminal Injuries Compensation Act 1995 (c. 53),
(b) arrangements made by the Secretary of State for compensation for criminal injuries in operation before the commencement of those schemes, or
(c) the scheme established under the Criminal Injuries (Northern Ireland) Order 2002 (S.I. 2002/796) (N.I.1), and
"personal injury" includes disease and impairment of physical or mental condition.

Persons entitled to exemptions for personal injury payments etc.

1.780

733.—The persons entitled to the exemptions given by sections 731(1) and 732(1) for payments are—

(a) the person entitled to the damages under the order, agreement, or to the compensation under the award in question ("A"),
(b) a person who receives the payment in question on behalf of A, and
(c) a trustee who receives the payment in question on trust for the benefit of A under a trust under which A is, while alive, the only person who may benefit.

Payments from trusts for injured persons

734.—(1) No liability to income tax arises for the persons specified in subsection (2) in respect of sums paid under a lifetime trust—
   (a) to the person ("A") who is entitled to—
      (i) a payment under an order, agreement or undertaking within section 731(2) or an annuity purchased or provided as mentioned in section 731(3), or
      (ii) compensation under an award within section 732(1), or
   (b) for the benefit of A.
(2) The persons are—
   (a) A, and
   (b) if subsection (1)(b) applies, a person who receives the sum on behalf of A.
(3) For the purposes of subsection (1), sums are paid under a lifetime trust if they are paid—
   (a) by the trustees of a trust under which A is, while alive, the only person who may benefit, and
   (b) out of payments within section 731(2) or (3) or 732(1) which are received by them on trust for A.

1.781

Health and employment insurance payments

Health and employment insurance payments

735.—(1) No liability to income tax arises under this Act in respect of an annual payment under an insurance policy if—
   (a) the payment is a benefit provided under so much of the policy as insures against a health or employment risk (see section 736),
   (b) no part of any premiums under the policy has been deductible in calculating the income of the insured for income tax purposes, and
   (c) the conditions in sections 737 and 738 and, so far as applicable, in sections 739 and 740 are met in relation to the policy.
(2) Subsection (1)(b) is subject to section 743.
(3) For the meaning of "the insured", see sections 742 and 743(2).

1.782

Health and employment risks and benefits

736.—(1) For the purposes of sections 735 and 737 to 743, a policy insures against a health risk if it insures against the insured becoming, or becoming in any specified way, subject—

1.783

(a) to any physical or mental illness, disability, infirmity or defect, or
(b) to any deterioration in a condition resulting from any such illness, disability, infirmity or defect.

(2) For the purposes of sections 735 and 737 to 743, a policy insures against an employment risk if it insures against circumstances arising as a result of which the insured ceases—
(a) to be employed or hold office, or
(b) to carry on any trade, profession or vocation.

(3) For the purposes of section 735, this section and sections 737 to 743, references to insurance against a risk include insurance providing for benefits payable otherwise than by way of indemnity if the circumstances insured against occur.

Payments to adopters

Payments to adopters, etc.: England and Wales

744.—(1) No liability to income tax arises in respect of the following payments —
  (a) any payment or reward falling within section 57(3) of the Adoption Act 1976 (c. 36) (payments authorised by the court) which is made to a person who has adopted or intends to adopt a child,
  (b) payments under section 57(3A)(a) of that Act (payments by adoption agencies of legal or medical expenses of persons seeking to adopt),
  (c) payments of allowances under regulations under section 57A of that Act (permitted allowances to persons who have adopted or intend to adopt children),
  (d) payments of financial support made in the course of providing adoption support services within the meaning of the Adoption and Children Act 2002 (c. 38) (see section 2(6) and (7) of that Act),
  (e) payments made under regulations under paragraph 3(1) of Schedule 4 to that Act (transitional and transitory provisions: adoption support services),
  (f) payments made under regulations under section 14F of the Children Act 1989 (special guardianship support services) to a person appointed as a child's special guardian,
  (g) payments made to a person under section 17 of that Act (provision of services for children in need, their families and others) by reason of that person being a person in whose favour a residence order with respect to a child is in force,
  (h) payments made to a person, in respect of a child, under paragraph 15 of Schedule 1 to that Act (local authority contribution to child's maintenance to recipients in whose favour residence order is in force), and
  (i) payments made in accordance with—
    (i) an order under that Schedule (orders for financial relief against parents etc), or
    (ii) a maintenance agreement,

(2005 c.5 s.744)

for the benefit of a child, to a person appointed as the child's special guardian or a person in whose favour a residence order with respect to the child is in force.

(2) But a payment is not within subsection (1)(f), (g), (h) or (i) if—
  (a) it is made to an excluded relative of the child,
  (b) it is made to a person appointed as the child's special guardian and an excluded relative is also appointed as the child's special guardian, or
  (c) it is made to a person in whose favour a residence order is in force with respect to the child and that order is also in favour of an excluded relative.

(3) In this section—

"excluded relative", in relation to a child, means—
  (a) a parent of the child, or
  (b) a person who is, or has been, the husband or wife or civil partner of a parent of the child;

"maintenance agreement" has the meaning given by paragraph 10(1) of Schedule 1 to the Children Act 1989;

"residence order" has the meaning given by section 8 of that Act.

Chapter 9

Other Income

Interest on damages for personal injury

751.—(1) No liability to income tax arises in respect of interest on damages for personal injury or death if— 1.785
  (a) it is included in a sum awarded by a court,
  (b) it does not relate to the period between the making and satisfaction of the award, and
  (c) in the case of an award by a court in a country outside the United Kingdom, it is exempt from any charge to tax in that place.

(2) No liability to income tax arises in respect of interest if—
  (a) it is included in a payment in satisfaction of a cause of action (including a payment into court), and
  (b) it would fall within subsection (1) if it were included in a sum awarded by a court in respect of a cause of action.

(3) In subsection (1)—

"damages" in Scotland includes solatium, and

"personal injury" includes disease and impairment of physical or mental condition.

Interest on repayment of student loan

753.—(1) No liability to income tax arises in respect of interest if— 1.786
  (a) it is paid to a person to whom a student loan has been made, and
  (b) it relates to an amount repaid to the person after being recovered from the person in respect of the loan.

(2) In this section "student loan" means a loan made under—
section 22 of the Teaching and Higher Education Act 1998 (c. 30),
section 73(f) of the Education (Scotland) Act 1980 (c. 44), or
Article 3 of the Education (Student Support) (Northern Ireland) Order 1998 (S.I. 1998/1760 (N.I. 14)).

Scholarship income

1.787   **776.**—(1) No liability to income tax arises in respect of income from a scholarship held by an individual in full-time education at a university, college, school or other educational establishment.

(2) This exemption is subject to section 215 of ITEPA 2003 (under which only the scholarship holder is entitled to the exemption if the scholarship is provided by reason of another person's employment).

(3) In this section "scholarship" includes a bursary, exhibition or other similar educational endowment.

Disabled person's vehicle maintenance grant

1.788   **780.**—(1) No liability to income tax arises in respect of a disabled person's vehicle maintenance grant.

(2) For this purpose a "disabled person's vehicle maintenance grant" means a grant to any person owning a vehicle that is made under—
  (a) paragraph 2 of Schedule 2 to the National Health Service Act 1977 (c. 49),
  (b) section 46(3) of the National Health Service (Scotland) Act 1978 (c. 29), or
  (c) Article 30 of the Health and Personal Social Services (Northern Ireland) Order 1972 (S.I. 1972/1265 (N.I. 14)), and Training Act (Northern Ireland) 1950 (c. 29 (N.I.)).

CHAPTER 10

GENERAL

General disregard of exempt income for income tax purposes

1.789   **783.**—(1) Amounts of income which are exempt from income tax as a result of this Part (whether because the type of income concerned is exempt from every charge to income tax or because it is exempt from every charge that is relevant to those particular amounts) are accordingly to be ignored for all other income tax purposes.

(2) An exception to this is that interest on deposits in ordinary accounts with the National Savings Bank which is exempt under this Part from every charge to income tax is not to be ignored for the purpose of providing information.

(3) This express exception to subsection (1) is without prejudice to the existence of any other implied or express exception to that subsection (whether in connection with the provision of information or otherwise).

(2005 c.5 s.784)

Part 7

Income Charged Under this Act: Rent-a-room and Qualifying Care Relief

Chapter 1

Rent-a-room Relief

Introduction

Overview of Chapter 1

784.—(1) This Chapter provides relief on income from the use of furnished accommodation in an individual's only or main residence. The relief is referred to in this Chapter as "rent-a-room relief".

(2) The form of relief depends on whether the individual's total rent-a-room amount exceeds the individual's limit (see sections 788 to 790).

(3) If it does not, the income is not charged to income tax unless the individual elects otherwise (see sections 791 to 794).

(4) If it does, the individual may elect for alternative methods of calculating the income (see sections 795 to 798).

1.790

Person who qualifies for relief

785.—(1) An individual qualifies for rent-a-room relief for a tax year if the individual—
  (a) has rent-a-room receipts for the tax year (see section 786), and
  (b) does not derive any taxable income other than rent-a-room receipts from a relevant trade, letting or agreement.

(2) "Taxable income" means receipts or other income in respect of which the individual is liable to income tax for the tax year.

(3) A relevant trade, letting or agreement is one from which the individual derives rent-a-room receipts for the tax year.

1.791

Basic definitions

Meaning of "rent-a-room receipts"

786.—(1) For the purposes of this Chapter an individual has rent-a-room receipts for a tax year if—
  (a) the receipts are in respect of the use of furnished accommodation in a residence in the United Kingdom or in respect of goods or services supplied in connection with that use,
  (b) they accrue to the individual during the income period for those receipts (see subsections (3) and (4)),
  (c) for some or all of that period the residence is the individual's only or main residence, and

1.792

(d) the receipts would otherwise be brought into account in calculating the profits of a trade or UK property business or chargeable to income tax under Chapter 8 of Part 5 (income not otherwise charged).

(2) Meals, cleaning and laundry are examples of goods or services supplied in connection with the use of furnished accommodation in a residence.

(3) If the receipts would otherwise be brought into account in calculating the profits of a trade, the income period is the basis period for the tax year (see Chapter 15 of Part 2).

(4) Otherwise the income period is the period which—
 (a) begins at the beginning of the tax year or, if later, the beginning of the letting in respect of which the receipts arise, and
 (b) ends at the end of the tax year or, if earlier, the end of that letting.

Meaning of "residence"

1.793 787.—(1) In this Chapter "residence" means—
 (a) a building, or part of a building, occupied or intended to be occupied as a separate residence, or
 (b) a caravan or houseboat.

(2) If a building, or part of a building, designed for permanent use as a single residence is temporarily divided into two or more separate residences, it is still treated as a single residence.

Meaning of "total rent-a-room amount"

1.794 788.—(1) For the purposes of this Chapter an individual's "total rent-a-room amount" for a tax year is the total of—
 (a) the individual's rent-a-room receipts for the tax year, and
 (b) any relevant balancing charges for the tax year (see section 802).

(2) In calculating the total rent-a-room amount, no deduction is allowed for expenses or any other matter.

Individual's limit

The individual's limit

1.795 789.—(1) For the purposes of this Chapter an individual's limit for a tax year depends on whether the individual meets the exclusive receipts condition for the tax year (see section 790).

(2) If the individual does, the individual's limit for the tax year is the basic amount for the tax year.

(3) If the individual does not, the individual's limit for the tax year is half that amount.

(4) The basic amount for a tax year is £4250.

(5) The Treasury may by order amend the sum for the time being specified in subsection (4).

(2005 c.5 s.803)

CHAPTER 2

QUALIFYING CARE RELIEF

Introduction

Overview of Chapter 2

803.—(1) This Chapter provides relief on income from the provision by an individual of qualifying care.
The relief is referred to in this Chapter as "qualifying care relief".
(2) The form of relief depends on whether the individual's total qualifying care receipts exceed the individual's limit (see sections 807 to 811).
(3) If they do not, the income is not charged to income tax (see sections 812 to 814).
(4) If they do, the individual may elect for an alternative method of calculating the income (see sections 815 to 819).
(5) If the qualifying care receipts are the receipts of a trade, special rules apply—
 (a) if the period of account of the trade does not end on 5th April (see sections 820 to 823), and
 (b) in relation to capital allowances (see sections 824 to 827).
(6) The provisions of this Chapter which are expressed to apply in relation to trades also apply in relation to professions and vocations.

Person who qualifies for relief

804.—(1) An individual qualifies for qualifying care relief for a tax year if the individual—
 (a) has qualifying care receipts for the tax year (see section 805), and
 (b) does not derive any taxable income, other than qualifying care receipts, from a relevant trade or arrangement.
(2) "Taxable income" means receipts or other income in respect of which the individual is liable to income tax for the tax year.
(3) A relevant trade or arrangement is one from which the individual derives qualifying care receipts for the tax year.
(4) Subsection (1) is subject to section 804A.

Shared lives care: further condition for relief

804A.—(1) This section applies if an individual ("N") has qualifying care receipts for a tax year in respect of the provision of shared lives care.
(2) N does not qualify for qualifying care relief in respect of those receipts if the placement cap is exceeded for the residence (or any of the residences) used by N to provide the care from which those receipts are derived.
(3) The placement cap is exceeded for a residence if, at any given time during the relevant period, shared lives care is being provided there (whether by N or anyone else) for more than 3 people in total.
(4) The relevant period, in relation to a residence, is the period for which the residence is N's only or main residence during the income period for the receipts (see section 805).

1.796

1.797

1.798

(5) If the placement cap is so exceeded but N also has qualifying care receipts for the tax year in respect of the provision of foster care, this Chapter is to apply to N for the tax year as if—
(a) references to qualifying care were to foster care, and
(b) accordingly, references (other than in this section) to qualifying care receipts did not include receipts in respect of the provision of shared lives care.

(6) In determining the number of people for whom shared lives care is being provided at any given time, brothers and sisters (including half-brothers and half-sisters) count as one person.

Basic definitions

Meaning of "qualifying care receipts"

1.799   **805.**—(1) For the purposes of this Chapter an individual has foster-care receipts for a tax year if—
(a) the receipts are in respect of the provision of qualifying care,
(b) they accrue to the individual during the income period for those receipts (see subsections (2) and (3)), and
(c) the receipts would otherwise be brought into account in calculating the profits of a trade or chargeable to income tax under Chapter 8 of Part 5 (income not otherwise charged).

(2) If the receipts would otherwise be brought into account in calculating the profits of a trade, the income period is the basis period for the tax year (see Chapter 15 of Part 2).

(3) Otherwise the income period is the tax year.

Meaning of providing qualifying care

1.800   **805A.**—For the purposes of this Chapter qualifying care is provided if an individual (alone or in partnership) provides—
(a) foster care but not shared lives care,
(b) shared lives care but not foster care, or
(c) both foster care and shared lives care.

Meaning of providing foster care

1.801   **806.**—(1) For the purposes of this Chapter foster care is provided if an individual—
(a) provides accommodation and maintenance for a child, and
(b) does so as a foster carer.

(2) An individual is a foster carer if the child is placed with the individual under any of the following enactments, unless the individual is excluded by subsection (5).

(3) The enactments are—
(a) section 23(2)(a) or 59(1)(a) of the Children Act 1989 (c. 41) (provision of accommodation for children by local authorities or voluntary organisations),
(b) regulations under section 5 of the Social Work (Scotland) Act 1968 (c. 49),
(c) section 70 of the Children (Scotland) Act 1995 (c. 36), and

(d) Article 27(2)(a) or 75(1)(a) of the Children (Northern Ireland) 1995 (S.I. 1995/755 (N.I. 2)) (provision of accommodation for children by authorities or voluntary organisations).

(4) An individual is also a foster carer if—
(a) the individual is approved as a foster carer by a local authority or a voluntary organisation in accordance with regulations under section 5 of the Social Work (Scotland) Act 1968 (c. 49), and
(b) the child in respect of whom the accommodation is provided is being "looked after" by a local authority within the meaning of section 17(6) of the Children (Scotland) Act 1995 (c. 36), unless the individual is excluded by subsection (5).

(5) The following are excluded individuals—
(a) a parent of the child,
(b) an individual who is not a parent of the child but who has parental responsibility (or, in Scotland, parental responsibilities) in relation to the child,
(c) if the child is in care and there was a residence order in force with respect to the child immediately before the care order was made, an individual in whose favour the residence order was made, and
(d) (in Scotland) if the child is in care and there was a residence order or contact order in force with respect to the child immediately before the child was placed in care, an individual in whose favour the residence order or contact order was made.

Meaning of providing shared lives care

806A.—(1) For the purposes of this Chapter shared lives care is provided by an individual if—
(a) the individual provides accommodation and care for an adult or child ("X") who has been placed with the individual, and
(b) the conditions in subsection (2) are met.

(2) The conditions are—
(a) the accommodation is in the individual's own home,
(b) the accommodation and care are provided on the basis that X will share the individual's home and daily family life during the placement,
(c) the placement is made under a specified social care scheme,
(d) the individual does not provide the accommodation and care as a foster carer, and
(e) the individual is not excluded within the meaning of section 806(5).

(3) Section 806(5) has effect for the purposes of subsection (2)(e) as if references to the child were to X (whatever X's age).

(4) "Specified social care scheme" means a social care scheme of a kind specified or described in an order made by the Treasury.

(5) An order under subsection (4) may make provision having effect in relation to the tax year current on the day on which the order is made.

(6) In this section—
"care" means personal care, including assistance and support;
"home" means an individual's only or main residence;
"social care scheme" means a scheme, service or arrangement for those who, by reason of age, illness, disability or other vulnerability, are in need of care.

Meaning of "residence"

1.803 806B.—(1) In this Chapter "residence" means—
(a) a building, or part of a building, occupied or intended to be occupied as a separate residence, or
(b) a caravan or houseboat.
(2) If a building, or part of a building, designed for permanent use as a single residence is temporarily divided into two or more separate residences, it is still treated as a single residence.

PART 10

GENERAL PROVISIONS

CHAPTER 1

INTRODUCTION

Overview of Part 10

1.804 864.—This Part—
(a) contains general rules which are of wider application than to a particular Part of this Act including certain calculation rules (see Chapter 2), and
(b) deals with supplementary matters including general definitions (see Chapter 3).

Social security contributions

Social security contributions: non-trades etc.

1.805 868.—(1) This section applies for the purpose of calculating profits or other income charged to income tax.
(2) For this purpose "profits or other income" does not include—
(a) the profits of a trade, profession, or vocation,
(b) the profits of a property business, or
(c) employment income,
but see subsection (6).
(3) No deduction is allowed for any contribution paid by any person under—
(a) Part 1 of the Social Security Contributions and Benefits Act 1992 (c.4), or
(b) Part 1 of the Social Security Contributions and Benefits (Northern Ireland) Act 1992 (c.7).
(4) But this prohibition does not apply to an employer's contribution.
(5) For this purpose "an employer's contribution" means—
(a) a secondary Class 1 contribution,
(b) a Class 1A contribution, or
(c) a Class 1B contribution,

(2005 c.5 s.868)

within the meaning of Part 1 of the Social Security Contributions and Benefits Act 1992 (c.4) or of the Social Security Contributions and Benefits (Northern Ireland) Act 1992 (c.7).

(6) Provision corresponding to that made by this section is made by—
  (a) section 53 (in relation to trades, professions and vocations),
  (b) section 272 (in relation to property businesses), and
  (c) section 360A of ITEPA 2003 (in relation to employment income).

Commissioners for Revenue and Customs Act 2005

(2005 c.11)

Arrangement of Sections

Commissioners and officers

1. The Commissioners
2. Officers of Revenue and Customs
3. Declaration of confidentiality
4. Her Majesty's Revenue and Customs

Functions

5. Commissioners' initial functions
7. Former Inland Revenue matters
9. Ancillary powers

Exercise of functions

12. Commissioners' arrangements
13. Exercise of Commissioners' functions by officers
14. Delegation

Information

17. Use of information
18. Confidentiality
23. Freedom of information

Offences

31. Obstruction
32. Assault
33. Power of arrest

General

50. Consequential amendments, &c.

Schedule 1 Former Inland Revenue Matters

INTRODUCTION AND GENERAL NOTE

1.807
This Act provides the necessary statutory machinery to bring about a major restructuring of the policy formation and administration of all UK taxes and of the tax credits, benefits and other matters formerly administered by the Commissioners (or Board) of Inland Revenue and the Commissioners of HM Customs and Excise. Although this may seem a major reform in the British context as it abolishes the oldest British government department, it is perhaps a catching-up exercise with others. The UK is the last of the EU states to bring together the collection of its direct and indirect taxes. The process was not simply a merger. The central policy teams of both the Inland Revenue and Customs and Excise were transferred to the Treasury, uniting the previously divided fiscal policy teams. Law enforcement has also been transferred elsewhere. The Act creates a separate Revenue and Customs Prosecution Office (under provisions not set out in this book), while some enforcement officers were transferred to the new Serious Crimes agency.

The opportunity was also taken to start the process of rationalising the powers of the previous two Departments, reflecting a process of integration that started some time before the formal merger took place in April 2005. The Inland Revenue Regulation Act 1890, set out in previous editions of this volume, has been repealed in entirety as have other administrative provisions dealing with the two Departments. Like its predecessors, the new Department, formally known as Her Majesty's Revenue and Customs (or HMRC), is headed by a body of Commissioners and not Ministers of the Crown. But for legal purposes the Commissioners for Revenue and Customs (as they are known) together are deemed to be a Minister of the Crown. As part of the merger, the hallowed (if not revered) status of Her Majesty's Inspector of Taxes has gone, as have other separate roles for individual officers of the two Departments. Instead, they now become "officers of Revenue and Customs"—though we doubt that the old practice of using initials (HMIT) will be used for the new name! One result is that the past custom of having the names of individual inspectors of tax on the names of court and tribunal cases has ended. All new tax, duty, tax credit and benefit cases will be taken in the name of HM Revenue and Customs.

The Act provides the relevant authority for HMRC to take over all existing responsibilities from the previous Boards and officers and for all necessary changes to be read into Acts of Parliament and subordinate legislation. We have adopted those revisions in this volume. References to "the Board" (meaning the Board of Inland Revenue) are therefore replaced by references to "the Commissioners", and references to "an officer of the Board" or similar by references to "an officer of Revenue and Customs". This will have the incidental effect of standardising widely variant language in past Acts. Further, wide powers of delegation are contained in this Act. In practice powers will be given to "the Commissioners" or "an officer of Revenue and Customs". But the former has authority to delegate almost all its functions to officers. An example of this delegation being standard practice is the delegation under the Tax Credits Act 2002. This Act replaces s.2 of that Act and, in effect, reads this Act into the administrative provisions relevant to that Act.

The Act was intended to come into effect on April 1, 2005, the beginning of the financial and tax year. The start was delayed a few days by the process leading up to the general election in May, but in effect HMRC may be regarded as being established with effect from the beginning of the 2005 tax year.

Commissioners and officers

The Commissioners

1.808
1.—(1) Her Majesty may by Letters Patent appoint Commissioners for Her Majesty's Revenue and Customs.

(2) The Welsh title of the Commissioners shall be Comisynwyr Cyllid a Thollau Ei Mawrhydi.

(3) A Commissioner—
(a) may resign by notice in writing to the Treasury, and
(b) otherwise, shall hold office in accordance with the terms and conditions of his appointment (which may include provision for dismissal).

(4) In exercising their functions, the Commissioners act on behalf of the Crown.

(5) Service as a Commissioner is service in the civil service of the State.

Officers of Revenue and Customs

2.—(1) The Commissioners may appoint staff, to be known as officers of Revenue and Customs.

(2) A person shall hold and vacate office as an officer of Revenue and Customs in accordance with the terms of his appointment (which may include provision for dismissal).

(3) An officer of Revenue and Customs shall comply with directions of the Commissioners (whether he is exercising a function conferred on officers of Revenue and Customs or exercising a function on behalf of the Commissioners).

(4) Anything (including anything in relation to legal proceedings) by or in relation to one officer of Revenue and Customs may be continued by or in relation to another.

(5) Appointments under subsection (1) may be made only with the approval of the Minister for the Civil Service as to terms and conditions of service.

(6) Service in the employment of the Commissioners is service in the civil service of the State.

(7) In Schedule 1 to the Interpretation Act 1978 (c. 30) (defined expressions) at the appropriate place insert—
" 'Officer of Revenue and Customs' has the meaning given by section 2(1) of the Commissioners for Revenue and Customs Act 2005."

Declaration of confidentiality

3.—(1) Each person who is appointed under this Act as a Commissioner or officer of Revenue and Customs shall make a declaration acknowledging his obligation of confidentiality under section 18.

(2) A declaration under subsection (1) shall be made—
(a) as soon as is reasonably practicable following the person's appointment, and
(b) in such form, and before such a person, as the Commissioners may direct.

(3) For the purposes of this section, the renewal of a fixed term appointment shall not be treated as an appointment.

"Her Majesty's Revenue and Customs"

4.—(1) The Commissioners and the officers of Revenue and Customs may together be referred to as Her Majesty's Revenue and Customs.

(2) The Welsh title of the Commissioners and the officers of Revenue and Customs together shall be Cyllid a Thollau Ei Mawrhydi.

(3) In Schedule 1 to the Interpretation Act 1978 (defined expressions) at the appropriate place insert—

" 'Her Majesty's Revenue and Customs' has the meaning given by section 4 of the Commissioners for Revenue and Customs Act 2005."

Functions

Commissioners' initial functions

5.—(1) The Commissioners shall be responsible for—
(a) the collection and management of revenue for which the Commissioners of Inland Revenue were responsible before the commencement of this section, and
(b) the collection and management of revenue for which the Commissioners of Customs and Excise were responsible before the commencement of this section, and
(c) the payment and management of tax credits for which the Commissioners of Inland Revenue were responsible before the commencement of this section.

(2) The Commissioners shall also have all the other functions which before the commencement of this section vested in—
(a) the Commissioners of Inland Revenue (or in a Commissioner), or
(b) the Commissioners of Customs and Excise (or in a Commissioner).

(3) This section is subject to section 35.

(4) In this Act "revenue" includes taxes, duties and national insurance contributions.

Former Inland Revenue matters

7.—(1) This section applies to the matters listed in Schedule 1.

(2) A function conferred by an enactment (in whatever terms) on any of the persons specified in subsection (3) shall by virtue of this subsection vest in an officer of Revenue and Customs—
(a) if or in so far as it relates to a matter to which this section applies, and
(b) in so far as the officer is exercising a function (whether or not by virtue of paragraph (a)) which relates to a matter to which this section applies.

(3) Those persons are—
(a) an officer of the Commissioners of Inland Revenue,
(b) an officer of the Board of Inland Revenue,
(c) an officer of inland revenue,
(d) a collector of Inland Revenue,
(e) an inspector of taxes,
(f) a collector of taxes,
(g) a person authorised to act as an inspector of taxes or collector of taxes for specific purposes,
(h) an officer having powers in relation to tax,
(i) a revenue official,
(j) a person employed in relation to Inland Revenue (or "the Inland Revenue"), and

(k) an Inland Revenue official.

(4) In so far as an officer of Revenue and Customs is exercising a function which relates to a matter to which this section applies, section 6(1) shall not apply.

(5) This section is subject to section 35.

Ancillary powers

9.—(1) The Commissioners may do anything which they think—
(a) necessary or expedient in connection with the exercise of their functions, or
(b) incidental or conducive to the exercise of their functions.

(2) This section is subject to section 35.

Commissioners' arrangements

12.—(1) The Commissioners shall make arrangements for—
(a) the conduct of their proceedings, and
(b) the conduct of the proceedings of any committee established by them.

(2) Arrangements under subsection (1) may, in particular—
(a) make provision for a quorum at meetings;
(b) provide that a function of the Commissioners—
 (i) may be exercised by two Commissioners, or
 (ii) may be exercised by a specified number of Commissioners (greater than two).

(3) A decision to make arrangements under subsection (1) must be taken with the agreement of more than half of the Commissioners holding office at the time.

Exercise of Commissioners' functions by officers

13.—(1) An officer of Revenue and Customs may exercise any function of the Commissioners.

(2) But subsection (1)—
(a) does not apply to the functions specified in subsection (3), and
(b) is subject to directions under section 2(3) and arrangements under section 12.

(3) The non-delegable functions mentioned in subsection (2)(a) are—
(a) making, by statutory instrument, regulations, rules or an order,
(b) approving an application for a warrant to search premises under section 20C of the Taxes Management Act 1970 (c. 9),
(c) approving an application for a warrant to enter premises under Part 7 of Schedule 13 to the Finance Act 2003 (c. 14), and
(d) giving instructions for the disclosure of information under section 20(1)(a), except that an officer of Revenue and Customs may give an instruction under section 20(1)(a) authorising disclosure of specified information relating to—
 (i) one or more specified persons,
 (ii) one or more specified transactions, or
 (iii) specified goods.

General Note

Subsections (3)(b) and (c) are to be repealed with effect from a date to be ordered by HM Treasury (Finance Act 2007 s.84 and Sch.27, Pt 5).

Delegation

1.818 14.—(1) Arrangements under section 12 may, in particular, enable the Commissioners,
or a number of Commissioners acting in accordance with arrangements by virtue of section 12(2)(b), to delegate a function of the Commissioners, other than a function specified in subsection (2) below—
  (a) to a single Commissioner,
  (b) to a committee established by the Commissioners (which may include persons who are neither Commissioners nor staff of the Commissioners nor officers of Revenue and Customs), or
  (c) to any other person.
(2) The non-delegable functions mentioned in subsection (1) are—
  (a) making, by statutory instrument, regulations, rules or an order, Commissioners for Revenue and Customs Act 2005
  (b) approving an application for a warrant to search premises under section 20C of the Taxes Management Act 1970, and
  (c) approving an application for a warrant to enter premises under Part 7 of Schedule 13 to the Finance Act 2003.
(3) The Commissioners may not delegate the function under section 20(1)(a) except to a single Commissioner.
(4) The delegation of a function by virtue of subsection (1) by the Commissioners or a number of Commissioners—
  (a) shall not prevent the exercise of the function by the Commissioners or those Commissioners, and
  (b) shall not, subject to express provision to the contrary in directions under section 2(3) or arrangements under section 12, prevent the exercise of the function by an officer of Revenue and Customs.
(5) Where the Commissioners or a number of Commissioners delegate a function
to a person by virtue of subsection (1)(c)—
  (a) the Commissioners or those Commissioners shall monitor the exercise of the function by that person, and
  (b) in the exercise of the function the delegate shall comply with any directions of the Commissioners or of those Commissioners.

GENERAL NOTE

1.819 This section has been added to this edition of the volume because of the use made by HMRC of s.14(1)(c). With effect from 2014, HMRC appointed SYNNEX-Concentrix UK Ltd, a wholly owned subsidiary of the US listed corporation SYNNEX Corporation, to act on its behalf in checking individual tax credits claims and awards. Concentrix is stated to have been authorised to make tax credit checks with claimants, employers and others on behalf of HMRC. According to the statement on the GOV.UK contract finder, the contract is for three years from May 6, 2014. The purpose of the contract is to provide HMRC with additional capacity and capability "to correct working tax credit claims that are potentially running with incorrect information . . . The price paid for the services will be based on commission on the losses prevented; which are estimated to be between £55 million to £75 million." The website sets out some further details of the contract. It is not clear how far that amounts to directions for the purpose of subs.(5).

(2005 c.11 s.16A)

Charter of standards and values

16A.—(1) The Commissioners must prepare a Charter.
(2) The Charter must include standards of behaviour and values to which Her Majesty's Revenue and Customs will aspire when dealing with people in the exercise of their functions.
(3) The Commissioners must –
(a) regularly review the Charter, and
(b) publish revisions, or revised versions, of it when they consider it appropriate to do so.
(4) The Commissioners must, at least once every year, make a report reviewing the extent to which Her Majesty's Revenue and Customs have demonstrated the standards of behaviour and values included in the Charter.]

Information

Use of information

17.—(1) Information acquired by the Revenue and Customs in connection with a function may be used by them in connection with any other function.
(2) Subsection (1) is subject to any provision which restricts or prohibits the use of information and which is contained in—
(a) this Act,
(b) any other enactment, or
(c) an international or other agreement to which the United Kingdom or Her Majesty's Government is party.
(3) In subsection (1) "the Revenue and Customs" means—
(a) the Commissioners,
(b) an officer of Revenue and Customs,
(c) a person acting on behalf of the Commissioners or an officer of Revenue and Customs,
(d) a committee established by the Commissioners,
(e) a member of a committee established by the Commissioners,
(f) the Commissioners of Inland Revenue (or any committee or staff of theirs or anyone acting on their behalf),
(g) the Commissioners of Customs and Excise (or any committee or staff of theirs or anyone acting on their behalf), and
(h) a person specified in section 6(2) or 7(3).
(4) In subsection (1) "function" means a function of any of the persons listed in subsection (3).
(5) In subsection (2) the reference to an enactment does not include—
(a) an Act of the Scottish Parliament or an instrument made under such an Act, or
(b) an Act of the Northern Ireland Assembly or an instrument made under such an Act.
(6) Part 2 of Schedule 2 (which makes provision about the supply and other use of information in specified circumstances) shall have effect.

Confidentiality

18.—(1) Revenue and Customs officials may not disclose information which is held by the Revenue and Customs in connection with a function of the Revenue and Customs.

(2) But subsection (1) does not apply to a disclosure—
(a) which—
    (i) is made for the purposes of a function of the Revenue and Customs, and
    (ii) does not contravene any restriction imposed by the Commissioners,
(b) which is made in accordance with section 20 or 21,
(c) which is made for the purposes of civil proceedings (whether or not within the United Kingdom) relating to a matter in respect of which the Revenue and Customs have functions,
(d) which is made for the purposes of a criminal investigation or criminal proceedings (whether or not within the United Kingdom) relating to a matter in respect of which the Revenue and Customs have functions,
(e) which is made in pursuance of an order of a court,
(f) which is made to Her Majesty's Inspectors of Constabulary, the Scottish inspectors or the Northern Ireland inspectors for the purpose of an inspection by virtue of section 27,
(g) which is made to the Independent Police Complaints Commission, or a person acting on its behalf, for the purpose of the exercise of a function by virtue of section 28, or
(h) which is made with the consent of each person to whom the information relates.
(3) Subsection (1) is subject to any other enactment permitting disclosure.
(4) In this section—
(a) a reference to Revenue and Customs officials is a reference to any person who is or was—
    (i) a Commissioner,
    (ii) an officer of Revenue and Customs,
    (iii) a person acting on behalf of the Commissioners or an officer of Revenue and Customs, or
    (iv) a member of a committee established by the Commissioners,
(b) a reference to the Revenue and Customs has the same meaning as in section 17,
(c) a reference to a function of the Revenue and Customs is a reference to a function of—
    (i) the Commissioners, or
    (ii) an officer of Revenue and Customs,
(d) a reference to the Scottish inspectors or the Northern Ireland inspectors has the same meaning as in section 27, and
(e) a reference to an enactment does not include—
    (i) an Act of the Scottish Parliament or an instrument made under such an Act, or
    (ii) an Act of the Northern Ireland Assembly or an instrument made under such an Act.

Freedom of information

1.823 **23.**—(1) Revenue and customs information relating to a person, the disclosure of which is prohibited by section 18(1), is exempt information by virtue of section 44(1)(a) of the Freedom of Information Act 2000 (c. 36) (prohibitions on disclosure) if its disclosure—

(a) would specify the identity of the person to whom the information relates, or
(b) would enable the identity of such a person to be deduced.

(2) Except as specified in subsection (1), information the disclosure of which is prohibited by section 18(1) is not exempt information for the purposes of section 44(1)(a) of the Freedom of Information Act 2000.

(3) In subsection (1) "revenue and customs information relating to a person" has the same meaning as in section 19.

Obstruction

31.—(1) A person commits an offence if without reasonable excuse he obstructs—
(a) an officer of Revenue and Customs,
(b) a person acting on behalf of the Commissioners or an officer of Revenue and Customs, or
(c) a person assisting an officer of Revenue and Customs.

(2) A person guilty of an offence under this section shall be liable on summary conviction to—
(a) imprisonment for a period not exceeding 51 weeks,
(b) a fine not exceeding level 3 on the standard scale, or
(c) both.

(3) In the application of this section to Scotland or Northern Ireland the reference in subsection (2)(a) to 51 weeks shall be taken as a reference to six months.

Assault

32.—(1) A person commits an offence if he assaults an officer of Revenue and Customs.

(2) A person guilty of an offence under this section shall be liable on summary conviction to—
(a) imprisonment for a period not exceeding 51 weeks,
(b) a fine not exceeding level 5 on the standard scale, or
(c) both.

(3) In the application of this section to Scotland or Northern Ireland the reference in subsection (2)(a) to 51 weeks shall be taken as a reference to six months.

Power of arrest

33.—(1) An authorised officer of Revenue and Customs may arrest a person without warrant if the officer reasonably suspects that the person—
(a) has committed an offence under section 30, 31 or 32,
(b) is committing an offence under any of those sections, or
(c) is about to commit an offence under any of those sections.

(2) In subsection (1) "authorised" means authorised by the Commissioners.

(3) Authorisation for the purposes of this section may be specific or general.

(4) In Scotland or Northern Ireland, a constable may arrest a person without warrant if the constable reasonably suspects that the person—
(a) has committed an offence under this Act,
(b) is committing an offence under this Act, or
(c) is about to commit an offence under this Act.

General

Consequential amendments, &c.

1.827   **50.**—(1) In so far as is appropriate in consequence of section 5 a reference in an enactment, instrument or other document to the Commissioners of Customs and Excise, to customs and excise or to the Commissioners of Inland Revenue (however expressed) shall be taken as a reference to the Commissioners for Her Majesty's Revenue and Customs.

(2) In so far as is appropriate in consequence of sections 6 and 7 a reference in an enactment, instrument or other document to any of the persons specified in section 6(2) or 7(3) (however expressed) shall be taken as a reference to an officer of Revenue and Customs.

SCHEDULE 1

FORMER INLAND REVENUE MATTERS

1.828
1 Capital gains tax.
2 Charities.
3 Child benefit.
4 Child tax credit.
5 Child trust funds.
6 Corporation tax (and amounts assessable or chargeable as if they were corporation tax).
7 Guardian's allowance.
8 Income tax.
9 Inheritance tax.
10 The issue of bank notes.
11 National insurance contributions.
12 The National Insurance Fund.
13 The national minimum wage.
14 Oil and gas royalties.
15 Payment of or in lieu of rates.
16 Payment in lieu of tax reliefs, in so far as the Commissioners of Inland Revenue were responsible before the commencement of section 5.
17 Pension schemes.
18 Petroleum revenue tax.
19 Rating lists.
20 Recovery of taxes due in other member States, in relation to matters corresponding to those for which the Commissioners of Inland Revenue were responsible before the commencement of section 5.
21 Stamp duty.
22 Stamp duty land tax.
23 Stamp duty reserve tax.
24 Statutory adoption pay.
25 Statutory maternity pay.
26 Statutory paternity pay.
27 Statutory sick pay.
28 Student loans.

(2005 c.11 Sch.1)

29   Valuation lists in relation to council tax.
30   Valuation of property.
31   Working tax credit.

Income Tax Act 2007

(2007 c.3)

ARRANGEMENT OF SELECTED SECTIONS

PART 1

OVERVIEW

1.	Overview of Income Tax Acts	1.829
2.	Overview of Act	

PART 2

BASIC PROVISIONS

CHAPTER 1

CHARGES TO INCOME TAX

3.   Overview of charges to income tax
4.   Income tax an annual tax

PART 14

INCOME TAX LIABILITY: MISCELLANEOUS RULES

CHAPTER 2

RESIDENCE

829.   Residence of individuals temporarily abroad
830.   Residence of individuals working abroad
831.   Foreign income of individuals in the United Kingdom for a temporary purpose
832.   Employment income of individuals in the United Kingdom for a temporary purpose

Income Tax Act 2007

CHAPTER 3

JOINTLY HELD PROPERTY

836. Jointly held property
837. Jointly held property: declarations of unequal beneficial interests

PART 16

INCOME TAX ACT DEFINITIONS, ETC

CHAPTER 1

DEFINITIONS

988. Overview of Chapter
989. The definitions
992. Meaning of "company"

CHAPTER 2

OTHER INCOME TAX ACTS PROVISIONS

1011. References to married persons, or civil partners, living together

(SCHEDULES OMITTED)

INTRODUCTION AND GENERAL NOTE

1.830 This Act came into effect on April 6, 2007. It is the fourth of the Acts produced as part of the Tax Law Rewrite Project. It brings to a close the complete rewrite of all primary legislation dealing with income tax save only for the areas (not relevant to this work) listed in s.1 below. As s.1 signposts, it is to be read with ITEPA and ITTOIA. Save as mentioned in that section, all the parts of the Income and Corporation Taxes Act 1988 that referred to income tax have now been repealed and replaced. The extracts from that Act previously in this volume have therefore been deleted. Only a few sections from this Act are relevant to this work, but s.2 is included to show the full and extensive contents of the Act. As with the other Tax Law Rewrite Acts, an extensive explanatory note (running for this Act to three volumes) was published with the Act. Anyone wishing to consider any reference to the Act further should look at that note as a starting point.

(2007 c.3 s.1)

Part 1

Overview

Overview of Income Tax Acts

1.—(1) The following Acts make provision about income tax—   1.831
 (a) ITEPA 2003 (which is about charges to tax on employment income, pension income and social security income and makes provision for the high income child benefit charge),
 (b) ITTOIA 2005 (which is about charges to tax on trading income, property income, savings and investment income and some other miscellaneous income), and
 (c) this Act (which contains the other main provisions about income tax).
(2) There are also provisions about income tax elsewhere: see in particular—
 (a) Part 18 of ICTA (double taxation relief),
 (b) CAA 2001 (allowances for capital expenditure), and
 (c) Part 4 of FA 2004 (pension schemes etc).
(3) Schedule 1 to the Interpretation Act 1978 (c.30) defines "the Income Tax Acts" (as all enactments relating to income tax).

Overview of Act

2.— (1) This Act has 17 Parts.   1.832
(2) Part 2 contains basic provisions about income tax including-
 (a) provision about the annual nature of income tax (Chapter 1),
 (b) the rates at which income tax is charged (Chapter 2), and
 (c) the calculation of income tax liability (Chapter 3).
(3) Part 3 is about taxpayers' personal reliefs including—
 (a) personal allowances (Chapter 2),
 (b) blind persons' allowances (Chapter 2), and
 (c) tax reductions for married couples and civil partners (Chapter 3).
(4) Part 4 is about loss relief including relief for—
 (a) trade losses (Chapters 2 and 3),
 (b) losses from property businesses (Chapter 4),
 (c) losses in an employment or office (Chapter 5),
 (d) losses on disposal of shares (Chapter 6), and
 (e) losses from miscellaneous transactions (Chapter 7).
(5) Part 5 is about relief under the enterprise investment scheme.
(6) Part 6 is about—
 (a) relief for investment in venture capital trusts, and
 (b) other matters relating to venture capital trusts.
(7) Part 7 is about community investment tax relief.
(8) Part 8 is about a variety of reliefs including relief for—
 (a) interest payments (Chapter 1),
 (b) gifts to charity including gift aid (Chapters 2 and 3),
 (c) annual payments and patent royalties (Chapter 4), and
 (d) maintenance payments (Chapter 5).
(9) Part 9 contains special rules about settlements and trustees including—

(a) general provision about settlements and trustees (Chapter 2),
(b) special income tax rates for trusts (Chapters 3, 4, 5 and 6),
(c) rules about trustees' expenses (Chapters 4 and 8),
(d) rules about trustees' discretionary payments (Chapter 7),
(e) rules about unauthorised unit trusts (Chapter 9), and
(f) rules about heritage maintenance settlements (Chapter 10).

(10) Part 10 contains special rules about charitable trusts etc.

(11) Part 11 is about manufactured payments and repos.

(12) Part 12 is about accrued income profits.

(13) Part 13 is about tax avoidance in relation to—
(a) transactions in securities (Chapter 1),
(b) transfers of assets abroad (Chapter 2),
(c) transactions in land (Chapter 3),
(d) sales of occupation income (Chapter 4), and
(e) trade losses (Chapter 5).

(14) Part 14 deals with some miscellaneous rules about income tax liability, including—
(a) limits on liability to income tax for non-UK residents (Chapter 1),
(b) special rules about residence (Chapter 2), and
(c) rules about jointly held property (Chapter 3).

(15) Part 15 is about the deduction of income tax at source.

(16) Part 16 contains definitions which apply for the purposes of the Income Tax Acts and other general provisions which apply for the purposes of those Acts.

(17) Part 17—
(a) contains provisions to be used in interpreting this Act,
(b) introduces Schedule 1 (minor and consequential amendments),
(c) introduces Schedule 2 (transitional provisions and savings),
(d) introduces Schedule 3 (repeals and revocations, including of spent enactments),
(e) introduces Schedule 4 (index of defined expressions that apply for the purposes of this Act),
(f) confers powers on the Treasury to make orders, and
(g) makes provision about the coming into force of this Act.

PART 2

BASIC PROVISIONS

CHAPTER 1

CHARGES TO INCOME TAX

Overview of charges to income tax

1.833   **3.**—(1) Income tax is charged under—
(a) Part 2 of ITEPA 2003 (employment income),
(b) Part 9 of ITEPA 2003 (pension income),
(c) Part 10 of ITEPA 2003 (social security income),

(d) Part 2 of ITTOIA 2005 (trading income),
(e) Part 3 of ITTOIA 2005 (property income),
(f) Part 4 of ITTOIA 2005 (savings and investment income), and
(g) Part 5 of ITTOIA 2005 (miscellaneous income).
(2) Income tax is also charged under other provisions, including—
(a) Chapter 5 of Part 4 of FA 2004 (registered pension schemes: tax charges),
(b) section 7 of F(No.2)A 2005 (social security pension lump sums),
(c) Part 10 of this Act (special rules about charitable trusts etc),
(d) Chapter 2 of Part 12 of this Act (accrued income profits), and
(e) Part 13 of this Act (tax avoidance).

Income tax an annual tax

4.—(1) Income tax is charged for a year only if an Act so provides.
(2) A year for which income tax is charged is called a "tax year".
(3) A tax year begins on 6 April and ends on the following 5 April.
(4) "The tax year 2007–08" means the tax year beginning on 6 April 2007 (and any corresponding expression in which two years are similarly mentioned is to be read in the same way).
(5) Every assessment to income tax must be made for a tax year.
(6) Subsection (5) is subject to Chapter 15 of Part 15 (by virtue of which an assessment may relate to a return period).

GENERAL NOTE

The Rewrite Acts retain the long-standing approach of providing framework legislation for income tax. It is the relevant section in each year's Finance Act that actually imposes the tax for the year. That section triggers s.4 and thence the charging sections in s.3 and in ITEPA and ITTOIA. The list of charging sections here may be compared with the similar—but not identical—list of chapters to the Tax Credits (Definition and Calculation of Income) Regulations 2002 below.

PART 14

INCOME TAX LIABILITY: MISCELLANEOUS RULES

CHAPTER 2

RESIDENCE

Residence of individuals temporarily abroad

829.—(1) This section applies if—
(a) an individual has left the United Kingdom for the purpose only of occasional residence abroad, and
(b) at the time of leaving the individual was both UK resident and ordinarily UK resident.
(2) Treat the individual as UK resident for the purpose of determining the individual's liability for income tax for any tax year during the whole or

Income Tax Act 2007

a part of which the individual remains outside the United Kingdom for the purpose only of occasional residence abroad.

GENERAL NOTE

1.837   This section and those that follow rewrite the former ss.334–336 of ICTA. They set out the only legislative meanings given to "resident" for income tax purposes. The detailed view of how HMRC assesses residence and ordinary residence in the light of these provisions and the relevant case law is set out in HMRC booklet IR20.

Residence of individuals working abroad

1.838   **830.**—(1) This section applies for income tax purposes if an individual works full-time in one or both of—
   (a) a foreign trade, and
   (b) a foreign employment.

(2) In determining whether the individual is UK resident ignore any living accommodation available in the United Kingdom for the individual's use.

(3) A trade is foreign if no part of it is carried on in the United Kingdom.

(4) An employment is foreign if all of its duties are performed outside the United Kingdom.

(5) An employment is also foreign if in the tax year in question—
   (a) the duties of the employment are in substance performed outside the United Kingdom, and
   (b) the only duties of the employment performed in the United Kingdom are duties which are merely incidental to the duties of the employment performed outside the United Kingdom in the year.

(6) In this section—
"employment" includes an office, and "trade" includes profession and vocation.

Foreign income of individuals in the United Kingdom for temporary purpose

1.839   **831.**—(1) Subsection (2) applies in relation to an individual if—
   (a) the individual is in the United Kingdom for some temporary purpose only and with no view to establishing the individual's residence in the United Kingdom, and
   (b) during the tax year in question the individual spends (in total) less than 183 days in the United Kingdom.

In determining whether an individual is within paragraph (a) ignore any living accommodation available in the United Kingdom for the individual's use.

(1A) In determining whether an individual is within subsection (1)(b) treat a day as a day spent by the individual in the United Kingdom if (and only if) the individual is present in the United Kingdom at the end of the day.

(1B) But in determining that issue do not treat as a day spent by the individual in the United Kingdom any day on which the individual arrives in the United Kingdom as a passenger if—
   (a) the individual departs from the United Kingdom on the next day, and

(b) during the time between arrival and departure the individual does not engage in activities that are to a substantial extent unrelated to the individual's passage through the United Kingdom.

(2) Apply the following rules in determining the individual's liability for income tax.

Rule 1

In relation to pension or social security income arising from a source outside the United Kingdom, treat the individual as non-UK resident for the purposes of the following—
  (a) Chapter 4 of Part 9 of ITEPA 2003 (tax on foreign pensions),
  (b) Chapter 5A of that Part (tax on pensions under registered pension schemes) but only if the income is an annuity under a registered pension scheme within paragraph 1(1)(f) of Schedule 36 to FA 2004,
  (c) Chapter 10 of that Part (tax on employment-related annuities),
  (d) Chapter 15 of that Part (tax on voluntary annual payments),
  (e) section 647 of ITEPA 2003 (meaning of "foreign residence condition") but only in its application for the purposes of section 651 of that Act (which provides an exemption for tax under Chapter 14 of Part 9 of that Act), and
  (f) Chapter 6 of Part 10 of ITEPA 2003 (taxable foreign benefits).

See sections 566 and 657 of ITEPA 2003 for the definitions of "pension income" and "social security income".

Rule 2

In relation to income arising from a source outside the United Kingdom, treat the individual as non-UK resident for the purposes of any charge under a provision mentioned in section 830(2) of ITTOIA 2005 (which contains a list of provisions under which relevant foreign income is charged).

In this rule "income" does not include income chargeable as a result of section 844 of ITTOIA 2005 (unremittable income: income charged on withdrawal of relief after source ceases).

(3) Paragraph (e) of Rule 1 in subsection (2) applies only if—
  (a) the individual makes a claim as mentioned in section 647(3)(a) of ITEPA 2003, and
  (b) the Commissioners are satisfied that subsection (2) of this section applies in relation to the individual.

(4) Subsection (5) applies in relation to an individual if subsection (2) would have applied in relation to the individual but for subsection (1)(b).

(5) Apply the rules set out in subsection (2) in determining the individual's liability for income tax.

But—
  (a) instead of treating the individual as non-UK resident in relation to the income and for the purposes mentioned in those rules, treat the individual as UK resident, and
  (b) ignore subsection (3).

Employment income of individuals in the United Kingdom for temporary purpose

832.—(1) Subsection (2) applies in relation to an individual if—
  (a) the individual is in the United Kingdom for some temporary purpose

only and with no intention of establishing the individual's residence in the United Kingdom, and

(b) during the tax year in question the individual spends (in total) less than 183 days in the United Kingdom.

In determining whether an individual is within paragraph (a) ignore any living accommodation available in the United Kingdom for the individual's use.

(1A) In determining whether an individual is within subsection (1)(b) treat a day as a day spent by the individual in the United Kingdom if (and only if) the individual is present in the United Kingdom at the end of the day.

(1B) But in determining that issue do not treat as a day spent by the individual in the United Kingdom any day on which the individual arrives in the United Kingdom as a passenger if—

(a) the individual departs from the United Kingdom on the next day, and

(b) during the time between arrival and departure the individual does not engage in activities that are to a substantial extent unrelated to the individual's passage through the United Kingdom.

(2) Treat the individual as non-UK resident for the purposes of Chapters 4 and 5 of Part 2 of ITEPA 2003 (which set out rules for determining taxable earnings from employment).

(3) Subsection (4) applies in relation to an individual if subsection (2) would have applied in relation to the individual but for subsection (1)(b).

(4) Treat the individual as UK resident for the purposes of the provisions mentioned in subsection (2).

CHAPTER 3

JOINTLY HELD PROPERTY

Jointly held property

1.841   836.—(1) This section applies if income arises from property held in the names of individuals—

(a) who are married to, or are civil partners of, each other, and

(b) who live together.

(2) The individuals are treated for income tax purposes as beneficially entitled to the income in equal shares.

(3) But this treatment does not apply in relation to any income within any of the following exceptions.

Exception A

Income to which neither of the individuals is beneficially entitled.

Exception B

Income in relation to which a declaration by the individuals under section 837 has effect (unequal beneficial interests).

Exception C

Income to which Part 9 of ITTOIA 2005 applies (partnerships).

Exception D

Income arising from a UK property business which consists of, or so far as it includes, the commercial letting of furnished holiday accommodation (within the meaning of Chapter 6 of Part 3 of ITTOIA 2005).

Exception E

Income consisting of a distribution arising from property consisting of—
  (a) shares in or securities of a close company to which one of the individuals is beneficially entitled to the exclusion of the other, or
  (b) such shares or securities to which the individuals are beneficially entitled in equal or unequal shares.

"Shares" and "securities" have the same meaning as in section 254 of ICTA.

Exception F

Income to which one of the individuals is beneficially entitled so far as it is treated as a result of any other provision of the Income Tax Acts as—
  (a) the income of the other individual, or
  (b) the income of a third party.

General Note

This section and the machinery section that follows should be read with s.1011 below. It sets out the general rule that couples living together are assumed to own any property, and therefore to receive any income from that property, in equal shares. Section 837 allows the couple to alter that position. However, that will make little difference to tax credits claims as entitlement is assessed on the total incomes of both members of the couple. Note that this rule does not apply to unmarried or unregistered couples, but again that does not affect tax credit entitlement. It does however affect income tax liability where the two members of the couple are liable to income tax at different rates at the margin.

Jointly held property: declarations of unequal beneficial interests

837.—(1) The individuals may make a joint declaration under this section if—
  (a) one of them is beneficially entitled to the income to the exclusion of the other, or
  (b) they are beneficially entitled to the income in unequal shares, and their beneficial interests in the income correspond to their beneficial interests in the property from which it arises.

(2) The declaration must state the beneficial interests of the individuals in—
  (a) the income to which the declaration relates, and
  (b) the property from which that income arises.

(3) The declaration has effect only if notice of it is given to an officer of Revenue and Customs—
  (a) in such form and manner as the Commissioners for Her Majesty's Revenue and Customs may prescribe, and
  (b) within the period of 60 days beginning with the date of the declaration.

(4) The declaration has effect in relation to income arising on or after the date of the declaration.

(5) The declaration continues to have effect until such time (if any) as there is a change in the beneficial interests of the individuals in either—
  (a) the income to which the declaration relates, or
  (b) the property from which that income arises.

Income Tax Act 2007

Part 16

Income Tax Acts Definitions, Etc

Chapter 1

Definitions

Overview of Chapter

1.844 **988.**—(1) This Chapter contains definitions which apply for the purposes of the Income Tax Acts, except where, in those Acts, the context otherwise requires.

(2) To find a definition go first to section 989, which sets out some of the definitions in full.

(3) If a definition is not set out in full in section 989, the section indicates where it is set out in full.

(4) In some cases it is stated that a definition does not apply for the purposes of specified provisions of the Income Tax Acts (see, for example, sections 990(2), 992(3) and 1007(4)).

(5) And in some cases it is stated that a definition has effect only for the purposes of specific provisions of the Income Tax Acts (see, for example, sections 991, 993, 995 and 1006).

The definitions

1.845 **989.**—The following definitions apply for the purposes of the Income Tax Acts—

"Act" has the meaning given by section 990,

. . .

"bank" is to be read in accordance with section 991,

. . .

"body of persons" means any body politic, corporate or collegiate and any company, fraternity, fellowship or society of persons whether corporate or not corporate,

. . .

"capital allowance" means any allowance under CAA 2001,

"the Capital Allowances Act" means CAA 2001,

"chargeable gain" has the same meaning as in TCGA 1992,

"chargeable period" means an accounting period of a company or a tax year,

"charity" means a body of persons or trust established for charitable purposes only,

. . .

"company" has the meaning given by section 992,

. . .

"dividend income" has the meaning given by section 19

. . .

394

"farming" has the meaning given by section 996,
"for accounting purposes" has the meaning given by section 997(4),
. . .
"generally accepted accounting practice" has the meaning given by section 997(1) and (3),
"grossing up" is to be read in accordance with section 998,
. . .
"international accounting standards" has the meaning given by section 997(5),
. . .
"non-UK resident" means not resident in the United Kingdom (and references to a non-UK resident or a non-UK resident person are to a person who is not resident there),
"normal self-assessment filing date", in relation to a tax year, means the 31 January following the tax year,
"notice" means notice in writing or in a form authorised (in relation to the case in question) by directions under section 118 of FA 1998,
. . .
"overseas property business" has the meaning given by Chapter 2 of Part 3 of ITTOIA 2005,
"period of account"—
(a) in relation to a person, means any period for which the person draws up accounts, and
(b) in relation to a trade, profession, vocation or other business, means any period for which the accounts of the business are drawn up,
. . .
"personal representatives" in relation to a person who has died, means—
(a) in the United Kingdom, persons responsible for administering the estate of the deceased, and
(b) in a territory outside the United Kingdom, those persons having functions under its law equivalent to those of administering the estate of the deceased,
"profits or gains" does not include chargeable gains,
. . .
"relevant foreign income" has the meaning given by section 830(1) to (3) of ITTOIA 2005 but also includes, for any purpose mentioned in any provision listed in section 830(4) of that Act, income treated as relevant foreign income for that purpose by that provision,
"research and development" is to be read in accordance with section 1006,
"retail prices index" means—
(a) the general index of retail prices (for all items) published by the Office for National Statistics, or
(b) if that index is not published for a relevant month, any substituted index or index figures published by that Office,
. . .
"Schedule A business" means any business the profits of which are chargeable to corporation tax under Schedule A, including the business in the course of which any transaction is (as a result of paragraph 1(2) of that Schedule) to be treated as entered into,
. . .

"settled property" (together with references to property comprised in a settlement) is to be read in accordance with section 466,
"settlor" is to be read in accordance with sections 467 to 473,
. . .
"stepchild", in relation to a civil partner, is to be read in accordance with section 246 of the Civil Partnership Act 2004 (c.33),
. . .
"tax" is to be read in accordance with section 832(3) of ICTA,
"tax credit" means a tax credit under section 397(1) of ITTOIA 2005,
"tax year" has the meaning given by section 4(2),
"the tax year 2007–08" (and any corresponding expression in which two years are similarly mentioned) has the meaning given by section 4(4),
"total income" has the meaning given by section 23 (see Step 1 in that section and also section 31),
"trade" includes any venture in the nature of trade,
"tribunal" means the First-tier Tribunal or, where determined by or under Tribunal Procedure Rules, the Upper Tribunal,
. . .
"UK generally accepted accounting practice" has the meaning given by section 997(2),
"UK property business" has the meaning given by Chapter 2 of Part 3 of ITTOIA 2005,
"UK resident" means resident in the United Kingdom (and references to a UK resident or a UK resident person are to a person who is resident there),
. . .
"year of assessment" means a tax year, and
"the year 1988–1989" means the tax year 1988–1989 (and any corresponding expression in which two years are similarly mentioned is to be read in the same way).

Meaning of "company"

1.846   992.—(1) In the Income Tax Acts "company" means any body corporate or unincorporated association, but does not include a partnership, a local authority or a local authority association.

(2) Subsection (1) needs to be with read with section 468 of ICTA (authorised unit trusts).
. . .

References to married persons, or civil partners, living together

1.847   1011.—Individuals who are married to, or are civil partners of, each other are treated for the purposes of the Income Tax Acts as living together unless—
  (a) they are separated under an order of a court of competent jurisdiction,
  (b) they are separated by deed of separation, or
  (c) they are in fact separated in circumstances in which the separation is likely to be permanent.

(2012 c.5)

Welfare Reform Act 2012

(2012 c.5)

ARRANGEMENT OF SELECTED SECTIONS

PART 1

UNIVERSAL CREDIT

33. Abolition of benefits   1.848

PART 3

OTHER BENEFIT CHANGES

76. Calculation of working tax credit

SCHEDULE 6

MIGRATION TO UNIVERSAL CREDIT

1. General
2. Claims before the appointed day
3. Claims after the appointed day
4. Awards
6. Tax credits

INTRODUCTION AND GENERAL NOTE

This Act started to come into effect so as to affect tax credits in February 2013 (when regulatory powers came into effect) and started replacing tax credits with the new universal credit with effect from April 6, 2013. On that date a small pilot scheme started in part of the North West of England under which claimants were paid universal credit in place of other benefits including any child tax credit or working tax credit to which they were previously entitled. Government announcements indicate that the extent of the pilot schemes is likely to be increased in 2013/14 but that tax credits will remain payable to nearly all current claimants until at least the following year. The relevant provisions are in Pt 1 of the Act.   1.849

Most of the rest of this lengthy Act is not relevant to the benefits in this volume. Only s.76 is relevant to tax credits of the material in Pts 2, 3, and 4. A number of provisions of Pt 5 are relevant as these deal with social security general administrative provisions. But not all of these have been brought into effect for 2013/14.

Welfare Reform Act 2012

Part 1

Universal Credit

Universal credit and other benefits

Abolition of benefits

1.850 **33.**—(1) The following benefits are abolished—
[...]
(f) child tax credit and working tax credit under the Tax Credits Act 2002.

General Note

1.851 This formally abolishes child tax credit and working tax credit. Part 1 of Sch.14 to the Act contains the necessary provision to repeal Pt 1 of the Tax Credit Act 2002 (but not Pts 2 or 3). Schedules 1 and 3 to the 2002 Act are also saved as they deal with relevant administration. However, as noted above, this abolition is taking place with initial pilots and then in stages. The pilot measures have started but the major dates for activation of this section and the related repeals have yet to be announced.

Migration to universal credit

1.852 **36.**—Schedule 6 contains provision about the replacement of benefits by universal credit.

Other Benefit Changes

Working tax credit

Calculation of working tax credit

1.853 **76.**—(1) Step 5 in regulation 7(3) of the 2002 Regulations has effect in relation to awards of working tax credit for the whole or part of the relevant year as if from the beginning of the day on 6 April 2011 the percentage to be applied under step 5 in finding the amount of the reduction were 41% (instead of 39%).

(2) Anything done by the Commissioners before the coming into force of this section in relation to awards of working tax credit for the whole or part of the relevant year is to be treated as having been duly done, if it would have been duly done but for being done on the basis that from the beginning of the day on 6 April 2011 the percentage to be applied under step 5 was 41%.

(3) In this section—
"the 2002 Regulations" means the Tax Credits (Income Thresholds and Determination of Rates) Regulations 2002 (S.I. 2002/2008);

(2012 c.5 s.76)

"the Commissioners" means the Commissioners for Her Majesty's Revenue and Customs;

"the relevant year" means the year beginning with 6 April 2011.

GENERAL NOTE

This is a deeming provision designed to validate retrospectively the failure to provide proper legislative authority at the correct time for the reduction rate of tax credits being increased under the emergency budget of 2010 from 39 per cent to 41 per cent.

1.854

SCHEDULE 6

MIGRATION TO UNIVERSAL CREDIT

General

1.—(1) Regulations may make provision for the purposes of, or in connection with, replacing existing benefits with universal credit.

(2) In this Schedule "existing benefit" means—
   (a) a benefit abolished under section 33(1);
   (b) any other prescribed benefit.

(3) In this Schedule "appointed day" means the day appointed for the coming into force of section 1.

1.855

Claims before the appointed day

2.—(1) The provision referred to in paragraph 1(1) includes—
   (a) provision for a claim for universal credit to be made before the appointed day for a period beginning on or after that day;
   (b) provision for a claim for universal credit made before the appointed day to be treated to any extent as a claim for an existing benefit;
   (c) provision for a claim for an existing benefit made before the appointed day to be treated to any extent as a claim for universal credit.

(2) The provision referred to in paragraph 1(1) includes provision, where a claim for universal credit is made (or is treated as made) before the appointed day, for an award on the claim to be made in respect of a period before the appointed day (including provision as to the conditions of entitlement for, and amount of, such an award).

1.856

Claims after the appointed day

3.—(1) The provision referred to in paragraph 1(1) includes—
   (a) provision permanently or temporarily excluding the making of a claim for universal credit after the appointed day by—
      (i) a person to whom an existing benefit is awarded, or
      (ii) a person who would be entitled to an existing benefit on making a claim for it;
   (b) provision temporarily excluding the making of a claim for universal credit after the appointed day by any other person;
   (c) provision excluding entitlement to universal credit temporarily or for a particular period;
   (d) provision for a claim for universal credit made after the appointed day to be treated to any extent as a claim for an existing benefit;
   (e) provision for a claim for an existing benefit made after the appointed day to be treated to any extent as a claim for universal credit.

(2) The provision referred to in paragraph 1(1) includes provision, where a claim for universal credit is made (or is treated as made) after the appointed day, for an award on the claim to be made in respect of a period before the appointed day (including provision as to the conditions of entitlement for, and amount of, such an award).

1.857

Awards

4.—(1) The provision referred to in paragraph 1(1) includes—
   (a) provision for terminating an award of an existing benefit;

1.858

(b) provision for making an award of universal credit, with or without application, to a person whose award of existing benefit is terminated.

(2) The provision referred to in sub-paragraph (1)(b) includes—
  (a) provision imposing requirements as to the procedure to be followed, information to be supplied or assessments to be undergone in relation to an award by virtue of that sub-paragraph or an application for such an award;
  (b) provision as to the consequences of failure to comply with any such requirement;
  (c) provision as to the terms on which, and conditions subject to which, such an award is made, including—
    (i) provision temporarily or permanently disapplying, or otherwise modifying, conditions of entitlement to universal credit in relation to the award;
    (ii) provision temporarily or permanently disapplying, or otherwise modifying, any requirement under this Part for a person to be assessed in respect of capability for work or work-related activity;
  (d) provision as to the amount of such an award;
  (e) provision that fulfilment of any condition relevant to entitlement to an award of an existing benefit, or relevant to the amount of such an award, is to be treated as fulfilment of an equivalent condition in relation to universal credit.

(3) Provision under sub-paragraph (2)(d) may secure that where an award of universal credit is made by virtue of sub-paragraph (1)(b)—
  (a) the amount of the award is not less than the amount to which the person would have been entitled under the terminated award, or is not less than that amount by more than a prescribed amount;
  (b) if the person to whom it is made ceases to be entitled to universal credit for not more than a prescribed period, the gap in entitlement is disregarded in calculating the amount of any new award of universal credit.

Work-related requirements and sanctions

1.859   5.—(1) The provision referred to in paragraph 1(1) includes—
[...]
  (b) provision relating to the application of sanctions.

(2) The provision referred to in sub-paragraph (1)(a) includes—
  (a) provision that a claimant commitment for a relevant benefit is to be treated as a claimant commitment for universal credit;
  (b) provision that a work-related requirement for a relevant benefit is treated as a work-related requirement for universal credit;
  (c) provision for anything done which is relevant to compliance with a work-related requirement for a relevant benefit to be treated as done for the purposes of compliance with a work-related requirement for universal credit;
  (d) provision temporarily disapplying any provision of this Part in relation to work-related requirements for universal credit.
[...]

Tax credits

1.860   6.—In relation to the replacement of working tax credit and child tax credit with universal credit, the provision referred to in paragraph 1(1) includes—
  (a) provision modifying the application of the Tax Credits Act 2002 (or of any provision made under it);
  (b) provision for the purposes of recovery of overpayments of working tax credit or child tax credit (including in particular provision for treating overpayments of working tax credit or child tax credit as if they were overpayments of universal credit).

Supplementary

1.861   7.—Regulations under paragraph 1(1) may secure the result that any gap in entitlement to an existing benefit (or what would, but for the provisions of this Part, be a gap in entitlement to an existing benefit) is to be disregarded for the purposes of provision under such regulations.

(2013 c.16)

Welfare Benefits Up-rating Act 2013

(2013 c.16)

ARRANGEMENT OF SELECTED SECTIONS

2. Up-rating of tax credits for tax years 2014–15 and 2015–16
Schedule: Meaning of the "relevant sums" and the "relevant amounts"

Up-rating of tax credits for tax years 2014–15 and 2015–16

2.—(1) The Treasury must, in each of the tax years ending with 5 April 2014 and 5 April 2015, make an order by statutory instrument increasing each of the relevant amounts by 1%. For the meaning of the "relevant amounts" see paragraph 2 of the Schedule.

(2) An order under this section must be framed so that it has effect in relation to awards of tax credits for the tax year following that in which the order is made.

(3) The Treasury may, in providing for an increase under subsection (1), adjust the amount of the increase so as to round any amount up or down to the extent the Treasury think appropriate.

(4) Subsection (1) does not apply in relation to a tax year if, on the review in that tax year under section 41 of the Tax Credits Act 2002, the Treasury determine that the general level of prices in the United Kingdom has not increased, or has increased by less than 1%, over the period under review.

(5) Where subsection (1) applies in relation to a tax year, the Treasury must not exercise any other power to vary any of the relevant amounts if that variation would take effect in relation to awards of tax credits for the tax year following that in which the order is made.

SCHEDULE

SECTIONS 1 AND 2

MEANING OF THE "RELEVANT SUMS" AND THE "RELEVANT AMOUNTS"

. . .

The "relevant amounts" for the purposes of section 2

2.—The "relevant amounts" for the purposes of section 2 are the monetary amounts—
   (a) specified in Schedule 2 to the Working Tax Credit (Entitlement and Maximum Rate) Regulations 2002 (S.I. 2002/2005) for the basic element, the 30-hour element, the second adult element and the lone parent element;
   (b) specified in regulation 7(4)(c) and (f) of the Child Tax Credit Regulations 2002 (S.I. 2002/2007).

GENERAL NOTE

With effect from April 6, 2014, s.2 of the Welfare Benefits Up-rating Act 2013 requires the Treasury to increase the non-disability elements of working and child tax credits in the annual up-rating exercise by no more than 1 per cent in 2014–15 and 2015–16. Schedule 2 to the Act details the specific elements affected.

PART II

TAX CREDITS

Tax Credits Act 2002 (Commencement No.3 and Transitional Provisions and Savings) Order 2003

(SI 2003/938)

The Treasury, in relation to articles 1 and 2, in exercise of the powers conferred upon them by section 61 of the Tax Credits Act 2002 and the Secretary of State for Work and Pensions, in relation to articles 1 and 3 to 5 in exercise of the powers conferred on him by s.62(1) of that Act and of all other powers enabling each of them in that behalf, hereby make the following Order:

ARRANGEMENT OF ARTICLES

1. Citation and interpretation.
2. Appointed day.
3. Saving provision.
4. Transitional application of sections 37 and 39A of the Contributions and Benefits Act.
5. Transitional application of section 154 of the Administration Act.

Schedule—Repeals specified in Schedule 6 to the 2002 Act which are commenced by this order.

Citation and interpretation

1.—(1) This Order may be cited as the Tax Credits Act 2002 (Commencement No.3 and Transitional Provisions and Savings) Order 2003.

(2) In this Order—
"the 2002 Act" means the Tax Credits Act 2002;
"the Administration Act" means the Social Security Administration Act 1992;
"the Contributions and Benefits Act" means the Social Security Contributions and Benefits Act 1992.

Appointed day

2. The day appointed for the coming into force of—
(a) section 1(3)(e) of the 2002 Act (abolition of increases in benefits in respect of children under sections 80 and 90 of the Contributions and Benefits Act);
(b) section 60 of, and Schedule 6, to, the 2002 Act, in so far as they repeal the provisions specified in the Schedule to this Order, is 6th April 2003.

Saving provision

3.—(1) Notwithstanding the coming into force of the specified provisions, the Contributions and Benefits Act and the Administration Act shall, in cases to which paragraph (2) applies, subject to paragraph (3), continue to have effect from the commencement date as if those provisions had not come into force.

(2) This paragraph applies where a person—
(a) is entitled to a relevant increase on the day before the commencement date; or
(b) claims a relevant increase on or after the commencement date and it is subsequently determined that he is entitled to a relevant increase in respect of a period which includes the day before the commencement date.

(3) The provisions saved by paragraph (1) shall continue to have effect until—
(a) subject to sub-paragraph (c), where a relevant increase ceases to be payable to a person to whom paragraph (2) applies for a period greater than 58 days beginning with the day on which it was last payable, on the day 59 days after the day on which it was last payable; or
(b) in any other case, subject to sub-paragraph (c), on the date on which entitlement to a relevant increase ceases;
(c) where regulation 6(19) or (23) of the Social Security (Claims and Payments) Regulations 1987 applies to a further claim for a relevant increase, on the date on which entitlement to that relevant increase ceases.

(4) In this article—
"the commencement date" means 6th April 2003;
"a relevant increase" means an increase under section 80 or 90 of the Contributions and Benefits Act;
"the specified provisions" means the provisions of the 2002 Act which are brought into force by article 2.

Transitional application of sections 37 and 39A of the Contributions and Benefits Act

4. For the purposes of the continuing application of sections 37 (widowed mother's allowance) and 39A (widowed parent's allowance) of the Contributions and Benefits Act in cases to which article 3(2) applies, those sections shall apply as if the amendments specified in paragraphs 26 and 28 of Schedule 3 to the 2002 Act had not come into force.

Transitional application of section 154 of the Administration Act

5. For the purposes of the continuing application of section 154(2)(c) of the Administration Act in cases to which article 3(2) applies, that section shall apply as if it had not been repealed in Schedule 6 to the 2002 Act and the reference to child benefit in that section shall be treated as including a reference to child tax credit under section 8 of the 2002 Act.

(SI 2003/938 Sch.)

Article 2   SCHEDULE

Repeals Specified in Schedule 6 to the 2002 Act Which are Commenced by this Order

Act	Provision
Contributions and Benefits Act	In section 20(1), the words "(with increase for child dependants)" (in each place) and in paragraph (f)(i), the words "and child". In section 30B(3), the word "80,". In section 56(1), the words "(and in particular to those of section 81 below)". Section 60(6). In sections 61(1) and (2), the words "on account of a child or an adult". In section 63(c) and (f)(i), the words "and child". In section 77(1), the words following paragraph (b). In section 78(4)(d), the word "80". Sections 80 and 81. In section 89(1), the words "section 80 and" and in the heading the words "child or". In section 90, the words "child or". In section 91(1)(b), the words "for an adult dependant". In Schedule 4, in Part IV, in column (1), the entries relating to widowed mother's allowance, widowed parent's allowance and child's special allowance and col.(2). In Schedule 5, in paragraph 2(5)(b) the word "80".
Administration Act	In section 3(3), the words "(together with any increase under section 80(5) of the Contributions and Benefits Act)". Section 150(1)(f).

Tax Credits Act 2002 (Commencement No.4, Transitional Provisions and Savings) Order 2003

(SI 2003/962 (c.51)) (as amended)

The Treasury, in exercise of the powers conferred upon them by sections 61 and 62(2) of the Tax Credits Act 2002, hereby make the following Order:

Arrangement of Articles

1. Citation and interpretation.
2. Commencement of provisions of the Act.
3. Savings.
4. Savings.
5. Transitional provisions.

Tax Credits Act 2002 (Commencement No.4) Order 2003

Schedule 1—Provisions of Sch.6 to the Act coming into force on 6th April 2003
Schedule 2—Provisions of Sch.6 to the Act coming into force on 8th April 2003

Citation and interpretation

2.9   **1.**—(1) This Order may be cited as the Tax Credits Act 2002 (Commencement No.4, Transitional Provisions and Savings) Order 2003.
(2) In this Order—
"the Act" means the Tax Credits Act 2002;
"the 1999 Act" means the Tax Credits Act 1999; and
"the superseded tax credits" means working families' tax credit and disabled person's tax credit.

Commencement of provisions of the Act

2.10   **2.**—(1) Subject to the provisions of articles 3 and 4 (savings and transitional provisions), the provisions of the Act specified in this article shall come into force in accordance with the following paragraphs of this article.
(2) Section 47 (consequential amendments), so far as it relates to paragraphs 4 to 7 of Schedule 3, shall come into force on 1st April 2003.
(3) The following provisions of the Act shall come into force on 6th April 2003—
   (a) section 1(3)(a) and (f) (abolition of children's tax credit under section 257AA of the Income and Corporation Taxes Act 1988 and employment credit);
   (b) section 47, so far as it relates to the provisions of Schedule 3 specified in sub-paragraph (d);
   (c) section 60 (repeals), so far as it relates to the provisions of Schedule 6 specified in sub-paragraph (e);
   (d) in Schedule 3 (consequential amendments)—
      (i) paragraphs 1 to 3,
      (ii) paragraphs 8 and 9, and
      (iii) paragraphs 13 to 59; and
   (e) in Schedule 6, the entries relating to the enactments specified in column 1 of Schedule 1 to this Order to the extent shown in column 2 of that Schedule.
(4) The following provisions of the Act shall come into force on 8th April 2003—
   (a) section 1(3)(b) and (c) (abolition of working families' tax credit and disabled person's tax credit);
   (b) section 47 so far as concerns the provisions of Schedule 3 mentioned in this paragraph;
   (c) section 60 so far as concerns the entries in Schedule 6 referred to in sub-paragraph (e);
   (d) paragraphs 10 to 12 of Schedule 3 to the Act; and
   (e) in Schedule 6 to the Act, the entries relating to the enactments specified in column 1 of Schedule 2 to this Order to the extent shown in column 2 of that Schedule.
(5) [[1]...]

(SI 2003/962 (c.51)) (as amended)

AMENDMENT

1. Tax Credits Act 2002 (Commencement and Transitional Provisions) (Partial Revocation) Order 2014 (SI 2014/1848) art.2 (July 14, 2014).

GENERAL NOTE

Section 1(3)(d) has never fully come into effect and will not as tax credits are now being replaced with universal credit under the Welfare Reform Act 2012. That Act abolishes both income support and jobseeker's allowance and both forms of tax credit as it comes into effect. Article 2(5) of this Order previously postponed the repeal of s.1(3)(d) of the 2002 Act but the latest amendment removes any commencement date.

The effect of the revocation of art.2(5) by SI 2014/1848 is to remove the time limit for the revocation of the child premia paid on some cases to beneficiaries of income support and jobseeker's allowance.

2.11

Tax Credits Act 2002 (Transitional Provisions) Order 2008

(SI 2008/3151)

The Treasury, in exercise of the powers conferred by section 62(2) of the Tax Credits Act 2002 make the following Order:

Citation

1. This Order may be cited as the Tax Credits Act 2002 (Transitional Provisions) Order 2008.

2.12

Deemed claims for tax credits

2.—[1. . .]

2.13

Amendments to the Tax Credits Act 2002 (Commencement No. 4, Transitional Provisions and Savings) Order 2003

3.—(1) The Tax Credits Act 2002 (Commencement No. 4, Transitional Provisions and Savings) Order 2003 shall be amended as follows:
 (2) [2. . .]
 (3) [1. . .]

2.14

AMENDMENTS

1. Tax Credits Act 2002 (Commencement and Transitional Provisions)(Partial Revocation) Order 2014 art.2 (July 14, 2014) (SI 2014/1848).
2. Tax Credits Act 2002 (Commencement and Transitional Provisions) (Partial Revocation) Order 2014 (SI 2014/1848) art.4 (July 14, 2014).

Tax Credits Act 2002 (Transitional Provisions) Order 2010

(SI 2010/644)

The Treasury make the following Order in exercise of the powers conferred by section 62(2) of the Tax Credits Act 2002.

Citation and commencement

2.15 1. This Order may be cited as the Tax Credits Act 2002 (Transitional Provisions) Order 2010 and shall come into force on 1st April 2010.

Interpretation

2.16 2.—(1) In this Order—
"benefit week" has the meaning given in—
  (a) regulation 2(1) of the Income Support Regulations 1987 in relation to income support, and
  (b) regulation 1(3) of the Jobseeker's Allowance Regulations 1996 in relation to income- based jobseeker's allowance;
"child premia" means the amounts in respect of income support or income-based jobseeker's allowance referred to in section 1(3)(d) of the Tax Credits Act 2002;
"polygamous unit" has the meaning given in regulation 2 of the Tax Credits (Polygamous Marriages) Regulations 2003;
"specified date" has the meaning given by paragraph (2);
"specified person" has the meaning given by paragraph (3).
(2) For the purposes of this Order the "specified date" is the day following the date notified to an officer of Revenue and Customs as the final day of the last benefit week for which the child premia is to be paid to the specified person—
  (a) by the Department for Work and Pensions, if the specified person is claiming in Great Britain, or
  (b) by the Department for Social Development, if the specified person is claiming in Northern Ireland.
(3) For the purposes of this Order a "specified person" is a person who—
  (a) until the specified date was receiving the child premia, and
  (b) has not made a claim for child tax credit.

Transitional provisions

2.17 3.—(1) Notwithstanding section 5(2) of the Tax Credits Act 2002, an award on a claim for child tax credit made by a person who until the specified date was receiving the child premia is for the period specified in paragraph (2)
(2) The period is a period beginning with the specified date and ending at the end of the tax year in which that date falls.
(3) Notwithstanding regulation 7 of the Tax Credits (Claims and Notifications) Regulations 2002, a person shall not be entitled to child tax credit in respect of any day prior to the day on which that person makes a claim for it ("the earlier day") if—
  (a) [1 . . .]

(b) the claimant is entitled, or in the case of a joint claim, either of the claimants is entitled, to the child premia on the earlier day.

AMENDMENT

1. Tax Credits Act 2002 (Commencement and Transitional Provisions)(Partial Revocation) Order 2014 art.3 (SI 2014/1848) (July 14, 2014).

Deemed claims for tax credits

4.—(1) A claim shall be deemed to be made under section 3(1) of the Tax Credits Act 2002 if Her Majesty's Revenue and Customs receive a claim for child tax credit from the Department of Work and Pensions or the Department for Social Development and the claim—
  (a) is in respect of a specified person,
  (b) complies with regulation 5(2) of the Tax Credits (Claims and Notifications) Regulations 2002, and
  (c) contains the information required in paragraphs (3) to (5) of regulation 3 of those Regulations.

(2) The claim shall be deemed to be made by the person in respect of whom it is made.

(3) If the specified person is a member of a married couple or an unmarried couple or a polygamous unit, the specified person and the other member of the couple or member or members of the polygamous unit are treated as making a joint claim.

(4) The specified person is treated as being responsible for the child or children or qualifying young person or persons to whom that person's entitlement to the child premia relates.

(5) The claim shall be deemed to be made on the specified date.

(6) This article is subject to article 3.

Working Tax Credit (Entitlement and Maximum Rate) Regulations 2002

(SI 2002/2005) (AS AMENDED)

Whereas a draft of this instrument, which prescribes the amount in excess of which, by virtue of subsection (2) of section 12 of the Tax Credits Act 2002, charges are not to be taken into account for the purposes of that subsection, and which also contains the first regulations made under sections 11 and 12 of that Act, has been laid before, and approved by resolution of, each House of Parliament:

Now, therefore, the Treasury, in exercise of the powers conferred upon them by sections 10, 11, 12, 65(1) and (7) and 67 of the Tax Credits Act 2002, hereby make the following Regulations:

Working Tax Credit (Entitlement and Maximum Rate) Regulations 2002

REGULATIONS

PART 1

GENERAL

2.19
1. Citation, commencement and effect.
2. Interpretation.
3. Other elements of working tax credit.

PART II

CONDITIONS OF ENTITLEMENT

BASIC ELEMENT

4. Entitlement to basic element of working tax credit: qualifying remunerative work.
5. Time off in connection with childbirth and adoption.
5A. Time off in connection with childbirth and placement for adoption: further provisions.
6. Periods of illness or incapacity for work.
7. Term-time and other seasonal workers.
7A. Strike periods.
7B. Persons suspended from work.
7C. Pay in lieu of notice.
7D. Ceasing to undertake work or working for less than 16 hours per week.
8. Gaps between jobs.

Disability element

9. Disability element and workers who are to be treated as at a disadvantage in getting a job.
9A. Initial claims.
9B. Training for work, etc.

30-hour element

10. 30-hour element.

Second-adult element

11. Second-adult element.

(SI 2002/2005) (as amended)

Lone-parent element

12. Lone-parent element.

Childcare element

13. Entitlement to childcare element of working tax credit.
14. Entitlement to childcare element of working tax credit.
15. Calculation of relevant childcare charges.
16. Change of circumstances.

Severe disability element

17. Severe disability element.

50 Plus element

18. 50 Plus element *(repealed)*

Death of a child or qualifying young person for whom the claimant is responsible

19. Entitlement after death of a child or qualifying young person for whom the claimant is responsible.

Part III

Maximum Rate

20. Maximum rates of elements of working tax credit.

Schedule 1—Disability which puts a person at a disadvantage in getting a job.
Schedule 2—Maximum rates of the elements of a working tax credit.

Part I

General

Citation, commencement and effect

1. These Regulations may be cited as the Working Tax Credit (Entitlement and Maximum Rate) Regulations 2002 and shall come into force—
  (a) for the purpose of enabling claims to be made, on 1st August 2002;
  (b) for the purpose of enabling decisions on claims to be made, on 1st January 2003; and
  (c) for all other purposes, on April 6, 2003;
and shall have effect for the tax year beginning on 6th April 2003 and subsequent tax years.

2.20

Definitions

  "claim"—see TCA 2002 s.3(8).
  "tax year"—see TCA 2002 s.47.

Working Tax Credit (Entitlement and Maximum Rate) Regulations 2002

GENERAL NOTE

2.21   These regulations give substance to ss.10 (entitlement) and 11 (maximum rate) of the TCA 2002. These are the only sections in the Act that apply specifically to the award and entitlement to working tax credit. Most of the provisions in those sections are enabling only. These are the regulations giving substance to working tax credit.

Interpretation

2.22   2.—(1) In these Regulations, except where the context otherwise requires—
"the Act" means the Tax Credits Act 2002, and a reference without more to a numbered section is a reference to the section of the Act bearing that number;
[¹⁰ "armed forces independence payment" means armed forces independence payment under the Armed Forces and Reserve Forces (Compensation Scheme) Order 2011;]
"the Board" means the Commissioners of Inland Revenue;
"the Contributions and Benefits Act" means the Social Security Contributions and Benefits Act 1992;
"child" has the same meaning as it has in the Child Tax Credit Regulations 2002;
"claim" means a claim for working tax credit and "joint claim" and "single claim" have the meanings respectively assigned in [¹section 3(8)];
"claimant" means the person making a claim and, in the case of a joint claim, means either of the claimants;
[⁶ "contributory employment and support allowance" means a contributory allowance under Part 1 of the Welfare Reform Act [¹¹ ("the 2007 Act") as amended by the provisions of Schedule 3, and Part 1 of Schedule 14, to the Welfare Reform Act 2012 that remove references to an income-related allowance, and a contributory allowance under Part 1 of the 2007 Act as that Part has effect apart from those provisions];]
[³"couple" has the meaning given by section 3(5A) of the Act;]
"the determination of the maximum rate" means the determination of the maximum rate of working tax credit;
[¹"employed", except in the expression "self-employed" means employed under a contract of service or apprenticeship where the earnings under the contract are chargeable to income tax as employment income under Parts II–VII of the Income Tax (Earnings and Pensions) Act 2003 [² otherwise than by reason of Chapter 8 of Part 2 of that Act (deemed employment in respect of arrangements made by intermediaries)];]
[⁴"employment zone" means an area within Great Britain—
(a) subject to a designation for the purposes of the Employment Zones Regulations 2003 by the Secretary of State, or
[⁵(b) listed in the Schedule to the Employment Zones (Allocation to Contractors) Pilot Regulations 2006],
pursuant to section 60 of the Welfare Reform and Pensions Act 1999.]
"employment zone programme" means a programme which is—
(a) established for one or more employment zones; and
(b) designed to assist claimants for a jobseeker's allowance to obtain sustainable employment;
[¹"initial claim" shall be construed in accordance with regulation 9A;]
"local authority" means—
(a) in relation to England, the council of a county or district, a

(SI 2002/2005 reg.2) (as amended)

metropolitan district, a London Borough, the Common Council of the City of London or the Council of the Isles of Scilly;
(b) in relation to Wales, the council of a county or county borough; or;
(c) in relation to Scotland, a council constituted under section 2 of the Local Government, etc. (Scotland) Act 1994;

[[1]"partner" means a member of a [[3]. . .] couple making a joint claim;]

"patient" means a person (other than a person who is serving a sentence, imposed by a court, in a prison or youth custody institution or, in Scotland, a young offenders' institution) who is regarded as receiving free in-patient treatment within the meaning of the Social Security (Hospital In-Patients) Regulations [[8]2005];

"period of award" shall be construed in accordance with [[1]section 5];

[[9] "personal independence payment" means personal independence payment under Part 4 of the Welfare Reform Act 2012;]

"qualifying young person" means a person who satisfies regulation 5 of the Child Tax Credit Regulations 2002;

"relevant childcare charges" has the meaning given by regulation 14;

[[1]. . .]

[[12] "self-employed" means engaged in carrying on a trade, profession or vocation on a commercial basis and with a view to the realisation of profits, either on one's own account or as a member of a business partnership and the trade, profession or vocation is organised and regular;]

"sports award" means an award made by one of the Sports Councils named in section 23(2) of the National Lottery etc. Act 1993 out of sums allocated to it for distribution under that section;

"surrogate child" means a child in respect of whom an order has been made under section 30 of the Human Fertilisation and Embryology Act 1990 [[7] (parental orders) or section 54 of the Human Fertilisation and Embryology Act 2008 (parental orders)];

[[1]. . .]

"training allowance" means an allowance (whether by way of periodical grants or otherwise) payable—
(a) out of public funds by a Government department or by or on behalf of the Secretary of State, Scottish Enterprise or Highlands and Islands Enterprise or the Department for Employment and Learning ("the relevant paying authority");
(b) to a person in respect of his maintenance or in respect of a member of his family; and
(c) for the period, or part of the period, during which he is following a course of training or instruction—
   (i) provided by, or in pursuance of arrangements made with, the relevant paying authority; or
   (ii) approved by the relevant paying authority in relation to him, but does not include an allowance, paid by a Government department, Northern Ireland department or the Scottish Executive to or in respect of a person by reason of the fact that he is training as a teacher, or is following a course of full-time education, other than under arrangements made under section 2 of the Employment and Training Act 1973, section 2 or 3 of the Disabled Persons (Employment) Act (Northern Ireland) 1945, or section 1(1) of the Employment and Training Act (Northern Ireland) 1950;

Working Tax Credit (Entitlement and Maximum Rate) Regulations 2002

[¹"training for work" shall be construed in accordance with regulation 9B;]
"week" means a period of seven days beginning with midnight between Saturday and Sunday.
[⁶ "the Welfare Reform Act" means the Welfare Reform Act 2007.]
(2) For the purposes of these Regulations a person is responsible for a child or qualifying young person if he is treated as being responsible for that child or qualifying young person in accordance with the rules contained in regulation 3 of the Child Tax Credit Regulations 2002.
(3) A reference in these Regulations to an enactment applying to Great Britain but not to Northern Ireland shall, unless the context otherwise requires, include a reference to the corresponding enactment applying in Northern Ireland.
[¹(4) In these Regulations as they apply to an office a reference to being employed includes a reference to being the holder of an office.]
[⁶ (5) For the purpose of these Regulations—
(a) two or more periods of entitlement to employment and support allowance are linked together if they satisfy the conditions in regulation 145 of the Employment and Support Allowance Regulations 2008 [¹¹or regulation 86 of the Employment and Support Allowance Regulations 2013]; and
(b) a period of entitlement to employment and support allowance is linked together with a period of entitlement to statutory sick pay if it follows that period within 12 weeks.]

AMENDMENTS

1. Working Tax Credit (Entitlement and Maximum Rate) (Amendment) Regulations 2003 (SI 2003/701) reg.3 (April 6, 2003).
2. Tax Credits (Miscellaneous Amendments No.2) Regulations 2003 (SI 2003/2815) reg.13 (November 26, 2003).
3. Civil Partnership Act 2004 (Tax Credits, etc.) (Consequential Amendments) Order 2005 (SI 2005/2919) art.2(2) (December 5, 2005).
4. Tax Credits (Miscellaneous Amendments) Regulations 2006 (SI 2006/766) reg.20(2) (April 6, 2006).
5. Tax Credits (Miscellaneous Amendments) Regulations 2007 (SI 2007/824) reg.3 (April 6, 2007).
6. Employment and Support Allowance (Consequential Provisions) (No.3) Regulations 2008 (SI 2009/1879) reg.20(2) (October 27, 2008).
7. Human Fertilisation and Embryology (Parental Orders) (Consequential, Transitional and Saving Provisions) Order 2010 (SI 2010/986) art.2 and Sch. para.7 (April 6, 2010).
8. Tax Credits (Miscellaneous Amendments) Regulations 2012 (SI 2012/848) reg.2(2)(b) (April 6, 2012).
9. Personal Independence Payment (Supplementary Provisions and Consequential Amendments) Regulations 2013 (SI 2013/388) reg.8 and Sch. para.28(2) (April 8, 2013).
10. Armed Forces and Reserve Forces Compensation Scheme (Consequential Provisions: Subordinate Legislation) Order 2013 (SI 2013/591) art.7 and Sch. para.24(2) (April 8, 2013).
11. Universal Credit (Consequential, Supplementary, Incidental and Miscellaneous Provisions) Regulations 2013 (SI 2013/630) reg.77(2) (April 29, 2013).
12. Working Tax Credit (Entitlement and Maximum Rate) (Amendment) Regulations 2015 (SI 2015/695) reg.3 (April 6, 2015).

(SI 2002/2005 reg.2) (as amended)

Definitions

See also TCA 2002 s.47. For definitions of terms used in income tax legislation see ITEPA 2003 Sch.1 and the index of definitions in ITA 2007 Sch.4 (not included in this work).

General Note

The definition of "self-employed" effective from April 6, 2015 replaces an earlier wider definition: "engaged in the carrying on of a trade profession or vocation". The new definition is deliberately narrower. HMRC explains this in *Revenue and Customs Brief 7 (2015)* as meaning that all new claimants "must show that they are trading on a commercial basis and their business is done with a view to achieving profits. The self-employment should also be structured, regular and ongoing."

The Brief indicates that HMRC intends to take a proactive approach to the new test:

"Self-employed WTC claimants with earnings below a threshold (this will be based on working hours and the National Minimum Wage) will be asked by HMRC to provide evidence that they are in a regular and organised trade, profession or vocation on a commercial basis and with a view to achieving profit.

The information we ask for should be available as part of normal business activity, for example receipts and expenses, records of sales and purchases. We may also ask for supporting documents such as a business plan, planned work, cash flow and profit projections."

The Chancellor added in the 2015 Budget:

"Autumn Statement 2014 announced measures to close down vulnerable gateways in the tax credit system to self-employed claimants. From 6 April 2015 a new test will require those Working Tax Credits (WTC) claimants relying on self-employment to meet the entitlement conditions to be undertaking an activity which is commercial and profitable, or working towards profitability. This test will apply to the working hours required to qualify for WTC as a self-employed claimant. The new requirement for the same claimants to register their self-employment for self-assessment purposes and provide a Unique Tax Reference number will begin from the following April. Throughout the 2015-16 tax year HMRC will be encouraging claimants to take the necessary action to meet this new requirement from 6 April 2016."

Other elements of working tax credit

3.—(1) For the purposes of determining the maximum rate of working tax credit, in addition to the basic element and the disability element, the following elements are prescribed—
(a) a 30 hour element;
(b) a second adult element;
(c) a lone parent element;
(d) a childcare element; [¹ and]
(e) a severe disability element; [¹ . . .]
(f) [¹ . . .].

(2) It is a condition of entitlement to the other elements of working tax credit that the person making the claim for working tax credit is entitled to the basic element.

(3) If the claim for working tax credit is a joint claim, and both members of the couple satisfy the conditions of entitlement for—
(a) the disability element; [¹ or]
(b) the severe disability element; [¹ . . .]

417

Working Tax Credit (Entitlement and Maximum Rate) Regulations 2002

(c) [¹ . . .]
the award must include two such elements.

AMENDMENT

1. Tax Credits (Miscellaneous Amendments) Regulations 2012 (SI 2012/848) reg.2(3) (April 6, 2012).

DEFINITIONS

"basic element"—see TCA 2002 s.11(4).
"claim"—see reg.2.
"joint claim"—see reg.2.

GENERAL NOTE

2.25 Section 11(2) of the TCA 2002 requires that all awards of working tax credit must contain a common element (known as the basic element—see s.11(4)). Section 11(3) requires that there be an element related to those with disabilities putting them at a disadvantage in getting a job. The list of other elements in s.11(6) is, however, permissive only. This regulation sets out the other elements to which claimants may for the time being be entitled as part of their working tax credit award, save one: the childcare element is not included because it is dealt with separately under s.12 of the TCA 2002.

The structure adopted is to require all claimants to show that they are entitled to the basic element in accordance with reg.4. Unless a claimant establishes that entitlement, he or she does not qualify for working tax credit at all. Once entitlement to the basic element is shown, a claimant may claim any or all of the other elements—subject, of course, to showing additional separate entitlement to each of them.

PART II

CONDITIONS OF ENTITLEMENT

Basic element

Entitlement to basic element of working tax credit: qualifying remunerative work

2.26 **4.**—(1) Subject to the qualification in paragraph (2), a person shall be treated as engaged in qualifying remunerative work if, and only if, he satisfies all of the following conditions [⁷ (and in the case of the Second condition, one of the variations in that condition)].

First condition

2.27 The person [⁹ is employed or self-employed and]—
   (a) is working at the date of the claim; or
   (b) has an offer of work which he has accepted at the date of the claim and the work is expected to commence within 7 days of the making of the claim.

In relation to a case falling within sub-paragraph (b) of this condition, references in the second third and fourth conditions below to work which the person undertakes are to be construed as references to the work which the person will undertake when it commences.

In such a case the person is only to be treated as being in qualifying remunerative work when he begins the work referred to in that subparagraph.

(SI 2002/2005 reg. 4) (as amended)

Second condition

[⁷ First variation: In the case of a single claim, the person—]
[¹(a) is aged at least 16 and—
   (i) undertakes work for not less than 16 hours per week,
   (ii) [⁷ . . .] is responsible for a child or qualifying young person, or he has a physical or mental disability which puts him at a disadvantage in getting a job and satisfies regulation 9(1)(c),]
(b) [⁷ . . .] [⁶ . . .]
(c) is aged at least 25 and undertakes not less than 30 hours work per week [⁶ . . .] [⁶; or
(d) is aged at least 60 and undertakes not less than 16 hours work per week]
[⁵[⁷ Second variation: In the case of a joint claim where neither person is responsible for a child or qualifying young person, the person—
(a) is aged at least 16 and undertakes work for not less than 16 hours per week and has a physical or mental disability which puts that person at a disadvantage in getting a job and satisfies regulation 9(1)(c);
(b) is aged at least 25 and undertakes work for not less than 30 hours per week; or
(c) is aged at least 60 and undertakes work for not less than 16 hours per week.
Third variation: In the case of a joint claim where a person or that person's partner is responsible for a child or qualifying young person, the person—
(a) is aged at least 16 and is a member of a couple where at least one partner undertakes work for not less than 16 hours per week and the aggregate number of hours for which the couple undertake work is not less than 24 hours per week;
(b) is aged at least 16 and undertakes work for not less than 16 hours per week and has a physical or mental disability which puts that person at a disadvantage in getting a job and satisfies regulation 9(1)(c);
(c) is aged at least 16 and undertakes work for not less than 16 hours per week and that person's partner is—
   (i) incapacitated and satisfies any of the circumstances in [⁸regulation 13(4) to (12)]; or
   (ii) an in-patient in hospital; or
   (iii) in prison (whether serving a custodial sentence or remanded in custody awaiting trial or sentence); or
   (iv) entitled to carer's allowance under section 70 of the Social Security Contributions and Benefits Act 1992(4);
(d) is aged at least 60 and undertakes work for not less than 16 hours per week.]].

2.28

Third condition

The work which the person undertakes is expected to continue for at least 4 weeks after the making of the claim or, in a case falling within sub-paragraph (b) of the first condition, after the work starts.

2.29

Working Tax Credit (Entitlement and Maximum Rate) Regulations 2002

Fourth condition

2.30 The work is done for payment or in expectation of payment. [⁷ . . .]
[⁵ A social security benefit is not payment for the purposes of satisfying this condition.]
[⁷ (1A) For the purposes of interpretation of paragraph (1)—
   (a) paragraphs (3) and (4) provide the method of determining the number of hours of qualifying remunerative work that a person undertakes;
   (b) regulations 5, 5A, 6 and 7A and 7B apply in relation to periods of absence from work connected with childbirth or adoption, sickness, strike periods or suspension from work;
   (c) regulations 7 and 7C apply to term time and seasonal workers and where pay is received in lieu of notice;
   (d) regulation 7D applies where a person or, in the case of a joint claim, one or both persons cease to work or reduce their hours to the extent that they no longer satisfy the Second condition in paragraph (1);
   (e) regulation 8 applies where there is a gap between jobs;
   (f) regulation 9 prescribes the conditions which must be satisfied by, or exist in relation to, a person so that he is to be treated as having a physical or mental disability which puts him at a disadvantage in getting a job.],
(2) A person who would otherwise satisfy the conditions in paragraph (1) shall not be regarded as engaged in qualifying remunerative work to the extent that he is—
   (a) engaged by a charitable or voluntary organisation, or is a volunteer, if the only payment received by him or due to be paid to him is a payment by way of expenses which falls to be disregarded under item 1 in Table 7 in regulation 19 of the Tax Credits (Definition and Calculation of Income) Regulations 2002;
   (b) engaged in caring for a person who is not a member of his household but is temporarily residing with him if the only payment made to him for providing that care is disregarded income by virtue of item 3 or 4 in Table 8 in regulation 19 of the Tax Credits (Definition and Calculation of Income) Regulations 2002;
   (c) engaged on a scheme for which a training allowance is being paid;
   (d) participating in the Intensive Activity Period specified in regulation 75(1)(a)(iv) of the Jobseeker's Allowance Regulations 1996 or the Preparation for Employment Programme specified in regulation 75(1)(a)(v) of the Jobseeker's Allowance Regulations (Northern Ireland) 1996;
   (e) engaged in an activity in respect of which—
      (i) a sports award has been made, or is to be made, to him, and
      (ii) no other payment is made, or is expected to be made, to him; or
   (f) participating in an employment zone programme, that is to say a programme established for one or more areas designated pursuant to section 60 of the Welfare Reform and Pensions Act 1999, and subject to the [³ Employment Zones 2003 and the Employment Zones (Allocation to Contractors) Pilot Regulations 2005] if he receives no payments under that programme other than—
      (i) discretionary payments disregarded in the calculation of a claimant's income under item 6(b) in [¹Table 6] in regulation

(SI 2002/2005 reg.4) (as amended)

    19 of the Tax Credits (Definition and Calculation of Income) Regulations 2002; or
   (ii) training premiums.
[⁴(g) a person who—
   (i) is serving a custodial sentence or has been remanded in custody awaiting trial or sentence, and
   (ii) is engaged in work (whether inside or outside a prison) while he is serving the sentence or remanded in custody.]

[²This is subject to the following qualification.

(2A) Neither sub-paragraph (c) nor sub-paragraph (d) of paragraph (2) applies if—
 (a) in a case falling within sub-paragraph (c), the training allowance, or
 (b) in a case falling within sub-paragraph (d), any payment made by the Secretary of State, or, in Northern Ireland, by the Department for Social Development, in connection with the Intensive Activity Period,
is chargeable to income tax as the profits of a trade, profession or vocation.]

(3) The number of hours for which a person undertakes qualifying remunerative work is—
 (a) in the case of an apprentice, employee or officeholder, the number of hours of such work which he normally performs—
  (i) under the contract of service or of apprenticeship under which he is employed, or
  (ii) in the office in which he is employed;
 (b) in the case of an agency worker, the number of hours in respect of which remuneration is normally paid to him by an employment agency with whom he has a contract of employment; or
 (c) in the case of a person who is self-employed, the number of hours he normally performs for payment or in expectation of payment.

This is subject to the following qualification.

(4) In reckoning the number of hours of qualifying remunerative work which a person normally undertakes—
 (a) any period of customary or paid holiday; and
 (b) any time allowed for meals or refreshment, unless the person is, or expects to be paid earnings in respect of that time, shall be disregarded.

[¹(5) In reckoning the number of hours of qualifying remunerative work which a person normally undertakes, any time allowed for visits to a hospital, clinic or other establishment for the purpose only of treating or monitoring the person's disability shall be included; but only if the person is, or expects to be, paid in respect of that time.]

[¹⁰ (6) In this regulation "work" shall be construed as a reference to any work that the person undertakes whether as a person who is employed or self-employed or both.]

AMENDMENTS

 1. Working Tax Credit (Entitlement and Maximum Rate) (Amendment) Regulations 2003 (SI 2003/701) reg.4 (April 6, 2003).
 2. Tax Credits (Miscellaneous Amendments) Regulations 2004 (SI 2004/762) reg.5 (April 6, 2004).
 3. Tax Credits (Miscellaneous Amendments) Regulations 2006 (SI 2006/766) reg.20(3) (April 6, 2006).
 4. Tax Credits (Miscellaneous Amendments) Regulations 2007 (SI 2007/824) reg.4 (April 6, 2007).

Working Tax Credit (Entitlement and Maximum Rate) Regulations 2002

5. Tax Credits (Miscellaneous Amendments) Regulations 2009 (SI 2009/697) reg.3 (April 6, 2009).
6. Tax Credits (Miscellaneous Amendments) (No.3) Regulations 2010 (SI 2010/2914) reg.11 (April 6, 2011).
7. Tax Credits (Miscellaneous Amendments) Regulations 2012 (SI 2012/848) reg.2(4) and (5) (April 6, 2012).
8. Working Tax Credit (Entitlement and Maximum Rate) (Amendment) Regulations 2013 (SI 2013/1736) reg.2 (August 5, 2013).
9. Working Tax Credit (Entitlement and Maximum Rate) (Amendment) Regulations 2015 (SI 2015/695) reg.4 (April 6, 2015).
10. Working Tax Credit (Entitlement and Maximum Rate) (Amendment) Regulations 2015 (SI 2015/695) reg.5 (April 6, 2015).

DEFINITIONS

"agency worker"—see ITEPA 2003 s.44.
"child"—see reg.2.
"claim"—see reg.2.
"employed"—see reg.2.
"Employment Zone programme"—see reg.2.
"office-holder"—see ITEPA 2003 s.5.
"partner"—see reg.2.
"qualifying young person"—see reg.2.
"responsible for a child"—see TCA 2002 s.48.
"self-employed"—see reg.2.
"sports award"—see reg.2.
"training allowance"—see reg.2.
"week"—see reg.2.

GENERAL NOTE

2.31 The structure of this key regulation is somewhat misleading. It suggests that there are four conditions for qualifying for entitlement to the basic element of working tax credit. This somewhat disguises the fact that there are four different and alternative bases for claiming working tax credit, all of which are wrapped up together in the "second condition", while the other three conditions are common to all groups of claimant. A fifth condition was added by amendment to the "second condition" in 2011.

First condition
2.32 Section 10(1) requires that all claimants for working tax credit must be in "qualifying remunerative work". This condition defines the scope of being "in" work. A claimant cannot receive working tax credit until he or she has started work (or, in the case of joint claimants or members of a polygamous unit, one of them has started work), or the work is to start within seven days. The addition of a specific mention of the self-employed to the first condition in April 2015 emphasises that self-employment must be shown to be current and ongoing. See the general note to reg.2 above.

As to whether the work concerned has to be in the United Kingdom, see the comments of Judge Rowland in *GC v HMRC (TC)* [2014] UKUT 251 (AAC) noted at para.2.424.

Second condition
2.33 This creates alternative conditions for, or routes to, entitlement. These routes have been modified in several ways with effect from April 6, 2012. The routes now are:

Route 1 is for a single claimant working 16 or more hours a week who is responsible for a child or qualifying young person. The requirement of responsibility for a child or qualifying young person is the same test as for child tax credit purposes, and the regulations adopt the same definitions. In practical terms, they are also the same tests as those for claiming child benefit. However, this does not apply to a person who is claiming child benefit only because he or she is contributing to the child's maintenance costs at the specified rate.

Route 2 is for a disabled claimant suffering prejudice in the job market. The test for work is again a 16-hour test.

Route 3 is for a couple making a joint claim where one is responsible for a child or qualifying young person. Here there are alternative requirements. The main rule is that the couple between them work 24 hours a week, with one of the couple working at least 16 hours. However, the test remains a 16-hour test if a claimant is entitled to the disability premium or the partner is incapacitated in one of the ways relevant for the childcare premium or is in hospital or in prison. The total of 24 hours for the couple together is new, although the minimum requirement remains that one of them must be working for 16 hours.

Route 4 is for single or joint claimants over 60 working 16 hours a week. There will be an interaction in some cases with state pension credit, as working tax credit counts as income for that purpose.

Route 5 is the safety net route. It applies to single or joint claimants who are over 25 and working 30 hours a week. In practice, this will be of benefit to those who are not working a full working week but are earning at the minimal level. This could also include the self-employed with low levels of profit despite continuing a work pattern of the required level.

The previous route for those over 50 has been repealed.

Third condition

This imposes a minimum level of continuity before working tax credit can be claimed. It is separate from, but to be read with, the 16- and 30-hour requirements of the second condition. In other words, it would seem that it has in cases of doubt to be shown that the work will be at a level of 16 or 30 hours a week for those four weeks. That will be a question of fact in all cases. The self-employed may have to show that they are, in that sense, "ordinarily self employed", which is the test for payment of Class 2 NI contributions. In the modern context of flexible employment and allegedly zero-hours contracts, close attention may have to be paid not only to the terms of agreement between the two parties to the work relationship but also to whether there is "an irreducible minimum of obligation on each side to create a contract of service": Stephenson LJ in *Nethermere (St Neots) Ltd v Gardiner* [1984] I.C.R. 612, CA. If there is, the question is then whether on the facts it is shown that it will (or, at the end of the year, did) last for four weeks at the required level. But there is a possible practical problem of timing for a claimant in this sort of work because of the interaction of this requirement with the terms of the first condition—requiring that the work start within seven days of the offer of work—and the backdating rule that prevents a claim being made more than three months after entitlement starts.

2.34

Fourth condition

This echoes the well known test from income support (reg.5 of the Income Support (General) Regulations 1987 (SI 1987/1967)). The test is that the work is done either for payment or in the expectation of it. There is considerable case law from the Courts and Commissioners on whether work is, in this sense, remunerative. The same test will apply to tax credits also. For the question whether work is remunerative, see in particular *R(IS) 22/95* and the decision of the Court of Appeal in *Chief Adjudication Officer v Ellis* (reported as the appendix to that decision). In *R(FIS) 1/86* it was established that the remuneration did not come from the work. That may cause other problems for tax credits, as it may not be clear whether money received in this way from work is "employment income". However, the courts have found, for example, that tips paid to a taxi driver are earnings from the driver's employment even though paid by third parties: see *Shilton v Wilmshurst* [1991] S.T.C. 88, HL. But the question whether the work is remunerative, and the question of the level of earnings from the work, are for separate determination.

2.35

Paragraph (2)

2.36 This paragraph lists seven specific activities that are excepted from "work" for working tax credit purposes. The addition of condition (g) in 2007 avoids claims that arose in individual cases from prisoners working in the community on day release.

The number of hours worked

2.37 Paragraphs (3)–(5), together with regs 5–8, help define the number of hours worked by a claimant or partner. Subject to the specific provisions, it is essentially a question of fact to be determined over the claim period which will (unlike for the previous benefits replaced by working tax credit) normally be a full year. The practical approach of *R(FC) 1/92* was to look at the hours actually worked, rather than the contractual requirements. The wording of this form of the rule would suggest that this is the proper approach to be taken.

Paragraph (3) provides the starting point for deciding the number of hours, but each category of work is tested against what is "normal". The main previous test was by reference to the hours worked in the week of claim, or either of the two previous weeks, or the following week, or the week next following any current holiday. Anyone meeting those tests was then assumed to be "normally" employed at the relevant level. This makes it clearer that the issue is one of fact, and is for most claimants a significant simplification of the rules. Paragraph (4) repeats the previous disregard of paid holidays and unpaid breaks, and para.(5) extends this to allow the inclusion of paid medical visits.

In *CTC/2103/2006*, a Deputy Commissioner decided that it was not correct to calculate the number of hours worked in a fluctuating situation by averaging hours across a month from a monthly pay slip. There was also no requirement in the legislation that 16 hours be worked every week. There was no set, or hard and fast, rule for deciding the number of hours worked. It is a question of fact in each case. However, it is one that causes repeated problems in administering tax credits. For this reason claimants are now required to notify HMRC within one month if their work hours change so that they stop working for 30, or 16, hours a week, as the case may be. See para.2.314, below. It will not always be easy to establish when that duty arises in cases of uncertainty such as that in *CTC/2103/2006*. But reg.7D below will provide a one-month period that deals with most cases.

In CTC/3443/2012 the Upper Tribunal applied the decision of the Court of Appeal in *R(IS) 22/95* to the appeal of a claimant arguing that he was undertaking work for 30 hours a week. The judge emphasised that this is a question of fact taking into account work necessary for a particular employment and that the work must be undertaken in expectation of payment for that work.

[¹ Time off in connection with [²childbirth] and adoption

2.38 **5.**—(1) This regulation applies for any period during which a person—
(a) is paid maternity allowance,
(b) is paid statutory maternity pay,
(c) is absent from work during an ordinary maternity leave period under section 71 of the Employment Rights Act 1996 or Article 103 of the Employment Rights (Northern Ireland) Order 1996;
[³(ca) is absent from work during the first 13 weeks of an additional maternity leave period under section 73 of the Employment Rights Act 1996 or article 105 of the Employment Rights (Northern Ireland) Order 1996,]
(d) is paid [⁵ statutory paternity pay [⁸. . .]]
[⁵ (da) [⁸. . .]
(e) is absent from work during [⁸ a] paternity leave period under sections 80A or 80B of the Employment Rights Act 1996 or Articles 112A or 112B of the Employment Rights (Northern Ireland) Order 1996,

(SI 2002/2005 reg.5) (as amended)

(ea) is absent from work during an additional paternity leave period under [⁸. . .] [⁹. . .]]
(f) is paid statutory adoption pay, [³. . .]
(g) is absent from work during an ordinary adoption leave period under section 75A of the Employment Rights Act 1996 or Article 107A of the Employment Rights (Northern Ireland) Order 1996. [³,or
(ga) is absent from work during the first 13 weeks of an additional adoption leave period under section 75B of the Employment Rights Act 1996 or article 107B of the Employment Rights (Northern Ireland) Order 1996]
[⁷ (h) is paid statutory shared parental pay,
(i) is absent from work during a period of shared parental leave under section 75E or 75G of the Employment Rights Act 1996.]

(2) For the purposes [⁴ of entitlement in this Part], the person is treated as being engaged in qualifying remunerative work during the period.

This is subject to [⁶ paragraphs (3), (3A) and regulation 7D].

(3) The person must have been engaged in qualifying remunerative work immediately before the beginning of the period.

[⁵ (3A) A person shall only be treated as being engaged in qualifying remunerative work by virtue of paragraph (1)(ea) for such period as that person would have been paid additional statutory paternity pay had the conditions of entitlement in [⁸. . .] Parts 2 or 3 of the Additional Statutory Paternity Pay (General) Regulations (Northern Ireland) 2010 been satisfied.]

[⁷ (3B) A person shall only be treated as being engaged in qualifying remunerative work by virtue of paragraph (1)(i) for such period as that person would have been paid statutory shared parental pay had the conditions of entitlement in Parts 2 or 3 of the Statutory Shared Parental Pay (General) Regulations 2014 been satisfied.]

(4) A person who is self-employed is treated as engaged in qualifying remunerative work for the requisite number of hours during any period for which paragraph (1) would have applied in his case but for the fact that the work he performed in the week immediately before the period began, although done for payment or in the expectation of payment, was not performed under a contract of service or apprenticeship.]

AMENDMENTS

1. Working Tax Credit (Entitlement and Maximum Rate) (Amendment) Regulations 2003 (SI 2003/701) reg.5 (April 6, 2003).
2. Tax Credits (Miscellaneous Amendments) Regulations 2004 (SI 2004/762) reg.6 (April 6, 2004).
3. Tax Credits (Miscellaneous Amendments) Regulations 2007 (SI 2007/824) reg.5 (April 6, 2007).
4. Tax Credits (Entitlement and Maximum Rate) (Amendment) Regulations 2009 (SI 2009/1829) regs 2 and 3 (July 31, 2009).
5. Tax Credits (Miscellaneous Amendments) (No.2) Regulations 2010 (SI 2010/2494) reg.3 (November 14, 2010).
6. Tax Credits (Miscellaneous Amendments) Regulations 2012 (SI 2012/848) reg.2(6) (April 6, 2012).
7. Shared Parental Leave and Statutory Shared Parental Pay (Consequential Amendments to Subordinate Legislation) Order 2014 (SI 2014/3255) art.11(2)(e) and (4) (December 31, 2014).
8. Shared Parental Leave and Statutory Shared Parental Pay (Consequential Amendments to Subordinate Legislation) Order 2014 (SI 2014/3255) art.11(2)(a)–(d) and (3) (April 5, 2015).

Working Tax Credit (Entitlement and Maximum Rate) Regulations 2002

9. Shared Parental Leave and Statutory Shared Parental Pay (Consequential Amendments to Subordinate Legislation) Order (Northern Ireland) 2015 (SR 2015/146) art.11(2) (April 5, 2015).

DEFINITIONS

"qualifying remunerative employment"—see reg.4.
"self-employed"—see reg.2.
"week"—see reg.2.

GENERAL NOTE

2.39   This regulation was rewritten to take account of the extended rights of mothers and fathers, including adoptive parents, to parental leave as from 2003. It is designed to stop an award of working tax credit being terminated by such leave. See also reg.5A.

[¹ Time off in connection with childbirth and placement for adoption: further provisions

2.40   **5A.**—(1) This regulation applies to a person for any period—
(a) which falls within a period to which regulation 5 applies; and
(b) which follows the birth or the placement for adoption of the child in connection with whose birth or placement entitlement to the allowance, pay or leave mentioned in regulation 5(1) arises.
(2) [³ A person who would have been treated as being engaged in qualifying remunerative work if they or, in the case of a joint claim, they or their partner had been responsible for a child or "qualifying young person"] immediately before the beginning of a period to which regulation 5 applies, shall be treated as [² being engaged in qualifying remunerative work for purposes of the conditions of entitlement in this Part] during the period mentioned in paragraph (1) above.
(3) Paragraph (4) of regulation 5 applies for the purpose of this regulation as it applies for the purpose of that regulation.]
[³ (4) This regulation is subject to regulation 7D.]

AMENDMENTS

1. Tax Credits (Miscellaneous Amendments) Regulations 2004 (SI 2004/762) reg.7 (April 6, 2004).
2. Working Tax Credit (Entitlement and Maximum Rate) (Amendment) Regulations 2009 (SI 2009/1829) regs 2 and 4 (July 31, 2009).
3. Tax Credits (Miscellaneous Amendments) Regulations 2012 (SI 2012/848) reg.2(7) (April 6, 2012).

GENERAL NOTE

2.41   This regulation reduces the number of hours, for which a person must have been engaged in qualifying remunerative work immediately before beginning a period of statutory leave in connection with the birth or placement for adoption of a child, in order to qualify for tax credit for so much of that period as follows the birth or placement for adoption of the relevant child.

[¹Periods of illness [², incapacity for work or limited capability for work]

2.42   **6.**—(1) This regulation applies for any period during which a person—
(a) is paid statutory sick pay;

(SI 2002/2005 reg.6) (as amended)

(b) is paid short-term incapacity benefit at the lower rate under sections 30A–30E of the Contributions and Benefits Act;
(c) is paid income support on the grounds of incapacity for work under paragraphs 7 and 14 of Schedule 1B to the Income Support (General) Regulations 1987,
[²(cc) is paid an employment and support allowance under Part 1 of the Welfare Reform Act, or]
(d) receives national insurance credits on the grounds of incapacity for work [² or limited capability for work] under reg.8B of the Social Security (Credits) Regulations 1975.

(2) For the purposes of the [³ conditions of entitlement in this Part], the person is treated as being engaged in qualifying remunerative work during the period.
This is subject to [⁴ paragraphs (3), (4) and regulation 7D].

(3) The person must have been engaged in qualifying remunerative work immediately before the beginning of the period.

(4) If the person is paid income support as specified in paragraph (1)(c) [² or employment and support allowance as specified in paragraph (1)(cc)] or receives national insurance credits as specified in paragraph (1)(d) he is treated as being engaged in qualifying remunerative work for a period of 28 weeks only, beginning with the day on which he is first paid income support [² or employment and support allowance] or receives national insurance credits (as the case may be).

(5) A person who is self-employed is treated as engaged in qualifying remunerative work for the requisite number of hours during any period for which paragraph (1) would have applied in his case but for the fact that the work he performed in the week immediately before the period began, although done for payment or in the expectation of payment, was not performed under a contract of service or apprenticeship.]

AMENDMENTS

1. Working Tax Credit (Entitlement and Maximum Rate) (Amendment) Regulations 2003 (SI 2003/701) reg.6 (April 6, 2003).
2. Employment and Support Allowance (Consequential Provisions) (No.3) Regulations 2008 (SI 2009/1879) reg.20(3) (October 27, 2008).
3. Working Tax Credit (Entitlement and Maximum Rate) (Amendment) Regulations 2009 (SI 2009/1829) regs 2 and 5) (July 31, 2009).
4. Tax Credits (Miscellaneous Amendments) Regulations 2012 (SI 2012/848) reg.2(8) (April 6, 2012).

DEFINITIONS

"incapacity for work"—see SSCBA 1992 s.171A.
"qualifying remunerative employment"—see reg.4.
"self-employed"—see reg.2.
"week"—see reg.2.

GENERAL NOTE

This paragraph allows continuity of a claim for working tax credit into a period of sickness or disability, provided that one of the alternative forms of benefit is received for the period. Paragraph 7 of Sch.1B to the Income Support (General) Regulations 1987 (SI 1987/1967) deal with those treated as incapable of work under the SSCBA 1992 and those entitled to statutory sick pay. Paragraph 14 deals with pregnant women who are incapable of work by reason of the pregnancy or are

2.43

Working Tax Credit (Entitlement and Maximum Rate) Regulations 2002

within 11 weeks before the expected date of confinement or seven weeks after the pregnancy ends. There is a 28-week limit on the overlap between working tax credit and either income support or contribution credits.

Term time and other seasonal workers

2.44   **7.**—(1) For the purposes of the [¹ conditions of entitlement in this Part], paragraph (2) applies if a person—
(a) works at a school, other educational establishment or other place of employment;
(b) there is a recognisable cycle to his employment there; and
(c) the length of that recognisable cycle is one year and includes periods of school holidays or similar vacations during which he does not work.
(2) If this paragraph applies, the periods mentioned in paragraph (1)(c) are disregarded in determining whether the [¹ conditions of entitlement in this Part] are satisfied.

AMENDMENT

1. Working Tax Credit (Entitlement and Maximum Rate) (Amendment) Regulations 2009 (SI 2009/1829) regs 2 and 6 (July 31, 2009).

GENERAL NOTE

2.45   This regulation deals with cyclical and "term time only" employment. To claim working tax credit the claimant must establish normal work of 16 hours a week. The income test is by reference to actual earnings over the entire year. As a consequence, this rule will operate to the advantage of those such as supply teachers, school learning support assistants and seasonal staff. They will continue to get their working tax credit throughout the year if the conditions of this regulation are met, while their earnings will be established without reference to assumed earnings during assumed hours of work. For example, someone working 20 hours a week for 40 weeks a year at, say, £125 a week, will meet the hours test for every week of the year if the conditions of this regulation are met, but will earn from that source only £5,000 so will be below the minimum figure of earnings for claiming working tax credit in full. This means also a continuing entitlement to claim childcare charges when appropriate. In addition, because child tax credit is now separated from working tax credit and will be separated from all other benefits, there will be no adverse effect on any child tax credit entitlement from fluctuating work patterns.

[¹Strike periods

2.46   **7A.**—(1) This regulation applies for any period during which a person is on strike.
(2) For the purposes of the [² conditions of entitlement in this Part], the person is treated as being engaged in qualifying remunerative work during the period.
This is subject to [³ paragraph (3) and regulation 7D].
(3) The person—
(a) must have been engaged in qualifying remunerative work immediately before the beginning of the period, and
(b) must not be on strike for longer than a period of 10 consecutive days on which he should have been working.]

(SI 2002/2005 reg.7A) (as amended)

AMENDMENTS

1. Working Tax Credit (Entitlement and Maximum Rate) (Amendment) Regulations 2003 (SI 2003/701) reg.7 (April 6, 2003).
2. Working Tax Credit (Entitlement and Maximum Rate) (Amendment) Regulations 2009 (SI 2009/1829) regs 2 and 7 (July 31, 2009).
3. Tax Credits (Miscellaneous Amendments) Regulations 2012 (SI 2012/848) reg.2(9) (April 6, 2012).

DEFINITION

"qualifying remunerative employment"—see reg.4.

GENERAL NOTE

2.47 This rule is a relaxation from the strict set of rules preventing workers benefitting during a strike. The effect of this regulation is to stop a break in entitlement occurring for a strike of 10 consecutive days or fewer.

[¹Persons suspended from work

2.48 **7B.**—(1) This regulation applies for any period during which a person is suspended from work while complaints or allegations against him are investigated.

(2) For the purposes of the [² conditions of entitlement in this Part], the person is treated as being engaged in qualifying remunerative work during the period.

This is subject to [³ paragraph (3) and regulation 7D].

(3) The person must have been engaged in qualifying remunerative work immediately before the beginning of the period.]

AMENDMENTS

1. Working Tax Credit (Entitlement and Maximum Rate) (Amendment) Regulations 2003 (SI 2003/701) reg.7 (April 6, 2003).
2. Working Tax Credit (Entitlement and Maximum Rate) (Amendment) Regulations 2009 (SI 2009/1829) regs 2 and 7 (July 31, 2009).
3. Tax Credits (Miscellaneous Amendments) Regulations 2012 (SI 2012/848) reg.2(9) (April 6, 2012).

DEFINITIONS

"qualifying remunerative employment"—see reg.4.

GENERAL NOTE

2.49 This deals with a practical problem similar in part to that behind reg.7A. However, in the case of someone is suspended from work, for example while a complaint is investigated, the period of suspension will often not be known.

[¹Pay in lieu of notice

2.50 **7C.**—(1) This regulation applies if a person stops work and receives pay in lieu of notice.

(2) For the purposes of the [³ conditions of entitlement in this Part], the person shall not be treated as being engaged in qualifying remunerative work during the period for which he receives the pay.]
[² (3) This regulation is subject to regulation 7D.]

Working Tax Credit (Entitlement and Maximum Rate) Regulations 2002

AMENDMENTS

1. Working Tax Credit (Entitlement and Maximum Rate) (Amendment) Regulations 2003 (SI 2003/701) reg.7 (April 6, 2003).
2. Working Tax Credit (Entitlement and Maximum Rate) (Amendment) Regulations 2007 (SI 2007/968) reg.2 (April 6, 2007).
3. Working Tax Credit (Entitlement and Maximum Rate) (Amendment) Regulations 2009 (SI 2009/1829) regs 2 and 7 (July 31, 2009)

DEFINITION

"qualifying remunerative employment"—see reg.4.

GENERAL NOTE

2.51   This deals in a pragmatic way with the problem caused when someone stops work before a period of notice has ended, but who receives pay in lieu of notice (often abbreviated to PILON). This regulation excludes the claimant from entitlement to working tax credit. But a problem may arise if the employee does not find other work during that period (and he or she may be prevented from doing so). The provisions about calculating earnings from employment for jobseeker's allowance purposes allow sums to be spread over the period for which they are paid, unless they are excluded from earnings for that purpose, and so may exclude entitlement to JSA. See regs 94 and 98 of the Jobseeker's Allowance Regulations 1996 (SI 1996/207) and the notes to them in Vol.II of this work. So the individual may be excluded from both working tax credit and jobseeker's allowance.

[¹Ceasing to undertake work or working for less than 16 [², 24] or 30 hours per week

2.52   **7D.**— (1) This regulation applies for the four-week period immediately after—
   (a) a person, not being a member of a couple, who is engaged in qualifying remunerative work for not less than 16 hours per week, ceases to work or starts to work less than 16 hours per week,
   (b) a person, being a member of a couple only one of whom is engaged in qualifying remunerative work for not less than 16 hours per week, ceases to work or starts to work less than 16 hours per week,
   (c) both members of a couple, each of whom is engaged in qualifying remunerative work for not less than 16 hours per week, cease to work or start to work less than 16 hours per week,
   (d) a person, being a member of a couple who is entitled to the childcare element of working tax credit each of whom is engaged in qualifying remunerative work for not less than 16 hours per week, ceases to work or start to work less than 16 hours per week, or
   (e) a person who satisfies paragraph (c) [² of the first variation or paragraph (b) of the second variation] of the second condition in regulation 4(1) and who is engaged in qualifying remunerative work for not less than 30 hours per week, ceases to work or starts to work less than 30 hours per week.
   [² (f) one or both members of a couple who satisfy paragraph (a) of the third variation of the Second condition in regulation 4(1) and are engaged in qualifying remunerative work cease to work or reduce their hours to the extent that they cease to meet the condition that one member of the couple works not less than 16 hours per week and

(SI 2002/2005 reg.7D) (as amended)

the aggregate number of hours for which the couple are engaged in qualifying remunerative work is not less than 24 hours per week.]
(2) For the purposes of the conditions of entitlement in this Part, the person is treated as being engaged in qualifying remunerative work during that period.]

AMENDMENTS

1. Working Tax Credit (Entitlement and Maximum Rate) (Amendment) Regulations 2009 (SI 2009/1829) reg.8 (July 31, 2009).
2. Tax Credits (Miscellaneous Amendments) Regulations 2012 (SI 2012/848) reg.2(10) (April 6, 2012).

GENERAL NOTE

This regulation provides for a four week run-on of WTC to those claimants whose hours fall below 16 hours a week. Where entitled, claimants will be eligible to claim income support or JSA whilst in receipt of WTC for the four week period (although the WTC will be treated as income for assessing entitlement to those benefits). The purpose of this rule is to reduce overpayments of tax credits and to ease the transition from tax credits to benefits. It is consistent with the shift from April 2007 of a mandatory reporting requirement on tax credits claimants to inform HMRC within a month of ceasing work.

Note that where the four week run-on applies, the claimant's child remains entitled to free school lunches by virtue of s.512ZB of the Education Act 1996 (see Education (Free School Lunches) (Working Tax Credit) (England) Order 2009 (SI 2009/830) art.2).

The new version of reg.7D, and the associated amendments to other regulations, introduce a more detailed test of hours worked, to include the hours worked by joint claimant couples as well as individual claimants.

See the note to reg.16 below about the relationship between this regulation and reg.16.

2.53

Gaps between jobs

8. For the purposes of the [¹ conditions of entitlement in this Part], a person shall be treated as being engaged in qualifying remunerative work for the requisite number of hours if he has been so engaged within the past seven days.

2.54

AMENDMENT

1. Working Tax Credit (Entitlement and Maximum Rate) (Amendment) Regulations 2009 regs 2 and 9 (July 31, 2009).

DEFINITION

"qualifying remunerative employment"—see reg.4.

2.55

GENERAL NOTE

Regulation 4 allows someone to make a claim for working tax credit if he or she has an offer of a job starting within seven days of the claim (see the first condition in reg.4). However, if there is a gap of not more than that period between jobs, this regulation allows the gap to be bridged so as to avoid the need to make a new claim. This is also consistent with the provisions of the Tax Credits (Claims and Notifications) Regulations 2002 (SI 2002/2014) reg.10, allowing claims for working tax credit seven days in advance.

Disability element

[¹Disability element and workers who are to be treated as at a disadvantage in getting a job

2.56 **9.**—(1) The determination of the maximum rate must include the disability element if the claimant, or, in the case of a joint claim, one of the claimants—
(a) undertakes qualifying remunerative work for at least 16 hours per week;
(b) has any of the disabilities listed in Part I of Schedule 1, or in the case of an initial claim, satisfies the conditions in Part II of Schedule 1; and
(c) is a person who satisfies any of Cases A to G on a day for which the maximum rate is determined in accordance with these Regulations.

[⁴ (2) Case A is where the person has, for at least one day in the preceding 182 days ("the qualifying day"), been in receipt of—
(a) higher rate short-term incapacity benefit;
(b) long-term incapacity benefit;
(c) severe disablement allowance; or
(d) employment and support allowance where entitlement to employment and support allowance or statutory sick pay [⁵ or a benefit or allowance mentioned in sub-paragraphs (a) to (c) or the income support payable under paragraph (3)(a)] has existed for a period of 28 weeks immediately preceding the qualifying day comprising one continuous period or two or more periods which are linked together.]

(3) Case B is where, for at least one day in the preceding 182 days, the person has been a person [² for whom at least one of the following benefits has been payable and for whom the applicable amount] included a higher pensioner or disability premium [²in respect of him] determined—
(a) in the case of income support, in accordance with [² paragraphs 10(1)(b) or (2)(b) or 11, and where applicable 12,] of Part III of Schedule 2 to the Income Support (General) Regulations 1987;
(b) in the case of income-based jobseeker's allowance, in accordance with [² paragraphs 12(1)(a), or (b)(ii), or (c), or 13, and where applicable 14 of Part 3 of] Schedule 1 to the Jobseeker's Allowance Regulations 1996;
(c) in the case of housing benefit, in accordance with [² [³paragraphs 11(1)(b) or 11(2)(b) or 12, and where applicable, 13 of Part 3 Schedule 3 of the Housing Benefit Regulations 2006];
(d) [⁹ . . .]
For the purposes of this Case "the applicable amount" has the meaning given by section 135 of the Contributions and Benefits Act.

(4) Case C is where the person is a person to whom at least one of the following is payable—
(a) a disability living allowance;
(b) an attendance allowance;
(c) a mobility supplement or a constant attendance allowance which is paid, in either case, in conjunction with a war pension or industrial injuries disablement benefit;
[⁶ (d) personal independence payment;]
[⁷ (e) armed forces independence payment.]

(SI 2002/2005 reg. 9) (as amended)

(5) Case D is where the person has an invalid carriage or other vehicle provided under—
   (a) section 5(2)(a) of, and Schedule 2 to, the National Health Service Act 1977,
   (b) section 46 of the National Health Service (Scotland) Act 1978; or
   (c) Article 30(1) of the Health and Personal Social Services (Northern Ireland) Order 1972.

(6) Case E is where the person—
[4 (a) has received—
   (i) on account of his incapacity for work, statutory sick pay, occupational sick pay, short-term incapacity benefit payable at the lower rate or income support, for a period of 140 qualifying days, or has been credited with Class 1 or Class 2 contributions under the Contributions and Benefits Act for a period of 20 weeks on account of incapacity for work, and where the last of those days or weeks (as the case may be) fell within the preceding 56 days; or
   (ii) on account of his [5 incapacity for work or] having limited capability for work, an employment and support allowance [5, or the pay or benefit mentioned in paragraph (i),] for a period of 140 qualifying days, or has been credited with Class 1 or Class 2 contributions under the Contributions and Benefits Act for a period of 20 weeks on account of [5 incapacity for work or] having limited capability for work, and where the last of those days or weeks (as the case may be) fell within the preceding 56 days;]
(b) has a disability which is likely to last for at least six months, or for the rest of his life if his death is expected within that time; and
(c) has gross earnings which are less than they were before the disability began by at least the greater of 20 per cent and £15 per week.

For the purpose of this Case "qualifying days" are days which form part of a single period of incapacity for work within the meaning of Part XI of the Contributions and Benefits Act [4 or a period of limited capability for work within the meaning of regulation 2(1) of the Employment and Support Allowance Regulations 2008].

(7) Case F is where the person—
(a) has undertaken training for work for at least one day in the preceding 56 days; and
[4 (b) has, within 56 days before the first day of that period of training for work, received—
   (i) higher rate short-term incapacity benefit;
   (ii) long-term incapacity benefit;
   (iii) severe disablement allowance; or
   (iv) contributory employment and support allowance where entitlement to that allowance or statutory sick pay [5 or a benefit or allowance mentioned in paragraphs (i) to (iii),] has existed for a period of 28 weeks comprising one continuous period or two or more periods which are linked together provided that, if the person received statutory sick pay, the person satisfied the first and second contribution conditions set out in paragraphs 1 and 2 of Schedule 1 to the Welfare Reform Act.]

[8(7A) In paragraph (7)(b)(iv), the reference to contributory employment and support allowance is a reference to an allowance under Part 1 of the Welfare Reform Act 2007 ("the 2007 Act") as amended by the provisions

Working Tax Credit (Entitlement and Maximum Rate) Regulations 2002

of Schedule 3, and Part 1 of Schedule 14, to the Welfare Reform Act 2012 that remove references to an income-based allowance, and a contributory allowance under Part 1 of the 2007 Act as that Part has effect apart from those provisions.]

(8) Case G is where the person was entitled, [² for at least one day in the preceding 56 days], to the disability element of working tax credit or to disabled person's tax credit by virtue of his having satisfied the requirements of Case A, B, E or F at some earlier time.

For the purposes of this Case a person is treated as having an entitlement to the disability element of working tax credit if that element is taken into account in determining the rate at which the person is entitled to a tax credit.

(9) For the purposes of the Act, a person who satisfies paragraph (1)(b) is to be treated as having a physical or mental disability which puts him at a disadvantage in getting a job.]

AMENDMENTS

1. Working Tax Credit (Entitlement and Maximum Rate) (Amendment) Regulations 2003 (SI 2003/701) reg.8 (April 6, 2003).
2. Tax Credits (Miscellaneous Amendments No.2) Regulations 2003 (SI 2003/2815) reg.14 (November 26, 2003).
3. Housing Benefit and Council Tax Benefit (Consequential Provisions) Regulations 2006 (SI 2006/217) reg.22(2) (March 6, 2006).
4. Employment and Support Allowance (Consequential Provisions) (No.3) Regulations 2008 (SI 2009/1879) reg.20(4) (October 27, 2008).
5. Tax Credits (Miscellaneous Amendments) Regulations 2012 (SI 2012/848) reg.2(11)(c), (12) and (13)(c) (April 6, 2012).
6. Personal Independence Payment (Supplementary Provisions and Consequential Amendments) Regulations 2013 (SI 2013/388) reg.8 and Sch. para.28(3) (April 8, 2013).
7. Armed Forces and Reserve Forces Compensation Scheme (Consequential Provisions: Subordinate Legislation) Order 2013 (SI 2013/591) art.7 and Sch. para.24(3) (April 8, 2013).
8. Universal Credit (Consequential, Supplementary, Incidental and Miscellaneous Provisions) Regulations 2013 (SI 2013/630) reg.77(3) (April 29, 2013).
9. Tax Credits (Miscellaneous Amendments) Regulations 2014 (SI 2014/658) reg.2 (April 6, 2014).

DEFINITIONS

"claim"—see reg.2.
"initial claim"—see reg.9A.
"joint claim"—see reg.2.
"qualifying remunerative employment"—see reg.4.
"training for work"—see reg.9B.
"week"—see reg.2.

GENERAL NOTE

2.57 This regulation, read with Sch.1, provides the tests for claiming working tax credit by Route 2, the route for those with disabilities. It imposes three separate sets of conditions, all of which must be met to meet the second condition in reg.4 of these Regulations. The first of the three conditions is the requirement that the claimant work 16 or more hours a week in qualifying remunerative work. This restates one of the requirements of the second condition, but with the specific addition of the reference to "qualifying remunerative" work. The other two conditions may be termed the "disability conditions".

(SI 2002/2005 reg.9) (as amended)

In *CTC/643/2005* a Commissioner decided that entitlement under reg.9(1) arises only during the period when a claimant is also entitled under one of the cases A to G. This follows from the reference in reg.9(1)(c) to the claimant satisfying any of Cases A to G "on a day for which the maximum rate is determined . . .". A claimant could not claim the disability element throughout a year unless he or she met the requirements of one of the cases throughout the year.

In *CSTC/76/2006* the Commissioner considered how the conditions are to be applied to joint claimants. She confirmed the view of HMRC that all the disablement conditions are to be met by the same individual and that individual must also undertake work for at least 16 hours a week. She rejected an attempt to argue a claim under this regulation where one of the joint claimants worked to the required extent and the other was disabled. This reflects the origin of this provision in the former disabled person's tax credit and disability working allowance. It is also consistent with the entitlement of a working partner to claim carer's allowance if caring for a disabled partner to the required level.

The revocation of reg.9(3)(d) removed a reference to council tax benefit following the abolition of that benefit.

First disability condition

To come within this condition, the claimant must have one or more of the disabilities listed in Pt 1 of Sch.1 to these Regulations (see below). Paragraph (5) emphasises that a person meeting this condition is to be treated as being put at a disadvantage by reason of the disability.

2.58

Second disability condition

To come within this condition, the claimant must meet the conditions of one or more of seven separate "cases" labelled Case A to Case G. Briefly these link with other benefits or activities as follows:

2.59

Case A: entitlement to long-term incapacity benefit, the higher rate of short-term incapacity benefit, severe disablement allowance or employment and support allowance and/or a limited capability for work credit when a benefit is no longer payable;

Case B: entitlement to a higher pension or disability premium of income support, income-based jobseeker's allowance, housing benefit and/or council tax benefit;

Case C: entitlement to disability living allowance, attendance allowance, mobility supplement or constant attendance allowance;

Case D: membership of the Motability scheme;

Case E: entitlement to occupational or statutory sick pay, short-term incapacity benefit, income support, employment and support allowance or "disability credits"; a continuing disability; and earnings that have reduced since the disability started by 20 per cent or £15 a week;

Case F: training for work linked with payment of the benefits in Case A;

Case G: immediate previous entitlement to the disability element of WTC or DPTC under Cases A, B, E or F.

There are special rules that apply to initial claims, noted under reg.9A below.

[¹Initial claims

9A.—(1) In regulation 9(1)(b) an "initial claim" means a claim which—
(a) is made for the disability element of working tax credit, and
(b) relates to a person who has not had an entitlement to that element or to disabled person's tax credit during the two years immediately preceding the making of the claim.

2.60

Working Tax Credit (Entitlement and Maximum Rate) Regulations 2002

(2) In paragraph (1) any reference to the making of a claim includes the giving of notification, in accordance with regulation 20 of the Tax Credits (Claims and Notifications) Regulations 2002, of a change of circumstances falling within that regulation.

(3) For the purposes of paragraph (1)(b), a person is treated as having an entitlement to the disability element of working tax credit if, by virtue of the person being a person who satisfies regulation 9, that element is taken into account in determining the rate at which the person is entitled to a tax credit.]

AMENDMENT

1. Working Tax Credit (Entitlement and Maximum Rate) (Amendment) Regulations 2003 (SI 2003/701) reg.8 (April 6, 2003).

DEFINITIONS

"claim"—see reg.2.
"claimant"—see reg.2.
"disability element"—see reg.9.

GENERAL NOTE

2.61 This regulation makes clear that an "initial claim" for the purposes of reg.9 is a first claim involving disability, or a notification that may involve the addition of a disability element to an award already made on other grounds. This clarifies the scope of reg.9(1), which extends the test of disability under the second disability condition for a first claim. An initial claim will have an extended relevance for working tax credit as compared with its predecessors as the claim will, in normal course of events, last for the balance of the tax year from the effective date of claim.

[¹Training for work, etc.

2.62 **9B.**—(1) In [²regulation 9], "training for work" means training for work received—
  (a) in pursuance of arrangements made under—
    (i) section 2(1) of the Employment and Training Act 1973,
    (ii) section 2(3) of the Enterprise and New Towns (Scotland) Act 1990, or
    (iii) section 1(1) of the Employment and Training Act 1950, or
  (b) on a course whose primary purpose is the teaching of occupational or vocational skills, and which the person attends for 16 hours or more a week.

(2) For the purposes of regulation 9(7), a period of training for work means a series of consecutive days of training for work, there being disregarded any day specified in paragraph (3).

(3) Those days are any day on which the claimant was—
  (a) on holiday;
  (b) attending court as a justice of the peace, a party to any proceedings, a witness or a juror;
  (c) suffering from some disease or bodily or mental disablement as a result of which he was unable to attend training for work, or his attendance would have put at risk the health of other persons;
  (d) unable to participate in training for work because—
    (i) he was looking after a child because the person who usually looked after that child was unable to do so;
    (ii) he was looking after a member of his family who was ill;

(SI 2002/2005 reg.9B) (as amended)

      (iii) he was required to deal with some domestic emergency; or
      (iv) he was arranging or attending the funeral of his partner or a relative; or
  (e) authorised by the training provider to be absent from training for work.

(4) For the purposes of paragraph (3)(d)(iv) "relative" means close relative, grandparent, grandchild, uncle, aunt, nephew or niece; and in this paragraph "close relative" means parent, parent-in-law, son, son-in-law, daughter, daughter-in-law, step-parent, step-son, step-daughter, brother, sister, or the spouse of any of the preceding persons or, if that person is one of an unmarried couple, the other member of that couple.]

AMENDMENTS

1. Working Tax Credit (Entitlement and Maximum Rate) (Amendment) Regulations 2003 (SI 2003/701) reg.8 (April 6, 2003).
2. Tax Credits (Miscellaneous Amendments) Regulations 2004 (SI 2004/762) reg.8 (April 6, 2004).

DEFINITIONS

  "claim"—see reg.2.
  "claimant"—see reg.2.
  "week"—see reg.2.

GENERAL NOTE

This definition is necessary to clarify the scope of Case F in reg.9(7).   2.63

30 hour element

30 hour element

10.—(1) The determination of the maximum rate must include a 30 hour element if the claimant, or in the case of a joint claim, at least one of the claimants, is engaged in qualifying remunerative work for at least 30 hours per week.   2.64

(2) The determination of the maximum rate must also include the 30-hour element if—
  (a) the claim is a joint claim,
  (b) at least one of the claimants is responsible for one or more children or qualifying young people,
  (c) the aggregate number of hours for which the couple engage in qualifying remunerative work is at least 30 hours per week, and
  (d) at least one member of the couple engages in qualifying remunerative work for at least 16 hours per week.
[^{1}(3) [^{2} . . .].]

AMENDMENTS

1. Working Tax Credit (Entitlement and Maximum Rate) (Amendment) Regulations 2003 (SI 2003/701) reg.9 (April 6, 2003).
2. Tax Credits (Miscellaneous Amendments) Regulations 2012 (SI 2012/848) reg.2(14) (April 6, 2012).

Working Tax Credit (Entitlement and Maximum Rate) Regulations 2002

DEFINITION

"child"—see reg.2.
"claim"—see reg.2.
"claimant"—see reg.2.
"couple"—see reg.2.
"joint claim"—see TCA 2002 s.3.
"qualifying remunerative work"—see reg.4.
"qualifying young person"—see reg.2.
"responsible"—see TCA 2002 s.48.
"week"—see reg.2.

GENERAL NOTE

2.65   An additional element of £800 a year is payable if the claimant or couple work 30 hours a week. Paragraphs (1) and (2) together ensure that the total of 30 hours can be worked by either of the couple or by both together if one or both of them are responsible for a child or qualifying young person.

Second adult element

[¹**Second adult element**

2.66   **11.**—(1) The determination of the maximum rate must include the second adult element if the claim is a joint claim.
This is subject to the following provisions of this regulation.
(2) [⁴ . . .]
(3) [⁴ . . .]
[² (4) The determination of the maximum rate shall [⁴ . . .] not include the second adult element if neither claimant has responsibility for a child or qualifying young person, and
   (a) one claimant is serving a custodial sentence of more than twelve months, or
   (b) one claimant is subject to immigration control within the meaning of [³ section 115(9)] of the Immigration and Asylum Act 1999.]
[³ (5) Paragraph (4)(b) does not apply where the claimant subject to immigration control is a person to whom Case 4 of regulations 3(1) of the Tax Credits (Immigration) Regulations 2003 applies.]

AMENDMENTS

1. Working Tax Credit (Entitlement and Maximum Rate) (Amendment) Regulations 2003 (SI 2003/701) reg.10 (April 6, 2003).
2. Tax Credits (Miscellaneous Amendments) Regulations 2009 (SI 2009/697) reg.4 (April 6, 2009).
3. Tax Credits (Miscellaneous Amendments) (No.2) Regulations 2009 (SI 2009/2887) reg.3 (October 30, 2009).
4. Tax Credits (Miscellaneous Amendments) Regulations 2012 (SI 2012/848) reg.2(15) (April 6, 2012).

DEFINITIONS

"50 Plus element"—see reg.18.
"child"—see reg.2.
"claimant"—see reg.2.
"joint claim"—see reg.2.
"qualifying remunerative work"—see reg.4.

(SI 2002/2005 reg.11) (as amended)

"qualifying young person"—see reg.2.
"responsible"—see TCA 2002 s.48.
"week"—see reg.2.

GENERAL NOTE

The value of the second adult element is a little above the value of the basic element. The deleted provisions related to the former 50 Plus credit. 2.67

Lone parent element

Lone parent element

12. The determination of the maximum rate must include the lone parent element if— 2.68
(a) the claim is a single claim; and
(b) the claimant is responsible for [¹a child or qualifying young person].

AMENDMENT

1. Working Tax Credit (Entitlement and Maximum Rate) (Amendment) Regulations 2003 (SI 2003/701) reg.11 (April 6, 2003).

DEFINITION

"child"—see reg.2.
"claim"—see reg.2.
"qualifying young person"—see reg.2.
"responsible"—see TCA 2002 s.48.

GENERAL NOTE

The value of the lone parent element is the same as that of the second adult element. 2.69

Childcare element

Entitlement to childcare element of working tax credit

13.—(1) The determination of the maximum rate must include a childcare element where that person, or in the case of a joint claim at least one of those persons, is incurring relevant childcare charges and— 2.70
  (a) is a person, not being a member of a [³. . .] couple, engaged in [¹qualifying remunerative work];
[¹(b) is a member or are members of a [³. . .] couple where both are engaged in qualifying remunerative work [⁵ for not less than 16 hours per week]; or
  (c) is a member or are members of a [³. . .] couple where one is engaged in qualifying remunerative work [⁵ for not less than 16 hours per week] and the other—
    (i) is incapacitated;
    (ii) is an in-patient in hospital; or
    (iii) is in prison (whether serving a custodial sentence or remanded in custody awaiting trial or sentence) [⁶; or]]
   [⁶ (iv) is entitled to carer's allowance under section 70 of the Social Security Contributions and Benefits Act 1992.]

Working Tax Credit (Entitlement and Maximum Rate) Regulations 2002

(2) For the purposes of paragraph (1), a person is not treated as incurring relevant childcare charges where the average weekly charge calculated in accordance with regulation 15 is nil or where an agreement within regulation 15(4) has not yet commenced.

[¹(3) [². . .]

(4) For the purposes of para.(1)(c)(i), the other member of a couple is incapacitated in any of the circumstances specified in [⁹paragraphs (5) to (12)].]

[⁹ (5) The circumstances specified in this paragraph are where housing benefit is payable under Part 7 of the Contributions and Benefits Act to the other member or the other member's partner and the applicable amount of the person entitled to the benefit includes a disability premium on account of the other member's incapacity or regulation 28(1)(c) of the Housing Benefit Regulations 2006 (treatment of child care charges) applies in that person's case.](c) of the Council Tax Benefit Regulations 2006] (treatment of childcare charges) applies in that person's case;

(6) The circumstances specified in this paragraph are where there is payable in respect of him one or more of the following pensions or allowances—
- (a) short-term incapacity benefit [¹payable at the higher rate] under section 30A of the Contributions and Benefits Act;
- (b) long-term incapacity benefit under section 40 or 41 of the Contributions and Benefits Act;
- (c) attendance allowance under section 64 of that Act;
- (d) severe disablement allowance under section 68 of that Act;
- (e) disability living allowance under section 71 of that Act;
- (f) increase of disablement pension under section 104 of that Act;
- (g) a pension increase under a war pension scheme or an industrial injuries scheme which is analogous to an allowance or increase of disablement pension under sub-paragraph (b), (d) or (e) above;
- [⁴ (h) contributory employment and support allowance where entitlement to that allowance or statutory sick pay [⁵ or a benefit or allowance mentioned in sub-paragraph (a) or (b) or (d),] has existed for a period of 28 weeks comprising one continuous period or two or more periods which are linked together provided that, if the person received statutory sick pay, the person satisfied the first and second contribution conditions set out in paragraphs 1 and 2 of Schedule 1 to the Welfare Reform Act;]
- [⁶ (i) personal independence payment.]
- [⁷ (j) armed forces independence payment.]

[⁸ (6A) In paragraph (6)(h), the reference to contributory employment and support allowance is a reference to an allowance under Part 1 of the Welfare Reform Act 2007 ("the 2007 Act") as amended by the provisions of Schedule 3, and Part 1 of Schedule 14, to the Welfare Reform Act 2012 that remove references to an income-related allowance, and a contributory allowance under Part 1 of the 2007 Act as that Part has effect apart from those provisions.]

(7) The circumstances specified in this paragraph are where a pension or allowance to which sub-paragraph [1 (c)], (d), (e) or (f) of paragraph (6) refers, was payable on account of his incapacity but has ceased to be payable only in consequence of his becoming a patient.

(8) The circumstances specified in this paragraph are where he has an invalid carriage or other vehicle provided to him under section 5(2)(a) of

(SI 2002/2005 reg.13) (as amended)

and Schedule 2 to the National Health Service Act 1977, section 46 of the National Health Service (Scotland) Act 1978; or Article 30(1) of the Health and Personal Social Services (Northern Ireland) Order 1972.

[9 (9) The circumstances specified in this paragraph are where, on 31st March 2013, council tax benefit was payable under Part 7 of the Contributions and Benefits Act (as then in force) to the other member or the other member's partner and the applicable amount of the person entitled to the benefit included a disability premium on account of the other member's incapacity.

(10) Paragraph (9) is subject to paragraphs (11) and (12).

(11) Paragraph (9) does not apply unless the other member of the couple was incapacitated (for the purposes of paragraph (1)(c)(i) and regulation 4(1) Second condition, Third variation (c)(i)) solely by virtue of that person or their partner having been in receipt, on 31st March 2013, of council tax benefit which included a disability premium on account of the other member's incapacity, and none of the other circumstances specified in paragraphs (5) to (8) applied on that date.

(12) If—
(a) the other member of the couple is incapacitated in the circumstances specified in paragraph (9), and
(b) the couple ceases to be entitled to working tax credit (for any reason) on or after 1st April 2013,

that member of the couple shall not be treated as incapacitated in the circumstances specified in paragraph (9) in relation to any subsequent claim.]

AMENDMENTS

1. Working Tax Credit (Entitlement and Maximum Rate) (Amendment) Regulations 2003 (SI 2003/701) reg.12 (April 6, 2003).
2. Tax Credits (Miscellaneous Amendments) Regulations 2004 (SI 2004/762) reg.9 (April 6, 2004).
3. Civil Partnership Act 2004 (Tax Credits, etc.) (Consequential Amendments) Order 2005 (SI 2005/2919) art.2(3) (December 5, 2005).
4. Employment and Support Allowance (Consequential Provisions) (No.3) Regulations 2008 (SI 2009/1879) reg.20(5) (October 27, 2008).
5. Tax Credits (Miscellaneous Amendments) Regulations 2012 (SI 2012/848) reg.2(16) and (17)(c)(iii) (April 6, 2012).
6. Personal Independence Payment (Supplementary Provisions and Consequential Amendments) Regulations 2013 (SI 2013/388) reg.8 and Sch. para.28(4) (April 8, 2013).
7. Armed Forces and Reserve Forces Compensation Scheme (Consequential Provisions: Subordinate Legislation) Order 2013 (SI 2013/591) art.7 and Sch. para.24(4) (April 8, 2013).
8. Universal Credit (Consequential, Supplementary, Incidental and Miscellaneous Provisions) Regulations 2013 (SI 2013/630) reg.77(4) (April 29, 2013).
9. Working Tax Credit (Entitlement and Maximum Rate) (Amendment) Regulations 2013 (SI 2013/1736) reg.3 (August 5, 2013).

DEFINITIONS

"child"—see reg.2.
"childcare"—see reg.14.
"couple"—see TCA 2002 s.3.
"claimant"—see reg.2.
"joint claim"—see reg.2.
"partner"—see reg.2.

"patient"—see reg.2.
"qualifying remunerative work"—see reg.4.
"relevant childcare charges"—see reg.14.

GENERAL NOTE

2.71　Specific provision is made for the childcare element in TCA 2002 s.12. The element may be claimed by those entitled to working tax credit and incurring relevant childcare charges for a child for whom a claimant is responsible in three circumstances:
(a) a lone parent working 16 hours a week;
(b) a couple both of whom are working 16 hours a week; or
(c) a couple, one of whom is working 16 hours a week and the other of whom is incapacitated, in hospital or in prison.

Incapacitated

2.72　The test of incapacity is set out in paras (4)–(8). Each of these tests refers to entitlement to a form of benefit to which only the disabled or incapacitated are entitled. This follows the policy of the tax credits legislation in relying on the determination by others of disability or incapacity in most cases. Paragraph (5) is by reference to housing benefit and council tax benefit, paras (6) and (7) by reference to benefits awarded by the Department for Work and Pensions, and para.(8) by reference to the Motability scheme.

Entitlement to childcare element of working tax credit

2.73　**14.**—(1) [¹Subject to paragraph (1A),] for the purposes of section 12 of the Act charges incurred for childcare are charges paid by the person, or in the case of a joint claim, by either or both of the persons, for childcare provided for any child for whom the person, or at least one of the persons, is responsible [² within the meaning of regulation 3 of the Child Tax Credit Regulations 2002].
In these Regulations, such charges are called "relevant childcare charges".
[¹(1A) Childcare charges do not include charges in respect of care provided by [⁴—
(a) a relative of the child, wholly or mainly in the child's home, or
(b) [¹² . . .]
[⁷(c) a provider mentioned in regulation 14(2)(c), in circumstances where the care is excluded from being qualifying chid care by article 4(2)(c) of the Tax Credits (Approval of Home Child Care Providers) Scheme (Northern Ireland) 2006.]
[⁸(d) a provider mentioned in [¹³ regulation 14(2)(f)(vii)], in circumstances where the care is excluded from being qualifying child care by Article 5(3)(d) of the Tax Credits (Approval of Child Care Providers) (Wales) Scheme 2007.]
[¹² [(e) a foster parent [¹³, a foster carer or a kinship carer] in respect of a child whom [¹³ that person is fostering or is looking after as the child's kinship carer]].
(1B) For the purposes of this regulation—
(a) "relative" means parent, grandparent, aunt, uncle, brother or sister whether by blood, half blood, marriage [⁵, civil patnership] or affinity;
(b) "the child's home" means the home of the person, or in the case of a joint claim of either or both of the persons, responsible for the child.]
[¹³ (c) "foster parent" in relation to a child—
(i) in relation to England, means a person with whom the child is placed under the Fostering Services Regulations 2002;

(SI 2002/2005 reg.14) (as amended)

  (ii) in relation to Wales, means a person with whom the child is placed under the Fostering Services (Wales) Regulations 2003;
  (iii) in relation to Northern Ireland, means a person with whom the child is placed under the Foster Placement (Children) Regulations (Northern Ireland) 1996; and
 (d) "foster carer" and "kinship carer" have the meanings given in regulation 2 of the Looked After Children (Scotland) Regulations 2009.]
(2) "Child care" means care provided for a child—
(a) in England [^{10} . . .]—
  (i) [^{12} . . .]
  (ii) [^{11} . . .]
[^{11} (iia) by a person registered under Part 3 of the Childcare Act 2006;]
[^{11} (iii) in respect of any period on or before the last day the child is treated as a child for the purpose of this regulation by or under the direction of the proprietor of a school on the school premises [^{12} (subject to paragraph 2(B))]]
  (iv) [^{9} . . .] [^{10} . . .]
 [^{3}(v) by a foster parent under the Fostering Services Regulations 2002 [^{10} . . .] in relation to a child other than one whom he is fostering;]
 [^{10}(vi) by a child care provider approved in accordance with the Tax Credits (Approval of Child Care Providers) Scheme 2005;
  (vii) by a domiciliary care worker under the Domiciliary Care Agencies Regulations 2002; or
  (viii) by a child care provider registered under the Childcare (Voluntary Registration) Regulations 2007;]
(b) in Scotland—
  (i) by a person in circumstances where the care service provided by him consists of child minding or of day care of children within the meaning of [^{15} schedule 12 to the Public Services Reform (Scotland) Act 2010 and is registered under Part 5 of that Act;]; [^{2}. . .]
 [^{7}(ia) by a child care agency where the service consists of or includes supplying, or introducing to persons who use the service, child carers within the meaning of [^{15} paragraph 5 of schedule 12 to the Public Services Reform (Scotland) Act 2010; or]]
  (ii) by a local authority in circumstances where the care service provided by the local authority consists of child minding or of day care of children within the meaning of [^{15} schedule 12 to the Public Services Reform (Scotland) Act 2010 and is registered under Part 5 of that Act; or] [^{2}[^{14} . . .]]
[^{3}[^{13} (iii) [^{14} . . .]]]
(c) in Northern Ireland—
  (i) by persons registered under Part XI of the Children (Northern Ireland) Order 1995; [^{2}. . .]
  (ii) by institutions and establishments exempt from registration under that Part by virtue of Article 121 of that Order; or
 [^{3}(iii) in respect of any period ending on or before the day on which he ceases to be a child for the purposes of this regulation, where the care is provided out of school hours by a school on school

premises or by an Education and Library Board or a Health and Social Services Trust; or
    (iv) [^14 . . .]
[^7(v) by a child care provider approved in accordance with the Tax Credits (approval of Home Child Care Providers) Scheme (Northern Ireland) 2006; [^14 or
    (vi) by a foster parent in relation to a child (other than one whom the foster parent is fostering) in circumstances where, but for the fact that the child is too old, the care would fall within one of the descriptions in paragraph (2C);]
  (d) [^1anywhere outside the United Kingdom]—
    (i) by a childcare provider approved by an accredited organisation within the meaning given by regulation 4 of the Tax Credit (New Category of Child Care Provider) Regulations 2002; or
    (ii) [^1. . .]
[^10 . . .]
[^10 (f) in Wales—
    (i) by persons registered under [^14 Part 2 of the Children and Families (Wales) Measure 2010;]
  [^14 (ii) by a person in circumstances where, but for article 11, 12 or 14 of the Child Minding and Day Care Exceptions (Wales) Order 2010(5), the care would be day care for the purposes of Part 2 of the Children and Families (Wales) Measure 2010;]
    (iii) in respect of any period on or before the last day he is treated as a child for the purposes of this regulation, where the care is provided out of school hours, by a school on school premises or by a local authority;
    (iv) by a child care provider approved by an accredited organisation within the meaning given by regulation 4 of the Tax Credit (New Category of Child Care Provider) Regulations 1999;
    (v) [^14 . . .]
    (vi) by a domiciliary care worker under the Domiciliary Care Agencies (Wales) Regulations 2004; [^14 . . .]
    (vii) by a child care provider approved under the Tax Credits (Approval of Child Care Providers) (Wales) Scheme 2007; [^14 or
    (viii) by a foster parent in relation to a child (other than one whom the foster parent is fostering) in circumstances where, but for the fact that the child is too old, the care would fall within one of the descriptions in paragraph (2D).]
[^11 (2A) In paragraph (2)(a)(iii)—
"proprietor", in relation to a school, means –
(a) the governing body incorporated under section 19 of the Education Act 2002, or
(b) if there is no such body, the person or body of persons responsible for the management of the school;
"school" means a school that Her Majesty's Chief Inspector of Education, Children's Services and Skills (the "Chief Inspector") is or may be required to inspect;
"school premises" means premises that may be inspected as part of an inspection of the school by the Chief Inspector.
  (2B) Care provided for a child in England is not [^12 child care] under paragraph (2)(a)(iii) if—

(SI 2002/2005 reg.14) (as amended)

(a) it is provided during school hours for a child who has reached compulsory school age, or
(b) it is provided in breach of a requirement to register under Part 3 of the Childcare Act 2006.]
[[14] (2C) The descriptions referred to in paragraph (2)(c)(vi) are—
(a) child minding or day care for the purposes of Part 11 of the Children (Northern Ireland) Order 1995(7); and
(b) qualifying child care for the purposes of the Tax Credits (Approval of Home Child Care Providers) Scheme (Northern Ireland) 2006(8).
(2D) The descriptions referred to in paragraph (2)(f)(viii) are—
(a) child minding, or day care, for the purposes of Part 2 of the Children and Families (Wales) Measure 2010; and
(b) qualifying child care for the purposes of the Tax Credits (Approval of Child Care Providers) (Wales) Scheme 2007.]
(3) For the purposes of this regulation a person is a child until the last day of the week in which falls 1st September following that child's 15th birthday (or 16th birthday if the child is disabled).
(4) For the purposes of paragraph (3), a child is disabled where—
(a) a disability living allowance is payable in respect of that child, or has ceased to be payable solely because he is a patient;
[[19] (b) the child is certified as severely sight impaired or blind by a consultant ophthalmologist;]
(c) the child ceased to be [[19] certified as severely sight impaired or blind by a consultant ophthalmologist] within the 28 weeks immediately preceding the date of claim; [[16] [[17]. . .]
(d) personal independence payment is payable in respect of that child, or would be payable but for regulations under section 86(1) (hospital in-patients) of the Welfare Reform Act 2012;] [[17] or
(e) armed forces independence payment is payable in respect of that child.]
(5) Charges paid in respect of the child's compulsory education or charges paid by a person to a partner or by a partner to the person in respect of any child for whom either or any of them is responsible are not relevant childcare charges.
(6) Where regulation 15(4) (agreement for the provision of future childcare) applies—
(a) the words "charges paid" in paragraph (1) include charges which will be incurred; and
(b) the words "childcare provided" in paragraph (1) include care which will be provided.
(7) [[2]. . .]
(8) Relevant childcare charges are calculated on a weekly basis in accordance with regulation 15.

AMENDMENTS

1. Working Tax Credit (Entitlement and Maximum Rate) (Amendment) Regulations 2003 (SI 2003/701) reg.13 (April 6, 2003).
2. Tax Credits (Miscellaneous Amendments) Regulations 2004 (SI 2004/762) reg.10 (April 6, 2004).
3. Working Tax Credit (Entitlement and Maximum Rate) (Amendment) Regulations 2004 (SI 2004/1276) reg.2 (June 1, 2004).
4. Working Tax Credit (Entitlement and Maximum Rate) (Amendment) Regulations 2005 (SI 2005/769) reg.4(b) (April 6, 2005).

Working Tax Credit (Entitlement and Maximum Rate) Regulations 2002

5. Civil Partnership Act 2004 (Tax Credits, etc.) (Consequential Amendments) Order 2005 (SI 2005/2919) art.2(4) (December 5, 2005).

6. Working Tax Credit (Entitlement and Maximum Rate) (Amendment) Regulations 2005 (SI 2005/769) reg.4(a) (January 1, 2006).

7. Tax Credits (Miscellaneous Amendments) Regulations 2006 (SI 2006/766) reg.20(4) (April 6, 2006).

8. Tax Credits (Miscellaneous Amendments) Regulations 2007 (SI 2007/824) reg.6 (April 6, 2007).

9. Working Tax Credit (Entitlement and Maximum Rate) (Amendment No.2) Regulations 2007 (SI 2007/2479) reg.2 (October 1, 2007).

10. Tax Credits (Miscellaneous Amendments) Regulations 2008 (SI 2008/604) reg.3 (April 6, 2008).

11. Tax Credits (Miscellaneous Amendments) (No.2) Regulations 2008 (SI 2008/2169) reg.2 (September 1, 2008).

12. Tax Credits (Miscellaneous Amendments) Regulations 2009 (SI 2009/697) reg.5 (April 6, 2009).

13. Tax Credits (Miscellaneous Amendments) (No.2) Regulations 2009 (SI 2009/2887) reg.4 (April 6, 2010).

14. Tax Credits (Miscellaneous Amendments) Regulations 2011 (SI 2011/721) reg.3 (April 6, 2011).

15. Public Services Reform (Scotland) Act 2010 (Consequential Modifications of Enactments) Order 2011 (SI 2011/2581) art.2 and Sch.2 para.36 (October 28, 2011).

16. Personal Independence Payment (Supplementary Provisions and Consequential Amendments) Regulations 2013 (SI 2013/388) reg.8 and Sch. para.28(5) (April 8, 2013).

17. Armed Forces and Reserve Forces Compensation Scheme (Consequential Provisions: Subordinate Legislation) Order 2013 (SI 2013/591) art.7 and Sch. para.24(5) (April 8, 2013).

18. Child Benefit (General) and Tax Credits (Miscellaneous Amendments) Regulations 2014 (SI 2014/2924) reg.4(2) (November 28, 2014).

DEFINITIONS

"child"—see reg.2.
"claim"—see reg.2.
"partner"—see reg.2.
"patient"—see reg.2.

GENERAL NOTE

2.74 The main content of this regulation is the definition of the main phrases on which reg.13 relies. "Child" receives a slightly limited definition compared with the standard approach for child tax credit and working tax credit, as para.(3) puts an upper limit on the relevant age of a child. The provision does not apply at all to those over 16, who are known as "qualifying young persons" for working tax credit and child tax credit purposes. There is an upwards extension of the age limit for disabled children in paras (3) and (4). This is by reference to payment of any level of disability living allowance or by blindness. There is also a limit applying to the youngest children. Paragraph (7) links with reg.13(3) to exclude a claim by someone on maternity, paternity or adoption leave by reference only to the child in respect of whom the leave is granted.

"Child care" is given an extensive definition. This is necessary because responsibility for childcare legislation is part of the devolved responsibilities of the Scottish and Northern Irish parliaments and the Welsh assembly. In addition, the definition has been extended to childcare outside the UK. This links with the provisions in the Tax Credits (Residence) Regulations 2003 (SI 2003/642) under which Crown servants outside the UK, and their partners, are regarded as being in the UK for tax credits purposes. Accordingly, staff provided with approved childcare facilities by, for example, defence establishments, can qualify for the childcare element of working tax credit. Any dispute about whether someone is providing "childcare" is for the authorities responsible for that particular set of registration rules.

"Relevant childcare charges" is defined by reference to charges for "childcare", with the important exception in para.(1A) of childcare provided by a (registered) relative in the child's home. It can, however, be provided in the carer's home even though the carer is, say, a grandparent. The condition ensures that both the carer, and the carer's premises, are open to inspection. Paragraph (5) excludes charges for education as against care, and payments made by one of a married or unmarried couple to the other (although the one to whom the payments are made may not be responsible for the child).

With regard to reg.14(2)(f), and with effect from October 1, 2103, minor amendments were made to the Tax Credits (Approval of Child Care Providers) (Wales) Scheme 2007 by SI 2013/2237. They affect only the information powers under the Scheme and do not make any changes to entitlement.

2.75

The scope of reg.14(5) was discussed by the deputy Commissioner in *CTC/3646/2007*, where the deputy Commissioner upheld a tribunal's decision to refuse to take account of apportioned fees for a "waiting class". Regulation 15(3) could not therefore be applied on the facts. The issue is further clarified by the addition of a definition of "full time education" to the Child Tax Credit Regulations by SI 2008/2169 reg.7(3) with effect from September 1, 2008.

Calculation of relevant childcare charges

15.—(1) Relevant childcare charges are calculated by aggregating the average weekly charge paid for childcare for each child in respect of whom charges are incurred [¹and rounding up the total to the nearest whole pound]. This is subject to [¹paragraphs (1A) and (2)].

2.76

[¹(1A) In any case in which the charges in respect of childcare are paid weekly, the average weekly charge for the purposes of paragraph (1) is established—
  (a) where the charges are for a fixed weekly amount, by aggregating the average weekly charge paid for childcare for each child in respect of whom charges are incurred in the most recent four complete weeks; or
  (b) where the charges are for variable weekly amounts, by aggregating the charges for the previous 52 weeks and dividing the total by 52.]

(2) In any case in which the charges in respect of childcare are paid monthly, the average weekly charge for the purposes of paragraph (1) is established—
  (a) where the charges are for a fixed monthly amount, by multiplying that amount by 12 and dividing the product by 52; or
  (b) where the charges are for variable monthly amounts, by aggregating the charges for the previous 12 months and dividing the total by 52.

(3) In a case where there is insufficient information for establishing the average weekly charge paid for childcare in accordance with paragraphs (1) and (2), an officer of the Board shall estimate the charge—
  (a) in accordance with information provided by the person or persons incurring the charges; and
  (b) by any method which in the officer's opinion is reasonable.

(4) If a person—
  (a) has entered into an agreement for the provision of childcare; and
  (b) will incur under that agreement relevant childcare charges in respect of childcare during the period of the award, the average weekly charge for childcare is based upon a written estimate of the future weekly charges provided by that person.

Working Tax Credit (Entitlement and Maximum Rate) Regulations 2002

AMENDMENT

1. Working Tax Credit (Entitlement and Maximum Rate) (Amendment) Regulations 2003 (SI 2003/701) reg.14 (April 6, 2003).

DEFINITIONS

"child"—see reg.14(3).
"childcare"—see reg.14(2).
"relevant childcare charges"—see reg.14(1).

GENERAL NOTE

2.77   This regulation sets out the methods to be used in calculating the amount of childcare charges on which the childcare element is to be based. The regulation was amended just before it came into effect because the previous form of the regulation was accepted as being seriously flawed. This created potential unfairness as between those who pay monthly for their childcare on an annualised basis and those who pay weekly on an actual basis. While the monthly payers usually have a steady pattern of payments, the weekly payers often pay more during school terms than during school holidays.

The rules deal with monthly payments by either using the fixed monthly charge, or the average of the last 12 monthly charges, to determine the weekly figure. Varying weekly charges are calculated by reference to the last 52 weeks, while fixed weekly charges are calculated by reference to the last four weeks. Presumably, however, regard must be had to more than four past weeks in applying this rule to avoid the problem of assessing the charges for the wrong four weeks.

There are two important provisos to these rules. The first is that HMRC may rely on estimates based on "any method . . . which is reasonable". This should allow a solution to the problem of increases in the charges that should be reflected in increases in the childcare element. The second proviso, in para.(4), allows an estimate of the future charges to be taken into account provided that the claimant has entered into a written agreement for the provision of childcare.

Change of circumstances

2.78   **16.**—(1) There is a relevant change in circumstances if—
   (a) [¹. . .]
   (b) [¹during the period of an award, the weekly relevant childcare charges, rounded up to the nearest whole pound]—
      (i) exceed the average weekly charge calculated in accordance with regulation 15 by £10 a week or more;
      (ii) are less than the average weekly charge calculated in accordance with regulation 15 by £10 a week or more; or
      (iii) are nil.
   If there is a relevant change in circumstances, the amount of the childcare element of working tax credit shall be recalculated with effect from the specified date.
   [¹(2) For the purposes of paragraph (1), the weekly relevant childcare charge—
   (a) where the childcare charges are for a fixed weekly amount, is the aggregate of the weekly charge paid for childcare for each child in respect of whom charges are incurred in each of the four consecutive weeks in which the change occurred; or
   (b) where the childcare charges are for variable weekly amounts, is established by aggregating the anticipated weekly charge paid for childcare for each child in respect of whom charges will be incurred for the following 52 weeks and dividing the total by 52.]

(SI 2002/2005 reg.16) (as amended)

(3) If in any case the charges in respect of childcare are paid monthly, the weekly relevant childcare charge for the purposes of paragraph (1) is established—
   (a) where the charges are for a fixed monthly amount, by multiplying that amount by 12 and dividing the product by 52; or
   (b) where the charges are for variable monthly amounts, by aggregating the [¹anticipated] charges for the [¹next] 12 months and dividing the total by 52.

(4) In a case where there is insufficient information for establishing the weekly relevant childcare charge paid for childcare in accordance with paragraphs (2) and (3), an officer of the Board shall estimate the charge—
   (a) in accordance with information provided by the person or persons incurring the charges; and
   (b) by any method which in the officer's opinion is reasonable.

(5) For the purpose of paragraph (1) the specified date is—
   (a) where the childcare charges are increased, the later of—
      (i) the first day of the week in which the change occurred, and
      (ii) the first day of the week in which falls the day which is [³ one month] prior to the date notification of the change is given,
[² (b) where the child care charges are decreased—
      (i) in a case where an award of child care charges is a fixed period, the length of which is known when the award is first made, the first day of the week following the end of that fixed period, and
      (ii) in all other cases, the first day of the week following the four consecutive weeks in which the change occurred.]

AMENDMENTS

1. Working Tax Credit (Entitlement and Maximum Rate) (Amendment) Regulations 2003 (SI 2003/701) reg.15 (April 6, 2003).
2. Working Tax Credit (Entitlement and Maximum Rate) (Amendment) Regulations 2010 (SI 2010/918) reg.3 (April 15, 2010).
3. Tax Credits (Miscellaneous Amendments) Regulations 2012 (SI 2012/848) reg.2(18) (April 6, 2012).

DEFINITIONS

"award"—see TCA 2002 s.14.
"change of circumstances"—see TCA 2002 s.6.

GENERAL NOTE

2.79 This regulation brings into play the mechanisms for amending or terminating an award of working tax credit. Section 6(3) of the TCA 2002 makes provision for regulations to impose a duty on a claimant to report a change of circumstances that may decrease the rate of entitlement to a tax credit. Regulation 21 of the Tax Credits (Claims and Notifications) Regulations 2002 (SI 2002/2014) imposes the requirement that notification of a change of circumstances as defined in this regulation must be given within one month of the change occurring. Regulations 22–24 of those Regulations set out how and by whom this is to be done.

Failure to notify may make the claimant liable to a penalty of £300 under s.32(3) of the TCA 2002.

In *HMRC v CB (TC)* [2013] UKUT 484 (AAC) the Upper Tribunal considered the interaction of reg.16 with reg.7D. The question in issue was the length of time for which entitlement to tax credits continued after a claimant who had been working 40 hours a week stopped working. The specific issue was the period for which the childcare element remained payable. There had been a timely notification of changes of circumstances. HMRC argued that the "run on" periods in reg.7D and reg.16 ran concurrently, while the appellant argued that they should be applied consecutively. Judge Ovey agreed with the appellant's arguments in part, noting that reg.13 determined the questions of entitlement to the childcare element and that reg.16 is concerned with actual changes only and with the date of any required recalculation. However, on the facts, this did not assist the appellant.

Severe disability element

Severe disability element

2.80   **17.**—(1) The determination of the maximum rate must include the severe disability element if the claimant, or, in the case of a joint claim, one of the claimants satisfies paragraph (2) [¹ or (3)] [² or (4)].

(2) A person satisfies this paragraph if a disability living allowance, attributable to the care component payable at the highest rate prescribed under section 72(3) of the Contributions and Benefits Act or an attendance allowance at the higher rate prescribed under section 65(3) of that Act—
 (a) is payable in respect of him; or
 (b) would be so payable but for a suspension of benefit by virtue of regulations under section 113(2) of the Contributions and Benefits Act (suspension during hospitalisation), or an abatement as a consequence of hospitalisation.

[¹ (3) A person satisfies this paragraph if the enhanced rate of the daily living component of personal independence payment under section 78(2) of the Welfare Reform Act 2012—
 (a) is payable in respect of that person; or
 (b) would be so payable but for regulations made under section 86(1) (hospital in-patients) of that Act.]

[² (4) A person satisfies this paragraph if an armed forces independence payment is payable in respect of him.]

AMENDMENTS

1. Personal Independence Payment (Supplementary Provisions and Consequential Amendments) Regulations 2013 (SI 2013/388) reg.8 and Sch. para.28(6) (April 8, 2013).

2. Armed Forces and Reserve Forces Compensation Scheme (Consequential Provisions: Subordinate Legislation) Order 2013 (SI 2013/591) art.7 and Sch. para.24(6) (April 8, 2013).

DEFINITIONS

"claimant"—see reg.2.
"joint claim"—see reg.2.

GENERAL NOTE

2.81   This provision is amended to deal with the replacement of disability living allowance with the new personal independence payment provided for in the Welfare Reform Act 2012. This is being introduced in stages. For the initial stages see: the Welfare Reform Act 2012 (Commencement No.8 and Savings and Transitional Provisions) Order 2013 (SI 2013/358).

This is separate from the disability element provided for in reg.9. It adds a further £1,255 to the entitlement of the claimant or claimants. But it is restricted to the case where the disabled individual is receiving the highest rate of the care component of disability living allowance (or the attendance allowance equivalent), which means that both day and night attention or supervision are needed.

There is no express provision dealing with interaction with the disability element. *CSTC/76/2006* makes it clear that the language of reg.9 requires that, in the case of a joint claim, the person who is disabled must also be the same person who is working 16 hours a week: see para.2.56, above. But this regulation does not repeat that language. Nor is this element dependent on the receipt of the disability element under reg.9. The mandatory language of reg.17 suggests that all joint claimants are entitled to the severe disability element if either of them meets the general conditions to claim WTC and either is in receipt of the highest rate of the care component of disability living allowance (or the higher rate of attendance allowance). It would follow that this element may be claimed by claimants following any of the four Routes noted at para.2.32, above, and not merely Route 2.

50 Plus element

50 Plus element

18.— [¹ ...]

AMENDMENT

1. Tax Credits (Miscellaneous Amendments) Regulations 2012 (SI 2012/848) reg.2(19) (April 6, 2012).

Death of a child or qualifying young person for whom the claimant is responsible

Entitlement after death of a child or qualifying young person for whom the claimant is responsible

19.—(1) Paragraph (2) applies if—
(a) the death occurs of a child or qualifying young person;
(b) working tax credit is payable to a person who was, or to a couple at least one of whom was, immediately before the death responsible for that child or qualifying young person;
(c) the prescribed conditions for an element of working tax credit were satisfied because the claimant, or at least one of the claimants, was responsible for that child or qualifying person, but would not have been satisfied but for that responsibility; and
(d) the prescribed conditions would have continued to be satisfied but for the death.

(2) If this paragraph applies, working tax credit shall continue to be payable, as if the child or qualifying young person had not died, for the period for which child tax credit continues to be payable in accordance with regulation 6 of the Child Tax Credit Regulations 2002.

DEFINITIONS

"child"—see reg.2.
"qualifying young person"—see reg.2.

GENERAL NOTE

Section 55 of the TCA 2002 provides an extension of the payment of child benefit for a period of eight weeks after the death of a child for whom the benefit is paid.

Working Tax Credit (Entitlement and Maximum Rate) Regulations 2002

Section 5(5) makes similar provision for child tax credit, and effect is given to this by reg.6 of the Child Tax Credit Regulations 2002 (SI 2002/2007). This regulation matches those extensions for working tax credit also, s.10(3)(d) of the TCA 2002 providing authority for this.

Claimants are required, from November 2006, to report the death of a child or qualifying young person for whom they are receiving additional credit within one month of the death. See para.2.313, below.

Part III

Maximum Rate

Maximum rates of elements of Working Tax Credit

2.85 20.—(1) The maximum annual rate of working tax credit (excluding the childcare element) payable to a single claimant or to a couple making a joint claim is the sum of whichever of the following elements are applicable—
- (a) the basic element specified in column.(2) of the table in Schedule 2 at paragraph 1;
- (b) in respect of a claimant who satisfies regulation 9(1), the disability element specified in column (2) of the table in Schedule 2 at paragraph 2;
- (c) the 30-hour element specified in column (2) of the table in Schedule 2 at paragraph 3 in respect of—
    - (i) a single claimant who works for not less than 30 hours per week;
    - (ii) a couple either or both of whom work for not less than 30 hours per week; or
    - (iii) a couple, at least one of whom is responsible for a child or a qualifying young person and at least one of whom works for 16 hours per week if their hours of work when aggregated amount to at least 30 hours per week;
- (d) the second-adult element specified in column (2) of the table in Schedule 2 at paragraph 4 where regulation 11 so provides;
- (e) the lone-parent element specified in column (2) of the table in Schedule 2 at paragraph 5 where regulation 12 applies; [4 and]
- (f) the severe disability element specified in column (2) of the table in Schedule 2 at paragraph 6—
    - (i) in respect of a single claimant who satisfies regulation 17; or
    - (ii) in respect of a member of a couple making a joint claim who satisfies regulation 17 [4 . . .]
- (g) [4 . . .].

(2) The maximum rate of the childcare element of a working tax credit is [³70 per cent] of the maxima specified in paragraph (3).

(3) The maxima are—
- (a) [²£175] per week, where the [¹claimant or, in the case of a joint claim, at least one of the claimants, is responsible for] only one child in respect of whom relevant childcare charges are paid; and
- (b) [²£300] per week where the [¹claimant or, in the case of a joint claim, at least one of the claimants, is responsible for] more than one child in respect of whom relevant childcare charges are paid.

(SI 2002/2005 reg.20) (as amended)

AMENDMENTS

1. Working Tax Credit (Entitlement and Maximum Rate) (Amendment) Regulations 2003 (SI 2003/701) reg.16 (April 6, 2003).
2. Tax Credits Up-rating Regulations 2005 (SI 2005/681) reg.3(1) (April 6, 2005).
3. Tax Credits Up-rating Regulations 2011 (SI 2011/1035) reg.3(2) (April 6, 2011).
4. Tax Credits (Miscellaneous Amendments) Regulations 2012 (SI 2012/848) reg.2(20) (April 6, 2012).

DEFINITIONS

"claimant"—see reg.2.
"joint claim"—see reg.2.

GENERAL NOTE

This regulation emphasises that the entitlement of a claimant or claimants to working tax credit is made up of each of the elements to which there is entitlement. It is "the sum of whichever of the . . . elements are applicable". However, as noted above, there must be entitlement under reg.4. to the basic element in all cases. Paragraph (1) provides the necessary drafting provision to tie each of the other elements (save for the childcare element), the conditions for which have been defined above, into the rate of award and entitlement to working tax credit to the claimant or claimants under s.11 of the TCA 2002.

2.86

Paragraphs (2) and (3) then provide the effective rate of the childcare element. They set the maximum weekly childcare element at £300 for care for two or more children, and £175 for care for a single child.

The current figures for the maximum rates of all elements other than the childcare element are in Sch.2.

The varying levels of working tax credit by reference to these differing elements and the different routes by which, under reg.4, claims can be made for working tax credit can be illustrated by some short examples. The examples show the maximum entitlement to working tax credit in each case. They do not take into account the income or benefit entitlements of the claimant(s).

2.87

Route 1: Lone-parent with three children, working 32 hours a week, and incurring childcare costs of £300 a week.

Basic element	£1,960
30-hour element	£800
Lone-parent element	£2,010
Childcare element	£10,920 (limited to 70 per cent of £300 a week)
Maximum entitlement	£15,690

The parent will also be entitled to child benefit.

Route 2: Lone claimant suffering prejudice in the job market, receiving disability living allowance, and working 20 hours a week.

Basic element	£1,960
Disability element	£2,970
Maximum entitlement	£4,930

Route 3: Couple with one child making joint claim, with one of the couple working 20 hours a week, and the other working 8 hours a week.

Basic element	£1,960
Second adult element	£2,010

Working Tax Credit (Entitlement and Maximum Rate) Regulations 2002

Childcare element	£6,370 (limited to 70 per cent of £175 a week)
Maximum entitlement	£10,340

The couple will also be entitled to child benefit.

Route 4: Single claimant over 60 working 16 hours a week.

Basic element	£1,960
Maximum entitlement	£1,960

The claimant may also be entitled to state pension credit.

Route 5: Single claimant over 25 working 30 hours a week.

Basic element	£1,960
Maximum entitlement	£1,960

SCHEDULE 1   **Regulation 9(1)**

DISABILITY WHICH PUTS A PERSON AT A DISADVANTAGE IN GETTING A JOB

PART I

2.88

1. When standing he cannot keep his balance unless he continually holds onto something.
2. Using any crutches, walking frame, walking stick, prosthesis or similar walking aid which he habitually uses, he cannot walk a continuous distance of 100 metres along level ground without stopping or without suffering severe pain.
3. He can use neither of his hands behind his back as in the process of putting on a jacket or of tucking a shirt into trousers.
4. He can extend neither of his arms in front of him so as to shake hands with another person without difficulty.
5. He can put neither of his hands up to his head without difficulty so as to put on a hat.
6. Due to lack of manual dexterity he cannot, with one hand, pick up a coin which is not more than $2^{1}/_{2}$ centimetres in diameter.
7. He is not able to use his hands or arms to pick up a full jug of 1 litre capacity and pour from it into a cup, without difficulty.
8. He can turn neither of his hands sideways through 180 degrees.
[[1] 9. He is certified as severely sight impaired or blind by a consultant ophthalmologist.]
10. He cannot see to read 16 point print at a distance greater than 20 centimetres, if appropriate, wearing the glasses he normally uses.
11. He cannot hear a telephone ring when he is in the same room as the telephone, if appropriate, using a hearing aid he normally uses.
12. In a quiet room he has difficulty in hearing what someone talking in a loud voice at a distance of 2 metres says, if appropriate, using a hearing aid he normally uses.
13. People who know him well have difficulty in understanding what he says.
14. When a person he knows well speaks to him, he has difficulty in understanding what that person says.
15. At least once a year during waking hours he is in a coma or has a fit in which he loses consciousness.
16. He has a mental illness for which he receives regular treatment under the supervision of a medically qualified person.
17. Due to mental disability he is often confused or forgetful.
18. He cannot do the simplest addition and subtraction.
19. Due to mental disability he strikes people or damages property or is unable to form normal social relationships.
20. He cannot normally sustain an 8-hour working day or a 5-day working week due to a medical condition or intermittent or continuous severe pain.

(SI 2002/2005 Sch.1) (as amended)

PART II

21. As a result of an illness or accident he is undergoing a period of habilitation or rehabilitation.

2.89

AMENDMENT

1. Child Benefit (General) and Tax Credits (Miscellaneous Amendments) Regulations 2014 (SI 2014/2924) reg.4(3) (November 28, 2014).

GENERAL NOTE

Under reg.9 of these Regulations, a person is treated as having a disability which puts him or her at a disadvantage in getting a job only if one of the paragraphs of this Schedule applies to him or her. If a paragraph does apply, reg.9 deems the claimant to be at a disadvantage in getting a job, whether or not the disability actually has that effect. See the notes to regs 9 and 9A for the application of these tests to initial and repeat claims.

2.90

The Schedule requires the exercise of a considerable amount of judgement. For instance, the words "without difficulty" frequently appear. The difficulty need not be severe and plainly a person may have difficulty with an action without necessarily suffering pain when performing it. Slowness may well be sufficient.

Attention is drawn to the final condition in para.20 before detailed comment is made on the specific disabilities. This is the overarching condition that a person cannot sustain a full working day or a full working week due either to a medical condition (of any nature, physical or mental) or intermittent or continuous severe pain. *R(S) 11/51* emphasised that this has to be determined by what a claimant can reasonably be expected to do with regard to his or her age, education, training and other personal factors. It is suggested that this should be the starting point for consideration of the application of this Schedule, with reference being made to the specific disabilities in that context.

Paragraph 2

Note that this test is not the same as the test prescribed in reg.12(1)(a)(ii) of the Social Security (Disability Living Allowance) Regulations 1991 (SI 1991/2890) in respect of the mobility component of disability living allowance. Not only is the distance of 100 metres prescribed, but the question is whether that distance can be walked "without stopping" or without "severe pain" (rather than "severe discomfort"). It should also be noted that only artificial aids which are habitually used are to be taken into account, so there is no need to consider whether an aid which is not used might be suitable. In *R(M) 2/89*, the Commissioner held that a person walks only when putting one foot in front of the other, so that a person who has to swing through crutches, rather than using them to help him or her move both legs separately, cannot walk.

2.91

Paragraph 6

Two-and-a-half centimetres (1 inch) is the diameter of a 50 pence coin. Since their reduction in size, other coins, apart from the £2 coin, are smaller. Note that the claimant satisfies the test (and so may qualify for benefit) if he or she can pick up a large coin in one hand but not the other. In *CDWA 3123/1997* the claimant had no thumb on his left hand and the terminal joint of his right thumb was missing. He maintained that he was only able to pick up a coin of 2.5 centimetres in diameter by pushing it across a surface and catching it in his hand. The Commissioner holds that the tests in Sch.1 were to be performed in the normal way and not by employing some unusual or awkward manoeuvre. The normal way of picking up coins with one hand was to use the pinch grip between the thumb and fingers. An ability to pick up with the fingers alone was irrelevant because that ability did not demonstrate the presence or absence of the pinch grip. The Commissioner also confirmed that para.6 would be satisfied if the claimant could not pick up a coin of the prescribed size with one hand even if he could with the other.

2.92

Paragraph 7

2.93   This is a test of both steadiness and strength, using both hands or arms at once if necessary. The Commissioner in *CDWA 3123/1997* confirmed that the position was different under para.7 (as compared with para.6) since, here, the question was whether the claimant could perform the pouring task using both hands and arms together. An inability to do so with either hand alone is immaterial if he or she can manage the task with both hands. But any realistic difficulty, however slight, in carrying out that task would satisfy the test in para.7. Arguably, an ability to pick up and pour with one hand alone, where the claimant has no use of the other arm at all, would mean that the claimant would not qualify under this paragraph, although that question did not arise in that case.

Paragraph 8

2.94   Presumably, this is a test of wrist movements and is intended to be performed with the elbows kept still.

Paragraph 9

2.95   This paragraph replaces from November 2014 the previous tests that relied on entries in registers maintained by local or health authorities. That process was becoming complicated with increasing divergences of approach in national and local governments as the issue is a devolved issue.

Paragraph 10

2.96   # 16 point print is 4 mm high. It is this size.

Paragraphs 12–14

2.97   If hearing or understanding is possible, but only with difficulty (perhaps after repetition), the claimant still qualifies. The precise relationship between paras 12 and 14 is unclear. Difficulty in understanding may arise for reasons other than loss of hearing and, indeed, a person without hearing may be able to understand through lip-reading. Can a person who can hear a loud voice, but not an ordinary conversational voice, at a distance of two metres qualify under para.14 if he or she cannot lip-read? In principle, the answer would seem to be "yes". That would not mean that para.12 had no effect because the person would only be able to qualify under para.14 if he or she was further disadvantaged by an inability to make use of other methods of comprehending speech.

Paragraph 16

2.98   Medication taken on prescription will be enough, provided that it is regular. Mental illness is not defined, but, if a person is receiving treatment there is likely to be a diagnosis of an illness and if it is an illness of the mind it will be mental illness.

Paragraph 17

2.99   Mental disability is not defined and neither is the extent of confusion or forgetfulness required. On one view, any confusion or forgetfulness suggests some disability of the mind and the question is whether the degree of confusion or forgetfulness is sufficient to warrant the view that the legislator intended such a claimant to qualify (see the approach of the Court Appeal in *W v L* [1974] Q.B. 711). On the other hand, in *R(A) 2/92*, a Commissioner considered that a specific diagnosis was required and that suggests that the first question is whether there is such a diagnosis. Only after that has been answered does one go on to consider whether there is any resulting confusion or forgetfulness.

Paragraph 19

2.100   See the note to para.17. The approach taken in *R(A) 2/92* would create real difficulties here given the view expressed there that "personality disorder" can be distinguished from "mental disability".

(SI 2002/2005 Sch.1) (as amended)

Paragraph 21
This applies only on an initial claim.

SCHEDULE 2   **Regulation 20(1)**

MAXIMUM RATES OF THE ELEMENTS OF A WORKING TAX CREDIT

[¹*Relevant element of working tax credit*	*Maximum annual rate*
1. Basic element	[³£1,960]
2. Disability element	[²£2,970]
3. 30-hour element	[³£800]
4. Second adult element	[³£2,010]
5. Lone-parent element	[³£2,010]
6. Severe disability element	[²£1,275]

AMENDMENTS

1. Tax Credits Up-rating Regulations 2013 (SI 2013/750) reg.3 (April 6, 2013).
2. Tax Credits Up-rating Regulations 2015 (SI 2015/451) reg.3 (April 6, 2015).
3. Child Benefit and Tax Credits Up-rating Order 2015 (SI 2015/567) art.4 (April 6, 2015).

Tax Credits (Definition and Calculation of Income) Regulations 2002

(SI 2002/2006) (AS AMENDED)

Whereas a draft of this instrument, which contains the first regulations made under section 7(8) and (9) of the Tax Credits Act 2002, has been laid before, and approved by resolution of, each House of Parliament:

Now, therefore, the Treasury, in exercise of the powers conferred upon them by sections 7(8) and (9), 65(1), (7) and (9) and 67 of the Tax Credits Act 2002, hereby make the following Regulations:

PART I

General provisions

1. Citation, commencement and effect.
2. Interpretation.

Tax Credits (Definition and Calculation of Income) Regulations 2002

PART II

INCOME FOR THE PURPOSES OF TAX CREDITS

General

3. Calculation of income of claimant.

CHAPTER 2

Employment income

4. Employment income.

CHAPTER 3

Pension income

5. Pension income.

CHAPTER 4

Trading income

6. Trading income.

CHAPTER 5

Social security income

7. Social security income.

CHAPTER 6

Student income

8. Student income.
9. Payments of income in connection with students to be disregarded for the purposes of regulation 3.

(SI 2002/2006) (as amended)

CHAPTER 7

Investment income

10. Investment income.

CHAPTER 8

Property income

11. Property income.

CHAPTER 9

Foreign income

12. Foreign income.

CHAPTER 10

Notional income

13. Introduction.
14. Claimants treated for any purpose as having income by virtue of the Income Tax Acts.
15. Claimants depriving themselves of income in order to secure entitlement.
16. Claimants to whom income becomes available upon the making of a claim.
17. Claimants providing services to other persons for less than full earnings.

CHAPTER 11

Miscellaneous income

18. Miscellaneous income.

Tax Credits (Definition and Calculation of Income) Regulations 2002

Part III

Sums disregarded in the calculation of income

General disregards in the calculation of income

19. General disregards in the calculation of income.

Introduction and General Note

2.104   Section 7 of TCA 2002 provides that entitlement to a tax credit is subject to an income test. These regulations provide the detail of that test. They do so by adopting, with some important modifications, the rules for deciding on the income of an individual in the rewritten income tax legislation adopted over the last few years by Parliament from the draft bills produced by the Tax Law Rewrite Project. The Acts produced by the Rewrite Project have modernised the language and presentation of income tax law, and parallel changes in annual Finance Acts have also rationalised parts of it. This has made it easier to abandon the previous approach of having a different set of defining rules of income for benefit purposes and to adopt the income tax rules into the benefit system.

The rewritten income tax law

2.105   With effect from April 6, 2007 all the former primary legislation dating back to the 1840s under which income tax was imposed and collected has been repealed and replaced by the new rewritten legislation. This is contained in three major Acts, the Income Tax (Earnings and Pensions) Act 2003, the Income Tax (Trading and Other Income) Act 2005 and the Income Tax Act 2007. In practice these contain all the income rules necessary for any tax credits calculation save for the rules about capital allowances in the Capital Allowances Act 2000, another rewrite measure.

A fundamental change in approach

2.106   The income test used for tax credits is fundamentally different to that used for the income-related benefits such as income support, jobseeker's allowance and housing benefit. The main differences are as follows:

(1) *There is no capital rule.* There has never been a wealth tax in the UK, save for that, in effect, imposed on those claiming means-tested benefits. The approach is to tax income from capital as (and if) it arises. This is the approach now adopted for tax credits.

(2) *Capital gains are irrelevant.* Income tax is supplemented for individuals by a separate capital gains tax, e.g. on the capital gain made on selling an asset. Capital gains are also ignored for tax credits purposes.

(3) *There are no rules deeming income from capital held.* The rules treating capital as income, and attributing tariff income to capital, have been abolished and not replaced.

(4) *There is no all-inclusive definition of income.* The previous approach was to base the calculation of non-earned income on "gross income and any capital treated as income". The income tax based approach is to calculate income from each named source and to then aggregate the totals to establish the relevant income. If income arises from a source that is not one of the named sources, it is excluded from the calculation.

(5) *Claimants may choose forms of income that avoid the calculation.* The rules generally follow the approach of income tax in looking at actual income

from capital, if any. They no longer follow the approach of the rules for the income-related benefits (perhaps more correctly the income and capital related benefits) of assuming income from capital at set rates while ignoring actual income from capital. They also leave any capital gains out of account. However, there remain some important anti-avoidance provisions based on the former family credit rules that take some account of capital and notional income. See regs 13–17 below.

Differences between tax credits income calculations and income tax assessments

The calculation of income for tax credits is based closely on the income tax approach. This allows HMRC to base its tax credits calculations on its income tax assessments or, in most cases, on the self-assessments of those individuals to income tax or the assessment and collection of income tax from employees by employers and agencies through the PAYE (Pay As You Earn) system. There are, however, some important differences from income tax assessments and these should also be noted: 2.107

(1) *Couples are assessed jointly, not separately.* The income tax system was transferred from a system in which married couples were assessed on their joint incomes in the name of the husband to a system of separate assessment of each partner in 1990. One reason for this was the growing concern about discrimination against couples who were married, and assessed jointly, as against those who were unmarried and separately assessed. The new rules require both married and unmarried couples to make joint applications for working tax credit and child tax credit. This is the first time that HMRC has been concerned to calculate the joint income of unmarried couples, and it will bring sharply into focus the need to look carefully at when two individuals are required to make a joint claim. The starting point in any calculation of income for tax credits purposes is therefore to establish who the claimant is or claimants are. If two people become a couple, or a couple breaks up, then that fact must be reported to HMRC and a new claim made.

(2) *The income tax personal allowances do not apply to tax credits.* Instead, claimants are entitled to the appropriate "elements". One important effect of this, combined with the first point, is that the widespread practice of transferring income from the working partner of a couple to the non-working partner, so as to claim the maximum value from personal allowances and to minimise higher-rate tax, and so to reduce income tax, will not work to reduce income for tax credits purposes.

(3) *The taxable forms of income are not identical to those used for income tax.* They are similar, but include some additional items, including rules dealing with income foregone and income of which a person has deprived himself or herself.

(4) *Claimants are taxed on worldwide income.* This is linked to (3). Tax credits may only be claimed by those who are ordinarily resident in the UK, but they are subject to the obligation to declare their full incomes, regardless of any reliefs by way of double taxation or exemption that they might receive under the Income Tax Acts or double taxation agreements.

(5) *Claimants are usually assessed on last year's income.* The income tax rules now use the current year's income from any source for almost all current year income tax assessments. From 2007, calculations of income for both awards of, and entitlement to, tax credit purposes were based usually on the previous year's income. They were changed to a current year basis when s.7(3) applied. However, from 2013/14 that subsection has been given greater importance because rises in total income from the previous year are now taken into account if they exceed £5,000 and falls in total income are taken into account if over £2,500.

(6) *The thresholds for income tax and each tax credit are different.* There is now a single personal allowance for income tax and NI contributions for all those

461

Tax Credits (Definition and Calculation of Income) Regulations 2002

under 65, with a higher figure for those over 65. But there are separate thresholds for working tax credit and child tax credit, and these are not linked to income tax.

(7) *Deductions and exclusions are not identical.* Nor are specific inclusions, so the assessment of income from employment for income tax purposes will not be identical, and nor will the total income.

The drafting techniques used in these Regulations are also those of the Rewrite Project, for example in the use of signposting provisions and the use of the "command" tense of verbs in taking the user step by step through a calculation. Following this approach, reg.3 lays down in clear terms how income is to be calculated. But it is, in practice, the fifth of five questions that need to be answered to establish the relevant income of a claimant or claimants.

The questions to be decided:

2.108
(1) Who is claiming?

(2) IS or JSA . . . or SPC?

(3) Which tax year?

(4) Are there any income changes during the tax year?

(5) What income?

The questions are as follows:

(1) Who is claiming?
2.109
Is the claim a single claim, a joint claim or a claim by a polygamous unit? The income of each claimant must be calculated.

(2) IS, JSA, SPC?
2.110
Automatic entitlement to child tax credit has yet to be introduced for those on income support and jobseeker's allowance, although it now exists for those of pensionable age receiving state pension credit instead. The 16-hour rule effectively prevents those on these benefits claiming working tax credit as well.

(3) Which tax year?
2.111
As noted above, in most cases the relevant income for tax credits is the income of the previous year not the current year income used for most income tax purposes. But attention must be paid to current income where there is a sharp increase in income between one year and the next. (This does not apply to capital gains, so will most often catch employees, as sums received from employment are seldom regarded as capital.)

(4) Are there any changes during the year?
2.112
The award of tax credit under ss.5 and 14 of the Act are by reference initially to the income of the previous year. But there may be relevant changes of circumstances that lead to a revision of the award if there is a notified change of circumstances under reg.6. The decision on entitlement is made only after the end of the tax year under s.19.

(5) What kinds of income?
2.113
This is determined by the current regulations.

CROSS-REFERENCES

2.114
The notes to each paragraph set out in full the Parts, Chapters and Section titles to all Chapters and Sections of the Taxes Act, ITEPA and Finance Acts referred to in these regulations. The regulations include cross references to a considerable number of income tax provisions, only some of which will be of more than

(SI 2002/2006) (as amended)

occasional importance to tax credits assessments. In addition, as explained below, major parts of both Acts are of no relevance to tax credits. The volume contains a selection of the more important provisions from both Acts, and the cross references supplement that by noting the full title of each Chapter and Section referred to in these Regulations.

PART I

General provisions

Citation, commencement and effect

1. These Regulations may be cited as the Tax Credits (Definition and Calculation of Income) Regulations 2002 and shall come into force—
(a) for the purpose of enabling claims to be made, on 1st August 2002;
(b) for the purpose of enabling awards to be made, on 1st January 2003; and
(c) for all other purposes, on 6th April 2003;
and shall have effect for the tax year beginning on 6th April 2003 and subsequent tax years.

2.115

DEFINITIONS

"award"—see TCA 2002 s.5.
"claim"—see TCA 2002 s.3.
"tax year"—see reg.2.

Interpretation

2.—(1) In these Regulations, unless the context otherwise requires—
"the Act" means the Tax Credits Act 2002;
"the Contributions and Benefits Act" means the Social Security Contributions and Benefits Act 1992; [³. . .]
"the Employment Act" means the Employment and Training Act 1973 [³; and
"the Northern Ireland Contributions and Benefits Act" means the Social Security Contributions and Benefits (Northern Ireland) Act 1992.]
(2) In these Regulations except where the context otherwise requires—
"the 1992 Fund" means moneys made available from time to time by the Secretary of State for Social Security for the benefit of persons eligible for payment in accordance with the provisions of a scheme established by him on 24th April 1992 as respects England and Wales and Northern Ireland and on 10th April 1992 as respects Scotland;
[⁶"the Board" means the Commissioners for Her Majesty's Revenue and Customs";]
"child" has the meaning given in the Child Tax Credit Regulations 2002;
"claim" means a claim for child tax credit or working tax credit and "joint claim" and "single claim" shall be construed in accordance with [²section 3(8)] of the Act and "claimant" shall be construed accordingly;

2.116

463

Tax Credits (Definition and Calculation of Income) Regulations 2002

[⁴"couple" has the meaning given by section 3(5A) of the Act;]
[¹"earnings" shall be construed in accordance with section 62 of the ITEPA;]
"the Eileen Trust" means the charitable trust of that name established on 29th March 1993 out of funds provided by the Secretary of State for Social Security for the benefit of persons eligible in accordance with its provisions;
[¹. . .];
[⁵"employment zone" means an area within Great Britain—
  (i) subject to a designation for the purposes of the Employment Zones Regulations 2003 by the Secretary of State, or
[⁷(ii) listed in the Schedule to the Employment Zones (Allocation to Contractors) Pilot Regulations 2006,]
  pursuant to section 60 of the Welfare Reform and Pensions Act 1999;]
"employment zone programme" means a programme which is—
  (a) established for one or more employment zones; and
  (b) designed to assist claimants for a Jobseeker's Allowance to obtain sustainable employment;
"family" means—
  (a) in the case of a joint claim, the [⁴. . .] couple by whom the claim is made and any child or qualifying young person for whom at least one of them is responsible, in accordance with regulation 3 of the Child Tax Credit Regulations 2002; and
  (b) in the case of a single claim, the claimant and any child or qualifying young person for whom he is responsible in accordance with regulation 3 of the Child Tax Credit Regulations 2002;
"the Independent Living Fund" means the charitable trust of that name established out of funds provided by the Secretary of State for Social Services for the purpose of providing financial assistance to those persons incapacitated by or otherwise suffering from very severe disablement who are in need of such assistance to enable them to live independently;
[⁹ "the Independent Living Fund (2006)" means the Trust of that name established by a deed dated 10th April 2006 and made between the Secretary of State for Work and Pensions of the one part and Margaret Rosemary Cooper, Michael Beresford Boyall and Marie Theresa Martin of the other part;]
"the Independent Living Funds" means the Independent Living Fund, [⁹ the Independent Living (Extension) Fund, the Independent Living (1993) Fund and the Independent Living Fund (2006)]
"the Independent Living (Extension) Fund" means the trust of that name established on 25th February 1993 by the Secretary of State for Social Security and Robin Glover Wendt and John Fletcher Shepherd;
"the Independent Living (1993) Fund" means the trust of that name established on 25th February 1993 by the Secretary of State for Social Security and Robin Glover Wendt and John Fletcher Shepherd;
[⁸ "ITA" means the Income Tax Act 2007]
[¹"ITEPA" means the Income Tax (Earnings and Pensions) Act 2003;]
[⁶"ITTOIA" means the Income Tax (Trading and Other Income) Act 2005;]
"the Macfarlane (Special Payments) Trust" means the trust of that name

(SI 2002/2006 reg.2) (as amended)

established on 29th January 1990 partly out of funds provided by the Secretary of State for Health for the benefit of certain persons suffering from haemophilia;

"the Macfarlane (Special Payments) (No.2) Trust" means the trust of that name established on 3rd May 1991 partly out of funds provided by the Secretary of State for Health for the benefit of certain persons suffering from haemophilia and other beneficiaries;

"the Macfarlane Trust" means the charitable trust established partly out of funds provided by the Secretary of State for Health to the Haemophilia Society for the relief of poverty or distress among those suffering from haemophilia;

"the Macfarlane Trusts" means the Macfarlane Trust, the Macfarlane (Special Payments) Trust and the Macfarlane (Special Payments) (No.2) Trust;

"pensionable age" has the meaning given by the rules in paragraph 1 of Schedule 4 to the Pensions Act 1995;

"pension fund holder", in relation to a [5registered pension scheme], means the trustees, managers or scheme administrators of the scheme [5. . .];

[12 "qualifying care receipts" has the meaning given to that expression by section 805 of the Income Tax (Trading and Other Income) Act 2005;]

"qualifying young person" has the meaning given in the Child Tax Credit Regulations 2002;

[5"registered pension scheme" has the meaning given by section 150(2) of the Finance Act 2004;]

[10 "Saving Gateway account" has the meaning given by section 1 of the Saving Gateway Accounts Act 2009;]

[5. . .]
[5. . .]
[6. . .];
[1. . .];
[11. . .]

"tax year" means a period beginning with the 6th April in one year and ending with 5th April in the next;

"the Taxes Act" means the Income and Corporation Taxes Act 1988;

"voluntary organisation" means a body, other than a public or local authority, the activities of which are carried on otherwise than for profit;

"war pension" has the meaning given in section 25(4) of the Social Security Act 1989.

(3) For the purposes of these Regulations, whether a person is responsible for a child or a qualifying young person is determined in accordance with regulaton 3 of the Child Tax Credit Regulations 2002.

(4) In these Regulations—

(a) a reference to a claimant's partner is a reference to a claimant's spouse [4or civil partner] or a person with whom the claimant lives as a spouse [4or civil partner]; and

(b) a reference to a claimant's former partner is a reference to a claimant's former spouse [4or civil partner] or a person with whom the claimant has lived as a spouse [4or civil partner]; and

(c) a reference in these Regulations to an Extra Statutory Concession is a reference to that Concession as published by the Inland Revenue on 1st July 2002.

Tax Credits (Definition and Calculation of Income) Regulations 2002

AMENDMENTS

1. Tax Credits (Definition and Calculation of Income) (Amendment) Regulations 2003 (SI 2003 No.732) reg.4 (April 6, 2003).
2. Tax Credits (Miscellaneous Amendments No.2) Regulations 2003 (SI 2003/2815) reg.3 (November 26, 2003).
3. Tax Credits (Miscellaneous Amendments) Regulations 2004 (SI 2004/762) reg.13 (April 6, 2004).
4. Civil Partnership Act 2004 (Tax Credits, etc.) (Consequential Amendments) Order 2005 (SI 2005/2919) art.3(2) (December 5, 2005).
5. Taxation of Pension Schemes (Consequential Amendments) Order 2006 (SI 2006/745) art.26(2) (April 6, 2006).
6. Tax Credits (Miscellaneous Amendments) Regulations 2006 (SI 2006/766) reg.7 (April 6, 2006).
7. Tax Credits (Miscellaneous Amendments) Regulations 2007 (SI 2007/824) reg.8 (April 6, 2007).
8. Tax Credits (Definition and Calculation of Income) (Amendment) Regulations 2007 (SI 2007/1305) reg.3 (May 16, 2007).
9. Independent Living Fund (2006) Order 2007 (SI 2007/2538) art.7 (October 1, 2007).
10. Tax Credits (Miscellaneous Amendments) Regulations 2010 (SI 2010/751) reg.3 (April 6, 2010).
11. Tax Credits (Miscellaneous Amendments) (No.3) Regulations 2010 (SI 2010/2914) reg.3 (December 31, 2010).
12. Tax Credits (Miscellaneous Amendments) Regulations 2011 (SI 2011/721) reg.2(2) (April 6, 2011).

GENERAL NOTE

2.117   See also the definitions in TCA 2002 ss.48 and 65 (above) and ITA 2007 Sch.4 (not included in this work).

PART II

INCOME FOR THE PURPOSES OF TAX CREDITS

CHAPTER 1

General

Calculation of income of claimant

2.118   **3.**—(1) The manner in which income of a claimant, or, in the case of a joint claim, the aggregate income of the claimants, is to be calculated for a tax year for the purposes of Part I of the Act is as follows.

Step 1

2.119   Calculate and then add together—
(a) the pension income (as defined in regulation 5(1));
(b) the investment income (as defined in regulation 10);
(c) the property income (as defined in regulation 11);
(d) the foreign income (as defined in regulation 12); and
(e) the notional income (as defined in regulation 13),
of the claimant, or, in the case of a joint claim, of the claimants.

(SI 2002/2006 reg.3) (as amended)

If the result of this step is £300 or less, it is treated as nil.
If the result of this step is more than £300, only the excess is taken into account in the following steps.

Step 2

Calculate and then add together— 2.120
  (a) the employment income (as defined in regulation 4);
  (b) the social security income (as defined in regulation 7);
  (c) the student income (as defined in regulation 8); and
  (d) the miscellaneous income (as defined in regulation 18), of the claimant, or in the case of a joint claim, of the claimants.

Step 3

Add together the results of steps 1 and 2. 2.121

Step 4

Calculate the trading income (as defined in regulation 6) of the claimant, or 2.122
in the case of a joint claim, of the claimants.
  Add the result of this step to that produced by step 3 [1 . . .] in the year.
  If there has been a trading loss in the year, [1 subtract] the amount of that loss from the result of step 3.
  [4A loss shall not be available for tax credit purposes, unless the trade was being carried on upon a commercial basis and with a view to the realisation of profits in the trade or, where the carrying on of the trade formed part of a larger undertaking, in the undertaking as a whole.]
  [2Any trading loss in the year not set off as a result of the calculations in Steps One to Four above due to an insufficiency of income may be carried forward and set off against trading income (if any) of the same trade, profession or vocation in subsequent years (taking earlier years first) for the purposes of calculation of income under this regulation.]
  (2) Subject to the qualifications in the following paragraphs of this regulation, and the provisions of Part III, the result of step 4 in paragraph (1) is the income of the claimant, or, in the case of a joint claim, of the claimants, for the purposes of the Act.
  (3) Income which—
  (a) arises in a territory outside the United Kingdom; and
  (b) is, for the time being, unremittable for the purposes of [4Chapter 4 of Part 8 of ITTOIA],
is disregarded in calculating the income of the claimant or, in the case of a joint claim, of the claimants.
  (4) Paragraph (5) applies in the case of a claimant who is [1, for income tax purposes]
  (a) resident [1and domiciled [7. . .] in the United Kingdom; [2. . .]
  (b) resident [7. . .] but not domiciled in the United Kingdom;
  [7. . .]
  (5) In the case of a person to whom this paragraph applies—
[1(a) any income arising outside the United Kingdom is to be taken into account, subject to any specific provision of these Regulations, regardless of the domicile or residence of the claimant; and;]
  (b) references to a sum being [1taken into account] are to be construed

as including a sum which would be taxable if he were resident [⁷...] and domiciled in the United Kingdom.

[¹(5A) Any income is to be taken into account, subject to any specific provision of these Regulations, notwithstanding the provision of any Order in Council under section 788 of the Taxes Act (double taxation agreements).]

(6) In the case of a claimant who would be chargeable to income tax but for some special exemption or immunity from income tax, income shall be calculated on the basis of the amounts which would be so chargeable but for that exemption or immunity.

[¹(6A) Income paid to a claimant in a currency other than sterling shall be converted into sterling at the average of the exchange rates applicable for the conversion of that currency into sterling in the period of 12 months [⁵ending on 31st March] in the tax year in which the income arises.]

(7) In calculating income under this Part there shall be deducted [¹...]—
  (a) [¹the amount of] any banking charge or commission payable in converting to sterling a payment of income which is made in a currency other than sterling;
  (b) [¹the grossed up amount of] any qualifying donation (within the meaning of [⁶ Chapter 2 of Part 8 of ITA (gift aid)]), made by the claimant or, in the case of a joint claim, by either or both of the claimants; [²...] [⁴...]
[³(c) the amount of any contribution made by the claimant, or in the case of a joint claim, by either or both of the claimants to a registered pension scheme together with the amount of any tax relief due on those contributions.]

[³...]

[²(8) If—
  (a) a claimant has sustained a loss in relation to a [⁴ UK property business] or an overseas property business; and
  (b) the relief to which he is entitled in accordance with [⁶ section 120 of ITA (deduction of property losses from general income)] exceeds the amount of his property income or foreign income for tax credits purposes, for the year in question;
the amount of his total income for tax credit purposes, computed in accordance with the preceding provisions of this regulation, shall be reduced by the amount of the excess.

[⁴In this paragraph "UK property business" and "overseas property business" have the same meaning as the have in the Taxes Act.]

AMENDMENTS

1. Tax Credits (Definition and Calculation of Income) (Amendment) Regulations 2003 (SI 2003/732) reg.5 (April 6, 2003).
2. Tax Credits (Miscellaneous Amendments No.2) Regulations 2003 (SI 2003/2815) reg.4 (November 26, 2003).
3. Taxation of Pension Schemes (Consequential Amendments) Order 2006 (SI 2006/745) art.26(3) (April 6, 2006).
4. Tax Credits (Miscellaneous Amendments) Regulations 2006 (SI 2006/766) reg.8 (April 6, 2006).
5. Tax Credits (Miscellaneous Amendments) Regulations 2007 (SI 2007/824) reg.9 (April 6, 2007).
6. Tax Credits (Definition and Calculation of Income) (Amendment) Regulations 2007 (SI 2007/1305) reg.4 (May 16, 2007).

(SI 2002/2006 reg.3) (as amended)

7. Tax Credits (Miscellaneous Amendments) Regulations 2014 (SI 2014/658) reg.4(2)–(4) (April 6, 2014).

GENERAL NOTE

Regulation 3(1) and (2) states that there are four steps to calculating the aggregate income of a claimant or joint claimants for a tax year, but it is suggested that this would be better presented as five steps. The four steps are:
(1) Add the totals of income from sources subject to the £300 discount and deduct that discount.
(2) Add the totals from all other sources, apart from trading income.
(3) Add the totals of (1) and (2).
(4) Add to, or subtract from, the total from (3) the net income (or net loss) from trading income.

The "fifth step" is then to deduct from that sum the various general deductions, exclusions, exemptions and disregards in these regulations. These are set out in reg.3(3) (unremittable income), reg.3(7) (other general deductions), reg.9 (exempt scholarship income) and the Tables 6, 7 and 8 in reg.19 (general disregards).

Paragraph (7) is part of the "fifth step", along with para.(3). It provides for two important deductions commonly made against income for income tax purposes. The first is to allow the deduction from income for tax credits purposes of any sums given to charities within the terms of the FA 1990 s.25. That is the provision authorising the tax deduction for "gift aid" payments for all non-refundable gifts of money to charities made otherwise than by covenant, the charity being treated as receiving the sum under deduction of tax at the basic rate. The other allows deductions from total income for contributions to registered pension schemes under the FA 2004 and related provisions.

Paragraphs (3)–(6) are a motley of provisions dealing with foreign elements. The combined effect of paras (4), (5), and (5A) includes all foreign income in the income to be used to calculate tax credits notwithstanding that for income tax purposes the income is excluded from a charge to income tax in the UK either because of the domicile of the taxpayer or because of a double tax agreement. It seems that para.(6) has, in part, the same aim, but it is not clear how it can override the tax exemptions applicable to diplomats and consuls under general international law and, in the UK, the Diplomatic Privileges Act 1964 and the Consular Relations Act 1968.

The amendments to paragraphs in 2014 reflect the abolition of the concept of "ordinary residence" for income tax purposes and other, minor, income tax changes.

CHAPTER 2

Employment income

Employment income

4.—(1) In these Regulations, "employment income" means—
(a) any [¹earnings] from an office or employment received in the tax year;
(b) so much of any payment made to a claimant in that year in respect of expenses as is chargeable to income tax [¹by virtue of section 62 or section 72 of ITEPA];
(c) [¹the cash equivalent of] any non-cash voucher received by the claimant in that year and chargeable to income tax under [¹section 87 of ITEPA];

Tax Credits (Definition and Calculation of Income) Regulations 2002

(d) [¹the cash equivalent of] any credit-token received by the claimant in that year and chargeable to income tax under [¹section 94 of ITEPA];
(e) [¹the cash equivalent of] any cash voucher received by the claimant in that year and chargeable to income tax under [¹section 81 of ITEPA];
[¹(f) any amount chargeable to tax under Chapter 3 of Part VI of ITEPA;]
(g) so much of a payment of statutory sick pay, received by the claimant during the year, as is subject to income tax [¹by virtue of section 660 of ITEPA;]
[¹³ (h) the amount (if any) by which a payment of statutory maternity pay, statutory paternity pay, statutory shared parental pay or statutory adoption pay exceeds £100 per week;]
(i) any amount charged to income tax for that year [¹under section 120 or section 149 of ITEPA;]
[¹(j) any sum to which section 225 of ITEPA applies;]
(k) any amount paid in that year by way of strike pay to the claimant as a member of a trade union;
[²(l) any amount charged to income tax for that year under Part 7 of ITEPA.]
[⁶(m) any amount paid to a person serving a custodial sentence or remanded in custody awaiting trial or sentence, for work done while serving the sentence or remanded in custody.]

For the purposes of this paragraph, references to the receipt of a payment of any description are references to its receipt by or on behalf of the claimant, or in the case of a joint claim of either of the claimants, in any part of the world.

This paragraph is subject to the following qualifications.

(2) Employment income does not include pension income.

[³(2A) [⁵ . . .]

(2B) [⁵ . . .]

[²(3) This paragraph applies if (apart from section 64 of ITEPA) the same benefit would give rise to two amounts ("A" and "B")—
(a) "A" being an amount of earnings from a claimant's employment as defined in section 62 of ITEPA, and
(b) "B" being an amount to be treated as earnings under any provision of Chapter 10 of Part 3 of ITEPA.

In such a case, the amount to be taken into account in computing the claimant's employment income is the greater of A and B, and the lesser amount shall be disregarded.]

(4) In calculating employment income, the payments and benefits listed in Table 1 shall be disregarded.

Table 1. Payments [¹and benefits] disregarded in the calculation of employment income

2.126

1. Any payment in respect of qualifying removal expenses, or the provision of any qualifying removal benefit, within the meaning of [¹Chapter 7 of Part 4 of ITEPA].

[¹2A. The payment or reimbursement of expenses incurred in the provision of transport to a disabled employee (as defined in section 246(4) of ITEPA) by his employer, if no liability to income tax arises in respect of that payment or reimbursement (as the case may be) by virtue of section 246 of ITEPA.

2B. The provision to a disabled employee (as defined in section 246(4) of ITEPA) by his employer of a car, the provision of fuel for the car, or the reimbursement of expenses incurred in connection with the car, if no liability to income tax arises in respect of that provision or reimbursement (as the case may be) by virtue of section 247 of ITEPA.

2C. The payment or reimbursement of expenses incurred on transport, if no liability to income tax arises in respect of that payment or reimbursement (as the case may be) by virtue of section 248 of ITEPA.]

3. Travel facilities provided for the claimant as a member of the naval, military or air forces of the Crown for the purpose of going on, or returning from, leave.

[[6]**3A.** The payment [[12]under a Royal Warrant made under section 333 of the Armed Forces Act 2006] of an operational allowance to a member of Her Majesty's forces in respect of service in an operational area specified by the Secretary of State for Defence.]

[[7]**3B.** A payment designated [[12]under a Royal Warrant made under section 333 of the Armed Forces Act 2006] as Council Tax Relief and made by the Secretary of State for Defence to a member of Her Majesty's forces.]

[[11]**3C.** The payment under a Royal Warrant made under section 333 of the Armed Forces Act 2006(2), of the Continuity of Education Allowance to or in respect of members of the armed forces of the Crown during their employment under the Crown or after their deaths.]

4. Payment or reimbursement of expenses in connection with the provision for, or use by, the claimant as a person holding an office or employment of a car-parking space at or near his place of work.

5. Any benefit or non-cash voucher provided to the claimant, or to any member of his family or household, [[1]in respect of which no liability to income tax arises by virtue of Chapter 5 of Part 4 of ITEPA.]

6. Any payment of incidental overnight expenses [[1]in respect of which no liability to income tax arises by virtue of section 240 of ITEPA.]

[[1]**7.** Food, drink and mess allowances for the armed forces and training allowances payable to members of the reserve forces in respect of which no liability to income tax arises by virtue of section 297 or 298 of ITEPA.]

8. The value of meal vouchers issued to the claimant as an employee [[1]if section 89 of ITEPA applies to the vouchers.]

9. Any cash payment received by the claimant as a miner in lieu of free coal, or the provision of the coal itself, [[1]in respect of which no liability to income tax arises by virtue of section 306 of ITEPA.]

10. An award made to the claimant as a director or employee by way of a testimonial to mark long service [[1]if, or to the extent that, no liability to income tax arises in respect of it by virtue of section 323 of ITEPA.]

11. Payment of a daily subsistence allowance [[1]in respect of which no liability to income tax arises by virtue of section 304 of ITEPA.].

[[1]**11A.** The payment or reimbursement of reasonable expenses incurred by an employee who has a permanent workplace at an offshore installation, on transfer transport, related accommodation and subsistence or local transport, if no liability to income tax arises in respect of that payment or reimbursement (as the case may be) by virtue of section 305 of ITEPA.

Tax Credits (Definition and Calculation of Income) Regulations 2002

For the purposes of this item, expressions which are defined in section 305 of ITEPA have the same meaning here as they do there.

11B. Payment of an allowance to a person in employment under the Crown in respect of which no liability to income tax arises by virtue of section 299 of ITEPA.

11C. The payment or reimbursement to an employee of any sum in connection with work-related training, or individual learning account training (as respectively defined in sections 251 and 256 of ITEPA) if no liability to income tax arises in respect of that payment or reimbursement (as the case may be) by virtue of any provision of Chapter 4 of Part 4 of ITEPA.

11D. The provision for an employee of a non-cash voucher or a credit-token, to the extent that liability to income tax does not arise in respect of that voucher or credit-token (as the case may be), under Chapter 4 of [²Part 3 of ITEPA, by virtue of any provision of Chapter 6 of Part 4 of ITEPA.]

11E. The provision for an employee of free or subsidised meal vouchers or tokens (within the meaning of section 317(5) of ITEPA), if no liability to income tax arises in respect of that provision by virtue of section 317 of ITEPA.]

[⁶**11F.** The provision of one mobile telephone for an employee in respect of which no liability to income tax arises by virtue of section 319 of ITEPA.]

12. An award made to the claimant under a Staff Suggestion Scheme, if the conditions specified in [¹sections 321 and 322 of ITEPA [³are satisfied].]

13. Travelling and subsistence allowances paid to or on behalf of the claimant by his employer [¹in respect of which no liability to income tax arises by virtue of section 245 of ITEPA.]

14. Any gift consisting of goods, or a voucher or token to obtain goods, [¹in respect of which no liability to income tax arises by virtue of section 270 or 324 of ITEPA.]

[¹**14A.** Any payment or reimbursement of expenses incurred in connection with an employment-related asset transfer (as defined in section 326(2) of ITEPA), if no liability to income tax arises in respect of that payment or reimbursement (as the case may be) by virtue of section 326 of ITEPA.

14B. Any payment of expenses incurred by an employee in connection with a taxable car if no liability to income tax arises in respect of the payment by virtue of section 239(2) of ITEPA.]

[²**14C.** The discharge of any liability of an employee in connection with a taxable car if no liability to income tax arises by virtue of section 239(1) of ITEPA.

14D. A benefit connected with a taxable car if no liability to income tax arises by virtue of section 239(4) of ITEPA.]

15. A cash voucher, non-cash voucher or credit-token to the extent that it is used by the recipient for the provision of childcare, the costs of which if borne by the recipient would be relevant childcare charges within the meaning of regulation 14 of the Working Tax Credit (Entitlement and Maximum Rate) Regulations 2002.

[³**16.** A payment made by the Department for Work and Pensions under section 2 of the Employment Act—
  (a) by way of In-Work Credit [⁸, Better Off In-Work Credit], Job Grant or Return to Work Credit, [⁸ . . .]

(SI 2002/2006 reg.4) (as amended)

(b) under the Employment Retention and Advancement Scheme or the Working Neighbourhoods Pilot.]

[⁸ (c) under the City Strategy Pathfinder Pilots,

(d) by way of an In-Work Emergency Discretion Fund payment pursuant to arrangements made by the Secretary of State, [⁹ . . .]

(e) by way of an Up-front Childcare Fund payment pursuant to arrangements made by the Secretary of State [⁹, or

(f) under the Future Capital pilot scheme.].]

[⁵**16A.** A payment made by the Department for Employment and Learning in Northern Ireland under section 1 of the Employment and Training Act (Northern Ireland) 1950 by way of Return to Work Credit.]

[⁸**16B.** Any In-Work Emergency Fund payment made to a person pursuant to arrangements made by the Department of Economic Development under section 1 of the Employment and Training Act (Northern Ireland) 1950.]

[²**17.** The payment or reimbursement of reasonable additional household expenses incurred by an employee who works from home, within the meaning of section 316A of ITEPA.

18. The payment or reimbursement of retraining course expenses within the meaning of the section 311 of ITEPA.]

[⁴**19.** Provision of computer equipment in respect of which no liability to income tax arises by virtue of section 320 of ITEPA.]

[⁸**20.** Pay As You Earn (PAYE) settlement agreements made under Part 6 of the Income Tax (PAYE) Regulations ("the PAYE Regulations") 2003.

For the purposes of this item the special arrangements under regulation 141 of the PAYE Regulations also apply.]

[¹¹**21.** The payment or reimbursement of a fee within section 326A(1) of ITEPA(3) (fees relating to vulnerable persons' monitoring schemes).]

[¹² **22.** The payment of a qualifying bonus within section 312A of ITEPA (limited exemption for qualifying bonus payments).]

(5) From the amount of employment income, calculated in accordance with the preceding provisions of this regulation, there shall be deducted the amount of any deduction permitted in calculating [¹calculating earnings by virtue of any provision of sections [²231 to 232,] 336–344, or s.346, 347, 351, 352, 362, 363, 367, 368, 370, 371, 373, 374, 376, 377 or 713 of ITEPA].

AMENDMENTS

1. Tax Credits (Definition and Calculation of Income) (Amendment) Regulations 2003 (SI 2003/732) reg.6 (April 6, 2003).

2. Tax Credits (Miscellaneous Amendments No.2) Regulations 2003 (SI 2003/2815) reg.5 (November 26, 2003).

3. Tax Credits (Miscellaneous Amendments) Regulations 2004 (SI 2004/762) reg.14 (April 6, 2004).

4. Tax Credits (Miscellaneous Amendments No.3) Regulations 2004 (SI 2004/2663) reg.2 (November 3, 2004).

5. Tax Credits (Miscellaneous Amendments) Regulations 2006 (SI 2006/766) reg.9 (April 6, 2006).

6. Tax Credits (Miscellaneous Amendments) Regulations 2007 (SI 2007/824) reg.10 (April 6, 2007).

Tax Credits (Definition and Calculation of Income) Regulations 2002

7. Tax Credits (Miscellaneous Amendments) Regulations 2008 (SI 2008/604) reg.2(2) (April 1, 2008).
8. Tax Credits (Miscellaneous Amendments) (No.2) Regulations 2008 (SI 2008/2169) reg.4 (September 1, 2008).
9. Tax Credits (Miscellaneous Amendments)(No.2) Regulations 2009 (SI 2009/2887) regs 5 and 6 (November 21, 2009).
10. Tax Credits (Miscellaneous Amendments) Regulations 2012 (SI 2012/848) reg.3(1) and (2) (April 6, 2012).
11. Tax Credits (Miscellaneous Amendments) Regulations 2014 (SI 2014/658) reg.4(5) (April 6, 2014).
12. Child Benefit (General) and Tax Credits (Miscellaneous Amendments) Regulations 2014 (SI 2014/2924) reg.5 (November 28, 2014).
13. Social Security and Tax Credits (Miscellaneous Amendments) Regulations 2015 (SI 2015/175) reg.7 (April 5, 2015).

CROSS-REFERENCES

The regulation adopts for tax credits purposes the following chapters and sections of ITEPA, all relating to employment income:

Pt 3: Employment income: Earnings and benefits, etc. treated as earnings
- s.62 Earnings

Pt 3: Ch.4: Taxable benefit: vouchers and credit-tokens
- s.72 Sums in respect of expenses treated as earnings
- s.81 Benefit of cash voucher treated as earnings
- s.87 Benefit of non-cash voucher treated as earnings
- s.89 Reduction for meal vouchers
- s.94 Benefit of credit-token treated as earnings

Pt 3: Ch.6: Taxable benefits: cars, vans and related vehicles
- s.120 Benefit of car treated as earnings
- s.149 Benefit of car fuel treated as earnings

Pt 3: Ch.10: Taxable benefits: residual liability to charge
- s.201 Employment-related benefits
- s.211 Special rules for scholarships: introduction

Pt 3: Ch.11: Taxable benefits: exclusion of lower-paid employments

Pt 3: Ch.12: Payments treated as earnings
- s.225 Payments for restrictive covenants

Pt 4: Employment income: exemptions
- s.239 Payments and benefits connected with taxable cars and vans and exempt heavy goods vehicles
- s.240 Incidental overnight expenses and benefits
- s.245 Travelling and subsistence during public transport strikes
- s.246 Transport between work and home for disabled employees
- s.247 Provision of cars for disabled employees
- s.248 Transport home: late-night working and failure of car-sharing arrangements

Pt 4: Ch.4: Exemptions: education and training
- s.251 Meaning of "work-related training"
- s.256 Meaning of "individual learning account training"

Pt 4: Ch.5: Exemptions; recreational benefits

Pt 4: Ch.6: Exemptions: non-cash vouchers and credit-tokens
- s.270 Exemptions of small gifts of vouchers and tokens from third parties

Pt 4: Ch.7: Exemptions: removal benefits and expenses
- s.297 Armed forces' food, drink and mess allowances
- s.298 Reserve and auxiliary forces' training allowances
- s.299 Crown employees' foreign service allowances
- s.304 Experts seconded to the European Commission
- s.305 Offshore oil and gas workers: mainland transfers

(SI 2002/2006 reg. 4) (as amended)

s.306	Miners, etc.: coal and allowances in lieu of coal
s.317	Subsidised meals
s.321	Suggestion awards
s.322	Suggestion awards: "the permitted maximum"
s.323	Long service awards
s.324	Small gifts from third parties
s.326	Expenses incidental to transfer of a kind not normally met by transferor

Pt 5: Employment income: deductions allowed from earnings

s.336	Deductions for expenses: the general rule
s.337	Travel in performance of duties
s.338	Travel for necessary attendance
s.339	Meaning of "workplace" and "permanent workplace"
s.340	Travel between group employments
s.341	Travel at start and finish of overseas employment
s.342	Travel between employments where duties performed abroad
s.343	Deduction for professional membership fees
s.344	Deduction for annual subscriptions
s.346	Deduction for employee liabilities
s.347	Payments made after leaving employment
s.351	Expenses of ministers of religion
s.352	Limited deduction for agency fees paid by entertainers
s.362	Deductions where non-cash voucher provided
s.363	Deductions where credit-token provided
s.367	Fixed sum deductions for repairing and maintaining work equipment
s.368	Fixed sum deductions from earnings payable out of public revenue
s.370	Travel costs and expenses where duties performed abroad: employee's travel
s.371	Travel costs and expenses where duties performed abroad: visiting spouse's or child's travel
s.373	non-domiciled employee's travel costs and expenses where duties performed in United Kingdom
s.374	Non-domiciled employee's spouse's or child's travel costs and expenses where duties performed in United Kingdom
s.376	Foreign accommodation and subsistence costs and expenses (overseas employments)
s.377	Costs and expenses in respect of personal security assets and sevices

Pt 6: Ch.3: Payments and benefits on termination of employment

s.660	Taxable benefits; United Kingdom benefits: Table A

Pt 12: Payroll giving

s.713	Donations to charity: payroll deduction scheme

GENERAL NOTE

This regulation defines "employment income" for the purposes of reg. 3. Although the result may be obvious in most cases, four questions have to be asked to set the context of a tax credits calculation of employment income when regard is had to a particular source of income:

What income is relevant?
What exemptions and deductions apply?
Whose income is it?
When is the income brought into calculation?

These are discussed in turn. The same pattern is followed in the notes on other regulations.

2.127

Tax Credits (Definition and Calculation of Income) Regulations 2002

What income is relevant? The scope of ITEPA and reg.4

2.128 In marginal cases it is always necessary to ask both if an income-generating activity is employment, self-employment or something else, and what earnings come from any employment, as against any other source.

Employment and self-employment

2.129 The common context of a dispute about whether an activity is or is not an employment is the contention by the individual concerned that he or she is self-employed. This issue is discussed in the general note to reg.6 below. "Office" used to be a separate provision in the old Sch.E, reflecting the antiquity of the phraseology used. ITEPA s.5 now relegates the status of office-holders (rightly in terms of relative importance) to a secondary status in the legislation. It also codifies the common law definition of "office". For all tax credits purposes, as for all ITEPA purposes, "employee" is to be read as including office holders, and "being employed" includes holding an office. "Office" is now defined (in words adopted from the income tax case of *GWR v Bater* [1920] 3 K.B. 266) as including "any position which has an existence independent of the person who holds it and may be filled by successive holders". For a discussion of that in the context of the borderline between holding an office and being self-employed see *Edwards v Clinch* [1982] A.C. 845.

Employment income

2.130 ITEPA deals with the income taxation of employment income in Pts 1–8 of the Act. For the structure of those Parts, see s.3 of ITEPA, and for the main charge to tax, see s.6. As can be seen from the list of cross-references, the policy and drafting approaches taken for the purposes of calculating employment income for tax credits purposes are to select from the provisions of those parts (ss.1–564), rather than simply to adopt the whole code, or those parts of the code felt appropriate. TCTM04101 directs HMRC officers to "Note that, although based on income tax law, not all of the additional rules for income chargeable to tax as employment income have been included in the tax credit employment income rules", and "not all of the general exemptions and reliefs from inclusion as income chargeable as employment income have been included . . .". This will also apply to ITEPA. The only major part of the code omitted as a whole is Pt 7 (Employment income: share-related income and exemptions—ss.417–554), although Pt 8 (relating to former employees) is also excluded. Elsewhere, close attention has to be paid to those charges and exemptions that are included (as listed in the cross-reference list derived from reg.3) and those that are excluded.

So, for example, while most sections in Pt 3 (Employment Income: earnings and benefits etc treated as earnings) are adopted, Ch.5 (taxable benefits: living accommodation) is not, nor is Ch.7 (taxable benefits: loans). Similarly, while most of the sections in Pt 4 (Employment income: exemptions) are allowed also as exemptions for tax credits purposes, again the approach has been to select those that are applied and those that are not. The same is true of Pt 5 (Employment income: deductions allowed from earnings). This reflects in part an assessment of the provisions that are not relevant (e.g. Pt 4, Ch.10 (exemptions on termination of employment)) are excluded as not relevant either to working tax credit or to child tax credit, but that does not always appear to explain the omission. For example, the exemption for subsidised meals in s.317 is applied, but not the exemption for care for children in s.318.

The resulting picture is one of some complexity, because one cannot simply adopt the income tax assessment of all employees for tax credits without looking through at least some of them to see on which sections of ITEPA the charge to tax is based or the exemption or deduction is claimed. In any case, other than the most straightforward, it may therefore be necessary to look at the breakdown of any charge to tax not based simply on earnings and the usual expenses and deductions. That also means that the approach of adopting a figure from the P45 or P60 supplied to an employee at the end of an employment or the end of a tax year may not be enough in those cases. While this might sound an over-exact approach to the calculation of income, it has to be borne in mind that the effective value of any charge or exemption for tax credit purposes is, at the margin, 41 per cent of the amount charged or claimed. So, a failure to allow a deduction for a £150 expense (which, if deductible at the basic rate of income tax, will have in effect cost the employee not £150 but £117) will "cost" the employee £61 in lost tax credits, or half the actual cost to the employee of the amount for which the deduction is claimed.

To follow that point with a relevant example, it would seem from the exclusion of s.317 that a claimant for WTC may claim for childcare charges if paid by the employee, but is liable to have the value of the advantage of employer-provided childcare taken into account as income for tax credits purposes although, of course, the employee will not be paying for, and therefore not able to claim for, that provision. However, this depends how the employer provides the advantage. If the employer provides childcare through the mechanism of providing the employee with a cash voucher, non-cash voucher or credit-token, the exclusion from calculation of that value by Table 1, Item 15, is broader than the income tax exclusion. As the working tax credit childcare element is not itself taxable to income tax (Taxes Act s.617A), the justification for this mismatch is not clear.

Differences between income tax assessments and tax credit calculations of employment income

The only full way of noting the differences between total net (i.e. after deductions) employment income for income tax purposes and for tax credits purposes is by precise reference to individual provisions in ITEPA. This must cover the ITEPA sections included in, and excluded from, reg.4 together with those provisions that are included in reg.4 but not by reference to specific provisions in ITEPA. Cross-references from reg.4 are not assisted by the reenactment of the employment income provisions since the regulation was drafted, as the previous drafting order of the regulation has been lost. As ITEPA is an immediately contemporary codification of employment income taxation, no reference for 2003–04 need be made to any other provision. In future years, it may be assumed that changes will, where appropriate, be made in parallel.

2.131

The full list of sections of ITEPA included by cross reference is set out above, and from that the obvious gaps can be identified. There are no differences with regard to cash earnings or equivalent (see ss.62 and 72 of ITEPA). But only some parts of the Pt 3 provisions on taxable benefits apply. Chapter 3 (expense payments), Ch.4 (vouchers and credit-tokens), Ch.6 (cars, vans and related benefits) and Ch.10 (residual liability) apply, but no part of Ch.5 (living accommodation), Ch.7 (loans), Ch.8 (notional loans in respect of acquisition of shares), or Ch.9 (disposals of shares for more than market value) apply. And of the six specific payments treated as earnings by Ch.12, only one (restrictive covenants under s.225) is expressly brought into the calculation.

Three kinds of income only are mentioned in reg.4 that are not related directly to specific provisions in ITEPA. Regulation 4(1)(h) requires inclusion of only the excess of statutory maternity pay over £100. For income tax purposes the sum is fully taxable. Regulation 4(1)(k) requires the inclusion of strike pay, whether or not that is otherwise taxable under this or any other head of income. These both reflect social security rules rather than income tax rules. Regulation 4(1)(m) adds prisoners' earnings.

What exemptions and deductions apply?

The exclusions from para.(4) are far harder to summarise. Part 4 deals with exemptions. Chapter 1 deals with general exemptions rules. Of the specific rules, Ch.2 (mileage allowances and passenger payments) is not within the scope of tax credits, and nor are many of the specific exemptions related to transport, travel and subsistence in Ch.3. Of ss.237–248 in that Chapter, only ss.239, 240 and 245–8 are permitted exclusions for tax credits calculations. Chapter 4 (education and training) exemptions are allowed, as are Ch.5 (recreational benefits) and Ch.7 (removal expenses). However, the exemptions in Ch.8 (special kinds of employees) and Ch.11 (miscellaneous exemptions) are included on a selected basis only. In

2.132

part, this selection excludes exemptions related to foreign elements, and to living accommodation (the benefit of which is excluded from the calculation of income), and so reflects the broader policy of the definition of relevant income. But there is no substitute in this Part of the Act for a detailed comparison of individual provisions.

There are only four groups of exemptions mentioned in reg.4 without express reference to ITEPA provisions. In the Table, Items 3, 3A and 3B (forces' payments) are defined broadly rather than in terms of s.296 of ITEPA, which is to the same effect. Item 4 (parking) is also broader than the equivalent s.237. Likewise, Item 15 (cash vouchers, etc.) is broader than ss.266–267. Items 16, 16A and 16B are tax-free public–funded payments.

By comparison, the deductions rules incorporated in para.(5) by section number follow closely the equivalent rules in Pt 5 of ITEPA, with only minor omissions. The differences are restricted largely to foreign issues or irrelevant categories of deduction, such as those related to (non-included) living accommodation.

2.133 TCTM confirms the HMRC view that most of the provisions in this regulation "mirror" or "are identical with" the equivalent ITEPA provisions. The guidance is to apply the same considerations for tax credits calculations in those cases as for income tax on employment income (and there are specific cross-references to the Inspectors Manual on employment income). It may in general be thought that the tax credits appeal authorities and tax appeal authorities would also strive to a common approach, as it may be predicted that that is the approach that superior courts would take if asked to consider the same rules in the different contexts.

In practice, HMRC relies on the information given by claimants to decide on any exemptions or deductions. If a claimant does not claim any expenses, then they will not usually be considered. And it will usually be too late to ask for them to be taken into account on an appeal, as the three-month rule applies to these changes as it does to all other aspects of a claim. See *CTC/2113/2006*.

Whose income is it?

2.134 This is rarely in issue in a tax credits context. One of the few practical problems arises where income is shared between husband and wife, but the joint claimant rules render that irrelevant here. The identity of the income tax payer, applying here also, is set out in ITEPA s.13. The taxable person, and therefore the person whose income it is for tax credits purposes, is the person to whose employment the earnings relate.

When is the income brought into calculation?

2.135 The employment income to be calculated for tax credits is the income "received by the claimant . . . in" or "paid to" the claimant in the tax year in question: para.(1). That tax year will either be the current year or the previous year, as determined under s.7(3) of the TCA 2002. The income for a tax year is therefore the income, in that sense, of the year. This is consistent with the general income tax rules for assessment on a current year basis. ITEPA s.19 provides for taxation to be based on the "net taxable earnings from an employment in the year". It is calculated when received, not when earned. That is a question of fact. This may be important for bonuses and other non-regular payments. In practice, that is also how the PAYE system operates.

CHAPTER 3

Pension income

Pension income

2.136 **5.**—[¹(1) In these Regulations, except where the context otherwise require, "pension income" means—

(SI 2002/2006 reg.5) (as amended)

(a) any pension to which section 577 or 629 of ITEPA applies;
(b) any pension to which section 569 of ITEPA applies;
(c) any voluntary annual payment to which section 633 of ITEPA applies;
[²(d) any pension, annuity or income withdrawal to which section 579A of ITEPA applies;
(e) any unauthorised member payments to which section 208(2)(a) or (b) of the Finance Act 2004 applies;]
(f) any periodical payment to which section 619 of ITEPA applies;
[². . .]
[². . .]
[². . .]
[². . .]
[²(k) any annuity paid under a retirement annuity contract to which Chapter 9 of Part 9 of ITEPA applies;]
(l) any annuity to which section 609, 610 or 611 of ITEPA applies;
[⁴ . . .]
[³(n) any social security lump sum to which section 7 of the Finance Act 2005 applies; and
(o) any lump sum to which section 636B or 636C of ITEPA applies.]

(2) In calculating the amount of a person's pension income there shall be disregarded any [¹payment or benefit mentioned] in Column 1 of Table 2 to the extent specified in the corresponding entry in Column 2.

Table 2. [¹Pensions, other payments and benefits] disregarded in the calculation of pension income

1. Payment	2. Extent of disregard
1. A wounds pension or disability pension to which [¹section 641 of ITEPA] applies.	So much of the payment as is disregarded by virtue of [¹section 641 of ITEPA].
2. An annuity or additional pension payable to a holder of the Victoria Cross, George Cross or any other decoration mentioned in [¹section 638 of ITEPA].	The whole of the annuity or additional pension and, if both are payable, the whole of both such annuity and additional pension.

1. Payment	2. Extent of disregard
3. A pension or allowance to which [¹section 639 of ITEPA] applies.	[¹The amount of the pension or allowance.]
4. A pension or allowance by reason of payment of which a pension or allowance specified in [¹section 639 of ITEPA] is withheld or abated.	[¹The amount treated as falling within section 639 of ITEPA by virtue of section 640(2) of that Act.]
5. [⁵. . .]	
6. A mobility supplement, or a payment in respect of attendance, paid in conjunction with a war pension.	The amount of the supplement or payment.

2.137

Tax Credits (Definition and Calculation of Income) Regulations 2002

1. Payment	2. Extent of disregard
7. [⁵. . .]	
8. A pension awarded at the supplementary rate under article 27(3) of the Personal Injuries (Civilians) Scheme 1983.	The amount for the time being specified in paragraph 1(c) of Schedule 4 to the Scheme.
9. A pension awarded on retirement through disability caused by injury on duty or by a work-related illness.	[¹The exempt amount of the pension calculated in accordance with section 644(3) of ITEPA.]
[¹10. A lump sum on which no liability to income tax arises by virtue of [² section 636A of ITEPA].	The amount of the lump sum.
11. Coal or smokeless fuel provided as mentioned in section 646(1) of ITEPA, or an allowance in lieu of such provision.	The amount on which no liability to income tax arises by virtue of that section.]

[¹(3) From the amount of pension income, calculated in accordance with the preceding provisions of this regulation, there shall be deducted any amount deductible for income tax purposes in computing pension income (as defined in ITEPA) under section 713 of that Act.]

AMENDMENTS

1. Tax Credits (Definition and Calculation of Income) (Amendment) Regulations 2003 (SI 2003/732) reg.7 (April 6, 2003).
2. Taxation of Pension Schemes (Consequential Amendments) Order 2006 (SI 2006/745) art.26(4) (April 6, 2006).
3. Tax Credits (Miscellaneous Amendments) Regulations 2006 (SI 2006/766) reg.10 (April 6, 2006).
4. Tax Credits (Miscellaneous Amendments) Regulations 2008 (SI 2008/604) reg.2(2) (April 6, 2008).
5. Tax Credits (Miscellaneous Amendments) (No.3) Regulations 2010 (SI 2010/2914) reg.4 (December 31, 2010).

GENERAL NOTE

2.138　This regulation defines "pension income" for the purposes of reg.3. "Pension income" is a new concept evolved by the Tax Law Rewrite Project and launched in ITEPA. Previously, taxation of pensions has mainly been as if pensions were emoluments, and therefore subject to Sch.E, with other rules bringing certain kinds of pension into various cases of Sch.D. The pension income provisions in ITEPA bring together most of the various charges to tax on different kinds of pensions, including some pensions payable to the former self-employed, and also pensions payable without reference to work of any kind. It also includes social security provisions by way of pension.

What income is relevant?

2.139　ITEPA Pt 9 rewrote the whole of the relevant provisions of the then income tax legislation dealing with income tax on pensions. However, no sooner had it

(SI 2002/2006 reg.5) (as amended)

been rewritten than much of it was rewritten again—by the Finance Act 2004. The provisions of FA 2004 came into effect on April 6, 2006. The amended Pt 9 applies to all pension income (including social security pensions from the UK and abroad, voluntary pensions, and pensions payable for ill-health retirements). The aim behind reg.5 is to include all pensions as income under this regulation for tax credits purposes.

What exemptions and deductions apply?

Again, the pattern is to adopt all relevant provisions in ITEPA Pt 9. Of the three chapters dealing with exemptions, Ch.16 (exemption for certain lump sums) applies fully. Chapter 17 (exemptions: any taxpayer) applies in large part. The sections not applied relate for the most part to foreign pensions, and are dealt with under the foreign income provision in reg.12. This also applies to Ch.18 (exemptions: non-UK resident taxpayers). The only other section not applied is ITEPA s.645 (social security pensions: increases for children), which does not apply by reason of the repeal of those provisions and their replacement by child tax credit by TCA 2002 (save for the oversight of the rare payments under s.85 of the SSCBA 1992 not being repealed by the Act).

2.140

Whose income is it?

ITEPA s.572 provides that the person liable for any tax charged is the person receiving or entitled to the pension. This is therefore the operative rule for inclusion of pension income for the calculation of tax credits income. It is the alternative to deal with those who are not entitled to a pension being received (as with voluntary pensions), but will rarely present problems. There is no significance for tax credits purposes in most cases about pensions to couples. If it is significant then, of course, entitlement is a question of law and receipt a question of fact.

2.141

When is the income brought into the calculation?

This also follows from s.572. As a result, pension income is to be included when entitlement arises. If there is no entitlement, as with voluntary pensions, then it is when the pension is received. That should follow the income tax treatment.

2.142

CHAPTER 4

Trading income

Trading income

6. The claimant's trading income is—
   (a) the amount of his taxable profits for the tax year from—
      (i) any trade carried on in the United Kingdom or elsewhere;
      (ii) any profession or vocation the income from which does not fall under any other provisions of these Regulations; or
   (b) if the claimant is a partner in the trade, profession or vocation, his taxable profit for the year arising from his share of the partnership's trading or professional income.
[¹ Here "taxable profits" has the same meaning as it has in Part 2 of ITTOIA but disregarding Chapter 16 of that Part (averaging profits of farmers and creative artists.]

2.143

AMENDMENT

1. Tax Credits (Miscellaneous Amendments) Regulations 2006 (SI 2006/766) reg.11 (April 6, 2006).

GENERAL NOTE

2.144   This regulation defines "trading income" for the purposes of reg.3. It does so, since 2006, by reference to the newly codified rules for taxing trading income set out in ITTOIA 2005. This now includes all income from trades, professions and vocations and some related forms of income. It covers income both sourced in the UK and sourced abroad.

Employment and self-employment

2.145   The critical distinction in the case of many of those with smaller incomes who claim to be traders or self-employed is whether that is a true description in both law and fact of the individual's status. This is directly relevant for the calculation of tax credits because it must be decided if regs 4 or 6 applies. Following from that decision are subsidiary questions about the exemptions and deductions that must be calculated in finding the net income; the question of which period of income is to be taken into account; and the provision in Step 4 of reg.3 allowing trading losses to be deducted from other income. The rules assume that there cannot be a net loss by way of employment income, and do not allow for it. But this is an important overall change in the tax credit rules because previously no income losses were allowed.

The status of employee or self-employed is important for several reasons besides the current context:

Income tax: employment income or trading income?
NI contributions: Class 1 or Class 2 contributions?
VAT: is the person carrying on registerable activities?
Benefits: is the individual entitled to benefits available only to employees?

In addition, there are other issues that arise from the employment status, such as the minimum wage, holiday entitlements, and employer liability, that are again to be decided separately.

2.146   Drawing a line between employment and self-employment has always been difficult. It is also wide open to abuse, for example to reduce NI contributions but to increase benefit entitlement. This has led to people claiming to be an employee for some purposes and self-employed for others, and to different government agencies in the past adopting different answers to an individual's status in different contexts.

One result has been a series of initiatives to concentrate the decision-making on this issue so as to avoid inconsistent official decisions. Another is a series of legislative initiatives to define more clearly where the borderline is and to deal with abusive situations.

As a result of various initiatives, HMRC are now the effective deciders, subject to appeal, of employment status. The Social Security (Transfer of Functions, etc.) Act 1999 transferred NI contribution administration to the Inland Revenue. In addition, s.8 of that Act transferred to the Inland Revenue the decision whether someone is employed or self-employed for most social security benefit purposes. Appeals from a HMRC decision under s.8, about contributions, and about income tax liability, all go to the tax appeal commissioners. In the case of the s.8 decisions, most of these were previously dealt with on appeal by social security appeal tribunals, so this was a transfer of appeal jurisdiction. HMRC has also inherited responsibility for the national minimum wage legislation.

There are several provisions that now provide that someone is, or is to be treated as, an employee rather than self-employed. Two of these deserve emphasis. The first is the category of workers who in practical terms are somewhere between the two main groups—agency workers. ITEPA Pt 1, Ch.7 deals with agency workers. Section 44 provides that in most such cases the worker is regarded as the employee of the agency even if that is not the formal status adopted. The second concerns

(SI 2002/2006 reg.6) (as amended)

Ch.8 of that Part, which codifies the controversial "IR35" rules for what are sometimes known as "pocket book companies". These rules provide that in stated situations an individual who is under an obligation to provide services to a third party via an intermediary in circumstances where the worker is not paid as an employee by the intermediary can be treated as being an employee of the intermediary with a deemed employment income from that intermediary. This is used, for example, where someone works for a genuine third party, but where the contractual relationship with the third party is, typically, through a company of which the individual is the only shareholder. The company then pays the individual in some indirect way—benefits, loans, dividends—which the individual claims (if asked) to be either not income at all or not employment income.

What income is relevant? What exemptions and deductions apply?
"Trade" is defined in the Taxes Act s.832 as "every trade, manufacture, adventure or concern in the nature of trade". There is considerable case law on this meaning, of which reference might be made in the marginal case to the decisions of the House of Lords in *Ransom v Higgs* [1974] 1 W.L.R. 1594 and *Ensign Tankers v Stokes* [1992] 1 A.C. 655. In *Ransom*, the House of Lords made clear the wide factual scope of "trade", in the light of the extending definition. The fact, for example, that no particular name could be given to the activity did not stop it being a trading activity if it was an economic or commercial activity aimed at generating profit (even if it did not do so). The converse of this is that activities that appear to be commercial but are not aimed at making a profit may be regarded in some cases as tax avoidance manoeuvres and not as trading (*Ensign Tankers*). Reference in marginal cases is usually made to the so-called "badges of trade". The badges were first identified by the Royal Commission on the Taxation of Income in 1952 as: **2.147**

(a) the subject-matter of the sale or realisation;
(b) the length of the period of ownership of assets realised;
(c) the frequency or number of similar transactions by that person;
(d) whether there was supplementary work on or in connection with the assets realised or the realisation;
(e) the reasons for the realisation of the assets; and
(f) motive.

Two other points should be emphasised. First, there is a need to distinguish activities generating capital from those generating income. For the calculation of tax credits income, all activities generating capital should be ignored. (This introduces into the tax credits context a much fought-over income tax borderline removed in part for income tax purposes by the introduction of capital gains tax.) Secondly, and seemingly by contrast to the first, a "one off" activity generating profit may be a trading activity. The statutory definition indicates that a single activity may be caught as an "adventure" or a "concern in the nature of trade". From these follow a third point: a payment is either a trading payment or it is capital. There is no middle ground. If a receipt is not a trading receipt, it cannot be brought into charge to income tax (and it is therefore suggested to tax credits either) under other income charging provisions. See *Jones v Leeming* [1930] A.C. 415.

As reg.6 reflects, the charge to income tax on the self-employed is based on the accounts of the business. Increasingly, both the legislative provision for, and the HMRC practice relating to, the taxation of commercial activity is accounts-based. The concern in calculating income for tax credits is therefore with the claimant's business accounts for any trade.

In practice, in simple cases, the accounts can be brief. HMRC will accept these for income tax purposes and presumably also for tax credits purposes. **2.148**

A simplified form of self-assessment tax return (SA103S) is available for those whose annual business turnover is under £79,000 (similar to the VAT registration level). This requires only total figures for:

(a) annual turnover;
(b) total allowable expenses;

Tax Credits (Definition and Calculation of Income) Regulations 2002

(c) net profits or losses; and
(d) capital allowances.

If turnover is over that limit, then full accounts itemising income and expenditure will need to be provided, or at least the individual will have to provide all the details required in the standard self-employment pages to the self-assessment form for income tax. In the more complex cases, there should be two sets of accounts: the ordinary working accounts produced for the business (be it company, partnership or individual) and the tax computations or adjustments necessary to change the accounts from the approach adopted for the business to the approach necessary for income tax purposes. For example, the standard item "depreciation" on capital assets held for the business must be removed and replaced by a claim for any specific capital allowances to which the taxpayer is entitled. A second and further set of such computations may be necessary for tax credits purposes—or at least points may need following up. It is common for a business run by a husband to make a payment to an otherwise-non-earning wife. That is a deduction for trading purposes, but must be added back in for the joint claim they should be making for tax credits purposes as earnings of the wife. The business may be paying rent for the accommodation to the owners of the premises used. If that is the jointly owned (or owned in common) home of the joint claimants, again the rental income needs to go back into the tax credits calculation as property income.

Whose income is it?

2.149   It is the income of the individual or partner running the business. The tax credits rules are silent as to partners' shares, so it will be the same share of the trading income as for income tax. That is based on the proposition that for English law purposes (but not Scottish law) a partnership is not a separate entity, so the trading income of the partnership is directly the trading income of the partners, divided as they decide or, by default, under the general rules of the Partnership Act 1890.

When is the income to be brought into the calculation?

2.150   The standard rule for income tax, and therefore tax credits, is that the tax payable in any one tax year (April 6 to April 5) is the income of that year. But for ongoing trades the tax is charged instead on the income of the "basis period" for that year. The basis period for a year is defined as the 12 months immediately following the basis period of the previous year. This is designed to prevent gaps occurring between tax years. In practice, this will be the 12 months accounts period for the business ending in that tax year. Many businesses end their accounting years on April 30. This creates the maximum convenient (for the business) gap between the accounts year and the tax year. Where a business using this practice ends its accounts, for example, on April 30, 2005, that will be the basis period for the tax year 2005–06.

There are special rules for the opening and closing years of a business, and anti-avoidance rules where a business changes its accounting year.

CHAPTER 5

Social security income

Social security income

2.151   **7.**—(1) The claimant's social security income is the total amount payable—
(a) under any provision of the Social Security Act 1988, the Contributions and Benefits Act [³, the Jobseekers Act 1995 or Part 1 of the Welfare Reform Act 2007] or under section 69 of the Child Support, Pensions and Social Security Act 2000;
(b) [¹. . .];

484

(SI 2002/2006 reg.7) (as amended)

(c) by the Secretary of State in respect of the non-payment of a payment which ought to have been made under a provision mentioned in sub-paragraph (a); and

(d) by way of an ex-gratia payment made by the Secretary of State, or in Northern Ireland by the Department for Social Development, in connection with a benefit, pension or allowance under the Contributions and Benefits Act.

This is subject to the following provisions of this regulation.

(2) Pensions under the Contributions and Benefits Act which are pension income by virtue of regulation 5(1)(a) are not social security income.

(3) In calculating the claimant's social security income the payments in Table 3 shall be disregarded.

Table 3. Payments under, or in connection with, the Act, the Social Security Act 1988, the Contributions and Benefits Act [³ the Jobseekers Act 1995 or Part 1 of the Welfare Reform Act 2007] disregarded in calculation of social security income

1. An attendance allowance under section 64 of the Contributions and Benefits Act.
2. A back to work bonus under section 26 of the Jobseekers Act 1995.
3. A bereavement payment under section 36 of the Contributions and Benefits Act.
4. Child benefit under Part II of the Act.
5. A Christmas bonus under section 148 of the Contributions and Benefits Act.
6. Council tax benefit under section 131 of the Contributions and Benefits Act.
7. A disability living allowance under section 71 of the Contributions and Benefits Act.
8. Disabled person's tax credit under section 129 of the Contributions and Benefits Act.
9. Any discretionary housing payment pursuant to regulation 2(1) of the Discretionary Financial Assistance Regulations 2001.
10. An ex-gratia payment by the Secretary of State or, in Northern Ireland, the Department for Social Development, to a person over pensionable age by way of supplement to incapacity benefit.
11. A guardian's allowance under section 77 of the Contributions and Benefits Act.
12. Housing benefit under section 130 of the Contributions and Benefits Act.
13. Income support under section 124 of the Contributions and Benefits Act, unless it is chargeable to tax under [¹section 665 of ITEPA.].

2.152

14. Incapacity benefit which is—
  (a) short term incapacity benefit payable at the lower rate; or
  (b) payable to a person who had received invalidity benefit before 13th April 1995 if the period of incapacity for work is treated, by virtue of regulation 2 of the Social Security (Incapacity Benefit) (Transitional) Regulations 1995 (days to be treated as days of incapacity for work) as having begun before that date.

15. Industrial injuries benefit [¹(except industrial death benefit)] under section 94 of the Contributions and Benefits Act.

16. A contribution-based jobseeker's allowance under the Jobseekers Act 1995 [⁷as amended by the provisions of Part 1 of Schedule 14 to the Welfare Reform Act 2012 that remove references to an income-based allowance, and a contribution-based allowance under the Jobseekers Act 1995 as that Act has effect apart from those provisions], to the extent that it exceeds the maximum contained in [¹section 674 of ITEPA.].

17. An income-based jobseeker's allowance under the Jobseekers Act 1995.

18. A maternity allowance under section 35 [⁸or section 35B(3)] of the Contributions and Benefits Act.

19. A severe disablement allowance under section 68 or 69 of the Contributions and Benefits Act

20. A social fund payment under Part VIII of the Contributions and Benefits Act.

[¹**20A.** Statutory adoption pay under Part XIIZB of the Contributions and Benefits Act.

21A. [⁵[¹⁰. . .] statutory paternity pay and [¹⁰. . .] under Part XIIZA of the Contributions and Benefits Act.]

[⁹ **21B.** Statutory shared parental pay under Part 12ZC of the Contributions and Benefits Act.]

21. Statutory maternity pay under Part XII of the Contributions and Benefits Act.

22. Statutory sick pay under Part IX of the Contributions and Benefits Act.

23. Working families' tax credit under section 128 of the Contributions and Benefits Act.

24. A payment by way of compensation for the non-payment of, or in respect of loss of entitlement (whether wholly or partly) of, income support, jobseeker's allowance, [²or housing benefit].

25. A payment in lieu of milk tokens or the supply of vitamins under the Welfare Food Regulations 1996.

[³ **26.** An income-related employment and support allowance payable under Part 1 of the Welfare Reform Act 2007.]

(SI 2002/2006 reg.7) (as amended)

> [⁴ **27.** A payment by way of health in pregnancy grant made pursuant to Part 8A of the Contributions and Benefits Act.]

> [⁶ **28.** Personal independence payment under Part 4 of the Welfare Reform Act 2012.]

(4) If an increase in respect of a child dependant is payable with an allowance, benefit, pension or other payment ("the main payment") listed in Table 3, the increase shall also be wholly disregarded in calculating the income of the recipient of the main payment.

(5) [¹. . .]

[¹(5A) From the amount of social security income, calculated in accordance with the preceding provisions of this regulation, there shall be deducted any amount deductible for income tax purposes in computing social security income (as defined in ITEPA) under section 713 of ITEPA.]

(6) A reference in this regulation to an enactment applying only in Great Britain includes a reference to a corresponding enactment applying in Northern Ireland.

AMENDMENTS

1. Tax Credits (Definition and Calculation of Income) (Amendment) Regulations 2003 (SI 2003/732) reg.8 (April 6, 2003).

2. Tax Credits (Miscellaneous Amendments No.2) Regulations 2003 (SI 2003/2815) reg.6 (November 26, 2003).

3. Employment and Support Allowance (Consequential Provisions) (No.3) Regulations 2008 (SI 2009/1879) reg.21 (October 27, 2008).

4. Tax Credits (Miscellaneous Amendments) Regulations 2009 (SI 2009/697) reg.7 (April 6, 2009).

5. Tax Credits (Miscellaneous Amendments) (No.2) Regulations 2010 (SI 2010/2494) reg.6 (November 14, 2010).

6. Personal Independence Payment (Supplementary Provisions and Consequential Amendments) Regulations 2013 (SI 2013/388) reg.8 and Sch., para.29 (April 8, 2013).

7. Universal Credit (Consequential, Supplementary, Incidental and Miscellaneous Provisions) Regulations 2013 (SI 2013/630) reg.78(2) (April 29, 2013).

8. Tax Credits (Miscellaneous Amendments) Regulations 2014 (SI 2014/658) reg.4(6) (April 6, 2014).

9. Shared Parental Leave and Statutory Shared Parental Pay (Consequential Amendments to Subordinate Legislation) Order 2014 (SI 2014/3255) art.12(3)(b) (December 31, 2014).

10. Shared Parental Leave and Statutory Shared Parental Pay (Consequential Amendments to Subordinate Legislation) Order 2014 (SI 2014/3255) art.12(3)(a) (April 6, 2015).

CROSS-REFERENCE

ITEPA s.713   Donations to charity: payroll giving scheme

GENERAL NOTE

This regulation defines "social security income" for the purposes of reg.3. "Social security income" is another creation of the Tax Law Rewrite Project. Like pension income, it forms a separate code in Pt 10 of ITEPA (ss.655–681). But, unlike the employment income and pensions income regulations, this regulation adopts the approach of parallel legislation to Pt 10 of ITEPA rather than adopting ITEPA provisions themselves. Nonetheless, the relevant ITEPA provisions are included in this volume both for cross-reference and for more general reference in handling social security benefits.

2.153

Tax Credits (Definition and Calculation of Income) Regulations 2002

Part 10 of ITEPA is in the following pattern. Chapter 1 sets out the structure of the Part. Chapter 2 deals with general points on tax on social security income, including a definition of the terms used. Chapter 3 lists the taxable UK social security benefits. This is in the form of Table A to s.660. Chapter 4 lists exemptions from the Ch.3 charge to specific benefits. Chapter 5 lists benefits wholly exempt from tax, in the form of Table B to s.677. Chapter 6 lists taxable foreign benefits, and Ch.7 lists exemptions from the benefits brought in under Ch.6. Of those chapters, Chs 6 and 7 are irrelevant to the head of the tax credits income calculation as it is limited to UK benefits only.

What income is relevant?

2.154 As just noted, reg.7 is expressly limited to benefits to which a claimant is entitled under UK legislation only. Foreign social security benefits are to be included under foreign income. There are two other limitations on social security income. The first, deriving from a parallel with ITEPA, is that state retirement benefits are treated as pension income not as social security income. The second, not deriving from that source, is the treatment of the statutory payments (sick, maternity, adoption, paternal) as employment income. ITEPA treats these as social security income (although this is a default rule—if they are taxed as employment income then they are excluded here: ITEPA s.660(2)).

With those exclusions, the other benefits that are taxable under Table A in ITEPA, and also relevant for calculating tax credit income, are:

    Widowed mother's/parent's allowance
    Carer's allowance
    Incapacity benefit (some)
    Income support (some)
    Jobseeker's allowance (some)

In each case there are provisions about how much of the income is taxed. In practice, much of that tax is collected under the PAYE scheme.

What exclusions and deductions apply?

2.155 The list in Table 3 parallels the list in Table B to s.677 of ITEPA (payments wholly exempt), along with the provisions, in particular, for jobseeker's allowance and incapacity benefit, save for the statutory payments (noted above) and the treatment of present and past tax credits. CTC and WTC are not taxable. The list is very extensive, and it leaves relevant to tax credits only the short list of benefits noted in the previous paragraph.

There is no specific provision in the regulations dealing with overpayments of benefit. In practice, this may not be a major problem because of the limited extent to which account is taken of benefits. But the position might arise where, say, a widowed parent's allowance was overpaid (perhaps because of the living together rule) so that income previously paid was required to be repaid. For income tax purposes, late account can be taken of this for up to five years after the event. For tax credits purposes, the reduction in income for the relevant period will be relevant only in so far as there can be a recalculation of the income for tax credits, and there is a timely claim made. As the main time-limit is three months, there will only be a limited extent to which such adjustments can be requested, even with the benefit of a rapid notification of the change of circumstances. The two benefits administered by HMRC, child benefit and guardian's allowance, are exempt in any event.

Social security beneficiaries may also set charitable giving against their income.

Whose income is it?

2.156 The regulation is silent on this point, which therefore falls to be decided by reference to the social security rules. ITEPA s.662 imposes the income tax on the person receiving or entitled to the benefit, so covering appointees as well as claimants.

(SI 2002/2006 reg.7) (as amended)

When is the income brought into the calculation?

The calculation is based on the amount actually received in the year, regardless of the period for which it is received.

2.157

CHAPTER 6

Student income

[¹Student Income

8. "Student income" means, in relation to a student—

2.158

[³ (a) in England, any adult dependant's grant payable [⁴ pursuant to regulations under section 22 of the Teaching and Higher Education Act 1998;]]

(b) in Scotland, any dependant's grant payable under regulation 4(1)(c) of the Students' Allowances (Scotland) Regulations [⁴ 2007]; [²...]

(c) in Northern Ireland, any grant which corresponds to income treated as student income in England [⁴...] by virtue of paragraph (a);] [² and

[³ (d) in Wales, any adult dependant's grant payable [⁴ pursuant to regulations under section 22 of the Teaching and Higher Education Act 1998.]]

AMENDMENTS

1. Tax Credits (Miscellaneous Amendments No.2) Regulations 2003 (SI 2003/2815) reg.7 (November 26, 2003).
2. Tax Credits (Miscellaneous Amendments) Regulations 2006 (SI 2006/766) reg.12 (April 6, 2006).
3. Tax Credits (Miscellaneous Amendments) (No.2) Regulations 2008 (SI 2008/2169) reg.5 (September 1, 2008).
4. Tax Credits (Miscellaneous Amendments) Regulations 2012 (SI 2012/848) reg.3(3) (April 6, 2012).

GENERAL NOTE

This regulation defines "student income" for the purposes of reg.3. "Student income" is not a head of taxation under the Taxes Act or under the scheme used by the Tax Law Rewrite Project. Instead, this is taken from social security law. It must be read with the exemptions in regs 9 and 19, and the general principles of income tax.

2.159

The effect of the narrow point in reg.8 with the various exemptions is to exclude most forms of income that students receive (other than earnings).

The award of student grants is now a devolved function, and differing rules now apply in the four countries of the United Kingdom. Only parts of the various forms of grant are included as student income, and most students' grants will be excluded. The equivalent income tax rules (in s.776 of ITTOIA) exempt most forms of scholarship income, subject to anti-avoidance provisions, on the principle that such income is a gift or grant, not taxable income. Interest on the reimbursement of student loan income is also exempt (s.753 of ITTOIA). (HMRC monitor this as it is the authority responsible for collecting repayments of student grants through earnings.) Regulation.9 applies these provisions to tax credit calculations.

Two other sources of student "income", in the widest sense, are or may be exempt from inclusion under general principles: loans and gifts. The extent to which this is so illustrates the difference between the means-tested benefits approach to assessing a claimant's income, and the rules for calculating tax credits income.

2.160

The question of the status of loans was discussed by the Court of Appeal at some length in *Morrell v Secretary of State for Work and Pensions* [2003] EWCA Civ 526. A claimant for income support had been receiving regular monthly sums from her mother by way of loan. Some of the money was paid by the mother to the claimant's landlord. The question was whether the sums were income for the purposes of income support. The Court of Appeal followed the recent decision of that Court in *Leeves v Chief Adjudication Officer* [1999] 1 E.L.R. 90. In that case the question was whether a student grant was to be treated as income for income support purposes. Potter LJ adopted the submission for the claimant that "income" should be given its ordinary and natural meaning, and that money accruing in respect of which there was an obligation of immediate and equivalent repayment was not income. On the facts, the student grant for maintenance was income but immediately repayable debts were not. The grant was income until the demand for repayment was made, when it ceased to be income.

But a further question arises for tax credits purposes. The payments must not only have the quality of income, but must fall under one of the kinds of income being taken into account. The definition of "student income" in reg.8 does not cover these loans, nor gifts, even if they are recurring. The question is whether such loans or gifts are income within any of the other kinds of income in the regulations. We shall return to that at para.2.182, below.

Further sources of income linked to education and training are exempt under the specific provisions listed in Table 6 of reg.19—items 4, 5, 6 and 7 are all relevant.

[¹Payments of income in connection with students to be disregarded for the purposes of regulation 3

2.161   **9.** Income which is exempt from income tax by virtue of section 753 or 776 of ITTOIA (which deal respectively with interest on the repayment of student loans and scholarship income) is disregarded in calculating a claimant's income under regulation 3.]

AMENDMENT

1. Tax Credits (Miscellaneous Amendments) Regulations 2006 (SI 2006/766) reg.13 (April 6, 2006).

GENERAL NOTE

2.162   This regulation is an exempting regulation only. See note to reg.8.

CHAPTER 7

Investment income

Investment income

2.163   **10.**—(1) In these Regulations, "investment income" means the gross amount of—
   (a) any interest of money whether yearly or otherwise, or any annuity or other annual payment, whether such payment is payable within or out of the United Kingdom, either as a charge on any property of the person paying it by virtue of any deed or will or otherwise, or as a reservation out of it, or as a personal debt or obligation by virtue of any contract, or whether the payment is received and payable half-yearly or at any shorter or longer periods, but not including property income;

(b) any discounts on securities;
(c) any income from securities payable out of the public revenues of the United Kingdom or Northern Ireland;
(d) dividends and other distributions of a company resident in the United Kingdom and any tax credit associated with that payment; and
(e) any amount treated as forming part of the individual's income for the year for income tax purposes by virtue of [³Chapter 9 of Part 4 of ITTOIA disregarding section 535 (top slicing relief)].

This is subject to the following qualification.

(2) In calculating investment income, there shall be disregarded—
(a) any amount listed in column 1 of Table 4 to the extent shown in the corresponding entry in column 2;
(b) any amount listed in column 1 of Table 5 during the period shown in the corresponding entry in column 2;
(c) any income arising from savings certificates, and interest on tax reserve certificates, exempted from tax by [³section 692, 693 or 750 of ITTOIA] (savings certificates and tax reserve certificates);
(d) the first £70 in any tax year of interest on deposits with National Savings and Investments, exempted from income tax by [³section 691 of ITTOIA (National Savings Bank ordinary account interest)];
(e) any payment to a claimant which does not form part of his income for the purposes of income tax by virtue of [³section 727 of ITTOIA (certain annual payments by individuals).]

Table 4. Payments disregarded in the calculation of investment income

1. Description of income to be disregarded	2. Extent of disregard
1. Any interest, dividends, distributions, profits or gains in respect of investments under— 　(a) a Personal Equity Plan; or 　(b) an Individual Savings Account; in respect of which the claimant is entitled to relief from income tax under [³Chapter 3 of Part 6 of ITTOIA] or which is taxed only in accordance with regulation 23 of the Individual Savings Account Regulations 1998.	The whole amount, unless it is interest under a personal equity plan to which regulation 17A(2) of the Personal Equity Plan Regulations 1989 applies. Interest to which that paragraph applies is disregarded only to the extent that it does not exceed the annual limit of £180 mentioned in that regulation.
2. [³. . .]	[³. . .]

Tax Credits (Definition and Calculation of Income) Regulations 2002

1. Description of income to be disregarded	2. Extent of disregard
[³**3.** Any interest payable under a certified SAYE savings arrangement for the purposes of Chapter 4 of Part 6 of ITTOIA.]	The whole amount.
4. Any winnings from betting, including pool betting, or lotteries or games with prizes.	The whole amount.
5. Any interest on a payment of £10,000 made by the Secretary of State to a person who was held prisoner by the Japanese during the Second World War or to the spouse of such a person, if the payment is held in a distinct account and no payment (other than interest) has been added to the account.	The whole amount of the interest.
6. Any interest on a payment made to the claimant by, or on behalf, of a government of a country outside the United Kingdom, either from its own resources or with contributions from any other organisation, by way of compensation for a victim of National Socialism if the payment is held in a distinct account and no payment (other than interest) has been added to the account. Here a reference to a victim of National Socialism is a reference to a person who was required to work as a slave or a forced labourer for National Socialists or their sympathisers during the Second World War, or suffered property loss, or suffered injury or is the parent of a child who died, at the hands of National Socialists or their sympathisers during the Second World War.	The whole amount of the interest.
7. Any monies paid to the claimant by a bank or building	The amount [⁴of interest exempted from income tax

(SI 2002/2006 reg.10) (as amended)

1. Description of income to be disregarded	2. Extent of disregard
society as compensation in respect of an unclaimed account held by a Holocaust victim and which vested in the Custodian of Enemy Property under section 7 of the Trading with the Enemy Act 1939 and treated as exempt from income tax by [⁴section 756A of ITTOIA]	under section 756A of ITTOIA.]

8. Any interest, or payment [³. . .], which is disregarded for income tax purposes by virtue of—
    [³(a) section 751 of ITTOIA (interest on damages for personal injury),or]
    (b) [³section 731 of ITTOIA (periodical payments of personal injury damages)] (personal injury damages in the form of periodical payments).
	The amount so disregarded.

[¹**9**]. Annuity payments under an award of compensation made under the Criminal Injuries Compensation Scheme (within the meaning of [³section 732(3) of ITTOIA].	The amount of any payment which is treated as not being income of the claimant or his partner by virtue of [³section 731 of ITTOIA.]
[¹**10**]. A payment under a life annuity.	The amount of interest eligible for relief under section 353 of the Taxes Act by virtue of section 365 of that Act.
[¹**11**]. Any interest, or payment in respect of interest, which is compensation to a person who is under the age of 18 years for the death of one or both of his parents.	The whole of the interest or payment.
12. A purchased life annuity to which [³Chapter 7 of Part 4 of ITTOIA] applies.	[³The amount exempted under section 717 of ITTOIA as calculated under section 719 of that Act.]
[³ **13.** Any payments which are exempt from Income tax by virtue of—	The whole amount.

493

Tax Credits (Definition and Calculation of Income) Regulations 2002

1. Description of income to be disregarded	2. Extent of disregard
(a) section 725 of ITTOIA (annual payments under immediate needs annuities), or (b) section 735 of ITTOIA (health and employment insurance payments).]	
[⁵ 14. Any income arising from or payment made in respect of a Saving Gateway account.	The whole amount.]

Table 5. Payments in connection with very severe disablement, Creutzfeldt–Jakob disease and haemophilia

2.165

1. Description of income to be disregarded	2. Applicable period
1. A trust payment made to — (a) a diagnosed person; (b) the diagnosed person's partner; or (c) the person who was his partner at the date of his death.	The period beginning on the date on which the trust payment is made and ending with the death of the person to whom the payment is made.
2. A trust payment made to a parent of a deceased diagnosed person, or a person acting in the place of his parent.	The period beginning on the date on which the trust payment is made and ending two years after that date.
3. The amount of any payment out of the estate of a person to whom a trust payment has been made, which is made to the person who was the diagnosed person's partner at the date of his death.	The period beginning on the date on which the payment is made and ending on the date on which that person dies.
4. The amount of any payment out of the estate of a person to whom a trust payment has been made, which is made to a parent of a deceased diagnosed person, or a person acting in the place of his parent.	The period beginning on the date on which the payment is made and ending two years after that date.

(SI 2002/2006 reg.10) (as amended)

(3) The amounts disregarded under Items 3 and 4 in Table 5 shall not exceed the total amount of any trust payments made to the person to whom the trust payment had been made.

(4) In this regulation, "diagnosed person" means—

(a) a person who has been diagnosed as suffering from, or who after his death has been diagnosed has having suffered from, variant Creutzfeldt–Jakob disease;

(b) a person who is suffering or has suffered from haemophilia; or

(c) a person in respect of whom a payment has been made from the 1992 Fund, the Eileen Trust or the Independent Living Funds; and a reference to a person being a member of the diagnosed person's household at the date of the diagnosed person's death includes a person who would have been a member of his household but for the diagnosed person being in residential accommodation, a residential care home or a nursing home on that date.

(5) In this regulation—

"relevant trust" means—

(a) a trust established out of funds provided by the Secretary of State in respect of persons who suffered, or who are suffering, from variant Creutzfeldt–Jakob disease for the benefit of persons eligible for payments in accordance with its provisions;

(b) the Macfarlane Trusts; or

(c) the 1992 Fund, the Eileen Trust or the Independent Living Funds.

"residential accommodation", "residential care home" and "nursing home" have the meanings given by regulation 2(1) of the Income Support (General) Regulations 1987; and

"trust payment" means a payment under a relevant trust.

AMENDMENTS

1. Tax Credits (Definition and Calculation of Income) (Amendment) Regulations 2003 (SI 2003/732) reg.9 (April 6, 2003).

2. Tax Credits (Miscellaneous Amendments No.2) Regulations 2003 (SI 2003/2815) reg.8 (November 26, 2003).

3. Tax Credits (Miscellaneous Amendments) Regulations 2006 (SI 2006/766) reg.14 (April 6, 2006).

4. Tax Credits (Miscellaneous Amendments) Regulations 2007 (SI 2007/824) reg.12 (April 6, 2007).

5. Tax Credits (Miscellaneous Amendments) Regulations 2010 (SI 2010/751) reg.4 (April 6, 2010).

GENERAL NOTE

This regulation was drafted ahead of, and anticipated, the relevant provisions of ITTOIA. But there were some changes to the Rewrite Bill after this regulation was brought into force, including the retitling of the relevant part of ITTOIA to cover "Savings and investment income". That accurately reflects the scope of this regulation. It completely reshapes the relevant provisions in the previous income tax legislation and, more than any other part of the Rewrite Acts, should be considered in the new form and not as a continuation of old history.

2.166

The relevant provisions in ITTOIA are in Pt 4, which has the following structure:

Chapter 1	Introduction
Chapter 2	Interest
Chapter 3	Dividends from UK resident companies

Tax Credits (Definition and Calculation of Income) Regulations 2002

Chapter 4	Dividends from non-UK resident companies
Chapter 5	Stock dividends from UK resident companies
Chapter 6	Release of loan to participator in close company
Chapter 7	Purchased life annuity payments
Chapter 8	Profits from deeply discounted securities
Chapter 9	Gains from contracts for life assurance
Chapter 10	Distributions from unauthorised unit trusts
Chapter 11	Transactions in deposits
Chapter 12	Disposals of futures and options involving guaranteed Returns
Chapter 13	Sales of foreign dividend coupons

Most of these chapters contain provisions designed to prevent avoidance, in particular by turning income into capital by one means or another. However, by bringing them all together the overall picture is now far clearer than it was before ITTOIA in that the full pattern of the scope of the income tax charges on forms of income from savings and investments can be seen from this list.

But reg.10 retains, at least for the time being, much of the flavour of the previous law, its wording still coming from the former s.18 of the Income and Corporation Taxes Act 1988.

2.167　Income from savings and investments is included in the calculation of income for tax credits purposes no account is taken of capital when someone claims a tax credit under the 2002 Act. In practice, however, some of the most popular forms of savings are shielded from an income tax charge, and assessment to tax credits, by the very important disregards listed out in Table 4. Interest and dividends received from saving held within an ISA (individual savings account) are protected not only from income tax but also tax credits assessment by item 1. Interest and bonuses paid under SAYE schemes (save as you earn) are protected by item 3. But interest on ordinary deposits with banks or building societies is taxable (subject to deduction of income tax at source).

Because reg.10 follows the former law, and not the present income tax law, express provision has been made to remove winnings from betting and lotteries. This is not an exemption but rather a limitation set by case law on the previous legislation. (Winnings were excluded to stop losses being claimed.)

CHAPTER 8

Property income

Property income

2.168　**11.**—(1) In these Regulations, "property income" means the annual taxable profits arising from a business carried on for the exploitation, as a source of rents or other receipts, of any estate, interest or rights in or over land in the United Kingdom.

Expressions which are used in this paragraph which are defined in [² Part 3 of ITTOIA] for the purposes of [² that Part] bear the same meaning here as they bear in [² that Part].

This paragraph is subject to the following [¹qualifications].

[² (2) In calculating property income there shall be disregarded any profits—
　(a)　treated as nil by section 791 to 794 of ITTOIA (full rent-a-room relief); or
　(b)　excluded from profits by section 795 to 798 of ITTOIA (alternative calculation of profits if amount exceeds limit).]

[¹(3) [² Where a property business (as defined in Part 3 of ITTOIA] makes

(SI 2002/2006 reg.11) (as amended)

a loss to which the relief provisions [³ contained in sections 118 (carry forward against subsequent property business profits) and 119 (how relief works) of ITA] apply, then such relief as may arise under [³ those sections] shall be applied in calculating property income for the purposes of this regulation.]

AMENDMENTS

1. Tax Credits (Miscellaneous Amendments No.2) Regulations 2003 (SI 2003/2815) reg.9 (November 26, 2003).
2. Tax Credits (Miscellaneous Amendments) Regulations 2006 (SI 2006/766) reg.15 (April 6, 2006).
3. Tax Credits (Definition and Calculation of Income) (Amendment) Regulations 2007 (SI 2007/1305) reg.6 (May 16, 2007).

GENERAL NOTE

This regulation reflects Pt 3 of ITTOIA under the same heading. However, the label is perhaps the least helpful of the new titles created by the Tax Law Rewrite Project. Part 3 and this regulation are limited to real property, and do not apply to any other kind of property. But it was thought better to avoid referring to income from land because the drafters wished to use popular terms and avoid legal complications.

2.169

The rules in Pt 3 remove another distinction in the former income tax law. Because taxation of income from land is usually sourced-based—that is, taxed where the land is—different rules used to apply to income from land in the UK and income received in the UK from land elsewhere. That distinction has now largely been removed in ITTOIA. But it has not been removed for tax credits purposes. Following the pattern of the old law, income from foreign land is foreign income within reg.12. In income tax practice, double taxation agreements normally reserve the taxation of income from land to the state where the land is, exempting it—or providing relief—elsewhere. But that does not apply for tax credits purposes. So someone who has, say, an apartment in Spain which is let for part of the year may not pay any UK income tax on the rent, but should have it taken into account for tax credits purposes under reg.12 alongside any income from UK land brought within reg.11.

CHAPTER 9

Foreign income

12.—(1) In these Regulations, "foreign income" means income arising, in the year in question, from [³a source outside the United Kingdom or from foreign holdings] which are not—

2.170

(a) employment income;
(b) trading income; or
(c) investment income falling within regulation 10(1)(e).

This is subject to the following provisions of this regulation.

[³(2) The reference in paragraph (1) to "foreign holdings" shall be construed in accordance with section 571 of ITTOIA.]

(3) In calculating the claimant's foreign income there shall be disregarded—

(a) any payment by way of an annuity or pension payable under any special provision for victims of National Socialist persecution which is made by the law of the Federal Republic of Germany, or any part of it, or of Austria;

[⁴(aa) any monies paid by a bank or building society which are exempted

from income tax under section 756A of ITTOIA (interest on certain deposits of victims of National-Socialist persecution).]
[³(b) the amount authorised to be deducted by the relevant provision if the claimant's foreign income comprises or includes a pension to which the following provisions of ITEPA apply—
   (i) sections 567(5) and 617 (deduction allowed for taxable pension income);
   (ii) section 575(2) (taxable pension income: foreign pensions);
   (iii) section 613(3) (taxable pension income: foreign annuities); and
   (iv) section 635(3) (taxable pension income: foreign voluntary annual payments); and]
(c) any amount which would be disregarded for the purposes of income tax by virtue of—
   (i) Extra Statutory Concession A10 (lumps sums paid by overseas pension schemes);
   (ii) [¹s.681 of ITEPA];
   (iii) [³section 751(1)(c) of ITTOIA] (interest on damages for personal injuries awarded by a foreign court); or
   (iv) Extra Statutory Concession A44 (education allowances payable to public officials of overseas territories); [³or
   (v) section 730 of ITTOIA (foreign maintenance payments)].

[²(4) Where an overseas property business ;[³(within the meaning of Part 3 of ITTOIA)] makes a loss to which the relief provisions [⁵ contained in sections 118 (carry forward against subsequent property business profits) and 119 (how relief works) of ITA apply], then such relief as may arise under [⁵ those sections] shall be applied in calculating foreign income for the purposes of this regulation.]

AMENDMENTS

1. Tax Credits (Definition and Calculation of Income) (Amendment) Regulations 2003 (SI 2003/732) reg.10 (April 6, 2003).
2. Tax Credits (Miscellaneous Amendments No.2) Regulations 2003 (SI 2003/2815) reg.10 (November 26, 2003).
3. Tax Credits (Miscellaneous Amendments) Regulations 2006 (SI 2006/766) reg.16 (April 6, 2006).
4. Tax Credits (Miscellaneous Amendments) Regulations 2007 (SI 2007/824) reg.13 (April 6, 2007).
5. Tax Credits (Definition and Calculation of Income) (Amendment) Regulations 2007 (SI 2007/1305) reg.7 (May 16, 2007).

GENERAL NOTE

2.171   The provisions in reg.3 above ensure that all forms of the foreign income of a tax credits claimant are potentially relevant to the calculation of income for tax credits purposes even if they would be exempt from income tax in the UK. "Foreign income" is not a specific head of charge for income tax purposes. And in practice most problems are dealt with not under the UK legislation but under the terms of the relevant double tax agreements. That approach and those agreements do not apply for tax credits purposes, so there is need to make express provision instead.
This regulation, as amended from 2006, provides for all foreign income charged to income tax to be relevant for tax credits save for specific exemptions. It also provides for the priorities between competing charges that arise, for example, where income is both foreign income and employment income, to prevent a double charge.

(SI 2002/2006 reg.12) (as amended)

The combination of exemptions and rules giving priority to other heads of assessment result in this head of charge still being of limited importance. But note that this provision will apply to some kinds of foreign pension and foreign savings or investment income.

"Foreign holdings" is defined in s.571 of ITTOIA as meaning shares and other securities outside the UK that are issued by a government or public authority of another country or by or on behalf of a body of persons not resident in the UK.

CHAPTER 10

Notional Income

Introduction

13. In these Regulations, "notional income" means income which, by virtue of regulations 14 to 17 a claimant is treated as having, but which he does not in fact have.

GENERAL NOTE

This regulation emphasises that the provisions of regs 14–17 are not parallels to income tax in the ordinary sense, in that the income is not in fact income of the claimant (or any of the joint claimants). It may, as the notes to the following regulations show, be the income of someone else.

Claimants treated for any purpose as having income by virtue of the Income Tax Acts

14.—(1) If an amount is treated for any purpose as the claimant's income under any provision mentioned in paragraph (2), he is to be treated as having that amount of income.

(2) The provisions mentioned in paragraph (1) are—
(a) the following provisions of the Taxes Act—
   [¹. . .];
   (ix) section 714 (transfers of securities: treatment of deemed sums and reliefs) or 716 (transfer of unrealised interest);
   (x) section 730 (transfer of income arising from securities);
   [² . . .]
   (xiv) section 761 (charge to income tax of offshore income gain); and
   [² . . .]
[¹(b) the following provisions of ITTOIA—
   (i) sections 277 to 283 (amounts treated as receipts: leases);
   (ii) Chapter 5 of Part 4 (stock dividends from UK resident companies);
   (iii) Chapter 6 of Part 4 (release of loan to participator in close company);
   (iv) section 427 (charge to tax on profits from deeply discounted securities);
   (v) Chapter 11 of Part 4 (transactions in securities);
   (vi) sections 624 to 628 (income treated as income of settlor: retained interests);

2.172

2.173

2.174

Tax Credits (Definition and Calculation of Income) Regulations 2002

  (vii) sections 629 to 632 (income treated as income of settlor: unmarried children);
  (viii) section 633 (capital sums paid to settlor by trustees of settlement);
  (ix) section 641 (capital sums paid to settlor by body connected with settlement);
  (x) section 652 (estate income: absolute interests in residue); and
  (xi) sections 654 to 655 (estate income: interests in residue);
[² (ba) the following provisions of ITA—
  (i) Chapter 5 of Part 11 (price differences under repos);
  (ii) Chapter 2 of Part 13 (transfer of assets abroad); and
  (iii) Chapter 3 of Part 13 (transactions in land).]
 (c) section 84 and Schedule 15 to the Finance Act 2004 (charge to income tax by reference to enjoyment of property previously owned).]

AMENDMENTS

1. Tax Credits (Miscellaneous Amendments) Regulations 2006 (SI 2006/766) reg.17 (April 6, 2006).
2. Tax Credits (Definition and Calculation of Income) (Amendment) Regulations 2007 (SI 2007/1305) reg.8 (May 16, 2007).

GENERAL NOTE

2.175 This regulation has been rewritten substantially with effect from the 2006–07 income tax year, but its contents remains broadly the same. It collects together a series of important income tax anti-avoidance provisions and includes them together as providing "notional income" for step 1 of the calculation of income for tax credits purposes under reg.3(1).

Note that this regulation is worded so that the assessment for tax credit purposes depends on self-assessment or an assessment for income tax purposes. A claimant who is treated as having an amount of any of these kinds of income for income tax purposes is treated as having that amount of income for the purposes of this regulation. It may therefore be assumed, it is suggested, that the issue will not arise for tax credits purposes unless it has already been identified for income tax purposes.

The regulation collects together both well-known and less well-known anti-avoidance provisions. The newest, in para.(2)(c), attracted considerable attention when enacted. It is the provision that deems someone who has given her or his property away (usually for inheritance tax purposes) but who continues to have a right to reside in the property to be in receipt of income and so liable to income tax on (broadly) the rent that could have been received from the property. That also applies for a tax credit assessment.

Claimants depriving themselves of income in order to secure entitlement

2.176 **15.** If a claimant has deprived himself of income for the purpose of securing entitlement to, or increasing the amount of, a tax credit, he is treated as having that income.

GENERAL NOTE

2.177 This is equivalent to Income Support (General) Regulations 1987 (SI 1987/1967) reg.42(1), and the note on that in Vol.II in this series should be consulted. Note, however, that this provision is defined by reference to deprivation for the purposes of securing or increasing entitlement to tax credits (and not, for example, income

(SI 2002/2006 reg.15) (as amended)

support). TCTM04920 gives the example of someone who transfers entitlement to an occupational pension to someone else by deed of gift. Without reference to authority, it emphasises that securing or increasing entitlement to tax credit may not be a claimant's main motive but it must be a significant one. That is a question of fact.

Claimants to whom income becomes available upon the making of a claim

16.—(1) If income would become available to a claimant upon the making of an application for that income, he is treated as having that income.

This is subject to the following qualification.

(2) Paragraph (1) does not apply in relation to income—
(a) under a trust derived from a payment made in consequence of a personal injury;
(b) under a personal pension scheme or retirement annuity contract;
(c) consisting in a sum to which Item 8 of Table 4 in regulation 10 refers (compensation for personal injuries which is administered by the Court); or
(d) consisting in a rehabilitation allowance made under section 2 of the Employment Act.

[1(3) Paragraph (1) also does not apply to income by way of—
(a) a Category A or Category B retirement pension,
(b) a graduated retirement benefit, or
(c) a shared additional pension,

payment of which has been deferred.

Here—

"Category A retirement pension" means a pension to which a person is entitled by virtue of section 44 of the Contributions and Benefits Act or the Northern Ireland Contributions and Benefits Act;

"Category B retirement pension" means a pension to which a person is entitled by virtue of any of sections 48A to 48C of the Contributions and Benefits Act or sections 48A to 48C of the Northern Ireland Contributions and Benefits Act;

"graduated retirement benefit" means a pension payable under—
(a) sections 36 and 37 of the National Insurance Act 1965; or
(b) sections 35 and 36 of the National Insurance Act (Northern Ireland) 1966; and

"shared additional pension" means a pension to which a person is entitled by virtue of section 55A of the Contributions and Benefits Act or section 55A of the Northern Ireland Contributions and Benefits Act.]

2.178

AMENDMENT

1. Tax Credits (Miscellaneous Amendments) Regulations 2004 (SI 2004/762) reg.15 (April 6, 2004).

DEFINITIONS

"Category A retirement pension"—see para.(3).
"Category B retirement pension"—see *ibid.*
"graduated retirement benefit"—see *ibid.*
"shared additional pension"—see *ibid.*

Tax Credits (Definition and Calculation of Income) Regulations 2002

GENERAL NOTE

2.179	See the note to the similar provision in Income Support (General) Regulations 1987 (SI 1987/1967) reg.42(2)–(4). The precise operative scope of this provision is not clear. For income support, sums not received may not count as earnings or other income. But most of the charges to income tax, as noted above, are on those "receiving or entitled to". So entitlement is enough to bring the sums in both for income tax purposes and tax credit purposes, even if they are not received. This regulation could, however, extend that to cover sums to which entitlement had not arisen, for example because no demand had been made for the sum under a contractual entitlement operative on such demand.

Claimants providing services to other persons for less than full earnings

2.180	**17.**—(1) If a claimant provides a service for another person and—
(a) the other person makes no payment of earnings or pays less than those paid for a comparable employment (including self-employment) in the area; and
(b) the Board are satisfied that the means of the other person are sufficient for him to pay for, or to pay more for, the service,
the claimant is to be treated as having such an amount of employment income, or in the case of a service provided in the course of a trade or business, such an amount of trading income as is reasonable for the employment of the claimant to provide the service.
This is subject to the following qualification.
(2) Paragraph (1) does not apply where—
(a) the claimant is a volunteer or is engaged to provide the service by a charitable or voluntary organisation and the Board are satisfied that it is reasonable for the claimant to provide the service free of charge; or
(b) the service is provided in connection with the claimant's participation in an employment or training programme—
  (i) [1(i) in Great Britain, which is approved by the Secretary of State;]; or
  (ii) in Northern Ireland in accordance with regulation 19(1)(p) of the Jobseeker's Allowance Regulations (Northern Ireland) 1996 other than where it is provided in connection with the claimant's participation in the Preparation for Employment Programme specified in regulation 75(1)(a)(v) of those Regulations.

AMENDMENT

1. Universal Credit (Consequential, Supplementary, Incidental and Miscellaneous Provisions) Regulations 2013 (SI 2013/630) reg.78(3) (April 29, 2013).

GENERAL NOTE

2.181	See the note in Vol.II in this series to the similar (though differently drafted) provision in Income Support (General) Regulations 1987 (SI 1987/1967) reg.42(6).

(SI 2002/2006 reg.18) (as amended)

Chapter 11

Miscellaneous income

Miscellaneous income

18. In these Regulations, "miscellaneous income" means income which does not fall within any other provision of these Regulations and which is subject to income tax under [¹ Part 5 of ITTOIA].

2.182

Amendment

1. Tax Credits (Miscellaneous Amendments) Regulations 2006 (SI 2006/766) reg.18 (April 6, 2006).

General Note

Part 5 of ITTOIA contains the "sweeper" provisions to bring within liability to income tax any forms of income that fall outside the specific charges to income tax. If, therefore, something can properly be regarded as employment income, trading income, savings and investment income, pension income, social security income or some other more specific form of income, then this provision does not apply. But it is not a "catch-all", and there is no global definition of "income" in UK income tax legislation.

2.183

Part 5 applies to "annual profits or gains" not otherwise charged to tax. It does not catch gifts or loans, nor does it catch single "one-off" payments unless they are of a trading or business nature. Nor does it catch receipts of capital sums, which in tax terms fall to be taxed under the Taxation of Chargeable Gains Act 2001, if at all. See the note to reg.6.

Part III

Sums disregarded in the calculation of income

General disregards in the calculation of income

19.—(1) For the purposes of regulation 3—
(a) the sums specified in Table 6 are disregarded in the calculation of income;
(b) the sums specified in column 1 of Table 7 are disregarded in the calculation of income if the condition in the corresponding entry in column 2 of that Table is satisfied; and
(c) the sums specified in column 1 of Table 8 are disregarded in the calculation of income to the extent specified in the corresponding entry in column 2 of that Table.

2.184

(2) In this regulation—
"the JSA Regulations" means the Jobseeker's Allowance Regulations 1996; and
"the JSA (NI) Regulations" means the Jobseeker's Allowance (Northern Ireland) Regulations 1996.

Tax Credits (Definition and Calculation of Income) Regulations 2002

Table 6. Sums disregarded in the calculation of income

2.185

1. Any payment of an employment credit under a scheme under section 2(2) of the Employment Act known as "New Deal 50 Plus" or the corresponding scheme under section 1 of the Employment and Training Act (Northern Ireland) 1950.
2. Any payment made— (a) under section 15 of the Disabled Persons (Employment Act) 1944 or section 15 of the Disabled Persons (Employment) Act (Northern Ireland) 1945; or (b) in accordance with arrangements made under section 2 of the Employment Act or section 1 of the Employment and Training Act (Northern Ireland) 1950 to assist disabled persons to obtain or retain employment despite their disability.
3. Any mandatory top-up payment made pursuant to— (a) section 2 of the Employment Act [³ or section 1 of the Employment and Training Act (Northern Ireland) 1950] in respect of the claimant's participation in— (i) an employment programme specified in regulation 75(1)(a)(ii)(bb) of the JSA Regulations or regulation 75(1)(a)(ii) of the JSA (NI) Regulations (Voluntary Sector Option of the New Deal); (ii) an employment programme specified in regulation 75(1)(a)(ii)(cc) of the JSA Regulations (Environmental Task Force Option of the New Deal) or regulation 75(1)(a)(iii) of the JSA (NI) Regulations; [⁵ . . .] [⁵ (iia) an employment programme specified in regulation 75(1)(a)(ii)(dd) of the JSA Regulations (Community Task Force);] (iii) the Intensive Activity Period of the New Deal Pilots for 25 Plus specified in regulation 75(1)(a)(iv) of the JSA Regulations or, in Northern Ireland, the Preparation for Employment Programme specified in regulation 75(1)(a)(v) of the JSA (NI) Regulations; [⁵ or (iv) the Backing Young Britain programme pursuant to arrangements made under section 2 of the Employment Act);] or (b) a written arrangement entered into between— (i) the Secretary of State and the person who has arranged for the claimant's participation in the Intensive Activity Period of the New Deal for 25 Plus and which is made in respect of his participation in that Period; or (ii) the Department for Employment and Learning and the person who has arranged for the claimant's participation in the Preparation for Employment Programme and which is made in respect of the claimant's participation in the Programme. [³This item applies only to the extent that the payment is not taxable as a profit of a trade, profession or vocation.]
4. Any discretionary payment pursuant to section 2 of the Employment Act, or, in Northern Ireland, section 1(1) of the Employment and Training Act (Northern Ireland) 1950 to meet, or help to meet, special needs in

(SI 2002/2006 reg.19) (as amended)

respect of the claimant's participation in the Full-Time Education and Training Option of the New Deal as specified in regulation 75(1)(b)(ii) of the JSA Regulations or of the JSA (NI) Regulations.

5. Any—
  (a) education maintenance allowance in accordance with regulations made under section 518 of the Education Act 1996 (payment of school expenses; grant of scholarships, etc.); or
  (b) payment (not within sub-paragraph (a)) in respect of a course of study attended by a child or qualifying young person payable—
    (i) in accordance with regulations made under section 518 of the Education (Scotland) Act 1980 (power to assist persons to take advantage of educational facilities) or section 12(2)(c) of the Further and Higher Education (Scotland) Act 1992 (provision of financial assistance to students); or
    (ii) by virtue of regulations made in Article 50, 51 or 55(1) of the Education and Libraries (Northern Ireland) Order 1986 (provisions to assist persons to take advantage of educational facilities).

6. Any payment made by an employment zone contractor payable in respect of the claimant's participation in the employment zone programme by way of—
  (a) a training premium;
  (b) a discretionary payment, being a fee, grant, loan or otherwise; or
  (c) any arrears of subsistence allowance paid as a lump sum.

7. [³. . .]

8. An amount of income equal to any qualifying maintenance payment within section 347B of the Taxes Act.

[⁹ **9.** Any payment by way of qualifying care receipts to the extent that those receipts qualify for relief under Chapter 2 of Part 7 of the Income Tax (Trading and Other Income) Act 2005(4).]

10. Any payment of maintenance, whether under a court order or not, which is made or due to be made by—
  (a) the claimant's former partner, or the claimant's partner's former partner; or
  (b) the parent of a child or qualifying young person where that child or qualifying young person is a member of the claimant's household except where that parent is the claimant or the claimant's partner.

11. Any payment in respect of a child or qualifying young person who is a member of the claimant's household made—
  [²(a) to adopters which is exempt from income tax by virtue of [⁴ sections 744 to 746 of ITTOIA];]
  (b) by a local authority in pursuance of paragraph 15(1) of Schedule 1 to the Children Act 1989 (local authority contribution to child's maintenance);
  [³(bb) by a local authority by way of special guardianship support services pursuant to regulations under section 14F(1)(b) of the Children Act 1989; or]
  (c) by an authority, as defined in Article 2 of the Children (Northern

Tax Credits (Definition and Calculation of Income) Regulations 2002

Ireland) Order 1995, in pursuance of Article 15 of, and paragraph 17 of Schedule 1 to, that Order (contribution by an authority to child's maintenance).
[⁸ 12. Any payment in respect of travelling expenses— (a) in relation to England under regulation 5, 6 or 12 of the National Health Service (Travel Expenses and Remission of Charges) Regulations 2003; (b) in relation to Wales under regulation 5, 6 or 11 of the National Health Service (Travelling Expenses and Remission of Charges) (Wales) Regulations 2007; (c) in relation to Scotland, under regulation 3, 5, or 11 of the National Health Service (Travelling Expenses and Remission of Charges) (Scotland) (No. 2) Regulations 2003; (d) in relation to Northern Ireland, under regulation 5, 6 or 11 of the Travelling Expenses and Remission of Charges Regulations (Northern Ireland) 2004; or (e) made by the Secretary of State for Health, the Scottish Ministers, the Welsh Ministers or the Department of Health, Social Services and Public Safety and which is analogous to a payment specified in paragraph (a), (b), (c) or (d).]
13. Any payment made by the Secretary of State or the Scottish Ministers under a scheme established to assist relatives and other persons to visit persons in custody.
[²14. Any payment under the Community Care (Direct Payments) Act 1996, section 57 of the Health and Social Care Act 2001, section 12B of the Social Work (Scotland) Act 1968, Article 15A of the Health and Personal Social Services (Direct Payments) (Northern Ireland) Order 1996 or section 8 of the Carers and Direct Payments Act (Northern Ireland) 2002.]
[¹14A. Any payment made under the "Supporting People" programme— (a) in England and Wales, under section 93 of the Local Government Act 2000; (b) in Scotland, under section 91 of the Housing (Scotland) Act 2001; or (c) in Northern Ireland, under Article 4 of the Housing Support Services (Northern Ireland) Order 2002.]
15. [¹Any payment or a voucher] provided under section 95 or 98 of the Immigration and Asylum Act 1999 for any former asylum-seeker or his dependants.
16. Any payment of a provident benefit by a trade union. Here— "provident benefit" has the meaning given in section 467(2) of the Taxes Act; and "trade union" has the meaning given in section 467(4) of the Taxes Act.

(SI 2002/2006 reg.19) (as amended)

[¹¹ **17.** Armed forces independence payment under the Armed Forces and Reserve Forces (Compensation Scheme) Order 2011.]

Table 7. Sums disregarded in calculating income if conditions are satisfied

1. Description of payment	*2. [³Conditions] that must be satisfied*
1. Any payment in respect of any expenses incurred by a claimant who is engaged by a charitable or voluntary organisation or is a volunteer.	The claimant does not receive remuneration or profit from the engagement and is not treated as possessing any employment income under regulation 17 in respect of that engagement.

2. A payment by way of—
  (a) travelling expenses reimbursed to the claimant;
  (b) a living away from home allowance under section 2(2)(d) of the Employment Act, section 2(4)(c) of the Enterprise and New Towns (Scotland) Act 1990 or section 1 of the Employment and Training Act (Northern Ireland) 1950;
  (c) training grant; [⁶ . . .]
  (d) childcare expenses reimbursed to the claimant in respect of his participation in—
    (i) a New Deal option;
    (ii) the Intensive Activity Period of the New Deal Pilots for 25 Plus; or
    (iii) the Preparation for Employment Programme.
  [⁵ (iv) the Flexible New Deal specified in regulation 75(1)(a)(v) of the [⁷ JSA Regulations 1996]];
	The claimant—
	  (a) participates in arrangements for training made under—
	    (i) section 2 of the Employment Act;
	    (ii) section 2 of the Enterprise and New Towns (Scotland) Act 1990; or
	    (iii) section 1 of the Employment and Training Act (Northern Ireland) 1950; or
	  (b) attends a course at an employment rehabilitation centre established under section 2 of the Employment Act.
	[³The payment is not taxable as a profit of a trade, profession or vocation.]

2.186

[⁷ (v)	the Community Task Force specified in regulation 75(1)(a)(ii)(dd) of the JSA Regulations;] [⁶ or
(e)	child care expenses under the Steps to Work Programme specified in regulation 75(1)(a)(vi) of the [⁷ JSA (NI) Regulations]].

Table 8. Sums partly disregarded in the calculation of income

2.187

Type of payment to be disregarded	Limit on, or exception to, the extent of disregard
1. Any discretionary payment made pursuant to section 2 of the Employment Act, or, in Northern Ireland, section 1(1) of the Employment and Training Act (Northern Ireland) 1950 to meet, or help meet, the claimant's special needs in undertaking a qualifying course within the meaning of regulation 17A(7) of the JSA Regulations or regulation 17A(7) of the JSA (NI) Regulations.	A payment is not within this item to the extent that it relates to travel expenses incurred as a result of the claimant's attendance on the course if an amount in respect of those expenses has already been disregarded pursuant to regulation 8.
2. Any payment made in respect of a career development loan paid pursuant to section 2 of the Employment Act.	A payment is not within this item to the extent that the loan has been applied for or paid in respect of living expenses for the period of education and training supported by the loan.

3. Any payment made to the claimant or his partner in respect of a person who is not normally a member of the claimant's household but is temporarily in his care, by—
    (a) a health authority;
    (b) a local authority;
    (c) a voluntary
    (c) organisation;
    (d) that person pursuant to section 26(3A) of
	A payment is only to be disregarded by virtue of this item if
	[¹(a)] any profits[⁴. . .] arising from the payment mentioned in col.1 are treated as nil by [⁴ section 791 to 794 of ITTOIA (full rent-a-room relief)]; or
	[¹(b)] excluded from profits [⁴by section 795 to 798 of ITTOIA

(SI 2002/2006 reg.19) (as amended)

	the National Assistance Act 1948; [¹⁰. . .]	(alternative calculation of profits if amount
[¹²(dza)	that person where the payment is for the provision of accommodation in respect of the meeting of that person's needs under section 18 or 19 of the Care Act 2014 (duty and power to meet needs for care and support);]	
[¹⁰(da)	a clinical commissioning group established under section 14D of the National Health Service Act 2006;	exceeds limit).]
(db)	the National Health Service Commissioning Board.]	

4. Any payment made in Northern Ireland to the claimant or his partner in respect of a person who is not normally a member of the claimant's household but is temporarily in his care—
   (a) pursuant to Article 36(7) of the Health and Personal Social Services (Northern Ireland) Order 1972 by an authority; a voluntary organisation; or the person concerned; or
   (b) by a training school within the meaning of section 137 of the Children and Young Persons Act (Northern Ireland) 1968.
 In this item "an authority" has the meaning given by Article 2 of the Children (Northern Ireland) Order 1995.
		A payment is only to be disregarded by virtue of this item if—
		 [¹(a)] any profits [⁴. . .] arising from the payment mentioned in column 1 are treated as nil by [⁴ section 791 to 794 of ITTOIA (full rent-a-room relief)]; or
		 [¹(b) excluded from profits [⁴by section 795 to 798 of ITTOIA (alternative calculation of profits if amount exceeds limit).]

5. Any payment under an insurance policy taken out to insure against the risk of being unable to maintain the repayments—		A payment is only to be disregarded by virtue of this item to the extent that it is used to— (a) maintain the

509

Tax Credits (Definition and Calculation of Income) Regulations 2002

Type of payment to be disregarded	Limit on, or exception to, the extent of disregard
(a) on a loan which is secured on the dwelling house which the claimant occupies as his home; or (b) under a regulated agreement or under a hire-purchase agreement or a conditional sale agreement. For the purposes of paragraph (b)— "regulated agreement" has the meaning given in the Consumer Credit Act 1974; and "hire-purchase agreement" and "conditional sale agreement" have the meanings given in Part 3 of the Hire-Purchase Act 1964.	repayments referred to in col.(1); and (b) meet any amount due by way of premiums on— (i) that policy; or (ii) in a case to which paragraph (a) of this item applies, an insurance policy taken out to insure against loss or damage to any building or part of a building which is occupied by the claimant as his home and which is required as a condition of the loan referred to in column (1).
[¹6]. Any payment in respect of the claimant's attendance at court as a juror or witness.	This item applies only to the extent that the payment is not compensation for loss of earnings or for the loss of payment of social security income.
[¹7]. Any payment of a sports award except to the extent that it has been made in respect of living expenses.	For the purposes of this item "living expenses" does not include— (a) the cost of vitamins, minerals or other special dietary supplements intended to enhance the performance of the claimant in the sport in respect of which the award was made; or (b) accommodation costs incurred as a consequence of living away from home whilst training for, or competing in, the

(SI 2002/2006 reg.19) (as amended)

Type of payment to be disregarded	Limit on, or exception to, the extent of disregard
	sport in respect of which the award was made.

AMENDMENTS

1. Tax Credits (Definition and Calculation of Income) (Amendment) Regulations 2003 (SI 2003/732) reg.11 (April 6, 2003).
2. Tax Credits (Miscellaneous Amendments No.2) Regulations 2003 (SI 2003/2815) reg.11 (November 26, 2003).
3. Tax Credits (Miscellaneous Amendments) Regulations 2004 (SI 2004/762) reg.16 (April 6, 2004).
4. Tax Credits (Miscellaneous Amendments) Regulations 2006 (SI 2006/766) reg.19 (April 6, 2006).
5. Tax Credits (Miscellaneous Amendments) Regulations 2009 (SI 2009/697) reg.8 (October 5, 2009).
6. Tax Credits (Miscellaneous Amendments) (No.2) Regulations 2009 (SI 2009/2887) reg.7(3) (November 21, 2009).
7. Tax Credits (Miscellaneous Amendments) Regulations 2010 (SI 2010/751) reg.5(3) (April 6, 2010).
8. Tax Credits (Miscellaneous Amendments) (No.3) Regulations 2010 (SI 2010/2914) reg.5 (December 31, 2010).
9. Tax Credits (Miscellaneous Amendments) Regulations 2011 (SI 2011/721) reg.2(3) (April 6, 2011).
10. National Treatment Agency (Abolition) and the Health and Social Care Act 2012 (Consequential, Transitional and Saving Provisions) Order 2013 (SI 2013/235) art.11 and Sch.2 para.55 (April 1, 2013).
11. Armed Forces and Reserve Forces Compensation Scheme (Consequential Provisions: Subordinate Legislation) Order 2013 (SI 2013/591) art.7 and Sch. para.25 (April 8, 2013).
12. Care Act 2014 (Consequential Amendments) (Secondary Legislation) Order 2015 (SI 2015/643) art.20 (April 1, 2015).

CROSS-REFERENCES

Taxes Act s.347B — Qualifying maintenance payments
F(2)A 1992 Sch.10 — Furnished Accommodation

GENERAL NOTE

This regulation adds to the exemptions and exceptions in regs 3 and 9 that apply generally to income. Exceptions, exemptions and deductions that are specific to one or more kinds of income, but not all kinds of income, are detailed under the specific regulations.

2.188

Table 6

This sets out the sums to be disregarded in total. For fuller notes, see the equivalent provisions to the similar items in Income Support (General) Regulations 1987 (SI 1987/1967) Sch.9 (in Vol.II in this series). Several of the provisions are wider than the equivalent provision in the Income Support (General) Regulations 1987 because these provisions also apply to Northern Ireland, while the Income Support (General) Regulations 1987 apply to Great Britain only.

2.189

Paragraph 1—see Sch.9 para.63.
Paragraph 2—see Sch.9 para.51.

Tax Credits (Definition and Calculation of Income) Regulations 2002

Paragraph 3—see Sch.9 para.62.
Paragraph 4—see Sch.9 para.13.
Paragraph 5—see Sch.9 para.11.
Paragraph 6—see Sch.9 para.72.
Paragraph 8—this excludes all sums within the scope of ITA 2007 ss.453–456 (certain periodic payments made by one party to a marriage or former marriage to the other party for the maintenance of the other party or their children under a court order or agreement).
Paragraph 9—Under Ch.2 of P.7 to ITTOIA, foster-care receipts are only taxable if they are more than the fixed amount for the tax year (£10,000) plus the amounts for children: £200 a week for a child under 11 and £250 for a child over 11.
Paragraph 10—this widens out the scope of para.8.
Paragraph 11—see Sch.9 para.25.
Paragraph 12—see Sch.9 para.48.
Paragraph 13—see Sch.9 para.50.
Paragraph 14—see Sch.9 para.58.
Paragraph 14A—this is a new provision.
Paragraph 15—this is specifically focussed on former asylum-seekers or dependants.
Paragraph 16—s.467 of the Taxes Act provides exemption from tax to trade unions that provide provident benefits to their members not exceeding £4,000 as a capital sum or £825 a year as an annuity during sickness, incapacity or old age, or after an accident, theft or death. The excludes the annuities from counting as income of claimants.

However, there are some differences between the tax credit provisions and the income support provisions listed. For example, the disregard in para.11 in Table 6 omits to mention local authority payments in Scotland under ss.34(6) or 50 of the Children Act 1975, whereas these payments are included in the equivalent income support rule: see Income Support (General) Regulations 1987 (SI 1987/1967) Sch.9 para.25(1)(b)). This would suggest that such payments in Scotland are disregarded for income support purposes but not for tax credits assessments. Note that, so far as England and Wales is concerned, the Children Act 1975 was repealed by the Children Act 1989, but this did not extend to Scotland: Children Act 1989 s.108(11).

Table 7

2.190 For item 1 see also the Income Support (General) Regulations 1987 (SI 1987/1967) Sch.9 para.2. For Item 2, see Sch.9 para.13.

Table 8

2.191 The final table lists those disregards that apply to part only of a payment. Item 1 is to the same effect as Income Support (General) Regulations 1987 (SI 1987/1967) Sch.9 para.65. Item 2 is based on Sch.9 para.59. Item 3 is similar to Sch.9 para.27, but excepts from it any payments that are or would be protected from income tax under the rent-a-room provisions (see reg.11). Item 4 is the equivalent provision for Northern Ireland. Item 5 parallels Sch.9 paras 29 and 30ZA. Item 6 is the same as Sch.9 para.43. Item 7 is based on Sch.9 para.69.

Child Tax Credit Regulations 2002

(SI 2002/2007) (AS AMENDED)

Whereas a draft of this instrument, which contains the first regulations made under section 9 of the Tax Credits Act 2002 has been laid before, and approved by resolution of, each House of Parliament:

Now, therefore, the Treasury, in exercise of the powers conferred on them by sections 8, 9, 65 and 67 of the Tax Credits Act 2002, hereby make the following Regulations:

(SI 2002/2007) (as amended)

ARRANGEMENT OF REGULATIONS

1. Citation, commencement and effect.
2. Interpretation.
3. Circumstances in which a person is or is not responsible for a child or qualifying young person.
4. Period for which a person who attains the age of 16 remains a child.
5. Maximum age and prescribed conditions for a qualifying young person.
6. Entitlement to child tax credit after death of child or qualifying young person.
7. Determination of the maximum rate at which a person or persons may be entitled to child tax credit.
8. Prescribed conditions for a disabled or severely disabled child or qualifying young person.

Citation, commencement and effect

1. These Regulations may be cited as the Child Tax Credit Regulations 2002 and shall come into force—
(a) for the purpose of enabling claims to be made, on 1st August 2002;
(b) for the purpose of enabling awards to be made, on 1st January 2003; and
(c) for all other purposes on 6th April 2003; and shall have effect for the tax year beginning on 6th April 2003 and subsequent tax years.

Interpretation

2.—(1) In these Regulations, unless the context otherwise requires—
"the Act" means the Tax Credits Act 2002;
"advanced education" means [^{12}...]—
(a) a course in preparation for a degree, a diploma of higher education, a higher national diploma, a higher national diploma or higher national certificate of Edexcel or the Scottish Qualifications Authority, or a teaching qualification; or
(b) any other course which is of a standard above ordinary national diploma, a national diploma or national certificate of Edexcel [^{2}...], a general certificate of education (advanced level), [^{2}or Scottish national qualifications at higher or advanced higher level];
[^{4}"approved training" has the meaning given by regulation 1(3) of the Child Benefit (General) Regulations 2006;]
[^{10}"armed forces independence payment" means armed forces independence payment under the Armed Forces and Reserve Forces (Compensation Scheme) Order 2011;]
[^{1}"the Board" means the Commissioners [^{4}for Her Majesty's Revenue and Customs];]
"the Careers Service" means—
(a) in England and Wales, a person with whom the Secretary of State or the National Assembly of Wales has made arrangements under s.10(1) of the Employment Act, and a [^{6}local authority] to whom the Secretary of State or the National Assembly of Wales has given a direction under section 10(2) of that Act;
(b) in Scotland, a person with whom the Scottish Ministers have made arrangements under section 10(1) of the Employment Act and any education authority to which a direction has been given by the Scottish Ministers under section 10(2) of that Act; and
(c) [^{1}...];

Child Tax Credit Regulations 2002

"child" means a person who has not attained the age of sixteen [5 . . .];

"claimant" has the meaning in section 9(8) of the Act, except in regulation 7, where that expression and "joint claimants" have the meanings given in regulation 7(1);

"the Connexions Service" means a person of any description with whom the Secretary of State has made an arrangement under section 114(2)(a) of the Learning and Skills Act 2000 and section 10(1) of the Employment Act, and any person to whom he has given a direction under section 114(2)(b) of the former Act and section 10(2) of the latter Act;

"the Contributions and Benefits Act" means the Social Security Contributions and Benefits Act 1992;

[3"couple" has the meaning given by section 3(5A) of the Act];

"custodial sentence"—
  (a) in England and Wales, has the meaning in section 76 of the Powers of Criminal Courts (Sentencing) Act 2000;
  (b) in Scotland, means detention under a sentence imposed by a court under section 44, 205, 207 or 208 of the Criminal Procedure (Scotland) Act 1995; and
  (c) in Northern Ireland, means a custodial sentence under the Criminal Justice (Children) (Northern Ireland) Order 1998;

"disability living allowance" means a disability living allowance under section 71 of the Contributions and Benefits Act;

"the Employment Act" means the Employment and Training Act 1973;

"the family element of child tax credit" and "the individual element of child tax credit" shall be construed in accordance with section 9(3) of the Act;

[12. . .]

"joint claim" and "single claim" shall be construed in accordance with section 3(8) of the Act;

"looked after by a local authority" has the meaning in section 22 of the Children Act 1989, section 17(6) of the Children (Scotland) Act 1995 or (in Northern Ireland) Article 25 of the Children (Northern Ireland) Order 1995 (with the modification that for the reference to a local authority there is substituted a reference to an authority within the meaning in Article 2 of that Order) [1, and (in Scotland) includes a child in respect of which a child assessment order within the meaning of section 35 of the Children's Hearings (Scotland) Act 2011 has been made or a child protection order within the meaning of section 37 of that Act has been made.];

the "main responsibility test" has the meaning given in rule 2.2. of regulation 3;

the "normally living with test" has the meaning given in rule 1.1. of regulation 3;

"Part I" means Part I of the Act;

"patient" means a person (other than a person who is serving a custodial sentence) who is regarded as receiving free in-patient treatment within the meaning of the Social Security (Hospital In-patients) Regulations 1975, or the Social Security (Hospital In-patients) Regulations (Northern Ireland) 1975;

[9"personal independence payment" means personal independence payment under Part 4 of the Welfare Reform Act 2012]

(SI 2002/2007 reg.2) (as amended)

[⁸ "placing for adoption" means placing for adoption in accordance with—
(a) the Adoption Agencies Regulations 2005,
(b) the Adoption Agencies (Wales) Regulations 2005,
(c) the Adoption Agencies (Scotland) Regulations 2009, or
(d) the Adoption Agencies Regulations (Northern Ireland) 1989;]
[⁵ "qualifying body" means–
  (a) the Careers Service or Connexions Service;
  (b) the Ministry of Defence;
  (c) in Northern Ireland, the Department for Employment and Learning or an Education and Library Board established under Article 3 of the Education and Libraries (Northern Ireland) Order 1986; or
  (d) for the purposes of applying Council Regulation (EEC) No. 1408/71 [⁷ and Regulation (EC) No.883/2004 of the European Parliament and of the Council], any corresponding body in another member state;]
"qualifying young person" means a person, other than a child, who—
  (a) has not attained the age of [⁴twenty]; and
  (b) satisfies the conditions in regulation 5(3) and (4);
[⁵ . . .]
"remunerative work" means work which is—
  (a) done for payment or in expectation of payment;
  (b) undertaken for not less than 24 hours a week, calculated in accordance with regulation 4(3) of the Working Tax Credit (Entitlement and Maximum Rate) Regulations 2002; and
  (c) not excluded from the meaning of engagement in remunerative work by regulation 4(2) of those Regulations;
and other expressions have the same meanings as defined in the Act.

(2) In the application of these Regulations to Northern Ireland, a reference to a provision of an enactment which applies only to Great Britain or England and Wales, shall be construed, so far as necessary, as including a reference to the corresponding enactment applying to Northern Ireland.

AMENDMENTS

1. Child Tax Credit (Amendment) Regulations 2003 (SI 2003/738) reg.3 (April 6, 2003).
2. Tax Credits (Miscellaneous Amendments No.2) Regulations 2003 (SI 2003/2815) reg.17 (November 26, 2003).
3. Civil Partnership Act 2004 (Tax Credits, etc.) (Consequential Amendments) Order 2005 (SI 2005/2919) art.4(2) (December 5, 2005).
4. Child Tax Credit (Amendment) Regulations 2006 (SI 2006/222) reg.3 (April 6, 2006).
5. Tax Credits (Miscellaneous Amendments) (No.2) Regulations 2008 (SI 2008/2169) reg.7 (September 1, 2008).
6. Local Education Authorities and Children's Services Authorities (Integration of Functions) (Local and Subordinate Legislation) Order 2010 (SI 2010/1172) art.4 and Sch.3 para.46 (May 5, 2010).
7. Tax Credits (Miscellaneous Amendments) (No.3) Regulations 2010 (SI 2010/2914) reg.9 (December 31, 2010).
8. Tax Credits (Miscellaneous Amendments) Regulations 2012 (SI 2012/848) reg.4(2) (April 6, 2012).
9. Personal Independence Payment (Supplementary Provisions and Consequential Amendments) Regulations 2013 (SI 2013/388) reg.8 and Sch. para.30(2) (April 8, 2013).

Child Tax Credit Regulations 2002

10. Armed Forces and Reserve Forces Compensation Scheme (Consequential Provisions: Subordinate Legislation) Order 2013 (SI 2013/591) art.7 and Sch. para.26(2) (April 8, 2013).
11. Children's Hearings (Scotland) Act 2011 (Consequential and Transitional Provisions and Savings) Order 2013 (SI 2013/1465) art.17 and Sch.1 para.19(2) (June 24, 2013).
12. Child Benefit (General) and Child Tax Credit (Amendment) Regulations 2014 (SI 2014/1231) reg.3 (June 4, 2014).

Circumstances in which a person is or is not responsible for a child or qualifying young person

2.195

3.—(1) For the purposes of child tax credit the circumstances in which a person is or is not responsible for a child or qualifying young person shall be determined in accordance with the following Rules.

Rule 1

1.1. A person shall be treated as responsible for a child or qualifying young person who is normally living with him (the "normally living with test").
1.2. This Rule is subject to rules 2 to 4.

Rule 2 (Competing claims)

2.1. This Rule applies where—
(a) a child or qualifying young person normally lives with two or more persons in—
 (i) different households; or
 (ii) the same household, where those persons are not limited to the members of a [² . . .] couple; or
 (iii) a combination of (i) and (ii); and
(b) two or more of those persons make separate claims (that is, not a single joint claim made by a [² . . .] couple) for child tax credit in respect of the child or qualifying young person.
2.2. The child or qualifying young person shall be treated as the responsibility of—
(a) only one of those persons making such claims; and
(b) whichever of them has (comparing between them) the main responsibility for him (the "main responsibility test");
subject to rules 3 and 4.

Rule 3

3.1. The persons mentioned in rule 2.2. (other than the child or qualifying young person) may jointly elect as to which of them satisfies the main responsibility test for the child or qualifying young person, and in default of agreement the Board may determine that question on the information available to them at the time of their determination.

Rule 4

4.1. A child or qualifying young person shall be treated as not being the responsibility of any person during any period in which any of the following Cases applies.

(SI 2002/2007 reg.3) (as amended)

Case A	The child or qualifying young person is provided with, or placed in, accommodation under Part III of the Children Act 1989, Part II of the Children (Scotland) Act 1995 [¹⁰ by virtue of a requirement in a child assessment order within the meaning of section 35 of the Children's Hearings (Scotland) Act 2011, a child protection order within the meaning of section 37 of that Act, a compulsory supervision order within the meaning of section 83 of that Act or an interim compulsory supervision order within the meaning of section 86 of that Act,] or Part IV of the Children (Northern Ireland) Order 1995, and the cost of that child's or qualifying young person's accommodation or maintenance is borne wholly or partly—
	  (i) out of local authority funds under [⁹ section 22C(10) or] section 23 of the Children Act 1989 or [⁸ regulation 33 of the Looked After Children (Scotland) Regulations 2009];
	  (ii) in Northern Ireland, by an authority, within the meaning in Article 2, and under Article 27, of that Order; or
	  (iii) out of other public funds.
	[⁴ . . .]

Case B	The child or qualifying young person— (i) is being looked after by a local authority; and (ii) has been placed for adoption by that authority in the home of a person proposing to adopt him, and a local authority is making a payment in respect of the child's or qualifying young person's accommodation or maintenance, or both, under [⁹ section 22C(10) or] section 23 of the Children Act 1989, [⁸ regulation 33 of the Looked After Children (Scotland) Regulations 2009] or Article 27 of the Children (Northern Ireland) Order 1995. This Case applies in Northern Ireland with the modification that for references to a local authority there are substituted references to an authority (within the meaning in Article 2 of that Order).

Case C	A custodial sentence—
	  (a) for life;
	  (b) without limit of time;
	  (c) of detention during Her Majesty's pleasure;
	  (d) in Northern Ireland, of detention during the pleasure of the Secretary of State; or
	  (e) for a term or period of more than four months,
	has been passed on the child or qualifying young person.

Case D	The [⁵ . . .] qualifying young person claims and is awarded child tax credit in his or her own right, in respect of a child for whom he or she is responsible, for that period.

[¹Case E	[⁵ . . .] The qualifying young person, claims incapacity benefit [⁶ or contributory employment and support allowance payable under Part 1 of the Welfare Reform Act 2007] in his or her own right and that benefit is paid to or in respect of him or her for that period.
	
	This Case does not apply at any time ("the later time") during a period of incapacity for work which began before 6th April 2004 in the case of a person in respect of whom, at a time—
	    (a) during that period of incapacity, and
	    (b) before that date,
	both incapacity benefit and child tax credit were payable, if child tax credit has been payable in respect of him or her continuously since 5th April 2004 until that later time. For the purposes of this Case "period of incapacity" shall be construed in accordance with section 30C of the 1992 Act (incapacity benefit: days and periods of incapacity for work) but disregarding subsections (5) and (5A) of that section.]

[³Case F	[⁵ . . .] The qualifying young person claims and receives working tax credit in his or her own right (whether alone or on a joint claim). [⁵ . . .]
[⁵ Case G	The qualifying young person has a spouse, civil partner or partner with whom they are living and the spouse, civil partner or partner is not in full-time education or approved training as provided for under regulation 5(3).
Case H	The responsible person is the spouse, civil partner or partner of a qualifying young person with whom they are living. [⁷ Cases G and H do] not apply to persons in receipt of child tax credit for a qualifying young person who is living with a partner on the day before 1st September 2008.]

[⁴ 4.2. Where a child or qualifying young person is in residential accommodation referred to in regulation 9 of the Child Benefit (General) Regulations 2006 and in the circumstances prescribed in paragraphs (a) or (b) of that regulation, he shall be treated as being the responsibility of any person who was treated as being responsible for him immediately before he entered that accommodation.]

(2) Where—
  (a) a claimant is treated as responsible for a child or qualifying young person by virtue of the preceding Rules, and
  (b) the child or qualifying young person has a child of his or her own, normally living with him or her,
the claimant shall also be treated as responsible for, and as having made a claim for child tax credit in respect of, the child of the child or qualifying young person (but without prejudice to the facts as to which of them is mainly responsible for that child).

(SI 2002/2007 reg.3) (as amended)

Amendments

1. Tax Credits (Miscellaneous Amendments) Regulations 2004 (SI 2004/762) reg.2 (April 6, 2004).
2. Civil Partnership Act 2004 (Tax Credits, etc.) (Consequential Amendments) Order 2005 (SI 2005/2919) art.4(3) (December 5, 2005).
3. Child Tax Credit (Amendment No.2) Regulations 2006 (SI 2006/1163) reg.2 (May 24, 2006).
4. Child Tax Credit (Amendment) Regulations 2007 (SI 2007/2151) reg.3 (August 16, 2007).
5. Tax Credits (Miscellaneous Amendments) (No.2) Regulations 2008 (SI 2008/2169) reg.8 (September 1, 2008).
6. Employment and Support Allowance (Consequential Provisions) (No.3) Regulations 2008 (SI 2009/1879) reg.22(2) (October 27, 2008).
7. Tax Credits (Miscellaneous Amendments) Regulations 2009 (SI 2009/697) reg.10 (April 6, 2009).
8. Adoption and Children (Scotland) Act 2007 (Consequential Modifications) Order 2011 (SI 2011/1740) art.2 and Sch.1 para.29(3) (July 15, 2011).
9. Tax Credits (Miscellaneous Amendments) Regulations 2012 (SI 2012/848) reg.4(3) (April 6, 2012).
10. Children's Hearings (Scotland) Act 2011 (Consequential and Transitional Provisions and Savings) Order 2013 (SI 2013/1465) art.17 and Sch.1 para.19(3) (June 24, 2013).

Definitions

"child"—see reg.2(1).
"claimant"—see *ibid*.
"custodial sentence"—see *ibid*.
"joint claim"—see *ibid*.
"looked after by a local authority"—see *ibid*.
"main responsibility test"—see *ibid*.
"normally living with test"—see *ibid*.
"placing for adoption"—see *ibid*.
"qualifying young person"—see *ibid*.

General Note

Section 8(1) of the TCA 2002 provides that entitlement to child tax credit is dependent upon the claimant (and/or his or her partner in the case of a joint claim) "being responsible for one or more children or qualifying young persons". The 2002 Act then provides that this expression may be defined further by regulations (s.8(2)). This regulation accordingly sets out a number of rules for determining whether a person is or is not responsible for a child or young person. The starting point is in r.1, namely that as a general rule, a person is responsible for a child or young person normally living with him or her. This presumption is then subject to r.2, which deals with competing claims, as well as r.3 (election by the parties or determination by HMRC in default of such agreement) and r.4 (special cases, principally involving children or young persons being accommodated at public expense and so not to be the subject of a child tax credit award). The Upper Tribunal rejected an attempt to challenge these rules as discriminatory against men in *HMRC v DH* [2005] UKUT 24 (AAC).

2.196

Paragraph (1)

Rule 1: The presumption is that a person is responsible for a child or qualifying young person "who is normally living with him" (r.1 para.1.1). This "normally living with test" has been inherited from WFTC (and, before that, family credit: see Family Credit (General) Regulations 1987 (SI 1987/1973) reg.7(1). The "normally living with test" was new to family credit, although the phrase "living with" the

2.197

claimant was (and still is) used in the child benefit legislation (SSCBA 1992 s.143 and see, in particular *R(F) 2/79* and *R(F) 2/81*).

In the context of family credit (and later WFTC), *CFC 1537/1995* decided that a child "normally lives with" a person for the purposes of reg.7(1) if he or she spent more time with that person than anyone else. This was the construction that made sense of reg.7(2) of the 1987 Regulations, which made provision for cases where a child either spent equal amounts of time in different households or there was doubt as to which household a child was living in. But reg.7(2) only applied in cases of real doubt; if there was simply a factual dispute this was not enough to bring it into play. Where reg.7(2) applied, there was then a series of tests. The first was receipt of child benefit, the rules for which include methods of establishing priorities between claimants. If no one was receiving child benefit then if only one person had claimed child benefit, that person had priority. If there had been no claims (or more than one claim), the final test was who had "primary responsibility".

In *GJ v HMRC (TC)* [2013] UKUT 561 (AAC), Judge Wikeley emphasised that the "normally living with" test bears its ordinary meaning and that the relevant facts take priority over the terms of a residence order stating what ought to be the case. Such cases are therefore essentially to be determined on the evidence before a tribunal about the actual arrangements within which a child normally lives at relevant times. This was followed by Judge McKenna in *CTC/135/2013* where it was again emphasised that the test was a question of fact, and not to be determined by legal concepts such as parental responsibility.

2.198 *Rule 2:* Rule 2, which applies to competing claims for child tax credit, adopts a slightly different approach to the old reg.7(2). Accordingly, it does not necessarily follow that *CFC 1537/1995* applies in precisely the same way. Rule 2 applies where two or more people (not being a couple) make child tax credit claims and the relevant child or qualifying young person "normally lives with two or more persons" *either* in different households *or* in the same household (other than in the case of a couple with a child in the same household) *or* in an arrangement that is a combination of these two first possibilities (r.2 para.2.1). Thus, r.2 only comes into play when the child or young person may, as a matter of fact, already be regarded as "normally" (but separately) living with at least two persons. For example, a child might spend weekdays living with one parent and weekends with the other parent in a different household. Although the child will spend more time living with the weekday parent, it is perfectly proper to say that he or she *also* normally lives with the weekend parent, at least for part of the week. This being so, the definition of "normally living with" applied in *CFC 1537/1995* (i.e. spending more time with one person than anyone else) cannot apply for the purposes of the meaning of "normally lives" in r.2 para.2.1, as that is specifically designed to deal with the situation where a child or young person by definition "normally" lives in more than one place. However, where r.2 does so apply, the general rule is that, as between the competing claimants, the child or young person is treated as the responsibility of the person with "main responsibility" for him or her (r.2 para.2.2). Thus, although *CFC 1537/1995* should be applied with care in this context, ultimately it may be a distinction without a difference.

Further factual complexity can arise where a couple who were previously living together in the same household with children start to maintain separate households but in the same dwelling with the children still present. See for example *JI v HMRC* [2013] UKUT 199 (AAC). And see the strong criticisms by the judge in that decision about unfairness that may arise if proper claims are not made to deal with a breakup of a couple's marriage or partnership.

As we have seen, the former reg.7(2) of the 1987 Regulations resolved problematic cases by reference first to the person in receipt of child benefit and then, in the absence of a child benefit claim, to the person with "primary responsibility" for the child or young person. Rule 2 makes no reference to the child benefit position. Instead, cases of shared care—as these will inevitably be—are to be determined by reference to who has "main responsibility" for the child or young person. This is presumably likely to be determined on a time basis, and so the weekdays parent

(SI 2002/2007 reg.3) (as amended)

in the example above is likely to be regarded as the one with such responsibility. As with the former reg.7(2), "responsibility" has no special meaning in the legislation and so must be determined according to the ordinary everyday meaning of the word. It would not seem that there is any material difference between "primary responsibility" (reg.7) and "main responsibility" (r.2). It would also appear that under r.2, as under the former reg.7, responsibility or the normality of living may be judged on an overall basis over a period. This is different from the income support provision, where the test of responsibility still has to be applied week by week (*CIS 49/1991* and *Whelan v Chief Adjudication Officer, The Independent*, November 14, 1994).

It will be evident from the analysis above that there is, under these Rules, no provision for the division of child tax credit between competing parents. The Rules are premised on establishing which claimant (or which couple of joint claimants) is entitled to child tax credit for a given child or young person, not on apportioning child tax credit entitlement between separated individual claimants (e.g. 5/7 to the weekdays parent and 2/7 to the weekend parent). Although the practical and administrative difficulties with such an arrangement are obvious, it did appear from the primary legislation that this might be a possibility (see, e.g. TCA 2002 ss.8(2) and 9(7)). There remains, therefore, the prospect of human rights challenges in this area, as with social security benefits which have elements related to a child or children's presence in a particular household for part-weeks in cases of shared care: see the General Note to Income Support (General) Regulations 1987 (SI 1987/1967) reg.15, in Vol.II in this series). See now *HMRC v DH* [2009] UKUT 24 (AAC) discussed in the commentary to s.9(7) of the Tax Credits Act 2002.

2.199

The Commissioners considered competing claims in joint care cases both for child benefit and child tax credit. *CTC/4390/2004* decided that a tribunal must decide between two seemingly equally placed claimants, perhaps by looking at the one who would benefit more from the claim. *CTC/4390/2004* was not followed, and was criticised, by an Upper Tribunal judge in *CM v HMRC (TC)* [2010] UKUT 400 (AAC) on the issue of whether one party would benefit more than the other party from the relative amounts that may be claimed by the parties. *CTC/1686/2007* emphasises that the discretion available to the Secretary of State in child benefit cases is not available for child tax credit. On an appeal the tribunal must decide on the facts, and has no discretion. However, the Commissioner endorsed the view of the tribunal that it is better if the two competing claimants can agree between themselves. HMRC has indicated that it will respect such agreements, including where the result is that the competing claimants "divide" the children between them for claim purposes.

The attribution of responsibility for a child or young person to a particular person under r.2 is itself subject to rr.3 and 4.

In *CTC/3096/2007* the Commissioner emphasised the need to apply the "main responsibility" test. See also *CTC/1686/2007* where the Commissioner compares these rules with those for child benefit and child support. See also *KN v HMRC* [2009] UKUT 79 (AAC), in which Judge Gamble emphasised that the test is "responsibility" not "care". He put weight on the person responsible when the child was at school. These decisions were followed by Judge Humphrey in the unreported case of *CTC/2409/2013*.

Rule 3: Where there are competing claims under r.2, the parties may by agreement notify HMRC as to which of them satisfies the main responsibility test for the child or young person in question. If the adults in question fail to agree, HMRC may determine that question on the information then available.

2.200

Rule 4: Rule 4 sets out a number of specific circumstances (or Cases) in which a child or young person is not to be treated as the responsibility of a tax credit claimant, even though any of rr.1–3 above might otherwise apply. Cases A–C all deal with situations in which a child or young person is being accommodated at public expense in one way or another and so payment of child tax credit is inappropriate. These are similar to the exclusions under the child benefit scheme. Case D covers

2.201

the special case of a child (aged at least 16) or young person who has herself been awarded child tax credit in respect of her own child (see also para.(2) where child tax credit has not been awarded in such circumstances to the young parent).

2.202   *Case A:* This exclusion covers children or young persons who are provided with or placed in accommodation under Pt III of the Children Act 1989 or associated legislation. The exception in reg.3 of the Child Benefit (General) Regulations 1976 (now Child Benefit (General) Regulations 2003 (SI 2003/493) reg.2) deals with children or young persons who are provided with residential accommodation on account of their disability.

2.203   *Case B:* This exclusion applies where: (i) a child or young person is being looked after by a local authority (in the sense that term is used under the Children Act 1989); (ii) he or she has been placed for adoption; and (iii) a fostering allowance is in payment.

2.204   *Case C:* CTC will continue to be paid unless the child or young person has been sentenced to detention for a period of four months or longer. This is more generous than the equivalent rules for income support and income-based jobseeker's allowance, under which benefit for the child or young person ceases immediately he or she is taken into custody (Income Support (General) Regulations 1987 (SI 1987/1967) reg.16(5)(f) and (6); see also reg.15(3) regarding home leave). It is also more generous than the former WFTC and DPTC rules, under which there was no entitlement to the elements of those tax credits relating to children where a custodial sentence had been passed (Family Credit (General) Regulations 1987 (SI 1987/1973) reg.8(2)(e)). The justifications for the change given by ministers are the extra costs associated with contact and the need to enable families to maintain contact with the child or young person for whom they are responsible, and to assist with that person's re-integration in the community. It is difficult to see how these arguments do not apply equally forcefully in the context of income support and income-based jobseeker's allowance.

2.205   *Case D:* See also para.(2) below.

2.206   *Case E:* The effect of this provision is that a person is not to be treated as responsible for a child or a qualifying young person in respect of whom incapacity benefit is payable. There is transitional protection during a period of incapacity which began before April 6, 2004 for cases where both incapacity benefit and child tax credit were in payment in respect of the child or qualifying young person before that date.

2.207   *Case F:* This exclusion means that a person is not to be treated as responsible for a child or qualifying young person who is receiving WTC in his or her own right, whether alone or as part of a joint claim, with a spouse or partner. It also provides for a period of transitional protection for some CTC recipients.

Cases G and H: These exclusions ensure alignment between the rules for CTC and those for child benefit.

2.208   *Paragraph (2):* This deals with the special case where a person (the claimant) is found to be responsible for a child or young person under rr.1–4 above (and so the exception in Case D of r.4 does not apply) and that child or young person herself has a child. In such circumstances, the claimant is treated as responsible for child tax credit purposes for both his or her child (or young person) and that child's own child.

[¹ Period for which a person who attains the age of sixteen is a qualifying young person

2.209   **4.**—(1) [² Subject to paragraph (1A), a] person who attains the age of sixteen is a qualifying young person from the date on which that person attained that age until 31st August which next follows that date.

(SI 2002/2007 reg.4) (as amended)

[² (1A) A person who attains the age of sixteen on 31st August is a qualifying young person from the date on which that person attained that age.]

(2) Paragraph (1) is subject to regulation 5 but as if there were no requirement to satisfy the first condition specified in paragraph (3) of that regulation.]

[² (2A) Paragraph (1A) is subject to regulation 5.]

AMENDMENTS

1. Tax Credits (Miscellaneous Amendments) (No.2) Regulations 2008 (SI 2008/2169) reg.9 (September 1, 2008).
2. Tax Credits (Miscellaneous Amendments) Regulations 2012 (SI 2012/848) reg.4(4) (April 6, 2012).

GENERAL NOTE

Section 8(3) of the TCA 2002 defines a child as a person who "has not attained the age of sixteen", but the same provision enables regulations to be made allowing a person to remain a "child" for tax credit purposes "for a prescribed period or until a prescribed date". This regulation provides that a child remains a child for both child tax credit and working tax credit purposes until August 31 following his or her 16th birthday.

Maximum age and prescribed conditions for a qualifying young person

5.—(1) For the purposes of Part I, a person ceases to be a qualifying young person (unless disqualified earlier under the following paragraphs) on the date on which he attains the age of [³twenty].

(2) A person who is not a child, but has not attained the age of [³twenty] years, is a qualifying young person for any period during which the following conditions are satisfied with regard to him [¹(and once a person falls within the terms of paragraph (3)(b), he shall be treated as having satisfied the first condition from the [⁴relevant leaving date] mentioned in that paragraph)].

(3) The first condition is that he is [³. . .]—
  (a) receiving full-time education, not being—
    (i) advanced education, or
    (ii) education received by that person by virtue of his employment or of any office held by him; [³. . .]
[³(ab) undertaking approved training [⁵, is enrolled or has been accepted to undertake such training,] which is not provided [⁷ by means of a contract of employment]; or]
  (b) under the age of eighteen years and—
    [²[³(i) he ceased to receive full-time education or to undertake approved training (the date of that event being referred to as "the relevant leaving date");]
    (ii) within three months of the [³relevant leaving date], he has notified the Board (in the manner prescribed by regulation 22 of the Tax Credits (Claims and Notifications) Regulations 2002) that he is registered for work or training with [⁷ a qualifying body]; and
    (iii) not more than 20 weeks has elapsed since the [³relevant leaving date.]

[³(3A) A person who has attained the age of nineteen years satisfies paragraph (3)(a) or (ab) only where the course of education or training began before he attained that age [⁵, or he enrolled or was accepted to undertake that course before he attained that age].]

(4) The second condition is that the period in question is not (and does not include)—

2.210

2.211

(a) a week in which he (having ceased to receive full-time education [³or approved training]) becomes engaged in remunerative work; [³or]
(b) [³. . .]
(c) a period in respect of which that person receives income support [⁸income-related employment and support allowance payable under Part 1 of the Welfare Reform Act 2007] [⁸,]income-based jobseeker's allowance within the meaning of section 1(4) of the Jobseekers Act 1995 [⁸or universal credit under Part 1 of the Welfare Reform Act 2012].

[⁷ (5) For the purposes of paragraphs (3) and (4) a person shall be treated as being in full-time education if full-time education is received by that person by undertaking a course—
(a) at a school or college, or
(b) where that person has been receiving that education prior to attaining the age of sixteen, elsewhere, if approved by the Board,]
where in pursuit of that course, the time spent receiving instruction or tuition, undertaking supervised study, examination or practical work or taking part in any exercise, experiment or project for which provision is made in the curriculum of the course, exceeds or exceeds on average 12 hours a week in normal term-time [⁵ . . .] [¹⁰ and shall include gaps between the ending of one course and the commencement of another, where the person enrols on and commences the latter course].

[⁹ (5A) If paragraph (5) does not apply, then for the purposes of paragraphs (3) and (4) a person shall be treated as being in full-time education if that person is being provided with "appropriate full-time education" in England within section 4 (appropriate full-time education or training) of the Education and Skills Act 2008.]

(6) In calculating the time spent in pursuit of the course, no account shall be taken of time occupied by meal breaks or spent on unsupervised study.

[³(7) In determining whether a person is undertaking a course of fulltime education or approved training, there shall be disregarded any interruption—
(a) for a period of up to 6 months, whether beginning before or after the person concerned attains age 16, to the extent that it is reasonable in the opinion of the Board to do so; and
(b) for any period due to illness or disability of the mind or body of the person concerned provided that it is reasonable in the opinion of the Board to do so.]

AMENDMENTS

1. Child Tax Credit (Amendment) Regulations 2003 (SI 2003/738) reg.4 (April 6, 2003).
2. Child Tax Credit (Amendment) Regulations 2003 (SI 2003/738) reg.5 (April 6, 2003).
3. Child Tax Credit (Amendment) Regulations 2006 (SI 2006/222) reg.4 (April 6, 2006).
4. Tax Credits (Miscellaneous Amendments) Regulations 2006 (SI 2006/766) reg.3 (April 6, 2006).
5. Child Tax Credit (Amendment) Regulations 2007 (SI 2007/2151) reg.4 (August 16, 2007).
6. Tax Credits (Miscellaneous Amendments) (No.2) Regulations 2008 (SI 2008/2169) reg.10 (September 1, 2008).
7. Employment and Support Allowance (Consequential Provisions) (No.3) Regulations 2008 (SI 2009/1879) reg.22(3) (October 27, 2008).

(SI 2002/2007 reg.5) (as amended)

8. Universal Credit (Consequential, Supplementary, Incidental and Miscellaneous Provisions) Regulations 2013 (SI 2013/630) reg.79 (April 29, 2013).
9. Child Benefit (General) and Child Tax Credit (Amendment) Regulations 2014 (SI 2014/1231) reg.3 (June 4, 2014).
10. Child Benefit (General) and Tax Credits (Miscellaneous Amendments) Regulations 2014 (SI 2014/2924) reg.3(2) (November 28, 2014).

DEFINITIONS

"advanced education"—see reg.2(1).
"Careers Service"—see *ibid.*
"Connexions Service"—see *ibid.*
"child"—see *ibid.*
"full-time education"—see para.(5).
"Pt I"—see reg.2(1).
"qualifying young person"—see *ibid.*
"recognised educational establishment"—see *ibid.*
"relevant training programme"—see *ibid.*
"remunerative work"—see *ibid.*

GENERAL NOTE

Section 8(4) of the TCA 2002 enables regulations to be made prescribing conditions to be met by a person in order to count as a "qualifying young person" (CTC being payable in respect of children and qualifying young persons (TCA 2002 s.8(1)). This regulation provides that the maximum age for a "qualifying young person" is the date on which he or she reaches the age of 20 (para.(1)). It also spells out the conditions which must be met by a person who is no longer a child (on which note the extended meaning of "child" in reg.4) in order to rank as a "qualifying young person" (paras (2)–(6)). Two conditions must be satisfied in this regard (they are cumulative and not alternative). First, the young person must *either* be receiving full-time education, as defined by para.(3)(a) (and see also paras (5) and (6)) *or* be aged under 18, have ceased to receive full-time education, be registered for work or training with one of the relevant official agencies, and have met the latter two criteria for no more than 20 consecutive weeks (para.(3)(b)). Secondly, the period in question must not be or include a week in which the young person becomes engaged in remunerative work (having ceased full-time education), or a period in which he or she received a training allowance under a training programme or received income support or income-based jobseeker's allowance (para.(4)).

These conditions are modelled on those that apply to child benefit, on which see SSCBA 1992 s.142 (and the commentary above). The definition of full-time education likewise is in identical terms to the relevant provision for child benefit purposes (Child Benefit (General) Regulations 2003 (SI 2003/493) reg.5.

In *JN v HMRC (TC)* [2010] UKUT 288 (AAC) the Upper Tribunal considered the meaning of "qualifying young person" before the 2008 amendments in a case where there was a gap in the education of the young person. The case concerned a young person who had left education in Kenya to come to Britain to continue studying here. The judge noted difficulties in treating the education in Kenya as taking place at a recognised establishment but accepted that the education itself could be recognised. On the facts tax credit was payable during the gap between leaving Kenya and starting a course in Britain.

In *ML v HMRC (TC)* [2015] UKUT 166 (AAC) detailed consideration was given to the meaning of "approved training" in para.(2)(ab). The condition is satisfied by training under the headings "access to apprenticeships" and "foundation learning". The First-tier Tribunal erred in leaving the second out of account. These derive from the definition of "approved training" in reg.1(3) of the Child Benefit (General) Regulations 2006 (see Part III of this volume). Note that this decision applies only in England—the tests are different in Scotland and Wales.

2.212

Entitlement to child tax credit after death of child or qualifying young person

6. If—
(a) a child or qualifying young person dies; and
(b) a person is (or would, if a claim had been made, have been) entitled to child tax credit in respect of the child or qualifying young person immediately before the death,

that person shall be entitled to child tax credit in respect of the child or qualifying young person for the period of eight weeks immediately following the death or, in the case of a qualifying young person, until the date on which he or she would have attained the age of [¹twenty] if earlier.

AMENDMENT

1. Child Tax Credit (Amendment) Regulations 2006 (SI 2006/222) reg.5 (April 6, 2006).

DEFINITIONS

"child"—see reg.2(1).
"qualifying young person"—see *ibid*.

GENERAL NOTE

Section 8(5) of the TCA 2002 enables regulations to be made allowing entitlement to child tax credit to continue for a prescribed period notwithstanding the death of the relevant child or qualifying young person. This regulation makes provision for the continued payment of child tax credit for a further eight weeks in such a situation. The same concession has been made in relation to child benefit (SSCBA 1992 s.145A, inserted by TCA 2002 s.55).

Determination of the maximum rate at which a person or persons may be entitled to child tax credit

7.—(1) In the following paragraphs—
(a) in the case of a single claim (but not a joint claim), the person making the claim is referred to as the "claimant"; and
(b) in the case of a joint claim, the members of the [¹. . .] couple making the claim are referred to as the "joint claimants".

(2) The maximum rate at which a claimant or joint claimants may be entitled to child tax credit shall be the aggregate of—
(a) the family element of child tax credit; and
(b) an individual element of child tax credit, in respect of each child or qualifying young person for whom—
   (i) the claimant; or
   (ii) either or both of the joint claimants;
   as the case may be, is or are responsible.

[² (3) The family element of child tax credit is £545.]

(4) The individual element of child tax credit for any child or qualifying young person referred to in paragraph (2)(b) above—
(a) where the child is disabled, is [³£5,920];
(b) where the child is severely disabled, is [³£7,195];
(c) in the case of any other child, is [⁴£2,780];
(d) where the qualifying young person is disabled, is [³£5,920];

(e) where the qualifying young person is severely disabled, is [³£7,195]; and
(f) in the case of any other qualifying young person, is [⁴£2,780].

AMENDMENTS

1. Civil Partnership Act 2004 (Tax Credits, etc.) (Consequential Amendments) Order 2005 (SI 2005/2919) art.4(4) (December 5, 2005).
2. Tax Credits Up-rating Regulations 2011 (SI 2011/1035) reg.2 (April 6, 2011).
3. Tax Credits Up-rating Regulations 2015 (SI 2015/451) reg.2(2) (April 6, 2015).
4. Child Benefit and Tax Credits Up-rating Order 2015 (SI 2015/567) art.3(2) (April 6, 2015).

DEFINITIONS

"child"—see reg.2(1).
"claimant"—see *ibid.* and para.(1)(a).
"the family element of child tax credit"—see reg.2(1).
"the individual element of child tax credit"—see *ibid.*
"joint claim"—see *ibid.*
"qualifying young person"—see *ibid.*
"single claim"—see *ibid.*

GENERAL NOTE

Section 9 of the TCA 2002 makes provision for the maximum rate of child tax credit. This regulation provides the detail on how this rate is to be arrived at (para. (2)). It also sets out the actual annual rates for the component elements (paras (3) and (4)). Claimants who are entitled to income support or income-based jobseeker's allowance are automatically entitled to the maximum child tax credit applicable in their circumstances (TCA 2002 s.7(2) and Tax Credits (Income Thresholds and Determination of Rates) Regulations 2002 (SI 2002/ 2008) reg.4). The entitlement of other claimants is dependent upon the operation of the thresholds and withdrawal rates specified in the Income Thresholds and Determination of Rates Regulations.

The amendment of subs.(3) removes, from April 6, 2011, previous entitlement for a double family element of £1,090 where the child or youngest child was under the age of one year and otherwise leaves the element at the same level as the previous year. Entitlement remains for those aged under one until April 5, 2011.

All other elements have been increased above inflation.

Prescribed conditions for a disabled or severely disabled child or qualifying young person

8.—(1) For the purposes of section 9 of the Act a child or qualifying young person—
(a) is disabled if he satisfies the requirements of paragraph (2); and
(b) is severely disabled if he satisfies the requirements of paragraph (3) [¹ or (4)] [² or (5)].
(2) A person satisfies the requirements of this paragraph if—
(a) disability living allowance is payable in respect of him, or has ceased to be so payable solely because he is a patient; or
[³ (b) he is certified as severely sight impaired or blind by a consultant ophthalmologist;]
(c) he ceased to be so [³. . .] certified as [³ severely sight impaired or] blind within the 28 weeks immediately preceding the date of claim [¹; or

2.216

2.217

(d) personal independence payment is payable in respect of that person, or would be so payable but for regulations made under section 86(1) (hospital in-patients) of the Welfare Reform Act 2012.]

(3) A person satisfies the requirements of this paragraph if the care component of disability living allowance—
 (a) is payable in respect of him; or
 (b) would be so payable but for either a suspension of benefit in accordance with regulations under section 113(2) of the Contributions and Benefits Act or an abatement as a consequence of hospitalisation,
at the highest rate prescribed under section 72(3) of that Act.

[1 (4) A person satisfies the requirements of this paragraph if the daily living component of personal independence payment—
 (a) is payable in respect of that person, or
 (b) would be so payable but for regulations made under section 86(1) (hospital in-patients) of the Welfare Reform Act 2012,
at the enhanced rate under section 78(2) of that Act.]

[2 (5) A person satisfies the requirements of this paragraph if an armed forces independence payment is payable in respect of him.]

AMENDMENTS

1. Personal Independence Payment (Supplementary Provisions and Consequential Amendments) Regulations 2013 (SI 2013/388) reg.8 and Sch. para.30(3) (April 8, 2013).

2. Armed Forces and Reserve Forces Compensation Scheme (Consequential Provisions: Subordinate Legislation) Order 2013 (SI 2013/591) art.7 and Sch. para.26(3) (April 8, 2013).

3. Child Benefit (General) and Tax Credits (Miscellaneous Amendments) Regulations 2014 (SI 2014/2924) reg.3(3) (November 28, 2014).

DEFINITIONS

"the Act"—see reg.2(1).
"child"—see *ibid.*
"the Contributions and Benefits Act"—see *ibid.*
"disability living allowance"—see *ibid.*
"patient"—see *ibid.*
"qualifying young person"—see *ibid.*

GENERAL NOTE

2.218 This provision is amended to adjust it to deal with the replacement of disability living allowance with the new personal independence payment provided for in the Welfare Reform Act 2012. This is being introduced in stages. For the initial stages see the Welfare Reform Act 2012 (Commencement No.8 and Savings and Transitional Provisions) Order 2013 (SI 2013/358).

Sections 9(5)(d) and (6) of the TCA 2002 make provision for a disabled child element and a severely disabled child element to be component parts of child tax credit. This regulation defines those terms. Thus, a child or qualifying young person is disabled if disability living allowance (DLA) is payable for them (or has ceased to be payable but only because he or she is now a patient) or if he or she is a registered blind person (or has ceased to be so registered in the immediately preceding 28 weeks) (para.(2)). A child or qualifying young person is severely disabled if they are entitled to the highest rate of the DLA care component (i.e. they satisfy both the "day" and "night" conditions in terms of their need for personal care or supervision): para.(3). The rates for these elements are set out in regs 8(4)(a) and (b).

The amendment to para.(2)(b) replaces from November 2014 the previous tests

(SI 2002/2007 reg.8) (as amended)

that relied on entries in registers maintained by local or health authorities. That was a process being made more difficult to operate in parallel with the approach adopted centrally for social security benefits as devolved governments adopt different approaches.

Tax Credits (Income Thresholds and Determination of Rates) Regulations 2002

(SI 2002/2008) (AS AMENDED)

Whereas a draft of this instrument, which contains the first regulations made under section 13(2) of the Tax Credits Act 2002, has been laid before, and approved by resolution of, each House of Parliament:

Now, therefore, the Treasury, in exercise of the powers conferred upon them by sections 8(1) to (3), 13(2) and (3), 65(1) and (7) and 67 of the Tax Credits Act 2002, hereby make the following Regulations:

Made by the Treasury under ss.8(1)–(3), 13(2) and (3), 65(1) and (7) and 67 of the Tax Credits Act 2002.

1. Citation, commencement and effect.
2. Interpretation.
3. Manner in which amounts to be determined for the purposes of section 7(1)(a) of the Act.
4. Social security benefits prescribed for the purposes of section 7(2) of the Act.
5. Amounts prescribed for the purposes of section 7(3) of the Act.
6. Manner of determining the rate at which a person is, or persons are, entitled to a tax credit.
7. Determination of rate of working tax credit.
8. Determination of rate of child tax credit.
9. Cases in which there is no rate of tax credit.

Citation, commencement and effect

1.—(1) These Regulations may be cited as the Tax Credits (Income Thresholds and Determination of Rates) Regulations 2002 and shall come into force—
 (a) for the purpose of enabling claims to be made, on August 1, 2002;
 (b) for the purpose of enabling decisions on claims to be made, on 1st January 2003; and
 (c) for all other purposes, on 6th April 2003.

(2) These Regulations shall have effect for the tax year beginning with 6th April 2003 and subsequent tax years.

DEFINITIONS

 "claim"—see TCA 2002 s.3.
 "decision on claim"—see TCA 2002 s.14.
 "tax year"—see reg.2.

Interpretation

2. In these Regulations—
 "the Act" means the Tax Credits Act 2002;

Tax Credits (Income Thresholds and Determination of Rates) Regulations 2002

"the income threshold" has the meaning given by section 7(1)(a) of the Act;
"period of award" shall be construed in accordance with section 5 of the Act;
"the relevant income" has the meaning given by section 7(3) of the Act;
"tax year" means a period beginning with 6th April in one year and ending with 5th April in the next.

Manner in which amounts to be determined for the purposes of section 7(1)(a) of the Act

2.222 **3.**—(1) This regulation prescribes the manner in which amounts are to be determined for the purposes of section 7(1)(a) of the Act.

(2) In the case of a person or persons entitled to working tax credit, the amount in relation to that tax credit is [[1]£6,420].

(3) In the case of a person or persons entitled to child tax credit, the amount in relation to that tax credit is [[2]£16,105].

AMENDMENTS

1. Tax Credits Up-rating Regulations 2005 (SI 2005/681) reg.4 (April 6, 2005).
2. Tax Credits Up-rating Regulations 2015 (SI 2015/451) reg.4(2) (April 6, 2015).

DEFINITION

"the Act"—see reg.2.

GENERAL NOTE

2.223 This regulation makes the necessary provision to give full operative effect to s.7(1) of the Act (income test).

HMRC does not use the term "income threshold". Instead it describes it in its literature as "taper start point". However, as the Commissioner noted in *CTC/2113/2006*, a failure to explain that this is how HMRC refers to the income thresholds can cause confusion.

Subsection (1)

2.224 Section 7(1) of TCA 2002 imposes an income test on all claimants for tax credits, the test being whether the relevant income of the claimant (or claimants) for the tax year exceeds "the amount" for that tax credit. If the relevant income does exceed the amount, then it must be calculated by how much it does so. This applies to all claimants apart from those within s.7(2) and reg.4 below. In other words, "the amount" is the income threshold for claiming that tax credit. Only those with no incomes or incomes below the threshold can claim the full tax credit for the year. The section allows, and this regulation provides, different thresholds for different tax credits.

The thresholds are reconsidered annually, and have been set at:

Year	CTC (£ pa)	WTC (£ pa)
2003–04	13,230	5,060
2004–05	13,480	5,060
2005–06	13,910	5,220
2006–07	14,155	5,220
2007–08	14,495	5,220
2008–09	15,575	6,420
2009–10	16,040	6,420
2010–11	16,190	6,420
2011–12	15,860	6,420

(SI 2002/2008 reg.3) (as amended)

2012–13	15,860	6,420
2013–14	15,910	6,420
2014–15	16,010	6,420
2015–16	16,105	6,420

The existence of separate thresholds means that in many cases separate calculations have to be made under s.7(1) about entitlement to each tax credit. The current thresholds have the effect that many more people are entitled to the child tax credit than to the working tax credit. Regulations 7 and 8 of these Regulations make provision for dealing with this.

Social security benefits prescribed for the purposes of section 7(2) of the Act

4. [4 (1) Subject to paragraph (2),] The following are social security benefits prescribed for the purposes of section 7(2) of the Act in relation to child tax credit and working tax credit—
  (a) income support under Part VII of the Social Security Contributions and Benefit Act 1992 other than income support to which a person is entitled only by virtue of regulation 6(2) and (3) of the Income Support (General) Regulations 1987;
  (b) income support under Part VII of the Social Security Contributions and Benefit (Northern Ireland) Act 1992 other than income support to which a person is entitled only by virtue of regulation 6(2) and (3) of the Income Support (General) Regulations (Northern Ireland) 1987;
  (c) an income-based jobseeker's allowance within the meaning of the Jobseekers Act 1995 or the Jobseekers (Northern Ireland) Order 1995.
  [1(d) state pension credit within the meaning of the State Pension Credit Act 2002 or the State Pension Credit Act (Northern Ireland) 2002.]
  [2(e) an income-related employment and support allowance payable under Part 1 of the Welfare Reform Act 2007 [3 or Part 1 of the Welfare Reform Act (Northern Ireland) 2007].]
  [4 (2) Paragraph (1) shall not apply in relation to working tax credit during the four-week period described in regulation 7D of the Working Tax Credit (Entitlement and Maximum Rate) Regulations 2002 (ceasing to undertake work or working for less than 16 or 30 hours per week).]

2.225

AMENDMENTS

1. Tax Credits (Miscellaneous Amendments No.2) Regulations 2003 (SI 2003/2815) reg.18 (November 26, 2003).
2. Employment and Support Allowance (Consequential Provisions) (No.3) Regulations 2008 (SI 2009/1879) reg.23 (October 27, 2008).
3. Employment and Support Allowance (Consequential Provisions No.2) Regulations (Northern Ireland) 2008 (SI 2008/412 (NI) reg.10 (October 27, 2008)).
4. Tax Credits (Miscellaneous Amendments) Regulations 2010 (SI 2010/751) reg.17(1) and (2) (April 6, 2010).

DEFINITION

  "the Act"—see reg.2.

GENERAL NOTE

Section 7(2) of the TCA 2002 provides that those entitled to any of the social security benefits prescribed for the purposes of that subsection are not to be subject to the income test in s.7(1). This does not apply to exclude the claimant from any other requirements for an award.

2.226

Tax Credits (Income Thresholds and Determination of Rates) Regulations 2002

Four benefits only have been prescribed by this regulation. They are:
(1) income support payable to any claimant. The exception applies to anyone who is a lone parent treated by regs 6(2) or (3) of the Income Support (General) Regulations 1987 (and its Northern Ireland equivalent) as being entitled to income support for the first 14 days of a period of remunerative work because he or she was a lone parent who was, for at least 26 weeks before the work started, receiving income support or income-based jobseeker's allowance;
(2) income-based jobseeker's allowance;
(3) state pension credit; and
(4) income-related employment and support allowance.

[¹ Amounts prescribed for the purposes of section 7(3) of the Act

2.227   5. The amount prescribed—
(a) for the purposes of section 7(3)(a) and (b) of the Act is [² £5,000]; and
(b) for the purposes of section 7(3)(c) and (d) of the Act is £2,500.]

AMENDMENTS

1. Tax Credits Up-rating Regulations 2012 (SI 2012/849) reg.4(2) and (3) (April 6, 2012).
2. Tax Credits Up-rating, etc. Regulations 2013 (SI 2013/750) reg.4(2) (April 6, 2013).

GENERAL NOTE

2.228   This regulation provides the detail for s.7(3) of the Act to operate. The amendments in 2012 and 2013 now bring that provision into general effect to deal with significant changes in total income of a claimant or couple between one tax year and the next. The provision allows an initial award of tax credit to be made on the income of the previous year. The confirmed entitlement will be adjusted from the figure awarded if, under these provisions, total income increases by over £5,000 in the current year for the award, or reduces by more than £2,500. Practical effect is, however, only given in most cases when entitlement is established at the end of the year, so in reality affecting what is received in the following year.

Manner of determining the rate at which a person is, or persons are, entitled to a tax credit

2.229   6. Regulations 7, 8 and 9 make provision as to the manner of determining the rate (if any) at which a person is, or persons are, entitled to a tax credit in any case where—
(a) the relevant income exceeds the income threshold; and
(b) his or their entitlement does not arise by virtue of section 7(2) of the Act.

DEFINITIONS

"entitlement"—see TCA 2002 ss.8 and 10.
"income threshold"—see reg.2.
"relevant income"—see reg.2.
"the Act"—see reg.2.

GENERAL NOTE

2.230   This is, on its face, purely a signposting regulation. It serves to remind the reader of the exception from the income test in s.7 of the TCA 2002, and also to tie in the £26 rule in reg.9 with the two main regulations: reg.7 dealing with working tax credit, and reg.8 dealing with child tax credit. As will be seen from those regulations,

(SI 2002/2008 reg.6) (as amended)

that order is intentional as entitlement to working tax credit, if any, must be calculated before entitlement to child tax credit.

There is, however, a drafting mismatch between the wording of this regulation and the approach of regs 7 and 8, which appears to deflect its intention. Regulation 6 states that the other regulations make provision for determining the rate of *entitlement* to tax credits. By contrast, regs 7 and 8 talk about periods of *award*. "Period of award" is defined in reg.2 of these Regulations by reference to s.5 of the TCA 2002 (entitled "periods of award"). And regs 7 and 8 of these Regulations refer to the elements of the credits to which a claimant "may be entitled" (regs 7(2)(a) and 8(2)).

The purpose of s.5 of TCA 2002 is to determine the period for which an award of tax credit is made. Awards are made under s.14 of the Act, and are made in advance of, or at the start of, the year of claim, using s.7(10) of the Act to estimate the income. At that point, the "period of award" can in most cases only be the whole tax year, or the balance of that year from the effective starting date of the award. Awards must ignore uncertain future changes as they are not then known. Regulations 7 and 8 set out in considerable detail how to deal with part-years. But, save for the case of claims made only part-way through a year, the "relevant period" for an award will always be the whole year, and the complexities of regs 7 and 8 are not needed.

The full calculations under regs 7 and 8 of these Regulations cannot be made until the end of the tax year, when the task of HMRC is to make entitlement decisions under s.18 of the Act. So why refer to periods of award rather than periods of entitlement? It would appear that this mismatch between *award* and *entitlement* is a leftover of the changes made to the Tax Credits Bill during its passage through Parliament (as discussed in the notes to those sections). It is suggested that, to make practical sense of this regulation, the definition of "period of award" as applied to both regs 7 and 8 has to take in periods of entitlement as well.

Determination of rate of working tax credit

7.—(1) In relation to a person or persons entitled to working tax credit, the rate shall be determined by finding the rate for each relevant period and, where necessary, adding together those rates.

2.231

(2) "Relevant period" means any part of the period of award throughout which—
  (a) the elements of working tax credit (other than the childcare element) to which the person or persons may be entitled, remain the same; and
  (b) there is no relevant change of circumstances for the purposes of the childcare element of working tax credit, within the meaning of reg.16(1) of the Working Tax Credit (Entitlement and Maximum Rate) Regulations 2002 (change of circumstances for the purposes of childcare element).

(3) The rate for each relevant period shall be found in accordance with the following steps—

Step 1—Finding the daily maximum rate for each element other than the childcare element

For each element of the tax credit (other than the childcare element) to be included in the case of the person or persons entitled to the tax credit, find the daily maximum rate using the following formula:

2.232

$$\frac{MR}{N1}$$

where:

533

Tax Credits (Income Thresholds and Determination of Rates) Regulations 2002

"MR" is the maximum rate in relation to that element for the tax year to which the claim for the tax credit relates;
"N1" is the number of days in that tax year.

Step 2—Finding the maximum rate for the relevant period for each element other than the childcare element

2.233　For each element of the tax credit to be so included, find the amount produced by multiplying the daily maximum rate (found under Step 1 and rounded up to the nearest penny) by the number of days in the relevant period.

Step 3—finding the income for the relevant period

2.234　Find the income for the relevant period by using the following formula:

$$\frac{I}{N1} \times N2$$

where:
"I" is the relevant income for the tax year to which the claim for the tax credit relates;
"N1" is the number of days in that tax year;
"N2" is the number of days in the relevant period.

Step 4—Finding the threshold for the relevant period

2.235　Find the threshold for the relevant period using the following formula:

$$\frac{[^1 £6,420]}{N1} \times N2$$

where:
"N1" is the number of days in that tax year;
"N2" is the number of days in the relevant period.

Step 5—Finding the amount of the reduction

2.236　Find the amount which is [¹ 41] per cent of the amount by which the income for the relevant period (found under Step 3 and rounded down to the nearest penny) exceeds the threshold for the relevant period (found under Step 4 and rounded up to the nearest penny).

Step 6—Reducing the elements of the tax credit (other than any childcare element)

2.237　If the amount found under Step 5 (rounded down to the nearest penny) is less than or equal to the total of the amounts found under Step 2 for the elements of the tax credit, deduct the amount found under Step 5 (rounded down to the nearest penny) from the total of those amounts found under Step 2.

Step 7—Finding the actual weekly childcare costs for the relevant period

2.238　Find the relevant childcare charges for the relevant period in accordance with reg.15 of the Working Tax Credit (Entitlement and Maximum Rate) Regulations 2002.

(SI 2002/2008 reg.7) (as amended)

Step 8—Finding the actual childcare costs for the relevant period

Multiply the result of Step 7 by $\frac{52}{N1} \times N2$

Here, N1 and N2 have the same meanings as in Step 3.
The result of this step is the amount of actual childcare costs for the relevant period.

Step 9—Finding the prescribed maximum childcare costs for the relevant period

Divide whichever of the maxima in reg.20(3) of the Working Tax Credit (Entitlement and Maximum Rate) Regulations 2002 is applicable by seven, round the result up to the nearest penny and multiply the resulting figure by the number of days in the relevant period.
The result of this is the prescribed maximum childcare costs for the relevant period.

Step 10—Finding the childcare element for the period

Take the lesser of the results of Steps 8 and 9.
Multiply that figure by [²70 per cent] and round the result up to the nearest penny.
The result of this step is the maximum rate of the childcare element for the relevant period.

Step 11—Reducing the elements of the tax credit (including any childcare element)

If the amount found under Step 5 (rounded down to the nearest penny) exceeds the total of the amounts found under Step 2 for the elements of the tax credit—
(a) deduct the excess from the amount found under Step 10 for any childcare element; and
(b) reduce the total of the amounts found under Step 2 for the other elements of the tax credit to nil.

Step 12—Finding the rate for the relevant period

Add together—
(a) the total of the amounts found under Step 2 for the elements of the tax credit (other than any childcare element) after reduction in accordance with Step 6 or Step 11; and
(b) the amount found under Step 10 for any childcare element after any reduction in accordance with Step 11.
This is the rate for the relevant period.
(4) "Child care element" has the meaning given by section 12(2) of the Act.

AMENDMENTS

1. Tax Credits Up-rating Regulations 2008 (SI 2008/796) reg.4(4) (April 6, 2008).
2. Tax Credits Up-rating Regulations 2011 (SI 2011/1035) reg.4(4) (April 6, 2011).
3. Tax Credits Up-rating Regulations 2012 (SI 2012/849) reg.4(4) (April 6, 2012).

Tax Credits (Income Thresholds and Determination of Rates) Regulations 2002

DEFINITIONS
"childcare element"—see TCA 2002 s.12.
"period of award"—see reg.2.
"rate"—see TCA 2002 s.13.

GENERAL NOTE

2.244   See the general note to reg.6 above. The effect of this regulation and reg.8—both together and separately—is to limit the amount of tax credit that a claimant can have to the relevant daily (or in the case of childcare element of working tax credit only, weekly) amount of the credit, if circumstances of a claimant change during a tax year. This approach is, as a result, less generous than the personal allowances for income tax, including children's tax credit. For example, the main personal allowance of an individual is the same amount for that individual throughout the year as is, for example, a bereaved person's allowance or a blind person's allowance. By contrast, the basis of calculation imposed by this regulation and reg.8 is that the elements of both working tax credit and child tax credit are payable only for the precise periods of the year for which the claimant can meet the requirement for that credit and element.

Paragraphs (1) and (2)
2.245   As noted above, "period of award" must be read as including also "period of entitlement" to make sense of this regulation. Likewise, the reference to "may be entitled" in para.(2) should include "is entitled".

Paragraph (3)
2.246   This paragraph is written in the "step-by-step" style, using the command tense of relevant verbs, that has been adopted as part of the Tax Law Rewrite approach to tax regulations. It is also written so that the rules in the paragraph can be operated in full by a computer.

Relevant periods of a full year
2.247   In most cases, as noted above, the complexities of this rule can be sidestepped because the question of an award of, or entitlement to, a tax credit can be judged by the full tax year. If the decision relates to a full year, then the steps can be telescoped as follows:

2.248   *Step 1 with Step 2:* Identify the annual amount of each element of working tax credit to which the claimant is entitled, apart from the childcare element, for that tax year.

2.249   *Step 3:* Identify the relevant income for the tax year (current year income or previous year income).

2.250   *Step 4 with Step 5 and Step 6:* If the income from Step 3 exceeds the annual amount from Steps 1 and 2, reduce the amounts from Steps 1 and 2 by 41 per cent. The result is the excess income for that year. The rate of reduction, originally 37 per cent, was increased to 39 per cent in 2006 when the income tax rate was lowered. Section 75 of the Welfare Reform Act 2012 provides power retrospectively to amend Step 5 in reg.7(3) of the Tax Credits (Income Thresholds and Determination of Rates) Regulations 2002 to provide for a reduction of 41 per cent from April 6, 2011 for all purposes. This gives effect to the announcement in the Emergency Budget of 2011. However, it was questionable whether there was authority in primary legislation to amend the figure in the way it was amended. Section 76 of the Welfare Reform Act 2012 now provides retrospective authority for the change.

(SI 2002/2008 reg.7) (as amended)

Step 7 with Step 8: Find the relevant childcare charges for the tax year. 2.251

Step 9 with Step 10: The maximum childcare element payable is reduced from 2011 to 70 per cent of £15,600 (£10,920) or of £9,100 for one child (£6,370) or, if less, 70 per cent of the actual charges paid. 2.252

Steps 11 and 12: If there is excess income for the tax year from Steps 4–6, reduce the annual amount from Steps 1 and 2 by the amount of that excess, if necessary to nil. If the excess is greater than that amount, next reduce the amount from Steps 9 and 10 by the amount by which that excess income exceeds the annual amount from Steps 1 and 2. If the excess income is greater than both amounts, then the amount of working tax credit for the tax year is nil. 2.253

Note from this that the childcare element of working tax credit is to be calculated on a weekly, not daily, basis in the event of any problem, and also is to be left in payment after the other elements have stopped being payable under these rules.

Relevant periods of less than a year

These periods arise only where there is a change of circumstances during a year that brings a relevant period to an end and/or starts a new one. Until 2006 this could cause problems where this happened in circumstances where claimants were not under a duty to report changes. The extension of the duty to report under reg.21 of the Tax Credits (Claims and Notifications) Regulations 2002, together with the reduction of the period in which the changes must be reported to one month, and the extension of award or entitlement by reg.7D of the Working Tax Credit (Entitlement and Maximum Rate) Regulations 2002 for four weeks after someone ceases work or works for less than 16 hours a week, have removed many of these problems. 2.254

CTC/2270/2007 confirms that the relevant income of a couple is their income for the year even if they only become a couple during the year. See the note to TCA 2002 s.7(4) above.

Determination of rate of child tax credit

8.—(1) In relation to a person or persons entitled to child tax credit, the rate shall be determined by finding the rate for each relevant period and, where necessary, adding together those rates. 2.255

(2) "Relevant period" means—
  (a) in the case of a person or persons entitled to child tax credit only, any part of the period of award throughout which the maximum rate at which he or they may be entitled to the tax credit remains the same;
  (b) in the case of a person or persons entitled to both child tax credit and working tax credit, any part of the period of award throughout which the maximum rate of child tax credit to which he or they may be entitled remains the same and both sub-paras (a) and (b) of reg.7(2) are met.

(3) The rate for each relevant period shall be found in accordance with the following steps—

Step 1—Finding the daily maximum rate for each element

For each element of the tax credit to be included in the case of the person or persons entitled to the tax credit, find the daily maximum rate using the following formula: 2.256

$$\frac{MR}{NI}$$

Tax Credits (Income Thresholds and Determination of Rates) Regulations 2002

where:
"MR" is the maximum rate in relation to that element for the tax year to which the claim for the tax credit relates;
"NI" is the number of days in that tax year.

Step 2—Finding the maximum rate for the relevant period for each element

2.257 For each element of the tax credit to be so included, find the amount produced by multiplying the maximum rate (found under Step 1 and rounded up to the nearest penny) by the number of days in the relevant period.

Step 3—Finding income for the relevant period

2.258 Find the income for the relevant period by using the following formula:

$$\frac{I}{NI} \times N2$$

where:
"I" is the relevant income for the tax year to which the claim for the tax credit relates;
"NI" is the number of days in that tax year;
"N2" is the number of days in the relevant period.

Step 4—Finding the threshold for the relevant period

2.259 Find the amount produced by the following formula:

$$\frac{[^3 £16,105]}{NI} \times N2$$

where:
"NI" is the number of days in that tax year;
"N2" is the number of days in the relevant period.
The threshold for the relevant period is—
  (a) in the case of a person or persons entitled to child tax credit only, that amount;
  (b) in the case of a person or persons entitled to both child tax credit and working tax credit—
    (i) that amount; or
    (ii) if greater, the lowest amount of income for the relevant period (found under Step 3) which, disregarding reg.9, would result in a determination in accordance with reg.7 providing for no rate of working tax credit in his or their case for that period.

Step 5—Finding the amount of the reduction of the elements of the tax credit [²...]

2.260 Find the amount (if any) which is [¹ 41 per cent] of the amount by which the income for the relevant period (found under Step 3 and rounded down to the nearest penny) exceeds the threshold for the relevant period (found under Step 4 and rounded up to the nearest penny).

(SI 2002/2008 reg.8) (as amended)

Step 6—Reducing the elements of the tax credit [² . . .]

If the amount found under Step 5 (rounded down to the nearest penny) is less than the total of the amounts found under Step 2 for the elements of the tax credit [² . . .], deduct the amount found under Step 5 (rounded down to the nearest penny) from the total of those amounts.

Step 7—Reducing the elements of the tax credit [² . . .] to nil

If the amount found under Step 5 (rounded down to the nearest penny) is equal to or exceeds the total of the amounts found under Step 2 for the elements of the tax credit [² . . .], reduce the total of those amounts to nil.
[² ...]

[² Step 8]—Finding the rate for the relevant period

[² The rate for the relevant period is the total of the amounts found under Step 2 for the elements of the tax credit after any reduction in accordance with Step 6 or Step 7.]
(4) "The family element" means the family element of child tax credit within the meaning given by section 9(3) of the Act.

AMENDMENTS

1. Tax Credits Up-rating Regulations 2011 (SI 2011/1035) reg.4(5) (April 6, 2011).
2. Tax Credits Up-rating Regulations 2012 (SI 2012/849) reg.4(5) (April 6, 2012).
3. Tax Credits Up-rating Regulations 2015 (SI 2015/451) reg.4(3) (April 6, 2015).

DEFINITIONS

"period of award"—see reg.2.
"the Act"—see reg.2.

GENERAL NOTE

See the general note to reg.6 above and the opening note to reg.7.

Paragraphs (1) and (2)
The same comments apply as those to paras (1) and (2) of reg.7.

Paragraph (3)
This appears to be the equivalent for child tax credit of reg.7, but it has two additional elements. First, the effect of the steps is to remove an award of or entitlement to working tax credit before that of child tax credit. This may be important where one of a couple is receiving one of the credits while the other is receiving the other tax credit. The effect is to take the credit from the earner (and the duty to pay from the employer) before it is taken from the carer.

Secondly, the family element is reduced, then removed, only after a second, higher income threshold. Before April 6, 2011 this was £50,000 and the withdrawal rate was gradual: 6.67 per cent. From April 6, 2011 the threshold is reduced to £40,000 and the same withdrawal rate is applied as to the lower threshold—now 41 per cent. This reduces the maximum income permitting a claim for child tax credit substantially—from around £66,000 to below £50,000, depending on the number of children.

Relevant periods of a full year

2.267 In parallel with reg.7, reg.8 is straightforward as applied to a period of award of a full year. Steps 1–6 require that the annual amount of all elements (including the family element) be found, that the income for the year also be found, and that the excess of the income over the £15,910 threshold, if any, be calculated. The maximum amount of child tax credit is found by reducing the annual amount of all elements *excluding* the family element by 41 per cent of the excess of the income over the threshold.

Relevant periods of less than a year

2.268 The changes noted in para.2.258, above, for the equivalent rule for WTC apply equally to CTC and have also removed most of the potential problems for this provision also.

Cases in which there is no rate of tax credit

2.269 **9.**—(1) In the case of a person or persons entitled to working tax credit only or child tax credit only, where the rate at which the person or persons would be entitled to the tax credit (as determined in accordance with reg.7 or 8) would be less than £26, there is no rate in his or their case.

(2) In the case of a person or persons entitled to both working tax credit and child tax credit, where the total of the rates at which the person or persons would be entitled to the tax credits (as determined in accordance with regulations 7 and 8) would be less than £26, there are no rates in his or their case.

GENERAL NOTE

2.270 This cut-off provision is authorised by s.13(3)(b) of the Act.

Tax Credits (Claims and Notifications) Regulations 2002

(SI 2002/2014) (AS AMENDED)

The Commissioners of Inland Revenue, in exercise of the powers conferred upon them by ss.4(1), 6, 14(2), 15(2), 16(3), 17(10), 19(2), 22(1)(b) and (2), 65(1), (2) and (7) and 67 of the Tax Credits Act 2002, hereby make the following Regulations:

ARRANGEMENT OF REGULATIONS

PART I

GENERAL

2.271
1. Citation, commencement and effect.
2. Interpretation.
3. Use of electronic communications to make claims or to give notices or notifications.

(SI 2002/2014) (as amended)

Part II

Claims

4. Interpretation of this Part.
5. Manner in which claims to be made.
6. Amended claims.
7. Time-limit for claims (if otherwise entitled to tax credit up to three months earlier).
7A. Time limit for claims—the Childcare Payments Act 2014.
8. Date of claims—disability element of working tax credit.
9. Advance claims before the year begins.
10. Advance claims—working tax credit.
11. Circumstances in which claims to be treated as made—notices containing provision under section 17(2)(a), (4)(a) or (6)(a) of the Act.
12. Circumstances in which claims to be treated as made—notices containing provision under section 17(2)(b), (4)(b) and (6)(b) of the Act.
13. Circumstances in which claims made by one member of a couple to be treated as also made by the other member of the couple.
14. Circumstances in which awards to be conditional and claims treated as made—decisions under section 14(1) of the Act made before 6th April 2003.
15. Persons who die after making a claim.
16. Persons who die before making joint claims.
17. Circumstances where one person may act for another in making a claim—receivers, etc.
18. Circumstances where one person may act for another in making a claim—other appointed persons.

Part III

Notifications of Changes of Circumstances

19. Interpretation of this Part.
20. Increases of maximum rate of entitlement to a tax credit as a result of changes of circumstances to be dependent on notification.
21. Requirement to notify changes of circumstances which may decrease the rate at which a person or persons is or are entitled to tax credit or mean that entitlement ceases.
22. Manner in which notifications to be given.
23. Person by whom notification may be, or is to be, given.
24. Amended notifications.
25. Date of notification—cases where change of circumstances which may increase the maximum rate.
26. Date of notification—disability element and severe disability element for working tax credit.
26A. Date of notification—disability element and severe disability element for child tax credit.
27. Advance notification.
28. Circumstances where one person may act for another in giving a notification—receivers, etc.
29. Circumstances where one person may act for another in giving a notification—other appointed persons.
29A. Form in which evidence of birth or adoption to be provided.

Tax Credits (Claims and Notifications) Regulations 2002

PART IV

NOTICES TO PROVIDE INFORMATION OR EVIDENCE

30. Employers.
31. Persons by whom childcare is provided.
32. Dates to be specified in notices under section 14(2), 15(2), 16(3), 18(10) or 19(2) of the Act.

PART V

FINAL DECISIONS

33. Dates to be specified in notices under section 17 of the Act.
34. Manner in which declaration or statement in response to a notice under section 17 of the Act to be made.
35. Circumstances where one person may act for another in response to a notice under section 17 of the Act—receivers, etc.
36. Circumstances where one person may act for another in response to a notice under section 17 of the Act.

PART I

GENERAL

Citation, commencement and effect

2.272   **1.**—(1) These Regulations may be cited as the Tax Credits (Claims and Notifications) Regulations 2002 and shall come into force on 12th August 2002.

(2) These Regulations have effect in relation to claims for a tax credit for periods of award beginning on or after 6th April 2003.

Interpretation

2.273   **2.**—In these Regulations—
"the Act" means the Tax Credits Act 2002;
[³ "appropriate office" means Comben House, Farriers Way, Netherton, Merseyside or any other office specified in writing by the Board;]
"the Board" means the Commissioners of Inland Revenue;
[²"couple" has the meaning given by section 3(5A) of the Act;]
"disability element" shall be construed in accordance with section 11(4) of the Act;
"joint claim" has the meaning given by section 3(8) of the Act;
[²...]
[⁴"personal independence payment" means personal independence payment under Part 4 of the Welfare Reform Act 2012;]

(SI 2002/2014 reg.2) (as amended)

[¹"relevant authority" means—
  (a) the Board;
  (b) the Secretary of State or the Department for Social Development in Northern Ireland; or
  (c) a person providing services to the Board, the Secretary of State or that Department in connection with tax credits;]
"severe disability element" has the meaning in regulation 17 of the Working Tax Credit Regulations;
"single claim" has the meaning given by section 3(8) of the Act;
"tax year" means a period beginning on 6th April in one year and ending with 5th April in the next;
[². . .]
"the Working Tax Credit Regulations" means the Working Tax Credit (Entitlement and Maximum Rate) Regulations 2002.

AMENDMENTS

1. Tax Credits (Claims and Notifications and Payments by the Board) (Amendment) Regulations 2003 (SI 2003/723) reg.3(1) (April 6, 2003).
2. Civil Partnership Act 2004 (Tax Credits, etc.) (Consequential Amendments) Order 2005 (SI 2005/2919) art.4(2) (December 5, 2005).
3. Tax Credits (Miscellaneous Amendments) Regulations 2009 (SI 2009/697) reg.12 (April 6, 2009).
4. Personal Independence Payment (Supplementary Provisions and Consequential Amendments) Regulations 2013 (SI 2013/388) reg.8 and Sch. para.31(2) (April 8, 2013).

Use of electronic communications to make claims or to give notices or notifications

3.—(1) In these Regulations "writing" includes writing produced by electronic communications that are approved by directions issued by or on behalf of the Board.

(2) If a claim which is required by these Regulations to be made to [¹a relevant authority at an appropriate office] is made in writing produced by electronic communications, it shall be treated for the purposes of these Regulations as having been made to, and received by, [¹a relevant authority at an appropriate office] on the date on which it is recorded on an official computer system.

(3) If a notice or notification which is required by these Regulations to be given to [¹a relevant authority at an appropriate office] is given in writing produced by electronic communications, it shall be treated for the purposes of these Regulations as having been given to, and received by, [¹a relevant authority at an appropriate office] on the date on which it is recorded on an official computer system.

(4) In this regulation—
  (a) "electronic communications" has the meaning given by section 132(10) of the Finance Act 1999;
  (b) "official computer system" means a computer system maintained by or on behalf of the Board to—
    (i) send or receive information, or
    (ii) process or store information.

2.274

AMENDMENT

1. Tax Credits (Claims and Notifications and Payments by the Board) (Amendment) Regulations 2003 (SI 2003/723) reg.3(2) (April 6, 2003).

DEFINITIONS

"appropriate office"—see reg.2.
"the Board"—see *ibid.*
"electronic communications"—see para.(4)(a).
"official computer system"—see para.(4)(b).
"relevant authority"—see reg.2.
"writing"—see para.(1).

GENERAL NOTE

2.275　See further the decision of Mr Commissioner Mesher in *CIS/995/2004*, discussed in the annotations to reg.4 below and Tax Credits Act 2002 s.14(2) above.

This regulation enables use of the internet and an official website for claims. The HMRC website claim facility was closed down after severe problems with fraud. The House of Commons Public Accounts Committee has since disclosed that the website was established outside recommended security procedures. It remains closed at the time of writing.

PART II

CLAIMS

Interpretation of this Part

2.276　4.—In this Part (and Part III) "the relevant date", in relation to a claim for a tax credit, means—
(a) in cases where regulation 6 applies, the date on which the claim would be treated as being made by that regulation disregarding [³ regulations 7, 7A and 8];
(b) in cases where sub-paragraph [²(d)] of regulation 11(3) applies, the date on which the claim would be treated as being made by that sub-paragraph disregarding [³ regulations 7, 7A and 8];
(c) in any other case, the date on which the claim is received by [¹ a relevant authority at an appropriate office].

AMENDMENTS

1. Tax Credits (Claims and Notifications and Payments by the Board) (Amendment) Regulations 2003 (SI 2003/723) reg.3(2) (April 6, 2003).
2. Tax Credits (Miscellaneous Amendments) Regulations 2009 (SI 2009/697) reg.13 (April 6, 2009).
3. Tax Credits (Claims and Notifications) (Amendment) Regulations 2015 (SI 2015/669) reg.3 (April 6, 2015).

DEFINITIONS

"appropriate office"—see reg.2.
"relevant authority"—see *ibid.*
"the relevant date"—see reg.4.

(SI 2002/2014 reg.4) (as amended)

General Note

2.277
The general rule is that the "relevant date" (or date of claim in social security terms) is the date on which the claim for tax credits is received by "a relevant authority at an appropriate office" (para.(c)). On the basis of the definition of these latter terms in reg.2, this will normally, but not always, be an HMRC office. For the date of receipt of electronic communications, e.g. online claims for tax credits, see reg.3. There are two modifications to the general rule in para.(c). First, amended claims are treated as made on the date on which the amended claim is received (see para.(a) and reg.6(3)). Secondly, where a claimant responds to a final notice under TCA 2002 s.17 within the specified time, the date of claim is the previous April 6 (reg.11(3)(a)). If the claimant's declaration is submitted beyond that time limit, then the date of claim is the latest date on which such declaration is received (see para.(b) and reg.11(3)(b)). Note that there are special rules governing the effective date of claim by refugees who have made a successful application for asylum and who subsequently make a retrospective claim for tax credits (see Tax Credits (Immigration) Regulations 2003 (SI 2003/653) regs 3 and 4).

Mr Commissioner Mesher's decision in *CIS/995/2004* deals with the complex interaction between tax credits and income support and what constitutes a claim for the former. Early in 2003 the claimant in *CIS/995/2004* claimed income support. On January 10, 2003, he also completed an online application form for child tax credit (CTC) and transmitted it to the Inland Revenue. In March 2003 the claimant received a TC602 letter from the Inland Revenue notifying him of his family's CTC entitlement for the 2003–04 tax year and asking him to sign and return the accompanying declaration. Having made further enquiries, the claimant discovered that he would be better off retaining entitlement to income support. He accordingly did not sign and return the TC602 declaration. However, the Revenue started making CTC payments in April 2003 and notified the DWP of this fact. This led the Secretary of State to decide that the claimant was no longer entitled to income support as his income exceeded his applicable amount.

The claimant appealed to a tribunal which disallowed his appeal, holding that reg.7 of the Social Security (Working Tax Credit and Child Tax Credit) Consequential Amendments Regulations 2003 (SI 2003/455) required the DWP to treat the claimant's income as including an amount equivalent to his CTC entitlement. Although finding error in the tribunal's reasoning in other respects, the Commissioner held that the tribunal had come to the only conclusion open to it as a matter of law and on the evidence before it. In particular, the Commissioner rejected the claimant's argument that he had only made a preliminary application for CTC which could not be completed until he had signed and returned the TC602 declaration. On the contrary, the online completion and transmission of the application form, notwithstanding the absence of any written confirmation at the time or later, amounted to a claim. Mr Commissioner Mesher thus held that the claimant had made a valid claim on January 10, 2003, whether in an approved electronic format (and so under regs 3 and 5(2)(a)—a point which did not have to be resolved) or alternatively under the wide power in reg.5(2)(b). A valid award of CTC had then followed. The Commissioner expressly left open the question whether an appeal tribunal or Commissioner has jurisdiction to go behind the Board's determination that a claim had been made.

The informality with which HMRC will accept renewals claims was emphasised in a public letter to the Institute of Chartered Accountants in England and Wales published on October 1, 2004. Speaking of renewal claims, the Deputy Chairman of the then Inland Revenue said:

"Claimants simply have to confirm or correct the information we hold about their circumstances and report their income for the year just finished. For those not in a position to provide actual income figures at the time they reply, an estimate will be accepted. The information necessary to renew can be accepted by telephone or through our e-portal or by filling in a short paper form."

He added:

"I should also make clear, in answer to a concern you raise, that renewals information is logged on receipt, even if it has not yet been processed, to make sure the payments continue."

Manner in which claims to be made

2.278 **5.**—(1) This regulation prescribes the manner in which a claim for a tax credit is to be made.

(2) A claim must be made to [¹a relevant authority at an appropriate office]—
   (a) in writing on a form approved or authorised by the Board for the purpose of the claim; or
[² (b) in such other manner as the Board may decide having regard to all the circumstances.]

(3) A claim must contain the information requested on the form (or such of that information as the Board may accept as sufficient in the circumstances of the particular case).

(4) In particular, a claim must include in respect of every person by whom the claim is made—
   (a) a statement of the person's national insurance number and information or evidence establishing that that number has been allocated to the person; or
   (b) information or evidence enabling the national insurance number that has been allocated to the person to be ascertained; or
   (c) an application for a national insurance number to be allocated to the person which is accompanied by information or evidence enabling such a number to be so allocated.

This paragraph is subject to [³ paragraphs (6) and (8)].

(5) "National insurance number" means the national insurance number allocated within the meaning of regulation 9 of the Social Security (Crediting and Treatment of Contributions, and National Insurance Numbers) Regulations 2001.

(6) Paragraph (4) does not apply if the Board are satisfied that the person or persons by whom the claim was made had a reasonable excuse for making a claim which did not comply with the requirements of that paragraph.

(7) At any time after a claim has been made but before the Board have given notice of their decision under section 14(1) of the Act in relation to the claim, the person or persons by whom the claim was made may amend the claim by giving notice orally or in writing to [¹a relevant authority at an appropriate office].

[³ (8) Paragraph (4) does not apply to any person who is subject to immigration control within the meaning set out in section 115(9)(a) of the Immigration and Asylum Act 1999 and to whom a national insurance number has not been allocated.]

AMENDMENTS

1. Tax Credits (Claims and Notifications and Payments by the Board) (Amendment) Regulations 2003 (SI 2003/723) reg.3(2) (April 6, 2003).

(SI 2002/2014 reg.5) (as amended)

2. Tax Credits (Miscellaneous Amendments) (No.2) Regulations 2008 (SI 2008/2169) reg.12 (September 1, 2008).

3. Tax Credits (Miscellaneous Amendments) Regulations 2009 (SI 2009/697) reg.14 (April 6, 2009).

DEFINITIONS

"the Act"—see reg.2.
"appropriate office"—see *ibid.*
"the Board"—see *ibid.*
"National insurance number"—see para.(5).
"relevant authority"—see reg.2.
"writing"—see reg.3(1).

GENERAL NOTE

See the note to s.14 of the 2002 Act, above against p.141, for a decision on appeals against decisions under this regulation.

2.279

Paragraph (2)

This rule is similar to, but not identical to, the standard social security provision in reg.4(1) of the Social Security (Claims and Payments) Regulations 1987 (SI 1987/1968). The fundamental difference is that it is not possible to make an oral claim for a social security benefit under reg.4(1) of the 1987 Regulations. This appears to be possible in the case of tax credits as the requirement that the claim be in writing appears only in para.(a), which will cover the great majority of cases, and not in the residual category envisaged by para.(b). And see the comments of Judge Rowland in *JI v HMRC* [2013] UKUT 199 (AAC) about the scope for treating a notification of a change of circumstances as a new claim (for example, when one member of a couple orally reports the breakdown of their relationship to HMRC).

2.280

Paragraphs (4)–(6)

The requirement to provide a national insurance number (or the information or evidence specified) mirrors the requirement for social security benefits set out in SSAA 1992 s.1(1B). Note however HMRC discretion not to apply this requirement if satisfied that the claimant had a reasonable excuse for making a claim which failed to comply with it (para.(6)). There is no equivalent discretion to disapply the requirement in the social security scheme.

2.281

Paragraph (7)

This provision is similar to the social security rule in reg.5(1) of the Social Security (Claims and Payments) Regulations 1987 (SI 1987/1968). However, a tax credits claim can be amended by giving oral notice, whereas the social security rule requires written notice. See further reg.6 on the determination of the date of claim for amended claims for tax credits.

2.282

Amended claims

6.—(1) In the circumstances prescribed by paragraph (2) a claim for a tax credit which has been amended shall be treated as having been made as amended and, subject to [² regulations 7, 7A and 8], as having been made on the date prescribed by paragraph (3).

2.283

(2) The circumstances prescribed by this paragraph are where a person has amended or persons have amended the claim in accordance with reg.5(7).

(3) The date prescribed by this paragraph is the date on which the claim being amended was received by [¹ a relevant authority at an appropriate office].

Tax Credits (Claims and Notifications) Regulations 2002

AMENDMENTS

1. Tax Credits (Claims and Notifications and Payments by the Board) (Amendment) Regulations 2003 (SI 2003/723) reg.3(2) (April 6, 2003).
2. Tax Credits (Claims and Notifications) (Amendment) Regulations 2015 (SI 2015/669) reg.3 (April 6, 2015).

DEFINITIONS

"appropriate office"—see reg.2.
"relevant authority"—see *ibid.*

Time-limit for claims (if otherwise entitled to tax credit up to [² [³ 31] days] earlier)

2.284   **7.**—(1) In the circumstances prescribed by paragraph (2), a claim for a tax credit received by [¹ a relevant authority at an appropriate office] shall be treated as having been made on the date prescribed by paragraph (3).

(2) The circumstances prescribed by this paragraph are those where the person or persons by whom the claim is made would (if a claim had been made) have been entitled to the tax credit either—
  (a) on the date falling [² [³ 31] days] before the relevant date (or on 6th April 2003, if later); or
  (b) at any later time in the period beginning on the date in subparagraph (a) and ending on the relevant date.

(3) The date prescribed by this paragraph is the earliest date falling within the terms of paragraph (2)(a) or (b) when the person or the persons by whom the claim is made would (if a claim had been made) have become entitled to the tax credit.

AMENDMENTS

1. Tax Credits (Claims and Notifications and Payments by the Board) (Amendment) Regulations 2003 (SI 2003/723) reg.3(2) (April 6, 2003).
2. Tax Credits (Miscellaneous Amendments)(No.2) Regulations 2009 (SI 2009/2887) reg.8 (November 21, 2009).
3. Tax Credits (Miscellaneous Amendments) Regulations 2012 (SI 2012/848) reg.5(2)(a) and (b) (April 6, 2012).

DEFINITIONS

"appropriate office"—see reg.2.
"relevant authority"—see *ibid.*

GENERAL NOTE

2.285   The standard rule until 2012/13 allowed backdating of claims for up to three months. From 2012/13, the rule has been changed to reduce the time limit to 31 days. This has given rise to a number of appeals, but there are no exceptions or discretions in the rule save for that in reg.8. Regulation 25 imposes a similar time limit on notifying changes of circumstances that may increase awards. This contrasts with the relevant income tax rule that allows corrections to be made (for example because no claim has been made for an allowance or no deduction for an expense) for up to six years after the relevant time. It also contrasts with the powers for HMRC to amend tax credits awards and entitlements to deal with overpayments.

Once a claim has been made, there may be an amendment to deal with corrections when the annual declaration is made ahead of the entitlement decision.

(SI 2002/2014 reg. 7) (as amended)

It is therefore better to make a claim if there may be entitlement rather than waiting to see. This has led to the widespread practice, accepted by HMRC, of protective claims, and also to the practice of HMRC reducing awards to nil rather than terminating them during the year where circumstances change. Statistics show that at any one time in recent years there are about ½ million nil or protective claims in the system.

In *AA v HMRC (TC)* [2012] UKUT 121 (AAC), Judge Turnbull held that there was no provision for backdating entitlement to tax credit for more than three months (the then maximum period allowed) in a case where the claimant had been granted indefinite leave to remain in the UK with retrospective effect for a longer period. The provisions for greater backdating in the case of refugees did not apply, and could not be made to apply by way of analogy to the claimant's situation.

[¹Time limit for claims – the Childcare Payments Act 2014

7A.—(1) Subject to paragraphs (3) and (4), regulation 7 does not apply where the claim for a tax credit made by a person or persons is received by a relevant authority at an appropriate office during an entitlement period where the person making the claim, or in the case of joint claimants either person, has for that entitlement period made a valid declaration of eligibility under section 4(2) of the Childcare Payments Act 2014 (declarations of eligibility).

(2) Subject to paragraphs (3) and (4), where a claim for tax credits is received by a relevant authority at an appropriate office during the period of 31 days beginning with the last day of the entitlement period for which the person making the claim or, in the case of joint claimants either person, has made a valid declaration of eligibility under section 4(2) of the Childcare Payments Act 2014, regulation 7 shall apply but the date prescribed by paragraph (3) of regulation 7 may be no earlier than the day following the last day of that entitlement period

(3) For the purposes of this regulation, the "appropriate date" is the date on which—

(a) Her Majesty's Revenue and Customs makes an account restriction order in accordance with section 24 of the Childcare Payments Act 2014 (imposing restrictions on childcare accounts) for the purposes of giving effect to a determination made under section 18(2) of that Act (cases where there is more than one eligible person) and regulations made thereunder,

(b) a childcare account is closed in accordance with regulations made under section 25 of the Childcare Payments Act 2014 (closure of childcare accounts), or

(c) a child ceases to be a "qualifying child" for the purposes of the Childcare Payments Act 2014 as defined in regulation 5 of the Childcare Payments (Eligibility) Regulations 2015 except in the case where they cease to be a "disabled child" as defined in regulation 5(5) of those Regulations.

(4) Where a claim for tax credits is received by a relevant authority at an appropriate office—

(a) during an entitlement period relating to a childcare account where the person making the claim, or in the case of joint claimants either person, has for that entitlement period made a valid declaration of eligibility under section 4(2) of the Childcare Payments Act 2014, or

(b) during the period of 31 days beginning with the day following the last day of that entitlement period, regulation 7 shall apply but the date prescribed in paragraph (3) of regulation 7 may be no earlier than the appropriate date.

(5) For the purposes of this regulation, the terms "childcare account" and "entitlement period" have the same meanings as they have for the purposes of the Childcare Payments Act 2014 and regulations made thereunder.]

AMENDMENT

1. Tax Credits (Claims and Notifications) (Amendment) Regulations 2015 (SI 2015/669) reg.2 (April 6, 2015).

DEFINITIONS

"appropriate date" —see para.(3).
"appropriate office" —see reg.2.
"childcare account" —see para.(5).
"entitlement period" —see para.(5).

GENERAL NOTE

2.287 The inserted reg.7A modifies the effect of the backdating provisions in reg.7 in circumstances where a claimant or, in the case of a joint claim, either or both of them, has made a declaration of eligibility under s.4(2) of the Childcare Payments Act 2014.

Paragraph (1)
2.288 This establishes the basic rule that where the claim for tax credits is made during an entitlement period under the Childcare Payments Act 2014, the backdating provisions in reg.7 do not apply. This is subject to specific provisions in paras (3) and (4).

Paragraph (2)
2.289 This provides that where the claim for tax credits is made within 31 days beginning with the last day of the entitlement period, the backdating provisions can only apply to the extent that they do not allow the backdating period to overlap with any day falling within that entitlement period. Again, this is made subject to the specific provisions in paras (3) and (4).

Paragraphs (3) and (4)
2.290 These paragraphs modify the backdating provisions in reg.7. They apply in three types of situation which may arise during an entitlement period for tax free childcare or during the period of 31 days beginning with the day following the last day of the entitlement period. The three circumstances are where: (1) HMRC makes an account restriction order under s.24 of the Childcare Payments Act 2014 (imposing restrictions on childcare accounts) in order to give effect to a determination made under s.18(2) of that Act (cases where there is more than one eligible person); (2) a tax free childcare account is closed in accordance with regulations made under s.25 of the 2014 Act (closure of childcare accounts); or (3) a child ceases to be a "qualifying child" for the purposes of the 2014 Act as defined by reg.5 of the Childcare Payments (Eligibility) Regulations 2015 (SI 2015/448) (unless the child ceases to be a qualifying child by no longer being a "disabled child" as defined in para.(5) of that regulation). In these exceptional cases the backdating rules in reg.7 do not allow the tax credits claim to be backdated any earlier than the date that the account restriction order is made, the childcare account is closed or the child ceases to be a "qualifying child" (as appropriate).

(SI 2002/2014 reg.8) (as amended)

[¹ Date of claims – disability element of working tax credit

8.—(1) In the circumstances prescribed by paragraph (2), the claim referred to in paragraph (2)(a) shall be treated as having been made on the date prescribed by paragraph (3).

(2) The circumstances prescribed by this paragraph are where—
(a) a claim for working tax credit including the disability element ("the tax credits claim") is made by a person or persons ("the claimants") which results in the Board making an award of working tax credit including the disability element;
(b) the claim is made within [² [³ 31] days] of the date that a claim for any of the benefits referred to in regulation 9(2) to (8) of the Working Tax Credit Regulations ("the benefits claim") is determined in favour of the claimants (or one of them); and
(c) the claimants would (subject to making a claim) have been entitled to working tax credit if (and only if) they had satisfied the requirements of regulation 9(1)(c) of the Working Tax Credit Regulations, on any day in the period—
  (i) beginning on the date of the benefits claim, and
  (ii) ending on the date of the tax credits claim.
(3) The date prescribed by this paragraph is—
(a) the first date in respect of which the benefit claimed is payable; or
(b) if later, the date falling [² [³ 31] days] before the claim for the benefit is made; or
(c) if later, the first day identified under paragraph (2)(c).]

2.291

AMENDMENTS

1. Tax Credits (Miscellaneous Amendments) Regulations 2009 (SI 2009/697) reg.15 (April 6, 2009).
2. Tax Credits (Miscellaneous Amendments)(No.2) Regulations 2009 (SI 2009/2887) reg.8 (November 21, 2009).
3. Tax Credits (Miscellaneous Amendments) Regulations 2012 (SI 2012/848) reg.5(2)(c) and (d) (April 6, 2012).

GENERAL NOTE

The new version of this regulation provides two special rules for claims for the disability element of a tax credit from 2009. In *SP v HMRC* [2009] UKUT 42 (AAC), *CTC/2878/2008* the Upper Tribunal upheld a ruling that under the previous rule a claimant for disability living allowance had to inform the Tax Credit Office separately of both the claim for the allowance and the award of the allowance if the claim to a disability element of a tax credit was to operate from the date of award of the allowance. In that case a claim was made, but refused and then awarded on appeal. Because the claimant had not notified the claim, the disability element of the tax credit could only be backdated for three months from notification of the award, not the full year back to the date when the allowance had first been awarded. The 2009 amending regulations recognised and changed the weak drafting of the original version, and so the decision no longer applies. A claimant need only notify an award to have the disability element backdated to start at the same time as the allowance, even if that is more than three months in the past.

2.292

Advance claims before the year begins

9.—(1) In the circumstances prescribed by paragraph (2) a claim for a tax credit may be made for a period after the relevant date.

2.293

Tax Credits (Claims and Notifications) Regulations 2002

(2) The circumstances prescribed by this paragraph are where a tax credit is claimed for a tax year by making a claim before the tax year begins.

(3) This regulation shall cease to have effect in relation to the tax year beginning on 6th April 2004 and subsequent tax years.

DEFINITIONS

"the relevant date"—see reg.4.
"tax year"—see reg.2.

GENERAL NOTE

2.294 This regulation provides, at least at the outset of the tax credits scheme, for claims for such credits to be made before the beginning of the tax year to which they relate (see also reg.14). There is further provision in reg.10 for advance claims for working tax credit where a person is about to start work.

Advance claims—working tax credit

2.295 **10.**—(1) In the circumstances prescribed by paragraph (2) a claim for a tax credit may be made for a period after the relevant date.

(2) The circumstances prescribed by this paragraph are where—
(a) the tax credit in question is working tax credit; and
(b) the case falls within sub-paragraph (b) of the First Condition in regulation 4(1) of the Working Tax Credit Regulations (person who has accepted an offer of work which is expected to commence within seven days).

(3) In the circumstances prescribed by paragraph (2)—
(a) an award on a claim for tax credit may be made subject to the condition that the requirements for entitlement are satisfied no later than the date prescribed by paragraph (4); and
(b) if those requirements are satisfied no later than that date, the claim shall be treated as being made on the date on which they are satisfied.

(4) The date prescribed by this paragraph is the date falling 7 days after the relevant date.

DEFINITIONS

"the relevant date"—see reg.4.
"the Working Tax Credit Regulations"—see reg.2.

GENERAL NOTE

2.296 This rule allows for working tax credit claims to be made up to seven days in advance where a person has accepted an offer of employment and is expected to commence within that week.

Circumstances in which claims to be treated as made—notices containing provision under section 17(2)(a), (4)(a) or (6)(a) of the Act

2.297 **11.**—(1) In the circumstances prescribed by paragraph (2), a claim for a tax credit is to be treated as made.

(2) The circumstances prescribed by this paragraph are where (in the case where there has been a previous single claim) a person has or (in the case where there has been a previous joint claim) [4 either person or] both persons have made a declaration in response to provision included in a notice under section 17 of the Act by virtue of—

552

(SI 2002/2014 reg.11) (as amended)

(a) subsection (2)(a) of that section;
(b) subsection (4)(a) of that section;
(c) subsection (6)(a) of that section; or
(d) any combination of those subsections.

The declaration made shall (subject to regulation 5(3)) be treated as a claim for tax credit by that person or persons for the tax year following that to which the notice relates.

[² (3) The claim shall be treated as made—
(a) in a case where the declaration is made by [⁴ the date specified on the section 17 notice], on 6th April [⁴ following the period to which the section 17 notice relates];

[³(aa) [⁴ . . .]]

(b) in a case where the declaration, not having been made by [⁴ the date specified on the section 17 notice], is made within 30 days following the date on the notice to the claimant that payments of tax credit under section 24(4) of the Act have ceased due to the claimant's failure to make the declaration, [³ on 6th April [⁴ . . .] following [⁴ the period to which the section 17 notice relates]];

(c) in a case where the declaration, not having been made by [⁴ the date specified on the section 17 notice] or within the 30 days specified in sub-paragraph (b), is made before [⁴ 31st January in the tax year following the period to which the section 17 notice relates], and, in the opinion of the Board, the claimant had good cause for not making the declaration as mentioned in sub-paragraphs (a) or (b), [⁴ on 6th April following the period to which the section 17 notice relates]; or

(d) in any other case, on the latest date on which the declaration is received by a relevant authority at an appropriate office (subject to the application of [⁵ regulations 7 and 7A]).]

[¹(4) Paragraph (3) does not apply—
(a) in the case where there has been a previous single claim (to which the notice referred to in paragraph (2) relates) if the person by whom it was made could no longer make a single claim; [⁴ . . .]

(b) in the case where there has been a previous joint claim (to which the notice referred to in paragraph (2) relates) if the persons by whom it was made could no longer make a joint claim [⁴ ; or

(c) in the case where the response to the notice referred to in paragraph (2) specifies that such response is not to be treated as a new claim for the tax year beginning 6th April following the period to which the section 17 notice relates].]

AMENDMENTS

1. Tax Credits (Miscellaneous Amendments) Regulations 2004 (SI 2004/762) reg.3(2) (April 6, 2004).
2. Tax Credits (Miscellaneous Amendments) Regulations 2008 (SI 2008/604) reg.4(2) (April 6, 2008).
3. Tax Credits (Miscellaneous Amendments) Regulations 2009 (SI 2009/697) reg.16 (April 6, 2009).
4. Tax Credits (Miscellaneous Amendments) Regulations 2010 (SI 2010/751) reg.7 (April 6, 2010).
5. Tax Credits (Claims and Notifications) (Amendment) Regulations 2015 (SI 2015/669) reg.4 (April 6, 2015).

DEFINITIONS

"the Act"—see reg.2.
"appropriate office"—see *ibid.*
"the Board"—see *ibid.*
"joint claim"—see *ibid.*
"relevant authority"—see *ibid.*
"single claim"—see *ibid.*
"tax year"—see *ibid.*

GENERAL NOTE

2.298   This allows the claimant's (or claimants') declaration in response to a HMRC final notice under various provisions of the TCA 2002 s.17, to be treated as a claim for tax credits. This effectively eases the process of making renewal claims for subsequent tax years. This assumes that the claimant(s) provide the necessary information as requested on the official form (para.(2) and reg.5(3)). The date of claim is the preceding April 6, i.e. the start of the tax year, assuming the declaration is returned within the designated time (para.(3)). There are further deeming rules under reg.12 in relation to s.17 final notices.

HMRC indicated at the Tax Credits Consultation Group meeting on January 15, 2008, in connection with late renewals after July 31, that: "claims could be renewed after July 31 if customers had good cause for the delay. Most cases are restored without difficulty but, for a small number, technical problems may prevent them being restored—where that happens, manual payments would be set up" (*http://www.hmrc.gov.uk/taxcredits/minutes150108.htm*). Legislative effect was given to this from April 6, 2008 by the replacement of para.(3). "Good cause" is the standard social security test derived from *R(S) 2/63*.

Circumstances in which claims to be treated as made—notices containing provision under section 17(2)(b), (4)(b) and (6)(b) of the Act

2.299   **12.**—(1) In either of the circumstances prescribed by paragraphs (2) and (4) a claim for a tax credit is to be treated as made.

(2) The circumstances prescribed by this paragraph are where a person is or persons are treated as having made a declaration in response to provision included in a notice under section 17 of the Act by virtue of—
   (a) subsection (2)(b) of that section; and
   (b) subsection (4)(b) of that section,
      or a combination of those subsections and subsection (6)(b) of that section.

(3) The declaration referred to in paragraph (2) shall (subject to regulation 5(3)) be treated as a claim by that person or persons for tax credit for the tax year following that to which the notice relates.

(4) The circumstances prescribed by this paragraph are where a person or any of the persons has—
   (a) made a statement under paragraph (b) of subsection (2) of section 17 of the Act in response to such a notice by the date specified for the purposes of that subsection; or
   (b) made a statement under paragraph (b) of subsection (4) of that section in response to such a notice by the date specified for the purposes of that subsection,
or a combination of any of those subsections and subsection (6)(b) of that section.

(SI 2002/2014 reg.12) (as amended)

(5) The notice referred to in paragraph (4), together with (and as corrected by) the statement or statements there referred to, shall (subject to regulation 5(3)) be treated as a claim for tax credit by that person or persons for the tax year following that to which the notice relates.

(6) The claim shall be treated as made on 6th April preceding the dates specified in the notice for the purposes of subsection (2) or (4) of section 17 of the Act.

(7) [² Paragraph (3) and (5) shall not apply]
- (a) in the case where there has been a previous single claim (to which the notice relates), the person by whom it was made could no longer make a single claim; [¹. . .]
- (b) in the case where there has been a previous joint claim (to which the notice relates), the persons by whom it was made could no longer jointly make a joint claim [¹ ; [². . .]

[² (c) in the case where, before the specified date, the person or persons to whom a notice under section 17 of the Act is given advise the Board that the person or persons do not wish to be treated as making a claim for tax credit for the tax year following that to which the notice relates; or]
- (d) in the case where there has been a previous single claim to which a notice under section 17 of the Act relates—
  - (i) a relevant notification is given to the person by whom the claim was made; and
  - (ii) the person fails to make a relevant request; and
- (e) in the case where there has been a previous joint claim to which a notice under section 17 of the Act relates—
  - (i) a relevant notification is given to the persons by whom the claim was made; and
  - (ii) they fail to make a relevant request.]

[³ (8) In this regulation—
- (a) "relevant notification" means a written notification to a person or persons by whom a claim for tax credit was made which—
  - (i) is given by the Board at least 35 days before the Board gives notice under section 17 of the Act to the person or persons;
  - (ii) states the date on which it is given;
  - (iii) advises that the Board intends to give such a notice to the person or persons; and
  - (iv) advises that this regulation will not have effect to treat the person or persons as making a claim for tax credit for the tax year following that to which the notice relates unless a relevant request is made;
- (b) "relevant request" means a request made to the Board by a person or persons to whom a relevant notification is given that—
  - (i) is made in response to the relevant notification within 30 days of the date on which it is given; and
  - (ii) requests that the person or persons will be treated by virtue of this regulation as making a claim for tax credit for the tax year following that to which the notice relates;
- (c) "specified date" means the date specified for the purposes of section 17(2) and (4) of the Act or, where different dates are specified, the later of them.]

Tax Credits (Claims and Notifications) Regulations 2002

AMENDMENTS

1. Tax Credits (Miscellaneous Amendments) Regulations 2010 (SI 2010/751) reg.8 (April 6, 2010).
2. Tax Credits (Miscellaneous Amendments) (No.3) Regulations 2010 (SI 2010/2914) reg.14 (December 31, 2010).
3. Tax Credits (Miscellaneous Amendments) (No.3) Regulations 2010 (SI 2010/2914) reg.15 (December 31, 2010).

DEFINITIONS

"the Act"—see reg.2.
"joint claim"—see *ibid*.
"single claim"—see *ibid*.
"tax year"—see *ibid*.

GENERAL NOTE

2.300   Regulation 11 makes provision for the claimant's declaration in response to an HMRC final notice to be treated as a claim for tax credits for the following tax year. This regulation makes similar provision for those cases in which the claimant is sent a final notice informing them that they will be treated as having declared that their circumstances as are specified in the notice. On the position of couples, see further reg.13.

The amendments from 2010 make express provision for the case where claimants notify HMRC that they do not wish to renew a tax credits claim, so as to prevent a deemed claim.

Circumstances in which claims made by one member of a couple to be treated as also made by the other member of the couple

2.301   **13.**—(1) In the circumstances prescribed by paragraph (2) [² or (3)] a claim for a tax credit made by one member of a [¹. . .] couple is to be treated as also made by the other member of the [¹. . .] couple.

(2) The circumstances prescribed by this paragraph are those where one member of a [¹. . .] couple is treated by [³ regulation 11 or] regulation 12 as having made a claim for a tax credit in response to a notice under section 17 of the Act given to both members of the couple.

[² (3) A claim for a tax credit made by one member of a couple is to be treated as also made by the other member of the couple in such manner and in such circumstances as the Board may decide.]

AMENDMENTS

1. Civil Partnership Act 2004 (Tax Credits, etc.) (Consequential Amendments) Order 2005 (SI 2005/2919) art.5(3) (December 5, 2005).
2. Tax Credits (Miscellaneous Amendments) (No.2) Regulations 2008 (SI 2008/2169) reg.13 (September 1, 2008).
3. Tax Credits (Miscellaneous Amendments) Regulations 2010 (SI 2010/751) reg.9 (April 6, 2010).

DEFINITIONS

"the Act"—see reg.2.
"couple"—see *ibid*.

GENERAL NOTE

HMRC has indicated that the new provision in para.(3) initially applies to telephone claims only. The effect is to require both partners to fill in the forms confirming the claims while validating the initial claim as a joint claim.

Circumstances in which awards to be conditional and claims treated as made—decisions under section 14(1) of the Act made before 6th April 2003

14.—*(transitional only—spent)*

Persons who die after making a claim

15.—(1) This regulation applies where any person who has made a claim for a tax credit dies—
  (a) before the Board have made a decision in relation to that claim under section 14(1) of the Act;
  (b) having given a notification of a change of circumstances increasing the maximum rate at which a person or persons may be entitled to the tax credit, before the Board have made a decision whether (and, if so, how) to amend the award of tax credit made to him or them; or
  (c) where the tax credit has been awarded for the whole or part of a tax year, after the end of that tax year but before the Board have made a decision in relation to the award under section 18(1), (5), (6) or (9) of the Act.

(2) In the case of a single claim, the personal representatives of the person who has died may proceed with the claim in the name of that person.

(3) In the case of a joint claim where only one of the persons by whom the claim was made has died, the other person with whom the claim was made may proceed with the claim in the name of the person who has died as well as in his own name.

(4) In the case of a joint claim where both the persons by whom the claim was made have died, the personal representatives of the last of them to die may proceed with the claim in the name of both persons who have died.

(5) For the purposes of paragraph (4), where persons have died in circumstances rendering it uncertain which of them survived the other—
  (a) their deaths shall be presumed to have occurred in order of seniority; and
  (b) the younger shall be treated as having survived the elder.

DEFINITIONS

"the Act"—see reg.2.
"the Board"—see *ibid.*
"joint claim"—see *ibid.*
"single claim"—see *ibid.*
"tax year"—see *ibid.*

GENERAL NOTE

This regulation makes provision as to how a claim is to proceed after the person or persons die after making it. In short, the personal representatives of the deceased person(s) may proceed with the claim (paras (2) and (4)), although in the case of a couple where only one partner has died the survivor may proceed with the claim in both their names (para.(3); see further reg.16). Paragraph (5) reflects the property law rule on contemporaneous deaths to be found in Law of Property Act 1925 s.184.

Persons who die before making joint claims

2.306   **16.**—(1) This regulation applies where one member of a [¹. . .] couple dies and the other member of the [¹. . .] couple wishes to make a joint claim for a tax credit.

(2) The member who wishes to make the claim may make and proceed with the claim in the name of the member who has died as well as in his own name.

(3) Any claim made in accordance with this regulation shall be for a tax credit for a period ending with—
   (a) the date of the death of the member of the [¹. . .] couple who has died; or
   (b) if earlier, 5th April in the tax year to which the claim relates.

AMENDMENT

1. Civil Partnership Act 2004 (Tax Credits, etc.) (Consequential Amendments) Order 2005 (SI 2005/2919) art.5(4) (December 5, 2005).

DEFINITIONS

"couple"—see reg.2.
"joint claim"—see *ibid*.

GENERAL NOTE

2.307   See note to reg.15.

Circumstances where one person may act for another in making a claim—receivers, etc.

2.308   **17.**—(1) In the circumstances prescribed by paragraph (2), any receiver or other person mentioned in sub-paragraph (b) of that paragraph may act for the person mentioned in sub-paragraph (a) of that paragraph in making a claim for a tax credit.

(2) The circumstances prescribed by this paragraph are where—
   (a) a person is, or is alleged to be, entitled to a tax credit but is unable for the time being to make a claim for a tax credit; and
   (b) there are any of the following—
      (i) a receiver appointed by the Court of Protection with power to make a claim for a tax credit on behalf of the person;
      (ii) in Scotland, a tutor, curator or other guardian acting or appointed in terms of law who is administering the estate of the person; and
      (iii) in Northern Ireland, a controller appointed by the High Court, with power to make a claim for a tax credit on behalf of the person.

(SI 2002/2014 reg.18) (as amended)

Circumstances where one person may act for another in making a claim—other appointed persons

18.—(1) In the circumstances prescribed by paragraph (2), any person mentioned in sub-paragraph (b) of that paragraph may act for the person mentioned in sub-paragraph (a) of that paragraph in making a claim for a tax credit.

(2) The circumstances prescribed by this paragraph are where—
  (a) a person is, or is alleged to be, entitled to a tax credit but is unable for the time being to make a claim for a tax credit; and
  (b) in relation to that person, there is a person appointed under—
     (i) regulation 33(1) of the Social Security (Claims and Payments) Regulations 1987;
     (ii) regulation 33(1) of the Social Security (Claims and Payments) Regulations (Northern Ireland) 1987; or
     (iii) paragraph (3).

(3) Where there is no person mentioned in regulation 17(2)(b) in relation to the person who is unable to act, the Board may appoint under this paragraph a person who—
  (a) has applied in writing to the Board to be appointed to act on behalf of the person who is unable to act; and
  (b) if a natural person, is aged 18 years or more.

(4) An appointment under paragraph (3) shall end if—
  (a) the Board terminate it;
  (b) the person appointed has resigned from the appointment having given one month's notice in writing to the Board of his resignation; or
  (c) the Board are notified that a receiver or other person mentioned in regulation 17(2)(b) has been appointed in relation to the person who is unable to make a claim.

DEFINITIONS

"the Board"—see reg.2.
"writing"—see reg.3(1).

GENERAL NOTE

HMRC has recently revised its procedures for recognising representatives. A claimant can authorise a representative to make a claim by filling in Form 64-8 (authorising your agent) for this and for tax purposes.

PART III

NOTIFICATIONS OF CHANGES OF CIRCUMSTANCES

Interpretation of this Part

19. In this Part "the notification date", in relation to a notification, means—
  (a) the date on which the notification is given to [¹a relevant authority at an appropriate office]; or

(b) in cases where regulation 24 applies, the date on which the notification would be treated by that regulation as being given disregarding regulations 25 and 26.

AMENDMENT

1. Tax Credits (Claims and Notifications and Payments by the Board) (Amendment) Regulations 2003 (SI 2003 No.723) reg.3(2) (April 6, 2003).

DEFINITIONS

"appropriate office"—see reg.2.
"relevant authority"—see *ibid*.

Increases of maximum rate of entitlement to a tax credit as a result of changes of circumstances to be dependent on notification

2.312   20.—(1) Any change of circumstances of a description prescribed by para.(2) which may increase the maximum rate at which a person or persons may be entitled to tax credit is to do so only if notification of it has been given in accordance with this Part.

(2) The description of changes of circumstances prescribed by this paragraph are changes of circumstances other than those in consequence of which the Board have given notice of a decision under section 16(1) of the Act in accordance with section 23 of the Act.

DEFINITIONS

"the Act"—see reg.2.
"the Board"—see *ibid.*

GENERAL NOTE

2.313   The effect of this provision is that increases in the maximum rate of entitlement to a tax credit, as a result of some relevant change of circumstances, are dependent upon notification. The normal rule is that changes which have the effect of increasing entitlement are backdated for a maximum of three months from the date of notification (reg.25).

The scope of this provision is potentially very wide. In *LV v HMRC (TC)* [2010] UKUT 483 (AAC) (see further para.2.317, below), the Judge commented that "it is clear that becoming disabled, receiving a diagnosis, claiming DLA and being awarded DLA can each be regarded as a change of circumstances. . .".

Requirement to notify changes of circumstances which may decrease the rate at which a person or persons is or are entitled to tax credit or mean that entitlement ceases

2.314   21.—(1) [¹Subject to paragraph (1A),] where a person has or persons have claimed a tax credit, notification is to be given within the time prescribed by paragraph (3) if there is a change of circumstances of the description prescribed by paragraph (2) which may decrease the rate at which he is or they are entitled to the tax credit or mean that he ceases or they cease to be entitled to the tax credit.

[¹(1A) Paragraph (1) does not apply where advance notification has been given under regulation [² 27(2), (2A) or (3)].]

(2) The changes of circumstances described by this paragraph are those where—

(SI 2002/2014 reg.21) (as amended)

(a) entitlement to the tax credit ceases by virtue of section 3(4), or regulations made under section 3(7), of the Act;
(b) there is a change in the relevant child care charges which falls within regulation 16(1)(b) (omitting paragraph (i)) of the Working Tax Credit Regulations;
(c) a person ceases to undertake work for at least 16 hours per week for the purposes of—
   (i) the Second Condition in regulation 4(1) (read with regulations 4(3) to (5) and 5 to 8) [⁴ except where that person falls within paragraph (a) of the third variation of the Second Condition], or
   (ii) regulation 13(1),
of the Working Tax Credit Regulations;
[⁴ (d) a person ceases to undertake work for at least 30 hours per week for the purposes of the first or second variation of the Second Condition in regulation 4(1) of the Working Tax Credit Regulations (read with regulations 4(3) to (5) and 5 to 8), except in a case where that person still falls within the terms of paragraph (a) or (d) of the first variation or paragraph (a) or (c) of the second variation of that Condition;]
(e) a person ceases to undertake, or engage in, qualifying remunerative work for at least 16 hours per week for the purposes of—
   (i) regulation 9(1)(a) (disability element), [⁴ or]
   (ii) regulation 10(2)(d) (30 hour element) [⁴ . . .]
   (iii) [⁴ . . .],
of the Working Tax Credit Regulations;
(f) a person ceases to engage in qualifying remunerative work for at least 30 hours per week, for the purposes of—
   (i) regulation 10(1) (30 hour element), or
   (ii) regulation 11(2)(c) (second adult element), in a case where the other claimant mentioned in that provision is not so engaged for at least 30 hours per week,
of the Working Tax Credit Regulations;
(g) a couple cease to engage in qualifying remunerative work for at least 30 hours per week, for the purposes of regulation 10(2)(c) (30 hour element) of the Working Tax Credit Regulations;
(h) a person ceases to be treated as responsible for a child or qualifying young person, for the purposes of child tax credit or of the Working Tax Credit Regulations;
(i) in a case where a person has given advance notification under regulation 27(2B) that a child is expected to become a qualifying young person, the child does not become a qualifying young person for the purposes of Part 1 of the Act;
(j) a person ceases to be a qualifying young person for the purposes of Part 1 of the Act, other than by attaining the age of twenty; or
(k) a child or qualifying young person dies.]
[⁴ (l) one or both members of a couple who satisfy paragraph (a) of the third variation of the Second Condition in regulation 4(1) of the Working Tax Credit Regulations (read with regulations 4(3) to (5) and 5 to 8) and are engaged in qualifying remunerative work cease to meet the condition that one member of the couple works not less than 16 hours per week and the aggregate number of hours for which the couple are engaged in qualifying remunerative work is not less than 24 hours per week, except in a case where the person or their

Tax Credits (Claims and Notifications) Regulations 2002

partner still falls within the terms of paragraph (b), (c) or (d) of the third variation of that Condition]

(3) The time prescribed by this paragraph is the period of [³ one] months beginning on the date on which the change of circumstances occurs or [²(except in the case of paragraph (2)(j))], if later, the period of [³one] months beginning on [² the date on which the person first becomes aware of the change in circumstances].

AMENDMENTS

1. Tax Credits (Claims and Notifications and Payments by the Board) (Amendment) Regulations 2003 (SI 2003/723) reg.4 (April 6, 2003).
2. Tax Credits (Claims and Notifications) (Amendment) Regulations 2006 (SI 2006/2689) regs 4 and 5 (November 1, 2006).
3. Tax Credits (Claims and Notifications) (Amendment) Regulations 2006 (SI 2006/2689) reg.6 (April 6, 2007).
4. Tax Credits (Miscellaneous Amendments) Regulations 2012 (SI 2012/848) reg.5(3) (April 6, 2012).

DEFINITIONS

"the Act"—see reg.2.
"Working Tax Credit Regulations"—see *ibid*.

GENERAL NOTE

2.315   The amendments to this regulation in 2006 significantly harden the previously relaxed regime about reporting changes that may terminate or decrease an award of credits. First, many more changes of circumstances must now be reported. Secondly, the time limit for reporting is reduced from three months to one month. The duty to notify is imposed by s.6(3) of TCA 2002 read with this regulation. Failure to comply with s.6(3) may incur a penalty not exceeding £300: s.32(3) of the Act. Fraudulently or negligently making an incorrect statement under that section can incur a penalty of up to £3,000: s.31(1)(a) of the Act. HMRC literature draws attention to these penalties.

In broad terms (and as stated by HMRC in the literature) the changes of circumstances that must now be reported within a month are:
For both tax credits:
- Getting married or becoming a civil partner.
- Living together with someone else as husband and wife or civil partners.
- Stopping living together with a spouse or civil partner or other partner.
- Leaving the UK for more than eight weeks.
- Death of child or young person for whom claimant is responsible.
- Child leaves home to live with someone else.

For CTC:
- Child does not become or stops being qualifying young person when 16 (e.g. leaves college or training) or until 20.
- Young person starts to claim benefits or credits personally.
- Child or young person stops being entitled to support from claimant.

For WTC:
- Claimant or partner stops working for 16 hours a week.
- Claimant or partner stops working for 30 hours a week.
- Claimant or partner stops paying for childcare or bill goes down by £10 a week.
- Being on strike for over 10 days.

The duty to report under this regulation also covers any other circumstance in which entitlement to or an award of tax credits should end under s.3(4) or (7) of TCA 2002. This includes changes in a polygamous relationship, ceasing to be entitled by reason of ceasing to be a resident of the UK, or adverse changes in immigration status. It does not include changes in disablement as for instance where disability living allowance stops being paid. This may be because HMRC is informed of this automatically by DWP. There is also no general duty to report changes of income if hours of work are not affected.

COP26 (set out in Pt VII below) indicates that HMRC also has 30 days to deal with notifications of changes of circumstances. After reminding readers of the duty to report changes as set out above, COP26 adds: "We also recommend that you report any changes in income as soon as possible to reduce the chance of receiving an overpayment." It also advises readers to notify HMRC of any failure to issue a new award notice after a change of circumstances within a month of the notification, or of any error in a new notice. COP26 sets these out as "your responsibilities". If a claimant fails in these responsibilities then COP26 indicates that any overpayment will normally be collected in full. The practical effect is to extend the duty to report beyond those set out in this regulation if recovery of any overpayment is to be avoided or reduced.

CIS/1813/2007 adds an additional reason for claimants ensuring they report changes promptly. In that case Deputy Commissioner Mark decided that where a claimant for income support had acted promptly and informed HMRC of a change in circumstances relating to tax credits, she was not to be penalised in connection with her claim for income support by delays on the part of HMRC to act on the information given. In that case the claimant properly notified HMRC that she had stopped work and no longer wished to claim working tax credit. HMRC took many weeks to stop payment. The overpayments were repayable to HMRC. The Deputy Commissioner was satisfied that the overpayments were not part of the claimant's income or, if that was incorrect, then that they were voluntary payments. He commented:

"For such payments to prevent the award of income support would mean that one branch of government could foist on a claimant money that the claimant does not want and that that branch could later reclaim, and so deprive the claimant of money that she could otherwise legitimately claim from another branch of government. Given that the payments are normally made directly into the claimant's bank account by standing order, it would be impossible for a claimant to prevent such payments being received except by closing the account. I do not consider that she is required to go to such an extreme."

In *JL v HMRC (TC)* [2013] UKUT 325 (AAC) the Upper Tribunal allowed an appeal concerning a job swap between a husband and wife. They were jointly claiming tax credits. At the start of the period the husband worked 16 hours a week. At the end of one week the husband stopped working at that work, and the wife took over, working the same hours and earning the same money. HMRC decided that this required the joint claim to stop and for a new claim to be made because there had been a change of circumstances within reg.21. The Judge could identify no provision in reg.21(2) that applied to the couple as there was no change in the working pattern (one of the couple working 16 hours a week) and no change in entitlement. Consequently there was no relevant change of circumstances. The HMRC decisions, affirmed by the First-tier Tribunal, that the joint claim had ended with the change, and that no new award could be made until a new claim was made, were set aside and entitlement throughout the relevant period confirmed.

Manner in which notifications to be given

22.—(1) This regulation prescribes the manner in which a notification is to be given.

(2) A notification must be given to [¹a relevant authority at an appropriate office].

(3) A notification may be given orally or in writing.

(4) At any time after a notification has been given but before the Board have made a decision under section 15(1) or 16(1) of the Act in

consequence of the notification, the person or persons by whom the notification was given may amend the notification by giving notice orally or in writing to [¹a relevant authority at an appropriate office].

AMENDMENT

1. Tax Credits (Claims and Notifications and Payments by the Board) (Amendment) Regulations 2003 (SI 2003 No.723) reg.3(2) (April 6, 2003).

DEFINITIONS

"the Act"—see reg.2.
"appropriate office"—see *ibid*.
"the Board"—see *ibid*.
"relevant authority"—see *ibid*.
"writing"—reg.3(1).

GENERAL NOTE

2.318 Problems of proof may emerge from the combination of reg.22(2) and (3) when linked in particular to penalty cases under s.32(3). Adequate notification to an "appropriate office" of a "relevant authority" would appear, from reg.2, to include notification given at a Jobcentre Plus office. This can give rise to disputes where an individual maintains that he or she has informed the local social security office and regards that as notification also to HMRC, particularly if the local office does not keep records in the same way as HMRC best practice. It is not clear whether local housing benefit services are regarded as persons providing services to the Secretary of State under the current regime by which investigations for housing benefit also include other benefits. There is a duty on such authorities to pass on information received. See Tax Credits (Administrative Arrangements) Regulations 2002 regs 3 and 5.

In *LV v HMRC (TC)* [2010] UKUT 483 (AAC) an Upper Tribunal judge decided that a mother who had reported by telephone on February 14, 2007 to an office of the Department for Works and Pensions that her son had now been diagnosed as disabled made a sufficient notification of the disablement for the purposes of regs 22 and 26A for payment of additional child tax credit to be made for the disabled child when, on October 15, 2007 a tribunal awarded disability living allowance to the child from February 14, 2007. HMRC had argued that the notification had to be to HMRC. The Judge decided that this was not required by the definition of "appropriate office" in reg.2. The judge commented that an alternative and narrower interpretation would be unfair because it would penalise the child in connection with the claim for tax credits because of the mistake made by the Secretary of State in handling the DLA claim. However, note that the definition of "appropriate office" has since been amended with effect from April 6, 2009.

Person by whom notification may be, or is to be, given

2.319 **23.**—(1) In the case of a single claim, notification is to be given by the person by whom the claim for a tax credit was made.

(2) In the case of a joint claim, notification may be given by either member of the [¹. . .] couple by whom the claim for a tax credit was made.

AMENDMENT

1. Civil Partnership Act 2004 (Tax Credits, etc.) (Consequential Amendments) Order 2005 (SI 2005/2919) art.5(5) (December 5, 2005).

(SI 2002/2014 reg.23) (as amended)

DEFINITIONS

"couple"—see reg.2.
"joint claim"—see *ibid.*
"single claim"—see *ibid.*

Amended notifications

24.—(1) In the circumstances prescribed by paragraph (2) a notification which has been amended shall be treated as having been given as amended and, subject to regulations [²25, 26 and 26A], as having been given on the date prescribed by paragraph(3).

(2) The circumstances prescribed by this paragraph are where the person or persons by whom the notification is given amends or amend the notification in accordance with regulation 22(4).

(3) The date prescribed by this paragraph is the date on which the notification being amended was given to [¹a relevant authority at an appropriate office].

AMENDMENTS

1. Tax Credits (Claims and Notifications and Payments by the Board) (Amendment) Regulations 2003 (SI 2003 No.723) reg.3(2) (April 6, 2003).
2. Tax Credits (Miscellaneous Amendments) Regulations 2004 (SI 2004/762) reg.3(3) (April 6, 2004).

DEFINITIONS

"appropriate office"—see reg.2.
"relevant authority"—see *ibid.*

Date of notification—cases where change of circumstances which may increase the maximum rate

25.—(1) Where a notification of a change of circumstances which may increase the maximum rate at which a person or persons may be entitled to tax credit is given in the circumstances prescribed by paragraph (2), that notification is to be treated as having been given on the date specified by paragraph (3).

(2) The circumstances prescribed by this paragraph are where notification is given to [¹a relevant authority at an appropriate office] of a change of circumstances which has occurred other than in the circumstances prescribed by [² regulations] 26(2) [² and 26A(2)].

(3) The date specified by this paragraph is—
(a) the date falling [³ one month] before the notification date; or
(b) if later, the date of the change of circumstances.

AMENDMENTS

1. Tax Credits (Claims and Notifications and Payments by the Board) (Amendment) Regulations 2003 (SI 2003/723) reg.3(2) (April 6, 2003).
2. Tax Credits (Miscellaneous Amendments) Regulations 2009 (SI 2009/697) reg.17 (April 6, 2009).
3. Tax Credits (Miscellaneous Amendments) Regulations 2012 (SI 2012/848) reg.5(4)(a) (April 6, 2012).

Tax Credits (Claims and Notifications) Regulations 2002

DEFINITIONS

"appropriate office"—see reg.2.
"the notification date"—see reg.19.
"relevant authority"—see reg.2.

GENERAL NOTE

2.322 Where a change in circumstances leads to an increase in the claimant's entitlement to tax credits, the change can be backdated for up to three months before the date of notification. The requirement for notification itself in such circumstances is contained in reg.20. See also notes on reg.7 (time limit for claims).

[¹ Date of notification—disability element and severe disability element of working tax credit

2.323 **26.**—(1) In the circumstances prescribed by paragraph (2), the notification of a change in circumstances is to be treated as having been given on the date prescribed by paragraph (3).
(2) The circumstances prescribed by this paragraph are where–
 (a) a notification is given of a change of circumstances in respect of a claim to working tax credit, which results in the Board making an award of the disability element or the severe disability element of working tax credit (or both of them) in favour of a person or persons; and
 (b) the notification date is within [² one month] of the date that a claim for any of the benefits referred to in regulation 9(2) to (8) or 17(2) of the Working Tax Credit Regulations is determined in favour of those persons (or one of them).
(3) The date prescribed by this paragraph is the latest of the following:
 (a) the first date in respect of which the benefit claimed was payable;
 (b) the date falling [² one month] before the claim for the benefit was made;
 (c) the date the claim for working tax credit was made (or treated as made under [³ regulations 7 and 7A]);
 (d) (for the purposes of the disability element only), the first date that the person or persons satisfied the conditions of entitlement for the disability element.]

AMENDMENTS

1. Tax Credits (Miscellaneous Amendments) Regulations 2009 (SI 2009/697) reg.18 (April 6, 2009).
2. Tax Credits (Miscellaneous Amendments) Regulations 2012 (SI 2012/848) reg.5(4)(b) and (c) (April 6, 2012).
3. Tax Credits (Claims and Notifications) (Amendment) Regulations 2015 (SI 2015/669) reg.4 (April 6, 2015).

GENERAL NOTE

2.324 This regulation was replaced in 2009 at the same time as reg.8. See the General Note to that regulation.
The requirement of para.(3) emphasises that both the date in respect of which DLA becomes payable and the date on which a claim for DLA is made constitute changes of circumstances. A claimant therefore needs to make multiple disclo-

sures when claiming for disablement to ensure timely and accurate payment of tax credit.

[¹ Date of notification—disability element and severe disability element of child tax credit

26A.—(1) In the circumstances prescribed by paragraph (2), the notification of a change in circumstances is to be treated as having been given on the date prescribed by paragraph (3).

(2) The circumstances prescribed by this paragraph are where–

(a) a notification is given of a change of circumstances in respect of a claim to child tax credit which results in the Board making an award of the disability element or the severe disability element of child tax credit (or both of those elements) in favour of a person or persons, in respect of a child; and

(b) the notification date is within [² one month] of the date that a claim for a disability living allowance [³ or personal independence payment] in respect of the child is determined in favour of those persons (or one of them).

(3) The date prescribed by this paragraph is the latest of the following:

(a) the first date in respect of which the disability living allowance [³ or personal independence payment] was payable;

(b) the date falling [² one month] before the claim for the disability living allowance [³ or personal independence payment] was made;

(c) the date the claim for child tax credit was made (or treated as made under [⁴ regulations 7 and 7A]).]

AMENDMENTS

1. Tax Credits (Miscellaneous Amendments) Regulations 2009 (SI 2009/697) reg.19 (April 6, 2009).
2. Tax Credits (Miscellaneous Amendments) Regulations 2012 (SI 2012/848) reg.5(4)(d) and (e) (April 6, 2012).
3. Personal Independence Payment (Supplementary Provisions and Consequential Amendments) Regulations 2013 (SI 2013/388) reg.8 and Sch. para.31(3) (April 8, 2013).
4. Tax Credits (Claims and Notifications) (Amendment) Regulations 2015 (SI 2015/669) reg.4 (April 6, 2015).

GENERAL NOTE

This provision is amended to adjust it to deal with the replacement of disability living allowance with the new personal independence payment provided for in the Welfare Reform Act 2012. This is being introduced in stages. For the initial stages see the Welfare Reform Act 2012 (Commencement No.8 and Savings and Transitional Provisions) Order 2013 (SI 2013/358).

The replacement of this regulation in 2009 was part of a package with regs 8 and 26. See the General Note to reg.8.

The requirement of para.(3) emphasises that both the date in respect of which DLA becomes payable and the date on which a claim for DLA is made constitute changes of circumstances. A claimant therefore needs to make multiple disclosures when claiming for a disabled child to ensure timely and accurate payment of tax credit. In *CTC/616/2011* an Upper Tribunal Judge commented on potential problems in applying this rule, but did not go beyond the particular facts of the decision in solving them.

Advance notification

27.—(1) In [¹any] of the circumstances prescribed by paragraphs (2) [¹, [² to]] and (3) a notification of a change of circumstances may be given for a period after the date on which it is given.

(2) The circumstances prescribed by this paragraph are those prescribed by regulation 10(2) (working tax credit: person who has accepted an offer of work expected to commence within seven days), the reference to "the claim" being read as a reference to the notification.

[¹(2A) The circumstances prescribed by this paragraph are where either regulation 15(4) (agreement for the provision of future childcare) or regulation 16(1) (relevant change in circumstances) of the Working Tax Credit Regulations applies.]

[² (2B) The circumstances prescribed by this paragraph are those where a child is expected to become a qualifying young person for the purposes of Part 1 of the Act.]

(3) The circumstances prescribed by this paragraph are where a tax credit has been claimed for the tax year beginning on 6th April 2003 by making a claim before that tax year begins, and the notification relates to that tax year and is given before that date.

(4) In the circumstances prescribed by paragraph (2), an amendment of an award of a tax credit in consequence of a notification of a change of circumstances may be made subject to the condition that the requirements for entitlement to the amended amount of the tax credit are satisfied at the time prescribed by paragraph (5).

(5) The time prescribed by this paragraph is the latest date which—
   (a) is not more than seven days after the date on which the notification is given; and
   (b) falls within the period of award in which the notification is given.

[¹(5A) In the circumstances prescribed by paragraph (2A), an amendment of an award of tax credit in consequence of a notification of a change of circumstances may be made subject to the condition that the requirements for entitlement to the amended amount of the tax credit are satisfied at the time prescribed by paragraph (5B).

(5B) The time prescribed by this paragraph is the first day of the week—
   (a) in which the agreement within regulation 15(4) of the Working Tax Credit Regulations commences or the relevant change of circumstances occurs; and
   (b) which is not more than seven days after the date on which notification is given and falls within the period of award in which the notification is given.

(5C) For the purposes of paragraph (5B), "week" means a period of 7 days beginning with midnight between Saturday and Sunday.]

(6) "Period of award" shall be construed in accordance with section 5 of the Act.

AMENDMENTS

1. Tax Credits (Claims and Notifications and Payments by the Board) (Amendment) Regulations 2003 (SI 2003/723) reg.5 (April 6, 2003).
2. Tax Credits (Claims and Notifications) (Amendment) Regulations 2006 (SI 2006/2689) reg.7 (November 1, 2006).

(SI 2002/2014 reg.27) (as amended)

DEFINITIONS

"the Act"—see reg.2.
"the claim"—see para.(2).
"period of award"—see para.(6).
"tax year"—see reg.2.
"week"—see para.(5C).

Circumstances where one person may act for another in giving a notification—receivers, etc.

28.—(1) In the circumstances prescribed by paragraph (2) any receiver or other person mentioned in sub-paragraph (b) of that paragraph may act for the person mentioned in sub-paragraph (a) of that paragraph in giving a notification.

(2) The circumstances prescribed by this paragraph are where—
(a) a person is unable for the time being to give a notification; and
(b) there are any of the following—
   (i) a receiver appointed by the Court of Protection with power to proceed with a claim for a tax credit on behalf of the person;
   (ii) in Scotland, a tutor, curator or other guardian acting or appointed in terms of law who is administering the estate of the person; and
   (iii) in Northern Ireland, a controller appointed by the High Court, with power to proceed with a claim for a tax credit on behalf of the person.

GENERAL NOTE

See also reg.35 in respect of receivers, etc. acting in response to final notices under TCA 2002 s.17.

Circumstances where one person may act for another in giving a notification—other appointed persons

29.—(1) In the circumstances prescribed by paragraph (2) any person mentioned in sub-paragraph (b) of that paragraph may act for the person mentioned in sub-paragraph (a) of that paragraph in giving a notification.

(2) The circumstances prescribed by this paragraph are where—
(a) a person is unable for the time being to give a notification; and
(b) in relation to that person, there is a person appointed under—
   (i) regulation 33(1) of the Social Security (Claims and Payments) Regulations 1987;
   (ii) regulation 33(1) of the Social Security (Claims and Payments) Regulations (Northern Ireland) 1987; or
   (iii) regulation 18(3);
and the provisions of regulation 18(3) shall apply to notifications and (under regulation 36) responses to notices under section 17 of the Act, as they apply to claims.

DEFINITION

"the Act"—see reg.2.

GENERAL NOTE

2.331 See also reg.36 in respect of appointees acting in response to final notices under TCA 2002 s.17.

[¹Form in which evidence of birth or adoption to be provided

2.332 **29A.** If the Board require the person, or either or both of the persons, by whom a claim is made to provide a certificate of a child's birth or adoption, the certificate so produced must be either an original certificate or a copy authenticated in such manner as would render it admissible in proceedings in any court in the jurisdiction in which the copy was made.]

AMENDMENT

1. Tax Credits (Miscellaneous Amendments No.2) Regulations 2004 (SI 2004/1241) reg.4 (May 1, 2004).

PART IV

NOTICES TO PROVIDE INFORMATION OR EVIDENCE

Employers

2.333 **30.**—(1) For the purposes of sections 14(2)(b), 15(2)(b), 16(3)(b) and 19(2)(b) of the Act the persons specified in paragraph (2) are prescribed, and, in relation to those persons, the information or evidence specified in paragraph (4) is prescribed.

(2) The persons specified in this paragraph are—
(a) any person named by a person or either of the persons by whom a claim for a tax credit is made as his employer or the employer of either of them; and
(b) any person whom the Board have reasonable grounds for believing to be an employer of a person or either of the persons by whom such a claim is made.

(3) "Employer" has the meaning given by section 25(5) of the Act.

(4) The information or evidence specified in this paragraph is information or evidence, including any documents or certificates, which relates to—
(a) the claim for the tax credit in question;
(b) the award of the tax credit in question; or
(c) any question arising out of, or under, that claim or award.

DEFINITIONS

"the Act"—see reg.2.
"the Board"—see *ibid.*
"employer"—see para.(3).

(SI 2002/2014 reg.31) (as amended)

Persons by whom childcare is provided

31.—(1) For the purposes of sections 14(2)(b), 15(2)(b), 16(3)(b) and 19(2)(b) of the Act the persons specified in paragraph (2) are prescribed, and, in relation to those persons, the information or evidence specified in paragraph (3) is prescribed.

(2) The persons specified in this paragraph are—
(a) any person named by a person or persons by whom a claim for the childcare element of working tax credit is made as being, in relation to him or either of them, a person by whom childcare is provided; and
(b) any person whom the Board have reasonable grounds for believing to be, in relation to a person or persons by whom such a claim is made, a person by whom childcare is provided.

(3) The information or evidence specified in this paragraph is information or evidence, including any documents or certificates, which relates to—
(a) the claim for the tax credit in question;
(b) the award of the tax credit in question; or
(c) any question arising out of, or under, that claim or award.

(4) "Child care" has the meaning given by regulation 14(2) of the Working Tax Credit Regulations.

DEFINITIONS

"the Act"—see reg.2.
"the Board"—see *ibid*.
"childcare"—see para.(4).

Dates to be specified in notices under section 14(2), 15(2), 16(3), 18(10) or 19(2) of the Act

32. In a notice under section 14(2), 15(2), 16(3), 18(10) or 19(2) of the Act, the date which may be specified shall not be less than 30 days after the date of the notice.

DEFINITION

"the Act"—see reg.2.

PART V

FINAL DECISION

[¹Dates to be specified in notices under section 17 of the Act

33. In a notice under section 17 of the Act—
(a) the date which may be specified for the purposes of subsection (2) or subsection (4) shall be not later than [²31st July] following the end of the tax year to which the notice relates, or 30 days after the date on which the notice is given, if later; and
(b) the date which may be specified for the purposes of subsection (8) shall be not later than 31st January following the end of the tax year to which the notice relates, or 30 days after the date on which the notice is given, if later.]

Tax Credits (Claims and Notifications) Regulations 2002

AMENDMENTS

1. Tax Credits (Miscellaneous Amendments) Regulations 2004 (SI 2004/762) reg.3(5) (April 6, 2004).
2. Tax Credits (Miscellaneous Amendments) Regulations 2007 (SI 2007/824) reg.14(3) (April 6, 2007).

DEFINITIONS

"the Act"—see reg.2.
"tax year"—see *ibid*.

[¹Manner in which declaration or statement in response to a notice under section 17 of the Act to be made

2.337   **34.**—(1) This regulation prescribes the manner in which a declaration or statement in response to a notice under section 17 of the Act must be made.
(2) A declaration or statement must be made—
(a) in writing in a form approved by the Board for that purpose;
(b) orally to an officer of the Board; or
(c) in such other manner as the Board may accept as sufficient in the circumstances of any particular case.
(3) In a case falling within paragraph (2)(b) one of two joint claimants may act for both of them in response to a notice under section 17 if, at the time the declaration or statement is made, a joint claim could be made by both of them.]

AMENDMENT

1. Tax Credits (Miscellaneous Amendments) Regulations 2004 (SI 2004/762) reg.3(5) (April 6, 2004).

DEFINITIONS

"the Act"—see reg.2.
"the Board"—see *ibid*.
"joint claim"—see *ibid*.

Circumstances where one person may act for another in response to a notice under section 17 of the Act—receivers, etc.

2.338   **35.**—(1) In the circumstances prescribed by paragraph (2) any receiver or other person mentioned in sub-paragraph (b) of that paragraph may act for the person mentioned in sub-paragraph (a) of that paragraph in response to a notice under section 17 of the Act.
(2) The circumstances prescribed by this paragraph are where—
(a) a person is unable for the time being to act in response to a notice under section 17 of the Act; and
(b) there are any of the following—
  (i) a receiver appointed by the Court of Protection with power to proceed with a claim for a tax credit on behalf of the person;
  (ii) in Scotland, a tutor, curator or other guardian acting or appointed in terms of law who is administering the estate of the person; and
  (iii) in Northern Ireland, a controller appointed by the High Court, with power to proceed with a claim for a tax credit and proceed with the claim on behalf of the person.

(SI 2002/2014 reg.35) (as amended)

DEFINITION

"the Act"—see reg.2.

Circumstances where one person may act for another in response to a notice under section 17 of the Act

36.—(1) In the circumstances prescribed by paragraph (2) any person mentioned in sub-paragraph (b) of that paragraph may act for the person mentioned in sub-paragraph (a) of that paragraph in response to a notice under section 17 of the Act.

(2) The circumstances prescribed by this paragraph are where—
(a) a person is unable for the time being to act in response to a notice under section 17 of the Act; and
(b) in relation to that person, there is a person appointed under—
    (i) regulation 33(1) of the Social Security (Claims and Payments) Regulations 1987;
    (ii) regulation 33(1) of the Social Security (Claims and Payments) Regulations (Northern Ireland) 1987; or
    (iii) regulation 18(3).

DEFINITION

"the Act"—see reg.2.

Tax Credits [¹(Payment by the Commissioners)] Regulations 2002

(SI 2002/2173) (AS AMENDED)

The Commissioners of Inland Revenue, in exercise of the powers conferred upon them by sections 24(2), (3), (4), (7) and (8), 65(1), (2) and (7) and 67 of the Tax Credits Act 2002, hereby make the following Regulations:

1. Citation, commencement and effect.
2. Interpretation.
3. Child tax credit and childcare element—member of a couple prescribed for the purposes of s.24(2) of the Act.
4. Working tax credit (excluding any childcare element)—member of a couple prescribed for the purposes of s.24(2) of the Act.
5. Member of a couple prescribed for the purposes of s.24(2) of the Act where one of the members of the couple has died.
6. Person prescribed for the purposes of s.24(3) of the Act where an award of a tax credit is made on a claim which is made by one person on behalf of another.
7. Prescribed circumstances for the purposes of s.24(4) of the Act.
8. Time of payment by way of a credit to a bank account or other account.
9. Time of payment other than by way of a credit to a bank account or other account, etc.
10. Single payment of small sums of tax credit.
11. Postponement of payment.
12. Amounts of payments.
12A. Recovery of overpayments of tax credits from other payments of tax credit.
13. Manner of payment.

14. Entitlement to tax credit or element dependent on a bank account or other account having been notified to the Board.

AMENDMENT

1. Tax Credit (Payment by Employers, etc.) (Amendment) Regulations 2005 (SI 2005/2200) reg.7(2) (August 29, 2005).

GENERAL NOTE

2.341   The original policy intention of making employers responsible for payments of WTC (other than the child care element) has now been abandoned. Since April 2006 HMRC has assumed responsibility for making all payments of both CTC and WTC. Accordingly the Working Tax Credit (Payment by Employers) Regulations 2002 (SI 2002/2172) have now been revoked: see Tax Credit (Payment by Employers, etc.) (Amendment) Regulations 2005 (SI 2005/2200) reg.9.

Citation, commencement and eVect

2.342   **1.**—(1) These Regulations may be cited as the Tax Credits (Payments by [²the Commissioners]) Regulations 2002 and shall come into force on 6th April 2003.

(2) These Regulations have effect in relation to payments of a tax credit, or any element of a tax credit, which must be made [¹. . .] in relation to the tax year beginning with 6th April 2003 and subsequent tax years.

[¹(3) Regulations 8 to 14 have effect only in relation to such payments as must be made by the Board.]

AMENDMENTS

1. Tax Credits (Claims and Notifications and Payments by the Board) (Amendment) Regulations 2003 (SI 2003/723) reg.7 (April 6, 2003).
2. Tax Credit (Payment by Employers, etc.) (Amendment) Regulations 2005 (SI 2005/2200) reg.7(2) (August 29, 2005).

Interpretation

2.343   **2.** In these Regulations—
"the Act" means the Tax Credits Act 2002;
[¹"the Commissioners" means Commissioners for Her Majesty's Revenue and Customs (see section 1 of the Commissioners for Revenue and Customs Act 2005);]
[²"couple" has the meaning given by section 3(5A) of the Act;]
"employee" and "employer" have the meaning given by section 25(5) of the Act;
[². . .];
"period of award" shall be construed in accordance with section 5 of the Act;
"the relevant tax year" means the whole or part of the tax year for which an award of a tax credit has been made to a person or persons (referred to in section 24(4) of the Act);
"tax year" means a period beginning with 6th April in one year and ending with 5th April in the next;
[². . .].

(SI 2002/2173 reg.2) (as amended)

AMENDMENTS

1. Tax Credit (Payment by Employers, etc.) (Amendment) Regulations 2005 (SI 2005/2200) reg.7(3) (August 29, 2005).
2. Civil Partnership Act 2004 (Tax Credits, etc.) (Consequential Amendments) Order 2005 (SI 2005/2919) art.6(2) (December 5, 2005).

Child tax credit and childcare element—member of a couple prescribed for the purposes of section 24(2) of the Act

3.—(1) This regulation has effect in relation to payments of—
(a) child tax credit; and
(b) any childcare element of working tax credit.

(2) Subject to regulation 5, the member of a [4couple] prescribed by paragraph (3) is prescribed for the purposes of section 24(2) of the Act.

(3) The member of a [4couple] [2prescribed by this paragraph is—
(a) where the [4couple] are for the time being resident at the same address—
　(i) the member who is identified by both members of the [4couple] as the main carer;
　(ii) in default of a member being so identified, the member who appears to [3 the Commissioner] to be the main carer; and
(b) where—
　(i) the members of the [4couple] are for the time being resident at different addresses, or
　(ii) one member of the [4couple] is temporarily absent from the address at which they live together,
　the member who appears to [3 the Commissioner] to be the main carer.
Here "main carer" means the member of the [4 couple] who is the main carer for the children and qualifying young persons for whom either or both of the members is or are responsible.]

(4) "Children" means persons who have not attained the age of 16 or who fall within the terms of regulation 4 of the Child Tax Credit Regulations 2002.

(5) "Qualifying young persons" means persons, other than children, who—
(a) have not attained the age of nineteen; and
(b) satisfy the conditions in regulation 5(3) and (4) of the Child Tax Credit Regulations 2002.

(6) Where payments are being made to the member of a [4couple] prescribed by virtue of paragraph (3) and the members of the [4couple] jointly give notice to [3 the Commissioners] that, as a result of a change of circumstances, the payments should be made to the other member as the main carer, the other member shall [2, except where the notice appears to [3the Commissioners] to be unreasonable,] be treated as prescribed by virtue of paragraph (3).

[1(7) For the purposes of this regulation, a person is responsible for a child or qualifying young person if he is treated as being responsible for that child or qualifying young person in accordance with the rules contained in regulation 3 of the Child Tax Credit Regulations 2002.]

Tax Credits [(Payment by the Commissioners)] Regulations 2002

AMENDMENTS

1. Tax Credits (Claims and Notifications and Payments by the Board) (Amendment) Regulations 2003 (SI 2003/723) reg.8 (April 6, 2003).
2. Tax Credits (Miscellaneous Amendments No.2) Regulations 2004 (SI 2004/1241) reg.5 (May 1, 2004).
3. Tax Credit (Payment by Employers, etc.) (Amendment) Regulations 2005 (SI 2005/2200) reg.7(4) (August 29, 2005).
4. Civil Partnership Act 2004 (Tax Credits, etc.) (Consequential Amendments) Order 2005 (SI 2005/2919) art.6(3) (December 5, 2005).

DEFINITIONS

"the Act"—see reg.2.
"children"—see para.(4).
"couple"—see reg.2.
"qualifying young persons"—see para.(5).

GENERAL NOTE

2.345 Section 24(2) of the TCA 2002 permits payments of tax credits, or elements within tax credits, in the case of a joint claim to whichever member of a married or unmarried couple is prescribed. This regulation deals with the payment of child tax credit and any childcare element of working tax credit by HMRC. It provides that such tax credits are payable by HMRC to the partner identified by the couple as the main carer of the children concerned or, in default, the partner identified as such by HMRC (para.(3)). The couple can ask HMRC to change the method of payment to the other partner as the main carer (para.(6)).

Working tax credit (excluding any childcare element)—member of a couple prescribed for the purposes of section 24(2) of the Act

2.346 **4.**—(1) This regulation has effect in relation to payments of working tax credit other than payments of any childcare element.

(2) Subject to regulation 5, the member of a [²couple] prescribed by para.(3) is prescribed for the purposes of section 24(2) of the Act.

(3) The member of a [²couple] prescribed by this paragraph is—
  (a) if only one member of the [²couple] is engaged in remunerative work, that member;
  (b) if both members of the [²couple] are engaged in remunerative work—
    (i) the member elected jointly by them; or
    (ii) in default of any election, such of them as appears to the Board to be appropriate.

(4) Where payments are being made to the member of [²couple] prescribed by virtue of paragraph (3)(b) and the members of the [²couple] jointly give notice to [¹the Commissioners] that, as a result of a change of circumstances, they wish payments to be made to the other member, the other member shall be treated as prescribed by virtue of paragraph (3)(b).

(5) For the purposes of paragraph (3), a member of a [²couple] is engaged in remunerative work if—
  (a) he is engaged in qualifying remunerative work; or
  (b) he works not less than 16 hours per week and the other member of the [²couple] is engaged in qualifying remunerative work.

(SI 2002/2173 reg.4) (as amended)

(6) "Qualifying remunerative work", and being engaged in it, have the meaning given by regulation 4 of the Working Tax Credit (Entitlement and Maximum Rate) Regulations 2002.

AMENDMENTS

1. Tax Credit (Payment by Employers, etc.) (Amendment) Regulations 2005 (SI 2005/2200) reg.7(4) (August 29, 2005).
2. Civil Partnership Act 2004 (Tax Credits, etc.) (Consequential Amendments) Order 2005 (SI 2005/2919) art.6(3) (December 5, 2005).

DEFINITIONS

"the Act"—see reg.2.
"couple"—see *ibid.*
"qualifying remunerative work"—see para.(6).

GENERAL NOTE

This deals with payment of working tax credit (excluding any childcare element, on which see reg.3) by HMRC. In the case of a couple, such working tax credit should be paid by HMRC to the member of the couple who is in remunerative work for working tax credit purposes (see paras (5) and (6)) or, if they both are, to the partner nominated jointly by the couple or, in default, as HMRC sees appropriate (para.(3)). As with reg.3, the couple have the option of changing their election (para. (4)).

2.347

Member of a couple prescribed for the purposes of section 24(2) of the Act where one of the members of the couple has died

5.—(1) This regulation applies where one of the members of a [¹couple] has died.

2.348

(2) The member of the [¹couple] prescribed by paragraph (3) is prescribed for the purposes of section 24(2) of the Act.

(3) The member of the [¹couple] prescribed by this paragraph is the member who survives.

(4) For the purposes of this regulation, where persons have died in circumstances rendering it uncertain which of them survived the other—
  (a) their deaths shall be presumed to have occurred in order of seniority; and
  (b) the younger shall be treated as having survived the elder.

AMENDMENT

1. Civil Partnership Act 2004 (Tax Credits, etc.) (Consequential Amendments) Order 2005 (SI 2005/2919) art.6(3) (December 5, 2005).

DEFINITIONS

"the Act"—see reg.2.
"couple"—see *ibid.*

GENERAL NOTE

This regulation is self-explanatory. Paragraph (4) follows the general property law rule on survivorship laid down by s.184 of the Law of Property Act 1925.

2.349

Tax Credits [(Payment by the Commissioners)] Regulations 2002

Person prescribed for the purposes of section 24(3) of the Act where an award of a tax credit is made on a claim which is made by one person on behalf of another

2.350

6.—For the purposes of section 24(3) of the Act, the person prescribed is—
(a) the person by whom the claim on behalf of another was made; or
(b) if at any time [¹the Commissioners] do not consider it appropriate for payments of the tax credit to be made to that person, the person on behalf of whom the claim was made.

AMENDMENT

1. Tax Credit (Payment by Employers, etc.) (Amendment) Regulations 2005 (SI 2005/2200) reg.7(4) (August 29, 2005).

DEFINITION

"the Act"—see reg.2.

GENERAL NOTE

2.351

See also regs 17, 18, 28 and 29 of the Tax Credits (Claims and Notifications) Regulations 2002 (SI 2002/2014).

Prescribed circumstances for the purposes of section 24(4) of the Act

2.352

7.—(1) Either of the circumstances prescribed by paragraphs (2) and (3) are prescribed circumstances for the purposes of section 24(4) of the Act.
(2) The circumstances prescribed by this paragraph are where—
(a) a claim for a tax credit for the next tax year has been made or treated as made by the person or persons by the date specified for the purposes of subsection (4) of section 17 of the Act in the notice given to him or them under that section in relation to the relevant tax year; and
(b) [¹the Commissioners] have not made a decision under section 14(1) of the Act in relation to that claim.
(3) The circumstances prescribed by this paragraph are where—
(a) a claim for a tax credit for the next tax year has not been made or treated as made by the person or persons; and
(b) [¹the Commissioners] have not made a decision under section 18(1) of the Act in relation to the person and persons for the relevant tax year.

AMENDMENT

1. Tax Credit (Payment by Employers, etc.) (Amendment) Regulations 2005 (SI 2005/2200) reg.7(4) (August 29, 2005).

DEFINITIONS

"the Act"—see reg.2.
"the relevant tax year"—see *ibid.*
"tax year"—see *ibid.*

(SI 2002/2173 reg.7) (as amended)

GENERAL NOTE

Section 24(4) of the TCA 2002 enables payments of tax credits to continue to be paid in a following tax year in the absence of a claim and award in certain circumstances. This regulation thus allows payments to continue to be made, without interruption, at the start of each tax year while claims are being renewed in two types of circumstances. The first is where a renewal claim has been made or treated as made but has yet to be determined by HMRC (para.(2)). The second is a step further back, where no such renewal claim has been made but HMRC similarly has yet to make its final decision on the previous year (para.(3)).

2.353

Time of payment by way of a credit to a bank account or other account

8.—(1) [³. . .] This regulation applies where the tax credit or element is to be paid by way of a credit to a bank account or other account notified to [²the Commissioners].

2.354

(2) [⁴Subject to paragraphs (2A) and (2B),] the tax credit or element shall be paid—

(a) each week; or

(b) every four weeks,

in accordance with any election given by the person to whom payment is to be made.

[¹(2A) If a person makes elections under paragraph (2) for child tax credit and any childcare element of working tax credit to be paid at differing intervals, the elections shall have no effect and [²the Commissioners] pay the child tax credit and any childcare element together either each week or every four weeks as appears to them to be appropriate.]

[⁴ (2B) Notwithstanding the terms of any election under paragraph (2), the Commissioners may pay the tax credit or element either each week or every four weeks as appears to them to be appropriate.]

(3) [³ . . .]

(4) This regulation is subject to regulations 10 and 11.

AMENDMENTS

1. Tax Credits (Claims and Notifications and Payments by the Board) (Amendment) Regulations 2003 (SI 2003/723) reg.9 (April 6, 2003).

2. Tax Credit (Payment by Employers, etc.) (Amendment) Regulations 2005 (SI 2005/2200) reg.7(4) (August 29, 2005).

3. Tax Credit (Payment by Employers, etc.) (Amendment) Regulations 2005 (SI 2005/2200) reg.9(2) (April 1, 2006).

4. Tax Credits (Miscellaneous Amendments) (No.3) Regulations 2010 (SI 2010/2914) reg.7 (December 31, 2010).

GENERAL NOTE

Employees paid tax credits by HMRC direct to their bank accounts have the option of having such payments paid weekly or four-weekly (para.(2)). However, it is not possible to have child tax credit and the childcare element of working tax credit paid at different intervals (para.(2A)). The intervals for payment via methods other than direct to a bank account are left to the discretion of HMRC (see reg.9). However, payment via bank accounts is clearly intended to be the standard method for HMRC to pay tax credits (see regs 13 and 14).

2.355

Tax Credits [(Payment by the Commissioners)] Regulations 2002

Time of payment other than by way of a credit to a bank account or other account, etc.

2.356

9.—(1) This regulation applies where—
(a) the tax credit or element is to be paid other than by way of a credit to a bank account or other account notified to [¹the Commissioners]; or
(b) [² . . .].

(2) The tax credit or element shall be paid at such times as appear to [¹the Commissioners] to be appropriate.

AMENDMENTS

1. Tax Credit (Payment by Employers, etc.) (Amendment) Regulations 2005 (SI 2005/2200) reg.7(4) (August 29, 2005).
2. Tax Credit (Payment by Employers, etc.) (Amendment) Regulations 2005 (SI 2005/2200) reg.9(2) (April 1, 2006).

[¹Single payment of small sums of tax credit

2.357

10.—The tax credit or element may be paid by way of a single payment, and at such time, and in such manner, as appear to [²the Commissioners] to be appropriate, in any of the following cases—
(a) where [²the Commissioners] are paying only child tax credit to a person and the weekly rate at which it is payable is less than £2;
(b) where [²the Commissioners] are paying both any childcare element (but no other element) of working tax credit and child tax credit to a person and the total weekly rate at which they are payable is less than £2;
(c) where [²the Commissioners] are paying only working tax credit (apart from any childcare element) to a person and the weekly rate at which it is payable (excluding any such childcare element) is less than £2;
(d) where [²the Commissioners] are paying both working tax credit (including elements other than, or in addition to, any childcare element) and child tax credit to a person who has elected under regulation 8(2) to have them paid at the same intervals and the total weekly rate at which they are payable is less than £2;
(e) where [²the Commissioners] are paying both working tax credit (apart from any childcare element) and child tax credit to a person who has elected under regulation 8(2) to have them paid at differing intervals and—
(i) the total weekly rate at which any such childcare element and the child tax credit are payable is less than £2; or
(ii) the weekly rate at which the working tax credit is payable (excluding any such childcare element) is less than £2.]

AMENDMENTS

1. Tax Credits (Claims and Notifications and Payments by the Board) (Amendment) Regulations 2003 (SI 2003/723) reg.10 (April 6, 2003).
2. Tax Credit (Payment by Employers, etc.) (Amendment) Regulations 2005 (SI 2005/2200) reg.7(4) (August 29, 2005).

(SI 2002/2173 reg.10) (as amended)

GENERAL NOTE

The original version of this regulation, which was substituted by the version above before it came into force, was just one sentence long: so much for simplicity. The basic principle, however, remains the same: if tax credits are payable at an aggregate level of less than £2 a week, then HMRC will pay them in such manner as it deems appropriate (typically by way of a lump sum).

2.358

Postponement of payment

11.—(1) [¹The Commissioners] may postpone payment of the tax credit or element in any of the circumstances specified in [⁴ paragraphs (2), (2A), (3) and (3A)].

2.359

(2) The circumstances specified in this paragraph are where there is a pending determination of an appeal against a decision of [² [³ the First-tier Tribunal, the appeal tribunal, the] Upper Tribunal, the Northern Ireland] Social Security Commissioner or a court relating to—
(a) the case in question; or
(b) another case where it appears to [¹the Commissioners] that, if the appeal were to be determined in a particular way, an issue would arise as to whether the award in the case in question should be amended or terminated under section 16(1) of the Act.

[⁴ (2A) The circumstances specified in this paragraph are where—
(a) a notice in writing has been given by the Commissioners to a person to notify a bank account or other account to which the Commissioners may make payment of a tax credit or element to which the person is entitled;
(b) a period of [⁵ four] weeks has elapsed since the day on which the Commissioners gave their notice; and
(c) no bank account or other account has been notified to the Commissioners pursuant to their notice.]

(3) The circumstances specified in this paragraph are where confirmation is pending of—
(a) the details of a bank account or other account by way of a credit to which payment is to be made; or
(b) the address of the person to whom payment is to be made, where it appears to [¹the Commissioners] that such details or address as were previously notified to them are incorrect.

[⁴ (3A) The circumstances specified in this paragraph are where—
(a) a notice under section 16(3) of the Tax Credits Act 2002 has been issued to the person, or either or both of the persons, to whom the tax credit or element was awarded, and
(b) such person or persons have not provided the information or evidence requested in that notice by the date specified in such notice.]

(4) For the purposes of paragraph (2), the circumstances where a determination of an appeal is pending include circumstances where a decision of [² [³ the First-tier Tribunal, the appeal tribunal, the] Upper Tribunal, the Northern Ireland] Social Security Commissioner or a court has been made and [¹the Commissioners]—
(a) are awaiting receipt of the decision;
(b) in the case of a decision by [² the [³ First-tier Tribunal or the appeal tribunal]], are considering whether to apply for a statement of

reasons or have applied for, and are awaiting receipt of, a statement of reasons; or
  (c) have received the decision or statement of reasons and are considering—
    (i) whether to apply for permission to appeal; or
    (ii) where permission is not needed or has been given, whether to appeal.

(5) "[³ Appeal tribunal]" has the meaning given by section 63(10) of the Act.

(6) "[² Northern Ireland Social] Security Commissioner" has the meaning given by section 63(13) of the Act.

[⁴ (7) The postponement of payment pursuant to the circumstances specified in paragraph (2A) shall cease at the earlier of the time when—
  (a) a bank account or other account is notified to the Commissioners; or
  (b) the entitlement to the tax credit or element ceases in accordance with regulation 14.]

AMENDMENTS

1. Tax Credit (Payment by Employers, etc.) (Amendment) Regulations 2005 (SI 2005/2200) reg.7(4) (August 29, 2005).
2. Tribunals, Courts and Enforcement Act 2007 (Transitional and Consequential Provisions) Order 2008 (SI 2008/2683) art.6 and Sch.1 para.205 (November 3, 2008).
3. Transfer of Tribunal Functions and Revenue and Customs Appeals Order 2009 (SI 2009/56) art.3(2) Sch.2 para.78 (April 1, 2009).
4. Tax Credits (Miscellaneous Amendments) Regulations 2010 (SI 2010/751) reg.10(1)–(5) (April 6, 2010).
5. Tax Credits (Miscellaneous Amendments) Regulations 2012 (SI 2012/848) reg.6(2) (April 6, 2012).

DEFINITIONS

"the Act"—see reg.2.
"Appeal tribunal"—see para.(5).
"Social Security Commissioner"—see para.(6).

GENERAL NOTE

2.360   This regulation sets out the two types of circumstances in which a payment of tax credits by HMRC may be postponed. The first is the straightforward situation where HMRC believes that either the bank details or recipient's address previously notified to them is incorrect (para.(3)). The second is where there is an appeal pending in relation either to the particular case or to another case in which the outcome might lead to the amendment or termination of the award in the instant case (para.(2)). This is, therefore, the tax credits equivalent of the anti-test case rule. (But note, however, that it is limited to the postponement of payment, and does not make provision for limiting the effect of test cases in terms of backdating entitlement to tax credits.) The "pending determination" must be one against a decision of an appeal tribunal, Social Security Commissioner or court (para.(2)). The notion of "pending" is defined by para.(4). There are no explicit time limits stated within this regulation on HMRC's consideration of whether or not to lodge an appeal, but there are, of course, fairly tight time constraints on the exercise of such a right in the first place.

Amounts of payments

12.—(1) The tax credit or element shall be paid in accordance with the most recent decision by [¹the Commissioners] under section 14(1), 15(1) or 16(1) of the Act.

(2) Where the tax credit or element is to be paid other than by way of a single payment, it shall be paid so far as possible in such amounts as will result in the person to whom payment is to be made receiving regular payments of similar amounts over the entire period of award.

(3) Where an award of tax credit is amended, the total amount paid prior to the award being amended [²may] be taken into account by [¹the Commissioners] in determining the amount of any further payments for the remainder of the period of award.

[³ (4) Where payments under section 24(4) of the Act are to be made the Commissioners may take any or both of the following factors into account in determining the amount of those payments—
   (a) the rate at which the person or persons were entitled to the tax credit for the relevant tax year;
   (b) the estimated amount of income the person or persons referred to above may receive in the current tax year.]

AMENDMENTS

1. Tax Credit (Payment by Employers, etc.) (Amendment) Regulations 2005 (SI 2005/2200) reg.7(4) (August 29, 2005).
2. Tax Credits (Miscellaneous Amendments) Regulations 2007 (SI 2007/824) reg.15 (April 6, 2007).
3. Tax Credits (Miscellaneous Amendments) Regulations 2008 (SI 2008/604) reg.5(2) (April 6, 2008).

DEFINITION

"the Act"—see reg.2.

GENERAL NOTE

This regulation provides for the amount of tax credits payable to be determined by HMRC's most recent relevant decision (para.(1)). Such payments should, so far as possible, be apportioned equally over regular payment intervals (para.(2)). The original formulation of para.(2) was mandatory in requiring HMRC to take prior payments into account in arriving at the appropriate amount due for payment following an amended award. Paragraph (2) now gives HMRC more flexibility in deciding the amount of any further tax credits where an award of tax credits is amended. Since April 2007, HMRC have been able to exercise a discretion in such cases. So, where claimants report a fall in income during the year, their tax credit payments will be adjusted for the rest of the year but will not include a one-off payment for the earlier part of the year. Their final award will be determined at the end of the year when their actual income is known, and any underpayment will be made good at that stage. Amounts of tax credits for subsequent years can be based on a preceding year's tax credit entitlement (para.(4); see further reg.7).

[¹Recovery of overpayments of tax credit from other payments of tax credit

12A.—(1) This regulation applies where notice is given to a person or persons under subsection (4) of section 29 of the Act (deduction of overpayments from payments of tax credit).

Tax Credits [(Payment by the Commissioners)] Regulations 2002

(2) The maximum rate at which an overpayment may be recovered from payments of tax credit is—
(a) where the only amount of tax credit to which the person is, or, in the case of a joint claim, the persons are, entitled, is the family element of child tax credit, 100% of that tax credit;
(b) where the total amount of tax credit to which the person is, or, in the case of a joint claim, the persons are, entitled is not subject to reduction—
(i) by virtue of section 7(2) of the Act; or
(ii) because their income for the relevant year does not exceed the relevant income threshold prescribed in his or their case in regulation 3 of the Tax Credits (Income Thresholds and Determination of Rates) Regulations 2002;
10% of that tax credit; and
(c) in any other case, 25% of the tax credit to which the person is, or in the case of a joint claim, the persons are, entitled.
(3) In paragraph (2) a reference to the amount to which a person is, or persons are, entitled is a reference to the amount to which they would be entitled but for the operation of that paragraph.]

AMENDMENT

1. Tax Credits (Miscellaneous Amendments) Regulations 2004 (SI 2004/762) reg.18 (April 6, 2004).

DEFINITION

"the Act"—see reg.2.

Manner of payment

2.364   **13.**—(1) Subject to paragraph (2), the tax credit or element shall be paid by way of a credit to a bank account or other account notified to [²the Commissioners] by the person to whom payment is to be made.
(2) Where [¹it does not appear to [²the Commissioners] to be appropriate] for the tax credit or element to be paid by way of a credit to a bank account or other account notified to [²the Commissioners] by the person to whom payment is to be made, the tax credit or element may be paid in such manner as appears to [²the Commissioners] to be appropriate.
(3) Subject to regulation 14, if no bank account or other account has been notified to [²the Commissioners], the tax credit or element shall be paid in such manner as appears to [²the Commissioners] to be appropriate.

AMENDMENTS

1. Tax Credits (Claims and Notifications and Payments by the Board) (Amendment) Regulations 2003 (SI 2003/723) reg.11 (April 6, 2003).
2. Tax Credit (Payment by Employers, etc.) (Amendment) Regulations 2005 (SI 2005/2200) reg.7(4) (August 29, 2005).

GENERAL NOTE

2.365   This regulation establishes the presumption in favour of payment by HMRC of tax credits to be direct to recipients' bank accounts.

(SI 2002/2173 reg.14) (as amended)

Entitlement to tax credit or element dependent on a bank account or other account having been notified to the Board

14.—[² (1) Subject to paragraph (3), where—
  (a) payment of a tax credit or element is postponed pursuant to the circumstances specified in regulation 11(2A), and
  (b) before the relevant time determined in accordance with this regulation, no bank account or other account is notified to the Commissioners by the person to whom a tax credit or element would have been paid if payment of it had not been postponed, that person shall cease to be entitled to the tax credit or element for the remainder of the period of the award beginning on the day from which the Commissioners decide to postpone payment.]

(2) [² . . .] an element by virtue of paragraph (1) subsequently notifies to [¹the Commissioners] a bank account or other account, paragraph (1)—
  (a) shall not have effect for the period of three months prior to the date on which [¹the Commissioners] receive the notification; and
  (b) shall cease to have effect for the remainder of the period of award.

(3) Where there are exceptional circumstances which are expected to result in a person not being able to obtain a bank account or other account throughout the period of award, paragraph (1) shall not have effect in relation to that person's entitlement to a tax credit or element for the period of award.

(4) [² . . .]

[² (4A) Subject to paragraphs (4C) and (4E), the relevant time is the earlier of—
  (a) three months after the time when the Commissioners decide to postpone payment of a tax credit or element; or
  (b) immediately after the end of the relevant tax year.

(4B) This paragraph applies where, before the time determined in accordance with paragraph (4A), the person entitled to payment of the tax credit or element—
  (a) requests from the Commissioners authority to open an account for which such authority is required; and
  (b) provides sufficient information from which the Commissioners can give that authority.

(4C) Subject to paragraph (4E), where paragraph (4B) applies, the relevant time is the later of—
  (a) the time determined in accordance with paragraph (4A); and
  (b) the expiry of the period of 3 weeks from the day on which the Commissioners give their authority following a request described in paragraph (4B)(a).

(4D) This paragraph applies where a person to whom a notice described in regulation 11(2A)(a) has been given has a reasonable excuse—
  (a) for not being able to take all necessary steps to obtain a bank account or other account before a time determined in accordance with paragraphs (4A) or (4C), or
  (b) for not being able to notify to the Commissioners the bank account or other account before a time determined in accordance with paragraphs (4A) or (4C).

(4E) Where paragraph (4D) applies, the relevant time is the later of—
  (a) the time determined in accordance with paragraph (4A);

(b) where paragraph (4B) applies, the time determined in accordance with paragraph (4C); and
(c) the date by which the account can reasonably be expected to be notified to the Commissioners.]

(5) "Writing" includes writing produced by electronic communications that are approved by [¹the Commissioners].

AMENDMENTS

1. Tax Credit (Payment by Employers, etc.) (Amendment) Regulations 2005 (SI 2005/2200) reg.7(4) (August 29, 2005).
2. Tax Credits (Miscellaneous Amendments) Regulations 2010 (SI 2010/751) reg.10(1) and (6)–(8) (April 6, 2010).

DEFINITIONS

"the relevant period"—see para.(4).
"writing"—see para.(5).

GENERAL NOTE

2.367 This regulation further demonstrates that entitlement to a tax credit is to be dependent on a bank account or other account having been notified to HMRC.

Tax Credits (Administrative Arrangements) Regulations 2002

(SI 2002/3036)

The Commissioners of Inland Revenue, in exercise of the powers conferred upon them by ss.58 and 65(1), (2), (7) and (9) of the Tax Credits Act 2002, hereby make the following Regulations:

ARRANGEMENT OF ARTICLES

2.368 1. Citation and commencement.
2. Interpretation.
3. Provision of information or evidence to relevant authorities.
4. Giving of information or advice by relevant authorities.
5. Recording, verification and holding, and forwarding, of claims, etc. received by relevant authorities.

GENERAL NOTE

2.369 Section 58 of the TCA 2002 provides for regulations to make provision as to the administrative arrangements to apply between a relevant authority (i.e. the Secretary of State, the equivalent Northern Ireland Department or a person providing services to either of these authorities: TCA 2002 s.58(3)) and HMRC, who have the care and management of tax credits (see TCA 2002 s.2). Section 58 applies where regulations under TCA 2002 ss.4 or 6 permit or require a claim or notification relating to a tax credit to be made or given to such a relevant authority. These Regulations have therefore been made under s.58 in order to provide for administrative arrangements in relation to claims and notifications made or given to a relevant authority in accordance with the Tax Credits

(Claims and Notifications) Regulations 2002 (SI 2002/2014). Regulation 5 of those Regulations requires claims to be made to "an appropriate office", which means an office of the Board, the DWP or its Northern Ireland equivalent (reg.2).

Citation and commencement

1. These Regulations may be cited as the Tax Credits (Administrative Arrangements) Regulations 2002 and shall come into force on 1st January 2003.

Interpretation

2. In these Regulations—
"the Board" means the Commissioners of Inland Revenue;
"the principal Regulations" means the Tax Credits (Claims and Notifications) Regulations 2002;
"relevant authority" means—
   (a) the Secretary of State;
   (b) the Department for Social Development in Northern Ireland; or
   (c) a person providing services to the Secretary of State or that Department.

Provision of information or evidence to relevant authorities

3.—(1) Information or evidence relating to tax credits which is held—
(a) by the Board; or
(b) by a person providing services to the Board, in connection with the provision of those services,
may be provided to a relevant authority for the purposes of, or for any purposes connected with, the exercise of that relevant authority's functions under the principal Regulations.

(2) Information or evidence relating to tax credits may be provided to a relevant authority by persons other than the Board (whether or not persons by whom claims or notifications relating to tax credits are or have been made or given).

DEFINITIONS

"the Board" —see reg.2.
"the principal Regulations"—see *ibid.*
"relevant authority"—see *ibid.*

Giving of information or advice by relevant authorities

4. A relevant authority to which a claim or notification is or has been made or given by a person in accordance with the principal Regulations may give information or advice relating to tax credits to that person.

DEFINITIONS

"the principal Regulations"—see reg.2.
"relevant authority"—see *ibid.*

Tax Credits (Administrative Arrangements) Regulations 2002

Recording, verification and holding, and forwarding, of claims etc. received by relevant authorities

5.—(1) A relevant authority may record and hold claims and notifications received by virtue of the principal Regulations and information or evidence received by virtue of regulation 3(2).

(2) Subject to paragraphs (3) and (4), a relevant authority must forward to the Board or a person providing services to the Board such a claim or notification, or such information or evidence, as soon as reasonably practicable after being satisfied that it is complete.

(3) Before forwarding a claim in accordance with paragraph (2), a relevant authority must verify—
  (a) that any national insurance number provided in respect of the person by whom the claim is made exists and has been allocated to that person;
  (b) that the matters verified in accordance with sub-paragraph (a) accord with—
    (i) its own records; or
    (ii) in the case of a person providing services to the Secretary of State or the Department for Social Development in Northern Ireland, records held by the Secretary of State or that Department; and
  (c) whether the details of any relevant claim for benefit that have been provided are consistent with those held by it.

(4) If a relevant authority cannot locate any national insurance number in respect of a person by whom such a claim is made, it must forward to the Board or a person providing services to the Board the claim (notwithstanding that it is not complete).

(5) "National insurance number" means the national insurance number allocated within the meaning of—
  (a) regulation 9 of the Social Security (Crediting and Treatment of Contributions, and National Insurance Numbers) Regulations 2001; or
  (b) regulation 9 of the Social Security (Crediting and Treatment of Contributions, and National Insurance Numbers) Regulations (Northern Ireland) 2001.

(6) "Claim for benefit" means a claim for—
  (a) a benefit in relation to which—
    (i) the Secretary of State has functions under the Social Security Contributions and Benefits Act 1992; or
    (ii) the Department for Social Development in Northern Ireland has functions under the Social Security Contributions and Benefits (Northern Ireland) Act 1992: [1. . .]
  (b) a jobseeker's allowance under—
    (i) the Jobseekers Act 1995; or
    (ii) the Jobseekers (Northern Ireland) Order 1995 [1. . .]; [1; or
  (c) universal credit under Part 1 of the Welfare Reform Act 2012]

AMENDMENT

1. Universal Credit (Consequential, Supplementary, Incidental and Miscellaneous Provisions) Regulations 2013 (SI 2013/630) reg.80 (April 29, 2013).

(SI 2002/3036 reg.5)

DEFINITIONS

"the Board"—see reg.2.
"the principal Regulations"—see *ibid.*
"relevant authority"—see *ibid.*

The Tax Credits (Appeals) (No.2) Regulations 2002

(SI 2002/3196) (AS AMENDED)

Made	*18th December 2002*
Coming into force	*1st January 2003*

ARRANGEMENT OF REGULATIONS

PART I

General

1. Citation, commencement, duration and interpretation
2. Service of notices or documents

2.375

PART II

General Appeal Matters

3. Other persons with a right of appeal or a right to make an application for a direction
4. Time within which an appeal is to be brought
5. Late appeals
6. (repealed)
7. (repealed)
8. Death of a party to an appeal or an application for a direction

PART III

Appeal Tribunals for Tax Credits

9–27. repealed

2.376

Whereas a draft of this instrument was laid before Parliament in accordance with section 80(1) of the Social Security Act 1998 and approved by a resolution of each House of Parliament.

Now, therefore, the Secretary of State for Work and Pensions, in exercise of the powers conferred upon him by sections 7(6), 12(2) and (7), 14(10) and (11), 16(1), 28(1), 39(1), 79(1) and (3) to (7) and 84 of, and paragraphs 11 and 12 of Schedule 1 and Schedule 5 to the Social Security Act 1998 and all other powers enabling him in that behalf, after consultation with the Council on Tribunals in accordance with section 8 of the Tribunals and Inquiries Act 1992, hereby makes the following Regulations:

The Tax Credits (Appeals) (No.2) Regulations 2002

Part I

General

Citation, commencement, duration and interpretation

1.—(1) These Regulations may be cited as the Tax Credits (Appeals) (No.2) Regulations 2002 and shall come into force on 1st January 2003.

(2) These Regulations shall cease to have effect on such day as is appointed by order made under section 63(1) of the Tax Credits Act 2002 (tax credits appeals etc.: temporary modifications).

(3) In these Regulations, unless the context otherwise requires—
"the Act" means the Social Security Act 1998;
"the 2002 Act" means the Tax Credits Act 2002;
"the Appeals Regulations" means the Tax Credits (Appeals) Regulations 2002;
"the Decisions and Appeals Regulations" means the Social Security and Child Support (Decisions and Appeals) Regulations 1999;
"the Working Tax Credit Regulations" means the Working Tax Credit (Entitlement and Maximum Rate) Regulations 2002;
"appeal" means an appeal under section 38 of the 2002 Act;
"an application for a direction" means an application for a direction to close down an enquiry made under section 19(9) of the 2002 Act;
[² . . .]
[² . . .]
[¹"couple" means—
  (a) a man and woman who are married to each other and are members of the same household;
  (b) a man and woman who are not married to each other but are living together as husband and wife;
  (c) two people of the same sex who are civil partners of each other and are members of the same household; or
  (d) two people of the same sex who are not civil partners of each other but are living together as if they were civil partners,
and for the purposes of paragraph (d), two people of the same sex are to be regarded as living together as if they were civil partners if, but only if, they would be regarded as living together as husband and wife were they instead two people of the opposite sex;]
"court" means the High Court, the Court of Appeal, the Court of Session, the High Court or Court of Appeal in Northern Ireland, the House of Lords or the Court of Justice of the European Community;
[² . . .]
[² . . .]
[² . . .]
"joint claim" means a claim made under section 3(3)(a) of the 2002 Act and any reference in these Regulations to "joint claimant" shall be construed accordingly;
[² . . .]
[² . . .]
[² . . .]
[² . . .]
[² . . .]

"partner" means, [¹. . .], the other member of [¹a] couple;
"party to the proceedings" means the Board and any other person—
  (a) who is an appellant in an appeal brought against a decision or determination set out in section 38 of the 2002 Act;
  (b) who is an applicant for a direction to close down an enquiry under section 19(9) of the 2002 Act;
  (c) who is a defendant (or defender) in penalty proceedings brought under paragraph 3 of Schedule 2 to the 2002 Act;
  (d) who is a person with a right of appeal or a right to make an application for a direction under regulation 3;
[² . . .]
[² . . .]
[² . . .]
"single claim" means a claim made under section 3(3)(b) of the 2002 Act;
"tax credit" means child tax credit or working tax credit, construing those terms in accordance with section 1(1) and (2) of the 2002 Act, and any reference in these Regulations to "child tax credit" or "working tax credit" shall be construed accordingly.

AMENDMENTS

1. Civil Partnership (Pensions, Social Security and Child Support) (Consequential, etc. Provisions) Order 2005 (SI 2005/2877) para.36(2) of Sch.3 (December 5, 2005).
2. Tribunals, Courts and Enforcement Act 2007 (Transitional and Consequential Provisions) Order 2008 (SI 2008/2683) art.6 and Sch.1 para.205 (November 3, 2008).

GENERAL NOTE

"party to the proceedings"
In *CTC/2612/2005*, the Commissioner pointed out that where only one member of a couple who should have been joint claimants had appealed, the other was not a party to the proceedings, which was unfair as she was potentially liable to repay an overpayment. The real problem was that it was unclear whether the Inland Revenue had issued a decision addressed to both of them. If they had, it is suggested that an appeal by one of member of the couple could have been treated as an appeal by both of them unless it was clear that only one of them wished to appeal (see *R(A) 2/06*).

2.378

It was pointed out in *PD v HMRC and CD (TC)* [2010] UKUT 159 (AAC) that *CTC/2612/2005* was decided under former procedures now replaced by the First-tier Tribunal (Social Entitlement Chamber) Rules 2008. Under those rules where one of a joint claim couple appeals a decision, the other is a respondent. The second claimant is therefore a party to the proceedings and should be notified of the proceedings and any proposal to deal with the appeal on the papers. This also applies to the decision in *CTC/2612/2005*. See now Tribunal Procedure (First-tier Tribunal) (Social Entitlement Chamber) Rules 2008 r.1 (definitions), 5 (case management powers), and 9 (substitution and addition of parties) in Vol.III of this work.

A more complex problem arose in *CTC/4390/2004*, where two separated parents each claimed child tax credit. It was pointed out that the legislation made no provision for them to be parties to a single appeal even though a decision could be binding only on the parties to it (see *CTC/2090/2004*). However, by the time the case reached the Commissioner, there were appeals by both parents (because the award to one parent had been terminated when the other parent won his appeal before the tribunal) and, with the agreement of the parties, the Commissioner, when allowing an appeal against the tribunal's decision, directed that the appeal be reheard at the same time as the other parent's appeal against the termination of her award.

In *CTC/1586/2007* an Upper Tribunal judge dealt with problems that can arise when a tribunal attempts to deal with split entitlement to child tax credits at a single hearing. The father was awarded child tax credit for one of his three children, the mother being awarded child tax credit for the other two. The father appealed against the award to the mother (that is, against the refusal to award him child tax credit for the other children), and the mother also appealed. But while the mother elected for an oral hearing, the father asked for a decision on the papers. At the hearing the tribunal took into account the mother's evidence to take away the award to the father. The Upper Tribunal Judge granted permission to appeal to the father on the grounds that this was unfair, as the father had not been put on notice that this might happen. At a hearing of the appeal, the parents agreed that the father should again be awarded child tax credit for the oldest child. This resulted in awards being made to both the mother and the father for the same child for a common period. Judge Lloyd-Davies offered the following more general guidance:

". . . where competing claims for tax credit in respect of a child or children are made by each parent, and the dispute is not otherwise resolved but proceeds to an appeal by both parents, then directions should be given which indicate that both appeals will be heard together, that an oral hearing will be held unless both parents agree to a paper hearing, and that, if an oral hearing is held, non-attendance by one parent may result in the evidence of the attending parent being accepted as evidence in the non-attending parent's appeal . . . HMRC . . . took issue with the fact that the mother in the present case had been joined as a party to the father's appeal and called a respondent, thereby possibly indicating that the mother would be bound by the result of the father's appeal when her award could not be affected by the outcome of the father's appeal: I agree and accept that the better course would have been to have invited the mother to give evidence, rather than become a party."

Service of notices or documents

2.379

2.—Where, by any provision of these Regulations—
(a) any notice or other document is required to be given or sent [¹ . . .] to the Board, that notice or document shall be treated as having been so given or sent on the day that it is received [¹ . . .] by the Board, and
(b) any notice or other document is required to be given or sent to any person other than [¹ . . .] the Board, that notice or document shall, if sent to that person's last known address, be treated as having been given or sent on the day that it was posted.

AMENDMENT

1. Tribunals, Courts and Enforcement Act 2007 (Transitional and Consequential Provisions) Order 2008 (SI 2008/2683) art.6 and Sch.1 para.206 (November 3, 2008).

DEFINITIONS

"the Board"—see s.39(1) of the Social Security Act 1998 as modified by reg.12 of the Tax Credits (Appeals) Regulations 2002.
"clerk to the appeal tribunal"—see reg.1(3).

GENERAL NOTE

2.380

A fax is received for the purposes of reg.2(a) when it is successfully transmitted to, and received by, a fax machine, irrespective of when it is actually collected from the fax machine (*R(DLA) 3/05*). Furthermore, the faxed request for a statement of reasons in that case was received by the clerk to the appeal tribunal when received at the tribunal venue, even though the clerk did not visit that venue until some days later. The Commissioner said that it would have been different if the venue had been a casual venue, such as local authority premises. Here, it was a dedicated venue and the fax number had been given to representatives precisely to enable them to communicate with the clerk. There was nothing in any document issued with the decision notice to indicate that the request for a statement of reasons had to be addressed to a different place.

The "last known address" to which documents must be sent for para.(b) to apply need not be the person's last known *residence* because the concepts are different. Moreover, the sender must consider the address to be reliable and, if he does not, should take reasonable steps to see whether a more reliable one exists (*CCS/2288/2005*). This approach exists to aid the innocent claimant and not the one who has failed to take reasonable steps to keep HMRC or the clerk to the tribunal aware of his whereabouts. Generally they are entitled to rely on a claimant to inform them of any move.

Deemed receipt of a document cannot cure a breach of the rules of natural justice so that, if a tribunal does not receive medical evidence submitted by the claimant in support of an application for a postponement, the decision of the tribunal can be set aside as being erroneous in point of law (*CG/2973/2004*). Decisions can also be set aside under reg.25 where documents go astray. That does not preclude an appeal, although an application for setting aside under reg.25 remains the more appropriate procedure (*CIB/303/1999*, declining to follow *R(SB) 55/83* but agreeing with *R(SB) 19/83*).

A provision similar to reg.2(b) relating to immigration appeals was held to be invalid in *R. (On the application of Saleem) v Secretary of State for the Home Department* [2001] 1 W.L.R. 443, but there are sufficient remedies in these Regulations for the injustice that reg.2(b) might otherwise cause and Commissioners have distinguished *Saleem* and held the equivalent provision relating to social security and child support appeals to be valid (*CCS/6302/1999* and *CIB/303/1999*).

PART II

GENERAL APPEAL MATTERS

Other persons with a right of appeal or a right to make an application for a direction

3.—For the purposes of section 12(2) of the Act (as applied and modified by the Appeals Regulations), where—

(a) a person has made a claim for a tax credit but is unable for the time being to make an appeal against a decision in respect of that tax credit; or

(b) a person is the person in respect of whom an enquiry has been initiated under section 19(1) of the 2002 Act, but is unable for the time being to make an application for a direction,

the following other persons have a right of appeal to [² the First-tier Tribunal] or a right to make an application for a direction—

(i) a receiver appointed by the Court of Protection with power to make a claim for a tax credit on behalf of the person;

(ii) in Scotland, a [¹judicial factor, or guardian acting or appointed under the Adults with incapacity (Scotland) Act 2000 who has

The Tax Credits (Appeals) (No.2) Regulations 2002

power to claim, or as the case may be, receive a tax credit on his behalf] who is administering the estate of the person;
(iii) a person appointed under regulation 33(1) of the Social Security (Claims and Payments) Regulations 1987 (persons unable to act);
(iv) where there is no person mentioned in sub-paragraph (iii) in relation to the person who is unable to act, a person who has applied in writing to the Board to be appointed to act on behalf of the person who is unable to act and, if a natural person, is aged 18 years or more and who has been so appointed by the Board for the purposes of this subparagraph.

AMENDMENTS

1. Social Security, Child Support and Tax Credits (Miscellaneous Amendments) Regulations 2005 (SI 2005/337) reg.4(2) (March 18, 2005).
2. Tribunals, Courts and Enforcement Act 2007 (Transitional and Consequential Provisions) Order 2008 (SI 2008/2683) art.6 and Sch.1 para.207 (November 3, 2008).

DEFINITIONS

"the Act"—see reg.1(3).
"the Appeals Regulations"—*ibid.*
"appeal"—*ibid.*
"an application for a direction"—*ibid.*
"the Board"—see s.39(1) of the Social Security Act 1998 as modified by reg.12 of the Tax Credits (Appeals) Regulations 2002.
"tax credit"—reg.1(3).

GENERAL NOTE

2.382 Section 12(2) of the Social Security Act 1998, mentioned in the opening words of this regulation, has actually been "modified" out of existence because it and subs. (1) have been replaced by a single subsection. This regulation is made under the substituted s.12(1)(d).

It is arguable that this regulation is at least partly unnecessary as those mentioned in it could submit appeals on the basis of their general authority to act on behalf of the real appellant.

Time within which an appeal is to be brought

2.383 **4.**—(1) Where a dispute arises as to whether an appeal was brought within the time limit specified in section 39(1) of the 2002 Act, the dispute shall be referred to, and be determined by, [¹ the First-tier Tribunal].

(2) The time limit specified in section 39(1) of the 2002 Act may be extended in accordance with regulation 5.

AMENDMENT

1. Tribunals, Courts and Enforcement Act 2007 (Transitional and Consequential Provisions) Order 2008 (SI 2008/2683) art.6 and Sch.1 para.208 (November 3, 2008).

(SI 2002/3196 reg.4) (as amended)

DEFINITIONS

"the 2002 Act"—see reg.1(3).
"appeal"—*ibid.*
"legally qualified panel member"—see reg.1(3).

GENERAL NOTE

The time limit specified in s.39(1) of the Tax Credits Act 2002 is the 30 days usual in tax cases rather than the month usual in social security cases. However, note that ss.39(1) and (2) have now been repealed in England, Wales and Scotland by SI 2014/886 (see General Note to s.39) with the result that appeal time limits are governed by tribunal procedural rules.

2.384

Late appeals

5.—(1) *[¹ The Board may treat a late appeal as made in time]* where the conditions specified in paragraphs *[¹(4)]* to (8) are satisfied, but no appeal shall in any event be brought more than one year after the expiration of the last day for appealing under section 39(1) of the 2002 Act.
[¹ . . .]
[¹ (4) An appeal may be treated as made in time if the Board is satisfied that it is in the interests of justice.]
(5) For the purposes of paragraph (4) it is not in the interests of justice to *[¹ treat the appeal as made in time unless the Board are]* satisfied that—
 (a) the special circumstances specified in paragraph (6) are relevant *[¹ . . .]*; or
 (b) some other special circumstances exist which are wholly exceptional and relevant *[¹ . . .]*,
and as a result of those special circumstances, it was not practicable for the appeal to be made within the time limit specified in section 39(1) of the 2002 Act.
(6) For the purposes of paragraph (5)(a), the special circumstances are that—
 (a) the *[¹ appellant]* or a partner or dependant of the *[¹ appellant]* has died or suffered serious illness;
 (b) the *[¹ appellant]* is not resident in the United Kingdom; or
 (c) normal postal services were disrupted.
(7) In determining whether it is in the interests of justice to *[¹ treat the appeal as made in time]*, regard shall be had to the principle that the greater the amount of time that has elapsed between the expiration of the time within which the appeal is to be brought under section 39(1) of the 2002 Act and the *[¹ submission of the notice of appeal]*, the more compelling should be the special circumstances.*]*
(8) In determining whether it is in the interests of justice to *[¹ treat the appeal as made in time]*, no account shall be taken of the following—
 (a) that the applicant or any person acting for him was unaware of or misunderstood the law applicable to his case (including ignorance or misunderstanding of the time limit imposed by section 39(1) of the 2002 Act); or
 (b) that *[¹ the Upper Tribunal]* or a court has taken a different view of the law from that previously understood and applied.
[¹ . . .]

2.385

AMENDMENT

1. Tribunals, Courts and Enforcement Act 2007 (Transitional and Consequential Provisions) Order 2008 (SI 2008/2683) art.6 and Sch.1 para.209 (November 3, 2008).

DEFINITIONS

"the 2002 Act"—see reg.1(3).
"appeal"—*ibid.*
"the Board"—see s.39(1) of the Social Security Act 1998 as modified by reg.12 of the Tax Credits (Appeals) Regulations 2002.
"court"—reg.1(3).
"legally qualified panel member"—*ibid.*
"panel member"—*ibid.*
"partner"—*ibid.*
"President"—*ibid.*

GENERAL NOTE

2.386   In an important and thorough decision, issued as *JI v HMRC* [2013] UKUT 199 (AAC), Upper Tribunal Judge Rowland decides that this regulation is invalid as there is no authority in primary legislation for it. In his view, after a careful analysis of the secondary legislation since 2002 including the provisions in these Regulations, he accepts a concession by HMRC that there is no power in legislation to allow any extension of the absolute time limit in s.39(1) either under these provisions or under the Tribunal Procedure Rules applying to the First-tier Tribunal and Upper Tribunal. He also recommends new legislation to deal with the issue. Section 39 is retained in italics in this edition for earlier appeals. It continues to apply in Northern Ireland.

See now the new s.39A of the 2002 Act added from April 1, 2014. See further the commentary to that section, above.

Death of a party to an appeal or an application for a direction

2.387   **8.**—(1) In any proceedings relating to an appeal or an application for a direction, on the death of a party to those proceedings (other than the Board) the following persons may proceed with the appeal or application for a direction in the place of such deceased party—
   (a) where the proceedings are in relation to a single claim, the personal representatives of the person who has died;
   (b) where the proceedings are in relation to a joint claim, where only one of the persons by whom the claim was made has died, the other person with whom the claim was made;
   (c) where the proceedings are in relation to a joint claim where both the persons by whom the claim was made have died, the personal representatives of the last of them to die;
   (d) for the purposes of paragraph (c), where persons have died in circumstances rendering it uncertain which of them survived the other—
      (i) their deaths shall be presumed to have occurred in order of seniority; and
      (ii) the younger shall be treated as having survived the elder.

(2) Where there is no person mentioned in paragraphs (1)(a) to (1)(c) to proceed with the appeal or application for a direction, the Board may appoint such person as they think fit to proceed with that appeal or that application in the place of such deceased party referred to in paragraph (1).

(3) A grant of probate, confirmation or letters of administration to the estate of the deceased party, whenever taken out, shall have no effect on an appointment made under paragraph (2).

(4) Where a person appointed under paragraph (2) has, prior to the date of such appointment, taken any action in relation to the appeal or application for a direction on behalf of the deceased party, the effective date

(SI 2002/3196 reg.8) (as amended)

of appointment by the Board shall be the day immediately prior to the first day on which such action was taken.

DEFINITIONS

"appeal"—see reg.1(3).
"an application for a direction"—*ibid.*
"the Board"—see s.39(1) of the Social Security Act 1998 as modified by reg.12 of the Tax Credits (Appeals) Regulations 2002.
"joint claimant"—reg.1(3).
"party to the proceedings"—*ibid.*
"single claimant"—*ibid.*

Tax Credits (Interest Rate) Regulations 2003

(SI 2003/123)

The Treasury, in exercise of the powers conferred upon them by ss.37(2) and (5), 65(1) and (8) and 67 of the Tax Credits Act 2002, hereby make the following Regulations:

ARRANGEMENT OF ARTICLES

1. Citation and commencement.
2. Interpretation.
3. Interest on overpayments of tax credit and penalties.
4. Prescribed rate of interest.

Citation and commencement

1. These Regulations may be cited as the Tax Credits (Interest Rate) Regulations 2003 and shall come into force on 18th February 2003.

GENERAL NOTE

The tax credits regime does not adopt quite the same approach to interest on overpayments as HMRC does for late payments of income tax. Whereas interest on late payments of income tax has long been a feature of revenue law, s.37 of the TCA 2002 adopts a compromise approach to tax credits. Thus, interest is charged on overpayments caused by fraud or neglect, but not otherwise. These regulations specify the rate of interest to be applied on such overpayments, and also on any penalty under ss.31–33 (penalties for incorrect statements, failure to comply with requirements, etc.).

Interpretation

2.—(1) In these Regulations—
"the Board" means the Commissioners of Inland Revenue;
"established rate" means—
  (a) on the coming into force of these Regulations, 6.5 per cent per annum;
  (b) in relation to any date after the first reference date after the coming into force of these Regulations, the reference rate found on the immediately preceding reference date;
"operative date" means the sixth day of each month;

2.388

2.389

2.390

2.391

"reference date" means the day of each month which is the 12th working day before the sixth day of the following month;

"tax credit" means child tax credit or, as the case may be, working tax credit, provision for which is made by the Tax Credits Act 2002;

"working day" means any day other than a non-business day within the meaning of section 92 of the Bills of Exchange Act 1882.

(2) For the purposes of regulation 4(2) the reference rate found on a reference date is the percentage per annum found by averaging the base lending rates at close of business on that date of—

(a) Bank of Scotland;
(b) Barclays Bank plc;
(c) Lloyds Bank plc;
(d) HSBC Bank plc;
(e) National Westminster Bank plc;
(f) The Royal Bank of Scotland plc,

and, if the result is not a whole number, rounding the result to the nearest such number, with any result midway between two whole numbers rounded down.

DEFINITION

"reference rate"—see reg.4(2).

Interest on overpayments of tax credit and penalties

2.392

3.—(1) Where the Board decide in accordance with section 37(1) of the Tax Credits Act 2002 that the whole or part of an overpayment of a tax credit which is attributable to fraud or neglect is to carry interest, the rate of interest for the purposes of section 37(2) of that Act is that prescribed by regulation 4.

(2) The rate of interest for the purposes of section 37(5) of the Tax Credits Act 2002 (interest on a penalty under any of sections 31–33 of that Act) is that prescribed by regulation 4.

DEFINITION

"the Board"—see reg.2(1).

Prescribed rate of interest

2.393

4.—(1) The rate of interest which is prescribed is, subject to paragraph (2), 6.5 per cent per annum.

(2) Where, on a reference date after the coming into force of these Regulations, the reference rate found on that date ("RR") differs from the established rate, the rate of interest which is prescribed shall, on and after the next operative date, be the percentage per annum found by applying the formula:

$$RR + 2.5.$$

DEFINITION

"established rate"—see reg.2(1).

(SI 2003/653)

Tax Credits (Immigration) Regulations 2003

(SI 2003/653)

The Treasury, in exercise of the powers conferred upon them by sections 42 and 65(1), (3), (7) and (9) of the Tax Credits Act 2002, hereby make the following Regulations:

ARRANGEMENT OF ARTICLES

1. Citation and commencement
2. Interpretation
3. Exclusion of persons subject to immigration control from entitlement to tax credits
4. Modifications of Part 1 of the Act for refugees whose asylum claims have been accepted
5. Transitional relief—claimants moving from income support and income based Jobseeker's Allowance to child tax credit

Citation and commencement

1.—These Regulations may be cited as the Tax Credits (Immigration) Regulations 2003 and shall come into force on 6th April 2003.

Interpretation

2.—In these Regulations—
"the Act" means the Tax Credits Act 2002;
"the Child Tax Credit Regulations" means the Child Tax Credit Regulations 2002;
[1"couple" has the meaning given by section 3(5A) of the Act;]
"immigration rules" has the meaning given by section 33 of the Immigration Act 1971;
"joint claim" has the meaning given by section 3(8) of the Act;
"limited leave" has the meaning given by section 33 of the Immigration Act 1971;
[1. . .]
"person subject to immigration control" has the meaning in section 115(9) of the Immigration and Asylum Act 1999;
"refugee" means a person who has been recorded by the Secretary of State as a refugee within the definition in Article 1 of the Convention relating to the Status of Refugees done at Geneva on 28th July 1951 as extended by Article 1(2) of the Protocol relating to the Status of Refugees done at New York on 31st January 1967;
"tax credit" refers to either child tax credit or working tax credit and references to tax credits are to both of them;
"the Working Tax Credit Regulations" means the Working Tax Credit (Entitlement and Maximum Rate) Regulations 2002.

AMENDMENT

1. Civil Partnership Act 2004 (Tax Credits, etc.) (Consequential Amendments) Order 2005 (SI 2005/2919) art.7(2) (December 5, 2005).

Tax Credits (Immigration) Regulations 2003

Exclusion of persons subject to immigration control from entitlement to tax credits

2.397	3.—(1) No person is entitled to child tax credit or working tax credit while he is a person subject to immigration control, except in the following Cases, and subject to paragraphs (2) to (9).

Case 1

2.398	He is a person who—
(a) has been given leave to enter, or remain in, the United Kingdom by the Secretary of State upon the undertaking of another person or persons, pursuant to the immigration rules, to be responsible for his maintenance and accommodation; and
(b) has been resident in the United Kingdom for a period of at least five years commencing on or after the date of his entry into the United Kingdom, or the date on which the undertaking was given in respect of him, whichever is the later.

Case 2

2.399	He is a person who—
(a) falls within the terms of paragraph (a) of Case 1; and
(b) has been resident in the United Kingdom for less than the five years mentioned in para.(b) of Case 1,
but the person giving the undertaking has died or, where the undertaking was given by more than one person, they have all died.

Case 3

2.400	[³. . .]

Case 4

2.401	Where the claim is for working tax credit, he is—
(a) a national of a state which has ratified the European Convention on Social and Medical Assistance (done in Paris on 11th December 1953) or of a state which has ratified the Council of Europe Social Charter (signed in Turin on 18th October 1961); and
(b) lawfully present in the United Kingdom.
The Case so described also applies where—
(a) the claim is for child tax credit;
(b) the award of child tax credit would be made on or after 6th April 2004; and
(c) immediately before the award is made (and as part of the transition of claimants entitled to elements of income support and income-based Jobseeker's Allowance, to child tax credit) the person is, or will on the making of a claim be, entitled to any of the amounts in relation to income support or income-based Jobseeker's Allowance which are described in section 1(3)(d) of the Act.

Case 5

2.402	Where the claim is for child tax credit, he is—
(a) a person who is lawfully working in the United Kingdom; and

(SI 2003/653 reg.3)

(b) a national of a State with which the Community has concluded an Agreement under Article 310 of the Treaty of Amsterdam amending the Treaty on European Union, the Treaties establishing the European Communities and certain related Acts providing, in the field of social security, for the equal treatment of workers who are nationals of the signatory State and their families.

(2) Where one member of a [1 . . .] couple is a person subject to immigration control, and the other member is not or is within any of Cases 1 to 5 or regulation 5—
  (a) the calculation of the amount of tax credit under the Act, the Child Tax Credit Regulations and the Working Tax Credit Regulations (including any second adult element or other element in respect of, or determined by reference to, that person);
  (b) the method of making (or proceeding with) a joint claim by the couple; and
  (c) the method of payment of the tax credit,
shall, subject to paragraph (3), be determined in the same way as if that person were not subject to such control.

(3) Where the other member is within Case 4 or 5 or regulation 5, para. (2) shall only apply to the tax credit to which he (in accordance with those provisions) is entitled.

(4) Where a person has submitted a claim for asylum as a refugee and in consequence is a person subject to immigration control, in the first instance he is not entitled to tax credits, subject to paragraphs (5) to (9).

(5) If that person—
  (a) is notified that he has been recorded by the Secretary of State as a refugee; and
  (b) claims tax credit within [2 one month] of receiving that notification,
paragraphs (6) to (9) and regulation 4 shall apply to him.

(6) He shall be treated as having claimed tax credits—
  (a) on the date when he submitted his claim for asylum; and
  (b) on every 6th April (if any) intervening between the date in sub-paragraph (a) and the date of the claim referred to in paragraph (5)(b),
rather than on the date on which he makes the claim referred to in paragraph (5)(b).

(7) [4 Regulations 7, 7A and 8] of the Tax Credits (Claims and Notifications) Regulations 2002 shall not apply to claims treated as made by virtue of paragraph (6).

(8) He shall have his claims for tax credits determined as if he had been recorded as a refugee on the date when he submitted his claim for asylum.

(9) The amount of support provided under—
  (a) section 95 or 98 of the Immigration and Asylum Act 1999;
  (b) regulations made under Schedule 9 to that Act, by the Secretary of State in respect of essential living needs of the claimant and his dependants (if any); or
  (c) regulations made under paragraph 3 of Schedule 8 to that Act,
(after allowing for any deduction for that amount under regulation 21ZB(3) of the Income Support (General) Regulations 1987) shall be deducted from any award of tax credits due to the claimant by virtue of paragraphs (6) and (8).

Amendments

1. Civil Partnership Act 2004 (Tax Credits, etc.) (Consequential Amendments) Order 2005 (SI 2005/2919) art.7(3) (December 5, 2005).
2. Tax Credits (Miscellaneous Amendments) Regulations 2012 (SI 2012/848) reg.7 (April 6, 2012).
3. Tax Credits (Miscellaneous Amendments) Regulations 2014 (SI 2014/658) reg.3 (April 6, 2014).
4. Tax Credits (Claims and Notifications) (Amendment) Regulations 2015 (SI 2015/669) reg.5 (April 6, 2015).

Definitions

"the Act"—see reg.2.
"the Child Tax Credit Regulations"—see *ibid*.
"couple"—see *ibid*.
"immigration rules"—see *ibid*.
"joint claim"—see *ibid*.
"limited leave"—see *ibid*.
"person subject to immigration control"—see *ibid*.
"refugee"—see *ibid*.
"tax credit"—see *ibid*.
"the Working Tax Credit Regulations"—see *ibid*.

General Note

2.403 These regulations are made under s.42(1) of the Tax Credits Act 2002, which enables regulations to make provision for the exclusion of "persons subject to immigration control" from entitlement to child tax credit or working tax credit (or both). For these purposes, a "person subject to immigration control" has the same meaning as in s.115 of the Immigration and Asylum Act 1999. Section 115(9) of the 1999 Act is the starting point for this definition, and defines a "person subject to immigration control" as a person who *either* requires leave to enter or remain in the UK but does not have it *or* has such leave but this is: (i) subject to a condition that he does not have recourse to public funds, or (ii) as a result of a maintenance undertaking, or (iii) through the continuation of leave pending certain appeals. For detailed commentary on this definition, see the annotations to reg.21(3) of the Income Support (General) Regulations 1987 (SI 1987/1967) in Vol.II in this series. It should be noted that a person who is a national of an EEA state (i.e. a national of an EU Member State or of Iceland, Liechtenstein or Norway) can *never* be a person subject to immigration control for the purposes of social security or tax credits.

The structure of reg.3 itself falls into three parts. Paragraph (1) sets out the general rule, along with certain exceptions. The position of couples, where one partner is a person subject to immigration control but the other is not, is dealt with in paras (2) and (3). Paragraphs (4)–(9) are concerned with the particular status of asylum seekers. These rules can never apply to British citizens. An individual who becomes a British citizen by naturalisation ceases to be subject to any immigration control on becoming a British citizen.

Paragraph (1)

2.404 The general rule is that a person subject to immigration control is not entitled to either child tax credit or working tax credit (para.(1)). This general rule is then subject to the exceptions listed in Cases 1–5. These Cases have been adapted from the exceptions to the general rule precluding persons subject to immigration control from being entitled to the various means-tested benefits, as set out in the Schedule to the Social Security (Immigration and Asylum) Consequential Amendments Regulations 2000 (SI 2000/636) see Vol.II in this series. Thus, Case 1 in para.(1) mirrors para.3 in Pt I of the Schedule to the 2000 Regulations; Case 2 follows para.2

of Pt I of the Schedule. These first two Cases operate as exceptions to the preclusionary rule for both child tax credit and working tax credit. The exception in Case 4 is in the same terms as para.4 in Pt I of the Schedule to the 2000 Regulations and applies to all working tax credit claims. It also applies to child tax credit claims in respect of awards made on or after April 6, 2004 where, immediately before the award the claimant was (or would have been) entitled to a child allowance or family or disabled child premium as part of an award of income support or income-based jobseeker's allowance. The exception in Case 5 is adapted from para.2 of Pt II of the Schedule to the 2000 Regulations, which deals with exceptions from the preclusionary rule in respect of certain noncontributory benefits.

There is also a special rule, applying to child tax credit only, which provides transitional relief for claimants moving from income support or income-based jobseeker's allowance to child tax credit (see reg.5).

Paragraphs (2) and (3)

Paragraph (2) provides that where only one member of a married or unmarried couple is a person subject to immigration control, and the other is not, entitlement to tax credits is determined in the same way as if neither of them were so subject. The same applies where the other member is either within one of the excepted cases in para.(1) or covered by the transitional provisions in reg.5 below. Note also the qualification in para.(3).

2.405

Paragraphs (4)–(9)

These provisions enable backdated claims to tax credits to be made where an asylum claim has been accepted. A claimant who has submitted a claim for asylum is a person subject to immigration control and so in the first instance is not entitled to tax credits (para.(4)). However, if such an application is accepted, the claimant may claim tax credits retrospectively (para.(5)). Any such retrospective claim must be made within three months of the notification from the IND (para.(5)(a)). This contrasts favourably with the 28 days allowed for retrospective claims for income support in similar situations (Income Support (General) Regulations 1987 (SI 1987/1967) reg.21ZB). In the event of a successful application for asylum, the claim for tax credits is treated as having been made on the date of the submission of the claim for asylum, not the post-acceptance date of the actual claim for tax credits (para.(6)(a)). The claim is also regarded as having been renewed on every intervening April 6, demonstrating an awareness of the delays which are well known in the system for determining asylum applications (para.(6)(b)). Accordingly, the normal time-limits in regs 7 and 8 of the Tax Credits (Claims and Notifications) Regulations 2002 (SI 2002/2014) for claiming tax credits are disapplied (para.(7)) and the claim treated as if the applicant had been recorded as a refugee on the date when the asylum application was actually made (para.(8)). Any arrears of tax credits which are due, following the application of these provisions, are then subject to an offset in recognition of any sums provided by way of asylum support under various statutory provisions (para.(9)).

2.406

Note that, by virtue of reg.4, the provisions of Pt I of the TCA 2002 apply to the determination of claims for tax credits made by refugees whose asylum claims have been accepted, subject to the omission of ss.14–17 and various modifications to ss.18 and 19 of the 2002 Act.

In *AA v HMRC (TC)* [2012] UKUT 121 (AAC), Judge Turnbull held that subs. (5), requiring additional backdating to tax credits in the case of a person "recorded by the Secretary of State as a refugee", did not permit backdating of entitlement to tax credit for more than three months (the then maximum) in a case where the claimant had been granted indefinite leave to remain in the UK with retrospective effect for a longer period. For cases with an EU dimension, see also *EG v HMRC (TC)* [2011] UKUT 467 (AAC), discussed in the note to TCA 2002 s.3(5A) above.

In *CTC/3692/2008* an Upper Tribunal Judge rejected a challenge to subss.(7)–(9)

2.407

as discriminatory and in breach of the Human Rights Act 1998. The Commissioner decided on the facts that while the rules were not discriminatory they also had not been applied properly. After outlining what should have happened, the appeal was sent back to HMRC for it to be redetermined.

In *FK v HMRC* [2009] UKUT 134 (AAC) Judge Jacobs considered the date from which a claim for child tax credit should start when a claimant has her status as a refugee confirmed. A mother claimed child tax credit on August 8, 2007, following confirmation of her status on July 3, 2007. She was awarded tax credits from 2005, when she was treated as making a new asylum claim, although she first claimed asylum unsuccessfully on arrival in 2000. Judge Jacobs agreed with a submission by HMRC supporting the mother's appeal against a First-tier Tribunal decision confirming the award only from the second claim. He cited art.24 of the Convention relating to the Status of Refugees 1951 as supporting the approach, previously adopted by a Social Security Commissioner in *R(IS) 9/98*, that the "grant" of asylum was recognition of the claimant's status, not the creation of that status. The status existed from the time the mother first arrived in the UK and her first, then unsuccessful, claim for asylum. Her claim was therefore operative from that time. The judge has examined this rule in two other decisions: *MI v HMRC* [2009] UKUT 73 (AAC) and *CTC/0838/2011* in the latter of which he noted that there had been no appeals against these decisions and that therefore a First-tier Tribunal was correct in applying them.

Modifications of Part I of the Act for refugees whose asylum claims have been accepted

2.408
4.—(1) For the purposes of claims falling within paragraph (2), Part I of the Act shall apply subject to the modifications set out in paras (3)–(5).

(2) A claim falls within this paragraph if it is a claim for tax credits which a person is treated as having made by virtue of regulation 3(6), other than a claim which he is treated as having made in the tax year in which he made his claim under regulation 3(5).

(3) Omit sections 14 to 17 (initial decisions, revised decisions and final notices).

(4) In section 18 (decisions after final notices)—
(a) in subsection (1) for "After giving a notice under section 17" substitute "In relation to each claim for a tax credit made by a person or persons for the whole or part of a tax year";
(b) omit subsections (2) to (9);
(c) for subsection (10) substitute—
"(10) Before making their decision the Board may by notice—
(a) require the person, or either or both of the persons, by whom the claim is made to provide any information or evidence which the Board consider they may need for making their decision; or
(b) require any person of a prescribed description to provide any information or evidence of a prescribed description which the Board consider they may need for that purpose,
by the date specified in the notice.";
(d) in subsection (11) omit—
(i) "any revision under subsection (5) or (9) and";
(ii) paragraph (a);
(iii) in paragraph (b), "in any other case,".

(5) In section 19 (enquiries)—

(SI 2003/653 reg.4)

   (a) in subsection (4), for paragraphs (a) and (b) substitute
      "one year after that decision or, if—
        (a) the person, or either of the persons, to whom the enquiry relates is required by section 8 of the Taxes Management Act 1970 to make a return; and
        (b) the return becomes final on a day more than one year after that decision,
      with that day (or, if both of the persons are so required and their returns become final on different days, with the later of those days).;"
   (b) in subsection (5) omit paragraph (a) and, in paragraph (b) "in any other case,";
   (c) omit subsection (6).

DEFINITIONS

"the Act"—see reg.2.
"tax credit"—see *ibid.*

GENERAL NOTE

See note to reg.3.

2.409

Transitional relief—claimants moving from income support and income-based jobseeker's allowance to child tax credit

5. In relation to child tax credit, a person is not treated for the purposes of these Regulations as subject to immigration control where—
   (a) the award of child tax credit would be made on or after 6th April 2004;
   (b) immediately before the award of child tax credit is made, he is, or will on the making of a claim be, entitled to any of the amounts in relation to income support or income-based jobseeker's allowance which are described in section 1(3)(d) of the Act; and
   (c) he is a person who, immediately before the award of child tax credit is made—
      (i) was receiving or entitled to income support by virtue of regulation 12(1) of the Social Security (Persons From Abroad) Miscellaneous Amendments Regulations 1996, and his claim for asylum has not been recorded by the Secretary of State as having been decided (other than on appeal) or abandoned; or
      (ii) was receiving or entitled to income support or income-based jobseeker's allowance by virtue of regulation 12(3) of the Social Security (Immigration and Asylum) Consequential Amendments Regulations 2000, and his claim for asylum has not been so recorded as having been decided (other than on appeal) or abandoned.

2.410

DEFINITIONS

"the Act"—see reg.2.
"person subject to immigration control"—see *ibid.*

General Note

2.411 This provides for transitional relief (on or after April 6, 2004) for claimants moving over from the specified elements of income support or income-based jobseeker's allowance to child tax credit.

Tax Credits (Residence) Regulations 2003

(SI 2003/654) (AS AMENDED)

The Treasury, in exercise of the powers conferred upon them by sections 3(7) and 65(1), (7) and (9) of the Tax Credits Act 2002, hereby make the following Regulations:

REGULATIONS

2.412
1. Citation and commencement
2. Interpretation
3. Circumstances in which a person is treated as not being in the United Kingdom
4. Persons temporarily absent from the United Kingdom
5. Crown servants posted overseas
6. Partners of Crown servants posted overseas
7. Transitional provision—income support and income-based Jobseeker's Allowance

Citation and commencement

2.413 **1.**—These Regulations may be cited as the Tax Credits (Residence) Regulations 2003 and shall come into force on 6th April 2003.

Interpretation

2.414 **2.**—(1) In these Regulations—
"the Act" means the Tax Credits Act 2002;
"child" has the same meaning as it has in the Child Tax Credit Regulations 2002;
[¹"couple" has the meaning given by section 3(5A) of the Act];
"Crown servant posted overseas" has the meaning given in regulation 5(2);
"partner" means where a person is a member of a [¹ . . .] couple, the other member of that couple;
"qualifying young person" has the meaning given in regulation 2, read with regulation 5, of the Child Tax Credit Regulations 2002;
"relative" means brother, sister, ancestor or lineal descendant.

(2) In these Regulations, a person is responsible for a child or qualifying young person if he is treated as being responsible for that child or qualifying young person in accordance with the rules contained in regulation 3 of the Child Tax Credit Regulations 2002.

(SI 2003/654 reg.2) (as amended)

AMENDMENT

1. Civil Partnership Act 2004 (Tax Credits, etc.) (Consequential Amendments) Order 2005 (SI 2005/2919) art.8(2) (December 5, 2005).

GENERAL NOTE

This regulation follows the pattern of all tax credit provisions in adopting the definitions of "child" and "qualifying young person" from the Child Tax Credit Regulations 2002 (SI 2002/2007).

Circumstances in which a person is treated as not being in the United Kingdom

3.—(1) A person shall be treated as not being in the United Kingdom for the purposes of Part I of the Act if he is not ordinarily resident in the United Kingdom.

(2) [5 Paragraphs (1) and (6) do] not apply to a Crown servant posted overseas or his partner.

(3) A person who is in the United Kingdom as a result of his deportation, expulsion or other removal by compulsion of law from another country to the United Kingdom shall be treated as being ordinarily resident in the United Kingdom [5 and paragraph (6) shall not apply].

(4) For the purposes of working tax credit, a person shall be treated as being ordinarily resident if he is exercising in the United Kingdom his rights as a worker pursuant to [3 Parliament and Council Regulation (EU) No 492/2011] or he is a person with a right to reside in the United Kingdom pursuant to [2 Council Directive No.2004/38/EC].

[1 (5) A person shall be treated as not being in the United Kingdom for the purposes of Part 1 of the Act where he—
  (a) makes a claim for child tax credit (other than being treated as making a claim under regulation 11 or 12 of the Tax Credits (Claims and Notifications) Regulations 2002 or otherwise), on or after 1st May 2004; and
 [4 (b) (i) does not have a right to reside in the United Kingdom; or
      (ii) has a right to reside in the United Kingdom under:
        — regulation 15A(1) of the Immigration (European Economic Area) Regulations 2006, but only in a case where the right exists under that regulation because the person satisfies the criteria in regulation 15A(4A) of those Regulations; or
        — Article 20 of the Treaty on the Functioning of the European Union (in a case where the right to reside arises because a British citizen would otherwise be deprived of the genuine enjoyment of the substance of their rights as a European Union citizen).]

[5 (6) Subject to paragraph (7), a person is to be treated as being in the United Kingdom for the purposes of Part 1 of the Act where he makes a claim for child tax credit only if that person has been living in the United Kingdom for 3 months before that claim plus any time taken into account by regulation 7 of the Tax Credits (Claims and Notifications) Regulations 2002 for determining for the purpose of that regulation when the claim is treated as having been made.

(7) Paragraph (6) shall not apply where the person—
  (a) most recently entered the United Kingdom before 1st July 2014;

(b) is a worker or a self-employed person in the United Kingdom for the purposes of Council Directive 2004/38/EC (rights of citizens of the European Union and their family members to move and reside freely within the territory of the Member States);

(c) retains the status of a worker or self-employed person in the United Kingdom pursuant to Article 7(3) of Council Directive 2004/38/EC;

(d) is treated as a worker in the United Kingdom pursuant to regulation 5 of the Accession of Croatia (Immigration and Worker Authorisation) Regulations 2013 (right of residence of a Croatian who is an "accession State national subject to worker authorisation");

(e) is a family member of a person referred to in sub-paragraphs (b), (c), (d) or (i);

(f) is a person to whom regulation 4 applies (persons temporarily absent from the United Kingdom) and who returns to the United Kingdom within 52 weeks starting from the first day of the temporary absence;

(g) returns to the United Kingdom after a period abroad of less than 52 weeks where immediately before departing from the United Kingdom that person had been ordinarily resident in the United Kingdom for a continuous period of 3 months;

(h) returns to the United Kingdom otherwise as a worker or self-employed person after a period abroad and where, otherwise than for a period of up to 3 months ending on the day of returning, that person has paid either Class 1 or Class 2 contributions pursuant to regulation 114, 118, 146 or 147 of the Social Security (Contributions) Regulations 2001 or pursuant to an Order in Council having effect under section 179 of the Social Security Administration Act 1992;

(i) is not a national of an EEA State and would be a worker or self-employed person in the United Kingdom for the purposes of Council Directive 2004/38/EC if that person were a national of an EEA State;

(j) is a refugee as defined in Article 1 of the Convention relating to the Status of Refugees done at Geneva on 28th July 1951, as extended by Article 1(2) of the Protocol relating to the Status of Refugees done at New York on 31st January 1967;

(k) has been granted leave, or is deemed to have been granted leave, outside the rules made under section 3(2) of the Immigration Act 1971 where that leave is—
 (i) granted by the Secretary of State with recourse to public funds, or
 (ii) deemed to have been granted by virtue of regulation 3 of the Displaced Persons (Temporary Protection) Regulations 2005;

(l) has been granted leave to remain in the United Kingdom by the Secretary of State pending an application for indefinite leave to remain as a victim of domestic violence;

(m) has been granted humanitarian protection by the Secretary of State under Rule 339C of Part 11 of the rules made under section 3(2) of the Immigration Act 1971.

(8) In this regulation, a "family member" means a person who is defined as a family member of another person in Article 2 of Council Directive 2004/38/EC.

(9) In this regulation, "EEA State", in relation to any time, means a state which at that time is a member State, or any other state which at that time is

(SI 2003/654 reg.3) (as amended)

a party to the agreement on the European Economic Area signed at Oporto on 2nd May, together with the Protocol adjusting that Agreement signed at Brussels on 17th March 1993, as modified or supplemented from time to time.]

AMENDMENTS

1. Tax Credits (Residence) (Amendment) Regulations 2004 (SI 2004/1243) reg.3 (May 1, 2004).
2. Tax Credits (Miscellaneous Amendments) Regulations 2006 (SI 2006/766) reg.4 (April 6, 2006).
3. Tax Credits (Miscellaneous Amendments) Regulations 2012 (SI 2012/848) reg.8 (April 6, 2012).
4. Child Benefit and Child Tax Credit (Miscellaneous Amendments) Regulations 2012 (SI 2012/2612) regs 5 and 6 (November 8, 2012).
5. Child Benefit (General) and the Tax Credits (Residence) (Amendment) Regulations 2014 (SI 2014/1511) regs 2 and 6 (July 1, 2014).

DEFINITIONS

"Crown servant posted overseas"—see reg.2.
"partner"—see reg.2.

GENERAL NOTE

Section 3(3) of the TCA 2002 makes it a requirement for entitlement to tax credits that the claimant is "in the United Kingdom". This regulation, authorised by s.3(7), imposes the income test of "ordinary residence" as an additional requirement for entitlement. Read together with the section, the regulations require that a claimant must show:

(a) ordinary residence in the UK, and
(b) presence in the UK or, if he or she is not present in the UK, that the absence is temporary.

The approach taken here is consistent with the general jurisdictional approach to income tax in the UK. In common with some other parts of the common law world, income tax is residence-based, rather than nationality-based (as in the United States) or source-based (as in other parts of Europe). Income tax uses two main tests: residence and ordinary residence. The Tax Credits (Definition and Calculation of Income) Regulations 2002 (SI 2002/2006) reg.3 removes the significance of both those tests for the purposes of defining the relevant income of a claimant. These Regulations impose the test at another level. Those Regulations also disapply the definitions of "residence" in the various UK double tax agreements (which, for income tax purposes, override the national legislation).

For full discussion of the rights under European law of a citizen of the European Union see Pt III of Vol.III of this work.

The Finance Act 2013 introduced a completely new and detailed tax regime for determining the residence and ordinary residence of individuals for income tax purposes, commencing for the tax year 2013–14 subject to transitional provisions. They therefore apply to income tax returns due for that and later years. The main change is one of approach. The former general case law-led factual approach is replaced by two extremely detailed sets of rules applying two new sets of tests. The first is a statutory residence test (or, rather, a set of parallel tests) applied by s.218 of, and Sch.45 to, the 2013 Act. The other is the abolition of the test of ordinary residence entirely by s.219 of, and Sch.46 to, the 2013 Act, the concept being replaced by specific statutory tests, such as a three-year non-residence test for employees. The legislation deals in considerable detail with the new tests for all relevant aspects of income tax, including split year rules. As these have no direct effect on tax credits legislation to date, none of the detailed amendments to the

2.417

Tax Credits (Residence) Regulations 2003

income tax legislation have been included in this volume. The guidance about the former income tax treatment remains fully relevant to tax credits. Booklet IR20 has been kept on the HMRC website for reference although it has no current relevance to income tax. (For current income tax purposes it has been replaced by Guidance Notes, in particular RDR1 on *Residence, Domicile and the Remittance Basis*.)

Ordinary residence

2.418 "Ordinary residence" was used as the test for WFTC (Family Credit (General) Regulations 1987 (SI 1987/1973) reg.3) where the test was worded as a requirement that the claimant be both present and ordinarily resident. In *R(M) 1/85*, the Commissioner followed *Shah* (below) for those purposes as defining the term. The new form of words appears to avoid the problem with the previous wording commented on in Vol.II of the 2002 edition of this work. One change, however, is that the test is now applied to the whole of the UK, as Northern Ireland no longer has a separate system for these purposes.

"Ordinary residence" is a question of fact, not law. For the only relevant provisions in income tax law, see the ITA 2007 ss.829–832. It is separate from the other test used for income tax, "residence". "Residence" is determined for income tax purposes by reference to each tax year. "Ordinary residence" is based on a longer view, though perhaps not so long a view as "habitual residence". It is clear from both case law and practice that a claimant can have two ordinary residences at the same time for income tax purposes, and that the status of ordinary residence can be acquired on arrival in the UK if the claimant arrives with the intention of staying. That may be compared with the approach often taken for social security purposes to "habitual residence". For the leading authorities on the approach to be taken to the test see *Levene v IRC* [1928] A.C. 217; *IRC v Lysaght* [1928] A.C. 234; and *Shah v Barnet LBC* [1983] 2 A.C. 309, HL.

HMRC has a code of practice, published as booklet IR20, which defines how HMRC treat disputed issues of ordinary residence. HMRC treat the question as partly one of intention and partly one of actual presence. The working practice is to treat someone as resident in the UK if he or she is present for more than 183 days in total in any one year (whenever that year starts), and to treat someone as ordinarily resident if present for more than an average of 91 days in each of four consecutive years. A new arrival who has a job lasting more than three years here and/or who buys a house here is likely to be treated as ordinarily resident on arrival, and the reverse will be true of those leaving. IR20 should be treated with some caution as it applies to tax credits. Commentators have taken the view on a number of occasions that the HMRC view is one that supports HMRC's own approach to the definitions, rather than necessarily takes a neutral view on the issues. Secondly, and linked with this, the HMRC code in IR20 is designed to include people who would probably prefer to be excluded from the charge to UK income tax. Will the same approach be applied where HMRC might wish to exclude the claimant, while the claimant's interest will be to be included? In other words, will HMRC apply its allegedly expansive view of its jurisdiction under IR20 in the same way when paying out tax credits as when collecting in tax? HMRC have now published a guidance leaflet that broadly follows the income tax approach: *Child and Working Tax Credits and Child Benefit: residence rules—Guidance for intermediaries*. It is on the HMRC website at *http://www.hmrc. gov.uk/taxcredits/residence-rules. htm*. The same approach is followed in the official manuals to HMRC staff.

In practice, problems will usually arise in the following situations:

(1) When someone who has been ordinarily resident in the UK goes overseas: the usual issue here will be that the claimant is no longer as a matter of fact "in" the United Kingdom to claim child tax credit for any children. Subject to the temporary absence rule in reg.4, and the rules for Crown servants in regs 5 and 6, the claimant will cease to qualify for tax credits. However, if the person (or one of two joint claimants leaving together) returns often enough to remain "present", then it will be a question of fact whether the claimant is ordinarily resident despite the overseas link.

(SI 2003/654 reg.3) (as amended)

Where one of two joint claimants goes overseas and the other does not, the claim should become a single claim.

(2) When someone arrives in the UK: the first practical requirement for working tax credit purposes is that the claimant has a job. If he or she has come to the UK to work and that work is likely to last at least three years, then current Revenue practice is to treat the person as ordinarily resident here on arrival. The position of the worker whose work here may not last that period but who has rights under EU law as a worker is protected by reg.3(4). It is suggested that if the person is accepted as ordinarily resident under either rule for working tax credit purposes then he or she should also be accepted as able to claim child tax credit as well. There will also be a practical argument in other cases that if the claimant is treated as liable to UK income tax, then he or she will expect UK tax credits. However, the liability to income tax may arise on residence alone before the individual becomes ordinarily resident in the UK.

(3) When someone has strong links with the UK and another state: there may be ordinary residence in both states. This will be a question of fact. Unlike regs 5 and 6 below, this regulation does not deal expressly with partners making joint claims. The position is clear from s.3 of the Act. A couple must make a joint claim if both are "in" the UK. If one of the couple is not present or ordinarily resident here, then only the other partner can make the claim. But this will have the effect of excluding the non-resident partner's income from the income calculation. It may therefore be in the interests of some claimants for child tax credit to claim, say, that the mother is present and ordinarily resident, but that the father is not. This is not now a concern for income tax purposes as all married couples are assessed to income tax separately.

The Treasury published a consultative document with the 2003 Budget about the tests of residence, ordinary residence and domicile, entitled: *Reviewing the residence and domicile rules as they affect the taxation of individuals: a background paper.* It is available on the HM Treasury website. It contains a valuable summary of current practice and the problems it generates. New income tax rules about residence are being introduced from 2013/14 under Finance Act 2013 ss.218–219.

Paragraphs (2) and (3)
Paragraph (2) relates to regs 5 and 6 below. Paragraph (3) deals with the problem that some of these individuals might not otherwise be regarded as ordinarily resident and so would be deprived of claims to either working tax credit or child tax credit. But see also the Tax Credits (Immigration) Regulations 2003 (SI 2003/653).

2.419

The amendments to reg.3 are parallel to amendments for child benefit. Both impose, with a lengthy list of exceptions, a general rule that anyone entering the United Kingdom from July 1, 2014 must be living here for three months before claiming.

Paragraphs (4) and (5)
Paragraph (4) provides a test for working tax credit, while para.(5) provides a test for child tax credit. They are different tests and it is important that they be considered separately.

2.420

Paragraph (4) makes express reference to legislation establishing the rights of freedom of movement of citizens of the European Union. For a full discussion of the relevant European Union law see Pt 3 of Vol.III of this work.

The rights of citizens of the European Union to claim child tax credit arise separately (and also separately from those for child benefit). Again, for full discussion see Vol.III.

It was intended to make para.(5) lapse on May 1, 2006 (see SI 2004/1243 reg.1), but the lapsing provision was itself revoked by SI 2006/766 reg.4, so continuing this paragraph in force without a time limit.

2.421

The paragraph therefore now introduces for all claims after May 1, 2004 the requirement that a claimant has a "right to reside" before making any child tax credit claim. It does not apply to working tax credit claims. It therefore does not apply to in-work benefits. It applies, in particular, to those who have moved to the UK from the new member states of the European Union ("A8 and A2" citizens), and their families, if they are not economically active.

"Right to reside" has superseded the previous test of "habitual residence" for social security benefits generally. See the Social Security (Habitual Residence) (Amendment) Regulations 2004 (SI 2004/1232), discussed in Vol. II of this work. The term is not defined by legislation. It does not apply to British citizens. Nor does it apply to any citizen of the European Economic Area legally working or self-employed in the UK or third country citizens with indefinite leave to remain in the UK. But it applies to any European Economic Area citizen who is economically inactive.

2.422 The test, including its application to child tax credit, was considered in a series of decisions taken by a Tribunal of Commissioners as decisions *CIS/3573/2005, CPC/2920/2005, CIS/2559/2005* and *CIS/2680/2005*. The Tribunal decided that the test of "right to reside" is a general test applying to all potentially within its scope. Further, the test is not met by reference to the other tests of lawful residence or actual habitual residence. Rather, it reflects the provisions of EU Council Directive 90/364 that Member States:

> "shall grant the right of residence to nationals of member states who do not enjoy this right under other provisions of Community Law . . . provided they . . . have sufficient resources to avoid becoming a burden on the social assistance system of the host member state during the period of their residence".

The Court of Appeal has dismissed an appeal against the decision of the Tribunal of Commissioners in *Abdirahman v Secrtary of State for Work and Pensions* [2007] EWCA Civ 657 *(R(IS)8/07)*; see further the commentary in Vol. II.

In *Zalewska v Department for Social Development* [2008] UKHL 67 the House of Lords upheld a decision of the Northern Ireland Court of Appeal and Social Security Commissioner that the use of the derogation from European Union law under which the test of "right to reside" was adopted was itself compatible with European Union law. The House of Lords also affirmed the decision of the Commissioner that, notwithstanding that the appellant in that case, who was Polish, was a worker, the Commissioner was correct in law in holding that the law permitted refusal of income support to the appellant in the circumstances of the case. The worker registration scheme was not disproportionate to its legitimate aims. The Commissioner's decision is *C6/05-06(IS)*.

HMRC guidance about the operation of the "right to reside" rule is included in its detailed *Child and Working Tax Credits and Child Benefit: residence rules guidance for intermediaries*. See *http://www.hmrc.gov.uk/taxcredits/residence-rules.htm*. Following the approach of the Tribunal of Commissioners, this states that groups subject to the "right to reside" must have "sufficient resources not to become a burden on the social assistance system of the UK". This may be expected to exclude most of those claiming or seeking to claim income support, jobseeker's allowance, or housing benefit. But it is suggested that it cannot exclude all claimants from elsewhere in the European Economic Area for child tax credit, given that the income text for child tax credit is such that it is payable to all but the highest earning parents responsible for children. Nor does it exclude those who do have direct rights under European law.

Persons temporarily absent from the United Kingdom

2.423 **4.**—(1) A person who is ordinarily resident in the United Kingdom and is temporarily absent from the United Kingdom shall be treated as being in the United Kingdom during the first—
  (a) 8 weeks of any period of absence; or
  (b) 12 weeks of any period of absence where that period of absence, or any extension to that period of absence, is in connection with—

(i) the treatment of his illness or physical or mental disability;
(ii) the treatment of his partner's illness or physical or mental disability;
(iii) the death of a person who, immediately prior to the date of death, was his partner;
(iv) the death, or the treatment of the illness or physical or mental disability, of a child or qualifying young person for whom either he or his partner is, or both of them are, responsible; or
(v) the death, or the treatment of the illness or physical or mental disability, of his or his partner's relative.

(2) A person is temporarily absent from the United Kingdom if at the beginning of the period of absence his absence is unlikely to exceed 52 weeks.

DEFINITIONS

"ordinarily resident"—see reg.3.
"partner"—see reg.2.

GENERAL NOTE

This regulation deals with the practical application of the requirement that a claimant be "in" the UK as well as ordinarily resident here. It adopts the approach long used in social security law of ignoring temporary absence. See, for comparison, Income Support (General) Regulations 1987 (SI 1987/1967) reg.4. The current rule appears reasonably generous as it ignores the first eight weeks of "any" period of absence. Presumably, a claimant could make a visit back to the UK before the end of eight (or 12) weeks to re-establish presence before starting a second period of absence, and so on. On the facts, this would also avoid the 52-week rule in para. (2). On the wording, it would seem that the 52-week rule reapplies at the beginning of each period of absence.

In *GC v HMRC (TC)* [2014] UKUT 251 (AAC) Judge Rowland allowed an appeal by an appellant who was refused working tax credit while working in Spain. The appellant had returned to the United Kingdom for periods during the year. In that context, no attention had been paid to the provisions of reg.4 of these Regulations allowing a person to continue to be regarded as being in the UK during the first eight weeks of a temporary absence. These should be considered to see if the appellant continued to be ordinarily resident in the United Kingdom. Further, there was nothing in the Working Tax Credit (Entitlement and Maximum Rate) Regulations 2002 (SI 2002/2005) requiring that the work had to be in the United Kingdom.

See reg.6 below for a modification of this regulation as it applies to the partners of Crown servants employed overseas. One problem with these provisions in practice is that they allow an individual to be treated as remaining in the UK, but they do not allow the individual to be treated as continuing to work here. One result is that although the main elements of tax credits remain payable, an individual going overseas for a short period can retain WTC but lose the childcare credit. This parallels reg.24 of the Child Benefit (General) Regulations 2006 (para.3.32, below) which makes similar provisions.

2.424

Crown servants posted overseas

5.—(1) A Crown servant posted overseas shall be treated as being in the United Kingdom.

(2) A Crown servant posted overseas is a person performing overseas the duties of any office or employment under the Crown in right of the United Kingdom—

2.425

Tax Credits (Residence) Regulations 2003

(a) who is, or was, immediately prior to his posting or his first of consecutive postings, ordinarily resident in the United Kingdom; or
(b) who, immediately prior to his posting or his first of consecutive postings, was in the United Kingdom in connection with that posting.

GENERAL NOTE

2.426   This regulation and reg.6 protect the position of British public servants and their partners (and therefore also their children) when working outside the UK. Section 44 of the TCA 2002 removes any doubt about the application of the tax credits scheme to Crown employees. See further reg.30 of the Child Benefit (General) Regulations 2006 (para.3.41, below) which makes similar provisions.

Partners of Crown servants posted overseas

2.427   **6.**—(1) The partner of a Crown servant posted overseas who is accompanying the Crown servant posted overseas shall be treated as being in the United Kingdom when he is either—
(a) in the country where the Crown servant is posted; or
(b) absent from that country in accordance with regulation 4 as modified by paragraphs (3) and (4).
(2) Regulation 4 applies to the partner of a Crown servant posted overseas with the modifications set out in paragraphs (3) and (4).
(3) Omit the words "ordinarily resident in the United Kingdom and is".
(4) In relation to a partner who is accompanying the Crown servant posted overseas the references to "United Kingdom" in the phrase "temporarily absent from the United Kingdom", in both places where it occurs, shall be construed as references to the country where the Crown servant is posted.

DEFINITIONS

"Crown servant posted overseas"—see reg.5.
"partner"—see reg.2.

Transitional provision—income support and income-based jobseeker's allowance

2.428   **7.**—A person is exempt from the requirement to be ordinarily resident in the United Kingdom (which is set out in regulation 3(1)) in respect of child tax credit on and for three years after the date on which the award of child tax credit is made where—
(a) the award of child tax credit would be made on or after 6th April 2004;
(b) immediately before the award of child tax credit is made, he is, or will be on the making of a claim, entitled to any of the amounts in relation to income support and income-based jobseeker's allowance which are described in section 1(3)(d) of the Act; and
(c) he is a person to which one or more of the following provisions applies—
    (i) paragraph (b) or (c) in the definition of "person from abroad" in regulation 21(3) of the Income Support (General) Regulations 1987;
    (ii) paragraph (b) or (c) in the definition of "person from abroad" in regulation 85(4) of the Jobseeker's Allowance Regulations 1996;
    (iii) paragraph (b) or (c) in the definition of "person from abroad" in regulation 21(3) of the Income Support (General) (Northern Ireland) Regulations 1987;

(SI 2003/654 reg.7) (as amended)

(iv) paragraph (b) or (c) in the definition of "person from abroad" in regulation 85(4) of the Jobseeker's Allowance Regulations (Northern Ireland)1996.

GENERAL NOTE

This is a narrow three-year transitional provision for child tax credit only. It took effect from or after April 6, 2004—the date when CTC was planned to replace the child additions to income support and jobseeker's allowance. It is limited to:
(a) claimants receiving either income support or income-based jobseeker's allowance including child additions immediately before the rule comes into effect; but only if
(b) they are claiming those benefits as refugees or following a grant of exceptional leave to enter or remain in the United Kingdom under the Immigration Acts.

It should be read with the Tax Credits (Immigration) Regulations 2003 (SI 2003/653).

2.429

Tax Credits (Official Error) Regulations 2003

(SI 2003/692)

The Commissioners of Inland Revenue, in exercise of the powers conferred upon them by sections 21 and 65(2), (3), (7) and (9) of the Tax Credits Act 2002 hereby make the following Regulations:

ARRANGEMENT OF REGULATIONS

1. Citation and commencement
2. Interpretation
3. (*Untitled*)

2.430

Citation and commencement

1.—These Regulations may be cited as the Tax Credits (Official Error) Regulations 2003 and shall come into force on 6th April 2003.

2.431

Interpretation

2.—(1) In these Regulations—
"the Board" means the Commissioners of Inland Revenue;
"official error" means an error relating to a tax credit made by—
(a) an officer of the Board;
(b) an officer of the Department for Work and Pensions;
(c) an officer of the Department for Social Development in Northern Ireland; or
(d) a person providing services to the Board or to an authority mentioned in paragraph (b) or (c) of this definition, in connection with a tax credit or credits,
to which the claimant, or any of the claimants, or any person acting for him, or any of them, did not materially contribute, excluding any error

2.432

Tax Credits (Official Error) Regulations 2003

of law which is shown to have been an error by virtue of a subsequent decision by a "Social Security Commissioner or by a court;"
"Social Security Commissioner" has the meaning given by section 63(13);
[¹ . . .]
(2) In these Regulations, references to a section are to that section of the Tax Credits Act 2002.

AMENDMENT

1. Tax Credits (Miscellaneous Amendments) Regulations 2010 (SI 2010/751) regs 11 and 12(1) (April 6, 2010).

GENERAL NOTE

2.433 The double inverted commas at the end of the very last line of the definition of "official error" are a typographical error in the HMSO version of these regulations. The lack of a heading to reg.3 is also unfortunate.

2.434 **3.**—(1) A decision under section 14(1), 15(1), 16(1), 18(1), (5), (6) or (9), 19(3) or 20(1) or (4) may be revised in favour of the person or persons to whom it relates if it is incorrect by reason of official error, subject to the following paragraphs.
(2) In revising a decision, the officer or person in question need not consider any issue that is not raised by the application for revision by the claimant or claimants or, as the case may be, did not cause him to act on his own initiative.
(3) A decision mentioned in paragraph (1) may be revised at any time not later than five years after [¹ the date of the decision].

AMENDMENT

1. Tax Credits (Miscellaneous Amendments) Regulations 2010 (SI 2010/751) regs 11 and 12(2) (April 6, 2010).

DEFINITIONS

"official error"—see reg.2(1).
"tax year"—see *ibid*.

GENERAL NOTE

2.435 These regulations, made under s.21 of the TCA 2002, provide for decisions under the various specified sections of the Act (see reg.3(1)) to be revised in favour of the claimant(s) if they are incorrect because of "official error". The definition of "official error" in reg.2(1) is identical in all material respects to that which applies in the social security scheme under the Social Security and Child Support (Decisions and Appeals) Regulations 1999 (SI 1999/991) (see reg.1(3) and the commentary in Vol. III of this series). However, whereas a social security decision may be revised on the basis of official error and arrears of benefit paid back to the date of the original claim (SSA 1998 s.9(3) and reg.3(5)(a) of the 1999 Regulations), a claim for tax credits is subject to a time limit of five years after the end of the tax year to which the decision relates (reg.3(3)).
In *JP v HMRC (TC)* [2013] UKUT 519 (AAC), the Upper Tribunal considered reg.3 of the Regulations in a case where a DWP official assisted a claimant in making a tax credits claim but in doing so omitted a claim for the disability of the claimant's child. Judge Turnbull accepted as correct an HMRC concession that the actions of the DWP official were official actions. However, the error had led to the award decision under s.14 of the 2002 Act. That had been replaced by an

entitlement decision under s.18. Following the decision in *CTC/262/2005*, the decision to be considered in the appeal was the s.18 decision, and the relevant question was whether the official error was the cause of that decision. On the facts, and applying a commonsense approach to causation as indicated in *R (Sier) v Cambridge CC HBRB* [2001] EWCA Civ 1523, it was decided that the original official error no longer operated to cause the error in the s.18 decision. The claimant had twice been warned to check the decision and had not done so.

Tax Credits (Provision of Information) (Functions Relating to Health) Regulations 2003

(SI 2003/731) (AS AMENDED)

The Commissioners of Inland Revenue, in exercise of the powers conferred upon them by sections 65(2) and 67 of, and paragraph 9(2) of Schedule 5 to, the Tax Credits Act 2002, hereby make the following Regulations:

ARRANGEMENT OF REGULATIONS

1. Citation and commencement
2. Interpretation
3. Prescribed functions relating to health

2.436

Citation and commencement

1.—These Regulations may be cited as the Tax Credits (Provision of Information) (Functions Relating to Health) Regulations 2003 and shall come into force on 6th April 2003.

2.437

GENERAL NOTE

Section 59 of and Sch.5 to the TCA 2002 make provision for the use and disclosure of information relating to claims by and between HMRC and government departments. These regulations prescribe functions for the purposes of para.9 of Sch.5 to the 2002 Act, which enables information relating to tax credits, child benefit or guardian's allowance to be provided by HMRC to the Department of Health, the National Assembly for Wales, the Scottish Ministers, or the Department of Health, Social Services and Public Safety in Northern Ireland for the purposes of such functions relating to health as may be prescribed. These functions are set out in reg.3. Information may also be provided to persons providing services to, or exercising functions on behalf of, those Departments or persons.

These regulations are supplemented by the Tax Credits (Provision of Information) (Functions Relating to Health) (No.2) Regulations 2003 (SI 2003/1650).

2.438

Interpretation

2.—In these Regulations—
"child tax credit" shall be construed in accordance with section 8 of the Tax Credits Act 2002;
[[1]"couple" has the meaning given by section 3(5A) of the Act;]

2.439

"disability element" means the disability element of working tax credit as specified in section 11(3) of the Tax Credits Act 2002;
"family" means—
- (a) in the case of a joint claim for a tax credit under the Tax Credits Act 2002, the [¹. . .] couple by whom the claim is made and any child or qualifying young person for whom at least one of them is responsible, in accordance with regulation 3 of the Child Tax Credit Regulations 2002;
- (b) in the case of a single claim for a tax credit under the Tax Credits Act 2002, the claimant and any child or qualifying young person for whom he is responsible in accordance with regulation 3 of the Child Tax Credit Regulations 2002;

"qualifying family" means a family—
[² (a) that has a relevant income of £16,190 or less, and
  (b) one member of which is a person who—
    (i) is receiving child tax credit, and
    (ii) is not eligible for working tax credit;]

"qualifying young person" has the meaning given by regulation 2(1), read with regulation 5(3) and (4), of the Child Tax Credit Regulations 2002;
"relevant income" has the same meaning as in section 7(3) of the Tax Credits Act 2002;
"working tax credit" shall be construed in accordance with section 10 of the Tax Credits Act 2002.

AMENDMENTS

1. Civil Partnership Act 2004 (Tax Credits, etc.) (Consequential Amendments) Order 2005 (SI 2005/2919) art.9(2) (December 5, 2005).
2. Tax Credits (Miscellaneous Amendments) Regulations 2011 (SI 2011/721) reg.4 (April 6, 2011).

Prescribed functions relating to health

2.440   3.—The following functions are prescribed for the purposes of paragraph 9 of Schedule 5 to the Tax Credits Act 2002 (provision of information by the Board of Inland Revenue for health purposes)—
- (a) the issue by or on behalf of the Secretary of State, the National Assembly for Wales, the Scottish Ministers or the Department of Health, Social Services, and Public Safety in Northern Ireland of a certificate confirming that the family is a qualifying family;
- (b) verification by or on behalf of the Secretary of State, the National Assembly for Wales, the Scottish Ministers or that Department at any time that a family is a qualifying family at that time;
- [¹ (ba) the provision of benefits by or on behalf of the Secretary of State or the Department of Health, Social Services and Public Safety under a scheme established pursuant to section 13 of the Social Security Act 1988(2) or article 13 of the Social Security (Northern Ireland) Order 1988 in so far as such a scheme relates to the health of pregnant women, mothers or children.]
- (c) [¹. . .]
- (d) [¹. . .]
- (e) [¹. . .]

(SI 2003/731 reg.3) (as amended)

DEFINITIONS

"family"—see reg.2.
"qualifying family"—see *ibid.*

AMENDMENTS

1. Tax Credits (Miscellaneous Amendments) Regulations 2011 (SI 2011/721) reg.4 (April 6, 2011).

The Tax Credits (Polygamous Marriages) Regulations 2003

(SI 2003/742) (AS AMENDED)

The Treasury, in exercise of the powers conferred upon them by sections 3(7), 7(8) and (9), 8, 10 to 12, 42, 43 and 65(1), (3), (7) and (9) of the Tax Credits Act 2002, and the Commissioners of Inland Revenue, in exercise of the powers conferred on them by sections 4(1), 6, 24 and 65(2), (3), (7) and (9) of that Act, and of all other powers enabling them in that behalf, hereby make the following Regulations:

ARRANGEMENT OF REGULATIONS

1. Citation, commencement and effect 2.441
2. Interpretation
3–21. Modifications to Pt I of the Act for members of polygamous units
22–25. Amendments to the Child Tax Credit Regulations 2002
26–34. Amendments to the Working Tax Credit (Entitlement and Maximum Rate) Regulations 2002
35–47. Amendments to the Tax Credits (Definition and Calculation of Income) Regulations 2002
39–47A. Amendments to the Tax Credits (Claims and Notifications) Regulations 2002
48–50. Amendments to the Tax Credits (Payment by the Board) Regulations 2002
51–52. Amendments to the Tax Credits (Residence) Regulations 2003
53–56. Amendments to the Tax Credits (Immigration) Regulations 2003

INTRODUCTION AND GENERAL NOTE

These regulations provide alternative language to that of single claims and joint claims, and the associated definitions for single and joint claims, in cases where the claimant is a party to a polygamous marriage. Part I of the TCA 2002 and all relevant regulations are altered to give consistent effect to the policy that all the members of a polygamous marriage, or "unit" as it is called, must jointly claim for and be responsible for any tax credits payable to any of them. This is a different approach from that usually taken for social security benefits purposes, under which polygamous marriages are usually ignored for benefit purposes unless they are in fact monogamous. See the Social Security and Family Allowances (Polygamous Marriages) Regulations 1975 (SI 1975/561) in Vol.I of this work. 2.442

Section 43(1) of the TCA 2002 empowers regulations to apply Pt I of that Act to persons who are parties to a polygamous marriage. "Party to a polygamous marriage" is defined by s.43(2) to include any marriage entered into under a law which permits polygamy and under which any party to the marriage has more than one spouse, that is, more than one husband or wife. The drafters have chosen to

619

adopt different language in these Regulations and the amendments made by these Regulations to the TCA 2002 and other regulations. Instead of "polygamous marriage", the term used throughout is "polygamous unit". The significance of this is discussed in reg.2 below.

The remaining regulations give effect to those modifications as necessary within the other regulations implementing the TCA 2002. Any necessary commentary is added to the relevant amended regulation.

Citation, commencement and effect

2.443   **1.**—(1) These Regulations may be cited as the Tax Credits (Polygamous Marriages) Regulations 2003 and shall come into force on 6th April 2003, immediately after the coming into force of the Child Tax Credit (Amendment) Regulations 2003.

(2) Regulations 22 to 56 only have effect in relation to members of polygamous units (and in the case of regulations 35 to 38, former members of such units).

Interpretation

2.444   **2.**—In these Regulations—
"the Act" means the Tax Credits Act 2002;
"polygamous couple" means a man and a woman who are married under a law which permits polygamy where—
  (a) they are not separated under a court order or in circumstances in which the separation is likely to be permanent; and
  (b) either of them has an additional spouse;
"polygamous unit" means—
  (a) a polygamous couple; and
  (b) any person who is married to either member of the polygamous couple and who is not separated from that member under a court order or in circumstances in which the separation is likely to be permanent.

GENERAL NOTE

2.445   Section 43(2) of the TCA 2002 provides that a person is a party to a polygamous marriage if:
  (a) he or she is a party to a marriage entered into under a law which permits polygamy; and
  (b) he or she has a spouse additional to any other party to the marriage.

The effect of this definition is to limit the scope of the operation of the modifications made under these Regulations to take account also of the definition of "married couple" in s.3(5) of the TCA 2002.

Modifications to Part I of the Act for members of polygamous units

2.446   **3.**—Regulations 4 to 21 prescribe modifications to Part I of the Act so far as it applies to members of polygamous units.

4.—In section 3—
  (a) in subsection (3)(a) after "United Kingdom", insert "(and neither of whom are members of a polygamous unit)";
  (b) after subsection (3)(a) insert—
    "(aa) jointly by the members of a polygamous unit all of whom are aged at least 16 and are in the United Kingdom, or";
  (c) in subsection (3)(b) after "paragraphs (a)", insert "or (aa)";

(SI 2003/742 reg.4) (as amended)

(d) after subsection (4)(a), insert—
"(aa) in the case of a joint claim under subsection (3)(a), if a member of the married or unmarried couple becomes a member of a polygamous unit; and
(ab) in the case of a joint claim under subsection (3)(aa), if there is any change in the persons who comprise the polygamous unit, and";
(e) after subsection (6), insert—
"(6A) In this Part 'polygamous unit' has the meaning given by regulation 2 of the Tax Credits (Polygamous Marriages) Regulations 2003.";
(f) in subsection (8), in the definition of "joint claim", after "para.(a)" insert "or para.(aa)".

5.—In section 4(1)(g)—
(a) for "member of a married couple or an unmarried couple", substitute "or more members of a polygamous unit";
(b) for "of the married couple or unmarried couple", substitute "or members".

6.—In section 7(2), for "either" substitute "any";

7.—In section 8(1), for "either or both" substitute "any or all".

8.—In section 9(2)(b), for "either or both" substitute "any or all".

9.—In section 10—
(a) in subsection (1), for "either or both" substitute "any or all";
(b) in subsection (3), for "either" wherever it appears substitute "any".

10.—In section 11—
(a) in subsection (3), for "either or both" substitute "any or all";
(b) in subsection (6)(a), for "either of the persons or the two" substitute "any of the persons or all";
(c) in subsection (6)(b), for "married couple or unmarried couple" substitute "polygamous unit";
(d) omit subsection (6)(c);
(e) in both subsection (6)(d) and (e), for "either or both" substitute "any or all".

11.—In both section 12(3) and (4)(a), for "either or both" substitute "any or all".

12.—In section 14(2)(a), for "either or both" substitute "any or all".

13.—In section 16(3)(a), for "either or both" substitute "any or all".

14.—In section 17(10)(b)—
(a) for "member of a married couple or an unmarried couple", substitute "or more members of a polygamous unit";
(b) for "married couple or unmarried couple", substitute "or members".

15.—In section 18(10), for "either or both" substitute "any or all".

16.—In section 19—
(a) in subsection (2)(a), for "either or both" substitute "any or all";
(b) in subsection (4)(a), for "either" substitute "any" and for "both" substitute "more than one";
(c) in subsection (9), for "either" substitute "any".

17.—In section 20(4)(b), for "either" (wherever it appears) substitute "any".

18.—In section 24(2)—
(a) for "married couple or an unmarried couple", substitute "polygamous unit";
(b) for "whichever of them" substitute "one or more of those persons as".

19.—In section 29(4), for "either or both" substitute "any or all".

The Tax Credits (Polygamous Marriages) Regulations 2003

20.—In section 31(2)—
(a) after "another" insert "or others";
(b) for "unless subsection (3) applies" substitute "or each of them unless subsection (3) applies to the person in question".

21.—In section 37(1), for "either or both" (in each place they appear) substitute "any or all".

Amendments to the Child Tax Credit Regulations 2002

2.447

22.—Amend the Child Tax Credit Regulations 2002 (for members of polygamous units only) as follows.

23. In regulation 2(1)—
(a) for the definition of "joint claim", substitute the following definition—
"'joint claim' means a claim under section 3(3)(aa) of the Act, as inserted by regulation 4(b) of the Tax Credits (Polygamous Marriages) Regulations 2003;";
(b) insert at the appropriate place the following definition—"'polygamous unit' has the meaning in the Tax Credits (Polygamous Marriages) Regulations 2003;".

24.—In regulation 3(1), in rule 2.1., for "married couple or unmarried couple" in each place it appears substitute "polygamous unit".

25. In regulation 7—
(a) in paragraph (1)(b), for "married couple or unmarried couple" substitute "polygamous unit";
(b) in paragraph (2)(b)(ii), for "either or both" substitute "any or all".

Amendments to the Working Tax Credit (Entitlement and Maximum Rate) Regulations 2002

2.448

26.—Amend the Working Tax Credit (Entitlement and Maximum Rate) Regulations 2002 (for members of polygamous units only) as follows.

27.—In regulation 2(1)—
(a) for the definition of "joint claim", substitute the following definition—" 'joint claim' means a claim under section 3(3)(aa) of the Act (as inserted by regulation 4(b) of the Tax Credits (Polygamous Marriages) Regulations 2003);";
(b) insert at the appropriate place the following definition—" 'polygamous unit' has the meaning in the Tax Credits (Polygamous Marriages) Regulations 2003;".

28.—In regulation 3(3)—
(a) for "both members of the couple satisfy", substitute "more than one member of the polygamous unit satisfies"; and
(b) for "two such elements", substitute "one such element for each of them that satisfies those conditions".

[² **29.**—In regulation 4(1) in the third variation of the Second Condition—
(a) in the introduction, for "that person's partner" substitute "any other member of the polygamous unit"; and
(b) in paragraph (a)—
(i) for "couple" (in both places) substitute "polygamous unit"; and
(ii) for "partner" substitute "member of the unit".]

30.—In regulation 10(2)—

(SI 2003/742 reg.30) (as amended)

(a) in sub-paragraph (c), for "couple" substitute "members of the polygamous unit";
(b) in sub-paragraph (d), for "couple" substitute "unit".

31.—In regulation 11—
(a) in paragraph (1), after "element" insert "(and an additional such element for each member of the polygamous unit exceeding two in number)";
(b) in paragraph (2)(c), for "neither of the claimants" substitute "no claimant";
(c) in paragraph (4), in the words preceding sub-paragraph (a), after "adult element" insert "for any claimant";
(d) in paragraph (4)(a), for "neither claimant" substitute "none of the claimants"; and
(e) in paragraph (4)(b), for "one claimant" substitute "the claimant in question".

32.—In regulation 13—
(a) omit paragraph (1)(a);
(b) in paragraph (1)(b), for "married or unmarried couple where both" substitute "polygamous unit where at least two of them";
(c) in paragraph (1)(c), for the words preceding paragraph (i) substitute "is a member or are members of a polygamous unit where at least one member is engaged in qualifying remunerative work and at least one other".
(d) in paragraph (4), for "the other member of a couple" substitute "another member of the polygamous unit";
(e) in paragraph (5), for "the other member or his partner" substitute "him or another member of the polygamous unit".

33.—In regulation 14—
(a) in paragraph (1), for "either or both" substitute "any or all";
(b) in paragraph (1B), for "either or both" substitute "any or all";
(c) in paragraph (5), for "a partner or by a partner" substitute "another member of the same polygamous unit or".

34.—In regulation 20—
(a) in paragraph (1), for "single claimant or to a couple" substitute "polygamous unit";
(b) omit paragraph (1)(c)(i);
(c) in paragraph (1)(c)(ii), for "a couple either or both" substitute "the members of a polygamous unit, any or all of whom";
(d) in paragraph (1)(c)(iii), for "a couple" substitute "the members of a polygamous unit";
(e) omit paragraph (1)(e);
(f) omit paragraph (1)(f)(i);
(g) in paragraph (1)(f)(ii), for "couple" substitute "polygamous unit".

Amendments to the Tax Credits (Definition and Calculation of Income) Regulations 2002

35.—Amend the Tax Credits (Definition and Calculation of Income) Regulations 2002 (for members or former members of polygamous units only) as follows.

2.449

36.—In regulation 2 (interpretation)—
(a) in paragraph (2), in the definition of "family" for "married or unmarried couple" substitute "members of the polygamous unit";

(b) in paragraph (2), insert at the appropriate places the following definitions—
"'joint claim' means a claim under section 3(3)(aa) of the Act, as inserted by regulation 4(b) of the Tax Credits (Polygamous Marriages) Regulations 2003; "polygamous unit" has the meaning in the Tax Credits (Polygamous Marriages) Regulations 2003;";
(c) in paragraph (4)(a), for the words from "a claimant's spouse" to the end substitute "another member of the same polygamous unit";
(d) in paragraph (4)(b), for the words from "claimant's former spouse" to the end substitute "person who was formerly a member with the claimant of the same polygamous unit".

37.—In regulation 3(7), (calculation of income of claimant)—
(a) in sub-paragraph (b), for "either or both" substitute "any or all";
(b) in sub-paragraph (c), for "either or both" substitute "any or all".

38. In regulation 4(1) (employment income), in the words succeeding sub-para.(k), for "either" substitute "any".

Amendments to the Tax Credits (Claims and Notifications) Regulations 2002

39.—Amend the Tax Credits (Claims and Notifications) Regulations 2002 (for members of polygamous units only) as follows.

40. In regulation 2 (interpretation)—
(a) for the definition of "joint claim" substitute the following definition—
" 'joint claim', means a claim under section 3(3)(aa) of the Act, as inserted by regulation 4(b) of the Tax Credits (Polygamous Marriages) Regulations 2003;";
(b) insert at the appropriate place the following definition—
"'polygamous unit' has the meaning in the Tax Credits (Polygamous Marriages) Regulations 2003;".

41.—In regulation 11(2), for "both" substitute "all of the".

42.—In regulation 13—
(a) in paragraph (1), for the words from "one member" to the end substitute "one or more members of a polygamous unit is to be treated as also made by the other member or members of that unit";
(b) in paragraph (2)—
(i) for "member of a married couple or an unmarried couple", substitute "or more members of a polygamous unit";
(ii) for "both members of the couple", substitute "all the members of the unit".

43.—In regulation 15—
(a) in paragraph (3) for the words from "only one" to the end, substitute "one or more members of a polygamous unit die, the other member or members of the unit may proceed with the claim in the name or names of the person or persons who have died, as well as in their own name or names";
(b) in paragraph (4), for "both" (in each place it appears) substitute "all of".

44.—In regulation 16—
(a) in paragraph (1), for the words from "member of a" to the end, sub-

stitute "or more members of a polygamous unit die and the other member or members of the unit wish to make a joint claim for a tax credit";
(b) for paragraph (2), substitute—
"(2) The survivor or survivors may make and proceed with the claim in the name of the member or members who have died as well as in his or their own names.;"
(c) in paragraph (3)(a)—
  (i) for "married couple or unmarried couple", substitute "polygamous unit";
  (ii) add at the end "(or the earliest such date if more than one)".

45.—In regulation 23(2), for "either member of the married couple or unmarried couple" substitute "any member of the polygamous unit".

46.—In regulation 30(2), for "either" (in each place it appears) substitute "any".

47.—In regulation 31(2)(a), for "either" substitute "any".

[¹**47A.** In regulation 34(3)—
(a) for "one of two joint claimants" substitute "any member of a polygamous unit"; and
(b) for "both" (in each place where it occurs) substitute "all".]

Amendments to the Tax Credits (Payment by the Board) Regulations 2002

48.—Amend the Tax Credits (Payments by the Board) Regulations 2002 (for members of polygamous units only) as follows.

49.—In regulation 2 (interpretation)—
(a) omit the definitions of "married couple" and "unmarried couple";
(b) insert at the appropriate place the following definition—
" 'polygamous unit' has the meaning in the Tax Credits (Polygamous Marriages) Regulations 2003;".

50.—In regulation 3—
(a) in the heading, for "couple" substitute "polygamous unit";
(b) for paragraphs (2) to (6) substitute—
"(2) There shall be established, for each particular child or qualifying young person for whom any or all of the members of the polygamous unit is or are responsible—
(a) the member of that unit who is (for the time being) identified by all the members of the unit as the main carer for that child or qualifying young person; or
(b) in default of such a member, the member of that unit who appears to the Board to be the main carer for that child or qualifying young person.

(3) The individual element of child tax credit for any child or qualifying young person shall be paid to the main carer of that child or qualifying young person.

(4) The family element of child tax credit for any polygamous unit shall be divided (pro rata) by the number of children and qualifying young persons for whom any or all of the members of that unit is or are responsible, and the proportion so attributable to each such child or qualifying young person shall be paid to the main carer of that child or qualifying young person.

(5) Any childcare element of working tax credit shall be divided (pro rata) by the number of children referred to in paragraph (2) in respect of whom

The Tax Credits (Polygamous Marriages) Regulations 2003

relevant childcare charges are paid, and the proportion so attributable to each such child shall be paid to the main carer of that child.

(6) In this regulation—

"child" has the meaning given by the Child Tax Credit Regulations 2002;

"qualifying young person" has the meaning given by those Regulations; and

"relevant childcare charges" has the meaning given by regulation 14(1) of the Working Tax Credit (Entitlement and Maximum Rate) Regulations 2002."

Amendments to the Tax Credits (Residence) Regulations 2003

2.452   **51.**—Amend the Tax Credits (Residence) Regulations 2003 (for members of polygamous units only) as follows.

52.—In regulation 2 (Interpretation)—

(a) in the definition of "partner", for the words from "married" to the end, substitute "polygamous unit, any other member of that unit";

(b) insert at the appropriate place the following definition—" 'polygamous unit' has the meaning in the Tax Credits (Polygamous Marriages) Regulations 2003;".

Amendments to the Tax Credits (Immigration) Regulations 2003

2.453   **53.**—Amend the Tax Credits (Immigration) Regulations 2003 (for members of polygamous units only) as follows.

54.—In regulation 2 (Interpretation)—

(a) for the definition of "joint claim", substitute the following definition— "joint claim" means a claim under section 3(3)(aa) of the Act, as inserted by regulation 4(b) of the "Tax Credits (Polygamous Marriages) Regulations 2003";

(b) insert at the appropriate place the following definition— "polygamous unit" has the meaning in the "Tax Credits (Polygamous Marriages) Regulations 2003;".

55.—In regulation 3(2)—

(a) for the words from "married couple" to "and the other", substitute "polygamous unit is a person subject to immigration control and any other";

(b) in sub-paragraph (b), for "couple" substitute "unit".

56.—In regulation 4(1) (modifications to the Tax Credits Act 2002), add at the end "(which, in the case of a claim by the members of a polygamous unit, are subject to the modifications made by regulations 4 to 21 of the Tax Credits (Polygamous Marriages) Regulations 2003)".

AMENDMENTS

1. Tax Credits (Miscellaneous Amendments) Regulations 2004 (SI 2004/762) reg.19 (April 6, 2004).

2. Tax Credits (Miscellaneous Amendments) Regulations 2012 (SI 2012/848) reg.9 (April 6, 2012).

(SI 2003/1650)

Tax Credits (Provision of Information) (Functions Relating to Health) (No.2) Regulations 2003

(SI 2003/1650)

The Commissioners of Inland Revenue, in exercise of the powers conferred upon them by sections 65(2) and 67 of, and paragraph 9 of Schedule 5 to the Tax Credits Act 2002 hereby make the following Regulations:

ARRANGEMENT OF REGULATIONS

1. Citation, commencement and extent
2. Prescribed functions relating to health

2.454

GENERAL NOTE

These regulations supplement the Tax Credits (Provision of Information) (Functions Relating to Health) Regulations 2003 (SI 2003/731).

2.455

Citation, commencement and extent

1.—(1) These Regulations may be cited as the Tax Credits (Provision of Information) (Functions Relating to Health) (No.2) Regulations 2003 and shall come into force on 17th July 2003.

(2) These Regulations do not extend to Northern Ireland.

2.456

Prescribed functions relating to health

2.—(1) The function specified in paragraph (2) is prescribed for the purposes of paragraph 9 of Schedule 5 to the Tax Credits Act 2002 (provision of information by the Board of Inland Revenue for health purposes).

(2) The function specified in this paragraph is the conduct, by a person providing services to the Secretary of State and the Scottish Ministers, of a survey of the mental health of persons in Great Britain who are under the age of 17 on 1st September 2003.

(3) Nothing in these Regulations limits the operation of the Tax Credits (Provision of Information Relating to Health) Regulations 2003.

2.457

Tax Credits (Provision of Information) (Function Relating to Employment and Training) Regulations 2003

(SI 2003/2041)

The Commissioners of Inland Revenue, in exercise of the powers conferred upon them by sections 65(2) and 67 of, and paragraph 5(2) of Schedule 5 to, the Tax Credits Act 2002, hereby make the following Regulations:

ARRANGEMENT OF REGULATIONS

1. Citation, commencement and extent
2. Prescribed function relating to employment and training

2.458

GENERAL NOTE

2.459 These regulations, made under para.5 of Sch.5 to the Tax Credits Act 2002, enable information relating to tax credits, child benefit or guardian's allowance to be provided by HMRC to the Secretary of State for the purposes of the operation of the Employment Retention and Advancement Scheme established under s.2 of the Employment and Training Act 1973.

Citation, commencement and extent

2.460 **1.**—(1) These Regulations may be cited as the Tax Credits (Provision of Information) (Function Relating to Employment and Training) Regulations 2003 and shall come into force on 29th August 2003.

(2) These Regulations do not extend to Northern Ireland.

Prescribed function relating to employment and training

2.461 **2.**—(1) The function specified in paragraph (2) is prescribed for the purposes of paragraph 5 of Schedule 5 to the Tax Credits Act 2002 (provision of information by the Board of Inland Revenue for employment and training purposes).

(2) The function specified in this paragraph is the operation of the Employment Retention and Advancement Scheme, that is to say the scheme for assisting persons to improve their job retention or career advancement, established by the Secretary of State under section 2 of the Employment and Training Act 1973.

Tax Credits Act 2002 (Child Tax Credit) (Transitional Provisions) Order 2003

(SI 2003/2170)

The Treasury, in exercise of the powers conferred upon them by section 62(2) of the Tax Credits Act 2002, make the following Order:

ARRANGEMENT OF ARTICLES

2.462   1. Citation and commencement
2. Transitional provision

GENERAL NOTE

2.463 Section 1(3)(d) of the Tax Credits Act 2002 provides for the abolition of various component elements of the applicable amount for the purposes of income support and income-based jobseeker's allowance (namely the child allowances, family premium, disabled child premium and enhanced disability premium for a child or young person). This Order makes transitional provision in connection with the introduction of child tax credit, but only for pensioners formerly in receipt of the minimum income guarantee in income support. The Order thus applies to persons who were in receipt of income support, were aged not less than 60 and were responsible for a child, throughout the period beginning on August 22, 2003 and ending

(SI 2003/2170)

on September 28, 2003 (art.2(1)). In such a case a person is deemed to have made a claim for child tax credit (a) on August 22, 2003 for the purpose of enabling a decision to be made by HMRC on the claim and (b) on the first day of the first benefit week beginning on or after September 29, 2003 for all other purposes, e.g. as regards payment (art.2(2)). This Order is thus associated with the introduction of state pension credit as from October 2003.

Citation and commencement

1. This Order may be cited as the Tax Credits Act 2002 (Child Tax Credit) (Transitional Provisions) Order 2003 and shall come into force on 22nd August 2003.

Transitional provision

2.—(1) This article applies in the case of a person who throughout the period beginning on 22nd August 2003 and ending on 28th September 2003 is—
   (a) in receipt of income support;
   (b) aged not less than 60; and
   (c) responsible for a child (within the meaning of regulation 3 of the Child Tax Credit Regulations 2002).
(2) Where this article applies to a person, he shall be treated as having made a claim for child tax credit in respect of the child for whom he is responsible as mentioned in paragraph (1)(c) of this article—
   (a) on 22nd August 2003 for the purposes of enabling the Board to make an initial decision on the claim; and
   (b) on the first day of the first benefit week in relation to income support beginning on or after 29th September 2003 for all other purposes.
(3) In paragraph (2) "benefit week" has the same meaning—
   (a) in relation to a person in Great Britain, as it bears in regulation 2(1) of the Income Support (General) Regulations 1987; and
   (b) in relation to a person in Northern Ireland, as it bears in regulation 2(1) of the Income Support (General) Regulations (Northern Ireland) 1987.

Tax Credits (Provision of Information) (Evaluation and Statistical Studies) Regulations 2003

(SI 2003/3308)

The Commissioners of Inland Revenue, in exercise of the powers conferred upon them by sections 65(2) and 67 of, and paragraph 4(2) of Schedule 5 to, the Tax Credits Act 2002 make the following Regulations:

Citation, commencement and extent

1.—(1) These Regulations may be cited as the Tax Credits (Provision of Information) (Evaluation and Statistical Studies) Regulations 2003 and shall come into force on 9th January 2004.
(2) These Regulations do not extend to Northern Ireland.

Purposes for which information may be provided

2.467　**2.**—The purposes of conducting evaluation and statistical studies in relation to—
(a) the education of children and young people under the age of 17; and
(b) the provision and use of child care,
are prescribed under paragraph 4 of Schedule 5 to the Tax Credits Act 2002 (provision of information by the Board of Inland Revenue for evaluation and statistical studies).

Here "child care" means any care provided for a child whether or not of a description prescribed for any purpose under the Act.

Tax Credits (Provision of Information) (Evaluation and Statistical Studies) (Northern Ireland) Regulations 2004

(SI 2004/1414)

The Commissioners of Inland Revenue, in exercise of the powers conferred upon them by sections 65(2) and 67 of, and paragraph 4(2) of Schedule 5 to, the Tax Credits Act 2002 make the following Regulations:

Citation, commencement and extent

2.468　**1.**—These Regulations may be cited as the Tax Credits (Provision of Information) (Evaluation and Statistical Studies) (Northern Ireland) Regulations 2004, shall come into force on 14th June 2004 and extend only to Northern Ireland.

Purposes for which information may be provided

2.469　**2.**—The purposes of conducting evaluation and statistical studies about community relations, education and employment of persons in Northern Ireland under the age of 18, are prescribed under paragraph 4 of Schedule 5 to the Tax Credits Act 2002 (provision of information by the Board of Inland Revenue for evaluation and statistical studies).

Tax Credits (Provision of Information) (Functions Relating to Health) (Scotland) Regulations 2004

(SI 2004/1895 (S.6))

The Commissioners of Inland Revenue, in exercise of the powers conferred upon them by sections 65(2) and 67 of, and paragraph 9 of Schedule 5 to, the Tax Credits Act 2002, make the following Regulations:

Citation, commencement and extent

2.470　**1.**—These Regulations may be cited as the Tax Credits (Provision of Information) (Functions Relating to Health) (Scotland) Regulations 2004, shall come into force on 11th August 2004 and extend only to Scotland.

(SI 2004/1895 (S.6) reg.2)

Purpose for which information may be provided

2.—(1) The purpose of conducting surveys of the health of children and young people under the age of 17 and their families, by the Scottish Ministers or persons providing services to them, or exercising functions on behalf of them, is prescribed under paragraph 9 of Schedule 5 to the Tax Credits Act 2002 (provision of information by the Board of Inland Revenue for health purposes).

(2) Nothing in these Regulations affects the operation of the Tax Credits (Provision of Information) (Functions Relating to Health) Regulations 2003 or the Tax Credits (Provision of Information) (Functions Relating to Health) (No.2) Regulations 2003.

2.471

Tax Credits (Provision of Information) (Function Relating to Employment and Training) Regulations 2005

(SI 2005/66)

The Commissioners of Inland Revenue, in exercise of the powers conferred upon them by sections 65(2) and 67 of, and paragraph 5(2) of Schedule 5 to, the Tax Credits Act 2002, make the following Regulations:

Citation and commencement

1.—These Regulations may be cited as the Tax Credits (Provision of Information) (Function Relating to Employment and Training) Regulations 2005 and shall come into force on 8th February 2005.

2.472

Prescribed function relating to employment and training

2.—(1) The function specified in paragraph (2) is prescribed for the purposes of paragraph 5 of Schedule 5 to the Tax Credits Act 2002 (provision of information by the Board of Inland Revenue for employment and training purposes).

(2) The function specified in this paragraph is evaluation of, and research in relation to, the employment and training programmes administered—
  (a) in Great Britain, by the Department for Work and Pensions; or
  (b) in Northern Ireland, the Department for Employment and Learning.

2.473

The Tax Credits (Child Care Providers) (Miscellaneous Revocation and Transitional Provisions) (England) Scheme 2007

(2007/2481)

ARRANGEMENT OF SCHEME

1. Citation, commencement and application
2. Interpretation
3. Partial revocation of the 1999 Regulations and transitional provision
4. Revocation of the 2005 Scheme and transitional provision

2.474

The Tax Credits (Child Care Providers) (Miscellaneous) Scheme 2007

The Secretary of State for Children, Schools and Families, being the appropriate national authority under section 12(6) of the Tax Credits Act 2002, and in exercise of the powers conferred by sections 12(5), (7) and (8) and 65(9) of that Act, makes the following Scheme:

Citation, commencement and application

2.475　**1.**—(1) This Scheme may be cited as the Tax Credits (Child Care Providers) (Miscellaneous Revocation and Transitional Provisions) (England) Scheme 2007.

(2) This Scheme comes into force—
(a) to the extent that it revokes the 2005 Scheme and the provisions of the 1999 Regulations other than regulations 11(a) and (b) and 12, on 1st October 2007; and
(b) to the extent that it revokes regulations 11(a) and (b) and 12 of the 1999 Regulations, on 1st October 2009.

(3) This Scheme applies in relation to England only.

Interpretation

2.476　**2.**—In this Scheme—
"the 1999 Regulations" means the Tax Credit (New Category of Child Care Provider) Regulations 1999;
"the 2005 Scheme" means the Tax Credits (Approval of Child Care Providers) Scheme 2005;
"the inspection provisions" means regulations 11(a) and (b) and 12 of the 1999 Regulations (access to information and records by officers of the Secretary of State and Her Majesty's Revenue and Customs); and
"the transitional period" means the period beginning on 1st October 2007 and ending on 1st October 2009.

Partial revocation of the 1999 Regulations and transitional provision

2.477　**3.**—(1) The 1999 Regulations are revoked to the extent that they make a Scheme for determining the description of persons by whom child care is provided, and whose charges fall to be taken into account in computing the child care element of working tax credit, subject to paragraph (3) of this article.

(2) Any accreditation of an organisation by the Secretary of State pursuant to the Scheme provided for by the 1999 Regulations, and any approval granted by such an organisation, shall lapse on 1st October 2007, except for the purposes of the inspection provisions.

(3) During the transitional period the inspection provisions shall have effect as if—
(a) the reference in regulation 11 to the period for which an organisation is accredited were a reference to the transitional period; and
(b) the reference in regulation 12 to the period during which a child care provider is approved by an accredited organisation were a reference to the transitional period.

DEFINITIONS

"the 1999 Regulations"—see art.2.
"the inspection provisions"—see *ibid.*
"the transitional period"—see *ibid.*

(2007/2481 reg.4)

Revocation of the 2005 Scheme and transitional provision

4.—(1) The 2005 Scheme is revoked, subject to paragraph (2).

(2) The provisions of the 2005 Scheme continue to have effect [¹ , with the modifications in paragraph (3),] in relation to—
  (a) any approval granted to a child care provider under that Scheme which is valid immediately before 1st October 2007; and
  (b) any application for approval under that Scheme which has not been granted before 1st October 2007.

[¹ (3) For the purposes of paragraph (2) the 2005 Scheme is amended as follows—
  (a) in article 2 omit the definitions of "the Tribunal" and "the Tribunal Regulations";
  (b) in article 11—
    (i) in paragraphs (1) and (5) for "Tribunal" substitute "First-tier Tribunal";
    (ii) for paragraph (2) substitute—
"(2) Tribunal Procedure Rules shall apply to an appeal under paragraph (1) as they apply to an appeal under section 79M of the 1989 Act."; and
  (c) omit paragraphs (3) and (4).]

2.478

AMENDMENT

1. Tribunals, Courts and Enforcement Act 2007 (Transitional and Consequential Provisions) Order 2008 (SI 2008/2683) art.6 and Sch.1 para.329 (November 3, 2008).

DEFINITION

"the 2005 Scheme"—see art.2.

GENERAL NOTE

This Scheme partially revokes the Tax Credit (New Category of Child Care Provider) Regulations 1999 (SI 1999/3110) and revokes the Tax Credits (Approval of Child Care Providers) Scheme 2005 (SI 2005/93), with transitional provisions (see 2007 main Vol.IV paras 2.578–2.590 for the 2005 Scheme). The new Scheme applies in relation to England only. For Wales, see the Tax Credits (Approval of Child Care Providers) (Wales) Scheme 2007 (SI 2007/226 (W.20), as amended by the Tax Credits (Approval of Child Care Providers) (Wales) (Amendment) Scheme 2007 SI 2008/2687 (W.237). The revocations provided for by the Scheme mostly came into force on October 1, 2007. Provision of a Scheme for Wales is now a devolved function with responsibility transferred to Welsh Ministers. Those powers were exercised with effect from November 1, 2011 to amend the 2007 Welsh Scheme. The principal amendment is the revocation of the power providing for decisions on claims to be made by a private contractor. All new claims from that date are to be decided by the Welsh Ministers: Tax Credits (Approval of Child Care Applications) (Wales) (Amendment) Scheme 2011 / Cynllun Credydau Treth (Cymeradwyau Darparwyr Gofal Plant) (Cymru) (Diwygio) 2011 (SI 2011/993).

Article 3(1) revokes the 1999 Regulations to the extent that they make a Scheme for determining the description of persons by whom child care is provided, and whose charges fall to be taken into account in computing the child care element of working tax credit. Article 3(2) makes various transitional provision concerning the access to information and records by HMRC officers and for allied matters.

2.479

Article 4(1) revokes the 2005 Scheme. Article 4(2) makes transitional provision to ensure that approvals granted under the 2005 Scheme that were valid immediately before October 1, 2007 continue to have effect until the end of their period of validity.

The 1999 Regulations and the 2005 Scheme have been revoked following the introduction of a system of voluntary registration for certain childcare providers under the Childcare Act 2006 (see the Childcare (Voluntary Registration) Regulations 2007 (SI 2007/730)).

The Loss of Tax Credits (Specified Day) Order 2013

(SI 2013/524)

The Treasury make the following Order in exercise of the powers conferred by sections 36A(10) and 36C(7) of the Tax Credits Act 2002:

Citation and commencement

2.480   1.—This Order may be cited as the Loss of Tax Credits (Specified Day) Order 2013 and shall come into force on 6th April 2013.

Specified day

2.481   2.—The day specified under sections 36A(10) and 36C(7) of the Tax Credits Act 2002 for the purposes of sections 36A to 36D that Act is 6th April 2013.

GENERAL NOTE

2.482   This Order specifies April 6, 2013 as the day for the purposes of ss.36A to 36D of the Tax Credits Act 2002. Where an offence within the scope of those sections is committed after this date, it is a "benefit offence" for the purposes of ss.36A to 36D of the Act.

The Loss of Tax Credits Regulations 2013

(SI 2013/715)

The Commissioners for Her Majesty's Revenue and Customs make these Regulations in the exercise of the powers conferred by sections 36A(5) and (6), 36C(4) and (5), 65(2) and 67 of the Tax Credits Act 2002. A draft of this instrument was laid before and approved by a resolution of each House of Parliament in accordance with section 66(1) and (2)(zb) of the Tax Credits Act 2002.

Citation, commencement and interpretation

2.483   1.—(1) These Regulations may be cited as the Loss of Tax Credits Regulations 2013 and come into force on 6th April 2013.

(2) In these Regulations, references to sections of the Act are to sections of the Tax Credits Act 2002.

(SI 2013/715 reg.2)

Loss of working tax credit for benefit offence and repeated benefit fraud: beginning of disqualification periods

2.—(1) For the purposes of section 36A(6) of the Act, the date on which the relevant period begins is the thirtieth day after the day on which the Commissioners for Her Majesty's Revenue and Customs ("the Commissioners") are notified of the disqualifying event mentioned in section 36A(1)—
  (a) in relation to England and Wales and Scotland, by the Secretary of State or by an authority which administers housing benefit or council tax benefit,
  (b) in relation to Northern Ireland, by the Department for Social Development, the Department of Finance and Personnel or the Northern Ireland Housing Executive.

(2) For the purposes of section 36C(5) of the Act, the prescribed date is the thirtieth day after the day on which the Commissioners are notified of the offender's conviction mentioned in that section, by the prosecuting authority responsible for bringing the current set of proceedings in which the offender was convicted.

Loss of working tax credit for benefit offence and repeated benefit fraud

3.—For the duration of any period—
  (a) comprised in the offender's disqualification period for the purposes of section 36A(4)(b) or 36C(3)(b) of the Act, and
  (b) not comprising any such disqualification period of the other member of the couple mentioned in either section,
the working tax credit in question shall be payable, but as if the amount payable were reduced by 50%.

GENERAL NOTE

These regulations provide for the date from which the disqualification period provided for in ss.36A to 36D of the 2002 Act operate.

Regulation 3 allows one of a joint couple to continue receiving half the previous working tax credit entitlement where the other of the couple has been convicted or is subject to a penalty under those sections.

The Tax Credits (Late Appeals) Order 2014

(SI 2014/885)

The Treasury make the following Order in exercise of the powers conferred by section 124(1), (2), (6) and (7) of the Finance Act 2008. A draft of this Order was laid before Parliament and approved by a resolution of each House of Parliament in accordance with section 124(9) of the Finance Act 2008.

Citation, commencement and extent

1.—(1) This Order may be cited as the Tax Credits (Late Appeals) Order 2014 and comes into force on the day after it is made.

(2) This Order extends to England and Wales and Scotland only.

Amendment of the Tax Credits Act 2002

2.488 **2.**—(1) The Tax Credits Act 2002 is amended as follows.

(2) [*inserts section 39A of the Tax Credits Act 2002*]

(3) Where, in respect of a late appeal made on or after 1 April 2013 and before this Order comes into force, the Commissioners for Her Majesty's Revenue and Customs have before this Order comes into force notified the appellant that they consider the appeal should proceed even though it was not made within the period specified in section 39(1) of the Tax Credits Act 2002, that notification is to have effect after this Order comes into force as a decision under section 39A to treat the appeal as made in time.

GENERAL NOTE

2.489 The Order adds the new s.39A to the 2002 Act. See the general note to that section. Article 2(3) gives retrospective effect to any admission of a late appeal by HMRC where that appeal was made on or after April 1, 2013, but before April 2, 2014, the day on which this Order took effect under art.1(2).

The Tax Credits, Child Benefit and Guardian's Allowance Reviews and Appeals Order 2014

(SI 2014/886)

The Treasury make this Order in exercise of the powers conferred by section 124(1), (2), (6) and (7) of the Finance Act 2008. A draft of this instrument was laid before and approved by resolution of the House of Commons in accordance with section 124(8) of that Act.

Citation, commencement and effect

2.490 **1.**—(1) This Order may be cited as the Tax Credits, Child Benefit and Guardian's Allowance Reviews and Appeals Order 2014 and comes into force on 6th April 2014.

(2) But articles 2(13), 3(2) to (6), 5(2), 5(7)(a), (c), (e), (g), (h), (j) and (l), and 5(9) only come

into force on a day appointed by an order of the Treasury made by statutory instrument, and the Treasury may so appoint different days for different purposes.

(3) Articles 2(12) and 3(1) extend to England and Wales and Scotland only.

(4) Articles 2(13) and 3(2) to (6) extend to Northern Ireland only.

(5) Any amendment made by this Order only has effect in relation to an HMRC decision made on or after the amendment comes into force.

Amendment of the Tax Credits Act 2002

2.491 **2.**—[*Amendments included in the Act above*]

(SI 2014/886 reg.3)

Revocation (for Great Britain) and amendment (for Northern Ireland) of the Tax Credits (Notice of Appeal) Regulations 2002

3.—(1) The Tax Credits (Notice of Appeal) Regulations 2002 are revoked (for England and Wales and Scotland).
. . .

Child benefit and guardian's allowance: amendment of the Social Security Act 1998 and the Social Security (Northern Ireland) Order 1998

4.—[*Amendments included in the 1998 Act above.*]

Amendment of the Child Benefit and Guardian's Allowance (Decisions and Appeals) Regulations 2003

5.—[*Amendments, so far as in force, included in the regulations above.*]

Tax Credits (Settlement of Appeals) Regulations 2014

(SI 2014/1933)

The Commissioners for Her Majesty's Revenue and Customs in exercise of the powers conferred by sections 63(8) and 65(2) and (6) of the Tax Credits Act 2002 and with the consent of the Lord Chancellor, the Department of Justice in Northern Ireland and the Scottish Ministers, make the following Regulations.

Citation, commencement and extent

1.—(1) These Regulations may be cited as the Tax Credits (Settlement of Appeals) Regulations 2014 and come into force on 12th August 2014
(2) These Regulations extend to England and Wales and Scotland only.

Interpretation

2.—In these Regulations—
"tax credits appeal" means an appeal which, by virtue of section 63 of the Tax Credits Act 2002 (tax credits appeals etc: temporary modifications), is to the First-tier Tribunal.

Application of section 54 of the Taxes Management Act 1970

3.—(1) Section 54 of the Taxes Management Act 1970 (settling of appeals by agreement) shall apply to a tax credits appeal, with the modifications prescribed by paragraphs (2) to (7).
(2) In subsection (1) for "tribunal" (in both places) substitute "First-tier Tribunal".
(3) In subsections (1) and (4) for "assessment" (in each place) substitute "determination".
(4) In subsections (1), (2) and (4)(a) for "the inspector or other proper officer of the Crown" substitute "an officer of Revenue and Customs".
(5) For subsection (3) substitute—
"(3) Where an agreement is not in writing—

(a) the preceding provisions of this section shall not apply unless the Board give notice, in such form and manner as they consider appropriate, to the appellant of the terms agreed between the officer of Revenue and Customs and the appellant; and
(b) the references in those preceding provisions to the time when the agreement was come to shall be construed as references to the date of that notice.".

(6) In subsection (4)(b) for "the inspector or other proper officer" substitute "an officer of Revenue and Customs".

(7) In subsection (4), in the words after paragraph (b), for "the inspector or other proper officer" substitute "an officer of Revenue and Customs".

Tax Credits (Exercise of Functions) Order 2014

(SI 2014/3280)

This Order in Council is made in exercise of the powers conferred by section 126(1), (2), (3)(a) and (b)(i) and (9) of the Welfare Reform Act 2012. Accordingly, Her Majesty is pleased, by and with the advice of Her Privy Council to order as follows:

Citation and commencement

2.498 1.—This Order may be cited as the Tax Credits (Exercise of Functions) Order 2014 and comes into force on 1st April 2015.

Interpretation

2.499 2.—(1) In this Order—
"the 2002 Act" means the Tax Credits Act 2002;
"the Administration Act" means the Social Security Administration Act 1992;
"the 2013 Regulations" means the Social Security (Overpayments and Recovery) Regulations 2013;
"notice" means a notice given under section 29 of the 2002 Act (recovery of overpayments of tax credits);
"penalty" means a penalty imposed under section 31 (incorrect statements etc.) or 32 (failure to comply with requirements) of the 2002 Act.

(2) Any interest carried under section 37 of the 2002 Act on an amount specified in a notice or on a penalty is to be regarded for the purpose of this Order as if it were specified in the notice or formed part of the penalty respectively.

Functions exercisable by the Secretary of State

2.500 3.—(1) The functions of the Commissioners under section 2 of the 2002 Act specified in paragraph (2) are to be exercisable concurrently with the Secretary of State.

(2) The functions are those that relate to—
(a) the recovery from a person to whom a notice has been given of the amount specified in a notice;

(SI 2014/3280 reg.3)

(b) the recovery from a person on whom a penalty has been imposed of the amount of the penalty.

Application of the Administration Act

4.—(1) Subject to paragraph (2), the amount specified in a notice or, as the case may be, the amount of a penalty is, for the purposes of the Administration Act, to be treated as if it were an amount recoverable under section 71ZB of that Act.

(2) Section 71ZB of the Administration Act has effect in relation to the amount specified in a notice or, as the case may be, the amount of a penalty, as if subsection (3) were omitted.

Application of the 2013 Regulations

5.—(1) The amount specified in a notice is, for the purposes of the 2013 Regulations, to be treated as if it were an overpayment as defined in regulation 2 of those Regulations.

(2) The amount of a penalty is, for the purposes of the 2013 Regulations, to be treated as if it were an amount recoverable under a provision of the Administration Act specified in regulation 3(2) of those Regulations.

Amendment of the 2013 Regulations

6.—In the definition of "overpayment" in regulation 2 of the 2013 Regulations (interpretation) omit paragraph (b).

2.501

2.502

2.503

PART III

CHILDREN AND GUARDIANS

The Child Benefit (General) Regulations 2006

(SI 2006/223)

ARRANGEMENT OF REGULATIONS

PART 1

INTRODUCTORY

1. Citation, commencement and interpretation.   **3.1**

PART 2

QUALIFYING YOUNG PERSONS: PRESCRIBED CONDITIONS

2. Introduction.
3. Education and training condition.
4. Continuation of entitlement until 31st August: 16 year olds.
5. Extension period: 16 and 17 year olds.
6. Interruptions.
7. Qualifying young person: terminal dates.
8. Child benefit not payable in respect of qualifying young person: other financial support.

PART 3

PERSON RESPONSIBLE FOR CHILD OR QUALIFYING YOUNG PERSON

9. Child or qualifying young person in residential accommodation in prescribed circumstances.
10. Days disregarded in determining whether child or qualifying young person living with someone.
11. Prescribed circumstances relating to contributions and expenditure in respect of child or qualifying young person.

PART 4

EXCLUSIONS AND PRIORITY

12. Child benefit not payable: qualifying young person living with another as member of couple.
13. Qualifying young person in a relevant relationship

The Child Benefit (General) Regulations 2006

14. Election under Schedule 10 to SSCBA and Schedule 10 to SSCB(NI)A
15. Modification of priority between persons entitled to child benefit
16. Child or qualifying young persons in detention, care etc.
17. Child or qualifying young person undergoing imprisonment or detention in legal custody
18. Child or qualifying young person in care
19. Interpretation of facts existing in a week

Part 5

Entitlement after Death of Child or Qualifying Young Person

20. Entitlement after death of child or qualifying young person

Part 6

Residence

21. Circumstances in which a child or qualifying young person treated as being in Great Britain
22. Application of regulation 24 where the person is in Northern Ireland
23. Circumstances in which person treated as not being in Great Britain
24. Persons temporarily absent from Great Britain
25. Circumstances in which a child or qualifying young person treated as being in Northern Ireland
26. Application of regulation 28 where person in Great Britain
27. Circumstances in which person treated as not being in Northern Ireland
28. Persons temporarily absent from Northern Ireland
29. Overlap of entitlement to child benefit under both the legislation of Northern Ireland and Great Britain
30. Crown servants posted overseas
31. Partners of Crown servants posted overseas
32. Child or qualifying young persons normally living with Crown servants posted overseas
33. Transitional provisions for Part 6

Part 7

General and Supplementary Provisions

34. Persons treated as residing together
35. Polygamous marriages
36. Right to child benefit of voluntary organisations
37. No requirement to state national insurance number
38. Exception to rules preventing duplicate payment
39. Use of electronic communications

(SI 2006/223 reg.1)

Part 1

Introductory

Citation, commencement and interpretation

1.—(1) These Regulations may be cited as the Child Benefit (General) Regulations 2006 and shall come into force on 10th April 2006 immediately after the Child Benefit Act 2005.

(2) In these Regulations—
"the 1989 Act" means the Children Act 1989;
"the 1995 Act" means the Children (Scotland) Act 1995;
"the 1995 Order" means the Children (Northern Ireland) Order 1995;
"SSCBA" means the Social Security Contributions and Benefits Act 1992;
"SSCB(NI)A" means the Social Security Contributions and Benefits (Northern Ireland) Act 1992.

(3) In these Regulations—
"advanced education" means full-time education for the purposes of—
  (a) a course in preparation for a degree, a diploma of higher education, [³ a higher national certificate,] a higher national diploma, or a teaching qualification; or
  (b) any other course which is of a standard above ordinary national diploma, a national diploma or national certificate of Edexcel, a general certificate of education (advanced level), or Scottish national qualifications at higher or advanced higher level;
[¹ "an appropriate office" means—
  (a) Waterview Park, Washington, Tyne and Wear; or
  (b) any other office specified in writing by the Commissioners.]
"approved training" means arrangements made by the Government—
[³ (a) in relation to England, known as "Foundation Learning" or "Access to Apprenticeships"];
  (b) in relation to Wales, known as "Skillbuild", "Skillbuild+" or [³ "Traineeships" or "Foundation Apprenticeships"];
[³ [⁴ (c) in relation to Scotland, known as "Employability Fund activity"; or,]]
[² [⁴ (d) in relation to Northern Ireland, known as "Training for Success" including "Programme Led Apprenticeships", the "Pathways for Young People" element of "Pathways for Success" or the "Collaboration and Innovation Programme";]]
"arrangements made by the Government" means arrangements—
  (a) in relation to England and Wales, made by the Secretary of State under section 2 of the Employment and Training Act 1973;
  (b) in relation to Scotland, made—
    (i) by the Scottish Ministers under section 2 of the Employment and Training Act 1973;
    (ii) by Scottish Enterprise or Highlands and Islands Enterprise under section 2 of the Enterprise and New Towns (Scotland) Act 1990; or
  (c) in relation to Northern Ireland, made by the Department

for Employment and Learning under [³ sections 1 and 3] of the Employment and Training Act (Northern Ireland) 1950;

"the Careers Service" means—
  (a) in England and Wales, a person with whom the Secretary of State or the National Assembly of Wales has made arrangements under section 10(1) of the Employment and Training Act 1973, and a [²local authority] to whom the Secretary of State or the National Assembly of Wales has given a direction under section 10(2) of that Act;
  (b) in Scotland, a person with whom the Scottish Ministers have made arrangements under section 10(1) of the Employment and Training Act 1973 and any education authority to which a direction has been given by the Scottish Ministers under section 10(2) of that Act; [³ . . .]
  (c) [³ . . .]

"child benefit" has the meaning given in section 141 of SSCBA and section 137 of SSCB(NI)A (child benefit);

"civil partnership" means two people of the same sex who are civil partners of each other and are neither—
  (a) separated under a court order; nor
  (b) separated in circumstances where the separation is likely to be permanent;

"cohabiting same sex couple" means two people of the same sex who are not civil partners of each other but are living together as if they were civil partners;

"the Commissioners" means the Commissioners for Her Majesty's Revenue and Customs (see section 1 of the Commissioners for Revenue and Customs Act 2005);

"the Connexions Service" means a person of any description with whom the Secretary of State has made an arrangement under section 114(2)(a) of the Learning and Skills Act 2000 and section 10(1) of the Employment and Training Act 1973, and any person to whom he has given a direction under section 114(2)(b) of the former, or section 10(2) of the latter, Act;

"couple" means two people—
  (a) of opposite sexes who are—
    (i) spouses residing together; or
    (ii) living together as if they were married to each other; or
  (b) of the same sex who are—
    (i) civil partners in a civil partnership; or
    (ii) a cohabiting same-sex couple;

"court" means any court in the United Kingdom, the Channel Islands or the Isle of Man;

"Crown servant posted overseas" has the meaning given in regulation 30(2);

"EEA State" means—
  (a) a member State, other than the United Kingdom, or
  (b) Norway, Iceland or Liechtenstein;

"full-time education" [⁴ except in regulation 3(2)(ab)]—
  (a) is education undertaken in pursuit of a course, where the average time spent during term time in receiving tuition, engag-

(SI 2006/223 reg.1)

ing in practical work, or supervised study, or taking examinations exceeds 12 hours per week; and

(b) in calculating the time spent in pursuit of the course, no account shall be taken of time occupied by meal breaks or spent on unsupervised study.

"hospital or similar institution" means a place in which persons suffering from mental disorders are or may be received for care or treatment but does not include a prison, a young offenders institution, Secure Training Centre, Local Authority Secure Unit, Juvenile Justice Centre, Young Offenders Centre or, if outside the United Kingdom, any comparable place;

"mental disorder" shall be construed as including references to any mental disorder within the meaning of the Mental Health Acts;

"the Mental Health Acts" means the Mental Health Act 1983, the Mental Health (Care and Treatment) (Scotland) Act 2003 or the Mental Health (Northern Ireland) Order 1986;

"partner" means, in relation to a person who is a member of a couple, the other member of that couple;

"penalty" means, in the case of any court in Great Britain or Northern Ireland—

(a) in England and Wales, a sentence of a detention and training order under section 100 of the Powers of Criminal Courts (Sentencing) Act 2000 or detention in a young offenders institution, and a sentence of detention under sections 90, 91, 92 and 93 of the Powers of Criminal Courts (Sentencing) Act 2000;

(b) in Scotland, a sentence of detention under sections 44, 205, 207, 208 or 216(7) of the Criminal Procedure (Scotland) Act 1995;

(c) in Northern Ireland, a sentence of imprisonment, or detention under Article 39, 41, 45 or 54 of, or paragraph 6 of Schedule 2 to, the Criminal Justice (Children) (Northern Ireland) Order 1998, or an order for detention in a juvenile justice centre or young offenders centre,

and in the case of any court outside the United Kingdom, any comparable sentence or order;

"relevant education" means education which is—

(a) full-time; and

(b) not advanced education;

"remunerative work" means work of not less than 24 hours a week—

(a) in respect of which payment is made; or

(b) which is done in expectation of payment;

"the Taxes Act" means the Income and Corporation Taxes Act 1988;

"writing" includes writing produced by electronic communications used in accordance with regulation 39.

(4) For the purposes of these Regulations, two people of the same sex are to be regarded as living together as if they were civil partners if, but only if, they would be regarded as living together as husband and wife were they instead two people of the opposite sex.

The Child Benefit (General) Regulations 2006

AMENDMENTS

1. Child Benefit and Guardian's Allowance (Miscellaneous Amendments) Regulations (SI 2009/3268) reg.5 (January 1, 2010).
2. Local Education Authorities and Children's Services Authorities (Integration of Functions) (Local and Subordinate Legislation) Order 2010 (SI 2010/1172) art.4 and Sch.3 para.66 (May 5, 2010).
3. Child Benefit (General) (Amendment) Regulations 2012 (SI 2012/818) regs 3–6 (April 6, 2012).
4. Child Benefit (General) and Child Tax Credit (Amendment) Regulations 2014 (SI 2014/1231) reg.2(2) (June 4, 2014).

PART 2

QUALIFYING YOUNG PERSONS: PRESCRIBED CONDITIONS

Introduction

3.3   **2.**—(1) Regulations 3 to 7 prescribe—
(a) the age which a person must not have attained, and
(b) the conditions which are to be satisfied,
for a person to be a qualifying young person.

(2) Where more than one of those regulations apply to a person, he is a qualifying young person until the last of them ceases to be satisfied.

(3) Regulations 3 to 7 are subject to the following qualifications.

(4) Regulation 8 prescribes an additional condition which must be satisfied for a person to be a qualifying young person in respect of a week.

(5) No-one who had attained the age of 19 before 10th April 2006 is a qualifying young person.

DEFINITIONS

"week"—SSCBA 1992 s.147.
"qualifying young person"—SSCBA 1992 s.142.

Education and training condition

3.4   **3.**—(1) This regulation applies in the case of a person who has not attained the age of 20.
(2) The condition is that the person—
(a) is undertaking a course of full-time education, which is not advanced education and which is not provided by virtue of his employment or any office held by him—
   (i) which is provided at a school or college; or
   (ii) which is provided elsewhere but is approved by the Commissioners;
[2 (ab) is being provided with "appropriate full-time education" in England within section 4 (appropriate full-time education or training) of the Education and Skills Act 2008, which is not—
   (i) a course in preparation for a degree, a diploma of higher education, a higher national certificate, a higher national diploma, a teaching qualification, any other course which is of a standard [3 above ordinary national diploma, a national diploma or national certificate] of Edexcel, a general certificate of

(SI 2006/223 reg.3)

education (advanced level), or Scottish national qualifications at higher or advanced higher level;
  (ii) provided by virtue of his employment or any office held by him;]
(b) having undertaken such a course as is mentioned in [² paragraph (a) or (ab)] [¹ has been accepted or is enrolled to undertake a further such course.]; or
(c) is undertaking approved training that is not provided by means of a contract of employment.
[¹or
(d) having undertaken a course mentioned in paragraph (a) or approved training mentioned in paragraph (c), has been accepted or is enrolled to undertake such approved training]

(3) A person is not a qualifying young person by virtue of paragraph (2)(a)(ii) unless he was receiving the education referred to in that paragraph as a child.

(4) A person who is aged 19 is only a qualifying young person by virtue of [² paragraph (2)(a), (2)(ab)] or (2)(c) if he began the education or training (as the case may be) referred to in that sub-paragraph [¹ or was accepted or enrolled to undertake that education or training] before attaining that age.

AMENDMENTS

1. Child Benefit (General) (Amendment) Regulations 2007 (SI 2007/2150) reg.4 (August 16, 2007).
2. Child Benefit (General) and Child Tax Credit (Amendment) Regulations 2014 (SI 2014/1231) reg.2(3) (June 4, 2014).
3. Child Benefit (General) and Tax Credits (Miscellaneous Amendments) Regulations 2014 (SI 2014/2924) reg.2 (November 28, 2014).

DEFINITIONS

"approved training"—see reg.1.
"full-time education"—see reg.1.

GENERAL NOTE

Full-time education is defined in reg.1. That definition includes time spent in "supervised study". The difference between supervised and unsupervised study was considered in *R(F) 1/93* where it was held that supervision required close attention to the pupil by a teacher, but a different conclusion, and a much wider interpretation has been held by the Court of Appeal to apply (in the context of university education), in relation to a claim for Carer's Allowance (see *Flemming v Secretary of State for Work and Pensions, R(G) 2/02*). The cautious approach that was adopted to this question by Judge Mesher in *AD v SSWP* [2009] UKUT 46 (AAC), a case also concerning Carer's Allowance, has been reversed in the Court of Appeal under the name of *Secretary of State v Deane* [2010] EWCA Civ 699.

3.5

Continuation of entitlement until 31st August: 16 year olds

4.—(1) This regulation applies in the case of a person who has not attained the age of 17 and who has left relevant education or training.

3.6

(2) The condition is that the 31st August next following the person's 16th birthday has not passed.

[¹ (3) In the case of a person who attains the age of 16 on 31 August in any year, the condition is that the 1st September immediately following has not passed.]

The Child Benefit (General) Regulations 2006

AMENDMENT

1. Child Benefit and Guardian's Allowance (Miscellaneous Amendments) Regulations (SI 2009/3268) reg.5 (January 1, 2010).

DEFINITION

"relevant education"—see reg.1.

Extension period: 16 and 17 year olds

5.—(1) This regulation applies in the case of a person who has not attained the age of 18.
(2) The condition is that—
(a) the person has ceased to be in education or training;
(b) the person is registered for work, education or for training with a qualifying body;
(c) the person is not engaged in remunerative work;
(d) the extension period which applies in the case of that person has not expired;
(e) immediately before the extension period begins, the person who is responsible for him is entitled to child benefit in respect of him without regard to this regulation; and
[1(f) the individual who is responsible for that person, within three months of that person's ceasing education or training, has made a request for the payment of child benefit during the extension period to the Commissioners, in writing, or by such other means as the Commissioners may accept.]
(3) For the purposes of paragraph (2) the extension period—
(a) begins on the first day of the week after that in which the person ceased to be in education or training; and
(b) ends 20 weeks after it started.
(4) In this regulation "qualifying body" means—
(a) the Careers Service or Connexions Service;
(b) the Ministry of Defence;
(c) in Northern Ireland, the Department for Employment and Learning or an Education and Library Board established under Article 3 of the Education and Libraries (Northern Ireland) Order 1986; or
(d) for the purposes of applying Council Regulation (EEC) No. 1408/71 [2 or Regulation (EC) No 883/2004 of the European Parliament and of the Council], any corresponding body in another member State.

AMENDMENTS

1. Child Benefit and Guardian's Allowance (Miscellaneous Amendments) Regulations (SI 2009/3268) reg.5 (January 1, 2010).
2. Child Benefit (General) (Amendment) Regulations 2012 (SI 2012/818) reg.7 (April 6, 2012).

DEFINITION

"remunerative work"—see reg.1.

(SI 2006/223 reg.6)

Interruptions

6.—(1) This regulation applies in the case of a person who has not attained the age of 20.

(2) If, immediately before the commencement of an interruption specified in paragraph (3)(a) or (b), a person was a qualifying young person by virtue of any other provision of these Regulations, he is such a person throughout a period of interruption during which he satisfies the condition specified in that sub-paragraph.

(3) The periods of interruption are—
   (a) one of up to six months (whether beginning before or after the person concerned became 16) but only to the extent to which, in the opinion of the Commissioners, that the interruption is reasonable; and
   (b) one attributable to the illness or disability of mind or body of the person concerned for such period as is reasonable in the opinion of the Commissioners.

This is subject to the following qualification.

(4) Paragraph (3) does not apply to an interruption which is, or is likely to be, followed immediately by a period during which—
   (a) provision is made for training of that person which is not approved training;
   (b) he is receiving advanced education;
   (c) he is receiving education by virtue of his employment or of any office held by him.

DEFINITION

"advanced education"—see reg.1.

GENERAL NOTE

Note that the overall test under this regulation is whether the interruption in education is, in the eyes of HMRC reasonable. Such reasonable interruptions are then disregarded for up to six months, or, if the reason for interruption is illness or disability for a longer period that is accepted as reasonable by HMRC. This provision is clearly appropriate to bridge any gap caused by school holidays and interval caused by a change of schools. In *R(F) 3/60* a gap of five months was accepted because there was difficulty in finding a suitable school for the child who suffered from a mental disability.

Qualifying young person: terminal dates

7.—(1) This regulation applies in the case of a person who has not attained the age of 20.

(2) The condition is that the period found in accordance with Cases 1 and 2 has not expired in his case.

Case 1

1.1 The period is from the date on which he ceases to receive relevant education or approved training, up to and including—
   (a) the week including the terminal date, or
   (b) if he attains the age of 20 on or before that date, the week including the last Monday before he attains that age.

1.2 For the purposes of this Case the "terminal date" means—
   (a) the last day in February,

(b) the last day in May,
(c) the last day in August,
(d) the last day in November,

whichever first occurs after the date on which the person's relevant education or approved training ceased (but subject to paragraph 1.3 of this Case).

1.3 In the case of a person in Scotland who—
  (a) undertakes the Higher Certificate or Advanced Higher Certificate immediately before ceasing relevant education, and
  (b) ceases relevant education on a date earlier than he would have done had he undertaken the comparable examination in England and Wales,

the terminal date shall be reckoned by reference to the date on which the cessation would have occurred had he undertaken the comparable examination.

Case 2

2.1. Where a person's name is entered as a candidate for any external examination in connection with relevant education which he is receiving at that time, so long as his name continues to be so entered before ceasing to receive such education, the prescribed period is—
  (a) from the later of—
    (i) date when that person ceased to receive relevant education, or
    (ii) the date on which he attained the age of 16,
  (b) up to and including—
    (i) whichever of the dates in paragraph 1.2 (as modified by paragraph 1.3 where appropriate) first occurs after the conclusion of the examination (or the last of the examinations if the person is entered for more than one), or
    (ii) the expiry of the week which includes the last Monday before his 20th birthday,
  whichever is the earlier.

This paragraph is subject to the following qualification.

(3) Child benefit is not payable in respect of a qualifying young person by virtue of this regulation for any week in which he is engaged in remunerative work.

DEFINITIONS

"approved training"—see reg.1.
"relevant education"—see reg.1.
"remunerative work"—see reg.1.
"week"—see SSCBA 1992 s.147.

GENERAL NOTE

3.11 Case 1 of this regulation extends entitlement to benefit in respect of a child who has left school for a period of up to three months ending on the quarterly dates prescribed. It is a corollary of the disentitlement to Income Support that applies to the same period. Case 2 similarly covers the period between the time a child leaves school and the time he sits external examinations for which he is entered. Note the extension continues only as long as he continues to be entered for an examination so that if he withdraws this route to qualification for child benefit ceases.

(SI 2006/223 reg.8)

Child benefit not payable in respect of qualifying young person: other financial support

8.—(1) This regulation applies in the case of a person who has not attained the age of 20 years.

(2) The condition is that the person is not in receipt, in a week, of—
(a) income support,
(b) income-based jobseeker's allowance within the meaning of section 1(4) of the Jobseekers Act 1995 or Article 3(4) of the Jobseekers (Northern Ireland) Order 1995,
(c) incapacity benefit by virtue of being a person to whom section 30A(1)(b) of SSCBA or section 30A(1)(b) of SSCB(NI)A applies, [¹. . .]
(d) tax credit under the Tax Credits Act 2002;
[¹ (e) employment and support allowance payable under Part 1 of the Welfare Reform Act 2007 [² or Part 1 of the Welfare Reform Act (Northern Ireland) 2007]] [³; or
(f) universal credit under Part 1 of the Welfare Reform Act 2012.]

3.12

AMENDMENTS

1. Employment and Support Allowance (Consequential Provisions) (No.3) Regulations 2008 (SI 2008/1897) reg.24 (October 27, 2008).
2. Employment and Support Allowance (Consequential Provisions No.2) Regulations (Northern Ireland) 2008 (SI 2008/412) reg.11 (October 27, 2008).
3. Universal Credit (Consequential, Supplementary, Incidental and Miscellaneous Provisions) Regulations 2013 (SI 2013/630) reg.84 (April 29, 2013).

PART 3

PERSON RESPONSIBLE FOR CHILD OR QUALIFYING YOUNG PERSON

Child or qualifying young person in residential accommodation in prescribed circumstances

9.—For the purposes of section 143(3)(c) of SSCBA and section 139(3)(c) of SSCB(NI)A (absence of child or qualifying young person in residential accommodation), the prescribed circumstances are that the residential accommodation has been provided solely—
(a) because of the disability of the child or qualifying young person, or
(b) because the child or qualifying young person's health would be likely to be significantly impaired, or further impaired, unless such accommodation were provided.

3.13

Days disregarded in determining whether child or qualifying young person living with someone

10.—(1) For the purpose of section 143(4) of SSCBA and section 139(4) of SSCB(NI)A (number of days that may be disregarded), the prescribed number of days is 84 consecutive days, calculated in accordance with paragraph (2).

3.14

(2) Two or more distinct relevant periods separated by one or more intervals each not exceeding 28 days are treated as a continuous period equal in duration to the total of such distinct periods and ending on the last day of the latter or last of such periods.

(3) In paragraph (2) "relevant periods" means periods to which—
  (a) section 143(3)(b) of SSCBA or section 139(3)(b) of SSCB(NI)A (absence of a child or qualifying young person undergoing medical or other treatment) applies;
  (b) section 143(3)(c) of SSCBA or section 139(3)(c) of SSCB(NI)A (absence of a child or qualifying young person in residential accommodation) applies.

Prescribed circumstances relating to contributions and expenditure in respect of child or qualifying young person

3.15 **11.**—(1) For the purposes of section 143(5)(a) of SSCBA and section 139(5)(a) of SSCB(NI)A (contributing to the cost of providing for a child or qualifying young person) the prescribed circumstances are that—
  (a) two or more persons are contributing to the cost of providing for the same child or qualifying young person;
  (b) the aggregate weekly amount of their contributions equals or exceeds, but the weekly amount of each of their individual contributions is less than, the weekly rate of child benefit which would be payable in respect of that child or qualifying young person had the aggregate weekly amount of their contributions been contributed by one only of them; and
  (c) they by agreement nominate in writing or, in default of such agreement, the Commissioners in their discretion determine, that the aggregate weekly amount of their contributions is to be treated as having been made by the person so nominated or determined.

This paragraph is subject to paragraph (3).

(2) The contribution subject to the nomination or determination made under paragraph (1) shall be treated as made by the person nominated or determined.

(3) Where pursuant to a nomination or determination made under paragraph (1) a person is awarded child benefit, the nomination or determination ceases to have effect in the week following that in which child benefit is awarded to that person (and accordingly thereafter the person shall be required to contribute to the maintenance of the child or qualifying young person at a rate which equals or exceeds the rate of child benefit payable in respect of that child or qualifying young person).

(4) Where spouses or civil partners are residing together a contribution made or expenditure incurred by one of them in respect of a child or qualifying young person shall if they agree, or in default of such agreement if the Commissioners in their discretion so determine, be treated as made or incurred by the other.

DEFINITIONS

"child or qualifying young person"—see SSCBA 1992 s.142.
"The Commissioners"—see reg.1.
"week"—see SSCBA 1992 s.147.
"writing"—see reg.1.

(SI 2006/223 reg.12)

PART 4

EXCLUSIONS AND PRIORITY

Child benefit not payable: qualifying young person living with another as member of couple

12.—(1) Child benefit is not payable to any person ("the claimant") in respect of a qualifying young person for any week in which the qualifying young person is living with another—
   (a) as if they were spouses, or
   (b) as a member of a cohabiting same-sex couple,
unless paragraph (2) applies.
The person with whom the qualifying young person is living is referred to in paragraph (2) as "the cohabitee".
   (2) This paragraph applies if—
   (a) the cohabitee is receiving relevant education or approved training; and
   (b) the claimant is not the cohabitee.

3.16

DEFINITIONS

"approved training"—see reg.1.
"cohabiting same-sex couple"—see reg.1.
"relevant education"—see reg.1.

GENERAL NOTE

The circumstances in which a couple are to regarded as living together are defined, in part, in reg.1(4).

3.17

Qualifying young person in a relevant relationship

13.—(1) A person ("the claimant") shall be entitled to child benefit in respect of a qualifying young person in a relevant relationship by virtue of paragraph 3 of Schedule 9 to SSCBA or paragraph 3 of Schedule 9 to SSCB(NI)A (entitlement: children or qualifying young persons who are married or civil partners) only if—
   (a) the claimant is not the spouse or civil partner of that qualifying young person; and
   (b) the qualifying young person is not residing with his spouse or civil partner, or, if he is, the spouse or civil partner is receiving relevant education or approved training.
   (2) In paragraph (1) "relevant relationship" means a marriage or a civil partnership.

3.18

DEFINITIONS

"approved training"—see reg.1.
"relevant education"—see reg.1.

Election under Schedule 10 to SSCBA and Schedule 10 to SSCB(NI)A

14.—(1) An election under Schedule 10 to SSCBA and Schedule 10 to SSCB(NI)A (any election under that Schedule to be made in the prescribed manner) shall be made by giving notice in writing to the Commissioners at an appropriate office on a form approved by the Commissioners [¹ or by telephone to an officer of Revenue and Customs at an appropriate office] or in such other manner being in writing as the Commissioners may accept as sufficient in the circumstances of any particular case or class of cases.

(2) An election is not effective to confer entitlement to child benefit in respect of a child or qualifying young person for any week earlier than the week following that in which it is made if the earlier week is one in respect of which child benefit has been paid in respect of that child or qualifying young person and has not been required to be repaid or voluntarily repaid or recovered.

(3) An election may be superseded by a subsequent election made in accordance with this regulation.

AMENDMENT

1. Child Benefit (General) (Amendment) Regulations 2007 (SI 2007/2150) reg.5 (August 16, 2007).

DEFINITIONS

"child or qualifying young person"—see SSCBA 1992 s.142.
"The Commissioners"—see reg.1.
"week"—see SSCBA 1992 s.147.
"writing"—see reg.1.

Modification of priority between persons entitled to child benefit

15.—(1) If a person entitled to child benefit in respect of a child or qualifying young person in priority to another person gives the Commissioners notice in writing at an appropriate office [¹ or gives an officer of the Inland Revenue and Customs notice by telephone at such an office] that he does not wish to have such priority, the provisions of Schedule 10 to SSCBA and Schedule 10 to SSCB(NI)A (priority between persons entitled) have effect with the modification that that person does not have such priority.

(2) A notice under paragraph (1)—
(a) is not effective in relation to any week, before the date on which the election becomes effective, for which child benefit in respect of that child or qualifying young person is paid to the person who made the election or to another person on his behalf; and
(b) ceases to have effect if the person who gave it makes a further claim to child benefit in respect of that child or qualifying young person.

AMENDMENT

1. Child Benefit (General) (Amendment) Regulations 2007 (SI 2007/2150) reg.6 (August 16, 2007).

(SI 2006/223 reg.15)

DEFINITIONS

"child or qualifying young person"—see SSCBA 1992 s.142.
"The Commissioners"—see reg.1.
"week"—see SSCBA 1992 s.147.
"writing"—see reg.1.

Child or qualifying young persons in detention, care etc.

16.—(1) Paragraph 1 of Schedule 9 to SSCBA and paragraph 1 of Schedule 9 to SSCB(NI)A do not apply to disentitle a person to child benefit in respect of a child or qualifying young person for any week—
- (a) unless that week is the 9th or a subsequent week in a series of consecutive weeks in which either of those paragraphs has applied to that child or qualifying young person; or
- (b) notwithstanding paragraph (a), if—
  - (i) that week is one in which falls the first day in a period of seven consecutive days in which the child or qualifying young person lives with that person for at least a part of the first day and throughout the following six days;
  - (ii) that week is one in which falls the first day in a period of seven consecutive days throughout which the child or qualifying young person lives with that person, being a period of seven consecutive days which immediately follows either a similar period of seven consecutive days or the period of seven consecutive days referred to in head (i) above;
  - (iii) that week is one in which falls the day, or the first day in a period of less than seven consecutive days, throughout which the child or qualifying young person lives with that person, being a day or days which immediately follow the period of seven consecutive days referred to in head (i) above or a period of seven consecutive days referred to in head (ii), or
  - (iv) as at that week that person establishes that he is a person with whom the child or qualifying young person ordinarily lives throughout at least one day in each week.

This paragraph is subject to the following qualifications.

(2) For the purposes of paragraph (1), a person shall not be regarded as having a child or qualifying young person living with him throughout any day or week unless he actually has that child or qualifying young person living with him throughout that day or week.

(3) Paragraph (1) does not apply for any day in any week to a person ("the carer") with whom a child or qualifying young person—
[² (a) is placed by a local authority in Great Britain in the carer's home in accordance with the provisions of—
  - (i) the Placement of Children (Wales) Regulations 2007,
  - (ii) the Review of Children's Cases (Wales) Regulations 2007,
  - (iii) the Care Planning, Placement and Case Review (England) Regulations 2010,
  - (iv) the Looked After Children (Scotland) Regulations 2009,
  - (v) the Fostering Services (England) Regulations 2011, or
  - (vi) the Fostering Services (Wales) Regulations 2003,

and that authority is making a payment, in respect of either the child or qualifying young person's accommodation or maintenance or both, under

section 22C(10) or 23 of the 1989 Act or under regulation 33 of the Looked After Children (Scotland) Regulations 2009;]
  (b) is placed by an authority in Northern Ireland, in the carer's home in accordance with the provisions of the Foster Placement (Children) Regulations (Northern Ireland) 1996 where the authority has a duty to provide accommodation and maintenance for the child under the Arrangements for Placement of Children (General) Regulations (Northern Ireland) 1996.

(4) Paragraph (1) does not apply in respect of any child or qualifying young person who—
  (a) is being looked after by a local authority in Great Britain or by an authority in Northern Ireland, and
  (b) has been placed for adoption by that authority in the home of a person proposing to adopt him,
provided that the local authority or authority is making a payment in respect of either the child or qualifying young person's accommodation or maintenance or both, under [² section 22C(10) or 23 of the 1989 Act, under regulation 33 of the Looked After Children (Scotland) Regulations 2009] or under Article 27 of the 1995 Order.

(5) For the purposes of paragraph (4), placing for adoption means placing for adoption in accordance with—
[² (a) the Adoption Agencies Regulations 2005,
  (aa) the Adoption Agencies (Wales) Regulations 2005,]
[¹ (b) the Adoption Agencies (Scotland) Regulations 2009, or]
  (c) the Adoption Agencies Regulations (Northern Ireland) 1989.

AMENDMENTS

1. Adoption and Children (Scotland) Act 2007 (Consequential Modifications) Order 2011 (SI 2011/1740) art.2 and Sch.1 para.43 (July 15, 2011).
2. Child Benefit (General) (Amendment) Regulations 2012 (SI 2012/818) regs 8–10 (April 6, 2012).

DEFINITIONS

"child or qualifying young person"—see SSCBA 1992 s.142.
"week"—see reg.19.

GENERAL NOTE

3.22   Schedule 9 para.(1) of the Act provides that no claim can be made in respect of a child who is in prison, detention, legal custody or in certain circumstances in local authority care. But this regulation relieves from that disqualification to some extent. Disqualification does not apply to the first eight weeks of the detention, etc. nor does it apply if the child actually lives with the claimant (as distinct from being maintained by the claimant) and does so for the whole week and, in effect, part weeks that commence or end a succession of whole weeks. Alternatively the claimant can retain benefit if the child ordinarily lives with him throughout at least one day each week. This means that the child must sleep at home two nights in the week. The relief outlined above does not apply if the child is placed by a local authority in a private home, is fostered, or is placed for adoption.

Child or qualifying young person undergoing imprisonment or detention in legal custody

3.23   17.—(1) For the purposes of paragraph 1(a) of Schedule 9 to SSCBA and paragraph 1(1)(a) of Schedule 9 to SSCB(NI)A, a child or qualifying

(SI 2006/223 reg.17)

young person is not regarded as undergoing imprisonment or detention in legal custody in any week unless—
   (a) in connection with a charge brought or intended to be brought against him in criminal proceedings at the conclusion of those proceedings, or
   (b) in the case of default of payment of a sum adjudged to be paid on conviction, in respect of such default,
a court imposes a penalty upon him.

(2) Subject to paragraph (3), paragraph 1(a) of Schedule 9 to SSCBA and paragraph 1(1)(a) of Schedule 9 to SSCB(NI)A do not apply to a child or qualifying young person in respect of any week in which that child or qualifying young person is liable to be detained in a hospital or similar institution in Great Britain or Northern Ireland as a person suffering from a mental disorder.

(3) Subject to paragraph (5), paragraph (2) does not apply where subsequent to the imposition of a penalty, the child or qualifying young person was removed to the hospital or similar institution while still liable to be detained as a result of that penalty and, in the case of a person who is liable to be detained in the hospital or similar institution by virtue of any provisions of the Mental Health Acts, a direction restricting his discharge has been given under any of those Acts and is still in force.

(4) In paragraph (3) a person who is liable to be detained by virtue of any provision of the Mental Health Acts shall be treated as if a direction restricting his discharge had been given under those Acts if he is to be so treated for the purposes of any of them.

(5) Where a certificate given by or on behalf of the Secretary of State shows the earliest date on which the child or qualifying young person would have been expected to be discharged from detention pursuant to the penalty if he had not been transferred to a hospital or similar institution, paragraph (3) shall not apply from the day following that date.

DEFINITIONS

"child or qualifying young person"—see SSCBA 1992 s.142.
"Court"—see reg.1.
"hospital or similar institution"—see reg.1.
"mental disorder"—see reg.1.
"the Mental Health Acts"—see reg.1.
"penalty"—see reg.1.
"week"—see reg.19.

GENERAL NOTE

This regulation provides that the disqualification from benefit in respect of a child who is in prison, detention in legal custody applies only if the child is sentenced to be detained.

This means that if benefit has been suspended during a period that the child is in custody on remand or awaiting sentence it may become payable if the child is not sentenced to a period of detention.

The disqualification does not apply if the child is detained as a result of a mental disorder, unless the child has been transferred to a hospital or similar institution after being sentenced to a period of detention, in which case, the disqualification continues only so long as the order for detention would have continued.

3.24

The Child Benefit (General) Regulations 2006

Child or qualifying young person in care

3.25   **18.**—For the purposes of paragraph 1(c) of Schedule 9 to SSCBA and paragraph 1(c) of Schedule 9 to SSCB(NI)A (child or qualifying young person in care in such circumstances as may be prescribed), the prescribed circumstances are that—
   (a) the child or qualifying young person is provided with, or placed in, accommodation under Part 3 of the 1989 Act, under Part 2 of the 1995 Act [¹, by virtue of a requirement in a child assessment order within the meaning of section 35 of the Children's Hearings (Scotland) Act 2011, a child protection order within the meaning of section 37 of that Act, a compulsory supervision order within the meaning of section 83 of that Act or an interim compulsory supervision order within the meaning of section 86 of that Act,] or under Part 4 of the 1995 Order and the cost of that child or qualifying young person's accommodation or maintenance is borne wholly or partly out of local authority funds, authority funds or any other public funds, and
   (b) the child or qualifying young person is not in residential accommodation in the circumstances prescribed in regulation 9.

AMENDMENT

1. Children's Hearings (Scotland) Act 2011 (Consequential and Transitional Provisions and Savings) Order 2013 (SI 2013/1465) art.17 Sch.1 para.25 (June 24, 2013).

DEFINITIONS

"child or qualifying young person"—see SSCBA 1992 s.142.
"the 1989 Act"—see reg.1.
"the 1995 Act"—see reg.1.
"the 1995 Order"—see reg.1.

Interpretation of facts existing in a week

3.26   **19.**—Where paragraph 1 of Schedule 9 to SSCBA or paragraph 1 of Schedule 9 to SSCB(NI)A applies, section 147(2) of SSCBA and section 143(2) of SSCB(NI)A (references to any condition being satisfied or any facts existing in a week to be construed as references to the condition being satisfied or the facts existing at the beginning of that week) has effect as if the words "at the beginning of that week" were substituted by "throughout any day in that week".

PART 5

ENTITLEMENT AFTER DEATH OF CHILD OR QUALIFYING YOUNG PERSON

Entitlement after death of child or qualifying young person

3.27   **20.**—The prescribed period for the purposes of section 145A of SSCBA and section 141A of SSCB(NI)A (entitlement after death of child or qualifying young person) is—
   (a) in the case of a child, eight weeks, and
   (b) in the case of a qualifying young person the shorter of—

(i) the period of eight weeks; and
(ii) the period commencing the week in which his death occurred and finishing on the Monday in the week following the week in which the qualifying young person would have attained the age of 20.

PART 6

RESIDENCE

Circumstances in which a child or qualifying young person treated as being in Great Britain

21.—(1) For the purposes of section 146(1) of SSCBA, a child or qualifying young person who is temporarily absent from Great Britain shall be treated as being in Great Britain during—
(a) the first 12 weeks of any period of absence;
(b) any period during which that person is absent by reason only of—
  (i) his receiving full-time education by attendance at a [¹ school or college] in an EEA State or in Switzerland; or
  (ii) his being engaged in an educational exchange or visit made with the written approval of the [¹ school or college] which he normally attends;
(c) any period as is determined by the Commissioners during which the child or qualifying young person is absent for the specific purpose of being treated for an illness or physical or mental disability which commenced before his absence began; or
(d) any period when he is in Northern Ireland.

(2) For the purposes of section 146(1) of SSCBA, where a child is born while his mother is absent from Great Britain in accordance with regulation 24, he shall be treated as being in Great Britain during such period of absence after his birth as is within 12 weeks of the date on which his mother became absent from Great Britain.

AMENDMENT

1. Child Benefit (General) (Amendment) Regulations 2007 (SI 2007/2150) reg.7 (August 16, 2007).

DEFINITIONS

"child or qualifying young person"—see SSCBA 1992 s.142.
"The Commissioners"—see reg.1.
"EEA State"—see reg.1.
"full time education"—see reg.1.

Application of regulation 24 where the person is in Northern Ireland

22.—If a person who is in Northern Ireland is treated as being in Great Britain in accordance with regulation 24, he is treated as not being in Northern Ireland for the purposes of section 142 of SSCB(NI)A.

The Child Benefit (General) Regulations 2006

Circumstances in which person treated as not being in Great Britain

3.30
23.—(1) A person shall be treated as not being in Great Britain for the purposes of section 146(2) of SSCBA if he is not ordinarily resident in the United Kingdom.
(2) [³ Paragraphs (1) and (5) do] not apply to a Crown servant posted overseas or his partner.
(3) A person who is in Great Britain as a result of his deportation, expulsion or other removal by compulsion of law from another country to Great Britain shall be treated as being ordinarily resident in the United Kingdom [³ and paragraph (5) shall not apply].
(4) A person shall be treated as not being in Great Britain for the purposes of section 146(2) of SSCBA where he [¹ makes a claim for child benefit on or after 1st May 2004] [² and
  (a) does not have a right to reside in the United Kingdom; or
  (b) has a right to reside in the United Kingdom by virtue of—
    (i) regulation 15A(1) of the Immigration (European Economic Area) Regulations 2006, but only in a case where the right exists under that regulation because the person satisfies the criteria in regulation 15A(4A) of those Regulations; or
    (ii) Article 20 of the Treaty on the Functioning of the European Union (in a case where the right to reside arises because a British citizen would otherwise be deprived of the genuine enjoyment of the substance of their rights as a European Union citizen).]
[³ (5) Subject to paragraph (6), a person is to be treated as being in Great Britain for the purposes of section 146(2) of SSCBA only if that person has been living in the United Kingdom for 3 months ending on the first day of the week referred to in that section.
(6) Paragraph (5) does not apply where the person—
(a) most recently entered the United Kingdom before 1st July 2014;
(b) is a worker or a self-employed person in the United Kingdom for the purposes of Council Directive 2004/38/EC (rights of citizens of the European Union and their family members to move and reside freely within the territory of the Member States);
(c) retains the status of a worker or self-employed person in the United Kingdom pursuant to Article 7(3) of Council Directive 2004/38/EC;
(d) is treated as a worker in the United Kingdom pursuant to regulation 5 of the Accession of Croatia (Immigration and Worker Authorisation) Regulations 2013 (right of residence of a Croatian who is an "accession State national subject to worker authorisation");
(e) is a family member of a person referred to in sub-paragraphs (b), (c), (d) or (i);
(f) is a person to whom regulation 24 applies (persons temporarily absent from Great Britain) and who returns to Great Britain within 52 weeks starting from the first day of the temporary absence;
(g) returns to the United Kingdom after a period abroad of less than 52 weeks where immediately before departing from the United Kingdom that person had been ordinarily resident in the United Kingdom for a continuous period of 3 months;
(h) returns to Great Britain otherwise than as a worker or self-employed

(SI 2006/223 reg.23)

person after a period abroad and where, otherwise than for a period of up to 3 months ending on the day of returning, that person has paid either Class 1 or Class 2 contributions by virtue of regulation 114, 118, 146 or 147 of the Social Security (Contributions) Regulations 2001 or pursuant to an Order in Council having effect under section 179 of the Social Security Administration Act 1992;

(i) is not a national of an EEA State and would be a worker or self-employed person in the United Kingdom for the purposes of Council Directive 2004/38/EC if that person were a national of an EEA State;

(j) is a refugee as defined in Article 1 of the Convention relating to the Status of Refugees done at Geneva on 28th July 1951, as extended by Article 1(2) of the Protocol relating to the Status of Refugees done at New York on 31st January 1967;

(k) has been granted leave, or is deemed to have been granted leave, outside the rules made under section 3(2) of the Immigration Act 1971 where the leave is—

(i) granted by the Secretary of State with recourse to public funds, or

(ii) deemed to have been granted by virtue of regulation 3 of the Displaced Persons (Temporary Protection) Regulations 2005;

(l) has been granted leave to remain in the United Kingdom by the Secretary of State pending an application for indefinite leave to remain as a victim of domestic violence;

(m) has been granted humanitarian protection by the Secretary of State under rule 339C of Part 11 of the rules made under section 3(2) of the Immigration Act 1971.

(7) In this regulation, a "family member" means a person who is defined as a family member of another person in Article 2 of Council Directive 2004/38/EC.]

AMENDMENTS

1. Child Benefit (General) (Amendment) Regulations 2007 (SI 2007/2150) reg.8 (August 16, 2007).

2. Child Benefit and Child Tax Credit (Miscellaneous Amendments) Regulations 2012 (SI 2012/2612) regs 2 and 3 (November 8, 2012).

3. Child Benefit (General) and the Tax Credits (Residence) (Amendment) Regulations 2014 (SI 2014/1511) regs 2 and 3 (July 1, 2014).

DEFINITIONS

"Crown servant posted overseas"—see regs 1 and 30.
"partner"—see regs 1 and 31.

GENERAL NOTE

For questions that involve persons either coming from or going to another country that is a part of the European Union reference should be made to the relevant sections of Vol.III of this work.

Paragraph (1) of s.146 requires that both the claimant and the child in respect of whom the claim is made should be present in the UK. This regulation extends the concept of presence into that of being "ordinarily resident". This concept is considered in the note to reg.4 of the Persons Abroad Regulations in Vol.I of this work. But in brief, it requires that a person has made this country his place of abode as a

3.31

voluntary and settled purpose in his life. Thus mere presence in the country is not enough. It must be legal presence, and at least for the time being, it should be his home. On cases involving EU nationals and the potential application of reg. 1408/71, see *JR v HMRC* [2009] UKUT 18 (AAC), confirmed by the Court of Appeal in *HMRC v Ruas* [2010] EWCA Civ 291; [2010] AACR 31 (see note to SSCBA 1992 s.146 at para.1.61, above).

Paragraph 2: disapplies this requirement in relation to a Crown servant who is posted overseas, his partner, and his child. These concepts are dealt with further in regs 30, 31 and 32.

Paragraph 3: affirms that a person who is in this country only because he has been deported from another country is, nevertheless, to be regarded as ordinarily resident here.

Paragraph 4: since 2004 a claimant must show, as well, that they have the right to reside in the UK. The right to reside is accorded automatically to all British citizens. It applies also to persons from the EEC countries (though subject to some restrictions) for an initial period as jobseekers and afterwards as workers; it can be acquired permanently after five years' residence without conditions. For a detailed account of the right to reside please refer to Vol.III of this work.

The requirement for a right to reside has been found to be lawful by the Court of Appeal of Northern Ireland in *Revenue and Customs v Spiridonova* [2014] NICA 63, reversing a decision of the Chief Commissioner for Northern Ireland (*AS v HMRC (CB)* [2013] NI Comm. 15).

See note to para.(3) of reg.27 below.

Persons temporarily absent from Great Britain

3.32

24.—(1) A person who is ordinarily resident in the United Kingdom and is temporarily absent from Great Britain shall be treated as being in Great Britain during the first—
  (a) 8 weeks of any period of absence; or
  (b) 12 weeks of any period of absence where that period of absence, or any extension to that period of absence, is in connection with—
     (i) the treatment of his illness or physical or mental disability;
     (ii) the treatment of his partner's illness or physical or mental disability;
     (iii) the death of a person who, immediately prior to the date of death, was his partner;
     (iv) the death, or the treatment of the illness or physical or mental disability, of a child or qualifying young person for whom either he or his partner is, or both of them are, responsible; or
     (v) the death, or the treatment of the illness or physical or mental disability, of his or his partner's relative.
Here "relative" means brother, sister, forebear or lineal descendant.

(2) A person is temporarily absent from Great Britain if at the beginning of the period of absence his absence is unlikely to exceed 52 weeks.

DEFINITIONS

"child or qualifying young person"—see SSCBA 1992 s.142.
"Partner"—see reg.1.

(SI 2006/223 reg.24)

GENERAL NOTE

A person may remain ordinarily resident and so for the purposes of s.146 "present" even though he is temporarily absent from the country. The concept of "temporary" absence is considered in the notes to reg.2 of the Persons Abroad Regulations in Vol.I of this work. This regulation limits temporary absence to an absence which at its outset must be unlikely to exceed 52 weeks, and then provides that the absence is, in any case, only waived for a period of eight weeks, or, if the reason for absence (or extended absence) is illness or death of one of the parties then a maximum of 12 weeks.

3.33

Circumstances in which a child or qualifying young person treated as being in Northern Ireland

25.—(1) For the purposes of section 142(1) of SSCB(NI)A a child or qualifying young person who is temporarily absent from Northern Ireland shall be treated as being in Northern Ireland during—

(a) the first 12 weeks of any period of absence;
(b) any period during which the child or qualifying young person is absent by reason only of—
   (i) his receiving full-time education by attendance at a [1 school or college] in an EEA State or in Switzerland; or
   (ii) his being engaged in an educational exchange or visit made with the written approval of the [1 school or college] which he normally attends;
(c) any period as is determined by the Commissioners during which the child or qualifying young person is absent for the specific purpose of being treated for an illness or physical or mental disability which commenced before his absence began; or
(d) any period when he is in Great Britain.

(2) For the purposes of section 142(1) of SSCB(NI)A, where a child is born while his mother is absent from Northern Ireland in accordance with regulation 28, he shall be treated as being in Northern Ireland during such period of absence after his birth as is within 12 weeks of the date on which his mother became absent from Northern Ireland.

3.34

AMENDMENT

1. Child Benefit (General) (Amendment) Regulations 2007 (SI 2007/2150) reg.9 (August 16, 2007).

DEFINITIONS

"child or qualifying young person"—see SSCBA 1992 s.142.
"The Commissioners"—see reg.1.
"EEA State"—see reg.1.
"full time education"—see reg.1.

Application of regulation 28 where person in Great Britain

26.—Where a person who is in Great Britain is treated as being in Northern Ireland in accordance with regulation 28, he is treated as not being in Great Britain for the purposes of section 146 of SSCBA.

3.35

Circumstances in which person treated as not being in Northern Ireland

27.—(1) A person shall be treated as not being in Northern Ireland for the purposes of section 142(2) of SSCB(NI)A if he is not ordinarily resident in the United Kingdom.

(2) A person who is in Northern Ireland as a result of his deportation, expulsion or other removal by compulsion of law from another country to Northern Ireland shall be treated as being ordinarily resident in the United Kingdom [[3] and paragraph (4) shall not apply].

(3) A person shall be treated as not being in Northern Ireland for the purposes of section 142(2) of SSCB(NI)A where he [[1] makes a claim for child benefit on or after 1st May 2004] [[2] and
  (a) does not have a right to reside in the United Kingdom; or
  (b) has a right to reside in the United Kingdom by virtue of—
    (i) regulation 15A(1) of the Immigration (European Economic Area) Regulations 2006, but only in a case where the right exists under that regulation because the person satisfies the criteria in regulation 15A(4A) of those Regulations; or
    (ii) Article 20 of the Treaty on the Functioning of the European Union (in a case where the right to reside arises because a British citizen would otherwise be deprived of the genuine enjoyment of the substance of their rights as a European Union citizen).]

[[3] (4) Subject to paragraph (5), a person is to be treated as being in Northern Ireland for the purposes of section 142(2) of SSCB(NI)A only if that person has been living in the United Kingdom for 3 months ending on the first day of the week referred to in that section.

(5) Paragraph (4) does not apply where the person—
  (a) most recently entered the United Kingdom before 1st July 2014;
  (b) is a worker or a self-employed person in the United Kingdom for the purposes of Council Directive 2004/38/EC;
  (c) retains the status of a worker or self-employed person in the United Kingdom pursuant to Article 7(3) of Council Directive 2004/38/EC;
  (d) is treated as a worker in the United Kingdom pursuant to regulation 5 of the Accession of Croatia (Immigration and Worker Authorisation) Regulations 2013 (right of residence of a Croatian who is an "accession State national subject to worker authorisation");
  (e) is a family member of a person referred to in sub-paragraphs (b), (c), (d) or (i);
  (f) is a person to whom regulation 28 applies (persons temporarily absent from Northern Ireland) and who returns to Northern Ireland within 52 weeks starting from the first day of the temporary absence;
  (g) returns to the United Kingdom after a period abroad of less than 52 weeks where immediately before departing from the United Kingdom that person had been ordinarily resident in the United Kingdom for a continuous period of 3 months;
  (h) returns to Northern Ireland otherwise than as a worker or self-employed person after a period abroad and where, otherwise than for a period of up to 3 months ending on the day of returning, that person has paid either Class 1 or Class 2 contributions by virtue of regulation 114, 118, 146 or 147 of the Social Security (Contributions)

(SI 2006/223 reg.27)

Regulations 2001 or pursuant to an Order in Council having effect under section 179 of the Social Security Administration Act 1992;
(i) is not a national of an EEA State and would be a worker or self-employed person in the United Kingdom for the purposes of Council Directive 2004/38/EC if that person were a national of an EEA State;
(j) is a refugee as defined in Article 1 of the Convention relating to the Status of Refugees done at Geneva on 28th July 1951, as extended by Article 1(2) of the Protocol relating to the Status of Refugees done at New York on 31st January 1967;
(k) has been granted leave, or is deemed to have been granted leave, outside the rules made under section 3(2) of the Immigration Act 1971 where that leave is—
   (i) granted by the Secretary of State with recourse to public funds, or
   (ii) deemed to have been granted by virtue of regulation 3 of the Displaced Persons (Temporary Protection) Regulations 2005;
(l) has been granted leave to remain in the United Kingdom by the Secretary of State pending an application for indefinite leave to remain as a victim of domestic violence;
(m) has been granted humanitarian protection by the Secretary of State under Rule 339C of Part 11 of the rules made under section 3(2) of the Immigration Act 1971.

(6) In this regulation, a "family member" means a person who is defined as a family member of another person in Article 2 of Council Directive 2004/38/EC.]

AMENDMENTS

1. Child Benefit (General) Amendment Regulations 2007 (SI 2007/2150) reg.10 (August 16, 2007).
2. Child Benefit and Child Tax Credit (Miscellaneous Amendments) Regulations 2012 (SI 2012/2612) regs 2 and 4 (November 8, 2012).
3. Child Benefit (General) and the Tax Credits (Residence) (Amendment) Regulations 2014 (SI 2014/1511) regs 2 and 4 (July 1, 2014).

GENERAL NOTE

Paragraph (3): Since 2004 a claimant must show, as well, that they have the right to reside in the UK. The right to reside is accorded automatically to all British citizens. It applies also to persons from the EEC countries (though subject to some restrictions) for an initial period as jobseekers and afterwards as workers; it can be acquired permanently after five years' residence without conditions. For a detailed account of the right to reside please refer to Vol.III of this work.

3.37

The requirement for a right to reside for CB was found to be lawful by the Court of Appeal of Northern Ireland in *Revenue and Customs v Spiridonova* [2014] NICA 63, reversing a decision of the Chief Commissioner for Northern Ireland (*AS v HMRC (CB)* [2013] NI Comm. 15).

In this case the claimant, a Latvian, had been living and working for almost all of 23 months in the country where she claimed CB in respect of a daughter living with her. Her claim was refused on the ground of right to reside because, at the time, Latvia was an A8 country which limited her right to claim. The Chief Commissioner had allowed her appeal on the ground that the right to reside requirement was directly discriminatory (as it would be satisfied automatically by a British citizen) and was therefore unlawful under art.3(1) of EC Regulation 1408/71 (now replaced by EC Regulation 883/04). In doing so he had distinguished the decision in *Patmalniece v SSWP* [2011] UKSC 11. The Commissioner went on to observe also, that if he were wrong in reaching this conclusion, that he would have found that the claimant had an alternative route to success derived from the *Patmalniece* decision on the basis that she was sufficiently integrated, economically and socially, to qualify anyway. So in the event that his finding of direct discrimination was not correct, the Chief Commissioner found that if the right to reside test was indirectly discriminatory, it was not objectively justified.

The Northern Ireland Court of Appeal reversed the Chief Commissioner's decision in *Revenue and Customs v Spiridonova* [2014] NICA 63. On the direct discrimination point, the Court of Appeal held that it was bound to follow the clear decision of the CJEU in *Bressol v Gouvernement de la Communaute Française* [2010] 3 C.M.L.R. 559, whatever its doubts about the CJEU's reasoning. As a result the conditions contained in reg.27(3) had to be viewed cumulatively. In this light the requirement under reg.27(3) that an accession state national had to have a right to reside in the UK in order to be eligible for CB was not directly discriminatory on the ground of nationality. Moreover, the fact that an accession state worker had achieved a certain degree of social and/or economic integration in the UK could not, of itself, operate as an exception to the right to reside test. It was, accordingly, still necessary to consider the specific statutory requirement that, to establish a right of residence in the UK as a worker, an accession state national had to be in continuous registered employment with an authorised employer in accordance with the Workers Registration Scheme, as established by the Accession (Immigration and Worker Registration) Regulations 2004. Since those Regulations were devised to apply to accession state workers, the fact that an individual had worked more or less continually for a period in Northern Ireland could not constitute an exception (*R. (on the application of D) v Secretary of State For Work and Pensions* [2004] EWCA Civ 1468 and *Zalewska v Department for Social Development* [2008] UKHL 67, [2008] 1 W.L.R. 2602 considered). The Chief Commissioner's decision that a degree of economic and/or social integration could operate as an exception to the right to reside requirement had inhibited him from any consideration of the specific statutory requirement that, to establish a right of residence in the UK as a worker, an accession state national had to be in continuous registered employment with an authorised employer under the Scheme. It followed that the Chief Commissioner did not make any finding as to whether the 2006 Regulations constituted a lawful means of attaining a legitimate objective and, if so, whether the means adopted were proportionate. In those circumstances, his conclusions as to indirect discrimination could not stand either.

Persons temporarily absent from Northern Ireland

3.38

28.—(1) A person who is ordinarily resident in the United Kingdom and is temporarily absent from Northern Ireland shall be treated as being in Northern Ireland during the first—

(a) 8 weeks of any period of absence; or
(b) 12 weeks of any period of absence where that period of absence, or any extension to that period of absence, is in connection with—
  (i) the treatment of his illness or physical or mental disability;
  (ii) the treatment of his partner's illness or physical or mental disability;
  (iii) the death of a person who, immediately prior to the date of death, was his partner;
  (iv) the death, or the treatment of the illness or physical or mental disability, of a child for whom either he or his partner is, or both of them are, responsible; or

(SI 2006/223 reg.28)

    (v) the death, or the treatment of the illness or physical or mental disability, of his or his partner's relative.

Here "relative" has the same meaning as in regulation 24.

(2) A person is temporarily absent from Northern Ireland if, at the beginning of the period of absence, his absence is unlikely to exceed 52 weeks.

DEFINITION

"partner"—see reg.1.

Overlap of entitlement to child benefit under both the legislation of Northern Ireland and Great Britain

29.—(1) Where by virtue of these Regulations two or more persons would be entitled to child benefit in respect of the same child or qualifying young person for the same week under both the legislation of Northern Ireland and Great Britain, one of them only shall be so entitled.

(2) Where the child is in Great Britain (except where regulation 25(1)(d) applies) or is treated as being in Great Britain, the question of which of the persons is entitled shall be determined in accordance with the legislation applying to Great Britain.

(3) Where the child is in Northern Ireland (except where regulation 21(1)(d) applies) or is treated as being in Northern Ireland, the question of which of the persons is entitled shall be determined in accordance with the legislation applying to Northern Ireland.

3.39

DEFINITIONS

"child or qualifying young person"—see SSCBA 1992 s.142.
"week"—see SSCBA 1992 s.147.

Crown servants posted overseas

30.—(1) For the purposes of section [² 146 (2)] of the Social Security and Contributions and Benefits Act, a Crown servant posted overseas shall be treated as being in Great Britain.

(2) A Crown servant posted overseas is a person performing overseas (but not in Northern Ireland) the duties of any office or employment under the Crown in right of the United Kingdom—
    (a) who is, or was, immediately prior to his posting or his first of consecutive postings, ordinarily resident in the United Kingdom; or
    (b) who, immediately prior to his posting or his first of consecutive postings, was in the United Kingdom in connection with that posting.

3.40

AMENDMENT

1. Child Benefit (General) (Amendment) Regulations 2007 (SI 2007/2150) reg.11 (August 16, 2007).

GENERAL NOTE

In *CF 1968/2007* Commissioner Williams held that the expression "Crown servant posted overseas" should include a consular correspondent who was appointed subsequently as an honorary consul of the UK. At all times, he said, the claimant

3.41

was fulfilling functions defined in the Vienna Convention on Consular Relations. (Adopted in the UK by the Consular Relations Act 1968.) In doing so he was performing the duties of an officer under the Crown required by reg.30. It did not matter whether the duties performed were included in the Convention. Nor did it matter that the claimant had been recruited whilst he was living in the overseas country, because, in the view of the Commissioner, the words "posted overseas" were only descriptive of the place where the duties were performed and not the process by which the claimant came to be there. There remained the matter of whether the claimant could show that he was, immediately before his posting, an ordinary resident in the United Kingdom; and on that the Commissioner referred the case for rehearing. There was some evidence that he may indeed have been an ordinary resident because he was a retired army officer who was paying UK income tax on his pension. Note, too, that although it will usually be necessary for the child in respect of whom the claim is made, to be resident in the UK there is an exception provided in reg.32; the child will be treated as being in Great Britain where he normally lives with a parent who is a Crown servant posted overseas.

Partners of Crown servants posted overseas

3.42

31.—(1) For the purposes of section [² 146 (2)] of the Social Security and Contributions and Benefits Act the partner of a Crown servant posted overseas who is accompanying the Crown servant posted overseas shall be treated as being in Great Britain when the partner is either—
 (a) in the country where the Crown servant is posted, or
 (b) absent from that country in accordance with regulation 24 as modified by paragraphs (3) and (4).

(2) Regulations 22 and 24 apply to the partner of a Crown servant posted overseas with the modifications set out in paragraphs (3) and (4).

(3) References to "Great Britain" in the phrase "temporarily absent from Great Britain" in paragraphs (1) and (2) of regulation 24 shall be construed as references to the country where the Crown servant is posted and regulation 21(2) shall apply, where appropriate, accordingly.

(4) In regulation 24 omit the words "ordinarily resident in the United Kingdom and is".

AMENDMENT

1. Child Benefit (General) (Amendment) Regulations 2007 (SI 2007/2150) reg.11 (August 16, 2007).

Child or qualifying young persons normally living with Crown servants posted overseas

3.43

32.—(1) For the purposes of section [¹ 146(1)] of the Social Security and Contributions and Benefits Act a child or qualifying young person who normally lives with a Crown servant posted overseas shall be treated as being in Great Britain when he is either—
 (a) in the country where the Crown servant is posted, or
 (b) absent from that country in accordance with regulation 21 as modified by paragraph (2).

(2) The reference to "Great Britain" in paragraph (1) of that regulation shall be construed as a reference to the country where the Crown servant is posted.

(SI 2006/223 reg.32)

AMENDMENT

1. Child Benefit (General) (Amendment) Regulations 2007 (SI 2007/2150) reg.11 (August 16, 2007).

DEFINITIONS

"child or qualifying young person"—see SSCBA 1992 s.142.
"Crown servant posted overseas"—see reg.1.

Transitional provisions for Part 6

33.—(1) In relation to a period of temporary absence which commenced before 7th April 2003, and continues after the coming into force of these Regulations, regulations 24 and 28 shall have effect subject to the modifications in paragraphs (2) and (3) respectively.

(2) For regulation 24(2) substitute—

"(2) A person is temporarily absent from Great Britain if at the beginning of the period of absence his absence was intended to be temporary and has throughout continued to be so intended.".

(3) For regulation 28(2) substitute—

"(2) A person is temporarily absent from Northern Ireland if at the beginning of the period of absence his absence was intended to be temporary and has throughout continued to be so intended.".

3.44

PART 7

GENERAL AND SUPPLEMENTARY PROVISIONS

Persons treated as residing together

34.—For the purposes of Part 9 of SSCBA and Part 9 of SSCB(NI)A, the prescribed circumstances in which persons are treated as residing together are that spouses, two persons who are civil partners of each other, or two persons who are parents of a child [¹ or, qualifying young person] are absent from one another—
(a) where such absence is not likely to be permanent; or
(b) by reason only of the fact that either of them is, or they both are, undergoing medical or other treatment as an in-patient in a hospital or similar institution whether such absence is temporary or not.

3.45

AMENDMENT

1. Child Benefit (General) (Amendment) Regulations 2007 (SI 2007/2150) reg.12 (August 16, 2007).

DEFINITIONS

"civil partners"—see reg.1.
"hospital or similar institution"—see reg.1.

The Child Benefit (General) Regulations 2006

GENERAL NOTE

3.46 The question whether parties are residing together may be important in determining priorities, and was formerly important in relation to one parent benefit.

This regulation provides a partial definition of what is meant by "residing together" by stating two instances in which they are not to be regarded as being apart. In the first, spouses or parents of a child who are not married are to be regarded as not being absent from each other (i.e. are residing together) so long as their absence is not permanent. There is no limit on the period of absence as long as it can still be regarded as temporary. In *R(F) 4/85* this rule was applied to a couple who had never lived together. They married while the husband was serving a term of imprisonment having met through the wife's involvement as a prison visitor. Nevertheless the Commissioner held that a similarly worded regulation meant that they must be regarded as residing together.

In the second instance they will be regarded as not absent (i.e. are residing together) if one or both of them is undergoing medical treatment. In this case they will be regarded as being together even if the separation is expected to be permanent. This will cover the case of a parent who is in a hospice receiving terminal care. But the concept of residing together still requires that the parties share a household rather than just a roof (*R(F)3/81*).

Polygamous marriages

3.47 **35.**—(1) For the purposes of Part 9 of SSCBA and Part 9 of SSCB(NI) A, a polygamous marriage is treated as having the same consequences as a monogamous marriage for any day, but only for any day, throughout which the polygamous marriage is in fact monogamous.

(2) In paragraph (1)—
  (a) "monogamous marriage" means a marriage celebrated under a law which does not permit polygamy;
  (b) "polygamous marriage" means a marriage celebrated under a law which, as it applies to the particular ceremony and to the parties in question, permits polygamy;
  (c) a polygamous marriage is referred to as being in fact monogamous when neither party to it has any spouse additional to the other; and
  (d) the day on which a polygamous marriage is contracted, or on which it terminates for any reason, shall be treated as a day throughout which that marriage was in fact monogamous if at all times on that day after the time at which it was contracted, or as the case may be, before it terminated, it was in fact monogamous.

DEFINITION

"a polygamous marriage"—see para.(2).

GENERAL NOTE

3.48 A polygamous marriage (celebrated after July 31, 1971) is void if either of the parties was at the time domiciled in the United Kingdom (Matrimonial Causes Act 1973). This regulation is therefore most likely to affect parties who have contracted a marriage in polygamous form before they settle in this country. The marriage will be recognised in relation to Child Benefit so long as it remains monogamous or, if it was once polygamous, once the extra spouse has died or been divorced.

(SI 2006/223 reg.36)

Right to child benefit of voluntary organisations

36.—(1) Subject to paragraph (4) and (5), for the purposes of section 147(6) of SSCBA and section 143(6) of SSCB(NI)A (right to child benefit of voluntary organisations), a voluntary organisation is regarded as the only person with whom a child is living for any week in which that child is—
- (a) living in premises which are provided or managed by the voluntary organisation, being premises which are required to be registered with a Government Department or local authority or which are otherwise regulated under or by virtue of any enactment relating to England and Wales, Scotland, or Northern Ireland; or
- (b) placed by the voluntary organisation in the home of any person in accordance with the provisions of the [1 Fostering Services (England) Regulations 2011, the Fostering Services (Wales) Regulations 2003, the Looked After Children (Scotland) Regulations 2009] or the Foster Placement (Children) Regulations (Northern Ireland) 1996.

(2) A voluntary organisation shall not be regarded as having ceased to have a child living with it by reason only of any temporary absence of that child—
- (a) if the child is undergoing medical or other treatment as an in-patient in a hospital, until such absence has lasted for more than 84 days; or
- (b) if the child is temporarily absent for any other reason, until such absence has lasted for more than 56 days.

(3) In calculating the period of 84 days for the purposes of paragraph (2)(a), two or more distinct periods of temporary absence separated by one or more intervals each not exceeding 28 days shall be treated as a continuous period equal in duration to the total of such distinct periods and ending on the last day of the latter or last of such periods.

(4) A voluntary organisation shall not be regarded as a person with whom a child or qualifying young person is living in any week if in that week—
- (a) that individual is in residential accommodation in the circumstances prescribed in regulation 3; or
- (b) paragraph 1 of Schedule 9 to SSCBA or paragraph 1 of Schedule 9 to SSCB(NI)A applies to that individual.

(5) Where immediately before the week in which paragraph (1) applies to a child or qualifying young person, that individual was living with a person who was then entitled to child benefit in respect of him, paragraph (1) shall have effect in relation to that person as if the words "the only person" were omitted for so long as the child or qualifying young person is treated as continuing to live with that person by virtue of section 143(2) of SSCBA or section 139(2) of SSCB(NI)A.

(6) Section 143(1)(b) of SSCBA and section 139(1)(b) of SSCB(NI)A (person to be treated as responsible for a child in any week if he is contributing to the cost of providing for the qualifying individual at a weekly rate not less than the weekly rate of child benefit payable in respect of the child or qualifying young person for that week) and regulation 16(1) (child or qualifying young person in detention) shall not apply to a voluntary organisation.

3.49

The Child Benefit (General) Regulations 2006

AMENDMENT

1. Child Benefit (General) (Amendment) Regulations 2012 (SI 2012/818) reg.11 (April 6, 2012).

DEFINITIONS

"child or qualifying young person"—see SSCBA 1992 s.142.
"voluntary organisation"—see SSCBA 1992 s.147.
"week"—see SSCBA 1992 s.147.

GENERAL NOTE

3.50 This regulation enables a voluntary organisation to claim benefit in respect of a child who is living in accommodation provided, managed or arranged by it. Living with a voluntary organisation will normally preclude a claim by any other person, except that a claim may continue to be made by a person who previously had the child living with him and subsequently has continued to maintain the child to the requisite extent. In such a case the original claimant will continue to be entitled but a claim made by the voluntary organisation would take priority under the usual rules as to priority.

No requirement to state national insurance number

3.51 **37.**—For the purposes of section 147(6) of SSCBA and section 143(6) of SSCB(NI)A, section 13(1A) of the Social Security Administration Act 1992 and section 11(1A) of the Social Security Administration (Northern Ireland) Act 1992 (requirement to state national insurance number) shall not apply to a claim for child benefit in respect of a child or qualifying young person who is treated as living with a voluntary organisation by virtue of regulation 36.

Exception to rules preventing duplicate payment

3.52 **38.**—(1) A person is not disentitled to child benefit in respect of a child or qualifying young person by virtue of section 13(2) of the Social Security Administration Act 1992 and section 11(2) of the Social Security Administration (Northern Ireland) Act 1992 (persons not entitled to benefit for any week if benefit already paid for that week to another person, whether or not that other person was entitled to it) if in respect of that week—
    (a) the determining authority has decided that the Commissioners are entitled to recover the child benefit paid in respect of that child or qualifying young person from a person in consequence of his misrepresentation of, or his failure to disclose, any material fact and, where that determining authority is one from whose decision an appeal lies, the time limit for appealing has expired and no appeal has been made; or
    (b) the child benefit paid to the other person has been voluntarily repaid to, or recovered by, the Commissioners in a case where the determining authority has decided under section 9 or 10 of the Social Security Act 1998 or under Article 10 or 11 of the Social Security (Northern Ireland) Order 1998 either—
        (i) that, while there was no entitlement to benefit, it is not recoverable, or
        (ii) that there was no entitlement to benefit but has made no decision as to its recoverability.

(2) In this regulation "determining authority" means, as the case may require—

(SI 2006/223 reg.38)

(a) the Commissioners;
(b) an appeal tribunal constituted under [¹ . . .] or Article 8 of the Social Security (Northern Ireland) Act 1998;
(c) the Chief or any other Social Security Commissioner, or a tribunal consisting of any three or more such Commissioners constituted in accordance with [¹ . . .] Article 16(7) of the Social Security (Northern Ireland) Act 1998;
[¹ (d) the First-tier Tribunal;
(e) the Upper Tribunal.]

AMENDMENT

1. Tribunals, Courts and Enforcement Act 2007 (Transitional and Consequential Provisions) Order 2008 art.6(1) and Sch.1 para.308 (November 3, 2008).

DEFINITIONS

"child or qualifying young person"—see SSCBA 1992 s.142.
"the Commissioners"—see reg.1.
"week"—see SSCBA 1992 s.147.

Use of electronic communications

39.—Schedule 2 to the Child Benefit and Guardian's Allowance (Administration) Regulations 2003 (use of electronic communications) applies to the delivery of information to or by the Commissioners which is authorised or required by these Regulations in the same manner as it applies to the delivery of information to or by the Commissioners which is authorised or required by those Regulations.

References in this regulation to the delivery of information shall be construed in accordance with section 132(8) of the Finance Act 1999.

3.53

PART 8

REVOCATIONS

Omitted

3.54

Child Benefit (Residence and Persons Abroad) Regulations 1976

(SI 1976/963) *(as amended)*

These regulations were revoked with effect from April 6, 2003 by the Tax Credits Act 2002. There was a saving in respect of regs 6 and 7 until April 2, 2006. Those provisions may be found in earlier editions of this book.

3.55

The Child Benefit (Rates) Regulations 2006

The Child Benefit (Rates) Regulations 2006

(SI 2006/965) *(as amended)*

ARRANGEMENT OF REGULATIONS

3.56
1. Citation, commencement and interpretation.
2. Rate of child benefit.
3. Saving
4. *Revocations omitted.*

Citation, commencement and interpretation

3.57
1. —(1) These Regulations may be cited as the Child Benefit (Rates) Regulations 2006 and shall come into force on 10th April 2006 immediately after the Child Benefit (General) Regulations 2006.
(2) In these Regulations—
"SSCBA" means the Social Security Contributions and Benefits Act 1992;
"SSCB(NI)A" means the Social Security Contributions and Benefits (Northern Ireland) Act 1992;
"qualifying young person" means a person—
(a) in Great Britain, who is such a person for the purposes of Part 9 of SSCBA; and
(b) in Northern Ireland, who is such a person for the purposes of Part 9 of SSCB(NI)A.
(3) References in these Regulations to any condition being satisfied or any facts existing shall be construed as references to the condition being satisfied or the facts existing at the beginning of that week.

Rate of child benefit

3.58
2. —(1) The weekly rate of child benefit payable in respect of a child or qualifying young person shall be—
(a) subject to paragraphs (2) to (5), in a case where in any week a child or qualifying young person is the only person or, if not the only person, the elder or eldest person in respect of whom child benefit is payable to a person, [^{1}[^{2} £20.70]] ("the enhanced rate");
(b) in any other case, [^{1}[^{2} £13.70]].
(2) If, in any week—
(a) a person is—
(i) living with his spouse or civil partner,
(ii) living with another person as his spouse or civil partner, or
(iii) a member of a polygamous marriage and is residing with other members of that marriage;
(b) child benefit would, but for this paragraph, be payable to that person in respect of a child or qualifying young person at the enhanced rate; and
(c) child benefit would, but for this paragraph, be payable at that rate to one of the other persons listed in paragraphs (i) to (iii) of sub-paragraph (a) in respect of another child or qualifying person,

(SI 2006/965 reg.2) (as amended)

the enhanced rate shall be payable in that week in respect of only the elder or eldest of the children and qualifying young persons referred to in sub-paragraphs (b) and (c).

(3) For the purposes of paragraph (2)(a) a person is a member of a polygamous marriage if—
 (a) during the subsistence of the marriage any party to it is married to more than one person; and
 (b) the ceremony of marriage took place under the law of a country which permits polygamy.

(4) Child benefit shall not be payable at the enhanced rate if the person to whom child benefit is payable is—
 (a) a voluntary organisation; or
 (b) a person residing (otherwise than as mentioned in paragraph (2)(a)) with a parent of the child or qualifying young person in respect of whom it is payable.

(5) If an allowance, or an increase of a benefit, pension or allowance, which is a specified benefit, is paid in respect of a week—
 (a) to a person, and
 (b) in respect of the only, elder or eldest child or qualifying young person in respect of whom that person is entitled to child benefit,
child benefit shall be payable at the enhanced rate for that week.

(6) The following are specified benefits—
 (a) any benefit under SSCBA receipt of which entitles the recipient to an increase specified in column 2 of the Table in Part 4 of Schedule 4 to that Act (increases for dependants);
 (b) any benefit under SSCB(NI)A receipt of which entitles the recipient to an increase specified in column 2 of the Table in Part IV of Schedule 4 to that Act (increases for dependants in Northern Ireland);
 (c) an allowance for a child or a qualifying young person granted in respect of the death of a person due to service or war injury—
  (i) under the Armed Forces and Reserve Forces (Compensation Scheme) Order 2005;
  (ii) under the Naval, Military and Air Forces Etc. (Disablement and Death) Service Pensions Order 1983;
  (iii) under the Pensions (Polish Forces) Scheme 1964;
  (iv) under the War Pensions (Mercantile Marine) Scheme 1964;
  (v) under the Warrant of 21st December 1964 concerning pensions and grants in respect of disablement or death due to service in the Home Guard;
  (vi) under the Order of 22nd December 1964 concerning pensions and grants in respect of disablement or death due to service in the Home Guard after 27th April 1952;
  (vii) under the Order by Her Majesty dated 4th January 1971 in respect of service in the Ulster Defence Regiment; or
  (viii) which the Commissioners for Her Majesty's Revenue and Customs accept as being analogous to an allowance for a child granted in respect of the death of a person due to service or war injury under any of the preceding provisions of this sub-paragraph.

The Child Benefit (Rates) Regulations 2006

AMENDMENTS

1. Child Benefit Up-rating Order 2010 (SI 2010/982) art.2 (April 12, 2010).
2. Child Benefit and Tax Credits Up-rating Order 2015 (SI 2015/567) art.2 (April 6, 2015).

Saving

3.59 **3.** —(1) Despite the revocation, by regulation 4 of these Regulations, of—
(a) the Child Benefit and Social Security (Fixing and Adjustment of Rates) Regulations 1976, and
(b) the Child Benefit and Social Security (Fixing and Adjustment of Rates) Regulations (Northern Ireland) 1976,
if the amount of child benefit which would have been payable under those Regulations would, by virtue of the relevant transitional provisions and savings (had they remained in force), be greater than the amount prescribed by these Regulations, the greater amount shall be payable.

(2) In paragraph (1) "the relevant transitional provisions and savings" means—
(a) in the case of child benefit payable under SSCBA, regulations 3 and 4 of the Child Benefit and Social Security (Fixing and Adjustment of Rates) (Amendment) Regulations 1998; and
(b) in the case of child benefit payable under SSCB(NI)A, regulations 3 and 4 of the Child Benefit and Social Security (Fixing and Adjustment of Rates) (Amendment) Regulations (Northern Ireland) 1998.

REVOCATIONS

3.60 **4.** *Omitted*

GENERAL NOTE

3.61 These regulations specify the rate of Child Benefit. Since April 8, 1991 it has been paid at a higher rate in respect of the first or only child of the family (though not if the claimant is a voluntary organisation). Where two families are living together so that there could be two eldest children, the higher rate will be paid only in respect of one (the older) of them.

Until July 6, 1998, reg.2 of the Fixing and Adjustment of Rates Regulations 1976 provided also for the payment of a supplement where the claimant was not living with a spouse. This benefit, generally known (though never labelled in the Regulations) as One Parent Benefit (OPB) was ended for new claimants from that date. Saving provisions for existing and continuing claims were contained in the Fixing and Adjustment of Rates (Amendment) Regulations 1998.

Guardian's Allowance (General) Regulations 2003

(SI 2003/495) (AS AMENDED)

ARRANGEMENT OF REGULATIONS

3.62
1. Citation and commencement.
2. Interpretation.
3. Modification to section 77(2) of the Act.

(SI 2003/495) (as amended)

4. Adopted children.
5. Illegitimate children.
6. Children of divorced parents.
7. Circumstances in which a person is to be treated as being in prison.
8. Rate of allowance and payment to the National Insurance Fund or the Northern Ireland National Insurance Fund.
9. Residence condition.
10. Prescribed manner of making an election under section 77(9) of the Act or section 77(9) of the Northern Ireland Act.
11. Omitted.

SCHEDULE

Revocations

Part 1—*Omitted.*
Part 2—*Omitted.*

The Treasury, in exercise of the powers conferred upon them by section 77(3), (8) and (9) of the Social Security Contributions and Benefits Act 1992, section 77(3), (8) and (9) of the Social Security Contributions and Benefits (Northern Ireland) Act 1992, and section 54(1) of the Tax Credits Act 2002 hereby make the following Regulations:

Citation and commencement

1.—These Regulations may be cited as the Guardian's Allowance (General) Regulations 2003 and shall come into force on 7th April 2003 immediately after the commencement of section 49 of the Tax Credits Act 2002.

Interpretation

2.—(1) In these Regulations—
"the Act" means the Social Security Contributions and Benefits Act 1992;
"adopted" means adopted pursuant to—
(a) an order made in the United Kingdom, the Channel Islands or the Isle of Man;
(b) an overseas adoption within the meaning of section 72(2) of the Adoption Act 1976;
(c) a Convention adoption order within the meaning of section 72(1) of the Adoption Act 1976; or
(d) a foreign adoption order within the meaning of section 4(3) of the Adoption (Hague Convention) Act (Northern Ireland) 1969.
"the Board" means the [1 Commissioners for Her Majesty's Revenue and Customs];
"the Northern Ireland Act" means the Social Security Contributions and Benefits (Northern Ireland) Act 1992.

Amendment

1. Guardian's Allowance (General) (Amendment) Regulations 2006 (SI 2006/204) (April 10, 2006).

3.63

3.64

3.65

Modification to section 77(2) of the Act

3.66 **3.**—Section 77(2) of the Act and section 77(2) of the Northern Ireland Act shall be treated as modified where regulations 4 to 6 apply.

Adopted children

3.67 **4.**—(1) Where a child [¹ or qualifying young person] has been adopted by two persons jointly, a reference in section 77(2) of the Act or section 77(2) of the Northern Ireland Act to [¹ the parents of the child or qualifying young person] shall be read as a reference to those two persons.

(2) Where a child [¹ or qualifying young person] has been adopted by one person only, the circumstances to be satisfied in section 77(2) of the Act or section 77(2) of the Northern Ireland Act are that that person is dead.

AMENDMENT

1. Guardian's Allowance (General) (Amendment) Regulations 2006 (SI 2006/204) (April 10, 2006).

DEFINITIONS

"adopted"—reg.2.
"child"—SSCBA 1992 s.122.

Illegitimate children

3.68 **5.**—Where—
(a) a child's parents are unmarried at the date of the birth; and
(b) paternity has not been established—
  (i) by a court of competent jurisdiction; or
  (ii) in the opinion of the determining authority,
  the circumstances to be satisfied in section 77(2) of the Act or section 77(2) of the Northern Ireland Act are that the mother of the child [¹ or qualifying young person] is dead.

AMENDMENT

1. Guardian's Allowance (General) (Amendment) Regulations 2006 (SI 2006/204) (April 10, 2006).

DEFINITION

"child"—SSCBA 1992 s.122.

Children of divorced parents

3.69 **6.**—(1) Where—
(a) [¹ the marriage or the civil partnership of a child's parents has been terminated by divorce or dissolved];
(b) at the death of one of the parents the child [² or qualifying young person] was not in the custody of or maintained by the other parent;
(c) there is no court order—
  [² (i) providing that child or qualifying young person is to reside with that other parent; or
  (ii) imposing any liability on him for [² the maintenance of the child or qualifying young person]; and

(SI 2003/495 reg.6) (as amended)

(d) there is no maintenance assessment or maintenance calculation, as defined by section 54 of the Child Support Act 1991, or, for Northern Ireland, Article 2(2) of the Child Support (Northern Ireland) Order 1991 in force in respect of that other parent and child [² or qualifying young person],

the circumstances to be satisfied in section 77(2) of the Act or section 77(2) of the Northern Ireland Act are that one of [² the parents of the child or qualifying young persons] is dead.

(2) Where a child [² or qualifying young person] has been adopted by two persons jointly, any reference in paragraph (1) above to [² the parents of the child or qualifying young person] shall be read as a reference to those two persons.

AMENDMENTS

1. Civil Partnership Act 2004 (Tax Credits, etc.) (Consequential Amendments) Order 2005 (SI 2005/2919) (December 5, 2005).
2. Guardian's Allowance (General) (Amendment) Regulations 2006 (SI 2006/204) (April 10, 2006).

DEFINITIONS

"adopted"—reg.2.
"child"—SSCBA 1992 s.122.

Circumstances in which a person is to be treated as being in prison

7.—(1) The circumstances in which a person is to be treated as being in prison for the purposes of section 77 of the Act or section 77 of the Northern Ireland Act are that he is—
   (a) serving a custodial sentence within the meaning of section 76 of the Powers of Criminal Courts (Sentencing) Act 2000, Article 2(2) of the Criminal Justice (Northern Ireland) Order 1996 or a sentence of detention or imprisonment within the meaning of section 307(1) of the Criminal Procedure (Scotland) Act 1995, with not less than 2 years remaining from the death of the other parent; or
   (b) detained in a hospital by order of the court under—
      (i) section 37(1), 38, or 45A of the Mental Health Act 1983;
      (ii) section 5 of the Criminal Procedure (Insanity) Act 1964;
      (iii) section 6 or 14 of the Criminal Appeal Act 1968;
      (iv) section 57, section [¹ 57A] or 59A of the Criminal Procedure (Scotland) Act 1995;
      (v) Article 44, 45, 50A, or 51(2) and (3) of the Mental Health (Northern Ireland) Order 1986; or
      (vi) section 11 or 13(5A) and (6) of the Criminal Appeal (Northern Ireland) Act 1980.

(2) In calculating the length of the sentence for the purposes of paragraphs (1)(a) above and (4) below—
   (a) disregard any reduction made to the length of the sentence to take account of any period spent in custody prior to sentencing; and
   (b) include any period spent in custody immediately prior to sentencing, save that where he is serving a custodial sentence or sentence of detention or imprisonment with the meaning of paragraph (1)(a) above immediately prior to sentencing, include only such

3.70

period of that sentence as remains following sentencing for the later sentence,

but nothing in this paragraph shall permit the payment of guardian's allowance in respect of any period in custody prior to sentencing.

(3) Subject to paragraph (4) below, a person shall not cease to be treated as being in prison in accordance with paragraph (1) above by virtue of the fact that he is temporarily released, unlawfully at large, or, in the case of a person serving a sentence, transferred to a hospital.

(4) A person serving a sentence in accordance with paragraph (1)(a) above shall cease to be treated as being in prison in accordance with that paragraph where—
- (a) he is released on licence, the remainder of his sentence is remitted, his sentence is reduced on appeal to a term of less than 2 years, or his conviction is quashed on appeal; or
- (b) he is not in custody and has not been in custody for a period at least equal to the remaining period of his sentence,

but that where a person to whom sub-paragraph (b) applies returns to prison to serve the remainder of the sentence, the length of the sentence for the purposes of paragraph (1)(a) above shall be the period of the remainder of the sentence.

(5) This regulation shall apply, subject to the necessary modifications, to a parent who is outside Great Britain or Northern Ireland and serving a custodial sentence with not less than 2 years remaining from the death of the other parent or detained in a hospital by a court order.

AMENDMENT

1. Mental Health (Care and Treatment) (Scotland) Act 2003 (Consequential Provisions) Order 2005 (SI 2005/2078) Sch.2 para.24 (October 5, 2005).

GENERAL NOTE

3.71   A claim for Guardian's Allowance can succeed where one parent is dead and the other is serving a sentence of imprisonment, or is in custody in a hospital or youth offenders institution, but only so long as the period of the sentence remaining at the time of the death is two years or more. Calculation of the period of sentence remaining is complicated.

Paragraph (2) provides for disregard of any reduction of the sentence to be made if the prisoner is on remand at the time of the death, but for the inclusion of that period as part of the two years remaining to be spent in prison. Where the prisoner is sentenced on separate occasions, to consecutive but overlapping sentences the period will include the earlier sentence only to the extent that it is not subsumed by the latter.

In any case no order for payment of benefit can be made in respect of the period spent in prison prior to the sentence being imposed. Benefit remains payable until the prisoner is released from prison. Payment is not stopped if the prisoner escapes or is transferred to a hospital for medical treatment, until the remaining period of the sentence has expired. If the prisoner is subsequently returned to prison the claim may be renewed in respect of the period then remaining to be served.

Where the child or young person has only one "parent" because he has been adopted by only one person or because he is illegitimate and paternity is not established, or because his parents are divorced and no custody or maintenance order is applicable, there is no entitlement to Guardian's Allowance if that one parent is imprisoned.

(SI 2003/495 reg.8) (as amended)

Rate of allowance and payment to the National Insurance Fund or the Northern Ireland National Insurance Fund

8.—(1) Where a person treated as being in prison for the purposes of section 77 of the Act or section 77 of the Northern Ireland Act contributes to the cost of providing for a child [¹ or qualifying young person], the weekly rate of any guardian's allowance payable shall be reduced by the amount of the contribution made in the week preceding the week for which any allowance is payable.

(2) In a case where entitlement to guardian's allowance is established by reference to a person being in prison, that person shall, on notice being given by the Board, pay to the National Insurance Fund or the Northern Ireland National Insurance Fund an amount equal to that paid by way of guardian's allowance.

3.72

AMENDMENT

1. Guardian's Allowance (General) (Amendment) Regulations 2006 (SI 2006/204) (April 10, 2006).

DEFINITIONS

"child"—SSCBA 1992 s.122.
"week"—SSCBA 1992 s.122.

GENERAL NOTE

This regulation ensures that where a child or young person is being supported by a payment of Guardian's Allowance as a result of a person being in prison that person should, where possible, contribute towards the child's up keep and that such contribution should then be used to offset the cost of Guardian's Allowance. The Regulation appears to allow for this to happen in either of two ways—Paragraph (1) allows for a reduction in the benefit paid to the claimant. Paragraph (2) provides for the payment of a sum equal to the benefit, to the NI.fund.

3.73

Residence condition

9.—(1) There shall be no entitlement to guardian's allowance in respect of a child [¹ or qualifying young person] unless at least one of [¹ the parents of that child or qualifying young person]—
  (a) was born in the United Kingdom; or
  (b) at the date of death of the parent whose death gives rise to the claim for guardian's allowance, has, in any two year period since the age of 16, spent at least 52 weeks of that period in Great Britain or Northern Ireland, as the case may require.

(2) For the purposes of paragraph (1)(b) above, a person shall be treated as being present in Great Britain or Northern Ireland (as the case may require) where—
  (a) his absence is by virtue of his employment—
    (i) as a serving member of the forces within the meaning of regulation 140 of the Social Security (Contributions) Regulations 2001;
    (ii) as an airman within the meaning of regulation 111 of those Regulations; or
    (iii) as a mariner within the meaning of regulation 115 of those Regulations; or

3.74

(b) his absence is by virtue of his employment and that employment is prescribed employment within the meaning of regulation 114(1) of those Regulations (continental shelf operations).

[¹ (3) Where a child or qualifying young person has been adopted by two persons jointly references in paragraph (1) above to the parents of the child or qualifying young person are to be read as references to those two persons.

(3A) Where a child or qualifying young person has been adopted by one person only, that person must satisfy the requirements of paragraph (1) above].

(4) Where regulation 5 applies, [¹ the mother of the child or qualifying young person] must satisfy the requirement of paragraph (1) above.

AMENDMENT

1. Guardian's Allowance (General) (Amendment) Regulations 2006 (SI 2006/204) (April 10, 2006).

DEFINITIONS

"adopted"—reg.2.
"child"—SSCBA 1992 s.122.
"employed"—SSCBA 1992 s.122.

Prescribed manner of making an election under section 77(9) of the Act or section 77(9) of the Northern Ireland Act

3.75   **10.**—(1) An election under section 77(9) of the Act or section 77(9) of the Northern Ireland Act (payment of guardian's allowance not to be made to a husband) must—
(a) be in writing, and
(b) be made either—
   (i) on a form approved by the Board, or
   (ii) in such other manner as the Board may accept as sufficient in the circumstances of the particular case.

[¹ (2) Notice of the election must be given at an appropriate office.
[² (3) In paragraph (2) "an appropriate office" means—
(a) Waterview Park, Washington, Tyne and Wear; or
(b) any other office specified in writing by the Board.]

(4) An election may be given by means of electronic communication in accordance with Schedule 2 to the Child Benefit and Guardian's Allowance (Administration) Regulations 2003.

AMENDMENTS

1. Guardian's Allowance (General) (Amendment) Regulations 2006 (SI 2006/204) (April 10, 2006).
2. Child Benefit and Guardian's Allowance (Miscellaneous Amendments) Regulations 2009 (SI 2009/3268) reg.6 (January 1, 2010).

DEFINITION

"the Board"—reg.2.

(SI 2003/495 reg.11) (as amended)

Revocations

11. *Omitted.*

Schedules omitted.

Guardian's Allowance Up-rating Order 2015

(SI 2015/439)

Citation and commencement

1.—This Order may be cited as the Guardian's Allowance Up-rating Order 2015 and comes into force on 6th April 2015.

Amendment of Schedule 4 to the Social Security Contributions and Benefits Act 1992

2.—In paragraph 5 of Part 3 of Schedule 4 to the Social Security Contributions and Benefits Act 1992 (weekly rate of guardian's allowance) for "£16.35" substitute "£16.55".

Guardian's Allowance Up-rating Regulations 2015

(SI 2015/545)

Citation, commencement and Interpretation

1.—(1) These Regulations may be cited as the Guardian's Allowance Up-rating Regulations 2015 and come into force on 6th April 2015.

(2) In these Regulations "the Up-rating Orders" means the Guardian's Allowance Up-rating Order 2015 and the Guardian's Allowance Up-rating (Northern Ireland) Order 2015.

Exceptions relating to payments of allowance by virtue of the Up-rating Orders

2.—Neither section 155(3) of the Social Security Administration Act 1992 nor section 135(3) of the Social Security Administration (Northern Ireland) Act 1992 shall apply if a questions arises as to either—
   (a) the weekly rate at which guardian's allowance is payable by virtue of either of the Uprating Orders, or
   (b) whether the conditions for receipt of that allowance at the altered rate are satisfied, until that question has been determined in accordance with the provisions of section 8 of the Social Security Act 1998 or article 9 of the Social Security (Northern Ireland) Order 1998.

Persons not ordinarily resident in either Great Britain or Northern Ireland

3.82   **3.**—Regulation 5 of the Social Security Benefit (Persons Abroad) Regulations 1975 and regulation 5 of the Social Security Benefit (Persons Abroad) Regulations (Northern Ireland) 1978 (application of disqualification in respect of up-rating of benefits) shall apply to any additional benefit payable by virtue of either of the Up-rating Orders.

PART IV

STATUTORY SICK PAY

Statutory Sick Pay (General) Regulations 1982

(SI 1982/894) (AS AMENDED)

The Secretary of State for Social Services, in exercise of the powers conferred upon him by sections 1(3) and (4), 3(5) and (7), 4(2), 5(5), 6(1), 8(1) to (3), 17(4), 18(1), 20 and 26(1) and (3) to (5) of, paragraph 1 of Schedule 1 to, and paragraphs 2(3) and 3(2) of Schedule 2 to, the Social Security and Housing Benefits Act 1982(a) and of all other powers enabling him in that behalf, hereby makes the following regulations.

ARRANGEMENT OF REGULATIONS

1. Citation, commencement and interpretation
2. Persons deemed incapable of work
2A. Linking periods of incapacity for work
3. Period of entitlement ending or not arising
3A. Maximum entitlement to Statutory Sick Pay in a period of entitlement (repealed)
4. Contract of service ended for the purpose of avoiding liability for statutory sick pay
5. Qualifying days
6. Calculation of entitlement limit
7. Time and manner of notification of incapacity for work
8. Manner in which statutory sick pay may not be paid
9. Time limits for paying statutory sick pay
9A. Liability of the Secretary of State for payments of statutory sick pay
9B. Insolvency of employer
9C. Payments by the Secretary of State
10. Persons unable to act
11. Rounding to avoid fractional amounts
12. Days not to be treated as, or as parts of, periods of interruption of employment
13. [*repealed*]
13A. Production of employer's records
14. Provision of information in connection with determination of questions
15. Provision of information by employers to employees
15A. Statements relating to the payment of statutory sick pay (repealed)
16. Meaning of "employee"
17. Meaning of "earnings"
18. Payments to be treated or not to be treated as contractual remuneration
19. Normal weekly earnings
20. Treatment of one or more employers as one
21. Treatment of more than one contract of service as one
21A. Election to be treated as different employers not to apply to recovery of statutory sick pay
22. [*repealed*]

Citation, commencement and interpretation

1.—(1) These regulations may be cited as the Statutory Sick Pay (General) Regulations 1982, and shall come into operation on 6th April 1983.

(2) In these regulations—

"the Act" means the Social Security and Housing Benefits Act 1982;

[¹"the Contributions and Benefits Act" means the Social Security Contributions and Benefits Act 1992;]

[²"income tax month" means the period beginning on the 6th day of any calendar month and ending on the 5th day of the following calendar month;]

(3) Unless the context otherwise requires, any reference—

(a) in these regulations to a numbered section or Schedule is a reference to the section or Schedule, as the case may be, of or to the Act bearing that number;

(b) in these regulations to a numbered regulation is a reference to the regulation bearing that number in these regulations; and

(c) in any of these regulations to a numbered paragraph is a reference to the paragraph bearing that number in that regulation.

AMENDMENTS

1. Social Security (Miscellaneous Provisions) Amendment (No.2) Regulations 1992 (SI 1992/2595) reg.14 (November 16, 1992).

2. Social Security Contributions, Statutory Maternity Pay and Statutory Sick Pay (Miscellaneous Amendments) Regulations 1996 (SI 1996/777) reg.2(2) (April 6, 1996).

GENERAL NOTE

The relevant provisions in Pt I of the Social Security and Housing Benefits Act 1982 have now been replaced by Pt XII of the SSCBA 1992.

Persons deemed incapable of work

2.—(1) A person who is not incapable of work of which he can reasonably be expected to do under a particular contract of service may be deemed to be incapable of work of such a kind by reason of some specific disease or bodily or mental disablement for any day on which either—

(a) (i) he is under medical care in respect of a disease or disablement as aforesaid,

(ii) it is stated by a registered medical practitioner that for precautionary or convalescent reasons consequential on such disease or disablement he should abstain from work, or from work of such a kind; and

(iii) he does not work under that contract of service; or

[¹(b) he is—

(i) excluded or abstains from work, or from work of such a kind, pursuant to a request or notice in writing lawfully made under an enactment; or

(ii) otherwise prevented from working pursuant to an enactment,

[² by reason of it being known or reasonably suspected that he is infected or contaminated by, or has been in contact with a case of, a relevant infection or contamination].]

(2) A person who at the commencement of any day is, or thereafter on that day becomes, incapable of work of such a kind by reason of some specific disease or bodily or mental disablement, and

(SI 1982/894 reg.2) (as amended)

   (a) on that day, under that contract of service, does no work, or no work except during a shift which ends on that day having begun on the previous day; and

   (b) does no work under that contract of service during a shift which begins on that day and ends on the next,

shall be deemed to be incapable of work of such a kind by reason of that disease or bodily or mental disablement throughout that day.

[¹(3) For the purposes of paragraph (1)(b)—

"enactment" includes an enactment comprised in, or in an instrument made under—

   (a) an Act; or

   (b) an Act of the Scottish Parliament; and

[² "relevant infection or contamination" means—

   (a) in England and Wales—

      (i) any incidence or spread of infection or contamination, within the meaning of section 45A(3) of the Public Health (Control of Disease) Act 1984 in respect of which regulations are made under Part 2A of that Act (public health protection) for the purpose of preventing, protecting against, controlling or providing a public health response to, such incidence or spread, or

      (ii) any disease, food poisoning, infection, infectious disease or notifiable disease to which regulation 9 (powers in respect of persons leaving aircraft) of the Public Health (Aircraft) Regulations 1979 applies or to which regulation 10 (powers in respect of certain persons on ships) of the Public Health (Ships) Regulations 1979 applies; and

   (b) in Scotland, any—

      (i) infectious disease within the meaning of section 1(5) of the Public Health etc (Scotland) Act 2008, or exposure to an organism causing that disease, or

      (ii) contamination within the meaning of section 1(5) of that Act, or exposure to a contaminant, to which sections 56 to 58 of that Act (compensation) apply.]

AMENDMENTS

1. Statutory Sick Pay (General) Amendment Regulations 2006 (SI 2006/799) reg.2 (April 10, 2006).

2. Social Security (Miscellaneous Amendments) (No.3) Regulations 2011 (SI 2011/2425) reg.6 (April 6, 2012).

DEFINITION

"contract of service"—see SSCBA 1992 s.163(1).

GENERAL NOTE

Paragraph (1)

Regulation 2 of the SSP (General) Regulations is in virtually identical terms to the former regs 3(1) and (2) of the old Unemployment, Sickness and Invalidity Benefit Regulations 1983 (SI 1983/1598), which covered deemed sickness for the purposes of sickness benefit (see the 1994 volume of *Bonner*, p.687). The relevant case law in that context revolved around the vexed question of whether the regulation covers a pregnant claimant who is herself fit for work but is recommended to refrain from work because of the danger of contracting a disease which would threaten the life of the foetus she is carrying. Earlier cases have involved school teachers who are pregnant when there is an outbreak of Rubella in the school.

There are two reported decisions under the old law which are worthy of note. In *R(S)24/54* it was held that a precautionary absence from work was not within sub-para.(a) of the regulation because she was not under medical care in respect of the disease during a period in which she had been advised to refrain from work simply to avoid contact with the disease. That decision was rejected by the Commissioner in *R(S)1/72* where the facts were identical, except that the claimant was awaiting the outcome of tests to determine whether she was immune to Rubella and could therefore return to work. In fact, the results of those tests were not available for about five weeks owing in part to a postal strike. The Commissioner found that during the whole of that time she was under medical care in respect of the disease and was, therefore, deemed to be incapable of work and entitled to benefit. Fortunately for her, the results showed that she was immune and she was able to return to work. No question arose as to whether she would have continued to qualify for benefit if she had not been immune and had been advised to remain off work. But, the line of the Commissioner's reasoning in that case and his rejection of *R(S)24/54* rather than any attempt to distinguish it suggest that he may well have held that the claimant would remain under medical care until the danger from the infection was past.

In *R(S)4/93* the claimant was an assistant in a veterinary practice, who was potentially in danger of infection by toxoplasmosis from handling cats. She was given certificates advising her to refrain from work over a period of about six weeks. Her claim for statutory sick pay was refused by her employer and she applied to an AO for a decision on her entitlement to statutory sick pay. The Commissioner adopted the reasoning in both of the earlier cases. Thus she found that the claimant was entitled to benefit for a period of five days while awaiting the outcome of tests, which were negative, but not entitled for a further period of five weeks for which a claim had been made. The Commissioner did not specifically address the point that there had been a change in wording to the regulation since the earlier cases. The regulation now specifically refers to absence which is recommended for "precautionary" reasons. But, given that such reasons must be "consequential on such disease", meaning one for which she is "under medical care", it is probable that the new words add nothing to the interpretation.

4.6 It is, on the face of it, a rather fine distinction to hold, as in *R(S)4/93*, that the claimant is under medical care while awaiting the outcome of the tests but not under medical care once they are known. Nor is it in point to observe, as does the Commissioner in *R(S)24/54*, that the claimant is not unfit for work, only unable to work in the particular place she was employed, because the whole point of this regulation is for a claimant to be *deemed* unfit even though she may be fit. No doubt some justice is done for a claimant whose contribution record qualifies her for contribution-based jobseeker's allowance (presumably she is not to be disqualified for voluntary leaving), but where the claimant does not have such an entitlement the loss of statutory sick pay will be hard felt.

A female claimant could also now potentially qualify for ESA because the regulations for that benefit specifically provide for a pregnant woman who has to refrain from work because of a danger to herself or her unborn child (see Employment and Support Allowance Regulations 2008 (SI 2008/794) reg.20(d)—see Vol.I in this series).

The amendments made in 2006, substituting a new subs.(1)(b) and inserting a new (3), do not change the original policy intention, but merely update these provisions to reflect modern public health legislation, as do the amendments effective from 2012.

(SI 1982/894 reg.2A) (as amended)

[¹Linking periods of incapacity for work

2A. In subsection (3) of section 2 of the 1982 Act (linking periods of incapacity for work), 8 weeks shall be substituted for 2 weeks.]

AMENDMENT

1. Statutory Sick Pay (General) Amendment Regulations 1986 (SI 1986/477) reg.2 (April 6, 1986).

GENERAL NOTE

Section 2 of the 1982 Act, along with the other original provisions relating to statutory sick pay, was repealed by the Social Security (Consequential Provisions) Act 1992 s.3 and Sch.1. The eight-week linking rule is now to be found in SSCBA 1992 s.152(3).

Period of entitlement ending or not arising

3.—(1) In a case where an employee is detained in legal custody or sentenced to a term of imprisonment (except where the sentence is suspended) on a day which in relation to him falls within a period of entitlement, that period shall end with that day.

(2) A period of entitlement shall not arise in relation to a period of incapacity for work if the employee in question is in legal custody or sentenced to or undergoing a term of imprisonment (except where the sentence is suspended).

[⁴(2A) A period of entitlement in respect of an employee who was entitled to incapacity benefit, maternity allowance or severe disablement allowance shall not arise in relation to any day within a period of incapacity for work beginning with the first day on which paragraph 2(d) of Schedule 11 to the Contributions and Benefits Act ceases to have effect where the employee in question is a person to whom regulation 13A of the Social Security (Incapacity for Work) (General) Regulations 1995 (welfare to work beneficiary) applies.]

[⁶(2B) Paragraph (2A) shall not apply, in the case of an employee who was entitled to incapacity benefit, where paragraph 2(d)(i) of Schedule 11 to the Contributions and Benefits Act ceases to have effect by virtue of paragraph 5A of that Schedule.]

[⁷ (2C) A period of entitlement in respect of an employee who was entitled to employment and support allowance shall not arise in relation to any day within a period of limited capability for work beginning with the first day on which paragraph 2(dd) of Schedule 11 to the Contributions and Benefits Act ceases to have effect where the employee in question is a person to whom regulation 148 of the Employment and Support Allowance Regulations 2008 (work and training beneficiaries) applies.]

[¹(3) A period of entitlement as between an employee and his employer shall end after 3 years if it has not otherwise ended in accordance with [³section 153(2) of the Contributions and Benefits Act] or with regulations (other than this paragraph) made under [³section 153(6) of the Contributions and Benefits Act].]

[²[³(4) Where a period of entitlement is current as between an employee and her employer and the employee—

(a) is pregnant or has been confined; and
(b) is incapable of work wholly or partly because of pregnancy or confinement on any day which falls on or after the beginning of the [⁵4th week] before the expected week of confinement; and
(c) is not by virtue of that pregnancy or confinement entitled to statutory maternity pay under Part XII of the Contributions and Benefits Act or to maternity allowance under section 35 of that Act;

the period of entitlement shall end on that day or, if earlier, on the day she was confined.]

[³(5) Where an employee—
(a) is pregnant or has been confined; and
(b) is incapable of work wholly or partly because of pregnancy or confinement on any day which falls on or after the beginning of the [⁵4th week] before the expected week of confinement; and
(c) is not by virtue of that pregnancy or confinement entitled to statutory maternity pay under Part XII of the Contributions and Benefits Act or to maternity allowance under section 35 of that Act;

a period of entitlement as between her and her employer shall not arise in relation to a period of incapacity for work where the first day in that period falls within 18 weeks of the beginning of the week containing the day referred to at (b) above or, if earlier, of the week in which she was confined.]

(6) In paragraphs (4) and (5), "confinement" and "confined" have the same, meanings as in [³section 171 of the Contributions and Benefits Act].]

AMENDMENTS

1. Statutory Sick Pay (General) Amendment Regulations 1986 (SI 1986/477) reg.3 (April 6, 1986).
2. Statutory Sick Pay (General) Amendment (No.2) Regulations 1987 (SI 1987/868) reg.2 (June 7, 1987).
3. Social Security Maternity Benefits and Statutory Sick Pay (Amendment) Regulations 1994 (SI 1994/1367) reg.9 (June 11, 1994).
4. Social Security (Welfare to Work) Regulations 1998 (SI 1998/2231) reg.6 (October 5, 1998).
5. Social Security, Statutory Maternity Pay and Statutory Sick Pay (Miscellaneous Amendments) Regulations 2002 (SI 2002/2690) reg.13 (November 24, 2002).
6. Employment Equality (Age) (Consequential Amendments) Regulations 2007 (SI 2007/825) reg.5(2) (April 6, 2007).
7. Employment and Support Allowance (Consequential Provisions) (No.2) Regulations 2008 (SI 2008/1554) reg.45 (October 27, 2008).

DEFINITIONS

"confined"—see para.(6).
"confinement"—see *ibid.*
"employee"—see SSCBA 1992 s.163(1) and reg.16.
"employer"—see SSCBA 1992 s.163(1).
"period of entitlement"—see *ibid.*
"period of incapacity for work"—see *ibid.*
"week"—see *ibid.*

(SI 1982/894 reg.3A) (as amended)

[¹Maximum entitlement to statutory sick pay in a period of entitlement

3A.—[² . . .]

AMENDMENTS

1. Statutory Sick Pay (General) Amendment Regulations 1986 (SI 1986/477) reg.4 (April 6, 1986).
2. Statutory Sick Pay (General) (Amendment) Regulations 2008 (SI 2008/1735) reg.3 (October 27, 2008).

Contract of service ended for the purpose of avoiding liability for statutory sick pay

4.—(1) The provisions of this regulation apply in any case where an employer's contract of service with an employee is brought to an end by the employer solely or mainly for the purpose of avoiding liability for statutory sick pay.

(2) Where a period of entitlement is current on the day on which the contract is brought to an end, the employer shall be liable to pay statutory sick pay to the employee until the occurrence of an event which, if the contract would have caused the period of entitlement to come to an end under section 3(2)(a), (b) or (d) or regulation 3(1) [¹of these regulations or regulation 10(2) of the Statutory Sick Pay (Mariners, Airmen and Persons Abroad) Regulations 1982], or (if earlier) until the date on which the contract would have expired.

AMENDMENT

1. Statutory Sick Pay (Mariners, Airmen and Persons Abroad) Regulations 1982 (SI 1982/1349) reg.10(3) (April 6, 1983).

DEFINITIONS

"contract of service"—see SSCBA 1992 s.163(1).
"employee"—see *ibid.* and reg.16.
"employer"—see SSCBA 1992 s.163(1).
"period of entitlement"—see *ibid.*

Qualifying days

5.—(1) In this regulation, "week" means a period of 7 consecutive days, beginning with Sunday.

(2) Where an employee and an employer of his have not agreed which day or days in any week are or were qualifying days [¹or where in any day or days are or were such as are referred to in paragraph (3)], the qualifying day or days in that week shall be—
  (a) the day or days on which it is agreed between the employer and employee that the employee is or was required to work (if not incapable) for that employer or, if it is so agreed that there is or was no such day;
  (b) the Wednesday, or, if there is no such agreement between and employee as mentioned in sub-paragraph (a);
  (c) every day, except that or those (if any) on which it is agreed between the employer and the employee that none of that employer's

employees are or were required to work (any agreement that all day such days being ignored).

[¹(3) No effect shall be given to any agreement between an employer to treat as qualifying days—
  (a) any day where the day is identified, whether expressly or reference to that or another day being a day of incapacity relation to the employee's contract of service with an employer;
  (b) any day identified, whether expressly or otherwise, by period of entitlement or to a period of incapacity for work.]

AMENDMENT

1. Statutory Sick Pay (General) Amendment Regulations 1985 (SI 1985/126) reg.2 (March 5, 1985).

DEFINITIONS

"contract of service"—see SSCBA 1992 s.163(1).
"employee"—see *ibid.* and reg.16.
"employer"—see SSCBA 1992 s.163(1).
"period of entitlement"—see *ibid.*
"period of incapacity for work"—see *ibid.*
"qualifying day"—see *ibid.*
"week"—see *ibid.*

GENERAL NOTE

4.13 This prescribes the manner in which qualifying days are to be determined in the absence of any effective agreement between employer on which days are to rank as such (see also SSCBA 1992 s.154). *R(SSP)1/85* decides that "required to work" in sub-paras (a) and (c) means obliged to work under one's terms of employment, and does not embrace the situation in which the employee was merely asked to work. Thus, there the employee's normal practice of working voluntary overtime on Saturdays could not turn Saturday into a qualifying day where the contract of service merely provided for 39 hours' work on Mon–Fri. That decision (at para.10) explains how what is now SSCBA 1992 s.154 and this paragraph interrelate to set out a series of alternatives, to be applied in turn as necessary, to determine qualifying days in any particular case. See also the decision of the EAT in *Moxon v Ipsos-RSL Ltd* [2002] All E.R. D 109 (Aug) (EAT/634/01), following and applying *R(SSP) 1/85*.

Paragraph (3)

4.14 This renders ineffective any agreement which, expressly or otherwise, identifies qualifying days by reference to it or another day being one of incapacity, or by reference to a period of entitlement or period of incapacity for work.

Calculation of entitlement limit

4.15 **6.**—(1) Where an employee's entitlement to statutory sick pay is calculated by reference to different weekly rates in the same period of entitlement [². . .], the entitlement limit shall be calculated in the manner described in paragraphs (2) and (3), or, as the case may be, (4) and (5); and where a number referred to in paragraph (2)(b) or (d) or (4)(a)(ii) or (d)(ii) is not a whole number [¹of thousandths, it shall be rounded up to the next thousandth].

(2) For the purpose of determining whether an employee has reached his

(SI 1982/894 reg.6) (as amended)

maximum entitlement to statutory sick pay in respect of a period of entitlement there shall be calculated—
- (a) the amount of statutory sick pay to which the employee became entitled during the part of the period of entitlement before the change in the weekly rate;
- (b) the number by which the weekly rate (before the change) must be multiplied in order to produce the amount mentioned in subparagraph (a);
- (c) the amount of statutory sick pay to which the employee has so far become entitled during the part of the period of entitlement after the change in the weekly rate; and
- (d) the number by which the weekly rate (after the change) must be multiplied in order to produce the amount mentioned in subparagraph (c);
- (e) the sum of the amounts mentioned in sub-paragraphs (a) and (c); and
- (f) the sum of the number mentioned in sub-paragraphs (b) and (d).

(3) When the sum mentioned in paragraph (2)(f) reaches [^{2}28], the sum mentioned in paragraph (2)(e) reaches the entitlement limit.

(4) [^{2}. . .]

(5) [^{2}. . .]

AMENDMENTS

1. Statutory Sick Pay (General) Amendment Regulations 1984 (SI 1984/385) reg.2(a) (April 16, 1984).
2. Statutory Sick Pay (General) Amendment Regulations 1986 (SI 1986/477) reg.9 (April 6, 1986).

DEFINITIONS

"employee"—see SSCBA 1992 s.163(1) and reg.16.
"period of entitlement"—see SSCBA 1992 s.163(1).

Time and manner of notification of incapacity for work

7.—(1) Subject to paragraph (2), notice of any day of incapacity for work shall be given by or on behalf of an employee to his employer—
- (a) in a case where the employer has decided on a time limit (not being one which requires the notice to be given earlier than [^{1}. . .] the first qualifying day in the period of incapacity for work which includes that day of incapacity for work [^{1}or by a specified time during that qualifying day]) and taken reasonable steps to make it known to the employee, within that time limit; and
- (b) in any other case, on or before the seventh day after that day of incapacity for work.

(2) Notice of any day of incapacity for work may be given [^{2}one month] later than as provided by paragraph (1) where there is good cause for giving it later [^{2}, or if in the particular circumstances that is not practicable, as soon as it is reasonably practicable thereafter] so however that it shall in any event be given on or before the 91st day after that day.

(3) A notice contained in a letter which is properly addressed and sent by prepaid post shall be deemed to have been given on the day on which it was posted.

(4) Notice of any day of incapacity for work shall be given by or on behalf of an employee to his employer—
  (a) in a case where the employer has decided on a manner in which it is to be given (not being a manner which imposes a requirement such as is specified in paragraph (5)) and taken reasonable steps to make it known to the employee, in that manner; and
  (b) in any other case, in any manner, so however that unless otherwise agreed between the employer and employee it shall be given in writing.

(5) The requirements mentioned in paragraph (4)(a) are that notice shall be given—
  (a) personally;
  (b) in the form of medical evidence;
  (c) more than once in every 7 days during a period of entitlement;
  (d) on a document supplied by the employer; or
  (e) on a printed form.

AMENDMENTS

1. Statutory Sick Pay (General) Amendment Regulations 1984 (SI 1984/385) reg.2(b) (April 16, 1984).

2. Social Security Contributions, Statutory Maternity Pay and Statutory Sick Pay (Miscellaneous Amendments) Regulations 1996 (SI 1996/777) reg.2(3) (April 6, 1996).

DEFINITIONS

"employee"—see SSCBA 1992 s.163(1) and reg.16.
"employer"—see SSCBA 1992 s.163(1).
"period of entitlement"—see *ibid.*
"period of incapacity for work"—see *ibid.*
"qualifying day"—see *ibid.*

Manner in which statutory sick pay may not be paid

8. Statutory sick pay may not be paid in kind or by way of the provision of board or lodging or of services or other facilities.

Time limits for paying statutory sick pay

9.—(1) In this regulation, "payday" means a day on which it has been agreed, or it is the normal practice, between an employer and an employee of his, that payments by way of remuneration are to be made, or, where there is no such agreement or normal practice, the last day of a calendar month.

(2) In any case where—
  (a) a decision has been made by an insurance officer, local tribunal or Commissioner in proceedings under Part I that an employee is entitled to an amount of statutory sick pay; and
  (b) the time for bringing an appeal against the decision has expired and either—
    (i) no such appeal has been brought; or
    (ii) such an appeal has been brought and has been finally disposed of, that amount of statutory sick pay is to be paid within the time specified in paragraph (3).

(3) Subject to paragraphs (4) and (5), the employer is required to pay the amount not later than the first pay day after—
   (a) where an appeal has been brought, the day on which the employer receives notification that it has been finally disposed of;
   (b) where leave to appeal has been refused and there remains no further opportunity to apply for leave, the day on which the employer receives notification of the refusal; and
   (c) in any other case, the day on which the time for bringing an appeal expires.

(4) Subject to paragraph (5), where it is impracticable, in view of the employer's methods of accounting for and paying remuneration, for the requirement of payment referred to in paragraph (3) to be met by the pay day referred to in that paragraph, it shall be met not later than the next following pay day.

(5) Where the employer would not have remunerated the employee for his work on the day of incapacity for work in question (if it had not been a day of incapacity for work) as early as the pay day specified in paragraph (3) or (if it applies) paragraph (4), the requirement of payment shall be met on the first day on which the employee would have been remunerated for his work on that day.

DEFINITIONS

"employee"—see SSCBA 1992 s.163(1) and reg.16.
"employer"—see SSCBA 1992 s.163(1).

[¹Liability of the Secretary of State for payments of statutory sick pay

9A.—(1) Notwithstanding the provisions of section 1 of the Act and subject to paragraph (4), where—
   (a) an adjudicating authority has determined that an employer is liable to
   (b) the time for appealing against the determination has expired; and
   (c) no appeal against the determination has been lodged or leave to appeal against the determination is required and has been refused,
then for any day of incapacity for work in respect of which it was determined the employer was liable to make those payments, and for any further days of incapacity for work which fall within the same spell of incapacity for work and in respect of which the employer was liable to make payments of statutory sick pay to that employee, the liability to make payments of statutory sick pay in respect of those days shall, to the extent that payment has not been made by the employer, be that of the Secretary of State and not the employer.

(2) For the purposes of this regulation a spell of incapacity for work consists of consecutive days of incapacity for work with no day of the week disregarded.

(3) In paragraph (1) above "adjudicating authority" means, as the case may be, the Chief or other adjudication officer, [² the First-tier Tribunal or the Upper Tribunal.]

(4) This regulation shall not apply to any liability of an employer to make a payment of statutory sick pay where the day of incapacity for work in

Statutory Sick Pay (General) Regulations 1982

respect of which the liability arose falls within a period of entitlement which commenced before 6th April 1987.]

AMENDMENTS

1. Statutory Sick Pay (General) Amendment Regulations 1987 (SI 1987/ 372) reg.2 (April 6, 1987).
2. Tribunals, Courts and Enforcement Act 2007 (Transitional and Consequential Provisions) Order 2008 (SI 2008/2683) art.6 and Sch.1 para.18 (November 3, 2008).

DEFINITIONS

"employee"—see SSCBA 1992 s.163(1) and reg.16.
"employer"—see SSCBA 1992 s.163(1).
"period of entitlement"—see *ibid.*
"week"—see *ibid.*

GENERAL NOTE

4.20 This regulation, together with regs 9B and 9C, prescribe the circumstances in which the liability to pay statutory sick pay is to be that of the Board of the Inland Revenue (now HMRC) and not the employer. (Although the regulation still refers to the Secretary of State, those functions were transferred—along with those under regs 9B and 9C—to the Board by s.1(2) of and Sch.2 to the Social Security Contributions (Transfer of Functions, etc.) Act 1999.) The relevant circumstances are where it is determined that statutory sick pay is payable but the employer neither pays the amount due nor appeals against the decision (reg.9A) and where the employer was insolvent at the time (reg.9B). Provision is also made (reg.9C) requiring HMRC to make the payments for which they are liable at weekly intervals.

[¹Insolvency of employer

4.21 **9B.**—(1) Notwithstanding the provisions of section 1 of the Act and subject to paragraph (3), any liability arising under Part I of the Act to make a payment of statutory sick pay in respect of a day of incapacity for work in relation to an employee's contract of service with his employer shall be that of the Secretary of State and not that of the employer where the employer is insolvent on that day.

(2) For the purposes of paragraph (1) an employer shall be taken to be insolvent if, and only if—
  (a) in England and Wales—
    (i) he has been adjudged bankrupt or has made a composition or arrangement with his creditors;
    (ii) he had died and his estate falls to be administered in accordance with an order under section 421 of the Insolvency Act 1986; or
    (iii) where an employer is a company, a winding-up order [². . .] is made or a resolution for voluntary winding-up is passed with respect to it [²or it enters administration], or a receiver or manager of its undertaking is duly appointed, or possession is taken by or on behalf of the holders of any debentures secured by a floating charge, or any property of the company comprised in or subject to the charge or a voluntary arrangement proposed for the purposes of Part 1 of the Insolvency Act 1986 is approved under that Part;

(SI 1982/894 reg.9B) (as amended)

    (b) in Scotland—
        (i) an award of sequestration is made on his estate or he executes a trust deed for his creditors or enters into a composition contract;
        (ii) he has died and a judicial factor appointed under section 11A of the Judicial Factors (Scotland) Act 1889 is required by that section to divide his insolvent estate among his creditors; or
        (iii) where the employer is a company, a winding-up order [^{2}. . .] is made or a resolution for voluntary winding-up is passed with respect to it [^{2}or it enters administration] or a receiver of its undertaking is duly appointed or a voluntary arrangement proposed for the purposes of Part 1 of the Insolvency Act 1986 is approved under that Part.
shall not apply where the employer became insolvent before 6th April 1987.]

AMENDMENTS

1. Statutory Sick Pay (General) Amendment Regulations 1987 (SI 1987/ 372) reg.2 (April 6, 1987).
2. Enterprise Act 2002 (Insolvency) Order 2003 (SI 2003/2096) art.5 and Sch.2 para.42 (September 15, 2003).

DEFINITIONS

"contract of service"—see SSCBA 1992 s.163(1).
"employee"—see *ibid.* and reg.16.
"employer"—see SSCBA 1992 s.163(1).

[^{1}Payments by the Secretary of State

9C. Where the Secretary of State becomes liable in accordance with regulation 9A or 9B to make payments of statutory sick pay to a person, the first payment shall be made as soon as reasonably practicable after he becomes so liable, and payments thereafter shall be made at weekly intervals, by means of an instrument of payment [^{2}, instrument for benefit payment] or by such other means as appears to the Secretary of State to be appropriate in the circumstances of the particular case.]

AMENDMENTS

1. Statutory Sick Pay (General) Amendment Regulations 1987 (SI 1987/372) reg.2 (April 6, 1987).
2. Social Security (Claims and Payments etc.) Amendment Regulations 1996 (SI 1996/672) reg.3 (April 4, 1996).

Persons unable to act

10.—(1) Where in the case of any employer—
(a) statutory sick pay is payable to him or he is alleged to be entitled to it;
(b) he is unable for the time being to act, and either—
    (i) no receiver has been appointed by the Court of Protection with power to receive statutory sick pay on his behalf; or
    (ii) in Scotland, his estate is not being administered by any tutor, curator or other guardian acting or appointed in terms of law,
the Secretary of State may, upon written application to him by a person who, if a natural person, is over the age of 18, appoint that person to

exercise, on behalf of the employee, any right to which he may be entitled under Part I and to deal on his behalf with any sums payable to him.

(2) Where the Secretary of State has made an appointment under paragraph (1)—

(a) he may at any time in his absolute discretion revoke it;
(b) the person appointed may resign his office after having given one month's notice in writing to the Secretary of State of his intention to do so; and
(c) the appointment shall terminate when the Secretary of State is notified that a receiver or other person to whom paragraph (1)(c) applies has been appointed.

(3) Anything required by Part I to be done by or to any employee who is unable to act may be done by or to the person appointed under this regulation to act on his behalf, and the receipt of the person so appointed shall be a good discharge to the employee's employer for any sum paid.

DEFINITIONS

"employee"—see SSCBA 1992 s.163(1) and reg.16.
"employer"—see SSCBA 1992 s.163(1).

GENERAL NOTE

4.24 The Secretary of State's functions under this regulation were transferred to the Board of the Inland Revenue (now HMRC) by s.1(2) of and Sch.2 to the Social Security Contributions (Transfer of Functions, etc.) Act 1999.

Rounding to avoid fractional amounts

4.25 11. Where any payment of statutory sick pay is made and the statutory sick pay due for the period for which the payment purports to be made includes a fraction of a penny, the payment shall be rounded up to the next whole number of pence.

Days not to be treated as, or as parts of, periods of interruption of employment

4.26 12. In a case to which paragraph 3 of Schedule 2 applies, the day of incapacity for work mentioned in sub-paragraph (1)(b) of that paragraph shall not be, or form part of, a period of interruption of employment where it is a day which, by virtue of section 17(1) or (2) of the Social Security Act 1975 or any regulations made thereunder, is not to be treated as a day of incapacity for work.

Records to be maintained by employers

4.27 13.—[1 . . .]

AMENDMENT

1. Statutory Sick Pay (Maintenance of Records) (Revocation) Regulations 2014 (SI 2014/55) reg.2 (April 6, 2014).

(SI 1982/894 reg.13A) (as amended)

[¹Production of employer's records

13A.—(1) An authorised officer of the Commissioners of Inland Revenue may by notice require an employer to produce to him at the place of keeping such records as are in the employer's possession or power and as (in the officer's reasonable opinion) contain, or may contain, information relevant to satisfy him that statutory sick pay has been paid and is being paid in accordance with these regulations to employees or former employees who are entitled to it.

(2) A notice referred to in paragraph (1) shall be in writing and the employer shall produce the records referred to in that paragraph within 30 days after the date of such a notice.

(3) The production of records in pursuance of this regulation shall be without prejudice to any lien which a third party may have in respect of those records.

(4) References in this regulation to "records" means—
(a) any wage sheet or deductions working sheet; or
(b) any other document which relates to the calculation or payment of statutory sick pay to his employees or former employees,
whether kept in written form, electronically, or otherwise.

(5) In paragraph (1), "place of keeping" means such place in Great Britain that an employer and an authorised officer may agree upon, or, in the absence of such agreement—
(a) any place in Great Britain where records referred to in paragraph (1) are normally kept; or
(b) if there is no such place, the employer's principal place of business in Great Britain.]

4.28

AMENDMENT

1. Statutory Maternity Pay (General) and Statutory Sick Pay (General) (Amendment) Regulations 2005 (SI 2005/989) reg.3(2) (April 6, 2005).

DEFINITIONS

"records"—see reg.13A(4).
"place of keeping"—see reg.13A(5).

Provision of information in connection with determination of questions

14. Any person claiming to be entitled to statutory sick pay, or any other person who is a party to proceedings arising under Part I, shall, if he receives notification from the Secretary of State that any information is required from him for the determination of any question arising in connection therewith, furnish that information to the Secretary of State within 10 days of receiving that notification.

4.29

GENERAL NOTE

The Secretary of State's functions under this regulation were transferred to the Board of the Inland Revenue (now HMRC) by s.1(2) of and Sch.2 to the Social Security Contributions (Transfer of Functions, etc.) Act 1999.

4.30

Provision of information by employers to employees

15.—(1) [³Subject to paragraph (1A),] in a case which falls within paragraph (a), (b) or (c) of section 18(3) (provision of information by employers

4.31

in connection with the making of claims for [²short term incapacity] and other benefits), the employer shall furnish to his employee, in writing on a form approved by the Secretary of State for the purpose [³, or in a form in which it can be processed by equipment operating automatically in response to instructions given for that purpose], the information specified in paragraphs (2), (3) or (4) below, respectively within the time specified in the appropriate one of those paragraphs.

[³(1A) For the purposes of paragraph (1), where, in the particular circumstances of a case, it is not practicable for the employer to furnish the information within the specified time mentioned in paragraph (2), (3), (4)(b)(ii) or (5), he shall, not later than the first pay day within the meaning of regulation 9(1) immediately following the relevant specified time, furnish the information to his employee.]

(2) In a case which falls within paragraph (a) (no period of entitlement arising in relation to a period of incapacity for work) of section 18(3)—
- (a) the information mentioned in paragraph (1) is a statement of all the reasons why, under the provisions of paragraph 1 of Schedule 1 and regulations made thereunder, a period of entitlement does not arise; and
- (b) it shall be furnished not more than 7 days after the day on which the employee's employer is notified by or on behalf of the employee of the incapacity for work on the fourth day of the period of incapacity for work.

(3) In a case which falls within paragraph (b) (period of entitlement ending but period of incapacity for work continuing) of section 18(3)—

[⁴ (a) the information mentioned in paragraph (1) above is a statement informing the employee of—
  - (i) the reason why the period of entitlement ended;
  - (ii) the date of the last day in respect of which the employer is or was liable to make a payment of statutory sick pay to him.]
- (b) the statement shall be furnished not more than 7 days after the day on which the period of entitlement ended, or, if earlier, on the day on which it is already required to be furnished under paragraph (4).]

(4) In a case which falls within paragraph (c) (period of entitlement expected to end before period of incapacity for work ends, on certain assumptions) of section 18(3)—

[¹[⁴ (a) the information mentioned in paragraph (1) above is a statement informing the employee of—
  - (i) the reason why the period of entitlement is expected to end;
  - (ii) the date of the last day in respect of which the employer is or was expected to be liable to make a payment of statutory sick pay to him.]
- (b) the statement shall be furnished—
  - (i) in a case where the period of entitlement is expected to end in accordance with section 3(2)(b) of the Act (maximum entitled to statutory sick pay), on or before the 42nd day before the period of entitlement is expected to end; or
  - (ii) in any other case, on or before the seventh day before the period of entitlement is expected to end

(SI 1982/894 reg.15) (as amended)

[³. . .].]
(5) For the purposes of section 18(3)(c)(i) (period for which the period of incapacity for work is to be assumed to continue to run) the prescribed period shall be 14 days.

AMENDMENTS

1. Statutory Sick Pay (General) Amendment Regulations 1986 (SI 1986/477) reg.6 (April 6, 1986).
2. Social Security (Incapacity Benefit) (Consequential and Transitional Amendments and Savings) Regulations 1995 (SI 1995/829) reg.15 (April 13, 1995).
3. Social Security Contributions, Statutory Maternity Pay and Statutory Sick Pay (Miscellaneous Amendments) Regulations 1996 (SI 1996/777) reg.2(5) (April 6, 1996).
4. Statutory Sick Pay (General) (Amendment) Regulations 2008 (SI 2008/1735) reg.2 (October 27, 2008).

DEFINITIONS

"employee"—see SSCBA 1992 s.163(1) and reg.16.
"employer"—see SSCBA 1992 s.163(1).
"period of entitlement"—see *ibid.*
"period of incapacity for work"—see *ibid.*
"prescribed"—see *ibid.*
"qualifying day"—see *ibid.*
"week"—see *ibid.*

GENERAL NOTE

The references to ss.3(2)(b) and 18(3) of the 1982 Act should now be read as referring to SSCBA 1992 s.153(2)(b) and SSAA 1992 s.130(3), respectively.

4.32

[¹Statements relating to the payment of statutory sick pay

15A.—[² . . .]

4.33

AMENDMENTS

1. Statutory Sick Pay (General) Amendment Regulations 1986 (SI 1986/477) reg.7 (April 6, 1986).
2. Statutory Sick Pay (General) (Amendment) Regulations 2008 (SI 2008/1735) reg.3 (October 27, 2008).

Meaning of "employee"

16.—(1) [²Subject to paragraph (1ZA),] in a case where, and in so far as, a person [². . .] is treated as an employed earner by virtue of the Social Security (Categorisation of Earners) Regulations 1978, he shall be treated as an employee for the purposes of Part I and in a case where, and in so far as, such a person is treated otherwise than as an employed earner by virtue of those regulations, he shall not be treated as an employee for the purposes of Part I.

[³(1ZA) Paragraph (1) shall have effect in relation to a person who—
(a) is under the age of 16; and
(b) would or, as the case may be, would not have been treated as an employed earner by virtue of the Social Security (Categorisation of Earners) Regulations 1978 had he been over that age,
as it has effect in relation to a person who is or, as the case may be, is not so treated.]

4.34

[¹(1A) Any person who is in employed earner's employment within the meaning of the Act under a contract of apprenticeship shall be treated as an employee for the purposes of Part I.]

(2) A person who is in employed earner's employment within the meaning of the Act but whose employer—
  (a) does not fulfil the conditions prescribed in regulation 119(1)(b) of the Social Security (Contributions) Regulations 1979 as to residence or presence in Great Britain, or
  (b) is a person who, by reason of any international treaty to which the United Kingdom is a party or of any international convention binding the United Kingdom—
    (i) is exempt from the provisions of the Act, or
    (ii) is a person against whom the provisions of that Act are not enforceable,
shall not be treated as an employee for the purposes of Part I.

AMENDMENTS

1. Statutory Sick Pay (Compensation of Employers) and Miscellaneous Provisions Regulations 1983 (SI 1983/376) reg.5(2) (April 6, 1983).
2. Employment Equality (Age) Regulations 2006 (SI 2006/1031) reg.49(1) and Sch.8 Pt 2 para.50 (October 1, 2006).
3. Employment Equality (Age) (Consequential Amendments) Regulations 2007 (SI 2007/825) reg.5(3) (April 6, 2007).

DEFINITIONS

"employee"—see SSCBA 1992 s.163(1) and reg.16.
"employer"—see SSCBA 1992 s.163(1).
"prescribed"—see *ibid*.

Meaning of "earnings"

17.—(1) [³. . .]

[⁴(2) For the purposes of section 163(2) of the Contributions and Benefits Act, the expression "earnings" refers to gross earnings and includes any remuneration or profit derived from a person's employment except any payment or amount which is—
  (a) excluded [⁸or disregarded in the calculation of a person's earnings under regulation 25, 27 or 123 of, or Schedule 3 to, the Social Security (Contributions) Regulations 2001] [⁷(or would have been so excluded had he not been under the age of 16)];
  (b) a chargeable emolument under section 10A of the Social Security Contributions and Benefits Act 1992, except where, in consequence of such a chargeable emolument being excluded from earnings, a person would not be entitled to statutory sick pay [⁷(or where such a payment or amount would have been so excluded and in consequence he would not have been entitled to statutory sick pay had he not been under the age of 16)].]

[¹(2A) [³. . .]]

(3) For the purposes of [⁵section 163(2) of the Contributions and Benefits Act] the expression "earnings" includes also—
[⁸(za) any amount retrospectively treated as earnings by regulations made by virtue of section 4B(2) of the Contributions and Benefits Act;]

(SI 1982/894 reg.17) (as amended)

    (a) any sum payable by way of maternity pay or payable by the Secretary of State in pursuance of section 40 of the Employment Protection (Consolidation) Act 1978 in respect of maternity pay;
    (b) any sum which is payable by the Secretary of State by virtue of section 122(3)(a) of that Act in respect of arrears of pay and which by virtue of section 42(1) of that Act is to go towards discharging a liability to pay maternity pay;
    (c) any sum payable in respect of arrears of pay in pursuance of an order for reinstatement or re-engagement under that Act;
    (d) any sum payable by way of pay in pursuance of an order under that Act for the continuation of a contract of employment;
    (e) any sum payable by way of remuneration in pursuance of a protective award under the Employment Protection Act 1975;
    (f) any sum payable to any employee under the Temporary Short time Working Compensation Scheme administered under powers conferred by the Employment Subsidies Act 1978;
    (g) any sum paid in satisfaction of any entitlement to statutory sick pay;
    [²(h) any sum payable by way of statutory maternity pay under Part V of the Social Security Act 1986, including sums payable in accordance with regulations made under section 46(8)(b) of that Act.]
    [⁶(i) any sum payable by way of statutory paternity pay, including any sums payable in accordance with regulations made under section 171ZD(3) of the Contributions and Benefits Act;
    (j) any sum payable by way of statutory adoption pay, including any sums payable in accordance with regulations made under section 171ZM(3) of the Contributions and Benefits Act;]
    [⁹(k) any sum payable by way of statutory shared parental pay, including any sums payable in accordance with regulations made under section 171ZX(3) of the Contributions and Benefits Act.]
    (4) [³. . .]
    (5) [³. . .]

AMENDMENTS

1. Statutory Sick Pay (Compensation of Employers) and Miscellaneous Provisions Regulations 1983 (SI 1983/376) reg.5(3) (April 6, 1983).
2. Statutory Sick Pay (General) Amendment (No.2) Regulations 1987 (SI 1987/868) reg.4 (June 7, 1987).
3. Social Security (Miscellaneous Provisions) Amendment (No.2) Regulations 1992 (SI 1992/2595) reg.15 (November 16, 1992).
4. Social Security Contributions, Statutory Maternity Pay and Statutory Sick Pay (Miscellaneous Amendments) Regulations 1999 (SI 1999/567) reg.13 (April 6, 1999).
5. Social Security, Statutory Maternity Pay and Statutory Sick Pay (Miscellaneous Amendments) Regulations 2002 (SI 2002/2690) reg.14(a) (November 24, 2002).
6. Social Security, Statutory Maternity Pay and Statutory Sick Pay (Miscellaneous Amendments) Regulations 2002 (SI 2002/2690) reg.14(b) (April 6, 2003).
7. Employment Equality (Age) Regulations 2006 (SI 2006/1031) reg.49(1) and Sch.8 Pt 2 para.51 (October 1, 2006).
8. Social Security, Occupational Pension Schemes and Statutory Payments (Consequential Provisions) Regulations 2007 (SI 2007/1154) reg.5(2) and (3) (April 6, 2007).

9. Shared Parental Leave and Statutory Shared Parental Pay (Consequential Amendments to Subordinate Legislation) Order 2014 (SI 2014/3255) art.3 (December 31, 2014).

DEFINITION

"employee"—see SSCBA 1992 s.163(1) and reg.16.

Payments to be treated or not to be treated as contractual remuneration

4.36   **18.** For the purposes of paragraph 2(1) and (2) of Schedule 2 to the Act, those things which are included within the expression "earnings" by regulation (except paragraph (3)(g) thereof) shall be, and those things which are excluded from that expression by that regulation shall not be, treated as contractual remuneration.

Normal weekly earnings

4.37   **19.**—(1) For the purposes of section 26, an employee's normal weekly earnings shall be determined in accordance with the provisions of this regulation.
(2) In this regulation—
"the critical date" means the first day of the period of entitlement in relation to which a person's normal weekly earnings fall to be determined, or, in a case to which paragraph 2(c) of Schedule 1 applies, the relevant date within the meaning of Schedule 1;
"normal pay day" means a day on which the terms of an employee's contract of service require him to be paid, or the practice in his employment is for him to be paid, if any payment is due to him; and
"day of payment" means a day on which the employee was paid.
(3) Subject to paragraph (4), the relevant period (referred to in section 26(2)) is the period between—
(a) the last normal pay day to fall before the critical date; and
(b) the last normal pay day to fall at least 8 weeks earlier than the normal pay day mentioned in sub-paragraph (a), including the normal pay day mentioned in sub-paragraph (a) but excluding that first mentioned in sub-paragraph (b).
(4) In a case where an employee has no identifiable normal pay day, paragraph (3) shall have effect as if the words "day of payment" were substituted for the words "normal pay day" in each place where they occur.
(5) In a case where an employee has normal pay days at intervals of, or approximating to one or more calendar months (including intervals of or approximating to a year) his normal weekly earnings shall be calculated by dividing his earnings in the relevant period by the number of calendar months in that period (or, if it is not a whole number, the nearest whole number), multiplying the result by 12 and dividing by 52.
(6) In a case to which paragraph (5) does not apply and the relevant period is not an exact number of weeks, the employee's normal weekly earnings shall be calculated by dividing his earnings in the relevant period by the number of days in the relevant period and multiplying the result by 7.
(7) In a case where the normal pay day mentioned in sub-paragraph (a) of paragraph (3) exists but that first mentioned in sub-paragraph (b) of that paragraph does not yet exist, the employee's normal weekly earnings shall be calculated as if the period for which all the earnings under his contract

(SI 1982/894 reg.19) (as amended)

of service received by him before the critical date represented payment were the relevant period.

(8) In a case where neither of the normal pay days mentioned in paragraph (3) yet exists, the employee's normal weekly earnings shall be the remuneration to which he is entitled, in accordance with the terms of his contract of service for, as the case may be—
(a) a week's work; or
(b) a number of calendar month's work, divided by that number of months multiplied by 12 and divided by 52.

DEFINITIONS

"contract of service"—see SSCBA 1992 s.163(1).
"employee"—see SSCBA 1992 s.163(1) and reg.16.
"period of entitlement"—see *ibid.*

GENERAL NOTE

For some of the difficulties in applying this regulation, see *R(SSP)1/89*. There, the relevant period for a school dinner lady extended from the end of one term until the last pay day before her period of incapacity began. This was 11 weeks, but as the relevant period began the day after the last pay day at the end of term it could not include the lump-sum payment that was made as a retainer throughout the vacation. Without that sum her average weekly earnings did not qualify her for statutory sick pay. See also *Spence v Commissioners for HMRC* [2012] UKFTT 213 (TC).

4.38

Treatment of one or more employers as one

20.—(1) In a case where the earnings paid to an employee in respect of 2 more employments are aggregated and treated as a single payment of earnings under regulation 12(1) of the Social Security (Contributions) Regulations 1979, the employers of the employee in respect of those employments shall be treated as one for all purposes of Part I.

4.39

(2) Where 2 or more employers are treated as one under the provisions of paragraph (1), liability for the statutory sick pay payable by them to the employee shall be apportioned between them in such proportions as they may agree or, in default of agreement, in the proportions which the employee's earnings from each employment bear to the amount of the aggregated earnings.

(3) [1Subject to paragraphs (4) and (5)] where a contract of service ("the current contract") was preceded by a contract of service entered into between the same employer and employee ("the previous contract"), and the interval between the date on which the previous contract ceased to have effect and that on which the current contract came into force was not more than 8 weeks, then, for the purposes of establishing the employee's maximum entitlement within the meaning of section 5 (limitation on entitlement to statutory sick pay in any one period of entitlement or tax year), the provisions of Part I shall not have effect as if the employer were a different employer in relation to each of those contracts of service.

[1(4) Where a contract of service ("the current contract") was preceded by two or more contracts of service entered into between the same employer and employee ("the previous contracts") and the previous contracts—
(a) existed concurrently for at least part of their length; and
(b) the intervals between the dates on which each of the previous contracts ceased to have effect and that on which the current contract came into force was not more than 8 weeks,

then, for the purposes of establishing the employee's maximum entitlement within the meaning of section 5 the provisions of Part I shall not have effect as if the employer were a different employer in relation to the current contract and whichever of the previous contracts was the contract by virtue of which the employer had become liable to pay the greatest proportion of statutory sick pay in respect of any tax year or period of entitlement.

(5) If, in any case to which paragraph (4) applies, the same proportion of the employer's liability for statutory sick pay becomes due under each of the previous contracts, then, for the purpose of establishing the employee's maximum entitlement within the meaning of section 5, the provisions of Part I shall have effect in relation to only one of the previous contracts.]

AMENDMENT

1. Statutory Sick Pay (Compensation of Employers) and Miscellaneous Provisions Regulations 1983 (SI 1983/376) reg.5(4) (April 6, 1983).

DEFINITIONS

"contract of service"—see SSCBA 1992 s.163(1).
"employee"—see SSCBA 1992 s.163(1) and reg.16.
"employer"—see SSCBA 1992 s.163(1).
"period of entitlement"—see *ibid.*

GENERAL NOTE

4.40 Specific provision is made in Statutory Sick Pay (National Health Service Employees) Regulations 1991 (SI 1991/589) in the case of NHS workers with divided contracts.

Treatment of more than one contract of service as one

4.41 **21.** Where 2 or more contracts of service exist concurrently between one employer and one employee, they shall be treated as one for all purposes of Part I except where, by virtue of regulation 11 of the Social Security (Contributions) Regulations 1979, the earnings from those contracts of service are not aggregated for the purposes of earnings-related contributions.

DEFINITIONS

"contract of service"—see SSCBA 1992 s.163(1).
"employee"—see SSCBA 1992 s.163(1) and reg.16.
"employer"—see SSCBA 1992 s.163(1).

[¹Election to be treated as different employers not to apply to recovery of statutory sick pay

4.42 **21A.**—(1) Paragraph (2) below applies for the purposes of section 159A of the Contributions and Benefits Act (power to provide for recovery by employers of sums paid by way of statutory sick pay) and of any order made under that section.

(2) Where an employer has made 2 or more elections under regulation 3 of the Income Tax (Employments) Regulations 1993 to be treated as a different employer in respect of each of the groups of employees specified in the election, the different employers covered by each of those elections shall be treated as one employer.]

(SI 1982/894 reg.21A) (as amended)

AMENDMENT

1. Statutory Sick Pay Percentage Threshold Order 1995 (Consequential) Regulations 1995 (SI 1995/513) reg.3 (April 6, 1995).

DEFINITIONS

"employee"—see SSCBA 1992 s.163(1) and reg.16.
"employer"—see SSCBA 1992 s.163(1).

[¹Offences

22. [². . .]

AMENDMENTS

1. Statutory Maternity Pay (General) and Statutory Sick Pay (General) (Amendment) Regulations 2001 (SI 2001/206) reg.2 (February 23, 2001).
2. Statutory Maternity Pay (General) and Statutory Sick Pay (General) (Amendment) Regulations 2005 (SI 2005/989) reg.3(3) (immediately before April 6, 2005).

GENERAL NOTE

The repeal of this provision was consequential upon the bringing into force of the National Insurance Contributions and Statutory Payments Act 2004.

Statutory Sick Pay (Mariners, Airmen and Persons Abroad) Regulations 1982

(SI 1982/1349) (AS AMENDED)

The Secretary of State for Social Services, in exercise of the powers conferred upon him by sections 3(5) and (7), 22(1) and 26(1) of and paragraph 1 of Schedule 1 to the Social Security and Housing Benefits Act 1982(a) and of all other powers enabling him in that behalf, hereby makes the following regulations.

ARRANGEMENT OF REGULATIONS

1. Citation, commencement and interpretation
2. Mariners—interpretation
3. Airmen—interpretation
4. Continental shelf—interpretation
5. Persons in other member States—meaning of "employee"
5A. Persons absent from Great Britain—meaning of "employee"
6. Mariners—meaning of "employee"
7. Airmen—meaning of "employee"
8. Continental shelf—meaning of "employee"
9. Meaning of "employee"—general
10. Persons abroad—general
11. *(repealed)*
12. *(repealed)*
13. *(repealed)*
14. Time for compliance with requirements of Part I and regulations

Statutory Sick Pay (Mariners, etc.) Regulations 1982

Citation, commencement and interpretation

4.46   **1.**—(1) These regulations may be cited as the Statutory Sick Pay (Mariners, Airmen and Persons Abroad) Regulations 1982, and shall come into operation on 6th April 1983.

(2) In these Regulations—

"the Act" means the Social Security and Housing Benefits Act 1982;

"Part I" means Part I of the Act;

[1"the Contributions and Benefits Act," means the Social Security Contributions and Benefits Act 1992;

"the Contributions Regulations" means the Social Security (Contributions) Regulations 1979;]

"the General Regulations" means the Statutory Sick Pay (General) Regulations 1982;

and other expressions, unless the context otherwise requires, have the same meanings as in Part I.

(3) Unless the context otherwise requires, any reference—

(a) in these regulations to a numbered regulation is a reference to the regulation bearing that number in these regulations; and

(b) in any of these regulations to a numbered paragraph is a reference to the paragraph bearing that number in that regulation.

AMENDMENT

1. Social Security Contributions, Statutory Maternity Pay and Statutory Sick Pay (Miscellaneous Amendments) Regulations 1996 (SI 1996/777) reg.3(2) (April 6, 1996).

GENERAL NOTE

4.47   These Regulations make special provision for statutory sick pay under what is now Pt XI of the SSCBA 1992 as it affects mariners, airmen, persons abroad and persons employed in operations on the Continental Shelf. Under s.163(1) of the SSCBA 1992, a person is not, as a rule, an "employee", and therefore not qualified to receive statutory sick pay, unless he or she is employed in Great Britain. Regulations 5–8 prescribe exceptions to this rule, so that certain persons who are employed in other Member States but who are subject to the legislation of the United Kingdom, certain mariners and airmen, and certain persons employed on the Continental Shelf, are "employees", though employed outside Great Britain; and so that certain limited classes of mariners and airmen are not "employees" though employed in Great Britain. Further general provision on the meaning of "employee" is made by reg.9, while reg.10 makes general provision regarding persons from abroad. Regulations 11–13, which provided for exceptions to reg.10, were repealed in 1996.

Some of the requirements of the Act and regulations made under it impose time-limits. Regulation 14 relaxes those requirements in their application to persons who are outside the United Kingdom and for that reason cannot comply with them.

It should be noted that these regulations have never been fully updated to include appropriate references to SSCBA 1992. Accordingly, all references to Pt I of the Social Security and Housing Benefits Act 1982 in these regulations should be read as references to Pt XI of SSCBA 1992.

Mariners—interpretation

4.48   **2.** In regulations 6 and 11, the expressions "British ship," "foreign-going ship" "managing owner," "mariner," "owner" and "radio officer" have the same meanings as in Case C of Part VIII of the Social Security

(SI 1982/1349 reg.2) (as amended)

(Contributions) Regulations 1979, and the expressions "ship" and "ship or vessel," except in regulation 6(2), include hovercraft.

GENERAL NOTE

The provisions relating to Case C of Pt VIII of the Social Security (Contributions) Regulations 1979 have been re-enacted in Case C of Pt IX of the Social Security Contributions Regulations 2001 (SI 2001/1004).

4.49

Airmen—interpretation

3. In regulations 7 and 12—

"airman" means a person who is, or has been, employed under a contract of service either as a pilot, commander, navigator or other member of the crew of any aircraft, or in any other capacity on board any aircraft where—
(a) the employment in that other capacity is for the purposes of the aircraft or its crew or of any passengers or cargo or mails carried thereby; and
(b) the contract is entered into in the United Kingdom with a view to its performance (in whole or in part) while the aircraft is in flight, but does not include a person in so far as his employment is as a serving member of the forces;

"British aircraft" means any aircraft belonging to Her Majesty and any aircraft registered in the United Kingdom of which the owner (or managing owner if there is more than one owner) resides or has his principal place of business in Great Britain, and references to the owner of an aircraft shall, in relation to an aircraft which has been hired, be taken as referring to the person for the time being entitled as hirer to possession and control of the aircraft by virtue of the hiring or any subordinate hiring.

4.50

DEFINITION

"contract of service"—see SSCBA 1992 s.163(1).

Continental shelf—interpretation

4. In this regulation and regulations 8 and 13—

"designated area" means any area which may from time to time be designated by Order in Council under the Continental Shelf Act 1964 as an area within which the rights of the United Kingdom with respect to the sea-bed and subsoil and their natural resources may be exercised;

"prescribed area" means an area over which Norway or any member State (other than the United Kingdom) exercises sovereign rights for the purpose of exploring the seabed and subsoil and exploiting their natural resources, being an area outside the territorial seas of Norway or that member State [¹or any other area which is from time to time specified under section 22(5) of the Oil and Gas (Enterprise) Act 1982];

"prescribed employment" means employment in a designated area or prescribed area in connection with [¹any activity mentioned in section 23(2) of the Oil and Gas (Enterprise) Act 1982 in any designated area or in any prescribed area.]

4.51

AMENDMENT

1. Social Security and Statutory Sick Pay (Oil and Gas (Enterprise) Act 1982) (Consequential) Regulations 1982 (SI 1982/1738) reg.5 (April 6, 1983).

DEFINITION

"prescribed"—see SSCBA 1992 s.163(1).

Persons in other member States—meaning of "employee"

4.52   5. Subject to regulations 6(2), 7(2) and 9, a person who is—
(a) gainfully employed in a member State other than the United Kingdom in such circumstances that if his employment were in Great Britain he would be an employee for the purposes of Part I or a person treated as such an employee under regulation 16 of the General Regulations; and
(b) subject to the legislation of the United Kingdom under Council Regulation (EEC) No. 1408/71;
notwithstanding that he is not employed in Great Britain, shall be treated as an employee for the purposes of Part I.

DEFINITIONS

"Pt I"—see reg.1(2).
"the General Regulations"—*ibid.*

[¹Persons absent from Great Britain—meaning of "employee"

4.53   5A. Subject to regulations 5, 6(2) and 9, where a person, while absent from Great Britain for any purpose, is gainfully employed by an employer who is liable to pay in respect of him secondary Class 1 contributions under section 6 of the Contributions and Benefits Act 1992 or regulation 120 of the Contributions Regulations, he shall be treated as an employee for the purposes of Part XI of the Contributions and Benefits Act.]

AMENDMENT

1. Social Security Contributions, Statutory Maternity Pay and Statutory Sick Pay (Miscellaneous Amendments) Regulations 1996 (SI 1996/777) reg.3(3) (April 6, 1996).

DEFINITIONS

"employer"—see SSCBA 1992 s.163(1).
"the Contributions and Benefits Act"—see reg.1(2).
"the Contributions Regulations"—*ibid.*

GENERAL NOTE

4.54   The Social Security Contributions Regulations 2001 (SI 2001/1004) have now revoked and superseded the Social Security Contributions Regulations 1979 (SI 1979/591). Regulation 146 of the 2001 Regulations is the parallel provision to reg.120 of the 1979 Regulations.

Mariners—meaning of "employee"

4.55   6.—(1) Subject to regulation 9, where a mariner—
(a) is employed as such and—

(SI 1982/1349 reg.6) (as amended)

    (i) the employment is on board a British ship; or
    (ii) the employment is on board a ship and the contract in respect of the employment is entered into the United Kingdom with a view to its performance (in whole or in part) while the ship or vessel is on her voyage; and
    (iii) in a case to which head (ii) applies, the person by whom the mariner's earnings are paid, or, in the case of employment as a master or member of the crewof a ship or vessel, either that person or the owner of the ship or vessel (or the managing owner if there is more than one owner) has a place of business in Great Britain; or
(b) is employed as a master, member of the crew or radio officer on board any ship or vessel, not being a mariner to whom the last preceding subparagraph applies; and
    (i) in the case of the employment being as a radio officer, if the contract under which the employment is performed is entered into in the United Kingdom, the employer or the person paying the radio officer his earnings for that employment has a place of business in Great Britain, or,
    (ii) in the case of the employment being as a master, member of the crew or radio officer, if the contract is not entered into in the United Kingdom, the employer or the person paying the earnings has his principal place of business in Great Britain,

then, unless he is a mariner to whom paragraph (2) applies, he shall, notwithstanding that he may not be employed in Great Britain, be treated as an employee for the purposes of Part I.

(2) A mariner who—
(a) is in employment (including any period of leave, other than leave for the purpose of study, accruing from the employment) as a master or member of the crew of a ship, where—
    (i) the employment is on a foreign-going ship; or
    (ii) the employment is partly on a foreign-going ship and partly otherwise than on such a ship, and it is a requirement of the contract of service which relates to that employment that any payment of earnings in respect of that employment is to be made during the employment on the foreign-going ship; or
(b) has been in such employment as is mentioned in sub-paragraph (a), where—
    (i) not more than thirteen weeks have elapsed since he was last in such employment;
    (ii) he continues to be employed by the employer by whom he was employed when he was last in such employment; and
    (iii) he is not employed (by that employer or any other) on terms which are inconsistent with his being able to resume such employment as is mentioned in sub-paragraph (a) after not more than thirteen weeks have elapsed since he was last in such employment;

shall, notwithstanding that he may be employed in Great Britain, not be treated as an employee for the purposes of Part I.

DEFINITIONS

    "British ship"—see reg.2.
    "contract of service"—see SSCBA 1992 s.163(1).

"employer"—*ibid.*
"foreign-going ship"—see reg.2.
"managing owner"—*ibid.*
"mariner"—*ibid.*
"owner"—*ibid.*
"Pt I"—see reg.1(2).
"radio officer"—see reg.2.
"ship"—*ibid.*
"ship or vessel"—*ibid.*
"week"—see SSCBA 1992 s.163(1).

Airmen—meaning of "employee"

4.56 7.—(1) Subject to regulation 9 and the following provisions of this regulation, where an airman is employed as such on board any aircraft, and the employer of that airman or the person paying the airman his earnings in respect of the employment (whether or not the person making the payment is acting as agent for the employer) or the person under whose directions the terms of the airman's employment and the amount of the earnings to be paid in respect thereof are determined has—
  (a) in the case of the aircraft being a British aircraft, a place of business in Great Britain; or
  (b) in any other case, his principal place of business in Great Britain, then, notwithstanding that he may not be employed in Great Britain, he shall be treated as an employee for the purposes of Part I.

(2) Subject to the provisions of paragraph (3), an airman shall not be treated as an employee for those purposes if he is not domiciled, and has no place of residence, in Great Britain.

(3) The provisions of paragraph (2) shall have effect subject to any Order in Council giving effect to any reciprocal agreement made under section 143 of the Social Security Act 1975 (reciprocity with other countries).

DEFINITIONS

"airman"—see reg.3.
"British aircraft"—*ibid.*
"employee"—see SSCBA 1992 s.163(1).
"employer"—*ibid.*
"Pt I"—see reg.1(2).

GENERAL NOTE

Paragraph (3)
4.57 Section 143 of the Social Security Act 1975 has now been replaced in similar terms by s.179 of the SSAA 1992.

Continental shelf—meaning of "employee"

4.58 8. Subject to regulation 9, a person in prescribed employment, notwithstanding that he may not be employed in Great Britain, shall be treated as an employee for the purposes of Part I.

DEFINITIONS

"employee"—see SSCBA 1992 s.163(1).
"Part I"—see reg.1(2).

(SI 1982/1349 reg.8) (as amended)

"prescribed employment"—see reg.4.
"prescribed"—see SSCBA 1992 s.163(1).

Meaning of "employee"—general

9. No person who, by virtue of regulation 16 of the General Regulations, would not be treated as an employee for the purposes of Part I if his employment were in Great Britain, shall be treated as an employee by virtue of any of regulations 5–8.

4.59

DEFINITIONS

"employee"—see SSCBA 1992 s.163(1).
"Part I"—see reg.1(2).
"the General Regulations"—*ibid.*

[¹Persons abroad—general

10. In a case where a mariner, an airman or a continental shelf employee, respectively, within the meaning of regulation 6(1), 7 or 8, or a person who, is an employee or, is treated as an employee under regulation 5 or 5A, is incapable of work during a period of entitlement to statutory sick pay while absent from Great Britain, his entitlement to statutory sick pay shall cease only if he fails to satisfy the conditions of entitlement under Part XI of the Contributions and Benefits Act notwithstanding that his employer ceases, during the period of entitlement, to be liable to pay, in respect of him, secondary Class 1 contributions under section 6 of the Contributions and Benefits Act or regulation 120 of the Contributions Regulations.]

4.60

AMENDMENT

1. Social Security Contributions, Statutory Maternity Pay and Statutory Sick Pay (Miscellaneous Amendments) Regulations 1996 (SI 1996/777) reg.3(4) (April 6, 1996).

DEFINITIONS

"employee"—see SSCBA 1992 s.163(1).
"employer"—*ibid.*
"period of entitlement"—*ibid.*
"the Contributions and Benefits Act"—see reg.1(2).
"the Contributions Regulations"—*ibid.*

GENERAL NOTE

See note to reg.5A.

4.61

Mariners—exception to regulation 10

11. [¹. . .]

4.62

AMENDMENT

1. Social Security Contributions, Statutory Maternity Pay and Statutory Sick Pay (Miscellaneous Amendments) Regulations 1996 (SI 1996/777) reg.3(5) (April 6, 1996).

Airmen—exception to regulation 10

4.63   12. [¹. . .]

AMENDMENT

1. Social Security Contributions, Statutory Maternity Pay and Statutory Sick Pay (Miscellaneous Amendments) Regulations 1996 (SI 1996/777) reg.3(6) (April 6, 1996).

Continental shelf—exception to regulation 10

4.64   13. [¹. . .]

AMENDMENT

1. Social Security Contributions, Statutory Maternity Pay and Statutory Sick Pay (Miscellaneous Amendments) Regulations 1996 (SI 1996/777) reg.3(7) (April 6, 1996).

Time for compliance with requirements of Part I and regulations

4.65   14. Where—
(a) an employee is outside the United Kingdom;
(b) Part I or regulations made there under require any act to be done forthwith or on the happening of a certain event or within a specified time; and
(c) because the employee is outside the United Kingdom he or his employer cannot comply with the requirement;

the employee or the employer, as the case may be, shall be deemed to have complied with it if he performs the act as soon as reasonably practicable.

DEFINITIONS

"employee"—see SSCBA 1992 s.163(1).
"employer"—*ibid.*
"Pt I"—see reg.1(2).

Statutory Sick Pay (Medical Evidence) Regulations 1985

(SI 1985/1604) (AS AMENDED)

The Secretary of State for Social Services, in exercise of the powers conferred upon him by section 17(2A) of the Social Security and Housing Benefits Act 1982, and of all other powers enabling him in that behalf, by this instrument, which contains only provisions consequential upon section 20 of the Social Security Act 1985 and regulations made under the aforesaid section 17(2A), makes the following regulations:

ARRANGEMENT OF ARTICLES

4.66   1.   Citation, commencement and interpretation
2.   Medical information

(SI 1985/1604) (as amended)

SCHEDULE 1—Part I—Rules
              Part II—Form of Doctor's Statement
              Part III—Notes
SCHEDULE 1A—Part I—Rules
              Part II—Form of Special Statement

Citation, commencement and interpretation

1.—(1) These regulations may be cited as the Statutory Sick Pay (Medical Evidence) Regulations 1985 and shall come into operation on 6th April 1986.

(2) In these regulations, unless the context otherwise requires
[2 "the 1992 Act" means the Social Security Administration Act 1992;]
"signature" means, in relation to a statement given in accordance with these regulations, the name by which the person giving that statement is usually known (any name other than the surname being either in full or otherwise indicated) written by that person in his own handwriting; and "signed" shall be construed accordingly.

(3) [1. . .]

AMENDMENTS

1. Social Security (Miscellaneous Provisions) Amendment Regulations 1992 (SI 1992/247) reg.6(2) (March 9, 1992).
2. Social Security (Medical Evidence) and Statutory Sick Pay (Medical Evidence) (Amendment) Regulations 2010 (SI 2010/137) reg.3(1) and (2) (April 6, 2010).

GENERAL NOTE

These Regulations and the rules in Sch.1 prescribe the form of the statement to be issued by a doctor advising an employee that he or she should refrain from work (or need not refrain from work) for a period up to six months, or longer in certain circumstances. Regulation 2(2) provides that medical information cannot be required in respect of an employee's first seven days in any spell of incapacity for work.

Medical information

2.—[2 (1) Medical information required under section 14(1) of the 1992 Act relating to incapacity for work shall be provided either—
  (a) in the form of a statement given by a doctor in accordance with the rules set out in Part 1 of Schedule 1 to these Regulations; or
  (b) by such other means as may be sufficient in the circumstances of any particular case.]

(2) An employee shall not be required under [1 section 14(1) of the 1992 Act] to provide medical information in respect of the first 7 days in any spell of incapacity for work; and for this purpose "spell of incapacity" means a continuous period of incapacity for work which is immediately preceded by a day on which the claimant either worked or was not incapable of work.

AMENDMENT

1. Social Security (Medical Evidence) and Statutory Sick Pay (Medical Evidence) (Amendment) Regulations 2010 (SI 2010/137) reg.3(1) and (3) (April 6, 2010).

4.67

4.68

4.69

Statutory Sick Pay (Medical Evidence) Regulations 1985

[1 "SCHEDULE 1   Regulation 2(1)(a)

Part 1

Rules

4.70   1. In these rules, unless the context otherwise requires—

"assessment" means either a consultation between a patient and a doctor which takes place in person or by telephone or a consideration by a doctor of a written report by another doctor or other health care professional;
"condition" means a specific disease or bodily or mental disability;
"doctor" means a registered medical practitioner, not being the patient;
"other health care professional" means a person (other than a registered medical practitioner and not being the patient) who is a registered nurse, a registered midwife, an occupational therapist or physiotherapist registered with a regulatory body established by an Order in Council under section 60 of the Health Act 1999, or a member of any profession regulated by a body mentioned in section 25(3) of the National Health Service Reform and Health Care Professions Act 2002;
"patient" means the person in respect of whom a statement is given in accordance with these rules.

2. Where a doctor issues a statement to a patient in accordance with an obligation arising under a contract, agreement or arrangement under Part 4 of the National Health Service Act 2006 or Part 4 of the National Health Service (Wales) Act 2006 or Part 1 of the National Health Service (Scotland) Act 1978 the doctor's statement shall be in a form set out at Part 2 of this Schedule and shall be signed by that doctor.

3. Where a doctor issues a statement in any case other than in accordance with rule 2, the doctor's statement shall be in the form set out in Part 2 of this Schedule or in a form to like effect and shall be signed by the doctor attending the patient.

4. A doctor's statement must be based on an assessment made by that doctor.

5. A doctor's statement shall be completed in ink or other indelible substance and shall contain the following particulars—
   (a) the patient's name;
   (b) the date of the assessment (whether by consultation or consideration of a report as the case may be) on which the doctor's statement is based;
   (c) the condition in respect of which the doctor advises the patient they are not fit for work;
   (d) a statement, where the doctor considers it appropriate, that the patient may be fit for work;
   (e) a statement that the doctor will or, as the case may be will not, need to assess the patient's fitness for work again;
   (f) the date on which the doctor's statement is given;
   (g) the address of the doctor,
and shall bear, opposite the words "Doctor's signature", the signature in ink of the doctor making the statement.

6. Subject to rule 8, the condition in respect of which the doctor is advising the patient is not fit for work or, as the case may be, which has caused the patient's absence from work shall be specified as precisely as the doctor's knowledge of the patient's condition at the time of the assessment permits.

7. Where a doctor considers that a patient may be fit for work the doctor shall state the reasons for that advice and where this is considered appropriate, the arrangements which the patient might make, with their employer's agreement, to return to work.

8. The condition may be specified less precisely where, in the doctor's opinion, disclosure of the precise condition would be prejudicial to the patient's well-being, or to the patient's position with their employer.

9. A doctor's statement may be given on a date after the date of the assessment on which it is based, however no further statement shall be furnished in respect of that assessment other than a doctor's statement by way of replacement of an original which has been lost, in which case it shall be clearly marked "duplicate".

10. Where, in the doctor's opinion, the patient will become fit for work on a day not later than 14 days after the date of the assessment on which the doctor's statement is based, the doctor's statement shall specify that day.

(SI 1985/1604 Sch.1) (as amended)

11. Subject to rules 12 and 13, the doctor's statement shall specify the minimum period for which, in the doctor's opinion, the patient will not be fit for work or, as the case may be, for which they may be fit for work.

12. The period specified shall begin on the date of the assessment on which the doctor's statement is based and shall not exceed 3 months unless the patient has, on the advice of a doctor, refrained from work for at least 6 months immediately preceding that date.

13. Where—
    (a) the patient has been advised by a doctor that they are not fit for work and, in consequence, has refrained from work for at least 6 months immediately preceding the date of the assessment on which the doctor's statement is based; and
    (b) in the doctor's opinion, the patient will not be fit for work for the foreseeable future,
instead of specifying a period, the doctor may, having regard to the circumstances of the particular case, enter, after the words "case for", the words "an indefinite period".

PART 2

FORM OF DOCTOR'S STATEMENT 4.71

**STATEMENT OF FITNESS FOR WORK
FOR SOCIAL SECURITY OR STATUTORY SICK PAY**

Patient's name: Mr, Mrs, Miss, Ms

I assessed your case on: / /

and, because of the following condition(s):

I advise you that:
☐ you are not fit for work.
☐ you may be fit for work taking account of the following advice:

If available, and with your employer's agreement, you may benefit from:
☐ a phased return to work   ☐ amended duties
☐ altered hours   ☐ workplace adaptations

Comments, including functional effects of your condition(s):

This will be the case for

or from / / to / /

I will/will not need to assess your fitness for work again at the end of this period.
(Please delete as applicable)

Doctor's signature

Date of statement / /

Doctor's address
]

Statutory Sick Pay (Medical Evidence) Regulations 1985

Amendment

1. Social Security (Medical Evidence) and Statutory Sick Pay (Medical Evidence) (Amendment) Regulations 2010 (SI 2010/137) reg.3(1) and (4) (April 6, 2010).

General Note

4.72   The new medical certificate for statutory sick pay was introduced at the same time as changes were made to the arrangements for medical certificates in respect of benefit claims generally and Employment and Support Allowance in particular (see Social Security (Medical Evidence) Regulations 1976 (SI 1976/615) as amended). The previous different forms have been consolidated into a single medical certificate. In addition, the new form enables a doctor to state not only that the patient is unfit for work but also whether the patient may be able to work with appropriate support. As part of the same package of reforms the previous Sch.1A was also repealed.

Statutory Sick Pay (National Health Service Employees) Regulations 1991

(SI 1991/589) (as amended)

The Secretary of State for Social Security in exercise of the powers conferred by sections 26(1) and (5A), 45(1) and 47 of the Social Security and Housing Benefits Act 1982 and of all other powers enabling him in that behalf, by this instrument, which contains only regulations consequential upon paragraph 16 of Schedule 6 to the Social Security Act 1990, hereby makes the following Regulations:

Arrangement of Regulations

4.73
1. Citation, commencement and interpretation
2. Treatment of more than one contract of employment as one contract
3. Notification of election
4. Provision of information by employees
5. Treatment of two or more employers as one
6. Time for which an election is to have effect

Citation, commencement and interpretation

4.74   **1.**—(1) These Regulations may be cited as the Statutory Sick Pay (National Health Service Employees) Regulations 1991 and shall come into force on 1st April 1991.

(2) In these Regulations, a "health authority" [²shall in relation to Wales have the same meaning it has in section 8] of the National Health Service Act 1977, and in relation to Scotland mean the health board within the meaning of section 2 of the National Health Service (Scotland) Act 1978.

[¹(3) [⁴ . . .]]
[²(4) [⁴ . . .]]

[³(5) In these Regulations, a reference to "NHS trust" shall be construed to include a reference to an NHS foundation trust within the meaning of section 1(1) of the Health and Social Care (Community Health and Standards) Act 2003 where the application for authorisation to become an NHS foundation trust was made by an NHS trust.]

(SI 1991/589 reg.1) (as amended)

AMENDMENTS

1. Health Act 1999 (Supplementary, Consequential etc. Provisions) (No.2) Order 2000 (SI 2000/694) art.3 and Sch. para.2(2) (April 1, 2000).
2. National Health Service Reform and Health Care Professions Act 2002 (Supplementary, Consequential etc. Provisions) Regulations 2002 (SI 2002/2469) reg.4 and Sch.1, Pt 2, para.50 (October 1, 2002).
3. Health and Social Care (Community Health and Standards) Act 2003 (Supplementary and Consequential Provision) (NHS Foundation Trusts) Order 2004 (SI 2004/696) art.3(17) and Sch.17 (April 1, 2004).
4. National Treatment Agency (Abolition) and the Health and Social Care Act 2012 (Consequential, Transitional and Saving Provisions) Order 2013 (SI 2013/235) art.11 and Sch.2 para.15(2) (April 1, 2013).

Treatment of more than one contract of employment as one contract

2. Where, in consequence of the establishment of one or more National Health Service Trusts under Part I of the National Health Service and Community Care Act 1990 or the National Health Service (Scotland) Act 1978, a person's contract of employment is treated by a scheme under that Part or Act as divided so as to constitute two or more contracts [^{1}[^{2} . . .]] he may elect for all those contracts to be treated as one contract for the purposes of Part I of the Social Security and Housing Benefits Act 1982.

4.75

AMENDMENTS

1. Health Act 1999 (Supplementary, Consequential etc. Provisions) (No.2) Order 2000 (SI 2000/694) art.3 and Sch. para.2(3) (April 1, 2000).
2. National Treatment Agency (Abolition) and the Health and Social Care Act 2012 (Consequential, Transitional and Saving Provisions) Order 2013 (SI 2013/235) art.11 and Sch.2 para.15(3) (April 1, 2013).

Notification of election

3. A person who makes an election under regulation 2 above shall give written notification of that election to each of his employers under the two or more contracts of service mentioned in that regulation, before the end of the fourth day of incapacity for work in the period of incapacity for work in relation to a contract of service with the employer with whom this day first occurs.

4.76

Provision of information by employees

4. A person who makes an election under regulation 2 above shall, as soon as is reasonably practicable after giving notice of that election, provide each of his employers under the two or more contracts of service mentioned in that regulation with the following information—
 (a) the name and address of each of his employers; and
 (b) the date his employment with each of those employers commenced; and
 (c) details of his earnings during the relevant period and for this purpose "earnings" and "relevant period" have the same meanings as they have for the purposes of section 26(2) of the Social Security and Housing Benefits Act 1982.

4.77

Statutory Sick Pay (National Health Service Employees) Regulations 1991

Treatment of two or more employers as one

5. The employer to be regarded for the purposes of statutory sick pay as the employee's employer under the one contract where 2 or more contacts of service are treated as one in accordance with regulation 2 above, shall be—
[¹(a) in the case of a person whose contract of employment is treated by a scheme under Part I of the National Health Service and Community Care Act 1990 or the National Health Service (Scotland) Act 1978 as divided—
  (i) the Health Authority [² . . .] from which the employee was transferred, in a case where any one of the employee's contracts of service is with that Health Authority [² . . .]; or
  (ii) the first NHS trust to which a contract of service was transferred in a case where none of the employee's contracts of service are with the Health Authority [² . . .] from which he was transferred.
[² . . .]

AMENDMENTS

1. Health Act 1999 (Supplementary, Consequential etc. Provisions) (No.2) Order 2000 (SI 2000/694) art.3 and Sch. para.2(4) (April 1, 2000).
2. National Treatment Agency (Abolition) and the Health and Social Care Act 2012 (Consequential, Transitional and Saving Provisions) Order 2013 (SI 2013/235) art.11 and Sch.2 para.15(4) (April 1, 2013).

Time for which an election is to have effect

6. An election made under regulation 2 shall lapse at the end of the period of incapacity for work in relation to the contract of service with the employer mentioned in regulation 5.

Statutory Sick Pay and Statutory Maternity Pay (Decisions) Regulations 1999

(SI 1999/776)

The Secretary of State for Social Security, in exercise of powers conferred by section 20(3) of the Social Security Administration Act 1992, sections 8(1)(f) and 25(3) of the Social Security Contributions (Transfer of Functions, etc.) Act 1999 and of all other powers enabling him in that behalf, with the concurrence of the Commissioners of Inland Revenue, hereby makes the following Regulations:

ARRANGEMENT OF REGULATIONS

1. Citation, commencement and interpretation
2. Application for the determination of any issue arising as to, or in connection with, entitlement to statutory sick pay or statutory maternity pay
3. Applications in connection with statutory sick pay or statutory maternity pay
4. Revocation of regulation 20 of the Social Security (Adjudication) Regulations 1995

(SI 1999/776 reg.1)

Citation, commencement and interpretation

1.—(1) These Regulations may be cited as the Statutory Sick Pay and Statutory Maternity Pay (Decisions) Regulations 1999 and shall come into force on 1st April 1999.

(2) In these Regulations—
(a) "the Contributions and Benefits Act" means the Social Security Contributions and Benefits Act 1992;
(b) "employee" and "employer" have, in relation to—
   (i) statutory sick pay, the meanings given by section 163(1) of the Contributions and Benefits Act;
   (ii) statutory maternity pay, the meanings given by section 171(1) of the Contributions and Benefits Act.

4.81

Application for the determination of any issue arising as to, or in connection with, entitlement to statutory sick pay or statutory maternity pay

2.—(1) An application for the determination of any issue arising as to, or in connection with, entitlement to statutory sick pay or statutory maternity pay may be submitted to an officer of the Board by—
(a) the Secretary of State; or
(b) the employee concerned.

(2) Such an issue shall be decided by an officer of the Board only on the basis of such an application or on his own initiative.

4.82

DEFINITION

"employee"—see reg.1(2).

Applications in connection with statutory sick pay or statutory maternity pay

3.—(1) An application for the determination of any issue referred to in regulation 2 above shall be made only in writing, in a form approved for the purpose by the Board, or in such other manner, being in writing, as an officer of the Board may accept as sufficient in the circumstances.

(2) Where such an application is made by an employee, it shall—
(a) be delivered or sent to an office of the Board within 6 months of the earliest day in respect of which entitlement to statutory sick pay or statutory maternity pay is in issue;
(b) state the period in respect of which entitlement to statutory sick pay or statutory maternity pay is in issue; and
(c) state the grounds (if any) on which the applicant's employer has denied liability for statutory sick pay or statutory maternity pay in respect of the period specified in the application.

4.83

DEFINITION

"employer"—see reg.1(2).

Revocation of regulation 20 of the Social Security (Adjudication) Regulations 1995

4. Regulation 20 of the Social Security (Adjudication) Regulations 1995 is hereby revoked.

4.84

Statutory Sick Pay Percentage Threshold (Revocations, Transitional and Saving Provisions) (Great Britain and Northern Ireland) Order 2014

(SI 2014/897)

4.85 A draft of this Order was laid before Parliament under section 176(1)(c) of the Social Security Contributions and Benefits Act 1992 and section 172(11A) of the Social Security Contributions and Benefits (Northern Ireland) Act 1992 and approved by a resolution of each House of Parliament.

The Secretary of State for Work and Pensions makes the following Order in exercise of the powers conferred by section 159A of the Social Security Contributions and Benefits Act 1992 and section 155A of the Social Security Contributions and Benefits (Northern Ireland) Act 1992.

ARRANGEMENT OF ARTICLES

1. Citation and commencement
2. Revocation
3. Transitional and saving provisions

Citation and commencement

4.86 1. This Order may be cited as the Statutory Sick Pay Percentage Threshold (Revocations, Transitional and Saving Provisions) (Great Britain and Northern Ireland) Order 2014 and comes into force on 6th April 2014.

Revocation

4.87 2. The following are revoked—
(a) the Statutory Sick Pay Percentage Threshold Order 1995,
(b) the Statutory Sick Pay Percentage Threshold Order (Northern Ireland) 1995.

Transitional and saving provisions

4.88 3. Notwithstanding the revocation of the Statutory Sick Pay Percentage Threshold Order 1995 and the Statutory Sick Pay Percentage Threshold Order (Northern Ireland) 1995, those Orders continue to have effect for the period of two years beginning with 6th April 2014 for the purposes of entitling an employer to recover an amount of statutory sick pay (whether paid before, on or after 6th April 2014) in respect of any day of incapacity for work falling before 6th April 2014.

GENERAL NOTE

4.89 See previous editions of this Volume for the Statutory Sick Pay Percentage Threshold Order 1995 (SI 1995/512), now revoked but subject to the transitional and saving provision in art.3.

PART V

STATUTORY MATERNITY PAY

Statutory Maternity Pay (General) Regulations 1986

(SI 1986/1960) (AS AMENDED)

The Secretary of State for Social Services, in exercise of the powers conferred by sections 46(4), (7) and (8), 47(1), (3), (6) and (7), 48(3) and (6), 50(1), (2), (4) and (5), 51(1)(g), (k), (n) and (r) and (4), 54(1), 83(1) and 84(1) of, and paragraphs 6, 8 and 12(3) of Schedule 4 to, the Social Security Act 1986(a), and of all other powers enabling him in that behalf, by this instrument, which contains only regulations made under the sections of the Social Security Act 1986 specified above and provisions consequential upon those sections and before the end of a period of 12 months from the commencement of those sections, makes the following regulations:

ARRANGEMENT OF REGULATIONS

PART I

INTRODUCTION

1. Citation, commencement and interpretation   5.1

PART II

ENTITLEMENT

2. The Maternity Pay Period
3. Contract of service ended for the purpose of avoiding liability for statutory maternity pay
4. Modification of entitlement provisions
5. Treatment of more than one contract of service as one
6. Prescribed rate of statutory maternity pay
7. Liability of Secretary of State to pay statutory maternity pay
8. Work after confinement
9. No liability to pay statutory maternity pay
9A. Working for not more than 10 days in the Maternity Pay Period
10. Death of woman

PART III

CONTINUOUS EMPLOYMENT AND NORMAL WORKING HOURS

11. Continuous employment
12. Continuous employment and unfair dismissal
13. Continuous employment and stoppages of work
14. Change of employer

15. Reinstatement after service with the armed forces
16. Normal working weeks
16A. Meaning of "week"

Part IV

General Provisions

17. Meaning of "employee"
18. Treatment of two or more employers as one
19. Payments to be treated as contractual remuneration
20. Meaning of "earnings"
21. Normal weekly earnings
21A. (*repealed*)
21B. Effect of maternity allowance on statutory maternity pay

Part V

Administration

22. Evidence of expected week of confinement
23. Notice of absence from work
24. Notification of employment after confinement
25. Provision of information in connection with determination of questions
25A. Provision of information relating to claims for certain other benefits
26. Records to be maintained by employers
26A. Production of employer's records

Part VI

Payment

27. Payment of statutory maternity pay
28. Rounding to avoid fractional amounts
29. Time when statutory maternity pay is to be paid
30. Payments by the Secretary of State
31. Persons unable to act

Part VII

Offences

32. (*repealed*)

(SI 1986/1960 reg.1) (as amended)

PART I

INTRODUCTION

Citation, commencement and interpretation

1.—(1) These regulations may be cited as the Statutory Maternity Pay (General) Regulations 1986 and shall come into operation in the case of regulations 1, 22 and 23 on 15th March, 1987, and in the case of the remainder of the regulations on 6th April, 1987.

(2) In these regulations, unless the context otherwise requires—
"the 1975 Act" means the Social Security Act 1975;
"the 1978 Act" means the Employment Protection (Consolidation) Act 1978;
"the 1986 Act" means the Social Security Act 1986.
[[1]"the Contributions and Benefits Act" means the Social Security Contributions and Benefits Act 1992.]
[[2]"statutory maternity leave" means ordinary maternity leave and any additional maternity leave under, respectively, sections 71 and 73 of the Employment Rights Act 1996.]

(3) Unless the context otherwise requires, any references in these regulations to—
(a) a numbered regulation is a reference to the regulation bearing that number in these regulations and any reference in a regulation to a numbered paragraph is a reference to the paragraph of that regulation bearing that number;
(b) any provision made by or contained in an enactment or instrument shall be construed as a reference to that provision as amended or extended by any enactment or instrument and as including a reference to any provision which it re-enacts or replaces, or which may reenact or replace it, with or without modifications.

AMENDMENTS

1. Social Security (Miscellaneous Provisions) Amendment (No.2) Regulations 1992 (SI 1992/2595) reg.12 (November 16, 1992).
2. Statutory Maternity Pay (General) (Amendment) Regulations 2005 (SI 2005/729) reg.2 (April 6, 2005).

GENERAL NOTE

The text of these Regulations pre-dates SSCBA 1992 and was not amended at the time of the SSCBA 1992 to reflect the provisions in the 1992 Act. The Regulations remain in force, of course, by virtue of s.17(2)(b) of the Interpretation Act 1978. As a result, regulations which survive unamended from the original text refer to the SSA 1975 and SSA 1986, whilst post-1992 amendments refer to the parallel provisions in SSCBA 1992. References to the 1975 Act should therefore be read as referring to SSCBA 1992, and those to Pt V of the SSA 1986 as referring to Pt XII of the SSCBA 1992.

Statutory Maternity Pay (General) Regulations 1986

Part II

Entitlement

The Maternity Pay Period

5.4 [¹ **2.**—(1) Subject to paragraphs (3) to (5), where—
(a) a woman gives notice to her employer of the date from which she expects his liability to pay her statutory maternity pay to begin; and
(b) in conformity with that notice ceases to work for him in a week which is later than the 12th week before the expected week of confinement,
the first day of the maternity pay period shall be the day on which she expects his liability to pay her statutory maternity pay to begin in conformity with that notice provided that day is not later than the day immediately following the day on which she is confined.
(2) The maternity pay period shall be a period of 39 consecutive weeks.
(3) In a case where a woman is confined—
(a) before the 11th week before the expected week of confinement; or
(b) after the 12th week before the expected week of confinement and the confinement occurs on a day which precedes that mentioned in a notice given to her employer as being the day on which she expects his liability to pay her statutory maternity pay to begin,
section 165 of the Contributions and Benefits Act shall have effect so that the first day of the maternity pay period shall be the day following the day on which she is so confined.
(4) In a case where a woman is absent from work wholly or partly because of pregnancy or confinement on any day—
(a) which falls on or after the beginning of the 4th week before the expected week of confinement; but
(b) not later than the day immediately following the day on which she is confined,
the first day of the maternity pay period shall be the day following the day on which she is so absent.
(5) In a case where a woman leaves her employment—
(a) at any time falling after the beginning of the 11th week before the expected week of confinement and before the start of the maternity pay period, but
(b) not later than the day on which she is confined,
the first day of the maternity pay period shall be the day following the day on which she leaves her employment.]

Amendment

1. Statutory Maternity Pay, Social Security (Maternity Allowance) and Social Security (Overlapping Benefits) (Amendment) Regulations 2006 (SI 2006/2379) reg.3(2) (October 1, 2006).

General Note

5.5 This regulation was substantially recast with a new version substituted with effect from October 1, 2006 which applies in relation to women whose expected week of

(SI 1986/1960 reg.2) (as amended)

confinement falls on or after April 1, 2007. The new version of the regulation was prompted by the enactment of the Work and Families Act 2006, which improved the SMP scheme. There are two main differences between the current and previous versions of the regulation.

First, SMP is now payable for 39 weeks as opposed to the 26 weeks that applied before October 1, 2006 (para.(2)); note that before November 24, 2002, the previous maximum period had been 18 weeks.

Secondly, before October 1, 2006 the maternity pay period for SMP purposes started from the week following the week that the woman ceased work in accordance with the requisite notice given to her employer. In practice this meant the Sunday following the day she stopped work in accordance with the notice. The new rule enables the maternity pay period to start on any day of the week as specified by the woman in her notice to the employer. This allows the start of the maternity pay period to match the start of the woman's maternity leave. Accordingly the general rule for determining the start of the maternity pay period is set out in para.(1). There are then a number of further special cases detailed in paras (3)–(5). Paragraph (3) covers those situations where the woman gives birth early. Paragraph (4) makes special provision to deal with the situation where the woman stops working because of a pregnancy-related absence in the four weeks before the expected week of confinement. Finally, para.(5) covers women who leave their employment after the start of the 11th week before the expected week of confinement, but before the maternity pay period commences and not later than day of actual confinement.

Paragraph (1)
"in conformity with that notice cases to work"

This expression was considered by the Upper Tribunal (Tax and Chancery Chamber) in *Wade and North Yorkshire Police Authority v HMRC (FTC/35/2009, FTC/42/2009* and *FTC/43/2009)* [2011] IRLR 393, where Mrs Wade claimed SMP in relation to pregnancies in 2005 and 2007. It was held that a woman might cease to work "in conformity with that notice" for the purposes of para.(1) even if she had previously ceased to work on some other basis. An analogy with the statutory maternity leave regime provided support for that approach. A woman eligible for statutory maternity leave could claim it from a date of her choosing, regardless of the basis for her period of leave, provided only that the date was no earlier than the 11th week before the expected week of confinement and during the last four weeks before the expected week of confinement she was not absent from work because of pregnancy in advance of the specified date. It was held that it made sense that she should be able to claim SMP from a similar date, especially given the symmetries between the two regimes. This interpretation also produced clarity for both employer and employee. The result was that the claimant was entitled to SMP from the fourth week before each expected week of confinement. It did not matter whether, in respect of the second pregnancy, it was para.(1) or para.(4) that governed the position.

5.6

Contract of service ended for the purpose of avoiding liability for statutory maternity pay

3.—(1) A former employer shall be liable to make payments of statutory maternity pay to any woman who was employed by him for a continuous period of at least eight weeks and whose contract of service with him was brought to an end by the former employer solely or mainly for the purpose of avoiding liability for statutory maternity pay.

5.7

(2) In order to determine the amount payable by the former employer—
(a) the woman shall be deemed for the purposes of Part V of the 1986 Act to have been employed by him from the date her employment with him ended until the end of the week immediately preceding the

Statutory Maternity Pay (General) Regulations 1986

14th week before the expected week of confinement on the same terms and conditions of employment as those subsisting immediately before her employment ended; and

(b) her normal weekly earnings for the period of 8 weeks immediately preceding the 14th week before the expected week of confinement shall for those purposes be calculated by reference to her normal weekly earnings for the period of 8 weeks ending with the last day in respect of which she was paid under her former contract of service.

GENERAL NOTE

5.8   This regulation, made under SSCBA 1992 s.164(8), sets out the principles governing entitlement to statutory maternity pay where an employer dismisses a woman with a view to avoiding liability to pay statutory maternity pay. In order for this provision to apply, the woman must have been continuously employed for at least eight weeks (para.(1)). Such action will also constitute an automatically unfair dismissal under Employment Rights Act 1999 s.99 and an act of sex discrimination.

Modification of entitlement provisions

5.9   **4.**—(1) [¹. . .]

(2) In relation to a woman in employed earner's employment who was confined before the 14th week before the expected week of confinement [¹section 164(2)(a) and (b) of the Contributions and Benefits Act] shall have effect as if for the conditions there set out, there were substituted the conditions that—

(a) she would but for her confinement have been in employed earner's employment with an employer for a continuous period of at least 26 weeks ending with the week immediately preceding the 14th week before the expected week of confinement; and

(b) her normal weekly earnings for the period of 8 weeks ending with the week immediately preceding the week of her confinement are not less than the lower earnings limit in force [¹under section 5(1)(a) of the Contributions and Benefits Act] immediately before the commencement of the week of her confinement.

[¹(3) In relation to a woman to whom paragraph (2) applies, section 166 of the Contributions and Benefits Act shall be modified so that subsection (2) has effect as if the reference to the period of 8 weeks immediately preceding the 14th week before the expected week of confinement was a reference to the period of 8 weeks immediately preceding the week in which her confinement occurred.]

AMENDMENT

1. Social Security Maternity Benefits and Statutory Sick Pay (Amendment) Regulations 1994 (SI 1994/1367) reg.3 (June 11, 1994).

GENERAL NOTE

Paragraph (2)

5.10   If the baby is born either before or in the qualifying week, statutory maternity pay is still payable so long as the woman would have been employed for 26 weeks by the end of the qualifying week, on the assumption that the baby had not in fact been born early.

(SI 1986/1960 reg.5) (as amended)

Treatment of more than one contract of service as one

5. Where 2 or more contracts of service exist concurrently between one employer and one employee, they shall be treated as one for the purposes of Part V of the 1986 Act, except where, by virtue of regulation 11 of the Social Security (Contributions) Regulations 1979 the earnings from those contracts of service are not aggregated for the purposes of earnings-related contributions.

[¹Prescribed rate of statutory maternity pay

6. The rate of statutory maternity pay prescribed under section 166(1)(b) of the Contributions and Benefits Act is a weekly rate of [²£139.58.]

AMENDMENTS

1. Social Security, Statutory Maternity Pay and Statutory Sick Pay (Miscellaneous Amendments) Regulations 2002 (SI 2002/2690) reg.3 (April 6, 2003).
2. Welfare Benefits Up-rating Order 2015 (SI 2015/15) art.4 (April 5, 2015)

Liability of Secretary of State to pay Statutory Maternity Pay

7.—(1) Where—
(a) an adjudicating authority has determined that an employer is liable to make payments of statutory maternity pay to a woman; and
(b) the time for appealing against that determination has expired; and
(c) no appeal against the determination has been lodged or leave to appeal against the determination is required and has been refused,
then for any week in respect of which the employer was liable to make payments of statutory maternity pay but did not do so, and for any subsequent weeks in the maternity pay period the liability to make those payments shall, notwithstanding section 46(3) of the 1986 Act, be that of the Secretary of State and not the employer.

(2) In paragraph (1) adjudicating authority means, as the case may be, the Chief or any other adjudication officer, [² the First-tier Tribunal or the Upper Tribunal.]

(3) Liability to make payments of statutory maternity pay shall, notwithstanding section 46(3) of the 1986 Act, be a liability of the Secretary of State and not the employer as from the week in which the employer first becomes insolvent until the end of the maternity pay period.

(4) For the purposes of paragraph (3) an employer shall be taken to be insolvent if, and only if—
(a) in England and Wales—
  (i) he has been adjudged bankrupt or has made a composition or arrangement with his creditors;
  (ii) he has died and his estate falls to be administered in accordance with an order under section 421 of the Insolvency Act 1986; or
  (iii) where an employer is a company, a winding-up order [¹. . .] is made or a resolution for voluntary winding-up is passed with respect to it [¹or it enter administration], or a receiver or manager of its undertaking is duly appointed, or possession is taken by or on behalf of the holders of any debentures secured by a floating charge, of any property of the company comprised in or subject to the charge or a voluntary arrangement proposed

for the purposes of Part 1 of the Insolvency Act 1986 is approved under that Part;
(b) in Scotland—
  (i) an award of sequestration is made on his estate or he executes a trust deed for his creditors or enters into a composition contract;
  (ii) he has died and a judicial factor appointed under section 1A of the Judicial Factors (Scotland) Act 1889 is required by that section to divide his insolvent estate among his creditors; or
  (iii) where the employer is a company, a winding-up order [1. . .] is made or a resolution for voluntary winding-up is passed with respect to it [1or it enter administration] or a receiver of its undertaking is duly appointed or a voluntary arrangement proposed for the purposes of Part 1 of the Insolvency Act 1986 is approved under that Part.

Amendments

1. Enterprise Act 2002 (Insolvency) Order 2003 (SI 2003/2096) art.5 and Sch.2 para.44 (September 15, 2003).
2. Tribunals, Courts and Enforcement Act 2007 (Transitional and Consequential Provisions) Order 2008 (SI 2008/2683) art.6 and Sch.1 para.42 (November 3, 2008).

General Note

5.14   The functions under this regulation were transferred from the Secretary of State for Social Security to the Board of the Inland Revenue (now HMRC) under s.1(2) of and Sch.2 to the Social Security (Transfer of Functions, etc.) Act 1999. References in this regulation to SSA 1986 s.46(3) should now be read as referring to SSCBA 1992 s.164(3). The various references to insolvency law provisions include the special administration regime under the Investment Bank Special Administration Regulations 2011 (SI 2011/245) (see reg.27 and Sch.6 Pt 1 of those Regulations).

Work after confinement

5.15   **8.**—(1) Where in the week immediately preceding the 14th week before the expected week of confinement a woman had two or more employers but one or more of them were not liable to make payments to her of statutory maternity pay ("non-liable employer"), section 47(6) of the 1986 Act shall not apply in respect of any week after the week of confinement but within the maternity pay period in which she works only for a non-liable employer.
(2) Where after her confinement a woman—
(a) works for an employer who is not liable to pay her statutory maternity pay and is not a non-liable employer, but
(b) before the end of her maternity pay period ceases to work for that employer, the person who before she commenced work was liable to make payments of statutory maternity pay to her shall, notwithstanding section 46 of the 1986 Act, not be liable to make such payments to her for any weeks in the maternity pay period after she ceases work.

General Note

5.16   References in this regulation to SSA 1986 ss.46 and 47(6) should now be read as referring to SSCBA 1992 ss.164 and 165(6).

(SI 1986/1960 reg.9) (as amended)

No liability to pay statutory maternity pay

9. Notwithstanding the provisions of section 46(1) of the 1986 Act, no liability to make payments of statutory maternity pay to a woman shall arise in respect of a week within the maternity pay period for any part of which she is detained in legal custody or sentenced to a term of imprisonment (except where the sentence is suspended), or of any subsequent week within that period.

GENERAL NOTE

The reference in this regulation to SSA 1986 s.46(1) should now be read as referring to SSCBA 1992 s.164(1).

[¹ Working for not more than 10 days in the Maternity Pay Period

9A. In a case where a woman does any work under a contract of service with her employer on any day, but for not more than 10 days (whether consecutive or not), during her maternity pay period, statutory maternity pay shall continue to be payable to the employee by the employer.]

AMENDMENT

1. Statutory Maternity Pay, Social Security (Maternity Allowance) and Social Security (Overlapping Benefits) (Amendment) Regulations 2006 (SI 2006/2379) reg.3(3) (October 1, 2006).

GENERAL NOTE

This provision applies in relation to women whose expected week of confinement falls on or after April 1, 2007. It enables a woman to work for up to 10 days under her contract during the statutory maternity pay period for the employer paying her SMP and still retain her SMP for that week—previously a week's SMP was lost for any week in which such work was undertaken.

Death of woman

10. An employer shall not be liable to make payments of statutory maternity pay in respect of a woman for any week within the maternity pay period which falls after the week in which she dies.

PART III

CONTINUOUS EMPLOYMENT AND NORMAL WORKING HOURS

Continuous employment

11.—(1) Subject to the following provisions of this regulation, where in any week a woman is, for the whole part of the week,—
  (a) incapable of work in consequence of sickness or injury; or
  (b) absent from work on account of a temporary cessation of work; or
  (c) absent from work in circumstances such that, by arrangement or custom, she is regarded as continuing in the employment of her employer for all or any purpose; or

Statutory Maternity Pay (General) Regulations 1986

(d) absent from work wholly or partly because of pregnancy or confinement, [²or
(e) absent from work in consequence of taking paternity leave, adoption leave [³, shared parental leave] or parental leave under Part 8 of the Employment Rights Act 1996,]

and returns to work for her employer after the incapacity for or absence from work, that week shall be treated for the purposes of Part V of the 1986 Act as part of a continuous period of employment with that employer, notwithstanding that no contract of service exists with that employer in respect of that week.

(2) Incapacity for work which lasts for more than 26 consecutive weeks shall not count for the purposes of paragraph (1)(a).

(3) Paragraph (1)(d) shall only apply to a woman who—
(a) has a contract of service with the same employer both before and after her confinement but not during any period of absence from work due to her confinement and the period between those contracts does not exceed 26 weeks; or
(b) returns to work in accordance with section 45(1) of the 1978 Act or in pursuance of an offer made in circumstances described in section 56A(2) of that Act after a period of absence from work wholly or partly occasioned by pregnancy or confinement.

[¹(3A) Where a woman who is pregnant—
(a) is an employee in an employed earner's employment in which the custom is for the employer—
  (i) to offer work for a fixed period of not more than 26 consecutive weeks;
  (ii) to offer work for such period on 2 or more occasions in a year for periods which do not overlap; and
  (iii) to offer the work available to those persons who had worked for him during the last or a recent such period, but
(b) is absent from work—
  (i) wholly or partly because of the pregnancy or her confinement; or
  (ii) because of incapacity arising from some specific disease or bodily or mental disablement,

then in her case paragraph (1) shall apply as if the words "and returns to work for an employer after the incapacity for or absence from work" were omitted and paragraph (4) shall not apply.]

(4) Where a woman is employed under a contract of service for part only of the week immediately preceding the 14th week before the expected week of confinement, the whole of that week shall count in computing any period of continuous employment for the purposes of Part V of the 1986 Act.

AMENDMENTS

1. Statutory Maternity Pay (General) Amendment Regulations 1990 (SI 1990/622) reg.2 (April 6, 1990).

2. Social Security, Statutory Maternity Pay and Statutory Sick Pay (Miscellaneous Amendments) Regulations 2002 (SI 2002/2690) reg.4 (April 6, 2003).

3. Shared Parental Leave and Statutory Shared Parental Pay (Consequential Amendments to Subordinate Legislation) Order 2014 (SI 2014/3255) art.4(2) (December 31, 2014).

DEFINITIONS

"the 1978 Act"—see reg.1(2).
"the 1986 Act"—*ibid.*

Continuous employment and unfair dismissal

12.—(1) This regulation applies to a woman in relation to whose dismissal an action is commenced which consists—
  (a) of the presentation by her of a complaint under section 67(1) of the 1978 Act; or
  (b) of her making a claim in accordance with a dismissals procedure agreement designated by an order under section 65 of that Act; or
  (c) of any action taken by a conciliation officer under section 134(3) of that Act; [¹or
  (d) of a decision arising out of the use of a statutory dispute resolution procedure contained in Schedule 2 to the Employment Act 2002 in a case where, in accordance with the Employment Act 2002 (Dispute Resolution) Regulations 2004, such a procedure applies.]
(2) If in consequence of an action of the kind specified in paragraph (1) a woman is reinstated or re-engaged by her employer or by a successor or associated employer of that employer the continuity of her employment shall be preserved for the purposes of Part V of the 1986 Act and any week which falls within the interval beginning with the effective date of termination and ending with the date of reinstatement or re-engagement, as the case may be, shall count in the computation of her period of continuous employment.
(3) In this regulation—
"successor" and "dismissals procedure agreement" have the same meanings as in section 30(3) and (4) of the Trade Union and Labour Relations Act 1974; and
"associated employer" shall be construed in accordance with section 153(4) of the 1978 Act.

AMENDMENT

1. Statutory Maternity Pay (General) and the Statutory Paternity Pay and Statutory Adoption Pay (General) (Amendment) Regulations 2005 (SI 2005/358) reg.3 (April 6, 2005).

DEFINITIONS

"the 1978 Act"—see reg.1(2).
"associated employer"—see para.(3).
"dismissals procedure agreement"—*ibid.*
"successor"—*ibid.*

Continuous employment and stoppages of work

13.—(1) Where for any week or part of a week a woman does no work because there is, within the meaning of section 19 of the 1975 Act a stoppage of work due to a trade dispute at her place of employment the continuity of her employment shall, subject to paragraph (2), be treated as continuing throughout the stoppage but, subject to paragraph (3), no such week shall count in the computation of her period of employment.
(2) Subject to paragraph (3), where during the stoppage of work a woman

is dismissed from her employment, the continuity of her employment shall not be treated in accordance with paragraph (1) as continuing beyond the commencement of the day she stopped work.

(3) The provisions of paragraph (1) to the extent that they provide that a week in which a stoppage of work occurred shall not count in the computation of a period of employment, and paragraph (2) shall not apply to a woman who proves that at no time did she have a direct interest in the trade dispute in question.

GENERAL NOTE

5.25 The reference in this regulation to SSA 1975 s.19 should now be read as referring to SSCBA 1992 s.27.

Change of employer

5.26 **14.** A woman's employment shall, notwithstanding the change of employer, be treated as continuous employment with the second employer where—
  (a) the employer's trade or business or an undertaking (whether or not it is an undertaking established by or under an Act of Parliament) is transferred from one person to another;
  (b) by or under an Act of Parliament, whether public or local and whenever passed, a contract of employment between any body corporate and the woman is modified and some other body corporate is substituted as her employer;
  (c) on the death of her employer, the woman is taken into the employment of the personal representatives or trustees of the deceased;
  (d) the woman is employed by partners, personal representatives or trustees and there is a change in the partners, or, as the case may be, personal representatives or trustees;
  (e) the woman is taken into the employment of an employer who is, at the time she entered his employment, an associated employer of her previous employer, and for this purpose "associated employer" shall be construed in accordance with section 153(4) of the 1978 Act;
  (f) on the termination of her employment with an employer she is taken into the employment of another employer and [¹those employers are the governors of a school maintained by a [²local authority (written the meaning of the Education Act 1996) and that authority].

AMENDMENTS

1. Statutory Maternity Pay (General) Amendment Regulations 1990 (SI 1990/622) reg.3 (April 6, 1990).
2. Local Educational Authorities and Children's Services Authorities (Integration of Functions) (Local and Subordinate Legislation) Order 2010 (SI 2010/1172) art.4 and Sch.3 para.11 (May 5, 2010).

DEFINITION

"the 1978 Act"—see reg.1(2).

Reinstatement after service with the armed forces, etc.

5.27 **15.** If a woman who is entitled to apply to her former employer under the Reserve Forces (Safeguard of Employment) Act 1985 enters the employment of that employer not later than the 6 month period mentioned in

(SI 1986/1960 reg.15) (as amended)

section 1(4)(b) of that Act, her previous period of employment with that employer (or if there was more than one such period, the last of those periods) and the period of employment beginning in the said period of 6 months shall be treated as continuous.

Normal working weeks

16.—(1) For the purposes of section 48(5) of the 1986 Act, a woman's contract of service shall be treated as not normally involving or having involved employment for less than 16 hours weekly where she is normally employed for 16 hours or more weekly.

(2) Where a woman's relations with her employer were governed for a continuous period of at least 2 years by a contract of service which normally involved employment for not less than 16 hours weekly and this period was followed by a further period, ending with the week immediately preceding the 14th week before the expected week of confinement, in which her relations with that employer were governed by a contract of service which normally involved employment for less than 16 hours, but not less than 8 hours weekly, then her contract of service shall be treated for the purpose of section 48(5) of the 1986 Act as not normally involving or having involved employment for less than 16 hours weekly.

(3) Where a woman's relations with her employer are or were governed for a continuous period of at least 2 years by a contract of service which involved—
 (a) for not more than 26 weeks in that period, employment for 8 hours or more but less than 16 hours weekly; and
 (b) for the whole of the remainder of that period employment for not less than 16 hours weekly, the contract of service shall be treated for the purposes of section 48(5) of the 1986 Act as not normally involving or having involved employment for less than 16 hours weekly.

5.28

GENERAL NOTE

The references in this regulation to SSA 1986 s.48(5) should now be read as referring to SSCBA 1992 s.166(5).

5.29

[¹**Meaning of "week"**

16A. Where a woman has been in employed earner's employment with the same employer in each of 26 consecutive weeks (but no more than 26 weeks) ending with the week immediately preceding the 14th week before the expected week of confinement then for the purpose of determining whether that employment amounts to a continuous period of at least 26 weeks, the first of those 26 weeks shall be a period commencing on the first day of her employment with the employer and ending at midnight on the first Saturday thereafter or on that day where her first day is a Saturday.]

5.30

AMENDMENT

1. Statutory Maternity Pay (General) Amendment Regulations 1990 (SI 1990/622) reg.4 (April 6, 1990).

Statutory Maternity Pay (General) Regulations 1986

Part IV

General Provisions

Meaning of "employee"

5.31   **17.**—(1) [¹Subject to paragraph (1A),] in a case where, and in so far as, a woman [¹. . .] is treated as an employed earner by virtue of the Social Security (Categorisation of Earners) Regulations 1978 she shall be treated as an employee for the purposes of Part V of the 1986 Act and in a case where, and in so far as, such a woman is treated otherwise than as an employed earner by virtue of those regulations, she shall not be treated as an employee for the purposes of Part V.

[²(1A) Paragraph (1) shall have effect in relation to a woman who—
(a) is under the age of 16; and
(b) would or, as the case may be, would not have been treated as an employed earner by virtue of the Social Security (Categorisation of Earners) Regulations 1978 had she been over that age,
as it has effect in relation to a woman who is, or, as the case may be, is not so treated.]

(2) Any woman who is in employed earner's employment within the meaning of the 1975 Act under a contract of apprenticeship shall be treated as the employee for the purposes of Part V.

(3) A woman who is in employed earner's employment within the meaning of the 1975 Act but whose employer—
(a) does not fulfil the conditions prescribed in regulation 119(1)(b) of the Social Security (Contributions) Regulations 1979 as to residence or presence in Great Britain, or
(b) is a woman who, by reason of any international treaty to which the United Kingdom is a party of any international convention binding the United Kingdom—
   (i) is exempt from the provisions of the 1975 Act, or
   (ii) is a woman against whom the provisions of that Act are not enforceable, shall not be treated as an employee for the purposes of Part V of the 1986 Act.

Amendments

1. Employment Equality (Age) Regulations 2006 (SI 2006/1031) reg.49(1) and Sch.8 Pt 2 para.53 (October 1, 2006).
2. Employment Equality (Age) (Consequential Amendments) Regulations 2007 (SI 2007/825) reg.6 (April 6, 2007).

Treatment of two or more employers as one

5.32   **18.**—(1) In a case where the earnings paid to a woman in respect of 2 or more employments are aggregated and treated as a single payment of earnings under regulation 12(1) of the Social Security (Contributions) Regulations 1979, the employers of the woman in respect of those employments shall be treated as one for all purposes of Part V of the 1986 Act.

(2) Where two or more employers are treated as one under the provisions of paragraph (1), liability for statutory maternity pay payable by them to a woman shall be apportioned between them in such proportions as they may

(SI 1986/1960 reg.18) (as amended)

agree or, in default of agreement, in the proportions which the woman's earnings from each employment bear to the amount of the aggregated earnings.

GENERAL NOTE

Specific provision is also made in the Statutory Maternity Pay (National Health Service Employees) Regulations 1991 (SI 1991/590) for NHS workers with divided contracts.

Payments to be treated as contractual remuneration

19. For the purposes of paragraph 12(1) and (2) of Schedule 4 to the 1986 Act, the payments which are to be treated as contractual remuneration are sums payable under the contract of service—
 (a) by way of remuneration;
 (b) for incapacity for work due to sickness or injury; and
 (c) by reason of pregnancy or confinement.

DEFINITION

"the 1986 Act"—see reg.1(2).

Meaning of "earnings"

20.—(1) [^{1}...]

[^{2}(2) For the purposes of section 171(4) of the Contributions and Benefits Act, the expression "earnings" refers to gross earnings and includes any remuneration or profit derived from a woman's employment except any payment or amount which is—
 (a) excluded [^{6}or disregarded in the calculation of a person's earnings under regulation 25, 27 or 123 of, or Schedule 3 to, the Social Security (Contributions) Regulations 2001] (payments to be disregarded and payments to directors to be disregarded respectively) [^{5}(or would have been so excluded had she not been under the age of 16)];
 (b) a chargeable emolument under section 10A of the Social Security Contributions and Benefits Act 1992, except where, in consequence of such a chargeable emolument being excluded from earnings, a woman would not be entitled to statutory maternity pay. [^{5}(or where such a payment or amount would have been so excluded and in consequence she would not have been entitled to statutory maternity pay had she not been under the age of 16)]]

(3) [^{1}...]

(4) For the purposes of section [^{3}section 171(4) of the Contributions and Benefits Act] the expression "earnings" includes also—
[^{6}(za) any amount retrospectively treated as earnings by regulations made by virtue of section 4B(2) of the Contributions and Benefits Act;]
 (a) any sum payable in respect of arrears of pay in pursuance of an order for reinstatement or re-engagement under the 1978 Act;
 (b) any sum payable by way of pay in pursuance of an order under the 1978 Act for the continuation of a contract of employment;
 (c) any sum payable by way of remuneration in pursuance of a protective award under the Employment Protection Act 1975;
 (d) any sum payable by way of statutory sick pay, including sums payable

Statutory Maternity Pay (General) Regulations 1986

in accordance with regulations made under section 1(5) of the Social Security and Housing Benefits Act 1982.

[4(e) any sum payable by way of statutory maternity pay, including sums payable in accordance with regulations made under section 164(9)(b) of the Contributions and Benefits Act;

(f) any sum payable by way of statutory paternity pay, including sums payable in accordance with regulations made under section 171ZD(3) of the Contributions and Benefits Act;

(g) any sum payable by way of statutory adoption pay, including sums payable in accordance with regulations made under section 171ZM(3) of the Contributions and Benefits Act;]

[7 (h) any sum payable by way of statutory shared parental pay, including any sums payable in accordance with regulations made under section 171ZX(3) of the Contributions and Benefits Act.]

(5) [1. . .]

(6) [1. . .]

AMENDMENTS

1. Social Security (Miscellaneous Provisions) Amendment (No.2) Regulations 1992 (SI 1992/2595) reg.13 (November 16, 1992).
2. Social Security Contributions, Statutory Maternity Pay and Statutory Sick Pay (Miscellaneous Amendments) Regulations 1999 (SI 1999/567) reg.12 (April 6, 1999).
3. Social Security, Statutory Maternity Pay and Statutory Sick Pay (Miscellaneous Amendments) Regulations 2002 (SI 2002/2690) reg.5(a) (November 24, 2002).
4. Social Security, Statutory Maternity Pay and Statutory Sick Pay (Miscellaneous Amendments) Regulations 2002 (SI 2002/2690) reg.5(b) (April 6, 2003).
5. Employment Equality (Age) Regulations 2006 (SI 2006/1031) reg.49(1) and Sch.8 Pt 2 para.53 (October 1, 2006, and in relation to any case where the expected week of confinement begins on or after January 14, 2007).
6. Social Security, Occupational Pension Schemes and Statutory Payments (Consequential Provisions) Regulations 2007 (SI 2007/1154) reg.4(2) and (3) (April 6, 2007).
7. Shared Parental Leave and Statutory Shared Parental Pay (Consequential Amendments to Subordinate Legislation) Order 2014 (SI 2014/3255) art.4(2) (December 31, 2014).

Normal weekly earnings

5.36   **21.**—(1) For the purposes of [1Part XII of the Contributions and Benefits Act], a woman's normal weekly earnings shall be calculated in accordance with the following provisions of this regulation.

(2) In this regulation—

"the appropriate date" means the first day of the 14th week before the expected week of confinement, or the first day in the week in which the woman is confined, whichever is the earlier. [1. . .]

"normal pay day" means a day on which the terms of a woman's contract of service require her to be paid, or the practice in her employment is for her to be paid, if any payment is due to her; and "day of payment" means a day on which the woman was paid.

(3) Subject to paragraph (4), the relevant period for the purposes of [1section 171(4) of the Contributions and Benefits Act] is the period between—

(SI 1986/1960 reg.21) (as amended)

(a) the last normal pay day to fall before the appropriate date; and
(b) the last normal pay day to fall at least eight weeks earlier than the normal pay day mentioned in sub-paragraph (a), including the normal pay day mentioned in sub-paragraph (a) but excluding that first mentioned in sub-paragraph (b).

(4) In a case where a woman has no identifiable normal pay day, paragraph (3) shall have effect as if the words "day of payment" were substituted for the words "normal pay day" in each place where they occur.

(5) In a case where a woman has normal pay days at intervals of or approximating to one or more calendar months (including intervals of or approximating to a year) her normal weekly earnings shall be calculated by dividing her earnings in the relevant period by the number of calendar months in that period (or, if it is not a whole number, the nearest whole number), multiplying the result by 12 and dividing by 52.

(6) In a case to which paragraph (5) does not apply and the relevant period is not an exact number of weeks, the woman's normal weekly earnings shall be calculated by dividing her earnings in the relevant period by the number of days in the relevant period and multiplying the result by 7.

[³(7) In any case where—
(a) a woman is awarded a pay increase (or would have been awarded such an increase had she not then been absent on statutory maternity leave); and
(b) that pay increase applies to the whole or any part of the period between the beginning of the relevant period and the end of her period of statutory maternity leave,

her normal weekly earnings shall be calculated as if such an increase applied in each week of the relevant period.]

AMENDMENTS

1. Social Security Maternity Benefits and Statutory Sick Pay (Amendment) Regulations 1994 (SI 1994/1367) reg.5 (June 11, 1994).
2. Statutory Maternity Pay (General) Amendment Regulations 1996 (SI 1996/1335) reg.2 (June 12, 1996).
3. Statutory Maternity Pay (General) (Amendment) Regulations 2005 (SI 2005/729) reg.3 (April 6, 2005).

GENERAL NOTE

The new reg.21(7) is designed to give effect to the ECJ judgment in *Alabaster v Woolwich Plc and the Secretary of State for Social Security* (C-147/02), [2004] I.R.L.R. 486). It ensures that employers must recalculate a woman's entitlement (or potential entitlement) to statutory maternity pay to reflect any pay rise that the woman would have received, but for her maternity leave, and which is effective at any time between the start of the period used to calculate her entitlement and the end of her maternity leave. For the Court of Appeal judgment following the decision of the ECJ, see *Alabaster v Barclays Bank Plc and the Secretary of State for Social Security* [2005] EWCA Civ 508; [2005] I.C.R. 1246.

5.37

[¹Effect of statutory maternity pay on [²incapacity benefit]

21A. [³. . .]

5.38

Amendments

1. Statutory Maternity Pay (General) Amendment Regulations 1988 (SI 1988/532) reg.3 (April 6, 1988).
2. Social Security (Incapacity Benefit) (Consequential and Transitional Amendments and Savings) Regulations 1995 (SI 1995/829) reg.18 (April 13, 1995).
3. Social Security, Statutory Maternity Pay and Statutory Sick Pay (Miscellaneous Amendments) Regulations 2002 (SI 2002/2690) reg.6 (November 24, 2002).

[¹Effect of maternity allowance on statutory maternity pay

5.39

21B. Where a woman, in any week which falls within the maternity pay period, is—
  (a) in receipt of maternity allowance pursuant to the provisions of sections 35 and 35A of the Contributions and Benefits Act; and
  (b) entitled to receive statutory maternity pay in consequence of [²—
      (i) receiving a pay increase referred to in regulation 21(7), or
      (ii) being treated as having been paid retrospective earnings under regulation 20(4)(za),]
the employer shall not be liable to make payments of statutory maternity pay in respect of such a week unless, and to the extent by which, the rate of statutory maternity pay exceeds the rate of maternity allowance received by her in that week.]

Amendments

1. Statutory Maternity Pay (General) (Amendment) Regulations 2005 (SI 2005/729) reg.4 (April 6, 2005).
2. Social Security, Occupational Pension Schemes and Statutory Payments (Consequential Provisions) Regulations 2007 (SI 2007/1154) reg.4(4) (April 6, 2007).

Part V

Administration

Evidence of expected week of confinement

5.40

22.—(1) A woman shall in accordance with the following provisions of this regulation, provide the person who is liable to pay her statutory maternity pay with evidence as to—
  (a) the week in which the expected date of confinement occurs, and
  (b) where her entitlement to statutory maternity pay depends upon the fact of her confinement, the week in which she was confined.

(2) For the purpose of paragraph (1)(b) a certificate of birth shall be sufficient evidence that the woman was confined in the week in which the birth occurred.

(3) The evidence shall be submitted to the person who will be liable to make payments of statutory maternity pay not later than the end of the third week of the maternity pay period so however that where the woman has good cause the evidence may be submitted later than that date but not later than the end of the 13th week of the maternity pay period.

(4) For the purposes of paragraph (3) evidence contained in an envelope

(SI 1986/1960 reg.22) (as amended)

which is properly addressed and sent by prepaid post shall be deemed to have been submitted on the day on which it was posted.

Notice of absence from work

23.—(1) Where a woman is confined before the beginning of the 14th week before the expected week of confinement, she shall be entitled to payments of statutory maternity pay only if—
  (a) she gives notice to the person who will be liable to pay it [²of the date on which she was confined], and
  (b) that notice is given within [²28 days] of the date she was confined or if in the particular circumstances that is not practicable, as soon as is reasonably practicable thereafter; and
  (c) where the person so requests, the notice in writing.

(2) Where a woman is confined before the date stated in a notice provided in accordance with [¹section 164(4) of the Contributions and Benefits Act] as being the date her absence from work is due to begin, she shall be entitled to payments of statutory maternity pay only if—
  (a) she gives a further notice to the person who will be liable to pay it specifying the date she was confined and the date her absence from work [². . .] began, and
  (b) that further notice is given within [²28 days] of the date she was confined or if in the particular circumstances that is not practicable, as soon as is reasonably practicable thereafter; and
  (c) where the person so requests, the notice is in writing.

(3) For the purposes of this regulation, a notice contained in an envelope which is properly addressed and sent by prepaid post shall be deemed to be given on the date on which it is posted.

[¹[²(4) Subject to paragraph (5), section 164(4) of the Contributions and Benefits Act (statutory maternity pay entitlement and liability to pay) shall not have effect in the case of a woman who leaves her employment with the person who will be liable to pay her statutory maternity pay after the beginning of the week immediately preceding the 14th week before the expected week of confinement.]

(5) A woman who is exempted from section 164(4) of the Contributions and Benefits Act by paragraph (4) but who is confined before the 11th week before the expected week of confinement shall only be entitled to statutory maternity pay if she gives the person who will be liable to pay it notice specifying the date she was confined.]

AMENDMENTS

1. Social Security Maternity Benefits and Statutory Sick Pay (Amendment) Regulations 1994 (SI 1994/1367) reg.6 (June 11, 1994).
2. Social Security, Statutory Maternity Pay and Statutory Sick Pay (Miscellaneous Amendments) Regulations 2002 (SI 2002/2690) reg.7 (November 24, 2002).

Notification of employment after confinement

24. A woman who after the date of confinement but within the maternity pay period commences work in employed earner's employment with a person who is not liable to make payments of statutory maternity pay to her and is not a non-liable employer for the purposes of regulation 8(1), shall within seven days of the day she commenced work inform any person who is so liable of the date she commenced work.

Provision of information in connection with determination of questions

25. Any woman claiming to be entitled to statutory maternity pay, or any other person who is a party to proceedings arising under the 1986 Act relating to statutory maternity pay, shall, if she receives notification from the Secretary of State that any information is required from her for the determination of any question arising in connection therewith, furnish that information to the Secretary of State within 10 days of receiving that notification.

DEFINITION

"the 1986 Act"—see reg.1(2).

GENERAL NOTE

The functions under this regulation were transferred from the Secretary of State for Social Security to the Board of the Inland Revenue (now HMRC) under s.1(2) of and Sch.2 to the Social Security (Transfer of Functions, etc.) Act 1999.

[¹Provision of information relating to claims for certain other benefits

25A.—(1) Where an employer who has been given notice in accordance with [³section 164(4)(a) or (9)(ea) of the Contributions and Benefits Act] or regulation 23 by a woman who is or has been an employee—
  (a) decides that he has no liability to make payments of statutory maternity pay to her; or
  (b) has made one or more payments of statutory maternity pay to her but decides, before the end of the maternity pay period and for a reason specified in paragraph (3), that he has no liability to make further payments to her,
then, in connection with the making of a claim by the woman for a maternity allowance [⁴, incapacity benefit or an employment and support allowance], he shall furnish her with the information specified in the following provisions of this regulation.

(2) Where the employer decides he has no liability to make payments of statutory maternity pay to the woman, he shall furnish her with details of the decision and the reasons for it.

(3) Where the employer decides he has no liability to make further payments of statutory maternity pay to the woman because [³ . . .] she has within the maternity pay period been detained in legal custody or sentenced to a term of imprisonment which was not suspended, [³ . . .], he shall furnish her with—
  (a) details of his decision and the reasons for it; and
  (b) details of the last week in respect of which a liability to pay statutory maternity pay arose and the total number of weeks within the maternity pay period in which such a liability arose.

(4) The employer shall—
  (a) return to the woman any maternity certificate provided by her in support of the notice referred to in paragraph (1); and
  (b) comply with any requirements imposed by the preceding provisions of this regulation—
    (i) in a case to which paragraph (2) applies, within 7 days of the decision being made, or, if earlier, within [³ 28 days] of the day

(SI 1986/1960 reg.25A) (as amended)

the woman gave notice of her intended absence or of her confinement if that had occurred; or
  (ii) in a case to which paragraph (3) refers, within 7 days of being notified of the woman's detention or sentence [³ . . .].
(5) In this regulation, 'incapacity benefit' means [²incapacity benefit] or a severe disablement allowance.]

AMENDMENTS

1. Statutory Maternity Pay (General) Amendment Regulations 1990 (SI 1990/622) reg.7 (April 6, 1990).
2. Social Security (Incapacity Benefit) (Consequential and Transitional Amendments and Savings) Regulations 1995 (SI 1995/829) reg.18 (April 13, 1995).
3. Social Security, Statutory Maternity Pay and Statutory Sick Pay (Miscellaneous Amendments) Regulations 2002 (SI 2002/2690) reg.8 (November 24, 2002).
4. Employment and Support Allowance (Consequential Provisions) (No.2) Regulations 2008 (SI 2008/1554) reg.46 (October 27, 2008).

Records to be maintained by employers

26.—(1) Every employer shall maintain for 3 years after the end of the tax year in which the maternity pay period ends a record in relation to any woman who is or was an employee of his of—
  (a) the date of the first day of absence from work wholly or partly because of pregnancy or confinement as notified by her and, if different, the date of the first day when such absence commenced;
  (b) the weeks in that tax year in which statutory maternity pay was paid and the amount paid in each week; and
  (c) any week in that tax year which was within her maternity pay period but for which no payment of statutory maternity pay was made to her and the reasons no payment was made.

(2) Except where he was not liable to make a payment of statutory maternity pay and subject to paragraphs (3) and (4), every employer shall retain for 3 years after the end of the tax year in which the maternity pay period ends any medical certificate or other evidence relating to the expected week of confinement, or as the case may be, the confinement which was provided to him by a woman who is or was an employee of his.

(3) Where an employer returns a medical certificate to an employee of his for the purpose of enabling her to make a claim for benefit under the 1975 Act, it shall be sufficient for the purposes of paragraph (2) if he retains a copy of that certificate.

(4) An employer shall not retain any certificate of birth provided to him as evidence of confinement by a woman who is or was an employee of his but shall retain a record of the date of birth.

5.46

DEFINITION

"the 1975 Act"—see reg.1(2).

[¹Production of employer's records

26A.—(1) An authorised officer of the Commissioners of Inland Revenue may by notice require an employer to produce to him at the place of keeping such records as are in the employer's possession or power and as (in the

5.47

officer's reasonable opinion) contain, or may contain, information relevant to satisfy him that statutory maternity pay has been paid and is being paid in accordance with these regulations to employees or former employees who are entitled to it.

(2) A notice referred to in paragraph (1) shall be in writing and the employer shall produce the records referred to in that paragraph within 30 days after the date of such a notice.

(3) The production of records in pursuance of this regulation shall be without prejudice to any lien which a third party may have in respect of those records.

(4) References in this regulation to "records" means—
  (a) any wage sheet or deductions working sheet; or
  (b) any other document which relates to the calculation or payment of statutory maternity pay to his employees or former employees,
whether kept in written form, electronically, or otherwise.

(5) In paragraph (1), "place of keeping" means such place in Great Britain that an employer and an authorised officer may agree upon, or, in the absence of such agreement—
  (a) any place in Great Britain where records referred to in paragraph (1) are normally kept; or
  (b) if there is no such place, the employer's principal place of business in Great Britain.]

AMENDMENT

1. Statutory Maternity Pay (General) and Statutory Sick Pay (General) (Amendment) Regulations 2005 (SI 2005/989) reg.2(2) (April 6, 2005).

PART VI

PAYMENT

Payment of statutory maternity pay

5.48   27. Payment of statutory maternity pay may be made in a like manner to payments of remuneration but shall not include payments in kind or by way of the provision of board or lodgings or of services or other facilities.

Rounding to avoid fractional amounts

5.49   [¹28. Where any payment of statutory maternity pay is paid for any week or part of a week and the amount due includes a fraction of a penny, the payment shall be rounded up to the next whole number of pence.]

AMENDMENT

1. Statutory Maternity Pay, Social Security (Maternity Allowance) and Social Security (Overlapping Benefits) (Amendment) Regulations 2006 (SI 2006/2379) reg.3(4) (October 1, 2006, and in relation to women whose expected week of confinement falls on or after April 1, 2007).

(SI 1986/1960 reg.29) (as amended)

Time when statutory maternity pay is to be paid

29.—(1) In this regulation, "payday" means a day on which it has been agreed, or it is the normal practice between an employer or former employer and a woman who is or was an employee of his, that payments by way of remuneration are to be made, or, where there is no such agreement or normal practice, the last day of a calendar month.

(2) In any case where—
(a) a decision has been made by an adjudication officer, appeal tribunal or Commissioner in proceedings under [Social Security Administration Act 1992] as a result of which a woman is entitled to an amount of statutory maternity pay; and
(b) the time for bringing an appeal against the decision has expired and either—
   (i) no such appeal has been brought; or
   (ii) such an appeal has been brought and has been finally disposed of that amount of statutory maternity pay shall be paid within the time specified in paragraph (3).

(3) Subject to paragraphs (4) and (5), the employer or former employer shall pay the amount not later than the first pay day after—
(a) where an appeal has been brought, the day on which the employer or former employer receives notification that it has been finally disposed of,
(b) where leave to appeal has been refused and there remains no further opportunity to apply for leave, the day on which the employer or former employer receives notification of the refusal; and
(c) in any other case, the day on which the time for bringing an appeal expires.

(4) Subject to paragraph (5), where it is impracticable, in view of the employer's or former employer's methods of accounting for and paying remuneration, for the requirement of payment referred to in paragraph (3) to be met by the pay day referred to in that paragraph, it shall be met not later than the next following pay day.

(5) Where the employer or former employer would not have remunerated the woman for her work in the week in question as early as the pay day specified in paragraph (3) or (if it applies) paragraph (4), the requirement of payment shall be met on the first day on which the woman would have been remunerated for her work in that week.

Payments by the Secretary of State

30. Where the Secretary of State becomes liable in accordance with regulation 7 to make payments of statutory maternity pay to a woman, the first payment shall be made as soon as reasonably practicable after he becomes so liable, and payments thereafter shall be made at weekly intervals, by means of an instrument of payment or by such other means as appears to the Secretary of State to be appropriate in the circumstances of any particular case.

GENERAL NOTE

The functions under this regulation were transferred from the Secretary of State for Social Security to the Board of the Inland Revenue (now HMRC) under s.1(2) of and Sch.2 to the Social Security (Transfer of Functions, etc.) Act 1999.

Persons unable to act

31.—(1) Where in the case of any woman—
(a) statutory maternity pay is payable to her or she is alleged to be entitled to it;
(b) she is unable for the time being to act;
(c) either—
  (i) no receiver has been appointed by the Court of Protection with power to receive statutory maternity pay on her behalf, or
  (ii) in Scotland, her estate is not being administered by any tutor, curator or other guardian acting or appointed in terms of law,

the Secretary of State may, upon written application to him by a person who, if a natural person, is over the age of 18, appoint that person to exercise, on behalf of the woman any right to which she may be entitled under Part V of the 1986 Act and to deal on her behalf with any sums payable to her.

(2) Where the Secretary of State has made an appointment under paragraph (1)—
(a) he may at any time in his absolute discretion revoke it;
(b) the person appointed may resign his office after having given one month's notice in writing to the Secretary of State of his intention to do so; and
(c) the appointment shall terminate when the Secretary of State is notified that a receiver or other person to whom paragraph (1)(c) applies has been appointed.

(3) Anything required by Part V of the 1986 Act to be done by or to any woman who is unable to act may be done by or to the person appointed under this regulation to act on her behalf, and the receipt of the person so appointed shall be a good discharge to the woman's employer or former employer for any sum paid.

GENERAL NOTE

The functions under this regulation were transferred from the Secretary of State for Social Security to the Board of the Inland Revenue (now HMRC) under s.1(2) of and Sch.2 to the Social Security (Transfer of Functions, etc.) Act 1999.

PART VII

OFFENCES

[1Offences

32. [2. . .]

GENERAL NOTE

See now ss.113A and 113B of the Social Security Administration Act 1992.

(SI 1987/235) (as amended)

Statutory Maternity Pay (Medical Evidence) Regulations 1987

(SI 1987/235) (AS AMENDED)

The Secretary of State for Social Services, in exercise of the powers conferred by sections 49 and 84(1) of and paragraph 6 of Schedule 4 to the Social Security Act 1986, and of all other powers enabling him in that behalf, by this instrument, which is made before the end of the period of 12 months from the commencement of the enactments contained in the 1986 Act under which it is made, makes the following regulations:

5.57

ARRANGEMENT OF REGULATIONS

1. Citation, commencement and interpretation
2. Evidence of pregnancy and confinement

SCHEDULE—Part I—Rules
             Part II—Form of certificate

Citation, commencement and interpretation

1.—(1) These regulations may be cited as the Statutory Maternity Pay (Medical Evidence) Regulations 1987 and shall come into force on 15th March 1987.

5.58

(2) In these regulations, unless the context otherwise requires—
"the Act" means the Social Security Act 1986;
[1"registered midwife" means a midwife who is registered as a midwife with the Nursing and Midwifery Council under the Nursing and Midwifery Order 2001;]
"doctor" means a registered medical practitioner;
"signature" means, in relation to any statement or certificate given in accordance with these regulations, the name by which the person giving that statement or certificate, as the case may be, is usually known (any name other than the surname being either in full or otherwise indicated) written by that person in his own handwriting; and
"signed" shall be construed accordingly.
[2[3 . . .]]

AMENDMENTS

1. Nursing and Midwifery Order 2001 (Consequential Amendments) Order 2002 (SI 2002/881) art.2 and Sch. para.2 (April 17, 2002).
2. National Health Service Reform and Health Care Professions Act 2002 (Supplementary, Consequential etc. Provisions) Regulations 2002 (SI 2002/2469) reg.11 and Sch.8 (October 1, 2002).
3. National Treatment Agency (Abolition) and the Health and Social Care Act 2012 (Consequential, Transitional and Saving Provisions) Order 2013 (SI 2013/235) art.11 and Sch.2 para.9(2) (April 1, 2013).

Evidence of pregnancy and confinement

5.59   2. The evidence as to pregnancy and the expected date of confinement which a woman is required to provide to a person who is liable to pay her statutory maternity pay shall be furnished in the form of a maternity certificate given by a doctor or by a registered midwife, not earlier than the beginning of the [¹20th week] before the expected week of confinement, in accordance with the rules set out in Part I of the Schedule to these regulations—
   (a) in the appropriate form as set out in Part II of that Schedule; or
   (b) in a form substantially to the like effect with such variations as the circumstances may require.

AMENDMENT

1. Social Security (Medical Evidence) and Statutory Maternity Pay (Medical Evidence) (Amendment) Regulations 2001 (SI 2001/2931) reg.3(2) (September 28, 2001).

DEFINITIONS

"doctor"—see reg.1(2).
"registered midwife"—see *ibid*.

SCHEDULE   Regulation 2

PART I

RULES

5.60   1. In these rules any reference to a woman is a reference to the woman in respect of whom a maternity certificate is given in accordance with these rules.
2. A maternity certificate shall be given by a doctor or registered midwife attending the woman and shall not be given by the woman herself.
3. The maternity certificate shall be on a form provided by the Secretary of State for the purpose and the wording shall be that set out in the appropriate part of the form specified in Part II of this Schedule.
4. Every maternity certificate shall be completed in ink or other indelible substance and shall contain the following particulars—
   (a) the woman's name;
   (b) the week in which the woman is expected to be confined or, if the maternity certificate is given after confinement, the date of that confinement and the date the confinement was expected to take place [¹. . .];
   (c) the date of the examination on which the maternity certificate is based;
   (d) the date on which the maternity certificate is signed; and
   [⁴(e) the address of the doctor or where the maternity certificate is signed by a registered midwife the personal identification number given to her on her registration in [⁶. . .] the register maintained by the Nursing and Midwifery Council [⁶("NMC") under article 5 of] the Nursing and Midwifery Order 2001 and the expiry date of that registration,]
and shall bear opposite the word "Signature", the signature of the person giving the maternity certificate written after there has been entered on the maternity certificate the woman's name and the expected date or, as the case may be, the date of the confinement.
5. After a maternity certificate has been given, no further maternity certificate based on the same examination shall be furnished other than a maternity certificate by way of replacement of an original which has been lost or mislaid, in which case it shall be clearly marked "duplicate".

(SI 1987/235 Sch.) (as amended)

[² PART II

FORM OF CERTIFICATE

MATERNITY CERTIFICATE

Please fill in this form in ink

Name of patient

Fill in this part if you are giving the certificate before the confinement.

Do not fill this in more [³than 20 weeks] before the week the baby is expected.

I certify that I examined you on the date given below. In my opinion you can expect to have your baby in the week that includes

.... / .... / ....

Week means period of 7 days starting on a Sunday and ending on a Saturday. Fill in this part if you are giving the certificate after the confinement.

I certify that I attended you in connection with the birth which took place on .... / .... / .... when you were delivered of a child [ ] children.

In my opinion your baby was expected in the week that includes ..../ .... / ....

Date of examination ..... / ..... / ......

Date of signing .... / .... / ....

Signature

Registered midwives

Please give your [⁶NMC] Personal Identification Number and the expiry date of your registration with the [⁶NMC].

Doctors
Please stamp your name and address here [⁷ . . .] [⁵ [⁷ unless the form has been stamped, in Wales, by the Local Health Board in whose medical performers list you are included or, in Scotland,] by the Health Board in whose primary medical services performers list you are included)].

AMENDMENTS

1. Social Security (Miscellaneous Provisions) Amendment Regulations 1991 (SI 1991/2284) reg.23 (November 1, 1991).
2. Social Security (Miscellaneous Provisions) Amendment Regulations 1991 (SI 1991/2284) reg.24 (November 1, 1991).

Statutory Maternity Pay (Medical Evidence) Regulations 1987

3. Social Security (Medical Evidence) and Statutory Maternity Pay (Medical Evidence) (Amendment) Regulations 2001 (SI 2001/2931) reg.3(3) (September 28, 2001).

4. Nursing and Midwifery Order 2001 (Consequential Amendments) Order 2002 (SI 2002/881) art.2 and Sch. para.3 (April 17, 2002).

5. General Medical Services and Personal Medical Services Transitional and Consequential Provisions Order 2004 (SI 2004/865) art.119 and Sch.1 para.5 (April 1, 2004).

6. Health Act 1999 (Consequential Amendments) (Nursing and Midwifery) Order 2004 (SI 2004/1771) art.3 and Sch. para.51 (August 1, 2004).

7. National Treatment Agency (Abolition) and the Health and Social Care Act 2012 (Consequential, Transitional and Saving Provisions) Order 2013 (SI 2013/235) art.11 and Sch.2 para.9(3) (April 1, 2013).

DEFINITIONS

"doctor"—see reg.1(2).
"registered midwife"—see *ibid.*
"signature"—see *ibid.*
"signed"—see *ibid.*

Statutory Maternity Pay (Persons Abroad and Mariners) Regulations 1987

(SI 1987/418) (AS AMENDED)

The Secretary of State for Social Services, in exercise of the powers conferred upon him by sections 80 and 84(1) of the Social Security Act 1986 and of all other powers enabling him in that behalf, by this instrument, which is made before the end of the period of 12 months from the commencement of the enactments under which it is made, makes the following Regulations:

ARRANGEMENT OF REGULATIONS

5.62
1. Citation, commencement and interpretation
2. Persons in other member States—meaning of "employee"
2A. Persons absent from Great Britain—meaning of "employee"
3. Meaning of "employee"—general
4. (*repealed*)
5. Women who worked in the European Community
6. Time for compliance with Part V of the 1986 Act and Regulations
7. Mariners
8. Continental shelf
9. (*repealed*)

Citation, commencement and interpretation

5.63   **1.**—(1) These Regulations may be cited as the Statutory Maternity Pay (Persons Abroad and Mariners) Regulations 1987 and shall come into force on 6th April 1987.

(SI 1987/418 reg.1) (as amended)

(2) In these Regulations, the "1986 Act" means the Social Security Act 1986;

[¹"the Contributions and Benefits Act" means the Social Security Contributions and Benefits Act 1992, "the Contributions Regulations" means the Social Security (Contributions) Regulations 1979"], and the "General Regulations" means the Statutory Maternity Pay (General) Regulations 1986.

(3) Unless the context otherwise requires, any reference in these Regulations to a numbered regulation is a reference to the regulation bearing that number in these Regulations and any reference in a regulation to a numbered paragraph is a reference to the paragraph of that regulation bearing that number.

AMENDMENT

1. Social Security Contributions, Statutory Maternity Pay and Statutory Sick Pay (Miscellaneous Amendments) Regulations 1996 (SI 1996/777) reg.4(2) (April 6, 1996).

GENERAL NOTE

These Regulations were made under the authority of what is now SSCBA 1992 s.170 and make special provision for statutory maternity pay as regards persons who are abroad or who are mariners. See also SMP (General) Regulations 1986 (SI 1986/1960) reg.17(3).

Persons in other member States—meaning of "employee"

2. Subject to regulation 3, a woman who is—
   (a) gainfully employed in a member State other than the United Kingdom in such circumstances that if her employment were in Great Britain she would be an employee for the purposes of Part V of the 1986 Act or a woman treated as such an employee under regulation 17 of the General Regulations; and
   (b) subject to the legislation of the United Kingdom under Council Regulation (EEC) No. 1408/71; notwithstanding that she is not employed in Great Britain, shall be treated as an employee for the purposes of Part V of the 1986 Act.

DEFINITIONS

"the 1986 Act"—see reg.1(2).
"the General Regulations"—see *ibid.*

[¹Persons absent from Great Britain—meaning of "employee"

2A. Subject to regulations 2, 3 and 7(3), where a woman, while absent from Great Britain for any purpose, is gainfully employed by an employer who is liable to pay in respect of her secondary Class 1 contributions under section 6 of the Contributions and Benefits Act or regulation 120 of the Contributions Regulations, she shall be treated as an employee for the purposes of Part XII of the Contributions and Benefits Act.]

AMENDMENT

1. Social Security Contributions, Statutory Maternity Pay and Statutory Sick Pay (Miscellaneous Amendments) Regulations 1996 (SI 1996/777) reg.4(3) (April 6, 1996).

Statutory Maternity Pay (Persons Abroad and Mariners) Regulations 1987

DEFINITIONS

"the Contributions and Benefits Act"—see reg.1(2).
"the Contributions Regulations"—see *ibid.*

Meaning of "employee"—general

5.67   **3.** No woman who, by virtue of regulation 17 of the General Regulations, would be treated as not being an employee for the purposes of Part V of the 1986 Act if her employment were in Great Britain, shall be treated as an employee by virtue of these Regulations.

DEFINITIONS

"the 1986 Act"—see reg.1(2).
"the General Regulations"—see *ibid.*

Women outside the European Community

5.68   **4.** [1. . .]

AMENDMENT

1. Social Security Contributions, Statutory Maternity Pay and Statutory Sick Pay (Miscellaneous Amendments) Regulations 1996 (SI 1996/777) reg.4(4) (April 6, 1996).

Women who worked in the European Community

5.69   **5.**—(1) A woman who is an employee or treated as an employee under regulation 2 and who—
(a) in the week immediately preceding the 14th week before the expected week of confinement was in employed earner's employment with an employer in Great Britain, and
(b) had in any week within the period of [1 26 weeks] immediately preceding that week been employed by the same employer in another member State,
shall be treated for the purposes of sections 46(2) and 48 of the 1986 Act as having been employed in employed earner's employment in those weeks in which she was so employed in the other member State.
(2) [1. . .]

AMENDMENT

1. Social Security Contributions, Statutory Maternity Pay and Statutory Sick Pay (Miscellaneous Amendments) Regulations 1996 (SI 1996/777) reg.4(5) (April 6, 1996).

DEFINITION

"the 1986 Act"—see reg.1(2).

Time for compliance with Part V of the 1986 Act and Regulations

5.70   **6.** Where—
(a) a woman is outside the United Kingdom;
(b) Part V of the 1986 Act or Regulations made under that Act or under Part III of the Social Security Act 1975 require any act to be done

(SI 1987/418 reg.6) (as amended)

forthwith or on the happening of a certain event or within a specified time; and
(c) because the woman is outside the United Kingdom she or her employer cannot comply with the requirement;

the woman or the employer, as the case may be, shall be deemed to have complied with it if the act is performed as soon as reasonably practicable.

DEFINITION

"the 1986 Act"—see reg.1(2).

Mariners

7.—(1) In this regulation, "foreign-going ship", "home-trade ship" and "mariner" have the same meanings as in Case C of Part VIII of the Social Security (Contributions) Regulations 1979 and the expressions "ship" and "ship or vessel", except in paragraph (3), include hovercraft.

(2) Subject to regulation 3, a mariner engaged in employment on board a home-trade ship with an employer who has a place of business within the United Kingdom shall be treated as an employee for the purposes of Part V of the 1986 Act, notwithstanding that she may not be employed in Great Britain.

(3) A mariner who is engaged in employment—
(a) on a foreign-going ship; or
(b) on a home-trade ship with an employer who does not have a place of business within the United Kingdom, shall not be treated as an employee for the purposes of Part V of the 1986 Act, notwithstanding that she may have been employed in Great Britain.

5.71

DEFINITIONS

"foreign-going ship"—see para.(1).
"home-trade ship"—see *ibid.*
"mariner"—see *ibid.*
"ship"—see *ibid.*
"ship or vessel"—see *ibid.*

Continental shelf

8.—(1) In this regulation—
"designated area" means any area which may from time to time be designated by Order in Council under the Continental Shelf Act 1964 as an area within which the rights of the United Kingdom with respect to the seabed and subsoil and their natural resources may be exercised;
"prescribed area" means an area over which Norway or any member State (other than the United Kingdom) exercises sovereign rights for the purpose of exploring the seabed and subsoil and exploiting their natural resources, being an area outside the territorial seas of Norway or that member State or any other area which is from time to time specified under section 22(5) of the Oil and Gas (Enterprise) Act 1982;
"prescribed employment" means employment in a designated area or prescribed area in connection with any activity mentioned in section 23(2) of the Oil and Gas (Enterprise) Act 1982 in any designated area or in any prescribed area.

5.72

Statutory Maternity Pay (Persons Abroad and Mariners) Regulations 1987

(2) Subject to regulation 3, a woman in prescribed employment shall be treated as an employee for the purposes of Part V of the 1986 Act notwithstanding that she may not be employed in Great Britain.

DEFINITIONS

"the 1986 Act"—see reg.1(2).
"designated area"—see para.(2).
"prescribed area"—see *ibid.*
"prescribed employment"—see *ibid.*

Persons Abroad—maternity pay period not commencing or ending

5.73 9. [1. . .]

AMENDMENT

1. Social Security Contributions, Statutory Maternity Pay and Statutory Sick Pay (Miscellaneous Amendments) Regulations 1996 (SI 1996/777) reg.4(6) (April 6, 1996).

Statutory Maternity Pay (National Health Service Employees) Regulations 1991

(SI 1991/590)

5.74 The Secretary of State for Social Security, in exercise of the powers conferred by sections 49, 50(2A), 84(1) of, and paragraph 6 of Schedule 4 to the Social Security Act 1986 and of all other powers enabling him in that behalf, by this instrument, which contains only Regulations consequential upon paragraph 22 of Schedule 6 to the Social Security Act 1990, makes the following Regulations:

ARRANGEMENT OF REGULATIONS

1. Citation, commencement and interpretation
2. Treatment of more than one contract of employment as one contract
3. Notification of election
4. Provision of information
5. Treatment of two or more employers as one
6. Time for which an election is to have effect

Citation, commencement and interpretation

5.75 1.—(1) These Regulations may be cited as the Statutory, Maternity Pay (National Health Service Employees) Regulations 1991 and shall come into force on 1st April 1991.

(2) In these Regulations, a "health authority" [2shall in relation to Wales have the same meaning it has in section 8] of the National Health Service Act 1977, and in relation to Scotland mean the health board within the meaning of section 2 of the National Health Service (Scotland) Act 1978.

[¹(3) [⁴ . . .]]
[²(4)[⁴ . . .]]
[³(5) In these Regulations, a reference to "NHS trust" shall be construed to include a reference to an NHS foundation trust within the meaning of section 1(1) of the Health and Social Care (Community Health and Standards) Act 2003 where the application for authorisation to become an NHS foundation trust was made by an NHS trust.]

AMENDMENTS

1. Health Act 1999 (Supplementary, Consequential, etc. Provisions) (No.2) Order 2000 (SI 2000/694) art.3 and Sch. para.3(2) (April 1, 2000).
2. National Health Service Reform and Health Care Professions Act 2002 (Supplementary, Consequential etc. Provisions) Regulations 2002 (SI 2002/2469) reg.4 and Sch.1 Pt 2 para.51 (October 1, 2002).
3. Health and Social Care (Community Health and Standards) Act 2003 (Supplementary and Consequential Provision) (NHS Foundation Trusts) Order 2004 (SI 2004/696) art.3(17) and Sch.17 (April 1, 2004).
4. National Treatment Agency (Abolition) and the Health and Social Care Act 2012 (Consequential, Transitional and Saving Provisions) Order 2013 (SI 2013/235) art.11 and Sch.2 para.16(2) (April 1, 2013).

Treatment of more than one contract of employment as one contract

2. Where, in consequence of the establishment of one or more National Health Service Trusts under Part I of the National Health Service and Community Care Act 1990, or the National Health Service (Scotland) Act 1978, a woman's contract of employment is treated by a scheme under that Part or Act as divided so as to constitute two or more contracts [¹ [² . . .]] she may elect for all those contracts to be treated as one contract for the purposes of Part V of the Social Security Act 1986.

5.76

AMENDMENTS

1. Health Act 1999 (Supplementary, Consequential etc. Provisions) (No.2) Order 2000 (SI 2000/694) art.3 and Sch. para.3(3) (April 1, 2000).
2. National Treatment Agency (Abolition) and the Health and Social Care Act 2012 (Consequential, Transitional and Saving Provisions) Order 2013 (SI 2013/235) art.11 and Sch.2 para.16(3) (April 1, 2013).

Notification of election

3. A woman who makes an election under regulation 2 above shall give written notification of that election to each of her employers under the two or more contracts of service mentioned in that regulation at least [¹28 days] before the first day she is going to be absent from work with any of her employers, wholly or partly because of pregnancy, or if in the particular circumstances that is not practicable, as soon as is reasonably practicable.

5.77

AMENDMENT

1. Social Security, Statutory Maternity Pay and Statutory Sick Pay (Miscellaneous Amendments) Regulations 2002 (SI 23002/2690) reg.11 (November 24, 2002).

Statutory Maternity Pay (National Health Service Employees) Regulations 1991

Provision of information

5.78　**4.** A woman who makes an election under regulation 2 above shall, within [¹28 days] of giving notice of that election or if in the particular circumstances that is not practicable, as soon as is reasonably practicable thereafter, provide each of her employers under the two or more contracts of service mentioned under that regulation with the following information—
 (a) the name and address of each of those employers; and
 (b) the date her employment with each of those employers commenced; and
 (c) details of her earnings during the relevant period from each employer and for this purpose the expressions "earnings" and "relevant period" have the same meanings as they have for the purposes of section 50(3) of the Social Security Act 1986.

AMENDMENT

1. Social Security, Statutory Maternity Pay and Statutory Sick Pay (Miscellaneous Amendments) Regulations 2002 (SI 2002/2690) reg.12 (November 24, 2002).

Treatment of two or more employers as one

5.79　**5.** The employer to be regarded for the purposes of statutory maternity pay as the employer under the one contract where 2 or more contracts of service are treated as one in accordance with regulation 2 above shall be—
 [¹(a) in the case of a woman whose contract of employment is treated by a scheme under Part I of the National Health Service and Community Care Act 1990 or the National Health Service (Scotland) Act 1978 as divided—
  (i) the Health Authority [² . . .] from which the woman was transferred, in a case where any one of the contracts of service is with that Health Authority [² . . .]; or
  (ii) the first NHS trust to which a contract of service was transferred in a case where none of the contracts of service are with the Health Authority [² . . .] from which she was transferred.
  [² . . .]]

AMENDMENTS

1. Health Act 1999 (Supplementary, Consequential etc. Provisions) (No.2) Order 2000 (SI 2000/694) art.3 and Sch. para.3(4) (April 1, 2000).
2. National Treatment Agency (Abolition) and the Health and Social Care Act 2012 (Consequential, Transitional and Saving Provisions) Order 2013 (SI 2013/235) art.11 and Sch.2 para.15(3) (April 1, 2013).

Time for which an election is to have effect

5.80　**6.** An election made under regulation 2 shall lapse at the end of the maternity pay period.

(SI 1994/1882) (as amended)

Statutory Maternity Pay (Compensation of Employers) and Miscellaneous Amendment Regulations 1994

(SI 1994/1882) (AS AMENDED)

The Secretary of State for Social Security, in exercise of powers conferred on him by sections 35(3), 167(1), (1A), (1B) and (4), 171(1) and 175(1) to (4) of the Social Security Contributions and Benefits Act 1992 and of all other powers enabling him in that behalf after agreement by the Social Security Advisory Committee that proposals in respect of regulation 9 should not be referred to it, hereby makes the following Regulations:

ARRANGEMENT OF REGULATIONS

1. Citation, commencement and interpretation
2. Meaning of "small employer"
3. Determination of the amount of additional payment to which a small employer shall be entitled
4. Right of employers to prescribed amount
5. Application for advance funding from the Board
6. Deductions from payments to the Board
6A. Payments to employers by the Board
7. Date when certain contributions are to be treated as paid
7A. Overpayments
8. Revocation
9. *Omitted*

Citation, commencement and interpretation

1.—(1) These Regulations may be cited as the Statutory Maternity Pay (Compensation of Employers) and Miscellaneous Amendment Regulations 1994 and regulations 2–7 shall have effect in relation to payments of statutory maternity pay due on or after 4th September 1994.

(2) This regulation and regulation 9 shall come into force on July 31, 1994.

(3) Regulations 2 to 8 shall come into force on 4th September 1994.

(4) In these Regulations—
[1"the Board" means the Commissioners of Inland Revenue;]
"the Contributions and Benefits Act" means the Social Security Contributions and Benefits Act 1992;
"the Maternity Allowance Regulations" means the Social Security (Maternity Allowance) Regulations 1987;
[1. . .];
[1"contributions payments" has the same meaning as in section 167(8) of the Contributions and Benefits Act;]
[1"the Contributions Regulations" means the Social Security (Contributions) Regulations 2001;]
"employer" shall include a person who was previously an employer of a woman to whom a payment of statutory maternity pay was made, whether or not that person remains her employer at the date any deduction from contributions payments is made by him in accordance

Statutory Maternity Pay and Miscellaneous Amendment Regulations 1994

with regulation 5 or, as the case may be, any payment is received by him in accordance with regulation 6;

[¹"the Employment Act" means the Employment Act 2002;]

"income tax month" means the period beginning on the 6th day of any calendar month and ending on the 5th day of the following calendar month;

[¹. . .];

[¹"income tax quarter" means, in any tax year, the period beginning on 6th April and ending on 5th July the period beginning on 6th July and ending on 5th October the period beginning on 6th October and ending on 5th January or the period beginning on 6th January and ending on 5th April;]

"qualifying day" means the first day in the week immediately preceding the 14th week before the expected week of confinement in which a woman who is or has been an employee first satisfies the conditions of entitlement to statutory maternity pay for which a deduction from a contributions payment is made by her employer in respect of a payment of statutory maternity pay made by him;

"qualifying tax year" means the tax year preceding the tax year in which the qualifying day in question falls.

[¹"statutory adoption pay" means any payment under section 171ZL of the Contributions and Benefits Act;

"statutory paternity pay" means any payment under section 171ZA or 171ZB of the Contributions and Benefits Act;

"tax year" means the period of 12 months beginning on 6th April in any year;

"writing" includes writing delivered by means of electronic communications approved by directions issued by the Board pursuant to regulations made under section 132 of the Finance Act 1999;]

[¹(5) Any reference in these Regulations to the employees of any employer includes, where the context permits, a reference to his former employees.]

(6) [¹. . .].

AMENDMENT

1. Statutory Maternity Pay (Compensation of Employers) Amendment Regulations 2003 (SI 2003/672) reg.2 (April 6, 2003).

GENERAL NOTE

5.83   These Regulations make provision for employers to be reimbursed for the cost of paying statutory maternity pay. The basic rule is that employers can recover 92 per cent of the total gross statutory maternity pay payments they make in any tax month (reg.4(a)). This is done by deducting such costs from tax payments, National Insurance contributions and other sums due to HMRC (reg.6). In certain circumstances employers may apply for advance funding from HMRC in order to meet their statutory maternity pay liabilities (reg.5; but see reg.7A regarding overpayments of such sums). Small employers—currently defined as those whose total National Insurance contributions do not exceed £45,000 in the previous tax year (reg.2(1))—are entitled to 100 per cent of the cost of their statutory maternity pay payments (reg.4(b)) together with a further 4.5 per cent of the total statutory maternity pay paid (reg.3). This additional amount is intended to compensate small employers for the cost of employers' National Insurance contributions on statutory maternity pay.

(SI 1994/1882 reg.1) (as amended)

Regulation 9 of these Regulations contained a miscellaneous amendment to reg.3(4) of the Social Security (Maternity Allowance) Regulations 1987 (SI 1987/416), which has itself subsequently been revoked, and so is not included in this volume (see Vol.I).

Meaning of "small employer"

2.—(1) Subject to the following provisions of this regulation, a small employer is an employer whose contributions payments for the qualifying tax year do not exceed [¹£45,000].

5.84

(2) For the purposes of this regulation, the amount of an employer's contributions payments shall be determined without regard to any deductions that may be made from them under any enactment or instrument.

(3) Where in the qualifying tax year an employer has made contributions payments in one or more, but less than 12, of the income tax months, the amount of his contributions payments for that tax year shall be estimated by adding together all of those payments, dividing the total amount by the number of those months in which he has made those payments and multiplying the resulting figure by 12.

(4) Where in the qualifying tax year an employer has made no contributions payments, but does have such payments in one or more income tax months which fall both—
(a) in the tax year in which the qualifying day falls; and
(b) before the qualifying day or, where there is more than one such day in that tax year, before the first of those days,

then the amount of his contributions payments for the qualifying tax year shall be estimated in accordance with paragraph (3) but as if the amount of the contributions payments falling in those months had fallen instead in the corresponding tax months in the qualifying tax year.

AMENDMENT

1. Statutory Maternity Pay (Compensation of Employers) Amendment Regulations 2004 (SI 2004/698) reg.2 (April 6, 2004).

DEFINITIONS

"contributions payments"—see reg.1(4).
"employer"—see *ibid.*
"qualifying day"—see *ibid.*
"qualifying tax year"—see *ibid.*

Determination of the amount of additional payment to which a small employer shall be entitled

3. In respect of any payment of statutory maternity pay [¹made in the tax year commencing [²6th April 2002], or in any subsequent tax year,] a small employer shall be [³entitled to recover an additional amount] being an amount equal to [²4.5 per cent.] of such payment, that percentage being the total amount of secondary Class 1 contributions estimated by the Secretary of State as to be paid in respect of statutory maternity pay by all employers in that year, expressed as a percentage of the total amount of statutory maternity pay estimated by him to be paid by all employers in that year.

5.85

765

Statutory Maternity Pay and Miscellaneous Amendment Regulations 1994

AMENDMENTS

1. Statutory Maternity Pay (Compensation of Employers) Amendment Regulations 1995 (SI 1995/566) reg.2 (April 6, 1995).
2. Statutory Maternity Pay (Compensation of Employers) Amendment Regulations 2002 (SI 2002/225) reg.2 (April 6, 2002).
3. Statutory Maternity Pay (Compensation of Employers) Amendment Regulations 2003 (SI 2003/672) reg.3 (April 6, 2003).

DEFINITIONS

"employer"—see reg.1(4).
"payment of statutory maternity pay"—see *ibid*.
"small employer"—see reg.2(1).

[¹**Right of employers to prescribed amount**

5.86   4. An employer who has made, or is liable to make, any payment of statutory maternity pay shall be entitled to recover—
   (a) an amount equal to 92 per cent of such payment; or
   (b) if he is a small employer—
       (i) an amount equal to such payment; and
       (ii) an additional amount under regulation 3, in accordance with the provisions of these Regulations.]

AMENDMENT

1. Statutory Maternity Pay (Compensation of Employers) Amendment Regulations 2003 (SI 2003/672) reg.4 (April 6, 2003).

DEFINITIONS

"employer"—see reg.1(4).
"payment of statutory maternity pay"—see *ibid*.
"small employer"—see reg.2(1).

[¹**Application for advance funding from the Board**

5.87   5.—(1) If an employer is entitled to recover an amount determined in accordance with regulation 4 in respect of statutory maternity pay which he is required to pay to an employee or employees in any income tax month or income tax quarter and the amount exceeds the aggregate of—
   (a) the total amount of tax which the employer is required to pay to the collector of taxes in respect of deductions from the emoluments of his employees in accordance with the Income Tax (Employments) Regulations 1993 for that income tax month or income tax quarter;
   (b) the total amount of deductions made by the employer from the emoluments of his employees for that income tax month or income tax quarter in accordance with regulations made under section 22(5) of the Teaching and Higher Education Act 1998 or section 73B of the Education (Scotland) Act 1980 or in accordance with Article 3(5) of the Education (Student Support) (Northern Ireland) Order 1988;
   (c) the total amount of contributions payments which the employer is required to pay to the collector of taxes in respect of the emoluments of his employees (whether by means of deduction or otherwise) in accordance with the Contributions Regulations for that income tax month or income tax quarter;

(SI 1994/1882 reg.5) (as amended)

   (d) the total amount of payments which the employer is required to pay to the collector of taxes in respect of deductions made on account of tax from payments to sub-contractors in accordance with section 559 of the Income and Corporation Taxes Act 1988 for that income tax month or income tax quarter; and
   (e) the statutory paternity pay, statutory adoption pay and statutory maternity pay which the employer is required to pay to his employees in that income tax month or income tax quarter,

the employer may apply to the Board in accordance with paragraph (2) for funds ("advance funding") to pay that excess (or so much of it as remains outstanding) to the employee or employees.

(2) Where—
   (a) the conditions in paragraph (1) are satisfied; or
   (b) the employer considers that the conditions in paragraph (1) will be satisfied on the date of any subsequent payment of emoluments to one or more employees who are entitled to a payment of statutory maternity pay,

the employer may apply to the Board for advance funding on a form approved for that purpose by the Board.

(3) An application by an employer under paragraph (2) shall be for an amount not exceeding the amount of statutory maternity pay which the employer is entitled to recover in accordance with regulation 4 and which he is required to pay to an employee or employees for the income tax month or income tax quarter to which the payment of emoluments relates.]

AMENDMENT

1. Statutory Maternity Pay (Compensation of Employers) Amendment Regulations 2003 (SI 2003/672) reg.4 (April 6, 2003).

DEFINITIONS

   "advance funding"—see para.(1).
   "the Board"—see reg.1(4).
   "the Contributions Regulations"—see *ibid.*
   "contributions payments"—see *ibid.*
   "employer"—see *ibid.*
   "income tax month"—see *ibid.*
   "income tax quarter"—see *ibid.*
   "statutory adoption pay"—see *ibid.*
   "statutory paternity pay"—see *ibid.*

[¹Deductions from payments to the Board

6. An employer who is entitled to recover an amount under regulation 4 may do so by making one or more deductions from the aggregate of the amounts specified in sub-paragraphs (a) to (e) of regulation 5(1), except where and insofar as—

   (a) those amounts relate to earnings paid before the beginning of the income tax month or income tax quarter in which the payment of statutory maternity pay was made;
   (b) those amounts are paid by him later than six years after the tax year in which the payment of statutory maternity pay was made;
   (c) the employer has received advance funding from the Board in accordance with an application under regulation 5; or

5.88

Statutory Maternity Pay and Miscellaneous Amendment Regulations 1994

(d) the employer has made a request in writing under regulation 5 that the amount which he is entitled to recover under regulation 4 be paid to him and he has not received notification by the Board that such request is refused.]

AMENDMENT

1. Statutory Maternity Pay (Compensation of Employers) Amendment Regulations 2003 (SI 2003/672) reg.4 (April 6, 2003).

DEFINITIONS

"advance funding"—reg.5(1).
"the Board"—see reg.1(4).
"employer"—see *ibid.*
"income tax month"—see *ibid.*
"income tax quarter"—see *ibid.*
"writing"—see *ibid.*

[¹Payments to employers by the Board

5.89   **6A.** If, in an income tax month or an income tax quarter—
(a) the total amount that the employer is entitled to deduct under regulation 6 is less than the amount which the employer is entitled to recover under regulation 4;
(b) the Board is satisfied that this is so; and
(c) the employer has so requested in writing, the Board shall pay to the employer the sum that the employer is unable to deduct under regulation 6.]

AMENDMENT

1. Statutory Maternity Pay (Compensation of Employers) Amendment Regulations 2003 (SI 2003/672) reg.4 (April 6, 2003).

DEFINITIONS

"the Board"—see reg.1(4).
"income tax month"—see *ibid.*
"income tax quarter"—see *ibid.*
"writing"—see *ibid.*

Date when certain contributions are to be treated as paid

5.90   **7.** Where an employer has made a deduction from a contributions payment under [¹regulation 6], the date on which it is to be treated as having been paid for the purposes of [¹section 167(6)] of the Contributions and Benefits Act (amount deducted to be treated as paid and received towards discharging liability in respect of Class 1 contributions) is—
(a) in a case where the deduction did not extinguish the contributions payment, the date on which the remainder of the contributions payment or, as the case may be, the first date on which any part of the remainder of the contributions payment was paid; and
(b) in a case where the deduction extinguished the contributions payment, the 14th day after the end of the income tax month during which there were paid the earnings in respect of which the contributions payment was payable.

(SI 1994/1882 reg.7) (as amended)

AMENDMENT

1. Statutory Maternity Pay (Compensation of Employers) Amendment Regulations 2003 (SI 2003/672) reg.5 (April 6, 2003).

DEFINITIONS

"the Contributions and Benefits Act"—see reg.1(4).
"contributions payments"—see *ibid.*
"employer"—see *ibid.*
"income tax month"—see *ibid.*

[¹Overpayments

7A.—(1) Where advance funding has been provided to an employer in accordance with an application under regulation 5, the Board may recover any part of it not used to pay statutory maternity pay ("the overpayment").

(2) An officer of the Board shall decide to the best of his judgement the amount of the overpayment and shall give notice in writing of his decision to the employer.

(3) A decision under paragraph (2) may be in respect of funding provided in accordance with regulation 5 for one or more income tax months or income tax quarters in a tax year—
- (a) in respect of one or more classes of employees specified in a decision notice (where a notice does not name any individual employee); or
- (b) in respect of one or more individual employees named in a decision notice.

(4) Subject to paragraphs (5), (6) or (7), Part 6 of the Taxes Management Act 1970 (collection and recovery) shall apply with any necessary modifications to a decision under this regulation as if the amount specified were an assessment and as if the amount set out in the notice were income tax charged on the employer.

(5) Where a decision under paragraph (2) relates to more than one employee, proceedings may be brought to recover the amount overpaid without distinguishing the sum to be repaid in respect of each employee and without specifying the employee in question.

(6) A decision to recover an amount made in accordance with this regulation shall give rise to one cause of action or matter of complaint for the purpose of proceedings under sections 65, 66 or 67 of the Taxes Management Act 1970.

(7) Nothing in paragraph (5) shall prevent separate proceedings being brought for the recovery of any amount which the employer is liable to repay in respect of each employee to whom the decision relates.]

DEFINITIONS

"the Board"—see reg.1(4).
"the overpayment"—see para.(1).
"advance funding"—see reg.5(1).
"employee"—see reg.1(5).
"employer"—see reg.1(4).
"income tax month"—see *ibid.*
"income tax quarter"—see *ibid.*
"tax year"—see *ibid.*
"writing"—see *ibid.*

Revocation

5.92   8. The Statutory Maternity Pay (Compensation of Employers) Regulations 1987 are hereby revoked.

Statutory Maternity Pay (General) (Modification and Amendment) Regulations 2000

(SI 2000/2883)

The Secretary of State for Social Security, in exercise of the powers conferred on him by sections 164(4), (9)(e) and (10), 165(1) and (3), 171(1) and 175(1) to (4) of the Social Security Contributions and Benefits Act 1992 and of all other powers enabling him in that behalf, after agreement by the Social Security Advisory Committee that proposals to make these Regulations should not be referred to it, hereby makes the following Regulations:

ARRANGEMENT OF REGULATIONS

5.93
1. Citation, commencement and interpretation
2. Modification of s.164(2)(a) of the Contributions and Benefits Act
3. Amendment of the Statutory Maternity Pay Regulations
4. Transitional provision

Citation, commencement and interpretation

5.94   **1.**—(1) These Regulations may be cited as the Statutory Maternity Pay (General) (Modification and Amendment) Regulations 2000 and shall come into force on 17th November 2000.

(2) In these Regulations—

"the Contributions and Benefits Act" means the Social Security Contributions and Benefits Act 1992;

"the Statutory Maternity Pay Regulations" means the Statutory Maternity Pay (General) Regulations 1986.

Modification of s.164(2)(a) of the Contributions and Benefits Act

5.95   **2.** Subject to regulation 4, in relation to a woman who is dismissed, or whose employment is otherwise terminated without her consent, after the beginning of the week immediately preceding the 14th week before the expected week of confinement, section 164(2)(a) of the Contributions and Benefits Act (conditions of entitlement to statutory maternity pay) shall be modified and have effect so that the words, "wholly or partly because of pregnancy or confinement" shall not apply.

DEFINITION

"Contributions and Benefits Act"—see reg.1(2).

GENERAL NOTE

5.96   In order to qualify for statutory maternity pay, the general rule under SSCBA 1992 s.164(2)(a) is that the claimant must have been continuously employed in an employed earner's employment for 26 weeks up to the 15th week before the expected week of confinement but has then ceased to work for the employer "wholly or partly because of pregnancy or confinement". This latter requirement caused problems for women who were dismissed for some other reason (e.g. redundancy). These Regulations were therefore enacted in 2000 (but with effect from March 4, 2001: reg.4) so as to extend the right to statutory maternity pay to all women, unless they left their job voluntarily.

Amendment of the Statutory Maternity Pay Regulations

3. . . . .

GENERAL NOTE

The amendments made by reg.3 have been incorporated into the text of the Statutory Maternity Pay (General) Regulations 1986 (SI 1986/1960) in this volume.

Transitional provision

4. In relation to a woman whose expected week of confinement begins before 4th March 2001, the Contributions and Benefits Act and the Statutory Maternity Pay Regulations shall have effect as if these Regulations were not in force.

DEFINITIONS

"Contributions and Benefits Act"—see reg.1(2).
"Statutory Maternity Pay Regulations"—see *ibid*.

Statutory Maternity Pay and Statutory Adoption Pay (Curtailment) Regulations 2014

(SI 2014/3054)

This instrument contains only regulations made by virtue of, or consequential upon, section 120(1), (4) and (6) of the Children and Families Act 2014 and is made before the end of the period of 6 months beginning with the coming into force of that enactment.

The Secretary of State for Work and Pensions, in exercise of the powers conferred by sections 165(3A), (3B), (3C) and (3D), 171ZN(2A), (2B), (2C) and (2D) and 175(1), (3) and (4) of the Social Security Contributions and Benefits Act 1992, makes the following Regulations:

Statutory Maternity Pay and SAP (Curtailment) Regulations 2014

Arrangement Of Regulations

Part 1

General

5.100
1. Citation and commencement
2. Interpretation
3. Notices

Part 2

Curtailment Of Maternity Pay Period

4. Curtailment of maternity pay period (statutory shared parental pay: M)
5. Curtailment of maternity pay period (statutory shared parental pay: P)
6. Curtailment of maternity pay period (shared parental leave: P)
7. Maternity pay period curtailment notice
8. Revocation (maternity pay period curtailment notice)

Part 3

Curtailment Of Adoption Pay Period

9. Curtailment of adoption pay period (statutory shared parental pay: A)
10. Curtailment of adoption pay period (statutory shared parental pay: AP)
11. Curtailment of adoption pay period (shared parental leave: AP)
12. Adoption pay period curtailment notice
13. Revocation (adoption pay period curtailment notice)

General Note

5.101   These Regulations allow eligible women to curtail their statutory maternity pay in accordance with s.165(3A) of the SSCBA 1992 in order to enable them to take statutory shared parental pay (ShPP) in accordance with s.171ZU of the 1992 Act. The Regulations also allow eligible women to curtail their statutory maternity pay in accordance with SSCBA 1992 s.165(3A), in order to allow their partner to take ShPP in accordance with SSCBA 1992 s.171ZU, or shared parental leave in accordance with s.75E of the Employment Rights Act 1996.

Regulation 3 prescribes how notices may be given under these Regulations. Regulation 4 applies to a woman curtailing her statutory maternity pay in order to take ShPP. Regulation 5 applies to a woman curtailing her SMP so that her partner can take ShPP. Regulation 6 allows a woman who is not eligible for statutory maternity leave to curtail her SMP so that her partner can take shared parental leave. In these circumstances, an eligible partner will be entitled to 52 weeks of shared parental leave less the amount of SMP the child's mother has taken at the point of curtailing the maternity pay period. Regulation 7 prescribes the requirements with which a maternity pay period curtailment notice must comply. Regulation 8 allows a woman to revoke a notice to curtail her SMP in specified circumstances and subject to certain conditions being satisfied.

These Regulations also make equivalent provisions for adopters. The Regulations allow eligible adopters to curtail their adoption pay period in accordance with SSCBA 1992 s.171ZN(2A) so as to enable them to take ShPP in accordance with SSCBA 1992 s.171ZV. The Regulations also allow eligible adopters to curtail their adoption pay period in accordance with s.171ZN(2A) to allow their partner to take ShPP in accordance with s.171ZV, or shared parental leave in accordance with s.75G of the Employment Rights Act 1996.

PART 1

GENERAL

Citation and commencement

1. These Regulations may be cited as the Statutory Maternity Pay and Statutory Adoption Pay (Curtailment) Regulations 2014 and come into force on 1st December 2014.

5.102

Interpretation

2. In these Regulations—
"the 1992 Act" means the Social Security Contributions and Benefits Act 1992;
"the 1996 Act" means the Employment Rights Act 1996;
"A" means a person who is entitled to statutory adoption pay;
"adoption pay curtailment date" means, subject to regulation 12(4), the date specified in an adoption pay period curtailment notice;
"adoption pay period curtailment notice" means a notice given in accordance with regulation 12;
"AP" means the person who is married to, or the civil partner or the partner of, A;
"C" means the child in respect of whom an entitlement to—
(a) shared parental leave arises under section 75E (entitlement to shared parental leave: birth) or 75G (entitlement to shared parental leave: adoption) of the 1996 Act;
(b) statutory shared parental pay arises under section 171ZU (entitlement: birth) or 171ZV (entitlement: adoption) of the 1992 Act;
"calendar week" means a period of seven days beginning with a Sunday;
"M" means the mother (or expectant mother) of C;
"maternity pay period curtailment date" means, subject to regulation 7(5), the date specified in a maternity pay period curtailment notice;
"maternity pay period curtailment notice" means a notice given in accordance with regulation 7 and regulation 8(5);
"P" means the father of C, or the person who is married to, or the civil partner or the partner of, M;
"partner" in relation to M or A, means a person (whether of a different sex or the same sex) who lives with M or A and with C in an enduring family relationship but is not M's or A's child, parent, grandchild, grandparent, sibling, aunt, uncle, niece or nephew;
"SPL Regulations" means the Shared Parental Leave Regulations 2014;
"ShPP Regulations" means the Statutory Shared Parental Pay (General) Regulations 2014;

5.103

"statutory adoption pay" has the meaning given in section 171ZL (entitlement) of the 1992 Act;
"statutory maternity pay" has the meaning given in section 164(1) (statutory maternity pay—entitlement and liability to pay) of the 1992 Act.

Notices

5.104

3. (1) Where a notice is to be given under these Regulations, it may be given—
  (a) where paragraph (2) applies, by electronic communication;
  (b) by post; or
  (c) by personal delivery.

(2) This paragraph applies where the person who is to receive the notice has agreed that the notice may be given to the person by being transmitted to an electronic address and in an electronic form specified by the person for the purpose.

(3) Where a notice is to be given under these Regulations it is to be taken to have been given—
  (a) if sent by electronic communication, on the day of transmission;
  (b) if sent by post in an envelope which is properly addressed and sent by prepaid post, on the day on which it is posted;
  (c) if delivered personally, on the day of delivery.

PART 2

CURTAILMENT OF MATERNITY PAY PERIOD

Curtailment of maternity pay period (statutory shared parental pay: M)

5.105

4. M's maternity pay period shall end on the maternity pay period curtailment date if—
  (a) M gives a maternity pay period curtailment notice (unless the notice is revoked under regulation 8);
  (b) M satisfies the conditions in sub-paragraphs (a) and (d) of regulation 4(2) (entitlement of mother to statutory shared parental pay (birth)) of the ShPP Regulations; and
  (c) P satisfies the conditions in sub-paragraph (b) of regulation 4(3) of the ShPP Regulations.

DEFINITIONS

"maternity pay period curtailment date"—reg.2.
"maternity pay period curtailment notice"—reg.2.
"ShPP Regulations"—reg.2.

Curtailment of maternity pay period (statutory shared parental pay: P)

5.106

5. M's maternity pay period shall end on the maternity pay period curtailment date if—

(a) M gives a maternity pay period curtailment notice (unless the notice is revoked under regulation 8);
(b) P satisfies the conditions in sub-paragraph (a) of regulation 5(2) (entitlement of father or partner to statutory shared parental pay (birth)) of the ShPP Regulations; and
(c) M satisfies the conditions in sub-paragraphs (b) and (c) of regulation 5(3) of the ShPP Regulations.

DEFINITIONS

"M"—reg.2.
"maternity pay period curtailment date"—reg.2.
"maternity pay period curtailment notice"—reg.2.
"P"—reg.2.
"partner"—reg.2.
"ShPP Regulations"—reg.2.

Curtailment of maternity pay period (shared parental leave: P)

6. M's maternity pay period shall end on the maternity pay period curtailment date if—
(a) M gives a maternity pay period curtailment notice (unless the notice is revoked under regulation 8);
(b) P satisfies the condition in sub-paragraph (a) of regulation 5(2) (father's or partner's entitlement to shared parental leave) of the SPL Regulations; and
(c) M satisfies the conditions in sub-paragraphs (a) and (c) of regulation 5(3) of the SPL Regulations.

DEFINITIONS

"M"—reg.2.
"P"—reg.2.
"maternity pay period curtailment date"—reg.2.
"maternity pay period curtailment notice"—reg.2.
"partner"—reg.2.
"ShPP Regulations"—reg.2.
"SPL Regulations"—reg.2.

Maternity pay period curtailment notice

7. (1) A maternity pay period curtailment notice must—
(a) be in writing;
(b) specify the date on which M's statutory maternity pay period is to end; and
(c) be given to the person who is liable to pay M's statutory maternity pay.
(2) The date specified in accordance with paragraph (1)(b) must be—
(a) the last day of a week;
(b) if M has the right to maternity leave under section 71 (ordinary maternity leave) of the 1996 Act, at least one day after the end of the compulsory maternity leave period, or, if M does not have that right, at least two weeks after the end of the pregnancy;
(c) at least eight weeks after the date on which M gave the maternity pay period curtailment notice; and

(d) at least one week before the last day of the maternity pay period.

(3) In paragraph (2) "the end of the compulsory maternity leave period" means whichever is the later of—
(a) the last day of the compulsory maternity leave period provided for in regulations under section 72(2) (compulsory maternity leave) of the 1996 Act; or
(b) where section 205 of the Public Health Act 1936 (women not to be employed in factories or workshops within four weeks after birth of a child) applies to M's employment, the last day of the period in which an occupier of a factory is prohibited from knowingly allowing M to be employed in that factory.

(4) If M has more than one entitlement to statutory maternity pay in relation to C, M must curtail the maternity pay period in relation to each (or none) of those entitlements, and in relation to each of those entitlements M must specify a maternity pay period curtailment date which falls in the same calendar week.

(5) Where M—
(a) returns to work before giving a notice in accordance with paragraph (1); and
(b) subsequently gives such a notice;
the "maternity pay period curtailment date" shall be the last day of the week in which that notice is given (irrespective of the date given in that notice under paragraph (1)).

(6) For the purposes of paragraphs (2)(a) and (5), "week" has the meaning given in section 165(8) (the maternity pay period) of the 1992 Act.

(7) In this regulation, M is treated as returning to work where statutory maternity pay is not payable to her in accordance with section 165(4) or (6) of the 1992 Act.

DEFINITIONS

"the 1992 Act"—see reg.2.
"the 1996 Act"—see reg.2.
"calendar week"—reg.2.
"C"—reg.2.
"M"—reg.2.
"P"—reg.2.
"maternity pay period curtailment date"—reg.2.
"maternity pay period curtailment notice"—reg.2.
"partner"—reg.2.
"ShPP Regulations"—reg.2.
"SPL Regulations"—reg.2.
"statutory maternity pay"—reg.2.
"week"—subs.(6).

Revocation (maternity pay period curtailment notice)

5.109

8.—(1) Subject to paragraph (2), M may revoke a maternity pay period curtailment notice by giving a notice ("a revocation notice") before the maternity pay period curtailment date if—
(a) she gave the maternity pay period curtailment notice before the birth of C; or
(b) P dies.

(2) Revocation is effective under paragraph (1) where M gives a

revocation notice to the person who is liable to pay M's statutory maternity pay that—
  (a) if given under paragraph (1)(a), is given within six weeks of the date of C's birth; or
  (b) if given under paragraph (1)(b), is given within a reasonable period from the date of P's death.
(3) A revocation notice must—
  (a) be in writing;
  (b) state that M revokes the maternity pay period curtailment notice; and
  (c) if given under paragraph (1)(b), state the date of P's death.
(4) Where in accordance with regulation 7(4) M has given a maternity pay period curtailment notice to more than one person, M must give a revocation notice to each of those persons.
(5) M may not give a maternity pay period curtailment notice in respect of the same maternity pay period subsequent to giving a revocation notice unless the revocation was made in accordance with paragraph (1)(a).

DEFINITIONS

"C"—reg.2.
"M"—reg.2.
"P"—reg.2.
"maternity pay period curtailment notice"—reg.2.
"revocation notice"—para.(1).
"statutory maternity pay"—reg.2.

PART 3

CURTAILMENT OF ADOPTION PAY PERIOD

Curtailment of adoption pay period (statutory shared parental pay: A)

9. A's adoption pay period shall end on the adoption pay curtailment date if—
  (a) A gives an adoption pay period curtailment notice (unless the notice is revoked under regulation 13);
  (b) A satisfies the conditions in sub-paragraphs (a) and (d) of regulation 17(2) (entitlement of adopter to statutory shared parental pay (adoption)) of the ShPP Regulations; and
  (c) AP satisfies the condition in sub-paragraph (b) of regulation 17(3) of the ShPP Regulations.

DEFINITIONS

"A"—reg.2.
"adoption pay period curtailment date"—reg.2.
"adoption pay period curtailment notice"—reg.2.
"AP"—reg.2.
"ShPP Regulations"—reg.2.

Curtailment of adoption pay period (statutory shared parental pay: AP)

5.111   **10.** A's adoption pay period shall end on the adoption pay curtailment date if—
(a) A gives an adoption pay period curtailment notice (unless the notice is revoked under regulation 13);
(b) AP satisfies the conditions in sub-paragraph (a) of regulation 18(2) (entitlement of adopter's partner to statutory shared parental pay (adoption)) of the ShPP Regulations; and
(c) A satisfies the conditions in sub-paragraphs (b) and (c) of regulation 18(3) of the ShPP Regulations.

DEFINITIONS

"A"—reg.2.
"adoption pay period curtailment date"—reg.2.
"adoption pay period curtailment notice"—reg.2.
"AP"—reg.2.
"partner"—reg.2.
"ShPP Regulations"—reg.2.

Curtailment of adoption pay period (shared parental leave: AP)

5.112   **11.** A's adoption pay period shall end on the adoption pay curtailment date if—
(a) A gives an adoption pay period curtailment notice (unless the notice is revoked under regulation 13);
(b) AP satisfies the condition in sub-paragraph (a) of regulation 21(2) (adopter's partner's entitlement to shared parental leave) of the SPL Regulations; and
(c) A satisfies the conditions in sub-paragraphs (a) and (c) of regulation 21(3) of the SPL Regulations.

DEFINITIONS

"A"—reg.2.
"adoption pay period curtailment date"—reg.2.
"adoption pay period curtailment notice"—reg.2.
"AP"—reg.2.
"partner"—reg.2.
"SPL Regulations"—reg.2.

Adoption pay period curtailment notice

5.113   **12.** (1) An adoption pay period curtailment notice must—
(a) be in writing;
(b) specify the date on which A's statutory adoption pay period is to end; and
(c) be given to the person who is liable to pay A's statutory adoption pay.
(2) The date specified in accordance with paragraph (1)(b) must be—
(a) the last day of a week;
(b) at least eight weeks after the date on which A gave the adoption pay period curtailment notice;

(SI 2014/3054 reg.12)

(c) at least two weeks after the first day of the adoption pay period; and
(d) at least one week before the last day of the adoption pay period.

(3) If A has more than one entitlement to statutory adoption pay in relation to C, A must curtail the adoption pay period in relation to each (or none) of those entitlements, and in relation to each of those entitlements A must specify an adoption pay curtailment date which falls in the same calendar week.

(4) Where A—
(a) returns to work before giving a notice in accordance with paragraph (1); and
(b) subsequently gives such a notice;
the adoption pay curtailment date shall be the last day of the week in which that notice is submitted (irrespective of the date given in that notice under paragraph (1)).

(5) For the purposes of paragraph (2)(a) and (4), "week" has the meaning given in section 171ZN(8) of the 1992 Act.

(6) In this regulation, A is treated as returning to work where statutory adoption pay is not payable to A in accordance with section 171ZN(3) or (5) of the 1992 Act.

DEFINITIONS

"the 1992 Act"—see reg.2.
"the 1996 Act"—see reg.2.
"A"—reg.2.
"adoption pay period curtailment date"—reg.2.
"adoption pay period curtailment notice"—reg.2.
"AP"—reg.2.
"calendar week"—reg.2.
"partner"—reg.2.
"SPL Regulations"—reg.2.
"statutory adoption pay"—reg.2.
"week"—para.(5).

Revocation (adoption pay period curtailment notice)

13. (1) Where AP dies before the adoption pay curtailment date, A may revoke an adoption pay period curtailment notice by giving a notice ("a revocation notice") in accordance with paragraph (2).

5.114

(2) A revocation notice must be given to the person who is liable to pay A statutory adoption pay within a reasonable period from the date of AP's death and before the adoption pay curtailment date.

(3) A revocation notice must—
(a) be in writing;
(b) state that A revokes the adoption pay period curtailment notice; and
(c) state the date of AP's death.

(4) Where in accordance with regulation 12(3) A has given an adoption pay period curtailment notice to more than one person, A must give a revocation notice to each of those persons.

(5) A may not give an adoption pay period curtailment notice subsequent to giving a revocation notice.

Statutory Maternity Pay and SAP (Curtailment) Regulations 2014

DEFINITIONS

"A"—reg.2.
"adoption pay period curtailment date"—reg.2.
"adoption pay period curtailment notice"—reg.2.
"AP"—reg.2.
"revocation notice"—para.(1).

PART VI

STATUTORY PATERNITY PAY AND STATUTORY ADOPTION PAY

Statutory Paternity Pay and Statutory Adoption Pay (Weekly Rates) Regulations 2002

(SI 2002/2818) (AS AMENDED)

Whereas a draft of the following Regulations was laid before Parliament in accordance with section 176(1)(a) of the Social Security Contributions and Benefits Act 1992 and approved by a resolution of each House of Parliament:

Now, therefore, the Secretary of State, in exercise of the powers conferred on her by sections 171ZE(1) and 171ZN(1) of the Social Security Contributions and Benefits Act 1992 and section 5(1)(l) of the Social Security Administration Act 1992, by this instrument, which contains only provision made by virtue of sections 2, 4 and 53 of and paragraphs 8 and 11 of Schedule 7 to the Employment Act 2002 and is made before the end of the period of 6 months from the coming into force of those enactments, hereby makes the following Regulations—

ARRANGEMENT OF REGULATIONS

1. Citation and commencement.
2. Weekly rate of payment of statutory paternity pay.
3. Weekly rate of payment of statutory adoption pay.
4. Rounding of fractional amounts.

Citation and commencement

1.—These Regulations may be cited as the Statutory Paternity Pay and Statutory Adoption Pay (Weekly Rates) Regulations and shall come into force on 8th December 2002.

GENERAL NOTE

These Regulations specify the weekly rate of statutory paternity pay and statutory adoption pay. In the current year, statutory paternity pay is the lower of £139.58 per week or 90 per cent of the employee's normal weekly earnings where the paternity pay period starts after that date (reg.2). Statutory adoption pay is set at the lower of £139.58 per week or 90 per cent of the employee's normal weekly earnings (reg.3). Fractional amounts are rounded in accordance with reg.4.

[[1]Weekly rate of payment of statutory paternity pay

2. The weekly rate of payment of statutory paternity pay shall be the smaller of the following two amounts—
  (a) [[2]£139.58];
  (b) 90 per cent. of the normal weekly earnings of the person claiming statutory paternity pay, determined in accordance with regulations 39 and 40 of the Statutory Paternity Pay and Statutory Adoption Pay (General) Regulations 2002.]

Statutory Paternity Pay and Statutory Adoption Pay Regulations 2002

AMENDMENTS

1. Statutory Paternity Pay and Statutory Adoption Pay (Weekly Rates) (Amendment) Regulations 2004 (SI 2004/925) reg.2 (April 4, 2004).
2. Welfare Benefits Up-rating Order 2015 (SI 2015/15) art.5(1)(a) (April 5, 2015).

Weekly rate of payment of statutory adoption pay

3. The weekly rate of payment of statutory adoption pay shall be the smaller of the following two amounts—
(a) [¹£138.58];
(b) 90 per cent of the normal weekly earnings of the person claiming statutory adoption pay, determined in accordance with regulations 39 and 40 of the Statutory Paternity Pay and Statutory Adoption Pay (General) Regulations 2002.

AMENDMENT

2. Welfare Benefits Up-rating Order 2015 (SI 2015/15) art.5(1)(b) (April 5, 2015).

Rounding of fractional amounts

[¹**4.** Where any payment of—
(a) statutory paternity pay is made on the basis of a calculation at—
  (i) the weekly rate specified in regulation 2(b); or
  (ii) the daily rate of one-seventh of the weekly rate specified in regulation 2(a) or (b); or
(b) statutory adoption pay is made on the basis of a calculation at—
  (i) the weekly rate specified in regulation 3(b); or
  (ii) the daily rate of one-seventh of the weekly rate specified in regulation 3(a) or (b),
and that amount includes a fraction of a penny, the payment shall be rounded up to the next whole number of pence.]

AMENDMENT

1. Statutory Paternity Pay and Statutory Adoption Pay (General) and the Statutory Paternity Pay and Statutory Adoption Pay (Weekly Rates) (Amendment) Regulations 2006 (SI 2006/2236) reg.4 (October 1, 2006).

GENERAL NOTE

The amended version of reg.4 applies in relation to an entitlement to SPP (birth) in respect of children whose expected week of birth begins on or after April 1, 2007 and to SPP (adoption) and SAP in respect of children expected to be placed for adoption, where the placement is expected to occur on or after April 1, 2007 (see reg.2 of SI 2006/2236).

(SI 2002/2819) (as amended)

Statutory Paternity Pay and Statutory Adoption Pay (National Health Service Employees) Regulations 2002

(SI 2002/2819) (AS AMENDED)

The Secretary of State, in exercise of the powers conferred on her by virtue of sections 171ZJ(9) and (10) and 171ZS(9) and (10) of the Social Security Contributions and Benefits Act 1992 and with the concurrence of the Commissioners of Inland Revenue by this instrument, which contains only provision made by virtue of sections 2 and 4 of the Employment Act 2002 and is made before the end of the period of 6 months from the coming into force of those enactments hereby makes the following Regulations—

ARRANGEMENT OF SECTIONS

1. Citation, commencement and interpretation.
2. Treatment of more than one contract of employment as one contract.
3. Notification of election.
4. Provision of information.
5. Treatment of two or more employers as one.
6. Time for which an election is to have effect.

Citation, commencement and interpretation

1.—(1) These Regulations may be cited as the Statutory Paternity Pay and Statutory Adoption Pay (National Health Service Employees) Regulations 2002 and shall come into force on 8th December 2002.
(2) In these Regulations—
"the Act" means the Social Security Contributions and Benefits Act 1992;
"the 1977 Act" means the National Health Service Act 1977;
"the 1978 Act" means the National Health Service (Scotland) Act 1978;
"the 1990 Act" means the National Health Service and Community Care Act 1990;
"the 2002 Act" means the National Health Service Reform and Health Care Professions Act 2002;
"Health Authority" means, in relation to Wales, a Health Authority established under section 8 of the 1977 Act and in relation to Scotland means a Health Board established under section 2 of the 1978 Act;
[[1]"NHS trust" shall be construed to include a reference to an NHS foundation trust within the meaning of section 1(1) of the Health and Social Care (Community Health and Standards) Act 2003 where the application for authorisation to become an NHS foundation trust was made by an NHS trust.]
[[2]...]
"statutory adoption pay period" means the period prescribed under section 171ZN(2) of the Act as the period in respect of which statutory adoption pay is payable to a person;
"statutory paternity pay period" means the period determined in

Statutory Paternity Pay and Statutory Adoption Pay Regulations 2002

accordance with section 171ZE(2) of the Act as the period in respect of which statutory paternity pay is payable to a person;
"Strategic Health Authority" means a Strategic Health Authority established under section 8 of the 1977 Act.

AMENDMENTS

1. Health and Social Care (Community Health and Standards) Act 2003 (Supplementary and Consequential Provision) (NHS Foundation Trusts) Order 2004 (SI 2004/696) art.3(1) and Sch.1 para.42 (April 1, 2004).
2. National Treatment Agency (Abolition) and the Health and Social Care Act 2012 (Consequential, Transitional and Saving Provisions) Order 2013 (SI 2013/235) art.11 and Sch.2 para.56(2) (April 1, 2013).

GENERAL NOTE

6.10   These Regulations, made under the authority of SSCBA 1992 ss.171ZJ(9) and (10) and 171ZS(9) and (10), make special provision for those NHS workers who are employed under two or more separate contracts of employment with different NHS Trusts. The regulations enable them to elect to have such contracts treated as one contract for the purposes of entitlement to statutory paternity pay and statutory adoption pay.

Treatment of more than one contract of employment as one contract

6.11   2. Where, in consequence of the establishment of one or more National Health Service Trusts under section 5 of the 1990 Act or section 12A of the 1978 Act, a person's contract of employment is treated by a scheme under section 6 of the 1990 Act or section 12B of the 1978 Act as divided so as to constitute two or more contracts [1. . .] he may elect for all those contracts to be treated as one contract for the purposes of Parts 12ZA and 12ZB of the Act.

AMENDMENT

1. National Treatment Agency (Abolition) and the Health and Social Care Act 2012 (Consequential, Transitional and Saving Provisions) Order 2013 (SI 2013/235) art.11 and Sch.2 para.56(3) (April 1, 2013).

DEFINITIONS

"the Act"—see reg.1(2).
"the 1977 Act"—see *ibid*.
"the 1978 Act"—see *ibid*.
"the 1990 Act"—see *ibid*.

Notification of election

6.12   3. A person who makes an election under regulation 2 above shall give written notification of that election to each of his employers under the two or more contracts of employment mentioned in that regulation at least 28 days before the beginning of the statutory paternity pay period or adoption pay period or, if in the particular circumstances that is not practicable, as soon as is reasonably practicable.

DEFINITIONS

"statutory adoption pay period"—see reg.1(2).
"statutory paternity pay period"—see *ibid*.

(SI 2002/2819 reg.4) (as amended)

Provision of information

4. A person who makes an election under regulation 2 above shall, within 28 days of giving notification of that election or, if in the particular circumstances that is not practicable, as soon as is reasonably practicable thereafter, provide each of his employers under the two or more contracts of employment mentioned in that regulation with the following information—

(a) the name and address of each of those employers;
(b) the date his employment with each of those employers commenced; and
(c) details of his normal weekly earnings during the relevant period from each employer, and for this purpose the expressions "normal weekly earnings" and "relevant period" have the same meanings as they have for the purposes of Parts 12ZA and 12ZB of the Act.

6.13

DEFINITIONS

"normal weekly earnings"—para.(c) and SSCBA 1992 ss.171ZJ(6) and 171ZS(6) and Statutory Paternity Pay and Statutory Adoption Pay (General) Regulations 2002 (SI 2002/2822) reg.40.
"relevant period"—para.(c) and SSCBA 1992 ss.171ZJ(7) and 171ZS(7) and Statutory Paternity Pay and Statutory Adoption Pay (General) Regulations 2002 (SI 2002/2822) reg.40(3).

Treatment of two or more employers as one

5. The employer to be regarded for the purposes of statutory paternity pay or statutory adoption pay as the employer under the one contract where two or more contracts are treated as one in accordance with regulation 2 above shall be—

(a) in the case of a person whose contract of employment is treated by a scheme under section 6 of the 1990 Act or section 12B of the 1978 Act as divided—
  (i) the Health Authority [1. . .] from which the person was transferred in a case where any one of the contracts of employment is with that Health Authority [1. . .]; or
  (ii) the first NHS trust to which a contract of employment was transferred in a case where none of the contracts of employment is with the Health Authority [1. . .]; [1. . .]
  [1. . .]

6.14

AMENDMENT

1. National Treatment Agency (Abolition) and the Health and Social Care Act 2012 (Consequential, Transitional and Saving Provisions) Order 2013 (SI 2013/235) art.11 and Sch.2 para.56(4) (April 1, 2013).

DEFINITIONS

"the 1977 Act"—see reg.1(2).
"the 1978 Act"—see *ibid.*
"Health Authority"—see *ibid.*
"Primary Care Trust"—see *ibid.*
"Strategic Health Authority"—see *ibid.*

Time for which an election is to have effect

6.15 **6.** An election made under regulation 2 shall lapse at the end of the statutory paternity pay period or, as the case may be, the adoption pay period.

DEFINITIONS

"statutory adoption pay period"—see reg.1(2).
"statutory paternity pay period"—see *ibid.*

Statutory Paternity Pay and Statutory Adoption Pay (Administration) Regulations 2002

(SI 2002/2820)

The Secretary of State, in exercise of the powers conferred on her by sections 7(1), (2)(a) and (b), (4)(a), (b) and (c) and (5), 8(1) and (2)(a), (b) and (c), 10(1) and (2) and 51(1) of the Employment Act 2002 and sections 8(1)(f) and (ga) and 25 of the Social Security Contributions (Transfer of Functions, etc.) Act 1999 and with the concurrence of the Commissioners of Inland Revenue, hereby makes the following Regulations—

ARRANGEMENT OF SECTIONS

6.16
1. Citation and commencement.
2. Interpretation.
3. Funding of employers' liabilities to make payments of statutory paternity or statutory adoption pay.
4. Application for funding from the Board.
5. Deductions from payments to the Board.
6. Payments to employers by the Board.
7. Date when certain contributions are to be treated as paid.
8. Overpayments.
9. Records to be maintained by employers.
10. Inspection of employers' records.
11. Provision of information relating to entitlement to statutory paternity pay or statutory adoption pay.
12. Application for the determination of any issue arising as to, or in connection with, entitlement to statutory paternity pay or statutory adoption pay.
13. Applications in connection with statutory paternity pay or statutory adoption pay.
14. Provision of information.

Citation and commencement

6.17 **1.** These Regulations may be cited as the Statutory Paternity Pay and Statutory Adoption Pay (Administration) Regulations 2002 and shall come into force on 8th December 2002.

GENERAL NOTE

6.18 These Regulations provide for employers to be reimbursed for the cost of making payments of statutory paternity pay and statutory adoption pay. They are therefore modelled in part on the Statutory Maternity Pay (Compensation of Employers) and Miscellaneous Amendment Regulations 1994 (SI 1994/1882). As with the regulations governing statutory maternity pay, they provide for employers to claim back 92 per cent of the total costs of their statutory paternity pay and statutory adoption pay payments, or 100 per cent in the case of small employers, with a small additional element in the latter instance (reg.3). Employers receive such monies by making deductions from income tax, National Insurance contributions and other payments that would otherwise be due to HMRC (reg.4). There is provision for HMRC to make a direct payment to an employer where such deductions would otherwise be insufficient (reg.6). HMRC also has the power to recover overpayments from employers (reg.8).

These Regulations also require employers to maintain relevant records (reg.9) and to permit HMRC officers to inspect such records (reg.10). Furthermore, employers who decide that they have no liability to pay statutory paternity pay or statutory adoption pay to an employee or ex-employee must give any such person details of that decision and the reasons for it (reg.11). Any question relating to entitlement to statutory paternity pay or statutory adoption pay may be submitted by the employee concerned to HMRC for decision (regs 12 and 13). HMRC has information-gathering powers as set out in reg.14.

Regulations 2 and 11 of these regulations are amended for the purposes of adoptions from overseas by the Statutory Paternity Pay (Adoption) and Statutory Adoption Pay (Adoptions from Overseas) (Administration) Regulations 2003 (SI 2003/1192).

Interpretation

2.—(1) In these Regulations—

"adopter", in relation to a child, means a person with whom the child is matched for adoption;

"adoption leave" means leave under section 75A of the Employment Rights Act 1996;

"adoption pay period" means the period prescribed under section 171ZN(2) of the Contributions and Benefits Act as the period in respect of which statutory adoption pay is payable to a person;

"the Board" means the Commissioners of Inland Revenue;

"the Contributions and Benefits Act" means the Social Security Contributions and Benefits Act 1992;

"contributions payments" has the same meaning as in section 7 of the Employment Act;

"the Contributions Regulations" means the Social Security (Contributions) Regulations 2001;

"the Employment Act" means the Employment Act 2002;

"income tax month" means the period beginning on the 6th day of any calendar month and ending on the 5th day of the following calendar month;

"income tax quarter" means the period beginning on the 6th day of April and ending on the 5th day of July, the period beginning on the 6th day of July and ending on the 5th day of October, the period beginning on the 6th day of October and ending on the 5th day of January or the period beginning on the sixth day of January and ending on the 5th day of April;

"paternity leave" means leave under section 80A or section 80B of the Employment Rights Act 1996;

"paternity pay period" means the period determined in accordance with section 171ZE(2) of the Contributions and Benefits Act as the period in respect of which statutory paternity pay is payable to a person;

"statutory adoption pay" means any payment under section 171ZL of the Contributions and Benefits Act;

"statutory paternity pay" means any payment under section 171ZA or section 171ZB of the Contributions and Benefits Act;

"tax year" means the 12 months beginning with 6th April in any year;

"writing" includes writing delivered by means of electronic communications approved by directions issued by the Board pursuant to regulations under section 132 of the Finance Act 1999;

(2) Any reference in these Regulations to the employees of an employer includes former employees of his.

Funding of employers' liabilities to make payments of statutory paternity or statutory adoption pay

3.—(1) An employer who has made any payment of statutory paternity pay or statutory adoption pay shall be entitled—
  (a) to an amount equal to 92 per cent of such payment; or
  (b) if the payment qualifies for small employer's relief by virtue of section 7(3) of the Employment Act—
    (i) to an amount equal to such payment; and
    (ii) to an additional payment equal to the amount to which the employer would have been entitled under section 167(2)(b) of the Contributions and Benefits Act had the payment been a payment of statutory maternity pay.

(2) The employer shall be entitled in either case (a) or case (b) to apply for advance funding in respect of such payment in accordance with regulation 4, or to deduct it in accordance with regulation 5 from amounts otherwise payable by him.

DEFINITIONS

"Contributions and Benefits Act"—see reg.2(1).
"Employment Act"—see *ibid.*
"statutory adoption pay"—see *ibid.*
"statutory paternity pay"—see *ibid.*

Application for funding from the Board

4.—(1) If an employer is entitled to a payment determined in accordance with regulation 3 in respect of statutory paternity pay or statutory adoption pay which he is required to pay to an employee or employees for an income tax month or income tax quarter, and the payment exceeds the aggregate of—
  (a) the total amount of tax which the employer is required to pay to the collector of taxes in respect of the deductions from the emoluments of his employees in accordance with the Income Tax (Employments) Regulations 1993 for the same income tax month or income tax quarter;
  (b) the total amount of the deductions made by the employer from the emoluments of his employees for the same income tax month or income tax quarter in accordance with regulations under section 22(5) of the Teaching and Higher Education Act 1998 or section

(SI 2002/2820 reg. 4)

    73B of the Education (Scotland) Act 1980 or in accordance with article 3(5) of the Education (Student Support) (Northern Ireland) Order 1998;
(c) the total amount of contributions payments which the employer is required to pay to the collector of taxes in respect of the emoluments of his employees (whether by means of deduction or otherwise) in accordance with the Contributions Regulations for the same income tax month or income tax quarter; and
(d) the total amount of payments which the employer is required to pay to the collector of taxes in respect of the deductions made on account of tax from payments to sub-contractors in accordance with section 559 of the Income and Corporation Taxes Act 1988 for the same income tax month or income tax quarter,

the employer may apply to the Board in accordance with paragraph (2) for funds to pay the statutory paternity pay or statutory adoption pay (or so much of it as remains outstanding) to the employee or employees.

    (2) Where—
(a) the condition in paragraph (1) is satisfied; or
(b) the employer considers that the condition in paragraph (1) will be satisfied on the date of any subsequent payment of emoluments to one or more employees who are entitled to payment of statutory paternity pay or statutory adoption pay,

the employer may apply to the Board for funding in a form approved for that purpose by the Board.

    (3) An application by an employer under paragraph (2) shall be for an amount up to, but not exceeding, the amount of the payment to which the employer is entitled in accordance with regulation 3 in respect of statutory paternity pay and statutory adoption pay which he is required to pay to an employee or employees for the income tax month or income tax quarter to which the payment of emoluments relates.

DEFINITIONS

    "the Board"—see reg.2(1).
    "contributions payments"—see *ibid.*
    "the Contributions Regulations"—see *ibid.*
    "income tax month"—see *ibid.*
    "income tax quarter"—see *ibid.*
    "statutory adoption pay"—see *ibid.*
    "statutory paternity pay"—see *ibid.*

Deductions from payments to the Board

    5. An employer who is entitled to a payment determined in accordance with regulation 3 may recover such payment by making one or more deductions from the aggregate of the amounts specified in subparagraphs (a) to (d) of regulation 4(1) except where and in so far as—
(a) those amounts relate to earnings paid before the beginning of the income tax month or income tax quarter in which the payment of statutory paternity pay or statutory adoption pay was made;
(b) those amounts are paid by him later than six years after the end of the tax year in which the payment of statutory paternity pay or statutory adoption pay was made;

(c) the employer has received payment from the Board under regulation 4; or
(d) the employer has made a request in writing under regulation 4 that the payment to which he is entitled in accordance with regulation 3 be paid to him and he has not received notification by the Board that the request is refused.

DEFINITIONS

"the Board"—see reg.2(1).
"income tax month"—see *ibid*.
"income tax quarter"—see *ibid*.
"statutory adoption pay"—see *ibid*.
"statutory paternity pay"—see *ibid*.
"tax year"—see *ibid*.
"writing"—see *ibid*.

Payments to employers by the Board

6.23 **6.** If the total amount which an employer is or would otherwise be entitled to deduct under regulation 5 is less than the payment to which the employer is entitled in accordance with regulation 3 in an income tax month or income tax quarter, and the Board are satisfied that this is so, then provided that the employer has in writing requested them to do so, the Board shall pay the employer such amount as the employer was unable to deduct.

DEFINITIONS

"the Board"—see reg.2(1).
"income tax month"—see *ibid*.
"income tax quarter"—see *ibid*.
"writing"—see *ibid*.

Date when certain contributions are to be treated as paid

6.24 **7.** Where an employer has made a deduction from a contributions payment under regulation 5, the date on which it is to be treated as having been paid for the purposes of section 7(5) of the Employment Act (when amount deducted from contributions payment to be treated as paid and received by the Board) is—
(a) in a case where the deduction did not extinguish the contributions payment, the date on which the remainder of the contributions payment or, as the case may be, the first date on which any part of the remainder of the contributions payment was paid; and
(b) in a case where the deduction extinguished the contributions payment, the 14th day after the end of the income tax month or income tax quarter during which there were paid the earnings in respect of which the contributions payment was payable.

DEFINITIONS

"the Board"—see reg.2(1).
"contributions payments"—see *ibid*.
"Employment Act"—see *ibid*.
"income tax month"—see *ibid*.
"income tax quarter"—see *ibid*.

(SI 2002/2820 reg.8)

Overpayments

8.—(1) This regulation applies where unds have been provided to the employer pursuant to regulation 4 in respect of one or more employees and it appears to an officer of the Board that the employer has not used the whole or part of those funds to pay statutory paternity pay or statutory adoption pay.

(2) An officer of the Board shall decide to the best of his judgement the amount of funds provided pursuant to regulation 4 and not used to pay statutory paternity pay or statutory adoption pay and shall serve notice in writing of his decision on the employer.

(3) A decision under this regulation may cover funds provided pursuant to regulation 4—
  (a) for any one income tax month or income tax quarter, or more than one income tax month or income tax quarter, in a tax year; and
  (b) in respect of a class or classes of employees specified in the decision notice (without naming the individual employees), or in respect of one or more employees named in the decision notice.

(4) Subject to the following provisions of this regulation, Part 6 of the Taxes Management Act 1970 (collection and recovery) shall apply with any necessary modifications to a decision under this regulation as if it were an assessment and as if the amount of funds determined were income tax charged on the employer.

(5) Where an amount of funds determined under this regulation relates to more than one employee, proceedings may be brought for the recovery of that amount without distinguishing the amounts making up that sum which the employer is liable to repay in respect of each employee and without specifying the employee in question, and the amount determined under this regulation shall be one cause of action or one matter of complaint for the purposes of proceedings under sections 65, 66 or 67 of the Taxes Management Act 1970.

(6) Nothing in paragraph (5) prevents the bringing of separate proceedings for the recovery of any amount which the employer is liable to repay in respect of each employee.

DEFINITIONS
  "the Board"—see reg.2(1).
  "income tax month"—see *ibid.*
  "income tax quarter"—see *ibid.*
  "statutory adoption pay"—see *ibid.*
  "statutory paternity pay"—see *ibid.*
  "tax year"—see *ibid.*
  "writing"—see *ibid.*

Records to be maintained by employers

9. Every employer shall maintain for three years after the end of a tax year in which he made payments of statutory paternity pay or statutory adoption pay to any employee of his a record of—
  (a) if the employee's paternity pay period or adoption pay period began in that year—
    (i) the date on which that period began; and

Statutory Paternity Pay and Statutory Adoption Pay Regulations 2002

(ii) the evidence of entitlement to statutory paternity pay or statutory adoption pay provided by the employee pursuant to regulations made under section 171ZC(3)(c) or section 171ZL(8)(c) of the Contributions and Benefits Act;

(b) the weeks in that tax year in which statutory paternity pay or statutory adoption pay was paid to the employee and the amount paid in each week; and

(c) any week in that tax year which was within the employee's paternity pay period or adoption pay period but for which no payment of statutory paternity pay or statutory adoption pay was made to him and the reason no payment was made.

DEFINITIONS

"adoption pay period"—see reg.2(1).
"the Contributions and Benefits Act"—see *ibid*.
"paternity pay period"—see *ibid*.
"statutory adoption pay"—see *ibid*.
"statutory paternity pay"—see *ibid*.
"tax year"—see *ibid*.

Inspection of employers' records

6.27 10.—(1) Every employer, whenever called upon to do so by any authorised officer of the Board, shall produce the documents and records specified in paragraph (2) to that officer for inspection, at such time as that officer may reasonably require, at the prescribed place.

(2) The documents and records specified in this paragraph are—

(a) all wages sheets, deductions working sheets, records kept in accordance with regulation 9 and other documents and records whatsoever relating to the calculation or payment of statutory paternity pay or statutory adoption pay to his employees in respect of the years specified by such officer; or

(b) such of those wages sheets, deductions working sheets, or other documents and records as may be specified by the authorised officer.

(3) The "prescribed place" mentioned in paragraph (1) means—

(a) such place in Great Britain as the employer and the authorised officer may agree upon; or

(b) in default of such agreement, the place in Great Britain at which the documents and records referred to in paragraph (2)(a) are normally kept; or

(c) in default of such agreement and if there is no such place as is referred to in sub-paragraph (b) above, the employer's principal place of business in Great Britain.

(4) The authorised officer may—

(a) take copies of, or make extracts from, any document or record produced to him for inspection in accordance with paragraph (1);

(b) remove any document or record so produced if it appears to him to be necessary to do so, at a reasonable time and for a reasonable period.

(5) Where any document or record is removed in accordance with paragraph (4)(b), the authorised officer shall provide—

(a) a receipt for the document or record so removed; and

(SI 2002/2820 reg.10)

(b) a copy of the document or record, free of charge, within seven days, to the person by whom it was produced or caused to be produced where the document or record is reasonably required for the proper conduct of a business.

(6) Where a lien is claimed on a document produced in accordance with paragraph (1), the removal of the document under paragraph (4)(b) shall not be regarded as breaking the lien.

(7) Where records are maintained by computer, the person required to make them available for inspection shall provide the authorised officer with all facilities necessary for obtaining information from them.

DEFINITIONS
"the Board"—see reg.2(1).
"prescribed place"—see para.(3).
"statutory adoption pay"—see reg.2(1).
"statutory paternity pay"—see *ibid.*

Provision of information relating to entitlement to statutory paternity pay or statutory adoption pay

11.—(1) Where an employer who has been given evidence of entitlement to statutory paternity pay or statutory adoption pay pursuant to regulations made under section 171ZC(3)(c) or section 171ZL(8)(c) of the Contributions and Benefits Act by a person who is or has been an employee decides that he has no liability to make payments of statutory paternity pay or statutory adoption pay to the employee, the employer shall furnish the employee with details of the decision and the reasons for it.

(2) Where an employer who has been given such evidence of entitlement to statutory adoption pay has made one or more payments of statutory adoption pay to the employee but decides, before the end of the adoption pay period, that he has no liability to make further payments to the employee because he has been detained in legal custody or sentenced to a term of imprisonment which was not suspended, the employer shall furnish the employee with—
(a) details of his decision and the reasons for it; and
(b) details of the last week in respect of which a liability to pay statutory adoption pay arose and the total number of weeks within the adoption pay period in which such a liability arose.

(3) The employer shall—
(a) return to the employee any evidence provided by him as referred to in paragraph (1) or (2); and
(b) comply with the requirements imposed by paragraph (1) within 28 days of—
   (i) in the case of entitlement to statutory paternity pay under section 171ZA(1) of the Contributions and Benefits Act, the day the employee gave notice of his intended absence or the end of the fifteenth week before the expected week of birth, whichever is the later; or
   (ii) in the case of entitlement to statutory paternity pay under section 171ZB(1) or of statutory adoption pay under section 171ZL(1) of the Contributions and Benefits Act, the end of the seven-day period that starts on the date on which the adopter is notified of having been matched with the child;

(c) comply with the requirements imposed by paragraph (2) within seven days of being notified of the employee's detention or sentence.

(4) For the purposes of paragraph (3)(b)(ii), an adopter is notified of having been matched with a child on the date on which he receives notification, under regulation 11(2) of the Adoption Agencies Regulations 1983 or [1 regulation 8(5) of the Adoption Agencies (Scotland) Regulations 2009] that an adoption agency has decided that he would be a suitable adoptive parent for the child.

[2 (4) For the purposes of paragraph (3)(b)(ii), an adopter is notified as having been matched with a child—
   (a) on the date that person receives notification of the adoption agency's decision under regulation 33(3)(a) of the Adoption Agencies Regulations 2005, regulation 28(3) of the Adoption Agencies (Wales) Regulations 2005 or regulation 8(5) of the Adoption Agencies (Scotland) Regulations 2009; or
   (b) on the date on which that person receives notification in accordance with regulation 12B(2)(a) of the Adoption Agencies Regulations 2005.

(5) In this regulation "adoption agency" has the meaning given, in relation to England and Wales, by section 2 of the Adoption and Children Act 2002 and, in relation to Scotland, by section 119(1) of the Adoption and Children (Scotland) Act 2007.]

AMENDMENTS

1. Adoption and Children (Scotland) Act 2007 (Consequential Modifications) Order 2011 (SI 2011/1740) art.2 and Sch.1 para.31 (July 15, 2011).

2. Statutory Paternity Pay and Statutory Adoption Pay (Parental Orders and Prospective Adopters) Regulations 2014 (SI 2014/2934) reg.11 (December 1, 2014, but have effect only in relation to children matched with a person who is notified of having been matched on or after April 5, 2015).

DEFINITIONS

"adopter"—see reg.2(1).
"adoption pay period"—see *ibid.*
"the Contributions and Benefits Act"—see *ibid.*
"statutory adoption pay"—see *ibid.*
"statutory paternity pay"—see *ibid.*

GENERAL NOTE

6.29   This regulation is modified for the purposes of adoptions from overseas by the Statutory Paternity Pay (Adoption) and Statutory Adoption Pay (Adoptions from Overseas) (Administration) Regulations 2003 (SI 2003/1192). The versions of paras (4) and (5) in italics have effect only in relation to children matched with a person who is notified of having been matched on or after April 5, 2015 (Statutory Paternity Pay and Statutory Adoption Pay (Parental Orders and Prospective Adopters) Regulations 2014 (SI 2014/2934) reg.3).

(SI 2002/2820 reg.12)

Application for the determination of any issue arising as to, or in connection with, entitlement to statutory paternity pay or statutory adoption pay

12.—(1) An application for the determination of any issue arising as to, or in connection with, entitlement to statutory paternity pay or statutory adoption pay may be submitted to an officer of the Board by the employee concerned.

(2) Such an issue shall be decided by an officer of the Board only on the basis of such an application or on his own initiative.

DEFINITIONS

"the Board"—see reg.2(1).
"statutory adoption pay"—see *ibid.*
"statutory paternity pay"—see *ibid.*

Applications in connection with statutory paternity pay or statutory adoption pay

13.—(1) An application for the determination of any issue referred to in regulation 12 shall be made in a form approved for the purpose by the Board.

(2) Where such an application is made by an employee, it shall—
(a) be made to an officer of the Board within six months of the earliest day in respect of which entitlement to statutory paternity pay or statutory adoption pay is in issue;
(b) state the period in respect of which entitlement to statutory paternity pay or statutory adoption pay is in issue; and
(c) state the grounds (if any) on which the applicant's employer had denied liability for statutory paternity pay or statutory adoption pay in respect of the period specified in the application.

DEFINITIONS

"the Board"—see reg.2(1).
"statutory adoption pay"—see *ibid.*
"statutory paternity pay"—see *ibid.*

Provision of information

14.—(1) Any person specified in paragraph (2) shall, where information or documents are reasonably required from him to ascertain whether statutory paternity pay or statutory adoption pay is or was payable, furnish that information or those documents within 30 days of receiving a notification from an officer of the Board requesting such information or documents.

(2) The requirement to provide such information or documents applies to—
(a) any person claiming to be entitled to statutory paternity pay or statutory adoption pay;
(b) any person who is, or has been, the spouse [¹, the civil partner] or partner of such a person as is specified in paragraph (a);
(c) any person who is, or has been, an employer of such a person as is specified in paragraph (a);

Statutory Paternity Pay and Statutory Adoption Pay Regulations 2002

(d) any person carrying on an agency or other business for the introduction or supply to persons requiring them of persons available to do work or to perform services; and
(e) any person who is a servant or agent of any such person as is specified in paragraphs (a) to (d).

DEFINITIONS

"the Board"—see reg.2(1).
"statutory adoption pay"—see *ibid.*
"statutory paternity pay"—see *ibid.*

AMENDMENT

1. Civil Partnership Act 2004 (Amendments to Subordinate Legislation) Order 2005 (SI 2005/2114) art.2(17) and Sch.17 para.2 (December 5, 2005).

Statutory Paternity Pay and Statutory Adoption Pay (Persons Abroad and Mariners) Regulations 2002

(SI 2002/2821) (AS AMENDED)

The Secretary of State, in exercise of the powers conferred upon her by virtue of sections 171ZI, 171ZJ(1), 171ZR and 171ZS(1) of the Social Security Contributions and Benefits Act 1992 and with the concurrence of the Treasury, by this instrument, which contains only provision made by virtue of sections 2 and 4 of the Employment Act 2002 and is made before the end of the period of 6 months from the coming into force of those enactments, hereby makes the following Regulations:

ARRANGEMENT OF REGULATIONS

6.33
1. Citation, commencement and interpretation.
2. Restriction on scope.
3. Treatment of persons in other EEA States as employees.
4. Treatment of certain persons absent from Great Britain as employees.
5. Entitlement to ordinary statutory paternity pay and additional statutory paternity pay where person has worked in an EEA State.
6. Entitlement to ordinary statutory adoption pay and additional statutory paternity paywhere person has worked in an EEA State.
7. Time for compliance with Parts XIIZA and XIIZB of the Act or regulations made under them.
8. Mariners.
9. Continental Shelf.
Schedule.

Citation, commencement and interpretation

6.34
1.—(1) These Regulations may be cited as the Statutory Paternity Pay and Statutory Adoption Pay (Persons Abroad and Mariners) Regulations 2002 and shall come into force on 8th December 2002.
(2) In these Regulations—
"the Act" means the Social Security Contributions and Benefits Act 1992;

(SI 2002/2821 reg.1) (as amended)

[¹ [³. . .]]
[¹ [² "adopter", in relation to a child, means the person with whom a child is, or is expected to be, placed for adoption under the law of the United Kingdom;]]
"the Contributions Regulations" means the Social Security Contributions Regulations 2001;
"EEA" means European Economic Area;
"EEA Agreement" means the Agreement on the European Economic Area signed at Oporto on 2nd May 1992 as adjusted by Protocol signed at Brussels on 17th March 1993;
"EEA State" means a State which is a contracting party to the EEA Agreement;
[¹ "foreign-going ship" means any ship or vessel which is not a home-trade ship;]
"the General Regulations" means the Statutory Paternity Pay and Statutory Adoption Pay (General) Regulations 2002;
[¹ "home-trade ship" includes—
 (a) every ship or vessel employed in trading or going within the following limits, that is to say, the United Kingdom (including for this purpose the Republic of Ireland), the Channel Islands, the Isle of Man, and the continent of Europe between the river Elbe and Brest inclusive;
 (b) every fishing vessel not proceeding beyond the following limits—
   on the South, Latitude 48°30'N,
   on the West, Longitude 12°W, and
   on the North, Latitude 61°N;
"mariner" means a person who is or has been in employment under a contract of service either as a master or member of the crew of any ship or vessel, or in any other capacity on board any ship or vessel where—
 (a) the employment in that other capacity is for the purposes of that ship or vessel or her crew or any passengers or cargo or mails carried by the ship or vessel; and
 (b) the contract is entered into in the United Kingdom with a view to its performance (in whole or in part) while the ship or vessel is on her voyage;
but does not include a person in so far as their employment is as a serving member of the forces;
"[³. . .] statutory paternity pay (adoption)" means statutory paternity pay payable in accordance with the provisions of Part 12ZA of the Act where the conditions specified in section 171ZB(2) of the Act are satisfied;
"[³. . .] statutory paternity pay (birth)" means statutory paternity pay payable in accordance with the provisions of Part 12ZA of the Act where the conditions specified in section 171ZA(2) of the Act are satisfied;
[² "placed for adoption" means—
(a) placed for adoption under the Adoption and Children Act 2002 or the Adoption and Children (Scotland) Act 2007; or
(b) placed in accordance with section 22C of the Children Act 1989 with a local authority foster parent who is also a prospective adopter;]

"serving member of the forces" means a person, other than one mentioned in Part 2 of the Schedule, who, being over the age of 16, is a member of any establishment or organisation specified in Part 1 of that Schedule (being a member who gives full pay service) but does not include any such person while absent on desertion;]

"week" means a period of 7 days beginning with Sunday.

[¹ [² (3) For the purposes of these Regulations—
(a) a person is matched with a child for adoption when an adoption agency decides that that person would be a suitable adoptive parent for the child;
(b) in a case where paragraph (a) applies, a person is notified as having been matched with a child on the date that person receives notification of the agency's decision, under regulation 33(3)(a) of the Adoption Agencies Regulations 2005, regulation 28(3) of the Adoption Agencies (Wales) Regulations 2005 or regulation 8(5) of the Adoption Agencies (Scotland) Regulations 2009;
(c) a person is also matched with a child for adoption when a decision has been made in accordance with regulation 22A of the Care Planning, Placement and Case Review (England) Regulations 2010 and an adoption agency has identified that person with whom the child is to be placed in accordance with regulation 12B of the Adoption Agencies Regulations 2005;
(d) in a case where paragraph (c) applies, a person is notified as having been matched with a child on the date on which that person receives notification in accordance with regulation 12B(2)(a) of the Adoption Agencies Regulations 2005.

(3A) The reference to "prospective adopter" in the definition of "placed for adoption" in paragraph (2) means a person who has been approved as suitable to adopt a child and has been notified of that decision in accordance with regulation 30B(4) of the Adoption Agencies Regulations 2005.

(3B) The reference to "adoption agency" in paragraph (3) has the meaning given, in relation to England and Wales, by section 2 of the Adoption and Children Act 2002 and in relation to Scotland, by section 119(1) of the Adoption and Children (Scotland) Act 2007.]

[¹ (4) For the purposes of these Regulations, the expressions "ship" and "ship or vessel" include hovercraft, except in regulation 8(3).]

AMENDMENTS

1. Statutory Paternity Pay and Statutory Adoption Pay (Persons Abroad and Mariners) Regulations 2002 (Amendment) Regulations 2010 (SI 2010/151) reg.3 (April 6, 2010).
2. Statutory Shared Parental Pay (Persons Abroad and Mariners) Regulations 2014 (SI 2014/3134) regs 12–14 (December 1, 2014).
3. Shared Parental Leave and Statutory Shared Parental Pay (Consequential Amendments to Subordinate Legislation) Order 2014 (SI 2014/3255) reg.13(2) (April 5, 2015).

GENERAL NOTE

6.35   These Regulations modify Pts XIIZA and XIIZB of the SSCBA 1992, which govern statutory paternity pay and statutory adoption pay respectively, in relation to persons abroad, those who work as mariners and persons who work on the Continental Shelf. They are modified in relation to adoptions from overseas by the

(SI 2002/2821 reg.1) (as amended)

Statutory Paternity Pay (Adoption) and Statutory Adoption Pay (Adoptions from Overseas) (Persons Abroad and Mariners) Regulations 2003 (SI 2003/1193).

Restriction on scope

2. A person who would not be treated under regulation 32 of the General Regulations as an employee for the purposes of Parts 12ZA [¹ ([³. . .] statutory paternity pay)] and 12ZB (statutory adoption pay) of the Act if his employment were in Great Britain shall not be treated as an employee under these Regulations.

AMENDMENTS

1. Statutory Paternity Pay and Statutory Adoption Pay (Persons Abroad and Mariners) Regulations 2002 (Amendment) Regulations 2010 (SI 2010/151) reg.4 (April 6, 2010).
2. Shared Parental Leave and Statutory Shared Parental Pay (Consequential Amendments to Subordinate Legislation) Order 2014 (SI 2014/3255) reg.13(3) (April 5, 2015).

DEFINITIONS

"the Act"—see reg.1(2).
"the General Regulations"—see *ibid.*

Treatment of persons in other EEA States as employees

3. A person who is—
   (a) gainfully employed in an EEA State other than the United Kingdom in such circumstances that, if his employment were in Great Britain, he would be an employee for the purposes of Parts 12ZA and 12ZB of the Act, or a person treated as such an employee under regulation 32 of the General Regulations; and
   (b) subject to the legislation of the United Kingdom under Council Regulation (EEC) No.1408/71,
notwithstanding that he is not employed in Great Britain, shall be treated as an employee for the purposes of Parts 12ZA and 12ZB of the Act.

DEFINITIONS

"the Act"—see reg.1(2).
"EEA"—see *ibid.*
"EEA State"—see *ibid.*
"the General Regulations"—see *ibid.*

Treatment of certain persons absent from Great Britain as employees

4. Subject to regulation 8(3), where a person, while absent from Great Britain for any purpose, is gainfully employed by an employer who is liable to pay secondary Class 1 contributions in respect of his employment under section 6 of the Act or regulation 146 of the Contributions Regulations, he shall be treated as an employee for the purposes of Parts 12ZA and 12ZB of the Act.

DEFINITIONS

"the Act"—see reg.1(2).
"the Contributions Regulations"—see *ibid.*

Statutory Paternity Pay and Statutory Adoption Pay Regulations 2002

[¹ Entitlement to [² statutory paternity pay] where person has worked in an EEA State

6.39

5.—(1) A person who is an employee or treated as an employee under regulation 3 and who—
  (a) in the week immediately preceding the 14th week before the expected week of the child's birth was in employed earner's employment with an employer in Great Britain; and
  (b) had in any week within the period of 26 weeks immediately preceding that week been employed by the same employer in another EEA State,

shall be treated for the purposes of section 171ZA of the Act [² (entitlement to statutory paternity pay (birth))] [². . .] as having been employed in employed earner's employment in those weeks in which the person was so employed in the other EEA State.

(2) A person who is an employee or treated as an employee under regulation 3 and who—
  (a) in the week in which the adopter is notified of being matched with the child for purposes of adoption was in employed earner's employment with an employer in Great Britain; and
  (b) had in any week within the period of 26 weeks immediately preceding that week been employed by the same employer in another EEA State,

shall be treated for the purposes of section 171ZB of the Act [² (entitlement to statutory paternity pay (adoption))] [². . .] as having been employed in employed earner's employment in those weeks in which the person was so employed in the other EEA State.]

AMENDMENTS

1. Statutory Paternity Pay and Statutory Adoption Pay (Persons Abroad and Mariners) Regulations 2002 (Amendment) Regulations 2010 (SI 2010/151) reg.5 (April 6, 2010).
2. Shared Parental Leave and Statutory Shared Parental Pay (Consequential Amendments to Subordinate Legislation) Order 2014 (SI 2014/3255) reg.13(4) (April 5, 2015).

DEFINITIONS

"the Act"—see reg.1(2).
"adopter"—see *ibid.*
"EEA"—see *ibid.*
"EEA State"—see *ibid.*
"statutory paternity pay (adoption)"—see *ibid.*
"statutory paternity pay (birth)"—see *ibid.*
"week"—see *ibid.*

Entitlement to statutory adoption pay where person has worked in an EEA State

6.40

6. A person who is an employee or treated as an employee under regulation 3 and who—
  (a) in the week in which he is notified that he has been matched with the child for the purposes of adoption was in employed earner's employment with an employer in Great Britain; and

(b) had in any week within the period of 26 weeks immediately preceding that week been employed by the same employer in another EEA State,

shall be treated for the purposes of section 171ZL of the Act (entitlement to statutory adoption pay) as having been employed in employed earner's employment in those weeks in which he was so employed in the other EEA State.

DEFINITIONS

"the Act"—see reg.1(2).
"EEA"—see *ibid.*
"EEA State"—see *ibid.*
"week"—see *ibid.*

Time for compliance with Parts 12ZA and 12ZB of the Act or regulations made under them

7. Where—
(a) a person is outside the United Kingdom;
(b) Parts 12ZA or 12ZB of the Act or regulations made under them require any act to be done forthwith or on the happening of a certain event or within a specified time; and
(c) because the person is outside the United Kingdom he or his employer cannot comply with the requirement,

the person or the employer, as the case may be, shall be deemed to have complied with it if the act is performed as soon as reasonably practicable.

DEFINITION

"the Act"—see reg.1(2).

Mariners

8.—(1) [¹ . . .]

(2) A mariner engaged in employment on board a home-trade ship with an employer who has a place of business within the United Kingdom shall be treated as an employee for the purposes of Parts 12ZA and 12ZB of the Act, notwithstanding that he may not be employed in Great Britain.

(3) A mariner who is engaged in employment—
(a) on a foreign-going ship; or
(b) on a home-trade ship with an employer who does not have a place of business within the United Kingdom,

shall not be treated as an employee for the purposes of Parts 12ZA and 12ZB of the Act, notwithstanding that he may have been employed in Great Britain.

AMENDMENT

1. Statutory Paternity Pay and Statutory Adoption Pay (Persons Abroad and Mariners) Regulations 2002 (Amendment) Regulations 2010 (SI 2010/151) reg.6 (April 6, 2010).

Statutory Paternity Pay and Statutory Adoption Pay Regulations 2002

DEFINITIONS

"the Act"—see reg.1(2).
"the Contributions Regulations"—see *ibid*.
"foreign-going ship"—see reg.1(2).
"home-trade ship"—see *ibid*.
"mariner"—see *ibid*.
"ship"—see *ibid*.
"ship or vessel"—see *ibid*.

Continental shelf

6.43

9.—(1) In this regulation—
"designated area" means any area which may from time to time be designated by Order in Council under section 1(7) of the Continental Shelf Act 1964 as an area within which the rights of the United Kingdom with respect to the seabed and subsoil and their natural resources may be exercised;
"prescribed employment" means any employment (whether under a contract of service or not) in a designated area in connection with continental shelf operations, as defined in section 120(2) of the Act.
(2) A person in prescribed employment shall be treated as an employee for the purposes of Parts 12ZA and 12ZB of the Act notwithstanding that he may not be employed in Great Britain.

DEFINITIONS

"the Act"—see reg.1(2).
"designated area"—see para.(1).
"prescribed employment"—see *ibid*.

[¹ SCHEDULE

PART 1

Establishments and organisations

6.44

1. Any of the regular naval, military or air forces of the Crown.
2. Royal Fleet Reserve.
3. Royal Naval Reserve.
4. Royal Marines Reserve.
5. Army Reserve.
6. Territorial Army.
7. Royal Air Force Reserve.
8. Royal Auxiliary Air Force.
9. The Royal Irish Regiment, to the extent that its members are not members of any force falling within paragraph 1.

(SI 2002/2821 reg.10) (as amended)

Part 2

Establishments and organisations of which Her Majesty's Forces shall not consist

10. Her Majesty's forces shall not be taken to consist of any of the establishments or organisations specified in Part 1 of this Schedule by virtue only of the employment in such establishment or organisation of the following persons—

(a) any person who is serving as a member of any naval force of Her Majesty's Forces and who (not having been an insured person under the National Insurance Act 1965 and not being a contributor under the Social Security Act 1975 or the Social Security Contributions and Benefits Act 1992) locally entered that force at an overseas base;

(b) any person who is serving as a member of any military force of Her Majesty's forces and who entered that force, or was recruited for that force outside the United Kingdom, and the depot of whose unit is situated outside the United Kingdom;

(c) any person who is serving as a member of any air force of Her Majesty's forces and who entered that force, or was recruited for that force, outside the United Kingdom, and is liable under the terms of his engagement to serve only in a specified part of the world outside the United Kingdom.]

6.45

Amendment

1. Statutory Paternity Pay and Statutory Adoption Pay (Persons Abroad and Mariners) Regulations 2002 (Amendment) Regulations 2010 (SI 2010/151) reg.7 and Sch. (April 6, 2010).

Note: the following version of the Statutory Paternity Pay and Statutory Adoption Pay (Persons Abroad and Mariners) Regulations 2002 (SI 2002/2821) is that as amended by the Ordinary Statutory Paternity Pay (Adoption), Additional Statutory Paternity Pay (Adoption) and Statutory Adoption Pay (Adoptions from Overseas) (Persons Abroad and Mariners) Regulations 2010 (SI 2010/150), which came into force on April 6, 2010 immediately after the coming into force of the Statutory Paternity Pay and Statutory Adoption Pay (Persons Abroad and Mariners) Regulations 2002 (Amendment) Regulations 2010 (SI 2010/151).

Statutory Paternity Pay and Statutory Adoption Pay (Persons Abroad and Mariners) Regulations 2002

(SI 2002/2821, AS AMENDED)

The Secretary of State, in exercise of the powers conferred upon her by virtue of sections 171ZI, 171ZJ(1), 171ZR and 171ZS(1) of the Social Security Contributions and Benefits Act 1992 and with the concurrence of the Treasury, by this instrument, which contains only provision made by virtue of sections 2 and 4 of the Employment Act 2002 and is made before the end of the period of 6

Statutory Paternity Pay and Statutory Adoption Pay Regulations 2002

months from the coming into force of those enactments, hereby makes the following Regulations:

Citation, commencement and interpretation

6.46   **1.**—(1) These Regulations may be cited as the Statutory Paternity Pay and Statutory Adoption Pay (Persons Abroad and Mariners) Regulations 2002 and shall come into force on 8th December 2002.

(2) In these Regulations—

"the Act" means the Social Security Contributions and Benefits Act 1992;

[¹ "additional statutory paternity pay (adoption)" means additional statutory paternity pay payable in accordance with the provisions of Part 12ZA of the Act where the conditions specified in section 171ZEB(2) of the Act are satisfied;

[². . .]]

[¹ [² "adopter", in relation to a child adopted from overseas, means—
  (a) a person by whom the child has been or is to be adopted, or
  (b) in a case where the child has been or is to be adopted by two people jointly, whichever of them has elected to take adoption leave under section 75A or 75B of the Employment Rights Act 1996 in respect of the child;]

"the Contributions Regulations" means the Social Security Contributions Regulations 2001;

"EEA" means European Economic Area;

"EEA Agreement" means the Agreement on the European Economic Area signed at Oporto on 2nd May 1992 as adjusted by Protocol signed at Brussels on 17th March 1993;

"EEA State" means a State which is a contracting party to the EEA Agreement;

[¹ "foreign-going ship" means any ship or vessel which is not a home-trade ship;]

"the General Regulations" means the Statutory Paternity Pay and Statutory Adoption Pay (General) Regulations 2002;

[¹. . .]

[¹ "home-trade ship" includes—
  (a) every ship or vessel employed in trading or going within the following limits, that is to say, the United Kingdom (including for this purpose the Republic of Ireland), the Channel Islands, the Isle of Man, and the continent of Europe between the river Elbe and Brest inclusive;
  (b) every fishing vessel not proceeding beyond the following limits—
on the South, Latitude 48°30'N,
on the West, Longitude 12°W, and
on the North, Latitude 61°N;

"mariner" means a person who is or has been in employment under a contract of service either as a master or member of the crew of any ship or vessel, or in any other capacity on board any ship or vessel where—
  (a) the employment in that other capacity is for the purposes of that ship or vessel or her crew or any passengers or cargo or mails carried by the ship or vessel; and
  (b) the contract is entered into in the United Kingdom with a view to its performance (in whole or in part) while the ship or vessel is on her voyage;
but does not include a person in so far as their employment is as a serving member of the forces;

(SI 2002/2821 reg.1) (as amended)

[² "official notification" means written notification, issued by or on behalf of the relevant central authority, that it is prepared to issue a certificate to the overseas authority concerned with the adoption of the child, or has issued a certificate and sent it to that authority, confirming, in either case, that the adopter is eligible to adopt and has been assessed and approved as being a suitable adoptive parent;]

"ordinary statutory paternity pay (adoption)" means statutory paternity pay payable in accordance with the provisions of Part 12ZA of the Act where the conditions specified in section 171ZB(2) of the Act are satisfied;

[² relevant central authority" means—
 (a) in the case of an adopter to whom Part 3 the Adoptions with a Foreign Element Regulations 2005 apply and who is habitually resident in Wales, the Welsh Ministers;
 (b) in the case of an adopter to whom [³ . . .] the Adoptions with a Foreign Element (Scotland) Regulations 2009 apply and who is habitually resident in Scotland, the Scottish Ministers; and
 (c) in any other case, the Secretary of State;]

[². . .];

"serving member of the forces" means a person, other than one mentioned in Part 2 of the Schedule, who, being over the age of 16, is a member of any establishment or organisation specified in Part 1 of that Schedule (being a member who gives full pay service) but does not include any such person while absent on desertion;]

"week" means a period of 7 days beginning with Sunday.

[¹ [² (3) References in these Regulations to provisions of Parts 12ZA and 12ZB of the Act are to be construed as references to those provisions as modified by the Social Security Contributions and Benefits Act 1992 (Application of Parts 12ZA and 12ZB to Adoptions from Overseas) Regulations 2003.]]

[¹ (4) For the purposes of these Regulations, the expressions "ship" and "ship or vessel" include hovercraft, except in regulation 8(3).]

AMENDMENTS

1. Statutory Paternity Pay and Statutory Adoption Pay (Persons Abroad and Mariners) Regulations 2002 (Amendment) Regulations 2010 (SI 2010/151) reg.3 (April 6, 2010).
2. Ordinary Statutory Paternity Pay (Adoption), Additional Statutory Paternity Pay (Adoption) and Statutory Adoption Pay (Adoptions from Overseas) (Persons Abroad and Mariners) Regulations 2010 (SI 2010/150) reg.4(2) and (3) (April 6, 2010).
3. Adoption and Children (Scotland) Act 2007 (Consequential Modifications) Order 2011 (SI 2011/1740) art.3 and Sch.2 Pt 3 (July 15, 2011).

Restriction on scope

2. *A person who would not be treated under regulation 32 of the General Regulations as an employee for the purposes of Parts 12ZA [¹ (ordinary and additional statutory paternity pay)] and 12ZB (statutory adoption pay) of the Act if his employment were in Great Britain shall not be treated as an employee under these Regulations.*

6.47

AMENDMENT

1. Statutory Paternity Pay and Statutory Adoption Pay (Persons Abroad and Mariners) Regulations 2002 (Amendment) Regulations 2010 (SI 2010/151) reg.4 (April 6, 2010).

Statutory Paternity Pay and Statutory Adoption Pay Regulations 2002

Treatment of persons in other EEA States as employees

6.48   3. A person who is—
(a) gainfully employed in an EEA State other than the United Kingdom in such circumstances that, if his employment were in Great Britain, he would be an employee for the purposes of Parts 12ZA and 12ZB of the Act, or a person treated as such an employee under regulation 32 of the General Regulations; and
(b) subject to the legislation of the United Kingdom under Council Regulation (EEC) No. 1408/71,
notwithstanding that he is not employed in Great Britain, shall be treated as an employee for the purposes of Parts 12ZA and 12ZB of the Act.

Treatment of certain persons absent from Great Britain as employees

6.49   4. Subject to regulation 8(3), where a person, while absent from Great Britain for any purpose, is gainfully employed by an employer who is liable to pay secondary Class 1 contributions in respect of his employment under section 6 of the Act or regulation 146 of the Contributions Regulations, he shall be treated as an employee for the purposes of Parts 12ZA and 12ZB of the Act.

[¹ Entitlement to ordinary statutory paternity pay and additional statutory paternity pay where person has worked in an EEA State

6.50   5.—(1) [². . .]
(2) A person who is an employee or treated as an employee under regulation 3 and who, [² in the week in which the person receives an official notification or completes 26 weeks' continuous employment with the person's employer, whichever is the later]—
(a) [². . .] was in employed earner's employment with an employer in Great Britain; and
(b) had in any week within the period of 26 weeks immediately preceding that week been employed by the same employer in another EEA State,
shall be treated for the purposes of section 171ZB of the Act (entitlement to ordinary statutory paternity pay (adoption)) and section 171ZEB of the Act (entitlement to additional statutory paternity pay (adoption)) as having been employed in employed earner's employment in those weeks in which the person was so employed in the other EEA State.]

AMENDMENT

1. Statutory Paternity Pay and Statutory Adoption Pay (Persons Abroad and Mariners) Regulations 2002 (Amendment) Regulations 2010 (SI 2010/151) reg.5 (April 6, 2010).
2. Ordinary Statutory Paternity Pay (Adoption), Additional Statutory Paternity Pay (Adoption) and Statutory Adoption Pay (Adoptions from Overseas) (Persons Abroad and Mariners) Regulations 2010 (SI 2010/150) reg.4(4) (April 6, 2010).

Entitlement to statutory adoption pay where person has worked in an EEA State

6.51   6. A person who is an employee or treated as an employee under regulation 3 and who [¹ , in the week in which the person receives an official notification or

(SI 2002/2821 reg.6) (as amended)

completes 26 weeks' continuous employment with the person's employer, whichever is the later]—
(a) [¹. . .] was in employed earner's employment with an employer in Great Britain; and
(b) had in any week within the period of 26 weeks immediately preceding that week been employed by the same employer in another EEA State,
shall be treated for the purposes of section 171ZL of the Act (entitlement to statutory adoption pay) as having been employed in employed earner's employment in those weeks in which [1 the person] was so employed in the other EEA State.

AMENDMENT

1. Ordinary Statutory Paternity Pay (Adoption), Additional Statutory Paternity Pay (Adoption) and Statutory Adoption Pay (Adoptions from Overseas) (Persons Abroad and Mariners) Regulations 2010 (SI 2010/150) reg.4(5) (April 6, 2010).

Time for compliance with Parts 12ZA and 12ZB of the Act or regulations made under them

7. Where— 6.52
(a) a person is outside the United Kingdom;
(b) Parts 12ZA or 12ZB of the Act or regulations made under them require any act to be done forthwith or on the happening of a certain event or within a specified time; and
(c) because the person is outside the United Kingdom he or his employer cannot comply with the requirement,
the person or the employer, as the case may be, shall be deemed to have complied with it if the act is performed as soon as reasonably practicable.

Mariners

8.—(1) [¹. . .] 6.53
(2) A mariner engaged in employment on board a home-trade ship with an employer who has a place of business within the United Kingdom shall be treated as an employee for the purposes of Parts 12ZA and 12ZB of the Act, notwithstanding that he may not be employed in Great Britain.
(3) A mariner who is engaged in employment—
(a) on a foreign-going ship; or
(b) on a home-trade ship with an employer who does not have a place of business within the United Kingdom,
shall not be treated as an employee for the purposes of Parts 12ZA and 12ZB of the Act, notwithstanding that he may have been employed in Great Britain.

AMENDMENT

1. Statutory Paternity Pay and Statutory Adoption Pay (Persons Abroad and Mariners) Regulations 2002 (Amendment) Regulations 2010 (SI 2010/151) reg.6 (April 6, 2010).

Continental shelf

9.—(1) In this regulation— 6.54
"designated area" means any area which may from time to time be designated by Order in Council under section 1(7) of the Continental Shelf Act 1964 as an area within which the rights of the United Kingdom with

Statutory Paternity Pay and Statutory Adoption Pay Regulations 2002

respect to the seabed and subsoil and their natural resources may be exercised;

"prescribed employment" means any employment (whether under a contract of service or not) in a designated area in connection with continental shelf operations, as defined in section 120(2) of the Act.

(2) A person in prescribed employment shall be treated as an employee for the purposes of Parts 12ZA and 12ZB of the Act notwithstanding that he may not be employed in Great Britain.

[¹ SCHEDULE

PART 1

Establishments and organisations

6.55

1. Any of the regular naval, military or air forces of the Crown.
2. Royal Fleet Reserve.
3. Royal Naval Reserve.
4. Royal Marines Reserve.
5. Army Reserve.
6. Territorial Army.
7. Royal Air Force Reserve.
8. Royal Auxiliary Air Force.
9. The Royal Irish Regiment, to the extent that its members are not members of any force falling within paragraph 1.

PART 2

Establishments and organisations of which Her Majesty's Forces shall not consist

6.56

10. Her Majesty's forces shall not be taken to consist of any of the establishments or organisations specified in Part 1 of this Schedule by virtue only of the employment in such establishment or organisation of the following persons—
  (a) any person who is serving as a member of any naval force of Her Majesty's forces and who (not having been an insured person under the National Insurance Act 1965 and not being a contributor under the Social Security Act 1975 or the Social Security Contributions and Benefits Act 1992) locally entered that force at an overseas base;
  (b) any person who is serving as a member of any military force of Her Majesty's forces and who entered that force, or was recruited for that force outside the United Kingdom, and the depot of whose unit is situated outside the United Kingdom;
  (c) any person who is serving as a member of any air force of Her Majesty's forces and who entered that force, or was recruited for that force, outside the United Kingdom, and is liable under the terms of his engagement to serve only in a specified part of the world outside the United Kingdom.]

(SI 2002/2821 reg.10) (as amended)

AMENDMENT

1. Statutory Paternity Pay and Statutory Adoption Pay (Persons Abroad and Mariners) Regulations 2002 (Amendment) Regulations 2010 (SI 2010/151) reg.7 and Sch. (April 6, 2010).

Statutory Paternity Pay and Statutory Adoption Pay (General) Regulations 2002

(SI 2002/2822) (AS AMENDED)

The Secretary of State, in exercise of the powers conferred on her by sections 171ZA(2)(a), 171ZB(2)(a), 171ZC(3)(a), (c), (d), (f) and (g), 171ZD(2) and (3), 171ZE(2)(a), (b)(i), (3), (7) and (8), 171ZG(3), 171ZJ(1), (3), (4), (7) and (8), 171ZL(8)(b) to (d), (f) and (g), 171ZM(2) and (3), 171ZN(2), (5) and (6), 171ZP(6), 171ZS(1), (3), (4), (7) and (8), and 175(4) of the Social Security Contributions and Benefits Act 1992 and section 5(1)(g), (i) and (p) of the Social Security Administration Act 1992 and with the concurrence of the Commissioners of Inland Revenue in so far as such concurrence is required, by this instrument, which contains only provision made by virtue of sections 2, 4 and 53 of and paragraphs 8 and 11 of Schedule 7 to the Employment Act 2002 and is made before the end of the period of 6 months from the coming into force of those enactments, hereby makes the following Regulations—

ARRANGEMENT OF REGULATIONS

PART 1

Introduction

1. Citation and commencement.
2. Interpretation.
3. Application.

6.57

PART 2

Statutory paternity pay (birth)

4. Conditions of entitlement to statutory paternity pay (birth): relationship with newborn child and child's mother.
5. Modification of entitlement conditions: early birth.
5A. Notice of entitlement to statutory paternity pay (birth).
6. Period of payment of statutory paternity pay (birth).
7. Additional notice requirements for statutory paternity pay (birth).
8. Qualifying period for statutory paternity pay (birth).
9. Evidence of entitlement to statutory paternity pay (birth).
10. Entitlement to statutory paternity pay (birth) where there is more than one employer.

Statutory Paternity Pay and Statutory Adoption Pay (General) Regs 2002

PART 3

Statutory paternity pay (adoption)

11. Conditions of entitlement to statutory paternity pay (adoption): relationship with child and with person with whom the child is placed for adoption.
11A. Notice of entitlement to statutory paternity pay (adoption).
12. Period of payment of statutory paternity pay (adoption).
13. Additional notice requirements for statutory paternity pay (adoption).
14. Qualifying period for statutory paternity pay (adoption).
15. Evidence of entitlement to statutory paternity pay (adoption).
16. Entitlement to statutory paternity pay (adoption) where there is more than one employer.

PART 4

Statutory paternity pay: provisions applicable to both statutory paternity pay (birth) and statutory paternity pay (adoption)

17. Work during a statutory paternity pay period.
18. Cases where there is no liability to pay statutory paternity pay.
19. Statutory paternity pay and contractual remuneration.
20. Avoidance of liability for statutory paternity pay.

PART 5

Statutory adoption pay

21. Adoption pay period.
22. Adoption pay period in cases where adoption is disrupted.
23. Additional notice requirements for statutory adoption pay.
24. Evidence of entitlement to statutory adoption pay.
25. Entitlement to statutory adoption pay where there is more than one employer.
26. Work during an adoption pay period.
27. Cases where there is no liability to pay statutory adoption pay.
27A. Working for not more than 10 days during an adoption pay period.
28. Statutory adoption pay and contractual remuneration.
29. Termination of employment before start of adoption pay period.
30. Avoidance of liability for statutory adoption pay.

PART 6

Statutory paternity pay and statutory adoption pay: provisions applicable to both statutory paternity pay and statutory adoption pay

31. Introductory.
32. Treatment of persons as employees.

33. Continuous employment.
34. Continuous employment and unfair dismissal.
35. Continuous employment and stoppages of work.
36. Change of employer.
37. Reinstatement after service with the armed forces, etc.
38. Treatment of one or more employers or two or more contracts of service as one.
39. Meaning of "earnings".
40. Normal weekly earnings.
41. Payment of statutory paternity pay and statutory adoption pay.
42. Time when statutory paternity pay and statutory adoption pay are to be paid.
43. Liability of the Board to pay statutory paternity pay or statutory adoption pay.
44. Liability of the Board to pay statutory adoption pay in cases of legal custody or imprisonment.
45. Payments by the Board.
46. Persons unable to act.
47. Service of notices by post.

PART 1

INTRODUCTION

Citation and commencement

1. These Regulations may be cited as the Statutory Paternity Pay and Statutory Adoption Pay (General) Regulations 2002 and shall come into force on 8th December 2002.

Interpretation

2.—(1) In these Regulations—
"the Act" means the Social Security Contributions and Benefits Act 1992;
"adopter", in relation to a child, means a person who has been matched with the child for adoption;
"adoption agency" has the meaning given, in relation to England and Wales, by section 1(4) of the Adoption Act 1976 and in relation to Scotland, by [¹ section 119(1) of the Adoption and Children (Scotland) Act 2007];
"the Board" means the Commissioners of Inland Revenue;
"the Contributions Regulations" means the Social Security (Contributions) Regulations 2001;
"expected week", in relation to the birth of a child, means the week, beginning with midnight between Saturday and Sunday, in which it is expected that the child will be born;
"statutory paternity pay (adoption)" means statutory paternity pay payable in accordance with the provisions of Part 12ZA of the Act where the conditions specified in section 171ZB(2) of the Act are satisfied;
"statutory paternity pay (birth)" means statutory paternity pay payable in accordance with the provisions of Part 12ZA of the Act where the conditions specified in section 171ZA(2) of the Act are satisfied.
(2) For the purposes of these Regulations—

6.58

6.59

Statutory Paternity Pay and Statutory Adoption Pay (General) Regs 2002

(a) a person is matched with a child for adoption when an adoption agency decides that that person would be a suitable adoptive parent for the child, either individually or jointly with another person; and
(b) a person is notified of having been matched with a child on the date on which he receives notification of the agency's decision, under regulation 11(2) of the Adoption Agencies Regulations 1983 or [1 regulation 8(5) of the Adoption Agencies (Scotland) Regulations 2009].

[2 (2) For the purposes of these Regulations—
(a) a person is matched with a child for adoption when an adoption agency decides that that person would be a suitable adoptive parent for the child;
(b) in a case where paragraph (a) applies, a person is notified as having been matched with a child on the date that person receives notification of the agency's decision, under regulation 33(3)(a) of the Adoption Agencies Regulations 2005, regulation 28(3) of the Adoption Agencies (Wales) Regulations 2005 or regulation 8(5) of the Adoption Agencies (Scotland) Regulations 2009;
(c) a person is also matched with a child for adoption when a decision is has been made in accordance with regulation 22A of the Care Planning, Placement and Case Review (England) Regulations 2010 and an adoption agency has identified that person with whom the child is to be placed in accordance with regulation 12B of the Adoption Agencies Regulations 2005.
(d) in a case where paragraph (c) applies, a person is notified as having been matched with a child on the date on which that person receives notification in accordance with regulation 12B(2)(a) of the Adoption Agencies Regulations 2005.

(3) A reference (however expressed) in these Regulations to "placed for adoption" means—
(a) placed for adoption under the Adoption and Children Act 2002 or the Adoption and Children (Scotland) Act 2007; or
(b) placed in accordance with section 22C of the Children Act 1989 with a local authority foster parent who is also a prospective adopter.

(4) The reference to "prospective adopter" in paragraph (3) means a person who has been approved as suitable to adopt a child and has been notified of that decision in accordance with regulation 30B(4) of the Adoption Agencies Regulations 2005.]

AMENDMENTS

1. Adoption and Children (Scotland) Act 2007 (Consequential Modifications) Order 2011 (SI 2011/1740) art.2 and Sch.1 para.32(2) (July 15, 2011).
2. *Statutory Paternity Pay and Statutory Adoption Pay (Parental Orders and Prospective Adopters) Regulations 2014 (SI 2014/2934) reg.4 (December 1, 2014, but have effect only in relation to children matched with a person who is notified of having been matched on or after April 5, 2015).*

GENERAL NOTE

6.60 The versions of paras (2) to (4) in italics have effect only in relation to children matched with a person who is notified of having been matched on or after April 5, 2015 (Statutory Paternity Pay and Statutory Adoption Pay (Parental Orders and Prospective Adopters) Regulations 2014 (SI 2014/2934) reg.3).

(SI 2002/2822 reg.2) (as amended)

Application

3.(1) Subject to the provisions of Part 12ZA of the Act (statutory paternity pay) and of these Regulations, there is entitlement to—
(a) statutory paternity pay (birth) in respect of children—
  (i) born on or after 6th April 2003; or
  (ii) whose expected week of birth begins on or after that date;
(b) statutory paternity pay (adoption) in respect of children—
  (i) matched with a person who is notified of having been matched on or after 6th April 2003; or
  (ii) placed for adoption on or after that date.
(2) Subject to the provisions of Part 12ZB of the Act (statutory adoption pay) and of these Regulations, there is entitlement to statutory adoption pay in respect of children—
(a) matched with a person who is notified of having been matched on or after 6th April 2003; or
(b) placed for adoption on or after that date.

DEFINITIONS

"the Act"—see reg.2(1).
"expected week"—see *ibid.*
"statutory paternity pay (adoption)"—see *ibid.*
"statutory paternity pay (birth)"—see *ibid.*

PART 2

STATUTORY PATERNITY PAY (BIRTH)

Conditions of entitlement to statutory paternity pay (birth): relationship with newborn child and child's mother

4. The conditions prescribed under section 171ZA(2)(a) of the Act are those prescribed in regulation 4(2)(b) and (c) of the Paternity and Adoption Leave Regulations 2002.

DEFINITION

"the Act"—see reg.2(1).

GENERAL NOTE

See the annotation to SSCBA 1992 s.171ZA.

Modification of entitlement conditions: early birth

5. Where a person does not meet the conditions specified in section 171ZA(2)(b) to (d) of the Act because the child's birth occurred earlier than the 14th week before the expected week of the birth, it shall have effect as if, for the conditions there set out, there were substituted the conditions that—
(a) the person would, but for the date on which the birth occurred, have been in employed earner's employment with an employer for a continuous period of at least 26 weeks ending with the week immedi-

Statutory Paternity Pay and Statutory Adoption Pay (General) Regs 2002

ately preceding the 14th week before the expected week of the child's birth;
(b) his normal weekly earnings for the period of 8 weeks ending with the week immediately preceding the week in which the child is born are not less than the lower earnings limit in force under section 5(1)(a) of the Act immediately before the commencement of the week in which the child is born.

DEFINITIONS

"the Act"—see reg.2(1).
"expected week"—see *ibid.*

[¹ Notice of entitlement to statutory paternity pay (birth)

6.64A

5A. The notice provided for in section 171ZC(1) of the Act must be given to the employer—
(a) in or before the 15th week before the expected week of the child's birth, or
(b) in a case where it was not reasonably practicable for the employee to give the notice in accordance with sub-paragraph (a), as soon as is reasonably practicable.]

AMENDMENT

1. Statutory Paternity Pay and Statutory Adoption Pay (General) (Amendment) Regulations 2014 (SI 2014/2862) regs 3 and 4 (December 1, 2014, but as regards entitlement only in respect of children whose expected week of birth begins on or after April 5, 2015 (SPP (birth)) or who are placed for adoption on or after April 5, 2015 ((SPP) adoption).

Period of payment of statutory paternity pay (birth)

6.65

6.—(1) Subject to paragraph (2) and regulation 8, a person entitled to statutory paternity pay (birth) may choose the statutory paternity pay period to begin on—
(a) the date on which the child is born or, where he is at work on that day, the following day;
(b) the date falling such number of days after the date on which the child is born as the person may specify;
(c) a predetermined date, specified by the person, which is later than the first day of the expected week of the child's birth.

(2) In a case where statutory paternity pay (birth) is payable in respect of a child whose expected week of birth begins before 6th April 2003, the statutory paternity pay period shall begin on a predetermined date, specified by the person entitled to such pay in a notice under section 171ZC(1) of the Act, which is at least 28 days after the date on which that notice was given, unless the person liable to pay statutory paternity pay (birth) agrees to the period beginning earlier.

(3) A person may choose for statutory paternity pay (birth) to be paid in respect of a period of a week.

[¹ (4) An employee who has made a choice in accordance with paragraph (1) may vary the date chosen provided that the employee gives the employer notice of the variation—

(SI 2002/2822 reg.6) (as amended)

(a) where the variation is to provide for the employee's statutory paternity pay period to begin on the date on which the child is born, or where he is at work on that day, the following day, at least 28 days before the first day of the expected week of the child's birth;
(b) where the variation is to provide for the employee's statutory paternity pay period to begin on a date that is a specified number of days (or a different specified number of days) after the date on which the child is born, at least 28 days before the date falling that number of days after the first day of the expected week of the child's birth;
(c) where the variation is to provide for the employee's statutory paternity pay period to begin on a predetermined date (or a different predetermined date), at least 28 days before that date,

or, if it is not reasonably practicable to give the notice at least 28 days before whichever day or date is relevant, as soon as is reasonably practicable.]

AMENDMENT

1. Statutory Paternity Pay and Statutory Adoption Pay (General) (Amendment) Regulations 2014 (SI 2014/2862) regs 3 and 5 (December 1, 2014, but as regards entitlement only in respect of children whose expected week of birth begins on or after April 5, 2015 (SPP (birth)) or who are placed for adoption on or after April 5, 2015 ((SPP) adoption)).

DEFINITIONS

"the Act"—see reg.2(1).
"expected week"—see *ibid.*
"statutory paternity pay (birth)"—see *ibid.*

Additional notice requirements for statutory paternity pay (birth)

7.—(1) Where the choice made by a person in accordance with paragraph (1) of regulation 6 and notified in accordance with section 171ZC(1) of the Act is that mentioned in sub-paragraph (a) or (b) of that paragraph, the person shall give further notice to the person liable to pay him statutory paternity pay, as soon as is reasonably practicable after the child's birth, of the date the child was born.

(2) Where the choice made by a person in accordance with paragraph (1) of regulation 6 and notified in accordance with section 171ZC(1) of the Act is that specified in sub-paragraph (c) of that paragraph, and the date of the child's birth is later than the date so specified, the person shall, if he wishes to claim statutory paternity pay (birth), give notice to the person liable to pay it, as soon as is reasonably practicable, that the period in respect of which statutory paternity pay is to be paid shall begin on a date different from that originally chosen by him.

(3) That date may be any date chosen in accordance with paragraph (1) of regulation 6.

6.66

DEFINITIONS

"the Act"—see reg.2(1).
"statutory paternity pay (birth)"—see *ibid.*

Qualifying period for statutory paternity pay (birth)

6.67 **8.** The qualifying period for the purposes of section 171ZE(2) of the Act (period within which the statutory paternity pay period must occur) is a period which begins on the date of the child's birth and ends—
(a) except in the case referred to in paragraph (b), 56 days after that date;
(b) in a case where the child is born before the first day of the expected week of its birth, 56 days after that day.

DEFINITIONS

"the Act"—see reg.2(1).
"expected week"—see *ibid.*

Evidence of entitlement to statutory paternity pay (birth)

6.68 **9.**—(1) A person shall provide evidence of his entitlement to statutory paternity pay (birth) by providing in writing to the person who will be liable to pay him statutory paternity pay (birth)—
(a) the information specified in paragraph (2);
(b) a declaration that he meets the conditions prescribed under section 171ZA(2)(a) of the Act and that it is not the case that statutory paternity pay (birth) is not payable to him by virtue of the provisions of section 171ZE(4) of the Act.
(2) The information referred to in paragraph (1)(a) is as follows—
(a) the name of the person claiming statutory paternity pay (birth);
(b) the expected week of the child's birth and, where the birth has already occurred, the date of birth;
(c) the date from which it is expected that the liability to pay statutory paternity pay (birth) will begin;
(d) whether the period chosen in respect of which statutory paternity pay (birth) is to be payable is a week.
[¹ (3) The information and declaration referred to in paragraph (1) shall be provided—
(a) in or before the 15th week before the expected week of the child's birth, or
(b) in a case where it was not reasonably practicable for the employee to provide it in accordance with sub-paragraph (a), as soon as is reasonably practicable.]
(4) Where the person who will be liable to pay statutory paternity pay (birth) so requests, the person entitled to it shall inform him of the date of the child's birth within 28 days, or as soon as is reasonably practicable thereafter.

AMENDMENT

1. Statutory Paternity Pay and Statutory Adoption Pay (General) (Amendment) Regulations 2014 (SI 2014/2862) regs 3 and 6 (December 1, 2014, but as regards entitlement only in respect of children whose expected week of birth begins on or after April 5, 2015 (SPP (birth)) or who are placed for adoption on or after April 5, 2015 ((SPP) adoption)).

DEFINITIONS

"the Act"—see reg.2(1).
"expected week"—see *ibid.*
"statutory paternity pay (birth)"—see *ibid.*

(SI 2002/2822 reg.9) (as amended)

GENERAL NOTE

The evidence of entitlement to statutory paternity pay (birth) is essentially a form of self-certification by the father or prospective father. This contrasts with the requirement to produce a medical certificate for statutory maternity pay purposes. The justification for the self-certification approach here is that it "balances the need for a light-touch procedure with the desire employers have expressed for some form of evidence to justify their payment of Statutory Paternity Pay" (*Government's Response on Simplification of Maternity Leave, Paternity Leave and Adoption Leave* (DTI, 2001), para.41).

6.69

Entitlement to statutory paternity pay (birth) where there is more than one employer

10. Statutory paternity pay (birth) shall be payable to a person in respect of a statutory pay week during any part of which he works only for an employer—
(a) who is not liable to pay him statutory paternity pay (birth); and
(b) for whom he has worked in the week immediately preceding the 14th week before the expected week of the child's birth.

6.70

DEFINITIONS

"expected week"—see *ibid.*
"statutory paternity pay (birth)"—see *ibid.*

PART 3

STATUTORY PATERNITY PAY (ADOPTION)

Conditions of entitlement to statutory paternity pay (adoption): relationship with child and with person with whom the child is placed for adoption

11.—(1) The conditions prescribed under section 171ZB(2)(a) of the Act are that a person—
(a) is married to [2, the civil partner] or the partner of a child's adopter (or in a case where there are two adopters, married to [2, the civil partner] or the partner of the other adopter); and
(b) has, or expects to have, the main responsibility (apart from the responsibility of the child's adopter, or in a case where there two adopters, together with the other adopter) for the upbringing of the child.
(2) For the purposes of paragraph (1), "partner" means a person (whether of a different sex or the same sex) who lives with the adopter and the child in an enduring family relationship but is not a relative of the adopter of a kind specified in paragraph [1(2A)].
[1(2A) The relatives of the adopter referred to in paragraph (2) are the adopter's parent, grandparent, sister, brother, aunt or uncle.]
(3) References to relationships in paragraph [1(2A)]—
(a) are to relationships of the full blood or half blood, or, in the case of an adopted person, such of those relationships as would exist but for the adoption; and

6.71

819

Statutory Paternity Pay and Statutory Adoption Pay (General) Regs 2002

(b) include the relationship of a child with his adoptive, or former adoptive parents but do not include any other adoptive relationships.

AMENDMENTS

1. Statutory Paternity Pay and Statutory Adoption Pay (Amendment) Regulations 2004 (SI 2004/488) reg.2 (April 6, 2004).
2. Civil Partnership Act 2004 (Amendments to Subordinate Legislation) Order 2005 (SI 2005/2114) art.2(17) and Sch.17 para.3 (December 5, 2005).

DEFINITIONS

"the Act"—see reg.2(1).
"adopter"—see *ibid.*
"partner"—see para.(2).

GENERAL NOTE

6.72 This regulation sets out the prescribed conditions for the purposes of SSCBA 1992 s.171ZB(2)(a), i.e. for the payment of statutory paternity pay in the case of adoption. The claimant must either be the adoptive parent's spouse or partner and expect to have the main responsibility (other than the adopter) for the child's upbringing. The definition of "partner" in para.(2) is innovative, in that it recognises that partners may be in a heterosexual or same sex relationship. The only qualifications are that the partner lives with the adopter and the child in "an enduring family relationship" and is not a relative of the adopter as defined in paras (2A) and (3). Guidance on the notion of "an enduring family relationship" in the context of a same-sex relationship might be sought in the decisions in *Fitzpatrick v Sterling Housing Association* [2001] A.C. 27 and *Ghaidan v Godin-Mendoza* [2004] UKHL 30; [2004] 3 W.L.R. 113. This explicit statutory recognition in English law of parity of treatment for heterosexual and same-sex couples pre-dated the Civil Partnership Act 2004.

[¹ Notice of entitlement to statutory paternity pay (adoption)

6.72A **11A.**—The notice provided for in section 171ZC(1) of the Act must be given to the employer—
(a) no more than seven days after the date on which the adopter is notified of having been matched with the child, or
(b) in a case where it was not reasonably practicable for the employee to give notice in accordance with sub-paragraph (a), as soon as is reasonably practicable.]

AMENDMENT

1. Statutory Paternity Pay and Statutory Adoption Pay (General) (Amendment) Regulations 2014 (SI 2014/2862) regs 3 and 7 (December 1, 2014, but as regards entitlement only in respect of children whose expected week of birth begins on or after April 5, 2015 (SPP (birth)) or who are placed for adoption on or after April 5, 2015 ((SPP) adoption)).

Period of payment of statutory paternity pay (adoption)

6.73 **12.**—(1) Subject to paragraph (2) and regulation 14, a person entitled to statutory paternity pay (adoption) may choose the statutory paternity pay period to begin on—
(a) the date on which the child is placed with the adopter or, where the person is at work on that day, the following day;

(SI 2002/2822 reg.12) (as amended)

 (b) the date falling such number of days after the date on which the child is placed with the adopter as the person may specify;
 (c) a predetermined date, specified by the person, which is later than the date on which the child is expected to be placed with the adopter.

(2) In a case where statutory paternity pay (adoption) is payable in respect of a child matched with an adopter who is notified of having been matched before 6th April 2003, the statutory paternity pay period shall begin on a predetermined date, specified by the person entitled to such pay in a notice under section 171ZC(1) of the Act, which is at least 28 days after the date on which that notice was given, unless the person liable to pay statutory paternity pay (birth) agrees to the period beginning earlier.

(3) A person may choose for statutory paternity pay (adoption) to be paid in respect of a period of a week.

[¹ (4) An employee who has made a choice in accordance with paragraph (1) may vary the date chosen provided that the employee gives the employer notice of the variation—

 (a) where the variation is to provide for the employee's statutory paternity pay period to begin on the date on which the child is placed with the adopter or, where the person is at work on that day, the following day, at least 28 days before the date provided under regulation 15(2)(b) as the date on which the child is expected to be placed for adoption;
 (b) where the variation is to provide for the employee's statutory paternity pay period to begin on a date that is a specified number of days (or a different specified number of days) after the date on which the child is placed with the adopter, at least 28 days before the date falling that number of days after the date provided under regulation 15(2)(b) as the date on which the child is expected to be placed for adoption;
 (c) where the variation is to provide for the employee's statutory paternity pay period to begin on a predetermined date, at least 28 days before that date,

or, if it is not reasonably practicable to give the notice at least 28 days before whichever date is relevant, as soon as is reasonably practicable.]

AMENDMENT

1. Statutory Paternity Pay and Statutory Adoption Pay (General) (Amendment) Regulations 2014 (SI 2014/2862) regs 3 and 8 (December 1, 2014, but as regards entitlement only in respect of children whose expected week of birth begins on or after April 5, 2015 (SPP (birth)) or who are placed for adoption on or after April 5, 2015 ((SPP) adoption)).

DEFINITIONS

 "the Act"—see reg.2(1).
 "adopter"—see *ibid.*
 "statutory paternity pay (adoption)"—see *ibid.*
 "statutory paternity pay (birth)"—see *ibid.*

Additional notice requirements for statutory paternity pay (adoption)

6.74

13.—(1) Where the choice made by a person in accordance with paragraph (1) of regulation 12 and notified in accordance with section 171ZC(1) of the Act is that mentioned in sub-paragraph (a) or (b) of that paragraph, the person shall give further notice to the person liable to pay him statutory paternity pay as soon as is reasonably practicable of the date on which the placement occurred.

(2) Where the choice made by a person in accordance with paragraph (1) of regulation 12 and notified in accordance with section 171ZC(1) of the Act is that mentioned in sub-paragraph (c) of that paragraph, or a date is specified under paragraph (2) of that regulation, and the child is placed for adoption later than the date so specified, the person shall, if he wishes to claim statutory paternity pay (adoption), give notice to the person liable to pay it, as soon as is reasonably practicable, that the period in respect of which statutory paternity pay is to be paid shall begin on a date different from that originally chosen by him.

(3) That date may be any date chosen in accordance with paragraph (1) of regulation 12.

DEFINITIONS

"the Act"—see reg.2(1).
"statutory paternity pay (adoption)"—see *ibid.*

Qualifying period for statutory paternity pay (adoption)

6.75

14. The qualifying period for the purposes of section 171ZE(2) of the Act (period within which the statutory pay period must occur) is a period of 56 days beginning with the date of the child's placement for adoption.

DEFINITION

"the Act"—see reg.2(1).

Evidence of entitlement for statutory paternity pay (adoption)

6.76

15.—(1) A person shall provide evidence of his entitlement to statutory paternity pay (adoption) by providing in writing to the person who will be liable to pay him statutory paternity pay (adoption)—
  (a) the information specified in paragraph (2);
  (b) a declaration that he meets the conditions prescribed under section 171ZB(2)(a) of the Act and that it is not the case that statutory paternity pay (adoption) is not payable to him by virtue of the provisions of section 171ZE(4) of the Act;
  (c) a declaration that he has elected to receive statutory paternity pay (adoption), and not statutory adoption pay under Part 12ZB of the Act.

(2) The information referred to in paragraph (1) is as follows—
  (a) the name of the person claiming statutory paternity pay (adoption);
  (b) the date on which the child is expected to be placed for adoption or, where the child has already been placed for adoption, the date of placement of the child;

(SI 2002/2822 reg.15) (as amended)

(c) the date from which it is expected that the liability to pay statutory paternity pay (adoption) will begin;
(d) whether the period chosen in respect of which statutory paternity pay (adoption) is to be payable is a week;
(e) the date the adopter was notified he had been matched with the child for the purposes of adoption.

[¹ (3) The information and declaration referred to in paragraph (1) shall be provided—
(a) no more than seven days after the date on which the adopter is notified of having been matched with the child, or
(b) in a case where it was not reasonably practicable for the employee to provide it in accordance with sub-paragraph (a), as soon as is reasonably practicable.]

(4) Where the person who will be liable to pay statutory paternity pay (adoption) so requests, the person entitled to it shall inform him of the date of the child's placement within 28 days, or as soon as is reasonably practicable thereafter.

AMENDMENT

1. Statutory Paternity Pay and Statutory Adoption Pay (General) (Amendment) Regulations 2014 (SI 2014/2862) regs 3 and 9 (December 1, 2014, but as regards entitlement only in respect of children whose expected week of birth begins on or after April 5, 2015 (SPP (birth)) or who are placed for adoption on or after April 5, 2015 ((SPP) adoption)).

DEFINITIONS

"the Act"—see reg.2(1).
"statutory paternity pay (adoption)"—see *ibid*.

Entitlement to statutory paternity pay (adoption) where there is more than one employer

16. Statutory paternity pay (adoption) shall be payable to a person in respect of a statutory pay week during any part of which he works only for an employer—
(a) who is not liable to pay him statutory paternity pay (adoption); and
(b) for whom he has worked in the week in which the adopter is notified of being matched with the child.

6.77

DEFINITIONS

"adopter"—see *ibid*.
"statutory paternity pay (adoption)"—see *ibid*.

PART 4

STATUTORY PATERNITY PAY: PROVISIONS APPLICABLE TO BOTH STATUTORY PATERNITY PAY (BIRTH) AND STATUTORY PATERNITY PAY (ADOPTION)

Work during a statutory paternity pay period

6.78 **17.**—(1) Where, in a case where statutory paternity pay is being paid to a person who works during the statutory paternity pay period for an employer who is not liable to pay him statutory paternity pay and who does not fall within paragraph (b) of regulation 10 or, as the case may be, paragraph (b) of regulation 16, there shall be no liability to pay statutory paternity pay in respect of any remaining part of the statutory paternity pay period.

(2) In a case falling within paragraph (1), the person shall notify the person liable to pay statutory paternity pay within seven days of the first day during which he works during the statutory pay period.

(3) The notification mentioned in paragraph (2) shall be in writing, if the person who has been liable to pay statutory paternity pay so requests.

Cases where there is no liability to pay statutory paternity pay

6.79 **18.** There shall be no liability to pay statutory paternity pay in respect of any week—
   (a) during any part of which the person entitled to it is entitled to statutory sick pay under Part 11 of the Act;
   (b) following that in which the person claiming it has died; or
   (c) during any part of which the person entitled to it is detained in legal custody or sentenced to a term of imprisonment (except where the sentence is suspended), or which is a subsequent week within the same statutory paternity pay period.

DEFINITION

"the Act"—see reg.2(1).

Statutory paternity pay and contractual remuneration

6.80 **19.** For the purposes of section 171ZG(1) and (2) of the Act, the payments which are to be treated as contractual remuneration are sums payable under a contract of service—
   (a) by way of remuneration;
   (b) for incapacity for work due to sickness or injury;
   (c) by reason of the birth or adoption of a child.

DEFINITION

"the Act"—see reg.2(1).

Avoidance of liability for statutory paternity pay

6.81 **20.**—(1) A former employer shall be liable to make payments of statutory paternity pay to a former employee in any case where the employee had

(SI 2002/2822 reg.20) (as amended)

been employed for a continuous period of at least 8 weeks and his contract of service was brought to an end by the former employer solely, or mainly, for the purpose of avoiding liability for statutory paternity pay.

(2) In a case falling within paragraph (1)—
(a) the employee shall be treated as if he had been employed for a continuous period ending with the child's birth or, as the case may be, the placement of the child for adoption;
(b) his normal weekly earnings shall be calculated by reference to his normal weekly earnings for the period of 8 weeks ending with the last day in respect of which he was paid under his former contract of service.

PART 5

Statutory adoption pay

Adoption pay period

21.—(1) Subject to paragraph (2), a person entitled to statutory adoption pay may choose the adoption pay period to begin—
(a) on the date on which the child is placed with him for adoption or, where he is at work on that day, on the following day;
(b) subject to paragraph (2), on a predetermined date, specified by him, which is no more than 14 days before the date on which the child is expected to be placed with him and no later than that date.

(2) In a case where statutory adoption pay is payable in respect of a child matched with an adopter who is notified of having been matched before 6th April 2003, the statutory adoption pay period shall begin on a predetermined date which is—
(a) on or after 6th April 2003; and
(b) no more than 14 days before the date on which the child is expected to be placed with the adopter.

(3) Subject to paragraph (4), where the choice made is that mentioned in sub-paragraph (b) of paragraph (1) or in a case where paragraph (2) applies, the adoption pay period shall, unless the employer agrees to the adoption pay period beginning earlier, begin no earlier than 28 days after notice under section 171ZL(6) of the Act has been given.

(4) Where the beginning of the adoption pay period determined in accordance with paragraph (3) is later than the date of placement, it shall be the date of placement.

(5) Subject to regulation 22, the duration of any adoption pay period shall be a continuous period of [[1]39] weeks.

(6) A choice made under paragraph (1), or a date specified under paragraph (2), is not irrevocable, but where a person subsequently makes a different choice, section 171ZL(6) of the Act shall apply to it.

6.82

AMENDMENT

1. Statutory Paternity Pay and Statutory Adoption Pay (General) and the Statutory Paternity Pay and Statutory Adoption Pay (Weekly Rates) (Amendment) Regulations 2006 (SI 2006/2236) reg.4 (October 1, 2006).

Statutory Paternity Pay and Statutory Adoption Pay (General) Regs 2002

DEFINITIONS

"the Act"—see reg.2(1).
"adopter"—see *ibid.*

Adoption pay period in cases where adoption is disrupted

6.83   **22.**—(1) Where—
(a) after a child has been placed for adoption—
   (i) the child dies;
   (ii) the child is returned to the adoption agency under section 30(3) of the Adoption Act 1976 or [¹, in Scotland, the child is returned to the adoption agency, adoption society or nominated person in accordance with section 25(6) of the Adoption and Children (Scotland) Act 2007];
   [² *(ii) the child is returned after being placed, or]*
(b) the adoption pay period has begun prior to the date the child has been placed for adoption, but the placement does not take place, the adoption pay period shall terminate in accordance with the provisions of paragraph (2).

(2) The adoption pay period shall, in a case falling within paragraph (1), terminate 8 weeks after the end of the week specified in paragraph (3).

(3) The week referred to in paragraph (2) is—
(a) in a case falling within paragraph (1)(a)(i), the week during which the child dies;
(b) in a case falling within paragraph (1)(a)(ii), the week during which the child is returned;
(c) in a case falling within paragraph (1)(b), the week during which the person with whom the child was to be placed for adoption is notified that the placement will not be made.

(4) For the purposes of paragraph (3), "week" means a period of 7 days beginning with Sunday.

[² *(5) In paragraph (1) "returned after being placed" means—*
(a) returned to the adoption agency under sections 31 to 35 of the Adoption and Children Act 2002;
(b) in Scotland, returned to the adoption agency, adoption society or nominated person in accordance with section 25(6) of the Adoption and Children (Scotland) Act 2007; or
(c) where the child is placed in accordance with section 22C of the Children Act 1989, returned to the adoption agency following termination of the placement.]

AMENDMENTS

1. Adoption and Children (Scotland) Act 2007 (Consequential Modifications) Order 2011 (SI 2011/1740) art.2 and Sch.1 para.32(3) (July 15, 2011).
2. *Statutory Paternity Pay and Statutory Adoption Pay (Parental Orders and Prospective Adopters) Regulations 2014 (SI 2014/2934) reg.5 (December 1, 2014, but have effect only in relation to children matched with a person who is notified of having been matched on or after April 5, 2015).*

DEFINITION

"week"—see para.(4).

(SI 2002/2822 reg.22) (as amended)

GENERAL NOTE

The versions of paras (1)(a)(ii) and (5) in italics have effect only in relation to children matched with a person who is notified of having been matched on or after April 5, 2015 (Statutory Paternity Pay and Statutory Adoption Pay (Parental Orders and Prospective Adopters) Regulations 2014 (SI 2014/2934) reg.3).

6.84

Additional notice requirements for statutory adoption pay

23.—(1) Where a person gives notice under section 171ZL(6) of the Act he shall at the same time give notice of the date on which the child is expected to be placed for adoption.

6.85

(2) Where the choice made in accordance with paragraph (1) of regulation 21 and notified in accordance with section 171ZL(6) of the Act is that mentioned in sub-paragraph (a) of that paragraph, the person shall give further notice to the person liable to pay him statutory adoption pay as soon as is reasonably practicable of the date the child is placed for adoption.

DEFINITION

"the Act"—see reg.2(1).

Evidence of entitlement to statutory adoption pay

24.—(1) A person shall provide evidence of his entitlement to statutory adoption pay by providing to the person who will be liable to pay it—

6.86

(a) the information specified in paragraph (2), in the form of one or more documents provided to him by an adoption agency, containing that information;
(b) a declaration that he has elected to receive statutory adoption pay, and not statutory paternity pay (adoption) under Part 12ZA of the Act.

(2) The information referred to in paragraph (1) is—
(a) the name and address of the adoption agency and of the person claiming payment of statutory adoption pay;
(b) the date on which the child is expected to be placed for adoption or, where the child has already been placed for adoption, the date of placement; and
(c) the date on which the person claiming payment of statutory adoption pay was informed by the adoption agency that the child would be placed for adoption with him.

(3) The information and declaration referred to in paragraph (1) shall be provided to the person liable to pay statutory adoption pay at least 28 days before the date chosen as the beginning of the adoption pay period in accordance with paragraph (1) of regulation 21, or, if that is not reasonably practicable, as soon as is reasonably practicable thereafter.

DEFINITIONS

"the Act"—see reg.2(1).
"adoption agency"—see *ibid.*
"statutory paternity pay (adoption)"—see *ibid.*

Entitlement to statutory adoption pay where there is more than one employer

6.87 **25.** Statutory adoption pay shall be payable to a person in respect of a week during any part of which he works only for an employer—
(a) who is not liable to pay him statutory adoption pay; and
(b) for whom he has worked in the week in which he is notified of being matched with the child.

Work during an adoption pay period

6.88 **26.**—(1) Where, in a case where statutory adoption pay is being paid to a person who works during the adoption pay period for an employer who is not liable to pay him statutory adoption pay and who does not fall within paragraph (b) of regulation 25, there shall be no liability to pay statutory adoption pay in respect of any remaining part of the adoption pay period.
(2) In a case falling within paragraph (1), the person shall notify the person liable to pay statutory adoption pay within 7 days of the first day during which he works during the adoption pay period.
(3) The notification contained in paragraph (2) shall be in writing if the person who has been liable to pay statutory adoption pay so requests.

Cases where there is no liability to pay statutory adoption pay

6.89 **27.**—(1) There shall be no liability to pay statutory adoption pay in respect of any week—
(a) during any part of which the person entitled to it is entitled to statutory sick pay under Part 9 of the Act;
(b) following that in which the person claiming it has died; or
(c) subject to paragraph (2), during any part of which the person entitled to it is detained in legal custody or sentenced to a term of imprisonment (except where the sentence is suspended).
(2) There shall be liability to pay statutory adoption pay in respect of any week during any part of which the person entitled to it is detained in legal custody where that person—
(a) is released subsequently without charge;
(b) is subsequently found not guilty of any offence and is released; or
(c) is convicted of an offence but does not receive a custodial sentence.

DEFINITION

"the Act"—see reg.2(1).

[1 Working for not more than 10 days during an adoption pay period

6.90 **27A.** In the case where an employee does any work under a contract of service with his employer on any day for not more than 10 such days during his adoption pay period, whether consecutive or not, statutory adoption pay shall continue to be payable to the employee by the employer.]

AMENDMENT

1. Statutory Paternity Pay and Statutory Adoption Pay (General) and the Statutory Paternity Pay and Statutory Adoption Pay (Weekly Rates) (Amendment) Regulations 2006 (SI 2006/2236) reg.5 (October 1, 2006).

(SI 2002/2822 reg.28) (as amended)

Statutory adoption pay and contractual remuneration

28. For the purposes of section 171ZP(4) and (5) of the Act, the payments which are to be treated as contractual remuneration are sums payable under a contract of service—
(a) by way of remuneration;
(b) for incapacity for work due to sickness or injury;
(c) by reason of the adoption of a child.

6.91

DEFINITION

"the Act"—see reg.2(1).

Termination of employment before start of adoption pay period

29.—(1) Where the employment of a person who satisfies the conditions of entitlement to statutory adoption pay terminates for whatever reason (including dismissal) before the adoption pay period chosen in accordance with regulation 21 has begun, the period shall begin 14 days before the expected date of placement or, where the termination occurs on, or within 14 days before, the expected date of placement, on the day immediately following the last day of his employment.

(2) In a case falling within paragraph (1), the notice requirements set out in section 171ZL(6) of the Act and these Regulations shall not apply.

6.92

DEFINITION

"the Act"—see reg.2(1).

Avoidance of liability for statutory adoption pay

30.—(1) A former employer shall be liable to make payments of statutory adoption pay to a former employee in any case where the employee had been employed for a continuous period of at least 8 weeks and his contract of service was brought to an end by the former employer solely, or mainly, for the purpose of avoiding liability for statutory adoption pay.

(2) In a case falling within paragraph (1)—
(a) the employee shall be treated as if he had been employed for a continuous period ending with the week in which he was notified of having been matched with the child for adoption; and
(b) his normal weekly earnings shall be calculated by reference to his normal weekly earnings for the period of 8 weeks ending with the last day in respect of which he was paid under his former contract of service.

6.93

Statutory Paternity Pay and Statutory Adoption Pay (General) Regs 2002

Part 6

Statutory Paternity Pay and Statutory Adoption Pay: Provisions Applicable to both Statutory Paternity Pay and Statutory Adoption Pay

Introductory

6.94   **31.**—(1) Subject to paragraph (2), the provisions of regulations 32–47 below apply to statutory paternity pay payable under Part 12ZA of the Act and to statutory adoption pay payable under Part 12ZB of the Act.
(2) The provisions of regulation 44 only apply to statutory adoption pay.

Definition

"the Act"—see reg.2(1).

Treatment of persons as employees

6.95   **32.**—(1) [¹Subject to paragraph (1A),] in a case where, and in so far as, a person [¹. . .] is treated as an employed earner by virtue of the Social Security (Categorisation of Earners) Regulations 1978 he shall be treated as an employee for the purposes of Parts 12ZA and 12ZB of the Act, and in a case where, and in so far as, such a person is treated otherwise than as an employed earner by virtue of those Regulations, he shall not be treated as an employee for the purposes of Parts 12ZA and 12ZB of the Act.
[²(1A) Paragraph (1) shall have effect in relation to a person who—
(a) is under the age of 16; and
(b) would or, as the case may be, would not have been treated as an employed earner by virtue of the Social Security (Categorisation of Earners) Regulations 1978 had he been over that age,
as it has effect in relation to a person who is or, as the case may be, is not so treated.]
(2) A person who is in employed earner's employment within the meaning of the Act under a contract of apprenticeship shall be treated as an employee for the purposes of Parts 12ZA and 12ZB of the Act.
(3) A person who is in employed earner's employment within the meaning of the Act but whose employer—
(a) does not fulfil the conditions prescribed in regulation 145(1) of the Contributions Regulations in so far as that provision relates to residence or presence in Great Britain; or
(b) is a person who, by reason of any international treaty to which the United Kingdom is a party or of any international convention binding the United Kingdom—
    (i) is exempt from the provisions of the Act; or
    (ii) is a person against whom the provisions of the Act are not enforceable,
shall not be treated as an employee for the purposes of Parts 12ZA and 12ZB of the Act.

(SI 2002/2822 reg.32) (as amended)

AMENDMENTS

1. Employment Equality (Age) Regulations 2006 (SI 2006/1031) reg.49(1) and Sch.8 Pt 2 para.60 (October 1, 2006).
2. Employment Equality (Age) (Consequential Amendments) Regulations 2007 (SI 2007/825) reg.7 (April 6, 2007).

DEFINITIONS

"the Act"—see reg.2(1).
"Contributions Regulations"—see *ibid.*

Continuous employment

33.—(1) Subject to the following provisions of this regulation, where in any week a person is, for the whole or part of the week—
(a) incapable of work in consequence of sickness or injury;
(b) absent from work on account of a temporary cessation of work;
(c) absent from work in circumstances such that, by arrangement or custom, he is regarded as continuing in the employment of his employer for all or any purposes,
and returns to work for his employer after the incapacity for or absence from work, that week shall be treated for the purposes of sections 171ZA, 171ZB and 171ZL of the Act as part of a continuous period of employment with that employer, notwithstanding that no contract of service exists with that employer in respect of that week.

(2) Incapacity for work which lasts for more than 26 consecutive weeks shall not count for the purposes of paragraph (1)(a).

(3) Where a person—
(a) is an employee in an employed earner's employment in which the custom is for the employer—
　(i) to offer work for a fixed period of not more than 26 consecutive weeks;
　(ii) to offer work for such period on two or more occasions in a year for periods which do not overlap; and
　(iii) to offer the work available to those persons who had worked for him during the last or a recent such period, but
(b) is absent from work because of incapacity arising from some specific disease or bodily or mental disablement,
then in that case paragraph (1) shall apply as if the words "and returns to work for his employer after the incapacity for or absence from work," were omitted and paragraph (4) shall not apply.

(4) Where a person is employed under a contract of service for part only of the relevant week within the meaning of subsection (3) of section 171ZL of the Act (entitlement to statutory adoption pay), the whole of that week shall count in computing a period of continuous employment for the purposes of that section.

DEFINITION

"the Act"—see reg.2(1).

Continuous employment and unfair dismissal

34.—(1) This regulation applies to a person in relation to whose dismissal an action is commenced which consists—

(a) of the presentation by him of a complaint under section 111(1) of the Employment Rights Act 1996;
(b) of his making a claim in accordance with a dismissals procedure agreement designated by an order under section 110 of that Act; [¹. . .]
(c) of any action taken by a conciliation officer under [² any of sections 18A to 18C] of the Employment Tribunals Act 1996; [¹or
(d) of a decision arising out of the use of a statutory dispute resolution procedure contained in Schedule 2 to the Employment Act 2002 in a case where, in accordance with the Employment Act 2002 (Dispute Resolution) Regulations 2004, such a procedure applies.]

(2) If, in consequence of an action of the kind specified in paragraph (1), a person is reinstated or re-engaged by his employer or by a successor or associated employer of that employer, the continuity of his employment shall be preserved for the purposes of Part 12ZA or, as the case may be, Part 12ZB of the Act, and any week which falls within the interval beginning with the effective date of termination and ending with the date of reinstatement or re-engagement, as the case may be, shall count in the computation of his period of continuous employment.

(3) In this regulation—
"successor" and "dismissal procedures agreement" have the same meanings as in section 235 of the Employment Rights Act 1996; and
"associated employer" shall be construed in accordance with section 231 of the Employment Rights Act 1996.

AMENDMENTS

1. Statutory Maternity Pay (General) and the Statutory Paternity Pay and Statutory Adoption Pay (General) (Amendment) Regulations 2005 (SI 2005/358) reg.4 (April 56, 2005).
2. Enterprise and Regulatory Reform Act 2013 (Consequential Amendments) (Employment) Order 2014 (SI 2014/386) art.2 Sch. para.19.

DEFINITIONS

"the Act"—see reg.2(1).
"associated employer"—see para.(3).
"dismissal procedures agreement"—see *ibid.*
"successor"—see *ibid.*

Continuous employment and stoppages of work

6.98   35.—(1) Where, for any week or part of a week a person does not work because there is a stoppage of work due to a trade dispute within the meaning of section 35(1) of the Jobseekers Act 1995 at his place of employment, the continuity of his employment shall, subject to paragraph (2), be treated as continuing throughout the stoppage but, subject to paragraph (3), no such week shall count in the computation of his period of employment.

(2) Subject to paragraph (3), where during the stoppage of work a person is dismissed from his employment, the continuity of his employment shall not be treated in accordance with paragraph (1) as continuing beyond the commencement of the day he stopped work.

(3) The provisions of paragraph (1), to the extent that they provide that a week in which the stoppage of work occurred shall not count in the

computation of a period of employment, and paragraph (2) shall not apply to a person who proves that at no time did he have a direct interest in the trade dispute in question.

Change of employer

36. A person's employment shall, notwithstanding a change of employer, be treated as continuous employment with the second employer where—
- (a) the employer's trade or business or an undertaking (whether or not it is an undertaking established by or under an Act of Parliament) is transferred from one person to another;
- (b) by or under an Act of Parliament, whether public or local and whenever passed, a contract of employment between any body corporate and the person is modified and some other body corporate is substituted as his employer;
- (c) on the death of his employer, the person is taken into employment of the personal representatives or trustees of the deceased;
- (d) the person is employed by partners, personal representatives or trustees and there is a change in the partners, or, as the case may be, personal representatives or trustees;
- (e) the person is taken into the employment of an employer who is, at the time he entered his employment, an associated employer of his previous employer, and for this purpose "associated employer" shall be construed in accordance with section 231 of the Employment Rights Act 1996;
- (f) on the termination of his employment with an employer he is taken into the employment of another employer and those employers are governors of a school maintained by a [¹local authority] and that authority.

6.99

AMENDMENT

1. Local Education Authorities and Children's Services Authorities (Integration of Functions) (Local Subordinate Legislation) Order 2010 (SI 2010/1172) art.4 and Sch.3 para.47 (May 5, 2010).

Reinstatement after service with the armed forces etc.

37. If a person who is entitled to apply to his employer under the Reserve Forces (Safeguard of Employment) Act 1985 enters the employment of that employer within the 6-month period mentioned in section 1(4)(b) of that Act, his previous period of employment with that employer (or if there was more than one such period, the last of those periods) and the period of employment beginning in that 6-month period shall be treated as continuous.

6.100

DEFINITION

"the Act"—see reg.2(1).

Treatment of two or more employers or two or more contracts of service as one

38.—(1) In a case where the earnings paid to a person in respect of two or more employments are aggregated and treated as a single payment of earnings under regulation 15(1) of the Contributions Regulations, the employers

6.101

of that person in respect of those employments shall be treated as one for the purposes of Part 12ZA or, as the case may be, Part 12ZB of the Act.

(2) Where two or more employers are treated as one under the provisions of paragraph (1), liability for statutory paternity pay or, as the case may be, statutory adoption pay, shall be apportioned between them in such proportions as they may agree or, in default of agreement, in the proportions which the person's earnings from each employment bear to the amount of the aggregated earnings.

(3) Where two or more contracts of service exist concurrently between one employer and one employee, they shall be treated as one for the purposes of Part 12ZA or, as the case may be, Part 12ZB of the Act, except where, by virtue of regulation 14 of the Contributions Regulations, the earnings from those contracts of service are not aggregated for the purposes of earnings-related contributions.

DEFINITIONS

"the Act"—see reg.2(1).
"Contributions Regulations"—see *ibid*.

Meaning of "earnings"

39.—(1) For the purposes of section 171ZJ(6) (normal weekly earnings for the purposes of Part 12ZA of the Act) and of section 171ZS(6) of the Act (normal weekly earnings for the purposes of Part 12ZB of the Act), the expression "earnings" shall be construed in accordance with the following provisions of this regulation.

(2) The expression "earnings" refers to gross earnings and includes any remuneration or profit derived from a person's employment except any payment or amount which is—
  (a) excluded from the computation of a person's earnings under regulation 25 of and Schedule 3 to, and regulation 123 of, the Contributions Regulations (payments to be disregarded) and regulation 27 of those Regulations (payments to directors to be disregarded) [¹(or would have been so excluded had he not been under the age of 16)];
  (b) a chargeable emolument under section 10A of the Act, except where, in consequence of such a chargeable emolument being excluded from earnings, a person would not be entitled to statutory paternity pay or, as the case may be, statutory adoption pay [¹(or where such a payment or amount would have been so excluded and in consequence he would not have been entitled to statutory paternity pay and statutory adoption pay had he not been under the age of 16)].

(3) For the avoidance of doubt, "earnings" includes—
[²(za) any amount retrospectively treated as earnings by regulations made by virtue of section 4B(2) of the Act;]
  (a) any sum payable in respect of arrears of pay in pursuance of an order for reinstatement or re-engagement under the Employment Rights Act 1996;
  (b) any sum payable by way of pay in pursuance of an order made under the Employment Rights Act 1996 for the continuation of a contract of employment;

(c) any sum payable by way of remuneration in pursuance of a protective award under section 189 of the Trade Union and Labour Relations (Consolidation) Act 1992;
(d) any sum payable by way of statutory sick pay, including sums payable in accordance with regulations made under section 151(6) of the Act;
(e) any sum payable by way of statutory maternity pay;
(f) any sum payable by way of statutory paternity pay;
(g) any sum payable by way of statutory adoption pay.

AMENDMENTS

1. Employment Equality (Age) Regulations 2006 (SI 2006/1031) reg.49(1) and Sch.8 Pt 2 para.61 (October 1, 2006).
2. Social Security, Occupational Pension Schemes and Statutory Payments (Consequential Provisions) Regulations 2007 (SI 2007/1154) reg.6 (April 6, 2007).

DEFINITIONS

"the Act"—see reg.2(1).
"Contributions Regulations"—see *ibid.*

Normal weekly earnings

40.—(1) For the purposes of Part 12ZA and Part 12ZB of the Act, a person's normal weekly earnings shall be calculated in accordance with the following provisions of this regulation.

(2) In this regulation—
"the appropriate date" means—
(a) in relation to statutory paternity pay (birth), the first day of the 14th week before the expected week of the child's birth or the first day in the week in which the child is born, whichever is the earlier;
(b) in relation to statutory paternity pay (adoption) and statutory adoption pay, the first day of the week after the week in which the adopter is notified of being matched with the child for the purposes of adoption;
"normal pay day" means a day on which the terms of a person's contract of service require him to be paid, or the practice in his employment is for him to be paid, if any payment is due to him; and
"day of payment" means a day on which the person was paid.

(3) Subject to paragraph (4), the relevant period for the purposes of sections 171ZJ(6) and 171ZS(6) is the period between—
(a) the last normal pay day to fall before the appropriate date; and
(b) the last normal pay day to fall at least 8 weeks earlier than the normal pay day mentioned in sub-paragraph (a),
including the normal pay day mentioned in sub-paragraph (a) but excluding that first mentioned in sub-paragraph (b).

(4) In a case where a person has no identifiable normal pay day, paragraph (3) shall have effect as if the words "day of payment" were substituted for the words "normal pay day" in each place where they occur.

(5) In a case where a person has normal pay days at intervals of or approximating to one or more calendar months (including intervals of or approximating to a year) his normal weekly earnings shall be calculated

6.103

Statutory Paternity Pay and Statutory Adoption Pay (General) Regs 2002

by dividing his earnings in the relevant period by the number of calendar months in that period (or, if it is not a whole number, the nearest whole number), multiplying the result by 12 and dividing by 52.

(6) In a case to which paragraph (5) does not apply and the relevant period is not an exact number of weeks, the person's normal weekly earnings shall be calculated by dividing his earnings in the relevant period by the number of days in the relevant period and multiplying the result by 7.

(7) In any case where a person receives a back-dated pay increase which includes a sum in respect of a relevant period, normal weekly earnings shall be calculated as if such a sum was paid in that relevant period even though received after that period.

DEFINITIONS

"the Act"—see reg.2(1).
"adopter"—see *ibid*.
"the appropriate date"—see para.(2).
"day of payment"— see *ibid*.
"expected week"—see reg.2(1).
"normal pay day"—see para.(2).
"statutory paternity pay (adoption)"—see reg.2(1).
"statutory paternity pay (birth)"—see *ibid*.

Payment of statutory paternity pay and statutory adoption pay

6.104   **41.** Payments of statutory paternity pay and statutory adoption pay may be made in a like manner to payments of remuneration but shall not include payment in kind or by way of the provision of board or lodgings or of services or other facilities.

Time when statutory paternity pay and statutory adoption pay are to be paid

6.105   **42.**—(1) In this regulation, "pay day" means a day on which it has been agreed, or it is the normal practice between an employer or former employer and a person who is or was an employee of his, that payments by way of remuneration are to be made, or, where there is no such agreement or normal practice, the last day of a calendar month.

(2) In any case where—
(a) a decision has been made by an officer of the Board under section 8(1) of the Social Security Contributions (Transfer of Functions, etc.) Act 1999 as a result of which a person is entitled to an amount of statutory paternity pay or statutory adoption pay; and
(b) the time for bringing an appeal against the decision has expired and either—
  (i) no such appeal has been brought; or
  (ii) such an appeal has been brought and has been finally disposed of,
that amount of statutory paternity pay or statutory adoption pay shall be paid within the time specified in paragraph (3).

(3) Subject to paragraphs (4) and (5), the employer or former employer shall pay the amount not later than the first pay day after—
(a) where an appeal has been brought, the day on which the employer or former employer receives notification that it has been finally disposed of;

(SI 2002/2822 reg.42) (as amended)

(b) where leave to appeal has been refused and there remains no further opportunity to apply for leave, the day on which the employer or former employer receives notification of the refusal; and

(c) in any other case, the day on which the time for bringing an appeal expires.

(4) Subject to paragraph (5), where it is impracticable, in view of the employer's or former employer's methods of accounting for and paying remuneration, for the requirement of payment referred to in paragraph (3) to be met by the pay day referred to in that paragraph, it shall be met not later than the next following pay day.

(5) Where the employer or former employer would not have remunerated the employee for his work in the week in question as early as the pay day specified in paragraph (3) or (if it applies) paragraph (4), the requirement of payment shall be met on the first day on which the employee would have been remunerated for his work in that week.

Definitions

"the Board"—see reg.2(1).
"pay day"—see para.(1).

Liability of the Board to pay statutory paternity pay or statutory adoption pay

43.—(1) Where—

(a) an officer of the Board has decided that an employer is liable to make payments of statutory paternity pay or, as the case may be, statutory adoption pay to a person;

(b) the time for appealing against the decision has expired; and

(c) no appeal against the decision has been lodged or leave to appeal against the decision is required and has been refused,

then for any week in respect of which the employer was liable to make payments of statutory paternity pay or, as the case may be, statutory adoption pay but did not do so, and for any subsequent weeks in the paternity pay period or, as the case may be, adoption pay period, the liability to make those payments shall, notwithstanding sections 171ZD and 171ZM of the Act, be that of the Board and not the employer.

(2) Liability to make payments of statutory paternity pay or, as the case may be, statutory adoption pay shall, notwithstanding sections 171ZD and 171ZM of the Act, be a liability of the Board and not the employer as from the week in which the employer first becomes insolvent until the end of the paternity pay or adoption pay period.

(3) For the purposes of paragraph (2), an employer shall be taken to be insolvent if, and only if—

(a) in England and Wales—
  (i) he has been adjudged bankrupt or has made a composition or arrangement with his creditors;
  (ii) he has died and his estate falls to be administered in accordance with an order made under section 421 of the Insolvency Act 1986; or
  (iii) where an employer is a company or a limited liability partnership, a winding-up order [1. . .] is made or a resolution for a voluntary winding-up is passed (or, in the case of a limited liability

6.106

partnership, a determination for a voluntary winding-up has been made) with respect to it [¹or it enters administration], or a receiver or a manager of its undertaking is duly appointed, or possession is taken, by or on behalf of the holders of any debentures secured by a floating charge, of any property of the company or limited liability partnership comprised in or subject to the charge, or a voluntary arrangement proposed for the purposes of Part 1 of the Insolvency Act 1986 is approved under that Part of that Act;

(b) in Scotland—
 (i) an award of sequestration is made on his estate or he executes a trust deed for his creditors or enters into a composition contract;
 (ii) he has died and a judicial factor appointed under section 11A of the Judicial Factors (Scotland) Act 1889 is required by that section to divide his insolvent estate among his creditors; or
 (iii) where the employer is a company or a limited liability partnership, a winding-up order [¹. . .] is made or a resolution for voluntary winding-up is passed (or, in the case of a limited liability partnership, a determination for a voluntary winding-up is made) with respect to it [¹or it enters administration], or a receiver of its undertaking is duly appointed, or a voluntary arrangement proposed for the purposes of Part 1 of the Insolvency Act 1986 is approved under that Part.

AMENDMENT

1. Enterprise Act 2002 (Insolvency) Order 2003 (SI 2003/2096) art.5 and Sch.2 para.79 (September 15, 2003).

DEFINITIONS

"the Act"—see reg.2(1).
"the Board"—see reg.2(1).

GENERAL NOTE

6.107 The various references to insolvency law provisions include the special administration regime under the Investment Bank Special Administration Regulations 2011 (SI 2011/245) (see reg.27 and Sch.6 Pt 1 of those Regulations).

Liability of the Board to pay statutory adoption pay in cases of legal custody or imprisonment

6.108 **44.** Where—
(a) there is liability to pay statutory adoption pay in respect of a period which is subsequent to the last week falling within paragraph (1)(c) of regulation 27; or
(b) there is liability to pay statutory adoption pay during a period of detention in legal custody by virtue of the provisions of paragraph (2) of that regulation,
that liability shall, notwithstanding section 171ZM of the Act, be that of the Board and not the employer.

(SI 2002/2822 reg.44) (as amended)

DEFINITIONS

"the Act"—see reg.2(1).
"the Board"—see reg.2(1).

Payments by the Board

45. Where the Board become liable in accordance with regulation 43 or 44 to make payments of statutory paternity pay or, as the case may be, statutory adoption pay to a person, the first payment shall be made as soon as reasonably practicable after they become so liable, and payments thereafter shall be made at weekly intervals, by means of an instrument of payment or by such other means as appears to the Board to be appropriate in the circumstance of any particular case.

6.109

DEFINITION

"the Board"—see reg.2(1).

Persons unable to act

46.—(1) Where in the case of any person—
(a) statutory paternity pay or, as the case may be, statutory adoption pay is payable to him or he is alleged to be entitled to it;
(b) he is unable for the time being to act; and
(c) either—
  (i) no receiver has been appointed by the Court of Protection with power to receive statutory paternity pay or, as the case may be, statutory adoption pay on his behalf; or
  (ii) in Scotland, his estate is not being administered by any tutor, curator or other guardian acting or appointed in terms of law,
the Board may, upon written application to them by a person who, if a natural person, is over the age of 18, appoint that person to exercise, on behalf of the person unable to act, any right to which he may be entitled under Part 12ZA or, as the case may be, Part 12ZB of the Act and to deal on his behalf with any sums payable to him.
(2) Where the Board have made an appointment under paragraph (1)—
(a) they may at any time in their absolute discretion revoke it;
(b) the person appointed may resign his office after having given one month's notice in writing to the Board of his intention to do so; and
(c) the appointment shall terminate when the Board are notified that a receiver or other person to whom paragraph (1)(c) applies has been appointed.
(3) Anything required by Part 12ZA or 12ZB of the Act to be done by or to any person who is unable to act may be done by or to the person appointed under this regulation to act on his behalf, and the receipt of the person so appointed shall be a good discharge to the person's employer or former employer for any sum paid.

6.110

DEFINITIONS

"the Act"—see reg.2(1).
"the Board"—see reg.2(1).

Service of notices by post

6.111 47. A notice given in accordance with the provisions of these Regulations in writing contained in an envelope which is properly addressed and sent by prepaid post shall be treated as having been given on the day on which it is posted.

Social Security Contributions and Benefits Act 1992 (Application of Parts 12ZA [¹, 12ZB and 12ZC] to Adoptions from Overseas) Regulations 2003

(SI 2003/499) (AS AMENDED)

The Secretary of State, in exercise of the powers conferred on her by sections 171ZK and 171ZT of the Social Security Contributions and Benefits Act 1992 by this instrument, which contains only provision made by virtue of sections 2 and 4 of the Employment Act 2002 and is made before the end of the period of 6 months from the coming into force of those enactments, hereby makes the following Regulations—

ARRANGEMENT OF REGULATIONS

6.112
1. Citation, commencement and interpretation.
2. Application of Part 12ZA of the Act to adoptions from overseas.
3. Application of Part 12ZB of the Act to adoptions from overseas.
4. Application of Part 12ZC of the Act to adoptions from overseas

Schedule 1—Application of Part 12ZA of the Act to adoptions from overseas.
Schedule 2—Application of Part 12ZB of the Act to adoptions from overseas.

AMENDMENT

1. Social Security Contributions and Benefits Act 1992 (Application of Parts 12ZA and 12ZB to Adoptions from Overseas) (Amendment) Regulations 2014 (SI 2014/2857) regs 2 and 3 (November 19, 2014).

Citation, commencement and interpretation

6.113 1.—(1) These Regulations may be cited as the Social Security Contributions and Benefits Act 1992 (Application of Parts 12ZA [¹ , 12ZB and 12ZC] to Adoptions from Overseas) Regulations 2003 and shall come into force, in so far as they apply powers to make regulations, on 10th March 2003, and for all other purposes on 6th April 2003.

(2) In these Regulations—

"adoption from overseas" means the adoption of a child who enters Great Britain from outside the United Kingdom in connection with or for the purposes of adoption which does not involve the placement of the child for adoption under the law of any part of the United Kingdom;

"the Act" means the Social Security Contributions and Benefits Act 1992.

AMENDMENT

1. Social Security Contributions and Benefits Act 1992 (Application of Parts 12ZA and 12ZB to Adoptions from Overseas) (Amendment) Regulations 2014 (SI 2014/2857) regs 2 and 4 (November 19, 2014).

GENERAL NOTE

These Regulations, made under provisions inserted into the SSCBA 1992 by the Employment Act 2002, apply Pts XIIZA and XIIZB of the 1992 Act, as modified by these Regulations, to adoptions from overseas. These are adoptions of children who enter Great Britain from outside the UK in connection with or for the purposes of adoption which does not involve the placement of a child for adoption under the law of any part of the UK. The relevant adoption law requirements are set out in the Adoption (Bringing Children into the United Kingdom) Regulations 2003 (SI 2003/1173). The regulations relating to statutory paternity pay and statutory adoption pay in connection with such overseas adoptions are the Statutory Paternity Pay (Adoption) and Statutory Adoption Pay (Adoptions from Overseas) Regulations 2003 (SI 2003/500).

6.114

Application of Part 12ZA of the Act to adoptions from overseas

2. Part 12ZA of the Act [^{1} ([^{2}. . .)] shall apply in relation to adoptions from overseas, with the modifications of sections 171ZB, 171ZE [^{1}, 171ZEB, 171ZEE] and 171ZJ of the Act specified in the second column of Schedule 1.

6.115

AMENDMENTS

1. Social Security Contributions and Benefits Act 1992 (Application of Parts 12ZA and 12ZB to Adoptions from Overseas) Regulations 2003 (Amendment) Regulations 2010 (SI 2010/153) reg.2(2) (April 6, 2010).
2. Shared Parental Leave and Statutory Shared Parental Pay (Consequential Amendments to Subordinate Legislation) Order 2014 (SI 2014/3255) reg.14(2) (April 5, 2015).

Application of Part 12ZB of the Act to adoptions from overseas

3. Part 12ZB of the Act shall apply in relation to adoptions from overseas, with the modifications of sections 171ZL and 171ZS of the Act specified in the second column of Schedule 2.

6.116

[^{1} Application of Part 12ZC of the Act to adoptions from overseas

4. Part 12ZC of the Act shall apply in relation to adoptions from overseas, with the modifications of section 171ZV of the Act specified in the second column of Schedule 3.]

AMENDMENT

1. Social Security Contributions and Benefits Act 1992 (Application of Parts 12ZA and 12ZB to Adoptions from Overseas) (Amendment) Regulations 2014 (SI 2014/2857) regs 2 and 5 (November 19, 2014).

SCHEDULE 1

Regulation 2

APPLICATION OF PART 12ZA OF THE ACT TO ADOPTIONS FROM OVERSEAS

Provision	Modification
Section 171ZB(2)	[1. . .] In paragraph (a)(i), for "who is placed for adoption under the law of any part of the United Kingdom" substitute "who is adopted from overseas".

Provision	Modification
	In paragraph (a)(ii), for "a person with whom the child is so placed for adoption" substitute "an adopter of the child". [1In paragraph (b), omit "ending with the relevant week".] In paragraph (d), for "the day on which the child is placed for adoption" substitute "the day on which the child enters Great Britain". In paragraph (e), for "a person with whom the child is placed for adoption" substitute "an adopter of the child".
Section 171ZB(3)	[1For subsection (3) substitute— "(3) The references in subsection (2)(c) and (d) to the relevant week are to— (a) the week in which official notification is sent to the adopter, or (b) the week at the end of which the person satisfies the condition in subsection (2)(b), whichever is the later."]
Section 171ZB(6)	For "the placement for adoption of more than one child as part of the same arrangement" substitute "the adoption from overseas of more than one child as part of the same arrangement".
Section 171ZB(7)	Omit subsection (7).
Section 171ZE(3)	In paragraph (b), for "with the date of the child's placement for adoption" substitute "with the date of the child's entry into Great Britain".
Section 171ZE(10)	For subsection (10) substitute— "(10) Where more than one child is the subject of adoption from overseas as part of the same arrangement, and the date of entry of each child is different, the reference in subsection (3)(b) to the date of the child's entry into Great Britain shall be interpreted as a reference to the date of the entry of the first child to enter Great Britain".
	[4. . .] [4. . .]
Section 171ZJ(1)	In the appropriate places in the alphabetical order, insert— "adopter", in relation to a child, means a person by whom the child has been or is to be adopted;" "adoption from overseas" means the adoption of a child who enters Great Britain from outside the United Kingdom in connection with or for the purposes of adoption which does not involve the placement of the child for adoption under the law of any part of the United Kingdom, and the references to a child adopted from overseas shall be construed accordingly;" "official notification" means written notification, issued by or on behalf of the relevant domestic authority, that it is prepared to issue a certificate to the overseas authority concerned with the adoption of the child, or has issued a certificate and sent it to that authority, confirming, in either case, that the adopter is

(SI 2003/499 Sch.1) (as amended)

Provision	Modification
	eligible to adopt and has been assessed and approved as being a suitable adoptive parent;" "relevant domestic authority" means— (a) in the case of an adopter to whom the Intercountry Adoption (Hague Convention) Regulations 2003 apply and who is habitually resident in Wales, the National Assembly of Wales; (b) in the case of an adopter to whom the [³Adoptions with a Foreign Element (Scotland) Regulations 2009] apply and who is habitually resident in Scotland, the Scottish Ministers; (c) in any other case, the Secretary of State".

AMENDMENTS

1. Statutory Paternity Pay and Statutory Adoption Pay (Amendment) Regulations 2004 (SI 2004/488) reg.3(2) (April 6, 2004).
2. Social Security Contributions and Benefits Act 1992 (Application of Parts 12ZA and 12ZB to Adoptions from Overseas) Regulations 2003 (Amendment) Regulations 2010 (SI 2010/153) reg.2(3) (April 6, 2010).
3. Adoptions with a Foreign Element (Scotland) Amendment Regulations 2011 (SSI 2011/159) reg.9(2) (March 21, 2011) (for Scotland) and Adoption and Children (Scotland) Act 2007 (Consequential Modifications) Order 2011 (SI 2011/1740) art.3 and Sch.2 para.7(2) (July 15, 2011) (for England, Wales and Northern Ireland).
4. Shared Parental Leave and Statutory Shared Parental Pay (Consequential Amendments to Subordinate Legislation) Order 2014 (SI 2014/3255) reg.14(3) (April 5, 2015).

SCHEDULE 2   **Regulation 3**

APPLICATION OF PART 12ZB OF THE ACT TO ADOPTIONS FROM OVERSEAS

6.118

Provision	Modification
Section 171ZL(2)	[¹. . .] In paragraph (a), for "with whom a child is, or is expected to be, placed for adoption under the law of any part of the United Kingdom" substitute "who is, or is expected to be, an adopter of a child from overseas". [¹In paragraph (b), omit "ending with the relevant week".]
Section 171ZL(3)	[¹For subsection (3) substitute— "(3) The reference in subsection (2)(d) to the relevant week is to— (a) the week in which official notification is sent to the adopter, or (b) the week at the end of which the person satisfies the condition in subsection (2)(b), whichever is the later."] [¹. . .]
Section 171ZL(4)	In paragraph (b), for "placed for adoption with him" substitute "adopted by him".
Section 171ZL(5)	For "the placement, or expected placement, for adoption of more than one child" substitute "the adoption, or expected adoption, from overseas of more than one child".
Section 171ZS(1)	In the appropriate places in the alphabetical order, insert— ""adopter", in relation to a child, means a person by whom a child has been or is to be adopted;"

Social Security Contributions and Benefits Act 1992 Regulations 2003

Provision	Modification
	"adoption from overseas" means the adoption of a child who enters Great Britain from outside the United Kingdom in connection with or for the purposes of adoption which does not involve the placement of the child for adoption under the law of any part of the United Kingdom, and the reference to an adopter from overseas shall be construed accordingly;" "official notification" means written notification, issued by or on behalf of the relevant domestic authority, that it is prepared to issue a certificate to the overseas authority concerned with the adoption of the child, or has issued a certificate and sent it to that authority, confirming, in either case, that the adopter is eligible to adopt and has been assessed and approved as being a suitable adoptive parent;" "relevant domestic authority" means— (a) in the case of an adopter to whom the Intercountry Adoption (Hague Convention) Regulations 2003 apply and who is habitually resident in Wales, the National Assembly of Wales; (b) in the case of an adopter to whom the [²Adoptions with a Foreign Element (Scotland) Regulations 2009] apply and who is habitually resident in Scotland, the Scottish Ministers; (c) in any other case, the Secretary of State".

AMENDMENTS

1. Statutory Paternity Pay and Statutory Adoption Pay (Amendment) Regulations 2004 (SI 2004/488) reg.3(3) (April 6, 2004).
2. Adoptions with a Foreign Element (Scotland) Amendment Regulations 2011 (SSI 2011/159) reg.9(3) (March 21, 2011) (for Scotland) and Adoption and Children (Scotland) Act 2007 (Consequential Modifications) Order 2011 (SI 2011/1740) art.3 and Sch.2 para.7(3) (July 15, 2011) (for England, Wales and Northern Ireland).

[¹ SCHEDULE 3   Regulation 4

APPLICATION OF PART 12ZC OF THE ACT TO ADOPTIONS FROM OVERSEAS

6.119

Provision	Modification
Section 171ZV	In subsection (1), for "with whom a child is, or is expected to be, placed for adoption under the law of any part of the United Kingdom" substitute "by whom a child is, or is expected to be, adopted from overseas".
	In paragraph (g) of subsection (2), for "placement for adoption of the child" substitute "adoption of the child from overseas".
	In paragraph (a) of subsection (4), for "with whom a child is, or is expected to be, placed for adoption under the law of any part of the United Kingdom" substitute "by whom a child is, or is expected to be, adopted from overseas".
	In paragraph (h) of subsection (4), for "placement for adoption of the child" substitute "adoption of the child from overseas".
	In subsection (16), for "placement for adoption" substitute "adoption from overseas".
	After subsection (16) insert—
	"(16A) For the purposes of this section, a person adopts a child from overseas if the person adopts a child who

(SI 2003/499 Sch.3) (as amended)

Provision	Modification
	enters Great Britain from outside the United Kingdom in connection with or for the purposes of adoption which does not involve the placement of the child for adoption under the law of any part of the United Kingdom.".
	Omit subsection (17).
	Omit subsection (18).]

AMENDMENT

1. Social Security Contributions and Benefits Act 1992 (Application of Parts 12ZA and 12ZB to Adoptions from Overseas) (Amendment) Regulations 2014 (SI 2014/2857) regs 2 and 6 (November 19, 2014).

Statutory Paternity Pay (Adoption) and Statutory Adoption Pay (Adoptions from Overseas) (Administration) Regulations 2003

(SI 2003/1192)

The Secretary of State, in exercise of the powers conferred on her by sections 7(1), 2(a) and (b), (4)(a), (b) and (c) and (5), 8(1) and (2)(a), (b) and (c), 10(1) and (2) and 51(1) of the Employment Act 2002 and sections 8(1)(f) and 25 of the Social Security Contributions (Transfer of Functions, etc.) Act 1999 and with the concurrence of the Commissioners of Inland Revenue, hereby makes the following Regulations:

ARRANGEMENT OF REGULATIONS

1. Citation and commencement.
2. Interpretation.
3. Application of the Statutory Paternity Pay and Statutory Adoption Pay (Administration) Regulations 2002 to adoptions from overseas.

6.120

Citation and commencement

1. These Regulations may be cited as the Statutory Paternity Pay (Adoption) and Statutory Adoption Pay (Adoptions from Overseas) (Administration) Regulations 2003 and shall come into force on 23rd May 2003.

6.121

GENERAL NOTE

These Regulations apply the Statutory Paternity Pay and Statutory Adoption Pay (Administration) Regulations 2002 (SI 2002/2820) to adoptions from overseas with the necessary modifications.

6.122

Interpretation

2. In these Regulations, "adoption from overseas" means the adoption of a child who enters Great Britain from outside the United Kingdom in connection with or for the purposes of adoption which does not involve the placement of the child for adoption under the law of any part of the United Kingdom.

6.123

Application of the Statutory Paternity Pay and Statutory Adoption Pay (Administration) Regulations 2002 to adoptions from overseas

6.124 3.—(1) The Statutory Paternity Pay and Statutory Adoption Pay (Administration) Regulations 2002 shall apply in the case of adoptions from overseas with the modifications set out in the following paragraphs of this regulation.

(2) In regulation 2(1) (interpretation)—
(a) in the definition of "adopter", for the words "with whom the child is matched for adoption" substitute "by whom the child has been or is to be adopted";
(b) after the definition of "income tax quarter", insert—
"official notification" means written notification, issued by or on behalf of the relevant domestic authority, that it is prepared to issue a certificate to the overseas authority concerned with the adoption of the child, or has issued a certificate and sent it to that authority, confirming, in either case, that the adopter is eligible to adopt and has been assessed and approved as being a suitable adoptive parent";
(c) in the definition of "paternity leave", insert at the end "as modified in its application to adoptions from overseas by the Employment Rights Act 1996 (Application of Section 80B to Adoptions from Overseas) Regulations 2003"; and
(d) after the definition of "paternity pay period" insert—
"relevant domestic authority means:—
(a) in the case of an adopter to whom the Intercountry Adoption (Hague Convention) Regulations 2003 apply and who is habitually resident in Wales, the National Assembly for Wales;
(b) in the case of an adopter to whom the [1Adoptions with a Foreign Element (Scotland) Regulations 2009] apply and who is habitually resident in Scotland, the Scottish Ministers; and
(c) in any other case, the Secretary of State;".

(3) After regulation 2(2), insert—
"(3) References in these Regulations to provisions of Parts 12ZA and 12ZB of the Contributions and Benefits Act are to be construed as references to those provisions as modified by the Social Security Contributions and Benefits Act 1992 (Application of Parts 12ZA and 12ZB to Adoptions from Overseas) Regulations 2003."

(4) In regulation 11(3)(b)(ii) (time within which an employer is required to give decision that he has no liability to make payments), for "the end of the seven-day period that starts on the date on which the adopter is notified of having been matched with the child" substitute "the date on which the employer's evidence was provided, or, where not all of the evidence referred to in paragraph (1) was provided on one date, the date on which the last of the evidence was provided".

(5) Omit regulation 11(4).

AMENDMENT

1. Adoptions with a Foreign Element (Scotland) Amendment Regulations 2011 (SSI 2011/159 reg.7 (March 21, 2011) (for Scotland) and Adoption and Children (Scotland) Act 2007 (Consequential Modifications) Order 2011 (SI 2011/1740) art.3 and Sch.2 para.9 (July 15, 2011) (for England, Wales and Northern Ireland).

(SI 2003/1194) (as amended)

Statutory Paternity Pay (Adoption) and Statutory Adoption Pay (Adoptions from Overseas) (No.2) Regulations 2003

(SI 2003/1194) (AS AMENDED)

The Secretary of State, in exercise of the powers conferred on her by sections 171ZB(2)(a), 171ZC(3)(a) to (d), (f) and (g), 171ZD(2) and (3), 171ZE(2)(a) and (b)(i), (3)(b), (7) and (8), 171ZG(3), 171ZJ(1), (3), (4), (7) and (8), 171ZL(8)(b) to (d), (f) and (g), 171ZM(2) and (3), 171ZN(2), (5) and (6), 171ZP(6), 171ZS(1), (3), (4), (7) and (8), and 175(4) of the Social Security Contributions and Benefits Act 1992, section 5(1)(g), (i) and (p) of the Social Security Administration Act 1992 and with the concurrence of the Commissioners of Inland Revenue in so far as such concurrence is required, by this instrument, which contains only provision made by virtue of sections 2, 4 and 53 and paragraphs 8 and 11 of Schedule 7 to the Employment Act 2002 and is made before the end of the period of 6 months from the coming into force of these enactments, hereby makes the following Regulations:

ARRANGEMENT OF REGULATIONS

General

1. Citation and commencement.
2. Interpretation and scope.
3. Application of the General Regulations to these Regulations.
4. Application.

Statutory paternity pay (adoption)

5. Conditions of entitlement to statutory paternity pay (adoption) in respect of adoptions from overseas: relationship with child and with adopter.
6. Period of payment of statutory paternity pay (adoption) in respect of adoptions from overseas.
7. Additional notice requirements for statutory paternity pay (adoption) in respect of adoptions from overseas.
8. Qualifying period for statutory paternity pay (adoption) in respect of adoptions from overseas.
9. Evidence of entitlement for statutory paternity pay (adoption) in respect of adoptions from overseas.
10. Entitlement to statutory paternity pay (adoption) where there is more than one employer in respect of adoptions from overseas.
11. Avoidance of liability for statutory paternity pay (adoption) in respect of adoptions from overseas.
12. Adoption pay period in respect of adoptions from overseas.

Statutory adoption pay

13. Adoption pay period in respect of adoptions from overseas where adoption is disrupted.
14. Additional notice requirements for statutory adoption pay in respect of adoptions from overseas.
15. Evidence of entitlement to statutory adoption pay in respect of adoptions from overseas.
16. Entitlement to statutory adoption pay in respect of adoptions from overseas where there is more than one employer.

Statutory Paternity Pay and Statutory Adoption Pay (No.2) Regs 2003

17. Termination of employment and liability to pay statutory adoption pay in respect of adoptions from overseas.
18. Avoidance of liability for statutory adoption pay in respect of adoptions from overseas.
19. Revocation.

General

Citation and commencement

6.127   **1.** These Regulations may be cited as the Statutory Paternity Pay (Adoption) and Statutory Adoption Pay (Adoptions from Overseas) (No.2) Regulations 2003 and shall come into force on 30th May 2003.

GENERAL NOTE

6.128   These Regulations, made under provisions inserted into the SSCBA 1992 by the Employment Act 2002, make provision relating to statutory paternity pay and statutory adoption pay in respect of adoptions from overseas. They should be read together with the Social Security Contributions and Benefits Act 1992 (Application of Pts XIIZA and XIIZB to Adoptions from Overseas) Regulations 2003 (SI 2003/499), which provide for Pts XIIZA and XIIZB of the 1992 Act to have effect, with the modification prescribed in those Regulations, in relation to cases which involve adoption, but not the placement of a child for adoption under the law of any part of the United Kingdom. Regulation 19 of these (No.2) Regulations revokes the Statutory Pay (Adoption) and Statutory Adoption Pay (Adoptions from Overseas) Regulations 2003 (SI 2003/500), which came into force on April 6, 2003 and originally made provision for paternity and adoption pay in the case of adoptions from overseas. The (No.2) Regulations are virtually in identical form to the original set. The main difference is the correction of "employee" to read "employer" in reg.11 where it first appears, but a number of other minor drafting amendments have also been made.

Interpretation and scope

6.129   **2.**—(1) In these Regulations—
"the Act" means the Social Security Contributions and Benefits Act 1992;
"adopter", in relation to a child, means a person by whom the child has been or is to be adopted;
"adoption from overseas" means the adoption of a child who enters Great Britain from outside the United Kingdom in connection with or for the purposes of adoption which does not involve the placement of the child for adoption under the law of any part of the United Kingdom;
"the Application Regulations" means the Social Security Contributions and Benefits Act 1992 (Application of Parts 12ZA and 12ZB to Adoptions from Overseas) Regulations 2003;
"the Board" means the Commissioners of Inland Revenue;
"enter Great Britain" means enter Great Britain from outside the United Kingdom in connection with or for the purposes of adoption, and cognate expressions shall be construed accordingly;
"the General Regulations" means the Statutory Paternity Pay and Statutory Adoption Pay (General) Regulations 2002;
"official notification" means written notification, issued by or on behalf of the relevant domestic authority, that it is prepared to issue a certificate to the overseas authority concerned with the adoption of the child,

or has issued a certificate and sent it to that authority, confirming, in either case, that the adopter is eligible to adopt, and has been assessed and approved as being a suitable adoptive parent;

"relevant domestic authority" means—

(a) in the case of an adopter to whom the Intercountry Adoption (Hague Convention) Regulations 2003 apply and who is habitually resident in Wales, the National Assembly for Wales;

(b) in the case of an adopter to whom the [1Adoptions with a Foreign Element (Scotland) Regulations 2009] apply and who is habitually resident in Scotland, the Scottish Ministers;

(c) in any other case, the Secretary of State;

"statutory paternity pay (adoption)" means statutory paternity pay payable in accordance with the provisions of Part 12ZA of the Act, as modified by the Application Regulations, where the conditions specified in section 171ZB(2) of the Act, as modified by the Application Regulations, are satisfied.

(2) References in these Regulations to the provisions of Parts 12ZA and 12ZB of the Act are to be construed as references to those provisions as modified by the Application Regulations.

(3) These Regulations apply to statutory paternity pay (adoption) and statutory adoption pay in respect of adoptions from overseas.

AMENDMENT

1. Adoptions with a Foreign Element (Scotland) Amendment Regulations 2011 (SSI 2011/159) reg. 6 (March 21, 2011) (for Scotland) and Adoption and Children (Scotland) Act 2007 (Consequential Modifications) Order 2011 (SI 2011/1740) art.3 and Sch.2 para.10 (July 15, 2011) (for England, Wales and Northern Ireland).

Application of the General Regulations to these Regulations

3.—(1) Subject to paragraph (2), the provisions of the General Regulations mentioned in paragraph (3) shall, in so far as they apply to statutory paternity pay (adoption) and statutory adoption pay, apply to adoptions from overseas.

(2) Any references to the provisions of Parts 12ZA or 12ZB of the Act in the regulations of the General Regulations mentioned in paragraph (3) shall be construed as references to those provisions as modified by the Application Regulations.

(3) The provisions of the General Regulations referred to in paragraph (1) are regulations 17 to 19, 26 to 28, 31 to 39, 41 to 47 and, subject to paragraph (4), regulation 40.

(4) In the General Regulations, the provisions of regulation 40 shall apply as if—

[1(a) in paragraph (2)(b), for "the week in which the adopter is notified of being matched with the child for the purposes of adoption" there were substituted—

"the week in which—

(i) official notification is sent to the adopter or

(ii) the person satisfies the condition in section 171ZB(2)(b) or 171ZL(2)(b) of the Act (26 weeks' continuous employment), whichever is the later;"]

(b) at the end of paragraph (2), there were added " 'official notification' has the same meaning in the Statutory Paternity Pay (Adoption)

Statutory Paternity Pay and Statutory Adoption Pay (No.2) Regs 2003

and Statutory Adoption Pay (Adoptions from Overseas) (No.2) Regulations 2003".

AMENDMENT

1. Statutory Paternity Pay and Statutory Adoption Pay (Amendment) Regulations 2004 (SI 2004/488) reg.4 (April 6, 2004).

DEFINITIONS

"the Act—see reg.2(1).
"adopter"—see *ibid*.
"adoption from overseas"—see *ibid*.
"the Application Regulation"—see *ibid*.
"the General Regulations"—see *ibid*.
"official notification"—see *ibid*.
"statutory paternity pay (adoption)"—see *ibid*.

Application

6.131 **4.**—(1) Subject to the provisions of Part 12ZA of the Act (statutory paternity pay), the provisions of the General Regulations mentioned in paragraph (3) of regulation 3 and these Regulations, there is entitlement to statutory paternity pay (adoption) in respect of children who enter Great Britain on or after 6th April 2003.
(2) Subject to the provisions of Part 12ZB of the Act (statutory adoption pay), the provisions of the General Regulations mentioned in paragraph (3) of regulation 3 and these Regulations, there is entitlement to statutory adoption pay in respect of children who enter Great Britain on or after 6th April, 2003.

DEFINITIONS

"the Act"—see reg.2(1).
"enter Great Britain"—see *ibid*.
"the General Regulation"—see *ibid*.
"Part XIIZA"—see reg.(2).
"Pt XIIZB"—see *ibid*.
"statutory paternity pay (adoption)"—see reg.2(1).

Statutory paternity pay (adoption)

Conditions of entitlement to statutory paternity pay (adoption) in respect of adoptions from overseas: relationship with child and with adopter

6.132 **5.**—(1) The conditions prescribed under section 171ZB(2)(a) of the Act are that a person—
(a) is married to [1, the civil partner] or the partner of a child's adopter (or in a case where there are two adopters, married to [1, the civil partner] or the partner of the other adopter); and
(b) has, or expects to have, the main responsibility (apart from the responsibility of the child's adopter or, in a case where there are two adopters, together with the other adopter) for the upbringing of the child.

(SI 2003/1194 reg.5) (as amended)

(2) For the purpose of paragraph (1), "partner" means a person (whether of a different sex or the same sex) who lives with the adopter and the child in an enduring family relationship but is not a relative of the adopter of a kind specified in paragraph (3).

(3) The relatives of a child's adopter referred to in the definition of "partner" in paragraph (2) are the adopter's parent, grandparent, sister, brother, aunt or uncle.

(4) References to relationships in paragraph (3)—
(a) are to relationships of the full blood or half blood or, in the case of an adopted person, such of those relationships as would exist but for the adoption; and
(b) include the relationship of a child with his adoptive, or former adoptive parents but do not include any other adoptive relationships.

AMENDMENT

1. Civil Partnership Act 2004 (Amendments to Subordinate Legislation) Order 2005 (SI 2005/2114) art.2(17) and Sch.17 para.6 (December 5, 2005).

DEFINITIONS

"the Act"—see reg.2(1).
"adopter"—see *ibid.*
"partner"—see para.(2).

Period of payment of statutory paternity pay (adoption) in respect of adoptions from overseas

6.—(1) Subject to notice under section 171ZC(1) of the Act, paragraph (92) and reg.8, a person entitled to statutory paternity pay (adoption) may choose the statutory paternity pay period to begin on—

(a) the date on which the child enters Great Britain or, where the person is at work on that day, the following day; or
(b) a pre-determined date, specified by the person, which is later than the date on which the child enters Great Britain.

(2) In a case where statutory paternity pay (adoption) is payable in respect of a child where the adopter has received official notification before 6th April 2003, the statutory paternity pay period shall begin on a predetermined date, later than the date of entry, specified by the person entitled to such pay in a notice under section 171ZC(1) of the Act, which is at least 28 days after the date on which that notice was given, unless the person liable to pay statutory paternity pay (adoption) agrees to the period beginning earlier.

(3) A person may choose for statutory paternity pay (adoption) to be paid in respect of a period of a week.

(4) A choice made in accordance with paragraph (1) is not irrevocable, but where a person subsequently makes a different choice in relation to the beginning of the statutory paternity pay period, section 171ZC(1) of the Act shall apply to it.

DEFINITIONS

"the Act"—see reg.2(1).
"adopter"—see *ibid.*
"enter Great Britain"—see *ibid.*

Statutory Paternity Pay and Statutory Adoption Pay (No.2) Regs 2003

"official notification"—see *ibid.*
"statutory paternity pay (adoption)"—see *ibid.*

Additional notice requirements for statutory paternity pay (adoption) in respect of adoptions from overseas

6.134 7.—(1) Where a person gives notice under section 171ZC(1) of the Act he shall give further notice of the following matters to the person liable to pay him statutory paternity pay (adoption)—
   (a) the date on which official notification was received, within 28 days of that date, or within 28 days of his completion of 26 weeks of continuous employment with that person, whichever is the later;
   (b) the date on which the child enters Great Britain, within 28 days of entry.
(2) Where the child has not entered Great Britain on the expected date, the person shall, if he wishes to claim statutory paternity pay (adoption), give notice to the person liable to pay it, as soon as is reasonably practicable, that the period in respect of which statutory paternity pay is to be paid shall begin on a date different from that originally chosen by him.
(3) That date may be any date chosen in accordance with paragraph (1) of regulation 6 or specified in accordance with paragraph (2) of that regulation.
(4) Where it becomes known to that person that the child will not enter Great Britain, he shall notify the person who would have been liable to pay statutory pay (adoption), as soon as is reasonably practicable.

DEFINITIONS

"the Act"—see reg.2(1).
"enter Great Britain"—see *ibid.*
"official notification"—see *ibid.*
"statutory paternity pay (adoption)"—see *ibid.*

Qualifying period for statutory paternity pay (adoption) in respect of adoptions from overseas

6.135 8. The qualifying period for the purposes of section 171ZE(2) of the Act (period within which the statutory pay period must occur) is a period of 56 days beginning with the date the child enters Great Britain.

DEFINITIONS

"the Act"—see reg.2(1).
"enter Great Britain"—see *ibid.*

Evidence of entitlement for statutory paternity pay (adoption) in respect of adoptions from overseas

6.136 9.—(1) A person shall produce evidence of his entitlement to statutory paternity pay (adoption) in respect of adoptions from overseas by providing in writing to the person who will be liable to pay him statutory paternity pay (adoption) the declarations specified in paragraph (2) and the information specified in paragraph (3).
(2) The declarations referred to in para.(1) are as follows—
   (a) that he meets the conditions prescribed under section 171ZB(2)
      (a) of the Act and that it is not the case that statutory paternity pay

(adoption) is not payable to him by virtue of the provisions of section 171ZE(4) of the Act;
(b) that he has elected to receive statutory paternity pay (adoption), and not statutory adoption pay under Part 12ZB of the Act;
(c) that official notification has been received.

(3) The information referred to in paragraph (1) is as follows—
(a) the name of the person claiming statutory paternity pay (adoption);
(b) the date on which it is expected that the child will enter Great Britain or, where the child has already entered Great Britain, that date;
(c) the date from which it is expected that the liability to pay statutory paternity pay (adoption) will begin;
(d) whether the period chosen in respect of which statutory paternity pay (adoption) is to be payable is a week.

(4) The declarations mentioned in paragraph (2) and information mentioned in paragraph (3) shall be provided to the person liable to pay statutory paternity pay (adoption) at least 28 days before the date mentioned in sub-paragraph (c) of paragraph (3) or, if that is not reasonably practicable, as soon as is reasonably practicable thereafter.

DEFINITIONS

"the Act"—see reg.2(1).
"adoption from overseas"—see *ibid*.
"enter Great Britain"—see *ibid*.
"official notification"—see *ibid*.
"Pt XIIZB"—see reg.2(2).
"statutory paternity pay (adoption)"—see reg.2(1).

Entitlement to statutory paternity pay (adoption) where there is more than one employer in respect of adoptions from overseas

10. Statutory paternity pay (adoption) shall be payable to a person in respect of a statutory pay week during any part of which he works only for an employer—
(a) who is not liable to pay him statutory paternity pay (adoption); and
(b) for whom he has worked in the week in which the adopter receives official notification.

6.137

DEFINITIONS

"adopter"—see reg.2(1).
"official notification"—see *ibid*.
"statutory paternity pay (adoption)"—see *ibid*.

Avoidance of liability for statutory paternity pay (adoption) in respect of adoptions from overseas

11.—(1) A former employer shall be liable to make payments of statutory paternity pay (adoption) to a former employee in any case where the employee has been employed for a continuous period of at least 8 weeks and his contract of service was brought to an end by the former employer solely, or mainly, for the purpose of avoiding liability for statutory paternity pay (adoption).

6.138

(2) In a case falling within paragraph (1)—
(a) the employee shall be treated as if he had been employed for a continuous period ending with the day the child enters Great Britain;
(b) his normal weekly earnings shall be calculated by reference to his normal weekly earnings for the period of 8 weeks ending with the last day in respect of which he was paid under his former contract of service.

DEFINITIONS

"enter Great Britain"—see reg.2(1).
"statutory paternity pay (adoption)"—see *ibid.*

Statutory adoption pay

Adoption pay period in respect of adoptions from overseas

12.—(1) Subject to paragraph (2), a person entitled to statutory adoption pay may choose the adoption pay period to begin—
(a) on the date on which the child enters Great Britain or, where the person is at work on that day, on the following day;
(b) on the pre-determined date, specified by him, which is no later than 28 days after the date the child enters Great Britain.

(2) In a case where statutory adoption pay is payable in respect of a child where the adopter has received official notification before 6th April 2003, the statutory adoption pay period shall begin on a predetermined date, later than the date of entry, specified by the person entitled to such pay in a notice under section 171ZL(6) of the Act, which is at least 28 days after the date on which that notice was given, unless the person liable to pay statutory adoption pay agrees to the period commencing earlier.

(3) Where the choice made is that mentioned in sub-paragraph (b) of paragraph (1) or in a case where paragraph (2) applies, the adoption pay period shall, unless the employer agrees to the adoption pay period beginning earlier, begin no earlier than 28 days after notice under section 171ZL(6) of the Act has been given.

(4) Subject to regulation 13, the duration of any adoption pay period shall be a continuous period of 26 weeks.

(5) A choice made under paragraph (1), or a date specified under paragraph (2), is not irrevocable, but where a person subsequently makes a different choice or specifies a different date in relation to the beginning of the statutory adoption pay period, section 171ZL(6) of the Act shall apply to it.

DEFINITIONS

"the Act"—see reg.2(1).
"adopter"—see *ibid.*
"enter Great Britain"—see *ibid.*
"official notification"—see *ibid.*

(SI 2003/1194 reg.13) (as amended)

Adoption pay period in respect of adoptions from overseas where adoption is disrupted

13.—(1) Where after a child enters Great Britain the child—

(a) dies; or

(b) ceases to live with the adopter,

the adoption pay period shall terminate in accordance with the provisions of paragraph (2).

(2) The adoption pay period shall, in a case falling within paragraph (1), terminate 8 weeks after the end of the week specified in paragraph (3).

(3) The week referred to in paragraph (2) is—

(a) in a case falling within paragraph (1)(a), the week during which the child dies;

(b) in a case falling within paragraph (1)(b), the week during which the child ceases to live with the adopter.

(4) For the purposes of paragraph (3), "week" means a period of 7 days beginning with Sunday.

6.140

DEFINITIONS

"adopter"—see reg.2(1).
"enter Great Britain"—see *ibid*.
"week"—see para.(4).

Additional notice requirements for statutory adoption pay in respect of adoptions from overseas

14.—(1) Where a person gives notice under section 171ZL(6) of the Act he shall give further notice of the following matters to the person liable to pay statutory adoption pay—

(a) the date on which official notification was received, within 28 days of that date, or within 28 days of his completion of 26 weeks of continuous employment, whichever is the later;

(b) the date on which the child enters Great Britain, within 28 days of entry.

(2) Where the child has not entered Great Britain on the expected date, the person shall, if he wishes to claim statutory adoption pay, give notice to the person liable to pay it, as soon as is reasonably practicable, that the period in respect of which statutory adoption pay is to be paid shall begin on a date different fromthat originally chosen by him.

(3) That date may be any date chosen in accordance with paragraph (1) of regulation 12 or specified in accordance with paragraph (2) of that regulation.

(4) Where it becomes known to the adopter that the child will not enter Great Britain, he shall notify the person who would have been liable to pay statutory adoption pay as soon as is reasonably practicable.

6.141

DEFINITIONS

"the act"—see reg.2(1).
"adopter"—see *ibid*.
"enter Great Britain"—see *ibid*.
"official notification"—see *ibid*.

855

Evidence of entitlement to statutory adoption pay in respect of adoptions from overseas

6.142   **15.**—(1) A person shall provide evidence of his entitlement to statutory adoption pay by providing, to the person who will be liable to pay it, a copy of the official notification and, in writing—
(a) the information specified in paragraph (2);
(b) a declaration that he has elected to receive statutory adoption pay, and not statutory paternity pay (adoption) under Part 12ZA of the Act;
(c) evidence, to be provided within 28 days of the child's entry into Great Britain, as to that date.
(2) The information referred to in paragraph (1) is—
(a) the name and address of the person claiming statutory adoption pay;
(b) the date on which it is expected that the child will enter Great Britain or, where he has already done so, the date of entry.
(3) The information and declaration referred to in paragraph (1) shall be provided to the person liable to pay statutory adoption pay at least 28 days before the date chosen as the beginning of the adoption pay period in accordance with paragraph (1) of regulation 12 or specified in accordance with paragraph (2) of that regulation or, if that is not reasonably practicable, as soon as is reasonably practicable thereafter.

DEFINITIONS

"the Act"—see reg.2(1).
"enter Great Britain"—see *ibid.*
"official notification"—see *ibid.*
"Pt XIIZA"—see reg.2(2).
"statutory paternity pay (adoption)"—see reg.2(1).

Entitlement to statutory adoption pay in respect of adoptions from overseas where there is more than one employer

6.143   **16.** Statutory adoption pay shall be payable to a person in respect of a week during any part of which he works for an employer—
(a) who is not liable to pay him statutory adoption pay; and
(b) for whom he has worked in the week in which he receives official notification.

DEFINITION

"official notification"—see reg.2(1).

Termination of employment and liability to pay statutory adoption pay in respect of adoptions from overseas

6.144   **17.**—(1) Where the employment of a person who satisfies the conditions of entitlement to statutory adoption pay in respect of adoptions from overseas terminates for whatever reason (including dismissal) before the adoption pay period chosen or specified by that person in accordance with regulation 12 has begun, the period shall begin on a date chosen by that person which is at least 28 days after notice has been given and within 28 days of the date of the child's entry into Great Britain.

(SI 2003/1194 reg.17) (as amended)

(2) Where the statutory adoption pay period has not commenced within a period of 6 months of the adopter's leaving his employer, liability to pay statutory adoption pay shall, notwithstanding section 171ZM(1) of the Act, pass to the Board.

(3) Where liability to pay statutory adoption pay has passed to the Board in accordance with paragraph (2) and the adopter, having started employment as an employed earner, becomes entitled to statutory adoption pay by virtue of that employment, the liability of the Board shall cease and section 171ZM(1) of the Act shall apply.

DEFINITIONS

"the Act"—see reg.2(1).
"adopter"—see *ibid.*
"adoption from overseas"—see *ibid.*
"the Board"—see *ibid.*

Avoidance of liability for statutory adoption pay in respect of adoptions from overseas

18.—(1) A former employer shall be liable to make payments of statutory adoption pay to a former employee in any case where the employee had been employed for a continuous period of at least 8 weeks and his contract of service was brought to an end by the former employer solely, or mainly, for the purpose of avoiding liability for statutory adoption pay.

(2) In a case falling within paragraph (1)—
(a) the employee shall be treated as if he had been employed for a continuous period ending with the week in which he received official notification; and
(b) his normal weekly earnings shall be calculated by reference to his normal weekly earnings for the period of 8 weeks ending with the last day in respect of which he was paid under his former contract of service.

DEFINITION

"official notification"—see reg.2(1).

Revocation

19. The Statutory Paternity Pay (Adoption) and Statutory Adoption Pay (Adoptions from Overseas) Regulations 2003 are hereby revoked.

Ordinary Statutory Paternity Pay (Adoption), Additional Statutory Paternity Pay (Adoption) and Statutory Adoption Pay (Adoptions from Overseas) (Persons Abroad and Mariners) Regulations 2010

(SI 2010/150)

ARRANGEMENT OF REGULATIONS

1. Citation and commencement
2. Interpretation

3. Revocation

4. Application of the Statutory Paternity Pay and Statutory Adoption Pay (Persons Abroad and Mariners) Regulations 2002 to adoptions from overseas

The Secretary of State makes the following Regulations in exercise of the powers conferred by sections 171ZI, 171ZJ(1), 171ZR and 171ZS(1) of the Social Security Contributions and Benefits Act 1992.

The Secretary of State makes these Regulations with the concurrence of the Treasury and after agreement by the Social Security Advisory Committee that the proposals in respect of these Regulations shall not be referred to it.

Citation and commencement

6.148　　**1.**—(1) These Regulations may be cited as the Ordinary Statutory Paternity Pay (Adoption), Additional Statutory Paternity Pay (Adoption) and Statutory Adoption Pay (Adoptions from Overseas) (Persons Abroad and Mariners) Regulations 2010.

(2) These Regulations come into force immediately after the coming into force of the Statutory Paternity Pay and Statutory Adoption Pay (Persons Abroad and Mariners) Regulations 2002 (Amendment) Regulations 2010.

Interpretation

6.149　　**2.** In these Regulations, "adoption from overseas" means the adoption of a child who enters Great Britain from outside the United Kingdom in connection with or for the purposes of adoption which does not involve the placement of the child for adoption under the law of any part of the United Kingdom.

Revocation

6.150　　**3.** The Statutory Paternity Pay (Adoption) and Statutory Adoption Pay (Adoptions from Overseas) (Persons Abroad and Mariners) Regulations 2003 are revoked.

Application of the Statutory Paternity Pay and Statutory Adoption Pay (Persons Abroad and Mariners) Regulations 2002 to adoptions from overseas

6.151　　**4.**—(1) The Statutory Paternity Pay and Statutory Adoption Pay (Persons Abroad and Mariners) Regulations 2002 shall have effect in relation to adoptions from overseas with the modifications set out in the following paragraphs of this regulation.

(2) In regulation 1(2) (interpretation)—
(a) omit the definitions of "additional statutory paternity pay (birth)" and "ordinary statutory paternity pay (birth);
(b) for the definition of "adopter", substitute—
""adopter", in relation to a child adopted from overseas, means—
(a) a person by whom the child has been or is to be adopted, or
(b) in a case where the child has been or is to be adopted by two people jointly, whichever of them has elected to take adoption leave under section 75A or 75B of the Employment Rights Act 1996 in respect of the child;";

(c) after the definition of "mariner", insert—
""official notification" means written notification, issued by or on behalf of the relevant
central authority, that it is prepared to issue a certificate to the overseas authority
concerned with the adoption of the child, or has issued a certificate and sent it to that
authority, confirming, in either case, that the adopter is eligible to adopt and has been
assessed and approved as being a suitable adoptive parent;";
(d) after the definition of "ordinary statutory paternity pay (adoption)", insert—
"relevant central authority" means—
(a) in the case of an adopter to whom Part 3 of the Adoptions with a Foreign Element Regulations 2005 apply and who is habitually resident in Wales, the Welsh Ministers;
(b) in the case of an adopter to whom [1 . . .] the Adoptions with a Foreign Element (Scotland) Regulations 2009 apply and who is habitually resident in Scotland, the Scottish Ministers; and
(c) in any other case, the Secretary of State;".

(3) For regulation 1(3), substitute—

"(3) References in these Regulations to provisions of Parts 12ZA and 12ZB of the Act are to be construed as references to those provisions as modified by the Social Security Contributions and Benefits Act 1992 (Application of Parts 12ZA and 12ZB to Adoptions from Overseas) Regulations 2003.".

(4) In regulation 5 (entitlement to ordinary statutory paternity pay and additional statutory paternity pay where person has worked in an EEA State)—
(a) omit paragraph (1);
(b) in the first line of paragraph (2), after "and who", insert ", in the week in which the person receives an official notification or completes 26 weeks' continuous employment with the person's employer, whichever is the later"; and
(c) in paragraph (2)(a) omit the words "in the week in which the adopter is notified of being matched with the child for the purposes of adoption".

(5) In regulation 6 (entitlement to statutory adoption pay where person has worked in an EEA State)—
(a) in the first line, after "and who", insert ", in the week in which the person receives an official notification or completes 26 weeks' continuous employment with the person's employer, whichever is the later";
(b) in paragraph (a), omit the words "in the week in which he is notified that he has been matched with the child for the purposes of adoption"; and
(c) in the full out, for the word "he", substitute "the person".

AMENDMENT

1. Adoptions with a Foreign Element (Scotland) Amendment Regulations 2011 (SSI 2011/159) reg.5 (March 21, 2011).

Additional Statutory Paternity Pay (National Health Service Employees) Regulations 2010

(SI 2010/152)

The Secretary of State in exercise of the powers conferred by section 171ZJ(9) and (10) of the Social Security Contributions and Benefits Act 1992 and with the concurrence of the Commissioners for Her Majesty's Revenue and Customs, by this instrument, which contains only provision consequential upon sections 6 to 10 of the Work and Families Act and is made before the end of the period of six months beginning with the coming into force of those enactments, makes the following Regulations.

ARRANGEMENT OF REGULATIONS

1. Citation, commencement and interpretation
2. Treatment of more than one contract of employment as one contract
3. Notification of election
4. Provision of information
5. Treatment of two or more employers as one
6. Time for which an election is to have effect

Citation, commencement and interpretation

1.—(1) These Regulations may be cited as the Additional Statutory Paternity Pay (National Health Service Employees) Regulations 2010 and come into force on 6th April 2010.

(2) In these Regulations—

"the 2006 Act" means the National Health Service Act 2006;

"the 2006 (Wales) Act" means the National Health Service (Wales) Act 2006;

"the Act" means the Social Security Contributions and Benefits Act 1992;

"additional statutory paternity pay" means additional statutory paternity pay payable in accordance with the provisions of Part 12ZA of the Act where the conditions specified in section 171ZEA(2) or 171ZEB(2) are satisfied;

"additional statutory paternity pay period" means the period, determined in accordance with section 171ZEE of the Act and with regulations made under that section, as the period in respect of which additional statutory paternity pay is payable;

"Local Health Board" means a Local Health Board established under section 11 of the 2006 (Wales) Act;

"Primary Care Trust" means a Primary Care Trust continuing in existence or established under section 18 of the 2006 Act;

"Special Health Authority" means, in relation to England, a Special Health Authority established under section 28 of the 2006 Act and, in relation to Wales, a Special Health Authority established under section 22 of the 2006 (Wales) Act; and

"Strategic Health Authority" means a Strategic Health Authority continuing in existence or established under section 13 of the 2006 Act.

(SI 2010/152 reg. 1)

(3) References in these Regulations to Part 12ZA of the Act are references to sections 171ZEA to 171ZEE and, in so far as they concern additional statutory paternity pay, to sections 171ZF to 171ZJ of the Act.

Treatment of more than one contract of employment as one contract

2. Where—　　　　　　　　　　　　　　　　　　　　　　　　　　　　　　　　6.154
 (a) in consequence of the establishment of one or more National Health Service trusts under section 25 of the 2006 Act or section 18 of the 2006 (Wales) Act, a person's contract of employment is treated by a scheme under paragraph 8 of Schedule 4 to the 2006 Act or paragraph 8 of Schedule 3 to the 2006 (Wales) Act as divided so as to constitute two or more contracts, or
 (b) an order under paragraph 26(1) of Schedule 3 to the 2006 Act provides that a person's contract is so divided, that person may elect for all those contracts to be treated as one contract for the purposes of Part 12ZA of the Act.

Notification of election

3. A person who makes an election under regulation 2 above shall give written notification of that election to each of their employers under the two or more contracts of employment mentioned in that regulation at least 28 days before the beginning of the additional statutory paternity pay period or, if in the particular circumstances that is not practicable, as soon as is reasonably practicable.　　　　　　　　　　　　　　　　　　　　　　6.155

Provision of information

4. A person who makes an election under regulation 2 above shall, within 28 days of giving notification of that election or, if in the particular circumstances that is not practicable, as soon as is reasonably practicable thereafter, provide each of their employers under the two or more contracts of employment mentioned in that regulation with the following information—　6.156
 (a) the name and address of each of those employers;
 (b) the date their employment with each of those employers commenced; and
 (c) details of their normal weekly earnings during the relevant period from each employer, and for this purpose the expressions "normal weekly earnings" and "relevant period" have the same meanings as they have for the purposes of Part 12ZA of the Act.

Treatment of two or more employers as one

5. The employer to be regarded for the purposes of additional statutory paternity pay as the employer under the one contract where two or more contracts of employment are treated as one in accordance with regulation 2 shall be—　　　　　　　　　　　　　　　　　　　　　　　　　　　　　6.157
 (a) in the case of a person whose contract of employment is treated by a scheme under paragraph 8 of Schedule 4 to the 2006 Act or paragraph 8 of Schedule 3 to the 2006 (Wales) Act as divided—
  (i) the Special Health Authority, Primary Care Trust or Local

Health Board from which the person was transferred, in a case where any one of the contracts is with such a body; or
  (ii) the first NHS trust to which a contract was transferred in a case where none of the contracts is with such a body; or
(b) in the case of a person whose contract of employment is divided as provided by an order under paragraph 26(1) of Schedule 3 to the 2006 Act—
  (i) the Strategic Health Authority, NHS trust or Primary Care Trust from which the person was transferred, in a case where any one of the contracts is with such a body; or
  (ii) the first Primary Care Trust to which a contract was transferred in a case where none of the contracts is with the body from which the person was transferred.

Time for which an election is to have effect

6. An election made under regulation 2 shall lapse at the end of the additional statutory paternity pay period.

Additional Statutory Paternity Pay (General) Regulations 2010

(SI 2010/1056)

The Secretary of State makes the following Regulations in exercise of the powers conferred by sections 171ZEA(1), (2), and (3), 171ZEB(1), (2) and (3), 171ZEC(1) and (3), 171ZED(2) and (3), 171ZEE(2), (4) and (7), 171ZG(3), 171ZJ(3), (4), (7) and (8) and 175(4) of the Social Security Contributions and Benefits Act 1992 and by section 5(1)(g)(i) and (p) of the Social Security Administration Act 1992 and with the concurrence of the Commissioners for Her Majesty's Revenue and Customs in so far as such concurrence is required.

This instrument contains only regulations made by virtue of, or consequential upon, sections 6 to 10 of the Work and Families Act 2006 and is made before the end of the period of 6 months beginning with the coming into force of those enactments. In accordance with section 176(1) of the Social Security Contributions and Benefits Act 1992, a draft of these Regulations was laid before Parliament and approved by a resolution of each House of Parliament.

ARRANGEMENT OF REGULATIONS

PART 1

INTRODUCTION

1. Citation and commencement
2. Interpretation
3. Application

Part 2

Additional Statutory Paternity Pay (Birth)

4. Entitlement to additional statutory paternity pay (birth)
5. Modification of entitlement conditions: early birth
6. Conditions to be satisfied by the child's mother
7. Additional statutory paternity pay period (birth)
8. Application for, and evidence of entitlement to, additional statutory paternity pay (birth)
9. Entitlement to additional statutory paternity pay (birth) in the event of the death of the mother
10. Application for, and evidence of entitlement to, additional statutory paternity pay (birth) in the event of the death of the mother
11. Entitlement to additional statutory paternity pay (birth) where there is more than one employer

Part 3

Additional Statutory Paternity Pay (Adoption)

12. Entitlement to additional statutory paternity pay (adoption)
13. Conditions to be satisfied by the child's adopter
14. Additional statutory paternity pay period (adoption)
15. Application for, and evidence of entitlement to, additional statutory paternity pay (adoption)
16. Entitlement to additional statutory paternity pay (adoption) in the event of the death of the adopter
17. Application for, and evidence of entitlement to, additional statutory paternity pay (adoption) in the event of the death of the adopter
18. Entitlement to additional statutory paternity pay (adoption) where there is more than one employer

Part 4

Additional Statutory Paternity Pay: Provisions Applicable to Both Additional Statutory Paternity Pay (Birth) and Additional Statutory Paternity Pay (Adoption)

19. Return to work
20. Work during the additional statutory paternity pay period
21. Cases where there is no liability to pay additional statutory paternity pay
22. Additional statutory paternity pay and contractual remuneration
23. Avoidance of liability for additional statutory paternity pay
24. Treatment of persons as employees
25. Continuous employment
26. Continuous employment and unfair dismissal
27. Continuous employment and stoppages of work
28. Change of employer
29. Reinstatement after service with the armed forces etc
30. Treatment of two or more employers or two or more contracts of service as one

Additional Statutory Paternity Pay (General) Regulations 2010

31. Meaning of "earnings"
32. Normal weekly earnings
33. Payment of additional statutory paternity pay
34. Time when additional statutory paternity pay is to be paid
35. Liability of the Commissioners to pay additional statutory paternity pay
36. Liability of the Commissioners to pay additional statutory paternity pay in cases of legal custody or imprisonment
37. Payments by the Commissioners
38. Persons unable to act
39. Service of notices by post

PART 1

INTRODUCTION

Citation and commencement

6.160   **1.** These Regulations may be cited as the Additional Statutory Paternity Pay (General) Regulations 2010 and come into force on 6th April 2010.

Interpretation

6.161   **2.**—(1) In these Regulations—
"the Act" means the Social Security Contributions and Benefits Act 1992;
"actual week of birth", in relation to a child, means the week beginning with midnight between Saturday and Sunday, in which the child is born;
"additional statutory paternity pay" means additional statutory paternity pay (adoption) or additional statutory paternity pay (birth);
"additional statutory paternity pay (adoption)" means additional statutory paternity pay payable in accordance with the provisions of Part 12ZA of the Act where the conditions specified in section 171ZEB(2) of the Act are satisfied;
"additional statutory paternity pay (birth)" means additional statutory paternity pay payable in accordance with the provisions of Part 12ZA of the Act where the conditions specified in section 171ZEA(2) of the Act are satisfied;
"additional statutory paternity pay period" means an additional statutory paternity pay period (adoption) or an additional statutory paternity pay period (birth);
"additional statutory paternity pay period (adoption)" means the period in respect of which additional statutory paternity pay (adoption) is payable;
"additional statutory paternity pay period (birth)" means the period in respect of which additional statutory paternity pay (birth) is payable;
"adopter", in relation to a child, means a person who has been matched with a child for adoption and who has elected to take adoption leave in order to care for the child;
"adoption agency" has the meaning given, in relation to England and Wales, by section 2 of the Adoption and Children Act 2002 and, in relation to Scotland, by section 119(1) of the Adoption and Children (Scotland) Act 2007;
"adoption leave" means ordinary adoption leave under section 75A of

the Employment Rights Act 1996 or additional adoption leave under section 75B of that Act;

"adoption pay period" has the meaning given by regulation 21 of the Statutory Paternity Pay and Statutory Adoption Pay (General) Regulations 2002;

"child" means a person who is, or when placed with an adopter for adoption was, under the age of eighteen;

"the Commissioners" means the Commissioners for Her Majesty's Revenue and Customs;

"the Contributions Regulations" means the Social Security (Contributions) Regulations 2001;

"expected week of birth", in relation to a child, means the week, beginning with midnight between Saturday and Sunday, in which, as appropriate, it is expected that the child will be born, or was expected that the child would be born;

"maternity allowance period" means the period for which maternity allowance is payable under section 35 of the Act;

"maternity pay period" has the meaning given by regulation 2 of the Statutory Maternity Pay (General) Regulations 1986;

"ordinary statutory paternity pay" means ordinary statutory paternity pay payable in accordance with the provisions of Part 12ZA of the Act where the conditions specified in section 171ZA(2) or 171ZB(2) are satisfied;

"partner", in relation to a child's mother or adopter, means a person (whether of a different sex or the same sex) who lives with the mother or adopter and the child in an enduring family relationship but is not a relative of the mother or adopter of a kind specified in paragraph (2); and

"processing", in relation to information, has the meaning given by section 1(1) of the Data Protection Act 1998.

(2) The relatives of a child's mother or adopter referred to in the definition of "partner" in paragraph (1) are the mother's or adopter's parent, grandparent, sister, brother, aunt or uncle.

(3) References to relationships in paragraph (2)—
(a) are to relationships of the full blood or half blood or, in the case of an adopted person, such of those relationships as would exist but for the adoption, and
(b) include the relationship of a child with his adoptive, or former adoptive parents, but do not include any other adoptive relationships.

(4) References to Part 12ZA of the Act in these Regulations are references to sections 171ZEA to 171ZEE and, in so far as they concern additional statutory paternity pay, to sections 171ZF to 171ZJ of the Act.

(5) For the purposes of these Regulations—
(a) a person is matched with a child for adoption when an adoption agency decides that that person would be a suitable adoptive parent for the child, and
(b) a person is notified of having been matched with a child on the date on which that person receives notification of the agency's decision, under regulation 33(3)(a) of the Adoption Agencies Regulations 2005, regulation 28(3) of the Adoption Agencies (Wales) Regulations 2005 or regulation 24 of the Adoption Agencies (Scotland) Regulations 2009.

Application

6.162   3. Subject to the provisions of Part 12ZA of the Act and of these Regulations, there is entitlement to—
(a) additional statutory paternity pay (birth) in respect of children whose expected week of birth begins on or after 3rd April 2011;
(b) additional statutory paternity pay (adoption) in respect of children matched with a person who is notified of having been matched on or after 3rd April 2011.

PART 2

ADDITIONAL STATUTORY PATERNITY PAY (BIRTH)

Entitlement to additional statutory paternity pay (birth)

6.163   4.—(1) A person ("P") is entitled to additional statutory paternity pay (birth) if—
(a) P satisfies the conditions–
    (i) as to relationship with a child ("C") and with C's mother ("M") specified in paragraph (2); and
    (ii) as to continuity of employment and normal weekly earnings specified in paragraph (3);
(b) M satisfies the conditions specified in regulation 6;
(c) P intends to care for C during the additional statutory paternity pay period (birth) in respect of C;
(d) M has signed the declaration referred to in regulation 8(1)(c); and
(e) P has complied with the requirements of regulation 8 including, where applicable, the requirements in regulation 8(3).
(2) The conditions referred to in paragraph (1)(a)(i) are that—
(a) P is either—
    (i) C's father; or
    (ii) is married to, or is the civil partner or the partner of, M but is not C's father; and
(b) P has, or expects to have, the main responsibility (apart from any responsibility of M) for the upbringing of C.
(3) Subject to regulation 5, the conditions referred to in paragraph (1)(a)(ii) are that—
(a) P has been in employed earner's employment with an employer for a continuous period of at least 26 weeks ending with the relevant week;
(b) P's normal weekly earnings for the period of eight weeks ending with the relevant week are not less than the lower earnings limit in force under section 5(1)(a) of the Act at the end of the relevant week; and
(c) P continues in employed earner's employment with the employer by reference to whom the condition in sub-paragraph (a) is satisfied for a continuous period beginning with the relevant week and ending with the week before the additional statutory paternity pay period (birth) in respect of C begins.
(4) The references in paragraph (3) to the relevant week are to the week immediately preceding the 14th week before C's expected week of birth.

(SI 2010/1056 reg. 5)

Modification of entitlement conditions: early birth

5.—(1) Where C's birth occurs earlier than the 14th week before C's expected week of birth, regulation 4(3) shall have effect as if, for the conditions set out there, there were susbstituted the conditions that—
  (a) P would have been in employed earner's employment with an employer for a continuous period of at least 26 weeks ending with the relevant week had C been born after the relevant week;
  (b) P's normal weekly earnings for the period of eight weeks ending with the week immediately preceding C's actual week of birth are not less than the lower earnings limit in force under section 5(1)(a) of the Act immediately before the commencement of C's actual week of birth; and
  (c) P continues in employed earner's employment with the employer by reference to whom the condition in sub-paragraph (a) is satisfied for a continuous period beginning with the date of C's birth and ending with the week before the additional statutory paternity pay period (birth) in respect of C begins.

(2) The references in paragraph 5(1)(a) to the relevant week are to the week immediately preceding the 14th week before C's expected week of birth.

6.164

Conditions to be satisfied by the child's mother

6. The conditions referred to in regulation 4(1)(b) are that M—
  (a) became entitled, by reference to becoming pregnant with C, to—
    (i) a maternity allowance, or
    (ii) statutory maternity pay;
  (b) has taken action constituting a return to work within the meaning of regulation 19;
  (c) has taken the action referred to in paragraph (b) not less than two weeks after the birth of C; and
  (d) has at least two weeks of her maternity allowance period or maternity pay period which remain unexpired.

6.165

Additional statutory paternity pay period (birth)

7.—(1) For the purposes of section 171ZEE(2)(a) of the Act, the date on which the additional statutory paternity pay period (birth) in respect of C begins is—
  (a) the date specified by P in accordance with regulation 8(2)(d) or last varied in accordance with regulation 8(6), or
  (b) if later, the date of M's taking action constituting a return to work within the meaning of regulation 19,
being, in either case, a date which falls no earlier than 20 weeks after the date of C's birth.

(2) For the purposes of section 171ZEE(2)(b)(ii) of the Act, the date on which the additional statutory paternity pay period (birth) in respect of C ends is the date specified by P in accordance with regulation 8(2)(e) or last varied in accordance with regulation 8(6).

(3) For the purposes of section 171ZEE(4)(a) of the Act, the additional statutory paternity pay period (birth) shall not last longer than 26 weeks.

(4) This paragraph applies instead of paragraph (2) where—
  (a) M dies after the beginning but before the end of the additional statutory paternity pay period (birth) in respect of C; and

6.166

Additional Statutory Paternity Pay (General) Regulations 2010

    (b) as soon as reasonably practicable after M's death, P gives the person paying P additional statutory paternity pay (birth) notice in writing of M's death.

(5) Where paragraph (4) applies, the date on which the additional statutory paternity pay period (birth) in respect of C ends is the date—
    (a) on which the maternity allowance period or maternity pay period in respect of C, which would have applied but for M's death, would have ended; or
    (b) if earlier, such date which, for the purposes of section 171ZEE(2)(b)(ii) of the Act, P may specify in the notice given under paragraph (4)(b).

Application for, and evidence of entitlement to, additional statutory paternity pay (birth)

6.167   **8.**—(1) P shall apply for additional statutory paternity pay (birth) to the person ("E") who will be liable to pay P such pay by providing to E—
    (a) the information, in writing, specified in paragraph (2);
    (b) a written declaration, signed by P–
        (i) that that information is correct;
        (ii) that P intends to care for C during the additional statutory paternity pay period (birth) in respect of C; and
        (iii) that P meets the conditions in regulation 4(2); and
    (c) a written declaration, signed by M—
        (i) that she has given notice to her employer that she is returning to work;
        (ii) that she satisfies the condition in regulation 6(a);
        (iii) specifying her name, address and National Insurance number;
        (iv) specifying the start date of her maternity allowance period or maternity pay period in respect of C;
        (v) specifying the date on which she intends to return to work;
        (vi) confirming that, in relation to C, P is, to M's knowledge, the sole applicant for additional statutory paternity pay; and
        (vii) providing M's consent as regards the processing by E of the information provided pursuant to paragraphs (i) to (vi).

(2) The information referred to in paragraph (1)(a) is as follows—
    (a) P's name;
    (b) C's expected week of birth;
    (c) C's date of birth;
    (d) the date on which P expects that E's liability to pay additional statutory paternity pay (birth) will begin; and
    (e) the date on which P expects that E's liability to pay additional statutory paternity pay (birth) will end.

(3) P shall also provide, if E so requests within 28 days of receiving the information and declarations referred to in paragraph (1)—
    (a) a copy of C's birth certificate; and
    (b) the name and business address of M's employer (or, if M is self-employed, her business address).

(4) The information and declarations referred to in paragraph (1) must be provided to E at least eight weeks before the date specified by P pursuant to paragraph (2)(d).

(5) P must give E what is requested under paragraph (3) within 28 days of E requesting it.

(6) P may, after applying for additional statutory paternity pay (birth) under paragraph (1), withdraw that application, vary the date on which it is expected that E's liability to pay additional statutory paternity pay (birth) will begin, or (before the additional statutory paternity pay period (birth) in respect of C has begun), vary the date on which it is expected that E's liability to pay additional statutory paternity pay will end, by notice in writing to E given—
  (a) if withdrawing an application, at least six weeks before the date specified by P pursuant to paragraph (2)(d), or
  (b) if varying the date on which it is expected that E's liability to pay additional statutory paternity pay (birth) will begin, at least six weeks before the earlier of the date varied or the new date, or
  (c) if varying the date on which it is expected that E's liability to pay additional statutory paternity pay (birth) will end, at least six weeks before the earlier of the date varied or the new date, or
  (d) in a case where it was not reasonably practicable to give notice in accordance with sub-paragraph (a), (b) or (c), as soon as is reasonably practicable.

(7) When P has applied for additional statutory paternity pay (birth) under paragraph (1), P must give E written notice as soon as reasonably practicable if at any time—
  (a) P no longer satisfies the conditions in regulation 4(2); or
  (b) M no longer intends to take action constituting a return to work within the meaning of regulation 19.

(8) When E has been provided with all of the information and the declarations referred to in paragraph (1) (together with, if applicable, what E has requested under paragraph (3)), E must, within 28 days, confirm the start and end dates of E's liability to pay P additional statutory paternity pay (birth) by notice in writing to P.

Entitlement to additional statutory paternity pay (birth) in the event of the death of the mother

9.—(1) In a case where M dies before the end of her maternity allowance period or maternity pay period in respect of C (but before the additional statutory paternity pay period (birth) in respect of C has begun)—
  (a) the provisions in regulations 4 to 6 shall apply, subject to the following modifications—
      (i) regulation 4(1)(d) shall not apply;
      (ii) regulation 4(1)(e) shall apply—
  (aa) as if the references to regulation 8 were references to regulation 10; and
  (bb) in a case where the date of which P informs E pursuant to regulation 10(1)(a) is earlier than the date by which P has complied with the other requirements of regulation 10, as if such other requirements had been complied with on such earlier date provided that they are complied with as soon as reasonably practicable thereafter;
      (iii) the condition in regulation 4(2)(a)(ii) shall be taken to be satisfied if it would have been satisfied but for the fact that M had died;
      (iv) the condition in regulation 6(a) shall be taken to be satisfied if M would have satisfied it but for the fact that M had died; and
      (v) regulation 6(b), (c) and (d) shall not apply;

Additional Statutory Paternity Pay (General) Regulations 2010

(b) regulation 7 shall not apply;
(c) for the purposes of section 171ZEE(2)(a) of the Act, the date on which the additional statutory paternity pay period (birth) in respect of C begins is such date, being the date of M's death or a later date, as P informs E of in accordance with regulation 10(1)(a) or as is last varied in accordance with regulation 10(7) or 10(8);
(d) for the purposes of section 171ZEE(2)(b)(ii) of the Act, the date on which the additional statutory paternity pay period (birth) in respect of C ends is, where earlier than the relevant date, the date specified by P in accordance with regulation 10(2)(d) or last varied in accordance with regulation 10(7) or 10(8);
(e) for the purposes of section 171ZEE(4)(a) of the Act, the additional statutory paternity pay period (birth) in respect of C shall not last longer than 39 weeks; and
(f) regulation 8 shall be replaced by regulation 10.

(2) In paragraph (1)(d), "the relevant date" means the date on which the maternity allowance period or maternity pay period in respect of C which would have applied but for M's death, would have ended.

(3) References in this regulation to M's maternity allowance period or maternity pay period in respect of C include, where M's death occurred before her maternity allowance period or maternity pay period in respect of C started, references to such period as would have existed but for the fact that M had died.

Application for, and evidence of entitlement to, additional statutory paternity pay (birth) in the event of the death of the mother

6.169   **10.**—(1) P shall apply for additional statutory paternity pay (birth) to the person ("E") who will be liable to pay P such pay by—
(a) informing E of the date on which P wishes the additional statutory paternity pay period (birth) in respect of C to begin or the date (if in the past) on which P wishes such period to have begun;
(b) providing E with the information, in writing, specified in paragraph (2); and
(c) providing E with a written declaration, signed by P—
  (i) that the information referred to in sub-paragraph (b) is correct;
  (ii) that P intends to care for C during the additional statutory paternity pay period (birth) in respect of C; and
  (iii) that P meets the conditions in regulation 4(2) (as modified by regulation 9(1)(a)(iii)).

(2) The information referred to in paragraph (1)(b) is as follows—
(a) P's name;
(b) C's expected week of birth;
(c) C's date of birth;
(d) the date on which P expects that E's liability to pay additional statutory paternity pay (birth) will end;
(e) M's name, address, and national insurance number;
(f) the start date of M's maternity pay period or maternity allowance period in respect of C, or, where M's death occurred before her maternity allowance period or maternity pay period in respect of C started, the date that that period would have started but for the fact that M had died; and

(g) the date of M's death.

(3) P shall also provide, if E so requests within 28 days of receiving the information and declaration referred to in paragraph (1)—
(a) a copy of C's birth certificate; and
(b) the name and business address of M's employer (or, if M was self-employed, her business address).

(4) Subject to paragraph (5), the information and declaration referred to in paragraph (1) must be provided to E as soon as reasonably practicable after, and in any event within eight weeks of, the date of M's death.

(5) If provided at least six weeks before the date of which P informs E pursuant to paragraph (1)(a), the information and declaration referred to in paragraph (1)(b) and (c) may be provided more than eight weeks after the date of M's death.

(6) P must give E what is requested under paragraph (3) within 28 days of E requesting it.

(7) Within eight weeks of the date of M's death, P may, after applying for additional statutory paternity pay (birth) under paragraph (1) and by giving E notice in writing, withdraw that application, vary the date (if in the future) on which P wishes the additional statutory paternity pay period (birth) in respect of C to begin, or (either before or after such period has begun) vary the date on which it is expected that E's liability to pay additional statutory paternity pay (birth) will end, with immediate effect.

(8) More than eight weeks after the date of M's death, P may, after applying for additional statutory paternity pay (birth) under paragraph (1), withdraw that application, vary the date (if in the future) on which P wishes the additional statutory paternity pay period (birth) in respect of C to begin, or (before such period has begun), vary the date on which it is expected that E's liability to pay additional statutory paternity pay (birth) will end, by notice in writing to E given—
(a) if withdrawing an application, at least six weeks before the date of which P has informed E pursuant to paragraph (1)(a), or
(b) if varying the date on which P wishes the additional statutory paternity pay period (birth) in respect of C to begin, at least six weeks before the earlier of the date varied or the new date, or
(c) if varying the date on which it is expected that E's liability to pay additional statutory paternity pay (birth) will end, at least six weeks before the earlier of the date varied or the new date, or
(d) in a case where it was not reasonably practicable to give notice in accordance with sub-paragraph (a), (b) or (c), as soon as is reasonably practicable.

(9) When E has been provided with all of the information and the declaration referred to in paragraph (1) (together with, if applicable, what E has requested under paragraph (3)), E must, within 28 days, confirm the date on which the additional statutory paternity pay period (birth) in respect of C begins or began and the date on which E's liability to pay P additional statutory paternity pay (birth) ends, by notice in writing to P.

Entitlement to additional statutory paternity pay (birth) where there is more than one employer

11.—(1) Additional statutory paternity pay (birth) shall be payable to a person in respect of a statutory pay week during any part of which that person works only for an employer—

(a) who is not liable to pay that person additional statutory paternity pay (birth); and
(b) for whom that person worked in the week immediately preceding the 14th week before the expected week of birth.

(2) In this regulation, "statutory pay week" means a week that that person has chosen as a week in respect of which additional statutory paternity pay (birth) shall be payable.

PART 3

ADDITIONAL STATUTORY PATERNITY PAY (ADOPTION)

Entitlement to additional statutory paternity pay (adoption)

6.171   **12.**—(1) A person ("P") is entitled to additional statutory paternity pay (adoption) if—
(a) P satisfies the conditions—
  (i) as to relationship with a child placed for adoption ("C") and the child's adopter ("A") specified in paragraph (2); and
  (ii) as to continuity of employment and normal weekly earnings specified in paragraph (3);
(b) A satisfies the conditions specified in regulation 13;
(c) P intends to care for C during the additional statutory paternity pay period (adoption) in respect of C;
(d) A has signed the declaration referred to in regulation 15(1)(c); and
(e) P has complied with the requirements in regulation 15, including, where applicable, the requirements in regulation 15(3).
(2) The conditions referred to in paragraph (1)(a)(i) are that—
(a) P is married to, or is the civil partner or the partner of, A; and
(b) P has been matched with C for adoption.
(3) The conditions referred to in paragraph (1)(a)(ii) are that—
(a) P has been in employed earner's employment with an employer for a continuous period of at least 26 weeks ending with the relevant week;
(b) P's normal weekly earnings for the period of eight weeks ending with the relevant week are not less than the lower earnings limit in force under section 5(1)(a) of the Act at the end of the relevant week; and
(c) P continues in employed earner's employment with the employer by reference to whom the condition in sub-paragraph (a) is satisfied for a continuous period beginning with the relevant week and ending with the week before the additional statutory paternity pay period (adoption) in respect of C begins.
(4) The references in paragraph (3) to the relevant week are to the week in which P was notified of having been matched with C.

Conditions to be satisfied by the child's adopter

6.172   **13.** The conditions referred to in regulation 12(1)(b) are that A—
(a) became entitled, by reference to the adoption of C, to statutory adoption pay;
(b) has taken action constituting a return to work within the meaning of regulation 19;

(SI 2010/1056 reg.13)

(c) has taken the action referred to in paragraph (b) not less than two weeks after the date C was placed for adoption with A; and
(d) has at least two weeks of their adoption pay period which remain unexpired.

Additional statutory paternity pay period (adoption)

14.—(1) For the purposes of section 171ZEE(2)(a) of the Act, the date on which the additional statutory paternity pay period (adoption) in respect of C begins is—
  (a) the date specified by P in accordance with regulation 15(2)(d) or last varied in accordance with regulation 15(6); or
  (b) if later, the date of A's taking action constituting a return to work within the meaning of regulation 19,
being, in either case, a date which falls no earlier than 20 weeks [¹after] the date on which C was placed for adoption.

(2) For the purposes of section 171ZEE(2)(b)(ii) of the Act, the date on which the additional statutory paternity pay period (adoption) in respect of C ends is the date specified by P in accordance with regulation 15(2)(e) or last varied in accordance with regulation 15(6).

(3) For the purposes of section 171ZEE(4)(a) of the Act, the additional statutory paternity pay period (adoption) in respect of C shall not last longer than 26 weeks.

(4) This paragraph applies instead of paragraph (2) where—
  (a) A dies after the beginning but before the end of the additional statutory paternity pay period (adoption) in respect of C; and
  (b) as soon as reasonably practicable after A's death, P gives the person paying P additional statutory paternity pay (adoption) notice in writing of A's death.

(5) Where paragraph (4) applies, the date on which the additional statutory paternity pay period (adoption) in respect of C ends is the date—
  (a) on which the adoption pay period in respect of C, which would have applied but for A's death, would have ended; or
  (b) if earlier, such date which, for the purposes of section 171ZEE(2)(b)(ii) of the Act, P may specify in the notice given under paragraph (4)(b).

6.173

AMENDMENT

1. Additional Statutory Paternity Pay (General) (Amendment) Regulations 2011 (SI 2011/678) reg.2 (April 1, 2011).

Application for, and evidence of entitlement to, additional statutory paternity pay (adoption)

15.—(1) P shall apply for additional statutory paternity pay (adoption) to the person ("E") who will be liable to pay P such pay by providing to E—
  (a) the information, in writing, specified in paragraph (2);
  (b) a written declaration, signed by P—
    (i) that that information is correct;
    (ii) that P intends to care for C during the additional statutory paternity pay period (adoption) in respect of C; and
    (iii) that P meets the conditions in regulation 12(2);

6.174

(c) a written declaration, signed by A—
  (i) that they have given notice to their employer that they are returning to work;
  (ii) that they satisfy the condition in regulation 13(a);
  (iii) specifying their name, address and National Insurance Number;
  (iv) specifying the start date of their adoption pay period in respect of C;
  (v) specifying the date on which they intend to return to work;
  (vi) confirming that, in relation to C, P is, to A's knowledge, the sole applicant for additional statutory paternity pay; and
  (vii) providing A's consent as regards the processing by E of the information provided pursuant to paragraphs (i) to (vi).

(2) The information referred to in paragraph (1)(a) is as follows—
  (a) P's name;
  (b) the date on which P was notified that they had been matched with C;
  (c) the date of C's placement for adoption;
  (d) the date on which P expects that E's liability to pay additional statutory paternity pay (adoption) will begin; and
  (e) the date on which P expects that E's liability to pay additional statutory paternity pay (adoption) will end.

(3) P shall also provide, if E so requests within 28 days of receiving the information and declarations referred to in paragraph (1)—
  (a) evidence, in the form of one or more documents issued by the adoption agency that matched P with C, of —
    (i) the name and address of the agency;
    (ii) the date on which P was notified that they had been matched with C; and
    (iii) the date on which the agency was expecting to place C with A and P; and
  (b) the name and business address of A's employer (or, if A is self-employed, A's business address).

(4) The information and declarations referred to in paragraph (1) must be provided to E at least eight weeks before the date specified by P pursuant to paragraph (2)(d).

(5) P must give E what is requested under paragraph (3) within 28 days of E requesting it.

(6) P may, after applying for additional statutory paternity pay (adoption) under paragraph (1), withdraw that application, vary the date on which it is expected that E's liability to pay additional statutory paternity pay (adoption) will begin, or (before the additional statutory paternity pay period (adoption) in respect of C has begun) vary the date on which it is expected that E's liability to pay additional statutory paternity pay (adoption) will end, by notice in writing to E given—
  (a) if withdrawing an application, at least six weeks before the date specified by P pursuant to paragraph (2)(d), or
  (b) if varying the date on which it is expected that E's liability to pay additional statutory paternity pay (adoption) will begin, at least six weeks before the earlier of the date varied or the new date, or
  (c) if varying the date on which it is expected that E's liability to pay additional statutory paternity pay (adoption) will end, at least six weeks before the earlier of the date varied or the new date, or
  (d) in a case where it was not reasonably practicable to give notice in

accordance with sub-paragraph (a), (b) or (c), as soon as is reasonably practicable.

(7) When P has applied for additional statutory paternity pay (adoption) under paragraph (1), P must give E written notice as soon as reasonably practicable if at any time—
  (a) P no longer satisfies the conditions in regulation 12(2); or
  (b) A no longer intends to take action constituting a return to work within the meaning of regulation 19.

(8) When E has been provided with all of the information and the declarations referred to in paragraph (1) (together with, if applicable, what E has requested under paragraph (3)), E must, within 28 days, confirm the start and end dates of E's liability to pay P additional statutory paternity pay (adoption), by notice in writing to P.

Entitlement to additional statutory paternity pay (adoption) in the event of the death of the adopter

16.—(1) In a case where A dies before the end of their adoption pay period in respect of C (but before the additional statutory paternity pay period (adoption) in respect of C has begun)—
  (a) the provisions in regulations 12 and 13 shall apply, subject to the following modifications—
    (i) regulation 12(1)(d) shall not apply;
    (ii) regulation 12(1)(e) shall apply—
  (aa) as if the references to regulation 15 were references to regulation 17; and
  (bb) in a case where the date of which P informs E pursuant to regulation 17(1)(a) is earlier than the date by which P has complied with the other requirements of regulation 17, as if such other requirements had been complied with on such earlier date provided that they are complied with as soon as reasonably practicable thereafter;
    (iii) the condition in regulation 12(2)(a) shall be taken to be satisfied if it would have been satisfied but for the fact that A had died;
    (iv) the condition in regulation 13(a) shall be taken to be satisfied if A would have satisfied it but for the fact that A had died; and.
    (v) regulation 13(b), (c) and (d) shall not apply;
  (b) regulation 14 shall not apply;
  (c) for the purposes of section 171ZEE(2)(a) of the Act, the date on which the additional statutory paternity pay period (adoption) in respect of C begins is such date, being the date of A's death or a later date, as P informs E of in accordance with regulation 17(1)(a) or as is last varied in accordance with regulation 17(7) or 17(8);
  (d) for the purposes of section 171ZEE(2)(b)(ii) of the Act, the date on which the additional statutory paternity pay period (adoption) in respect of C ends is, where earlier than the relevant date, the date specified by P in accordance with regulation 17(2)(d) or last varied in accordance with regulation 17(7) or 17(8);
  (e) for the purposes of section 171ZEE(4)(a) of the Act, the additional statutory paternity pay period (adoption) in respect of C shall not last longer than 39 weeks; and
  (f) regulation 15 shall be replaced by regulation 17.

Additional Statutory Paternity Pay (General) Regulations 2010

(2) In paragraph (1)(d), "the relevant date" means the date on which the adoption pay period in respect of C which would have applied but for A's death, would have ended.

(3) References in this regulation to A's adoption pay period in respect of C include, where A's death occurred before A's adoption pay period in respect of C started, references to such period as would have existed but for the fact that A had died.

Application for, and evidence of entitlement to, additional statutory paternity pay (adoption) in the event of the death of the adopter

6.176   **17.**—(1) P shall apply for additional statutory paternity pay (adoption) to the person ("E") who will be liable to pay P such pay by—
  (a) informing E of the date on which P wishes the additional statutory paternity pay period (adoption) in respect of C to begin or the date (if in the past) on which P wishes such period to have begun;
  (b) providing E with the information, in writing, specified in paragraph (2); and
  (c) providing E with a written declaration, signed by P—
    (i) that the information referred to in sub-paragraph (b) is correct;
    (ii) that P intends to care for C during the additional statutory paternity pay period (adoption) in respect of C; and
    (iii) that P meets the conditions in regulation 12(2) (as modified by regulation 16(1)(a)(iii)).

(2) The information referred to in paragraph (1)(b) is as follows—
  (a) P's name;
  (b) the date on which P was notified that they had been matched with C;
  (c) the date of C's placement for adoption;
  (d) the date on which P expects that E's liability to pay additional statutory paternity pay (adoption) will end;
  (e) A's name, address, and National Insurance number;
  (f) the start date of A's adoption pay period in respect of C or, where A's death occurred before their adoption pay period in respect of C started, the date that that period would have started but for the fact that A had died; and
  (g) the date of A's death.

(3) P shall also provide, if E so requests within 28 days of receiving the information and declaration referred to in paragraph (1)—
  (a) evidence, in the form of one or more documents issued by the adoption agency that matched P with C, of
    (i) the name and address of the agency;
    (ii) the date on which P was notified that they had been matched with C; and
    (iii) the date on which the agency was expecting to place C with A and P; and
  (b) the name and business address of A's employer (or, if A was self-employed, A's business address).

(4) Subject to paragraph (5), the information and declaration referred to in paragraph (1) must be provided to E as soon as reasonably practicable after, and in any event within eight weeks of, the date of A's death.

(5) If provided at least six weeks before the date of which P informs E pursuant to paragraph (1)(a), the information and evidence referred to in

paragraph (1)(b) and (c) may be provided more than eight weeks after the date of A's death.

(6) P must give E what is requested under paragraph (3) within 28 days of E requesting it.

(7) Within eight weeks of the date of A's death, P may, after applying for additional statutory paternity pay (adoption) under paragraph (1) and by giving E notice in writing, withdraw that application, vary the date (if in the future) on which P wishes the additional statutory paternity pay period (adoption) in respect of C to begin, or (either before or after such period has begun) vary the date on which it is expected that E's liability to pay additional statutory paternity pay (adoption) will end, with immediate effect.

(8) More than eight weeks after the date of A's death, P may, after applying for additional statutory paternity pay (adoption) under paragraph (1), withdraw that application, vary the date (if in the future) on which P wishes the additional statutory paternity pay period (adoption) in respect of C to begin, or (before such period has begun), vary the date on which it is expected that E's liability to pay additional statutory paternity pay (adoption) will end, by notice in writing to E given—

(a) if withdrawing an application, at least six weeks before the date of which P informs E pursuant to paragraph (1)(a), or
(b) if varying the date on which P wishes the additional statutory paternity pay period (adoption) in respect of C to begin, at least six weeks before the earlier of the date varied or the new date, or
(c) if varying the date on which it is expected that E's liability to pay additional statutory paternity pay (adoption) will end, at least six weeks before the earlier of the date varied or the new date, or
(d) in a case where it was not reasonably practicable to give notice in accordance with sub-paragraph (a), (b) or (c), as soon as is reasonably practicable.

(9) When E has been provided with all of the information and the declaration referred to in paragraph (1) (together with, if applicable, what E has requested under paragraph (3)), E must, within 28 days, confirm the date on which the additional statutory paternity pay period (adoption) in respect of C begins or began and the date on which E's liability to pay P additional statutory paternity pay (adoption) ends, by notice in writing to P.

Entitlement to additional statutory paternity pay (adoption) where there is more than one employer

18.—(1) Additional statutory paternity pay (adoption) shall be payable to a person in respect of a statutory pay week during any part of which that person works only for an employer—

(a) who is not liable to pay that person additional statutory paternity pay (adoption); and
(b) for whom that person worked in the week immediately preceding the 14th week before the expected week of the placement for adoption.

(2) In this regulation "statutory pay week" means a week that that person has chosen in respect of which additional statutory paternity pay (adoption) shall be payable.

Additional Statutory Paternity Pay (General) Regulations 2010

Part 4

Additional Statutory Paternity Pay: Provisions Applicable to Both Additional Statutory Paternity Pay (Birth) and Additional Statutory Paternity Pay (Adoption)

Return to work

6.178   **19.** For the purposes of these Regulations, a mother or adopter is treated as returning to work if one of the following situations applies—
    (a) in a case where a mother is entitled to maternity allowance, that allowance is not payable to her by virtue of regulations made under section 35(3)(a)(i) of the Act;
    (b) in a case where an adopter is entitled to statutory adoption pay, that payment is not payable to that person in accordance with section 171ZN(3) or (5) of the Act;
    (c) in a case where a mother is entitled to statutory maternity pay, that payment is not payable to her in accordance with section 165(4) or (6) of the Act.

Work during the additional statutory paternity pay period

6.179   **20.**—(1) In a case where additional statutory paternity pay is being paid to a person who works during the additional statutory paternity pay period for an employer who is not liable to pay that person additional statutory paternity pay and who does not fall within, as appropriate, regulation 11(1)(b) or regulation 18(1)(b), there shall be no liability to pay additional statutory paternity pay in respect of the week in which the person does that work.

(2) In a case falling within paragraph (1), the person shall notify the person liable to pay additional statutory paternity pay within seven days of the first day during which the former works during the additional statutory paternity pay period.

(3) The notification mentioned in paragraph (2) shall be in writing, if the person who has been liable to pay additional statutory paternity pay so requests.

(4) In a case where an employee does any work on any day, under a contract of service with an employer who is liable to pay that employee additional statutory paternity pay, for not more than ten such days during the employee's additional statutory paternity pay period, whether consecutive or not, additional statutory paternity pay shall continue to be payable to the employee by the employer.

Cases where there is no liability to pay additional statutory paternity pay

6.180   **21.**—(1) There shall be no liability to pay additional statutory paternity pay in respect of any week—
    (a) during any part of which the person entitled to it is entitled to statutory sick pay under Part 11 of the Act;
    (b) following that in which the person claiming it has died; or
    (c) subject to paragraph (2), during any part of which the person enti-

tled to it is detained in legal custody or sentenced to a term of imprisonment (except where the sentence is suspended).

(2) There shall be liability to pay additional statutory paternity pay in respect of any week during any part of which the person entitled to it is detained in legal custody where that person—
  (a) is released subsequently without charge;
  (b) is subsequently found not guilty of any offence and is released; or
  (c) is convicted of an offence but does not receive a custodial sentence.

Additional statutory paternity pay and contractual remuneration

22.—(1) For the purposes of section 171ZG(1) and (2) of the Act (as such provisions apply to additional statutory paternity pay), the payments which are to be treated as contractual remuneration are sums payable under a contract of service—
  (a) by way of remuneration;
  (b) for incapacity for work due to sickness or injury; and
  (c) by reason of birth or adoption of a child.

Avoidance of liability for additional statutory paternity pay

23.—(1) A former employer shall be liable to make payments of additional statutory paternity pay to a former employee in any case where the employee had been employed for a continuous period of at least eight weeks and the employee's contract of service was brought to an end by the former employer solely, or mainly, for the purpose of avoiding liability for additional statutory paternity pay or ordinary statutory paternity pay, or both.

(2) In a case falling within paragraph (1)—
  (a) the employee shall be treated as if they had been employed for a continuous period ending with the earliest date that they could have been entitled to additional statutory paternity pay; and
  (b) their normal weekly earnings shall be calculated by reference to their normal weekly earnings for the period of eight weeks ending with the last day in respect of which they were paid under their former contract of service.

Treatment of persons as employees

24.—(1) Subject to paragraph (2), in a case where, and in so far as, a person is treated as an employed earner by virtue of the Social Security (Categorisation of Earners) Regulations 1978 that person shall be treated as an employee for the purposes of Part 12ZA of the Act, and in a case where, and in so far as, such a person is treated otherwise than as an employed earner by virtue of those regulations, that person shall not be treated as an employee for the purposes of Part 12ZA of the Act.

(2) Paragraph (1) shall have effect in relation to a person who—
  (a) is under the age of 16; and
  (b) would or, as the case may be, would not have been treated as an employed earner by virtue of the Social Security (Categorisation of Earners) Regulations 1978 had they been over that age,
as it has effect in relation to a person who is or, as the case may be, is not so treated.

(3) A person who is in employed earner's employment under a contract

Additional Statutory Paternity Pay (General) Regulations 2010

of apprenticeship shall be treated as an employee for the purposes of Part 12ZA of the Act.
 (4) A person who is in employed earner's employment but whose employer—
 (a) does not fulfil the conditions prescribed in regulation 145(1) of the Contributions Regulations in so far as that provision relates to residence or presence in Great Britain; or
 (b) is a person who, by reason of any international treaty to which the United Kingdom is a party or of any international convention binding the United Kingdom—
  (i) is exempt from the provisions of the Act; or
  (ii) is a person against whom the provisions of the Act are not enforceable,
shall not be treated as an employee for the purposes of Part 12ZA of the Act.

Continuous employment

6.184 **25.**—(1) Subject to the following provisions of this regulation, where in any week a person is, for the whole or part of the week—
 (a) incapable of work in consequence of sickness or injury;
 (b) absent from work on account of a temporary cessation of work;
 (c) absent from work in circumstances such that, by arrangement or custom, that person is regarded as continuing in the employment of their employer for all or any purposes,
and returns to work for their employer after the incapacity for or absence from work, that week shall be treated for the purposes of sections 171ZEA and 171ZEB of the Act as part of a continuous period of employment with that employer, notwithstanding that no contract of service exists with that employer in respect of that week.
 (2) Incapacity for work which lasts for more than 26 consecutive weeks shall not count for the purposes of paragraph (1)(a).
 (3) Where a person—
 (a) is an employee in employed earner's employment in which the custom is for the employer—
  (i) to offer work for a fixed period of not more than 26 consecutive weeks;
  (ii) to offer work for such period on two or more occasions in a year for periods which do not overlap; and
  (iii) to offer the work available to those persons who had worked for the employer during the last or a recent such period, but
 (b) is absent from work because of incapacity arising from some specific disease or bodily or mental disablement,
then in that case paragraph (1) shall apply as if the words "and returns to work for their employer after the incapacity for or absence from work," were omitted.

Continuous employment and unfair dismissal

6.185 **26.**—(1) This regulation applies to a person in relation to whose dismissal an action is commenced which consists—
 (a) of the presentation by that person of a complaint under section 111(1) of the Employment Rights Act 1996;
 (b) of their making a claim in accordance with a dismissal procedures agreement designated by an order under section 110 of that Act; or

(c) of any action taken by a conciliation officer under [¹ any of sections 18A to 18C] of the Employment Tribunals Act 1996.

(2) If, in consequence of an action of the kind specified in paragraph (1), a person is reinstated or re-engaged by their employer or by a successor or associated employer of that employer, the continuity of their employment shall be preserved for the purposes of Part 12ZA of the Act, and any week which falls within the interval beginning with the effective date of termination and ending with the date of reinstatement or re-engagement, as the case may be, shall count in the computation of their period of continuous employment.

(3) In this regulation—

"dismissal procedures agreement" and "successor" have the same meanings as in section 235 of the Employment Rights Act 1996; and

"associated employer" shall be construed in accordance with section 231 of the Employment Rights Act 1996.

AMENDMENT

1. Enterprise and Regulatory Reform Act 2013 (Consequential Amendments) (Employment) Order 2014 (SI 2014/386) art.2 Sch. para.67.

Continuous employment and stoppages of work

27.—(1) Where, for any week or part of a week a person does not work because there is a stoppage of work due to a trade dispute within the meaning of section 35(1) of the Jobseekers Act 1995 at their place of employment, that person's continuity of employment shall, subject to paragraph (2), be treated, for the purposes of Part 12ZA of the Act, as continuing throughout the stoppage but, subject to paragraph (3), no such week shall count in the computation of their period of employment.

(2) Subject to paragraph (3), where during the stoppage of work a person is dismissed from their employment, that person's continuity of employment shall not be treated in accordance with paragraph (1) as continuing beyond the commencement of the day they stopped work.

(3) The provisions of paragraph (1), to the extent that they provide that a week in which the stoppage of work occurred shall not count in the computation of a period of employment, and paragraph (2) shall not apply to a person who proves that at no time did they have a direct interest in the trade dispute in question.

Change of employer

28. A person's employment shall, notwithstanding a change of employer, be treated, for the purposes of Part 12ZA of the Act, as continuous employment with the second employer where—
(a) the employer's trade or business or an undertaking (whether or not it is an undertaking established by or under an Act of Parliament) is transferred from one person to another;
(b) by or under an Act of Parliament, whether public or local and whenever passed, a contract of employment between any body corporate and the person is modified and some other body corporate is substituted as that person's employer;
(c) on the death of their employer, the person is taken into the employment of the personal representatives or trustees of the deceased;
(d) the person is employed by partners, personal representatives or

Additional Statutory Paternity Pay (General) Regulations 2010

trustees and there is a change in the partners, or, as the case may be, personal representatives or trustees;
(e) the person is taken into the employment of an employer who is, at the time they entered that employer's employment, an associated employer of their previous employer, and for this purpose "associated employer" shall be construed in accordance with section 231 of the Employment Rights Act 1996; or
(f) on the termination of the person's employment with an employer they are taken into the employment of another employer and those employers are governors of a school maintained by a local education authority.

Reinstatement after service with the armed forces etc

6.188   **29.** If a person who is entitled to apply to their employer under the Reserve Forces (Safeguard of Employment) Act 1985 enters the employment of that employer within the six month period mentioned in section 1(4)(b) of that Act, their previous period of employment with that employer (or if there was more than one such period, the last of those periods) and the period of employment beginning in that six-month period shall be treated as continuous.

Treatment of two or more employers or two or more contracts of service as one

6.189   **30.**—(1) In a case where the earnings paid to a person in respect of two or more employments are aggregated and treated as a single payment of earnings under regulation 15(1) of the Contributions Regulations, the employers of that person in respect of those employments shall be treated as one for the purposes of Part 12ZA of the Act.

(2) Where two or more employers are treated as one under the provisions of paragraph (1), liability for additional statutory paternity pay shall be apportioned between them in such proportions as they may agree, or in default of agreement, in the proportions which the person's earnings from each employment bear to the amount of the aggregated earnings.

(3) Where two or more contracts of service exist concurrently between one employer and one employee, they shall be treated as one for the purposes of Part 12ZA of the Act, except where, by virtue of regulation 14 of the Contributions Regulations, the earnings from those contracts of service are not aggregated for the purposes of earnings-related contributions.

Meaning of "earnings"

6.190   **31.**—(1) For the purposes of section 171ZJ(6) of the Act (as such provision applies to additional statutory paternity pay) (normal weekly earnings for the purposes of Part 12ZA of the Act), the expression "earnings" shall be construed in accordance with the following provisions of this regulation.

(2) The expression "earnings" refers to gross earnings and includes any remuneration or profit derived from a person's employment except any payment or amount which is—
(a) excluded from the computation of a person's earnings under regulation 25 of and Schedule 3 to, and regulation 123 of, the Contributions

Regulations (payments to be disregarded) and regulation 27 of those Regulations (payments to directors to be disregarded) (or would have been so excluded had they not been under the age of 16);
(b) a chargeable emolument under section 10A of the Act except where, in consequence of such a chargeable emolument being excluded from earnings, a person would not be entitled to additional statutory paternity pay (or where such a payment or amount would have been so excluded and in consequence the person would not have been entitled to additional statutory paternity pay had they not been under the age of 16).

(3) For the avoidance of doubt, "earnings" includes—
(a) any amount retrospectively treated as earnings by regulations made by virtue of section 4B(2) of the Act;
(b) any sum payable in respect of arrears of pay in pursuance of an order for reinstatement or re-engagement under the Employment Rights Act 1996;
(c) any sum payable by way of pay in pursuance of an order made under the Employment Rights Act 1996 for the continuation of a contract of employment;
(d) any sum payable by way of remuneration in pursuance of a protective award under section 189 of the Trade Union and Labour Relations (Consolidation) Act 1992;
(e) any sum payable by way of statutory sick pay, including sums payable in accordance with regulations made under section 151(6) of the Act;
(f) any sum payable by way of statutory maternity pay;
(g) any sum payable by way of ordinary statutory paternity pay;
(h) any sum payable by way of additional statutory paternity pay; and
(i) any sum payable by way of statutory adoption pay.

Normal weekly earnings

32.—(1) For the purposes of Part 12ZA of the Act, a person's normal weekly earnings shall be calculated in accordance with the following provisions of this regulation.

(2) In this regulation—
"the appropriate date" means—
(a) in relation to additional statutory paternity pay (birth), the first day of the 14th week before the expected week of the child's birth or the first day in the week in which the child is born, whichever is the earlier;
(b) in relation to additional statutory paternity pay (adoption), the first day of the week after the week in which the adopter is notified of being matched with the child for the purposes of adoption;
"day of payment" means a day on which the person was paid; and
"normal pay day" means a day on which the terms of a person's contract of service require that person to be paid, or the practice in that person's employment is for that person to be paid, if any payment is due to them.

(3) Subject to paragraph (4), the relevant period for the purposes of section 171ZJ(6) (as such provision applies to additional statutory paternity pay) is the period between—

(a) the last normal pay day to fall before the appropriate date; and
(b) the last normal pay day to fall at least eight weeks earlier than the normal pay day mentioned in sub-paragraph (a),

including the normal pay day mentioned in sub-paragraph (a) but excluding that first mentioned in sub-paragraph (b).

(4) In a case where a person has no identifiable normal pay day, paragraph (3) shall have effect as if the words "day of payment" were substituted for the words "normal pay day" in each place where they occur.

(5) In a case where a person has normal pay days at intervals of or approximating to one or more calendar months (including intervals of or approximating to a year) that person's normal weekly earnings shall be calculated by dividing their earnings in the relevant period by the number of calendar months in that period (or, if it is not a whole number, the nearest whole number), multiplying the result by 12 and dividing by 52.

(6) In a case to which paragraph (5) does not apply and the relevant period is not an exact number of weeks, the person's normal weekly earnings shall be calculated by dividing their earnings in the relevant period by the number of days in the relevant period and multiplying the result by seven.

(7) In any case where a person receives a back-dated pay increase which includes a sum in respect of a relevant period, normal weekly earnings shall be calculated as if such a sum was paid in that relevant period even though received after that period.

Payment of additional statutory paternity pay

6.192   **33.** Payments of additional statutory paternity pay may be made in a like manner to payments of remuneration but shall not include payment in kind or by way of the provision of board or lodgings or of services or other facilities.

Time when additional statutory paternity pay is to be paid

6.193   **34.**—(1) In this regulation, "pay day" means a day on which it has been agreed, or it is the normal practice between an employer or former employer and a person who is or was an employee of theirs, that payments by way of remuneration are to be made, or, where there is no such agreement or normal practice, the last day of a calendar month.

(2) In any case where—
(a) a decision has been made by an officer of Revenue and Customs under section 8(1) of the Social Security Contributions (Transfer of Functions, etc) Act 1999 as a result of which a person is entitled to an amount of additional statutory paternity pay; and
(b) the time for bringing an appeal against the decision has expired and either—
   (i) no such appeal has been brought; or
   (ii) such an appeal has been brought and has been finally disposed of,

that amount of additional statutory paternity pay shall be paid within the time specified in paragraph (3).

(3) Subject to paragraphs (4) and (5), the employer or former employer shall pay the amount not later than the first pay day after—
(a) where an appeal has been brought, the day on which the employer or former employer receives notification that it has been finally disposed of;

(b) where leave to appeal has been refused and there remains no further opportunity to apply for leave, the day on which the employer or former employer receives notification of the refusal; and

(c) in any other case, the day on which the time for bringing an appeal expires.

(4) Subject to paragraph (5), where it is impracticable, in view of the employer's or former employer's methods of accounting for and paying remuneration, for the requirement of payment referred to in paragraph (3) to be met by the pay day referred to in that paragraph, it shall be met not later than the next following pay day.

(5) Where the employer or former employer would not have remunerated the employee for their work in the week in question as early as the pay day specified in paragraph (3) or (if it applies) paragraph (4), the requirement of payment shall be met on the first day on which the employee would have been remunerated for his work in that week.

Liability of the Commissioners to pay additional statutory paternity pay

35.—(1) Where—
(a) an officer of Revenue and Customs has decided that an employer is liable to make payments of additional statutory paternity pay;
(b) the time for appealing against the decision has expired; and
(c) no appeal against the decision has been lodged or leave to appeal against the decision is required and has been refused,

then for any week in respect of which the employer was liable to make payments of additional statutory paternity pay but did not do so, and for any subsequent weeks in the additional statutory paternity pay period, the liability to make those payments shall, notwithstanding section 171ZED of the Act, be that of the Commissioners and not the employer.

(2) Liability to make payments of additional statutory paternity pay shall, notwithstanding section 171ZED of the Act, be a liability of the Commissioners and not the employer as from the week in which the employer first becomes insolvent until the end of the additional statutory paternity pay period.

(3) For the purposes of paragraph (2) an employer shall be taken to be insolvent if, and only if—
(a) in England and Wales—
   (i) the employer has been adjudged bankrupt or has made a composition or arrangement with its creditors;
   (ii) the employer has died and the employer's estate falls to be administered in accordance with an order made under section 421 of the Insolvency Act 1986; or
   (iii) where an employer is a company or a limited liability partnership, a winding-up order is made or a resolution for a voluntary winding-up is passed (or, in the case of a limited liability partnership, a determination for a voluntary winding-up has been made) with respect to it, or it enters administration, or a receiver or a manager of its undertaking is duly appointed, or possession is taken, by or on behalf of the holders of any debentures secured by a floating charge, of any property of the company or limited liability partnership comprised in or subject to the charge, or a

voluntary arrangement proposed for the purposes of Part 1 of the Insolvency Act 1986 is approved under that Part of that Act;
(b) in Scotland—
  (i) an award of sequestration is made on the employer's estate or the employer executes a trust deed for its creditors or enters into a composition contract;
  (ii) the employer has died and a judicial factor appointed under section 11A of the Judicial Factors (Scotland) Act 1889 is required by that section to divide the employer's insolvent estate among the employer's creditors; or
  (iii) where the employer is a company or a limited liability partnership, a winding-up order is made or a resolution for voluntary winding-up is passed (or, in the case of a limited liability partnership, a determination for a voluntary winding-up is made) with respect to it, or it enters administration, or a receiver of its undertaking is duly appointed, or a voluntary arrangement proposed for the purposes of Part 1 of the Insolvency Act 1986 is approved under that Part.

GENERAL NOTE

6.195 The various references to insolvency law provisions include the special administration regime under the Investment Bank Special Administration Regulations 2011 (SI 2011/245) (see reg.27 and Sch.6 Pt 1 of those Regulations).

Liability of the Commissioners to pay additional statutory paternity pay in cases of legal custody or imprisonment

6.196 **36.**—(1) Where—
(a) there is liability to pay additional statutory paternity pay in respect of a period which is subsequent to the last week falling within paragraph (1)(c) of regulation 21, or
(b) there is liability to pay additional statutory paternity pay during a period of detention in legal custody by virtue of the provisions of paragraph (2) of that regulation,
that liability, notwithstanding section 171ZED of the Act, shall be that of the Commissioners and not the employer.

Payments by the Commissioners

6.197 **37.** Where the Commissioners become liable in accordance with regulation 35 or 36 to make payments of additional statutory paternity pay to a person, the first payment shall be made as soon as reasonably practicable after they become so liable, and payments thereafter shall be made at weekly intervals, by means of an instrument of payment or by such other means as appears to the Commissioners to be appropriate in the circumstance of any particular case.

Persons unable to act

6.198 **38.**—(1) Where to any person—
(a) additional statutory paternity pay is payable or it is alleged that additional statutory paternity pay is payable;
(b) that person is unable for the time being to act; and

(c) either—
    (i) no deputy has been appointed by the Court of Protection with power to receive additional statutory paternity pay on their behalf, or
    (ii) in Scotland, their estate is not being administered by a guardian acting or appointed under the Adults with Incapacity (Scotland) Act 2000,

the Commissioners may, upon written application to the Commissioners by a person who, if a natural person, is over the age of 18, appoint that person to exercise, on behalf of the person unable to act, any right to which the person unable to act may be entitled under Part 12ZA of the Act and to deal on behalf of the person unable to act with any sums payable to the person unable to act.

(2) Where the Commissioners have made an appointment under paragraph (1)—
  (a) they may at any time in their absolute discretion revoke it;
  (b) the person appointed may resign their office after having given one month's notice in writing to the Commissioners of their intention to do so; and
  (c) the appointment shall terminate when the Commissioners are notified that a deputy or other person to whom paragraph (1)(c) applies has been appointed.

(3) Anything required by Part 12ZA of the Act to be done by or to any person who is unable to act may be done by or to the person appointed under this regulation to act on behalf of the person unable to act, and the receipt of the person so appointed shall be a good discharge to the employer or former employer of the person unable to act for any sum paid.

Service of notices by post

39. A notice given in accordance with the provisions of these Regulations in writing contained in an envelope which is properly addressed and sent by prepaid post shall be treated as having been given on the day on which it is posted.

Additional Statutory Paternity Pay (Adoptions from Overseas) Regulations 2010

(SI 2010/1057)

ARRANGEMENT OF REGULATIONS

1. Citation and commencement
2. Interpretation and scope
3. Application of the General Regulations to these Regulations
4. Application
5. Entitlement to additional statutory paternity pay (adoption) in respect of adoptions from Overseas
6. Conditions to be satisfied by the child's adopter

Additional Statutory Paternity Pay (Adoptions from Overseas) Regulations 2010

7. Additional statutory paternity pay period (adoption) in respect of adoptions from overseas
8. Application for, and evidence of entitlement to, additional statutory paternity pay (adoption) in respect of adoptions from overseas
9. Entitlement to additional statutory paternity pay (adoption) in respect of adoptions from overseas in the event of the death of the adopter
10. Application for, and evidence of entitlement to, additional statutory paternity pay (adoption) in respect of adoptions from overseas in the event of the death of the adopter
11. Entitlement to additional statutory paternity pay (adoption) in respect of adoptions from overseas where there is more than one employer
12. Return to work

The Secretary of State makes the following Regulations in exercise of the powers conferred by sections 171ZEB(1), (2) and (3), 171ZEC(1) and (3), 171ZED(2) and (3), 171ZEE(2), (4) and (7), 171ZG(3), 171ZJ (3), (4), (7) and (8) and 175(4), of the Social Security Contributions and Benefits Act 1992, and with the concurrence of the Commissioners for Her Majesty's Revenue and Customs in so far as such concurrence is required.

This instrument contains only regulations made by virtue of, or consequential upon, sections 7 to 10 of the Work and Families Act 2006 and is made before the end of the period of six months beginning with the coming into force of those enactments. In accordance with section 176(1) of the Social Security Contributions and Benefits Act 1992, a draft of these Regulations was laid before Parliament and approved by a resolution of each House of Parliament.

Citation and commencement

6.201   1. These Regulations may be cited as the Additional Statutory Paternity Pay (Adoptions from Overseas) Regulations 2010 and come into force on 9th April 2010.

Interpretation and scope

6.202   2.—(1) In these Regulations—
"the Act" means the Social Security Contributions and Benefits Act 1992;
"additional statutory paternity pay (adoption)" means additional statutory paternity pay payable in accordance with the provisions of Part 12ZA of the Act where the conditions specified in section 171ZEB(2) of the Act are satisfied;
"additional statutory paternity pay period (adoption)" means the period in respect of which additional statutory paternity pay (adoption) is payable;
"adopter", in relation to a child, means a person by whom the child has been or is to be adopted or, in a case where the child has been or is to be adopted by two people jointly, whichever of them has elected to take adoption leave in respect of the child;
"adoption from overseas" means the adoption of a child who enters Great Britain from outside the United Kingdom in connection with or for the purposes of adoption which does not involve the placement of the child for adoption under the law of any part of the United Kingdom;
"adoption leave" means ordinary adoption leave under section 75A

(SI 2010/1057 reg.2)

of the Employment Rights Act 1996 or additional adoption leave under section 75B of that Act;

"adoption pay period" has the meaning given by regulation 12 of the Statutory Paternity Pay (Adoption) and Statutory Adoption Pay (Adoptions from Overseas) (No.2) Regulations 2003;

"the Application Regulations" means the Social Security Contributions and Benefits Act 1992 (Application of Parts 12ZA and 12ZB to Adoptions from Overseas) Regulations 2003;

"child" means a person who is, or when entering Great Britain was, under the age of eighteen;

"enter Great Britain" means enter Great Britain from outside the United Kingdom in connection with or for the purposes of adoption, and cognate expressions shall be construed accordingly;

"the General Regulations" means the Additional Statutory Paternity Pay (General) Regulations 2010;

"official notification" means written notification, issued by or on behalf of the relevant central authority, that it is prepared to issue a certificate to the overseas authority concerned with the adoption of the child, or that it has issued a certificate and sent it to that authority, confirming, in either case, that the adopter is eligible to adopt, and has been assessed and approved as being a suitable adoptive parent;

"partner", in relation to a child's adopter, means a person (whether of a different sex or the same sex) who lives with the adopter and the child in an enduring family relationship, but is not a relative of the adopter of a kind specified in paragraph (2);

"processing", in relation to information, has the meaning given by section 1(1) of the Data Protection Act 1998; and

"relevant central authority" means—
(a) in the case of an adopter to whom Part 3 of the Adoptions with a Foreign Element Regulations 2005 apply and who is habitually resident in Wales, the Welsh Ministers;
(b) in the case of an adopter to whom [1 . . .] the Adoptions with a Foreign Element (Scotland) Regulations 2009 apply and who is habitually resident in Scotland, the Scottish Ministers; and
(c) in any other case, the Secretary of State.

(2) The relatives of a child's adopter referred to in the definition of "partner" in paragraph (1) are the adopter's parent, grandparent, sister, brother, aunt or uncle.

(3) References to relationships in paragraph (2)—
(a) are to relationships of the full blood or half blood or, in the case of an adopted person, such of those relationships as would exist but for the adoption, and
(b) include the relationship of a child with his adoptive, or former adoptive parents, but do not include any other adoptive relationships.

(4) References in these Regulations to Part 12ZA of the Act are references to sections 171ZEA to 171ZEE and, in so far as they concern additional statutory paternity pay, to sections 171ZF to 171ZJ of the Act.

(5) References in these Regulations to any of the provisions referred to in paragraph (4) are to be construed as references to those provisions as modified, where appropriate, by the Application Regulations.

(6) These Regulations apply to additional statutory paternity pay (adoption) in respect of adoptions from overseas.

Additional Statutory Paternity Pay (Adoptions from Overseas) Regulations 2010

AMENDMENT

1. Adoptions with a Foreign Element (Scotland) Amendment Regulations 2011 (SSI 2011/159) reg. 4 (March 21, 2011) (for Scotland) and Adoption and Children (Scotland) Act 2007 (Consequential Modifications) Order 2011 (SI 2011/1740) art.3 and Sch.2 Pt 3 (July 15, 2011) for England, Wales and Northern Ireland).

Application of the General Regulations to these Regulations

6.203　**3.**—(1) Subject to paragraph (2), the provisions of the General Regulations mentioned in paragraph (3) shall, in so far as they apply to additional statutory paternity pay (adoption), apply to adoptions from overseas.

(2) Any references to the provisions of Part 12ZA of the Act in the provisions of the General Regulations mentioned in paragraph (3) shall be construed as references to the provisions of Part 12ZA as modified, where appropriate, by the Application Regulations.

(3) The provisions of the General Regulations referred to in paragraph (1) are regulations 21, 22, 24 to 31, 33 to 39 and, subject to paragraphs (4) and (5) respectively, regulations 20 and 32.

(4) In the General Regulations, the provisions of regulation 20 shall apply as if for ", as appropriate, regulation 11(1)(b) or regulation 18(1)(b),", there were substituted "regulation 11(1)(b) of the Additional Statutory Paternity Pay (Adoptions from Overseas) Regulations 2010,".

(5) In the General Regulations, the provisions of regulation 32 shall apply as if—
　(a) in paragraph (2)(b), for "the week in which the adopter is notified of being matched with the child for the purposes of adoption" there were substituted—
　　"(b) the week in which—
　　　(i) official notification is sent to the adopter, or
　　　(ii) the person satisfies the condition in regulation 5(3)(a) of the Additional Statutory Paternity Pay (Adoptions from Overseas) Regulations 2010 (26 weeks' continuous employment),
　　whichever is the later"; and
　(b) at the end of paragraph (2), there were added ""official notification" has the same meaning as in the Additional Statutory Paternity Pay (Adoptions from Overseas) Regulations 2010".

Application

6.204　**4.** Subject to the provisions of Part 12ZA of the Act and of these Regulations, there is entitlement to additional statutory paternity pay (adoption) in respect of adoptions from overseas of children who enter Great Britain on or after 3rd April 2011.

Entitlement to additional statutory paternity pay (adoption) in respect of adoptions from overseas

6.205　**5.**—(1) A person ("P") is entitled to additional statutory paternity pay (adoption) in respect of an adoption from overseas if—
　(a) P satisfies the conditions—
　　(i) as to relationship with a child ("C") and the child's adopter ("A") specified in paragraph (2); and

(ii) as to continuity of employment and normal weekly earnings specified in paragraph (3);
(b) A satisfies the conditions specified in regulation 6;
(c) P intends to care for C during the additional statutory paternity pay period (adoption) in respect of C;
(d) A has signed the declaration referred to in regulation 8(1)(c); and
(e) P has complied with the requirements in regulation 8, including, where applicable, the requirements in regulation 8(3).

(2) The conditions referred to in paragraph (1)(a)(i) are that—
(a) P is married to, or is the civil partner or the partner of, A; and
(b) P has, or expects to have, the main responsibility (apart from any responsibility of A) for the upbringing of C.

(3) The conditions referred to in paragraph (1)(a)(ii) are that—
(a) P has been in employed earner's employment with an employer for a continuous period of at least 26 weeks prior to the date on which C enters Great Britain;
(b) P's normal weekly earnings for the period of eight weeks ending with the prescribed week are not less than the lower earnings limit in force under section 5(1)(a) of the Act at the end of the prescribed week; and
(c) P continues in employed earner's employment with the employer by reference to whom the condition in sub-paragraph (a) above is satisfied for a continuous period beginning with the prescribed week and ending with the week before the additional statutory paternity pay period (adoption) in respect of C begins.

(4) The references in paragraph (3) to the "prescribed week" are to the week in which—
(a) official notification is sent to A; or
(b) P satisfies the condition in paragraph (3)(a) (26 weeks' continuous employment); whichever is the later.

Conditions to be satisfied by the child's adopter

6. The conditions referred to in regulation 5(1)(b) are that A—
(a) became entitled, by reference to the adoption of C, to statutory adoption pay;
(b) has taken action constituting a return to work within the meaning of regulation 12;
(c) has taken the action referred to in paragraph (b) not less than two weeks after the date C enters Great Britain; and
(d) has at least two weeks of their adoption pay period which remain unexpired.

Additional statutory paternity pay period (adoption) in respect of adoptions from overseas

7.—(1) For the purposes of section 171ZEE(2)(a) of the Act, the date on which the additional statutory paternity pay period (adoption) in respect of C begins is—
(a) the date specified by P in accordance with regulation 8(2)(d) or last varied in accordance with regulation 8(6); or
(b) if later, the date of A's taking action constituting a return to work within the meaning of regulation 12;

Additional Statutory Paternity Pay (Adoptions from Overseas) Regulations 2010

being, in either case, a date which falls no earlier than 20 weeks after the date on which C enters Great Britain.

(2) For the purposes of section 171ZEE(2)(b)(ii) of the Act, the date on which the additional statutory paternity pay period (adoption) in respect of C ends is the date specified by P in accordance with regulation 8(2)(e) or last varied in accordance with 8(6).

(3) For the purposes of section 171ZEE(4)(a) of the Act, the additional statutory paternity pay period (adoption) in respect of C shall not last longer than 26 weeks.

(4) This paragraph applies instead of paragraph (2) where—
   (a) A dies after the beginning but before the end of the additional statutory paternity pay period (adoption) in respect of C; and
   (b) as soon as reasonably practicable after A's death, P gives the person paying P additional statutory paternity pay (adoption) notice in writing of A's death.

(5) Where paragraph (4) applies, the date on which the additional statutory paternity pay period (adoption) in respect of C ends is the date—
   (a) on which the adoption pay period in respect of C, which would have applied but for A's death, would have ended; or
   (b) if earlier, such date which, for the purposes of section 171ZEE(2)(b)(ii) of the Act, P may specify in the notice given under paragraph (4)(b).

Application for, and evidence of entitlement to, additional statutory paternity pay (adoption) in respect of adoptions from overseas

6.208

8.—(1) P shall apply for additional statutory paternity pay (adoption) to the person ("E") who will be liable to pay P such pay by providing to E—
   (a) the information, in writing, specified in paragraph (2);
   (b) a written declaration, signed by P—
      (i) that that information is correct;
      (ii) that P intends to care for C during the additional statutory paternity pay period (adoption) in respect of C; and
      (iii) that P meets the conditions in regulation 5(2);
   (c) a written declaration, signed by A—
      (i) that they have given notice to their employer that they are returning to work;
      (ii) that they satisfy the condition in regulation 6(a);
      (iii) specifying their name, address and National Insurance Number;
      (iv) specifying the start date of their adoption pay period in respect of C;
      (v) specifying the date on which they intend to return to work;
      (vi) confirming that, in relation to C, P is, to A's knowledge, the sole applicant for additional statutory paternity pay; and
      (vii) providing A's consent as regards the processing by E of the information provided pursuant to paragraphs (i) to (vi).

(2) The information referred to in paragraph (1)(a) is as follows—
   (a) P's name;
   (b) the date on which the official notification in respect of C was sent to A;
   (c) the date of C's entry into Great Britain;
   (d) the date on which P expects that E's liability to pay additional statutory paternity pay (adoption) will begin; and

(e) the date on which P expects that E's liability to pay additional statutory paternity pay (adoption) will end.

(3) P shall also provide, if E so requests within 28 days of receiving the information and declarations referred to in paragraph (1)—
  (a) a copy of the official notification in respect of C; and
  (b) evidence of the date that C entered Great Britain; and
  (c) the name and business address of A's employer (or, if A is self-employed, A's business address).

(4) The information and declarations referred to in paragraph (1) must be provided to E at least eight weeks before the date specified by P pursuant to paragraph (2)(d).

(5) P must give E what is requested under paragraph (3) within 28 days of E requesting it.

(6) P may, after applying for additional statutory paternity pay (adoption) under paragraph (1), withdraw that application, vary the date on which it is expected that E's liability to pay additional statutory paternity pay (adoption) will begin, or (before the additional statutory paternity pay period (adoption) in respect of C has begun), vary the date on which it is expected that E's liability to pay additional statutory paternity pay (adoption) will end, by notice in writing to E given—
  (a) if withdrawing an application, at least six weeks before the date specified by P pursuant to paragraph (2)(d), or
  (b) if varying the date on which it is expected that E's liability to pay additional statutory paternity pay (adoption) will begin, at least six weeks before the earlier of the date varied or the new date, or
  (c) if varying the date on which it is expected that E's liability to pay additional statutory paternity pay (adoption) will end, at least six weeks before the earlier of the date varied or the new date, or
  (d) in a case where it was not reasonably practicable to give notice in accordance with subparagraph (a), (b) or (c), as soon as is reasonably practicable.

(7) When P has applied for additional statutory paternity pay (adoption) under paragraph (1), P must give E written notice as soon as reasonably practicable if at any time—
  (a) P no longer satisfies the conditions in regulation 5(2); or
  (b) A no longer intends to take action constituting a return to work within the meaning of regulation 12.

(8) When E has been provided with all of the information and the declarations referred to in paragraph (1) (together with, if applicable, what E has requested under paragraph (3)), E must, within 28 days, confirm the start and end dates of E's liability to pay P additional statutory paternity pay (adoption), by notice in writing to P.

Entitlement to additional statutory paternity pay (adoption) in respect of adoptions from overseas in the event of the death of the adopter

9.—(1) In a case where A dies before the end of their adoption pay period in respect of C (but before the additional statutory paternity pay period (adoption) in respect of C has begun)—
  (a) the provisions in regulations 5 and 6 shall apply, subject to the following modifications—
    (i) regulation 5(1)(d) shall not apply;

Additional Statutory Paternity Pay (Adoptions from Overseas) Regulations 2010

  (ii) regulation 5(1)(e) shall apply—
    (aa) as if the references to regulation 8 were references to regulation 10; and
    (bb) in a case where the date of which P informs E pursuant to regulation 10(1)(a) is earlier than the date by which P has complied with the other requirements of regulation 10, as if such other requirements had been complied with on such earlier date provided that they are complied with as soon as reasonably practicable thereafter;
  (iii) the condition in regulation 5(2)(a) shall be taken to be satisfied if it would have been satisfied but for the fact that A had died;
  (iv) the condition in regulation 6(a) shall be taken to be satisfied if A would have satisfied it but for the fact that A had died; and
  (v) regulation 6(b), (c) and (d) shall not apply;
 (b) regulation 7 shall not apply;
 (c) for the purposes of section 171ZEE(2)(a) of the Act, the date on which the additional statutory paternity pay (adoption) in respect of C begins is such date, being the date of A's death or a later date, as P informs E of in accordance with regulation 10(1)(a) or as is last varied in accordance with regulation 10(7) or 10(8);
 (d) for the purposes of section 171ZEE(2)(b)(ii) of the Act, the date on which the additional statutory paternity pay period (adoption) in respect of C ends is, where earlier than the relevant date, the date specified by P in accordance with regulation 10(2)(d) or last varied in accordance with regulation 10(7) or 10(8);
 (e) for the purposes of section 171ZEE(4)(a) of the Act, the additional statutory paternity pay period (adoption) in respect of C shall not last longer than 39 weeks; and
 (f) regulation 8 shall be replaced by regulation 10.

(2) In paragraph (1)(d), "the relevant date" means the date on which the adoption pay period in respect of C which would have applied but for A's death, would have ended.

(3) References in this regulation to A's adoption pay period in respect of C include, where A's death occurred before A's adoption pay period in respect of C started, references to such period as would have existed but for the fact that A had died.

Application for, and evidence of entitlement to, additional statutory paternity pay (adoption) in respect of adoptions from overseas in the event of the death of the adopter

10.—(1) P shall apply for additional statutory paternity pay (adoption) to the person ("E") who
will be liable to pay P such pay by—
 (a) informing E of the date on which P wishes the additional statutory paternity pay period (adoption) in respect of C to begin or the date (if in the past) on which P wishes such period to have begun;
 (b) providing E with the information, in writing, specified in paragraph (2); and
 (c) by providing E with a written declaration, signed by P—
  (i) that the information referred to in sub-paragraph (b) is correct;
  (ii) that P intends to care for C during the additional statutory paternity pay period (adoption) in respect of C; and

(iii) that P meets the conditions in regulation 5(2) (as modified by regulation 9(1)(a)(iii));

(2) The information referred to in paragraph (1)(a) is as follows—
(a) P's name;
(b) the date the official notification in respect of C sent to A;
(c) the date of C's entry into Great Britain;
(d) the date on which P expects that E's liability to pay additional statutory paternity pay (adoption) will end;
(e) A's name, address, and National Insurance number;
(f) the start date of A's adoption pay period in respect of C or, in a case where A's death occurred before A's adoption pay period in respect of C started, the date that that period would have started but for the fact that A had died; and
(g) the date of A's death.

(3) P shall also provide, if E so requests within 28 days of receiving the information and declaration referred to in paragraph (1)—
(a) a copy of the official notification in respect of C;
(b) evidence of the date that C entered Great Britain; and
(c) the name and business address of A's employer (or, if A was self-employed, A's business address).

(4) Subject to paragraph (5), the information and declaration referred to in paragraph (1) must be provided to E as soon as reasonably practicable after, and in any event within eight weeks of, the date of A's death.

(5) If provided at least six weeks before the date of which P informs E pursuant to paragraph (1)(a), the information and evidence referred to in paragraph (1)(b) and (c) may be provided more than eight weeks after the date of A's death.

(6) P must give E what is requested under paragraph (3) within 28 days of E requesting it.

(7) Within eight weeks of the date of A's death, P may, after applying for additional statutory paternity pay (adoption) under paragraph (1) and by giving E notice in writing, withdraw that application, vary the date (if in the future) on which P wishes the additional statutory paternity pay period (adoption) in respect of C to begin, or (either before or after such period has begun) vary the date on which it is expected that E's liability to pay additional statutory paternity pay (adoption) will end, with immediate effect.

(8) More than eight weeks after the date of A's death, P may, after applying for additional statutory paternity pay (adoption) under paragraph (1), withdraw that application, vary the date (if in the future) on which P wishes the additional statutory paternity pay period (adoption) in respect of C to begin, or (before such period has begun), vary the date on which it is expected that E's liability to pay additional statutory paternity pay (adoption) will end, by notice in writing to E given—
(a) if withdrawing an application, at least six weeks before the date of which P informs E pursuant to paragraph (1)(a), or
(b) if varying the date on which P wishes the additional statutory paternity pay period (adoption) in respect of C to begin, at least six weeks before the earlier of the date varied or the new date, or
(c) if varying the date on which it is expected that E's liability to pay

additional statutory paternity pay (adoption) will end, at least six weeks before the earlier of the date varied or the new date, or

(d) in a case where it was not reasonably practicable to give notice in accordance with subparagraph (a), (b) or (c), as soon as is reasonably practicable.

(9) When E has been provided with all of the information and the declaration referred to in paragraph (1) (together with, if applicable, what E has requested under paragraph (3)), E must, within 28 days, confirm the date on which the additional statutory paternity pay period (adoption) in respect of C begins or began and the date on which E's liability to pay P additional statutory paternity pay (adoption) ends, by notice in writing to P.

Entitlement to additional statutory paternity pay (adoption) in respect of adoptions from overseas where there is more than one employer

6.211　11.—(1) Additional statutory paternity pay (adoption) shall be payable to a person in respect of a statutory pay week during any part of which that person works only for an employer—
(a) who is not liable to pay that person additional statutory paternity pay (adoption); and
(b) for whom that person worked in the week in which the adopter of a child from overseas received the relevant official notification.

(2) In this regulation "statutory pay week" means a week that person has chosen in respect of which additional statutory paternity pay (adoption) shall be payable.

Return to work

6.212　12. For the purposes of these Regulations, an adopter entitled to statutory adoption pay is treated as returning to work if that payment is not payable to that person in accordance with section 171ZN(3) or (5) of the Act.

Additional Statutory Paternity Pay (Weekly Rates) Regulations 2010

(SI 2010/1060)

Arrangement of Regulations

6.213　1. Citation and commencement
2. Weekly rate of payment of additional statutory paternity pay
3. Rounding of fractional amounts

6.214　The Secretary of State makes the following Regulations in exercise of the powers conferred by section 171ZEE(1) of the Social Security Contributions and Benefits Act 1992 and section 5(1)(l) of the Social Security Administration Act 1992.

(SI 2010/1060)

This instrument contains only regulations made by virtue of, or consequential upon, sections 10 and 11 of, and paragraph 24 of Schedule 1 to, the Work and Families Act 2006 and is made before the end of the period of 6 months before the coming into force of those enactments.

In accordance with section 176(1) of the Social Security Contributions and Benefits Act 1992, a draft of these Regulations was laid before Parliament and approved by resolution of each House of Parliament.

Citation and commencement

1. These Regulations may be cited as the Additional Statutory Paternity Pay (Weekly Rates) Regulations 2010 and come into force on 6th April 2010.

Weekly rate of payment of additional statutory paternity pay

2. The weekly rate of payment of additional statutory paternity pay shall be the smaller of the following two amounts—
(a) [¹ £139.58];
(b) 90% of the normal weekly earnings of the person claiming additional statutory paternity pay, determined in accordance with regulations 31 and 32 of the Additional Statutory Paternity Pay (General) Regulations 2010.

AMENDMENT

1. Welfare Benefits Up-rating Order 2015 (SI 2015/30) art.5(2) (April 5, 2015)

Rounding of fractional amounts

3. Where any payment of additional statutory paternity pay is made on the basis of a calculation at—
(a) the weekly rate specified in regulation 2(b); or
(b) the daily rate of one-seventh of the weekly rate specified in regulation 2(a) or (b),
and that amount includes a fraction of a penny, the payment shall be rounded up to the nearest whole number of pence.

Social Security Contributions and Benefits Act 1992 (Application of Parts 12ZA, 12ZB and 12ZC to Parental Order Cases) Regulations 2014

(SI 2014/2866)

This instrument contains only regulations made by virtue of, or consequential upon, sections 119(1) and 122(5)(c) and (6)(c) of the Children and Families Act 2014 and is made before the end of the period of 6 months beginning with the coming into force of that enactment.

The Secretary of State, in exercise of the powers conferred by sections 171ZK(2), 171ZT(2) and 171ZZ5(2) of the Social Security Contributions and Benefits Act 1992, makes the following Regulations:

Social Security Contributions and Benefits Act 1992 Regulations 2014

ARRANGEMENT OF REGULATIONS

6.218
1. Citation, commencement and application
2. Interpretation
3. Application of Part 12ZA of the Act to parental order parents
4. Application of Part 12ZB of the Act to parental order parents
5. Application of Part 12ZC of the Act to parental order parents

Sch.1. Application of Part 12ZA of the Act to parental order cases
Sch.2. Application of Part 12ZB of the Act to parental order cases
Sch.3 Application of Part 12ZC of the Act to parental order cases

GENERAL NOTE

6.219 These Regulations apply Pts 12ZA, 12ZB and 12ZC of the SSCBA 1992, as modified by these Regulations, to parental order parents. A "parental order parent" is a person who has applied, or intends to apply, with another person, under s.54 of the Human Fertilisation and Embryology Act 2008 for a parental order in respect of a child or someone who has such an order. Part 12ZA provides for entitlement to statutory paternity pay. Part 12ZB provides for entitlement to statutory adoption pay. Part 12ZC (inserted into SSCBA 1992 by Pt 7 of the Children and Families Act 2014) provides for entitlement statutory shared parental pay. Official estimates are that the numbers of employees likely to be affected by these Regulations are very small; for example, in 2013 only 185 parental orders were granted. Of those who apply or intend to apply for a parental order (regardless of whether they subsequently obtain one), only a proportion will meet the eligibility requirements to be entitled to adoption leave and pay, paternity leave and pay or to be able to opt into shared parental leave and pay.

Citation, commencement and application

6.220 **1.**—(1) These Regulations may be cited as the Social Security Contributions and Benefits Act 1992 (Application of Parts 12ZA, 12ZB and 12ZC to Parental Order Cases) Regulations 2014.

(2) Subject to paragraphs (3) and (4), these Regulations come into force on 19th November 2014.

(3) The modification of section 171ZA of the Social Security Contributions and Benefits Act 1992 by the insertion of subsection (3C) as set out in Schedule 1 to these Regulations comes into force on the date that section 171ZA(2)(ba) comes into force.

(4) The modification of section 171ZL of the Social Security Contributions and Benefits Act 1992 by the insertion of subsection (3B) as set out in Schedule 2 to these Regulations comes into force on the date that section 171ZL(2)(ba) comes into force.

(5) Regulation 4 does not have effect in cases involving children whose expected week of birth ends on or before 4th April 2015.

Interpretation

6.221 **2.**—In these Regulations—
"the Act" means the Social Security Contributions and Benefits Act 1992;
"intended parent", in relation to a child, means a person who, on the day of the child's birth—

(SI 2014/2866 reg.2)

(a) applies, or intends to apply during the period of 6 months beginning with that day, with another person for a parental order in respect of the child, and

(b) expects the court to make a parental order on that application in respect of the child;

"parental order" means an order under section 54(1) of the Human Fertilisation and Embryology Act 2008; and

"parental order parent" means a person—

(a) on whose application the court has made a parental order in respect of a child, or

(b) who is an intended parent of a child.

Application of Part 12ZA of the Act to parental order parents

3.—Part 12ZA of the Act (statutory paternity pay) has effect in relation to parental order parents with the modifications of sections 171ZA, 171ZB and 171ZE of the Act specified in the second column of Schedule 1 to these Regulations.

6.222

Application of Part 12ZB of the Act to parental order parents

4.—Part 12ZB of the Act (statutory adoption pay) has effect in relation to parental order parents with the modifications of sections 171ZL and 171ZN of the Act specified in the second column of Schedule 2 to these Regulations.

6.223

Application of Part 12ZC of the Act to parental order parents

5.—Part 12ZC of the Act (statutory shared parental pay) has effect in relation to parental order parents with the modifications of section 171ZV of the Act specified in the second column of Schedule 3 to these Regulations.

6.224

SCHEDULE 1   Regulation 3

Application of Part 12ZA of the Act to parental order cases

6.225

Provision	Modification
Section 171ZA	After subsection (4) insert— "(4A) A person who satisfies the conditions in section 171ZB(2)(a) to (d) in relation to a child is not entitled to statutory paternity pay under this section in respect of that child.".

Section 171ZB	For paragraph (a) of subsection (2) substitute—
	"(a) that he satisfies prescribed conditions as to being a person—
	  (i) on whose application the court has made a parental order in respect of a child, or
	  (ii) who is an intended parent of a child;
	(ab) that he satisfies prescribed conditions as to relationship with the other person on whose application the parental order was made or who is an intended parent of the child;".
	In paragraph (d) of subsection (2), for "placed for adoption" substitute "born".
	In paragraph (e) of subsection (2), omit "where he is a person with whom the child is placed for adoption,".
	For subsection (3) substitute—

Provision	Modification

	"(3) The references in this section to the relevant week are to the week immediately preceding the 14th week before the expected week of the child's birth.".
	After subsection (3) insert—
	"(3B) In a case where a child is born earlier than the 14th week before the expected week of the child's birth—
	  (a) subsection (2)(b) shall be treated as satisfied in relation to a person if, had the birth occurred after the end of the relevant week, the person would have been in employed earner's employment with an employer for a continuous period of at least 26 weeks ending with the relevant week;
	  (b) subsection (2)(c) shall be treated as satisfied in relation to a person if the person's normal weekly earnings for the period of 8 weeks ending with the week immediately preceding the week in which the child is born are not less than the lower earnings limit in force under section 5(1)(a) immediately before the commencement of the week in which the child is born; and
	  (c) subsection (2)(d) shall not apply.
	(3C) In a case where a child is born before the end of the relevant week, subsection (2)(ba) shall be treated as satisfied in relation to a person if, had the birth occurred after the end of the relevant week, the person would have been entitled to be in the relevant employment at the end of the relevant week.
	In this subsection "the relevant employment" means the employment by reference to which the person satisfies the condition in subsection (2)(b).".
	In subsection (6), for "placement for adoption of more than one child as part of the same arrangement" substitute "birth, or expected birth, of more than one child as a result of the same pregnancy".
	For subsection (7) substitute—
	"(7) In this section—
	"intended parent", in relation to a child, means a person who, on the day of the child's birth—
	  (a) applies, or intends to apply during the period of 6 months beginning with that day, with another person for a parental order in respect of the child, and
	  (b) expects the court to make a parental order on that application in respect of the child; and
	"parental order" means an order under section 54(1) of the Human Fertilisation and Embryology Act 2008.".
	Omit subsection (8).
	Omit subsection (9).

Section 171ZE	In paragraph (b) of subsection (3), for "placement for adoption" substitute "birth".
	In subsection (4)—
	  (a) in paragraph (a), for "sub-paragraph (i) of section 171ZA(2)(a)" substitute "section 171ZA(2)(a)(i)";
	  (b) in paragraph (b), for "sub-paragraph (ii) of that provision" substitute "section 171ZA(2)(a)(ii) or 171ZB(2)(ab)".
	In subsection (9), for "the reference in subsection (3)(a) to the date of the child's birth shall be read as a reference" substitute "the references in subsection (3)(a) and (b) to the date of the child's birth shall be read as references".
	Omit subsection (10).
	Omit subsection (12).

(SI 2014/2866 Sch. 2)

SCHEDULE 2

Regulation 4

Application of Part 12ZB of the Act to parental order cases

6.226

Provision	Modification
Section 171ZL	For paragraph (a) of subsection (2) substitute— "(a) that he is— 　(i) a person on whose application the court has made a parental order in respect of a child, or 　(ii) an intended parent of a child;".
	For subsection (3) substitute— "(3) The references in this section to the relevant week are to the week immediately preceding the 14th week before the expected week of the child's birth.". After subsection (3) insert— "(3A) In a case where a child is born earlier than the 14th week before the expected week of the child's birth— 　(a) subsection (2)(b) shall be treated as satisfied in relation to a person if, had the birth occurred after the end of the relevant week, the person would have been in employed earner's employment with an employer for a continuous period of at least 26 weeks ending with the relevant week; and 　(b) subsection (2)(d) shall be treated as satisfied in relation to a person if the person's normal weekly earnings for the period of 8 weeks ending with the week immediately preceding the week in which the child is born are not less than the lower earnings limit in force under section 5(1)(a) immediately before the commencement of the week in which the child is born. (3B) In a case where a child is born before the end of the relevant week, subsection (2)(ba) shall be treated as satisfied in relation to a person if, had the birth occurred after the end of the relevant week, the person would have been entitled to be in the relevant employment at the end of the relevant week. In this subsection "the relevant employment" means the employment by reference to which the person satisfies the condition in subsection (2)(b).". For paragraph (b) of subsection (4), substitute— "(b) the other person on whose application the court has made a parental order in respect of the child or who is an intended parent of the child— 　(i) is a person to whom the conditions in subsection (2) above apply, and 　(ii) has elected to receive statutory adoption pay.". Omit subsection (4A). Omit subsection (4B). In subsection (5), for "placement, or expected placement, for adoption of more than one child as part of the same arrangement" substitute "birth, or expected birth, of more than one child as a result of the same pregnancy". After subsection (8) insert— "(8A) In this section— 　"intended parent", in relation to a child, means a person who, on the day of the child's birth— 　(a) applies, or intends to apply during the period of 6 months beginning with that day, with another person for a parental order in respect of the child, and 　(b) expects the court to make a parental order on that application in respect of the child; and

Social Security Contributions and Benefits Act 1992 Regulations 2014

Provision	Modification
	"parental order" means an order under section 54(1) of the Human Fertilisation and Embryology Act 2008.". Omit subsection (9). Omit subsection (10).
Section 171ZN	In subsection (2F) (5), for "in which the person is notified that the person has been matched with a child for the purposes of adoption" substitute "immediately preceding the 14th week before the expected week of the child's birth". Omit subsection (9).

SCHEDULE 3   **Regulation 5**

6.227   Application of Part 12ZC of the Act to parental order cases

Provision	Modification

Section 171ZV	In subsection (1), for "with whom a child is, or is expected to be, placed for adoption under the law of any part of the United Kingdom" substitute "on whose application the court has made a parental order in respect of a child or who is an intended parent of a child".
	In paragraph (a) of subsection (2), for "another person" substitute "the other person on whose application the court has made a parental order in respect of the child or who is an intended parent of the child".
	In paragraph (g) of subsection (2), for "the placement for adoption of the child" substitute "being a person on whose application the court has made a parental order in respect of the child or being an intended parent of the child".
	In paragraph (a) of subsection (4), for "with whom a child is, or is expected to be, placed for adoption under the law of any part of the United Kingdom" substitute "on whose application the court has made a parental order in respect of a child or who is an intended parent of a child".
	In paragraph (h) of subsection (4), for "the placement for adoption of the child" substitute "being a person on whose application the court has made a parental order in respect of the child or being an intended parent of the child".
	In subsection (16), for "the placement for adoption of more than one child as part of the same arrangement" substitute "the birth of more than one child as a result of the same pregnancy".
	After subsection (16) insert—
	"(16A) In this section—
	    "intended parent", in relation to a child, means a person who, on the day of the child's birth—
	      (a) applies, or intends to apply during the period of 6 months beginning with that day, with another person for a parental order in respect of the child, and
	      (b) expects the court to make a parental order on that application in respect of the child; and
	"parental order" means an order under section 54(1) of the Human Fertilisation and Embryology Act 2008.".
	Omit subsection (17).
	Omit subsection (18).

(SI 2014/2934)

Statutory Paternity Pay and Statutory Adoption Pay (Parental Orders and Prospective Adopters) Regulations 2014

(SI 2014/2934)

This instrument contains only regulations made by virtue of, or consequential upon, section 119 of the Children and Families Act 2014 and is made before the end of the period of 6 months beginning with the coming into force of that enactment.

The Secretary of State in exercise of the powers conferred by sections 171ZB(2)(a), 171ZC(1A) and (3)(a), (c), (d), (f) and (g), 171ZD(2) and (3), 171ZE(2), (3), (7) and (8), 171ZG(3), 171ZJ(1), (3), (4), (7) and (8), 171ZL(8)(b) to (d), (f) and (g), 171ZM(2) and (3), 171ZN(2), (5) and (6), 171ZP(6), 171ZS(1), (3), (4), (7) and (8) and 175(4) of the Social Security Contributions and Benefits Act 1992, section 5(1)(g), (i) and (p) of the Social Security Administration Act 1992 and sections 8(1) and (2)(c) and 51(1) of the Employment Act 2002 and with the concurrence of the Commissioners for Her Majesty's Revenue and Customs, in so far as such concurrence is required, makes the following Regulations:

PART I

General

1. Citation and commencement
2.–3. Interpretation

PART 2

AMENDMENT OF THE PAY REGULATIONS

4.–5. Amendment of the Pay Regulations [*omitted*]

PART 3

APPLICATION AND MODIFICATION OF THE PAY REGULATIONS IN PARENTAL ORDER CASES

6.–24. Application of the Pay regulations to intended parents and parental order parents

Statutory Paternity Pay and Statutory Adoption Pay Regulations 2014

PART 4

AMENDMENT OF THE ADMINISTRATION REGULATIONS

25. Amendment of the Administration Regulations [*omitted*]

PART 5

MODIFICATION OF THE ADMINISTRATION REGULATIONS IN PARENTAL ORDER CASES

26. Modification of the Administration Regulations in parental order cases

GENERAL NOTE

6.229   Part 1 of these Regulations deals with citation, commencement and interpretation issues.

Part 2 of these Regulations amends the Statutory Paternity Pay and Statutory Adoption Pay (General) Regulations (SI 2002/2822) to make provision for a new right to statutory adoption pay for local authority foster parents who are prospective adopters if they have been notified that a child is to be placed with them under s.22C of the Children Act 1989 (following consideration in accordance with s.22C(9B)(c)). The amendments made also make provision for new rights to statutory paternity pay to the spouses, civil partners and partners of these prospective adopters.

Part 3 of these Regulations make provision for an entitlement to statutory adoption pay and statutory paternity pay (adoption) in respect of cases which involve a person who has applied with another person for a parental order under s.54 of the Human Fertilisation and Embryology Act 2008. Under s.54 a court may make an order providing for a child of a surrogate mother to be treated as the child of the applicants if certain conditions are satisfied. Part 3 needs to be read in conjunction with the Social Security Contributions and Benefits Act 1992 (Application of Pts 12ZA, 12ZB and 12ZC to Parental Order Cases) Regulations 2014 (SI 2014/2866). This Part should also be read in conjunction with the Statutory Paternity Pay and Statutory Adoption Pay (General) Regulations (SI 2002/2822) which this Part applies with modifications.

Part 4 amends to Statutory Paternity Pay and Statutory Adoption Pay (Administration) Regulations 2002 (SI 2002/2820) to cover the situation where statutory paternity pay or statutory adoption pay is paid to local authority foster parents who are prospective adopters. Part 5 modifies those 2002 Regulations in a case where statutory paternity pay or statutory adoption pay is paid to a person who has applied with another person for a parental order.

(SI 2014/2934 reg.1)

Part 1

General

Citation and commencement

1.—These Regulations may be cited as the Statutory Paternity Pay and Statutory Adoption Pay (Parental Orders and Prospective Adopters) Regulations 2014 and come into force on 1st December 2014.

Interpretation

2.—In these Regulations—
"Administration Regulations" means the Statutory Paternity Pay and Statutory Adoption Pay (Administration) Regulations 2002;
"parental order parent" means a person on whose application the court has made a parental order in relation to a child;
"Pay Regulations" means the Statutory Paternity Pay and Statutory Adoption Pay (General) Regulations 2002.

3.—(1) The amendments made in Part 2 and 4 of these Regulations have effect only in relation to children matched with a person who is notified of having been matched on or after 5th April 2015.

(2) For the purposes of paragraph (1)—
(a) a person is matched with a child for adoption when an adoption agency decides that that person would be a suitable adoptive parent for the child;
(b) in a case where paragraph (a) applies, a person is notified as having been matched with a child on the date that person receives notification of the agency's decision, under regulation 33(3)(a) of the Adoption Agencies Regulations 2005, regulation 28(3) of the Adoption Agencies (Wales) Regulations 2005 or regulation 8(5) of the Adoption Agencies (Scotland) Regulations 2009;
(c) a person is also matched with a child for adoption when a decision has been made in accordance with regulation 22A of the Care Planning, Placement and Case Review (England) Regulations 2010 and an adoption agency has identified that person with whom the child is to be placed in accordance with regulation 12B of the Adoption Agencies Regulations 2005;
(d) in a case where paragraph (c) applies, a person is notified as having been matched with a child on the date on which that person receives notification in accordance with regulation 12B(2)(a) of the Adoption Agencies Regulations 2005.

(3) In paragraph (2) "adoption agency" has the meaning given, in relation to England and Wales, by section 2 of the Adoption and Children Act 2002 and in relation to Scotland, by section 119(1) of the Adoption and Children (Scotland) Act 2007.

Statutory Paternity Pay and Statutory Adoption Pay Regulations 2014

Part 2

Amendment Of The Pay Regulations

[*The amendments made by regs 4 and 5 are incorporated into the Statutory Paternity Pay and Statutory Adoption Pay (General) Regulations 2002 (SI 2002/2822)*].

Part 3

Application And Modification Of The Pay Regulations In Parental Order Cases

Application of the Pay Regulations to intended parents and parental order parents

6.233 **6.**—(1) The provisions of the Pay Regulations in so far as they apply to statutory paternity pay (adoption) and statutory adoption pay shall apply to an intended parent or a parental order parent with the modifications set out in this Part of these Regulations.
(2) In this regulation—
"statutory adoption pay" means statutory adoption pay payable in accordance with the provisions of Part 12ZB of the Social Security Contributions and Benefits Act 1992;
"statutory paternity pay (adoption)" means statutory paternity pay payable in accordance with the provisions of Part 12ZA of the Social Security Contributions and Benefits Act 1992 where the conditions specified in section 171ZB of that Act are satisfied.

Application of the Pay Regulations to intended parents and parental order parents

6.234 **7.**—In regulation 2 (interpretation) of the Pay Regulations as they apply to an intended parent or a parental order parent—
  (a) paragraph (1) shall read as if—
    (i) the definition of "adopter" were omitted;
    (ii) there were the following definitions—
""Parent A" in relation to a child means the intended parent or parental order parent who has elected to be Parent A;
"parental order parent" means a person on whose application the court has made an order in respect of the child under section 54(1) of the Human Fertilization and Embryology Act 2008;
"statutory shared parental pay" means statutory shared parental pay payable in accordance with Part 12ZC of the Act;";
  (b) paragraph (2) shall apply as if that paragraph read—
    "(2) An intended parent or a parental order parent elects to be Parent A in relation to a child if that person (A) agrees with the other intended parent or parental order parent of the child (B) that A and not B will be parent A.".

(SI 2014/2934 reg. 8)

Application of the Pay Regulations to intended parents and parental order parents

8.—In regulation 3 (application) of the Pay Regulations as they apply an intended parent or a parental order parent—

(a) paragraph (1)(b) shall read as if sub-paragraphs (i) and (ii) were omitted and replaced by—

"whose expected week of birth begins on or after 5th April 2015".

(b) paragraph (2) shall read as if sub-paragraphs (a) and (b) were omitted and replaced by—

"whose expected week of birth begins on or after 5th April 2015".

6.235

Application of the Pay Regulations to intended parents and parental order parents

9.—In regulation 11 (conditions of entitlement) of the Pay Regulations as they apply to an intended parent or a parental order parent—

(a) paragraph (1) shall apply as if sub-paragraphs (a) and (b) were omitted and replaced by—

"(a) is an intended parent or parental order parent in relation to the child;
(b) is married to, the civil partner or the partner of Parent A; and
(c) has or expects to have the main responsibility for the upbringing of the child (apart from the responsibility of Parent A)."

(b) paragraph (2) shall read as if the words "the adopter" in both places where those words occur were "Parent A";

(c) paragraph (2A) shall read as if the words "the adopter" in both places where those words occur were "Parent A".

6.236

Application of the Pay Regulations to intended parents and parental order parents

10.—Regulation 11A (notice of entitlement to statutory paternity pay (adoption)) of the Pay Regulations as they apply to an intended parent or a parental order parent shall apply as if paragraphs (a) and (b) read—

"(a) in or before the 15th week before the expected week of the child's birth; or

(b) in a case where it was not reasonably practicable for the employee to give the notice in accordance with paragraph (a), as soon as reasonably practicable.".

6.237

Application of the Pay Regulations to intended parents and parental order parents

11.—In regulation 12 (period of payment of statutory paternity pay (adoption)) of the Pay Regulations as they apply to an intended parent or a parental order parent—

(a) paragraph (1) shall apply as if that paragraph read—

"(1) Subject to regulation 14, a person entitled to statutory paternity pay (adoption) may choose the statutory pay period to begin—

(a) on the date on which the child is born or, where the person is at work on that day, the following day;

(b) the date falling such number of days after the date on which the child is born as the person may specify; or

6.238

(c) a predetermined date, specified by the person which is later than the expected week of the child's birth.";
(b) paragraph (2) shall not apply;
(c) paragraph (4) shall apply as if sub-paragraphs (a) to (c) read—
"(a) where the variation is to provide for the employee's statutory paternity pay period to begin on the date on which the child is born, or where the employee is at work on that day, the following day, at least 28 days before the first day of the expected week of the child's birth,
(b) where the variation is to provide for the employee's statutory paternity pay period to begin on a date that is a specified number of days (or a different specified number of days) after the date on which the child is born, at least 28 days before the date falling that number of days after the first day of the expected week of the child's birth,
(c) where the variation is to provide for the employee's statutory paternity pay period to begin on a predetermined date (or a different predetermined date), at least 28 days before that date, ".

Application of the Pay Regulations to intended parents and parental order parents

6.239   12.—In regulation 13 (additional notice requirements for statutory paternity pay (adoption)) of the Pay Regulations as they apply to an intended parent or a parental order parent—
(a) paragraph (1) shall read as if the words "the date on which the placement occurred" were "the date on which the child was born";
(b) paragraph (2) shall read as if the words "is placed for adoption" were "is born".

Application of the Pay Regulations to intended parents and parental order parents

6.240   13.—In regulation 14 (qualifying period for statutory paternity pay (adoption)) of the Pay Regulations as they apply to an intended parent or a parental order parent shall read as if the words "of 56 days" to the end were omitted and replaced by—
"which begins on the date of the child's birth and ends—
(a) except in the case referred to in paragraph (b), 56 days after that date;
(b) in a case where the child is born before the first day of the expected week of its birth, 56 days after that day.".

Application of the Pay Regulations to intended parents and parental order parents

6.241   14.—In regulation 15 (evidence of entitlement for statutory paternity pay (adoption)) of the Pay Regulations as they apply to an intended parent or a parental order parent—
(a) paragraph (2)(b) shall apply as if that paragraph read—
"(b) the expected week of the child's birth;";
(b) paragraph (2)(e) shall apply as if that paragraph read—
"(e) the date on which the child was born";
(c) paragraph (3) shall apply as if sub-paragraphs (a) and (b) read—
"(a) in or before the 15th week before the expected week of the child's birth;

(b) in a case where it was not reasonably practicable for the employee to provide it in accordance with sub-paragraph (a), as soon as reasonably practicable.";
(d) paragraph (4) shall read as if the words "child's placement" were "child's birth".

Application of the Pay Regulations to intended parents and parental order parents

15.—In regulation 16 (entitlement to statutory paternity pay (adoption) where there is more than one employer) of the Pay Regulations as they apply to an intended parent or a parental order parent, paragraph (b) shall read as if the words "in which the adopter is notified of being matched with the child" were "immediately preceding the 14th week before the expected week of the child's birth".

Application of the Pay Regulations to intended parents and parental order parents

16.—In regulation 20 (avoidance of liability for statutory paternity pay) of the Pay Regulations as they apply to an intended parent or a parental order parent, paragraph (2)(a) shall read as if the words "or, as the case may be, the placement of the child for adoption" were omitted.

Application of the Pay Regulations to intended parents and parental order parents

17.—(1) In regulation 21 (adoption pay period) of the Pay Regulations as they apply to an intended parent or a parental order parent, paragraph (1) shall read as if that paragraph read—
"(1) The adoption pay period in respect of a person entitled to statutory adoption pay shall begin on the day on which the child is born or, where the person is at work on that day, the following day."
(2) Paragraph (2), (3), (4) and (6) shall not apply.

Application of the Pay Regulations to intended parents and parental order parents

18.—In regulation 22 (adoption pay period in cases where adoption is disrupted) of the Pay Regulations as they apply to an intended parent or a parental order parent—
(a) paragraph (1) shall apply as if that paragraph read—
"(1) The adoption pay period shall terminate in accordance with the provisions of paragraph (2) where—
(a) the child dies;
(b) the person entitled to statutory adoption pay does not apply for a parental order in respect of the child within the time limit set in section 54(3) of the Human Fertilisation and Embryology Act 2008; or
(c) the that person's application for a parental order in respect of the child is refused, withdrawn or otherwise terminated and any time limit for an appeal or a new application has expired;"
(b) in paragraph (3)—
(i) sub-paragraph (a) shall apply as if the reference to paragraph (1)(a)(i) were a reference to paragraph (1)(a);

(ii) sub-paragraph (b) shall apply as if that sub-paragraph read—
"(b) in a case falling within paragraph (1)(b) the week during which the time limit in section 54(3) of the Human Fertilisation and Embryology Act 2008 for an application for a parental order for the child expires;";
(iii) sub-paragraph (c) shall apply as if that sub-paragraph read—
"(c) in a case falling within paragraph (1)(c) the week during which the person's application for a parental order is refused, withdrawn or otherwise terminated without the order being granted."

Application of the Pay Regulations to intended parents and parental order parents

6.246 **19.**—In regulation 23 (additional notice requirements for statutory adoption pay) of the Pay Regulations as they apply to an intended parent or a parental order parent—
(a) paragraph (1) shall read as if the words "the date on which the child is expected to be placed for adoption" were "the expected week of the child's birth";
(b) paragraph (2) shall read as if—
(i) the words from "Where the choice" to "sub-paragraph (a) of that paragraph," were omitted;
(ii) the words "the date the child is placed for adoption" were "the date on which the child is born".

Application of the Pay Regulations to intended parents and parental order parents

6.247 **20.**—In regulation 24 (evidence of entitlement to statutory adoption pay) of the Pay Regulations as they apply to an intended parent or a parental order parent—
(a) in paragraph (1), sub-paragraph (a) shall apply as if that sub-paragraph read—
"(a) a statutory declaration specified in paragraph (2) where the person who will be liable to pay the statutory adoption pay requests it in accordance with paragraph (3)";
(b) paragraph (2) shall apply as if that paragraph read—
"(2) The statutory declaration referred to in paragraph (1)(a) is a statutory declaration stating that the person making the declaration—
(a) has applied, or intends to apply, under section 54 of the Human Fertilisation and Embryology Act 2008 with another person for a parental order in respect of the child within the time limit for making such an application; and
(b) expects the court to make a parental order on that application in respect of the child.";
(c) paragraph (3) shall apply as if that paragraph read—
"(3) The declaration in referred to—
(a) in paragraph (1)(a) shall be provided to the person liable to pay statutory adoption pay within 14 days of that person requesting that declaration where the person requests it within 14 days of receiving the notice under section 171ZL(6) of the Act;
(b) in paragraph (1)(b) shall be provided to the person liable to pay statutory adoption pay at least 28 days before the beginning of the

(SI 2014/2934 reg.20)

adoption pay period, or if that is not reasonably practicable , as soon as reasonably practicable after that date."

Application of the Pay Regulations to intended parents and parental order parents

21.—In regulation 25 (entitlement to statutory adoption pay where there is more than one employer) of the Pay Regulations as they apply to an intended parent or a parental order parent, paragraph (b) shall read as if the words "in which he is notified of being matched with the child" were "immediately preceding the 14th week before the expected week of the child's birth".

Application of the Pay Regulations to intended parents and parental order parents

22.—In regulation 29 (termination of employment before start of adoption pay period) of the Pay Regulations as they apply to an intended parent or a parental order parent, paragraph (1) shall apply as if—
(a) the words "chosen in accordance with regulation 21" were omitted;
(b) the words "14 days before the expected date of placement" to the end were "on the day on which the child is born".

Application of the Pay Regulations to intended parents and parental order parents

23.—In regulation 30 (avoidance of liability for statutory adoption pay) of the Pay Regulations as they apply to an intended parent or a parental order parent, in paragraph (2), sub-paragraph (a) shall read as if the words "in which he was notified of having been matched with the child for adoption" read "immediately preceding the 14th week before the expected week of the child's birth".

Application of the Pay Regulations to intended parents and parental order parents

24.—In regulation 40 (normal weekly earnings) of the Pay Regulations as they apply to an intended parent or a parental order parent, in paragraph (2), the definition of "the appropriate date" shall read—

""the appropriate date" means in relation to statutory paternity pay (adoption) and statutory adoption pay , the first day of the 14th week before the expected week of the child's birth or the first day in the week in which the child is born, whichever is earlier;".

PART 4

AMENDMENT OF THE ADMINISTRATION REGULATIONS

[*The amendments made by reg.25 are incorporated into the Statutory Paternity Pay and Statutory Adoption Pay (Administration) Regulations 2002 (SI 2002/2820).*]

Statutory Paternity Pay and Statutory Adoption Pay Regulations 2014

Part 5

Modification Of The Administration Regulations In Parental Order Cases

6.252   **26.**—In the case of entitlement to statutory paternity pay or statutory adoption pay under section 171ZB or 171ZL of the Social Security Contributions and Benefits Act 1992 as those sections apply to an intended parent or to a parental order parent—
(a) paragraph (3)(b)(ii) of regulation 11 (provision of information) of the Administration Regulations shall read as if the words from "the end of the seven day period that starts on the date on which the adopter is notified of having been matched with the child" were—
"the day the employee gave notice of the employee's intended absence or the end of the fifteenth week before the expected week of birth, whichever is later;"
(b) paragraph (4) and (5) of that regulation shall not apply.

Statutory Maternity Pay and Statutory Adoption Pay (Curtailment) Regulations 2014

(SI 2014/3054)

6.253   For the text of these Regulations, see Part V above.

PART VII

STATUTORY SHARED PARENTAL PAY

Statutory Shared Parental Pay (Administration) Regulations 2014

(SI 2014/2929)

The Secretary of State makes these Regulations in exercise of powers conferred by sections 7, 8, 10 and 51(1) of the Employment Act 2002 and sections 8(1)(f) and (ga) and 25(3) and (6) of the Social Security Contributions (Transfer of Functions, etc.) Act 1999 with the concurrence of the Commissioners for Her Majesty's Revenue and Customs:

ARRANGEMENT OF REGULATIONS

1. Citation and commencement
2. Interpretation
3. Funding of employers' liabilities to make payments of statutory shared parental pay
4. Applications for funding from the Commissioners
5. Deductions from payments to the Commissioners
6. Payments to employers by the Commissioners
7. Date when certain contributions are to be treated as paid
8. Overpayments
9. Records to be maintained by employers
10. Inspection of employers' records
11. Provision of information relating to entitlement to statutory shared parental pay
12. Application for the determination of any issue arising as to, or in connection with, entitlement to statutory shared parental pay
13. Applications in connection with statutory shared parental pay
14. Provision of information

GENERAL NOTE

Part 7 of the Children and Families Act 2014 inserted a new Pt 12ZC into the SSCBA 1992 giving the Secretary of State the power to make regulations to create an entitlement to statutory shared parental pay (ShPP). These Regulations provide for the funding of employers' liabilities to make ShPP payments and also impose obligations on employers in connection with such payments and confer powers on the Commissioners for HMRC. Under reg.3, an employer is entitled to an amount equal to 92 per cent of ShPP payments made by the employer, or the whole of such payments if the employer is a small employer. Regulations 4 to 7 provide for employers to be reimbursed through deductions from income tax, national insurance and other payments that they would otherwise make to HMRC (and for HMRC to fund payments to the extent that employers cannot be fully reimbursed in this way). Regulation 8 enables HMRC to recover overpayments to employers. Regulation 9 requires employers to maintain records relevant to ShPP payments to employees or former employees, while reg.10 empowers HMRC officers to inspect, copy or remove employers' payment records. Regulation 11 requires an employer who decides not to make any (or any further) ShPP payments to an employee (or former employee) to give that person the details of the decision and the reasons for it. Regulations 12 and 13 provide for HMRC officers to determine issues relating to a person's ShPP entitlement. Regulation 14 provides for employers, employment agencies, ShPP claimants and others to furnish information or documents to HMRC officers on request.

Statutory Shared Parental Pay (Administration) Regulations 2014

Citation and commencement

7.03   **1.**—These Regulations may be cited as the Statutory Shared Parental Pay (Administration) Regulations 2014 and come into force on 1st December 2014.

Interpretation

7.04   **2.**—(1) In these Regulations—

"the 1992 Act" means the Social Security Contributions and Benefits Act 1992;

"the Commissioners" means the Commissioners for Her Majesty's Revenue and Customs;

"contributions payments" has the same meaning as in section 7 of the Employment Act 2002;

"the Contributions Regulations" means the Social Security (Contributions) Regulations 2001;

"income tax month" means the period beginning on the 6th day of any calendar month and ending on the 5th day of the following calendar month;

"income tax quarter" means the period beginning on—
(a) the 6th day of April and ending on the 5th day of July;
(b) the 6th day of July and ending on the 5th day of October;
(c) the 6th day of October and ending on the 5th day of January;
(d) the 6th day of January and ending on the 5th day of April;

"period of payment of statutory shared parental pay" means each week during which statutory shared parental pay is payable to a person under section 171ZY(2) of the 1992 Act;

"statutory shared parental pay" means statutory shared parental pay payable in accordance with the provisions of Part 12ZC of the 1992 Act;

"tax year" means the 12 months beginning with 6th April in any year;

"writing" includes writing delivered by means of electronic communications to the extent that the electronic communications are approved by directions issued by the Commissioners pursuant to regulations under section 132 of the Finance Act 1999.

(2) Any reference in these Regulations to the employees of an employer includes the employer's former employees.

Funding of employers' liabilities to make payments of statutory shared parental pay

7.05   **3.**—(1) An employer who has made any payment of statutory shared parental pay shall be entitled—
(a) to an amount equal to 92% of such payment; or
(b) if the payment qualifies for small employer's relief by virtue of section 7(3) of the Employment Act 2002—
  (i) to an amount equal to such payment; and
  (ii) to an additional payment equal to the amount to which the employer would have been entitled under section 167(2)(b) of the 1992 Act had the payment been a payment of statutory maternity pay.

(2) The employer shall be entitled in either case (a) or case (b) to apply for advance funding in respect of such payment in accordance with

regulation 4, or to deduct it in accordance with regulation 5 from amounts otherwise payable by the employer.

DEFINITION

"statutory shared parental pay"—reg.2(1).

Applications for funding from the Commissioners

4.—(1) An employer may apply to the Commissioners for funds to pay the statutory shared parental pay (or so much of it as remains outstanding) to the employee or employees in a form approved for that purpose by the Commissioners where—
- (a) the conditions in paragraph (2) are satisfied; or
- (b) the condition in paragraph (2)(a) is satisfied and the employer considers that the condition in paragraph (2)(b) will be satisfied on the date of any subsequent payment of emoluments to one or more employees who are entitled to payment of statutory shared parental pay.

(2) The conditions in this paragraph are—
- (a) the employer is entitled to a payment determined in accordance with regulation 3 in respect of statutory shared parental pay which the employer is required to pay to an employee or employees for an income tax month or income tax quarter; and
- (b) the payment exceeds the aggregate of—
  - (i) the total amount of tax which the employer is required to pay to the collector of taxes in respect of the deduction from the emoluments of employees in accordance with the Income Tax (Pay as You Earn) Regulations 2003 for the same income tax month or income tax quarter;
  - (ii) the total amount of the deductions made by the employer from the emoluments of employees for the same income tax month or income tax quarter in accordance with regulations under section 22(5) of the Teaching and Higher Education Act 1998 or under section 73B of the Education (Scotland) Act 1980 or in accordance with article 3(5) of the Education (Student Support) (Northern Ireland) Order 1998;
  - (iii) the total amount of contributions payments which the employer is required to pay to the collector of taxes in respect of the emoluments of employees (whether by means of deduction or otherwise) in accordance with the Contributions Regulations for the same income tax month or income tax quarter; and
  - (iv) the total amount of payments which the employer is required to pay to the collector of taxes in respect of the deductions made on account of tax from payments to sub-contractors in accordance with section 61 of the Finance Act 2004 for the same income tax month or income quarter.

(3) An application by an employer under paragraph (1) shall be for an amount up to, but not exceeding, the amount of the payment to which the employer is entitled in accordance with regulation 3 in respect of statutory shared parental pay which the employer is required to pay to an employee or employees for the income tax month or income tax quarter to which the payment of emoluments relates.

Statutory Shared Parental Pay (Administration) Regulations 2014

DEFINITIONS

"the Commissioners"—reg.2(1).
"contributions payments"—reg.2(1).
"the Contributions Regulations"—reg.2(1).
"income tax month"—reg.2(1).
"income tax quarter"—reg.2(1).
"statutory shared parental pay"—reg.2(1).

Deductions from payments to the Commissioners

7.07 **5.**—An employer who is entitled to a payment determined in accordance with regulation 3 may recover such payment by making one or more deductions from the aggregate of the amounts specified in sub-paragraphs (i) to (iv) of regulation 4(2)(b) except where and in so far as—
  (a) those amounts relate to earnings paid before the beginning of the income tax month or income tax quarter in which the payment of statutory shared parental pay was made;
  (b) those amounts are paid by the employer later than six years after the end of the tax year in which the payment of statutory shared parental pay was made;
  (c) the employer has received payment from the Commissioners under regulation 4; or
  (d) the employer has made a request in writing under regulation 4 that the payment to which the employer is entitled in accordance with regulation 3 be paid and the employer has not received notification by the Commissioners that the request is refused.

DEFINITIONS

"the Commissioners"—reg.2(1).
"income tax month"—reg.2(1).
"income tax quarter"—reg.2(1).
"statutory shared parental pay"—reg.2(1).
"tax year"—reg.2(1).
"writing"—reg.2(1).

Payments to employers by the Commissioners

7.08 **6.**—The Commissioners shall pay the employer such amount as the employer was unable to deduct where—
  (a) the Commissioners are satisfied that the total amount which the employer is or would otherwise be entitled to deduct under regulation 5 is less than the payment to which the employer is entitled in accordance with regulation 3 in an income tax month or income tax quarter; and
  (b) the employer has in writing requested the Commissioners to do so.

DEFINITIONS

"the Commissioners"—reg.2(1).
"income tax month"—reg.2(1).
"income tax quarter"—reg.2(1).
"writing"—reg.2(1).

Date when certain contributions are to be treated as paid

7.—Where an employee has made a deduction from a contributions payment under regulation 5, the date on which it is to be treated as having been paid for the purposes of subsection (5) of section 7 (funding of employers' liabilities) of the Employment 2002 is—
  (a) in a case where the deduction did not extinguish the contributions payment, the date on which the remainder of the contributions payment or, as the case may be, the first date on which any part of the remainder of the contributions payment was paid; and
  (b) in a case where deduction extinguished the contributions payment, the 14th day after the end of the income tax month or income tax quarter during which there were paid the earnings in respect of which the contributions payment was payable.

DEFINITIONS

"contributions payments"—reg.2(1).
"income tax month"—reg.2(1).
"income tax quarter"—reg.2(1).

Overpayments

8.—(1) This regulation applies where funds have been provided to the employer pursuant to regulation 4 in respect of one or more employees and it appears to an officer of Revenue and Customs that the employer has not used the whole or part of those funds to pay statutory shared parental pay.

(2) An officer of Revenue and Customs shall decide to the best of the officer's judgement the amount of funds provided pursuant to regulation 4 and not used to pay statutory shared parental pay and shall serve notice in writing of this decision on the employer.

(3) A decision under this regulation may cover funds provided pursuant to regulation 4—
  (a) for any one income tax month or income tax quarter, or more than one income tax month or income tax quarter, in a tax year; and
  (b) in respect of a class or classes of employees specified in the decision notice (without naming the individual employees), or in respect of one or more employees named in the decision notice.

(4) Subject to the following provisions of this regulation, Part 6 of the Taxes Management Act 1970 (collection and recovery) shall apply with any necessary modifications to a decision under this regulation as if it were an assessment and as if the amount of funds determined were income tax charged on the employer.

(5) Where an amount of funds determined under this regulation relates to more than one employee, proceedings may be brought for the recovery of that amount without distinguishing the amounts making up that sum which the employer is liable to repay in respect of each employee and without specifying the employee in question, and the amount determined under this regulation shall be one cause of action or one matter of complaint for the purposes of proceedings under section 65, 66 or 67 of the Taxes Management Act 1970.

(6) Nothing in paragraph (5) prevents the bringing of separate proceedings for the recovery of any amount which the employer is liable to repay in respect of each employee.

Statutory Shared Parental Pay (Administration) Regulations 2014

Definitions

"employee"—reg.2(2).
"income tax month"—reg.2(1).
"income tax quarter"—reg.2(1).
"statutory shared parental pay"—reg.2(1).

Records to be maintained by employers

7.11   9.—Every employer shall maintain for three years after the end of a tax year in which the employer made payments of statutory shared parental pay to any employee a record of—
  (a) if the employee's period of payment of statutory shared parental pay began in that year—
    (i) the date of which that period began; and
    (ii) the evidence of entitlement to statutory shared parental pay provided by the employee pursuant to regulations made under section 171ZW(1)(b) of the 1992 Act;
  (b) the weeks in that tax year in which statutory shared parental pay was paid to the employee and the amount paid in each week;
  (c) any week in that tax year which was within the employee's period of payment of statutory shared parental pay but for which no payment of statutory shared parental pay was made to the employee and the reason no payment was made.

Definitions

"employee"—reg.2(2).
"period of payment of statutory shared parental pay"—reg.2(1).
"statutory shared parental pay"—reg.2(1).
"tax year"—reg.2(1).
"writing"—reg.2(1).

Inspection of employers' records

7.12   10.—(1) Every employer, whenever called upon to do so by any authorised officer of Revenue and Customs, shall produce the documents and records specified in paragraph (2) to that officer for inspection, at such time as that officer may reasonably require, at the prescribed place.
  (2) The documents and records specified in this paragraph are—
  (a) all wage sheets, deductions working sheets, records kept in accordance with regulation 9 and other documents relating to the calculation or payment of statutory shared parental pay to employees in respect of the years specified by such officer; or
  (b) such of those wages sheets, deductions working sheets, or other documents and records as may be specified by the authorised officer.
  (3) The "prescribed place" mentioned in paragraph (1) means—
  (a) such place in Great Britain as the employer and the authorised officer may agree upon; or
  (b) in default of such agreement, the place in Great Britain at which the documents and records referred to in paragraph (2)(a) are normally kept; or
  (c) in default of such agreement and if there is no such place as it referred to in sub-paragraph (b), the employer's principal place of business in Great Britain.

(SI 2014/2929 reg.10)

(4) The authorised officer may—
(a) take copies of, or make extracts from, any document or record produced to the authorised officer for inspection in accordance with paragraph (1); and
(b) remove any document or record so produced if it appears to the authorised officer to be necessary to do so, at a reasonable time and for a reasonable period.

(5) Where any document or record is removed in accordance with paragraph (4)(b), the authorised officer shall provide—
(a) a receipt for the document or record so removed; and
(b) a copy of the document or record, free of charge, within seven days, to the person by whom it was produced or caused to be produced where the document or record is reasonably required for the proper conduct of business.

(6) Where a lien is claimed on a document produced in accordance with paragraph (1), the removal of the document under paragraph (4)(b) shall not be regarded as breaking the lien.

(7) Where records are maintained by computer, the person required to make them available for inspection shall provide the authorised officer with all facilities necessary for obtaining information from them.

DEFINITIONS

"employee"—reg.2(1).
"prescribed place"—para.(3).
"statutory shared parental pay"—reg.2(1).

Provision of information relating to entitlement to statutory shared parental pay

11.—(1) An employer shall furnish the employee with details of a decision that the employer has no liability to make payments of statutory shared parental pay to the employee and the reason for it where the employer—
(a) has been given evidence of entitlement to statutory shared parental pay pursuant to regulations made under section 171ZW(1)(b) of the 1992 Act; and
(b) decides that they have no liability to make payments of statutory shared parental pay to the employee.

(2) An employer who has been given such evidence of entitlement to statutory shared parental pay shall furnish the employee with the information specified in paragraph (3) where the employer—
(a) has made one or more payments of statutory shared parental pay to the employee but,
(b) decides, before the end of the period of payment of statutory shared parental pay, that they have no liability to make further payments to the employee because the employee has been detained in legal custody or sentenced to a term of imprisonment which was not suspended.

(3) The information specified in this paragraph is—
(a) details of the employer's decision and the reasons for it; and
(b) details of the last week in respect of which a liability to pay statutory shared parental pay arose and the total number of weeks within the period of payment of statutory shared parental pay in which such liability arose.

7.13

(4) The employer shall—
(a) return to the employee any evidence provided by the employee as referred to in paragraph (1) or (2);
(b) comply with the requirements imposed by paragraph (1) within 28 days of the day the employee gave evidence of entitlement to statutory shared parental pay pursuant to regulations made under section 171ZW(1)(b) of the 1992 Act; and
(c) comply with the requirements imposed by paragraph (2) within seven days of being notified of the employee's detention or sentence.

DEFINITIONS

"employee"—reg.2(2).
"period of payment of statutory shared parental pay"—reg.2(1).
"statutory shared parental pay"—reg.2(1).

Application for the determination of any issue arising as to, or in connection with, entitlement to statutory shared parental pay

7.14   **12.**—(1) An application for the determination of any issue arising as to, or in connection with, entitlement to statutory shared parental pay may be submitted to an officer of Revenue and Customs by the employee concerned.
(2) Such an issue shall be decided by an officer of Revenue and Customs only on the basis of such an application or on their own initiative.

DEFINITION

"statutory shared parental pay"—reg.2(1).

Applications in connection with statutory shared parental pay

7.15   **13.**—(1) An application for the determination of any issue referred to in regulation 12 shall be made in a form approved for the purpose by the Commissioners.
(2) Where such an application is made by an employee, it shall—
(a) be made to an officer of Revenue and Customs within six months of the earliest day in respect of which entitlement to statutory shared parental pay is an issue;
(b) state the period in respect of which entitlement to statutory shared parental pay is in issue; and
(c) state the grounds (if any) on which the applicant's employer had denied liability for statutory shared parental pay in respect of the period specified in the application.

DEFINITIONS

"Commissioners"—reg.2(1).
"employee"—reg.2(2).
"statutory shared parental pay"—reg.2(1).

Provision of information

7.16   **14.**—(1) Where an officer of Revenue and Customs—
(a) reasonably requires information or documents from a person specified in paragraph (2) to ascertain whether statutory shared parental pay is or was payable, and

(SI 2014/2929 reg.14)

(b) gives notification to that person requesting such information or documents, that person shall furnish that information within 30 days of receiving the notification.

(2) The requirement to provide such information or documents applies to—

(a) any person claiming to be entitled to statutory shared parental pay;
(b) any person who is, or has been, the spouse, civil partner or partner of such a person as is specified in sub-paragraph (a);
(c) any person who is, or has been, an employer of such a person as is specified in sub-paragraph (a);
(d) any person carrying on an agency or other business for the introduction or supply of persons available to do work or to perform services to persons requiring them; and
(e) any person who is a servant or agent of any such person as is specified in sub-paragraphs (a) to (d).

DEFINITIONS

"statutory shared parental pay"—reg.2(1).

Statutory Shared Parental Pay (General) Regulations 2014

(SI 2014/3051)

A draft of these Regulations was laid before Parliament in accordance with section 176(1) of the Social Security Contributions and Benefits Act 1992 and approved by resolution of each House of Parliament.

This instrument contains only regulations made by virtue of, or consequential upon, section 119 of the Children and Families Act 2014 and is made before the end of the period of 6 months beginning with the coming into force of that enactment.

The Secretary of State, in exercise of the powers conferred by sections 171ZU(1), (2), (3), (4), (5), (12), (13), (14) and (15), 171ZV(1), (2), (3), (4), (5), (12), (13), (14), (15) and (17), 171ZW(1)(a) to (f), 171ZX(2) and (3), 171ZY(1), (3), (4) and (5), 171ZZ1(3), 171ZZ4(3), (4), (7) and (8) and 175(3) of the Social Security Contributions and Benefits Act 1992 and by section 5(1)(g), (i), (l) and (p) of the Social Security Administration Act 1992 and with the concurrence of the Commissioners for Her Majesty's Revenue and Customs in so far as such concurrence is required, makes the following Regulations:

ARRANGEMENT OF REGULATIONS

PART 1

1. Citation and commencement
2. Definitions
3. Application

7.17

Part 2

4. Entitlement of mother to statutory shared parental pay (birth)
5. Entitlement of father or partner to statutory shared parental pay (birth)
6. Notification and evidential requirements relating to the mother
7. Notification and evidential requirements relating to the father or partner
8. Variation of number of weeks of pay to be claimed and of periods when pay is to be claimed
9. Modification of notice conditions in case of early birth
10. Extent of entitlement to statutory shared parental pay (birth)
11. When statutory shared parental pay (birth) is not to be paid
12. Work during period of payment of statutory shared parental pay (birth)
13. Care of child during period of payment of statutory shared parental pay
14. Other cases where there is no liability to pay statutory shared parental pay
15. Conditions of entitlement to statutory shared parental pay: absence from work
16. Entitlement to statutory shared parental pay (birth) in cases relating to death

Part 3

17. Entitlement of adopter to statutory shared parental pay (adoption)
18. Entitlement of partner to statutory shared parental pay (adoption)
19. Notification and evidential requirements relating to the adopter
20. Notification and evidential requirements relating to the partner
21. Variation of number of weeks of pay to be claimed and of periods when pay is to be claimed
22. Extent of entitlement to statutory shared parental pay (adoption)
23. When statutory shared parental pay (adoption) is not to be paid
24. Work during period of payment of statutory shared parental pay (adoption)
25. Care of child during period of payment of statutory shared parental pay
26. Other cases where there is no liability to pay statutory shared parental pay
27. Conditions of entitlement to statutory shared parental pay: absence from work
28. Entitlement to statutory shared parental pay (adoption) in cases relating to death

Part 4

29. Conditions relating to employment and earnings of a claimant's partner
30. Conditions as to continuity of employment and normal weekly earnings relating to a claimant for statutory shared parental pay (birth)
31. Conditions as to continuity of employment and normal weekly earnings in relation to a claimant for statutory shared parental pay (adoption)
32. Normal weekly earnings of a claimant for statutory shared parental pay
33. Treatment of persons as employees
34. Continuous employment
35. Continuous employment and unfair dismissal
36. Continuous employment and stoppages of work
37. Change of employer
38. Reinstatement after service with the armed forces etc
39. Treatment of two or more employers or two or more contracts of service as one

Part 5

40. Weekly rate of payment of statutory shared parental pay
41. Statutory shared parental pay and contractual remuneration
42. Avoidance of liability for statutory shared parental pay
43. Payment of statutory shared parental pay
44. Time when statutory shared parental pay is to be paid
45. Liability of the Commissioners to pay statutory shared parental pay
46. Liability of the Commissioners to pay statutory shared parental pay in case of legal custody or imprisonment
47. Payments by the Commissioners
48. Persons unable to act
49. Service of notices

    Schedule   Statutory Shared Parental Pay in Special Circumstances

General Note

These Regulations introduce a new entitlement for mothers, fathers or the partners of mothers who are employed earners and for adopters and their partners who are employed earners to receive a statutory payment from their employers called statutory shared parental pay (ShPP). Part 7 of the Children and Families Act 2014 inserted a new Chapter 1B into Pt 8 of the Employment Rights Act 1996, giving the Secretary of State the power to make regulations to create an entitlement to shared parental leave. Part 7 of the 2014 Act also inserts a new Pt 12ZC into the SSCBA 1992 giving the Secretary of State the power to make regulations to create an entitlement to ShPP. Eligible employees will be able to share up to 50 weeks of shared parental leave and up to 37 weeks of ShPP. Shared parental leave and pay can be taken at any time between the birth of a child or the placement of a child for adoption or with prospective adopters. ShPP must be taken before the child's first birthday or the first anniversary of the placement.

7.18

Part 1 of the Regulations is introductory and in particular specifies for what children the new entitlement arises by reference to the time of their expected week of birth or placement for adoption.

Part 2 (regs 4–16) relates to entitlement to ShPP in connection with the birth of a child. Regulations 4 and 5 set out the conditions which a mother, mother's partner or father must satisfy in order to be entitled to this pay. Regulations 6 and 7 detail what notices and information the claimant mother, mother's partner or father must provide. Regulation 8 provides for the claimants to vary their entitlement once they have claimed it. Regulation 9 provides for the modification of the notice provisions in the case of an early birth. Regulation 10 details how many weeks of ShPP are available to claimants. Regulation 11 sets out when ShPP is not to be paid. Regulations 12 to 15 deal with further circumstances relating to such matters as work or absence from work which mean that pay may, or may not be, payable.

Part 3 (regs 17–28) concerns ShPP in connection with adoption. The provisions correspond to the provisions in Pt 2.

Part 4 (regs 29–39) sets out the conditions relating to employment and earnings that a claimant and the claimant's partner (or child's father) must satisfy in order for the claimant to be entitled to ShPP (regs 29–32). This Part also contains further provisions relating to employment (regs 33–39).

Part 5 (regs 40–48) contains provisions as to the rate of ShPP, how it is paid, when it is paid and who pays it.

The Schedule contains provisions modifying the regulations in various cases where a claimant, a claimant's partner or father of the child dies or where the child dies or, in the case of adoption, is returned after being placed.

Note also that these Regulations are modified for certain special purposes by two sets of other regulations. First, the Statutory Shared Parental Pay (Adoption from

Statutory Shared Parental Pay (General) Regulations 2014

Overseas) Regulations 2014 (SI 2014/3093) make provision relating to ShPP in respect of adoptions from overseas. Secondly, the Statutory Shared Parental Pay (Parental Order Cases) Regulations 2014 (SI 2014/3097) provide an entitlement to ShPP in cases which involve a person who has applied with another person for a parental order under s.54 of the Human Fertilisation and Embryology Act 2008.

PART 1

Citation and commencement

7.19   **1.**—These Regulations may be cited as the Statutory Shared Parental Pay (General) Regulations 2014 and come into force on 1st December 2014.

Definitions

7.20   **2.**—(1) In these Regulations—
"1992 Act" means the Social Security Contributions and Benefits Act 1992;
"A" means a person with whom C is, or is expected to be, placed for adoption under the law of any part of the United Kingdom;
"AP" means a person who at the date C is placed for adoption is married to, or is the civil partner of, or is the partner of A;
"C" means the child in relation to whom entitlement to statutory shared parental pay arises;
"M" means the mother (or expectant mother) of C;
"P" means the father of C or a person who at the date of C's birth is married to, or is the civil partner of, or is the partner of M;
"actual week of birth", in relation to a child, means the week beginning with midnight between Saturday and Sunday, in which the child was born;
"adoption agency" has the meaning given, in relation to England and Wales, by section 2 of the Adoption and Children Act 2002 and in relation to Scotland, by section 119(1) of the Adoption and Children (Scotland) Act 2007;
"child", in relation to A, means a person who is, or when placed with A for adoption was, under the age of 18;
"the Commissioners" means the Commissioners for Her Majesty's Revenue and Customs;
"expected week of birth", in relation to a child, means the week, beginning with midnight between Saturday and Sunday, in which, as appropriate, it is expected that the child will be born, or was expected that the child would be born;
"partner", in relation to M or A, means a person (whether of a different sex or the same sex) who lives with, as the case may be, M or A as well as C in an enduring family relationship but is not a relative of M or A of a kind specified in paragraph (2);
"placed for adoption" means—
(a) placed for adoption under the Adoption and Children Act 2002 or the Adoption and Children (Scotland) Act 2007; or
(b) placed in accordance with section 22C of the Children Act 1989 with a local authority foster parent who is also a prospective adopter;

(SI 2014/3051 reg.2)

"processing", in relation to information, has the meaning given by section 1(1) of the Data Protection Act 1998;

"shared parental leave" means leave under section 75E or 75G of the Employment Rights Act 1996;

"statutory shared parental pay" means statutory shared parental pay payable in accordance with Part 12ZC of the 1992 Act;

"statutory shared parental pay (adoption)" means statutory shared parental pay payable where entitlement to that pay arises under regulation 17 or 18;

"statutory shared parental pay (birth)" means statutory shared parental pay payable where entitlement to that pay arises under regulation 4 or 5;

"week" in Parts 2, 3 and 5 means a period of seven days.

(2) The relatives of M or A referred to in the definition of "partner" in paragraph (1) are M's, or, A's parent, grandparent, sister, brother, aunt, uncle, child, grandchild, niece or nephew.

(3) References to relationships in paragraph (2)—
(a) are to relationships of the full-blood or half-blood or, in the case of an adopted person, such of those relationships as would exist but for the adoption; and
(b) include the relationship of a child with his adoptive, or former adoptive parents, but do not include any other adoptive relationship.

(4) For the purpose of these Regulations—
(a) a person is matched with a child for adoption when an adoption agency decides that that person would be a suitable adoptive parent for the child;
(b) in a case where paragraph (a) applies, a person is notified as having been matched with a child on the date that person receives notification of the agency's decision, under regulation 33(3)(a) of the Adoption Agencies Regulations 2005, regulation 28(3) of the Adoption Agencies (Wales) Regulations 2005 or regulation 8(5) of the Adoption Agencies (Scotland) Regulations 2009;
(c) a person is also matched with a child for adoption when a decision has been made in accordance with regulation 22A of the Care Planning, Placement and Case Review (England) Regulations 2010 and an adoption agency has identified that person with whom the child is to be placed in accordance with regulation 12B of the Adoption Agencies Regulations 2005;
(d) in a case where paragraph (c) applies, a person is notified as having been matched with a child on the date on which that person receives notification in accordance with regulation 12B(2)(a) of the Adoption Agencies Regulations 2005.

(5) The reference to "local authority foster parent" in the definition of "placed for adoption" in paragraph (1) means a person approved as a local authority foster parent in accordance with regulations made by virtue of paragraph 12F of Schedule 2 to the Children Act 1989.

(6) The reference to "prospective adopter" in the definition of "placed for adoption" in paragraph (1) means a person who has been approved as suitable to adopt a child and has been notified of that decision in accordance with regulation 30B(4) of the Adoption Agencies Regulations 2005.

Statutory Shared Parental Pay (General) Regulations 2014

General Note

7.21　This regulation is modified for certain special cases by the Statutory Shared Parental Pay (Adoption from Overseas) Regulations 2014 (SI 2014/3093) and the Statutory Shared Parental Pay (Parental Order Cases) Regulations 2014 (SI 2014/3097).

Application

7.22　**3.**—These Regulations apply in relation to—
(a) statutory shared parental pay (birth) in respect of children whose expected week of birth begins on or after 5th April 2015;
(b) statutory shared parental pay (adoption) in respect of children placed for adoption on or after 5th April 2015.

Definitions

"child"—reg.2(1).
"expected week of birth"—reg.2(1).
"placed for adoption"—reg.2(1).
"statutory shared parental pay (adoption)"—reg.2(1).
"statutory shared parental pay (birth)"—reg.2(1).

General Note

7.23　This regulation is modified for certain special cases by the Statutory Shared Parental Pay (Adoption from Overseas) Regulations 2014 (SI 2014/3093) and the Statutory Shared Parental Pay (Parental Order Cases) Regulations 2014 (SI 2014/3097).

Part 2

Entitlement of mother to statutory shared parental pay (birth)

7.24　**4.**—(1) M is entitled to statutory shared parental pay (birth) if M satisfies the conditions specified in paragraph (2) and if P satisfies the conditions specified in paragraphs (3).
(2) The conditions referred to in paragraph (1) are that—
(a) M satisfies the conditions as to continuity of employment and normal weekly earnings specified in regulation 30;
(b) M has at the date of C's birth the main responsibility for the care of C (apart from the responsibility of P);
(c) M has complied with the requirements specified in regulation 6 (notification and evidential requirements of M);
(d) M became entitled by reference to the birth or expected birth of C to statutory maternity pay in respect of C;
(e) the maternity pay period that applies as a result of M's entitlement to statutory maternity pay is, and continues to be, reduced under section 165(3A) of the 1992 Act;
(f) it is M's intention to care for C during each week in respect of which statutory shared parental pay (birth) is paid to her;
(g) M is absent from work during each week in respect of which statutory shared parental pay (birth) is paid to her (except in the cases

referred to in regulation 15 (entitlement to shared parental pay: absence from work)); and
(h) where M is an employee (within the meaning of the Employment Rights Act 1996) M's absence from work as an employee during each week that statutory shared parental pay (birth) is paid to her is absence on shared parental leave in respect of C;
(3) The conditions referred to in paragraph (1) are that—
(a) P has at the date of C's birth the main responsibility for the care of C (apart from the responsibility of M); and
(b) P satisfies the conditions relating to employment and earnings in regulation 29 (conditions as to employment and earnings of claimant's partner).

DEFINITIONS

"1992 Act"—reg.2(1).
"C"—reg.2(1).
"expected week of birth"—reg.2(1).
"M"—reg.2(1).
"P"—reg.2(1).
"partner"—reg.2(1).
"statutory shared parental pay (birth)"—reg.2(1).
"week"—reg.2(1).

Entitlement of father or partner to statutory shared parental pay (birth)

5.—(1) P is entitled to statutory shared parental pay (birth) if P satisfies the conditions specified in paragraph (2) and M satisfies the conditions specified in paragraph (3).

(2) The conditions specified in paragraph (1) are that—
(a) P satisfies the conditions as to continuity of employment and normal weekly earnings specified in regulation 30;
(b) P has at the date of C's birth the main responsibility for the care of C (apart from the responsibility of M);
(c) P has complied with the requirements specified in regulation 7 (notification and evidential requirements of P);
(d) it is P's intention to care for C during each week in respect of which statutory shared parental pay (birth) is paid to P;
(e) P is absent from work during each week in respect of which statutory shared parental pay (birth) is paid to P (except in the cases referred to in regulation 15 (entitlement to statutory shared parental pay: absence from work)); and
(f) where P is an employee (within the meaning of the Employment Rights Act 1996 P's absence from work as an employee during each week that statutory shared parental pay (birth) is paid to P is absence on shared parental leave in respect of C.

(3) The conditions specified in paragraph (1) are—
(a) M has at the date of C's birth the main responsibility for the care of C (apart from the responsibility of P);
(b) M meets the conditions as to employment and earnings in regulation 29 (conditions as to employment and earnings of claimant's partner);

(c) M became entitled by reference to the birth, or expected birth, of C to statutory maternity pay or maternity allowance; and
(d) the maternity pay period or the maternity allowance period which applies to M as a result of her entitlement to statutory maternity pay or maternity allowance is, and continues to be, reduced under sections 35(3A) or 165(3A) of the 1992 Act.

DEFINITIONS

"1992 Act"—reg.2(1).
"C"—reg.2(1).
"expected week of birth"—reg.2(1).
"M"—reg.2(1).
"P"—reg.2(1).
"partner"—reg.2(1).
"statutory shared parental pay (birth)"—reg.2(1).
"week"—reg.2(1).

Notification and evidential requirements relating to the mother

6.—(1) The notice and evidential requirements referred to in regulation 4(2)(c) are that M gives the employer who will be liable to pay statutory shared parental pay (birth) to M the notice and information specified in—
(a) paragraphs (2) and (3)(a), (b), (d) and (e) at least 8 weeks before the beginning of the first period specified by M pursuant to paragraph (2)(d);
(b) paragraph (3)(c) at least 8 weeks before the beginning of the first period specified by M pursuant to paragraph (2)(d) or, where C is not born by that time, as soon as reasonably practicable after the birth of C but in any event before the beginning of that first period; and
(c) paragraph (4) within 14 days of that employer requesting that information where the employer requests it within 14 days of receiving the notice and information specified in paragraph (2) and (3) (a),(b),(d) and (e).
(2) The notice specified in this paragraph is notice of—
(a) the number of weeks in respect of which M would be entitled to claim statutory shared parental pay (birth) in respect of C if entitlement were fully exercised disregarding any intention of P to claim statutory shared parental pay in respect of C;
(b) the number of weeks out of those specified under sub-paragraph (a) in respect of which M intends to claim statutory shared parental pay (birth) in respect of C;
(c) the number of weeks out of those specified under sub-paragraph (a) in respect of which P intends to claim statutory shared parental pay (birth) in respect of C;
(d) the period or periods during which M intends to claim statutory shared parental pay (birth) in respect of C.
(3) The information specified in this paragraph is—
(a) a written declaration signed by P who in connection with M's claim is required to satisfy the conditions specified in regulation 4(3)—
(i) that P consents to M's intended claim for statutory shared parental pay;

(SI 2014/3051 reg. 6)

    (ii) that P meets, or will meet, the conditions in regulation 4(3) (conditions to be satisfied by P);
    (iii) specifying P's name, address and national insurance number or, if P has no national insurance number, stating that P has no such number; and
    (iv) providing P's consent as regards the processing by the employer who will be liable to pay statutory shared parental pay (birth) to M of the information in the written declaration;
(b) C's expected week of birth;
(c) C's date of birth;
(d) M's name;
(e) a written declaration signed by M—
    (i) that the information given by M under paragraphs (2) and (3) is correct;
    (ii) that M meets, or will meet, the conditions in regulation 4(2);
    (iii) that M will immediately inform the person who will be liable to pay statutory shared parental pay (birth) if M ceases to meet the condition in regulation 4(2)(e); and
    (iv) specifying the date on which M's maternity pay period or maternity allowance period in respect of C began and the number of weeks by which it is, or will be, reduced.
(4) The information specified in this paragraph is—
(a) a copy of C's birth certificate or, if one has not been issued, a declaration signed by M which states that it has not been issued; and
(b) the name and address of P's employer or, if P has no employer, a written declaration signed by M that P has no employer.

DEFINITIONS

"C"—reg.2(1).
"expected week of birth"—reg.2(1).
"M"—reg.2(1).
"P"—reg.2(1).
"partner"—reg.2(1).
"processing"—reg.2(1).
"statutory shared parental pay (birth)"—reg.2(1).
"week"—reg.2(1).

Notification and evidential requirements relating to the father or partner

7.—(1) The notification and evidential requirements referred to in regulation 5(2)(c), are that P gives the employer who will be liable to pay statutory shared parental pay (birth) to P the notice and information specified in—
(a) paragraphs (2) and (3)(a), (b), (d) and (e) at least 8 weeks before the beginning of the first period specified by P pursuant to paragraph (2)(d);
(b) paragraph 3(c) at least 8 weeks before the beginning of the first period specified by P pursuant to paragraph (2)(d) or, where C is not born by that time, as soon as reasonably practicable after the birth of C but in any event before the beginning of that first period; and
(c) paragraph (4) within 14 days of that employer requesting that information where the employer requests it within 14 days of receiving all

the notices and information specified in paragraphs (2) and (3)(a), (b), (d) and (e).
(2) The notice specified in this paragraph is notice of—
(a) the number of weeks in respect of which P would be entitled to claim statutory shared parental pay (birth) in respect of C if entitlement were fully exercised disregarding any intention of M to claim statutory shared parental pay in respect of C;
(b) the number of weeks out of those specified under sub-paragraph (a) in respect of which P intends to claim statutory shared parental pay (birth) in respect of C;
(c) the number of weeks out of those specified under sub-paragraph (a) in respect of which M intends to claim statutory shared parental pay (birth) in respect of C;
(d) the period or periods during which P intends to claim statutory shared parental pay (birth) in respect of C.
(3) The information specified in this paragraph is—
(a) a written declaration signed by M who in connection with P's claim is required to satisfy the conditions specified in regulation 5(3)—
  (i) that M consents to P's intended claim for statutory shared parental pay;
  (ii) that M meets, or will meet, the conditions in regulation 5(3) (conditions to be satisfied by M);
  (iii) that M will immediately inform P if M ceases to meet the condition in regulation 5(3)(d);
  (iv) specifying M's name, address and national insurance number or, if M has no national insurance number, stating that M has no such number;
  (v) specifying the date on which M's maternity pay period or maternity allowance period in respect of C began and the number of weeks by which it is, or will be, reduced; and
  (vi) providing M's consent as regards the processing by the person who is, or will be, liable to pay statutory shared parental pay (birth) to P under section 171ZX(1) of the 1992 Act of the information in the written declaration;
(b) C's expected week of birth;
(c) C's date of birth;
(d) P's name;
(e) a written declaration signed by P—
  (i) that the information given by P is correct;
  (ii) that P meets, or will meet, the conditions in regulation 5(2); and
  (iii) that P will immediately inform the person who will be liable to pay statutory shared parental pay (birth) if M ceases to meet the condition in regulation 5(3)(d).
(4) The information specified in this paragraph is—
(a) a copy of C's birth certificate or, if one has not been issued, a declaration signed by P which states that it has not been issued; and
(b) the name and address of M's employer (or, if M has no employer a written declaration signed by P that M has no employer.

(SI 2014/3051 reg.7)

DEFINITIONS

"C"—reg.2(1).
"expected week of birth"—reg.2(1).
"M"—reg.2(1).
"P"—reg.2(1).
"partner"—reg.2(1).
"statutory shared parental pay (birth)"—reg.2(1).
"week"—reg.2(1).

Variation of number of weeks of pay to be claimed and of periods when pay is to be claimed

8.—(1) M or, as the case may be, P may vary the period or periods during which they intend to claim statutory shared parental pay (birth) by notice in writing given to the employer who will be liable to pay that pay to M or P at least 8 weeks before the beginning of the first period specified in that notice.

(2) M may vary the number of weeks in respect of which M intends to claim statutory shared parental pay (birth) by notice in writing given to the employer who will be liable to pay statutory shared parental pay (birth) to M—
  (a) of the number of weeks during which M and P have exercised, or intend to exercise, an entitlement to statutory shared parental pay (birth) in respect of C; and
  (b) which is accompanied by a written declaration signed by P who in connection with M's claim is required to satisfy the conditions specified in regulation 4(3) that P consents to that variation.

(3) P may vary the number of weeks in respect of which P intends to claim statutory shared parental pay (birth) by notice in writing given to the employer who will be liable to pay statutory shared parental pay (birth) to P—
  (a) of the number of weeks during which P and M have exercised, or intend to exercise, an entitlement to statutory shared parental pay (birth) in respect of C; and
  (b) which is accompanied by a written declaration by M who in connection with P's claim is required to satisfy the conditions specified in regulation 5(3) that M consents to that variation.

7.28

DEFINITIONS

"C"—reg.2(1).
"M"—reg.2(1).
"P"—reg.2(1).
"statutory shared parental pay (birth)"—reg.2(1).
"week"—reg.2(1).

Modification of notice conditions in case of early birth

9.—(1) This paragraph applies where—
  (a) one or more of the periods specified in a notice given under regulation 6, 7, or 8 during which M or, as the case may be, P intends to claim statutory shared parental pay (birth) start in the 8 weeks following the first day of C's expected week of birth;
  (b) C's date of birth is before the first day of the expected week of birth; and

7.29

Statutory Shared Parental Pay (General) Regulations 2014

(c) M or, as the case may be, P varies by notice under regulation 8(1) the period or periods referred to in sub-paragraph (a) so that that period or those periods start the same length of time following C's date of birth as that period or those periods would have started after the first day of the expected week of birth.

(2) Where paragraph (1) applies the requirement in regulation 8(1) to give notice at least 8 weeks before the first period specified in the notice is satisfied if such notice is given as soon as reasonably practicable after C's date of birth.

(3) This paragraph applies where—

(a) C is born more than 8 weeks before the first day of the expected week of birth; and

(b) M or, as the case may be, P has not given the notice and information under regulations 6 or 7 before the date of C's birth.

(4) Where paragraph (3) applies and M, or as the case may be, P specifies in a notice under regulation 6 or 7 a period or periods of statutory shared parental pay (birth) which start in the 8 weeks following C's date of birth, then the following modifications apply—

(a) in regulation 6—

(i) paragraph (1)(a) shall apply as if it read—

"(a) paragraphs (2) and (3) as soon as reasonably practicable after the date of C's birth but in any event before the first period specified by M pursuant to paragraph (2)(d);";

(ii) paragraph (1)(b) and (c) shall not apply;

(iii) paragraph (4) shall not apply.

(b) in regulation 7—

(i) paragraph (1)(a) shall apply as if it read—

"(a) paragraphs (2) and (3) as soon as reasonably practicable after the date of C's birth but in any event before the first period specified by P pursuant to paragraph (2)(d). ";

(ii) paragraph (1)(b) and (c) shall not apply;

(iii) paragraph (4) shall not apply.

DEFINITIONS

"C"—reg.2(1).
"expected week of birth"—reg.2(1).
"M"—reg.2(1).
"P"—reg.2(1).
"statutory shared parental pay (birth)"—reg.2(1).
"week"—reg.2(1).

Extent of entitlement to statutory shared parental pay (birth)

7.30   10.—(1) The number of weeks in respect of which M or P is entitled to payments of statutory shared parental pay (birth) in respect of C is 39 weeks less—

(a) the number of weeks—

(i) in respect of which maternity allowance or statutory maternity pay is payable to M in respect of C up to the time M has returned to work (where M has returned to work without satisfying the condition in regulations 4(2)(e) or 5(3)(d) (condition as to reduction of the maternity pay period or the maternity allowance period)); or

(SI 2014/3051 reg.10)

 (ii) in any other case, to which the maternity allowance period is reduced by virtue of section 35(3A) of the 1992 Act or, as the case may be, the maternity pay period is reduced by virtue of section 165(3A); and
(b) the number of weeks of statutory shared parental pay in respect of C which—
 (i) in the case of M, P has notified P's intention to claim under regulation 7 or 8; or
 (ii) in the case of P, M has notified M's intention to claim under regulation 6 or 8.

(2) In a case where—
(a) P was entitled to payments of statutory shared parental pay (birth) in respect of C; and
(b) P ceases to be so entitled because M ceases to satisfy the condition in regulation 5(3)(d); and
(c) P becomes entitled again to such payments as a result of M satisfying the condition in regulation 5(3)(d);
the number of weeks in which P claimed statutory shared parental pay (birth) up to the time P ceases to be so entitled is also to be deducted from the number of weeks specified in paragraph (1).

(3) Where paragraph (2) applies the number of weeks of statutory shared parental pay (birth) which P notified P's intention to claim under regulation 7(2)(b) (as varied under regulation 8(3)) before P ceases to be entitled to statutory shared parental pay (birth) is to be disregarded for the purposes of this regulation.

(4) In the case where M has more than one entitlement to statutory maternity pay in respect of C and in relation to all those entitlements she returns to work without satisfying the conditions in regulation 4(2)(e) or (5)(3)(d), paragraph (1)(a)(i) shall apply as though it read—
 "(i) in respect of which statutory maternity pay is payable to M in respect of C up to the last day M returns to work;".

(5) In the case where M has more than one entitlement to statutory maternity pay in respect of C and the maternity pay periods which apply as a result of those entitlements are all reduced by virtue of section 165(3A) of the 1992 Act before she returns to work, paragraph (1)(a)(ii) shall apply as though it read—
 "(ii) falling in the period beginning with the first day of the maternity pay period which is the earliest to begin and ending on the last day of the maternity pay period which is the last to end;".

(6) In the case where M has more than one entitlement to statutory maternity pay in respect of C and—
(a) M returns to work in relation to one or more of those entitlements without satisfying the condition regulation 4(2)(e) or 5(3)(d), and
(b) in relation to one or more of the maternity pay periods which apply as a result of those entitlements that period or those periods are reduced by virtue of section 165(3A) before M returns to work,
paragraph (1)(a) shall apply as though it read—
 "(a) the number of weeks falling within the period beginning with the first day of the maternity pay period which is the earliest to begin and ending with the later of—
  (i) the last day of the maternity pay period which is reduced by virtue of section 165(3A) before M returns to work (or, where

there is more than one such period, the last of those periods); and

(ii) the day on which M returned to work without satisfying the condition in regulation 4(2)(e) or 5(3)(d) in relation to that period (or, where there is more than one such period, the last of those periods);".

(7) In a case where P has more than one entitlement to statutory shared parental pay in respect of C, paragraph (1)(b)(i) shall apply as though it read—

"(i) in the case of M, P has notified P's intention to claim under regulation 7 or 8 falling within the period beginning with the first day of the earliest period so notified and ending with the last day of the latest period so notified;".

(8) In a case where M has more than one entitlement to statutory shared parental pay in respect of C, paragraph (1)(b)(ii) shall apply as though it read—

"(ii) in the case of P, M has notified M's intention to claim under regulations 6 or 8 falling within the period beginning with the first day of the earliest period so notified and ending with the last day of the latest period so notified;".

(9) In a case where P has more than one entitlement to statutory shared parental pay in respect of C, paragraph (2) shall apply as though the number of weeks referred to were the number of weeks which P claimed statutory shared parental pay in respect of C falling within the period beginning with the first day of the earliest period P claimed statutory shared parental pay and ending with the time P ceases to be so entitled.

(10) In this regulation a person is treated as returning to work if one of the following situations apply—

(a) in a case where the person is entitled to maternity allowance, the allowance is not payable to her by virtue of regulations made under section 35(3)(a)(i) of the 1992 Act;

(b) in a case where the person is entitled to statutory maternity pay, that payment is not payable to her in accordance with section 165(4) or (6) of the 1992 Act.

(11) In determining in paragraph (1)(a)(i) the number of weeks in respect of which maternity allowance is payable to M in respect of C up to the time M has returned to work, part of a week in respect of which maternity allowance is payable is to be treated as a whole week.

(12) In paragraph (1)(a)(ii), (6), (7), (8) and (9) part of a week is to be treated as a whole week.

(13) In paragraph (1)(a) "week" has the meaning given by section 122(1) of the 1992 Act, in relation to maternity allowance, or the meaning given by section 165(8) in relation to statutory maternity pay.

DEFINITIONS

"1992 Act"—reg.2(1).
"C"—reg.2(1).
"expected week of birth"—reg.2(1).
"M"—reg.2(1).
"P"—reg.2(1).
"statutory shared parental pay (birth)"—reg.2(1).
"week"—reg.2(1) and para.(13).

(SI 2014/3051 reg.11)

When statutory shared parental pay (birth) is not to be paid

11.—(1) Statutory shared parental pay (birth) is not payable after the day before C's first birthday (or where more than one child is born as a result of the same pregnancy the first birthday of the first child so born).

(2) Statutory shared parental pay (birth) is not payable to M before the end of M's maternity pay period.

DEFINITIONS

"C"—reg.2(1).
"child"—reg.2(1).
"M"—reg.2(1).
"statutory shared parental pay (birth)"—reg.2(1).

Work during period of payment of statutory shared parental pay (birth)

12.—(1) Despite section 171ZY(4) of the 1992 Act (statutory shared parental pay not payable to a person in respect of a week during any part of which the person works for any employer) statutory shared parental pay (birth) is payable to M or, as the case may be, P—
  (a) in respect of a statutory pay week during any part of which M or, as the case may be, P works only for an employer—
    (i) who is not liable to pay that person statutory shared parental pay; and
    (ii) for whom that person worked in the week immediately preceding the 14th week before the expected week of birth; or,
  (b) where M or, as the case may be, P does any work on any day under a contract of service with an employer during a statutory pay week during which that employer is liable to pay that person statutory shared parental pay (birth) in respect of C and where that day and any previous days so worked do not exceed 20.

(2) Where statutory shared parental pay (birth) is paid to M or P in respect of any week falling within a period specified in a notice under regulation 6, 7, and 8 during which M or P works for an employer falling within paragraph (1)(a)(i) but not paragraph (1)(a)(ii), M or, as the case may be, P shall notify the employer liable to pay statutory shared parental pay (birth) within seven days of the first day during which the former does such work.

(3) The notification mentioned in paragraph (2) shall be in writing, if the employer who has been liable to pay statutory shared parental pay (birth) so requests.

(4) In this regulation "statutory pay week" means a week in respect of which that person has chosen to exercise an entitlement to statutory shared parental pay (birth).

DEFINITIONS

"1992 Act"—reg.2(1).
"C"—reg.2(1).
"expected week of birth"—reg.2(1).
"M"—reg.2(1).
"P"—reg.2(1).
"statutory pay week"—para.(4).
"statutory shared parental pay (birth)"—reg.2(1).
"week"—reg.2(1).

Care of child during period of payment of statutory shared parental pay

7.33 13.—Despite section 171ZY(3) of the 1992 Act (statutory shared parental pay not payable to a person in respect of a week if it is not the person's intention at the beginning of the week to care for C) statutory shared parental pay (birth) is payable in the cases referred to in paragraph 6 of the Schedule (death of child).

DEFINITIONS

"1992 Act"—reg.2(1).
"C"—reg.2(1).
"expected week of birth"—reg.2(1).
"statutory shared parental pay (birth)"—reg.2(1).
"week"—reg.2(1).

Other cases where there is no liability to pay statutory shared parental pay

7.34 14.—(1) There is no liability to pay statutory shared parental pay (birth) to M or, as the case may be, P in respect of any week—
   (a) during any part of which the person who is entitled to that pay is entitled to statutory sick pay under Part 11 of the 1992 Act;
   (b) following that in which the person who is claiming that pay has died; or
   (c) during any part of which the person who is entitled to that pay is detained in legal custody or sentenced to a term of imprisonment except where the sentence is suspended (but see paragraph (2)).

(2) There is liability to pay statutory shared parental pay (birth) to M or, as the case may be, P in respect of any week during any part of which the person who is entitled to that pay is detained in legal custody where that person—
   (a) is released subsequently without charge;
   (b) is subsequently found not guilty of any offence and is released; or
   (c) is convicted of an offence but does not receive a custodial sentence.

DEFINITIONS

"1992 Act"—reg.2(1).
"M"—reg.2(1).
"P"—reg.2(1).
"statutory shared parental pay (birth)"—reg.2(1).
"week"—reg.2(1).

Conditions of entitlement to statutory shared parental pay: absence from work

7.35 15.—(1) The condition in regulation 4(2)(g) and 5(2)(e) does not apply where M or, as the case may be, P—
   (a) during any part of a statutory pay week works other than for an employer;
   (b) during any part of a statutory pay week works only for an employer who falls within paragraph (1)(a) of regulation 12 (work during period payment of statutory shared parental pay);
   (c) works in circumstance where paragraph (1)(b) of regulation 12 applies.

(SI 2014/3051 reg.15)

(2) In this regulation "statutory pay week" means a week in respect of which that person has chosen to exercise an entitlement to statutory shared parental pay (birth).

DEFINITIONS
"M"—reg.2(1).
"P"—reg.2(1).
"statutory pay week"—para.(2).
"statutory shared parental pay (birth)"—reg.2(1).
"week"—reg.2(1).

Entitlement to statutory shared parental pay (birth) in cases relating to death

16.—The Part 1 of the Schedule (statutory shared parental pay in special circumstances) has effect.

7.36

PART 3

Entitlement of adopter to statutory shared parental pay (adoption)

17.—(1) A is entitled to statutory shared parental pay (adoption) if A satisfies the conditions specified in paragraph (2) and AP satisfies the conditions specified in paragraph (3).

7.37

(2) The conditions referred to in paragraph (1) are that—
(a) A satisfies the conditions as to continuity of employment and normal weekly earnings specified in regulation 31 (conditions as to claimant's continuity of employment and normal weekly earnings);
(b) A has at the date of C's placement for adoption the main responsibility for the care of C (apart from the responsibility of AP);
(c) A has complied with the requirements specified in regulation 19 (notification and evidential requirements);
(d) A became entitled to statutory adoption pay by reference to the placement for adoption of C;
(e) the adoption pay period that applies as a result of A's entitlement to statutory adoption pay is, and continues to be, reduced under section 171ZN(2A) of the 1992 Act;
(f) it is A's intention to care for C during each week in respect of which statutory shared parental pay (adoption) is paid to A;
(g) A is absent from work during each week in respect of which statutory shared parental pay is paid to A (except in the cases referred to in regulation 27 (entitlement to statutory shared parental pay (adoption): absence from work); and
(h) where A is an employee (within the meaning of the Employment Rights Act 1996) A's absence from work as an employee during each week that statutory shared parental pay is paid to A is absence on shared parental leave in respect of C.

(3) The conditions referred to in paragraph (1) are that—
(a) AP has at the date of C's placement for adoption the main responsibility for the care of C (apart from the responsibility of A); and
(b) AP satisfies the employment and earnings conditions in regulation 29

(conditions relating to employment and earnings of claimant's partner).

DEFINITIONS

"1992 Act"—reg.2(1).
"A"—reg.2(1).
"AP"—reg.2(1).
"C"—reg.2(1).
"statutory shared parental pay (adoption)"—reg.2(1).
"week"—reg.2(1).

GENERAL NOTE

7.38 This regulation is modified for certain special cases by the Statutory Shared Parental Pay (Adoption from Overseas) Regulations 2014 (SI 2014/3093) and the Statutory Shared Parental Pay (Parental Order Cases) Regulations 2014 (SI 2014/3097).

Entitlement of partner to statutory shared parental pay (adoption)

7.39 **18.**—(1) AP is entitled to statutory shared parental pay (adoption) if AP satisfies the conditions specified in paragraph (2) and A satisfies the conditions specified in paragraph (3).
(2) The conditions specified in paragraph (1) are that—
(a) AP satisfies the conditions as to continuity of employment and normal weekly earnings specified in regulation 31 (conditions as to continuity of employment and normal weekly earnings);
(b) AP has at the date of C's placement for adoption the main responsibility for the care of C (apart from the responsibility of A);
(c) AP has complied with the requirements specified in regulation 20 (notification and evidential requirements);
(d) it is AP's intention to care for C during each week in respect of which statutory shared parental pay (adoption) is paid to AP;
(e) AP is absent from work during each week in respect of which statutory shared parental pay (adoption) is paid to AP (except in the cases referred to in regulation 27 (entitlement to statutory shared parental pay: absence from work)); and
(f) where AP is an employee (within the meaning of the Employment Rights Act 1996) AP's absence from work as an employee during each week that statutory shared parental pay is paid to AP is absence on shared parental leave in respect of C.
(3) The conditions specified in paragraph (1) are that—
(a) A has at the date of C's placement for adoption the main responsibility for the care of C (apart from any responsibility of AP);
(b) A satisfies the employment and earnings conditions in regulation 29;
(c) A became entitled to statutory adoption pay by reference to the placement for adoption of C; and
(d) the adoption pay period that applies as a result A's entitlement to statutory adoption pay is, and continues to be, reduced under section 171ZN(2A) of the 1992 Act.

DEFINITIONS

"1992 Act"—reg.2(1).
"A"—reg.2(1).

"AP"—reg.2(1).
"C"—reg.2(1).
"statutory shared parental pay (adoption)"—reg.2(1).
"week"—reg.2(1).

GENERAL NOTE

This regulation is modified for certain special cases by the Statutory Shared Parental Pay (Adoption from Overseas) Regulations 2014 (SI 2014/3093) and the Statutory Shared Parental Pay (Parental Order Cases) Regulations 2014 (SI 2014/3097).

Notification and evidential requirements relating to the adopter

19.—(1) The notification and evidential requirements referred to in regulation 17(2)(c) are that A gives the employer who will be liable to pay statutory shared parental pay (adoption) to A the notice and information specified in—
  (a) paragraphs (2) and (3)(a), (b), (d) and (e) at least 8 weeks before the beginning of the first period specified by A pursuant to paragraph (2)(d);
  (b) paragraph (3)(c) at least 8 weeks before the beginning of the first period specified by A pursuant to paragraph (2)(d) or, if C is not placed for adoption by that time, as soon as reasonably practicable after the placement of C but in any event before the beginning of that first period; and
  (c) paragraph (4) within 14 days of that employer requesting that information where the employer requests it within 14 days of receiving the notice and information specified in paragraph (2) and (3)(a), (b), (d) and (e).
(2) The notice specified in this paragraph is notice of—
(a) the number of weeks in respect of which A would be entitled to claim statutory shared parental pay (adoption) in respect of C if entitlement were fully exercised disregarding any intention of AP to claim statutory shared parental pay (adoption) in respect of C;
(b) the number of weeks (out of those specified under paragraph (2)(a)) in respect of which A intends to claim statutory shared parental pay (adoption) in respect of C;
(c) the number of weeks (out of those specified under paragraph (2)(a)) in respect of which AP intends to claim statutory shared parental pay (adoption) in respect of C; and
(d) the period or periods during which A intends to claim statutory shared parental pay (adoption) in respect of C.
(3) The information specified in this paragraph is—
(a) a written declaration signed by AP who in connection with A's claim is required to satisfy the conditions specified in regulation 17(3)—
  (i) that AP consents to A's intended claim for statutory shared parental pay;
  (ii) that AP meets or will meet the conditions in regulation 17(3) (conditions to be satisfied by AP);
  (iii) specifying AP's name, address and national insurance number or, if AP has no national insurance number, stating that AP has no such number; and

Statutory Shared Parental Pay (General) Regulations 2014

           (iv) providing AP's consent as regards the processing by the employer who will be liable to pay statutory shared parental pay (adoption) to A of the information in the written declaration;
    (b) the date on which A was notified that A had been matched with C;
    (c) the date of C's placement for adoption;
    (d) A's name; and
    (e) a written declaration signed by A—
        (i) that the information given by A under paragraph (2) and (3) is correct;
        (ii) that A meets or will meet the conditions in regulation 17(2); and
        (iii) that A will immediately inform the person who will be liable to pay statutory shared parental pay (adoption) if A ceases to meet the condition in regulation 17(2)(e); and
        (iv) specifying the date on which A's adoption pay period in respect of C began and the number of weeks by which it is, or will be, reduced.

(4) The information specified in this paragraph is—
    (a) evidence, in the form of one or more documents issued by the adoption agency that matched A with C, of—
        (i) the name and address of the adoption agency;
        (ii) the date on which A was notified that A had been matched with C; and
        (iii) the date on which the adoption agency was expecting to place C with A; and
    (b) the name and address of AP's employer or, if AP has no employer, a written declaration signed by A that AP has no employer.

DEFINITIONS

"A"—reg.2(1).
"AP"—reg.2(1).
"adoption agency"—reg.2(1).
"C"—reg.2(1).
"placed for adoption"—reg.2(1).
"processing"—reg.2(1).
"statutory shared parental pay (adoption)"—reg.2(1).
"week"—reg.2(1).

GENERAL NOTE

7.42   This regulation is modified for certain special cases by the Statutory Shared Parental Pay (Adoption from Overseas) Regulations 2014 (SI 2014/3093) and the Statutory Shared Parental Pay (Parental Order Cases) Regulations 2014 (SI 2014/3097).

Notification and evidential requirements relating to the partner

7.43   **20.**—(1) The notification and evidential conditions referred to in regulation 18(2)(c) are that AP gives the employer who will be liable to pay statutory shared parental pay (adoption) to AP the notice and information specified in—
    (a) paragraphs (2) and (3)(a), (b), (d) and (e) at least 8 weeks before the beginning of the first period specified by AP pursuant to paragraph (2)(d);

(SI 2014/3051 reg.20)

- (b) paragraph (3)(c) at least 8 weeks before the beginning of the first period specified by AP pursuant to paragraph (2)(d) or if C is not placed for adoption by that time, as soon as reasonably practicable after the placement of C but in any event before that first period; and
- (c) paragraph (4) (where applicable) within 14 days of that employer requesting this information where the employer requests it within 14 days of receiving all the notice and information specified in paragraph (2) and (3)(a), (b), (d) and (e).

(2) The notice specified in this paragraph is notice of—
- (a) the number of weeks in respect of which AP would be entitled to claim statutory shared parental pay (adoption) in respect of C if entitlement were fully exercised disregarding any intention of A to claim statutory shared parental pay (adoption) in respect of C;
- (b) the number of weeks (out of those specified under paragraph (2)(a)) in respect of which AP intends to claim statutory shared parental pay (adoption) in respect of C;
- (c) the number of weeks (out of those specified under paragraph (2)(a)) in respect of which A intends to claim statutory shared parental pay (adoption) in respect of C;
- (d) the period or periods during which AP intends to claim statutory shared parental pay (adoption) in respect of C.

(3) The information specified in this paragraph is—
- (a) a written declaration signed by A who in connection with AP's claim is required to satisfy the conditions in regulation 18(3)—
    - (i) that A consents to AP's intended claim for statutory shared parental pay (adoption);
    - (ii) that A meets, or will meet, the conditions in regulation 18(3) (conditions to be satisfied by A);
    - (iii) that A will immediately inform AP if A ceases to meet the conditions in regulation 18(3)(d);
    - (iv) specifying A's name, address and national insurance number or, if A has no national insurance number, stating that A has no such number;
    - (v) specifying the date on which A's adoption pay period in respect of C began and the number of weeks by which it is, or will be, reduced; and
    - (vi) providing A's consent as regards the processing by the employer who is, or will be, liable to pay statutory shared parental pay (adoption) to AP of the information in the written declaration;
- (b) the date on which A was notified that A had been matched with C;
- (c) the date of C's placement for adoption;
- (d) AP's name;
- (e) a written declaration signed by AP—
    - (i) that the information given by AP is correct;
    - (ii) that AP meets, or will meet, the conditions in regulation 18(2); and
    - (iii) that AP will immediately inform the person who will be liable to pay statutory shared parental pay (adoption) if A ceases to meet the condition 18(3)(d).

(4) The information specified in this paragraph is—
- (a) evidence, in the form of one or more documents issued by the adoption agency that matched A with C, of —

(i) the name and address of the adoption agency;
(ii) the date on which A was notified that A had been matched with C; and
(iii) the date on which the adoption agency was expecting to place C for adoption with A; and
(b) the name and address of A's employer or, if A has no employer, a written declaration signed by AP that A has no employer.

Definitions

"A"—reg.2(1).
"AP"—reg.2(1).
"adoption agency"—reg.2(1).
"C"—reg.2(1).
"placed for adoption"—reg.2(1).
"processing"—reg.2(1).
"statutory shared parental pay (adoption)"—reg.2(1).
"week"—reg.2(1).

General Note

7.44   This regulation is modified for certain special cases by the Statutory Shared Parental Pay (Adoption from Overseas) Regulations 2014 (SI 2014/3093) and the Statutory Shared Parental Pay (Parental Order Cases) Regulations 2014 (SI 2014/3097).

Variation of number of weeks of pay to be claimed and of periods when pay is to be claimed

7.45   **21.**—(1) A or, as the case may be, AP may vary the period or periods during which they intend to claim statutory shared parental pay (adoption) by notice in writing given to the employer who will be liable to pay that pay to A or AP at least 8 weeks before the beginning of the first period specified in that notice.

(2) A may vary the number of weeks in respect of which A intends to claim statutory shared parental pay (adoption) by notice in writing given to the employer who will be liable to pay that pay to A—
  (a) of the number of weeks during which A and AP have exercised, or intend to exercise, an entitlement to statutory shared parental pay in respect of C; and
  (b) which contains a written declaration signed by AP who in connection with A's claim is required to satisfy the conditions in regulation 17(3) that AP consents to that variation.

(3) AP may vary the number of weeks in respect of which AP intends to claim statutory shared parental pay (adoption) by notice in writing given to the employer who will be liable to pay that pay to AP—
  (a) of the number of weeks during which AP and A have exercised, or intend to exercise, an entitlement to statutory shared parental pay (adoption) in respect of C; and
  (b) which is accompanied by a written declaration by A who in connection with AP's claim is requires to satisfy the conditions in regulation 18(3) that A consents to that variation.

(SI 2014/3051 reg.21)

DEFINITIONS

"A"—reg.2(1).
"AP"—reg.2(1).
"C"—reg.2(1).
"statutory shared parental pay (adoption)"—reg.2(1).
"week"—reg.2(1).

Extent of entitlement to statutory shared parental pay (adoption)

22.—(1) The number of weeks in respect of which A or, as the case may be, AP is entitled to payments of statutory shared parental pay (adoption) in respect of C is 39 weeks less— 7.46
   (a) the number of weeks—
      (i) in respect of which statutory adoption pay is payable to A in respect of C up to the time that person has returned to work (where that person has returned to work without satisfying the conditions in regulations 17(2)(e) or 18(3)(d)) (condition as to reduction in adoption pay period); or
      (ii) in any other case, to which the adoption pay period is reduced by virtue of section 171ZN(2A) of the 1992 Act; and
   (b) the number of weeks of statutory shared parental pay (adoption) in respect of C which—
      (i) in the case of A, AP has notified AP's intention to claim under regulation 20 or 21; or
      (ii) in the case of AP, A has notified A's intention to claim under regulation 19 or 21.

(2) In the case where A has more than one entitlement to statutory adoption pay in respect of C and in relation to all those entitlements A returns to work without satisfying the conditions in regulation 17(2)(e) or 18(3)(d), paragraph (1)(a)(i) shall apply as though it read—

"(i) in respect of which statutory adoption pay is payable to A in respect of C up to the last day A returns to work;".

(3) In the case where A has more than one entitlement to statutory adoption pay in respect of C and the adoption pay periods which apply as a result of those entitlements are all reduced by virtue of section 171ZN(2A) of the 1992 Act before A returns to work, paragraph (1)(a)(ii) shall apply as though it read—

"(ii) falling in the period beginning with the first day of the adoption pay period which is the earliest to begin and ending with the last day of the adoption pay period which is the last to end;".

(4) In a case where A has more than one entitlement to statutory adoption pay in respect of C and—
   (a) A returns to work in relation to one or more of those entitlements without satisfying the conditions in regulation 17(2)(e) or 18(3)(d), and
   (b) in relation to one or more of the adoption pay periods which apply as a result of those entitlements that period or those periods are reduced by virtue of section 171ZN(2A) of the 1992 Act before A returns to work,

paragraph (1)(a) shall apply as though it read—

"(a) the number of weeks falling within the period beginning with the first day of the adoption pay period which is the earliest to begin and ending with the later of—

(i) the last day of the adoption pay period which is reduced by virtue of section 171ZN(2A) of the 1992 Act before A returns to work (or, where there is more than one such period, the last of those periods); and

(ii) the day on which A returned to work without satisfying the conditions in regulation 17(2)(e) or 18(3)(d) in relation to that period (or, where there is more than one such period, the last of those periods);".

(5) In the case where AP has more than one entitlement to statutory shared parental pay in respect of C, paragraph (1)(b)(i) shall apply as though it read—

"(i) in the case of A, AP has notified AP's intention to claim under regulation 20 or 21 falling within the period beginning with the first day of the earliest period so notified and ending with the last day of the latest period so notified;".

(6) In the case where A has more than one entitlement to statutory shared parental pay in respect of C, paragraph (1)(b)(ii) shall apply as though it read—

"(ii) in the case of AP, A has notified A's intention to claim under regulation 19 or 21 falling within the period beginning with the first day of the earliest period so notified and ending with the last day of the latest period so notified;".

(7) In this regulation a person is treated as returning to work if statutory adoption pay is not payable to A in accordance with section 171ZN(3) or (5) of the 1992 Act.

(8) In paragraph (1)(a)(ii), (4), (5) and (6) part of a week is to be treated as a whole week.

(9) In paragraph (1)(a) "week" has the meaning given by section 171ZN(8) of the 1992 Act.

DEFINITIONS

"1992 Act"—reg.2(1).
"A"—reg.2(1).
"AP"—reg.2(1).
"C"—reg.2(1).
"statutory shared parental pay (adoption)"—reg.2(1).
"week"—reg.2(1) and para.(9).

When statutory shared parental pay (adoption) is not to be paid

23.—(1) Statutory shared parental pay (adoption) is not payable after the day before the first anniversary of the date on which C was placed for adoption (or where more than one child is placed for adoption through a single placement, the first anniversary of the date of placement of the first child).

(2) Statutory shared parental pay (adoption) is not payable to A before the end of A's adoption pay period.

DEFINITIONS

"A"—reg.2(1).
"C"—reg.2(1).
"child"—reg.2(1).
"placed for adoption"—reg.2(1).
"statutory shared parental pay (adoption)"—reg.2(1).

(SI 2014/3051 reg.23)

GENERAL NOTE

This regulation is modified for certain special cases by the Statutory Shared Parental Pay (Adoption from Overseas) Regulations 2014 (SI 2014/3093) and the Statutory Shared Parental Pay (Parental Order Cases) Regulations 2014 (SI 2014/3097).

7.48

Work during period of payment of statutory shared parental pay (adoption)

24.—(1) Despite section 171ZY(4) of the 1992 Act (statutory shared parental pay not payable to a person in respect of a week during any part of which person works for any employer) statutory shared parental pay (adoption) is payable to A or, as the case may be, AP—
  (a) in respect of a statutory pay week during any part of which A or, as the case may be, AP works only for an employer—
      (i) who is not liable to pay that person statutory shared parental pay; and
      (ii) for whom that person worked in the week immediately preceding the 14th week before the expected week of the placement for adoption; or
  (b) where A or, as the case may be, AP does any work on any day under a contract of service with an employer during a statutory pay week during which that employer is liable to pay that person statutory shared parental pay (adoption) in respect of C and where that day and any previous days so worked do not exceed 20.

(2) Where statutory shared parental pay (adoption) is paid to A or AP in respect of any week falling within a period specified in a notice under regulation 19, 20 or 21 during which A or AP works for an employer falling within paragraph (1)(a)(i) but not paragraph (1)(a)(ii) A or, as the case may be, AP shall notify the employer liable to pay statutory shared parental pay within seven days of the first day during which the former does such work.

(3) The notification mentioned in paragraph (2) shall be in writing, if the employer who has been liable to pay statutory shared parental pay so requests.

(4) In this regulation "statutory pay week" means a week in respect of which that person has chosen to exercise an entitlement to statutory shared parental pay (adoption).

7.49

DEFINITIONS

"1992 Act"—reg.2(1).
"A"—reg.2(1).
"AP"—reg.2(1).
"C"—reg.2(1).
"statutory pay week"—para.(4).
"statutory shared parental pay (adoption)"—reg.2(1).
"week"—reg.2(1).

GENERAL NOTE

This regulation is modified for certain special cases by the Statutory Shared Parental Pay (Adoption from Overseas) Regulations 2014 (SI 2014/3093) and the Statutory Shared Parental Pay (Parental Order Cases) Regulations 2014 (SI 2014/3097).

7.50

Care of child during period of payment of statutory shared parental pay

7.51   **25.**—Despite section 171ZY(3) of the 1992 Act (statutory shared parental pay not payable to a person in respect of a week if it is not the person's intention at the beginning of the week to care for C) statutory shared parental pay (adoption) is payable in the cases set out in paragraph 12 of the Schedule (disrupted placement or death of child).

DEFINITIONS

"1992 Act"—reg.2(1).
"C"—reg.2(1).
"child"—reg.2(1).
"statutory shared parental pay (adoption)"—reg.2(1).
"week"—reg.2(1).

Other cases where there is no liability to pay statutory shared parental pay

7.52   **26.**—(1) There is no liability to pay statutory shared parental pay (adoption) to A or, as the case may be, AP in respect of any week—
   (a) during any part of which the person who is entitled to that pay is entitled to statutory sick pay under Part 11 of the 1992 Act;
   (b) following that in which the person who is claiming that has died; or
   (c) during any part of which the person who is entitled to it is detained in legal custody or sentenced to a term of imprisonment except where the sentence is suspended (but see paragraph (2)).

(2) There is liability to pay statutory shared parental pay to A or, as the case may be, AP in respect of any week during any part of which the person entitled to that pay is detained in legal custody where that person—
   (a) is released subsequently without charge;
   (b) is subsequently found not guilty of any offence and is released; or
   (c) is convicted of an offence but does not receive a custodial sentence.

DEFINITIONS

"1992 Act"—reg.2(1).
"A"—reg.2(1).
"AP"—reg.2(1).
"statutory shared parental pay (adoption)"—reg.2(1).
"week"—reg.2(1).

Conditions of entitlement to statutory shared parental pay: absence from work

7.53   **27.**—(1) The condition in regulations 17(2)(g) and 18(2)(e) does not apply are where A or, as the case may be, AP—
   (a) during any part of a statutory pay week works other than for an employer;
   (b) during any part of a statutory pay week works only for an employer who falls within paragraph (1)(a) of regulation 24 (work during period payment of statutory shared parental pay);
   (c) works in circumstances where paragraph (1)(b) of regulation 24 applies.

(2) In this regulation "statutory pay week" means a week in respect of

(SI 2014/3051 reg.27)

which that person has chosen to exercise an entitlement to statutory shared parental pay (adoption).

DEFINITIONS

"A"—reg.2(1).
"AP"—reg.2(1).
"statutory pay week"—para.(2).
"statutory shared parental pay (adoption)"—reg.2(1).
"week"—reg.2(1).

Entitlement to statutory shared parental pay (adoption) in cases relating to death

28.—Part 2 of the Schedule (statutory shared parental pay in special circumstances) has effect.

7.54

PART 4

Conditions relating to employment and earnings of a claimant's partner

29.—(1) In relation to the entitlement of M, P, A or AP to statutory shared parental pay a person satisfies the conditions as to earnings and employment specified in regulations 4(3)(b), 5(3)(b), 17(3)(b) and 18(3)(b) if that person—

(a) has been engaged in employment as an employed or self-employed earner for any part of the week in the case of at least 26 of the 66 weeks immediately preceding the calculation week; and

(b) has average weekly earnings (determined in accordance with paragraph (2)) of not less than the amount set out in section 35A(6A) (state maternity allowance) of the 1992 Act in relation to the tax year before the tax year containing the calculation week.

(2) A person's average weekly earnings are determined by dividing by 13 the specified payments made, or treated as being made, to or for the benefit of that person in the 13 weeks (whether or not consecutive) in the period of 66 weeks immediately preceding the calculation week in which the payments are greatest.

(3) Where a person receives any pay after the end of the period in [¹ paragraph (2)] in respect of any week falling [¹ within] that period, the average weekly amount is to be determined as if such sum had been paid in that period.

(4) Where a person is not paid weekly, the payments made or treated as made for that person's benefit for the purposes of [¹ paragraph (2)], are to be determined by dividing the total sum paid to that individual by the nearest whole number of weeks in respect of which that sum is paid.

(5) In this regulation—

"calculation week" means in relation to—

(a) statutory shared parental pay (birth) the expected week of birth of C; and

(b) statutory shared parental pay (adoption), the week in which A was notified as having been matched for adoption with C;

7.55

"employed earner" has the meaning given by section 2 of the 1992 Act, subject for these purposes to the effect of regulations made under section 2(2)(b) of that Act;

"self-employed earner" has the meaning given by section 2 of the 1992 Act, subject for these purposes to the effect of regulations made under section 2(2)(b) of that Act;

"specified payments"—
(a) in relation to a self-employed earner who satisfies the conditions in paragraph (6), are to be treated as made to the self-employed earner at an amount per week equal to the amount set out in section 35(6A) of the 1992 Act that is in force at the end of the week;
(b) in relation to an employed earner, are all payments made to the employed earner or for that employed earner's benefit as an employed earner specified in regulation 2 (specified payments for employed earners) of the Social Security (Maternity Allowance) (Earnings) Regulations 2000;

"tax year" means the 12 months beginning with the 6th April in any year.

(6) The conditions referred to in paragraph (a) of the definition of "specified payments" are that, in respect of any week, the self-employed earner—
(a) does not hold a certificate of exception issued pursuant to regulation 44(1) of the Social Security (Contributions) Regulations 2001 and has paid a Class 2 contribution (within the meaning of section 1 of the 1992 Act), or
(b) holds such a certificate of exception.

AMENDMENT

1. Statutory Shared Parental Pay (General) (Amendment) Regulations 2015 (SI 2015/189), reg.2(2) (March 8, 2015).

DEFINITIONS

"1992 Act"—reg.2(1).
"A"—reg.2(1).
"AP"—reg.2(1).
"calculation week"—para.(5).
"employed earner"—para.(5).
"M"—reg.2(1).
"self-employed earner"—para.(5).
"specified payments"—para.(5).
"tax year"—para.(5).
"week"—reg.2(1).

GENERAL NOTE

7.56 This regulation is modified for certain special cases by the Statutory Shared Parental Pay (Adoption from Overseas) Regulations 2014 (SI 2014/3093) and the Statutory Shared Parental Pay (Parental Order Cases) Regulations 2014 (SI 2014/3097).

Conditions as to continuity of employment and normal weekly earnings relating to a claimant for statutory shared parental pay (birth)

7.57 30.—(1) The conditions as to continuity of employment and normal weekly earnings referred to in regulation 4(2)(a) and 5(2)(a) are—

(SI 2014/3051 reg.30)

- (a) the person has been in employed earner's employment with an employer for a continuous period of at least 26 weeks ending with the relevant week;
- (b) the person's normal weekly earnings (see regulation 32) with the employer by reference to which the condition in sub-paragraph (a) is satisfied for the period of eight weeks ending with the relevant week are not less than the lower earnings limit in force under sub-section (1)(a) of section 5 (earnings limits and thresholds for class 1 contributions) of the 1992 Act at the end of the relevant week;
- (c) the person continues in employed earner's employment with the employer by reference to which the condition in sub-paragraph (a) is satisfied for a continuous period beginning with the relevant week and ending with the week before the first week falling within the relevant period relating to that person under section 171ZY(2) of the 1992 Act.

(2) Where C's birth occurs earlier than the 14th week before C's expected week of birth paragraph (1) shall have effect as if, for the conditions set out there, there were substituted conditions that—

- (a) the person would have been in employed earner's employment for a continuous period of at least 26 weeks ending with the relevant week had C been born after the relevant week;
- (b) the person's normal weekly earnings for the period of eight weeks ending with the week immediately preceding C's actual week of birth are not less than the lower earnings limit in force under section 5(1)(a) of the 1992 Act immediately before the commencement of C's actual week of birth; and
- (c) the person continues in employed earner's employment with the employer by reference to whom the condition in sub-paragraph (a) is satisfied for a continuous period beginning with the date of C's birth and ending with the week before the first week falling within the relevant period relating to that person under section 171ZY(2) of the 1992 Act.

(3) The references in this regulation to the relevant week are to the week immediately preceding the 14th week before C's expected week of birth.

(4) Where more than one child is born as a result of the same pregnancy the date the first child is born is to be used to determine C's actual week of birth or the date of C's birth.

DEFINITIONS

"1992 Act"—reg.2(1).
"actual week of birth"—reg.2(1).
"C"—reg.2(1).
"expected week of birth"—reg.2(1).
"M"—reg.2(1).
"week"—reg.2(1).

Conditions as to continuity of employment and normal weekly earnings in relation to a claimant for statutory shared parental pay (adoption)

31.—(1) The conditions as to continuity of employment and normal weekly earnings referred to in regulations 17(2)(a) and 18(2)(a) relating

Statutory Shared Parental Pay (General) Regulations 2014

to the entitlement of A and AP to statutory shared parental pay (adoption) are—
(a) the person has been in employed earner's employment with an employer for a continuous period of at least 26 weeks ending with the relevant week;
(b) the person's normal weekly earnings (see regulation 32) with the employer by reference to which the condition in sub-paragraph (a) is satisfied for the period of eight weeks ending with the relevant week are not less than the lower earnings limit in force under subsection (1)(a) of section 5 (earnings limits and thresholds for class 1 contributions) of the 1992 Act at the end of the [¹ relevant week];
(c) the person continues in employed earner's employment with the employer by reference to which the condition in sub-paragraph (a) is satisfied for a continuous period beginning with the relevant week and ending with the week before the first week falling within the relevant period relating to that person under section 171ZY(2) of the 1992 Act.
(2) The references in paragraph (1) to the relevant week are to the week in which A was notified of having been matched with C.

AMENDMENT

1. Statutory Shared Parental Pay (General) (Amendment) Regulations 2015 (SI 2015/189) reg.2(3) (March 8, 2015).

DEFINITIONS

"1992 Act"—reg.2(1).
"A"—reg.2(1).
"AP"—reg.2(1).
"statutory shared parental pay (adoption)"—reg.2(1).
"week"—reg.2(1).

GENERAL NOTE

7.59   This regulation is modified for certain special cases by the Statutory Shared Parental Pay (Adoption from Overseas) Regulations 2014 (SI 2014/3093) and the Statutory Shared Parental Pay (Parental Order Cases) Regulations 2014 (SI 2014/3097).

Normal weekly earnings of a claimant for statutory shared parental pay

7.60   **32.**—(1) For the purpose of section 171ZZ4(6) (which defines normal weekly earnings for the purposes of Part 12ZC of the 1992 Act) "earnings" and "relevant period" have the meanings given in this regulation.
(2) The relevant period is the period—
(a) ending on the last normal pay day to fall before the appropriate date; and
(b) beginning with the day following the last normal pay day to fall at least eight weeks earlier than the normal pay day mentioned in sub-paragraph (a).
(3) In a case where a person has no identifiable normal pay day, paragraph (2) shall have effect as if the words "day of payment" were substituted for the words "normal pay day" in each place where they occur.

(4) In a case where a person has normal pay days at intervals of or approximating to one or more calendar months (including intervals of or approximating to a year) that person's normal weekly earnings shall be calculated by dividing their earnings in the relevant period by the number of calendar months in that period (or, if it is not a whole number, the nearest whole number), multiplying the result by 12 and dividing by 52.

(5) In a case to which paragraph (4) does not apply and the relevant period is not an exact number of weeks, the person's normal weekly earnings shall be calculated by dividing their earnings in the relevant period by the number of days in the relevant period and multiplying the result by seven.

(6) In any case where a person receives a back-dated pay increase which includes a sum in respect of a relevant period, normal weekly earnings shall be calculated as if such a sum was paid in that relevant period even though received after that period.

(7) The expression "earnings" refers to gross earnings and includes any remuneration or profit derived from a person's employment except any amount which is—
- (a) excluded from the computation of a person's earnings under regulation 25 (payments to be disregarded) of, and Schedule 3 to, the Social Security (Contributions) Regulations 2001 and regulation 27 (payments to directors to be disregarded) of those Regulations (or would have been so excluded had they not been made under the age of 16);
- (b) a chargeable emolument under section 10A (class 1B contributions) of the 1992 Act except where, in consequence of such a chargeable emolument being excluded from earnings, a person would not be entitled to statutory shared parental pay (or where such a payment or amount would have been so excluded and in consequence the person would not have been entitled to statutory shared parental pay had they not been aged under the age of 16).

(8) The expression "earnings" includes—
- (a) any amount retrospectively treated as earnings by regulations made by virtue of section 4B(2) of the 1992 Act;
- (b) any sum payable in respect of arrears of pay in pursuance of an order for reinstatement or re-engagement under the Employment Rights Act 1996;
- (c) any sum payable by way of pay in pursuance of an order made under the Employment Rights Act 1996 for the continuation of a contract of employment;
- (d) any sum payable by way of remuneration in pursuance of a protective award under section 189 of the Trade Union and Labour Relations (Consolidation) Act 1992;
- (e) any sum payable by way of statutory sick pay, including sums payable in accordance with regulations made under section 151(6) of the 1992 Act;
- (f) any sum payable by way of statutory maternity pay;
- (g) any sum payable by way of statutory paternity pay;
- (h) any sum payable by way of statutory shared parental pay; and
- (i) any sum payable by way of statutory adoption pay.

(9) In paragraphs (2) to (4)—
- (a) "the appropriate date" means—

(i) in relation to statutory shared parental pay (birth), the first day of the 14th week before the expected week of the child's birth or the first day in the week in which the child is born, whichever is earlier (but see paragraph (10)),

(ii) in relation to statutory shared parental pay (adoption) the first day of the week after the week in which A is notified of being matched with the child for the purposes of adoption;

(b) "day of payment" means a day on which the person was paid; and

(c) "normal pay day" means a day on which the terms of a person's contract of service require the person to be paid, or the practice in that person's employment is for that person to be paid if any payment is due to them.

(10) Where more than one child is born as a result of the same pregnancy, the date the first child is born is to be used to determine the week in which the child is born.

DEFINITIONS

"1992 Act"—reg.2(1).
"A"—reg.2(1).
"the appropriate date"—para.(9).
"day of payment"—para.(9).
"earnings"—para.(1).
"normal pay day"—para.(9).
"relevant period"—para.(1).
"statutory shared parental pay"—reg.2(1).
"week"—reg.2(1).

GENERAL NOTE

7.61 This regulation is modified for certain special cases by the Statutory Shared Parental Pay (Adoption from Overseas) Regulations 2014 (SI 2014/3093) and the Statutory Shared Parental Pay (Parental Order Cases) Regulations 2014 (SI 2014/3097).

Treatment of persons as employees

7.62 **33.**—(1) A person is treated as an employee for the purposes of Part 12ZC of the 1992 Act (even though not falling within the definition of 'employee' in section 171ZZ4(2) of that Act) where, and in so far as, that person is treated as an employed earner by virtue of the Social Security (Categorisation of Earners) Regulations 1978 (but see paragraph (3)).

(2) A person shall not be treated as an employee for the purposes of Part 12ZC of the 1992 Act (even though falling within the definition of 'employee' in section 171ZZ4(2) of that Act) where, and in so far as, that person is not treated as an employed earner by virtue of those Regulations (but see paragraph (3)).

(3) Paragraphs (1) and (2) shall have effect in relation to a person who—
(a) is under the age of 16; and
(b) would, or as the case may be, would not have been treated as an employed earner by virtue of those Regulations had they been over that age;

as they have effect in relation to a person who is, or as the case may be, is not treated as an employed earner by virtue of those Regulations.

(SI 2014/3051 reg.33)

(4) A person is treated as an employee for the purpose of Part 12ZC of the 1992 Act (even though not falling within the definition of 'employee' in section 171ZZ4(2) of that Act) where that person is in employed earner's employment under a contract of apprenticeship.

(5) A person is not to be treated as an employee for the purposes of Part 12ZC of the 1992 Act (even though falling within the definition of 'employee' in section 171ZZ4(2) of that Act) where that person is in employed earner's employment but that person's employer—
(a) does not fulfil the conditions prescribed in regulation 145(1) (conditions as to residence or presence) of the Social Security (Contributions) Regulations 2001 in so far as that provision relates to residence or presence in Great Britain; or
(b) is a person who, by reason of any international treaty to which the United Kingdom is a party or of any international convention binding the United Kingdom—
   (i) is exempt from the provisions of the 1992 Act; or
   (ii) is a person against whom the provisions of the 1992 Act are not enforceable.

DEFINITION

"1992 Act"—reg.2(1).

Continuous employment

34.—(1) A week is to be treated for the purposes of sections 171ZU and 171ZV of the 1992 Act (see also regulations 30 and 31) as part of a period of continuous employment with the employer even though no contract of service exists with that employer in respect of that week in the circumstances mentioned in paragraph (2) and subject to paragraphs (3) and (4).

(2) The circumstances mentioned in paragraphs (1) are that in any week the person is, for the whole or part of the week—
(a) incapable of work in consequence of sickness or injury;
(b) absent from work on account of a temporary cessation of work; or
(c) absent from work in circumstances such that, by arrangement or custom, that person is regarded as continuing in the employment of their employer for all or any purposes;
and returns to work for their employer after the incapacity for or absence from work.

(3) Incapacity for work which lasts for more than 26 consecutive weeks shall not count for the purposes of paragraph (2)(a).

(4) Where a person—
(a) is an employee in employed earner's employment in which the custom is for the employer—
   (i) to offer work for a fixed period of not more than 26 consecutive weeks;
   (ii) to offer work for such period on two or more occasions in a year for periods which do not overlap; and
   (iii) to offer the work available to those persons who had worked for the employer during the last or a recent such period; but
(b) is absent from work because of incapacity arising from some specific disease or bodily or mental disablement;
then in that case paragraph (2) shall apply as if the words "and returns

7.63

Statutory Shared Parental Pay (General) Regulations 2014

to work for their employment for their employer after the incapacity for or absence from work" were omitted.

Definition

"1992 Act"—reg.2(1).

Continuous employment and unfair dismissal

7.64   35.—(1) Where in consequence of specified action in relation to a person's dismissal, the person is reinstated or re-engaged by their employer or by a successor or associated employer of that employer then—
   (a) the continuity of their employment shall be preserved for the purposes of sections 171ZU and [¹ 171ZV] of the 1992 Act (see also regulations 30 and 31) for the period beginning with the effective date of termination and ending with the date of reinstatement or re-engagement; and
   (b) any week which falls within the interval beginning with the effective date of termination and ending with the date of reinstatement or re-engagement, as the case may be, shall count in the computation of their period of continuous employment.
(2) In this regulation—
   (a) "associated employer" shall be construed in accordance with section 231 of the Employment Rights Act 1996;
   (b) "dismissal procedures agreement" and "successor" have the same meanings as in section 235 of the Employment Rights Act 1996;
   (c) "specified action in relation to a person's dismissal" means action which consists of—
      (i) the presentation by that person of a complaint under section 111(1) (complaints to employment tribunal) of the Employment Rights Act 1996;
      (ii) that person making a claim in accordance with a dismissal procedure agreement designated by an order under section 110 of that Act; or
      (iii) any action taken by a conciliation officer under section 18 (conciliation) of the Employment Tribunals Act 1996.

Amendment

1. Statutory Shared Parental Pay (General) (Amendment) Regulations 2015 (SI 2015/189) reg.2(4) (March 8, 2015).

Definitions

"1992 Act"—reg.2(1).
"associated employer"—para.(2)(a).
"dismissal procedures agreement"—para.(2)(b).
"specified action in relation to a person's dismissal"—para.(2)(c).
"successor"—para.(2)(b).
"week"—reg.2(1).

Continuous employment and stoppages of work

7.65   36.—(1) Where a person does not work for any week or part of a week because there is a stoppage of work at that person's place of employment due to a trade dispute within the meaning of section 35(1) of the Jobseekers Act 1995 then—

(a) that person's continuity of employment shall be treated as continuing throughout the stoppage (but see paragraph (2)[1]) for the purposes of sections 171ZU and [1 171ZV] of the 1992 Act (see also regulations 30 and 31); and

(b) no such week shall count in the computation of their period of continuous employment (but see paragraph(3)).

(2) Where during the stoppage of work a person is dismissed from their employment, that person's continuity of employment shall not be treated under paragraph (1) as continuing beyond the commencement of the day that person stopped work (but see paragraph (3)).

(3) Paragraph (1)(b) and paragraph (2) do not apply to a person who proves that at no time did they have a direct interest in the trade dispute in question.

AMENDMENT

1. Statutory Shared Parental Pay (General) (Amendment) Regulations 2015 (SI 2015/189) reg.2(5) (March 8, 2015).

DEFINITIONS

"1992 Act"—reg.2(1).
"week"—reg.2(1).

Change of employer

37.—(1) Where a person's employer changes, a person's employment is to be treated for the purposes of sections 171ZU and 171ZV of the 1992 Act (see also regulations 30 and 31) as continuous employment with the second employer in the following circumstances—

(a) the employer's trade or business or an undertaking (whether or not it is an undertaking established by or under an Act of Parliament) is transferred from one person to another;

(b) a contract of employment between any body corporate and the person is modified by or under an Act of Parliament, whether public or local and whenever passed and some other body corporate is substituted as that person's employer;

(c) on the death of the employer, the person is taken into the employment of the personal representatives or trustees of the deceased;

(d) the person is employed by partners, personal representatives or trustees and there is a change in the partners, or as the case may be, personal representatives or trustees;

(e) the person is taken into the employment of an employer who is, at the time the person entered into to the employer's employment, an associated employer of the person's previous employer; or

(f) on the termination of the person's employment with an employer that person is taken into the employment of another employer and those employers are governors of a school maintained by a local education authority.

(2) In paragraph (1)(e) "associated employer" shall be construed in accordance with section 231 of the Employment Rights Act 1996.

DEFINITIONS

"1992 Act"—reg.2(1).
"associated employer"—para.(2).

Reinstatement after service with the armed forces etc

7.67   **38.**—Where a person—
  (a) is entitled to apply to their employer under the Reserve Forces (Safeguard of Employment) Act 1985; and
  (b) enters the employment of that employer within the six month period mentioned in section 1(4)(b) (obligation to reinstate) of that Act;
that person's previous period of employment with that employer (or if there was more than one such period, the last of those periods) and the period of employment beginning in that six month period shall be treated as continuous for the purposes of sections 171ZU and 171ZV of the 1992 Act (see also regulations 30 and 31).

DEFINITION

"1992 Act"—reg.2(1).

Treatment of two or more employers or two or more contracts of service as one

7.68   **39.**—(1) In a case where the earnings paid to a person in respect of two or more employments are aggregated and treated as a single payment of earnings under regulation 15(1) (aggregation of earnings paid in respect of different employed earner's employments by different persons) of the Social Security (Contributions) Regulations 2001, the employers of that person in respect of those employments shall be treated as one for the purposes of Part 12ZC of the 1992 Act (and these Regulations).

(2) Where two or more employers are treated as one under the provisions of paragraph (1), liability for statutory shared parental pay shall be apportioned between them in such proportions as they may agree, or in default of agreement, in the proportions which the person's normal weekly earnings from each employment bear to the amount of the aggregated normal weekly earnings over the relevant period as defined in regulation 32(2).

(3) Where two or more contracts of service exist concurrently between one employer and one employee, they shall be treated as one for the purposes of Part 12ZC of the 1992 Act (and these Regulations) except where, by virtue of regulation 14 (aggregation of earnings paid in respect of separate employed earner's employments under the same employer) of the Social Security (Contributions) Regulations 2001, the earnings from those contracts of service are not aggregated for the purpose of earnings-related contributions.

DEFINITION

"1992 Act"—reg.2(1).

PART 5

Weekly rate of payment of statutory shared parental pay

7.69   **40.**—(1) The weekly rate of payment of statutory shared parental pay is the smaller of the following two amounts—
  (a) [¹£139.58];

(SI 2014/3051 reg.40)

(b) 90% of the normal weekly earnings of the individual claiming statutory shared parental pay determined in accordance with section 171ZZ4(6) of the 1992 Act and regulation 32).

(2) Where the amount of any payment of statutory shared parental pay is calculated by reference to—

(a) the weekly rate specified in paragraph (1)(b), or
(b) the daily rate of one-seventh of the weekly rate specified in paragraph (1)(a) or (b),

and that amount includes a fraction of a penny, the payment shall be rounded up to the nearest whole number of pence.

AMENDMENT

1. Welfare Benefits Up-rating Order 2015 (SI 2015/30) art.5(3) (April 5, 2105).

DEFINITIONS

"1992 Act"—reg.2(1).
"statutory shared parental pay"—reg.2(1).

Statutory shared parental pay and contractual remuneration

41.—For the purposes of section 171ZZ1(1) and (2) (payment of contractual remuneration to go towards discharging liability to pay statutory shared parental pay and payment of statutory shared parental pay to go towards discharging liability to pay contractual remuneration) the payments which are to be treated as contractual remuneration are sums payable under a contract of service—

(a) by way of remuneration;
(b) for incapacity for work due to sickness or injury; and
(c) by reason of birth, adoption or care of a child.

7.70

Avoidance of liability for statutory shared parental pay

42.—(1) A former employer is liable to make payments of statutory shared parental pay to a former employee in any case where the employee has been employed for a continuous period of at least eight weeks and the employee's contract of service was brought to an end by the former employer solely, or mainly, for the purpose of avoiding liability for statutory shared parental pay.

7.71

(2) In a case falling within paragraph (1)—

(a) the employee shall be treated as if the employee had been employed for a continuous period ending with the period of seven days beginning with Sunday before the first week falling within the relevant period relating to that employee under section 171ZY(2) of the 1992 Act; and
(b) regulation 32(2) (relevant period for the purpose of the calculation of normal weekly earnings) shall apply as if it read—

"(2) The relevant period is the period—

(a) ending on the last day of payment under the former contract of employment; and
(b) beginning with the day following the day of payment under that contract to fall at least 8 weeks earlier than the day of payment mentioned in sub-paragraph (a).".

Statutory Shared Parental Pay (General) Regulations 2014

DEFINITIONS

"1992 Act"—reg.2(1).
"statutory shared parental pay"—reg.2(1).
"week"—reg.2(1).

Payment of statutory shared parental pay

7.72 **43.**—Payments of statutory shared parental pay may be made in like manner to payments of remuneration but shall not include payment in kind or by way of the provision of board and lodgings.

DEFINITION

"statutory shared parental pay"—reg.2(1).

Time when statutory shared parental pay is to be paid

7.73 **44.**—(1) In any case where—
(a) a decision has been made by an officer of Revenue and Customs under section 8(1) (decisions by officers) of the Social Security Contributions (Transfer of Functions, etc) Act 1999 as a result of which a person is entitled to an amount of statutory shared parental pay; and
(b) the time for bringing an appeal against the decision has expired and either—
(i) no such appeal has been brought; or
(ii) such appeal has been brought and has been finally disposed of;
that amount of statutory shared parental pay shall be paid within the time specified in paragraph (2).

(2) The employer or former employer shall pay the amount not later than the first pay day after the following days (but see paragraphs (3) and (4))—
(a) where an appeal has been brought, the day on which the employer or former employer receives notification that it has been finally disposed of;
(b) where leave to appeal has been refused, and there remains no further opportunity to apply for leave, the day on which the employer or former employer receives notification of the refusal; and
(c) in any other case, the day on which the time for bringing an appeal expires.

(3) Where it is impracticable, in view of the employer's or former employer's methods of accounting for and paying remuneration, for the requirement of payment referred to in paragraph (2) to be met by the pay day referred to in that paragraph, it shall be met not later than the next following pay day (but see paragraph (4)).

(4) Where the employer or former employer would not have remunerated the employee for their work in the week in respect of which statutory shared parental pay is payable as early as the pay day specified in paragraph (2) or (if it applies) paragraph (3), the requirement of payment shall be met on the first day on which the employee would have been remunerated for his work in that week.

(5) In this regulation "pay day" means a day on which it has been agreed, or it is the normal practice between an employer or former employer to agree and a person who is or was an employee of theirs, that payments by

(SI 2014/3051 reg.44)

way of remuneration are to be made, or, where there is no such agreement or normal practice, the last day of a calendar month.

DEFINITIONS

"statutory shared parental pay"—reg.2(1).
"pay day"—para.(5).

Liability of the Commissioners to pay statutory shared parental pay

45.—(1) Despite section 171ZX(1) of the 1992 Act (liability to make payments of statutory shared parental pay is liability of the employer) where the conditions in paragraph (2) are satisfied, liability to make payments of statutory shared parental pay to a person is to be liability of the Commissioners and not the employer for—

(a) any week in respect of which the employer was liable to pay statutory shared parental pay to that person but did not do so; and
(b) for any subsequent weeks that person is entitled to payments of statutory shared parental pay.

(2) The conditions in this paragraph are that—

(a) an officer of the Revenue and Customs has decided under section 8(1) of the Social Security Contributions (Transfer of Functions, etc) Act 1999 that an employer is liable to make payments of statutory shared parental pay;
(b) the time for appealing against the decision has expired; and
(c) no appeal against the decision has been lodged or leave to appeal against the decision is required and has been refused.

(3) Despite section 171ZX(1) of the 1992 Act, liability to make payments of statutory shared parental pay to a person is to be a liability of the Commissioners and not the employer as from the week in which the employer first becomes insolvent (see paragraphs 4 and 5) until the last week that person is entitled to payment of statutory shared parental pay.

(4) For the purposes of paragraph (3) an employer shall be taken to be insolvent if, and only if, in England and Wales—

(a) the employer has been adjudged bankrupt or has made a composition or arrangement with its creditors;
(b) the employer has died and the employer's estate falls to be administered in accordance with an order made under section 421 Insolvency Act 1986; or
(c) where an employer is a company or a limited liability partnership—
  (i) a winding-up order is made or a resolution for a voluntary winding-up is passed (or, in the case of a limited liability partnership, a determination for voluntary winding-up has been made) with respect to it,
  (ii) it enters administration,
  (iii) a receiver or manager of its undertaking is duly appointed,
  (iv) possession is taken, by or on behalf of the holders of any debentures secured by a floating charge, of any property of the company or limited liability partnership comprised in or subject to the charge, or
  (v) a voluntary arrangement proposed for the purposes of Part 1 of the Insolvency Act 1986 is approved under that Part.

(5) For the purposes of paragraph (3) an employer shall be taken to be insolvent if, and only if, in Scotland—

7.74

(a) an award of sequestration is made on the employer's estate;
(b) the employer executes a trust deed for its creditors;
(c) the employer enters into a composition contract;
(d) the employer has died and a judicial factor appointed under section 11A of the Judicial Factors (Scotland) Act 1889 is required by that section to divide the employer's insolvent estate among the employer's creditors; or
(e) where the employer is a company or a limited liability partnership—
   (i) a winding-up order is made or a resolution for voluntary winding-up is passed (or in the case of a limited liability partnership, a determination for a voluntary winding-up is made) with respect to it,
   (ii) it enters administration,
   (iii) a receiver of its undertaking is duly appointed, or
   (iv) a voluntary arrangement proposed for the purposes of Part I of the Insolvency Act 1986 is approved under that Part.

DEFINITIONS

"1992 Act"—reg.2(1).
"Commissioners"—reg.2(1).
"statutory shared parental pay"—reg.2(1).
"week"—reg.2(1).

Liability of the Commissioners to pay statutory shared parental pay in case of legal custody or imprisonment

7.75   **46.**—Where there is liability to pay statutory shared parental pay—
(a) in respect of a period which is subsequent to the last week falling within paragraph (1)(c) of regulations 14 and 26 (cases where there is no liability to pay statutory shared parental pay); or
(b) during a period of detention in legal custody by virtue of paragraph (2) of those regulations;
that liability, despite section 171ZX(1) of the 1992 Act, shall be that of the Commissioners and not the employer.

DEFINITIONS

"1992 Act"—reg.2(1).
"Commissioners"—reg.2(1).
"statutory shared parental pay"—reg.2(1).

Payments by the Commissioners

7.76   **47.**—Where the Commissioners become liable in accordance with regulation 45 (liability of the Commissioners to pay statutory shared parental pay) or regulation 46 (liability of the Commissioners to pay statutory shared parental pay in case of legal custody or imprisonment) then—
(a) the first payment is to be made as soon as reasonably practicable after they become so liable; and
(b) subsequent payments are to be made at weekly intervals;
by means of an instrument of payment or by such other means as appear to the Commissioners to be appropriate in the circumstances of any particular case.

DEFINITIONS

"Commissioners"—reg.2(1).
"statutory shared parental pay"—reg.2(1).

Persons unable to act

48.—(1) This regulation applies where—
(a) statutory shared parental pay is payable to a person or it is alleged that statutory shared parental pay is payable to a person;
(b) that person is unable for the time being to act;
(c) no deputy has been appointed by the Court of Protection with power to receive [¹ statutory shared parental pay] on their behalf or, in Scotland, their estate is not being administered by a guardian acting or appointed under the Adults with Incapacity (Scotland) Act 2000; and
(d) a written application has been made to the Commissioners by a person, who, if a natural person, is over the age of 18 to exercise any right, or deal with any sums payable, under Part 12ZC of the 1992 Act on behalf of the person unable to act.

(2) Where this regulation applies the Commissioners may appoint the person referred to in paragraph (1)(d)—
(a) to exercise, on behalf of the person unable to act, any right which the person unable to act may be entitled under Part 12ZC of the 1992 Act; and
(b) to deal, on behalf of the person unable to act, with any sums payable to the person unable to act under Part 12ZC of the 1992 Act.

(3) Where the Commissioners have made an appointment under paragraph (2)—
(a) they may at any time revoke it;
(b) the person appointed may resign their office after having given one month's notice in writing to the Commissioners of that person's intention to do so; and
(c) the appointment shall end when the Commissioners are notified that a deputy or other person to whom paragraph (1)(c) applies has been appointed.

(4) Anything required by Part 12ZC of the 1992 Act to be done by or to the person who is unable to act may be done by or to the person appointed under this regulation to act on behalf of the person unable to act, and the receipt of the person so appointed shall be a good discharge to the employer or former employer of the person unable to act for any sum paid.

AMENDMENT

1. Statutory Shared Parental Pay (General) (Amendment) Regulations 2015 (SI 2015/189) reg.2(6) (March 8, 2015).

DEFINITIONS

"1992 Act"—reg.2(1).
"Commissioners"—reg.2(1).
"statutory shared parental pay"—reg.2(1).

Service of notices

7.78   **49.**—(1) Where a notice is to be given under these Regulations, it may be given—
(a) where paragraph (2) applies, by electronic communication;
(b) by post; or
(c) by personal delivery.

(2) This paragraph applies where the person who is to receive the notice has agreed that the notice may be given to the person by being transmitted to an electronic address and in an electronic form specified by the person for that purpose.

(3) Where a notice is to be given under these Regulations it is to be taken to have been given—
(a) if sent by electronic communication, on the day of transmission;
(b) if sent by post in an envelope which is properly addressed and sent by prepaid post, on the day on which it is posted;
(c) if delivered personally, on the day of delivery.

SCHEDULE Regulations 16 and 28

Statutory Shared Parental Pay In Special Circumstances

Part 1

Statutory Shared Parental Pay (Birth)

Entitlement of father or partner to statutory shared parental pay (birth) in the event of the death of M before curtailment

7.79   1.—(1) In a case where M dies—
(a) before the end of her maternity allowance period in respect of C and without reducing that period under section 35(3A) of the 1992 Act, or
(b) before the end of her maternity pay period in respect of C and without reducing that period under section 165(3A) of the 1992 Act,

then these Regulations shall apply, in respect of any period after M dies, subject to the modifications in the following provisions of this paragraph.

(2) In regulation 2(1) a person is to be regarded as falling within the definition of P if that person would have done so but for the fact that M had died.

(3) In regulation 5 (entitlement of father or partner)—
(a) paragraph (3)(d) shall not apply;
(b) in a case where M dies before her maternity allowance period or maternity pay period in respect of C starts then the condition in paragraph (3)(c) shall be taken to be satisfied if it would have been satisfied but for the fact that M had died.

(4) In regulation 7 (notification and evidential requirements relating to father or mother's partner)—
(a) paragraph (1)(a) shall apply as if it read—
"(a) paragraphs (2) and (3) at least 8 weeks before the beginning of the first period specified by P pursuant to paragraph (2)(d) or, where it is not reasonably practicable for P to satisfy this requirement, as soon as reasonably practicable after the death of M, but in any event before that period;";
(b) paragraph (1)(b) and (c) shall not apply;
(c) in paragraph (2)—
(i) sub-paragraph (a) shall apply as if the words "disregarding any intention of M to claim statutory shared parental pay (birth) in respect of C" were omitted; and
(ii) sub-paragraph (c) shall not apply;
(d) in paragraph (3)—
(i) sub-paragraph (a) shall not apply;
(ii) sub-paragraph (d) shall apply as if it read—
"(d) the following information relating to P and M—

(i) P's name, M's name and national insurance number (where this number is known to P), M's address immediately before she died and the date of M's death; and
　　　(ii) the start date of M's maternity pay period or maternity allowance period in respect of C or, where M's death occurred before her maternity allowance period or maternity pay period in respect of C started, the date that period would have started but for the fact that M had died;"; and
　　　(iii) sub-paragraph (e)(iii) shall not apply;
　(e) paragraph (4) shall not apply.
(5) In regulation 8(3) (variation)—
　(a) sub-paragraph (a) shall apply as if the reference to M were omitted; and
　(b) sub-paragraph (b) shall not apply.
(6) In regulation 10 (extent of entitlement), paragraph (1)(a) shall apply as if the number of weeks referred to is the number of weeks in which maternity allowance or statutory maternity pay was payable to M in respect of C up to the time of M's death.

Notification And Variation: Death Of Mother Or Partner After Curtailment
2.—(1) In the case where—
　(a) P, who in connection with a claim by M would be required to satisfy the conditions specified in regulation 4(3), dies after M has reduced her maternity allowance period in respect of C under section 35(3A) of the 1992 Act or her maternity pay period in respect of C under section 165(3A) of the 1992 Act; and
　(b) before P dies M has not given the notices and information specified in regulation 6 (notice and evidential requirements relation to the mother),
then these Regulations apply in respect of any period after P dies, subject to the modifications in the following provisions of this paragraph.
(2) In regulation 6 (notification and evidential requirements relating to the mother)—
　(a) paragraph (1)(a) shall apply as if it read—
"(a) paragraphs (2) and (3) at least 8 weeks before the beginning of the first period specified by M pursuant to paragraph (2)(d) or where it is not reasonably practicable for M to satisfy this requirement as soon as reasonably practicable after the death of P, but in any event before that period;";
　(b) paragraph (1)(b) and (c) shall not apply;
　(c) in paragraph (2)—
　　　(i) sub-paragraph (a) shall apply as if the words "disregarding any intention of P to claim statutory shared parental pay in respect of C" were omitted;
　　　(ii) sub-paragraph (c) shall not apply;
　(d) in paragraph (3)—
　　　(i) sub-paragraph (a) shall not apply;
　　　(ii) sub-paragraph (d) shall apply as if it read—
"(d) M's name, P's name and national insurance number (where this number is known to M), P's address immediately before P died and the date of P's death";
　(e) paragraph (4) shall not apply.
(3) In regulation 8 (variation)—
　(a) paragraph (2)(a) shall apply as if it read—
"(a) of the number of weeks during which M and P have exercised, and the number of weeks M intends to exercise, an entitlement to statutory shared parental pay (birth) in respect of C";
　(b) paragraph (2)(b) shall not apply.
(4) In regulation 10 (extent of entitlement)—
　(a) paragraph (1)(b)(i) shall apply as if the words "P has notified P's intention to claim" to the end read "the number of weeks in which P claimed statutory shared parental pay (birth) in respect of C up to the time of P's death.";
　(b) paragraph (7) shall apply as if the words "the last day of the latest period so notified" were "the time of P's death".

3.—(1) In the case where—
　(a) P, who in connection with M's claim is required to satisfy the conditions specified in regulation 4(3), dies after M has reduced her maternity allowance period in respect of C under section 35(3A) of the 1992 Act or her maternity pay period in respect of C under section 165(3A) of the 1992 Act, and
　(b) before P dies M has given the notices and information specified in regulation 6 (notification and evidential requirements relating to the mother),
then these Regulations apply in respect of any period after P dies, subject to the modifications in the following provisions of this paragraph.

Statutory Shared Parental Pay (General) Regulations 2014

(2) In regulation 8 (variation)—
(a) paragraph (1) shall apply in relation to the first notice made under that paragraph following P's death as if at the end of that paragraph there is added—
"or, where it is not reasonably practicable for M to satisfy this requirement, by notice in writing given to that employer as soon as reasonably practicable after the death of P, but in any event before that period and which states the date of P's death";
(b) paragraph (2)(a) shall apply as if it read—
"(a) of the number of weeks during which M and P have exercised, and the number of weeks M intends to exercise, an entitlement to statutory shared parental pay (birth) in respect of C";
(c) paragraph (2)(b) shall not apply.
(3) In regulation 10—
(a) paragraph (1)(b)(i) shall apply as if the words "P has notified P's intention to claim" to the end read—
"the number of weeks in which P claimed statutory shared parental pay (birth) in respect of C up to the time of P's death;";
(b) paragraph (7) shall apply as if the words "the last day of the latest period so notified" were "the time of P's death".

7.82 4.—(1) In the case where—
(a) M dies after she has reduced her maternity allowance period in respect of C under section 35(3A) of the 1992 Act or her maternity pay period in respect of C under section 165(3A) of the 1992 Act, and
(b) before M dies P has not given the notices and information specified in regulation 7 (notification and evidential requirements relating to father or partner),
then these Regulations apply in respect of any period after M dies, subject to the modifications in the following provisions of this paragraph.
(2) In regulation 2(1) (definitions) a person is to be regarded as falling within the definition of P if that person would have done so but for the fact that M has died.
(3) In regulation 7 (notification and evidential requirements relating to P)—
(a) in paragraph (1)—
(i) sub-paragraph (a) shall apply as if it read—
"(a) paragraphs (2) and (3) at least 8 weeks before the beginning of the first period specified by P pursuant to paragraph (2)(d) or where it is not reasonably practicable for P to satisfy this requirement as soon as reasonably practicable after the death of M, but in any event before that period;";
(ii) sub-paragraphs (b) and (c) shall not apply;
(b) in paragraph (2)—
(i) sub-paragraph (a) shall apply as if the words "disregarding any intention of M to claim statutory shared parental pay in respect of C" were omitted;
(ii) sub-paragraph (c) shall not apply;
(c) in paragraph (3)—
(i) sub-paragraph (a) shall not apply;
(ii) sub-paragraph (d) shall apply as if it read—
"(d) P's name, M's name and national insurance number (where this number is known to P), M's address immediately before she died and the date of M's death";
(iii) sub-paragraph (e)(iii) shall not apply;
(d) paragraph (4) shall not apply.
(4) In regulation 8(variation), in paragraph (3)—
(a) sub-paragraph (a) shall apply as if it read—
"(a) of the number of weeks during which P and M have exercised, and the number of weeks P intends to exercise, an entitlement to statutory shared parental pay (birth) in respect of C";
(b) sub-paragraph (b) shall not apply.
(5) In regulation 10 (extent of entitlement)—
(a) paragraph (1)(b)(ii) shall apply as if the words "M has notified M's intention to claim" to the end read—
"the number of weeks in which M claimed statutory shared parental pay (birth) in respect of C up to the time of M's death;";
(b) paragraph (8) shall apply as if the words "the last day of the latest period" were "the time of M's death".

7.83 5.—(1) In the case where—
(a) M dies after she has reduced her maternity allowance period in respect of C under

section 35(3A) of the 1992 Act or her maternity pay period in respect of C under section 165(3A) of the 1992 Act, and
(b) before M dies P has given the notice and information specified in regulation 7 (notification and evidential requirements relating to father or mother's partner),
then these Regulations apply in in respect of any period after M dies subject to the modifications in the following provisions of this paragraph.
(2) In regulation 8 (variation)—
(a) paragraph (1) shall apply in relation to the first notice made under that regulation following M's death as if at the end of that paragraph there is added—
"or, where it is not reasonably practicable for P to satisfy this requirement, by notice in writing given to that employer as soon as reasonably practicable after the death of M, but in any event before that period and which states the date of M's death";
(b) paragraph (3)(a) shall apply as if it read—
"(a) of the number of weeks during which P and M have exercised, and the number of weeks P intends to exercise, an entitlement to statutory shared parental pay (birth) in respect of C";
(c) paragraph (3)(b) shall not apply.
(3) In regulation 10 (extent of entitlement)—
(a) paragraph (1)(b)(ii) shall apply as if the words "M has notified M's intention to claim" to the end read—
"the number of weeks in which M claimed statutory shared parental pay (birth) in respect of C up to the time of M's death";
(b) paragraph (8) shall apply as if the words "the last day of the latest period" were "the time of M's death".

Death Of Child

6.—(1) In the case where M has given the notice and information in accordance with regulation 6(1) and then C dies, then in respect of any period after C dies paragraph (2)(f) of regulation 4 (entitlement of mother to statutory shared parental pay), shall not apply, and regulation 8 shall apply in accordance with sub-paragraph (3).

(2) In the case where P has given the notices and information in accordance with regulation 7(1) and then C dies, then in respect of any period after C dies paragraph (2)(d) of regulation 5 (entitlement of father or partner to statutory shared parental pay) shall not apply and regulation 8 shall apply in accordance with sub-paragraph (3).

(3) Where paragraph (1) or (2) applies, regulation 8 (variation) shall apply as if it read—
"(1) M, or as the case may be, P may cancel the period or periods during which they intend to claim statutory shared parental pay (birth) by notice in writing which is given at least 8 weeks before the first period to be cancelled, or, if this is not reasonably practicable, as soon as reasonably practicable after the death of C, but in any event before that period to the employer who will be liable to pay statutory shared parental pay (birth) to M or P.
(2) M and P may each only give one notice under paragraph (1).".
(4) Where more than one child is born of the same pregnancy—
(a) sub-paragraphs (2) and (3) only apply where all the children die; and
(b) a reference in this paragraph relating to the death of C (however expressed) is to the death of the last of those children to die.

PART 2

Statutory Shared Parental Pay (Adoption)

Entitlement Of Adopter's Partner To Statutory Shared Parental Pay (Adoption) In The Event Of The Death Of Adopter Before Curtailment

7.—(1) In a case where A dies before the end of A's adoption pay period in respect of C and without reducing that period under section 171ZN(2A) of the 1992 Act then these Regulations apply in respect of any period after

A dies, subject to the modifications in the following provisions of this paragraph.

(2) In regulation 2 a person is to be regarded as falling within the definition of AP if that person would have done so but for the fact that A had died.

(3) In regulation 18 (entitlement of partner to statutory shared parental pay (adoption))—
(a) paragraph (3)(d) shall not apply;
(b) in the case where A dies before A's adoption pay period in respect of C starts, then the condition in paragraph (3)(c) shall be taken to be satisfied if it would have been satisfied but for the fact that A had died.

(4) In regulation 20 (notification and evidential requirements relating to partner)—
(a) paragraph (1)(a) shall apply as if it read—
"(a) paragraphs (2) and (3) at least 8 weeks before the beginning of the first period specified by AP pursuant to paragraph (2)(d) or, where it is not reasonably practicable for AP to satisfy this requirement, as soon as reasonably practicable after the death of A, but in any event before that week";
(b) paragraph (1)(b) and (c) shall not apply;
(c) in paragraph (2)—
　(i) sub-paragraph (a) shall apply as if the words "disregarding any intention of A to claim statutory shared parental pay (adoption) in respect of C" were omitted,
　(ii) sub-paragraph (c) shall not apply;
(d) in paragraph (3)—
　(i) sub-paragraph (a) shall not apply,
　(ii) sub-paragraph (d) shall apply as if it read—
"(d) the following information about AP and A—
　(i) AP's name, A's name and national insurance number (where this number is known to AP), A's address immediately before she died and the date of A's death; and
　(ii) the start date of A's adoption pay period in respect of C;",
　(iii) sub-paragraph (e)(iii) shall not apply;
(e) paragraph (4) shall not apply.

(5) In regulation 21(variation), in paragraph (3)—
(a) sub-paragraph (a) shall apply as if the reference to A were omitted;
(b) sub-paragraph (b) shall not apply.

(6) In regulation 22 (extent of entitlement), paragraph (1)(a) shall apply as if the number of weeks referred to is the number of weeks in which statutory adoption pay was payable to A in respect of C up to the time of A's death.

Notification Or Variation: Death Of Adopter Or Adopter's Partner After Curtailment

8.—(1) In the case where—
(a) AP who in connection with a claim by A would be required to satisfy the conditions in regulation 17(3), dies after A has reduced A's adoption pay period in respect of C under section 171ZN(2A) of the 1992 Act, and

(b) before AP dies A has not given the notice and information specified in regulation 19 (notification and evidential requirements relating to the adopter),

then these Regulations apply in respect of any period after AP dies, subject to the modifications in the following provisions of this paragraph.

(2) In regulation 19 (notification and evidential requirements relating to the adopter)—

(a) paragraph (1)(a) shall apply as if it read—

"(a) paragraphs (2) and (3) at least 8 weeks before the beginning of the first period specified by A pursuant to paragraph (2)(d) or, where it is not reasonably practicable for A to satisfy this requirement, as soon as reasonably practicable after the death of AP but in any event before that period;";

(b) paragraph (1)(b) and (c) shall not apply;

(c) paragraph (2)(a) shall apply as if the words "disregarding any intention of AP to claim statutory shared parental pay (adoption) in respect of C" were omitted;

(d) paragraph (2)(c) shall not apply;

(e) paragraph (3)(a) shall not apply;

(f) paragraph (3)(d) shall apply as if it read—

"(d) A's name, AP's name and national insurance number (where this number is known to A), AP's address immediately before AP died and the date of AP's death";

(g) paragraph (4) shall not apply.

(3) In regulation 21 (variation), in paragraph (3) sub-paragraph (a) shall apply as if it read—

"(a) of the number of weeks during which A and AP have exercised, and the number of weeks A intends to exercise, an entitlement to statutory shared parental pay (adoption) in respect of C;";

(a) paragraph (b) shall not apply.

(4) In regulation 22 (extent of entitlement to statutory shared parental pay (adoption))—

(a) paragraph (1)(b)(i) shall apply as if the words "AP has notified AP's intention to claim" to the end read—

"the number of weeks in which AP claimed statutory shared parental pay (adoption) in respect of C up to the time of AP's death;";

(b) paragraph (5) shall apply as if the words "the last day of the latest period so notified" were "the time of AP's death".

9.—(1) In the case where—

(a) AP, who in connection with A's claim is required to satisfy the conditions specified in regulation 17(3), dies after A has reduced A's adoption pay period under section 171ZN(2A) of the 1992 Act, and

(b) before AP dies A has given the notices and information specified in regulation 19 (notification and evidential requirements relating to the adopter),

then these Regulations apply in respect of any period after AP dies, subject to the modifications in the following provisions of this paragraph.

(2) In regulation 21 (variation)—

(a) paragraph (1) shall apply in relation to the first notice made under that paragraph following AP's death as if at the end of that paragraph there is added—

"or, where it is not reasonably practicable for A to satisfy this requirement, by notice in writing given to that employer as soon as reasonably practicable after the death of AP, but in any event before that period and which states the date of AP's death";

(b) paragraph (2)(a) shall apply as if it read—

"(a) of the number of weeks during which A and AP have exercised, and the number of weeks A intends to exercise, an entitlement to statutory shared parental pay (adoption) in respect of C;";

(c) paragraph (2)(b) shall not apply.

(3) In regulation 22 (extent of entitlement)—

(a) paragraph (1)(b)(i) shall apply as if the words "AP has notified AP's intention to claim" to the end read "the number of weeks in which AP claimed statutory shared parental pay (adoption) in respect of C up to the time of AP's death;";

(b) paragraph (5) shall apply as if the words "the last day of the latest period so notified" were "the time of AP's death".

7.88   10.—(1) In the case where—

(a) A dies after A has reduced A's adoption pay period in respect of C under section 171ZN(2A) of the 1992 Act, and

(b) before A dies AP has not given the notice and information specified in regulation 20 (notification and evidential requirements relating to adopter's partner);

then the Regulations apply in respect of any period after A dies subject to the modifications in the following provisions of this paragraph.

(2) In regulation 2(1) (definitions) a person is to be regarded as falling within the definition of AP if that person would have done so but for the fact that A has died.

(3) In regulation 20 (notification and evidential requirements relating to partner)—

(a) paragraph (1)(a) shall apply as if it read—

"(a) paragraphs (2) and (3) at least 8 weeks before the beginning of the first period specified by AP pursuant to paragraph (2)(d) or if it is not reasonably practicable for AP to satisfy this requirement as soon as reasonably practicable after the death of A, but in any event before that period;";

(b) paragraph (1)(b) and (c) shall not apply;

(c) paragraph (2)(a) shall apply as if the words "disregarding any intention of A to claim statutory shared parental pay (adoption) in respect of C" were omitted;

(d) paragraph (2)(c) shall not apply;

(e) paragraph (3)(a) shall not apply;

(f) paragraph (3)(d) shall apply as if it read—

"(d) AP's name, A's name and national insurance number (where this number is known to AP), A's address immediately before A died and the date of A's death;";

(g) paragraph (4) shall not apply.

(4) In regulation 21 (variation), in paragraph (3)—

(a) sub-paragraph (a) shall apply as if it read—

"(a) of the number of weeks during which AP and A have exercised, and the number of weeks AP intends to exercise, an entitlement to statutory shared parental pay (adoption) in respect of C";

(b) sub-paragraph (b) shall not apply.

(5) In regulation 22 (extent of entitlement)—

(a) paragraph (1)(b)(ii) shall apply as if the words "A has notified A's intention to claim" to the end read—
"the number of weeks in which A claimed statutory shared parental pay (adoption) in respect of C up to the time of A's death;".
(b) paragraph (6) shall apply as if the words "the last day of the latest period so notified" were "the time of A's death".

11.—(1) In the case where—

(a) A dies after A has reduced A's adoption pay period in respect of C under section 171ZN(2A) of the 1992 Act; and
(b) before A dies AP has given the notice and information specified in regulation 20 (notification and evidential requirements relating to the partner);

then these Regulations apply in respect of any period after A dies subject to the modifications in the following provisions of this paragraph.

(2) In regulation 21 (variation)—
(a) paragraph (1) shall apply in relation to the first notice made under that regulation following A's death as if at the end of that paragraph there is added—
"or, where is it not reasonably practicable for AP to satisfy this requirement, by notice in writing given to that employer as soon as reasonably practicable after the death of A, but in any event before that period and which states the date of A's death;";
(b) paragraph (3)(a) shall apply as it is read—
"(a) of the number of weeks during which AP and A have exercised, and the number of weeks AP intends to exercise, an entitlement to statutory shared parental pay (adoption) in respect of C";
(c) paragraph (3)(b) shall not apply.
(3) In regulation 22 (extent of entitlement)—
(a) paragraph (1)(b)(ii) shall apply as if the words "A has notified A's intention to claim" to the end read—
"the number of weeks in which A claimed statutory shared parental pay (adoption) in respect of C up to the time of A's death.".
(b) paragraph (6) shall apply as if the words "the last day of the latest period so notified" were "the time of A's death".

Death Of Child Or Disrupted Placement

12.—(1) In the case where A has given the notices and information specified in regulation 19(1) and then C dies or is returned after being placed then in respect of any period after C dies or is returned after being placed paragraph (2)(f) of regulation 17 (entitlement of adopter to statutory shared parental pay) shall not apply and regulation 21 shall apply in accordance with sub-paragraph (3).

(2) In the case where AP has given the notices and information specified in regulation 20(1) and then C dies or is returned after being placed then in respect of any period after C dies or is returned after being placed paragraph (2)(d) of regulation 18 (entitlement of adopter to statutory shared parental pay) shall not apply and regulation 21 shall apply in accordance with sub-paragraph (3).

(3) Where paragraph (1) or (2) applies, regulation 21 (variation) shall apply as if it read—
"(1) A or, as the case may be, AP may cancel the period or periods during which they intend to claim statutory shared parental pay (adoption) by

notice in writing which is given at least 8 weeks before the first period to be cancelled or, if this is not reasonably practicable, as soon as reasonably practicable after the death of C or after C is returned after being placed, but in any event before that period to the employer who will be liable to pay statutory shared parental pay (adoption) to A or AP.

(2) A and AP may each only give one notice under paragraph (1).".

(4) Where more than one child is placed for adoption as a result of the same placement—
  (a) sub-paragraphs (1) and (2) only apply where all the children die or, as the case may be, all the children are returned after being placed;
  (b) a reference in this paragraph to the death of C or to the return of C after being placed (however expressed) is to the death of the last of those children to die or is to the last of those children to be returned after being placed.

(5) In this paragraph "returned after being placed" means—
  (a) returned to the adoption agency under sections 31 to 35 of the Adoption and Children Act 2002;
  (b) in Scotland, returned to the adoption agency, adoption society or nominated person in accordance with section 25(6) of the Adoption and Children (Scotland) Act 2007; or
  (c) where the child is placed in accordance with section 22C of the Children Act 1989, returned to the adoption agency following termination of the placement.

GENERAL NOTE

7.91   This Schedule is modified for certain special cases by the Statutory Shared Parental Pay (Adoption from Overseas) Regulations 2014 (SI 2014/3093) and the Statutory Shared Parental Pay (Parental Order Cases) Regulations 2014 (SI 2014/3097).

Statutory Shared Parental Pay (Adoption From Overseas) Regulations 2014

(SI 2014/3093)

A draft of these Regulations was laid before Parliament in accordance with section 176(1) of the Social Security Contributions and Benefits Act 1992 and approved by resolution of each House of Parliament.

This instrument contains only regulations made by virtue of, or consequential upon, section 119(1) of the Children and Families Act 2014 and is made before the end of the period of 6 months beginning with the coming into force of that enactment.

The Secretary of State, in exercise of the powers conferred by sections 171ZV(1) to (5), and (12) to (15), 171ZW(1), 171ZX(2) and (3), 171ZY(1), and (3) to (5), 171ZZ1(3), 171ZZ4(3), (4), (7) and (8), and 175(3) of the Social Security Contributions and Benefits Act 1992 and by section 5(1)(g), (i), (l) and (p) of the Social Security Administration Act 1992 and with the concurrence of the Commissioners for Her Majesty's Revenue and Customs in so far as such concurrence is required, makes the following Regulations.

(SI 2014/3051 Sch.)

ARRANGEMENT OF REGULATIONS

1. Citation and commencement
2. Interpretation
3. Application of the General Regulations to adoptions from overseas
4.–16. Modifications to the General Regulations for the purposes of adoptions from overseas

7.92

Citation and commencement

1.—These Regulations may be cited as the Statutory Shared Parental Pay (Adoption from Overseas) Regulations 2014 and come into force on 5th April 2015.

7.93

Interpretation

2.—In these Regulations—
"1992 Act" means the Social Security Contributions and Benefits Act 1992;
"the Application Regulations" means the Social Security Contributions and Benefits Act 1992 (Application of Parts 12ZA, 12ZB and 12ZC to Adoptions from Overseas) Regulations 2003;
"the General Regulations" means the Statutory Shared Parental Pay (General) Regulations 2014; and
"statutory shared parental pay (adoption)" means any pay payable in accordance with the provisions of Part 12ZC of the 1992 Act where the conditions in section 171ZV of that Act are satisfied.

7.94

Application of the General Regulations to adoptions from overseas

3.—(1) The provisions of the General Regulations mentioned in paragraph (2), in so far as they apply to statutory shared parental pay (adoption), apply to adoptions from overseas, subject to paragraphs (3) and (4) and the modifications set out in regulations 4 to 16 below.
(2) The relevant provisions are—
(a) regulation 2;
(b) regulation 3(b);
(c) Parts 3 to 5;
(d) Part 2 of the Schedule.
(3) Any references in the provisions of the General Regulations mentioned in paragraph (2) to the provisions of Part 12ZC of the 1992 Act must be construed as references to the provisions of Part 12ZC as modified by the Application Regulations.
(4) Any references in the provisions of the General Regulations mentioned in paragraph (2) to other provisions of the General Regulations must be construed as references to those provisions as modified by these Regulations.

7.95

Modifications to the General Regulations for the purposes of adoptions from overseas

4.—The General Regulations are modified as follows.

7.96

Modifications to the General Regulations for the purposes of adoptions from overseas

7.97 5.—(1) Regulation 2 (definitions) is modified as follows.
(2) In paragraph (1)—
(a) for the definition of "A" substitute—
""A", in relation to C, means the person by whom C has been or is to be adopted;" and
(b) insert the following definitions in the appropriate places alphabetically—
""enter Great Britain" means enter Great Britain from outside the United Kingdom in connection with or for the purposes of adoption;";
""official notification" means written notification, issued by or on behalf of the relevant central authority, that it is prepared to issue a certificate to the overseas authority concerned with the adoption of C, or that it has issued a certificate and sent it to that authority, confirming, in either case, that A is eligible to adopt, and has been assessed and approved as being a suitable adoptive parent;";
""relevant central authority" means—
(a) in the case of an adopter to whom Part 3 of the Adoptions with a Foreign Element Regulations 2005(1) applies and who is habitually resident in Wales, the Welsh Ministers;
(b) in the case of an adopter to whom the Adoptions with a Foreign Element (Scotland) Regulations 2009(2) apply and who is habitually resident in Scotland, the Scottish Ministers; and
(c) in any other case, the Secretary of State.".

Modifications to the General Regulations for the purposes of adoptions from overseas

7.98 6.—In regulation 3 (application), for paragraph (b) substitute—
"(b) statutory shared parental pay (adoption) in respect of children who enter Great Britain on or after 5th April 2015.".

Modifications to the General Regulations for the purposes of adoptions from overseas

7.99 7.—(1) Regulation 17 (entitlement of adopter to statutory shared parental pay (adoption)) is modified as follows.
(2) In paragraphs (2)(b) and (3)(a) for "date of C's placement for adoption" substitute "date C enters Great Britain".
(3) In paragraph (2)(d) for "the placement for adoption of C" substitute "the adoption of C".

Modifications to the General Regulations for the purposes of adoptions from overseas

7.100 8.—(1) Regulation 18 (entitlement of partner to statutory shared parental pay (adoption)) is modified as follows.
(2) In paragraphs (2)(b) and (3)(a) for "date of C's placement for adoption" substitute "date C enters Great Britain".
(3) In paragraph 3(c) for "the placement for adoption of C" substitute "the adoption of C".

(SI 2014/3093 reg.3)

Modifications to the General Regulations for the purposes of adoptions from overseas

9.—(1) Regulation 19 (notification and evidential requirements relating to the adopter) is modified as follows.

(2) In paragraph (1)(b)—
(a) for "if C is not placed for adoption by that time" substitute "if C has not entered Great Britain by that time";
(b) for "placement of C" substitute "date of C's entry into Great Britain".

(3) In paragraph (3)(b) for "A was notified that A had been matched with C" substitute "A received the official notification".

(4) In paragraph (3)(c) for "date of C's placement for adoption" substitute "date of C's entry into Great Britain".

(5) For paragraph (4)(a) substitute—
"(a) the date on which A expects C to enter Great Britain; and".

7.101

Modifications to the General Regulations for the purposes of adoptions from overseas

10.—(1) Regulation 20 (notification and evidential requirements relating to the partner) is modified as follows.

(2) In paragraph (1)(b)—
(a) for "if C is not placed for adoption by that time" substitute "if C has not entered Great Britain by that time";
(b) for "placement of C" substitute "date of C's entry into Great Britain".

(3) In paragraph (3)(b) for "A was notified that A had been matched with C" substitute "A received the official notification".

(4) In paragraph (3)(c) for "date of C's placement for adoption" substitute "date of C's entry into Great Britain".

(5) For paragraph (4)(a) substitute—
"(a) the date on which A expects C to enter Great Britain; and".

7.102

Modifications to the General Regulations for the purposes of adoptions from overseas

11.—In regulation 23 (period of payment of statutory shared parental pay), in paragraph (1), for "C was placed for adoption (or where more than one child is placed for adoption as a result of the same arrangement, the date of placement of the first child to be placed as part of the arrangement)" substitute "C entered Great Britain (or where more than one child is adopted as a result of the same arrangement, the date on which the first child entered Great Britain)".

7.103

Modifications to the General Regulations for the purposes of adoptions from overseas

12.—In regulation 24 (work during a period of statutory shared parental pay), in paragraph (1)(a)(ii), for "immediately preceding the 14th week before the expected week of the placement for adoption" substitute "in which A received the official notification".

7.104

Modifications to the General Regulations for the purposes of adoptions from overseas

7.105   **13.**—In regulation 29 (conditions relating to employment and earnings of claimant's partner), in paragraph (5), for the definition of "calculation week" substitute—

""calculation week" means the week in which A received the official notification;".

Modifications to the General Regulations for the purposes of adoptions from overseas

7.106   **14.**—In regulation 31 (conditions as to continuity of employment and earnings), in paragraph (2), for "A was notified of having been matched with C" substitute "A received the official notification".

Modifications to the General Regulations for the purposes of adoptions from overseas

7.107   **15.**—In regulation 32 (normal weekly earnings of a claimant), in paragraph (9), in the definition of "appropriate date" for "the week in which A is notified of being matched with the child for the purposes of adoption" substitute "the week in which the official notification is sent to A".

Modifications to the General Regulations for the purposes of adoptions from overseas

7.108   **16.**—(1) Paragraph 12 (death of child) of the Schedule is modified as follows.

(2) In sub-paragraphs (1) and (2) for "or is returned after being placed" substitute "or regulation 28 of the Adoptions with a Foreign Element Regulations 2005 or regulation 31 of the Adoptions with a Foreign Element (Scotland) Regulations 2009 applies,".

(3) In sub-paragraph (3) for "the death of C or after C is returned after being placed" substitute "the date on which C dies or regulation 28 of the Adoptions with a Foreign Element Regulations 2005 or regulation 31 of the Adoptions with a Foreign Element (Scotland) Regulations 2009 applies".

(4) In sub-paragraph (4)—
(a) for "placed for adoption as a result of the same placement" substitute "adopted as a result of the same arrangement";
(b) for "all the children are returned after being placed" substitute "regulation 28 of the Adoptions with a Foreign Element Regulations 2005 or regulation 31 of the Adoptions with a Foreign Element (Scotland) Regulations 2009 applies in relation to all of the children";
(c) for paragraph (b) substitute—
"(b) a reference in this paragraph to the death of C or to the application of regulation 28 of the Adoptions with a Foreign Element Regulations 2005 or regulation 31 of the Adoptions with a Foreign Element (Scotland) Regulations 2009 (however expressed) is to the death of the last of those children to die or is to the last of those children in relation to whom those regulations applied.".

(5) Omit sub-paragraph (5).

(SI 2014/3093 reg.11)

Statutory Shared Parental Pay (Parental Order Cases) Regulations 2014

(SI 2014/3097)

A draft of these Regulations was laid before Parliament in accordance with section 176(1) of the Social Security Contributions and Benefits Act 1992 and approved by resolution of each House of Parliament.

This instrument contains only regulations made by virtue of, or consequential upon, section 119(1) of the Children and Families Act 2014 and is made before the end of the period 6 months beginning with the coming into force of that enactment.

The Secretary of State, in exercise of the powers conferred by sections 171ZV(1), (2), (3), (4), (5), (12), (13), (14) and (15), 171ZW(1)(a) to (f), 171ZX(2) and (3), 171ZY(1), (3), (4) and (5), 171ZZ1(3), 171ZZ4(3), (4), (7) and (8) and 175(3) of the Social Security Contributions and Benefits Act 1992 and by section 5(1)(g), (i), (l) and (p) of the Social Security Administration Act 1992 and with the concurrence of the Commissioners for Her Majesty's Revenue and Customs, in so far as such concurrence is required, makes the following Regulations:

ARRANGEMENT OF REGULATIONS

1. Commencement and Citation
2. Interpretation
3. Application of the Pay Regulations to an intended parent or a parental order parent
4.–16. Modifications of the Pay Regulations as they apply to an intended parent or a parental order parent

7.109

GENERAL NOTE

These Regulations provide an entitlement to statutory shared parental pay in respect of cases which involve a person who has applied, with another person, for a parental order under s.54 of the Human Fertilisation and Embryology Act 2008. Under s.54 a court may make an order providing for a child of a surrogate mother to be treated as the child of the applicants for the order if certain conditions are satisfied. These Regulations need to be read in conjunction with the Social Security Contributions and Benefits Act 1992 (Application of Parts 12ZA, 12ZB and 12ZC to Parental Order Cases) Regulations 2014 (SI 2014/2866). They should also be read in conjunction with the Statutory Shared Parental Pay (General) Regulations 2014 (SI 2014/3051) which they apply with modifications.

7.110

PART 1

INTRODUCTION

Citation and commencement

1.—These Regulations may be cited as the Statutory Shared Parental Pay (Parental Order Cases) Regulations 2014 and come into force on 1st December 2014.

7.111

Interpretation

7.112 **2.**—In these Regulations—
"A" and "AP" have the same meanings as in the Pay Regulations as modified by these Regulations;
"C", "expected week of birth" and "statutory shared parental pay (adoption)" have the same meanings as under the Pay Regulations;
"parental order parent" means a person on whose application the court has made a parental order in respect of C;
"parental statutory declaration" means a statutory declaration stating that the person making the declaration—
(a) has applied, or intends to apply, under section 54 of the Human Fertilisation and Embryology Act 2008 with another person for a parental order in respect of C within the time limit for making such an application; and
(b) expects the court to make a parental order on that application in respect of C;
"Pay Regulations" means the Statutory Shared Parental Pay (General) Regulations 2014.

Application of the Pay Regulations to an intended parent or a parental order parent

7.113 **3.**—The provisions of the Pay Regulations in so far as they apply to statutory shared parental pay (adoption) shall apply to an intended parent or a parental order parent with the modifications set out in Part 2 of these Regulations.

PART 2

Modifications of the Pay Regulations as they apply to an intended parent or a parental order parent

7.114 **4.**—Regulation 2 (interpretation) of the Pay Regulations as they apply to an intended parent or a parental order parent shall read as if—
(a) in paragraph (1)—
(i) the definition of "A" read "means the intended parent or parental order parent in relation to C who has elected to receive statutory adoption pay under section 171ZL(2)(e) of the 1992 Act and to whom the conditions in that subsection apply;";
(ii) the definition of "AP" read "means the intended parent or parental order parent in relation to C who at the date of C's birth is married to, or is the civil partner of, or is the partner of A;";
(iii) the definition of "child" were omitted;
(iv) there was the following definition—
""parental order parent" means a person on whose application the court has made an order in respect of C under section 54(1) of the Human Fertilization and Embryology Act 2008;";
(v) the definitions of "placed for adoption" and "adoption agency" were omitted;

(b) paragraphs (4), (5) and (6) were omitted.

5.—In regulation 3 (application) of the Pay Regulations as they apply to an intended parent or a parental order parent paragraph (b) shall read as if the words in that paragraph were—

"statutory shared parental pay (adoption) in respect of children whose expected week of birth begins on or after 5th April 2015.".

6.—In regulation 17 (entitlement of adopter to statutory shared parental pay (adoption)) of the Pay Regulations as they apply to an intended parent or a parental order parent—
(a) in paragraph (2)—
　(i) sub-paragraph (b) shall read as if the words in that sub-paragraph were—

"A has, or expects to have, at the date of C's birth the main responsibility for the care of C (apart from the responsibility of AP);";

　(ii) sub-paragraph (d) shall read as if the words "to the placement for adoption of C" read "to being the intended parent or parental order parent of C";
(b) in paragraph (3), sub-paragraph (a) shall read as if the words in that sub-paragraph were—

"AP has, or expects to have, at the date of C's birth the main responsibility for the care of C (apart from the responsibility of A);".

7.—In regulation 18 (entitlement of partner to statutory shared parental pay (adoption)) of the Pay Regulations as they apply to an intended parent or a parental order parent—
(a) in paragraph (2), sub-paragraph (b) shall read as if the words in that sub-paragraph were—

"AP has, or expects to have, at the date of C's birth the main responsibility for the care of C (apart from the responsibility of A)";

(b) in paragraph (3)—
　(i) sub-paragraph (a) shall read as if the words in that sub-paragraph were—

"A has, or expects to have, at the date of C's birth the main responsibility for the care of C (apart from the responsibility of A);";

　(ii) sub-paragraph (c) shall read as if the words "to the placement for adoption of C" read "to being the intended parent or parental order parent of C".

8.—(1) In regulation 19 (notification and evidential requirements relating to the adopter) of the Pay Regulations as they apply to an intended parent or a parental order parent—
(a) paragraph (1)(b) shall read as if the words "if C is not placed for adoption by that time as soon as reasonably practicable after the placement of C" were "if C is not born by that time as soon as reasonably practicable after the birth of C";
(b) in paragraph (3)—
　(i) sub-paragraph (b) shall read as if the words in that sub-paragraph were "the expected week of birth of C";
　(ii) sub-paragraph (c) shall read as if the words in that sub-paragraph were "C's date of birth";
　(iii) that paragraph shall apply as if there were also specified a parental statutory declaration by A unless the condition in paragraph (2)(a) or (b) of this regulation is satisfied;
(c) paragraph (4) shall apply as if—

Statutory Shared Parental Pay (Parental Order Cases) Regulations 2014

  (i) sub-paragraph (a) were omitted;
  (ii) there were also specified a copy of C's birth certificate or, if one has not been issued, a written declaration signed by A which states that it has not been issued;
  (iii) where A has not provided a parental statutory declaration as a result of the condition in paragraph (2)(a) of this regulation being satisfied, there were specified a parental statutory declaration.

(2) The conditions referred to in paragraph (1)(b)(iii) and (c)(iii) are—
 (a) that A has given the employer who will be liable to pay statutory shared parental pay (adoption) to A a statutory declaration as evidence of A's entitlement to statutory adoption pay in respect of C in accordance with regulation 24 of the Statutory Paternity Pay and Statutory Adoption Pay (General) Regulations 2002;
 (b) that A is a parental order parent and has given the employer a copy of the order in respect of C made under section 54(1) of the Human Fertilisation and Embryology Act 2008.

7.119 **9.**—In regulation 20 (notification and evidential requirements relating to the partner) of the Pay Regulations as they apply to an intended parent or a parental order parent—
 (a) paragraph (1)(b) shall read as if the words "if C is not placed for adoption by that time as soon as reasonably practicable after the placement of C " were "if C is not born by that time as soon as reasonably practicable after the birth of C";
 (b) in paragraph (3)—
  (i) sub-paragraph (b) shall read as if the words in that sub-paragraph were "the expected week of birth of C";
  (ii) sub-paragraph (c) shall read as if the words in that sub-paragraph were "C's date of birth";
  (iii) sub-paragraph (e) shall read as if the written declaration signed by AP was also required to contain the statement that A and AP are the intended parents or the parental order parents of C;
 (c) paragraph (4) shall apply as if—
  (i) sub-paragraph (a) were omitted; and
  (ii) there were specified a copy of C's birth certificate or, if one has not been issued, a written declaration signed by AP which states that it has not been issued.

7.120 **10.**—(1) The Pay Regulations apply to an intended parent or a parental order parent with the modification provided for in paragraph (2) where—
 (a) one or more of the periods specified in a notice under regulation 19, 20 or 21 of the Pay Regulations during which A or, as the case may be, AP intends to claim statutory shared parental pay (adoption) start in the 8 weeks following the first day of C's expected week of birth;
 (b) C's date of birth is before the first day of the expected week of birth; and
 (c) A or, as the case may be, AP varies by notice under regulation 21(1) the period or periods referred to in sub-paragraph (a) so that that period or those periods start the same length of time following C's date of birth as that period or those periods would have started after the first day of the expected week of birth.

(2) The modification in this paragraph is that the requirement in regula-

tion 21(1) to give notice at least 8 weeks before the first period specified in the notice is satisfied if such notice is given as soon as reasonably practicable after C's date of birth.

(3) The Pay Regulations apply to an intended parent or a parental order parent with the modifications provided for in paragraph (4) where—
(a) C is born more than 8 weeks before the first day of the expected week of birth;
(b) A or, as the case may be, AP has not given the notice and information under regulations 19 or 20 of the Pay Regulations before the date of C's birth; and
(c) A or, as the case may be, AP specifies in a notice under regulations 19 or 20 a period or periods of statutory shared parental pay (adoption) which start in the 8 weeks following C's date of birth.
(4) The modifications in this paragraph are—
(a) in regulation 19—
  (i) paragraph (1)(a) shall read as if the words in that sub-paragraph were—
"paragraphs (2) and (3) as soon as reasonably practicable after the date of C's birth but in any event before the first period specified by A pursuant to paragraph (2)(d) ";
  (ii) paragraph (1)(b) and (c) shall not apply;
  (iii) paragraph (4) shall not apply.
(b) in regulation 20—
  (i) paragraph (1)(a) shall read as if the words in that sub-paragraph were—
"paragraphs (2) and (3) as soon as reasonably practicable after the date of C's birth but in any event before the first period specified by AP pursuant to paragraph (2)(d)";
  (ii) paragraph (1)(b) and (c) shall not apply;
  (iii) paragraph (4) shall not apply.

11.—In regulation 23 (when statutory shared parental pay (adoption) is not to be paid) of the Pay Regulations as they apply to an intended parent or a parental order parent, paragraph (1) shall read—
"Statutory shared parental pay (adoption) is not payable after the day before the date of C's first birthday (or, where more than one child is born of the same pregnancy, the birthday of the first child so born).".

12.—In regulation 24 (work during period of payment of statutory shared parental pay) of the Pay Regulations as they apply to an intended parent or a parental order parent, paragraph (1)(a)(ii) shall read as if the words "the expected week of placement for adoption" read "the expected week of birth".

13.—In regulation 29 (conditions relating to employment and earnings of a claimant's partner) of the Pay Regulations as they apply to an intended parent or a parental order parent, in paragraph (5), the definition of "calculation week" shall read—
""calculation week" means the expected week of birth of C;".

14.—Regulation 31 (conditions as to continuity of employment and normal weekly earnings in relation to a claimant) of the Pay Regulations as they apply to an intended parent or a parental order parent, shall read as if—
(a) the words in paragraph (2) were—
"Where C's birth occurs earlier than the 14th week before C's expected

Statutory Shared Parental Pay (Parental Order Cases) Regulations 2014

week of birth paragraph (1) shall have effect as if, for the conditions set out there, there were substituted conditions that—
(a) the person would have been in employer earner's employment for a continuous period of at least 26 weeks ending with the relevant week had C been born after the relevant week;
(b) the person's normal weekly earnings for the period of eight weeks ending with the week immediately preceding C's actual week of birth are not less than the lower earnings limit in force under section 5(1)(a) of the 1992 Act immediately before the commencement of C's actual week of birth; and
(c) the person continues in employed earner's employment with the employer by reference to whom the condition in sub-paragraph (a) is satisfied for a continuous period beginning with the date of C's birth and ending with the week before the first week falling within the relevant period relating to that person under section 171ZY(2) of the 1992 Act.".
(b) the following paragraphs were added—
"(3) The references in this regulation to the relevant week are to the week immediately preceding the 14th week before C's expected week of birth.
(4) Where more than one child is born as a result of the same pregnancy the date the first child is born is to be used to determine C's actual week of birth or the date of C's birth.".

7.125 **15.**—In regulation 32 (normal weekly earnings of a claimant for statutory shared parental pay) of the Pay Regulations as they apply to an intended parent or a parental order parent, in paragraph (9), sub-paragraph (a), the definition of "the appropriate date" shall read—
""the appropriate date" means the first day of the 14th week before the expected week of the child's birth or the first day in the week in which the child is born, whichever is earlier (but see paragraph (10)).".

7.126 **16.**—In the Schedule (statutory shared parental pay in special circumstances) to the Pay Regulations as they apply to an intended parent or a parental order parent, in paragraph 12—
(a) sub-paragraphs (1) and (2) shall read as if the words "is returned after being placed" (in each place where they occur) read "the parental order does not proceed";
(b) sub-paragraph (4) shall read as if the words in that sub-paragraph were—
"Where more than one child is born of the same pregnancy—
(a) sub-paragraphs (1) and (2) only apply where all the children die or the parental order does not proceed in respect of all the children; and
(b) a reference in this paragraph relating to the death of C (however expressed) is to the death of the last of those children to die.".
(c) sub-paragraph (5) shall read as if the words in that sub-paragraph were—
"For the purpose of this paragraph a parental order does not proceed if—
(a) A and AP have not made an application for an order in respect of C under section 54(1) of the Human Fertilisation and Embryology Act 2008 within the time limit for such an application under section 54(3) of that Act; or
(b) an application made for such an order in respect of C is refused,

Statutory Shared Parental Pay (Persons Abroad and Mariners) Regulations 2014

(SI 2014/3134)

The Secretary of State, in exercise of the powers conferred by sections 171ZZ3(1) and 171ZZ4(3)(b) of the Social Security Contributions and Benefits Act 1992, and with the concurrence of the Treasury, makes the following Regulations.

This instrument contains only regulations made by virtue of, or consequential upon, section 119 of the Children and Families Act 2014 and is made before the end of the period of 6 months beginning with the coming into force of that enactment.

ARRANGEMENT OF REGULATIONS

1. Citation and commencement
2. Interpretation
3. Application
4. Restriction on scope
5. Treatment of persons in other EEA states as employees
6. Treatment of certain persons absent from Great Britain as employees
7. Entitlement to statutory shared parental pay where person has worked in an EEA state
8. Time for compliance with Part 12ZC of the Act or regulations made under it
9. Mariners
10. Continental Shelf
11. Adoptions from overseas
12.–14. Statutory Paternity Pay and Statutory Adoption Pay
Sch.1. Establishments and organisations
Sch.2. Adoptions from Overseas

GENERAL NOTE

These Regulations relate to the treatment under Pt 12ZC of the SSCBA 1992 of persons abroad, persons who work as mariners and persons who work on the continental shelf. The effect is that persons who would otherwise not fulfil the qualifying conditions for entitlement to statutory shared parental pay (ShPP) because of the nature of their employment or the fact that they are outside the United Kingdom will have an entitlement to such pay.

Statutory Shared Parental Pay (Parental Order Cases) Regulations 2014

PART 1

GENERAL

Citation and commencement

7.129   1.—These Regulations may be cited as the Statutory Shared Parental Pay (Persons Abroad and Mariners) Regulations 2014 and come into force on 1st December 2014.

PART 2

STATUTORY SHARED PARENTAL PAY

Interpretation

7.130   2.—(1) In these Regulations—
"the Act" means the Social Security Contributions and Benefits Act 1992;
"adopter", in relation to a child, means the person with whom a child is, or is expected to be, placed for adoption under the law of the United Kingdom;
"adoption from overseas" means the adoption of a child who enters Great Britain from outside the United Kingdom in connection with or for the purposes of adoption which does not involve the placement of the child for adoption under the law of any part of the United Kingdom;
"EEA" means European Economic Area;
"foreign-going ship" means any ship or vessel which is not a home-trade ship;
"General Regulations" means the Statutory Shared Parental Pay (General) Regulations 2014;
"home-trade ship" includes—
(a) every ship or vessel employed in trading or going within the following limits—
   (i) the United Kingdom (including for this purpose the Republic of Ireland),
   (ii) the Channel Islands,
   (iii) the Isle of Man, and
   (iv) the continent of Europe between the river Elbe and Brest inclusive;
(b) every fishing vessel not proceeding beyond the following limits—
   (i) on the South, Latitude 48°30 N,
   (ii) on the West, Longitude 12°W, and
   (iii) on the North, Latitude 61°N;
"mariner" means a person who is or has been in employment under a contract of service either as a master or member of the crew of any ship or vessel, or in any other capacity on board any ship or vessel where—
(a) the employment in that other capacity is for the purposes of that ship or vessel or her crew or any passengers or cargo or mails carried by the ship or vessel; and

(b) the contract is entered into in the United Kingdom with a view to its performance (in whole or in part) while the ship or vessel is on her voyage,

but does not include a person in so far as their employment is as a serving member of the forces;

"placed for adoption" means—
(a) placed for adoption under the Adoption and Children Act 2002 or the Adoption and Children (Scotland) Act 2007; or
(b) placed in accordance with section 22C of the Children Act 1989 with a local authority foster parent who is also a prospective adopter;

"serving member of the forces" means a person, other than one mentioned in Part 2 of Schedule 1, who, being over the age of 16, is a member of any establishment or organisation specified in Part 1 of that Schedule (being a member who gives full pay service) but does not include any such person while absent on desertion;

"statutory shared parental pay (adoption)" means statutory shared parental pay payable where entitlement to that pay arises under regulation 17 or 18 of the General Regulations;

"statutory shared parental pay (birth)" means statutory shared parental pay payable where entitlement to that pay arises under regulation 4 or 5 of the General Regulations.

(2) For the purposes of these regulations, the expressions "ship" and "ship or vessel" include hovercraft, except in regulation 9(2).

(3) For the purposes of these Regulations—
(a) a person is matched with a child for adoption when an adoption agency decides that that person would be a suitable adoptive parent for the child;
(b) in a case where paragraph (a) applies, a person is notified as having been matched with a child on the date that person receives notification of the agency's decision, under regulation 33(3)(a) of the Adoption Agencies Regulations 2005, regulation 28(3) of the Adoption Agencies (Wales) Regulations 2005 or regulation 8(5) of the Adoption Agencies (Scotland) Regulations 2009;
(c) a person is also matched with a child for adoption when a decision has been made in accordance with regulation 22A of the Care Planning, Placement and Case Review (England) Regulations 2010 and an adoption agency has identified that person with whom the child is to be placed in accordance with regulation 12B of the Adoption Agencies Regulations 2005;
(d) in a case where paragraph (c) applies, a person is notified as having been matched with a child on the date on which that person receives notification in accordance with regulation 12B(2)(a) of the Adoption Agencies Regulations 2005.

(4) The reference to "prospective adopter" in the definition of "placed for adoption" in paragraph (1) means a person who has been approved as suitable to adopt a child and has been notified of that decision in accordance with regulation 30B(4) of the Adoption Agencies Regulations 2005.

(5) The reference to "adoption agency" in paragraph (3) has the meaning given, in relation to England and Wales, by section 2 of the Adoption and Children Act 2002 and in relation to Scotland, by section 119(1) of the Adoption and Children (Scotland) Act 2007.

Application

7.131 **3.**—These Regulations apply in relation to—
(a) statutory shared parental pay (birth) in respect of children whose expected week of birth begins on or after 5th April 2015;
(b) statutory shared parental pay (adoption) in respect of children placed for adoption on or after 5th April 2015.

DEFINITIONS

"statutory shared parental pay (adoption)"—reg.2(1).
"statutory shared parental pay (birth)"—reg.2(1).

Restriction on scope

7.132 **4.**—A person who would not be treated under regulation 33 (treatment of persons as employees) of the General Regulations as an employee for the purposes of Part 12ZC (statutory shared parental pay) of the Act if that person's employment were in Great Britain shall not be treated as an employee under these Regulations.

DEFINITION

"General Regulations"—reg.2(1).

Treatment of persons in other EEA states as employees

7.133 **5.**—A person who is—
(a) gainfully employed in an EEA state other than the United Kingdom in such circumstances that, if the employment were in Great Britain, the person would be an employee for the purposes of Part 12ZC of the Act, or a person treated as such an employee under regulation 33 of the General Regulations; and
(b) subject to the legislation of the United Kingdom under Council Regulation (EEC) No.1408/71,
notwithstanding that person not being employed in Great Britain, shall be treated as an employee for the purposes of Parts 12ZC of the Act.

DEFINITIONS

"EEA"—reg.2(1).
"General Regulations"—reg.2(1).

Treatment of certain persons absent from Great Britain as employees

7.134 **6.**—Subject to regulation 9(2), where a person, while absent from Great Britain for any purpose, is gainfully employed by an employer who is liable to pay secondary Class 1 contributions (within the meaning of section 1(2) of the Act) in respect of that person's employment under section 6 of the Act or regulation 146 of the Social Security Contributions Regulations 2001, that person shall be treated as an employee for the purposes of Part 12ZC of the Act.

(SI 2014/3134 reg.2)

Entitlement to statutory shared parental pay where person has worked in an EEA state

7.—(1) A person who—
(a) is an employee or treated as an employee under regulation 5;
(b) in the week immediately preceding the 14th week before the expected week of the child's birth was in employed earner's employment with an employer in Great Britain; and
(c) had in any week within the period of 26 weeks immediately preceding that week been employed by the same employer in another EEA state,

shall be treated for the purposes of section 171ZU of the Act (entitlement to shared parental pay: birth) as having been employed in employed earner's employment with an employer in those weeks in which the person was so employed in the other EEA state.

(2) A person who—
(a) is an employee or treated as an employee under regulation 5;
(b) in the week in which the adopter is notified of having been matched with the child for the purposes of adoption was in employed earner's employment with an employer in Great Britain; and
(c) had in any week within the period of 26 weeks immediately preceding that week been employed by the same employer in another EEA State,

shall be treated for the purposes of section 171ZV of the Act (entitlement to shared parental pay: adoption) as having been employed in employed earner's employment in those weeks in which the person was so employed in the other EEA State.

DEFINITIONS

"EEA"—reg.2(1).
"statutory shared parental pay (adoption)"—reg.2(1).
"statutory shared parental pay (birth)"—reg.2(1).

Time for compliance with Part 12ZC of the Act or regulations made under it

8.—Where—
(a) a person is outside the United Kingdom;
(b) Part 12ZC of the Act or regulations made under it require any act to be done forthwith or on the happening of a certain event or within a specified time; and
(c) because the person is outside the United Kingdom that person or that person's employer cannot comply with the requirement,

the person or the employer, as the case may be, shall be deemed to have complied with the requirement if the act is performed as soon as reasonably practicable.

Mariners

9.—(1) A mariner engaged in employment on board a home-trade ship with an employer who has a place of business within the United Kingdom shall be treated as an employee for the purposes of Part 12ZC of the Act, notwithstanding that he may not be employed in Great Britain.

(2) A mariner who is engaged in employment—
(a) on a foreign-going ship; or
(b) on a home-trade ship with an employer who does not have a place of business within the United Kingdom,

shall not be treated as an employee for the purposes of Part 12ZC of the Act, notwithstanding that the mariner may have been employed in Great Britain.

DEFINITIONS

"foreign-going ship"—reg.2(1).
"home-trade ship"—reg.2(1).
"mariner"—reg.2(1).

Continental shelf

10.—(1) In this regulation—
"designated area" means any area which may from time to time be designated by Order in Council under section 1(7) of the Continental Shelf Act 1964 as an area within which the rights of the United Kingdom with respect to the seabed and subsoil and their natural resources may be exercised;
"prescribed employment" means any employment (whether under a contract of service or not) in a designated area in connection with continental shelf operations, as defined in section 120(2) of the Act.
(2) A person in prescribed employment shall be treated as an employee for the purposes of Part 12ZC of the Act notwithstanding that that person may not be employed in Great Britain.

Adoptions from overseas

11.—Schedule 2 applies to adoptions from overseas.

PART 3

STATUTORY PATERNITY PAY AND STATUTORY ADOPTION PAY

12.—The Statutory Paternity Pay and Statutory Adoption Pay (Persons Abroad and Mariners) Regulations 2002 are amended as follows.

13.—(1) Paragraph (2) of regulation 1 is amended as follows
(2) For the definition "adopter" substitute—
""adopter", in relation to a child, means the person with whom a child is, or is expected to be, placed for adoption under the law of the United Kingdom;".
(3) Before the definition of "serving member of the forces" insert—
""placed for adoption" means—
(a) placed for adoption under the Adoption and Children Act 2002 or the Adoption and Children (Scotland) Act 2007; or

(SI 2014/3134 reg. 8)

(b) placed in accordance with section 22C of the Children Act 1989 with a local authority foster parent who is also a prospective adopter;".

14.—For paragraph (3) of regulation 1 substitute—

"(3) For the purposes of these Regulations—
(a) a person is matched with a child for adoption when an adoption agency decides that that person would be a suitable adoptive parent for the child;
(b) in a case where paragraph (a) applies, a person is notified as having been matched with a child on the date that person receives notification of the agency's decision, under regulation 33(3)(a) of the Adoption Agencies Regulations 2005, regulation 28(3) of the Adoption Agencies (Wales) Regulations 2005 or regulation 8(5) of the Adoption Agencies (Scotland) Regulations 2009;
(c) a person is also matched with a child for adoption when a decision has been made in accordance with regulation 22A of the Care Planning, Placement and Case Review (England) Regulations 2010 and an adoption agency has identified that person with whom the child is to be placed in accordance with regulation 12B of the Adoption Agencies Regulations 2005;
(d) in a case where paragraph (c) applies, a person is notified as having been matched with a child on the date on which that person receives notification in accordance with regulation 12B(2)(a) of the Adoption Agencies Regulations 2005.

(3A) The reference to "prospective adopter" in the definition of "placed for adoption" in paragraph (2) means a person who has been approved as suitable to adopt a child and has been notified of that decision in accordance with regulation 30B(4) of the Adoption Agencies Regulations 2005.

(3B) The reference to "adoption agency" in paragraph (3) has the meaning given, in relation to England and Wales, by section 2 of the Adoption and Children Act 2002 and in relation to Scotland, by section 119(1) of the Adoption and Children (Scotland) Act 2007.".

SCHEDULE 1   Regulation 2(1)

PART 1

Establishments and organisations
1. Any of the regular, naval, military or air forces of the Crown.
2. Royal Fleet Reserve.
3. Royal Naval Reserve.
4. Royal Marines Reserve.
5. Army Reserve.
6. Territorial Army.
7. Royal Air Force Reserve.
8. Royal Auxiliary Air Force.
9. The Royal Irish Regiment, to the extent that its members are not members of any force falling within paragraph 1.

Part 2

Establishments And Organisations Of Which Her Majesty's Forces Shall Not Consist

7.143　10.—Her Majesty's forces shall not be taken to consist of any of the establishments or organisations specified in Part 1 of this Schedule by virtue only of the employment in such establishment or organisation of the following persons –
  (a) any person who is serving as a member of any naval force of Her Majesty's forces and who (not having been an insured person under the National Insurance Act 1965 and not being a contributor under the Social Security Act 1975 or the Social Security Contributions and Benefits Act 1992) locally entered that force at an overseas base;
  (b) any person who is serving as a member of any military force of Her Majesty's forces and who entered that force, or was recruited for that force outside the United Kingdom, and the depot of whose unit is situated outside the United Kingdom;
  (c) any person who is serving as a member of any air force of Her Majesty's forces and who entered that force, or was recruited for that force, outside the United Kingdom, and is liable under the terms of his engagement to serve only in a specified part of the world outside the United Kingdom.

SCHEDULE 2　　　　　　　　　　　　　　　　Regulation 11

Adoptions from Overseas

Interpretation

7.144　1.—In this Schedule "the Application Regulations" means the Social Security Contributions and Benefits Act 1992 (Application of Parts 12ZA, 12ZB and 12ZC to Adoptions from Overseas) Regulations 2003.

Application to adoptions from overseas

7.145　2.—(1) The provisions of these Regulations, in so far as they apply to statutory shared parental pay (adoption) apply to adoptions from overseas with the modifications set out in paragraphs 3 to 6 and subject to sub-paragraphs (2) and (3).
　(2) Any references in these Regulations to the provisions of Part 12ZC of the Act must be construed as references to the provisions of Part 12ZC as modified by the Application Regulations.

Modifications of the Regulations for the purposes of adoptions from overseas

7.146　3.—The Regulations are modified as follows.
7.147　4.—(1) Regulation 2 (interpretation) is modified as follows.
　(2) In paragraph 1—
　　(a) for the definition of "adopter" substitute—
""adopter", in relation to C, means the person by whom C has been or is to be adopted; ";
　　(b) for the definition of "statutory shared parental pay (adoption)" substitute—
""statutory shared parental pay (adoption)" means statutory shared parental pay payable where entitlement to that pay arises under regulation 17 or 18 of the General Regulations as modified by the Statutory Shared Parental Pay (Adoption from Overseas) Regulations 2014;";
　　(c) insert the following definitions in the appropriate places alphabetically—
""enter Great Britain" means enter Great Britain from outside the United Kingdom in connection with or for the purposes of adoption;";
""official notification" means written notification, issued by or on behalf of the relevant

central authority, that it is prepared to issue a certificate to the overseas authority concerned with the adoption of the child, or that it has issued a certificate and sent it to that authority, confirming, in either case, that the adopter is eligible to adopt, and has been assessed and approved as being a suitable adoptive parent;";

""relevant central authority" means—
- (a) in the case of an adopter to whom Part 3 of the Adoptions with a Foreign Element Regulations 2005 apply and who is habitually resident in Wales, the Welsh Ministers;
- (b) in the case of an adopter to whom the Adoptions with a Foreign Element (Scotland) Regulations 2009 apply and who is habitually resident in Scotland, the Scottish Ministers; and
- (c) in any other case, the Secretary of State;".

5.—In Regulation 3 (application), for paragraph (1)(b) substitute—

"(b)statutory shared parental pay (adoption) in respect of children who enter Great Britain on or after 5th April 2015.".

6.—(1) In regulation 7 (entitlement to shared parental pay where person has worked in an EEA State), for paragraph (2) substitute—

"(2) A person who—
- (a) is an employee or treated as an employee under regulation 5;
- (b) in the week in which the adopter received the official notification was in employed earner's employment with an employer in Great Britain; and
- (c) had in any week within the period of 26 weeks immediately preceding that week been employed by the same employer in another EEA State,

shall be treated for the purposes of section 171ZV of the Act (entitlement to shared parental pay: adoption) as modified by the Application Regulations as having been employed in employed earner's employment in those weeks in which the person was so employed in the other EEA State.".

PART VIII

CHILD TRUST FUNDS

Child Trust Funds Act 2004 (Commencement No.1) Order 2004

(SI 2004/2422)

The Treasury, in exercise of the powers conferred upon them by section 27 of the Child Trust Funds Act 2004, make the following Order:

ARRANGEMENT OF ARTICLES

1. Citation and interpretation
2. Commencement of certain provisions of the Act

Citation and interpretation

1.—(1) This Order may be cited as the Child Trust Funds Act 2004 (Commencement No.1) Order 2004.

(2) In this Order—

"account" means an account which (from the appointed day) is capable of being a child trust fund (within the meaning in the Act);

"the Act" means the Child Trust Funds Act 2004;

"the appointed day" means the day appointed under section 27 of the Act for the purposes of sections 8 and 9 of the Act.

Commencement of certain provisions of the Act

2. The following provisions of the Act shall come into force on 1st January 2005 for the purposes mentioned in relation to each provision:

Provision	Purposes
Section 1(3) of the Act	All purposes
Section 3(1) and (3) of the Act	All purposes (save that an account may only be a child trust fund from the appointed day)
Section 3(2), (4) to (9) and (12) of the Act	To allow accounts to be opened, and contracts with an account provider for their management to be signed, save that the account is only to be: (a) a child trust fund, or (b) subscribed to and operated, from the appointed day.
Section 5(1) and (2) of the Act	To ensure an orderly introduction of accounts, by issuing some vouchers before the appointed day.
Section 5(3) to (5) of the Act	Where a voucher has been issued before the appointed day under section 5(1) of the Act, to allow

Child Trust Funds Act 2004 (Commencement No.1) Order 2004

Provision	Purposes
	accounts to be opened, save that the account is only to be: (a) a child trust fund, or (b) subscribed to and operated, from that day.
Section 15(1), (2)(a) and (3) of the Act	So far as those provisions relate to the persons referred to in section 15(2)(a) of the Act
Section 17 of the Act	All purposes
Section 18 of the Act	All purposes
Section 20(1) (except paragraphs (b) and (c)), (2) to (6), (7) (except paragraph (c)), (8) and (9) of the Act	All purposes (except for the purposes of sections 6, 7, 9, 10 or 13 of the Act)
Section 21 of the Act	For the purposes of the provisions of section 20 of the Act which are commenced by this Order
Section 22(1) and (6) of the Act	All purposes
Section 23(1) to (3) of the Act	For the purposes of section 22(1) and (6) of the Act
Section 24(1) (except paragraph (c)), (2) and (3) of the Act	For the purposes of section 22(1) and (6) of the Act
Section 24(5) to (7) of the Act	All purposes

Child Trust Funds Act 2004 (Commencement No.2) Order 2004

(SI 2004/3369)

The Treasury, in exercise of the powers conferred upon them by section 27 of the Child Trust Funds Act 2004, make the following Order:

Arrangement of Articles

1. Citation and interpretation
2. Commencement of provisions of the Act

Citation and interpretation

8.3   **1.**—(1) This Order may be cited as the Child Trust Funds Act 2004 (Commencement No.2) Order 2004.
(2) In this Order—
"the Act" means the Child Trust Funds Act 2004;

(SI 2004/3369 reg.1)

"the earlier Order" means the Child Trust Funds Act 2004 (Commencement No. 1) Order 2004.

Commencement of provisions of the Act

2.—(1) Sections 1 to 24 of the Act shall come into force on 6th April 2005, subject to the following paragraphs.

(2) Paragraph (1) does not apply to provisions brought into force for all purposes by the earlier Order.

(3) Section 23(1) of the Act shall come into force for all purposes on 1st January 2005.

(4) Where a provision of the Act (other than section 23(1)) was partially brought into force by the earlier Order, that provision shall come into force for all other purposes on 6th April 2005.

Child Trust Funds Regulations 2004

(SI 2004/1450) (AS AMENDED)

ARRANGEMENT OF REGULATIONS

PART 1

Introductory

1. Citation and commencement
2. Interpretation
3. Vouchers
4. Descriptions of accounts
5. Opening of account by responsible person or the child
6. Opening of account by Inland Revenue—(Revenue allocated accounts)
7. Government contributions
7A. *(repealed)*
7B. Yearly disability payments

PART 2

Other requirements to be satisfied in relation to accounts

8. General requirements for accounts
9. Annual limit on subscriptions
10. Statements for an account
11. General investment rules
12. Qualifying investments for an account
13. Conditions for application by responsible person or the child to open an account (and changes to an account)
14. Account provider—qualifications and Board's approval
15. Account provider—appointment of tax representative
16. Account provider—withdrawal by Board of approval

17. Account provider—appeal against non-approval or withdrawal of Board's approval
18. Permitted withdrawals from an account
18A. Permitted withdrawals from an account where the child is terminally ill
19. Account provider's intention to make a bulk transfer of accounts or to cease to act as an account provider
19A. Account provider ceasing to accept Revenue allocated accounts
20. Account provider ceasing to qualify
20A. Transfers to other accounts for children
21. Transfer of accounts to other account providers
22. Recoupment of Inland Revenue contributions to void accounts (and other accounts)
23. "Repair" of invalid accounts

PART 3

Tax and administration of accounts

24. Exemption from tax of account income and gains
25. Tax liabilities and reliefs—account provider to act on behalf of the named child
26. Repayments in respect of tax to account provider—interim tax claims
27. Repayments in respect of tax to account provider—annual tax claims
28. Account provider's tax claims—supplementary provisions
29. Assessments for withdrawing relief and recovering tax
30. Fortnightly claim and financial returns
31. Records to be kept by account provider
32. Returns of information by account provider
33. Information about "looked after children" from Local Authorities
33A. The Official Solicitor or Accountant of Court to be the person who has the authority to manage an account
34. *(repealed)*
35. *(repealed)*
36. Capital gains tax—adaptation of enactments
37. Administration of tax in relation to accounts—supplementary
38. Application of the provisions of Chapter 2 of Part 13 of the Taxes Act and of Chapter 9 of Part 4 of ITTOIA 2005 to policies

Schedule — Stakeholder Accounts
Description of stakeholder account
Characteristics of stakeholder account etc
Stakeholder accounts—charges etc

The Treasury, in exercise of the powers conferred upon them by sections 3(1) to (5) and (7), 5(1), (4) and (5), 6, 7, 8(1), 9(2) and (10)(b), 11(1), 12(2), 13, 15, 16, 23(1) and 28(1) to (4) of the Child Trust Funds Act 2004, hereby make the following Regulations:

(SI 2004/1450 reg.1) (as amended)

PART 1

INTRODUCTORY

Citation and commencement

1. These Regulations may be cited as the Child Trust Funds Regulations 2004 and shall come into force for the purposes of—
   (a) issuing vouchers (see regulation 3),
   (b) completing account-opening formalities (see regulation 5),
   (c) applications under regulation 13 to open an account with effect from the appointed day,
   (d) applications under regulation 14 to be approved as an account provider to manage accounts from the appointed day,
   (e) regulation 17, so far as it relates to applications referred to in paragraph (d), [¹ . . .]
   (f) [¹ . . .]
on 1st January 2005, and for all other purposes on the appointed day.

AMENDMENT

1. Child Trust Funds (Amendment) Regulations 2013 (SI 2013/263) reg.2(4)(a) (March 16, 2013).

Interpretation

2.—(1) In these Regulations—
  (a) the following expressions have the meanings given in the Child Trust Funds Act 2004 ("the Act")—
   "child"
   "child trust fund"
   "eligible child"
   [⁵ "the income threshold" (see section 9(6) of the Act)]
   "Inland Revenue"
   "Inland Revenue contributions" (see section 11(2) of the Act),
   "parental responsibility" (see section 3(9) of the Act);
   [⁵ "the relevant income" (see section 9(6) of the Act)]
   "relevant person" (see section 15(2) of the Act),
   [⁵ "relevant social security benefit" (see section 9(6) of the Act)]
   "responsible person", in relation to a child under 16 (see section 3(8) of the Act),
   [⁵ "tax year" (see section 9(6) of the Act)]
   "the person entitled to child benefit in respect of the child" (see section 2(1)(a), (4) and (6) of the Act);
  (b) except where the context otherwise requires—
   "account" means a scheme of investment which (except in regulation 22(1)) qualifies as a child trust fund, other than in the cases of—
     (i) an account with a deposit-taker,
     (ii) a share or deposit account with a building society, or
     (iii) a deposit account with a person falling within [¹² section 991(2) of the Income Tax Act 2007], or a [⁶ credit union];

Child Trust Funds Regulations 2004

an "account investment" is an investment under the account which is a qualifying investment for an account within the meaning of regulation 12;

an "account provider" is a person who fulfils the conditions of these Regulations and is approved by the Board for the purpose of these Regulations as an account provider;

[6 "adoption order" has the meaning in section 46(1) of the Adoption and Children Act 2002 or section 28 of the Adoption and Children (Scotland) Act 2007 or of "Adoption Order" in Article 2(2) of the Adoption (Northern Ireland) Order 1987, as the case may be, and includes any corresponding order under the Adoption (Scotland) Act 1978, and any order of a court in the Isle of Man or any of the Channel Islands which, under section 108 of the Adoption and Children Act 2002, is declared to correspond to an adoption order made under that Act;]

"appointed day" means the day appointed, under section 27 of the Act, for the purposes of sections 8 and 9 of the Act;

"assurance undertaking" has the meaning in Article 2 of the Council Directive of 5th November 2002 concerning life assurance (2002/83/EC);

[1"Bank of England base rate" means the rate announced from time to time by the Monetary Policy Committee of the Bank of England as the official dealing rate, being the rate at which the Bank is willing to enter into transactions for providing short-term liquidity in the money markets;]

[3"the Board" means the Commissioners for Her Majesty's Revenue and Customs;]

"building society" means a building society within the meaning of the Building Societies Act 1986, or the Irish Building Societies Act 1989;

[4"building society bonus", except in regulation 24(a)(i), excludes any bonus, distribution of funds or the conferring of rights in relation to shares—
(a) in connection with an amalgamation, transfer of engagements or transfer of business of a building society, and
(b) mentioned in section 96 or 100 of the Building Societies Act 1986,
and "payment under a building society bonus scheme" shall be construed accordingly;]

"company", except in regulation 12(4)(a), means any body corporate having a share capital other than—
  (i) an open-ended investment company, within the meaning given by section 236 of the Financial Services and Markets Act 2000,
  (ii) a UCITS,
  (iii) [13 a registered society], or
  (iv) a body corporate which is a 51 per cent. subsidiary of any [13 registered society];

[2"credit union" means a society registered as a credit union under the Industrial and Provident Societies Act 1965 or the Credit Unions (Northern Ireland) Order 1985;]

"deposit-taker" has the meaning given by [6 section 853 (as extended under section 854) of ITA 2007];

(SI 2004/1450 reg.2) (as amended)

"the Director of Savings" has the same meaning as in the National Debt Act 1972;
"the Distance Marketing Directive" means Directive 2002/65/EC of the European Parliament and of the Council of 23rd September 2002, and includes any provisions by which an EEA State or the United Kingdom has transposed the Directive or has corresponding obligations in its domestic law, and "distance contract" has the meaning in that Directive;
"electronic communications" includes any communications by means of a telecommunication system (within the meaning in the Telecommunications Act 1984);
[[10] "EEA Agreement" means the agreement on the European Economic Area signed at Oporto on 2nd May 1992, together with the Protocol adjusting that Agreement signed at Brussels on 17th March 1993, as modified or supplemented from time to time;
"EEA State", in relation to any time, means a state which at that time is a member State, or any other state which at that time is a party to the EEA Agreement;]
"European institution" means an EEA firm of the kind mentioned in [[12] paragraph 5(a) to (d), (f) and (h)] of Schedule 3 to the Financial Services and Markets Act 2000 which is an authorised person for the purposes of that Act as a result of qualifying for authorisation under paragraph 12 [[12] (1) to (4) and (7)] of that Schedule;
"51 per cent. subsidiary" and "75 per cent. subsidiary" have the meanings given by section 838 of the Taxes Act;
[[6] "FISMA 2000" means the Financial Services and Markets Act 2000(**9**)";
"gains", except in regulations 22(1) to (3), 24(a)(ii), (iii) and (v), 37(5) and 38, means "chargeable gains" within the meaning in the 1992 Act;
"gilt-edged securities" has the meaning given by paragraphs 1 and 1A of Schedule 9 to the 1992 Act;
[[6] "guardian" means a guardian of a child within the meaning in section 5 of the Children Act 1989, section 7 of the Children (Scotland) Act 1995 or Article 2(2) of the Children (Northern Ireland) Order 1995, as the case may be;]
"incorporated friendly society" means a society incorporated under the Friendly Societies Act 1992;
[[13] . . .];
"investments under the account" has the same meaning as investments under a child trust fund in the Act;
[[12] "investment trust" refers to a company that is such a trust for the purposes of the Corporation Tax Acts(2), or would be such a trust but for section 1158(3) of the Corporation Tax Act 2010;]
[[6] "ITA 2007" means the Income Tax Act 2007;]
[[6] "ITTOIA 2005" means the Income Tax (Trading and Other Income) Act 2005;]
"the Management Act" means the Taxes Management Act 1970;
"market value" shall be construed in accordance with section 272 of the 1992 Act;
[[3][[6] . . .];

[9 "non-UCITS retail scheme"—
(a) has the meaning in COLL (that is, a scheme to which, or to whose authorised fund manager and depositary, sections 5.1, 5.4 and 5.6 of COLL apply),
(b) includes a "recognised scheme" by virtue of section 270 or 272 of FISMA 2000, which would fall within paragraph (a) of this definition if it were an authorised fund, and
(c) includes a sub-fund of an umbrella which the terms of the scheme identify as a sub-fund which would fall within paragraph (a) or (b) of this definition if it were itself an authorised fund or a recognised scheme.

In this definition, expressions defined in the Glossary of the Financial Conduct Authority Handbook have those defined meanings;]

"the 1992 Act" means the Taxation of Chargeable Gains Act 1992;

"notice" except in regulations 12(12) and 37(6)(a), means notice in writing;

[3"qualifying units in or shares of a non-UCITS retail scheme" means that—
(a) the instrument constituting the scheme secures that redemption of the units or shares in question shall take place no less frequently than bi-monthly (see [9section] 6.2.16(6) of the [6. . .] [9 COLL] omitting the words "Except where (7) applies, and", read with [9section] 6.3.4(1), whether or not those [9sections] apply to the scheme), and
(b) a provision for suspension of dealings in exceptional conditions in accordance with [9section] 7.2 of [9 the COLL] (or any foreign procedure which is a direct foreign equivalent of that [9section]) shall not be treated as a provision contrary to paragraph (a) of this definition;]

"recognised stock exchange" has the same meaning as in [10 section 1005 of ITA 2007]

"registered friendly society" has the meaning given by the Friendly Societies Act 1992 and includes any society that by virtue of section 96(2) of that Act is to be treated as a registered friendly society;

[13 "registered society" means—
(a) a registered society within the meaning given by section 1(1) of the Co-operative and Community Benefit Societies Act 2014; or
(b) a society registered or deemed to be registered under the Industrial and Provident Societies Act (Northern Ireland) 1969;]

[6 "relevant authorised person" means a firm mentioned in section 697(2)(b) of ITTOIA 2005];

[6. . .]

"security" means any loan stock or similar security of a company whether secured or unsecured;

[6 "special guardian" has the meaning in section 14A of the Children Act 1989;]

"subscriptions" has the meaning in section 12(1) of the Act (but excluding Inland Revenue contributions and income or gains arising from investments under the account);

(SI 2004/1450 reg.2) (as amended)

"tax" where neither income tax nor capital gains tax is specified means either of those taxes;

"the Taxes Act" means the Income and Corporation Taxes Act 1988;

"year", except in the expression "subscription year" in regulations 9, 21(5)(b) and 32(2)(b)(iv), means a year of assessment (within the meaning in section 832(1) of the Taxes Act, or section 288(1) of the 1992 Act, as the case may be);

(c) "authorised fund" means—
  (i) an authorised unit trust, or
  (ii) an open-ended investment company [6. . .] in the case of which an authorisation order made [9. . .] under regulation 14 of the Open-Ended Investment Companies Regulations 2001 is in force;

"authorised unit trust" means a unit trust scheme in the case of which an authorisation order made [9. . .] under section 243 of the Financial Services and Markets Act 2000 is in force;

[9 "COLL" means the Collective Investment Schemes Sourcebook made by the Financial Conduct Authority under FISMA 2000;]

"depositary interest" means the rights of the person mentioned in paragraph (ii), under a certificate or other record (whether or not in the form of a document) acknowledging—
  (i) that a person holds relevant investments or evidence of the right to them, and
  (ii) that another person is entitled to rights in or in relation to those or identical relevant investments, including the right to receive such investments, or evidence of the right to them or the proceeds from such investments, from the person mentioned in paragraph (i),

where "relevant investments" means investments which are exclusively qualifying investments for an account falling within regulation 12(2)(a) to (i), and the rights mentioned in paragraph (ii) are exclusively rights in or in relation to relevant investments;

[7. . .]

[7 "insolvency event" means the procedures listed in the definition of "insolvency event" in regulation 19(15) of the Payment Services Regulations 2009;]

"open-ended investment company" [7 means a company to which section 236 of FISMA 2000 applies], and "shares" in relation to an open-ended investment company, includes shares of any class and of any denomination of a given class and, in relation to a part of an umbrella company, means shares in the company which confer for the time being rights in that part;

[7 "recognised UCITS" means—
(a) a collective investment scheme constituted in an EEA State, which is a "recognised scheme" under section 264 of FISMA 2000, and complies with the requirements to be a "UCITS scheme" for the purposes of the [9COLL], or
(b) a part of a recognised UCITS mentioned in paragraph (a) of this definition, which would be a sub-fund of an umbrella scheme which is a recognised UCITS;]

[7. . .]

[⁷ "UK UCITS" means—
(a) a collective investment scheme [⁹ with Part 4A permission under FISMA 2000], which complies with the requirements to be a "UCITS scheme" for the purposes of [⁹ COLL], or
(b) a part of a UK UCITS mentioned in paragraph (a) of this definition which would be a sub-fund of an umbrella scheme which is a UK UCITS;]
"umbrella scheme" means an authorised fund which according to the terms of the scheme is an umbrella scheme belonging to the category under that name established by the [⁹ Financial Conduct Authority], and—
  (i) in the case of an authorised fund which is an authorised unit trust, references to a part of an umbrella scheme shall be construed in accordance with subsection (8) of section 468 of the Taxes Act, [⁷ and paragraphs (6) and (7) of regulation 7 of the Authorised Investment Funds (Tax) Regulations 2006 shall apply for the purposes of these Regulations as they apply for the purposes of those Regulations]
  (ii) in the case of an authorised fund which is an open-ended investment company, references to a part of an umbrella scheme shall be construed in accordance with [⁷ subsection (4) of section 468A of the Taxes Act, and paragraphs (2) and (3) of regulation 7 of the Authorised Investment Funds (Tax) Regulations 2006 shall apply for the purposes of these Regulations as they apply for the purposes of those Regulations];
[⁷. . .]
"units", in relation to an authorised unit trust, means the rights or interests (however described) of the unit holders in that unit trust and, in relation to a part of an umbrella scheme, means the rights or interests for the time being of the unit holders in that part;
[⁷ "units in, or shares of, a UK UCITS or recognised UCITS" means the rights (however described) of the holders of the units or shares in that UK UCITS or recognised UCITS;]
[⁷. . .]
[¹¹ (1A) In these Regulations-
(a) a "bulk transfer of accounts" occurs where two or more accounts are transferred, without a break in the management of the accounts, by an account provider ("the transferor") direct to another account provider ("the transferee")—
  (i) pursuant to an agreement made between the transferor and the transferee where the transfers are not made pursuant to requests made by the person who is the registered contact in relation to the accounts transferred; or
  (ii) pursuant to an insurance business transfer scheme or a banking business transfer scheme under Part 7 (Control of Business Transfers) of FISMA 2000;
(b) [¹⁴. . .]
(c) [¹⁴. . .]
(2) The table below indexes other definitions in these Regulations—

(SI 2004/1450 reg.2) (as amended)

Term defined	Regulation
"the applicant"	5
"the commencement date"	7(8)
"description" of an account	4
"the disqualifying circumstances"	16
[⁸...]	[⁸...]
[⁸...]	[⁸...]
"initial contribution"	7(1)
"interim tax claim"	26(2)
"local authority"	33(1)
"looked after child"	33(1)
"management agreement"	5
"the named child"	5 and 8(1)
"qualifying circumstances"	14
"qualifying investments for an account"	12
"registered contact"	8(1)(d)
[⁸...]	[⁸...]
"special contribution"	7(1)
"subscription year"	9(2)
"supplementary contribution"	7(5)
"the termination event"	12(12)
"the transfer instructions"	8(2)(h)
"the internal transfer instructions"	8(2)(i)

AMENDMENTS

1. Child Trust Funds (Amendment) Regulations 2004 (SI 2004/2676) reg.3 (April 6, 2005).
2. Child Trust Funds (Amendment No.2) Regulations 2005 (SI 2005/909) reg.3 (April 6, 2005).
3. Child Trust Funds (Amendment No.3) Regulations 2005 (SI 2005/3349) reg.3 (December 27, 2005).
4. Child Trust Funds (Amendment No.3) Regulations 2006 (SI 2006/3195) reg.3 (January 1, 2007).
5. Child Trust Funds (Amendment) Regulations 2009 (SI 2009/475) reg.3 (April 6, 2009, but have effect where the Child Benefit commencement date for the child (first day for which child benefit was paid in respect of the child) is on or after April 6, 2008).
6. Child Trust Funds (Amendment) Regulations 2010 (SI 2010/582) reg.3(1) (April 6, 2010).
7. Child Trust Funds (Amendment) Regulations 2010 (SI 2010/582) reg.3(2) (April 6, 2010).
8. Child Trust Funds (Amendment) Regulations 2013 (SI 2013/263) reg.2(4)(b) (March 16, 2013).
9. Financial Services Act 2012 (Consequential Amendments and Transitional Provisions) Order 2013 (SI 2013/472) art.3 and Sch.2 para.93(a) and (b) (April 1, 2013).
10. Child Trust Funds (Amendment No. 2) Regulations 2013 (SI 2013/1744) reg.3 (August 5, 2013).
11. Child Trust Funds (Amendment No. 2) Regulations 2013 (SI 2013/1744) reg.4 (August 5, 2013).
12. Child Trust Funds (Amendment) Regulations 2014 (SI 2014/649) reg.3 (April 6, 2014).
13. Co-operative and Community Benefit Societies and Credit Unions Act 2010

(Consequential Amendments) Regulations 2014 (SI 2014/1815) reg.2 and Sch. para.13 (August 1, 2014).

14. Child Trust Funds (Amendment No.2) Regulations 2015 (SI 2015/876) regs. 2 and 3 (April 6, 2015).

Vouchers

3.—(1) The voucher to be issued under section 5(1) of the Act shall contain the following particulars—
(a) the full name of the child,
(b) his date of birth,
(c) his unique reference number,
(d) the [² short expiry date] of the voucher, and
(e) the amount of the initial contribution (see regulation 7(1)),
and a statement that the voucher cannot be exchanged for money.

(2) The voucher shall be sent to the person who is entitled to child benefit in respect of the child (or, in the case of a child who is an eligible child because of section 2(3) of the Act, to a responsible person in relation to the child) by post.

(3) The expiry date [¹. . .] shall be whichever is the earlier of—
(a) the date 12 months from the date of issue of the voucher, or
(b) where the child is over 17 years of age, the date on which he will attain the age of 18 years.

[² (4) But for references in these Regulations to the short expiry date of the voucher paragraph (3) applies with "60 days" instead of "12 months".]

AMENDMENTS

1. Child Trust Funds (Amendment) Regulations 2006 (SI 2006/199) reg.3 (February 7, 2006).
2. Child Trust Funds (Amendment No.3) Regulations 2011 (SI 2011/2447) reg.3 (November 1, 2011).

DEFINITIONS

"child"—see reg.2(1)(a).
"eligible child"—see *ibid*.
"responsible person"—see *ibid*.

Descriptions of accounts

4.—(1) An account may be of either of the following descriptions—

Stakeholder account

Where the account meets the characteristics and conditions in the Schedule to these Regulations.

Non-stakeholder account

Where any of those characteristics or conditions is not met.

(2) Accounts opened by the Inland Revenue (see regulation 6) must be stakeholder accounts.

DEFINITION

"account"—see reg.2(1)(b).

(SI 2004/1450 reg.5) (as amended)

Opening of account by responsible person or the child

5.—(1) For the purposes of these Regulations, subject to [¹paragraphs (1A) and (2)], an account is opened for a child ("the named child") with an account provider on the date the last of the following conditions is satisfied (in any order), where "the applicant" means—
- (a) if the named child is 16 or over, the child; and
- (b) in any other case, a responsible person in relation to the named child.

Condition 1

The applicant gives the voucher relating to the named child to the account provider [¹not later than 7 days after its [³ short expiry date] [² or, where the account provider has chosen to open accounts without sight of the relevant voucher, the applicant gives the following information to the account provider:
- (a) the [³ short expiry date] of the voucher,
- (b) the amount of the initial contribution as specified on the voucher, and
- (c) where the date of birth shown on the voucher differs from the actual date of birth of the child (see regulation 13(5)(c)), the date of birth shown on the voucher]

Condition 2

The applicant enters into an agreement with the account provider (the "management agreement") for the management of the account (see regulation 8(1) and (2)), which includes the application and declaration required by regulation 13.

Condition 3

Where that application is not in writing the applicant has agreed, or is treated as having agreed, the contents of the copy of the declaration required by regulation 13(3).

Condition 4

- (a) In any case where the management agreement is a distance contract, the agreement must be an initial service agreement for the purposes of the Distance Marketing Directive, and contain the instructions required by regulation 8(1)(f), and
- (b) in every case where there is any right to cancel (or automatic cancellation of) the management agreement, the period during which it may be exercised or occur has expired without that right being exercised or cancellation occurring.

(2) An account must satisfy the requirements that—
- (a) no subscription to the account is accepted by the account provider until the account has been opened in accordance with paragraph (1); and
- (b) where the account is so opened before the appointed day, it shall not be treated as open for the purpose of accepting subscriptions until the appointed day.

[¹(1A) The application to open the account must be made, and Condition 2 satisfied, not later than the [³ short expiry date] of the voucher.]

8.10

AMENDMENTS

1. Child Trust Funds (Amendment) Regulations 2006 (SI 2006/199) reg.4 (February 7, 2006).
2. Child Trust Funds (Amendment No.2) Regulations 2009 (SI 2009/694) reg.3 (April 6, 2009).
3. Child Trust Funds (Amendment No.3) Regulations 2011 (SI 2011/2447) reg.4 (November 1, 2011).

DEFINITIONS

"account"—see reg.2(1)(b).
"account provider"—see *ibid.*
"appointed day"—see *ibid.*
"child"—see reg.2(1)(a).
"the Distance Marketing Directive"—see reg.2(1)(b).
"responsible person"—see reg.2(1)(a).
"subscriptions"—see reg.2(1)(b).

GENERAL NOTE

Note that the amendments made by SI 2011/2447 only have effect in relation to vouchers issued on or after January 1, 2012 (reg.1(2)).

Opening of account by Inland Revenue—(Revenue allocated accounts)

8.11   **6.**—(1) The Board shall apply to open an account for a child to whom section 6 of the Act applies, by forwarding to an account provider the particulars which would be required for a voucher (see regulation 3), but omitting paragraph (1)(d) of that regulation.

(2) The account provider shall immediately open a stakeholder account in the name of the child, which shall have the same effect as if a responsible person for the child (or the child if aged 16 or over) had entered into the account provider's standard management agreement for the stakeholder account in question, including the terms mentioned in Condition 2 of regulation 5(1) (but treating the reference to the application and declaration required by regulation 13 as a reference to the authorisation required by regulation 13(4)) and regulation 8(1)(f).

(3) The Inland Revenue shall maintain (and update from time to time) a list of account providers who have agreed to accept Revenue allocated accounts under this regulation, in the order of the date of their agreement, and the account provider shall be selected in rotation from the current list.

(4) Where the account provider offers two or more types of stakeholder account [²—
  (a) the account provider shall select the type or types to be used for the purposes of this regulation (subject to sub-paragraph (b)),
  (b) any type selected must be offered to the general public at the time of opening a Revenue allocated account of that type, and
  (c) if more than one type has been selected, the account to be opened shall be chosen by the account provider in rotation between the selected types of accounts.]

[¹(5) The Inland Revenue shall write to the person who is entitled to child benefit in respect of the child (or, in the case of a child who is an eligible child because of section 2(3) of the Act, to a responsible person in relation to the child) to inform them of the opening of the account and particulars of it.]

(SI 2004/1450 reg.6) (as amended)

AMENDMENTS

1. Child Trust Funds (Amendment) Regulations 2004 (SI 2004/2676) reg.4 (April 6, 2005).
2. Child Trust Funds (Amendment No.3) Regulations 2005 (SI 2005/3349) reg.4 (December 27, 2005).

DEFINITIONS

"account"—see reg.2(1)(b).
"account provider"—see *ibid.*
"child"—see reg.2(1)(a).
"eligible child"—see *ibid.*
"responsible person"—see *ibid.*

Government contributions

7.—(1) The amounts of the contribution for the purposes of section 8(1) of the Act are set out in paragraphs (2) to [⁴(4B)], (the amounts set out in paragraphs [⁴(2), (4)(a) and 4(A)] to be known as the "initial contribution", and the amounts set out in paragraphs [⁴(3), (4)(b) and 4(B)] as the "special contribution").

8.12

(2) Where the child is an eligible child on the appointed day by virtue of section 2(1)(a) of the Act (by reason of a child benefit award), and—
  (i) was born after 31st August 2002 but before 6th April 2003, the amount is £277,
  (ii) was born between 6th April 2003 and 5th April 2004, the amount is £268, and
  (iii) was born between 6th April 2004 and the day preceding the appointed day, the amount is £256.

(3) Where the child is an eligible child on the appointed day by virtue of section 2(1)(b) of the Act (by reason of being a child in the care of a local authority at that date) and—
  (i) was born after 31st August 2002 but before 6th April 2003, the amount is £554,
  (ii) was born between 6th April 2003 and 5th April 2004, the amount is £536, and
  (iii) was born between 6th April 2004 and the day preceding the appointed day, the amount is £512.

(4) [⁴Subject to paragraphs (4A) and (4B), where] the child [¹becomes an eligible child] on or after the appointed day and—
(a) is first an eligible child by virtue of section 2(1)(a) of the Act, the amount is £250, and
(b) is first an eligible child by virtue of section 2(1)(b) of the Act, the amount is £500.

[⁴ (4A) Where a child—
(a) is first an eligible child by virtue of section 2(1)(a) of the Act, and
(b) the commencement date for the child (see paragraph (8)) is after the relevant 2010 date (see paragraph (10E)),
the amount is £50.

(4B) Where a child—
(a) is first an eligible child by virtue of section 2(1)(b) of the Act, and
(b) either—
  (i) is born on or after the relevant 2010 date, or
  (ii) is first in the United Kingdom (other than temporarily) on or after the relevant 2010 date, or

(iii) becomes an eligible child on or after 3 months (less one day) after the relevant 2010 date,

the amount is £100.]

(5) The amounts of the supplementary contribution for the purposes of section 9(2) of the Act (to be known as the "supplementary contribution") are set out in paragraphs (6) and (7).

(6) Where the child is an eligible child on the appointed day (and is a child to whom section 9 of the Act applies), the amount—
  (a) if the commencement date was after 31st August 2002 but before 6th April 2003, is £266,
  (b) if the commencement date was between 6th April 2003 and 5th April 2004, is £258,
  (c) if the commencement date was between 6th April 2004 and the appointed day, is £250.

(7) [4Subject to pragraphs (7A), where] the child becomes an eligible child after the appointed day (and is a child to whom section 9 of the Act applies), the amount is £250.

[4 (7A) Where the child is one to whom section 9 of the Act applies, and the commencement date for the child is after the relevant 2010 date, the amount is £50.]

(8) The "commencement date", in relation to a child, means the first day for which child benefit was paid (under a decision mentioned in section 2(6) of the Act) in respect of the child, except that—
  (a) where entitlement to child benefit is wholly excluded by a directly applicable Community provision, it means the date on which that exclusion took effect, [4. . .]
  (b) [4. . .]

[1(9) The Inland Revenue shall, following final determination of entitlement to child tax credit, write to the person who is entitled to child benefit in respect of the child (or, in the case of a child who is an eligible child because of section 2(3) of the Act, to a responsible person in relation to the child) to inform them that the supplementary contribution is being paid into the child's account.]

[2(10) A further contribution under section 10 of the Act of [4£50] is due for any child where—
  (a) the commencement date (for child benefit: see paragraph (8)) in relation to that child is after 5th April 2005, and
  (b) income support or income-based jobseeker's allowance was paid for that commencement date to a person whose applicable amount included an amount in respect of the child.

[3 (10A) A further contribution under section 10 of the Act of [4£50] is due for any child if—
  (a) an account is held by the child,
  (b) the child was first an eligible child by virtue of section 2(1)(a) of the Act,
  (c) section 9 of the Act does not apply to the child,
  (d) a contribution is not, and has not been, due for the child under paragraph (10),
  (e) the child is an eligible child on the day identified under the provisions of paragraph (10B) or (10C) as the case may be, and
  (f) the condition in paragraph (10B) or (10C) is satisfied in relation to the child.

(10B) The condition in this paragraph is that it has been determined in

accordance with the provision made by and by virtue of sections 18 to 21 of the Tax Credits Act 2002—
  (a) that a person was, or persons were, entitled to child tax credit in respect of the child for any day falling—
    (i) after the commencement date, but
    (ii) not later than three months immediately preceding the expiry date of the voucher for the child (see regulation 3), and
  (b) that either the relevant income of the person or persons for the tax year in which that day fell does not exceed the income threshold or the person, or either of those persons, was entitled to a relevant social security benefit for that day,
and that determination has not been overturned.

(10C) The condition in this paragraph is that income support, or income-based jobseeker's allowance, was paid for any day falling—
  (a) after the commencement date, but
  (b) not later than one month immediately preceding the expiry date of the voucher for the child (see regulation 3),
to a person whose applicable amount included an amount in respect of the child.]

[[4] (10D) Her Majesty's Revenue and Customs must inform the account provider holding the child's account where an amount is payable to the account under paragraph (10) or (10A).

(10E) In this regulation, "the relevant 2010 date" means—
  (a) 2nd August 2010; or
  (b) if later, the day on which regulation 3 of the Child Trust Funds (Amendment No.3) Regulations 2010 came into force.]

(11) On receipt of the further contribution [[3] mentioned in paragraph (10) or (10A)] from the Inland Revenue the account provider must credit the account held by the child with the amount of the payment.]

AMENDMENTS

1. Child Trust Funds (Amendment) Regulations 2004 (SI 2004/2676) reg.5 (April 6, 2005).
2. Child Trust Funds (Amendment) Regulations 2005 (SI 2005/383) reg.3 (April 6, 2005).
3. Child Trust Funds (Amendment) Regulations 2009 (SI 2009/475) reg.4 (April 6, 2009, but have effect where the Child Benefit commencement date for the child (first day for which child benefit was paid in respect of the child) is on or after April 6, 2008).
4. Child Trust Funds (Amendment No.3) Regulations 2010 (SI 2010/1894) reg.3 (August 2, 2010).

DEFINITIONS

"account"—see reg.2(1)(b).
"account provider"—see *ibid*.
"appointed day"—see *ibid*.
"child"—see reg.2(1)(a).
"eligible child"—see *ibid*.
"responsible person"—see *ibid*.

Child Trust Funds Regulations 2004

GENERAL NOTE

8.13   Note that the amended and reduced amount of £50 under para.(10) and (10A) has effect where the commencement date for the child (within the meaning of reg.7(8) of the Child Trust Funds Regulations 2004, as amended by reg.3(7) of the Child Trust Funds (Amendment No.3) Regulations 2010) is after the day on which reg.3 of those Regulations comes into force in accordance with reg.1(3) (see reg.1(4) of the 2010 Regulations).

[¹Age 7 payments

8.14   7A.—[² . . .]

AMENDMENTS

1. Child Trust Funds Amendment Regulations 2009 (SI 2009/475) reg.5 (April 6, 2009).
2. Child Trust Funds (Amendment No. 3) Regulations 2010 (SI 2010/1894) reg.4 (August 1, 2010).

[¹Yearly disability payments

8.15   7B.—(1) A further contribution under section 10 of the Act is due for any eligible child who is entitled in [²the year 2009/10 or 2010/11] to a disability living allowance, in accordance with paragraphs (2) to (4).

(2) Where it has been determined that the child is entitled to the care component of a disability living allowance at the highest weekly rate (see section 72(4)(a) of either the Social Security Contributions and Benefits Act 1992 or the Social Security Contributions and Benefits (Northern Ireland) Act 1992), at any time in the year (whether it is paid or not), the contribution payable for the year shall be £200.

(3) In any other case where it has been determined that the child is entitled to a disability living allowance at any time in the year (whether it is paid or not), the contribution payable for the year shall be £100.

(4) [² . . .]

(5) Her Majesty's Revenue and Customs must inform the account provider holding the child's account where an amount is payable to that account under this regulation.

(6) On receipt of each further contribution from Her Majesty's Revenue and Customs, the account provider must credit the child's account with the amount of the payment.]

AMENDMENTS

1. Child Trust Funds (Amendment No. 2) Regulations 2010 (SI 2010/836) reg.3 (April 1, 2010).
2. Child Trust Funds (Amendment No. 3) Regulations 2010 (SI 2010/1894) reg.5 (August 1, 2010).

GENERAL NOTE

8.16   This regulation provides for *yearly* government contributions into the Child Trust Fund accounts of disabled and severely disabled children. It applies only to children who became entitled to disability living allowance (DLA) on or after April 6, 2009 (see Child Trust Funds (Amendment No.2) Regulations 2010 (SI 2010/836) reg.1(2)). It makes provision for the yearly disability payments into the fund of £200 where the child is entitled to the highest rate care component of DLA (para.(2)) and of £100 in other cases (para.(3)). The provision rests on "entitlement" to disability living allowance, rather than actual payment, in order to cover certain children in hospital in respect of whom payment is not made, but who would remain formally entitled to DLA.

PART 2

OTHER REQUIREMENTS TO BE SATISFIED IN RELATION TO ACCOUNTS

General requirements for accounts

8.—(1) An account must satisfy the requirements that—
(a) it is the account for a single child ("the named child");
(b) the named child is or has been an eligible child;
(c) no child may hold more than one account;
(d) at any time—
  (i) where the named child is under 16, only a single responsible person in relation to the named child, or
  (ii) where the named child is 16 or over, only the child,
  ("the registered contact") may give instructions to the account provider with respect to its management;
(e) the account must at all times be managed in accordance with these Regulations by an account provider and, subject to regulation 6(2), under terms agreed and recorded in a management agreement made between the account provider and the registered contact (on behalf of the named child where appropriate); and
(f) the management agreement must include instructions to the provider as to the manner in which Inland Revenue contributions and any subscriptions made are to be invested under the account.

(2) Apart from other requirements of these Regulations the terms so agreed shall include the conditions that—
(a) the account investments shall be in the beneficial ownership of the named child;
(b) the title to all account investments, except those falling within regulation 12(2)(k), (l) or (m), shall be vested in the account provider or his nominee, subject to sub-paragraph (f);
(c) where a share certificate or other document evidencing title to an account investment is issued, it shall be held by the account provider or as he may direct, subject to sub-paragraph (f);
(d) in relation to qualifying investments falling within regulation 12(2)(a), (b) and (f) to (j), the account provider shall, if the registered contact so elects (and subject to any charge for the arrangement), arrange for the registered contact to receive a copy of the annual report and accounts issued to investors by every company, unit trust, open-ended investment company or other entity in which account investments are held;
(e) in relation to qualifying investments falling within regulation 12(2)(a), (b) and (f) to (j), the account provider shall, if the registered

8.17

Child Trust Funds Regulations 2004

contact so elects (subject to any charge for the arrangement, and to any provisions made under any enactment), be under an obligation to arrange for the registered contact to be able—
  (i) to attend any meetings of investors in companies, unit trusts, open-ended investment companies and other entities in which account investments are held,
  (ii) to vote, and
  (iii) to receive, in addition to the documents referred to in sub-paragraph (d), any other information issued to investors in such companies, unit trusts, open-ended investment companies and other entities;
(f) if and so long as a person falling within regulation 14(2)(d)(iv) acts as account provider of an account, and the account investments include a policy of life insurance—
  (i) the title to all such policies shall be vested in the registered contact, and
  (ii) where a policy document or other document evidencing title to such policies of life insurance is issued, it shall be held by the registered contact;
(g) the account provider shall satisfy himself that any person to whom he delegates any of his functions or responsibilities under the management agreement is competent to carry out those functions or responsibilities;
(h) on the instructions of the registered contact ("the transfer instructions") and within such time as is stipulated by the registered contact in the transfer instructions, the whole of an account, with all rights and obligations of the parties to it, shall be transferred free of expense (except any incidental expenses) to another account provider subject to and in accordance with regulation 21;
[1(ha) where the account is or has been transferred to the account provider by a transfer under regulation 21, that no charges or expenses are due in respect of that transfer, except in accordance with sub-paragraph (h);]
[2(hb) any transfer under regulation 20A shall be free of expense (except any incidental expenses);]
(i) where the account provider offers accounts of another description or type, on the instructions of the registered contact ("the internal transfer instructions") and within such time as is stipulated by the registered contact in the internal transfer instructions, the account shall become (free of expense, except any incidental expenses) an account of that other description or type (any necessary change in the investments being made accordingly); and
(j) the account provider shall notify the registered contact if by reason of any failure to satisfy the provisions of these Regulations an account is or will become no longer exempt from tax by virtue of regulation 24.

(3) Where the transfer instructions or internal transfer instructions, or any new management agreement entered into by the registered contact with the account provider (or a new account provider) under regulation 8(1)(e), is a distance contract, the transfer or internal transfer shall only take effect once those contracts satisfy Condition 4 in regulation 5(1).

(4) The time stipulated in transfer instructions or internal transfer instructions shall be subject to any reasonable business period (not

(SI 2004/1450 reg.8) (as amended)

exceeding 30 days) of the account provider required for the practical implementation of the instructions.

(5) In this regulation, "incidental expenses" means stamp duty and other dealing costs of disposing of or acquiring investments.

AMENDMENTS

1. Child Trust Funds (Amendment) Regulations 2004 (SI 2004/2676) reg.6 (April 6, 2005).
2. Child Trust Funds (Amendment No.2) Regulations 2015 (SI 2015/876) regs 2 and 4 (April 6, 2015).

DEFINITIONS

"account"—see reg.2(1)(b).
"account investment"—see *ibid.*
"account provider"—see *ibid.*
"child"—see reg.2(1)(a).
"company"—see reg.2(1)(b).
"incidental expenses"—see reg.8(5).
"open-ended investment company"—see reg.2(1)(c).
"responsible person"—see reg.2(1)(a).
"subscriptions"—see reg.2(1)(b).
"tax"—see *ibid.*

Annual limit on subscriptions

9.—(1) Any person (including the child) may make subscriptions to a child's account, subject to paragraphs (2) and (3).

(2) Subscriptions to an account made during any subscription year, that is—
(a) the period beginning with the day on which the account is opened (or if opened before the appointed day, opened for the purpose of accepting subscriptions under regulation 5(2)(b)), and ending immediately before the child's next birthday, and
(b) any succeeding period of twelve months,
shall not in aggregate exceed the sum of [²£4.080].

(3) Where the aggregate of subscriptions in any year falls short of [²£4.080] or is nil, there shall be no addition to the amount for any succeeding year.

8.18

AMENDMENTS

1. Child Trust Funds (Amendment No.3) Regulations 2011 (SI 2011/2447) reg.5 (November 1, 2011).
2. Child Trust Funds Amendment Regulations 2015 (SI 2015/600) regs 2 and 3 (April 6, 2015).

DEFINITIONS

"account"—see reg.2(1)(b).
"appointed day"—see *ibid.*
"child"—see reg.2(1)(a).
"subscriptions"—see reg.2(1)(b).

Statements for an account

10.—[² (1) The account provider must produce a statement for the account—

8.19

(a) subject to paragraphs (6) and (7), annually ("an annual statement"), and
(b) where an account is transferred [³ . . .] under regulation [³ 20A or] 21, as at the transfer date ("a transfer statement").

(2) References in paragraphs (2A)(b), (3), (4), (5), (6) and (8) to a statement (without more) shall be construed as references to any statement required to be produced in accordance with this regulation.

(2A) The account provider must produce an annual statement at a date (a "relevant date") not later than 12 months from the latest of—
(a) the date of the opening of the account;
(b) the date at which the most recent statement was produced; and
(c) the last date at which, but for paragraph (6), a previous annual statement would have had to have been produced.]

(3) [² A statement required to be produced in accordance with this regulation] shall be sent—
(a) where the named child is the registered contact, to the child,
(b) where a responsible person is the registered contact, to the named child care of the registered contact,
(c) where the Official Solicitor or Accountant of Court has been appointed under section 3(10) of the Act, to the Official Solicitor or Accountant of Court, on behalf of the child, and
(d) in any other case, to the named child,
within 30 days of the [² date specified in paragraph (3A)].

[² (3A) The date specified in this paragraph is—
(a) in relation to an annual statement, the relevant date;
(b) in relation to a transfer statement, the transfer date; or
(c) where paragraph (7) applies, the later of the relevant date in relation to the annual statement requested and the date that the request is received by the account provider.]

(4) Statements shall include the following information—
(a) the full name of the child;
(b) his address;
(c) his date of birth;
(d) his unique reference number;
(e) the description of the account (see regulation 4);
(f) the name of the registered contact (if any);
(g) the [² relevant date];
[² (h) the total market value of the investments under the account at the date at which the most recent statement was produced (if any);]
(i) the amount of any Government contributions [¹(see regulation 7) received by the account provider], during the period between—
[² (i) the date at which the most recent statement was produced, or the opening of the account (whichever is the later), and]
(ii) the [² relevant date];
(j) the aggregate amount of subscriptions (if any) received during the period in sub-paragraph (i);
(k) the total amount of deductions (including management charges) made during the period in sub-paragraph (i);
(l) the total market value of the investments under the account at the [² relevant date];
(m) the number or amount, description and market value of each of the investments under the account at the [² relevant date];

(SI 2004/1450 reg.10) (as amended)

(n) the basis used in calculating the market value of each investment under the account (together with a statement of any change from a basis used in the previous statement); and
(o) the exchange rate used where any investment is, or is denominated in, a currency other than sterling.

[¹(5) As an alternative to the information in paragraph (4)(k), the statement may include, in relation to any management charges or other incidental expenses deducted from the account during the period in paragraph (4)(i)—
(a) the rate, expressed as an annual percentage rate, at which, and the period in relation to which, such deductions were made, or
(b) where such deductions were made in relation to different periods at different rates—
  (i) each rate, expressed as an annual percentage rate, at which those deductions were made; and
  (ii) the period in relation to which they were made at that rate.]

[² (6) Where, in relation to an annual statement, at a relevant date—
(a) the aggregate market value of the account investments held under the account is less than £300, or
(b) no subscriptions under regulation 9 have been made to the account during the relevant period,
then, subject to paragraph (7), the account provider need only produce the annual statement if it would be the first statement to be produced following the child's fourth, tenth or fifteenth birthday.

(7) Paragraph (6) shall not apply where any potential recipient of an annual statement (see paragraph (3)) requests such a statement.

(8) "The relevant period" means the period—
(a) beginning on the latest of—
  (i) the date of the opening of the account;
  (ii) the date at which the most recent statement was produced; and
  (iii) the last date as at which, but for paragraph (6), an annual statement would have had to have been produced; and
(b) ending on the relevant date.]

AMENDMENTS

1. Child Trust Funds (Amendment) Regulations 2004 (SI 2004/2676) reg.7 (April 6, 2005).
2. Child Trust Funds (Amendment No.2) Regulations 2011 (SI 2011/992) reg.2 (April 20, 2011).
3. Child Trust Funds (Amendment No.2) Regulations 2015 (SI 2015/876) regs 2 and 5 (April 6, 2015).

DEFINITIONS

"account"—see reg.2(1)(b).
"account provider"—see *ibid.*
"child"—see reg.2(1)(a).
"investments under the account"—see reg.2(1)(b).
"market value"—see *ibid.*
"responsible person"—see reg.2(1)(a).
"subscriptions"—see reg.2(1)(b).

General investment rules

11.—(1) All transactions by way of purchase by an account provider of investments under an account shall be made—

8.20

(a) in the case of an authorised fund which is a dual priced unit trust, at the [³ maximum sale price of a unit of the relevant class at the relevant valuation point] within the meaning of, and complying with the requirements of, [³ [⁴ paragraphs] 6.3.5 and 6.3.5B] of the [⁴ COLL];
(b) in the case of an authorised fund which is a single priced unit trust or an open-ended investment company, at the price of a unit [³ of the relevant class at the relevant valuation point] within the meaning of, and complying with the requirements of, [³ [⁴ paragraphs] 6.3.5 and 6.3.5A] of the [⁴ COLL]; and
(c) in the case of all other account investments, at the price for which those investments might reasonably be expected to be purchased in the open market.

(2) In paragraph (1)—

"a dual priced unit trust" means an authorised unit trust in respect of which the manager gives different prices for buying and selling units at the same time;

"a single priced unit trust" means an authorised unit trust in respect of which the manager gives the same price for buying and selling units at the same time.

(3) All other transactions by way of sale or otherwise by an account provider in investments under an account shall be made at the price for which those investments might reasonably be expected to be sold or otherwise transacted, as the case may be, in the open market.

(4) Investments, or rights in respect of investments, may not at any time—
(a) be purchased or made otherwise than out of cash which an account provider holds under an account at that time; or
(b) be purchased from—
   (i) the named child, or
   (ii) the spouse [³or civil partner] of the named child,
   so as to become account investments under the account.

(5) Subject to paragraph (6), contributions, subscriptions and any other cash held by an account provider under an account shall be held only in sterling and be deposited in an account with a deposit-taker [¹(including for this purpose a credit union)], or a deposit account or a share account with a building society, which is designated as a CTF account for the purposes of these Regulations only.

(6) An account provider who is a European institution, a relevant authorised person or an assurance undertaking may hold an account investor's cash subscription and other cash held under an account in the currency of the EEA State in which he has his principal place of business and may deposit such cash in an account, which is designated as mentioned in paragraph (5), with any person authorised under the law of that State to accept deposits.

AMENDMENTS

1. Child Trust Funds (Amendment No.2) Regulations 2005 (SI 2005/909) reg.4 (April 6, 2005).
2. Civil Partnership Act 2004 (Tax Credits, etc.) (Consequential Amendments) Order 2005 (SI 2005/2919) art.15 (December 5, 2006).

(SI 2004/1450 reg.11) (as amended)

3. Child Trust Funds (Amendment) Regulations 2010 (SI 2010/582) reg.4 (April 6, 2010).

4. Financial Services Act 2012 (Consequential Amendments and Transitional Provisions) Order 2013 (SI 2013/472) art.3 and Sch.2 para.93(c) (April 1, 2013).

DEFINITIONS

"account"—see reg.2(1)(b).
"account investment"—see *ibid.*
"account provider"—see *ibid.*
"assurance undertaking"—see *ibid.*
"authorised fund"—see reg.2(1)(c).
"building society"—see reg.2(1)(b).
"child"—see reg.2(1)(a).
"Collective Investment Schemes Sourcebook"—see reg.2(1)(c).
"credit union"—see reg.2(1)(b).
"deposit taker"—see *ibid.*
"dual priced unit trust"—see reg.11(2).
"EEA State"—see reg.2(1)(b).
"European institution"—see *ibid.*
"investments under the account"—see *ibid.*
"open-ended investment company"—see reg.2(1)(c).
"relevant authorised person"—see reg.2(1)(b).
"single priced unit trust"—see reg.11(2).
"subscriptions"—see reg.2(1)(b).
"units"—see reg.2(1)(c).

Qualifying investments for an account

12.—(1) This regulation specifies the kind of investments ("qualifying investments for an account") which may be purchased, made or held under an account.

8.21

(2) Qualifying investments for an account to which paragraph (1) refers are—
  (a) shares, not being shares in an investment trust, issued by a company wherever incorporated and [⁵either officially listed on a recognised stock exchange or, in the European Economic Area, admitted to trading on a recognised stock exchange (see paragraph (3))]
  (b) securities—
      (i) issued by a company wherever incorporated, [³ and]
      (ii) which satisfy at least one of the conditions specified in paragraph (5)
      [³. . .]
  (c) gilt-edged securities;
  (d) any securities issued by or on behalf of a government of any EEA State;
  (e) any securities which, in relation to a security mentioned in sub-paragraph (d), would be a strip of that security if "strip" had the same meaning as in section 47 of the Finance Act 1942, with the omission of the words "issued under the National Loans Act 1968";
  (f) shares in an investment trust [⁶. . .][³. . .];
  (g) [³. . .]
  (h) [³. . .]
  [³ (i) units in, or shares of, a UK UCITS or recognised UCITS;]
  (j) a depositary interest;

Child Trust Funds Regulations 2004

  (k) cash deposited in a deposit account with a building society, or a person falling within [³ section 991 of ITA 2007 (including for this purpose a credit union)], subject to paragraph (8);
  (l) cash deposited in a share account with a building society, subject to paragraph (8);
  (m) policies of life insurance which satisfy the conditions specified in paragraphs (9) and (10);
  (n) any securities issued under the National Loans Act 1968—
      (i) for the purpose of or in connection with raising money under the auspices of the Director of Savings within the meaning of section 11(1)(a) of the National Debt Act 1972, and
      (ii) other than national savings certificates, premium savings bonds, national savings stamps and national savings gift tokens,
      which, according to the terms and conditions subject to which they are issued and purchased, are expressly permitted to be held under an account.
[²(o) arrangements falling within section 47 of the Finance Act 2005 (alternative finance arrangements) under which the person referred to in that section as Y is a financial institution;
  (p) arrangements falling within section 49 of that Act;
  (q) qualifying units in or shares of a non-UCITS retail scheme;]
[⁷ (r) core capital deferred shares within the meaning of regulation 2 of the Building Societies (Core Capital Deferred Shares) Regulations 2013, provided that such shares are listed on the official list of a recognised stock exchange.]

(3) [⁶An investment in shares fulfils the conditions as to official listing and admission to trading in paragraph (2)(a)] or (f) [⁵, or the condition as to admission to trading in paragraph (2)(a),] if—
  (a) in pursuance of a public offer, the account provider applies for the allotment or allocation to him of shares in a company [⁶ . . .] which are due to be admitted to such listing [⁵or admitted to such trading] within 30 days of the allocation or allotment, and which, when admitted to such listing [⁵ or trading], would be qualifying investments for an account, and
  (b) the shares are not allotted or allocated to the account provider in the circumstances specified in paragraph (4).

(4) The circumstances specified in this paragraph are where—
  (a) the allotment or allocation of the shares was connected with the allotment or allocation of—
      (i) shares in the company or investment trust of a different class, or
      (ii) rights to shares in the company or investment trust of a different class, or
      (iii) shares or rights to shares in another company or investment trust, or
      (iv) units in or shares in, or rights to units in or shares in, an authorised fund or a part of an umbrella scheme, or
      (v) securities or rights to securities of the company or investment trust, or of another company or investment trust,
  to the account provider, the registered contact or any other person; and
  (b) the terms on which the first-mentioned shares in this paragraph were offered were significantly more favourable to the account provider

(SI 2004/1450 reg.12) (as amended)

or the named child than they would have been if their allotment or allocation had not been connected as described in sub-paragraph (a).

(5) The conditions specified in this paragraph are—
(a) that the shares in the company issuing the securities are listed on the official list of a recognised stock exchange;
(b) that the securities are so listed;
(c) that the company issuing the securities is a 75 per cent subsidiary of a company whose shares are so listed.

(6) [³. . .]

(7) In paragraph (4)(a), "company" means any body corporate having a share capital.

[⁴ (8) A deposit account or share account which is a qualifying investment for an account falling within paragraph (2)(k) or (l) must not be connected with any other investment, held by the named child or any other person.

(8A) For the purposes of paragraph (8), a deposit account or share account described in that paragraph, is connected with another investment if—
(a) either was opened or acquired with reference to the other, or with a view to enabling the other to be opened or acquired on particular terms, or with a view to facilitating the opening or acquisition of the other on particular terms,
(b) the terms on which the deposit account or share account was opened would have been significantly less favourable to the holder if the other investment had not been held, and
(c) the other investment is not a tax exempt investment.

(8B) The following are tax exempt investments for the purposes of paragraph (8A)—
(a) an account investment held under a child trust fund;
(b) an account investment within the meaning given in the Individual Savings Account Regulations 1998 held under an account opened (or treated as opened) in accordance with regulation 12 or 12A of those regulations.]

(9) The conditions specified in this paragraph are that—
(a) the insurance is on the life of the named child only;
(b) the terms and conditions of the policy provide—
   (i) that the policy may only be owned or held as a qualifying investment for an account which satisfies the provisions of these Regulations;
   (ii) that the policy shall automatically terminate if it comes to the notice of the account provider, in any manner, that the event specified in paragraph (11) has occurred in relation to the policy;
   (iii) for an express prohibition of any payment of the proceeds from the termination of the policy or a partial surrender of the rights conferred by the policy, to the named child (while he is still a child) [¹except in accordance with regulation 18A (terminal illness)]; and
   (iv) that the policy, the rights conferred by the policy and any share or interest in the policy or rights respectively, shall not be capable of assignment or (in Scotland) assignation, other than that they may be vested in the named child's personal representatives, and that the title to the policy may be transferred

Child Trust Funds Regulations 2004

to a new account provider subject to and in accordance with regulations 8(2)(f) and 21;
(c) the policy evidences or secures a contract of insurance which—
  (i) falls within paragraph 1 or 3 of Part 2 of Schedule 1 to the Financial Services and Markets Act 2000 (Regulated Activities) Order 2001, or
  (ii) would fall within either of those paragraphs if the insurer were a company with permission under Part 4 of the Financial Services and Markets Act 2000 to effect or carry out contracts of insurance;
(d) the policy is not—
  (i) a contract to pay an annuity on human life,
  (ii) a personal portfolio bond within the meaning given by [³ section 516 of ITTOIA 2005], or
  (iii) a contract, the effecting and carrying out of which constitutes "pension business" within the meaning given by section 431B(1) of the Taxes Act; and
(e) after the first payment in respect of a premium in relation to the policy has been made, there is no contractual obligation on any person to make any other such payment.

(10) The condition specified in this paragraph is that no sum may at any time, at or after the making of the insurance, be lent to or at the direction of the named child or registered contact by or by arrangement with the insurer for the time being responsible for the obligations under the policy.

(11) The event specified in this paragraph is that—
(a) there has been a breach of any of the conditions in paragraph (9) or (10), or any of those conditions was not satisfied at the date on which the insurance was made; and
(b) the breach or non-compliance cannot be remedied in accordance with regulation 23, or (in any other case), has not been remedied within a reasonable time.

(12) Where the event specified in paragraph (11) occurs in relation to a policy, the policy shall nevertheless be treated, for the purposes of these Regulations, excepting paragraphs (9)(b)(ii) and (11), and regulations 37(6) and 38, as if it had satisfied the conditions in paragraphs (9) and (10) during the period—
(a) commencing at the time when that specified event occurred, and
(b) ending immediately before—
  [³ (i) the end of the final insurance year in relation to the policy, within the meaning given by section 499 of ITTOIA 2005,]
  (ii) the time at which that specified event came to the notice of the account provider,
whichever first occurs (the "termination event").

AMENDMENTS

1. Child Trust Funds (Amendment) Regulations 2004 (SI 2004/2676) reg.8 (April 6, 2005).
2. Child Trust Funds (Amendment No.3) Regulations 2005 (SI 2005/3349) reg.5 (December 27, 2005).
3. Child Trust Funds (Amendment) Regulations 2010 (SI 2010/582) reg.5 (April 6, 2010).
4. Child Trust Funds (Amendment) Regulations 2012 (SI 2012/1870) reg.2 (August 8, 2012).

(SI 2004/1450 reg.12) (as amended)

5. Child Trust Funds (Amendment No. 2) Regulations 2013 (SI 2013/1744) reg.5 (August 5, 2013).
6. Child Trust Funds (Amendment) Regulations 2014 (SI 2014/649) reg.5 (April 6, 2014).
7. Child Trust Funds (Amendment No.2) Regulations 2014 (SI 2014/1453) regs 2 and 4 (July 1, 2014).

DEFINITIONS

"account"—see reg.2(1)(b).
"account provider"—see *ibid.*
"authorised fund"—see reg.2(1)(c).
"building society"—see reg.2(1)(b).
"child"—see reg.2(1)(a).
"company"—see regs.2(1)(b) and 12(7).
"credit union"—see reg.2(1)(b).
"depositary interest"—see reg.2(1)(c).
"EEA State"—see reg.2(1)(b).
"European institution"—see *ibid.*
"fund of funds scheme"—see reg.2(1)(c).
"gilt-edged securities"—see reg.2(1)(b).
"investments under the account"—see *ibid.*
"investment trust"—see *ibid.*
"money market scheme"—see reg.2(1)(c).
"recognised stock exchange"—see reg.2(1)(b).
"relevant European institution"—see *ibid.*
"securities scheme"—see reg.2(1)(c).
"security"—see reg.2(1)(b).
"the Taxes Act"—see *ibid.*
"UCITS"—see reg.2(1)(c).
"umbrella scheme"—see *ibid.*
"units"—see *ibid.*
"warrant scheme"—see *ibid.*
"year"—see reg.2(1)(b).

Conditions for application by responsible person or the child to open an account (and changes to an account)

13.—(1) An application by a responsible person in relation to a child or the child if 16 or over, as the case may be, ("the applicant") to open an account for the child with an account provider must be made to the account provider in a statement which must satisfy the conditions specified in paragraphs (2) to (6).

(2) An application must specify the description of account applied for.

(3) An application must incorporate a declaration by the applicant that he—
(a) is aged 16 years of age or over,
(b) is—
  (i) (where the child is under 16) a responsible person in relation to the named child (that is, that he has parental responsibility [¹or, in Scotland, parental responsibilities] in relation to the child), or
  (ii) the child if 16 or over, and
(c) is to be the registered contact for the account;
and where the application is not in writing, must authorise the account

8.22

provider to record the terms of the declaration in a written declaration made on behalf of the applicant.

(4) The applicant must authorise the account provider (on behalf of the named child where appropriate)—
- (a) to hold the child's Inland Revenue contributions, subscriptions, account investments, interest, dividends and any other rights or proceeds in respect of those investments and cash, and
- (b) to make on his behalf any claims to relief from tax in respect of account investments,

and the authority must continue until a further application and declaration is made in accordance with paragraph (10).

(5) An application must contain—
- (a) the applicant's full name,
- (b) his address, including postcode,
- (c) the named child's full name [1and date of birth],
- (d) his address, including postcode, and
- (e) the child's unique reference number on the voucher.

(6) There may be only one declaration and authorisation under paragraphs (3) to (5) in force for an account at any time.

(7) Except in the case—
- (a) of the death or incapacity of the registered contact,
- (b) where the registered contact cannot be contacted,
- (c) of the bringing to an end of a Court order, under which he is a responsible person for the named child,
- (d) of the named child attaining the age of 16 years,
- [3 (da) where the new registered contact has been appointed to be a guardian or special guardian of the named child,
- (db) where the new registered contact is the adopter of the named child under an adoption order,]
- (e) where the Official Solicitor or Accountant of Court is appointed under section 3(10) of the Act, or
- (f) where a Court so orders,

any change in the identity of the registered contact shall require confirmation by the current registered contact that his declaration and authorisation under paragraphs (3)(c) and (4) is cancelled [3, and in the cases in sub-paragraphs (a) to (f) it shall be treated as automatically cancelled].

(8) An account provider must decline to accept an application if he has reason to believe that—
- (a) the voucher has expired, or is not or might not be genuine, or
- (b) the applicant has given untrue information in his application.

(9) Where the application is not in writing, the account provider shall make the written declaration referred to in paragraph (3), and notify the applicant of its contents, and such declaration shall take effect from the date on which the applicant agrees the contents (subject to any corrections), and if he neither agrees or disagrees with the contents within 30 days, he shall be treated as having agreed them.

(10) Where—
- (a) there is a change in the identity of the registered contact, the new registered contact, or
- (b) an account has been opened by the Inland Revenue under regulation 6 (Revenue allocated accounts) and a responsible person in relation to the child (or the child, if 16 or over) subsequently

(SI 2004/1450 reg.13) (as amended)

applies to the account provider to be the registered contact for the account, he,
shall make the application and declaration required by paragraphs (3) to (5).

[¹(11) Where the new registered contact is the Official Solicitor or the Accountant of Court, he shall make the declaration and authorisation required by paragraphs (3)(c) and (4) [²and shall be treated as a party to the existing management agreement for the account in question].]

AMENDMENTS

1. Child Trust Funds (Amendment) Regulations 2004 (SI 2004/2676) reg.9 (April 6, 2005).
2. Child Trust Funds (Amendment No.2) Regulations 2004 (SI 2004/3382) reg.3 (April 6, 2005).
3. Child Trust Funds (Amendment) Regulations 2010 (SI 2010/582) reg.6 (April 6, 2010).

DEFINITIONS

"account"—see reg.2(1)(b).
"account investment"—see *ibid.*
"account provider"—see *ibid.*
"child"—see reg.2(1)(a).
"parental responsibility"—see *ibid.*
"responsible person"—see *ibid.*
"subscriptions"—see reg.2(1)(b).
"tax"—see *ibid.*

Account provider—qualifications and Board's approval

14.—(1) This regulation specifies the circumstances ("qualifying circumstances") in which a person may be approved by the Board as an account provider.

(2) The qualifying circumstances are the following—
(a) the person must make an application to the Board for approval in a form specified by the Board;
(b) the person must undertake with the Board—
   (i) to either offer stakeholder accounts to the general public (whether or not accounts of another description are offered), or to fulfil the requirements in paragraph (3),
   (ii) to accept vouchers from any responsible person or the child if 16 or over (subject to [²paragraph (iia) and] regulation 13(8)),
   [³(iia) in the case of a credit union, to accept vouchers from any responsible person or the child if 16 or over, if the child to which the voucher relates is a member, or fulfils or is treated as fulfilling a qualification for admission to membership, of the credit union (subject to regulation 13(8))]
   (iii) where the person accepts Revenue allocated accounts, to allow instructions for their management to be made or given by post (whether or not other methods are allowed),
   (iv) to publicise (and up-date where appropriate) statements of the minimum amount which may be subscribed to an account on a single occasion, and the permitted means of payment of subscriptions,
   (v) to inform persons proposing to make subscriptions to an

account (other than the named child) that the subscription is a gift to the child,
- (vi) to publicise (and up-date where appropriate) statements of the extent to which social, environmental or ethical decisions are taken into account in selecting, retaining or realising investments,
- (vii) that a child's unique reference number shall only be used for the purposes of the child's account (and of fulfilling the requirements of these Regulations with regard to that account), and
- (viii) that whether there is an initial contribution or special contribution to an account, whether there is a supplementary contribution to the account, and whether the account is a Revenue allocated account is information held for the purposes mentioned in paragraph (vii) only, and shall not be used for other purposes (including marketing other products);
- (c) [7 . . .];
- (d) an account provider must be—
  - (i) an authorised person within the meaning of [8 FISMA 2000], who has permission to carry on one or more of the activities specified in Articles 14, 21, 25, 37, 40, 45, 51, 53 and (in so far as it applies to any of those activities) 64 of the Financial Services and Markets Act 2000 (Regulated Activities) Order 2001, but excluding any person falling within paragraph (iv) below;
- [4[5(iia) in the case of a credit union, an authorised person within the meaning of [9 FISMA 2000], who has permission to carry on one or more of the activities specified in Article 5 of the Financial Services and Markets Act 2000 (Regulated Activities) Order 2001;]
  - (ii) a European institution which carries on one or more of those activities;
  - (iii) a building society [6 or a person falling within section 991 of ITA 2007 (including for this purpose a credit union)]; or
  - (iv) an insurance company within the meaning given by section 431(2) of the Taxes Act, an incorporated friendly society or a registered friendly society, or any other assurance undertaking;
- [8 (e) an account provider must not be prevented from acting as such by any requirement imposed under Part 4A of FISMA 2000, or by any prohibition or prohibition order in or made under that Act; and]
- (f) an account provider who—
  - (i) is a European institution or a relevant authorised person and who does not have a branch or business establishment in the United Kingdom, or has such a branch or business establishment but does not intend to carry out all his functions as an account provider at that branch or business establishment, or
  - (ii) falls within the expression "any other assurance undertaking" in sub-paragraph (d)(iv),

must fulfil one of the three requirements specified in regulation 15.

(3) The requirements in this paragraph are that the person provides to any potential applicant for a child trust fund ([1before commencement of completion of] any application under regulation 13)—
- (a) a statement that a stakeholder account is available from a named alternative account provider who offers it on the terms in paragraph (2)(b)(i) (omitting the words from ", or to" to the end);

(b) a detailed description of that stakeholder account; and
(c) sufficient information (according to the method of communication used, and including documentation where appropriate) to put the potential applicant in the position to make an application to that alternative account provider, complying with regulation 13.

(4) The terms of the Board's approval may include conditions designed to ensure that the provisions of these Regulations are satisfied.

AMENDMENTS

1. Child Trust Funds (Amendment) Regulations 2004 (SI 2004/2676) reg.10 (April 6, 2005).
2. Child Trust Funds (Amendment No.2) Regulations 2005 (SI 2005/909) reg.6 (April 6, 2005).
3. Child Trust Funds (Amendment No.2) Regulations 2005 (SI 2005/909) reg.7 (April 6, 2005).
4. Child Trust Funds (Amendment No.2) Regulations 2005 (SI 2005/909) reg.8 (April 6, 2005).
5. Child Trust Funds (Amendment No.3) Regulations 2005 (SI 2005/3349) reg.6 (December 27, 2005).
6. Child Trust Funds (Amendment) Regulations 2010 (SI 2010/582) reg.7 (April 6, 2010).
7. Child Trust Funds (Amendment) Regulations 2013 (SI 2013/263) reg.2(4)(c) (March 16, 2013).
8. Financial Services Act 2012 (Consequential Amendments and Transitional Provisions) Order 2013 (SI 2013/472) art.3 and Sch.2 para.93(d) (April 1, 2013).
9. Financial Services Act 2012 (Consequential Amendments and Transitional Provisions) (No. 3) Order 2013 (SI 2013/1765) reg.8 (September 1, 2013).

DEFINITIONS

"account"—see reg.2(1)(b).
"account provider"—see *ibid.*
"applicant"—see reg.5.
"assurance undertaking"—see reg.2(1)(b).
"building society"—see *ibid.*
"child"—see reg.2(1)(a).
"child trust fund"—see *ibid.*
"company"—see reg.2(1)(b).
"credit union"—see *ibid.*
"European institution"—see *ibid.*
"incorporated friendly society"—see *ibid.*
"registered friendly society"—see *ibid.*
"relevant authorised person"—see *ibid.*
"relevant European institution"—see *ibid.*
"responsible person"—see reg.2(1)(a).
"subscriptions"—see reg.2(1)(b).
"the Taxes Act"—see *ibid.*

Account provider—appointment of tax representative

15.—(1) This regulation specifies the requirements mentioned in regulation 14(2)(f).

(2) The first requirement specified in this regulation is that—
(a) a person who falls within [¹ section 698(2)(b) of ITTOIA 2005] is for the time being appointed by the account provider to be

8.24

responsible for securing the discharge of the duties prescribed by paragraph (5) which fall to be discharged by the account provider, and
  (b) his identity and the fact of his appointment have been notified to the Board by the account provider.

(3) The second requirement specified in this regulation is that there are for the time being other arrangements with the Board for a person other than the account provider to secure the discharge of such duties.

(4) The third requirement specified in this regulation is that there are for the time being other arrangements with the Board designed to secure the discharge of such duties.

(5) The duties prescribed by this paragraph are those that fall to be discharged by an account provider under these Regulations.

(6) The appointment of a person in pursuance of the first requirement shall be treated as terminated in circumstances where—
  (a) the Board have reason to believe that the person concerned—
    (i) has failed to secure the discharge of any of the duties prescribed by paragraph (5), or
    (ii) does not have adequate resources to discharge those duties, and
  (b) the Board have notified the account provider and that person that they propose to treat his appointment as having terminated with effect from the date specified in the notice.

(7) Where, in accordance with the first requirement, a person is at any time responsible for securing the discharge of duties, the person concerned—
  (a) shall be entitled to act on the account provider's behalf for any of the purposes of the provisions relating to the duties;
  (b) shall secure (where appropriate by acting on the account provider's behalf) the account provider's compliance with and discharge of the duties; and
  (c) shall be personally liable in respect of any failure of the account provider to comply with or discharge any such duty as if the duties imposed on the account provider were imposed jointly and severally on the account provider and the person concerned.

AMENDMENT

1. Child Trust Funds (Amendment) Regulations 2010 (SI 2010/582) reg.8 (April 6, 2010).

DEFINITIONS

"account provider"—see reg.2(1)(b).
"notice"—see *ibid.*
"the Taxes Act"—see *ibid.*

Account provider—withdrawal by Board of approval

16.—(1) This regulation specifies the circumstances ("the disqualifying circumstances") in which the Board may by notice withdraw their approval of a person as an account provider in relation to an account.

(2) The disqualifying circumstances are that the Board have reason to believe—
  (a) that any provision of the Act or these Regulations, or any term of an undertaking given in accordance with regulation 14(2)(b) or

(SI 2004/1450 reg.16) (as amended)

condition under regulation 14(4), is not or at any time has not been satisfied, either in respect of an account managed by the account provider or otherwise; or

(b) that a person to whom they have given approval to act as an account provider is not qualified so to act.

[² (2A) Where paragraph (2B) applies, a term of an undertaking given in accordance with regulation 14(2)(b) shall not be taken as not satisfied only by reason that the person to whom the Board's approval as an account provider has been given does not accept vouchers.

(2B) This paragraph applies where—
(a) a person does not accept any voucher after a day specified by that person; and
(b) no less than 30 days before the specified day, notice in writing is given to the Board of the person's intention not to accept vouchers after that day.]

(3) The notice to which paragraph (1) refers shall specify—
(a) the date from which the Board's approval is withdrawn; and
(b) the disqualifying circumstances.

[¹ (4) On receiving the notice referred to in paragraph (1), subject to any appeal under section 22(1)(b) of the Act, the account provider shall notify the registered contact (or, if there is no registered contact, the named child) of the right to transfer the account under regulation 21, and of his or her rights under regulation 20(3).]

AMENDMENTS

1. Child Trust Funds (Amendment) Regulations 2010 (SI 2010/582) reg.9 (April 6, 2010).
2. Child Trust Funds (Amendment No. 4) Regulations 2010 (SI 2010/2599) reg.3(1) (November 16, 2010).

DEFINITIONS

"account"—see reg.2(1)(b).
"account provider"—see *ibid*.
"notice"—see *ibid*.

Account provider—appeal against non-approval or withdrawal of Board's approval

17. A person who has been notified of a decision by the Board not to approve that person as an account provider, or an account provider to whom notice of withdrawal of approval has been given under regulation 16, may appeal against the decision by notice given to the Board within 30 days after the date of the notification or notice.

8.26

DEFINITIONS

"account provider"—see reg.2(1)(b).
"notice"—see *ibid*.

Permitted withdrawals from an account

18. Withdrawals from an account before the date on which the named child attains the age of 18 years may only be made—
(a) by the account provider, to settle any management charges and other

8.27

1029

incidental expenses, which are due by or under the management agreement, or
[¹(ab) in accordance with regulation 18A, or]
(b) where the account provider is satisfied that the named child has died under that age.

AMENDMENT

1. Child Trust Funds (Amendment) Regulations 2004 (SI 2004/2676) reg.11 (April 6, 2005).

DEFINITIONS

"account"—see reg.2(1)(b).
"account provider"—see *ibid*.
"child"—see reg.2(1)(a).

[¹Permitted withdrawals from an account where the child is terminally ill

18A.—(1) A person with parental responsibility (or, in Scotland, parental responsibilities) for the named child (including a local authority, but excluding a person under 16), or the named child if 16 or over, may make a claim to the Board, for withdrawals from an account to be permitted in accordance with this regulation.
(2) The claim shall be—
(a) made in a manner prescribed by the Board, which shall include the giving of any consent necessary for the verification or consideration of the claim, and
(b) accepted in either of the following cases:

[² *Case 1*

The child:
(i) in England and Wales or Scotland falls within either section 72(5) of the Social Security Contributions and Benefits Act 1992 (special rules for terminally ill person's entitlement to care component of disability living allowance) or section 82(4) of the Welfare Reform Act 2012 (terminal illness); or
(ii) in Northern Ireland, falls within section 72(5) of the Social Security Contributions and Benefits (Northern Ireland) Act 1992 (the care component).]

Case 2

Evidence that the named child is terminally ill has been supplied to the satisfaction of the Board.
(3) The Board shall issue a letter to the claimant authorising withdrawals from the account under this regulation [² . . .]
(4) Once a claim has been accepted, withdrawals may be made by the registered contact (on behalf of the named child, where he is not the child) at any time—
(a) provided that, immediately following any withdrawal, a balance sufficient to keep the account open is maintained in the account, and

(SI 2004/1450 reg.18A) (as amended)

(b) excepting any transfer of a policy of life insurance (as opposed to the proceeds from such a policy).

(5) Where account investments are withdrawn in a form other than sterling currency, regulation 36(1)(b) shall apply (with any necessary modifications) to any such investment immediately before it is withdrawn.

(6) In this regulation, "terminally ill" has the meaning [²(a) for England, Wales and Scotland,] in section 66(2)(a) of the Social Security Contributions and Benefits Act 1992 [² or in section 82(4) of the Welfare Reform Act 2012 (terminal illness); or (b) for Northern Ireland, in section 72(5) of the Social Security Contributions and Benefits (Northern Ireland) Act 1992 (the care component)].]

AMENDMENTS

1. Child Trust Funds (Amendment) Regulations 2004 (SI 2004/2676) reg.12 (April 6, 2005).
2. Child Trust Funds (Amendment) Regulations 2014 (SI 2014/649) reg.6 (April 6, 2014).

DEFINITIONS

"account"—see reg.2(1)(b).
"account investment"—see *ibid*.
"account provider"—see *ibid*.
"child"—see reg.2(1)(a).
"parental responsibility"—see *ibid*.

[¹ Account provider's intention to make a bulk transfer of accounts or to cease to act as an account provider

19.—(1) An account provider must give notice to the Board if the account provider—
(a) intends to cease to act as an account provider; or
(b) intends to make a bulk transfer of accounts.

(2) An account provider must give notice to the person who is the registered contact (or, if there is no registered contact, the named child) if the account provider—
(a) intends to cease to act as an account provider; or
(b) intends that the account will be one of the accounts transferred in a bulk transfer of accounts.

(3) The notices described in paragraphs (1) and (2) must—
(a) specify whether the account provider—
  (i) intends to cease to act as an account provider; or
  (ii) intends to make a bulk transfer of accounts;
(b) where the notice specifies an intention to cease to act as an account provider—
  (i) specify the day on or after which the account provider intends to cease to act as an account provider; and
  (ii) be given no less than 30 days before that day;
(c) where the notice specifies an intention to make a bulk transfer of accounts—
  (i) specify the day on or after which the account provider intends to make the first transfer in the bulk transfer of accounts;
  (ii) be given no less than 30 days before that day; and

8.29

(iii) advise the name and address of the person to whom the account provider intends to transfer accounts.
(4) The notice described in paragraph (2) must also—
(a) identify the account to which it relates;
(b) in the case of a notice under paragraph (2)(a), advise the registered contact of the right to transfer the account under regulation 21 and of his rights under regulation 20(3);
(c) in the case of a notice under paragraph (2)(b) —
(i) advise the registered contact that the account may be transferred otherwise than in a bulk transfer of accounts, such that regulation 21 applies, if sufficient instructions are provided to enable the account provider to do so; and
(ii) advise the day by which the account provider must receive sufficient instructions for the account to be transferred otherwise than in a bulk transfer of accounts.

(5) Where an account provider intends to make a bulk transfer of accounts in consequence of an intention to cease to act as an account provider, such intention may be specified in a single notice to the Board or to a registered contact (or, if there is no registered contact, the named child) (as appropriate, respectively) provided the requirements of paragraphs (3), (4)(a) and (c) are met.

AMENDMENT

1. Child Trust Funds (Amendment No.2) Regulations 2013 (SI 2013/1744) reg.6 (August 5, 2013).

[¹ Account provider ceasing to accept Revenue allocated accounts

19A. A person shall give notice to the Board of his intention to cease to accept further Revenue allocated accounts under regulation 6, not less than 30 days before he so ceases.]

AMENDMENT

1. Child Trust Funds (Amendment No.2) Regulations 2013 (SI 2013/1744) reg.6 (August 5, 2013).

Account provider ceasing to qualify

20.—(1) A person shall cease to qualify as an account provider and shall notify the Board within 30 days of the relevant event in sub-paragraphs (a) to (f), of that relevant event, where—
(a) the person no longer fulfils the conditions of regulation 14;
[¹ (b) there is an insolvency event in relation to the account provider;
[² (ba) a debt relief order is made in respect of the person (under Part 7A of the Insolvency Act 1986);]
(c) an application has been made for a bank insolvency order or a bank administration order;]
(d) in the case of a building society, a person falling [¹ section 991 of ITA 2007 or a credit union]—
(i) it ceases to be a building society or to fall within [¹ section 991 of ITA 2007 or to be a credit union], as the case may be;
(ii) its directors have made a proposal under Part 1 of the Insolvency

Act 1986 for a composition in satisfaction of its debts or a scheme of arrangement of its affairs; or
(iii) a receiver or manager of its property has been appointed; or
(f) in the case of a European institution, a relevant authorised person or an assurance undertaking which falls within regulation 14(2)(d)(iv), action corresponding to any described in sub-paragraph (b) to (e) has been taken by or in relation to the institution, person or undertaking under the law of an EEA State.

(2) On giving the notice referred to in paragraph (1), the person shall also notify the registered contact (or, if there is no registered contact, the named child) of the right to transfer the account under regulation 21, and the notice shall inform the recipient of the rights under paragraph (3).

(3) Where a registered contact—
(a) receives a notice under paragraph (2), or regulation [¹ 16(4) or] [³ 19(2)(9)], and
(b) within 30 days of the sending of the notice, transfers the account to another account provider pursuant to regulation 21,

the period between the transferor ceasing to act or qualify as an account provider, and the transfer to the transferee, shall be ignored in determining whether the account has at all times been managed by an account provider.

AMENDMENTS

1. Child Trust Funds (Amendment) Regulations 2010 (SI 2010/582) reg.10 (April 6, 2010).
2. Tribunals, Courts and Enforcement Act 2007 (Consequential Amendments) Order 2012 (SI 2012/2404) art.3(3) and Sch.3 para.34 (October 1, 2012).
3. Child Trust Funds (Amendment No. 2) Regulations 2013 (SI 2013/1744) reg.7 (August 5, 2013).

DEFINITIONS

"account"—see reg.2(1)(b).
"account provider"—see *ibid.*
"assurance undertaking"—see *ibid.*
"building society"—see *ibid.*
"child"—see reg.2(1)(a).
"company"—see reg.2(1)(b).
"EEA State"—see *ibid.*
"European institution"—see *ibid.*
"notice"—see *ibid.*
"relevant authorised person"—see *ibid.*
"relevant European institution"—see *ibid.*
"the Taxes Act"—see *ibid.*

[¹ Transfers to other accounts for children

20A.—(1) An account provider must at the request of the registered contact—
(a) transfer all the investments under the child trust fund, or an amount representing their value in cash, to a protected child account that is provided by a person chosen by the registered contact, and
(b) when all the investments have been transferred, close the child trust fund.

Child Trust Funds Regulations 2004

(2) An account is only a protected child account for the purposes of section 7A(2) of the Act if it satisfies the condition of being a junior ISA account within regulation 2B of the Individual Savings Account Regulations 1998.]

AMENDMENT

1. Child Trust Funds (Amendment No.2) Regulations 2015 (SI 2015/876) regs 2 and 6 (April 6, 2015).

DEFINITIONS

"account"—see reg.2(1)(b).
"account provider"—see *ibid.*
"registered contact"—reg.8(1)(d).

Transfer of accounts [⁵ . . .]

8.31   21.—(1) Where—
(a) arrangements are made by a registered contact to transfer the whole of the investments under an account from one account provider ("the transferor") to another account provider ("the transferee"), [⁴ . . .]
(b) the whole of the investments under an account are so transferred in consequence of an account provider ("the transferor") ceasing to act or to qualify as an account provider, [⁴ [⁵ . . .]
[⁵ (ba) there is a transfer under regulation 20A to a protected child account, or]
[⁴(c) an account is transferred in a bulk transfer of accounts [⁵ . . .],]
the transfer shall be treated as a transfer of the account.

(2) The account and its description under regulation 4 shall not be affected for the purposes of these Regulations by reason of the transfer [⁵ in paragraph (1)(a), (b) or (c)], save that, where the registered contact specifies in accordance with paragraph (3)(a) an account of a different description, the account shall, on the transfer, become an account of that other description.

(3) The registered contact shall make—
(a) the application required by regulation 13(2) (modified as if the words "applied for" were replaced with [¹ following the transfer]), and
(b) the application and declaration required by regulation 13(3) to (5),
to the transferee.

[⁴(3A) Paragraph (3) does not apply where an account is transferred [⁵ under regulation 20A or] in a bulk transfer of accounts.

(3B) [⁵ . . .]
(3C) [⁵ . . .]
(3D) [⁵ . . .]
(3E) [⁵ . . .]
(3F) [⁵ . . .]

(3G) An account transferred in accordance with this regulation in a bulk transfer of accounts is an account opened pursuant to an application in accordance with regulation 13 for the purposes of these Regulations [⁵ . . .].

[¹[⁴(3H) Where a registered contact applies in accordance with paragraph (3) to a potential transferee for a transfer under this regulation, specifying

(SI 2004/1450 reg.21) (as amended)

a stakeholder account offered by the transferee, the transferee shall not decline to accept that application (or the transfer in consequence of it) except where—
- (a) the transferee has reason to believe that the registered contact has given untrue information in his application;
- (b) the transferee demonstrates to the satisfaction of the Board that acceptance of transfers, or a class of transfers, during a particular period would jeopardise his ability to prevent any of the matters mentioned in regulation 16(2)(a); or
- (c) the transferor does not give the transferee the notice in accordance with paragraph (4).]

(4) The transferor shall on the date of the transfer give the transferee a notice containing the information specified in paragraph (5) and the declaration specified in paragraph (6).

[5 (4A) In relation to paragraph (1)(ba), the account provider shall on the date of the transfer give the person providing the protected child account a notice containing the information specified in paragraph (5)(a) and (b)(i), (ii) and (iv) and the declaration specified in paragraph (6) (with references to "transferor" changed to "account provider" and references to "transferee" changed to "person providing the protected child account").]

(5) The information specified in this paragraph is—
- (a) as regards the named child—
  - (i) his full name,
  - (ii) his date of birth,
  - (iii) his unique reference number;
- (b) as regards the account—
  - (i) the description of the account,
  - (ii) the date of the transfer,
  - (iii) the total amount subscribed to the account during the period from the beginning of the subscription year in which the transfer takes place to the date of the transfer,
  - (iv) any amount which has been claimed from the Board under regulations [3 26 or 27] and which has not been paid at the date of the transfer; [2, and
  - (v) the total amount subscribed to the account during the previous subscription year, where that subscription year ended later than the 5th April preceding the date of the transfer.]
- (c) the full name and address, including postcode, of the registered contact who has made the transfer arrangements.

(6) The declaration specified in this paragraph is a declaration by the transferor that—
- (a) he has fulfilled all his obligations to the named child, the Board or otherwise, which are imposed by these Regulations;
- (b) he has transferred to the transferee or his nominee all the account investments and that, where registration of any such transfer is required, he has taken the necessary steps to ensure that those account investments can be registered in the name of the transferee or nominee;
- (c) he will forward any further payment received in respect of those account investments to the transferee, on receipt of the payment, and
- (d) the information contained in the notice is correct.

AMENDMENTS

1. Child Trust Funds (Amendment) Regulations 2004 (SI 2004/2676) reg.13 (April 6, 2005).
2. Child Trust Funds (Amendment) Regulations 2010 (SI 2010/582) reg.11 (April 6, 2010).
3. Child Trust Funds (Amendment) Regulations 2013 (SI 2013/263) reg.2(4)(d) (March 16, 2013).
4. Child Trust Funds (Amendment No.2) Regulations 2013 (SI 2013/1744) reg.8 (August 5, 2013).
5. Child Trust Funds (Amendment No.2) Regulations 2015 (SI 2015/876) regs 2, 7 and 8 (April 6, 2015).

DEFINITIONS

"account"—see reg.2(1)(b).
"account investment"—see *ibid.*
"account provider"—see *ibid.*
"child"—see reg.2(1)(a).
"eligible child"—see *ibid.*
"notice"—see reg.2(1)(b).

Recoupment of Inland Revenue contributions to void accounts (and other accounts)

8.32   22.—(1) Where—
(a) the named child has never been an eligible child (see regulation 8(1)(b)), or
(b) there is a breach of regulation 8(1)(c) in relation to an account,
the account is void, and the persons mentioned in paragraph (3) shall account to the Inland Revenue for Inland Revenue contributions paid in respect of the account, together with income and gains which have arisen in consequence of the crediting of any of those payments to the account.

(2) Where—
(a) the condition in section 9(5) of the Act [² or regulation 7(10B) or 7A(4)] was satisfied in relation to a child, but the determination under sections 18 to 21 of the Tax Credits Act 2002 has been overturned, or
(b) the condition in section 9(8) of the Act was satisfied in relation to a child, but it has subsequently been determined that payment of the relevant benefit or tax credit mentioned in that subsection should not have been made, or that the applicable amount or tax credit should not have included an amount or credit in respect of the child, [¹or
(c) the requirements of regulation 7(10) [², or the condition in regulation 7(10C) [³, 7A(5) or 7B(1)] was,] were satisfied in relation to a child, but it has subsequently been determined that payment of the relevant benefit mentioned in [² the relevant provision] should not have been made, or that the applicable amount should not have included an amount in respect of that child,]
the persons mentioned in paragraph (3) shall account to the Inland Revenue for any supplementary contribution [¹, or further contribution, as the case may be,] paid in respect of the account, together with income and gains which have arisen in consequence of the crediting of any such payment to the account.

(3) The persons mentioned in paragraphs (1) and (2) are—

(SI 2004/1450 reg.22) (as amended)

 (a) the account provider (to the extent that he has assets in his possession or control),
 (b) the registered contact,
 (c) the named child, and
 (d) any person in whom the Inland Revenue contributions, income or gains, or any property directly or indirectly representing any of them, is vested (whether beneficially or otherwise)
and they shall be jointly and severally liable.

(4) Where a person accountable under this regulation is notified by the Inland Revenue that an amount is due from him under it, that amount shall be treated for the purposes of Part 6 of the Management Act (collection and recovery) as if it were tax charged in an assessment on that person, and due and payable.

AMENDMENTS

1. Child Trust Funds (Amendment) Regulations 2005 (SI 2005/383) reg.4 (April 6, 2005).
2. Child Trust Funds (Amendment) Regulations 2009 (SI 2009/475) reg.6 (April 6, 2009).
3. Child Trust Funds (Amendment No. 2) Regulations 2010 (SI 2010/836) reg.4 (April 1, 2010).

DEFINITIONS

 "account"—see reg.2(1)(b).
 "account provider"—see *ibid.*
 "child"—see reg.2(1)(a).
 "eligible child"—see *ibid.*
 "the Management Act"—see reg.2(1)(b).
 "tax"—see *ibid.*

"Repair" of invalid accounts

23.—(1) Except in the case of a breach of regulation 8(1)(b) or (c) (where no repair of an account is possible), it is an overriding requirement to be satisfied in relation to an account that the account provider and registered contact, as the case may be, take any steps necessary to remedy any breach of these Regulations. **8.33**

(2) Where a breach is remedied as mentioned in paragraph (1), the account shall, to the extent of that breach, be treated as having been a valid account at all times, except for determining whether there has been a breach of these Regulations for the purposes of section 20 of the Act (penalties).

DEFINITIONS

 "account"—see reg.2(1)(b).
 "account provider"—see *ibid.*

Child Trust Funds Regulations 2004

PART 3

TAX AND ADMINISTRATION OF ACCOUNTS

Exemption from tax of account income and gains

8.34   24.—Subject to compliance with these Regulations (and in particular regulation 9)—
- (a) no tax shall be chargeable on the account provider or his nominee, or on the named child or registered contact (on his behalf)—
    - (i) in respect of interest, dividends, distributions or gains in respect of account investments [²(excluding any building society bonus)],
    - [¹(ia) in respect of alternative finance return or profit share return paid by a financial institution (within the meanings in Chapter 5 of Part 2 of the Finance Act 2005);]
    - [²(ib) in respect of a payment under a building society bonus scheme, so far as the payment is calculated by reference to account investments (and if paid directly by the society into the account, the payment shall not count towards the subscription limit in regulation 9);]
    - (ii) on any annual profits or gains treated [⁴ under Part 12 of ITA 2007] as having been received by any of them in respect of account investments,
    - (iii) on an offshore income gain to which a disposal made by any of them of an account investment gives rise, which is treated by section 761(1) of the Taxes Act as constituting profits or gains,
    - [⁴ (iv) on a profit on the disposal of a deeply discounted security within the meaning given by section 430 of ITTOIA 2005;] or
    - (v) in respect of gains treated [⁴ under Chapter 9 of Part 4 of ITTOIA 2005] as arising in connection with a policy of life insurance which is an account investment;
- (b) losses accruing on any disposal of account investments shall be disregarded for the purposes of capital gains tax;
- [³(ba) any gain or loss accruing on and attributable to a payment within paragraph (ib) of sub-paragraph (a) shall not be a chargeable gain or allowable loss for capital gains tax purposes;]
- (c) [⁴ section 935 of ITA 2007] shall apply with the following modifications—
    - (i) for references to a plan manager, substitute references to an account provider,
    - (ii) for references to a plan, substitute references to an account, and
    - (iii) for the reference to [¹Chapter 3 of Part 6 of ITTOIA 2005], substitute a reference to the Act;
- (d) [⁴ a deficiency arising in a tax year and falling within section 539(1) of ITTOIA 2005], so far as it relates to a policy of life insurance which is an account investment, shall not be allowable as a deduction from the total income of the named child;
- (e) relief in respect of tax shall be given in the manner and to the extent provided by these Regulations; and

(f) income arising from account investments shall not be regarded as income for any income tax purposes (including [¹section 629 of ITTOIA 2005]).

AMENDMENTS

1. Child Trust Funds (Amendment No.3) Regulations 2005 (SI 2005/3349) reg.7 (December 27, 2005).
2. Child Trust Funds (Amendment No.3) Regulations 2006 (SI 2006/3195) reg.4 (January 1, 2007).
3. Child Trust Funds (Amendment No.3) Regulations 2006 (SI 2006/3195) reg.5 (January 1, 2007).
4. Child Trust Funds (Amendment) Regulations 2010 (SI 2010/582) reg.12 (April 6, 2010).

DEFINITIONS

"account"—see reg.2(1)(b).
"account investment"—see *ibid.*
"account provider"—see *ibid.*
"child"—see reg.2(1)(a).
"gains"—see reg.2(1)(b).
"security"—see *ibid.*
"tax"—see *ibid.*
"the Taxes Act"—see *ibid.*
"year"—see *ibid.*

Tax liabilities and reliefs—account provider to act on behalf of the named child

25.—(1) An account provider may under these Regulations make tax claims, conduct appeals and agree on behalf of the named child (or of the registered contact in respect of the child) liabilities for and reliefs from tax in respect of an account.

(2) Tax claims shall be made to the Board in accordance with the provisions of regulations 26 and 27.

(3) Where any relief or exemption from tax previously given in respect of an account has by virtue of these Regulations become excessive, in computing the relief due on any claim there shall be deducted (so that amounts equal to that excess are set-off or repaid to the Board, as the case may be) notwithstanding that those amounts have been invested, any other amount of tax due to the Board by the account provider in respect of any tax liability in respect of account investments under an account including (but without prejudice to the making of an assessment under that Schedule) any amount falling due in respect of a liability under [¹ Chapter 9 of Part 15 of ITA 2007].

AMENDMENT

1. Child Trust Funds (Amendment) Regulations 2010 (SI 2010/582) reg.13 (April 6, 2010).

DEFINITIONS

"account"—see reg.2(1)(b).
"account investment"—see *ibid.*
"account provider"—see *ibid.*
"child"—see reg.2(1)(a).

"tax"—see *ibid.*
"the Taxes Act"—see *ibid.*

Repayments in respect of tax to account provider—interim tax claims

8.36   **26.**—(1) Notwithstanding the provisions of any other enactment, the Board shall not be under an obligation to make any repayment in respect of tax under these Regulations earlier than the end of the month following the month in which the claim for the repayment is received.

(2) A claim for repayment in respect of tax which is not an annual claim ("interim tax claim") may be made only for a period of a month (or a number of months not exceeding six) beginning on the 6th day of the month and ending on the 5th day of the relevant following month.

(3) No claim for repayment may be made for the month ending 5th October or any subsequent month in a year until the annual claim due under regulation 27(2) in respect of an account for the preceding year has been duly made by the account provider and received by the Board.

(4) Where, on the occasion of a claim, there is due to the Board an amount in respect of tax, that amount shall be recoverable by the Board in the same manner as tax charged by an assessment on the account provider which has become final and conclusive.

(5) This regulation and regulation 27 shall not apply to any repayment in respect of tax on account investments falling within regulation 12(2)(m) (life insurance), or on distributions and other rights or proceeds in respect of those investments.

DEFINITIONS

"account"—see reg.2(1)(b).
"account investment"—see *ibid.*
"account provider"—see *ibid.*
"tax"—see *ibid.*
"year"—see *ibid.*

Repayments in respect of tax to account provider—annual tax claims

8.37   **27.**—(1) An annual tax claim is a claim for repayment in respect of tax for a year and may not be made at any time more than six years after the end of the year.

(2) Where the account provider—
(a) has made at least one interim tax claim during a year, or
(b) wishes to reclaim tax, or there is due to the Board an amount in respect of tax, following the end of the year,
the account provider shall within six months after the end of the year make an annual tax claim to establish the total of tax repayments due under an account for that year.

(3) Where the aggregate of the repayments in respect of interim tax claims for the year shown by an annual tax claim exceeds the amount of tax repayable for the year shown on the claim, the account provider shall repay the amount of the excess to the Board with the claim.

(4) If an account provider fails to make the annual tax claim required under paragraph (2)(a) within the time limited, the Board may issue a

notice to the account provider showing the aggregate of payments in respect of the interim tax claims for the year, and stating that the Board are not satisfied that the amount due to the account provider for that year exceeds the lower amount stated in the notice.

(5) If an annual tax claim is not delivered to the Board within 14 days after the issue of a notice under paragraph (4) the amount of the difference between the aggregate and the lower amount stated in the notice shall immediately become recoverable by the Board in the same manner as tax charged by an assessment on the account provider which has become final and conclusive.

(6) Where an annual tax claim has been made and the account provider subsequently discovers that an error or mistake has been made in the claim the account provider may make a supplementary annual claim within the time allowed in paragraph (1).

DEFINITIONS

"account"—see reg.2(1)(b).
"account provider"—see *ibid.*
"notice"—see *ibid.*
"tax"—see *ibid.*
"year"—see *ibid.*

Account provider's tax claims—supplementary provisions

28.—(1) Section 42 of the Management Act shall not apply to tax claims under these Regulations.

(2) No appeal shall lie from the Board's decision on an interim tax claim.

(3) An appeal [¹ . . .] from the Board's decision on an annual tax claim, [¹. . .] shall be brought by giving notice to the Board within 30 days of receipt of notice of the decision.

(4) No payment or repayment made or other thing done on or in relation to an interim tax claim or a notice under regulation 27(4) shall prejudice the decision on an annual tax claim.

(5) The provisions contained in Part 5 of the Management Act (appeals and other proceedings) shall apply to an appeal under paragraph (3) above, [¹ and, on an appeal that is notified to the tribunal, the tribunal] may vary the decision appealed against whether or not the variation is to the advantage of the appellant.

(6) All such assessments, payments and repayments shall be made as necessary to give effect to the Board's decision on an annual tax claim or to any variation of that decision on appeal.

(7) Claims under these Regulations shall be in such form and contain such particulars as the Board prescribe and, subject to regulation 32(1), shall be signed by the account provider, and forms prescribed for annual claims may require a report to be given by a person qualified for appointment as auditor of a company.

AMENDMENT

1. Transfer of Tribunal Functions and Revenue and Customs Appeals Order 2009 (SI 2009/56) art.3(2) and Sch.2 para.127 (April 1, 2009).

DEFINITIONS

"account provider"—see reg.2(1)(b).
"company"—see *ibid*.
"the Management Act"—see *ibid*.
"notice"—see *ibid*.
"tax"—see *ibid*.

Assessments for withdrawing relief and recovering tax

8.39   29.—(1) Where—
(a) any relief or exemption from tax given in respect of income or gains under an account is found not to be due or to be excessive, or
(b) the full amount of tax in respect of the income or gains under an account has not otherwise been fully accounted for and paid to the Board on behalf of the named child,
an assessment to tax may be made by the Board in the amount or further amount which in their opinion ought to be charged.

(2) An assessment to which paragraph (1) refers may be made on the account provider or on the registered contact (in respect of the child where the child is under the age of 16).

(3) If the assessment is made to recover tax in respect of income under an account it shall be made under Case VI of Schedule D.

(4) [1 ...].

AMENDMENT

1. Child Trust Funds, Registered Pension Schemes and Stamp Duty Reserve Tax (Consequential Amendments) Regulations 2012 (SI 2012/886) reg.2 (April 6, 2012).

DEFINITIONS

"account"—see reg.2(1)(b).
"account provider"—see *ibid*.
"child"—see reg.2(1)(a).
"gains"—see reg.2(1)(b).
"the Management Act"—see *ibid*.
"tax"—see *ibid*.

Fortnightly claim and financial returns

8.40   30.—[1. . .]

AMENDMENT

1. Child Trust Funds (Amendment) Regulations 2013 (SI 2013/263) reg.2(3) (March 16, 2013).

Records to be kept by account provider

8.41   31.—(1) An account provider shall at all times keep sufficient records in respect of an account to enable the requirements of these Regulations to be satisfied.

(2) In particular, an account provider shall produce (when required to do so by an officer of the Board) any—
(a) application made under regulation 13(1) or (10),

(SI 2004/1450 reg.31) (as amended)

   (b) voucher given to him,
   (c) annual statement issued by him, and
   (d) transfer notice given to him under regulation 21(4),
or electronic copies, within the period of 3 years from when it was made, issued or given (notwithstanding any transfer of the account under regulation [² 20A or] 21).
   [¹ (3) [² . . .]
   (4) [² . . .]]

AMENDMENTS

1. Child Trust Funds (Amendment No. 2) Regulations 2013 (SI 2013/1744) reg.9 (August 5, 2013).
2. Child Trust Funds (Amendment No.2) Regulations 2015 (SI 2015/876) regs 2 and 9 (April 6, 2015).

DEFINITIONS

   "account"—see reg.2(1)(b).
   "account provider"—see *ibid.*
   "notice"—see *ibid.*
   "year"—see *ibid.*

Returns of information by account provider

32.—(1) An account provider shall within 60 days after the end of each year in which he acts as an account provider, and after ceasing to act or to qualify as an account provider, deliver by means of electronic communications to the Board a return for that year, or for the part of that year in which he so acted or qualified, in a form specified by the Board, which contains the information specified in paragraph (2).

(2) The information specified in this paragraph is information relating to each account in respect of which he acted as account provider, in the year or the part of the year for which the return is made, other than accounts transferred [³ . . .] under regulation [³ 20A or] 21 in that year or part of a year, as to—
   (a) as regards the named child—
      (i) [¹. . .]
      (ii) [¹. . .]
      (iii) his unique reference number;
   (b) as regards each such account—
      (i) whether or not the account is a stakeholder account,
      (ii) whether or not there is a registered contact for the account,
      (iii) the aggregate market value of the account investments held under the account, subject to paragraph (3), the value of each account investment being determined either as at 5th April in that year, or any other valuation date not falling earlier than 5th October in that year, and
      (iv) the total amount of cash subscribed to the account, in the subscription year ending during the year or the part of the year for which the return is made.

[² (2A) Where, during the year or part of the year, the named child reaches the age of 18 years or dies, there shall be substituted for paragraph (2)(b)(iii)—

8.42

("iii) the aggregate market value of the account investments held under the account immediately before the relevant event mentioned in paragraph (2A),"]

(3) The reference in paragraph (2)(b)(iii) to market value shall be construed—
- (a) in the case of policies of life insurance, as a reference to their surrender value, and
- (b) as referring to separate values for—
    - (i) cash falling within regulation 12(2)(k) or (l), and
    - (ii) policies of life insurance and all other account investments.

(4) No claim for repayment, or repayment, may be made under regulations 26 and 27 until the returns which have become due under this regulation have been duly made by the account provider and received by the Board.

AMENDMENTS

1. Child Trust Funds (Amendment No.2) Regulations 2005 (SI 2005/909) reg.9 (April 6, 2005).
2. Child Trust Funds (Amendment) Regulations 2010 (SI 2010/582) reg.14 (April 6, 2010).
3. Child Trust Funds (Amendment No.2) Regulations 2015 (SI 2015/876) regs 2 and 10 (April 6, 2015).

DEFINITIONS

"account"—see reg.2(1)(b).
"account investment"—see *ibid*.
"account provider"—see *ibid*.
"child"—see reg.2(1)(a).
"electronic communications"—see reg.2(1)(b).
"market value"—see *ibid*.
"year"—see *ibid*.

Information about "looked after children" from Local Authorities

8.43   **33.**—[1. . .]

AMENDMENT

1. Child Trust Funds (Amendment) Regulations 2011 (SI 2011/781) reg.3 (April 7, 2011).

[1 The Official Solicitor or Accountant of Court to be the person who has the authority to manage an account

8.44   **33A.**—[4 (1) Every local authority shall be under a duty to—
- (a) identify any child who—
    - (i) is born after 31st August 2002 and before 3rd January 2011,
    - (ii) is under 16 years of age at the end of the return period, and
    - (iii) during the return period falls within the circumstances specified in paragraph (2) for the first time since the child became looked after (in Scotland, looked after and accommodated) by the local authority; and
- (b) deliver to the Board, within 10 days of the end of each return period and by means of electronic communications, a return for that period in a form specified by the Board containing the information specified in paragraph (2A) for each child identified under sub-paragraph (a).]

(SI 2004/1450 reg.33A) (as amended)

(2) The circumstances specified are where—
(a) the child is looked after (in Scotland, looked after and accommodated) by the local authority, and
(b) at least one of the following conditions is satisfied.

Condition 1

There is no person, or no person other than the local authority, who has parental responsibility (in Scotland, parental responsibilities) for the child.

Condition 2

It is part of the care plan for the child that—
(a) the child will live indefinitely away from home (or his former home), and
(b) the child will not have face to face contact with any parent having parental responsibility (in Scotland, parental responsibilities) for the child.

Condition 3

An order has been made under section 34(4) of the Children Act 1989 or Article 53(4) of the Children (Northern Ireland) Order 1995, authorising the local authority to refuse to allow contact between the child and any person with parental responsibility [⁶(or, in Scotland, a compulsory supervision order or an interim compulsory supervision order is in force and contains a direction regulating contact to the effect that the child has no contact with a person who has parental responsibilities in relation to that child)], and there is no other individual with parental responsibility (in Scotland, parental responsibilities) for the child to act as registered contact.
[⁶ In this Condition—
(a) "compulsory supervision order" has the meaning given by section 83 of the Children's Hearings (Scotland) Act 2011;
(b) "interim compulsory supervision order" has the meaning given by section 86 of that Act; and
(c) "contact direction" means a measure mentioned in section 83(2)(g) of that Act and contained within a compulsory supervision order or an interim compulsory supervision order.]

Condition 4

The Court of Protection has—
(a) appointed a [³ deputy] for a person with parental responsibility for the child, or
[³ (b) determined that such a person lacks capacity within the meaning of the Mental Capacity Act 2005 (c.9) to manage the child's property and affairs]
and there is no other individual with parental responsibility for the child to act as registered contact.
In Scotland, in this Condition for—
(a) "Court of Protection" substitute "Sheriff",
(b) [³ "deputy"] substitute "guardian appointed under section 58 of the Adults with Incapacity (Scotland) Act 2000",

(c) the reference to a [³ person lacking capacity], substitute "incapable for the purposes of the Adults with Incapacity (Scotland) Act 2000," and
(d) "parental responsibility" substitute "parental responsibilities".

Condition 5

The child has been lost or abandoned, and there is no prospect for the foreseeable future of reunification of the child with a parent having parental responsibility (in Scotland, parental responsibilities) for the child.
In this Condition, "lost or abandoned"—
(a) in England and Wales, has the meaning in section 20(1)(b) of the Children Act 1989;
(b) in Northern Ireland, has the meaning in Article 21(1)(b) of the Children (Northern Ireland) Order 1995; and
(c) in Scotland, has the meaning in section 25(1)(b) of the Children (Scotland) Act 1995.

[²Condition 6

In England and Wales, an adoption agency or local authority has been authorised to place the child for adoption under section 19, or by a placement order under section 21, of the Adoption and Children Act 2002, or in Northern Ireland, an Order has been made under Article 17 or 18 of the Adoption (Northern Ireland) Order 1987 to free the child for adoption.]
[⁴ (2A) The information specified in this paragraph is—
(a) the name, address and unique identifier of the local authority making the return;
(b) the name of the local authority officer responsible for the return;
(c) the full name, sex and date of birth of the child;
(d) the full name and address of the child's mother, if known by the local authority (or failing that the full name and address of the child's father, if known), unless the local authority considers the child's situation to be particularly sensitive;
(e) any information that the local authority has about whether the child is or may be a person subject to immigration control within the meaning of section 115(9) of the Immigration and Asylum Act 1999(1), and the nature of that information;
(f) a correspondence address for the child; and
(g) if known by the local authority, the child's unique reference number as stated on the voucher issued under section 5(1) of the Child Trust Funds Act 2004(2) (if any).]
[⁵ (2B) The unique identifier of a local authority as referred to in paragraph (2A)(a) is the number allocated to the local authority by the Board for the purpose of these Regulations.]
(3) Where—
[⁴ (a) the local authority delivers to the Board a return under this regulation in respect of any child, and]
(b) the Board (subject to checking and if necessary correcting the contents of the form) delivers it to the Official Solicitor (where the child is in England and Wales or Northern Ireland) or the Accountant of Court (where the child is in Scotland),

(SI 2004/1450 reg.33A) (as amended)

the Official Solicitor or Accountant of Court, as the case may be, shall be the person who has the authority to manage the child's account for the purposes of section 3(6)(b) of the Act.

(4) The Official Solicitor or Accountant of Court shall cease to be the person who has the authority to manage the child's account (and shall be discharged from the duties of registered contact) where—
   (a) the child attains the age of 16,
   (b) in any case where the child is under 16 and still looked after (in Scotland, looked after and accommodated) by a local authority—
      (i) the local authority confirms to the Official Solicitor or Accountant of Court that there is a named responsible person in relation to the child, who is able to be the registered contact for the child's account, and that none of the Conditions in paragraph (2) applies, and
      (ii) the Official Solicitor or Accountant of Court cancels his declaration and authorisation in accordance with regulation 13(7) and is replaced as registered contact by that responsible person, in accordance with regulation 13(10), or
   (c) in any case where the child is under 16 and is not looked after (in Scotland, looked after and accommodated) by a local authority—
      (i) a responsible person for the child provides evidence to the satisfaction of the Official Solicitor or Accountant of Court, as the case may be, that he has parental responsibility for the child, and
      (ii) the Official Solicitor or Accountant of Court cancels his declaration and authorisation in accordance with regulation 13(7) and is replaced as registered contact by that responsible person, in accordance with regulation 13(10).

(5) A local authority shall, for the purposes of paragraph (4), confirm to the Official Solicitor or Accountant of Court, as the case may be—
   (a) whether the child is still looked after (in Scotland, looked after and accommodated) by the authority, and
   (b) the identity of the person or persons who had parental responsibility for the child at the date when he ceased to be looked after (in Scotland, looked after and accommodated) by the authority (or, at the option of the authority, any later date).

[4 (6) In this regulation—

"local authority" includes an authority within the meaning of the Children (Northern Ireland) Order 1995(3);

"looked after and accommodated child", in Scotland, means a child who is—
   (a) both looked after, and provided with or placed in accommodation, by a local authority within the meaning of those expressions in Part 2 of the Children (Scotland) Act 1995(4), or
   (b) accommodated by a local authority under section 22 of that Act,
and related expressions shall be construed accordingly;

"looked after child"—
   (a) in England and Wales, has the meaning given in section 22(1) of the Children Act 1989(5), extended to include a child accommodated by a local authority under section 17 of that Act, and

Child Trust Funds Regulations 2004

(b) in Northern Ireland, means a child accommodated under Part 4 of the Children (Northern Ireland) Order 1995,

and related expressions shall be construed accordingly;

"return period" means a period—

(a) beginning on 7th April 2011 and ending on 6th May 2011, and

(b) each succeeding period of one month.]

AMENDMENTS

1. Child Trust Funds (Amendment No.2) Regulations 2004 (SI 2004/3382) reg.5 (April 6, 2005).

2. Child Trust Funds (Amendment No.2) Regulations 2006 (SI 2006/2684) reg.5 (October 31, 2006).

3. Mental Capacity Act 2005 (Transitional and Consequential Provisions) Order 2007 (SI 2007/1898) art.6 and Sch.1 para.33 (October 1, 2007).

4. Child Trust Funds (Amendment) Regulations 2011 (SI 2011/781) reg.4 (April 7, 2011).

5. Child Trust Funds (Amendment No.3) Regulations 2011 (SI 2011/2447) reg.6 (November 1, 2011).

6. Children's Hearings (Scotland) Act 2011 (Consequential and Transitional Provisions and Savings) Order 2013 (SI 2013/1465) Sch.1 para.21 (June 24, 2013).

DEFINITIONS

"account"—see reg.2(1)(b).
"child"—see reg.2(1)(a).
"parental responsibility"—see *ibid*.
"responsible person"—see *ibid*.

Information to be provided to the Board

8.45   **34.** [¹ . . .]

AMENDMENT

1. Child Trust Funds (Amendment) Regulations 2010 (SI 2010/582) reg.16 (April 6, 2010).

Inspection of records by officer of the Board

8.46   **35.**—[¹ . . .]

AMENDMENT

1. Child Trust Funds (Amendment) Regulations 2010 (SI 2010/582) reg.16 (April 6, 2010).

Capital gains tax—adaptation of enactments

8.47   **36.**—(1) For the purposes of capital gains tax—

(a) any assets held by a named child as account investments shall be regarded as held by the child in a separate capacity from that in which he holds any other assets of the same description; and

(b) the named child shall be treated as having sold all the account investments, and as having reacquired them in his personal capacity, for a consideration equal to their market value, immediately before he attains the age of 18 years (and ceases to be a child).

(2) Sections 127 to 131 of the 1992 Act shall not apply in relation to

qualifying investments falling within any of sub-paragraphs (a), (b), and (f) to (i) of regulation 12(2) which are held under an account if there is by virtue of any allotment for payment as is mentioned in section 126(2) of that Act a reorganisation affecting those assets.

DEFINITIONS

"account"—see reg.2(1)(b).
"account investment"—see *ibid.*
"child"—see reg.2(1)(a).
"market value"—see reg.2(1)(b).
"the 1992 Act"—see *ibid.*

Administration of tax in relation to accounts—supplementary

37.—(1) Nothing in these Regulations shall be taken to prejudice any powers conferred or duties imposed by or under any enactment in relation to the making of returns of income or gains, or for the recovery of tax, penalties or interest by means of an assessment or otherwise.

(2) Notwithstanding the provisions of these Regulations an account provider shall not be released from obligations under these Regulations in relation to an account except under conditions agreed in writing with and notified to that person by the Board.

(3) The provisions contained in the Management Act shall apply to any assessment under these Regulations as if it were an assessment to tax for the year in which, apart from these Regulations, the named child would have been liable (by reason of his ownership of the investments).

(4) No obligation as to secrecy imposed by statute or otherwise shall preclude the Board from disclosing to an account provider or registered contact that any provision of these Regulations has not been satisfied or that relief has been given or claimed in respect of investments under an account.

(5) If—
(a) a chargeable event, within the meaning given by [¹ Chapter 9 of Part 4 of ITTOIA 2005], has happened in relation to a policy of life insurance which is an account investment, and
(b) the body by whom the policy was issued is satisfied that no gain is to be treated as chargeable to tax on the happening of the event by virtue of regulation 24(a)(v),

the body shall not be obliged to deliver the certificates mentioned in section 552(1) of [¹ the Taxes Act].

This paragraph does not prevent the operation of section 552(1) in a case to which regulation 38(1) applies.

(6) Where—
(a) it comes to the notice of the account provider, in any manner, that the event specified in regulation 12(11) has occurred in relation to a policy, and
(b) the account provider is not the insurer for the time being responsible for the obligations under the policy or, where the policy is not still in existence, the person who was the last such insurer,

the account provider shall, within 30 days of the event coming to his notice give notice to that insurer, specifying the event mentioned in sub-paragraph (a) and the termination event.

AMENDMENT

1. Child Trust Funds (Amendment) Regulations 2010 (SI 2010/582) reg.17 (April 6, 2010).

DEFINITIONS

"account"—see reg.2(1)(b).
"account investment"—see *ibid.*
"account provider"—see *ibid.*
"child"—see reg.2(1)(a).
"gains"—see reg.2(1)(b).
"the Management Act"—see *ibid.*
"notice"—see *ibid.*
"tax"—see *ibid.*
"the Taxes Act"—see *ibid.*
"year"—see *ibid.*

Application of the provisions of Chapter 2 of Part 13 of the Taxes Act [¹ and of Chapter 9 of Part 4 of ITTOIA 2005] to policies

8.49 38.—(1) This paragraph applies to a case where—
(a) the event specified in regulation 12(11) has occurred in relation to a policy of life insurance, and
(b) a termination event within the meaning in regulation 12(12) occurs in relation to that policy.

(2) Where—
(a) there is a case to which paragraph (1) applies, and
(b) a chargeable event in relation to the policy, within the meaning given by section 540 of the Taxes Act, has occurred prior to the time at which the termination event mentioned in paragraph (1)(b) occurs,
the named child shall cease to be, and shall be treated as not having been, entitled to relief from tax under regulation 24(a)(v), in respect of gains treated as arising on the occurrence of any chargeable event mentioned in sub-paragraph (b).

(3) The provisions of Chapter 2 of Part 13 of the Taxes Act shall apply, in a case to which paragraph (1) applies, to—
(a) the termination event mentioned in paragraph (1)(b), and
(b) any chargeable event mentioned in paragraph (2)(b),
with the modifications provided for in paragraphs (4) to (8) of this regulation, and the registered contact and the account provider shall account to the Board in accordance with this regulation for tax from which relief under regulation 24 has been given on the basis that the named child was so entitled, or in circumstances such that the named child was not so entitled.

(4) A termination of a policy of insurance pursuant to regulation 12(9)(b)(ii) shall be treated as the surrender [¹ of all rights under the policy for the purposes of section 484(1)(a)(i) of ITTOIA 2005].

[¹ (5) Section 530 of ITTOIA 2005 does not apply to a gain in a case to which paragraph (1) applies.]

(6) Relief under section 550 of the Taxes Act shall be computed as if paragraph (5) had not been enacted.

(7) In section 552 of the Taxes Act—
(a) in subsection (1)(b) for "policy holder" substitute "named child";
(b) in subsection (3)—

(SI 2004/1450 reg.38) (as amended)

   (i) omit "(or, where the appropriate policy holder is a company, the corresponding financial year)";
   (ii) for "the name and address of the appropriate policy holder" substitute "the name and address of the named child";
   (iii) omit "and the corresponding financial year,";
  (c) in subsection (5)—
   (i) for "the appropriate policy holder" substitute "the named child";
   (ii) omit sub-paragraph (b)(ii);
   (iii) omit paragraph (c);
   (iv) in paragraph (d) omit "except where paragraph (c) above applies,";
   (v) omit paragraph (f);
  (d) in subsection (6)—
   (i) omit paragraph (b);
   (ii) for paragraph (c) substitute—
    "(c) if the event is a death, the period of three months beginning with the receipt of written notification of the death;";
   (iii) after paragraph (c) insert—
    "(d) if the event is—
     (i) a termination event, or
     (ii) a chargeable event preceding a termination event (as mentioned in regulation 38(2) of the Child Trust Funds Regulations 2004),
    the period of three months beginning with the date on which the insurer received notice under regulation 37(6) of those Regulations or, if earlier, actual notice of the termination event.";
  (e) in subsection (7)—
   (i) in paragraph (a) omit ", or, where the policy holder is a company, the financial year,";
   (ii) omit paragraph (b);
   (iii) for paragraph (c) substitute—
    "(c) if the event is a death, the period of three months beginning with the receipt of written notification of the death;";
   (iv) after paragraph (c) insert—
    "(ca) if the event is—
     (i) a termination event, or
     (ii) a chargeable event preceding such a termination event (as mentioned in regulation 38(2) of the Child Trust Funds Regulations 2004,
    the period of three months beginning with the date on which the insurer received notice under regulation 37(6) of those Regulations or, if earlier, actual notice of the termination event."; and
   (v) in paragraph (d) after "paragraph (c)" insert "or (ca)";
  (f) in subsection (8)—
   (i) in paragraph (b) for "policy holder" substitute "named child in respect";
   (ii) in paragraph (c) omit the words from "or" to the end;
  (g) in subsection (9) omit "or financial year" in each place where they occur;

(h) in subsection (10)—
  (i) before the definition of "amount" insert—
    "'named child' has the same meaning as in the Child Trust Funds Regulations 2004;";
  (ii) omit the definitions of "appropriate policy holder" and "financial year";
  (iii) for the definition of "the relevant year of assessment" substitute—
    "'the relevant year of assessment', in the case of any gain, means the year of assessment to which the gain is attributable;"; and
  (iv) after the definition of "section 546 excess" insert—
    "'termination event' has the same meaning as in the Child Trust Funds Regulations 2004;"; and
  (v) omit subsection (11).
(8) In section 552ZA of the Taxes Act—
(a) in subsection (2)(b) omit the words "or an assignment"; and
(b) omit subsections (3) and (4).
(9) The account provider shall account for and pay income tax at the [¹ basic] rate in force for the year in which the termination event, or the chargeable event mentioned in paragraph (2)(b) occurred, as the case may be, and any amount so payable—
  (a) may be set off against any repayment in respect of tax due under regulation 26 or 27 and subject thereto,
  (b) shall be treated as an amount of tax due not later than 6 months after the end of the year in which the event specified in regulation 12(11) came to the notice of the account provider, and
  (c) shall be payable without the making of an assessment.
(10) Where tax is charged in accordance with paragraph (3)(a) or (b)—
  (a) an assessment to income tax at the [¹ basic] rate in force for the relevant year may be made on the account provider or on the registered contact (on behalf of the named child), and
  (b) an assessment to income tax at the higher rate within the meaning of [¹ section 10(3) of ITA 2007], for that year, may be made on the registered contact (on behalf of the named child) within five years after the 31st January next following that year, and regulation 29 shall not apply.

AMENDMENT

1. Child Trust Funds (Amendment) Regulations 2010 (SI 2010/582) reg.18 (April 6, 2010).

DEFINITIONS

"account provider"—see *ibid.*
"child"—see reg.2(1)(a).
"company"—see reg.2(1)(b).
"notice"—see *ibid.*
"tax"—see *ibid.*
"the Taxes Act"—see *ibid.*
"year"—see *ibid.*

(SI 2004/1450 Sch.) (as amended)

SCHEDULE

STAKEHOLDER ACCOUNTS

Description of stakeholder account

1. An account is a stakeholder account where it has the characteristics and complies with the conditions set out in paragraph 2.

8.50

Characteristics of stakeholder account etc

2.—(1) A stakeholder account must have the characteristics set out in sub-paragraph (2) and must comply with the conditions set out in sub-paragraphs (3) to (5).

8.51

(2) The characteristics of a stakeholder account are—
- (a) the account does not directly hold investments of any of the following kinds—
    - (i) those referred to in regulation 12(2)(f) (shares in an investment trust);
    - (ii) securities of an investment trust;
    - (iii) rights in with-profits endowment policies;
    - (iv) rights, under a contract of insurance, in a with-profits fund;
    - (v) units or shares in a relevant collective investment scheme unless it is a requirement of that scheme that the purchase and sale price of those units or shares shall, at any given time, not differ from each other and that the price must be made available to the public on a daily basis;
    - (vi) rights under a contract of insurance which are expressed as shares in funds held by the insurer unless it is a requirement of the contract of insurance that the purchase and sale price of those shares shall, at any given time, not differ from each other and that the price must be made available to the public on a daily basis;
    - [¹(via) shares referred to in regulation 12(2)(a) (shares issued by a company wherever incorporated and officially listed on a recognised stock exchange [⁴ or, in the European Economic Area, admitted to trading on a recognised stock exchange])]
    - (vii) depositary interests, where the investments concerned are investments of any of the kinds listed above in this paragraph;
- (b) [¹the requirement is fulfilled that] the account provider, and any relevant person, [¹. . .] ensure that, subject to the other provisions of this paragraph, the account has exposure to equities [¹. . .];
- [¹(ba) interest accrues on investments referred to in regulation 12(2)(k) and (l) (cash deposited in a deposit account or in a share account) on a daily basis at a rate that is not less than the Bank of England base rate minus 1 per cent per annum [³, except where cash is held temporarily on deposit in the course of dealing in investments under the account];
- [²(baa) when the Bank of England base rate increases, the interest rate on investments referred to in regulation 12(2)(k) and (l) (cash deposited in a deposit account or in a share account) must be raised within one month of the date of that increase;]
- (bb) in relation to qualifying investments which are securities (other than in an investment trust) or a depositary interest where the relevant investments (within the meaning in that definition) are such securities, the requirement is fulfilled that—
    - (i) the securities fall within regulation 12(2)(c) [², (d) or (e)], or
    - (ii) where the securities fall within regulation 12(2)(b) [². . .] or (n), the contract under which the securities are or have been acquired, or any other transaction entered into by the registered contact or any other person, has the effect that the named child is not exposed, or not exposed to a significant extent, to the risk of loss from fluctuations in the value of the securities exceeding 20% of the capital consideration paid or payable for the acquisition of those securities, during the period when the securities in question are held in the account.]
- (c) [¹the requirement is fulfilled that] the account provider and any relevant person [¹. . .] have regard to—
    - (i) the need for diversification of investments of the account, in so far as is appropriate to the circumstances of the account; and
    - (ii) the suitability for the purposes of the account of any investment, investment strategy or investment option proposed; and
- (d) except where otherwise instructed by the registered contact, the account is subject to lifestyling.

1053

(3) The account provider must permit payment of subscriptions to the account by—
 (a) cheque;
 (b) direct debit;
 (c) standing order;
 (d) direct credit (other than standing order).
[¹For the purposes of this sub-paragraph, those means of payment do not include payments by cash, credit card or debit card or any combination including a payment by cash, credit card or debit card.]

(4) The minimum amount which may be subscribed to the account on a single occasion is £10 except where the account provider permits a smaller amount.

(5) Deductions from the account may only be made in the circumstances, and to the extent, set out in paragraph 3.

(6) In this paragraph—

"equities" means shares issued by a company wherever incorporated and officially listed on a recognised stock exchange [⁴ or, in the European Economic Area, admitted to trading on a recognised stock exchange];

"insurer" means—
 (a) a person who has permission under Part 4 of the Financial Services and Markets Act 2000 to effect or carry out contracts of insurance, or
 (b) an EEA firm of the kind mentioned in paragraph 5(d) of Schedule 3 to that Act, which has permission under paragraph 15 of that Schedule (as a result of qualifying for authorisation under paragraph 12 of that Schedule) to effect or carry out contracts of insurance;

"lifestyling" means the process beginning from a date on or before the child is [⁵ 15] years of age, or from when the account is opened, whichever is later, and continuing until the child is 18 years of age, by which the account provider, and any relevant person, adopts an investment strategy which aims progressively to minimise the variation or potential variation in capital value of the account caused by market conditions from time to time;

"relevant collective investment scheme" means an authorised unit trust scheme, an authorised open-ended investment company or a recognised scheme, as the case may be, as defined in section 237(3) of the Financial Services and Markets Act 2000;

"relevant person" means any person to whom the account provider has delegated any of his functions or responsibilities under the management agreement; and

"with-profits fund" means a fund maintained by an insurer in respect of a particular part of its long-term business for which—
 (a) separate accounting records are maintained by the insurer in respect of all income and expenditure relating to that part of its business; and
 (b) the benefits payable in respect of policies allocated to that fund are determined partly by reference to a discretion exercisable by any person.

(7) In this paragraph, the definitions of "contract of insurance" and "insurer" must be read with—
 (a) section 22 of the Financial Services and Markets Act 2000,
 (b) any relevant order made under that section, and
 (c) Schedule 2 to that Act.

Stakeholder accounts—charges etc

8.52 **3.**—(1) Deductions from a stakeholder account may only be made to the extent set out in this paragraph.

(2) Subject to sub-paragraph (5), charges for the management of, and other expenses in connection with, a stakeholder account may be recovered from the account to the extent that they do not exceed whichever is the greater of—
 (a) 3/730 per cent of the value of the child's rights in the account for each day on which the account is held; or
 (b) 3/730 per cent of the value of the investments under the account for each day on which the account is held.

(3) For the purposes of sub-paragraph (2)—
 (a) the frequency, which must be daily, weekly or monthly, with which rights or investments are to be valued; and
 (b) where valuation is to take place weekly or monthly, the day of the week or, as the case may be, the date in the month on which it is to take place,

must be specified in advance in writing by the account provider to the registered contact, and the specification may not be amended during the period of 12 months after the date on which it is made.

(4) When calculating the value of a child's rights or of investments for the purposes of sub-paragraph (2), where the account provider has specified under sub-paragraph (3) that they are to be valued weekly or monthly—
- (a) where they are to be valued weekly, they are to be valued on such day of the week ("the specified day") as has been so specified by the account provider (except that, where that day is not a working day, the rights are to be valued on the next working day), and the value of the rights on each subsequent day prior to the next specified day is to be taken to be the value of the rights on the previous specified day; and
- (b) where they are to be valued monthly, they are to be so valued on such date in each month ("the specified date") as has been so specified by the account provider (except that, where that date is not a working day, the rights are to be valued on the next working day), and the value of the rights on each subsequent day prior to the next specified date is to be taken to be the value of the rights on the previous specified date.

(5) The following charges and expenses may be deducted in full from the account and are not subject to and do not count towards the limit provided for in sub-paragraph (2)—
- (a) any stamp duty, stamp duty reserve tax [1, value added tax] or other charges [1(including any dilution levy)] incurred by the account provider directly or indirectly in the sale or purchase of investments held under the account;
- [1(aa) where any amount of tax is paid or anticipated to be payable in respect of income received or capital gains realised by the account provider in respect of investments held for the purposes of the account, the amount so deducted or anticipated;]
- (b) any charges or expenses incurred by the account provider directly or indirectly in complying with an order of the court or any other requirements imposed by law; and
- (c) expenses incurred by the account provider in complying with its obligations under regulation 8(2)(d) and (e).

(6) Valuations for the purpose of sub-paragraph (2) shall be after the deduction of any charges or expenses properly deducted from the account under sub-paragraph (5).

AMENDMENTS

1. Child Trust Funds (Amendment) Regulations 2004 (SI 2004/2676) reg.15 (April 6, 2005).

2. Child Trust Funds (Amendment No.2) Regulations 2004 (SI 2004/3382) reg.6 (April 6, 2005).

3. Child Trust Funds (Amendment No.2) Regulations 2006 (SI 2006/2684) reg.6 (October 31, 2006).

4. Child Trust Funds (Amendment No.2) Regulations 2013 (SI 2013/1744) reg.10 (August 5, 2013).

5. Child Trust Funds (Amendment No.2) Regulations 2015 (SI 2015/876) regs 2 and 11 (April 6, 2015).

DEFINITIONS

"account"—see reg.2(1)(b).
"account provider"—see *ibid.*
"Bank of England base rate"—see *ibid.*
"child"—see reg.2(1)(a).
"company"—see reg.2(1)(b).
"contract of insurance"—see para.2(7).
"depositary interest"—see reg.2(1)(c).
"equities"—see para.2(6).
"insurer"—see *ibid.*, and para.2(7).
"investments under the account"—see reg.2(1)(b).
"investment trust"—see *ibid.*
"lifestyling"—see para.2(6).
"open-ended investment company"—see reg.2(1)(c).
"recognised stock exchange"—see reg.2(1)(b).

"relevant collective investment scheme"—see para.2(6).
"relevant person"—see reg.2(1)(a) and para.2(6).
"subscriptions"—see reg.2(1)(b).
"tax"—see *ibid.*
"units"—see reg.2(1)(c).
"with-profits fund"—see para.2(6).

Child Trust Funds (Insurance Companies) Regulations 2004

(SI 2004/2680)

The Treasury, in exercise of the powers conferred upon them by section 333B of the Income and Corporation Taxes Act 1988 as extended by section 14(1) of the Child Trust Funds Act 2004, hereby make the following Regulations:

ARRANGEMENT OF REGULATIONS

8.53
1. Citation and commencement
2. Interpretation
3. Child trust fund business
4.–17. Modifications of the Taxes Act
18.–19. Modification of the Taxation of Chargeable Gains Act 1992
20.–21. Modification of the Capital Allowances Act 2001
22. Amendments to the Insurance Companies Regulations

Citation and commencement

8.54 **1.**—These Regulations may be cited as the Child Trust Funds (Insurance Companies) Regulations 2004 and shall come into force on the day appointed under section 27 of the Child Trust Funds Act 2004, for the purposes of sections 8 and 9 of that Act.

Interpretation

8.55 **2.**—In these Regulations—
"child trust fund business" has the meaning given by regulation 3;
"individual savings account business" has the meaning given in the Insurance Companies Regulations;
"the Insurance Companies Regulations" means the Individual Savings Account (Insurance Companies) Regulations 1998;
"the principal Regulations" means the Child Trust Funds Regulations 2004;
"the Taxes Act" means the Income and Corporation Taxes Act 1988.

Child trust fund business

8.56 **3.**—For the purposes of these Regulations "child trust fund business", in relation to an insurance company, means so much of that company's life assurance business as is referable to any policy of life insurance, or to the reinsurance of liabilities under any such policy, where the policy is, on the date on which the insurance is made, a qualifying investment for an account within the meaning of regulation 12 of the principal Regulations.

Modifications of the Taxes Act

4.—Regulations 5 to 17 specify modifications of provisions of the Taxes Act so far as concerns the child trust fund business (and, in the case of regulations 11(b) and (c), 13 and 14, the individual savings account business) of insurance companies.

5.—In section 431(2) insert at the appropriate place the following definition—

"'child trust fund business' has the meaning given by regulation 3 of the Child Trust Funds (Insurance Companies) Regulations 2004;".

6.—In both of sections 431C(1) and 431D(1) after "pension business" insert ", child trust fund business".

7.—In section 431F after "pension business," insert "child trust fund business,".

8.—In section 432A(2) (as modified by the Insurance Companies Regulations) after paragraph (aa) insert—

"(ab) child trust fund business;".

9.—In section 432AA(4) (as modified by the Insurance Companies Regulations) after paragraph (aa) insert—

"(ab) child trust fund business;".

10.—In both of sections 432C(1) and 432D(1) after "pension business," insert "child trust fund business,".

11.—In section 436—
(a) after the words "pension business", in each place where they occur, insert "or child trust fund business";
(b) in subsection (1)(a) for "that business" substitute "the business of each such category".
(c) after subsection (3)(c) insert—
"(ca) there may be set off (so far as it has not been set off under paragraph (c)), against the profits of child trust fund business any loss, to be computed on the same basis as the profits, which has arisen from individual savings account business, in the same or any previous accounting period;
(cb) there may be set off (so far as it has not been set off under paragraph (c)), against the profits of individual savings account business any loss, to be computed on the same basis as the profits, which has arisen from child trust fund business, in the same or any previous accounting period;".

12.—In section 438(1) add at the end "or child trust fund business".

13.—In section 440(4)(a) add at the end, "individual savings account business or child trust fund business, or assets linked to any of those categories but not to any other category of business".

14.—In section 440A(2)(a)(i) after "pension business" insert ", individual savings account business or child trust fund business or any of those categories of business".

15.—In section 466(2) insert at the appropriate place the following definition—

"'child trust fund business' shall be construed in accordance with section 431(2);".

16.—In section 755A (as modified by the Insurance Companies Regulations) after paragraph (aa) in each of subsections (4) and (13) insert—

"(ab) child trust fund business,".

Child Trust Funds (Insurance Companies) Regulations 2004

17.—In paragraph 5(5) of Schedule 19AA after "pension business," insert "child trust fund business,".

Modification of the Taxation of Chargeable Gains Act 1992

8.58 18.—Regulation 19 specifies a modification of section 212 of the Taxation of Chargeable Gains Act 1992 so far as concerns child trust fund business of insurance companies.

19.—In section 212(2) after "pension business" insert, "child trust fund business".

Modification of the Capital Allowances Act 2001

8.59 20.—Regulation 21 specifies a modification of section 256 of the Capital Allowances Act 2001 so far as concerns child trust fund business of insurance companies.

21.—In section 256(3)(a) after "pension business" insert, "child trust fund business".

Amendments to the Insurance Companies Regulations

8.60 22.—Regulations 13(b), 15 and 16 of the Insurance Companies Regulations (which are superseded by regulations 11(b), 13 and 14 of these Regulations) shall cease to have effect.

GENERAL NOTE

8.61 These Regulations make various technical modifications to revenue law provisions. They provide for the exemption from corporation tax of income and gains made by an insurance company providing child trust funds, so far as they relate to the company's child trust fund business. They also provide for the profit from operating child trust fund business to be taxed in the same way as profits from the company's Individual Savings Account (ISA) business, and for losses arising one category to be set off against profits from the other.

The Child Trust Funds (Non-tax Appeals) Regulations 2005

(SI 2005/191)

Made   *3 February 2005*
Laid before Parliament   *4 February 2005*
Coming into force   *25 February 2005*

8.62 The Treasury, in exercise of the powers conferred upon them by sections 23(1), 24(5) and 28(1) to (4) of the Child Trust Funds Act 2004, make the following Regulations:

Citation, commencement and duration

8.63 1.—(1) These Regulations may be cited as the Child Trust Funds (Non-tax Appeals) Regulations 2005 and shall come into force on 25 February 2005.

(2) [¹ . . .]

1058

(SI 2005/191 reg.1)

AMENDMENT

1. Transfer of Tribunal Functions and Revenue and Customs Appeals Order 2009 (SI 2009/56) art.3(2) Sch.2 para.132 (April 1, 2009).

Interpretation

2. *Omitted.*

Prescribed manner of notice of appeal

3.—(1) The prescribed manner of giving notice of appeal [¹, in respect of an appeal to an appeal tribunal,] to the Inland Revenue under section 23(1) of the Child Trust Funds Act 2004 is as follows.
(2) The notice must—
(a) be given in writing,
(b) contain sufficient information to identify the appellant and the decision against which the appeal is being made, and
(c) be signed by or on behalf of the appellant.
(3) In paragraph (2)(a) "writing" includes writing produced by electronic communications if those electronic communications are approved by the Commissioners of Inland Revenue.
(4) In paragraph (2)(c) "signed", where the notice is in writing produced by electronic communications, means authenticated in any manner approved by those Commissioners.

AMENDMENT

1. Tribunals, Courts and Enforcement Act 2007 (Transitional and Consequential Provisions) Order 2008 (SI 2008/2683) art.6(1) and Sch.1 para. 262 (November 3, 2008).

DEFINITIONS

"Inland Revenue"—see Child Trust Funds Act 2004 s.29, but see the note below.
"signed"—see para.(4).
"writing"—see para.(3).

GENERAL NOTE

For what amounts to a signature, see the annotation to reg.2 of the Tax Credits (Notice of Appeal) Regulations 2002. Also, see para.(4) for signatures on electronic documents.
The functions of the Commissioners of Inland Revenue have been transferred to the Commissioners for Her Majesty's Revenue and Customs (Commissioners for Revenue and Customs Act 2005 s.5(2)(a)).

4.–15. *Omitted.*

The Child Trust Funds (Appeals) Regulations 2005

(SI 2005/990)

Made   24th March 2005
Coming into force in accordance with regulation 1(1)

The Child Trust Funds (Appeals) Regulations 2005

8.68   Whereas a draft of this instrument was laid before Parliament in accordance with section 80(1) of the Social Security Act 1998 and approved by resolution of each House of Parliament.

Now therefore, the Secretary of State for Work and Pensions, in exercise of the powers conferred upon him by sections 7(6) and (7), 12(7), 14(10) (a) and (11), 16(1) and (3)(a), 28(1), 79(1) and (4) to (7) and 84 of, and paragraphs 7, 11 and 12 of Schedule 1 to, and paragraphs 1 to 6 of Schedule 5 to, the Social Security Act 1998, after consultation with the Council on Tribunals in accordance with section 8 of the Tribunals and Inquiries Act 1992, hereby makes the following Regulations:

Citation, commencement, duration and interpretation

8.69   **1.**—(1) These Regulations may be cited as the Child Trust Funds (Appeals) Regulations 2005 and shall come into force on the day after they are made.

(2) [² . . .]

(3) In these Regulations, unless the context otherwise requires—

"the Act" means the Social Security Act 1998;

"the 2004 Act" means the Child Trust Funds Act 2004;

"appeal" means an appeal under section 22 of the 2004 Act to [¹ the First-tier Tribunal];

"the Board" means the Commissioners of Inland Revenue;

[¹ . . .]

[¹ . . .]

[¹ . . .]

[¹ . . .]

"notification period" has the meaning given in regulation 3;

"party to the proceedings" means the Board and any person who brings an appeal;

[¹ . . .]

(4) [¹ . . .]

AMENDMENTS

1. Tribunals, Courts and Enforcement Act 2007 (Transitional and Consequential Provisions) Order 2008 (SI 2008/2683) art.6(1) and Sch.1 para.291 (November 3, 2008).

2. Transfer of Tribunal Functions and Revenue and Customs Appeals Order 2009 (SI 2009/56) art.3(2) and Sch.2 para.136 (April 1, 2009).

GENERAL NOTE

Paragraph (3)—"the Board"

8.70   The functions of the Commissioners of Inland Revenue have been transferred to the Commissioners for Her Majesty's Revenue and Customs (Commissioners for Revenue and Customs Act 2005 s.5(2)(a)).

Service of notices or documents

8.71   **2.**—Where by any provision of these Regulations—

(a) any notice or other document is required to be given or sent to [¹ . . .] the Board, that notice or document shall be treated as having been so given or sent on the day that it is received by [¹ . . .] by the Board, and

(b) any notice or other document is required to be given or sent to any person other than [¹ . . .] the Board, that notice or document shall, if sent to that person's last known address, be treated as having been given or sent on the day that it was posted.

AMENDMENT

1. Tribunals, Courts and Enforcement Act 2007 (Transitional and Consequential Provisions) Order 2008 (SI 2008/2683) art.6(1) and Sch.1 para.292 (November 3, 2008).

DEFINITION

"the Board"—see reg.1(3), but see also the note below.

GENERAL NOTE

The functions of the Commissioners of Inland Revenue ("the Board") have been transferred to the Commissioners for Her Majesty's Revenue and Customs (Commissioners for Revenue and Customs Act 2005 s.5(2)(a)).

Disputes about notices of appeal

3.—Where a dispute arises as to whether notice of an appeal was given to the Board within the period of thirty days specified in section 23(1) of the 2004 Act ("the notification period") the dispute shall be referred to, and be determined by, [¹ the First-tier Tribunal].

AMENDMENT

1. Tribunals, Courts and Enforcement Act 2007 (Transitional and Consequential Provisions) Order 2008 (SI 2008/2683) art.6(1) and Sch.1 para.293 (November 3, 2008).

DEFINITIONS

"the 2004 Act"—see reg.1(3).
"the Board"—*ibid.* but see also the note below.

GENERAL NOTE

The functions of the Commissioners of Inland Revenue ("the Board") have been transferred to the Commissioners for Her Majesty's Revenue and Customs (Commissioners for Revenue and Customs Act 2005 s.5(2)(a)).

Late appeals

4.—(1) Where the conditions specified in paragraphs [¹ (4) to (8) are satisfied, the Board may treat an appeal as made in time where an appeal is] brought within a period of one year after the expiration of the notification period.

(2) [¹ . . .]
(3) [¹ . . .]
[¹ (4) The Board must not treat the appeal as made in time unless the Board is satisfied that it is in the interests of justice.]
(5) For the purposes of paragraph (4) it is not in the interests of justice to [¹ treat the appeal as made in time unless the Board are] satisfied that—
   (a) the special circumstances specified in paragraph (6) are relevant [¹ . . .]; or

1061

(b) some other special circumstances exist which are wholly exceptional and relevant [¹ . . .],

and as a result of those special circumstances, it was not practicable for the appeal to be brought within the notification period.

(6) For the purposes of paragraph (5)(a), the special circumstances are that—
- (a) the [¹ appellant] or a partner or dependant of the [¹ appellant] has died or suffered serious illness;
- (b) the [¹ appellant] is not resident in the United Kingdom; or
- (c) normal postal services were disrupted.

(7) In determining whether it is in the interests of justice to [¹ treat the appeal as made in time], regard shall be had to the principle that the greater the amount of time that has elapsed between the expiration of the notification period and the [¹ submission of the notice of appeal, the more compelling should be the special circumstances.]

(8) In determining whether it is in the interests of justice to [¹ treat the appeal as made in time] no account shall be taken of the following—
- (a) that the [¹ appellant] or any person acting for him was unaware of or misunderstood the law applicable to his case (including ignorance or misunderstanding of the notification period); or
- (b) that [¹the Upper Tribunal] or a court has taken a different view of the law from that previously understood and applied.

(9) [¹ . . .]
(10) [¹ . . .]
(11) As soon as practicable after the decision is made a copy of the decision shall be sent or given to every party to the proceedings.

AMENDMENT

1. Tribunals, Courts and Enforcement Act 2007 (Transitional and Consequential Provisions) Order 2008 (SI 2008/2683) art.6(1) and Sch.1 para.294 (November 3, 2008).

DEFINITIONS

"the 2004 Act"—see reg.1(3).
"appeal"—*ibid.*
"the Board"—*ibid.* but see also the note below.
"notification period"—*ibid.*
"party to the proceedings"—*ibid.*

GENERAL NOTE

8.76 See the note to reg.5 of the Tax Credit (Appeals) (No.2) Regulations 2002.
The functions of the Commissioners of Inland Revenue ("the Board") have been transferred to the Commissioners for Her Majesty's Revenue and Customs (Commissioners for Revenue and Customs Act 2005 s.5(2)(a)).

Death of a party to an appeal

8.77 **5.**—In any proceedings relating to an appeal under section 22(2), (4), (5) or (6) of the 2004 Act, on the death of a party to the proceedings (other than the Board) the personal representative of the person who has died may represent him at any hearing.

(SI 2005/990 reg.5)

DEFINITIONS

"the 2004 Act"—see reg.1(3).
"appeal"—*ibid.*
"the Board"—*ibid.* but see also the note below.
"party to the proceedings"—*ibid.*

GENERAL NOTE

The functions of the Commissioners of Inland Revenue ("the Board") have been transferred to the Commissioners for Her Majesty's Revenue and Customs (Commissioners for Revenue and Customs Act 2005 s.5(2)(a)). **8.78**

PART IX

HMRC CODES OF PRACTICE AND GUIDANCE

NOTE

HMRC policy is to publish manuals, guides and forms dealing with all parts of the law under its management. As part of this policy, HMRC publishes a series of leaflets and factsheets about tax credits together with most of the relevant forms. These are now accessible through the GOV.UK lists of HMRC leaflets and forms. Hard copies are available through the helpline 0345 3003900.

All the guides are official publications. But none in this field carry the force of law. Nonetheless some of them are particularly important as they set out the terms on which HMRC exercises discretions (for example as to overpayments and penalties). They also detail the administrative procedures and standards that HMRC sets itself. The key guides to the way in which HMRC deals with overpayments and penalties are set out in this volume. They are marked in bold in the following list of leaflets:

How HMRC handle Tax Credit Overpayments	A leaflet available for advisers to download and print
Tax Credit Annual Review Help Sheets	(helpsheet for people who help and advise others on the tax credits renewals process—for download and print.)
WTC1	Child Tax Credit and Working Tax Credit An introduction
WTC2	A guide to Child Tax Credit and Working Tax Credit
WTC5	Working Tax Credit—Help with the costs of childcare
WTC5/CP	Working Tax Credit—The childcare element—Information for childcare providers
WTC7	Tax Credits penalties
WTC8	Child Tax Credit and Working Tax Credit—How do overpayments happen?
WTC/AP	Child Tax Credit and Working Tax Credit: how to appeal against a tax credit decision or award
WTC/FS1	Tax credits enquiry
WTC/FS2	Tax credits examinations
WTC/FS3	Tax credits formal request for information
WTC/FS4	Tax credits meetings
WTC/FS5	Tax credits—coming to the United Kingdom
WTC/FS6	Tax credits—leaving the United Kingdom

Note

WTC/FS9	Tax credits—suspension of payments
WTC/FS10	Tax credits checks
COP26	What happens if we have paid you too much tax credit?

The key standard forms are available to download from the site above. They are:

TC600	Tax Credits claim form
TC602	Checking a tax credits award
TC603R	Tax Credits renewal pack
TC603RD	Tax Credits renewal and annual declaration
TC689	Authority for intermediary to act
TC825	Working sheet for gift aid payments, pension contributions and trading losses
TC846	Form to dispute a tax credit overpayment
TC956	Disability working sheet

The standard manuals issued to staff are:

CCM	New Tax Credits Claimant Compliance Manual
NTC Manual	Clerical procedures
TCTM	Tax Credits Technical Manual

All are available on the site above (although some paragraphs are withheld under the Freedom of Information Act exemptions).

LEAFLET WTC7

TAX CREDIT PENALTIES

WHAT HAPPENS AT THE END OF A CHECK

This leaflet tells you about the penalties you may get if your claim for tax credits is not correct. It also explains how to appeal against those penalties.

Introduction

When you claim Child Tax Credit or Working Tax Credit you are responsible for making sure that the information on your claim is correct. 9.1

This leaflet is for anyone who may be charged a penalty after we have carried out a check on their tax credits claim. It does not tell you everything about penalties, but it does tell you what is likely to happen and what you can do if we charge you a penalty.

Information about how and why we carry out tax credits checks is in the factsheet. We normally give these to customers when we start a check.

Why do we charge penalties?

We charge penalties to: 9.2

- encourage people to be careful and make sure their claims are correct in future

- stop customers from giving us incorrect information in the future and

- penalise people who try to defraud the system.

Your penalty

We can charge you a penalty of up to £3,000 if you deliberately gave the wrong information. This includes the information you give: 9.3

- in your claim

- on any notification of a change in circumstances

- in response to a particular request for information during our checks.

We calculate penalties as a percentage of the tax credits when you over-claimed as a result of the incorrect award if you made a deliberate error.

We will explain why we believe that you have deliberately given us incorrect information. If you do not accept our explanation you can ask an independent tribunal to decide.

We will not charge you a penalty if you have taken reasonable care to give us the correct information, even if you make a mistake which results in you claiming too much tax credits.

If we believe you may have committed a criminal offence, we may carry out an investigation and prosecute you. If this happens, we will not charge you a penalty.

What is a deliberate error?

9.4 Deliberate error is where a claimant has deliberately given the wrong information to claim for an element of tax credits they are not entitled to or to increase an element by making a false statement about their circumstances. This can include:

- giving us incorrect working hours information such as
  - claiming to be working when not actually working
  - claiming to be working over 16 or 30 hours when not doing so
  - for couples with children, claiming to be working a combined total of 24 hours when the claimants do not work those hours, have not done so in the recent past and have no intention of doing so
- claiming to be in prison, an inpatient in hospital or incapacitated when they are not
- claiming to be entitled to carers allowance when they are not
- claiming for the disability element with no basis to support such a claim
- understatement of income where there was no basis for the amount of income declared
- failing to tell us about a source of income
- claiming as a single person when a partner is present and a joint claim should have been submitted
- any other wrong declarations where the information concerns the claimant's own circumstances which they can be reasonably expected to know.

Couples

9.5 If you have made a joint claim with your partner, you are both responsible for the information you provide in your claim.

We may charge you a penalty as a couple where:

- either of you could have told us about any change in circumstances, or
- you were both responsible for giving us incorrect information.

If the incorrect information relates to one partner and the other person could not have reasonably known that it was not correct, we will only charge the penalty on that partner.

The maximum penalty for a joint claim is no more than the maximum penalty for an individual claim.

The amount of your penalty

9.6 When working out the amount of your penalty, we will take into account:

- the amount of tax credits overclaimed
- whether it is your first, second or third or subsequent offence
- the behaviour that led to the overclaim.

The level of the penalty depends on the behaviour that led to you claiming too much tax credits. For example, how careful you were in making your claim or whether it was a deliberate attempt to get money you were not entitled to. The penalty levels for deliberate overclaims are:

- for a first offence, a penalty of 30% of the overclaimed tax credits
- for a second offence, a penalty of 50% of the overclaimed tax credits
- for a third or subsequent offence, a penalty of 100% of the overclaimed tax credits up to a maximum of £3,000.

If you do not understand our explanation of the penalty, you can ask us to put it in writing so that you can seek independent advice.

Interest

We may charge you interest if you pay a penalty late We will contact you if we think that you have become liable to a penalty. We can do this: 9.7

- by phone
- in a meeting
- in writing.

We will explain why we are charging you a penalty and tell you both the maximum amount we can charge and the amount of the penalty we propose to charge. We are always willing to discuss with you the amount of the penalty and the reasons for it.

Paying your penalty

We will discuss the arrangements for payment covering: 9.8

- any overpaid tax credits
- the penalty
- any interest due.

It is quick and easy to pay by phone. You can pay by debit card, credit card or Direct Debit. You can also pay using the internet and telephone banking. For more information on how to pay go to **www.hmrc.gov.uk/payinghmrc**

Co-operation

The extent to which you co-operate and give us information is entirely up to you. If you are not sure whether to give us the information or if you are reluctant to co-operate, we suggest you get independent advice before deciding what to do. We may decide to reduce or stop your current tax credits payments based on the information we hold. A number of independent organisations offer help with tax credits, such as the Citizens Advice. You will find them in *The Phone Book*. 9.9

Your right to appeal

9.10 You have the right to appeal if we:

- ask you to pay penalties or interest, or
- change your award.

Our leaflet WTC/AP *What to do if you think our decision is wrong* gives more information about how to appeal. If we charge you a penalty you will get a copy of this leaflet with our decision notice.

We will not treat your right of appeal as non-cooperation.

Independent tribunals

9.11 If we can't change our decision, we will send your appeal to an independent tribunal. They will listen to both of us and decide whether you will have to pay the penalty and how much you will have to pay.

Help with tax credits

9.12 For more information:

- go to **www.hmrc.gov.uk/taxcredits**
- phone the helpline on **0345 300 3900**
- textphone the helpline (for people with hearing or speech difficulties) on **0345 300 3909**
- write to us at

  Tax Credit Office
  PRESTON
  PR1 4AT.

When you get in touch with us please tell us:

- your full name
- your National Insurance number
- a daytime phone number.

Your rights and obligations

9.13 *Your Charter* explains what you can expect from us and what we expect from you. For more information go to **www.hmrc.gov.uk/charter** and have a look at *Your Charter*.

Complaints

9.14 For more information about complaints procedures go to **www.hmrc.gov.uk** and under *Quick links* select *Complaints and appeals*

We have a range of services for people with disabilities, including guidance in Braille, audio and large print. Most of our forms are also available in large print. Please contact us on any of our phone helplines if you need these services.

CODE OF PRACTICE 26

WHAT HAPPENS IF WE'VE PAID YOU TOO MUCH TAX CREDIT?

This leaflet explains why overpayments happen and how to pay them back. It also tells you when you don't have to pay them back and how to dispute an overpayment.

Introduction

Mandatory reconsideration

An overpayment means we've paid you more money than you're entitled to.

9.15

If you think the amount of tax credits you were awarded was wrong, you can ask us to look at the decision again. This is called mandatory reconsideration and you must normally contact us within 30 days of the date shown on your decision notice. You can also ask us to look at any penalty we have imposed in connection with your tax credits claim or if we decided to charge interest on your overpayment.

When we have looked at the decision again we will send you a Mandatory Reconsideration Notice explaining what we have done. This will include all the information you need to appeal to HM Courts and Tribunals Service in England, Scotland and Wales or The Appeals Service in Northern Ireland, if you are still unhappy with our decision.

Appeals to the Tribunal or Appeals Service must be made in writing and within 30 days of the date of the Mandatory Reconsideration Notice.

We will put any recovery action on hold while we carry out the reconsideration or while your appeal is being considered.

To find out more, see our leaflet WTC/AP, 'What to do if you think your Child Tax Credit or Working Tax Credit is wrong'. You can get a copy of this leaflet:

- online, go to **www.hmrc.gov.uk/leaflets/wtc_ap.pdf**
- by phoning our helpline on 0345 300 3900.

When you should dispute an overpayment

If you think our decision is right, but you don't agree that you should repay the overpayment, you should dispute our decision to recover the overpayment.

9.16

For more information on how to dispute an overpayment and by when, read page 8 of this leaflet. Please contact us (read page 17) if you:

- don't agree that you have been overpaid
- don't know if you should ask us to look at the decision that generated the overpayment again under mandatory reconsideration or dispute the decision to recover an overpayment

What happens if we've paid you too much tax credit?

How we work out the amount of your tax credits

9.17　Tax credits depend on your income and your family circumstances. When your income or family circumstances change then your entitlement or the amount we pay you may change.

We pay you tax credits for a tax year – from 6 April one year to 5 April the next. When we first work out what to pay you, we look at your family's circumstances now and your income for the previous tax year. If you think your income for the current tax year is going to be lower than in the previous year you can give us an estimate of what it will be. If we use this lower figure it is important you tell us if your income is going to be higher. If you don't, you are likely to be overpaid.

After 5 April each year, we send you a renewal pack asking you to:

- check the information we hold about you
- tell us how much income you had in the previous tax year

If your tax credits award is renewed automatically and you are in PAYE employment, we may have used income figures provided to us by your employer. It is important that you check that these figures are the correct figures for tax credits. Your renewal notes will help. Please contact us if you think they are not and tell us why.

You should fill in and return your renewal form as quickly as possible. We'll then work out the actual amount due to you for the year that has just ended and also the amount for the year that started on 6 April.

How an overpayment happens

9.18　An overpayment can happen if:

- you don't give us the right information either when you claim or when you renew your claim at the end of the year
- you're late telling us about a change in your circumstances
- your income in 2015 to 2016 is more than £5,000 higher than it was in 2014 to 2015 (more than £10,000 prior to 2012 to 2013 or more than £25,000 prior to 2011 to 2012)
- you tell us an estimated current year income which turns out to be too low
- you give us wrong information when you tell us about a change in your circumstances or income
- we make a mistake when we record the information you give us
- we don't act on information you give us

Changes in your circumstances or income

9.19　You should keep us up to date with any changes in your income and your family circumstances. The law says that you must tell us about certain changes within **1 month** of them happening.

Sometimes it might not be clear exactly when there has been a change so you must tell us **within 1 month** of the date when you realised a change has happened.

You should use the checklist that we sent with your award notice to check what changes you need to tell us about. If you need to tell us about a change, you may find it helpful to keep a note of the date you contacted us, the name of the person you spoke to and details of the change.

After you tell us about a change we'll work out the new amount of tax credits payments you're due and send you a new award notice.

Where a change of circumstances results in you having already received more than we estimate for your full year entitlement, normally tax credits will stop. Normal hardship rules will still apply and be assessed on a case by case basis (read page 14, 'Financial Hardship').

If you start living with a partner, you separate from your partner or your partner dies

You must let us know within 1 month if: 9.20

- you marry or enter into a civil partnership or start living with someone as though you are married or in a civil partnership

- you are married, or in a civil partnership, and you separate legally or in circumstances likely to be permanent How an overpayment happens Changes in your circumstances or income If you start living with a partner, you separate from your partner or your partner dies 4 COP26 What happens if we've paid you too much tax credits

- you stop living with someone as though you are married or in a civil partnership

- your partner dies

Your claim will legally end in these circumstances. If you can still claim tax credits, you will need to make a new claim. If you do make a new claim, it may be backdated up to 1 month.

The longer you delay telling us about this type of change, the bigger any overpayment may be. If you have started a new claim we may consider reducing the amount that you have to pay back. We will work out how much you would have been paid in your new claim if you had told us about the change on time and take that amount off your overpayment.

Our responsibilities and yours

To help get your award right and to help avoid building up an overpayment, it's important that we meet our responsibilities and you meet yours.   9.21

Our responsibilities

When you contact us for information we should give you correct advice based on the information you give us. We'll offer you support, for example, if you want us to explain your award notice to you, we'll talk you through it in detail.   9.22

When you make or renew your claim we should accurately record and use the information you give us to work out your tax credits and pay you the correct amount.

When we send you an award notice we should include information you've given us about your family and your income. If you tell us that there is a mistake or something missing on your award notice, we should put it right and send you a corrected award notice.

When you contact us to tell us about a change of circumstance, we should accurately record what you've told us and send you a new award notice within 30 days. The 30 days doesn't start until we get all of the information we need from you to make the change. It is therefore important that you give us all of the information when you tell us about a change.

Your responsibilities

9.23   When you make or renew your claim you should give us accurate, complete and up-to-date information.

You should tell us about any changes of circumstance throughout the year so we have accurate and up-to-date information. The law says you must tell us about certain changes within 1 month of them happening. You should use the checklist we sent with your award notice to check what these changes are. To reduce the chance of building up an overpayment, we recommend that you tell us about any changes in income as soon as possible.

Each time you get an award notice you should use the checklist we send with it. You should check all the items listed and tell us if anything is wrong, missing or incomplete. You must tell us about some changes within **1 month** of them happening – these are listed on the back of the checklist.

The main details we expect you to check are:

- whether it's a joint award (for you and your partner) or a single award (based on your individual circumstances)
- the hours you work
- whether you get Income Support, income-based Jobseeker's Allowance, income-related Employment and Support Allowance or Pension Credit
- that a disability element is shown if you, or anyone in the household, is entitled to it
- the number and age of any children in your household
- any childcare costs
- your total household income for the period shown on the award notice

We'll send you a corrected award notice if you tell us anything is wrong, missing or incomplete. **If you don't get an award notice within 30 days of telling us about a change in circumstance let us know as soon as possible.**

You should check that the payments you get match what we said they should be on your award notice. You should tell us if you get any payments that don't match what is shown on your award notice.

If anything is wrong, missing or incomplete you must tell us within 30 days of the date on your award notice. Please make a note of when you got your award notice and when you told us about the mistake. We may ask you for this information to show that you acted **within 30 days.**

If you had difficult personal circumstances that meant you couldn't check your award notice or bank payments, for example, a member of your family has been seriously ill, let us know as soon as possible.

CODE OF PRACTICE 26

If you don't understand any award notice, phone our helpline (read page 17).

If we fail to meet our responsibilities

If we fail to meet our responsibilities, but you meet all of yours, we won't ask you to pay back all of an overpayment caused by our failure. 9.24

However – you must tell us about any mistakes on your award notice within 30 days of the date on your award notice. If you do, then you won't be responsible for an overpayment caused by our mistake. If you tell us about a mistake **more than 30 days** after the date on your award notice we may ask you to pay back an overpayment up to the date you contacted us.

Example 1

On 1 September you tell us about a change in your circumstances but we don't change your award until 16 October. We won't collect back any overpayment that arises **after** 30 September. 9.25

Example 2

On 12 August you tell us about a change in your income. We send you a new award notice which you get on 19 August, but we haven't correctly recorded the information you gave us. If you spot this and tell us about the mistake by 18 September (30 days from 19 August) we won't collect any overpayment caused by our mistake. 9.26

Example 3

On 12 August you tell us about a change in your income. We send you a new award notice which you get on 19 August, but we haven't correctly recorded the information you gave us. If you spot this and don't tell us about the mistake until 27 September (38 days from 19 August) you may be responsible for the overpayment up to the date you contacted us. 9.27

Whenever you tell us about a mistake we won't collect an overpayment that may build up if we fail to correct our mistake from this time.

If you fail to meet your responsibilities

If you fail to meet your responsibilities, but we meet all of ours, we'll normally ask you to pay back all of an overpayment. For example, if you tell us about a mistake on your award notice **more than 30 days** after the date on your award notice, then you may have to pay back an overpayment which has built up until the time you contacted us. But also read 'Exceptional circumstances' below. 9.28

If we both fail to meet our responsibilities

If we both fail to meet one or more of our responsibilities, we'll look at the circumstances of your case and may write off parts of an overpayment. 9.29

What happens if we've paid you too much tax credit?

If it takes you some time to tell us we didn't meet our responsibilities

9.30 We ask you to tell us about any mistakes we've made **within 30 days** of the date on your award notice. If you don't tell us **within 30 days**, we'll ask you to pay back an overpayment up to the date you told us. **We won't ask you to pay back an overpayment, which is caused by our mistake, after the date you told us.**

Exceptional circumstances

9.31 We understand that exceptional circumstances may prevent you from meeting your responsibilities on time. For example, you or a close family member may have been seriously ill so you couldn't report a change, check your award notice or tell us about our mistake **within 30 days** of the date on your award notice. Please let us know, as soon as it becomes possible, if you think this applies to you, or if you're not sure whether we've made a mistake.

If you don't understand why there is an overpayment, please contact us. We can give you an explanation over the phone or in writing. Our leaflet WTC8, 'Why overpayments happen' gives more information about things that can cause overpayments. You can get a copy:

You can get a copy:

- online, go to **www.hmrc.gov.uk/leaflets/wtc8.pdf**

- by phoning our helpline (read page 17) if you don't have access to the internet

Appointees

9.32 We know that some customers may not be able to manage their own affairs, handle money or understand or complete forms. In such circumstances another person may act on their behalf. These people are called appointees.

Appointees can sometimes be appointed by a court or government department but can also be appointed by an individual who decides that they need help in dealing with their affairs. The appointee could be a family member, a friend, a carer, a voluntary sector organisation or a mental health or social care professional who would be able to act in all dealings with us. For more information, go to **www.hmrc.gov.uk/manuals/tct-manual/tctm06109.htm**

Challenging the recovery of an overpayment

How to dispute an overpayment

9.33 If you don't agree that we should ask you to pay back an overpayment you can ask us to look at this again. We call this disputing an overpayment. To do this, we recommend you fill in form TC846, 'Tax credits overpayment'. You can get a copy:

- online, go to **www.hmrc.gov.uk/forms/tc846.pdf**

- by phoning our helpline (read page 17) if you don't have access to the internet

You may write to us instead, but you'll need to give us all of your details, and tell us:

- in what tax year the overpayment being disputed happened
- if and when you contacted us
- why you think the overpayment happened
- why you think you shouldn't have to pay back the overpayment

Usually you have to dispute recovery of an overpayment within 3 months from the date of:

- your final decision notice
- the decision on your Annual Review notice (if your award is renewed automatically)
- your Statement of Account
- the letter which gives you our decision of your mandatory reconsideration
- the letter from the Tribunal or Appeals Service which gives you their decision on your appeal

You can only dispute recovery of an overpayment that happened in the tax year the notice or letter relates to. You will not normally be able to dispute overpayments from earlier tax years. We will only accept a late dispute in exceptional circumstances, for example, if you were in hospital for that 3-month period. If you do send us a dispute, we will continue to seek recovery of the overpayment while we are considering your dispute.

If your decision is later revised and you receive another decision notice for the same year, you have 3 months from the date of that notice.

Example 4

Mary and Alan have overpayments from 2010 to 2011 and 2011 to 2012 tax years. They are paying the overpayments back from their tax credits award in 2014 to 2015. They were late reporting a change of circumstances in 2014 to 2015 and there is a new overpayment shown on their final 2014 to 2015 award notice. Their final award notice also shows the overpayments from the earlier tax years.

Mary and Alan have 3 months from the date of their 2014 to 2015 decision notice to dispute the new overpayment only. But they will not be able to dispute the overpayments from 2010 to 2011 and 2011 to 2012 tax years.

9.34

Historic debt

If you no longer get tax credits, you will have been informed on past notices that, if you want to dispute an overpayment, you should do so as quickly as possible. If you have failed to do so you can no longer dispute overpayments from previous awards, where it has been more than 3 months since you received your final decision notice. However, if you can show there are exceptional circumstances why you haven't previously disputed the overpayment, such as being in hospital, we will consider the dispute.

If you are no longer in receipt of tax credits, but have received a final

9.35

decision notice from us in the last 3 months you will only be able to dispute the overpayment occurring in the tax year the notice relates to.

If you have reclaimed tax credits and are receiving payments, we will tell you if we are recovering historic debts from your ongoing award. You will only be able to dispute the overpayment in the 3 months after you received the final decision notice relating to your previous award. Read page 12 'Paying back an overpayment'.

Example 5

9.36 You receive your tax credits renewal pack on 21 May 2015 which requires you to confirm family details and income for the previous 12 months ending in April 2015. You check your household details and decide you have no changes to report. We send out a final decision notice on 15 August 2015. The letter shows you have been overpaid tax credits because your eldest child left school in September 2014 though your award was only changed in January 2015.

You do not notice the information about the overpayment until December 2015 when you realise your monthly tax credits payments are being reduced to automatically pay it back. You agree there has been an overpayment but believe you should not have to pay it back because you told HM Revenue & Customs about your daughter leaving school in September 2014 and we did not change your award until January 2015. You have 3 months to dispute the overpayment from 15 August 2015. This means that you need to send us your dispute against the overpayment by 15 November 2015. As you are now out of time you cannot dispute the overpayment unless you can show there are exceptional circumstances for missing the deadline, such as being in hospital.

Where we got a decision wrong

9.37 In some cases we may revise the decision which caused the overpayment. We can only do this where the decision is incorrect as a result of an error by us and we find that you did not materially contribute to the error. We call this type of error an 'official error'. However, we will not revise a decision which is incorrect due to official error if more than 5 years have passed from the date of the decision, or if the revised decision would not be in your favour.

Where a dispute is found in your favour, we will refund the amount already recovered.

Example 6

9.38 You have received Working Tax Credit since 2009. You became entitled to Disability Living Allowance in 2010 and asked us whether you were entitled to the disability element of Working Tax Credit.

We wrongly advised you and said you were not entitled to the disability element. In 2014 you visited Citizens Advice with a query about your tax credits award. The adviser noticed that you qualified for the disability element but it was not included on your award. You contacted us and asked about our original advice. Since our decision was wrong, solely because of our error, your awards would be revised all the way back to 2010.

CODE OF PRACTICE 26

How we decide whether you should pay back some or all of an overpayment

We'll check: 9.39

- that we accurately recorded and acted on any information you gave us **within 30 days** of you telling us about a change of circumstance
- that we accurately worked out and paid you your correct entitlement
- that the information we included on your award notice was accurate at the date of the notice
- what you told us if you contacted us, and whether the advice we gave you based on that information was correct
- whether you contacted us to discuss any queries on your award notice, and whether we answered them correctly
- that you gave us accurate and up-to-date information when you claimed tax credits
- that you told us about any changes of circumstance at the right time
- that you checked your award notice **within 30 days** of the date on your award notice and if and when you told us about any mistakes
- that you checked that the payments you got matched the amounts on your award notice and if not, that you told us **within 30 days** of the date on your award notice
- whether you told us of any exceptional circumstances that meant you couldn't tell us about a change of circumstance or about our mistake **within 30 days**

Once we've checked whether we've met our responsibilities and you've met yours, we'll decide whether an overpayment should be paid back.

We'll decide whether you must pay back all or only part of an overpayment. We'll give you our decision, along with our reasons, normally in writing. However, we won't stop collecting an overpayment while we do this.

We may not ask you to pay back an overpayment if you contacted us to tell us that your exceptional personal circumstances meant you couldn't check your award notice or bank payments. For example, a member of your family may have been seriously ill. If this is the case please let us know as soon as possible.

If you still think you shouldn't pay back an overpayment

If you're still unhappy that we have decided to continue collecting an overpayment you can ask us to look at the decision again if you give us new and relevant information. You can only ask us to review this decision once and you will have to do this within 30 days of receiving your dispute decision letter. We will only accept a late request for a review in exceptional circumstances, for example, if you were in hospital for that 30-day period. However, we won't stop collecting an overpayment while we do this. 9.40

If you don't have any new information to give us, but you're still unhappy

What happens if we've paid you too much tax credit?

with our decision, you may wish to contact a professional adviser or organisation, for example, Citizens Advice. You can consider what options are open to you, including any through the courts.

If you're not happy with our service, please read 'Customer service' on page 17.

Paying back an overpayment

9.41 We may collect back an overpayment from you in a number of ways. We may:

- reduce your payments from an ongoing tax credits award
- ask you to make direct payments to us
- adjust your tax code
- reduce your payments from an ongoing Universal Credit award

In some exceptional cases we may ask you to do more than one of the above.

From an ongoing tax credits award

9.42 If you're still getting tax credits payments we'll automatically reduce these payments to recover an overpayment from your ongoing tax credits. Overpayments we will recover may be from:

- awards you or your partner have had as single people
- awards you and your partner have had together either now or previously

We will not recover from your ongoing tax credits any overpayments from awards you or your partner have had with other partners.

How much we reduce your payments by will depend on how much you're getting. We reduce awards at different levels, read the table below.

Recovery from an on-going tax credits award only takes place where an overpayment is established at the end of the year and that overpayment falls for cross year recovery.

If an overpayment still exists at the end of the year it will be recovered at the rates below from the award starting at 6 April of the following year.

If you want help understanding which recovery rate applies to you, please contact us (read page 17).

Your tax credits award	The most we'll take back
If you're getting the maximum tax credits with no reduction due to income	10%
All other awards – for example, those entitled to Child Tax Credit, or Working Tax Credit below the maximum	25%

By direct payment

If you're no longer entitled to tax credits, we'll ask you to make a direct payment to us. We'll also ask you to make a direct payment to us if your tax credits award has ended (this might happen if there is a change in your household, for example, you were in a couple and now you're single).

9.43

From an ongoing tax credits award and by direct payment

This may happen if you have an overpayment from an old award which ended and you have an overpayment from a current award. For example, you and your partner separated and you then made another claim as a single person or in a new couple. We could ask you to pay back an overpayment from your current award as well From an ongoing tax credits award as a direct payment from your previous award. If this applies to you, you can ask for the direct payment to be put on hold until you've paid back the overpayment from your ongoing tax credits payments.

If you do have an outstanding overpayment from an old claim, in some circumstances we may recover this from your ongoing award, instead of asking you to pay this overpayment back directly.

9.44

Asking for more time to pay back a direct payment

If we've asked you to pay back an overpayment from a previous award directly, but you need more time to pay it back, please phone our Payment Helpline on **0345 302 1429** as soon as possible. We can arrange for you to pay it back in equal instalments. If you would like more details on different direct payment options, tell us when you phone.

9.45

By an adjustment to your tax code

If you are in PAYE employment or getting pension income and have a tax credits overpayment we may be able to adjust your tax code to collect your overpayment. We will write to you and let you know if we can collect your overpayment this way. If we do write to you and you would prefer not to have your tax code adjusted, you can contact us to pay in full or to agree an instalment arrangement. The amount that is recovered depends on your income.

9.46

From an ongoing Universal Credit award

If you're getting Universal Credit we may ask the Department for Work and Pensions to reduce your payments of Universal Credit to recover your tax credits overpayment. How much they reduce your payments by will depend on how much you are getting.

9.47

Financial hardship

If you need to discuss financial hardship with us, please try and phone us to explain this.

When you phone we may ask you about any family circumstances that may lead to extra living costs. For example, if you're looking after someone who is chronically ill or disabled. In some exceptional circumstances, we may cancel an overpayment altogether.

9.48

What happens if we've paid you too much tax credit?

If you can't pay for your essential living expenses

9.49　If you can't pay for your essential living expenses such as your rent, gas or electricity and:

- you're paying back an overpayment directly

- we've reduced your ongoing payments so you can pay back an overpayment

- we've asked you to pay back an overpayment phone our Payment Helpline on **0345 302 1429**. We'll ask you about your circumstances in more detail.

If you can't pay for your essential living expenses and you are getting Universal Credit, you should contact the Department for Work and Pensions.

Whether you are repaying your overpayment from a reduction in your tax credits payments or through a direct payment, we may offer you an option for extending the period over which you pay back the overpayment. We can do this by reducing the amount being recovered each month or stopping recovery in exceptional circumstances.

If we do reduce the amount of your repayments, it will take you longer to pay off an overpayment.

In some exceptional circumstances, we may cancel an overpayment altogether.

If you and your partner separate

9.50　If you and your partner separate and your joint claim ends, we'll work out if you've been overpaid. If you have, we'll write to you both, usually at the end of the tax year to:

- tell you how much we've overpaid you by

- ask you to contact us to arrange to pay back the money

You and your ex-partner are both responsible for paying back an overpayment from your joint claim. The letter sent to each of you will show the total overpayment that you both owe.

You should first of all try to agree with your ex-partner how much each of you should pay. The options are that:

- each of you pays half

- each of you pays a different amount

- one of you pays the full amount

When you have reached an agreement with your ex-partner, you should phone the Payment Helpline on **0345 302 1429** to arrange repaying the overpayment. You will then get a letter confirming what you have to pay back. You might not be able to talk it over with your ex-partner, either because you don't want to contact them or you don't know where they are. Even if you do speak to them you might not be able to agree on what each of you should pay back.

If this happens, you should still speak to the Payment Helpline as quickly as possible. You will then be asked to pay back half of the overpayment, with your partner being asked to pay back the rest. You will not be asked to pay back more than half of the overpayment.

You can make a new claim as a single person or with a new partner. To make a claim, please phone our helpline (read page 17).

We can't reduce your payments from your new claim to collect back an overpayment that you had with your previous partner. You must pay this overpayment back directly by ringing the Payment Helpline.

However, if you get back together with your ex-partner and claim again, we can reduce your payments to recover the overpayment.

Contact us

When you contact us please tell us: 9.51

- your full name
- your National Insurance number
- a daytime phone number

By phone

- Tax Credits Helpline **0345 300 3900**
- Payment Helpline **0345 302 1429**
- Textphone **0345 300 3909**
- If you prefer to speak in Welsh, phone **0300 200 1900**
- If you are abroad and can't get through on the helpline, please phone **+44 2890 538 192**

In writing

- You can write to the address shown on your award notice, or to the address below. 9.52
  — Tax Credit Office
  PRESTON
  PR1 4AT

Customer service

For information about our complaints procedure, go **to www.gov.uk/complain-to-hm-revenue-and-customs** 9.53
Your rights and obligations
'Your Charter' explains what you can expect from us and what we expect from you. For more information, go to **www.gov.uk/hmrc/your-charter**

INDEX

This index has been prepared using Sweet and Maxwell's Legal Taxonomy. Main index entries conform to keywords provided by the Legal Taxonomy except where references to specific documents or non-standard terms (denoted by quotation marks) have been included. These keywords provide a means of identifying similar concepts in other Sweet & Maxwell publications and online services to which keywords from the Legal Taxonomy have been applied. Readers may find some minor differences between terms used in the text and those which appear in the index. Suggestions to *sweetandmaxwell.taxonomy@thomson.com*.

(All references are to paragraph number)

Accounting date
trading income, 1.730
Additional statutory paternity pay
adoption
common provisions, 6.178–6.199
entitlement, 1.122, 6.171–6.177
overseas adoptions, 6.202–6.212
adoption (entitlement)
applications, 6.174
conditions to be satisfied by child's adopter, 6.172
death of the adopter, and, 6.175–6.176
evidence of entitlement, 6.174
generally, 6.171
more than one employer, where, 6.177
pay period, 6.173
statutory provision, 1.122
applications
adoption, 6.174
birth, 6.167
overseas adoptions, 6.208
avoidance of liability, 6.182
birth
common provisions, 6.178–6.199
entitlement, 1.121, 6.163–6.170
birth (entitlement)
applications, 6.167
conditions to be satisfied by child's mother, 6.165
death of the mother, and, 6.168–6.169
early birth, 6.164
evidence of entitlement, 6.167
generally, 6.163
modification of conditions, 6.163
more than one employer, where, 6.170
pay period, 6.166
statutory provision, 1.121
change of employer, 6.187
Commissioners
liability to pay, 6.194–6.196
payment, 6.197
conditions to be satisfied

adoption, 6.172
birth, 6.165
overseas adoptions, 6.206
continuous employment
generally, 6.184
stoppages of work, and, 6.186
unfair dismissal, and, 6.185
contracting out, 1.126–1.127
contractual remuneration, and
generally, 6.181
statutory provision, 1.128–1.129
death
adoption, 6.175–6.176
birth, 6.168–6.169
overseas adoptions, 6.209–6.210
definitions, 6.161
'earnings', 6.190
entitlement
adoption, 1.122, 6.171–6.177
birth, 1.121, 6.163–6.170
statutory provision, 1.121–1.123
evidence of entitlement
adoption, 6.174
birth, 6.167
liability of Commissioners
generally, 6.194–6.195
legal custody or imprisonment, 6.196
statutory provision, 1.124
more than one employer
adoption, 6.177
birth, 6.170
overseas adoptions, 6.211
NHS employees
notification of election, 6.155
provision of information, 6.156
timing of election, 6.158
treatment of more than one contract of employment, 6.154
treatment of more than one employer, 6.157
no liability to pay, 6.180
normal weekly earnings, 6.191

1087

overseas adoptions
  application of General Regulations
    2010, 6.203
  application of other Regulations, 6.151
  application of SSCBA 1992, 6.204
  applications, 6.208
  conditions of entitlement, 6.206
  death of adopter, 6.209–6.210
  definitions, 6.202
  entitlement, 6.205
  entitlement where more than one
    employer, 6.211
  evidence of entitlement, 6.208
  pay period, 6.207
  return to work, 6.212
pay period
  adoption, 6.173
  birth, 6.166
  overseas adoptions, 6.207
  statutory provision, 1.125
payment
  generally, 6.192
  liability of Commissioners,
    6.194–6.197
  statutory provision, 1.124
  timing, 6.193
persons unable to act, 6.198
rate, 1.125
return to work
  generally, 6.178
  overseas adoptions, 6.212
service of notices by post, 6.199
service with armed forces, 6.188
stoppages of work, 6.186
timing of payment, 6.193
treatment of more than one contract of
  employment, 6.189
treatment of more than one employer,
  6.189
treatment of persons as employees, 6.183
unfair dismissal, 6.185
weekly rates
  generally, 6.216
  rounding, 6.217
work during pay period, 6.179
**Additional Statutory Paternity Pay
(Adoption), etc Regulations 2010**
arrangement, 6.147
citation, 6.148
commencement, 6.148
definitions, 6.149
general provision, 6.151
revocation, 6.150
**Additional Statutory Paternity Pay
(Adoptions from Overseas)
Regulations 2010**
application, 6.203–6.204
arrangement, 6.200
citation, 6.201
commencement, 6.201
definitions, 6.202
general provisions, 6.205–6.212
scope, 6.202

**Additional Statutory Paternity Pay
(General) Regulations 2010**
application, 6.162
arrangement, 6.159
citation, 6.160
commencement, 6.160
definitions, 6.161
general provisions, 6.163–6.199
**Additional Statutory Paternity Pay
(NHS Employees) Regulations
2010**
arrangement, 6.152
citation, 6.153
commencement, 6.153
definitions, 6.153
general provisions, 6.154–6.158
**Additional Statutory Paternity Pay
(Weekly Rates) Regulations 2010**
arrangement, 6.213
citation, 6.215
commencement, 6.215
general provisions, 6.216–6.217
recitals, 6.214
Administration
See **Administrative requirements**
**Administrative requirements (statutory
adoption pay)**
adoption from overseas, 6.120–6.124
determination of entitlement issues
  application, 6.30
  form of application, 6.31
employers' records
  generally, 6.26
  inspection, 6.27
funding of liabilities
  application to Revenue, 6.21
  date of payment of contributions, 6.24
  generally, 6.20
  method, 6.22–6.23
  overpayments, 6.25
provision of information, 6.32
**Administrative requirements (statutory
maternity pay)**
employer's records
  maintenance, 5.46
  production, 5.47
expected week of confinement, 5.40
notice of absence from work, 5.41
notification of employment after
  confinement, 5.42
provision of information
  claims for other benefits, 5.45
  determination of questions, 5.43–5.44
**Administrative requirements (statutory
paternity pay)**
adoption from overseas, 6.120–6.124
determination of entitlement issues
  application, 6.30
  form of application, 6.31
employers' records
  generally, 6.26
  inspection, 6.27
funding of liabilities

Index

application to Revenue, 6.21
date of payment of contributions, 6.24
generally, 6.20
method, 6.22–6.23
overpayments, 6.25
provision of information, 6.32
Administrative requirements (tax credits)
definitions, 2.371
general note, 2.369
forwarding of claims, 2.374
holding of claims, 2.374
provision of information
by authorities, 2.373
to authorities, 2.372
recording of claims, 2.374
statutory provision, 1.415–1.416
Adopted children
child benefit
Regulations, 3.21
guardian's allowance
Regulations, 3.67
statutory provision, 1.40
Adopters
annual payments, 1.784
meaning, 6.34
Adoption
statutory paternity pay
conditions of entitlement, 6.71–6.72
evidence of entitlement, 6.76
notice of entitlement, 6.72A
notice requirements, 6.74
payment period, 6.73
qualifying period, 6.75
statutory provisions, 1.113–1.114
treatment of more than one employer, 6.77
statutory shared parental pay
conditions, 7.55–7.68
definitions, 7.20–7.21
entitlement, 7.37–7.54
general note, 7.18
working tax credit, 2.38–2.41
Adoption from overseas
See **Intercountry adoption**
Adoption pay
See **Statutory adoption pay**
Advance claims
generally, 2.293–2.294
working tax credit, 2.295–2.296
"Advance funding"
statutory maternity pay, 5.87
Age
statutory pay, 1.168
"Age 7 payments"
child trust funds, 8.14
Agency workers
employment income, 1.494
Air crew
statutory adoption pay, 1.151–1.152
statutory maternity pay, 1.104
statutory paternity pay, 1.132–1.133
statutory sick pay

definitions, 4.50, 4.56–4.57, 4.63
general note, 4.47
statutory provision, 1.88
time for compliance, 4.65
Allocations (contributions)
child benefit, 3.5
Amendments
claims, 2.283
Amendments (tax returns)
Revenue, by
during enquiry, 1.10
generally, 1.7
taxpayer, by
during enquiry, 1.9
generally, 1.6
Amount treated as income of settlor
See **Settlement income**
Annual payments
adopters, to, 1.784
employment insurance payments, 1.782–1.783
foreign maintenance payments, 1.777
health insurance payments, 1.782–1.783
pension income, 2.136
periodical payments of personal injury damages
compensation awards, 1.779
generally, 1.778
persons entitled, 1.780
trusts, from, 1.781
Annual reports
tax credits, 1.396–1.397
"Annual review"
tax credits, 1.398–1.399
Annuities
life annuity payments
charge to tax, 1.761
income charged, 1.763
meaning, 1.762
person liable, 1.764
pension income, 2.136–2.137
Appeal notices
child trust funds
disputes concerning, 8.73–8.74
prescribed form, 8.65–8.66
service, 8.71–8.72
signature, 8.65–8.66
statutory provision, 1.686
Appeals
child trust funds, and
appealable decisions, 1.684–1.685
exercise of right, 1.686
general regulations, 8.68–8.78
notice of appeal, 8.62–8.67
penalties, 1.683
temporary modifications, 1.687
First-tier Tribunal, to, 1.223–1.224
late appeals
child trust fund appeals, 8.75–8.76
tax credit appeals, 2.385–2.386
tax returns, 1.18–1.20
tax credits
appealable decisions, 1.385–1.390

1089

Index

exercise of right, 1.391–1.392
general regulations, 2.375–2.387
late appeals, 1.393–1.395
temporary modifications, 1.425–1.426
verification of claims, 2.374
Appeals (child trust funds)
assessment of tax returns, 1.19–1.20
death of party, 8.77–8.78
decisions of Board, 1.233–1.234
definitions, 8.69–8.70
exercise of right
generally, 1.235–1.238, 1.686
regulations, 1.239–1.240
general regulations
citation, 8.69
commencement, 8.69
definitions, 8.69–8.70
duration, 8.69
general provisions, 8.71–8.78
recitals, 8.68
late appeals, 8.75–8.76
notice of appeal
disputes concerning, 8.73–8.74
prescribed form, 8.65–8.66
service, 8.71–8.72
signature, 8.65–8.66
statutory provision, 1.686
penalties, 1.683
Regulations
general, 8.68–8.78
notice of appeal, 8.62–8.67
service of notices or documents, 8.71–8.72
temporary modifications, 1.687
time limits, 8.75–8.76
Appeals (tax credits)
appealable decisions, 1.385–1.390
assessment of tax returns, 1.19–1.20
death of party, 2.387
decisions of Board, 1.235–1.238
definitions, 2.377–2.378
directions
death of party, 2.387
exercise of right
generally, 1.391–1.392
other persons, 2.381–2.382
extensions of time, 2.385–2.386
general regulations
general matters, 2.381–2.387
service of notices, 2.379–2.380
late appeals
generally, 1.393–1.395
other persons, 2.385–2.386
'party to the proceedings', 2.387–2.378
Regulations
general, 2.375–2.387
right of appeal
decisions of Board, 1.235–1.238
generally, 1.391–1.392
other persons, 2.381–2.382
service of notices, 2.379–2.380
settlement, 2.495–2.497
temporary modifications, 1.425–1.426

time limits
extension, 2.385–2.386
generally, 2.383–2.384
Approval of Child Care Providers Scheme
See **Childcare Approval Scheme**
Aspect enquiries
amendment by taxpayer, 1.9
completion, 1.12
correction by Revenue, 1.10
notice, 1.8
Assault
officers of Revenue and Customs, 1.825
Assignment
tax credits, 1.406–1.407
Asylum seekers
definitions, 2.396
exclusion from entitlement, 2.397–2.409
general note, 2.403
modifications of Act, 2.408–2.409
statutory provision, 1.400–1.401
transitional relief, 2.410–2.411
Attendance allowance
social security income, 2.152
"Avoidance of liability"
statutory adoption pay
adoption from overseas, 6.145
generally, 6.93
statutory maternity pay, 5.7–5.8
statutory paternity pay
adoption from overseas, 6.138
generally, 6.81
statutory sick pay, 4.11
Back to work bonus
social security income, 2.152
Bad debts
trading income, 1.722
Bankruptcy
tax credits, 1.406–1.407
Basic element
See also **Working tax credit**
adoption, 2.38–2.41
ceasing to undertake work, 2.52–2.53
childbirth, 2.38–2.41
gaps between jobs, 2.54–2.55
ill health, 2.42–2.43
pay in lieu of notice, 2.50–2.51
qualifying remunerative work, and
excepted activities, 2.36
generally, 2.26–2.32
hours worked, 2.37
minimum level of continuity, 2.34
remunerative work, 2.35
routes to entitlement, 2.33
seasonal work, 2.44–2.45
strike periods, 2.46–2.47
suspension from work, 2.48–2.49
term-time work, 2.44–2.45
working less than 16 hours a week, 2.52–2.53
Basis periods
accounting date, 1.730

normal rules, 1.731
professions and vocations, 1.729
"Benefits code"
See also **Employment income, Taxable benefits**
definitions, 1.499
dispensations, 1.498
meaning, 1.496
relationship with earnings, 1.497
Bereavement payment
social security income, 2.152
"Betting winnings"
investment income, 2.164
Birth
evidence
statutory paternity pay, 6.68–6.69
tax credits, 2.332
statutory paternity pay
conditions of entitlement, 6.62–6.64
evidence of entitlement, 6.68–6.69
notice of entitlement, 6.64A
notice requirements, 6.66
payment period, 6.65
qualifying period, 6.67
statutory provisions, 1.107–1.112
treatment of more than one employer, 6.70
tax credits, 2.332
working tax credit, 2.38–2.41
Board of Inland Revenue
See **Commissioners for Revenue and Customs**
Breach of regulations
See **Enforcement**
Building societies (dividends)
savings and investment income, 1.753
Business entertainment
trading income, 1.724
Capital
general rule, 2.106
Capital expenditure
trading income, 1.720
Capital gains
generally, 2.106
Capital receipts
trading income, 1.727
Care (children)
child benefit
Regulations, 3.21, 3.25
statutory basis, 1.170
Careers services
generally, 3.2
Carers
remunerative work, 2.36
Carer's allowance
social security income, 2.154
Cash vouchers
See **Vouchers**
"Ceasing to undertake work"
working tax credit, 2.52–2.53
Change of circumstances (tax credits)
advance, in, 2.327
amendment, 2.320

automatic, 2.289
childcare element (working tax credit), 2.78–2.79
date of, 2.321–2.326
decrease of rate, 2.314–2.317
definitions, 2.211
discretionary, 1.288
evidence of birth or adoption, 2.332
failure to report, 1.290
generally, 1.284–1.285
increase of maximum rate, 2.312–2.313
mandatory, 1.287
method, 2.317–2.318
person acting on behalf of another, by, 2.328–2.331
relevant changes, 1.286
relevant person, 2.319
"Change of employer"
statutory adoption pay, 6.99
statutory maternity pay, 5.26
statutory paternity pay
additional pay, 6.187
generally, 6.99
Charge to tax (income tax)
emoluments (offices and employment)
general note, 1.476–1.477
employment income
agency workers, 1.494
deductions from earnings, 1.532–1.543
earnings, 1.495
'employment', 1.483–1.484
exemptions, 1.525–1.531
general note, 1.476–1.477
introductory provision, 1.481–1.482
nature, 1.486–1.488
office-holders, 1.485
operation, 1.489–1.493
taxable benefits, 1.496–1.524
general note
ITA 2007, 1.830
ITEPA 2003, under, 1.476–1.477
general rule
ITA 2007, 1.833–1.835
ITTOIA 2005, 1.697–1.699
ITEPA 2003, under, 1.479
miscellaneous income
income not otherwise charged, 1.773
settlements, 1.768–1.772
pension income
amount charged, 1.547
general note, 1.545
general rules, 1.549–1.553
introductory provision, 1.544
nature of charge, 1.546
person liable to tax, 1.548
social security pensions, 1.554–1.557
property income
generally, 1.740
income charged, 1.742
person liable, 1.743
territorial scope, 1.741
savings and investments income

1091

dividends from non-resident UK
  companies, 1.758
dividends from UK resident companies,
  1.755
interest, 1.750
purchased life annuity payments,
  1.761
Schedule E (offices and employment
  emoluments)
  general note, 1.476–1.477
social security income
  amount charged, 1.564
  definitions, 1.597–1.598
  exempt benefits, 1.573–1.588
  foreign benefits, 1.593–1.596
  general note, 1.559
  introductory provision, 1.558
  nature of charge, 1.560–1.561
  person liable to tax, 1.565
  taxable benefits, 1.566–1.572
  wholly exempt benefits, 1.589–1.592
trading income
  generally, 1.705
  income charged, 1.707
  person liable, 1.708
  territorial scope, 1.706
Charitable work
See **Voluntary work**
Charters
  Revenue and Customs, 1.820
"Cheque vouchers"
  meaning, 1.509
Child
See **Children**
Child benefit
  adopted children, 3.21
  advanced education, child in, 3.4–3.5
  allocation of contributions, 3.5
  care
    Regulations, 3.21, 3.25
    statutory basis, 1.170
  'child', 1.45
  child in care
    Regulations, 3.21, 3.25
    statutory basis, 1.170
  child in detention
    Regulations, 3.21–3.24
    statutory basis, 1.170
  child treated as being in GB, 3.28
  child treated as being in Northern Ireland,
    3.34
  civil partnership, 3.18
  continuation of entitlement, 3.6
  Crown servants posted overseas
    child, 3.43
    generally, 3.40–3.41
    partners, 3.42
  days of absence, 3.4
  death of child, after
    Regulations, 3.27
    statutory basis, 1.56
  definitions, 1.60–1.61
  detention, child in

    Regulations, 3.21–3.24
    statutory basis, 1.170
  duplicate payments, 3.52
  education and training condition, 3.4–3.5
  election, 3.19
  election not to receive, 1.207–1.208
  electronic communications, use of, 3.53
  entitlement
    child, 1.45
    death of child, after, 1.56
    exclusions, 1.53–1.54
    generally, 1.41–1.44
    person responsible for child, 1.46–1.52
    persons subject to immigration control,
      1.59
    presence in GB, 1.57–1.58
    priority, 1.53–1.54
    qualifying young person, 1.45
  exclusions
    care, child in, 1.170
    detention, child in, 1.170
    generally, 1.53–1.54
    imprisoned child, 1.170
    married child, 1.171
    Regulations, 3.16–3.26
  extension period, 3.7
  full-time education, child in, 3.4–3.5
  imprisoned child
    Regulations, 3.24
    statutory basis, 1.170
  incapacity benefit, child receiving, 3.12
  income support, child receiving, 3.12
  increases for dependants, and
    persons entitled treated as not entitled,
      3.47–3.48
    persons not entitled treated as entitled,
      3.45–3.46
  interruptions, 3.8–3.9
  jobseeker's allowance, child receiving,
    3.12
  living with partner as spouse, 3.16–3.17
  married child
    Regulations, 3.18
    statutory basis, 1.171
  NI number, and, 3.51
  overpayments, 1.211–1.212
  person responsible for child
    Regulations, 3.13–3.15
    statutory basis, 1.46–1.52
  person temporarily absent
    from GB, 3.32–3.33
    from Northern Ireland, 3.38
  person treated as not being resident
    in GB, 3.30–3.31
    in Northern Ireland, 3.36–3.37
  persons subject to immigration control,
    1.59
  polygamous marriages, 3.47–3.48
  prescribed conditions
    continuation of entitlement, 3.6
    education and training condition,
      3.4–3.5
    extension period, 3.7

1092

Index

interruptions, 3.8–3.9
introduction, 3.3
terminal dates, 3.10–3.11
presence in GB, 1.57–1.58
priority
  generally, 1.53–1.54
  miscellaneous provisions, 1.174–1.182
Regulations, 3.20
qualifying young person
  continuation of entitlement, 3.6
  definition, 1.45
  education and training condition, 3.4–3.5
  extension period, 3.7
  interruptions, 3.8–3.9
  introduction, 3.3
  other financial support, 3.12
  person responsible for child, 3.13–3.15
  prescribed conditions, 3.3–3.12
  terminal dates, 3.10–3.11
rate
  generally, 1.55
  weekly rates, 3.56–3.61
residence
  child treated as being in GB, 3.28
  child treated as being in Northern Ireland, 3.34
  Crown servants posted overseas, 3.40–3.43
  overlap of entitlement, 3.39
  person temporarily absent from GB, 3.32–3.33
  person temporarily absent from Northern Ireland, 3.38
  person treated as not being in GB, 3.30–3.31
  person treated as not being in Northern Ireland, 3.36–3.37
  transitional provisions, 3.44
residential accommodation, child in, 3.3
residing together, persons treated as, 3.45–3.46
social security income, 2.152
temporary absence
  from GB, 3.32–3.33
  from Northern Ireland, 3.38
terminal dates, 3.10–3.11
training scheme, child in, 3.4–3.5
unmarried couples, 3.45–3.46
voluntary organisations, 3.49–3.50
'week', 1.61
Child Benefit (General) Regulations 2006
arrangement, 3.1
citation, 3.2
commencement, 3.2
definitions, 3.2
general provisions, 3.3–3.54
Child Benefit (Rates) Regulations 2006
arrangement, 3.56
citation, 3.57
commencement, 3.57
definitions, 3.57

general note, 3.61
general provisions, 3.58
saving, 3.59
Child Benefit (Residence and Persons Abroad) Regulations 1976
general note, 3.55
Child maintenance
See **Child support**
Child maintenance bonus
social security income
  income support, 1.576
  jobseeker's allowance, 1.581
Child support
disregards, 2.185
Child tax credit
See also **Appeals (tax credits)**
abolition, 1.850–1.851
administrative arrangements
  definitions, 2.371
  general note, 2.369
  provision of information, 2.372–2.373
  recording, etc. of claims, 2.374
  statutory provisions, 1.415–1.416
age of child, 2.209–2.210
annual reports, 1.396–1.397
annual review, 1.398–1.399
appeals
  appealable decisions, 1.385–1.390
  exercise of right, 1.391–1.392
  general regulations, 2.375–2.387
  late appeals, 1.393–1.395
  temporary modifications, 1.425–1.426
assignment, 1.406–1.407
bankruptcy, 1.406–1.407
changes of circumstances
  advance, in, 2.327
  amendment, 2.320
  automatic, 1.289
  date of, 2.321–2.326
  decrease of rate, 2.314–2.317
  definitions, 2.211
  discretionary, 1.288
  failure to report, 1.290
  generally, 1.284–1.285
  increase of maximum rate, 2.312–2.313
  mandatory, 1.287
  method, 2.317–2.318
  person acting on behalf of another, by, 2.328–2.331
  relevant changes, 1.286
  relevant person, 2.319
child care providers scheme, 2.474–2.479
claims
  definitions, 2.276–2.277
  generally, 2.278–2.310
  statutory provisions, 1.267–1.281
Codes of Practice
  overpayments, 9.15–9.53
Crown employment, 1.404–1.405
death of child, after, 2.213–2.214
decisions
  discovery, on, 1.336–1.337
  final decision, 1.331–1.332

1093

final notice, 1.329–1.330
  information requirements, 1.344–1.345
  initial decision, 1.317–1.322
  notice of, 1.346–1.347
  official error, subject to, 1.338–1.339
  other revised decisions, 1.325–1.328
  power to enquire, 1.333–1.335
  review, 1.340–1.343
  revision after notifications, 1.323–1.324
definitions
  regulations, in, 2.194
  statute, in, 1.412–1.413
determination of rate
  cut-off provisions, 2.269–2.270
  full year periods, 2.267
  generally, 2.255–2.266
  introduction, 2.229–2.230
  short periods, 2.268
development of system, 1.257
disabled child, 2.217–2.218
disclosure of information, 1.417–1.418
duration, 1.282–1.283
entitlement, 1.299–1.301
evidence of birth or adoption, 2.332
failure to comply with requirements, 1.366–1.369
forwarding of claims, 2.374
fraud, and
  generally, 1.371–1.372
  powers relating to documents, 1.373–1.374
functions of Commissioners, 1.265–1.266
general note, 1.255
holding of claims, 2.374
inalienability, 1.406–1.407
income test
  calculation, 2.118–2.124
  definitions, 2.116–2.117
  disregards, 2.184–2.191
  employment income, 2.125–2.135
  foreign income, 2.170–2.171
  general note, 2.104–2.114
  investment income, 2.163–2.167
  miscellaneous income, 2.182–2.183
  notional income, 2.172–2.181
  pension income, 2.136–2.142
  property income, 2.168–2.169
  social security income, 2.151–2.157
  statutory provision, 1.291–1.298
income thresholds, 2.222–2.224
incorrect statements
  conduct of penalty cases, 1.363
  fraudulently or negligently, 1.362
  generally, 1.359–1.361
  level of penalties, 1.364–1.365
interest
  definitions, 2.391
  general note, 2.390
  overpayments, on, 2.392
  prescribed rate, 2.393
  statutory provision, 1.383–1.384
  student income, 2.158–2.162
  trading income, 2.143–2.150

maximum rate
  generally, 2.215–2.216
  statutory provision, 1.302–1.304
means testing, 2.104
Northern Ireland, 1.427–1.428
notices by Board, 1.408–1.409
notices to provide information
  childcare provider, to, 2.334
  dates to be specified, 2.335
  definitions, 2.273
  electronic communications, 2.274–2.275
  employers, to, 2.333
  s.17 TCA 2002, under, 2.336–2.339
notification of change of circumstances
  advance, in, 2.327
  amendment, 2.320
  automatic, 1.289
  date of, 2.321–2.326
  decrease of rate, 2.314–2.317
  definitions, 2.211
  discretionary, 1.288
  evidence of birth or adoption, 2.332
  failure to report, 1.290
  generally, 1.284–1.285
  increase of maximum rate, 2.312–2.313
  mandatory, 1.287
  method, 2.317–2.318
  person acting on behalf of another, by, 2.328–2.331
  relevant changes, 1.286
  relevant person, 2.319
official errors
  definitions, 2.432–2.433
  general note, 2.435
  generally, 2.434
overpayments
  Code of Practice, 9.15–9.53
  generally, 1.352–1.353
  method of recovery, 2.363
  recovery, 1.354–1.356
payment
  employees' rights, 1.350–1.351
  generally, 1.348–1.349
payment by Revenue and Customs
  amount, 2.361–2.362
  bank account requirement, 2.366–2.367
  definitions, 2.343
  general note, 2.341
  joint claims, for, 2.344–2.349
  method, 2.364–2.365
  person acting on behalf of another, for, 2.350–2.351
  postponement, 2.359–2.360
  recovery of overpayments, 2.363
  renewal claims, 2.352–2.353
  single payments, 2.357–2.358
  timing, 2.354–2.356
penalties
  determination, 1.435
  failure to comply with requirements, 1.366–1.369
  general note, 1.440–1.443

Guidance, 9.1–9.14
incorrect statements, etc., 1.359–1.365
mitigation, 1.437
proceedings before Commissioners, 1.436
recovery, 1.439
supplementary, 1.370
time limits, 1.438
period of award, 1.282–1.283
persons subject to immigration control
  definitions, 2.396
  exclusion from entitlement, 2.397–2.409
  general note, 2.403
  modifications of Act, 2.408–2.409
  statutory provision, 1.400–1.401
  transitional relief, 2.410–2.411
polygamous marriages
  definitions, 2.444–2.445
  general note, 2.442
  modification of Regulations, 2.447–2.453
  modification of TCA 2002, 2.446
  statutory provision, 1.402–1.403
provision of information
  authorities, by, 2.373
  authorities, to, 2.372
  functions relating to employment, 2.461, 2.473
  functions relating to health, 2.438–2.440, 2.457, 2.471
  functions relating to training, 2.461, 2.473
qualifying young person
  definition, 2.194
  maximum age, 2.211–2.212
rate, 1.315–1.316
recording of claims, 2.374
recovery of overpayments
  generally, 1.354–1.356
  method, 2.363
residence requirements
  Crown servants posted overseas, 2.425–2.427
  definitions, 2.414–2.415
  ordinary residence, 2.418–2.419
  person treated as not being in UK, 2.416–2.422
  temporary absence from UK, 2.423–2.424
  tests, 2.420–2.422
  transitional provision, 2.428–2.429
responsibility for child
  competing claims, 2.199–2.200
  excepted cases, 2.201–2.207
  generally, 2.195–2.197
  normally living with test, 2.198
  special case, 2.208
review of decisions
  generally, 1.340–1.341
  late application, 1.342–1.343
severely disabled child, 2.217–2.218
statutory provisions

appeals, 1.385–1.395
child tax credit, 1.299–1.304
decisions, 1.317–1.347
fraud, 1.371–1.374
generally, 1.263–1.298
interest, 1.383–1.384
payment, 1.348–1.358
penalties, 1.359–1.371
rate, 1.315–1.316
supplementary, 1.396–1.413
working tax credit, 1.305–1.314
transitional provisions, 2.462–2.465
underpayments, 1.357–1.358
use of information, 1.417–1.418
verification of claims, 2.374

Child Tax Credit Regulations 2002
arrangement, 2.192
citation, 2.193
commencement, 2.193
definitions, 2.194
effect, 2.193
general provisions, 2.195–2.218
modifications to, 2.447

Child trust funds
See also **Child trust funds (appeals)**
account providers
  appeal against non-approval or withdrawal of approval, 8.26
  appointment of tax representative, 8.24
  approval, 1.620–1.622
  ceasing to accept Revenue allocated accounts, 8.29
  ceasing to act, 8.29
  ceasing to qualify, 8.30
  definition, 1.693
  generally, 1.620
  intention to make bulk transfer of accounts, 8.29
  introduction, 1.600
  provision of information, 1.671–1.672
  qualifying circumstances, 8.23–8.26
  types of account, 1.621–1.623
  withdrawal of approval, 8.25
age 7 payments, 8.14
appeals
  appealable decisions, 1.684–1.685
  exercise of right, 1.686
  general regulations, 8.68–8.78
  notice of appeal, 8.62–8.67
  penalties, 1.683
  temporary modifications, 1.687
approval of account providers
  appeals, 8.26
  appointment of tax representative, 8.24
  disqualifying circumstances, 8.25
  generally, 1.620–1.622
  qualifying circumstances, 8.23
  withdrawal, 8.25
assignment of investments, 1.628–1.629
background, 1.600
bankruptcy of child, 1.628–1.629
bulk transfer of accounts, 8.29
capital gains tax

1095

Index

adaptation of enactments, 8.47
generally, 1.668–1.669
characteristics
  eligible child, 1.608–1.617
  introduction, 1.603–1.607
  requirements to be satisfied, 1.618–1.627
charge over investments, 1.628–1.629
child benefit, 1.610
child in care, 1.611
Commissioners of Inland Revenue, and
  General Commissioners, 8.60–8.63
  Special Commissioners, 8.64–8.67
contributions
  further, 1.659–1.663
  generally, 8.12–8.13
  initial, 1.649–1.650
  non-monetary subscriptions, 1.666–1.667
  recoupment, 1.664–1.665
  supplementary, 1.651–1.658
corporation tax, 1.670
date of birth, 1.610
death of child, and
  payments to parent, 1.679–1.680
  withdrawal of fund, 1.623
definitions, 1.693
descriptions of accounts, 8.9
eligible child
  meaning, 1.608–1.617
  opening of fund, 1.630–1.636
further contributions, 1.659–1.663
future, 1.601
general note, 1.600–1.601
generally, 1.603–1.607
government contributions
  further, 1.659–1.663
  generally, 8.12–8.13
  initial, 1.649–1.650
  non-monetary subscriptions, 1.666–1.667
  recoupment, 1.664–1.665
  supplementary, 1.651–1.658
HM Revenue and Customs
  opening of fund, 1.637–1.643
  status and role, 1.607
inalienability, 1.628–1.629
income tax, 1.668–1.669
information
  account providers, from, 1.671–1.672
  child in care of authority, about, 1.673–1.674
  disclosure of, 1.677–1.678
  use of, 1.675–1.676
initial contributions, 1.649–1.650
insurance companies, 8.53–8.61
intention to make bulk transfer of accounts, 8.29
invalid accounts, repair of, 8.33
investment rules
  generally, 8.20
  qualifying investments, 8.21
jurisdiction of Commissioners
  General Commissioners, 8.60–8.63
  Special Commissioners, 8.64–8.67
looked after child
  authority to manage account, 8.44
  generally, 1.611
  information from local authorities, 8.43
management of, 1.625
meaning, 1.603–1.607
migrant workers' children, 1.613
Northern Ireland, 1.688–1.689
objectives, 1.600
opening by eligible child
  conditions for application, 8.22
  generally, 8.10
  statutory provision, 1.630–1.636
opening by HM Revenue and Customs
  generally, 8.11
  statutory provision, 1.637–1.643
opening by responsible person
  conditions for application, 8.22
  generally, 8.10
  statutory provision, 1.630–1.636
parental responsibility, 1.618
payments to parent, 1.679–1.680
penalties
  appeals, 1.683
  decisions, 1.683
  generally, 1.681–1.682
  mitigation, 1.683
  recovery, 1.683
permitted withdrawals from fund
  child is terminally ill, where, 8.28
  generally, 8.27
  statutory provision, 1.623
powers to safeguard interests of children, 1.648
recoupment of IR contributions
  generally, 8.32
  statutory provision, 1.664–1.665
repair of invalid accounts, 8.33
repayments of tax to account provider
  annual claims, 8.37
  interim claims, 8.36
requirements to be satisfied
  generally, 8.17
  statutory provision, 1.618–1.627
residence, 1.613–1.614
responsible person
  meaning, 1.626–1.627
  opening of fund, 1.630–1.636
revenue allocated accounts
  account provider ceases to accept, where, 8.29
  generally, 8.11
  statutory provision, 1.637–1.643
Revenue and Customs
  opening of fund, 1.637–1.643
  status and role, 1.607
safeguarding interests of children, 1.648
stakeholder accounts
  characteristics, 8.51

Index

charges, 8.52
description, 8.50
generally, 8.9
statements of account, 8.18
subscription limits
  generally, 8.18
  statutory provision, 1.666–1.667
supplementary contributions, 1.651–1.658
tax
  account provider to act on behalf of named child, 8.35
  account provider's tax claims, 8.36–8.37
  administration, 8.48
  application of Taxes Act, 8.49
  assessment for withdrawal of relief, 8.39
  capital gains tax, 1.668–1.669
  corporation tax, 1.670
  fortnightly claims, 8.40
  generally, 8.34
  income tax, 1.668–1.669
  information about looked after children, 8.43–8.44
  information to be provided to Board, 8.45
  inspection of records, 8.46
  records, 8.41
  repayments to account provider, 8.36–8.37
  returns of information, 8.42
  tax returns, 8.40
transfers
  account provider ceases to act, where, 8.29
  account provider ceases to qualify, where, 8.30
  child reaching 18, on, 1.647
  generally, 1.644–1.645
  intention to make bulk transfer of accounts, 8.29
  other accounts for children, to, 1.646, 8.31
  statutory provision, 1.644–1.648
vouchers
  generally, 8.8
  statutory provision, 1.631–1.634
withdrawals from fund
  child is terminally ill, where, 8.28
  generally, 8.27
  statutory provision, 1.623
yearly disability payments, 8.15–8.16
Child Trust Funds Act 2004
arrangement of sections, 1.599
commencement
  introduction, 1.602
  Order No.1, 8.1–8.2
  Order No.2, 8.3–8.4
definitions, 1.693
extent, 1.602
general note, 1.600–1.601
general provisions, 1.603–1.687
supplementary, 1.688–1.695

Child trust funds (appeals)
assessment of tax returns, 1.19–1.20
death of party, 8.77–8.78
decisions of Board, 1.233–1.234
definitions, 8.69–8.70
exercise of right
  generally, 1.235–1.238, 1.686
  regulations, 1.239–1.240
general regulations
  citation, 8.69
  commencement, 8.69
  definitions, 8.69–8.70
  duration, 8.69
  general provisions, 8.71–8.78
  recitals, 8.68
late appeals, 8.75–8.76
notice of appeal
  disputes concerning, 8.73–8.74
  prescribed form, 8.65–8.66
  service, 8.71–8.72
  signature, 8.65–8.66
  statutory provision, 1.686
penalties, 1.683
Regulations
  general, 8.68–8.78
  notice of appeal, 8.62–8.67
service of notices or documents, 8.71–8.72
temporary modifications, 1.687
time limits, 8.75–8.76
Child Trust Funds (Appeals) Regulations 2005
citation, 8.69
commencement, 8.69
definitions, 8.69–8.70
duration, 8.69
general provisions, 8.71–8.78
recitals, 8.68
Child Trust Funds (Insurance Companies) Regulations 2004
arrangement, 8.53
citation, 8.54
commencement, 8.54
definitions, 8.55
general provisions, 8.56–8.61
Child Trust Funds (Non-tax Appeals) Regulations 2005
citation, 8.63
commencement, 8.63
definitions, 8.64
general provisions, 8.65–8.67
recitals, 8.62
Child Trust Funds Regulations 2004
arrangement, 8.5
citation, 8.6
commencement, 8.6
definitions, 8.7
general provisions, 8.8–8.49
schedule, 8.50–8.52
Childbirth
See **Birth**
Childcare
See also **Child Approval Scheme**

1097

claims time limits, 2.286–2.290
employer-contracted and provided
   'care', 1.530
   'child', 1.530
   employer-contracted, 1.527–1.528
   employer-provided, 1.525–1.526
   introductory note, 1.482
   'parental responsibility', 1.530
   'qualifying child care', 1.531
   'relevant earnings', 1.529
   regulations, 2.132–2.133
   'required time', 1.529
notice to provide information by provider, 2.334

Childcare Approval Scheme
revocation provisions, 2.474–2.479

Childcare element
See also **Working tax credit**
calculation of childcare charges, 2.76–2.77
change of circumstances, 2.78–2.79
'child', 2.73–2.75
'childcare', 2.73–2.75
generally, 2.70–2.72
incapacitation, 2.72
payment by Revenue and Customs, 2.344–2.345
qualifying young persons, 2.75
'relevant childcare charges', 2.73–2.75
statutory provision, 1.313–1.314

Childcare Payments Act 2014
disregards, 2.185
time limits for claims, 2.286–2.290

Childcare vouchers
meaning, 1.509

Children
childcare element (working tax credit), 2.73–2.75

Christmas bonus
social security income, 2.152

Civil partners
references in Income Tax Acts, 1.847

Civil partnerships
child benefit, 3.18

Civil penalties
See **Penalties**

CJD
See **Creuzfeld-Jakob Disease**

Claims
administrative arrangements
   definitions, 2.371
   general note, 2.369
   provision of information, 2.372–2.373
   recording, etc. of claims, 2.374
advance, in
   generally, 2.293–2.294
   working tax credit, 2.295–2.296
amendment, 2.283
conditional, 2.303
dead applicants, on behalf of
   generally, 2.304–2.305
   joint claims, for, 2.306–2.307
deeming provision
   one member of couple on behalf of both, 2.301–2.302
   revenue final notices, in response to, 2.297–2.300
definitions
   generally, 2.273
   relevant date, 2.276–2.277
disability element of WTC, 2.291–2.292
electronic communications, 2.274–2.275
forwarding of, 2.374
holding of, 2.374
method, 2.278–2.282
person acting on behalf of another, by
   generally, 2.308
   other appointed persons, 2.309–2.310
polygamous marriages, 2.450
provision of information
   by authorities, 2.373
   to authorities, 2.372
recording, 2.374
statutory provisions
   generally, 1.267–1.279
   supplementary, 1.280–1.281
time limits
   Childcare Payments Act 2014, under, 2.286–2.290
   generally, 2.284–2.285
verification, 2.374

Clerical errors
tax returns
   during enquiry, 1.10
   generally, 1.7

Closure notices
tax return enquiries, 1.12

Codes of practice
overpayments, 9.15–9.53

Cohabitation
child benefit
   living with another, 3.16–3.17
   residing together, 3.45–3.46
references in Income Tax Acts, 1.111

Co-habiting child
See **Cohabitation**

Collective investment schemes
child trust funds, 8.7

Commissioners for Revenue and Customs
administration of taxes, 1.3
appointment, 1.808
assault, 1.825
Charter of standards and values, 1.820
child trust funds, and
   General Commissioners, 8.60–8.63
   Special Commissioners, 8.64–8.67
conduct of proceedings, 1.815
decisions
   amendment of existing legislation, 1.245–1.246
   appeals, 1.233–1.246
   definitions, 1.247–1.249
   generally, 1.227–1.228
   matters arising, 1.241–1.242
   regulations, 1.229–1.230

Secretary of State's delegated functions, 1.243–1.244
supersession of earlier decisions, 1.231–1.232
tax credits, 1.317–1.347
verification of claims, 2.374
variation of earlier decisions, 1.231–1.232
declaration of confidentiality, 1.810
delegation of functions, 1.818–1.819
exercise of functions, 1.816–1.817
former Inland Revenue matters
  generally, 1.813
  schedule, 1.828
freedom of information, 1.823
functions
  ancillary powers, 1.814
  Charter of standards and values, 1.820
  conduct of proceedings, 1.815
  delegation, 1.818–1.819
  exercise by officers, 1.816–1.817
  former Inland Revenue matters, 1.813
  generally, 1.265–1.266
  initial functions, 1.812
general note, 1.807
information
  confidentiality, 1.822
  freedom of information, 1.823
  use, 1.821
initial functions, 1.812
ITEPA 2003, 1.478
notices
  tax credits, 1.408–1.409
obstruction, 1.824
offences
  assault, 1.825
  obstruction, 1.824
  power of arrest, 1.826
payments
  amount, 2.361–2.362
  bank account requirement, 2.366–2.367
  definitions, 2.343
  general note, 2.341
  joint claims, for, 2.344–2.349
  method, 2.364–2.365
  person acting on behalf of another, for, 2.350–2.351
  postponement, 2.359–2.360
  recovery of overpayments, 2.363
  renewal claims, 2.352–2.353
  single payments, 2.357–2.358
  timing, 2.354–2.356
resignation, 1.808
responsibility for certain taxes, 1.3
staff appointments, 1.809
supply of information
  statutory adoption pay, 1.460
  statutory paternity pay, 1.460
tax credits
  functions, 1.265–1.266
  notices, 1.408–1.409
transfer of property, 1.827
use of information
  statutory adoption pay, 1.462

Commissioners for Revenue and Customs Act 2005
arrangement of sections, 1.806
consequential amendments, 1.827
general provisions, 1.808–1.826
introduction, 1.807
schedule, 1.828

Commissioners of Inland Revenue
See **Commissioners for Revenue and Customs**

Compensation of employers (statutory maternity pay)
additional payment to small employers, 5.85
advance funding, 5.87
date of payment of contributions, 5.90
definitions
  generally, 5.82
  'small employer', 5.84
general note, 5.83
method
  deduction from payments to Revenue, 5.88
  payments to employer by Revenue, 5.89
overpayments, 5.91
prescribed amount, 5.86

"Conditional claims"
generally, 2.303

"Connexions Service"
definition, 3.2

Continental shelf (employees)
statutory adoption pay
  definitions, 6.34
  general note, 6.35
  generally, 6.43
statutory maternity pay
  definitions, 5.63
  general note, 5.64
  generally, 5.72
  statutory provisions, 1.104
statutory paternity pay
  definitions, 6.34
  general note, 6.35
  generally, 6.43
  statutory provisions, 1.132–1.133
statutory shared parental pay, 7.138
statutory sick pay
  definitions, 4.51, 4.58, 4.64
  general note, 4.47
  statutory provision, 1.88
  time for compliance, 4.65

Continuity of employment
statutory adoption pay
  change of employer, 6.99
  generally, 6.96
  reinstatement after service with armed forces, 6.100
  stoppages of work, 6.98
  unfair dismissal, 6.97
statutory maternity pay
  change of employer, 5.26

1099

generally, 5.22
stoppages of work, 5.24–5.25
unfair dismissal, 5.23
statutory paternity pay
change of employer, 6.99
generally, 6.96
reinstatement after service with armed forces, 6.100
stoppages of work, 6.98
unfair dismissal, 6.97
statutory shared parental pay
adoption, 7.58–7.59
birth, 7.57
change of employer, 7.66
'continuous employment', 7.63
service with armed forces, 7.67
stoppages of work, 7.65
unfair dismissal, and, 7.64
Continuous employment
See **Continuity of employment**
Contracting out
statutory adoption pay, 1.145–1.146
statutory paternity pay, 1.126–1.127
Contractual remuneration
See **Remuneration**
Contribution-based jobseekers' allowance
social security income, 2.152
Correction of errors
See **Clerical errors**
Council tax benefit
social security income, 2.152
Credit tokens
application of provisions, 1.511
benefit treated as earnings, 1.513
disregard for money, goods or services obtained, 1.514
meaning, 1.512
"Creuzfeldt-Jakob disease"
investment income, 2.165
Crime prevention (fraud)
statutory adoption pay
generally, 1.458–1.459
procedure and appeals, 1.466–1.474
statutory paternity pay
generally, 1.458–1.459
procedure and appeals, 1.466–1.474
tax credits
generally, 1.371–1.372
powers relating to documents, 1.373–1.374
supply of information by tax authorities, 1.216
Crown servants
child benefit
child, 3.43
generally, 3.40–3.41
partners, 3.42
'Crown servant posted overseas', 3.2
overseas employees
generally, 2.425–2.426
partners, 2.427
statutory adoption pay, 1.149–1.150

statutory maternity pay, 1.103
statutory paternity pay, 1.130–1.131
statutory shared parental pay, 1.163
statutory sick pay, 1.87
tax credits, 1.404–1.405
"Curtailment of pay period"
statutory adoption pay
definitions, 5.103
general note, 5.101
notice, 5.113
revocation notice, 5.114
service of notices, 5.104
shared parental leave: AP, 5.112
statutory shared parental pay: A, 5.110
statutory shared parental pay: AP, 5.111
statutory maternity pay
definitions, 5.103
general note, 5.101
notice, 5.108
revocation notice, 5.109
service of notices, 5.104
shared parental leave: P, 5.107
statutory shared parental pay: M, 5.105
statutory shared parental pay: P, 5.106
"Days of absence"
child benefit, 3.4
Death
child benefit
Regulations, 3.27
statutory basis, 1.56
child tax credit, 2.213–2.214
child trust fund appeals, 8.77–8.78
statutory maternity pay, 5.21
statutory shared parental pay
entitlement (adoption), 7.54
entitlement (birth), 7.36
tax credit appeals, 2.387
tax credits
generally, 2.304–2.305
joint claims, for, 2.306–2.307
working tax credit, 2.83–2.84
Debts
trading income
debts incurred and later released, 1.728
doubtful debts, 1.722
Decisions (Commissioners for Revenue and Customs)
amendment of existing legislation, 1.245–1.246
appeals
exercise of right, 1.235–1.238
generally, 1.233–1.234
regulations, 1.239–1.240
definitions, 1.247–1.249
generally, 1.227–1.228
matters arising, 1.241–1.242
regulations, 1.229–1.230
review of decisions
generally, 1.340–1.341
late application, 1.342–1.343
Secretary of State's delegated functions, 1.243–1.244

Index

supersession of earlier decisions, 1.231–1.232
tax credits
  discovery, on, 1.336–1.337
  final decision, 1.331–1.332
  final notice, 1.329–1.330
  information requirements, 1.344–1.345
  initial decision, 1.317–1.322
  notice of, 1.346–1.347
  official error, subject to, 1.338–1.339
  other revised decisions, 1.325–1.328
  power to enquire, 1.333–1.335
  review, 1.340–1.343
  revision after notifications, 1.323–1.324
verification of claims, 2.374
variation of earlier decisions, 1.231–1.232

Deductions
application of provisions, 1.532
'deductibility provisions', 1.537
employment income, 2.132–2.133
expenses, 1.540
expenses paid by employee
  effect of reimbursement, 1.539
  generally, 1.538
general rules
  double deductions, 1.535
  income from which be made, 1.533
  maximum amount, 1.534
  order for making, 1.536
pension income, 2.140
regulations, 2.132–2.133
social security income, 2.155
trading income
  bad debts, 1.722
  business entertainment and gifts, 1.724
  capital expenditure, 1.720
  doubtful debts, 1.722
  generally, 2.147–2.148
  professions and vocations, 1.719
  relationship between rules, 1.718
  social security contributions, 1.725
  unconnected losses, 1.721
  unpaid remuneration, 1.723
  wholly and exclusively rules, 1.721
travel expenses
  necessary attendance, for, 1.542
  performance of duties, in, 1.541
  'workplace', 1.543

"Deemed income from capital"
generally, 2.106

"Depriving self of income to secure entitlement"
notional income, 2.176–2.177

Detention
child benefit
  Regulations, 3.21–3.24
  statutory basis, 1.170
statutory maternity pay, 5.17–5.18
statutory paternity pay, 6.108
statutory shared parental pay, 7.75
statutory sick pay. 4.9

"Determination of rate"
child tax credit
  full year periods, 2.267
  generally, 2.255–2.266
  short periods, 2.268
cut-off provisions, 2.269–2.270
generally, 2.229–2.230
working tax credit
  full year periods, 2.247–2.253
  generally, 2.231–2.246
  short periods, 2.254

Directions
tax credit appeals
  death of party, 2.387

Disability element (working tax credit)
Cases A to G, 2.59
date of claim, 2.291–2.292
generally, 2.56–2.58
initial claims, 2.60–2.61
relevant disabilities, 2.88–2.101
'training for work', 2.62–2.63

"Disability periods "
working tax credit, 2.42–2.43

Disability living allowance
social security income, 2.152

Disability pension
See **Pension income**

Disability working allowance
working tax credit, 2.57

Disabled persons
child tax credit, 2.217–2.218

Disabled persons tax credit
social security income, 2.152

Disabled persons' vehicles
maintenance grant, 1.788

Disclosure (information)
statutory maternity pay, 1.220
statutory sick pay, 1.218
tax credits, 1.417–1.418

Discretionary payments
disregards, 2.185
social security income, 2.152

Disregards
conditional exclusions, 2.190
employment income, 2.126
generally, 2.184–2.188
investment income, 2.164
partial disregard, 2.191
pension income, 2.137
social security income, 2.152
student income, 2.161–2.162
total disregard, 2.189

Divided contracts
statutory adoption pay
  general note, 6.10
  generally, 6.87
  lapse of election, 6.15
  notification of election, 6.12
  provision of information, 6.13
  relevant employer, 6.14, 6.101
statutory maternity pay
  generally, 5.11
  relevant employer, 5.32–5.33
statutory maternity pay (National Health Service)

1101

lapse of election, 5.80
notification of election, 5.77
provision of information, 5.78
treatment of more than one contract as one, 5.76
treatment of two or more employers as one, 5.79
statutory paternity pay
  adoption of child, on, 6.77
  birth of child, on, 6.70
  general note, 6.10
  lapse of election, 6.15
  notification of election, 6.12
  provision of information, 6.13
  relevant employer, 6.14, 6.101
statutory sick pay
  generally, 4.41
  relevant employer, 4.39–4.40
statutory sick pay (National Health Service)
  lapse of election, 4.79
  notification of election, 4.76
  provision of information, 4.77
  treatment of more than one contract as one, 4.75
  treatment of two or more employers as one, 4.78
Dividends
non-resident UK companies, from
  charge to tax, 1.758
  income charged, 1.759
  person liable, 1.760
savings and investment income, 1.80
UK resident companies, from
  charge to tax, 1.755
  income charged, 1.756
  introduction, 1.754
  person liable, 1.757
Divorcees
guardian's allowance, 3.69
Doubtful debts
See **Debts**
Duplication of payments
child benefit, 3.52
Earnings
employment income, 1.495
statutory adoption pay
  generally, 6.102
  normal weekly earnings, 6.103
statutory maternity pay
  generally, 5.35
  normal weekly earnings, 5.36–5.37
statutory paternity pay
  generally, 6.102
  normal weekly earnings, 6.103
statutory shared parental pay
  generally, 7.60
  normal weekly earnings, 7.57–7.61
statutory sick pay
  excepted payments, 4.36
  generally, 4.35
  normal weekly earnings, 4.37–4.38

Education
child benefit
  definition, 3.2
  generally, 3.4–3.5
Education maintenance allowance
disregards, 2.185
Eileen Trust
tax credits, 2.165
Election
child benefit
  generally, 3.19
  not to receive, 1.207–1.208
guardian's allowance, 3.75
Electronic communications
child benefit, 3.53
claims and notifications, 2.274–2.275
Employed earners
See **Employees**
Employees
statutory maternity pay, 5.31
statutory paternity pay, 6.95
Employer-contracted childcare
See **Childcare**
Employers
notice to provide information, 2.333
payment of WTC, 2.341
provision of information, and
  statutory maternity pay, 1.221
  statutory sick pay, 1.219
Employment records
statutory adoption pay
  generally, 6.26
  inspection, 6.27
statutory maternity pay
  maintenance, 5.46
  production, 5.47
statutory paternity pay
  generally, 6.26
  inspection, 6.27
statutory sick pay
  maintenance, 4.27
  production, 4.28
Employment Act 2002
arrangement of sections, 1.445
general note, 1.446
general provisions
  maternity, 1.464–1.465
  paternity and adoption, 1.447–1.463
schedule, 1.466–1.474
"Employment functions"
provision of information, and
  general note, 2.459
  generally, 2.461, 2.473
Employment income
agency workers, 1.494
benefits code
  definitions, 1.499
  dispensations, 1.498
  meaning, 1.496
  relationship with earnings, 1.497
cash vouchers
  application of provisions, 1.503–1.504
  benefit treated as earnings, 1.507

Index

disregard for money, goods or services obtained, 1.514
meaning, 1.505
sickness-benefits related, 1.506
charge to tax
  agency workers, 1.494
  'employment', 1.483–1.484
  exemptions, 1.482
  introductory provision, 1.481–1.482
  nature, 1.486–1.488
  office-holders, 1.485
  operation, 1.489–1.493
credit tokens
  application of provisions, 1.511
  benefit treated as earnings, 1.513
  disregard for money, goods or services obtained, 1.514
  meaning, 1.512
deductions from earnings
  application of provisions, 1.532
  'deductibility provisions', 1.537
  expenses, 1.540
  expenses paid by employee, 1.538–1.539
  general rules, 1.533–1.536
  regulations, 2.132–2.133
  travel expenses, 1.541–1.543
definitions
  'employment', 1.483–1.484
  'employment income', 1.487
  'exempt income', 1.488
  'general earnings', 1.487
  'net taxable earnings', 1.491
  'net taxable specific income', 1.492
  'paid', 1.501
  'put at disposal', 1.501
  'specific employment income', 1.487
  'taxable earnings', 1.490
  'taxable specific income', 1.490
differences from tax assessments, 2.131
disregarded payments, 2.126
earnings, 1.495
employer-contracted and provided childcare
  'care', 1.530
  'child', 1.530
  definitions, 1.530–1.531
  employer-contracted, 1.527–1.528
  employer-provided, 1.525–1.526
  introductory note, 1.482
  'parental responsibility', 1.530
  'qualifying child care', 1.531
  'relevant earnings', 1.529
  regulations, 2.132–2.133
  'required time', 1.529
'employment', 1.483–1.484
employment-related benefits
  cash equivalent treated as earnings, 1.517
  cost of benefit, 1.518
  excluded benefits, 1.516
  meaning, 1.515
exemptions
  'care', 1.530
  'child', 1.530
  definitions, 1.530–1.531
  employer-contracted childcare, 1.527–1.528
  employer-provided childcare, 1.525–1.526
  introductory note, 1.482
  'parental responsibility', 1.530
  'qualifying child care', 1.531
  'relevant earnings', 1.529
  regulations, 2.132–2.133
  'required time', 1.529
expenses payments
  definitions, 1.501
  relevant sums, 1.500
  sums treated as earnings, 1.502
general note
  regulations, 2.127
  statutory provisions, 1.476–1.477
generally, 2.125
identity of taxpayer, 2.134
lower-paid employment
  calculation of earnings rate, 1.523
  excluded provisions of benefits code, 1.521
  extra amounts relating to car, 1.524
  meaning, 1.522
meaning, 1.487
minor benefits, 1.519–1.520
nature, 2.130
nature of charge to tax
  definitions, 1.487–1.488
  generally, 1.486
non-cash vouchers
  application of provisions, 1.508
  benefit treated as earnings, 1.510
  disregard for money, goods or services obtained, 1.514
  meaning, 1.509
office-holders, 1.485
operation of tax charge
  amount of income charged, 1.489
  definitions, 1.490–1.492
  person liable to tax, 1.493
scope, 2.128
self-employment, 2.129
sickness-benefits related vouchers, 1.506
statutory provisions
  charge to tax, 1.481–1.494
  deductions from earnings, 1.532–1.543
  earnings, 1.495
  general note, 1.476–1.477
  taxable benefits, 1.496–1.524
taxable benefits
  benefits code, 1.496–1.499
  cash vouchers, 1.503–1.507
  credit tokens, 1.511–1.514
  expenses payments, 1.500–1.502
  lower-paid employees, 1.521–1.524
  minor benefits, 1.519–1.520
  non-cash vouchers, 1.508–1.510

residual liability, 1.515–1.518
vouchers, 1.503–1.510
time of calculation, 2.135
travel expenses
necessary attendance, for, 1.542
performance of duties, in, 1.541
'workplace', 1.543
vouchers
cash vouchers, 1.503–1.507
non-cash vouchers, 1.508–1.510
"Employment insurance"
annual payments, 1.782–1.783
Employment records
statutory adoption pay
generally, 6.26
inspection, 6.27
statutory maternity pay
maintenance, 5.46
production, 5.47
statutory paternity pay
generally, 6.26
inspection, 6.27
statutory sick pay
maintenance, 4.27
production, 4.28
"Employment-related benefits"
cash equivalent treated as earnings, 1.517
cost of benefit, 1.518
excluded benefits, 1.516
meaning, 1.515
Employment zones
disregards, 2.185
remunerative work, 2.36
Enforcement
statutory maternity pay
breach of regulations, 1.213–1.214
fraud, 1.215
negligence, 1.215
statutory sick pay
breach of regulations, 1.213–1.214
fraud, 1.215
negligence, 1.215
Enquiries into tax returns
See **Tax enquiries**
Entitlement
additional statutory paternity pay (adoption)
applications, 6.174
conditions to be satisfied by child's adopter, 6.172
death of the adopter, and, 6.175–6.176
evidence of entitlement, 6.174
generally, 6.171
more than one employer, where, 6.177
pay period, 6.173
additional statutory paternity pay (birth)
applications, 6.167
conditions to be satisfied by child's mother, 6.165
death of the mother, and, 6.168–6.169
early birth, 6.164
evidence of entitlement, 6.167
generally, 6.163

modification of conditions, 6.163
more than one employer, where, 6.170
pay period, 6.166
statutory adoption pay
determination of issues, 6.30–6.31
evidence, 6.86
provision of information, 6.28–6.29
statutory provisions, 1.139–1.140
statutory maternity pay
evidence, 5.59
generally, 1.91–1.93
statutory paternity pay
adoption of child, on, 6.71–6.77
birth of child, on, 6.62–6.70
determination of issues, 6.30–6.31
evidence, 6.62–6.64, 6.71–6.72
provision of information, 6.28–6.29
statutory provisions, 1.107–1.116
statutory sick pay
employer's liability, 1.64–1.68
evidence, 4.67–4.72
general note, 1.62–1.63
limitations, 1.80–1.81
qualifying conditions, 1.69–1.79
Error by officials
See **Official errors**
Errors
See **Clerical errors**
"Evaluation studies"
generally, 2.467
Northern Ireland, 2.469
Evidence
admissibility not affected by offer of settlement, 1.25
Evidence
See also **Medical evidence**
statutory adoption pay, 6.86
statutory maternity pay, 5.59
statutory paternity pay
adoption of child, on, 6.71–6.72
birth of child, on, 6.62–6.64
statutory sick pay
definitions, 4.67
doctor's statement, 4.70–4.72
general note, 4.68
information required, 4.69
Ex gratia payments
social security income, 2.152
Exempt income
annual payments
adopters, to, 1.784
employment insurance payments, 1.782–1.783
foreign maintenance payments, 1.777
health insurance payments, 1.782–1.783
periodical payments of personal injury damages, 1.778–1.781
employment income, 1.488
employment insurance payments, 1.782–1.783
foreign maintenance payments, 1.777

general disregard, 1.789
health insurance payments, 1.782–1.783
introduction, 1.697–1.698
overview, 1.776
payments to adopters, 1.784
periodical payments of personal injury damages
  compensation awards, 1.779
  generally, 1.778
  persons entitled, 1.780
  trusts, from, 1.781
statutory overview, 1.700
tax credits
  employment income, 2.132–2.133
  pension income, 2.140
  social security income, 2.155
  trading income, 2.147–2.148

"Expected week of confinement"
statutory maternity pay, 5.40

Expenses
definitions, 1.501
relevant sums, 1.500
sums treated as earnings, 1.502

Extensions of time
child trust fund appeals, 8.75–8.76
tax credit appeals, 2.385–2.386

Failure to comply with requirements
See **Non-compliance**

Failure to disclose
overpayments, 1.211–1.212

Farming
trading income, 1.709

50-plus element
working tax credit, 2.82

First-tier Tribunal
appeals to, 1.223–1.224

Foreign income
introduction, 1.697–1.698
social security income
  application of provisions, 1.593–1.594
  person liable to tax, 1.596
  taxable income, 1.595
statutory overview, 1.700
tax credits, 2.170–2.171

"Foreign maintenance"
annual payments, 1.777

"Former Inland Revenue matters"
generally, 1.813
schedule, 1.828

Foster care relief
definitions
  providing foster care, 1.801
  providing qualifying care, 1.800
  qualifying care receipts, 1.799
  residence, 1.803
overview, 1.796
qualifying person, 1.797

"Forwarding claims"
administrative arrangements, 2.374

Fraud
loss of tax credits, and
  generally, 1.379–1.380
  introduction, 1.261–1.262

Regulations, 2.483–2.486
specified day, 2.480–2.482
supplementary, 1.381–1.382
statutory adoption pay
  generally, 1.458–1.459
  procedure and appeals, 1.466–1.474
statutory maternity pay, 1.215
statutory paternity pay
  generally, 1.458–1.459
  procedure and appeals, 1.466–1.474
statutory sick pay, 1.215
tax credits
  generally, 1.371–1.372
  introduction, 1.261–1.262
  loss of tax credit, 1.375–1.382
  powers relating to documents, 1.373–1.374
  supply of information by tax authorities, 1.216
tax returns, 1.17

Fraud prevention
See **Crime prevention (fraud)**

Freedom of information
Her Majesty's Revenue and Customs, 1.823

Full-time students
child benefit
  definition, 3.2
  generally, 3.4–3.5

Funding of legal services
See **Legal advice and funding**

Further education
child benefit, 3.4–3.5
definition, 3.2

Gambling
investment income, 2.164

"Gaps between jobs"
working tax credit, 2.54–2.55

"General earnings"
employment income, 1.487

Generally accepted accounting practice
trading income, 1.713

Gifts
trading income, 1.724

Guardian's allowance
See also **Non-contributory benefits**
adopted child
  Regulations, 3.67
  statutory provision, 1.40
divorced persons, child of, 3.69
election, 3.75
entitlement
  conditions, 1.32–1.40
  generally, 1.30–1.31
illegitimate child, 3.68
imprisoned person, child of, 3.70–3.71
overpayments, 1.211–1.212
prisoner, child of, 3.70–3.71
residence, 3.74
social security income, 2.152
uprating
  Order 2015, 3.78–3.79
  Regulations 2015, 3.80–3.82

1105

Index

Guardian's Allowance (General) Regulations 2003
arrangement, 3.62
citation, 3.64
commencement, 3.64
definitions, 3.65
general provisions, 3.66–3.76
recitals, 3.63
schedule, 3.77
Haemophilia
investment income, 2.165
Health
provision of information, and
definitions, 2.439
general note, 2.438
generally, 2.440, 2.457
Northern Ireland, 2.471
Health insurance
annual payments, 1.782–1.783
Her Majesty's Revenue and Customs
See **Revenue and Customs**
"Holding claims"
administrative arrangements, 2.374
Hospitals
definition, 3.2
"Hours worked"
qualifying remunerative work, 2.37
Housing benefit
social security income, 2.152
Identity of taxpayer
See **Taxable persons**
Ill health
working tax credit, 2.42–2.43
Illegitimacy
guardian's allowance, 3.68
Immigrants
definitions, 2.396
exclusion from entitlement, 2.397–2.409
general note, 2.403
modifications of Act, 2.408–2.409
polygamous marriages, 2.453
statutory provision, 1.400–1.401
transitional relief, 2.410–2.411
Immigration control
See **Immigrants**
Imprisonment
child benefit
Regulations, 3.24
statutory basis, 1.170
guardian's allowance, 3.70–3.71
statutory maternity pay, 5.17–5.18
statutory paternity pay, 6.108
statutory sick pay, 4.9
"Inalienability"
tax credits, 1.406–1.407
"Incapacitation"
childcare element (working tax credit), 2.72
Incapacity benefit
child benefit, 3.12
social security income
long-term, 1.573
short-term, 1.574

statutory maternity pay
generally, 5.38
statutory provision, 1.204
statutory sick pay, 1.198–1.199
working tax credit, 2.152
Incapacity for work
statutory sick pay
notification, 4.16
persons deemed incapable, 4.4–4.6
persons unable to act, 4.23–4.24
working tax credit, 2.42–2.43
Income
calculation, 2.118–2.124
capital, 2.106
deemed income from capital, 2.106
definitions, 2.116–2.117
disregards
conditional exclusions, 2.190
generally, 2.184–2.188
partial disregard, 2.191
total disregard, 2.189
employment income
deductions, 2.132–2.133
differences from tax assessments, 2.131
disregarded payments, 2.126
exemptions, 2.132–2.133
general note, 2.127
generally, 2.125
identity of taxpayer, 2.134
nature, 2.130
scope, 2.128
self-employment, 2.129
time of calculation, 2.135
foreign income, 2.170–2.171
general note
change in approach, 2.106
cross-references, 2.114
differences from tax assessments, 2.107
introduction, 2.104
questions to be decided, 2.108–2.113
Tax Law Rewrite Project, 2.105
investment income
disregarded payments, 2.164
general note, 2.166–2.167
generally, 2.163
very severe disablement payments, 2.165
miscellaneous income, 2.182–2.183
not otherwise charged
charge to tax, 1.773
income charged, 1.774
person liable, 1.775
notional income
depriving self of income to secure entitlement, 2.176–2.177
entitlement to sums, 2.178–2.179
generally, 2.172–2.173
provision of services for less than full earnings, 2.180–2.181
sums treated as income under Taxes Acts, 2.174–2.175
pension income
deductions, 2.140

1106

Index

disregarded payments, 2.137
exemptions, 2.140
general note, 2.138
generally, 2.136
identity of taxpayer, 2.141
relevant income, 2.139
time of calculation, 2.142
polygamous marriages, 2.449
property income, 2.168–2.169
social security income
  deductions, 2.155
  disregarded payments, 2.152
  exemptions, 2.155
  general note, 2.153
  generally, 2.151
  identity of taxpayer, 2.156
  relevant income, 2.154
  time of calculation, 2.157
statutory provision, 1.291–1.298
student income
  disregarded payments, 2.161–2.162
  generally, 2.158–2.160
tax-exempt savings, 2.106
thresholds
  definitions, 2.221
  generally, 2.222–2.224
trading income
  deductions, 2.147–2.148
  exemptions, 2.147–2.148
  general note, 2.144
  generally, 2.143
  identity of taxpayer, 2.149
  relevant income, 2.147–2.148
  self-employment, 2.145–2.146
  time of calculation, 2.150
voluntary work, 2.179–2.180
"Income not otherwise charged"
charge to tax, 1.773
income charged, 1.774
person liable, 1.775
Income support
child benefit, 3.12
generally, 2.225–2.226
income test, 2.110
social security income
  amount in excess of taxable maximum, 1.577
  child maintenance bonus, 1.576
  definitions, 1.579–1.580
  general rule, 1.575
  generally, 2.152
  taxable maximum, 1.578
  trade disputes, 1.575
Income tax
assessment, 2.107
charge to tax, 1.833–1.835
definitions
  civil partners, 1.847
  'company', 1.846
  general list, 1.845
  living together, 1.847
  married persons, 1.847
  overview, 1.844

employment income, 1.481–1.543
exempt income, 1.776–1.789
foster care relief
  foster care receipts, 1.799
  overview, 1.796
  providing foster care, 1.801
  providing qualifying care, 1.800
  providing shared lives care, 1.802
  qualifying person, 1.797
  residence, 1.803
general note
  ITA 2007, 1.830
  ITEPA 2003, 1.476–1.477
  ITTOIA 2005, 1.697–1.699
general provisions, 1.804–1.805
individuals in UK for temporary purpose
  employment income, 1.830
  foreign income, 1.829
individuals temporarily abroad, 1.826–1.827
individuals working abroad, 1.828
jointly held property
  declarations of unequal beneficial interests, 1.843
  generally, 1.841–1.842
miscellaneous income, 1.765–1.775
overview
  ITA 2007, 1.831–1.832
  ITEPA 2003, 1.479–1.480
  ITTOIA 2005, 1.700–1.701
pension income, 1.544–1.557
property income, 1.732–1.744
rent-a-room relief, 1.790–1.795
residence
  individuals in UK for temporary purpose, 1.829–1.830
  individuals temporarily abroad, 1.826–1.827
  individuals working abroad, 1.828
returns, 1.4–1.28
savings and investment income, 1.745–1.764
social security income, 1.558–1.596
trading income, 1.702–1.731
Income Tax Act 2007
See also **Income tax**
arrangement of sections, 1.829
definitions, 1.844–1.847
general note, 1.830
general provisions
  charge to tax, 1.833–1.835
  jointly held property, 1.841–1.843
  overview, 1.831–1.832
  residence, 1.836–1.840
Income tax (charge to tax)
emoluments (offices and employment)
  general note, 1.476–1.477
employment income
  agency workers, 1.494
  deductions from earnings, 1.532–1.543
  earnings, 1.495
  'employment', 1.483–1.484
  exemptions, 1.525–1.531

1107

general note, 1.476–1.477
introductory provision, 1.481–1.482
nature, 1.486–1.488
office-holders, 1.485
operation, 1.489–1.493
taxable benefits, 1.496–1.524
general note
  ITA 2007, 1.830
  ITEPA 2003, under, 1.476–1.477
general rule
  ITA 2007, 1.833–1.835
  ITTOIA 2005, 1.697–1.699
  ITEPA 2003, under, 1.479
miscellaneous income
  income not otherwise charged, 1.773
  settlements, 1.768–1.772
pension income
  amount charged, 1.547
  general note, 1.545
  general rules, 1.549–1.553
  introductory provision, 1.544
  nature of charge, 1.546
  person liable to tax, 1.548
  social security pensions, 1.554–1.557
property income
  generally, 1.740
  income charged, 1.742
  person liable, 1.743
  territorial scope, 1.741
savings and investments income
  dividends from non-resident UK companies, 1.758
  dividends from UK resident companies, 1.755
  interest, 1.750
  purchased life annuity payments, 1.761
Schedule E (offices and employment emoluments)
  general note, 1.476–1.477
social security income
  amount charged, 1.564
  definitions, 1.597–1.598
  exempt benefits, 1.573–1.588
  foreign benefits, 1.593–1.596
  general note, 1.559
  introductory provision, 1.558
  nature of charge, 1.560–1.561
  person liable to tax, 1.565
  taxable benefits, 1.566–1.572
  wholly exempt benefits, 1.589–1.592
trading income
  generally, 1.705
  income charged, 1.707
  person liable, 1.708
  territorial scope, 1.706

Income Tax (Earnings and Pensions) Act 2003 (ITEPA)
See also **Income tax**
arrangement of sections, 1.475
definitions, 1.597–1.598
general note
  CRCA 2005, 1.478
  introduction, 1.476–1.477

general provisions
  employment income, 1.481–1.543
  overview, 1.479–1.480
  pension income, 1.544–1.557
  social security income, 1.558–1.596

Income tax (tax returns)
amendment by taxpayer
  during enquiry, 1.9
  generally, 1.6
appeals, 1.18–1.24
assessment
  appeals, 1.18–1.24
  discovery of loss of tax, on, 1.13
  loss, destruction or damage, 1.26
  relief for excessive assessments, 1.14–1.15
  time limits, 1.16–1.17
  want of form, 1.27
closure notices, 1.12
correction by Revenue
  during enquiry, 1.10
  generally, 1.7
definitions, 1.28
destruction, etc., 1.22
enquiry
  amendment by taxpayer, 1.9
  completion, 1.12
  correction by Revenue, 1.10
  notice, 1.8
fraudulent conduct, 1.17
generally, 1.4
loss, destruction or damage, 1.26
negligent conduct, 1.17
notice of enquiry, 1.8
penalties, 1.25
records, 1.11
relief for excessive assessments
  double assessment, 1.14
  recovery of overpaid tax etc, 1.15
self-assessment, 1.5
time limits
  fraudulent conduct, 1.17
  negligent conduct, 1.17
  ordinary period, 1.16
want of form, 1.27

Income Tax (Trading and Other Income) Act 2005
See also **Income tax**
arrangement of sections, 1.696
general note, 1.697–1.699
general provisions
  exempt income, 1.776–1.789
  foster care relief, 1.796–1.803
  general rules, 1.804–1.805
  miscellaneous income, 1.765–1.775
  overview, 1.700–1.701
  property income, 1.732–1.744
  rent-a-room relief, 1.790–1.795
  savings and investment income, 1.745–1.764
  trading income, 1.702–1.731

Income test
See **Income**

1108

Incorrect statements
See **Misstatements**
Individual savings accounts
　income test, 2.106
　investment income, 2.164
Industrial injuries benefits
　social security income, 2.152
Information
　administrative arrangements, and
　　by authorities, 2.373
　　to authorities, 2.372
　employers, by
　　statutory maternity pay, 1.221
　　statutory sick pay, 1.219
　functions relating to employment
　　general note, 2.459
　　generally, 2.461, 2.473
　functions relating to health
　　definitions, 2.439
　　general note, 2.438
　　generally, 2.440, 2.457
　　Scotland, 2.471
　functions relating to training
　　general note, 2.459
　　generally, 2.461, 2.473
　Secretary of State, by
　　statutory maternity pay, 1.220
　　statutory sick pay, 1.218
　statutory adoption pay
　　entitlement, as to, 6.28–6.29
　　generally, 6.32
　statutory maternity pay, 5.41
　　claims for other benefits, 5.45
　　determination of questions, 5.43–5.44
　statutory paternity pay
　　entitlement, as to, 6.28–6.29
　　generally, 6.32
　statutory sick pay
　　employee to Secretary of State, by, 4.29–4.30
　　employer to employee, by, 4.31–4.32
　tax authorities, by
　　contributions purposes, for, 1.217
　　fraud prevention, for, 1.216
　tax credits
　　generally, 2.467
　　Northern Ireland, 2.469
Inland Revenue
See **Revenue and Customs**
Insolvency (employers)
　statutory sick pay, 4.21
"Intensive Activity Period"
　remunerative work, 2.36
Intercountry adoption
　additional statutory paternity pay
　　application of General Regulations 2010, 6.203
　　application of SSCBA 1992, 6.204
　　applications, 6.208
　　conditions of entitlement, 6.206
　　death of adopter, 6.209–6.210
　　definitions, 6.202
　　entitlement, 6.205
　　entitlement where more than one employer, 6.211
　　evidence of entitlement, 6.208
　　pay period, 6.207
　　return to work, 6.212
　pay period, 6.139–6.140
　statutory adoption pay
　　administration, 6.120–6.124
　　application of General Regulations 2002, 6.130
　　application of SSCBA 1992, 6.112–6.119
　　avoidance of liability, 6.145
　　definitions, 6.129
　　evidence of entitlement, 6.142
　　general note, 6.128
　　notice requirements, 6.141
　　pay period, 6.139–6.140
　　termination of employment, 6.144
　　treatment of more than one employer, 6.143
　statutory paternity pay
　　administration, 6.120–6.124
　　application of General Regulations 2002, 6.130
　　application of SSCBA 1992, 6.112–6.119
　　avoidance of liability, 6.138
　　conditions of entitlement, 6.132
　　definitions, 6.129
　　evidence of entitlement, 6.136
　　general note, 6.128
　　notice requirements, 6.134
　　pay period, 6.133
　　qualifying period, 6.135
　　treatment of more than one employer, 6.137
　statutory shared parental pay
　　application of General Regulations, 7.95
　　definitions, 7.94
　　modification of General Regulations, 7.96–7.108
Interest
　charge to tax, 1.750
　income charged, 1.751
　person liable, 1.752
　tax credits
　　definitions, 2.391
　　general note, 2.390
　　generally, 1.383–1.384
　　overpayments, on, 2.392
　　prescribed rate, 2.393
　territorial scope, 1.749
　trading income, 1.717
"Interruption of employment"
　statutory sick pay, 4.26
Investment income
　building society dividends, 1.753
　dividends from non-resident UK companies
　　charge to tax, 1.758
　　income charged, 1.759
　　person liable, 1.760

1109

dividends from UK resident companies
  charge to tax, 1.755
  income charged, 1.756
  introduction, 1.754
  person liable, 1.757
general note, 1.746
interest
  charge to tax, 1.750
  income charged, 1.751
  person liable, 1.752
  territorial scope, 1.749
introduction, 1.697–1.698
overview, 1.745
priority rules
  generally, 1.747–1.748
  introduction, 1.701
purchased life annuity payments
  charge to tax, 1.761
  income charged, 1.763
  meaning, 1.762
  person liable, 1.764
statutory overview
  introduction, 1.700
  priority rules, 1.701
tax credits
  disregarded payments, 2.164
  general note, 2.166–2.167
  generally, 2.163
  very severe disablement payments, 2.165
territorial scope of charge, 1.749
ISAs
  See **Individual investment accounts**
Jobseekers' allowance
child benefit, 3.12
child maintenance bonus, 1.581
generally, 2.225–2.226
income test, 2.110
Intensive Activity Period, 2.36
social security income
  amount in excess of taxable maximum, 1.582
  child maintenance bonus, 1.581
  definitions, 1.586
  generally, 2.152
  taxable maximum, 1.583–1.585
taxable maximum
  amount in excess of, 1.582
  contribution-based JSA, 1.585
  definitions, 1.586
  general, 1.583
  income-based JSA, 1.584
Joint property
declarations of unequal beneficial interests, 1.843
generally, 1.841–1.842
"Late appeals"
child trust funds, 8.75–8.76
tax credits
  generally, 1.393–1.395
  invalid regulation, 2.385–2.386
  Order, 2.487–2.489

Lifetime annuities
  charge to tax, 1.761
  income charged, 1.763
  meaning, 1.762
  person liable, 1.764
Linking periods
  statutory sick pay. 4.7–4.8
"Living away from home allowance"
  disregards, 2.185
"Living together"
  references in Income Tax Acts, 1.847
Lone-parent element
  working tax credit, 2.68–2.69
"Lottery winnings"
  investment income, 2.164
"Lower-paid employment"
  calculation of earnings rate, 1.523
  excluded provisions of benefits code, 1.521
  extra amounts relating to car, 1.524
  meaning, 1.522
Macfarlane Trust
  tax credits, 2.165
Maintenance
  disregards, 2.185
Mariners
  See **Seafarers**
Market gardening
  trading income, 1.709
"Married child"
  child benefit
    Regulations, 3.18
    statutory basis, 1.171
Married persons
  See **Spouses**
Maternity allowance
  statutory maternity pay, 5.39
  working tax credit, 2.152
Maternity pay
  See **Statutory maternity pay**
Means testing
  capital, 2.106
  general rule, 2.104
Medical evidence
  maternity
    definitions, 5.58
    evidence of pregnancy and confinement, 5.59
    form of certificate, 5.60–5.61
  sickness
    definitions, 4.67
    doctor's statement, 4.70–4.72
    general note, 4.68
    information required, 4.69
Milk tokens
  See **Welfare food**
"Miscellaneous income"
  amount treated as income of settlor
    settlements, 1.768–1.772
  income not otherwise charged
    charge to tax, 1.773
    income charged, 1.774
    person liable, 1.775

introduction, 1.697–1.698
overview, 1.765
priority rules
  generally, 1.766–1.767
  introduction, 1.701
settlements
  charge to tax, 1.768–1.769
  income charged, 1.771
  person liable, 1.772
  'settlement', 1.770
statutory overview
  introduction, 1.700
  priority rules, 1.701
tax credits
  general note, 2.183
  generally, 2.182
territorial scope, 1.768

Misrepresentation
overpayments, 1.211–1.212

Misstatements
statutory adoption pay, 1.458–1.459
statutory paternity pay, 1.458–1.459
tax credits
  conduct of penalty cases, 1.363
  fraudulently or negligently, 1.362
  generally, 1.359–1.361
  level of penalties, 1.364–1.365

Mistakes
See **Clerical errors**

Mobility supplement
See **War pensioner's mobility supplement**

National insurance contributions
trading income, 1.725

National insurance numbers
child benefit, 3.51

National Savings
income test, 2.106

Negligence
statutory maternity pay, 1.215
statutory sick pay, 1.215
tax returns, 1.17

"Net taxable earnings"
employment income, 1.491

"Net taxable specific income"
employment income, 1.492

New Deal
disregards, 2.185

NHS employees (divided contracts)
statutory maternity pay
  lapse of election, 5.80
  notification of election, 5.77
  provision of information, 5.78
  treatment of more than one contract as one, 5.11, 5.76
  treatment of two or more employers as one, 5.32–5.33, 5.79
statutory paternity pay
  general note, 6.10
  lapse of election, 6.15
  notification of election, 6.12
  provision of information, 6.13
  relevant employer, 6.14

statutory sick pay
  generally, 4.41
  lapse of election, 4.79
  notification of election, 4.76
  provision of information, 4.77
  relevant employer, 4.39–4.40
  treatment of more than one contract as one, 4.75
  treatment of two or more employers as one, 4.78

Non-cash vouchers
See **Vouchers**

Non-compliance
failure to comply with requirements
  statutory adoption pay, 1.456–1.457
  statutory paternity pay, 1.456–1.457
  tax credits, 1.366–1.369

Non-disclosure
overpayments, 1.211–1.212

Normal weekly income
additional statutory paternity pay, 6.191
statutory adoption pay
  'earnings', 6.102
  generally, 6.103
statutory maternity pay
  'earnings', 5.35
  generally, 5.36–5.37
statutory paternity pay
  'earnings', 6.102
  generally, 6.103
statutory shared parental pay
  adoption, 7.58–7.59
  'appropriate date', 7.60
  birth, 7.57
  'day of payment', 7.60
  'earnings', 7.60
  meaning, 7.60–7.61
  'normal pay day', 7.60
  'relevant period', 7.60

"Normal working weeks"
statutory maternity pay
  generally, 5.28–5.29
  'week', 5.30

"Normally living with test"
child tax credit, 2.198

Northern Ireland
tax credits
  evaluation and statistical studies, 2.468–2.469
  generally, 1.427–1.428

Notices
absence from work
  statutory maternity pay, 5.41
child trust fund appeals
  disputes concerning, 8.73–8.74
  prescribed form, 8.65–8.66
  service, 8.71–8.72
  signature, 8.65–8.66
  statutory provision, 1.686
enquiries in returns, 1.8
provision of information
  childcare provider, to, 2.334
  dates to be specified, 2.335

Index

definitions, 2.273
electronic communications,
  2.274–2.275
employers, to, 2.333
s.17 TCA 2002, under, 2.336–2.339
tax credits, 1.408–1.409
tax returns, 1.8
Notification
change of circumstances
  definitions, 2.273
  electronic communications,
    2.274–2.275
  generally, 2.312–2.332
  polygamous marriages, 2.450
employment after confinement, 5.42
incapacity for work, 4.16
statutory maternity pay, 5.42
statutory sick pay, 4.16
Notification (change of circumstances)
advance, in, 2.327
amendment, 2.320
date
  disability element of CTC, 2.325–2.326
  disability element of WTC,
    2.323–2.324
  increase of maximum rate,
    2.321–2.322
decrease of rate, 2.314–2.317
definitions
  generally, 2.273
  notification date, 2.211
disability element of CTC, 2.325–2.326
disability element of WTC, 2.323–2.324
electronic communications, 2.274–2.275
evidence of birth or adoption, 2.332
increase of maximum rate, and
  date of notification, 2.321–2.322
  general rule, 2.312–2.313
method, 2.317–2.318
person acting on behalf of another, by
  generally, 2.328–2.329
  other appointed persons, 2.330–2.331
polygamous marriages, 2.450
relevant person, 2.319
Notional income
depriving self of income to secure
  entitlement, 2.176–2.177
entitlement to sums, 2.178–2.179
generally, 2.172–2.173
provision of services for less than full
  earnings, 2.180–2.181
sums treated as income under Taxes Acts,
  2.174–2.175
Obstruction
officers of Revenue and Customs, 1.824
Officeholders
employment income, 1.485
Officers of Revenue and Customs
See **Revenue and Customs officers**
"Official errors"
definitions, 2.432–2.433
general note, 2.435
generally, 2.434

Offshore workers
statutory adoption pay
  definitions, 6.34
  general note, 6.35
  generally, 6.43
statutory maternity pay
  definitions, 5.63
  general note, 5.64
  generally, 5.72
  statutory provisions, 1.104
statutory paternity pay
  definitions, 6.34
  general note, 6.35
  generally, 6.43
  statutory provisions, 1.132–1.133
statutory sick pay
  definitions, 4.51, 4.58, 4.64
  general note, 4.47
  statutory provision, 1.88
  time for compliance, 4.65
Ordinary residence
Crown servants posted overseas
  generally, 2.425–2.426
  partners, 2.427
definitions, 2.414–2.415
meaning, 2.418–2.419
person treated as not being in UK,
  2.416–2.422
temporary absence from UK,
  2.423–2.424
tests, 2.420–2.422
transitional provision, 2.428–2.429
**Ordinary Statutory Paternity Pay
(Adoption), etc Regulations
2010**
arrangement, 6.147
citation, 6.148
commencement, 6.148
definitions, 6.149
general provision, 6.151
revocation, 6.150
Overpayments
child benefit, 1.211–1.212
Code of Practice, 9.15–9.53
failure to disclose, 1.211–1.212
guardian's allowance, 1.211–1.212
interest, 2.392
misrepresentation, 1.211–1.212
statutory adoption pay, 6.25
statutory maternity pay, 5.91
statutory paternity pay, 6.25
tax credits
  generally, 1.352–1.353
  method of recovery, 2.363
  recovery, 1.354–1.356
Overseas adoption
See **Intercountry adoption**
Overseas employees
Crown servants
  generally, 2.425–2.426
  partners, 2.427
"Paid"
employment income, 1.501

1112

Index

Parental orders
application of Parts 12ZA, 12ZB and 12ZC SSCBA 1992
Regulations, 6.218–6.227
meaning, 6.221
statutory adoption pay, and
application of Part 12ZB SSCBA 1992, 6.223, 6.226
definitions, 6.221
Regulations, 6.228–6.253
statutory paternity pay, and
application of Part 12ZB SSCBA 1992, 6.222, 6.225
definitions, 6.221
Regulations, 6.228–6.253
statutory shared parental pay, and
application of Part 12ZB SSCBA 1992, 6.224, 6.227
application of Pay Regulations, 7.113
definitions, 6.221, 7.112
general note, 7.110
modification of Pay Regulations, 7.114–7.126

Partnership income
introduction, 1.697–1.698
statutory overview, 1.700

Paternity pay
see **Statutory paternity pay**

Payments in lieu of notice
working tax credit, 2.50–2.51

"Pay period"
additional statutory paternity pay
adoption, 6.173
birth, 6.166
overseas adoptions, 6.139–6.140
statutory adoption pay
disrupted adoption, 6.83–6.84
generally, 6.82
statutory provision, 1.143–1.144
treatment of more than one contract, 6.85
statutory maternity pay
generally, 5.4–5.6
statutory provision, 1.94–1.95
statutory paternity pay
adoption of child, on, 6.73
birth of child, on, 6.65
statutory provision, 1.119–1.120
work during
statutory adoption pay, 6.88
statutory paternity pay, 6.78

Payments (employers) (statutory adoption pay)
funding
application to Revenue, 6.21
date of payment of contributions, 6.24
generally, 6.20
method, 6.22–6.23
overpayments, 6.25
generally, 6.104
period
adoption of child, on, 6.73
birth of child, on, 6.65
persons acting on behalf of another, to, 6.110
timing, 6.105

Payments (employers) (statutory maternity pay)
funding
additional payment to small employers, 5.85
advance funding, 5.87
date of payment of contributions, 5.90
deduction from payments to Revenue, 5.88
definitions, 5.82
general note, 5.83
overpayments, 5.91
payments to employer by Revenue, 5.89
prescribed amount, 5.86
'small employer', 5.84
generally, 5.48
persons acting on behalf of another, to, 5.53–5.54
rounding, 5.49
Secretary of State, by, 5.51–5.52
timing, 5.50

Payments (employers) (statutory paternity pay)
funding
application to Revenue, 6.21
date of payment of contributions, 6.24
generally, 6.20
method, 6.22–6.23
overpayments, 6.25
generally, 6.104
period
adoption of child, on, 6.73
birth of child, on, 6.65
persons acting on behalf of another, to, 6.110
timing, 6.105

Payments (employers) (statutory sick pay)
liability of Secretary of State, 4.19–4.20
method, 4.17
Secretary of State, by, 4.22
statements relating to, 4.33
time limits, 4.18

Payments (Revenue and Customs)
statutory adoption pay
generally, 6.109
liability, 6.106–6.108
statutory maternity pay, 5.89
statutory paternity pay
generally, 6.109
liability, 6.106–6.107

Payments (Revenue and Customs) (tax credits)
amount, 2.361–2.362
bank account requirement, 2.366–2.367
child care element of WTC, 2.344–2.345
definitions, 2.343
general note, 2.341
introduction, 2.341
joint claims, for

1113

child tax credit, 2.344–2.345
child care element of WTC, 2.344–2.345
death of one of couple, 2.348–2.349
working tax credit, 2.346–2.347
method, 2.364–2.365
person acting on behalf of another, for, 2.350–2.351
polygamous marriages, 2.451
postponement, 2.359–2.360
recovery of overpayments
generally, 1.354–1.356
method, 2.363
renewal, on, 2.352–2.353
single payments, 2.357–2.358
timing
bank account, 2.354–2.355
other than to bank account, 2.356
working tax credit, and
generally, 2.346–2.347
introduction, 2.341

Penalties
child trust funds
appeals, 1.683
decisions, 1.683
generally, 1.681–1.682
mitigation, 1.683
recovery, 1.683
failure to comply with requirements
statutory adoption pay, 1.456–1.457
statutory paternity pay, 1.456–1.457
tax credits, 1.366–1.369
incorrect statements
statutory adoption pay, 1.458–1.459
statutory paternity pay, 1.458–1.459
tax credits, 1.359–1.32
incorrect statements (tax credits)
conduct of penalty cases, 1.363
fraudulently or negligently, 1.362
generally, 1.359–1.361
level of penalties, 1.364–1.365
statutory adoption pay
appeals, 1.468
definitions, 1.474
determination, 1.466–1.467
failure to comply, 1.456–1.457
fraud, 1.458–1.459
incorrect statements, 1.458–1.459
interest, 1.473
mitigation, 1.471
proceedings before Commissioners, 1.469
proceedings before court, 1.470
time limits, 1.472
statutory maternity pay
breach of regulations, 1.213–1.214
fraud, 1.215
negligence, 1.215
statutory paternity pay
appeals, 1.468
definitions, 1.474
determination, 1.466–1.467
failure to comply, 1.456–1.457
fraud, 1.458–1.459
incorrect statements, 1.458–1.459
interest, 1.473
mitigation, 1.471
proceedings before Commissioners, 1.469
proceedings before court, 1.470
time limits, 1.472
statutory sick pay
breach of regulations, 1.213–1.214
fraud, 1.215
negligence, 1.215
tax credits
determination, 1.435
failure to comply with requirements, 1.366–1.369
Guidance, 9.1–9.14
incorrect statements, 1.359–1.365
mitigation, 1.437
proceedings before Commissioners, 1.436
recovery, 1.439
supplementary, 1.370–1.371
time limits, 1.438
tax returns, 1.21
Taxes Management Act 1970, 1.25

Pension income
annual payments, 2.136
charge to tax
amount charged, 1.547
nature, 1.546
person liable to tax, 1.548
deductions, 2.140
disregarded payments, 2.137
exemptions, 2.140
general note
regulations, 2.138
statutory provisions, 1.545
general rules
application of provisions, 1.549–1.550
'pension', 1.551
person liable to tax, 1.553
taxable pension income, 1.552
generally, 2.136
identity of taxpayer, 2.141
relevant income, 2.139
state retirement pension
application of provisions, 1.554–1.555
person liable to tax, 1.557
taxable pension income, 1.556
statutory provisions
charge to tax, 1.546–1.548
general note, 1.545
general rules, 1.549–1.553
introductory provision, 1.544
social security pensions, 1.554–1.557
time of calculation, 2.142

Periodical payments (personal injury)
compensation awards, 1.779
generally, 1.778
persons entitled, 1.780
trusts, from, 1.781

Index

"Person responsible for child"
child benefit, 3.13–3.15
Person temporarily absent
See **Temporary absence**
"Person treated as not being resident"
child benefit
in GB, 3.30–3.31
in Northern Ireland, 3.36–3.37
Personal allowances
income test, 2.107
Personal equity plans
investment income, 2.164
Personal injury (damages)
exempt income
compensation awards, 1.779
generally, 1.778
persons entitled, 1.780
trusts, from, 1.781
interest, 1.785
Persons abroad
statutory adoption pay
absent from Great Britain, 6.38
definitions, 6.34
general note, 6.35
has worked in other EEA States, 6.39
in other EEA States, 6.37
time for compliance, 6.41
statutory maternity pay
absent from Great Britain, 5.66
definitions, 5.63
'employee', 5.67
general note, 5.64
in other Member States, 5.65
time for compliance, 5.70
women who worked in the EC, 5.69
statutory paternity pay
absent from Great Britain, 6.38
definitions, 6.34
general note, 6.35
has worked in other EEA States, 6.39
in other EEA States, 6.37
time for compliance, 6.41
statutory sick pay
absent from Great Britain, 4.53–4.54
definitions, 4.48–4.59
employees, 4.60
general note, 4.47
persons abroad, 4.60–4.61
in other Member States, 4.52
time for compliance, 4.65
"Persons residing together"
child benefit, 3.16–3.17
Persons subject to immigration control
See **Immigrants**
Pilots
statutory adoption pay, 1.151–1.152
statutory maternity pay, 1.104
statutory paternity pay, 1.132–1.133
statutory sick pay
definitions, 4.50, 4.56–4.57, 4.63
general note, 4.47
statutory provision, 1.88
time for compliance, 4.65

"Placed for adoption"
meaning, 6.34
Polygamy
child benefit, 3.47–3.48
tax credits
amendment of Regulations, 2.447–2.453
amendment of TCA 2002, 2.446
definitions, 2.444–2.445
general note, 2.442
statutory provision, 1.402–1.403
Postponement
payments, 2.359–2.360
Premium savings bonds
income test, 2.106
"Presence in Great Britain"
guardian's allowance, 3.74
Priorities
child benefit
generally, 1.53–1.54
miscellaneous provisions, 1.174–1.182
Regulations, 3.20
Professions
basic rules, 1.712
basis periods, 1.729
receipts, 1.719
rules restricting deductions, 1.719
Property income
calculation of profits, 1.744
charge to tax
generally, 1.740
income charged, 1.742
person liable, 1.743
territorial scope, 1.741
generating income from land, 1.739
introduction, 1.697–1.698
overseas property business, 1.738
overview, 1.732–1.733
priority rules
generally, 1.734–1.735
introduction, 1.701
profits
generally, 1.740
income charged, 1.742
person liable, 1.743
territorial scope, 1.741
property businesses
introduction, 1.736–1.739
profits, 1.740–1.744
statutory overview
introduction, 1.700
priority rules, 1.701
tax credits
general note, 2.169
generally, 2.168
UK property business, 1.737
Provision of information
administrative arrangements, and
by authorities, 2.373
to authorities, 2.372
employers, by
statutory maternity pay, 1.221
statutory sick pay, 1.219

1115

Index

functions relating to employment
  general note, 2.459
  generally, 2.461, 2.473
functions relating to health
  definitions, 2.439
  general note, 2.438
  generally, 2.440, 2.457
  Scotland, 2.471
functions relating to training
  general note, 2.459
  generally, 2.461, 2.473
Secretary of State, by
  statutory maternity pay, 1.220
  statutory sick pay, 1.218
statutory adoption pay
  Board, by, 1.460
  entitlement, as to, 6.28–6.29
  generally, 6.32
  Secretary of State, by, 1.461
statutory maternity pay, 5.41
  claims for other benefits, 5.45
  determination of questions, 5.43–5.44
statutory paternity pay
  Board, by, 1.460
  entitlement, as to, 6.28–6.29
  generally, 6.32
  Secretary of State, by, 1.461
statutory sick pay
  employee to Secretary of State, by, 4.29–4.30
  employer to employee, by, 4.31–4.32
tax authorities, by
  statutory adoption pay, 1.460–1.461
  statutory paternity pay, 1.460–1.461
  tax credits, 1.216–1.217
tax credits
  contributions purposes, for, 1.217
  fraud prevention, for, 1.216
  generally, 2.467
  Northern Ireland, 2.469
"Purchased life annuity payments"
  charge to tax, 1.761
  income charged, 1.763
  meaning, 1.762
  person liable, 1.764
"Put at disposal"
  employment income, 1.501
Qualifying care relief
  See **Foster care relief, Shared lives care relief**
"Qualifying days"
  statutory sick pay
    generally, 4.12–4.14
    statutory provision, 1.78–1.79
Qualifying periods
  statutory paternity pay
    adoption of child, on, 6.75
    birth of child, on, 6.67
"Qualifying remunerative work"
  excepted activities, 2.36
  generally, 2.26–2.32
  hours worked, 2.37
  minimum level of continuity, 2.34

remunerative work, 2.35
routes to entitlement, 2.33
Qualifying young persons (child benefits)
care, in
  generally, 3.25
  statutory basis, 1.170
continuation of entitlement, 3.6
definition, 1.45
detention, in
  generally, 3.21–3.24
  statutory basis, 1.170
education and training condition, 3.4–3.5
extension period, 3.7
interruptions, 3.8–3.9
introduction, 3.3
living with another as a couple, where, 3.16–3.17
other financial support, 3.12
person responsible for child, 3.13–3.15
prescribed conditions, 3.3–3.12
relevant relationship, in, 3.18
terminal dates, 3.10–3.11
youth training, in, 3.21–3.24
Qualifying young persons (tax credits)
definition, 2.194
maximum age, 2.211–2.212
working tax credit, and
  childcare element, 2.75
  death, 2.83–2.84
Rate of payment
child benefit
  generally, 1.55
  weekly rates, 3.56–3.61
Receipts
basic rules, 1.715–1.716
capital receipts, 1.727
debts incurred and later released, 1.728
professions and vocations, 1.726
Records
administrative arrangements
  claims, 2.374
statutory adoption pay
  generally, 6.26
  inspection, 6.27
statutory maternity pay
  maintenance, 5.46
  production, 5.47
statutory paternity pay
  generally, 6.26
  inspection, 6.27
statutory sick pay
  maintenance, 4.27
  production, 4.28
Taxes Management Act 1970, 1.11
Recovery of payments
  See **Repayments**
Reinstatement
service with armed services
  statutory maternity pay, 5.27
"Relevant income"
  generally, 2.227–2.228

1116

Index

Remuneration
statutory adoption pay
  generally, 6.91
  statutory provision, 1.147–1.148
statutory maternity pay
  generally, 5.34
  statutory provision, 1.205
statutory paternity pay
  additional, 6.181
  generally, 6.80
  statutory provision, 1.128–1.129
statutory sick pay, 1.197
Rent-a-room relief
definitions
  rent-a-room amount, 1.794
  rent-a-room receipts, 1.792
  residence, 1.793
individual's limit, 1.795
introduction, 1.697–1.698
overview, 1.790
qualifying person, 1.791
statutory overview, 1.700
trading income, 1.711
Repayments (statutory maternity pay)
additional payment to small employers, 5.85
advance funding, 5.87
date of payment of contributions, 5.90
definitions
  generally, 5.82
  'small employer', 5.84
general note, 5.83
method
  deduction from payments to Revenue, 5.88
  payments to employer by Revenue, 5.89
overpayments, 5.91
prescribed amount, 5.86
Repayments (statutory sick pay)
generally, 4.85–4.89
statutory provisions, 1.83–1.85
Repayments (tax credits)
generally, 1.354–1.356
method, 2.363
Representation
See **Professional representation**
Residence
child benefit
  child treated as being in GB, 3.28
  child treated as being in Northern Ireland, 3.34
  Crown servants posted overseas, 3.40–3.43
  overlap of entitlement, 3.39
  person temporarily absent from GB, 3.32–3.33
  person temporarily absent from Northern Ireland, 3.38
  person treated as not being in GB, 3.30–3.31
  person treated as not being in Northern Ireland, 3.36–3.37
  transitional provisions, 3.44

Crown servants posted overseas
  generally, 2.425–2.426
  partners, 2.427
definitions, 2.414–2.415
guardian's allowance, 3.74
individuals in UK for temporary purpose
  employment income, 1.830
  foreign income, 1.829
individuals temporarily abroad, 1.826–1.827
individuals working abroad, 1.828
ordinary residence, 2.418–2.419
person treated as not being in UK, 2.416–2.422
polygamous marriages, 2.452
temporary absence from UK, 2.423–2.424
tests, 2.420–2.422
transitional provision, 2.428–2.429
Residential accommodation
child benefit, 3.3
Respondent's observations
See **Observations**
"Responsibility for child"
competing claims, 2.199–2.200
excepted cases, 2.201–2.207
generally, 2.195–2.197
normally living with test, 2.198
special case, 2.208
Returns of income
See **Tax returns**
Revenue and Customs
ancillary powers, 1.814
appointments
  Commissioners, 1.808
  officers, 1.809
assault on officers, 1.825
Charter of standards and values, 1.820
Commissioners
  appointment, 1.808
  Charter of standards and values, 1.820
  declaration of confidentiality, 1.810
  functions, 1.812–1.819
  staff appointments, 1.809
conduct of proceedings, 1.815
confidentiality, 1.822
declaration of confidentiality, 1.810
delegation of functions, 1.818–1.819
former Inland Revenue matters
  generally, 1.813
  schedule, 1.828
freedom of information, 1.823
functions
  ancillary powers, 1.814
  Charter of standards and values, 1.820
  conduct of proceedings, 1.815
  delegation, 1.818–1.819
  exercise by officers, 1.816–1.817
  former Inland Revenue matters, 1.813
  initial, 1.812
general note, 1.807
information
  confidentiality, 1.822

1117

freedom of information, 1.823
use, 1.821
initial functions, 1.812
ITEPA 2003, 1.478
meaning, 1.811
obstruction, 1.824
offences
  assault, 1.825
  obstruction, 1.824
  power of arrest, 1.826
officers
  appointment, 1.809
  assault, 1.825
  declaration of confidentiality, 1.810
  exercise of functions, 1.816–1.817
  obstruction, 1.824
  power of arrest, 1.826
payments by
  general note, 2.341
  generally, 2,421–2.367
  introduction, 2.341
resignation, 1.808
staff appointments, 1.809
transfer of property, 1.827

Revenue and Customs officers
appointment, 1.809
assault, 1.825
declaration of confidentiality, 1.810
exercise of Commissioners functions, 1.816–1.817
generally, 1.809
obstruction, 1.824
power of arrest, 1.826

Revenue and Customs (payments)
amount, 2.361–2.362
bank account requirement, 2.366–2.367
child care element of WTC, 2.344–2.345
definitions, 2.343
general note, 2.341
introduction, 2.341
joint claims, for
  child tax credit, 2.344–2.345
  child care element of WTC, 2.344–2.345
  death of one of couple, 2.348–2.349
  working tax credit, 2.346–2.347
method, 2.364–2.365
person acting on behalf of another, for, 2.350–2.351
postponement, 2.359–2.360
recovery of overpayments
  generally, 1.354–1.356
  method, 2.363
renewal, on, 2.352–2.353
single payments, 2.357–2.358
timing
  bank account, 2.354–2.355
  other than to bank account, 2.356
working tax credit, and
  generally, 2.346–2.347
  introduction, 2.341

Rounding
statutory adoption pay, 6.6–6.7
statutory maternity pay, 5.49
statutory paternity pay, 6.6–6.7

Savings income
building society dividends, 1.753
dividends from non-resident UK companies
  charge to tax, 1.758
  income charged, 1.759
  person liable, 1.760
dividends from UK resident companies
  charge to tax, 1.755
  income charged, 1.756
  introduction, 1.754
  person liable, 1.757
general note, 1.746
interest
  charge to tax, 1.750
  income charged, 1.751
  person liable, 1.752
  territorial scope, 1.749
introduction, 1.697–1.698
overview, 1.745
priority rules
  generally, 1.747–1.748
  introduction, 1.701
purchased life annuity payments
  charge to tax, 1.761
  income charged, 1.763
  meaning, 1.762
  person liable, 1.764
statutory overview
  introduction, 1.700
  priority rules, 1.701
territorial scope of charge, 1.749

Schedules
See also **Income tax**
ITEPA 2003, 1.476–1.477
ITTOIA 2005, 1.697–1.698

Scholarship income
other income, 1.787
tax credits, 2.161–2.162

Seafarers
statutory adoption pay
  definitions, 6.34
  general note, 6.35
  generally, 6.42
statutory maternity pay
  definitions, 5.63
  general note, 5.64
  generally, 5.71
  statutory provisions, 1.104
statutory paternity pay
  definitions, 6.34
  general note, 6.35
  generally, 6.42
  statutory provisions, 1.132–1.133
statutory shared parental pay
  definitions, 7.130
  general note, 7.128
  general provisions, 7.137–7.138
statutory sick pay

definitions, 4.48–4.49, 4.55, 4.62
general note, 4.47
statutory provision, 1.88
time for compliance, 4.65
Seasonal workers
working tax credit, 2.54–2.55
Second-adult element
working tax credit, 2.66–2.67
Self-assessment
tax returns, 1.5
Self-employment
employment income, 2.129
trading income, 2.145–2.146
Service (notices)
child trust fund appeals, 8.71–8.72
statutory adoption pay, 6.111
statutory paternity pay, 6.111
tax credit appeals, 2.379–2.380
Settlement income
charge to tax, 1.768–1.769
income charged, 1.771
person liable, 1.772
'settlement', 1.770
Severe disability element
working tax credit, 2.80–2.81
Severe disablement allowance
investment income, 2.165
social security income, 2.152
Severely disabled persons
child tax credit, 2.217–2.218
Shared lives care relief
definitions
providing qualifying care, 1.800
providing shared lives care, 1.802
qualifying care receipts, 1.799
residence, 1.803
further condition for relief, 1.798
overview, 1.796
qualifying person, 1.797
Shared parental leave
curtailment of pay period
statutory adoption pay: AP, 5.112
statutory maternity pay: P, 5.107
Sick pay
See **Statutory sick pay**
Sickness benefits (vouchers)
taxable benefits, 1.506
"Sickness periods"
working tax credit, 2.42–2.43
Social fund
social security income, 2.152
Social Security Act 1998
general provisions
appeals, 1.223–1.224
recitals, 1.222
Social Security Administration Act 1992
arrangement of sections, 1.206
general provisions
claims and payments, 1.207–1.210
enforcement, 1.213–1.215
information, 1.216–1.221
overpayments, 1.211–1.212

Social security administration (statutory adoption pay)
adoption from overseas, 6.120–6.124
determination of entitlement issues
application, 6.30
form of application, 6.31
employers' records
generally, 6.26
inspection, 6.27
funding of liabilities
application to Revenue, 6.21
date of payment of contributions, 6.24
generally, 6.20
method, 6.22–6.23
overpayments, 6.25
provision of information, 6.32
Social security administration (statutory maternity pay)
employer's records
maintenance, 5.46
production, 5.47
expected week of confinement, 5.40
notice of absence from work, 5.41
notification of employment after confinement, 5.42
provision of information
claims for other benefits, 5.45
determination of questions, 5.43–5.44
Social security administration (statutory paternity pay)
adoption from overseas, 6.120–6.124
determination of entitlement issues
application, 6.30
form of application, 6.31
employers' records
generally, 6.26
inspection, 6.27
funding of liabilities
application to Revenue, 6.21
date of payment of contributions, 6.24
generally, 6.20
method, 6.22–6.23
overpayments, 6.25
provision of information, 6.32
Social security contributions
See **National insurance contributions**
Social Security Contributions and Benefits Act 1992
application, 1.167
arrangement of sections, 1.29
definitions, 1.168–1.169
general note, 1.29
general provisions
child benefit, 1.41–1.61
guardian's allowance, 1.30–1.40
statutory adoption pay, 1.138–1.155
statutory maternity pay, 1.91–1.105
statutory paternity pay, 1.106–1.137
statutory shared parental pay, 1.155–1.166
statutory sick pay, 1.62–1.90
modifications to
adoptions from overseas, 6.112–6.119

1119

dismissal for reasons of pregnancy, 5.95–5.96
parental orders, 6.218–6.227
schedules, 1.170–1.205
Social Security Contributions (Transfer of Functions, etc.) Act 1999
arrangement of sections, 1.226
definitions, 1.249
general provisions, 1.227–1.247
long title, 1.225
miscellaneous provisions, 1.248–1.250
Social security income
charge to tax
amount charged, 1.564
definitions, 1.562–1.563
nature of charge, 1.560–1.561
person liable to tax, 1.565
child maintenance bonus
income support, 1.576
jobseeker's allowance, 1.581
deductions, 2.155
disregarded payments, 2.152
exemptions
generally, 2.155
incapacity benefit, 1.573–1.574
income support, 1.575–1.580
increases in respect of children, 1.581
jobseeker's allowance, 1.581–1.586
foreign benefits, 1.593–1.596
general note
regulations, 2.153
statutory provisions, 1.559
generally, 2.151
identity of taxpayer, 2.156
incapacity benefit
long-term, 1.573
short-term, 1.574
income support
amount in excess of taxable maximum, 1.577
child maintenance bonus, 1.576
definitions, 1.579–1.580
general rule, 1.575
taxable maximum, 1.578
trade disputes, 1.575
jobseeker's allowance
amount in excess of taxable maximum, 1.582
child maintenance bonus, 1.581
definitions, 1.586
taxable maximum, 1.583–1.585
relevant income, 2.154
statutory provisions
charge to tax, 1.560–1.565
exempt benefits, 1.573–1.588
foreign benefits, 1.593–1.596
general note, 1.559
introductory provision, 1.558
taxable benefits, 1.566–1.572
wholly exempt benefits, 1.589–1.592
Table A benefits, 1.566–1.568
Table B benefits, 1.589–1.592
taxable benefits

exemptions, 1.573–1.588
person liable to tax, 1.571–1.572
Table A, 1.566–1.568
taxable income, 1.569–1.570
taxable foreign benefits
application of provisions, 1.593–1.594
person liable to tax, 1.596
taxable income, 1.595
time of calculation, 2.157
wholly exempt benefits, 1.589–1.592
Social security pensions
See **Pension income, State retirement pension**
"Specific employment income"
employment income, 1.487
"Sports awards"
remunerative work, 2.36
Spouses
references in Income Tax Acts, 1.847
State pension credit
generally, 2.226
income test, 2.110
State retirement pension
See also **Pension income**
application of provisions, 1.554–1.555
person liable to tax, 1.557
taxable pension income, 1.556
Statistical evidence
generally, 2.467
Northern Ireland, 2.469
Statutory adoption pay
administration
determination of entitlement issues, 6.28–6.31
employers' records, 6.26–6.27
funding of liabilities, 6.20–6.25
provision of information, 6.32
statutory provision, 1.447–1.455
adoption without placement, 1.154–1.155
avoidance of liability, 6.93
benefits, 1.147–1.148
continental shelf employees
definitions, 6.34
general note, 6.35
generally, 6.43
statutory provision, 1.151–1.152
continuous employment
change of employer, 6.99
generally, 6.96
reinstatement after service with armed forces, 6.100
stoppages of work, 6.98
unfair dismissal, 6.97
contracting out restrictions, 1.145–1.146
contractual remuneration, and
generally, 6.91
statutory provision, 1.151–1.152
Crown employment, 1.149–1.150
curtailment of pay period
definitions, 5.103
general note, 5.101
notice, 5.113
revocation notice, 5.114

Index

service of notices, 5.104
shared parental leave: AP, 5.112
statutory shared parental pay: A, 5.110
statutory shared parental pay: AP, 5.111
definitions, 1.153
determination of entitlement issues
  application, 6.30
  form of application, 6.31
divided contracts
  general note, 6.10
  lapse of election, 6.15
  notification of election, 6.12
  provision of information, 6.13
  relevant employer, 6.14
earnings, 6.102
employed earners, 6.95
employer's liability
  funding, 1.449–1.450
  generally, 1.141–1.142
employers' records
  generally, 6.26
  inspection, 6.27
entitlement
  determination of issues, 6.30–6.31
  provision of information, 6.28–6.29
  statutory provisions, 1.139–1.140
evidence of entitlement, 6.86
excepted cases, 6.89
failure to comply, 1.456–1.457
fraud
  generally, 1.458–1.459
  procedure and appeals, 1.466–1.474
funding of liabilities
  application to Revenue, 6.21
  date of payment of contributions, 6.24
  generally, 6.20
  method, 6.22–6.23
  overpayments, 6.25
general note, 1.138
incorrect statements, 1.458–1.459
information
  power to require, 1.454–1.455
  supply, 1.460–1.461
  use by Board, 1.462
liability of Revenue, 6.106–6.108
mariners
  definitions, 6.34
  general note, 6.35
  generally, 6.42
  statutory provision, 1.151–1.152
NHS employees
  general note, 6.10
  lapse of election, 6.15
  notification of election, 6.12
  provision of information, 6.13
  relevant employer, 6.14
normal weekly earnings
  earnings, 6.102
  generally, 6.103
notice requirements, 6.85
overseas adoptions
  administration, 6.120–6.124
  application of General Regulations 2002, 6.130
  application of SSCBA 1992, 6.112–6.119
  avoidance of liability, 6.145
  definitions, 6.129
  evidence of entitlement, 6.142
  general note, 6.128
  notice requirements, 6.141
  pay period, 6.139–6.140
  termination of employment, 6.144
  treatment of more than one employer, 6.143
parental orders, and
  application of Part 12ZB SSCBA 1992, 6.223, 6.226
  definitions, 6.221
  Regulations, 6.228–6.253
pay period
  disrupted adoption, 6.83–6.84
  generally, 6.82
  statutory provision, 1.143–1.144
  treatment of more than one contract, 6.85
payment
  generally, 6.104
  liability of Revenue, 6.106–6.108
  persons acting on behalf of another, to, 6.110
  Revenue, by, 6.109
  statutory provisions, 1.451–1.452
  timing, 6.105
penalties
  appeals, 1.468
  definitions, 1.474
  determination, 1.466–1.467
  failure to comply, 1.456–1.457
  fraud, 1.458–1.459
  incorrect statements, 1.458–1.459
  interest, 1.473
  mitigation, 1.471
  proceedings before Commissioners, 1.469
  proceedings before court, 1.470
  time limits, 1.472
persons abroad
  absent from Great Britain, 6.38
  definitions, 6.34
  general note, 6.35
  has worked in other EEA States, 6.40
  in other EEA States, 6.37
  time for compliance, 6.41
provision of information
  entitlement, as to, 6.28–6.29
  generally, 6.32
rate, 1.143–1.144
relationship with benefits, 1.147–1.148
rounding, 6.6–6.7
service of notices, 6.111
special classes of person, 1.151–1.152
statutory provisions
  administration, 1.447–1.455

1121

adoption without placement,
1.154–1.155
contracting out restrictions,
1.1451–1.146
Crown employment, 1.149–1.150
definitions, 1.153
employer's liability, 1.141–1.142
entitlement, 1.139–1.140
general note, 1.138
information, 1.460–1.462
pay period, 1.143–1.144
penalties, 1.456–1.459
rate, 1.143–1.144
relationship with benefits, 1.147–1.148
relationship with remuneration,
1.147–1.148
special classes of person, 1.151–1.152
supplementary, 1.153
supply of information
Board, by, 1.460
Secretary of State, by, 1.461
ten days or less working in pay period, 6.90
termination of employment before start of period, 6.92
treatment of more than one contract
general note, 6.10
generally, 6.87
lapse of election, 6.15
notification of election, 6.12
provision of information, 6.13
relevant employer, 6.14, 6.101
weekly rates
general note, 6.3
generally, 6.5
rounding, 6.6–6.7
work during pay period, 6.88
working tax credits
social security income, 2.152
working 10 days or less in pay period,
6.90

Statutory Adoption Pay (Administration) Regulations 2002
application
Adoption from Overseas Regulations, to, 6.120–6.124
arrangement, 6.16
citation, 6.17
commencement, 6.17
definitions, 6.19
general note, 6.18
general provisions, 6.20–6.32

Statutory Adoption Pay (Adoptions from Overseas) (No.2) Regulations 2003
application, 6.131
arrangement, 6.125
citation, 6.127
commencement, 6.127
definitions, 6.129
general note, 6.128
general provisions, 6.139–6.145
revocation provision, 6.146

Statutory Adoption Pay (Adoptions from Overseas) (Persons Abroad and Mariners) Regulations 2010
arrangement, 6.147
citation, 6.148
commencement, 6.148
definitions, 6.149
general provision, 6.151
revocation, 6.150

Statutory Adoption Pay (Curtailment) Regulations 2014
arrangement, 5.100
citation, 5.102
commencement, 5.102
definitions, 5.103
general note, 5.101
general provisions, 5.104–5.113
revocation, 5.114

Statutory Adoption Pay (General) Regulations 2002
amendment
Parental Orders and Prospective Adopters Regulations 2014, by, 6.228–6.252
application
Adoption from Overseas (No.2) Regulations, to, 6.130
generally, 6.61
arrangement, 6.57
citation, 6.58
commencement, 6.58
definitions, 6.59–6.60
general provisions, 6.82–6.111

Statutory Adoption Pay (NHS Employees) Regulations 2002
arrangement, 6.8
citation, 6.9
commencement, 6.9
definitions, 6.9
general note, 6.10
general provisions, 6.11–6.15

Statutory Adoption Pay (Parental Orders and Prospective Adopters) Regulations 2014
arrangement, 6.228
citation, 6.230
commencement, 6.230
general note, 6.231
general provisions, 6.232–6.252

Statutory Adoption Pay (Persons Abroad and Mariners) Regulations 2002
amended form, 6.46–6.56
application to overseas adoptions,
6.151
arrangement, 6.33
citation, 6.34
commencement, 6.34
definitions, 6.34
general note, 6.35
general provisions, 6.36–6.43
schedules, 6.44–6.45

Index

Statutory Adoption Pay (Weekly Rates) Regulations 2002
  arrangement, 6.1
  citation, 6.2
  commencement, 6.2
  general note, 6.3
  general provisions, 6.4–6.7
Statutory maternity pay
  administration
    employer's records, 5.46–5.47
    expected week of confinement, 5.40
    notice of absence from work, 5.41
    notification of employment after confinement, 5.42
    provision of information, 5.43–5.45
  avoidance of liability, 5.7–5.8
  benefits, and
    generally, 1.101–1.102
    miscellaneous provision, 1.203–2.194
  breach of regulations, 1.213–1.214
  change of employer, 5.26
  civil penalties
    breach of regulations, 1.213–1.214
    fraud, 1.215
    negligence, 1.215
  compensation of employers
    additional payment to small employers, 5.85
    advance funding, 5.87
    date of payment of contributions, 5.90
    deduction from payments to Revenue, 5.88
    definitions, 5.82
    general note, 5.83
    overpayments, 5.91
    payments to employer by Revenue, 5.89
    prescribed amount, 5.86
    'small employer', 5.84
  continental shelf employees
    definitions, 5.63
    general note, 5.64
    generally, 5.72
    statutory provisions, 1.104
  continuous employment
    change of employer, 5.26
    generally, 5.22
    stoppages of work, 5.24–5.25
    unfair dismissal, 5.23
  contractual remuneration, as
    generally, 5.34
    statutory provision, 1.205
  Crown employment, 1.103
  curtailment of pay period
    definitions, 5.103
    general note, 5.101
    notice, 5.108
    revocation notice, 5.109
    service of notices, 5.104
    shared parental leave: P, 5.107
    statutory shared parental pay: M, 5.105
    statutory shared parental pay: P, 5.106
  death of woman, 5.21
  definitions
    'earnings', 5.35
    'employee', 5.31
    generally, 5.2–5.3
    statutory provisions, 1.105
    'week', 5.30
  detention in custody, 5.17–5.18
  determination of entitlement
    application, 4.82
    definitions, 4.81
    procedure, 4.83
  divided contracts (general Regulations)
    treatment of more than one contract as one, 5.11
    treatment of two or more employers as one, 5.32–5.33
  divided contracts (NHS Regulations)
    lapse of election, 5.80
    notification of election, 5.77
    provision of information, 5.78
    treatment of more than one contract as one, 5.76
    treatment of two or more employers as one, 5.79
  employee, 5.31
  employee's duties, 1.210
  employer's records
    maintenance, 5.46
    production, 5.47
  employment contract terminated to avoid liability, 5.7–5.8
  enforcement
    breach of regulations, 1.213–1.214
    fraud, 1.215
    negligence, 1.215
  entitlement, 1.91–1.93
  expected week of confinement, 5.40
  fraud, 1.215
  funding of employers' liabilities, 1.99–1.100
  imprisonment, 5.17–5.18
  incapacity benefit, and
    generally, 5.38
    statutory provision, 1.204
  information
    disclosure by Secretary of State, 1.220
    employers, by, 1.221
  liability of Secretary of State to pay
    generally, 5.13–5.14
    statutory provision, 1.91–1.93
  mariners
    definitions, 5.63
    general note, 5.64
    generally, 5.71
    statutory provisions, 1.104
  maternity allowance, 5.39
  medical evidence
    definitions, 5.58
    evidence of pregnancy and confinement, 5.59
    form of certificate, 5.60–5.61
  modification of provisions, 5.9–5.10
  national health service employees
    lapse of election, 5.80

1123

notification of election, 5.77
provision of information, 5.78
treatment of more than one contract as one, 5.76
treatment of two or more employers as one, 5.79
negligence, 1.215
normal working earnings
'earnings', 5.35
generally, 5.36–5.37
normal working weeks
generally, 5.28–5.29
'week', 5.30
notice of absence from work, 5.41
notification of employment after confinement, 5.42
offences, 5.55–5.56
pay period
generally, 5.4–5.6
statutory provision, 1.94–1.95
payment
generally, 5.48
persons acting on behalf of another, to, 5.53–5.54
rounding, 5.49
Secretary of State, by, 5.51–5.52
timing, 5.50
persons abroad
absent from Great Britain, 5.66
definitions, 5.63
'employee', 5.67
general note, 5.64
in other Member States, 5.65
time for compliance, 5.70
women who worked in the EC, 5.69
persons acting on behalf of another, to, 5.53–5.54
provision of information
claims for other benefits, 5.45
determination of questions, 5.43–5.44
rate
generally, 5.12
statutory provision, 1.96–1.98
recovery of payments, 1.99–1.100
reinstatement after service with armed services, 5.27
relationship with benefits
generally, 1.101–1.102
miscellaneous provision, 1.203–2.194
rounding fractional amounts, 5.49
special classes of persons, 1.104
statutory provisions
Crown employment, 1.103
definitions, 1.105
entitlement, 1.91–1.93
pay period, 1.94–1.95
rate, 1.96–1.98
recovery of payments, 1.99–1.100
relationship with benefits, 1.101–1.102
special classes of persons, 1.104
stoppages of work, 5.24–5.25
ten days or less work in pay period, 5.19–5.20

treatment of more than one contract of service
generally, 5.11
NHS employees, 5.76
relevant employer, 5.32–5.33
unfair dismissal, 5.23
work after confinement, 5.15–5.16
working tax credits
social security income, 2.152
working 10 days or less in pay period, 5.19–5.20
Statutory Maternity Pay (Compensation of Employers) and Miscellaneous Amendment Regulations 1994
arrangement, 5.81
citation, 5.82
commencement, 5.82
definitions, 5.82
general note, 5.83
general provisions, 5.84–5.91
revocations, 5.92
Statutory Maternity Pay (Curtailment) Regulations 2014
arrangement, 5.100
citation, 5.102
commencement, 5.102
definitions, 5.103
general note, 5.101
general provisions, 5.104–5.113
revocation, 5.114
Statutory Maternity Pay (Decisions) Regulations 1999
arrangement, 4.80
citation, 4.81
commencement, 4.81
definitions, 4.81
general provisions, 4.82–4.83
revocations, 4.84
Statutory Maternity Pay (General) Regulations 1986
amendments to
2000 Regulations, 5.93–5.99
arrangement, 5.1
citation, 5.2
commencement, 5.2
definitions, 5.2–5.3
general provisions
administration, 5.40–5.47
employee, 5.31
entitlement, 5.4–5.21
miscellaneous, 5.31–5.39
normal working weeks, 5.28–5.30
offences, 5.55–5.56
payment, 5.48–5.54
Statutory Maternity Pay (Medical Evidence) Regulations 1987
arrangement, 5.57
citation, 5.58
commencement, 5.58
definitions, 5.58
general provisions, 5.59
schedule, 5.60–5.61

Index

Statutory Maternity Pay (National Health Service Employees) Regulations 1991
arrangement, 5.74
citation, 5.75
commencement, 5.75
definitions, 5.75
general provisions, 5.76–5.80

Statutory Maternity Pay (Persons Abroad and Mariners) Regulations 1987
arrangement, 5.62
citation, 5.63
commencement, 5.63
definitions, 5.63
general note, 5.64
general provisions, 5.65–5.73

Statutory paternity pay
additional pay
  common provisions, 6.178–6.199
  entitlement (adoption), 6.171–6.177
  entitlement (birth), 6.163–6.170
  overseas adoptions, 6.200–6.212
  statutory provision, 1.121–1.127
administration
  determination of entitlement issues, 6.28–6.31
  employers' records, 6.26–6.27
  funding of liabilities, 6.20–6.25
  provision of information, 6.32
  statutory provision, 1.447–1.455
adoption of child, on
  conditions of entitlement, 6.71–6.72
  evidence of entitlement, 6.76
  notice of entitlement, 6.72A
  notice requirements, 6.74
  payment period, 6.73
  qualifying period, 6.75
  statutory provisions, 1.113–1.114
  treatment of more than one employer, 6.77
adoption without placement, 1.136–1.137
avoidance of liability, 6.81
birth of child, on
  conditions of entitlement, 6.62–6.64
  evidence of entitlement, 6.68–6.69
  notice of entitlement, 6.64A
  notice requirements, 6.66
  payment period, 6.65
  qualifying period, 6.67
  statutory provisions, 1.107–1.112
  treatment of more than one employer, 6.70
conditions of entitlement
  adoption of child, on, 6.71–6.72
  birth of child, on, 6.62–6.64
continental shelf employees
  definitions, 6.34
  general note, 6.35
  generally, 6.43
continuous employment
  change of employer, 6.99
  generally, 6.96
  reinstatement after service with armed forces, 6.100
  stoppages of work, 6.98
  unfair dismissal, 6.97
contractual remuneration, and
  generally, 6.80
  statutory provision, 1.128–1.129
definitions, 1.134–1.135
detention in custody, 6.108
determination of entitlement issues
  application, 6.30
  form of application, 6.31
divided contracts
  general note, 6.10
  lapse of election, 6.15
  notification of election, 6.12
  provision of information, 6.13
  relevant employer, 6.14
earnings, 6.102
employed earners, 6.95
employer's liability, 1.117–1.118
employers' records
  generally, 6.26
  inspection, 6.27
entitlement
  adoption of child, on, 6.71–6.77
  birth of child, on, 6.62–6.70
  determination of issues, 6.30–6.31
  provision of information, 6.28–6.29
  statutory provisions, 1.107–1.116
evidence of entitlement
  adoption of child, on, 6.71–6.72
  birth of child, on, 6.62–6.64
excepted cases, 6.79
failure to comply, 1.456–1.457
fraud
  generally, 1.458–1.459
  procedure and appeals, 1.466–1.474
funding of liabilities
  application to Revenue, 6.21
  date of payment of contributions, 6.24
  generally, 6.20
  method, 6.22–6.23
  overpayments, 6.25
imprisonment, 6.108
incorrect statements, 1.458–1.459
information
  power to require, 1.454–1.455
  supply, 1.460–1.461
  use by Board, 1.462
liability of Revenue to pay
  detention in custody, 6.108
  generally, 6.106–6.107
  imprisonment, 6.108
mariners
  definitions, 6.34
  general note, 6.35
  generally, 6.42
NHS employees
  general note, 6.10
  lapse of election, 6.15
  notification of election, 6.12

1125

Index

provision of information, 6.13
relevant employer, 6.14
normal weekly earnings
  earnings, 6.102
  generally, 6.103
notice requirements
  adoption of child, on, 6.74
  birth of child, on, 6.66
  statutory provisions, 1.115–1.116
overseas adoptions
  administration, 6.120–6.124
  application of General Regulations 2002, 6.130
  application of SSCBA 1992, 6.112–6.119
  avoidance of liability, 6.138
  conditions of entitlement, 6.132
  definitions, 6.129
  evidence of entitlement, 6.136
  general note, 6.128
  notice requirements, 6.134
  pay period, 6.133
  qualifying period, 6.135
  treatment of more than one employer, 6.137
parental orders, and
  application of Part 12ZB SSCBA 1992, 6.222, 6.225
  definitions, 6.221
  Regulations, 6.228–6.253
pay period
  adoption of child, on, 6.73
  birth of child, on, 6.65
  statutory provision, 1.119–1.120
payment
  generally, 6.104
  liability of Revenue, 6.106–6.108
  persons acting on behalf of another, to, 6.110
  Revenue, by, 6.109
  timing, 6.105
penalties
  appeals, 1.468
  definitions, 1.474
  determination, 1.466–1.467
  failure to comply, 1.456–1.457
  fraud, 1.458–1.459
  incorrect statements, 1.458–1.459
  interest, 1.473
  mitigation, 1.471
  proceedings before Commissioners, 1.469
  proceedings before court, 1.470
  time limits, 1.472
persons abroad
  absent from Great Britain, 6.38
  definitions, 6.34
  general note, 6.35
  has worked in other EEA States, 6.39
  in other EEA States, 6.37
  time for compliance, 6.41
provision of information

entitlement, as to, 6.28–6.29
generally, 6.32
qualifying period
  adoption of child, on, 6.75
  birth of child, on, 6.67
rate, 1.119–1.120
rounding, 6.6–6.7
service of notices, 6.111
special classes of persons, 1.132–1.133
statutory provisions
  additional pay, 1.121–1.125
  administration, 1.447–1.455
  adoption without placement, 1.136–1.137
  contracting out restrictions, 1.126–1.127
  Crown employment, 1.130–1.131
  definitions, 1.134–1.135
  employer's liability, 1.117–1.118
  entitlement, 1.107–1.116
  general note, 1.106–1.106A
  information, 1.460–1.462
  pay period, 1.119–1.120
  penalties, 1.456–1.459
  rate, 1.119–1.120
  relationship with contractual remuneration, 1.128–1.129
  special classes of persons, 1.132–1.133
  supplementary, 1.134
supply of information
  Board, by, 1.460
  Secretary of State, by, 1.461
treatment of more than one contract
  adoption of child, on, 6.77
  birth of child, on, 6.70
  general note, 6.10
  lapse of election, 6.15
  notification of election, 6.12
  provision of information, 6.13
  relevant employer, 6.14, 6.101
weekly rates
  general note, 6.3
  generally, 6.4
  rounding, 6.6–6.7
work during pay period, 6.78
working tax credits
  social security income, 2.152
Statutory Paternity Pay (Administration) Regulations 2002
application
  Adoption from Overseas Regulations, to, 6.120–6.124
arrangement, 6.16
citation, 6.17
commencement, 6.17
definitions, 6.19
general note, 6.18
general provisions, 6.20–6.32
Statutory Paternity Pay (Adoption from Overseas) (No.2) Regulations 2003
application, 6.131
arrangement, 6.125
citation, 6.127

Index

commencement, 6.127
definitions, 6.129
general note, 6.128
general provisions, 6.132–6.138
revocation provision, 6.146
Statutory Paternity Pay (General) Regulations 2002
amendment
Parental Orders and Prospective Adopters Regulations 2014, by, 6.228–6.252
application
Adoption from Overseas (No.2) Regulations, to, 6.130
generally, 6.61
arrangement, 6.57
citation, 6.58
commencement, 6.58
definitions, 6.59–6.60
general provisions
adoption, 6.71–6.77
birth, 6.62–6.70
common provisions, 6.78–6.81
miscellaneous, 6.94–6.111
Statutory Paternity Pay (NHS Employees) Regulations 2002
arrangement, 6.8
citation, 6.9
commencement, 6.9
definitions, 6.9
general note, 6.10
Statutory Paternity Pay (Parental Orders and Prospective Adopters) Regulations 2014
arrangement, 6.228
citation, 6.230
commencement, 6.230
general note, 6.231
general provisions, 6.232–6.252
general provisions, 6.10–6.15
Statutory Paternity Pay (Persons Abroad and Mariners) Regulations 2002
amended form, 6.46–6.56
application to overseas adoptions, 6.151
arrangement, 6.33
citation, 6.34
commencement, 6.34
definitions, 6.34
general note, 6.35
general provisions, 6.36–6.43
schedules, 6.44–6.45
Statutory Paternity Pay (Weekly Rates) Regulations 2002
arrangement, 6.1
citation, 6.2
commencement, 6.2
general note, 6.3
general provisions, 6.4–6.7
Statutory shared parental pay
absence from work
entitlement (adoption), 7.53
entitlement (birth), 7.35

administration
applications, 7.14–7.15
definitions, 7.04
funding employers' liabilities, 7.05–7.10
general note, 7.02
provision of information as to entitlement, 7.13
records by employers, 7.11–7.12
adoption
conditions, 7.55–7.68
definitions, 7.20–7.21
entitlement, 7.37–7.54
general note, 7.18
adoption (entitlement)
absence from work, 7.53
adopter, of, 7.37–7.38
care of child during period of payment, 7.51
death, and, 7.54
evidential requirements, 7.41–7.44
extent, 7.46
notification requirements, 7.41–7.44
number of weeks of pay to be claimed, 7.45
other cases where no liability to pay, 7.52
partner, of, 7.39–7.40
periods when pay is to be claimed, 7.45
statutory provision, 1.157
variation of number of weeks of pay to be claimed, 7.45
when not to be paid, 7.47
work during period of payment, 7.49–7.50
adoption from overseas
application of General Regulations, 7.95
definitions, 7.94
modification of General Regulations, 7.96–7.108
avoidance of liability, 7.71
birth
conditions, 7.55–7.68
definitions, 7.20–7.21
entitlement, 7.24–7.36
general note, 7.18
birth (entitlement)
absence from work, 7.35
care of child during period of payment, 7.33
death, and, 7.36
evidential requirements, 7.26–7.27
extent, 7.30
father, of, 7.25
modification of notice conditions where early birth, 7.29
mother, of, 7.24
notification requirements, 7.26–7.27
number of weeks of pay to be claimed, 7.28
other cases where no liability to pay, 7.34
partner, of, 7.25

1127

Index

periods when pay is to be claimed, 7.28
statutory provision, 1.156
variation of number of weeks of pay to be claimed, 7.28
when not to be paid, 7.31
work during period of payment, 7.32
care of child during period of payment
  entitlement (adoption), 7.51
  entitlement (birth), 7.33
conditions of entitlement
  'continuous employment', 7.63–7.67
  continuity of employment of claimant, 7.57–7.59
  'employees', 7.62
  employment and earnings of claimant's partner, 7.55–7.56
  multiple employers, 7.68
  normal weekly earnings of claimant, 7.57–7.61
continental shelf, 7.138
continuity of employment of claimant
  adoption, 7.58–7.59
  birth, 7.57
  change of employer, 7.66
  'continuous employment', 7.63
  service with armed forces, 7.67
  stoppages of work, 7.65
  unfair dismissal, and, 7.64
contracting out, 1.161
contractual remuneration, and
  generally, 7.70
  statutory provision, 1.162
Crown employment, 1.163
curtailment of adoption pay period
  A, 5.110
  AP, 5.111
curtailment of maternity pay period
  M, 5.105
  P, 5.106
'day of payment', 7.60
date when contributions treated as paid, 7.09
death, and
  entitlement (adoption), 7.54
  entitlement (birth), 7.36
deductions from payments to Commissioners, 7.07
definitions
  administration regulations, 7.04
  general regulations, 7.20–7.21
  statute, 1.165
'earnings', 7.60
entitlement
  adoption, 1.157, 7.37–7.54
  application for determination of issues arising, 7.14–7.15
  birth, 1.156, 7.24–7.36
  conditions, 7.55–7.68
  definitions, 7.20–7.21
  general note, 7.18
  provision of information as to, 7.13
  statutory provisions, 1.156–1.158
entitlement (adoption)
  absence from work, 7.53
  adopter, of, 7.37–7.38
  care of child during period of payment, 7.51
  death, and, 7.54
  evidential requirements, 7.41–7.44
  extent, 7.46
  notification requirements, 7.41–7.44
  number of weeks of pay to be claimed, 7.45
  other cases where no liability to pay, 7.52
  partner, of, 7.39–7.40
  periods when pay is to be claimed, 7.45
  statutory provision, 1.157
  variation of number of weeks of pay to be claimed, 7.45
  when not to be paid, 7.47
  work during period of payment, 7.49–7.50
entitlement (birth)
  absence from work, 7.35
  care of child during period of payment, 7.33
  death, and, 7.36
  evidential requirements, 7.26–7.27
  extent, 7.30
  father, of, 7.25
  modification of notice conditions where early birth, 7.29
  mother, of, 7.24
  notification requirements, 7.26–7.27
  number of weeks of pay to be claimed, 7.28
  other cases where no liability to pay, 7.34
  partner, of, 7.25
  periods when pay is to be claimed, 7.28
  statutory provision, 1.156
  variation of number of weeks of pay to be claimed, 7.28
  when not to be paid, 7.31
  work during period of payment, 7.32
evidential requirements
  entitlement (adoption), 7.41–7.44
  entitlement (birth), 7.26–7.27
fathers
  entitlement, 7.25
funding employers' liabilities
  applications, 7.06
  date when contributions treated as paid, 7.09
  deductions from payments, 7.07
  generally, 7.05
  overpayments, 7.10
  payments to employers, 7.08
  records by employers, 7.11–7.12
imprisonment, in case of, 7.75
liability to pay, 1.159
mariners
  definitions, 7.130
  general note, 7.128
  general provisions, 7.137–7.138

Index

mothers
  entitlement, 7.24
'normal pay day', 7.60
normal weekly earnings of claimant
  adoption, 7.58–7.59
  'appropriate date', 7.60
  birth, 7.57
  'day of payment', 7.60
  'earnings', 7.60
  meaning, 7.60–7.61
  'normal pay day', 7.60
  'relevant period', 7.60
notification requirements
  entitlement (adoption), 7.41–7.44
  entitlement (birth), 7.26–7.27
number of weeks of pay to be claimed
  entitlement (adoption), 7.45
  entitlement (birth), 7.28
other cases where no liability to pay
  entitlement (adoption), 7.52
  entitlement (birth), 7.34
overpayments, 7.10
parental orders, and
  application of Part 12ZB SSCBA 1992, 6.224, 6.227
  application of Pay Regulations, 7.113
  definitions, 6.221, 7.112
  general note, 7.110
  modification of Pay Regulations, 7.114–7.126
partners
  entitlement (adoption), 7.39–7.40
  entitlement (birth), 7.25
pay period, 1.160
payment
  avoidance of liability, 7.71
  Commissioners, by, 7.74–7.76
  contractual remuneration, and, 7.70
  method, 7.72
  parental orders, and, 7.114–7.126
  persons unable to act, where, 7.77
  timing, 7.73
  weekly rate, 7.69
payment by Commissioners
  custody or imprisonment, in case of, 7.75
  generally, 7.76
  liability, 7.74–7.75
payments to employers by Commissioners, 7.08
periods when pay is to be claimed
  entitlement (adoption), 7.45
  entitlement (birth), 7.28
persons abroad
  definitions, 7.130
  general note, 7.128
  general provisions, 7.131–7.136
persons unable to act, where, 7.77
power to apply Part 12ZC, 1.166
provision of information
  entitlement, as to, 7.13
  generally, 7.16
rate, 1.160

records by employers
  generally, 7.11
  inspection, 7.12
'relevant period', 7.60
remuneration, and, 1.162
service of notices, 7.78
service with armed forces, 7.67
special circumstances, in
  adoption, 7.85–7.91
  birth, 7.79–7.84
special classes of person, 1.164
stoppages of work, 7.65
unfair dismissal, and, 7.64
variation of number of weeks of pay to be claimed
  entitlement (adoption), 7.45
  entitlement (birth), 7.28
weekly rate, 7.69
when not to be paid
  entitlement (adoption), 7.47
  entitlement (birth), 7.31
work during period of payment
  entitlement (adoption), 7.49–7.50
  entitlement (birth), 7.32
Statutory Shared Parental Pay (Administration) Regulations 2014
arrangement, 7.01
citation, 7.03
commencement, 7.03
definitions, 7.04
general note, 7.02
general provisions, 7.05–7.16
Statutory Shared Parental Pay (Adoption from Overseas) Regulations 2014
arrangement, 7.92
citation, 7.93
commencement, 7.93
definitions, 7.94
general provisions, 7.94–7.108
Statutory Shared Parental Pay (General) Regulations 2014
application, 7.22–7.23
arrangement, 7.17
citation, 7.19
commencement, 7.19
definitions, 7.20–7.21
general note, 7.18
general provisions
  adoption, 7.37–7.54
  birth, 7.24–7.36
  conditions of entitlement, 7.55–7.68
  payment, 7.69–7.78
  schedule, 7.79–7.91
Statutory Shared Parental Pay (Parental Order Cases) Regulations 2014
arrangement, 7.109
citation, 7.111
commencement, 7.111
definitions, 7.112
general note, 7.110
general provisions, 7.113–7.126

1129

Statutory Shared Parental Pay (Persons Abroad and Mariners) Regulations 2014
application, 7.131
arrangement, 7.127
citation, 7.129
commencement, 7.129
definitions, 7.130
general note, 7.128
general provisions, 7.132–7.142
schedule, 7.143–7.149

Statutory sick pay
air crew
  definitions, 4.50, 4.56–4.57, 4.63
  general note, 4.47
  statutory provision, 1.88
  time for compliance, 4.65
avoidance of liability, 4.11
benefits, and
  generally, 1.86
  miscellaneous provisions, 1.196–1.202
breach of regulations, 1.213–1.214
calculation of limit, 4.15
civil penalties
  breach of regulations, 1.213–1.214
  fraud, 1.215
  negligence, 1.215
continental shelf employees
  definitions, 4.51, 4.58, 4.64
  general note, 4.47
  statutory provision, 1.88
  time for compliance, 4.65
contractual remuneration, 1.197
Crown employment, 1.87
definitions
  earnings, 4.35
  employee, 4.34
  generally, 4.2–4.3
  statutory provisions, 1.89–1.90
detention in custody. 4.9
determination of entitlement
  application, 4.82
  definitions, 4.81
  procedure, 4.83
divided contracts (general Regulations)
  generally, 4.41
  relevant employer, 4.39–4.40
divided contracts (NHS Regulations)
  lapse of election, 4.79
  notification of election, 4.76
  provision of information, 4.77
  treatment of more than one contract as one, 4.75
  treatment of two or more employers as one, 4.78
earnings
  excepted payments, 4.36
  generally, 4.35
  normal weekly earnings, 4.37–4.38
employee's duties, 1.209
employer's liability, 1.64–1.68
employment contract terminated to avoid liability, 4.11

enforcement
  breach of regulations, 1.213–1.214
  fraud, 1.215
  negligence, 1.215
entitlement
  employer's liability, 1.64–1.68
  general note, 1.62–1.63
  limitations, 1.80–1.81
  qualifying conditions, 1.69–1.118
fraud, 1.215
general note, 1.62–1.63
imprisonment, 4.9
incapacity benefit, 1.198–1.199
information
  disclosure by Secretary of State, 1.218
  employers, by, 1.219
insolvency of employer, 4.21
interruption of employment
  excepted days, 4.26
limitations on entitlement, 1.80–1.81
linking periods of incapacity. 4.7–4.8
mariners
  definitions, 4.48–4.49, 4.55, 4.62
  general note, 4.47
  statutory provision, 1.88
  time for compliance, 4.65
maximum entitlement, 4.10
medical evidence
  definitions, 4.67
  doctor's statement, 4.70–4.72
  general note, 4.68
  information required, 4.69
method of payment, 4.17
national health employees
  lapse of election, 4.79
  notification of election, 4.76
  provision of information, 4.77
  treatment of more than one contract as one, 4.75
  treatment of two or more employers as one, 4.78
negligence, 1.215
notification of incapacity for work
  generally, 4.16
  statutory provisions, 1.81
offences, 4.43–4.44
payment
  liability of Secretary of State, 4.19–4.20
  method, 4.17
  Secretary of State, by, 4.22
  statements relating to, 4.33
  time limits, 4.18
percentage threshold, 4.85–4.89
period of entitlement, 1.71–1.77, 1.183–1.195
period of incapacity for work, 1.69–1.70
persons abroad
  absent from Great Britain, 4.53–4.54
  definitions, 4.48–4.59
  employees, 4.60
  general note, 4.47
  persons abroad, 4.60–4.61

in other Member States, 4.52
time for compliance, 4.65
persons deemed incapable of work, 4.4–4.6
persons unable to act, 4.23–4.24
provision of information
  employee to Secretary of State, by, 4.29–4.30
  employer to employee, by, 4.31–4.32
qualifying conditions
  period of entitlement, 1.71–1.77, 1.183–1.195
  period of incapacity for work, 1.69–1.70
  qualifying days, 1.78–1.79
qualifying days
  generally, 4.12–4.14
  statutory provisions, 1.78–1.79
rate of payment, 1.82
records
  maintenance, 4.27
  production, 4.28
recovery of statutory sick pay
  generally, 4.85–4.89
  statutory provisions, 1.83–1.85
relationship with benefits
  generally, 1.86
  miscellaneous provisions, 1.196–1.202
'relevant infection or contamination', 4.4
rounding fractional amounts, 4.25
special classes of person, 1.88
statutory provisions
  Crown employment, 1.87
  definitions, 1.89–1.90
  employer's liability, 1.64–1.68
  general note, 1.29
  limitations on entitlement, 1.80–1.81
  qualifying conditions, 1.65–1.79
  rates of payment, 1.82
  recovery of payments, 1.83–1.85
  relationship with benefits, 1.86
  special classes of person, 1.88
time limits for payment, 4.18
treatment of two or more contracts as one
  generally, 4.41
  NHS employees, 4.75
  relevant employer, 4.39–4.40
unemployability supplement, 1.200
Statutory Sick Pay (Decisions) Regulations 1999
arrangement, 4.80
citation, 4.81
commencement, 4.81
definitions, 4.81
general provisions, 4.82–4.83
revocation, 4.84
Statutory Sick Pay (General) Regulations 1982
arrangement, 4.1
citation, 4.2
commencement, 4.2
definitions, 4.2–4.3
general provisions, 4.4–4.44

Statutory Sick Pay (Mariners, Air crew and Person Abroad) Regulations 1982
arrangement, 4.45
citation, 4.46
commencement, 4.46
definitions, 4.46
general note, 4.47
general provisions, 4.48–4.65
Statutory Sick Pay (Medical Evidence) Regulations 1985
arrangement, 4.66
citation, 4.67
commencement, 4.67
definitions, 4.67
general note, 4.68
general provisions, 4.69
schedules, 4.70–4.72
Statutory Sick Pay (NHS Employees) Regulations 1985
arrangement, 4.73
citation, 4.74
commencement, 4.74
definitions, 4.74
general provisions, 4.75–4.79
Statutory Sick Pay Percentage Threshold (etc.) Order 2014
arrangement, 4.85
citation, 4.86
commencement, 4.86
revocations, 4.87
transitional and saving provisions, 4.88–4.89
Stoppages of work
See **Strikes**
Strikes
statutory maternity pay, 5.24–5.25
working tax credit, 2.46–2.47
Student income
disregarded payments, 2.161–2.162
generally, 2.158–2.160
Student loans
other income, 1.786
tax credits, 2.161–2.162
Supersession
decisions of Board, 1.231–1.232
Supply of information
See **Provision of income**
Suspension from work
working tax credit, 2.48–2.49
"Table A benefits"
social security income, 1.566–1.568
"Table B benefits"
social security income, 1.589–1.592
Tax credits
See also **Child tax credit; Working tax credit**
administrative arrangements, 1.415–1.416
annual reports, 1.396–1.397
annual review, 1.398–1.399
anti-fraud measures, 1.261–1.262
appeals
  appealable decisions, 1.385–1.390

1131

Index

exercise of right, 1.391–1.392
general regulations, 2.375–2.387
late appeals, 1.393–1.395
settlement, 2.495–2.497
temporary modifications, 1.425–1.426
assignment, 1.406–1.407
bankruptcy, 1.406–1.407
changes of circumstances
  automatic notification, 1.289
  discretionary notification, 1.288
  failure to report, 1.290
  generally, 1.284–1.285
  mandatory notification, 1.287
  relevant changes, 1.286
child tax credit
  abolition, 1.850–1.851
  entitlement, 1.299–1.301
  general note, 1.255
  maximum rate, 1.302–1.304
claims
  generally, 1.267–1.279
  supplementary, 1.280–1.281
Codes of Practice
  overpayments, 9.15–9.53
Crown employment, 1.404–1.405
decisions
  discovery, on, 1.336–1.337
  final decision, 1.331–1.332
  final notice, 1.329–1.330
  information requirements, 1.344–1.345
  initial decision, 1.317–1.322
  notice of, 1.346–1.347
  official error, subject to, 1.338–1.339
  other revised decisions, 1.325–1.328
  power to enquire, 1.333–1.335
  review, 1.340–1.343
  revision after notifications, 1.323–1.324
definitions, 1.412–1.413
development of system, 1.257
disclosure of information, 1.417–1.418
duration, 1.282–1.283
evaluation studies
  generally, 2.467
  Northern Ireland, 2.469
exercise of functions
  definitions, 2.499
  Secretary of State, by, 2.500–2.501
failure to comply with requirements, 1.366–1.369
fraud, and
  generally, 1.371–1.372
  introduction, 1.261–1.262
  loss of tax credit, 1.375–1.382
  powers relating to documents, 1.373–1.374
functions of Board, 1.265–1.266
general note
  anti-fraud measures, 1.261–1.262
  changes to Act, 1.260
  child tax credit, 1.255
  development of system, 1.257
  generally, 1.254
  problems with Act, 1.259

repeal of Act, 1.253
scheme of Act, 1.252
working tax credit, 1.256
generally, 1.263–1.264
inalienability, 1.406–1.407
income test, 1.291–1.298
incorrect statements
  conduct of penalty cases, 1.363
  fraudulently or negligently, 1.362
  generally, 1.359–1.361
  level of penalties, 1.364–1.365
interest, 1.383–1.384
loss of
  generally, 1.375–1.376
  Regulations, 2.483–2.486
  repeated benefit fraud, for, 1.379–1.382
  specified day, 2.480–2.482
  supplementary, 1.377–1.378
Northern Ireland
  evaluation and statistical studies, 2.468–2.469
  generally, 1.427–1.428
notices by Board, 1.408–1.409
overpayments
  Code of Practice, 9.15–9.53
  generally, 1.352–1.353
  method of recovery, 2.363
  recovery, 1.354–1.356
payment
  employees' rights, 1.350–1.351
  generally, 1.348–1.349
penalties
  determination, 1.435
  failure to comply with requirements, 1.366–1.369
  Guidance, 9.1–9.14
  incorrect statements, 1.359–1.365
  mitigation, 1.437
  proceedings before Commissioners, 1.436
  recovery, 1.439
  supplementary, 1.370–1.371
  time limits, 1.438
period of award, 1.282–1.283
persons subject to immigration control, 1.400–1.401
polygamous marriages, 1.402–1.403
provision of information
  evaluation studies, 2.467
  statistical studies, 2.467
rate, 1.315–1.28
repeal of Act, 1.253
repeated benefit fraud, and
  generally, 1.379–1.380
  introduction, 1.261–1.262
  Regulations, 2.483–2.486
  specified day, 2.480–2.482
  supplementary, 1.381–1.382
review of decisions
  generally, 1.340–1.341
  late application, 1.342–1.343
settlement of appeals

definitions, 2.496
general provisions, 2.497
statistical studies
  generally, 2.467
  Northern Ireland, 2.469
underpayments, 1.357–1.358
Universal Credit, and, 1.261–1.262
use of information, 1.417–1.418
Welfare Reform Act 2012, and, 1.261–1.262
working tax credit
  abolition, 1.850–1.851
  childcare element, 1.313–1.314
  entitlement, 1.305–1.310
  general note, 1.256
  maximum rate, 1.311–1.312
Tax Credits Act 2002
arrangement of sections, 1.251
commencement
  generally, 1.421–1.422
  introduction, 1.258
  Order No. 3, 2.1–2.7
  Order No. 4, 2.8–2.11
consequential amendments, 1.410–1.411
definitions
  general, 1.431–1.432
  tax credits, 1.412–1.413
general note, 1.252–1.262
general provisions, 1.263–1.413
modifications
  persons subject to immigration control, 2.408–2.409
  polygamous marriages, 2.446
Northern Ireland, 1.427–1.428
Parliamentary control, 1.430
regulations, orders and schemes, 1.429
repeal of provisions, 1.253
repeals
  generally, 1.419–1.420
  Order No. 3, 2.7
savings
  generally, 1.423–1.424
  Order No. 3, 2.4
schedules, 1.435–1.444
supplementary provisions, 1.415–1.418
tax credits
  appeals, 1.385–1.395
  child tax credit, 1.299–1.304
  decisions, 1.317–1.347
  fraud, 1.371–1.374
  generally, 1.263–1.298
  interest, 1.383–1.384
  loss of tax credit, 1.375–1.382
  payment, 1.348–1.358
  penalties, 1.359–1.371
  rate, 1.315–1.316
  supplementary, 1.396–1.413
  working tax credit, 1.305–1.314
temporary modifications, 1.425–1.426
transitional provisions
  child tax credit, 2.462–2.465
  generally, 1.423–1.424
  Order No. 3, 2.5–2.6

Order 2008, 2.12–2.14
Order 2010, 2.15–2.18
tax year 2003/04, 2.4–2.5
Tax Credits (Administrative Arrangements) Regulations 2002
arrangement, 2.368
citation, 2.370
commencement, 2.370
definitions, 2.371
general note, 2.369
general provisions, 2.372–2.374
Tax credits (appeals)
appealable decisions, 1.385–1.390
assessment of tax returns, 1.19–1.20
death of party, 2.387
decisions of Board, 1.235–1.238
definitions, 2.377–2.378
directions
  death of party, 2.387
  exercise of right
    decisions of Board, 1.235–1.238
    generally, 1.391–1.392
    other persons, 2.381–2.382
extensions of time, 2.385–2.386
general regulations
  general matters, 2.381–2.387
  service of notices, 2.379–2.380
late appeals
  generally, 1.393–1.395
  invalid regulation, 2.385–2.386
  Order, 2.487–2.489
Orders
  late appeals, 2.487–2.489
'party to the proceedings', 2.387–2.378
Regulations
  general, 2.375–2.387
right of appeal
  decisions of Board, 1.235–1.238
  generally, 1.391–1.392
  other persons, 2.381–2.382
service of notices, 2.379–2.380
temporary modifications, 1.425–1.426
time limits
  extension, 2.385–2.386
  generally, 2.383–2.384
Tax Credits (Appeals) (No. 2) Regulations 2002
arrangement, 2.375
citation, 2.377
commencement, 2.377
definitions, 2.377–2.378
duration, 2.377
general provisions
  general matters, 2.381–2.387
  service of notices, 2.379–2.380
recitals, 2.376
Tax Credits (Approval of Child Care Providers) Scheme 2005
revocation provisions, 2.474–2.479
Tax Credits, Child Benefit and Guardian's Allowance Reviews and Appeals Order 2014
citation, 2.490

1133

Index

commencement, 2.490
general provisions, 2.490–2.494
Tax Credits (Claims and Notifications) Regulations 2002
arrangement, 2.271
citation, 2.272
commencement, 2.272
definitions, 2.273
effect, 2.272
general provisions
  claims, 2.276–2.310
  electronic communications, 2.274–2.275
  final decisions, 2.336–2.339
  notice to provide information, 2.333–2.335
  notifications, 2.311–2.332
modifications to, 2.450
Tax Credits (Definition and Calculation of Income) Regulations 2002
arrangement, 2.103
citation, 2.115
commencement, 2.115
definitions, 2.116–2.117
effect, 2.115
general note
  change in approach, 2.106
  cross-references, 2.114
  differences between calculations and tax assessments, 2.107
  introduction, 2.104
  questions to be decided, 2.108–2.113
  Tax Law Rewrite Project, 2.105
general provisions
  disregards, 2.184–2.191
  income, 2.118–2.183
modifications to, 2.449
Tax Credits (Exercise of Functions) Order 2014
citation, 2.498
commencement, 2.498
definitions, 2.499
general provisions, 2.500–2.503
Tax Credits (Immigration) Regulations 2003
arrangement, 2.394
citation, 2.395
commencement, 2.395
definitions, 2.396
general provisions, 2.397–2.411
modifications to, 2.453
Tax Credits (Income Thresholds and Determination of Rates) Regulations 2002
arrangement, 2.219
citation, 2.220
commencement, 2.220
definitions, 2.221
effect, 2.220
general provisions, 2.222–2.270
Tax Credits (Interest Rate) Regulations 2003
arrangement, 2.388

citation, 2.389
commencement, 2.389
definitions, 2.391
general note, 2.390
general provisions, 2.392–2.393
Tax Credits (Late Appeals) Order 2014
citation, 2.487
commencement, 2.487
general provisions, 2.502–2.489
Tax Credits (Official Error) Regulations 2003
arrangement, 2.430
citation, 2.431
commencement, 2.431
definitions, 2.432–2.433
general note, 2.435
general provision, 2.434
Tax Credits (Payments by the Commissioners) Regulations 2002
arrangement, 2.340
citation, 2.342
commencement, 2.342
definitions, 2.343
effect, 2.342
general note, 2.341
general provisions, 2.344–2.367
modifications to, 2.451
Tax Credits (Polygamous Marriages) Regulations 2003
arrangement, 2.441
citation, 2.443
commencement, 2.443
definitions, 2.444–2.445
effect, 2.443
general note, 2.442
general provision, 2.446–2.453
Tax Credits (Provision of Information) (Evaluation and Statistical Studies) Regulations 2003
citation, 2.466
commencement, 2.466
general provision, 2.467
Tax Credits (Provision of Information) (Evaluation and Statistical Studies) (Northern Ireland) Regulations 2004
citation, 2.468
commencement, 2.468
general provision, 2.469
Tax Credits (Provision of Information) (Functions Relating to Employment and Training) Regulations 2003
arrangement, 2.458
citation, 2.460
commencement, 2.460
general note, 2.459
general provision, 2.461
Tax Credits (Provision of Information) (Functions Relating to Employment and Training) Regulations 2005
citation, 2.472

Index

commencement, 2.472
general provision, 2.473
Tax Credits (Provision of Information) (Functions Relating to Health) Regulations 2003
arrangement, 2.436
citation, 2.437
commencement, 2.437
definitions, 2.439
general note, 2.438
general provision, 2.440
Tax Credits (Provision of Information) (Functions Relating to Health) (Scotland) Regulations 2004
citation, 2.470
commencement, 2.470
general provision, 2.471
Tax Credits (Provision of Information) (Functions Relating to Health) (No.2) Regulations 2003
arrangement, 2.454
citation, 2.456
commencement, 2.456
general note, 2.455
general provision, 2.457
Tax Credits (Residence) Regulations 2003
arrangement, 2.412
citation, 2.413
commencement, 2.413
definitions, 2.414–2.415
general provisions, 2.416–2.427
modifications to, 2.452
transitional provision, 2.428–2.429
Tax Credits (Settlement of Appeals) Regulations 2014
citation, 2.495
commencement, 2.495
definitions, 2.496
general provisions, 2.497
Tax enquiries
amendment by taxpayer, 1.9
completion, 1.11
correction by Revenue, 1.10
notice, 1.8
"Tax-exempt savings"
income test, 2.106
investment income, 2.164
voluntary work, 2.179–2.180
Tax reform
Tax Law Rewrite Project
calculation of income, 2.105
Tax returns
amendment by taxpayer
during enquiry, 1.9
generally, 1.6
appeals, 1.18–1.24
assessment
appeals, 1.18–1.24
discovery of loss of tax, on, 1.13
loss, etc., 1.26
relief for excessive assessments, 1.14–1.15

time limits, 1.16–1.17
want of form, 1.27
closure notices, 1.12
correction by Revenue
during enquiry, 1.10
generally, 1.7
definitions, 1.28
destruction, etc., 1.22
enquiry
amendment by taxpayer, 1.9
completion, 1.12
correction by Revenue, 1.10
notice, 1.8
fraudulent conduct, 1.17
generally, 1.4
loss, etc., 1.26
negligent conduct, 1.17
notice of enquiry, 1.8
penalties, 1.25
records, 1.11
relief for excessive assessments
double assessment, 1.14
recovery of overpaid tax etc, 1.15
self-assessment, 1.5
time limits
fraudulent conduct, 1.17
negligent conduct, 1.17
ordinary period, 1.16
want of form, 1.27
Taxable benefits
benefits code
definitions, 1.499
dispensations, 1.498
meaning, 1.496
relationship with earnings, 1.497
cash vouchers
application of provisions, 1.503–1.504
benefit treated as earnings, 1.507
disregard for money, goods or services obtained, 1.514
meaning, 1.505
sickness-benefits related, 1.506
credit tokens
application of provisions, 1.511
benefit treated as earnings, 1.513
disregard for money, goods or services obtained, 1.514
meaning, 1.512
employment-related benefits
cash equivalent treated as earnings, 1.517
cost of benefit, 1.518
excluded benefits, 1.516
meaning, 1.515
expenses payments
definitions, 1.501
relevant sums, 1.500
sums treated as earnings, 1.502
foreign benefits
application of provisions, 1.593–1.594
person liable to tax, 1.596
taxable income, 1.595

1135

general note
  regulations, 2.127
  statutory provisions, 1.476–1.477
lower-paid employment
  calculation of earnings rate, 1.523
  excluded provisions of benefits code, 1.521
  extra amounts relating to car, 1.524
  meaning, 1.522
minor benefits, 1.519–1.520
non-cash vouchers
  application of provisions, 1.508
  benefit treated as earnings, 1.510
  disregard for money, goods or services obtained, 1.514
  meaning, 1.509
sickness-benefits related vouchers, 1.506
social security income
  exemptions, 1.573–1.588
  person liable to tax, 1.571–1.572
  Table A, 1.566–1.568
  taxable income, 1.569–1.570
vouchers
  cash vouchers, 1.503–1.507
  non-cash vouchers, 1.508–1.510

Taxable income
employment income, 1.490

"Taxable maximum"
income support
  amount in excess of, 1.577
  general, 1.578
jobseeker's allowance, and
  amount in excess of, 1.582
  contribution-based JSA, 1.585
  definitions, 1.586
  general, 1.583
  income-based JSA, 1.584

Taxable persons
See also **Income test**
employment income, 2.134
pension income, 2.141
social security income, 2.156
trading income, 2.149

"Taxable specific income"
employment income, 1.490

Taxes Management Act 1970
arrangement of sections, 1.1
definitions, 1.28
general note, 1.2
general provisions
  administration, 1.3
  appeals, 1.18–1.24
  assessment and claims, 1.12–1.17
  penalties, 1.25
  records, 1.11
  returns of income and gains, 1.4–1.10
miscellaneous provisions
  documents, 1.26–1.27

Temporary absence
child benefit
  from GB, 3.32–3.33
  from Northern Ireland, 3.38
residence requirements, 2.423–2.424

"Term-time work"
working tax credit, 2.44–2.45

Territorial waters
statutory pay, 1.167

TESSAs
investment income, 2.164

30-hour element
working tax credit, 2.64–2.65

Time
See also **Time limits**
calculation of income
  employment income, 2.135
  pension income, 2.142
  social security income, 2.157
  trading income, 2.150

Time limits
child trust fund appeals, 8.75–8.76
claims
  Childcare Payments Act 2014, under, 2.286–2.290
  generally, 2.284–2.285
statutory sick pay, 4.18
tax credit appeals
  extension, 2.385–2.386
  generally, 2.383–2.384
tax credits, 2.284–2.285

Top-up payments
disregards, 2.185
time limits for claims, 2.286–2.290

Trading income
accounting date, 1.730
bad debts, 1.722
basic rules
  calculation of losses, 1.714
  deductions, 1.718
  GAAP, 1.713
  interest, 1.717
  professions and vocations, 1.712
  receipts and expenses, 1.715–1.716
basis periods
  accounting date, 1.730
  normal rules, 1.731
  professions and vocations, 1.729
business entertainment and gifts, 1.724
calculation of losses, 1.714
capital expenditure, 1.720
capital receipts, 1.727
charge to tax
  generally, 1.705
  income charged, 1.707
  person liable, 1.708
  territorial scope, 1.706
debts incurred and later released, 1.728
deductions
  relationship between rules, 1.718
  rules restricting, 1.719–1.725
doubtful debts, 1.722
farming, 1.709
foster care relief, 1.711
generally accepted accounting practice, 1.713
income treated as trade profits

Index

charge to tax, 1.705–1.708
  starting and cessation, 1.710
interest, 1.717
introduction, 1.697–1.698
market gardening, 1.709
overview, 1.702–1.703
priority rules
  generally, 1.704
  introduction, 1.701
professions and vocations
  basic rules, 1.712
  basis periods, 1.729
  receipts, 1.719
  rules restricting deductions, 1.719
receipts
  basic rules, 1.715–1.716
  capital receipts, 1.727
  debts incurred and later released, 1.728
  professions and vocations, 1.726
rent-a-room relief, 1.711
rules restricting deductions
  bad debts, 1.722
  business entertainment and gifts, 1.724
  capital expenditure, 1.720
  doubtful debts, 1.722
  professions and vocations, 1.719
  social security contributions, 1.725
  unconnected losses, 1.721
  unpaid remuneration, 1.723
  wholly and exclusively rules, 1.721
social security contributions, 1.725
statutory overview
  introduction, 1.700
  priority rules, 1.701
tax credits
  deductions, 2.147–2.148
  exemptions, 2.147–2.148
  general note, 2.144
  generally, 2.143
  identity of taxpayer, 2.149
  relevant income, 2.147–2.148
  self-employment, 2.145–2.146
  time of calculation, 2.150
trade profits
  basic rules, 1.712–1.718
  basis periods, 1.729–1.731
  income treated as, 1.705–1.710
  receipts, 1.726–1.728
  rules restricting deductions, 1.719–1.725
unconnected losses, 1.721
unpaid remuneration, 1.723
wholly and exclusively rules, 1.721
Training
child benefit, 3.4–3.5
disability element (working tax credit), 2.62–2.63
provision of information, and
  general note, 2.459
  generally, 2.461, 2.473
remunerative work, 2.36
working tax credit, 2.62–2.63

Training allowance
remunerative work, 2.36
"Training grants"
disregards, 2.186
Transfer of assets
Revenue and Customs, 1.827
"Transport vouchers"
meaning, 1.509
Travelling expenses
disregards, 2.185–2.186
necessary attendance, for, 1.542
performance of duties, in, 1.541
'workplace', 1.543
"Treatment of more than one contract"
statutory adoption pay
  general note, 6.10
  generally, 6.87
  lapse of election, 6.15
  notification of election, 6.12
  provision of information, 6.13
  relevant employer, 6.14, 6.101
statutory maternity pay
  generally, 5.11
  relevant employer, 5.32–5.33
statutory paternity pay
  adoption of child, on, 6.77
  birth of child, on, 6.70
  general note, 6.10
  lapse of election, 6.15
  notification of election, 6.12
  provision of information, 6.13
  relevant employer, 6.14, 6.101
statutory sick pay
  generally, 4.41
  relevant employer, 4.39–4.40
"Unconnected losses"
trading income, 1.721
Underpayments
tax credits, 1.357–1.358
Unemployability supplement
statutory sick pay, 1.200
Universal credit
migration to
  general provisions, abolition, 1.855–1.861
  introduction, 1.852
Unfair dismissal
statutory maternity pay, 5.23
Unmarried couples
child benefit, 3.45–3.46
"Unpaid remuneration"
trading income, 1.723
Uprating
guardian's allowance
  Order 2015, 3.78–3.79
  Regulations 2015, 3.80–3.82
generally, 1.863
'relevant amounts', 1.864–1.865
Variation
decisions of Board, 1.231–1.232
Vehicle maintenance grant
See **Disabled persons' vehicles**

Index

Verification
  claims, 2.374
Vocations
  See **Professions**
Voluntary organisations
  child benefit, 3.49–3.50
Voluntary work
  income test, 2.179–2.180
  remunerative work, 2.36
Vouchers
  cash
    application of provisions, 1.503–1.504
    benefit treated as earnings, 1.507
    disregard for money, goods or services obtained, 1.514
    meaning, 1.505
    sickness-benefits related, 1.506
  child trust funds
    generally, 8.8
    statutory provision, 1.631–1.634
  non-cash
    application of provisions, 1.508
    benefit treated as earnings, 1.510
    disregard for money, goods or services obtained, 1.514
    meaning, 1.509
  sickness benefits related, 1.506
  transport vouchers, 1.509
War pensioner's mobility supplement
  pension income, 2.137
"Weekly rates"
  additional statutory paternity pay
    generally, 6.216
    rounding, 6.217
  statutory adoption pay
    general note, 6.3
    generally, 6.4
    rounding, 6.6–6.7
  statutory paternity pay
    additional, 6.213–6.217
    general note, 6.3
    generally, 6.4
    rounding, 6.6–6.7
Welfare Benefits Up-rating Act 2013
  arrangement of sections, 1.862
  general provisions, 1.863
  schedule, 1.864–1.865
Welfare food
  milk tokens, 2.152
Welfare Reform Act 2012
  arrangement of sections, 1.848
  general note, 1.849
  general provisions
    other benefit changes, 1.853–1.854
    universal credit, 1.850–1.852
  schedule
    universal credit, 1.855–1.861
"Wholly and exclusively"
  trading income, 1.721
"Wholly exempt benefits"
  social security income, 1.589–1.592
Widowed mother's allowance
  social security income, 2.154

Widowed parent's allowance
  social security income, 2.154
"Winnings"
  investment income, 2.164
"Work after confinement"
  statutory maternity pay, 5.15–5.16
"Work during pay period"
  statutory adoption pay, 6.88
  statutory paternity pay, 6.78
"Working less than 16 hours a week"
  working tax credit, 2.52–2.53
Working tax credit
  50-plus element, 2.82
  abolition, 1.850–1.851
  administrative arrangements
    definitions, 2.371
    general note, 2.369
    provision of information, 2.372–2.373
    recording, etc. of claims, 2.374
    statutory provision, 1.415–1.416
  adoption, 2.38–2.41
  annual reports, 1.396–1.397
  annual review, 1.398–1.399
  anti-fraud measures, 1.261–1.262
  appeals
    appealable decisions, 1.385–1.390
    exercise of right, 1.391–1.392
    general regulations, 2.375–2.387
    late appeals, 1.393–1.395
    temporary modifications, 1.425–1.426
  assignment, 1.406–1.407
  bankruptcy, 1.406–1.407
  basic element
    adoption, 2.38–2.41
    ceasing to undertake work, 2.52–2.53
    childbirth, 2.38–2.41
    gaps between jobs, 2.54–2.55
    ill health, 2.42–2.43
    pay in lieu of notice, 2.50–2.51
    qualifying remunerative work, 2.26–2.37
    seasonal work, 2.44–2.45
    strike periods, 2.46–2.47
    suspension from work, 2.48–2.49
    term-time work, 2.44–2.45
    working less than 16 hours a week, 2.52–2.53
  benefit offences, and
    generally, 1.375–1.376
    introduction, 1.261–1.262
    Regulations, 2.483–2.486
    specified day, 2.480–2.482
    supplementary, 1.377–1.378
  capital rule, 2.106
  carers, 2.36
  ceasing to undertake work, 2.52–2.53
  change of circumstances
    advance, in, 2.327
    amendment, 2.320
    automatic, 1.289
    date of, 2.321–2.326
    decrease of rate, 2.314–2.317
    definitions, 2.211

1138

Index

discretionary, 1.288
evidence of birth or adoption, 2.332
failure to report, 1.290
generally, 1.284–1.285
increase of maximum rate, 2.312–2.313
mandatory, 1.287
method, 2.317–2.318
person acting on behalf of another, by, 2.328–2.331
relevant changes, 1.286
relevant person, 2.319
charitable work, 2.36
child care providers, 2.474–2.479
childbirth, 2.38–2.41
childcare element
   calculation of childcare charges, 2.76–2.77
   change of circumstances, 2.78–2.79
   'child', 2.73–2.75
   'childcare', 2.73–2.75
   generally, 2.70–2.72
   incapacitation, 2.72
   qualifying young persons, 2.75
   'relevant childcare charges', 2.73–2.75
   statutory provisions, 1.313–1.314
claims
   definitions, 2.276–2.277
   generally, 2.278–2.310
   statutory provision, 1.267–1.281
Codes of Practice
   overpayments, 9.15–9.53
conditions of entitlement
   basic element, 2.26–2.63
   childcare element, 2.70–2.79
   death of child, after, 2.83–2.84
   disability element, 2.56–2.63
   50-plus element, 2.82
   lone-parent element, 2.68–2.69
   second-adult element, 2.66–2.67
   severe disablement, 2.80–2.81
   30-hour element, 2.64–2.65
Crown employment, 1.404–1.405
death of child, after, 2.83–2.84
decisions
   discovery, on, 1.336–1.337
   final decision, 1.331–1.332
   final notice, 1.329–1.330
   information requirements, 1.344–1.345
   initial decision, 1.317–1.322
   notice of, 1.346–1.347
   official error, subject to, 1.338–1.339
   other revised decisions, 1.325–1.328
   power to enquire, 1.333–1.335
   review, 1.340–1.343
   revision after notifications, 1.323–1.324
definitions
   regulations, in, 2.22–2.23
   statute, in, 1.412–1.413
determination of rate
   cut-off provisions, 2.269–2.270
   full year periods, 2.247–2.253
   generally, 2.231–2.246

introduction, 2.229–2.230
short periods, 2.254
development of system, 1.257
disability element
   Cases A to G, 2.59
   generally, 2.56–2.58
   initial claims, 2.60–2.61
   relevant disabilities, 2.88–2.101
   'training for work', 2.62–2.63
disability periods, 2.42–2.43
disability work allowance, 2.57
disclosure of information, 1.417–1.418
duration, 1.282–1.283
elements of credit
   basic element, 2.26–2.63
   childcare element, 2.70–2.79
   death of child, after, 2.83–2.84
   disability element, 2.56–2.63
   50-plus element, 2.82
   generally, 2.24–2.25
   lone-parent element, 2.68–2.69
   second-adult element, 2.66–2.67
   severe disability element, 2.80–2.81
   30-hour element, 2.64–2.65
employment zone programme, 2.36
entitlement, 1.305–1.310
excepted activities, 2.36
failure to comply with requirements, 1.366–1.369
50-plus element, 2.82
fraud, and
   generally, 1.371–1.372
   introduction, 1.261–1.262
   loss of tax credit, 1.375–1.382
   powers relating to documents, 1.373–1.374
forwarding of claims, 2.374
functions of Board, 1.265–1.266
gaps between jobs, 2.54–2.55
general note, 1.256
holding of claims, 2.374
hours worked, 2.37
ill health, 2.42–2.43
inalienability, 1.406–1.407
incapacity for work, 2.42–2.43
income test
   calculation, 2.118–2.124
   definitions, 2.116–2.117
   disregards, 2.184–2.191
   employment income, 2.125–2.135
   foreign income, 2.170–2.171
   general note, 2.104–2.114
   investment income, 2.163–2.167
   miscellaneous income, 2.182–2.183
   notional income, 2.172–2.181
   pension income, 2.136–2.142
   property income, 2.168–2.169
   social security income, 2.151–2.157
   statutory provision, 1.291–1.298
   student income, 2.158–2.162
   trading income, 2.143–2.150
income thresholds, 2.222–2.224

1139

incorrect statements
  conduct of penalty cases, 1.363
  fraudulently or negligently, 1.362
  generally, 1.359–1.361
  level of penalties, 1.364–1.365
Intensive Activity Period, 2.36
interest
  definitions, 2.391
  general note, 2.390
  overpayments, on, 2.392
  prescribed rate, 2.393
  statutory provision, 1.383–1.384
lone-parent element, 2.68–2.69
loss of tax credits, and
  benefit offences, for, 1.375–1.378
  Regulations, 2.483–2.486
  repeated benefit fraud, for, 1.379–1.382
  specified day, 2.480–2.482
maximum rate
  amount, 2.102
  generally, 2.85–2.87
  statutory provision, 1.311–1.312
means testing, 2.104
minimum level of continuity, 2.34
Northern Ireland, 1.427–1.428
notices by Board, 1.408–1.409
notices to provide information, and
  childcare provider, to, 2.334
  dates to be specified, 2.335
  definitions, 2.273
  electronic communications, 2.274–2.275
  employers, to, 2.333
  s.17 TCA 2002, under, 2.336–2.339
notification of change of circumstances
  advance, in, 2.327
  amendment, 2.320
  automatic, 1.289
  date of, 2.321–2.326
  decrease of rate, 2.314–2.317
  definitions, 2.211
  discretionary, 1.288
  evidence of birth or adoption, 2.332
  failure to report, 1.290
  generally, 1.284–1.285
  increase of maximum rate, 2.312–2.313
  mandatory, 1.287
  method, 2.317–2.318
  person acting on behalf of another, by, 2.328–2.331
  relevant changes, 1.286
  relevant person, 2.319
official errors
  definitions, 2.432–2.433
  general note, 2.435
  generally, 2.434
overpayments
  Code of Practice, 9.15–9.53
  generally, 1.352–1.353
  method of recovery, 2.363
  recovery, 1.354–1.356
pay in lieu of notice, 2.50–2.51
payment
  employees' rights, 1.350–1.351
  generally, 1.348–1.349
payment by Revenue and Customs
  child care element, 2.344–2.345
  generally, 2.346–2.347
  introduction, 2.341
penalties
  determination, 1.435
  failure to comply with requirements, 1.366–1.369
  Guidance, 9.1–9.14
  incorrect statements, 1.359–1.365
  mitigation, 1.437
  proceedings before Commissioners, 1.436
  recovery, 1.439
  supplementary, 1.370–1.371
  time limits, 1.438
period of award, 1.282–1.283
persons subject to immigration control
  definitions, 2.396
  exclusion from entitlement, 2.397–2.409
  general note, 2.403
  modifications of Act, 2.408–2.409
  statutory provision, 1.400–1.401
  transitional relief, 2.410–2.411
polygamous marriages
  definitions, 2.444–2.445
  general note, 2.442
  modification of Regulations, 2.447–2.453
  modification of TCA 2002, 2.446
  statutory provision, 1.402–1.403
provision of information
  authorities, by, 2.373
  authorities, to, 2.372
  functions relating to employment, 2.461, 2.473
  functions relating to health, 2.438–2.440, 2.457, 2.471
  functions relating to training, 2.461, 2.473
qualifying remunerative work
  excepted activities, 2.36
  generally, 2.26–2.32
  hours worked, 2.37
  minimum level of continuity, 2.34
  remunerative work, 2.35
  routes to entitlement, 2.33
qualifying young persons
  childcare element, 2.75
  death, 2.83–2.84
rate, 1.315–1.316
recording of claims, 2.374
remunerative work, 2.35
repeated benefit fraud, and
  generally, 1.379–1.380
  introduction, 1.261–1.262
  Regulations, 2.483–2.486

specified day, 2.480–2.482
supplementary, 1.381–1.382
residence requirements
  Crown servants posted overseas, 2.425–2.427
  definitions, 2.414–2.415
  ordinary residence, 2.418–2.419
  person treated as not being in UK, 2.416–2.422
  tests, 2.420–2.422
  temporary absence from UK, 2.423–2.424
review of decisions
  generally, 1.340–1.341
  late application, 1.342–1.343
routes to entitlement, 2.33
seasonal work, 2.44–2.45
second-adult element, 2.66–2.67
severe disability element, 2.80–2.81
sickness, 2.42–2.43
sports award, 2.36
statutory provisions
  appeals, 1.385–1.395
  child tax credit, 1.299–1.304
  decisions, 1.317–1.347
  fraud, 1.371–1.374
  generally, 1.263–1.298
  interest, 1.383–1.384
  loss of tax credit, 1.375–1.382
  payment, 1.348–1.358
  penalties, 1.359–1.371
  rate, 1.315–1.316
  supplementary, 1.396–1.413
  working tax credit, 1.305–1.314
strike periods, 2.46–2.47
suspension from work, 2.48–2.49
term-time work, 2.44–2.45
30-hour element, 2.64–2.65
training allowance, 2.59
underpayments, 1.357–1.358
use of information, 1.417–1.418
verification of claims, 2.374
voluntary work, 2.36
working less than 16 hours a week, 2.52–2.53

Working Tax Credit (Entitlement and Maximum Rate) Regulations 2002
arrangement, 2.19
citation, 2.20
commencement, 2.20
definitions, 2.22–2.23
effect, 2.20–2.21
general note, 2.21
general provisions
  conditions of entitlement, 2.26–2.84
  elements of credit, 2.24–2.25
  maximum rate, 2.85–2.87
modifications to, 2.448
schedules
  disabilities, 2.88–2.101
  maximum rates, 2.102
Working Tax Credit (Payment by Employers) Regulations 2002
general note, 2.341
"Wounds pension"
pension income, 2.137
"Yearly disability payments"
child trust funds, 8.15–8.16
Young persons (child benefit)
care, in
  generally, 3.25
  statutory basis, 1.170
continuation of entitlement, 3.6
definition, 1.45
detention, in
  generally, 3.21–3.24
  statutory basis, 1.170
education and training condition, 3.4–3.5
extension period, 3.7
interruptions, 3.8–3.9
introduction, 3.3
living with another as a couple, where, 3.16–3.17
other financial support, 3.12
person responsible for child, 3.13–3.15
prescribed conditions, 3.3–3.12
relevant relationship, in, 3.18
terminal dates, 3.10–3.11
youth training, in, 3.21–3.24

1141